The Delaware Law of Corporations & Business Organizations Statutory Deskbook 2012 Edition

The Delaware Law of Corporations and Business Organizations Statutory Deskbook, which is compact and easily portable, is designed to facilitate research into matters of statutory scope and construction. The *Statutory Deskbook* brings you the complete text, with all current amendments of the principal Delaware business organization statutes and case law annotations, including:

- The Delaware General Corporation Law;
- Limited Liability Company Act;
- Statutory Trust Statute;
- Revised Uniform Limited Partnership Act;
- The Delaware Revised Uniform Partnership Act;
- The Uniform Unincorporated Nonprofit Association Act;
- Other related provisions of the State of Delaware Constitution, Franchise Tax Law, and Code.

Also included are analyses of the 2011 Amendments to the Delaware General Corporation Law; Limited Liability Company Act; Revised Uniform Limited Partnership Act, Revised Uniform Partnership Act and Statutory Trust Act.

2012 Edition Highlights

This 2012 Edition brings you, included in your subscription price, an electronic version of the deskbook on CD-ROM.

For questions concerning this shipment, billing, or other customer service matters, call our Customer Service Department at 1-800-234-1660.

For toll-free ordering, please call 1-800-638-8437.

Copyright © 2012 CCH Incorporated. All Rights Reserved.

Wolters Kluwer
Law & Business

ASPEN PUBLISHERS

THE DELAWARE LAW OF CORPORATIONS & BUSINESS ORGANIZATIONS

STATUTORY DESKBOOK

2012 EDITION

R. Franklin Balotti
Jesse A. Finkelstein

Wolters Kluwer
Law & Business

This publication is designed to provide accurate and authoritative information in regard to the subject matter covered. It is sold with the understanding that the publisher and the author(s) are not engaged in rendering legal, accounting, or other professional services. If legal advice or other professional assistance is required, the services of a competent professional should be sought.

>
—From a *Declaration of Principles* jointly adopted by
> a Committee of the American Bar Association and
> a Committee of Publishers and Associations.

Copyright © 2012, 2011-1996 CCH Incorporated. All Rights Reserved.

No part of this publication may be reproduced or transmitted in any form or by any means, including electronic, mechanical, photocopying, recording, or utilized by any information storage or retrieval system, without written permission from the publisher. For information about permissions or to request permissions online, visit us at *www.aspenpublishers.com/licensing/default.aspx*, or a written request may be faxed to our permissions department at 212-771-0803.

Published by Wolters Kluwer Law & Business in New York.

Wolters Kluwer Law & Business serves customers worldwide with CCH, Aspen Publishers and Kluwer Law International products.

Printed in the United States of America

ISBN 978-0-7355-1016-6

1 2 3 4 5 6 7 8 9 0

SUMMARY TABLE OF CONTENTS

2011 Amendments to the General Corporation Law of the State of Delaware—Analysis	GCL-i
Index	Corp.—1
Constitution of the State of Delaware	Corp.—51
Delaware General Corporation Law	Corp.—101
Delaware Corporation Franchise Tax	Corp.—501
Delaware Professional Service Corporations	Corp.—551
2011 Amendments to the Delaware Limited Liability Company Act—Analysis	LLC-i
Delaware Limited Liability Company Act	Corp.—601
2011 Amendments to the Delaware Statutory Trust Act—Analysis	DSTA-i
Delaware Statutory Trusts	Corp.—701
Delaware Code Provisions	Corp.—801
Delaware Court of Chancery Rules	Corp.—901
2011 Amendments to the Delaware Revised Uniform Limited Partnership Act—Analysis	DRULPA-i
Delaware Revised Uniform Limited Partnership Act	DE-35
2011 Amendments to the Delaware Revised Uniform Partnership Act—Analysis	DRUPA-i
Delaware Revised Uniform Partnership Act	DRUPA-1
Uniform Unincorporated Nonprofit Association Act	DE-NPC-1
Selected Taxes and Fees For Delaware Corporations	DE-TAX-1

INTRODUCTION

This statutory booklet contains the State of Delaware Constitution, Delaware General Corporation Law Annotated including Franchise Tax Law, the Limited Liability Company Act, selected Delaware Code Provisions including the Treatment of Statutory Trusts, the Revised Uniform Limited Partnership Act, the Delaware Revised Uniform Partnership Act, and the Uniform Unincorporated Nonprofit Association Act.

This statutory booklet is designed to be a convenient guide to Delaware corporations, limited partnerships, and limited liability companies and is able to be easily transported by the user as an extension of the current three-volume **The Delaware Law of Corporations and Business Organizations, Third Edition**. In addition, the accompanying CD-ROM contains the full contents of the statutory booklet, with a search mechanism that allows the user to make research more efficient.

* * * * *

Neither the authors nor the firm of Richards, Layton & Finger have prepared the annotations which appear in this book. The annotations were prepared by the staff of Aspen Publishers.

2011 AMENDMENTS TO THE GENERAL CORPORATION LAW OF THE STATE OF DELAWARE — ANALYSIS

By Jesse A. Finkelstein
and
Brigitte V. Fresco
Richards, Layton & Finger, P.A.
Wilmington, Delaware

I. Introduction

Legislation amending the General Corporation Law of the State of Delaware (the "DGCL") was adopted by the Delaware General Assembly and was signed by the Governor of the State of Delaware on July 7, 2011. The DGCL amendments became effective on August 1, 2011. The DGCL amendments are designed to keep Delaware law current and address issues raised by practitioners, the judiciary and legislators with respect to the current language or interpretation of the DGCL.

II. Formation; Foreign Corporations

—Contents of Certificate of Incorporation [8 Del. C. § 102] and Corporations Using "trust" in Name [8 Del. C. § 395]. Section 102 of the DGCL sets forth the required contents of a certificate of incorporation. Under Section 102(a)(1) of the DGCL, the name of a corporation (i) shall contain certain "corporate" endings, such as "company," "corporation" or "incorporated" (or abbreviations thereof) unless waived by the Division of Corporations in the Department of State upon the certification by the corporation that its total assets are not less than $10,000,000; (ii) shall be distinguishable upon the records in the office of the Divisions of Corporation in the Department of State from the names that are reserved and from the names on records for other entities; and (iii) shall not contain the word "bank" or any variation thereof, except in certain circumstances. Section 102(a)(1) was amended in two respects.

First, Section 102(a)(1) was amended to allow the Division of Corporations in the Department of State, in its sole discretion, to waive the requirement that a corporation's name contain certain "corporate" endings (or abbreviations thereof) if the corporation is both a nonprofit nonstock corporation and an association of professionals.

Second, Section 102(a)(1) was amended, in conjunction with amendments to Section 395 of the DGCL, to give the Director of the Division of Corporations and the State Bank Commissioner the discretion to waive certain requirements and restrictions that apply when a corporation uses the word "trust" in its name, so long as the use of the word "trust" is clearly not purporting to refer to a trust business. In that connection, Section 102(a)(1) was amended to specifically provide that, except as provided in Section 395 of the DGCL, the name of a corporation shall not include the word "trust."

Section 395 of the DGCL, which sets forth when a Delaware corporation may use the word "trust" in its name, was also amended. The amendments to Section 395 include adding a new subsection (d) providing that the limitations on the use of the word "trust" as part of the corporation's name shall not apply to a corporation that is not subject to the supervision of the State Bank Commissioner of the State of Delaware and that is not regulated under the Bank Holding Company Act of 1956 or section 10 of the Home Owners' Loan Act, and where the use of the word "trust" clearly (i) does not refer to a trust business; (ii) is not likely to mislead the public into believing that the nature of the business of the corporation includes activities that fall under the supervision of the State Bank Commissioner of the State of Delaware or that are regulated under the Bank Holding Company Act of 1956 or section 10 of the Home Owners' Loan Act; and (iii) will not otherwise lead to a pattern and practice of abuse that might cause harm to the interests of the public or the State of Delaware, as determined by the Director of the Division of Corporations and the State Bank Commissioner. The amendments to Section 395 also updated statutory references to the Savings and Loan Holding Company Act, which was moved to section 10 of the Home Owners' Loan Act.

—*Contents of Certificate of Incorporation [8 Del. C. § 102]; Execution, Acknowledgement, Filing, Recording and Effective Date of Original Certificate of Incorporation and Other Instruments; Exceptions [Section 103]; Registered Office in State [8 Del. C. § 131]; and Annual Report [8 Del. C. § 374].* Prior to the amendments, under Section 102(a)(2) of the DGCL, a corporation's certificate of incorporation had to include the address (which was to include the street, number, city and county) of the corporation's registered office in the State of Delaware and the name of the registered agent at such address. Section 102(a)(2) was amended in connection with the amendment to Section 131 of the DGCL. Section 102(a)(2) now requires the address of the registered office to be stated in accordance with Section 131(c) of the DGCL, which added the requirement that the postal code be included in such address.

Section 103 of the DGCL sets forth the requirements to file documents with the Secretary of State of the State of Delaware (the "Secretary of State"). Section 103 was amended in connection with the amendments to Sections 102(a)(2), 131 and 374 of the DGCL by adding a new subjection (j) to clarify that it is not necessary for a Delaware corporation to amend its certificate of incorporation, or any other document, that has been filed with the Secretary of State prior to August 1, 2011, to add the postal code to the address of its registered office as is required pursuant to the amendments to Sections 102(a)(2), 131 and 374. However, any certificate or other document filed on or after August 1, 2011 that changes the address of the registered agent must comply with Section 131(c) (*i.e.*, such address must include the postal code).

Section 131 of the DGCL provides that every corporation must maintain a registered office in the State of Delaware. Section 131 was amended to add a new subsection (c) which provides that the address of the registered office contained in any certificate of incorporation or other document filed with the Secretary of State shall include the street, number, city, county and postal code. Sections 102(a)(2) and Section 374 were both amended to cross reference Section 131(c) with respect to the contents of the address of the registered office of the corporation.

Section 374 requires a foreign corporation doing business in the State of Delaware to file an annual report with the Secretary of State. Such annual report must include, among other things, the address of the corporation's registered office in the State of Delaware. Section 374 was amended to add a cross reference to new Section 131(c) to clarify that the address of the registered office must contain all the information required by Section 131(c), which now must include the postal code.

III. Directors and Officers

—Indemnification of Officers, Directors, Employees and Agents; Insurance [8 Del. C. § 145]. Section 145 of the DGCL provides that a Delaware corporation may provide indemnification and advancement of expenses to its officers, directors, employees and agents. In 2009, Section 145(f) was amended to provide that a right to indemnification and advancement of expenses under a provision in the certificate of incorporation or bylaws could not be eliminated or impaired by an amendment to such provision after the occurrence of the act or omission giving rise to the indemnification or advancement claim, unless the provision contained, at the time of the act or omission, an explicit provision permitting such elimination or limitation. Section 145(f) was amended to clarify that indemnification and advancement of expenses under a provision of a certificate of incorporation or bylaw cannot be eliminated or impaired by an

amendment to the certificate of incorporation or the bylaws after the occurrence of the act or omission to which the indemnification or advancement of expenses relates, unless the provision, at the time of the act or omission, explicitly authorizes such elimination or limitation. Thus, for example, a corporation may not circumvent an indemnification or advancement of expenses provision in a bylaw by adopting an amendment to its certificate of incorporation.

IV. Merger, Consolidation or Conversion; Domestication and transfer

—Conversion of Other Entities to a Domestic Corporation [8 Del. C. § 265] and Domestication of Non-United States Entities [8 Del. C. § 388]. Section 265 of the DGCL permits "other entities" to convert to a Delaware corporation by filing a certificate of conversion and a certificate of incorporation with the Secretary of State. Section 388 of the DGCL permits a non-United States entity to become domesticated as a Delaware corporation by filing a certificate of corporate domestication and a certificate of incorporation with the Secretary of State. Both Section 265(b) and Section 388(b) were amended to clarify that the certificate of incorporation and the certificate of conversion or certificate of corporate domestication, as applicable, must be filed simultaneously with the Secretary of State and, to the extent such certificate of incorporation and certificate of conversion or certificate of corporate domestication, as applicable, are to have a post-filing effective date or time, such certificates must provide for the same effective date or time.

V. Sale of Assets; Dissolution and Winding Up

—Payment of Franchise Taxes Before Dissolution or Merger [8 Del. C. § 277]. Prior to the amendments, Section 277 of the DGCL provided that no corporation shall be dissolved or merged until all franchise taxes due or assessable, including all franchise taxes that would be due or assessable for the entire

calendar month during which the dissolution or merger becomes effective, have been paid. Section 277 was amended to also include conversions of corporations to other entities pursuant to Section 266 of the DGCL and transfers to foreign jurisdictions (without continuing its existence as a corporation of the State of Delaware) pursuant to Section 390 of the DGCL. The amendment also clarified that the corporation must file all annual franchise tax reports, including the final franchise tax report for the year in which the dissolution, merger, transfer or conversion becomes effective. Notwithstanding the foregoing, the amendments to Section 277 provide that if the Secretary of State certifies an instrument effecting a dissolution, merger, transfer or conversion, the corporation will be dissolved, merged, transferred or converted at the effective time of the instrument.

VI. Renewal, Revival, Extension and Restoration of Certificate of Incorporation or Charter; Miscellaneous Provisions; Corporation Franchise Tax

—Renewal of Certificate of Incorporation or Charter of Religious, Charitable, Educational, etc., Corporations [8 Del. C. § 313]; Taxes and Fees Payable to the Secretary of State upon Filing Certificate or Other Paper [8 Del. C. § 391]; and Corporations Subject to and Exempt from Franchise Taxes [8 Del. C. § 501]. Section 313 of the DGCL governs how religious, charitable, educational and certain other corporations whose purpose is for the public welfare may renew its certificate of incorporation that has become inoperative or void. In order to conform Section 313 to the amendments made to Section 501(b), Section 313 was amended to use the term "exempt corporation."

Section 391 of the DGCL sets forth the taxes and fees payable to the Secretary of State in connection with the filing of certain documents with the Secretary of State. Like Section 313, Section 391(a)(3) was amended to use the term "exempt corporations" instead of "corporations created solely for religious and charitable purposes" in order to conform Section 391 to the amendments made to Section 501.

Section 501 of the DGCL sets forth which corporations are subject to annual franchise taxes and which corporations are exempt from annual franchise taxes. Section 501 was amended in two ways. First, Section 501(a) was amended to clarify that captive insurance companies licensed under chapter 69 of Title 18 of the Delaware Code are not required to pay annual franchise taxes. Second, Section 501(b)(5) was amended to clarify that the definition of "exempt corporation" includes a religious corporation or purely charitable or educational association, and a company, association or society, which, by its certificate of incorporation, has for its object the assistance of sick, needy or disabled members, or the defraying of funeral expenses of deceased members, or to provide for the wants of the widows and families after the death of its members.

# DELAWARE
TABLE OF CONTENTS

Editor's Note: In cases where the state legislature has not provided section titles, they have been prepared by the editorial staff of Aspen Publishers and are set off in brackets.

	Page
Index	1
Constitution (Const)	51
General Corporation Law (GCL)	101
Corporate Franchise Tax	501
Professional Service Corporations	551
Limited Liability Company Act	601
Statutory Trusts	701
Delaware Code (Code)	801
Court of Chancery Rules	901

CONSTITUTION

	Section
Jurisdiction of supreme court	Art. IV, §11
[No loan of credit by municipal to private corporation; municipal corporation cannot be stockholder in private corporation]	Art. VIII, §8
[Corporations must be organized under general laws]	Art. IX, §1
[Pre-existing corporations must accept provisions of constitution before amendment or renewal of charter]	Art. IX, §2
[Stock must be issued for cash, labor, or property]	Art. IX, §3
[Reservation protective of existing corporate rights]	Art. IX, §4
[Foreign corporations, before doing business in state, must appoint agent for service of process]	Art. IX, §5
[Shares of non-residents shall not be taxed]	Art. IX, §6

GENERAL CORPORATION LAW (Title 8)

Formation

Incorporators; how corporation formed; purposes	101
Contents of certificate of incorporation	102
Execution, acknowledgment, filing, recording and effective date of original certificate of incorporation and other instruments; exceptions	103
Certificate of incorporation; definition	104
Certificate of incorporation and other certificates; evidence	105
Commencement of corporate existence	106
Powers of incorporators	107
Organization meeting of incorporators or directors named in certificate of incorporation	108
Bylaws	109
Emergency bylaws and other powers in emergency	110
Jurisdiction to interpret, apply, enforce or determine the validity of corporate instruments and provisions of this title	111
Access to proxy solicitation materials	112
Proxy expense reimbursement	113
Application of chapter to nonstock corporations	114

Powers

General powers	121
Specific powers	122
Powers respecting securities of other corporations or entities	123
Effect of lack of corporate capacity or power; ultra vires	124
Conferring academic or honorary degrees	125
Banking power denied	126
Private foundation; powers and duties	127

© 2010 Aspen Publishers. All Rights Reserved.

GENERAL CORPORATION LAW (Title 8) (continued):

Registered office and registered agent

Registered office in state; principal office or place of business in state 131
Registered agent in state; resident agent 132
Change of location of registered office; change of registered agent ... 133
Change of address or name of registered agent 134
Resignation of registered agent coupled with appointment of successor 135
Resignation of registered agent not coupled with appointment of successor 136

Directors and officers

Board of directors; powers; number, qualifications, terms and quorum; committees; classes of directors; nonstock corporations; reliance upon books; action without meeting; removal 141
Officers; titles, duties, selection, term; failure to elect; vacancies. 142
Loans to employees and officers; guaranty of obligations of employees and officers 143
Interested directors; quorum 144
Indemnification of officers, directors, employees and agents; insurance 145
Submission of matters for stockholder vote 146

Stock and dividends

Classes and series of stock; redemption; rights 151
Issuance of stock; lawful consideration; fully paid stock 152
Consideration for stock 153
Determination of amount of capital; capital, surplus and net assets defined 154
Fractions of shares 155
Partly paid shares 156
Rights and options respecting stock 157
Stock certificates; uncertificated shares 158
Shares of stock; personal property, transfer and taxation 159
Corporation's powers respecting ownership, voting, etc., of its own stock; rights of stock called for redemption 160
Issuance of additional stock; when and by whom 161
Liability of stockholder or subscriber for stock not paid in full 162
Payment for stock not paid in full 163
Failure to pay for stock; remedies 164
Revocability of preincorporation subscriptions 165
Formalities required of stock subscriptions 166
Lost, stolen or destroyed stock certificates; issuance of new certificate or uncertificated shares 167
Judicial proceedings to compel issuance of new certificate or uncertificated shares 168
Situs of ownership of stock 169
Dividends; payment; wasting asset corporations 170
Special purpose reserves 171
Liability of directors and committee members as to dividends or stock redemption 172
Declaration and payment of dividends 173
Liability of directors for unlawful payment of dividend or unlawful stock purchase or redemption; exoneration from liability; contribution among directors; subrogation 174

GENERAL CORPORATION LAW (Title 8) (continued):

Stock transfers

	Section
Transfer of stock, stock certificates and uncertificated stock	201
Restrictions on transfer and ownership of securities	202
Business combinations with interested stockholders	203

Meetings, elections, voting and notice

Meetings of stockholders	211
Voting rights of stockholders; proxies; limitations	212
Fixing date for determination of stockholders of record	213
Cumulative voting	214
Voting rights of members of nonstock corporations; quorum; proxies	215
Quorum and required vote for stock corporations	216
Voting rights of fiduciaries, pledgors and joint owners of stock	217
Voting trusts and other voting agreements	218
List of stockholders entitled to vote; penalty for refusal to produce; stock ledger	219
Inspection of books and records	220
Voting, inspection and other rights of bondholders and debenture holders	221
Notice of meetings and adjourned meetings	222
Vacancies and newly created directorships	223
Form of records	224
Contested election of directors; proceedings to determine validity	225
Appointment of custodian or receiver of corporation on deadlock or for other cause	226
Powers of court in elections of directors	227
Consent of stockholders or members in lieu of meeting	228
Waiver of notice	229
Exception to requirements of notice	230
Voting procedures and inspectors of elections	231
Notice by electronic transmission	232
Notice to stockholders sharing an address	233

Amendment of certificate of incorporation; changes in capital and capital stock

Amendment of certificate of incorporation before receipt of payment for stock	241
Amendment of certificate of incorporation after receipt of payment for stock; nonstock corporations	242
Retirement of stock	243
Reduction of capital	244
Restated certificate of incorporation	245

Merger, consolidation or conversion

Merger or consolidation of domestic corporations	251
Merger or consolidation of domestic and foreign corporations; service of process upon surviving or resulting corporation	252
Merger of parent corporation and subsidiary or subsidiaries	253
Merger or consolidation of domestic corporation and joint-stock or other association	254
Merger or consolidation of domestic nonstock corporations	255
Merger or consolidation of domestic and foreign nonstock corporations; service of process upon surviving or resulting corporation	256

Section

GENERAL CORPORATION LAW (Title 8) (continued):
Merger, consolidation or conversion (continued):
Merger or consolidation of domestic stock and nonstock
corporations 257
Merger or consolidation of domestic and foreign stock and
nonstock corporations 258
Status, rights, liabilities, etc. of constituent and surviving or
resulting corporations following merger or consolidation 259
Powers of corporation surviving or resulting from merger or
consolidation; issuance of stock, bonds or other indebtedness 260
Effect of merger upon pending actions 261
Appraisal rights 262
Merger or consolidation of domestic corporations and partnerships 263
Merger or consolidation of domestic corporation and limited
liability company 264
Conversion of other entities to a domestic corporation 265
Conversion of a domestic corporation to other entities 266
Merger of parent entity and subsidiary corporation or
corporations 267

Sale of assets, dissolution and winding up
Sale, lease or exchange of assets; consideration; procedure 271
Mortgage or pledge of assets 272
Dissolution of joint venture corporation having 2
stockholders 273
Dissolution before issuance of shares or beginning of
business; procedure 274
Dissolution generally; procedure 275
Dissolution of nonstock corporation; procedure 276
Payment of franchise taxes before dissolution, merger,
transfer or conversion 277
Continuation of corporation after dissolution for purposes of
suit and winding up affairs 278
Trustees or receivers for dissolved corporations; appointment;
powers; duties 279
Notice to claimants; filing of claims 280
Payment and distribution to claimants and stockholders 281
Liability of stockholders of dissolved corporations 282
Jurisdiction 283
Revocation or forfeiture of charter; proceedings 284
Dissolution or forfeiture of charter by decree of court; filing 285

Insolvency; receivers and trustees
Receivers for insolvent corporations; appointment and powers 291
Title to property; filing order of appointment; exception 292
Notices to stockholders and creditors 293
Receivers or trustees; inventory; list of debts and report 294
Creditors' proofs of claims; when barred; notice 295
Adjudication of claims; appeal 296
Sale of perishable or deteriorating property 297
Compensation, costs and expenses of receiver or trustee 298
Substitution of trustee or receiver as party; abatement of actions 299
Employee's lien for wages when corporation insolvent 300
Discontinuance of liquidation 301
Compromise or arrangement between corporation and
creditors or stockholders 302
Proceeding under the Federal Bankruptcy Code of the United States;
effectuation 303

GENERAL CORPORATION LAW (Title 8) (continued):
Renewal, revival, extension and restoration of certificate of incorporation or charter
Revocation of voluntary dissolution 311
Renewal, revival, extension and restoration of certificate of incorporation 312
Renewal of certificate of incorporation or charter of exempt corporations 313
Status of corporation 314

Suits against corporations, directors, officers or stockholders
Service of process on corporations 321
Failure of corporation to obey order of court; appointment of receiver 322
Failure of corporation to obey writ of mandamus; quo warranto proceedings for forfeiture of charter 323
Attachment of shares of stock or any option, right or interest therein; procedure; sale; title upon sale; proceeds 324
Actions against officers, directors or stockholders to enforce liability of corporation; unsatisfied judgment against corporation 325
Action by officer, director or stockholder against corporation for corporate debt paid 326
Stockholder's derivative action; allegation of stock ownership 327
Effect of liability of corporation on impairment of certain transactions 328
Defective organization of corporation as defense 329
Usury; pleading by corporation 330

Close corporations; special provisions
Law applicable to close corporation 341
Close corporation defined; contents of certificate of incorporation 342
Formation of a close corporation 343
Election of existing corporation to become a close corporation 344
Limitations on continuation of close corporation status 345
Voluntary termination of close corporation status by amendment of certificate of incorporation; vote required 346
Issuance or transfer of stock of a close corporation in breach of qualifying conditions 347
Involuntary termination of close corporation status; proceeding to prevent loss of status 348
Corporate option where a restriction on transfer of a security is held invalid 349
Agreements restricting discretion of directors 350
Management by stockholders 351
Appointment of custodian for close corporation 352
Appointment of a provisional director in certain cases 353
Operating corporation as partnership 354
Stockholders' option to dissolve corporation 355
Effect of this subchapter on other laws 356

Foreign corporations
Definition; qualification to do business in state; procedure 371
Additional requirements in case of change of name, change of business purpose or merger or consolidation 372
Exceptions to requirements 373
Annual report 374

GENERAL CORPORATION LAW (Title 8) (continued):
Foreign corporations (continued):
Failure to file report 375
Service of process upon qualified foreign corporations 376
Change of registered agent 377
Penalties for noncompliance 378
Banking powers denied 379
Foreign corporation as fiduciary in this state 380
Withdrawal of foreign corporation from state; procedure;
   service of process on secretary of state 381
Service of process on nonqualifying foreign corporations 382
Actions by and against unqualified foreign corporations 383
Foreign corporations doing business without having
   qualified; injunctions 384
Filing of certain instruments with recorder of deeds not required. 385

Domestication and transfer
Domestication of non-United States entities 388
Temporary transfer of domicile into this state 389
Transfer, domestication or continuance of domestic corporations. 390

Miscellaneous provisions
Taxes and fees payable to secretary of state upon filing
   certificate or other paper 391
Rights, liabilities and duties under prior statutes 393
Reserved power of state to amend or repeal chapter; chapter
   part of corporation's charter or certificate of incorporation. 394
Corporations using "trust" in name, advertisements and
   otherwise; restrictions; violations and penalties; exceptions 395
Publication of chapter by secretary of state; distribution 396
Penalty for unauthorized publication of chapter 397
Short title 398

CORPORATION FRANCHISE TAX
Corporations subject to and exempt from franchise tax 501
Annual franchise tax report; contents; failure to file and pay tax;
   duties of secretary of state 502
Rates and computation of franchise tax 503
Collection and disposition of tax; tentative return and tax;
   penalty interest; investigation of annual franchise tax
   report; notice of additional tax due 504
Review and refund; jurisdiction and power of the secretary of
   state; appeal 505
Collection of tax; preferred debt 507
Injunction against exercise of franchise or transacting business. 508
Further remedy in court of chancery; appointment of receiver
   or trustee; sale of property 509
Failure to pay tax or file a complete annual report for 1 year;
   charter void; extension of time 510
Repeal of charters of delinquent corporations;
   report to governor and proclamation 511
Filing and publication of proclamation 512
Acting under proclaimed charter; penalty 513
Mistakes in proclamation; correction 514
Annual report of secretary of state 515
Retaliatory taxation and regulation; imposition 516
Duties of attorney general 517
Relief for corporations with assets in certain unfriendly nations. 518

PROFESSIONAL SERVICE CORPORATIONS

	Section
Legislative intent	601
Short title	602
Definitions	603
Exemptions	604
Authority to organize; law governing	605
Number of directors; officers	606
Rendition of professional services through licensed officers, employees and agents	607
Chapter not to affect professional relationship; legal liabilities and standards for professional conduct; negligence; attachment of assets	608
Engaging in other business prohibited	609
Issuance of capital stock to licensed individuals; voting trust agreements prohibited; holding of stock by shareholder's estate	610
Disqualification of officer, shareholder, agent or employee	611
Sale or transfer of shares	612
Price for shares	613
Perpetual corporate existence	614
Conversion into business corporation	615
Time for transfer of shares upon death or disqualification	616
Corporate name	617
Applicability of general corporation law; consolidation or merger of corporations; annual report	618
Construction of chapter	619

LIMITED LIABILITY COMPANY ACT (Title 6)

General provisions

Definitions	18-101
Name set forth in certificate	18-102
Reservation of name	18-103
Registered office; registered agent	18-104
Service of process on domestic limited liability companies	18-105
Nature of business permitted; powers	18-106
Business transactions of member or manager with the limited liability company	18-107
Indemnification	18-108
Service of process on managers and liquidating trustees	18-109
Contested matters relating to managers; contested votes	18-110
Interpretation and enforcement of limited liability company agreement	18-111

Formation; certificate of formation

Certificate of formation	18-201
Amendment to certificate of formation	18-202
Cancellation of certificate	18-203
Execution	18-204
Execution, amendment or cancellation by judicial order	18-205
Filing	18-206
Notice	18-207
Restated certificate	18-208
Merger and consolidation	18-209
Contractual appraisal rights	18-210
Certificate of correction	18-211
Domestication of non-United States entities	18-212
Transfer or continuance of domestic limited liability companies	18-213
Conversion of certain entities to a limited liability company	18-214

LIMITED LIABILITY COMPANY ACT (Title 6) (continued):
  Formation; certificate of formation (continued):
    Series of members, managers, limited liability company
      interests or assets 18-215
    Approval of conversion of a limited liability company 18-216
  Members
    Admission of members 18-301
    Classes and voting 18-302
    Liability to third parties 18-303
    Events of bankruptcy 18-304
    Access to and confidentiality of information; records 18-305
    Remedies for breach of limited liability company agreement
      by member 18-306
  Managers
    Admission of managers 18-401
    Management of limited liability company 18-402
    Contributions by a manager 18-403
    Classes and voting 18-404
    Remedies for breach of limited liability company agreement
      by manager 18-405
    Reliance on reports and information by member, manager
      or liquidating trustee 18-406
    Delegation of rights and powers to manage 18-407
  Finance
    Form of contribution 18-501
    Liability for contribution 18-502
    Allocation of profits and losses 18-503
    Allocation of distributions 18-504
    Defense of usury not available 18-505
  Distributions and resignation
    Interim distributions 18-601
    Resignation of manager 18-602
    Resignation of member 18-603
    Distribution upon resignation 18-604
    Distribution in kind 18-605
    Right to distribution 18-606
    Limitations on distribution 18-607
  Assignment of limited liability company interests
    Nature of limited liability company interest 18-701
    Assignment of limited liability company interest 18-702
    Member's limited liability company interest subject to
      charging order 18-703
    Right of assignee to become member 18-704
    Powers of estate of deceased or incompetent member 18-705
  Dissolution
    Dissolution 18-801
    Judicial dissolution 18-802
    Winding up 18-803
    Distribution of assets 18-804
    Trustees or receivers for limited liability companies;
      appointment; powers; duties 18-805
    Revocation of dissolution 18-806
  Foreign limited liability companies
    Law governing 18-901
    Registration required; application 18-902
    Issuance of registration 18-903
    Name; registered office; registered agent 18-904

LIMITED LIABILITY COMPANY ACT (Title 6) (continued):
  Foreign limited liability companies (continued):
    Amendments to application 18-905
    Cancellation of registration 18-906
    Doing business without registration 18-907
    Foreign limited liability companies doing business without
      having qualified; injunctions 18-908
    Execution; liability 18-909
    Service of process on registered foreign limited liability companies... 18-910
    Service of process on unregistered foreign limited liability companies .. 18-911
    Activities not constituting doing business 18-912
  Derivative actions
    Right to bring action 18-1001
    Proper plaintiff 18-1002
    Complaint 18-1003
    Expenses 18-1004
  Miscellaneous
    Construction and application of chapter and limited liability
      company agreement 18-1101
    Short title 18-1102
    Severability 18-1103
    Cases not provided for in this chapter 18-1104
    Fees 18-1105
    Reserved power of State of Delaware to alter or repeal chapter...... 18-1106
    Taxation of limited liability companies 18-1107
    Cancellation of certificate of formation for failure to pay taxes...... 18-1108
    Revival of domestic limited liability company 18-1109

STATUTORY TRUSTS
  Domestic statutory trusts
    Definitions .... T. 12, §3801
    Contributions by beneficial owners .... T. 12, §3802
    Liability of beneficial owners and trustees .... T. 12, §3803
    Legal proceedings .... T. 12, §3804
    Rights of beneficial owners and trustees in trust property .... T. 12, §3805
    Management of statutory trust .... T. 12, §3806
    Trustee in State; registered agent .... T. 12, §3807
    Existence of statutory trust .... T. 12, §3808
    Applicability of trust law .... T. 12, §3809
    Certificate of trust; amendment; restatement; cancellation .... T. 12, §3810
    Execution of certificate .... T. 12, §3811
    Filing of certificate .... T. 12, §3812
    Fees .... T. 12, §3813
    Use of names regulated .... T. 12, §3814
    Merger and consolidation .... T. 12, §3815
    Derivative actions .... T. 12, §3816
    Indemnification .... T. 12, §3817
    Treasury interests .... T. 12, §3818
    Access to and confidentiality of information; records .... T. 12, §3819
    Conversion of other business entities to a statutory trust ..... T. 12, §3820
    Conversion of a statutory trust .... T. 12, §3821
    Domestication of non-United States entities .... T. 12, §3822
    Transfer or continuance of domestic statutory trusts .... T. 12, §3823
    Reserved power of State to amend or repeal chapter .... T. 12, §3824
    Construction and application of chapter and governing
      instrument .... T. 12, §3825
    Short title .... T. 12, §3826

STATUTORY TRUSTS (continued):
Foreign statutory trusts
Law governing .... T. 12, §3851
Registration required; application .... T. 12, §3852
Issuance of registration .... T. 12, §3853
Name; registered office; registered agent .... T. 12, §3854
Amendments to application .... T. 12, §3855
Cancellation of registration .... T. 12, §3856
Doing business without registration .... T. 12, §3857
Foreign statutory trusts doing business without having
    qualified; injunctions .... T. 12, §3858
Execution; liability .... T. 12, §3859
Service of process on registered foreign statutory trusts ..... T. 12, §3860
Service of process on unregistered foreign statutory trusts ... T. 12, §3861
Fees .... T. 12, §3862
Activities not constituting doing business .... T. 12, §3863

DELAWARE CODE
Antitrust
Restraint of trade unlawful .... T. 6, §2103
Actions by attorney general for violations; civil penalty;
    equitable relief .... T. 6, §2107
Actions for equitable relief and damages; suits parens patriae... T. 6, §2108
Interest
Defense of usury as available to certain entities and associations... T. 6, §2306
Contracts
Choice of law .... T. 6, §2708
Voluntary alternative dispute resolution
Short title; purpose .... T. 6, §7701
Definitions .... T. 6, §7702
How ADR is selected .... T. 6, §7703
Contents of certificate .... T. 6, §7704
Place of filing .... T. 6, §7705
Filing fee .... T. 6, §7706
Revocation of ADR .... T. 6, §7707
Qualifications of ADR specialist .... T. 6, §7708
Selection of ADR specialist .... T. 6, §7709
Initiation of ADR proceeding .... T. 6, §7710
Participation by other parties .... T. 6, §7711
Scheduling of ADR proceedings .... T. 6, §7712
Compensation of ADR specialist .... T. 6, §7713
Conduct of the ADR proceedings .... T. 6, §7714
Conclusion of ADR .... T. 6, §7715
Confidentiality .... T. 6, §7716
Immunity .... T. 6, §7717
Attendance at ADR .... T. 6, §7718
Enforcement of ADR rights .... T. 6, §7719
Tolling of limitations .... T. 6, §7720
Effect of commencing litigation .... T. 6, §7721
Court of chancery
Technology disputes .... T. 10, §346
Mediation proceedings for business disputes .... T. 10, §347
Compelling appearance of defendant in absence of personal
    service .... T. 10, §365
Compelling appearance of nonresident defendant .... T. 10, §366

DELAWARE CODE (continued):
Superior court
Mediation and arbitration proceedings for business disputes ..... T. 10, §546
Process; commencement of actions
Personal jurisdiction by acts of nonresidents .... T. 10, §3104
Actions against corporations; service of process .... T. 10, §3111
Service of process on nonresident directors, trustees
 or members of the governing body of Delaware
 corporations .... T. 10, §3114
Attachments
Domestic attachment; when writ may be issued .... T. 10, §3501
Corporations subject to attachment and garnishment .... T. 10, §3502
Foreign attachment against foreign corporations .... T. 10, §3507
Pleading and practice
Proof of incorporation or corporate existence .... T. 10, §3915
Executions
Employees of insolvent corporation .... T. 10, §4935
Personal actions
Corporate officers' bonds .... T. 10, §8114
Procedure
Deposit for cost .... T. 10, §9525
Escheats
Other property escheated .... T. 12, §1197
Definitions .... T. 12, §1198
Report by holders of abandoned property .... T. 12, §1199
Payment or delivery of abandoned property .... T. 12, §1201
Periods of limitation not a bar .... T. 12, §1202
Effect of payment and delivery .... T. 12, §1203
Sale of abandoned property .... T. 12, §1204
Deposit and disbursement of funds .... T. 12, §1205
Claims for abandoned property paid or delivered;
 determination of claims; appeals .... T. 12, §1206
Rules and regulations .... T. 12, §1208
No private escheats .... T. 12, §1210
Trusts
Transfer of stocks, bonds or other corporate securities by
 trustee; certificate of register in chancery .... T. 12, §3532
Limits on campaign contributions and expenditures
Contribution limits generally .... T. 15, §8012
Form, acknowledgment and proof of deeds and other legal instruments
Acknowledgment of corporate deeds; other instruments ...... T. 25, §127
Titles and conveyances
Deeds by foreign corporations .... T. 25, §305
Secretary of state
Disposition of moneys received; division of corporations
 corporate revolving fund; secretary of state special
 operations fund .... T. 29, §2311
Fees .... T. 29, §2315

COURT OF CHANCERY RULES   Rule
Process 4
Derivative actions by shareholders 23.1

INDEX TO DELAWARE STATUTES

(Section numbers in bold face type refer to sections of the General Corporation Law; section numbers in light face type refer to sections of the Constitution and to sections from the Delaware Code.)

———— All References Are to Statute Section (§) Numbers ————

—A—

ABANDONED PROPERTY. ESCHEATS, INFRA
ACKNOWLEDGMENTS, Title 25, §127
ADJOURNED MEETINGS, **222**
ALTERATIONS AND CORRECTIONS
  Certificate of incorporation, infra
  Certificate of trust, statutory trusts, Title 12, §3810
  Charter of corporation, Const Art IX, §2
ALTERNATIVE DISPUTE RESOLUTION
  Application of chapter, Title 6, §7721
  Attendance of parties, Title 6, §7718
  Certificate of agreement to select
    generally, Title 6, §7703
    contents of, Title 6, §7704
    filing, infra this group
  Compensation of specialist, Title 6, §7713
  Conclusion of, Title 6, §7715
  Confidentiality of, Title 6, §7716
  Contents of certificate of agreement, Title 6, §7704
  Definitions, Title 6, §7702
  Enforcement of rights, Title 6, §7719
  Fee for filing certificate of agreement, Title 6, §7706
  Filing of certificate of agreement
    fee, Title 6, §7706
    place of, Title 6, §7705
  Immunity of specialist, Title 6, §7717
  Notice as initiation of proceeding, Title 6, §7710
  Other parties, participation by, Title 6, §7711
  Place for filing certificate of agreement, Title 6, §7705
  Purpose, Title 6, §7701
  Qualifications of specialist, Title 6, §7713
  Revocation of, Title 6, §7707
  Scheduling of proceedings, Title 6, §7712
  Selection of specialist, Title 6, §7709
  Short title, Title 6, §7701
  Specialist
    compensation of, Title 6, §7713
    immunity of, Title 6, §7717
    qualifications of, Title 6, §7708
    selection of, Title 6, §7709
  Tolling of statute of limitations, Title 6, §7720
ANNUAL REPORT
  Foreign corporations, infra
  Professional service corporations, **618**
ANTITRUST
  Attorney General, actions by, Title 6, §§2107, 2108
  Restraint of trade unlawful, Title 6, §2103
APPLICATION OF LAW
  Close corporations, **341**
  General laws, corporations organized under, Const Art IX, §1
  Limited liability companies, Title 6, §18-1101
  Statutory trusts, Title 12, §§3809, 3821
  Voluntary Alternative Dispute Resolution Act, Title 6, §7721
APPLICATION TO NONSTOCK CORPORATIONS, **114**
APPRAISAL RIGHTS, **262**
ASSIGNMENT. LIMITED LIABILITY COMPANIES, INFRA

ATTACHMENT
  Corporations subject to attachment and garnishment, Title 10, §3502
  Domestic attachment, Title 10, §3501
  Foreign attachment against foreign corporations, Title 10, §3507
  Stock, attachment of, **324**
ATTORNEY GENERAL
  Antitrust actions by, Title 6, §§2107, 2108
  Duties with regard to franchise tax, **517**

—B—

BENEFICIAL OWNERS. STATUTORY TRUSTS, INFRA
BONDHOLDERS AND DEBENTURE HOLDERS
  Voting and inspection rights of, **221**
BUSINESS COMBINATIONS
  Interested stockholders, business combinations with, **203**
  Merger and consolidation, infra
BUSINESS DISPUTES
  Mediation and arbitration proceedings, Title 10, §546
BYLAWS
  Generally, **109**
  Emergency bylaws, **110**
  Enforcement, **111**
  Interpretation, **111**

—C—

CAMPAIGN CONTRIBUTIONS, LIMITATIONS, Title 15, §8012
CANCELLATION. TERMINATION, INFRA
CAPITAL
  Liability of corporation, effect of increase or decrease in capital on, **328**
  Reduction of, **244**
CERTIFICATE OF AGREEMENT. ALTERNATIVE DISPUTE RESOLUTION, SUPRA
CERTIFICATE OF FORMATION. LIMITED LIABILITY COMPANIES, INFRA
CERTIFICATE OF INCORPORATION
  Acknowledgment, **103**
  Amendment
    after receipt of payment for stock, **242**
    before receipt of payment for stock, **241**
    nonstock corporations, **242**
    restated certificate of incorporation, **245**
  Close corporations, infra
  Contents, **102**
  Definition, **104**
  Enforcement, **111**
  Evidence of, **105**
  Execution, **103**
  Exempt corporations, renewal of certificate of incorporation, **313**
  Extension of, **312**
  Filing and recording, infra
  Interpretation, **111**

II—Corp. DELAWARE Index 8-15-11

───────── All References Are to Statute Section (§) Numbers ─────────

CERTIFICATE OF INCORPORATION (continued):
Nonstock corporations, amendment of certificate, 242
Payment for stock
 amendment of certificate after, 242
 amendment of certificate before, 241
Renewal
 generally, 312
 exempt corporations, 313
 status of corporation after, 314
Restated certificate of incorporation, 245
Restoration of, 312
Revival of, 312
Status of corporation after renewal, 314
CERTIFICATE OF TRUST. STATUTORY TRUSTS, SUPRA
CHOICE OF LAW, Title 6, §2708
CLAIMANTS. DISSOLUTION, INFRA
CLOSE CORPORATIONS
 Application of law, 341
 Certificate of incorporation
  contents, 342
  termination by amendment to, 346
 Contents of certificate of incorporation, 342
 Conversion to, 344
 Definition, 342
 Directors, agreements restricting discretion of, 350
 Dissolution by stockholders, 355
 Formation, 343
 Involuntary termination, 348
 Issuance or transfer of stock
  invalid transfer, corporate option, 349
  restrictions, 347
 Management by stockholders, 351
 Option of corporation pursuant to invalid issue or transfer, 349
 Other laws, effect of subchapter on, 356
 Partnership, operating close corporation as, 354
 Restrictions on issue or transfer of stock, 347
 Status, limitations on, 345
 Stockholders
  dissolution of corporation by, 355
  management by, 351
 Termination
  involuntary, 348
  voluntary termination by amendment of certificate of incorporation, 346
COMPENSATION
 Payment, infra
 Specialist for alternative dispute resolution, Title 6, §7713
CONSIDERATION. STOCKS AND STOCKHOLDERS, INFRA
CONSOLIDATION. MERGER AND CONSOLIDATION, INFRA
CONSTITUTIONAL PROVISIONS
 Charter, no amendment or renewal before acceptance of constitutional provisions, Const Art IX, §2
 Existing corporate rights protected, Const Art IX, §4
 Foreign corporations; appointment of agent for service of process, Const Art IX, §5
 General laws, corporations organized under, Const Art IX, §1
 Issuance of stock for cash, labor or property only, Const Art IX, §3
 Municipal corporations, Const Art VIII, §8
 Non-residents, shares not taxed, Const Art IX, §6

CONTRACTS
 Choice of law, Title 6, §2708
CONTRIBUTIONS
 Campaign contributions, limitations, Title 15, §8012
 Limited liability companies, infra
 Statutory trusts, contributions by beneficial owners, Title 12, §3802
CONVERSION
 Close corporation, conversion to, 344
 Domestic corporation to other entities, 266
 Other entities to domestic corporation, 265
 Professional service corporation, conversion into business corporation, 615
CORRECTIONS. ALTERATIONS AND CORRECTIONS, SUPRA
COSTS AND FEES
 Alternative dispute resolution, filing fees, Title 6, §7706
 Insolvent corporation, compensation, costs and expenses of receiver or trustee, 298
 foreign, Title 12, §3862
 Limited liability companies, infra
 Secretary of state, fees charged by, Title 29, §2315
 Statutory trusts, Title 12, §3813
 Taxation, infra
COURT ACTIONS
 Alternative dispute resolution, supra
 Attachment, supra
 Bond of officer, Title 10, §8114
 Compelling appearance of defendant
  absence of personal service, Title 10, §365
  nonresident defendant, Title 10, §366
 Defective organization no defense, 329
 Derivative actions, infra
 Directors and officers
  actions for reimbursement of corporate debt paid, 326
 Directors, officers and stockholders
  liability of corporation, actions against to enforce, 325
 Insolvency, infra
 Liability of corporation, actions against directors and officers to enforce, 325
 Mediation proceedings, Title 10, §§347, 546
 New stock certificate or uncertificated shares, judicial proceedings to compel issuance, 167
 Nonresident defendant, compelling appearance of, Title 10, §366
 Order of court, failure of corporation to obey, 322
 Personal jurisdiction by acts of nonresidents, Title 10, §3104
 Personal service, compelling appearance of defendant without, Title 10, §365
 Proof of incorporation or corporate existence, Title 10, §3915
 Quo warranto proceedings, 323
 Reimbursement for corporate debt paid, actions by directors and officers, 326
 Statutory trusts, Title 12, §3804
 Technology disputes, Title 10, §346
 Usury, pleading by corporation, 330
 Writ of mandamus, failure of corporation to obey, 323
COURT OF CHANCERY RULES
 Derivative actions by shareholders, Rule 23.1
 Process, Rule 4
CUMULATIVE VOTING, 214

DELAWARE Index — Corp.—III

All References Are to Statute Section (§) Numbers

CUSTODIANS AND RECEIVERS
 Appointment of, **226**
 Dissolution, appointment of receivers for, **279**
 Insolvency, infra

—D—

DEEDS
 Foreign corporations, Title 25, §305
DEFINITIONS
 Alternative dispute resolution, Title 6, §7702
 Certificate of incorporation, **104**
 Close corporation, **342**
 Escheats, Title 12, §1198
 Foreign corporations, **371**
 Limited liability companies, Title 6, §18-101
 Professional service corporations, **603**
 Statutory trusts, Title 12, §3801
DERIVATIVE ACTIONS
 Allegation of stock ownership, **327**
 Limited liability companies, infra
 Prosecution by officer or employee, Title 10, §9525
 Shareholders, Rule 23.1
 Statutory trusts, Title 12, §3816
DIRECTORS AND OFFICERS
 Action without meeting, **141**
 Capital, reduction of by resolution of directors, **244**
 Classes of directors, **141**
 Close corporations, agreements restricting discretion of directors, **350**
 Committees, **141**
 Contested election, **225**
 Court actions, supra
 Cumulative voting for, **214**
 Dividends, infra
 Elections and voting
  contested election, **225**
  court, powers of in election of directors, **227**
 Employees and agents
  indemnification, **145**
  loans, **143**
 Indemnification, **145**
 Interested directors, **144**
 Judicial powers in election, **227**
 Loans to employees and officers, **143**
 Number of directors, **141**
 Officers
  generally, **142**
  indemnification, **145**
  loans, **143**
  prosecution of derivative action by, Title 10, §9525
 Organization meeting, **108**
 Powers, **141**
 Prosecution of derivative actions by officer, Title 10, §9525
 Qualifications, **141**
 Quorum
  generally, **141**
  interested directors, **144**
 Records of corporation, reliance of directors on, **141**
 Redemption of stock, liability of directors for, **173**
 Removal, **141**
 Retirement of stock by resolution of directors, **243**
 Terms of directors, **141**
 Vacancies, **223**
 Vote
  submitting matter for, **146**

DIRECTORS, OFFICERS AND STOCKHOLDERS
 Actions by against corporation for corporate debt paid, **326**
DISSOLUTION
 Claimants
  notice of dissolution; filing of claims, **280**
  payment and distribution to, **281**
 Continuation of corporation after dissolution, **278**
 Courts
  decree of court, dissolution by, **285**
  jurisdiction of, **284**
 Decree of court, dissolution by, **285**
 Franchise taxes, payment of before dissolution, merger, transfer or conversion, **277**
 Issuance of shares, dissolution before, **274**
 Joint venture corporation having two stockholders, **273**
 Jurisdiction of the court, **283**
 Limited liability companies, infra
 Nonstock corporation, **276**
 Procedure
  generally, **275**
  nonstock corporation, **276**
 Revocation
  forfeiture of charter, revocation of, **284**
  voluntary dissolution, revocation of, **311**
 Stocks and stockholders, infra
 Trustees or receivers; appointment, powers and duties, **279**
 Winding up, infra
DISTRIBUTIONS. LIMITED LIABILITY COMPANIES, INFRA
DIVIDENDS
 Generally, **170**
 Declaration and payment, **173**
 Liability of directors
  records of corporation, reliance on, **173**
  unlawful dividends, liability for, **174**
 Reliance on records in declaring, liability of directors, **173**
 Special purpose reserves, **171**
 Unlawful dividends, liability of directors for, **174**
DOMESTICATION
 Generally, **388**
 Limited liability companies, infra
 Temporary transfer of domicile into state, **389**
 Transfer, domestication or continuance of domestic corporations, **390**
DURATION, STATUTORY TRUSTS, TITLE 12, §3808

—E—

ELECTIONS AND VOTING
 Bondholders and debenture holders, **221**
 Directors and officers, supra
 Inspectors of elections, **231**
 Limited liability companies, infra
 Nonstock corporations, **215**
 Quorum and required vote, **216**
 Stocks and stockholders, infra
ELECTRONIC TRANSMISSION, **232**
EMPLOYEES AND AGENTS
 Directors and officers, supra
 Insolvent corporations, employee's lien for wages, **300**

ESCHEATS
Claims for property, Title 12, §1206
Definitions, Title 12, §1198
Deposit and disbursement of funds, Title 12, §1205
Limitations period not a bar, Title 12, §1202
Other property escheated, Title 12, §1197
Payment or delivery of abandoned property
  generally, Title 12, §1201
  effect of, Title 12, §1203
Private escheats prohibited, Title 12, §1210
Reports by holders of abandoned property, Title 12, §1199
Rules and regulations, Title 12, §1208
Sale of abandoned property, Title 12, §1204
EXCHANGE OF ASSETS. SALE, LEASE OR EXCHANGE OF ASSETS, INFRA
EXECUTION
Certificate of incorporation, **103**

—F—

FEES. COSTS AND FEES, SUPRA
FIDUCIARIES
Foreign corporations as, **380**
Voting rights, **217**
FILING AND RECORDING
Generally, **103**
Certificate of agreement. Alternative dispute resolution, supra
Certificate of incorporation, effect of filing, **106**
Certificate of trust, statutory trusts, Title 12, §3812
Limited liability companies, infra
FOREIGN STATUTORY TRUSTS
Amendments to application, Title 12, §3855
Doing business without registration, Title 12, §3857
Doing business without having qualified, Title 12, §3858
Execution, Title 12, §3859
Fees, Title 12, §3862
Law governing, Title 12, §3851
Name, Title 12, §3854
Registered agent, Title 12, §3854
Registered office, Title 12, §3854
Registration, Title 12, §3852
  cancellation, Title 12, §3856
  issuance, Title 12, §3853
Service of process
  registered foreign statutory trusts, Title 12, §3860
  unregistered foreign statutory trusts, Title 12, §3861
FOREIGN CORPORATIONS
Annual report
  generally, **374**
  failure to file, **375**
Attachment against, Title 10, §3507
Banking powers denied, **379**
Definition, **371**
Domestic corporations, merger with, **252, 256**
Exceptions to requirements, **373**
Failure to file annual report, **375**
Fiduciaries, foreign corporations as, **380**
Instruments need not be filed with recorder of deeds, **385**

FOREIGN CORPORATIONS (continued):
Merger or consolidation
  domestic corporation, merger or consolidation with, **252, 256**
  procedure, **372**
Name, change of, **372**
Noncompliance with subsection, penalties for, **378**
Procedure for merger or consolidation, **372**
Purpose, change of, **372**
Qualification to do business in state, **371**
Registered agent, change of, **377**
Service of process on
  generally, **376**, Rule 4
  agent for service of process, Const Art IX, §5
  nonqualifying foreign corporations, service on, **382**
Title to property, Title 25, §305
Unqualified foreign corporations
  actions by and against, **383**
  injunctions against, **384**
  service of process on, **382**
Withdrawal, **381**
FRANCHISE TAX
Generally, **501**
Annual franchise tax report
  generally, **502**
  investigation of, 502
Annual report by secretary of state, 515
Attorney general, duties, 517
Charter void for failure to pay tax, 510
Collection and disposition of tax, 504
Correction of mistake in repealing charter for unpaid taxes, 514
Dissolution, payment of tax before, **281**
Injunction against transacting business, 508
Investigation of annual franchise report, 504
Notice
  additional tax due, 504
  repeal of charter for unpaid taxes, 512
Penalty for acting where charter repealed for unpaid taxes, 513
Penalty interest for unpaid tax, 504
Preferred debt of unpaid taxes in case of insolvency, 507
Proclamation, filing and publication, 512
Rates and computation of, 503
Receiver or trustee appointed for failure to pay taxes, 509
Refund, fund for payment of, 506
Relief for corporations with assets in unfriendly nations, 518
Retaliatory taxation, 516
Review and refund, 505
Unpaid taxes
  charter void, 510
  correction of mistake in repealing charter, 514
  penalty for acting under repealed charter, 513
  preferred debt in case of insolvency, 507
  receiver or trustee appointed, 509
  repeal of charter by governor
    generally, 511
    mistakes; correction of repeal, 514
    notice of repeal, 512
    penalty for acting under repealed charter, 513

—I—

IMMUNITY
Alternative dispute resolution, immunity of specialist, Title 6, §7717
INCORPORATION
Certificate of incorporation, supra
Close corporation, formation of, **343**
Defective organization no defense to claim, **329**
Dissolution by incorporators, **274**
Formation of corporation, **101**
Incorporators
    generally, **101**
    dissolution before issuance of stock, **274**
    organization meeting, **108**
    powers, **107**
Organization meeting of incorporators or directors, **108**
Powers of incorporators, **107**
Proof of incorporation or corporate existence, Title 10, §3915
Purposes of corporation, **101**
INCORPORATORS. INCORPORATION, SUPRA
INDEMNIFICATION
Directors and officers, supra
Limited liability companies, Title 6, §18-108
Statutory trusts, Title 12, §3817
INSOLVENCY
Abatement of action against receiver or trustee, **299**
Appointment of trustee, **291**
Claims, adjudication of and appeals, **296**
Compensation, costs and expenses of receiver or trustee, **298**
Creditors
    notices given by receiver or trustee, **293**
    proofs of claims, **295**
Discontinuance of liquidation, **301**
Employee's lien for wages, **300**, Title 10, §4935
Filing
    lists of assets and debts by receivers and trustees, **294**
    order of appointment of receiver or trustee, **292**
Notice to stockholders and creditors by receivers and trustees, **293**
Perishable or deteriorating property, sale of, **297**
Powers of trustee, **291**
Proceeding under federal Bankruptcy Code, **303**
Proofs of claims by creditors, **295**
Proceeding under federal Bankruptcy Code, **303**
Receivers and trustees
    abatement of action against, **299**
    appointment and powers, **291**
    assets and debts, filing of lists, **294**
    compensation, costs and expenses, **298**
    notices to stockholders and creditors, **293**
    order of appointment, filing of, **292**
    substitution as party, **299**
    title of property in, **292**
Substitution of receivers and trustees as plaintiff, **299**
Title of property in receivers and trustees, **292**
INSPECTION. RECORDS AND REPORTS, INFRA
INSPECTORS OF ELECTIONS, 231
INTERESTED DIRECTORS, 144

INTERESTED TRANSACTIONS
Limited liability companies, members and managers, Title 6, §18-107

—J—

JURISDICTION
Dissolution, **283**
Personal jurisdiction by acts of nonresidents, Title 10, §3104
Supreme Court, Const Art IV, §11

—L—

LEASE. SALE, LEASE OR EXCHANGE OF ASSETS, INFRA
LIABILITIES
Dividends, supra
Limited liability companies, infra
Prior statutes, liabilities under, **393**
Redemption, infra
Sale, lease, or exchange of assets, effect on liabilities of corporation, **328**
Statutory trusts, liability of beneficial owners and trustees, Title 12, §3803
LIENS
Insolvent corporation, employees' lien against, **300**, Title 10, §4935
LIMITATIONS
Campaign contributions, Title 15, §8012
Limited liability companies, infra
Stock transfers, **202**
LIMITED LIABILITY COMPANIES
Access of members to records, Title 6, §18-305
Admission
    managers, Title 6, §18-401
    members, Title 6, §18-301
Agreement, interpretation and enforcement of, Title 6, §18-111
Amendment
    application for registration of foreign limited liability company, Title 6, §18-905
    certificate of correction, Title 6, §18-211
    certificate of formation, infra this group
Application for registration of foreign limited liability company
    generally, Title 6, §18-901
    amendment, Title 6, §18-905
Application of law, Title 6, §18-1101
Assignment
    generally, Title 6, §18-702
    assignee, right to become member, Title 6, §18-704
    member's limited liability company interest, Title 6, §18-703
Bankruptcy, events of, Title 6, §18-304
Breach of limited liability company agreement, remedies for
    managers, Title 6, §18-405
    members, Title 6, §18-306
Cancellation
    certificate of formation, infra this group
    registration of foreign limited liability company, cancellation of, Title 6, §18-906
Certificate of correction, Title 6, §18-211

VI—Corp.　　　　　　　　　　DELAWARE Index　　　　　　　　　　10-1-07

——————————— All References Are to Statute Section (§) Numbers ———————————

LIMITED LIABILITY COMPANIES (continued):
Certificate of formation
　generally, Title 6, §18-201
　amendment
　　generally, Title 6, §18-202
　　certificate of correction, Title 6, §18-211
　　judicial order, amendment by, Title 6, §18-205
　　restated certificate, Title 6, §18-208
　cancellation
　　generally, Title 6, §18-203
　　failure to pay taxes, cancellation for, Title 6, §18-1108
　　judicial order, cancellation by, Title 6, §18-205
　certificate of correction, Title 6, §18-211
　execution
　　generally, Title 6, §18-204
　　judicial order, execution by, Title 6, §18-205
　filing
　　generally, Title 6, §18-206
　　notice of formation, filing of certificate as, Title 6, §18-207
　judicial order, execution, amendment or cancellation by, Title 6, §18-205
　notice of formation, filing of certificate as, Title 6, §18-207
　restated certificate, Title 6, §18-208
Classes and voting
　managers, Title 6, §18-404
　members, Title 6, §18-302
Complaint for derivative action, Title 6, §18-1003
Contested matters relating to managers, Title 6, §18-110
Contractual appraisal rights pursuant to merger or consolidation, Title 6, §18-210
Contributions
　form of, Title 6, §18-501
　liability for contribution, Title 6, §18-502
　managers, contributions by, Title 6, §18-403
Conversion
　approval, Title 6, §18-216
　certain entities, Title 6, §18-214
Costs and fees
　generally, Title 6, §18-1005
　derivative action, expenses for, Title 6, §18-1004
Deceased or incompetent member, powers of estate, Title 6, §18-705
Definitions, Title 6, §18-101
Delegation of rights and powers by managers, Title 6, §18-407
Derivative actions
　complaint, Title 6, §18-1003
　expenses, Title 6, §18-1004
　proper plaintiff, Title 6, §18-1002
　right to bring action, Title 6, §18-1001
Dissolution
　generally, Title 6, §18-801
　distribution of assets upon winding up, Title 6, §18-804
　judicial dissolution, Title 6, §18-802
　revocation, Title 6, §18-806
　winding up
　　generally, Title 6, §18-803
　　distribution of assets, Title 6, §18-804
Distribution of assets upon winding up, Title 6, §18-804

LIMITED LIABILITY COMPANIES (continued):
Distributions
　allocation of, Title 6, §18-504
　in kind distributions, Title 6, §18-605
　interim distributions, Title 6, §18-601
　limitations on, Title 6, §18-607
　resignation, distribution upon, Title 6, §18-604
　right to, Title 6, §18-606
Doing business, activities not constituting, Title 6, §18-912
Domestic corporation, merger or consolidation with limited liability company, Title 6, §18-209
Domestication of non-U.S. entities, Title 6, §18-212
Elections. Classes and voting, supra this group
Equity applicable where case not covered, Title 6, §18-1104
Execution. Certificate of formation, supra this group
Expenses for derivative action, Title 6, §18-1004
Failure of foreign limited liability company to register, Title 6, §18-907
Fees. Costs and fees, supra this group
Filing. Certificate of formation, supra
Foreign limited liability companies
　activities not constituting doing business, Title 6, §18-912
　amendment to application for registration, Title 6, §18-905
　application for registration, Title 6, §18-901
　cancellation of registration, Title 6, §18-906
　execution of documents, Title 6, §18-909
　failure to register, Title 6, §18-907
　issuance of registration, Title 6, §18-903
　law governing, Title 6, §18-901
　name, Title 6, §18-904
　process and service of process
　　registered foreign companies, Title 6, §18-910
　　unregistered foreign companies, Title 6, §18-911
　registered office and registered agent, Title 6, §18-904
　registration
　　amendment to application for registration, Title 6, §18-905
　　application for
　　　generally, Title 6, §18-902
　　　amendment to application, Title 6, §18-905
　　cancellation of, Title 6, §18-906
　　failure to register, Title 6, §18-907
　　issuance of, Title 6, §18-903
　　unqualified foreign limited liability companies enjoined from doing business, Title 6, §18-908
　　unregistered foreign companies, service on, Title 6, §18-911
Form of contribution, Title 6, §18-501
In kind distributions, Title 6, §18-605
Indemnification, Title 6, §18-108
Interest in company, nature of, Title 6, §18-701
Interested transactions of member or manager, Title 6, §18-107
Interim distributions, Title 6, §18-601
Issuance of registration for foreign limited liability companies, Title 6, §18-903
Judicial dissolution, Title 6, §18-802
Judicial order, execution, amendment or cancellation of certificate of formation by, Title 6, §18-205

All References Are to Statute Section (§) Numbers

LIMITED LIABILITY COMPANIES (continued):
Law governing foreign limited liability companies, Title 6, §18-901
Liabilities
  contributions, liability for, Title 6, §18-502
  third parties, liability of members to, Title 6, §18-303
Limitations on distributions, Title 6, §18-607
Liquidation trustees, reports and information, reliance on, Title 6, §18-406
Managers
  admission of, Title 6, §18-401
  breach of limited liability company agreement, remedies for, Title 6, §18-405
  classes and voting, Title 6, §18-404
  contested matters, Title 6, §18-110
  contributions by, Title 6, §18-403
  delegation of rights and powers to manage, Title 6, §18-407
  indemnification, Title 6, §18-108
  interested transactions, Title 6, §18-107
  management of company, Title 6, §18-402
  reports and information, reliance on, Title 6, §18-406
  resignation, infra this group
  service of process on, Title 6, §18-109
Members
  admission of, Title 6, §18-301
  assignee, right to become member, Title 6, §18-704
  bankruptcy, events of, Title 6, §18-304
  breach of limited liability company agreement, remedies for, Title 6, §18-306
  classes and voting, Title 6, §18-302
  derivative action, right to bring, Title 6, §18-1001
  indemnification, Title 6, §18-108
  interested transactions, Title 6, §18-107
  liability to third parties, Title 6, §18-303
  records, access to and confidentiality of, Title 6, §18-305
  reports and information, reliance on, Title 6, §18-406
  resignation, infra this group
Merger and consolidation
  generally, Title 6, §18-209
  contractual appraisal rights, Title 6, §18-210
  domestic corporation, merger or consolidation with, **264**
Name
  generally, Title 6, §18-102
  foreign limited liability companies, Title 6, §18-904
  reservation of name, Title 6, §18-103
Notice of formation, filing of certificate of formation as, Title 6, §18-207
Powers and purposes, Title 6, §18-106
Process and service of process
  domestic limited liability companies, service of process on, Title 6, §18-105
  foreign limited liability companies, supra
  managers and liquidating trustees, service of process on, Title 6, §18-109
Profits and losses, allocation of, Title 6, §18-503
Proper plaintiff to derivative action, Title 6, §18-1002
Receivers, Title 6, §18-805

LIMITED LIABILITY COMPANIES (continued):
Records and reports
  access of members to and confidentiality of, Title 6, §18-305
  reliance on, Title 6, §18-406
Registered foreign limited liability companies, service on, Title 6, §18-910
Registered office and registered agent
  generally, Title 6, §18-104
  foreign limited liability companies, Title 6, §18-904
Registration. Foreign limited liability companies, supra this group
Reliance on reports and information by member, manager, or liquidation trustee, Title 6, §18-406
Reservation of name, Title 6, §18-103
Reservation of power, Title 6, §18-1106
Resignation
  distribution upon, Title 6, §18-604
  manager, Title 6, §18-602
  member, Title 6, §18-602
Restated certificate of formation, Title 6, §18-208
Revival of company canceled for failure to pay taxes, Title 6, §18-1109
Right to distributions, Title 6, §18-606
Series of members or managers or limited liability company interests, Title 6, §18-215
Severability of Act, Title 6, §18-1103
Short title, Title 6, §18-1102
Taxation
  generally, Title 6, §18-1107
  cancellation of certificate of formation for failure to pay taxes, Title 6, §18-1108
  revival of company canceled for failure to pay taxes, Title 6, §18-1109
Third parties, liability of members to, Title 6, §18-303
Transfer or domestication of limited liability companies, Title 6, §18-213
Trustees, Title 6, §18-805
Unqualified foreign limited liability companies enjoined from doing business, Title 6, §18-908
Unregistered foreign limited liability companies, service on, Title 6, §18-911
Usury, not available as defense, Title 6, §18-505
Voting. Classes and voting, supra this group
Winding up. Dissolution, supra this group

LIQUIDATION
Dissolution, supra
Insolvency, supra

LOANS
Employees and officers of corporation, loans to, **143**

—M—

MANAGERS. LIMITED LIABILITY COMPANIES, SUPRA
MEDIATION PROCEEDINGS
For business disputes, Title 10, §§347, 546
MEETINGS. STOCKS AND STOCKHOLDERS, INFRA
MEMBERS. LIMITED LIABILITY COMPANIES, SUPRA

MERGER AND CONSOLIDATION
Appraisal rights, **262**
Domestic corporations
generally, **251, 263**
foreign corporations, merger or consolidation with, **252, 256**
joint-stock association, merger or consolidation with, **254**
Effect of merger or consolidation
pending actions, effect of merger on, **261**
powers or corporation surviving or resulting from merger or consolidation, **260**
status, rights, liabilities of constituent and surviving or resulting corporations, **259**
Foreign corporations, merger or consolidation with domestic corporations, **252, 256**
Joint-stock association, merger or consolidation of domestic corporation with, **254**
Liability of corporation, effect on, **328**
Limited liability companies, supra
Nonstock corporations, infra
Parent corporation and subsidiary, **253**
Parent entity and subsidiary corporation, **267**
Professional service corporations, **618**
Statutory trusts, Title 12, §3815
MORTGAGE. SALE, LEASE OR EXCHANGE OF ASSETS, INFRA
MUNICIPAL CORPORATIONS, Const Art VIII, §8

—N—

NAME
Foreign corporations, change of name, **372**
Limited liability companies, supra
Professional service corporation, **617**
Statutory trusts, Title 12, §3814
foreign, Title 12, §3854
"Trust" as part of, **395**
NONSTOCK CORPORATIONS
Application of chapter to, **114**
Amendment of certificate of incorporation, **242**
Dissolution, **276**
Elections and voting, **215**
Merger and consolidation
generally, **255**
domestic stock corporations, merger or consolidation with, **257**
foreign corporations, merger or consolidation with nonstock corporations, **256**
stock corporations, **258**
NOTICE AND PUBLICATION
Alternative dispute resolution, Title 6, §7710
Certificate of formation. Limited liability companies, supra
Dissolution, **280**
Insolvent corporations, notice to stockholders and creditors, **293**
Secretary of state, publication of chapter by, **396**
Stocks and stockholders, infra
Unauthorized publication of chapter, penalty, **397**
NUMBER
Directors, **141**

—O—

OFFICERS. DIRECTORS AND OFFICERS, SUPRA
ORGANIZATION MEETING, **108**

—P—

PAYMENT
Consideration for issuance of stock. Stocks and stockholders, infra
Dissolution, payment to claimants and stockholders, **281**
Escheats, supra
Insolvent corporation, compensation, costs and expenses of receiver or trustee, **298**
PENALTY
Repealed charter, penalty for acting under, **513**
Unauthorized publication of chapter, penalty, **397**
PLEDGE. SALE, LEASE OR EXCHANGE OF ASSETS, INFRA
POWERS. PURPOSES AND POWERS, INFRA
PRIOR STATUTES, RIGHTS, LIABILITIES AND DUTIES UNDER, **393**
PROCEEDING UNDER FEDERAL BANKRUPTCY CODE, **303**
PROCESS AND SERVICE OF PROCESS
Generally, **321**, Title 10, §3111, Rule 4
Limited liability companies, supra
Non-resident directors, trustees or members, Title 10, §3114
Personal service, compelling appearance of defendant without, Title 10, §365
PROFESSIONAL SERVICE CORPORATIONS
Annual report, **618**
Application of General Corporation Law, **618**
Authority to organize, **605**
Capital stock, issuance of, **610**
Consolidation or merger, **618**
Construction of chapter, **619**
Conversion into business corporation, **615**
Death or disqualification of stockholder, time for transfer of shares, **616**
Definitions, **603**
Disqualification of officer, shareholder, agent or employee, **611**
Duration, **614**
Estate of shareholders, holding of stock by, **610**
Exemptions, **604**
Law governing, **605**
Legislative intent, **601**
License required for officers, employees and agents, **607**
Name, **617**
Number of directors and officers, **606**
Other businesses prohibited, **609**
Price for shares, **613**
Relationship unaffected by chapter, **608**
Sale or transfer of shares, **612**
Short title, **602**
Stocks and stockholders
death or disqualification of stockholder, time for transfer of shares, **616**
disqualification of stockholder, **611**
estate of stockholders, holding of stock by, **610**
issuance of capital stock, **610**
price for stock, **613**
sale or transfer of stock, **612**
voting trust agreements prohibited, **610**
Voting trust agreements prohibited, **610**

PROPERTY
Escheats, supra
Insolvent corporations, sale of perishable or deteriorating property, **297**

PROXIES
Access to proxy solicitation materials, **112**
Proxy expense reimbursement, **113**

PUBLICATION, SERVICE BY, Rule 4

PURPOSES AND POWERS
Alternative dispute resolution, purpose of, Act, Title 6, §7701
Banking power of corporation denied, **126**
Confer academic or honorary degrees, power of corporation to, **125**
Corporation
  general powers, **121**
  banking power denied, **126**
  confer academic or honorary degrees, **125**
  foreign corporation, change of purpose, **372**
  private foundations, **127**
  purpose of formation, **101**
  securities of other entities, powers respecting, **123**
  specific powers, **122**
  ultra vires, **124**
Foreign corporation, change of purpose, **372**
Incorporators, powers, **107**
Limited liability companies, Title 6, §18-106
Private foundations, powers and duties, **127**
Securities of other entities, powers of corporation respecting, **123**
Specific powers of corporation, **122**
Trustee, insolvent corporations, **291**
Ultra vires, **124**

— Q —

QUALIFICATIONS
Foreign corporation, qualification to do business in state, **371**
Specialist in alternative dispute resolution, Title 6, §7713

QUO WARRANTO, 323

QUORUM
Stockholders, **212**

— R —

RECEIVERS. CUSTODIANS AND RECEIVERS, SUPRA

RECORDS AND REPORTS
Abandoned property, reports by holders, Title 12, §1199
Form of records, **224**
Inspection of books and records
  generally, **220**
  bondholders and debenture holders, **221**
Limited liability companies, supra
Reliance on by directors, **141**
Statutory trusts, Title 12, §3819

REDEMPTION
Liability of directors
  records of corporation, no liability when relied on, **173**
  unlawful redemption, **174**
Unlawful redemption, liability of directors for, **174**

REGISTERED OFFICE AND REGISTERED AGENT
Change of office or agent
  registered agent, change by, **134**
  resolution of corporation, change by, **133**
Limited liability companies, supra
Principal office or place of business, **131**
Resident agent, **132**
Resignation of registered agent
  appointment of successor coupled with, **135**
  without appointment of successor, **136**
Statutory business trusts, Title 12, §3854
Successor to registered agent
  appointed by resigning agent, **135**
  resignation without appointment, **136**

REMOVAL
Directors, **141**

RENEWAL
Certificate of incorporation, supra

REPEAL. CHARTER, FRANCHISE TAX, SUPRA

REPORTS. RECORDS AND REPORTS, SUPRA

RESERVATION OF POWER
Limited Liability Company Act, Title 6, §18-1106

RESERVATION TO AMEND OR APPEAL, 394

RESIGNATION. REGISTERED OFFICE AND REGISTERED AGENT, SUPRA

RESTATED CERTIFICATE OF INCORPORATION, 245

RETIREMENT OF STOCK, 243

REVOCATION
Alternative dispute resolution, Title 6, §7707
Dissolution, supra
  limited liability company, supra
Limited liability company revived after cancellation for failure to pay taxes, Title 6, §18-1109
Preincorporation subscriptions, **165**

RULES. COURT OF CHANCERY RULES, SUPRA

— S —

SALE, LEASE OR EXCHANGE OF ASSETS
Generally, **271**
Abandoned property, sale of, Title 12, §1204
Liability of corporation, effect on, **328**
Mortgage or pledge of assets, **272**

SECRETARY OF STATE
Disposition of moneys received, Title 29, §2311
Fees, Title 29, §2315

SERVICE OF PROCESS. PROCESS AND SERVICE OF PROCESS, SUPRA

SEVERABILITY
Limited Liability Company Act, Title 6, §18-1103

SHARES AND SHAREHOLDERS. STOCKS AND STOCKHOLDERS, INFRA

SHORT TITLE
General Corporation Law, **398**
Limited Liability Company Act, Title 6, §18-1102
Professional Service Corporation Act, **602**
Statutory Trust Act, Title 12, §3826
Voluntary Alternative Dispute Resolution Act, Title 6, §7701

X—Corp.   DELAWARE Index   5-1-09

─────────── **All References Are to Statute Section (§) Numbers** ───────────

SPECIALIST. ALTERNATIVE DISPUTE RESOLUTION, SUPRA
STATUTE OF LIMITATIONS
    Alternative dispute resolution, tolling of statute, Title 6, §7720
STATUTORY TRUSTS
    Activities not constituting doing business, Title 12, §3863
    Amendment of certificate of trust, Title 12, §3810
    Application of law, Title 12, §§3809, 3825
    Beneficial owners
       liability, Title 12, §3803
       rights, Title 12, §3805
    Cancellation of certificate of trust, Title 12, §3810
    Certificate of trust
       generally, Title 12, §3810
       amendment, Title 12, §3810
       cancellation, Title 12, §3810
       execution, Title 12, §3811
       filing, Title 12, §3812
       restatement, Title 12, §3810
    Contributions by beneficial owners, Title 12, §3802
    Conversion to statutory trust, Title 12, §3820
       approval of, Title 12, §3821
    Definitions, Title 12, §3801
    Derivative actions, Title 12, §3816
    Domestication of non-U.S. entities, Title 12, §3822
    Duration, Title 12, §3808
    Execution of certificate of trust, Title 12, §3811
    Filing of certificate of trust, Title 12, §3812
    Foreign, infra
    Indemnification, Title 12, §3817
    Legal proceedings, Title 12, §3804
    Liability of beneficial owners and trustees, Title 12, §3803
    Management, Title 12, §3806
    Merger and consolidation, Title 12, §3815
    Name, regulation of, Title 12, §3814
    Records, access to and confidentiality of, Title 12, §3819
    Reservation of power to amend or appeal, Title 12, §3824
    Restatement of certificate of trust, Title 12, §3810
    Rights of beneficial owners and trustees, Title 12, §3805
    Short title, Title 12, §3826
    Transfer on continuance of domestic statutory trusts, Title 12, §3823
    Treasury interests, Title 12, §3818
    Trustee in state, Title 12, §3807
STOCK SUBSCRIPTIONS. STOCKS AND STOCKHOLDERS, INFRA
STOCK TRANSFERS. STOCKS AND STOCKHOLDERS, INFRA
STOCKS AND STOCKHOLDERS
    Adjourned meetings, 222
    Appraisal rights, 262
    Attachment of stock, 324
    Capital, determination of amount, 154
    Certificates for stock
       lost, stolen or destroyed certificates, infra this group
       uncertificated shares, 158
    Classes and series of stock, 151

STOCKS AND STOCKHOLDERS (continued):
    Close corporations, supra
    Consent in lieu of meeting, 228
    Consideration for issuance of stock
       generally, 153
       capital, determination of amount, 154
       cash, labor or property only, Const Art IX, §3
       failure to pay for stock; remedies, 164
       partly paid stock, infra this group
    Court actions, supra
    Cumulative voting, 214
    Derivative actions
       allegation of stock ownership, 327
       by stockholders, Rule 23.1
    Directors
       provisional director, appointment of, 353
    Dissolution
       liability of stockholders of dissolved corporations, 282
       payment to stockholders, 281
    Elections and voting
       generally, 212
       cumulative voting, 214
       fiduciaries, pledgors and joint owners of stock, 217
       list of stockholders entitled to vote, 219
       voting trusts, 218
    Exception to requirement of notice, 230
    Failure to pay for stock; remedies, 164
    Fiduciaries, pledgors and joint owners of stock, voting rights, 217
    Formalities required for stock subscriptions, 166
    Fractions of shares, 155
    Insolvency, notices given by receiver or trustee, 293
    Interested stockholders, business combinations with, 203
    Issuance of stock
       generally, 152
       consideration for issuance of stock, supra this group
       dissolution before, 274
       fractions of shares, 155
       lost, stolen or destroyed certificates, infra this group
       partly paid shares, infra this group
    Judicial proceedings to compel issuance of new certificate or uncertificated shares, 168
    Liability of stockholders where stock not paid in full, 162
    List of stockholders entitled to vote, 219
    Lost, stolen or destroyed certificates
       issuance of new certificate or uncertificated shares, 167
       judicial proceedings to compel issuance of new certificate or uncertificated shares, 168
    Meetings
       generally, 211
       adjourned meetings, 222
       consent in lieu of meeting, 228
       electronic transmission, 232
       exception to requirement of notice, 230
       notice
          exception to requirement of notice, 230
          waiver of notice, 229
       notice of meeting, 222, 232

― All References Are to Statute Section (§) Numbers ―

STOCKS AND STOCKHOLDERS (continued):
  Meetings (continued):
    record date, **213**
    waiver of notice, **229**
  Notice
    meetings, infra this group
    stockholders sharing an address, **233**
  Options, **157**
  Partly paid shares
    generally, **156**
    liability of stockholder for, **162**
    payment for stock not paid in full, **163**
  Payment for stock not paid in full, **163**
  Professional service corporations, supra
  Quorum, **212**
  Redemption of stock, **160**
  Retirement of stock, **243**
  Revocation of preincorporation subscriptions, **165**
  Situs of ownership of stock, **169**
  Subscriptions for stock
    formalities required, **166**
    revocability of preincorporation subscriptions, **165**
  Taxation of stock, **159**
  Transfer of stock, **159**
    generally, **201**
    restrictions on, **202**
  Uncertificated shares, **158**
  Unissued stock, **161**
  Voting trusts, **218**
  Waiver of notice of meeting, **229**
SUCCESSORS. REGISTERED OFFICE AND REGISTERED AGENT, SUPRA
SUITS, DERIVATIVE, Rule 23.1
SUPREME COURT
  Jurisdiction, Const Art IV, §11

—T—

TAXATION
  Generally, **391**
  Franchise tax, supra
  Limited liability companies, supra
  Non-residents, Const Art IX, §6
  Stockholders, taxation of stock, Const Art IX, §6
TERMINATION
  Alternative dispute resolution, conclusion of proceeding, Title 6, §7715

TERMINATION (continued):
  Certificate of formation, cancellation of. Limited liability companies, supra
  Certificate of trust, cancellation of, Title 12, §3810
  Close corporations, supra
  Dissolution, supra
  Withdrawal, foreign corporations, **381**
TERMS, DIRECTORS, **141**
TRUSTEES
  Dissolution, **279**
  Statutory trusts, supra
  Transfer of corporate securities by, Title 12, §3532

—U—

ULTRA VIRES, **124**
UNCLAIMED PROPERTY. ESCHEATS, SUPRA
UNISSUED STOCK, **161**
UNPAID TAXES. FRANCHISE TAX, SUPRA
UNQUALIFIED FOREIGN CORPORATIONS. FOREIGN CORPORATIONS, SUPRA
USURY
  Generally, Title 6, §2306
  Limited liability companies, usury not available as defense, Title 6, §18-505
  Pleading by corporation, **330**

—V—

VACANCIES, DIRECTORS, **223**
VOLUNTARY ALTERNATIVE DISPUTE RESOLUTION ACT. ALTERNATIVE DISPUTE RESOLUTION, SUPRA
VOTING TRUSTS, **218**

—W—

WINDING UP
  Continuing of corporation after dissolution for purposes of winding up, **278**
  Dissolution, supra
  Limited liability companies, supra
WITHDRAWAL
  Foreign corporations, **381**

[The page following this is Corp.—51]

CONSTITUTION OF THE STATE OF DELAWARE
(As Amended)
ARTICLE IV. JUDICIARY

11 JURISDICTION OF SUPREME COURT.—The Supreme Court shall have jurisdiction as follows:

(1)(a) To receive appeals from the Superior Court in civil causes and to determine finally all matters of appeal in the interlocutory or final judgments and other proceedings of said Superior Court in civil causes: Provided that on appeal from a verdict of a jury, the findings of the jury, if supported by evidence, shall be conclusive.

(1)(b) To receive appeals from the Superior Court in criminal causes, upon application of the accused in all cases in which the sentence shall be death, imprisonment exceeding one month, or fine exceeding One Hundred Dollars, and in such other cases as shall be provided by law; and to determine finally all matters of appeal on the judgments and proceedings of said Superior Court in criminal causes: Provided, however, that appeals from the Superior Court in cases of prosecution under Section 8 of Article V of this Constitution shall be governed by the provisions of that Section.

(1)(c) Notwithstanding any provisions of this Section to the contrary, to receive appeals from the Superior Court in criminal causes, upon application by the State in all causes in which the Superior Court, or any inferior court an appeal from which lies to the Superior Court, has granted an accused any of the following: a new trial or judgment of acquittal after a verdict, modification of a verdict, arrest of judgment, relief in any post-conviction proceeding or in any action collaterally attacking a criminal judgment, or a new punishment hearing in a capital case after the court has imposed a sentence of death, or any order or judgment declaring any act of the General Assembly, or any portion of any such act, to be unconstitutional under either the Constitution of the United States or the State of Delaware, inoperative or unenforceable, except that no appeal shall lie where otherwise prohibited by the double jeopardy clause of the Constitution of the United States or of this State. Notwithstanding anything in this Article to the contrary, the General Assembly may by statute implement the jurisdiction herein conferred.

(2) Wherever in this Constitution reference is made to a writ of error or a proceeding in error to the Superior Court, such reference shall be construed as referring to the appeal provided for in Section (1)(a) and Section (1)(b) of this Article.

(3) To receive appeals from the Superior Court in cases of prosecution under Section 8 of Article V of this Constitution and to determine finally all matters of appeal in such cases.

(4) To receive appeals from the Court of Chancery and to determine finally all matters of appeal in the interlocutory or final decrees and other proceedings in chancery.

(5) To issue writs of prohibition, quo warranto, certiorari and mandamus to the Superior Court, and the Court of Chancery, or any of the Judges of the said courts and also to any inferior court or courts established or to be established by law and to any of the Judges thereof and to issue all orders, rules and processes proper to give effect to the same. The General Assembly shall have power to provide by law in what manner the jurisdiction and power hereby conferred may be exercised in vacation and whether by one or more Justices of the Supreme Court.

(6) To issue such temporary writs or orders in causes pending on appeal, or on writ of error, as may be necessary to protect the rights of parties and any Justice of the Supreme Court may exercise this power when the court is not in session.

(7) To exercise such other jurisdiction by way of appeal, writ of error or of certiorari as the General Assembly may from time to time confer upon it.

(8) To hear and determine questions of law certified to it by other Delaware courts, the Supreme Court of the United States, a Court of Appeals of the United States, a United States District Court, the United States Securities and Exchange Commission, or the highest appellate court of any other state, where it appears to the Supreme Court that there are important and urgent reasons for an immediate determination of such questions by it. The Supreme Court may, by rules, define generally the conditions under which questions may be certified to it and prescribe methods of certification. (Last amended by Ch. 37, L. '07, eff. 5-3-07.)

ARTICLE VIII. REVENUE AND TAXATION

8 [NO LOAN OF CREDIT BY MUNICIPAL TO PRIVATE CORPORATION; MUNICIPAL CORPORATION CANNOT BE STOCKHOLDER IN PRIVATE CORPORATION].—No county, city, town or other municipality shall lend its credit or appropriate money to, or assume the debt of, or become a shareholder or joint owner in or with any private corporation or any person or company whatever.

.1 Constitution paramount law.—In construing a constitution, conflicting statutory or by-law provisions cannot prevail over constitutional provisions. *Gaskill v Gladys Belle Oil Co, 146 A 337 (1929); Brooks v State, 79 A 790 (1911).*

.2 Private authority.—Parking authority is not *private* corporation so city may lend its credit. *Wilmington Parking Authority v Ranken, 105 A2d 614 (1954).*

ARTICLE IX. CORPORATIONS

1 [CORPORATIONS MUST BE ORGANIZED UNDER GENERAL LAWS].— No corporation shall hereafter be created, amended, renewed or revised by special act, but only by or under general law, nor shall any existing corporate charter be amended, renewed or revived by special act, but only by or under general law; but the foregoing provisions shall not apply to municipal corporations, banks or corporations for charitable, penal, reformatory, or educational purposes, sustained in whole or in part by the State. The General Assembly shall, by general law, provide for the revocation or forfeiture of the charters of all corporations for the abuse, misuse, or non-user of their corporate powers, privileges or franchises. Any proceeding for such revocation or forfeiture, shall be taken by the Attorney General, as may be provided by law. No general incorporation law, nor any special act of incorporation, shall be enacted without the concurrence of two-thirds of all the members elected to each House of the General Assembly.

.1 General corporation laws and special acts.—At common law and prior to enactment of general corporation laws, corporations were created by special act of the legislature. In Delaware, organization under the General Corporation Law is equivalent to creation by special act of the legislature. *State v Penn-Beaver Oil Co, 143 A 257 (1926).*

Adoption of Constitution of 1897 did not abrogate any corporate charters granted by special act of legislature. Whether or not the corporate organization had been completed prior to the adoption of the Constitution does not affect validity of charter. *State ex rel White v Hancock, 45 A 851 (1899).*

Provisions of pre-existing general corporation laws do not apply to corporations incorporated under General Corporation Law. *In re Powell, 58 A 831 (1904).* (The general corporation law before court in that case was the act of 1883.)

.2 Power of revocation.—Power of revocation in an earlier constitution (Const. 1831, Art. 2, §17) construed: *Wilmington City Ry Co v Wilmington & Brandywine Springs Co, 46 A 12 (1900),* and *Mayor v Addioks, 47 A 366 (1900).* See, also, *State v Levy Court, 43 A 522 (1899).*

Under Constitution of 1831 legislature can revoke corporate charters. *Wilmington & Reading R Co v Downward, 14 A 720, 38 A 133 (1888).*

Nothing in this section is intended to deprive state of its vested right, under Constitution of 1831, to revoke in whole or in part the corporate charters of concerns incorporated thereunder. *Wilmington City Ry Co v People's Ry Co, 47 A 245 (Ch Ct 1990).*

.3 Applicability to preexisting corporations.—The constitution and GCL are applicable to corporations organized prior to their adoption and enactment even though such corporations never filed acceptance of provisions of constitution and never had their charters amended under GCL. *Bay State Gas Co v State ex rel Content, 56 A 1114, 1120 (1904).*

.4 Same—acceptance of constitution.—Pre-existing corporation that filed its acceptance of constitutional provisions is bound by general corporation law and subject to the penalties provided therein. *State v Front & Union St Ry Co, 104 A 154 (1918).*

.5 Status of private corporations.—Whether corporation is public is not determined by nature or purpose of its business, but by character of its origin and policy of the law. Whatever may be its intended purpose, whether for private profit or public good, offices of corporation are public in sense that state is enabled, by proper remedies, to compel obedience to its laws. *Brooks v State, 79 A 791 (1911).*

Laws governing formation of boulevard corporations do not violate this section. *Clendaniel v Conrad, 83 A 1036 (1912).*

.6 Amendment of charter.—Legislature cannot amend GCL, so as to enlarge scope of subjects which corporations theretofore existing may alter by amending their charters, and thus to effect changes which, when the corporations were created, they could not effectuate against the will of an objecting stockholder. *Keller v Wilson & Co, Inc, 190 A 115 (1936),* reversing *180 A 584,* cited and followed in *Consolidated Film Industries, Inc v Johnson, 192 A 603 (1937); Johnson v Consolidated Film Industries, Inc, 194 A 844 (1937)* (held that corporation formed after amendment of the GCL was not authorized to make charter amendments which would have retroactive effect), aff'd, *Consolidated Film Industries, Inc v Johnson, 197 A 489 (1938).*

2 [PRE-EXISTING CORPORATIONS MUST ACCEPT PROVISIONS OF CONSTITUTION BEFORE AMENDMENT OR RENEWAL OF CHARTER].—No corporation in existence at the adoption of this Constitution shall have its charter amended or renewed without first filing, under the corporate seal of said corporation, and duly attested, in the office of the Secretary of State, an acceptance of the provisions of this Constitution.

3 [STOCK MUST BE ISSUED FOR CASH, LABOR, OR PROPERTY].— (Repealed by Ch. 281, L. '04, eff. 8-1-04.)

Decisions Under Repealed Law

.1 Services.—Corporation may issue stock for services rendered and money spent in promotion of corporation. *Shore v Union Drug Co, 156 A 204 (1931); Yasik v Wachtel, 17 A2d 309 (1941); Diamond State Brewery, Inc v De La Rigaudiere, 17 A2d 313 (1941).*

.2 Future services.—Agreement to render future services as director and secretary, or lending of one's name to the corporation, is not sufficient consideration for issuance of full-paid, nonassessable stock. *Bowen v Imperial Theatres Inc, 115 A 918 (1922); Blair v F H Smith Co, 156 A 207 (1931).* See also, *Du Pont v Deputy, 22 FSupp 589 (D Del 1938),* record remanded, with instructions to amend judgment by increasing amount of recovery allowed, *103 F2d 257 (3d Cir 1939),* rev'd, *Deputy v Du Pont, 308 US 488 (1940).*

.3 Money or property for stock.—Giving check for stock does not satisfy this section, when check is not backed by sufficient funds. *Champion v Commissioner of Internal Revenue, 303 F2d 887 (5th Cir 1962).*

Stock not properly issued. *Baker v Banker's Mtge Co, 133 A 698 (1926).*

Stock properly issued under this section. *Henderson v Plymouth Oil Co, 131 A 165 (1925); Alexander v Phillips Petroleum Co, 130 F2d 593 (10th Cir 1942).* See, *Bodell v Gen Gas & Elec Corp, 139 A 442 (1926).*

Corporation can cancel stock given to promoter for property which he then failed to deliver to it. In the absence of actual fraud in the issuance of the stock, the judgment of the directors as to value is conclusive. *Diamond State Brewery, Inc v De Larigaudier, 17 A2d 313 (1941).* See also, *Yasik v Wachtel and Diamond State Brewery, Inc, 17 A2d 309 (1941).*

Unconditional license to use patent is property within the meaning of this section for which corporate stock ordinarily may be issued. *West v Sirian Lamp Co, 37 A2d 835 (1944), 42 A2d 883 (Ch Ct 1945), 44 A2d 658 (1945).*

Preincorporation services (promotional or underwriting) are good considerations for stock issuance. *Blish v Thompson Automatic Arms Corp, 64 A2d 581 (1948),* comment *63 Harvard L R 351 (Dec 1949).*

Release of valid unliquidated claim against corporation is adequate consideration for stock issuance; board's judgment as to amount thereof is conclusive. *Blish v Thompson Automatic Arms Corp, 64 A3d 581 (1948),* comment *63 Harv L R 351 (Dec 1949).*

Where stock is issued for property, in absence of actual fraud, judgment of director as to value of property received in exchange for stock is conclusive. *Alexander v Phillips Petroleum Co, 130 F2d 593 (10th Cir 1942).*

.4 Note.—Maker of note for stock who paid interest thereon did not thereby become stockholder, so as to be entitled to dividends before paying a judgment on the note. *Reason:* Having paid interest maker of note was in same position as if it had paid for stock when purchased and corporation could not retain both interest on note and dividends on stock. *A M Andrews Inv Corp v Translux Daylight Picture Screen Corp, 277 NY 620, 14 NE2d 191 (1938).*

Promissory note, secured only by issued stock, is not legal consideration for issuance of the stock. *Sohland v Baker, 141 A 277 (1927); Arndt v Abbott, 32 NE2d 342 (Ill App Ct 1941).*

.5 Consideration.—Where the consideration for which stock is issued meets test of the law, the stock will not be cancelled. *AINSCOW v Potter, 193 A 926 (1937).*

If values underlying old stock are at least equal to total of capital value of par value stock and declared value of the no par value stock issued in exchange or in substitution for old stock, legal requirements as to the quantity of consideration are complied with. *Topkis v Delaware Hardware Co, 2 A2d 114 (1938).*

Constitutional and statutory exactions as to quality of consideration for which corporation issues stock are not offended against if company, with assent of all stockholders, creates new shares and gives them in exchange for all its theretofore outstanding stock. *Topkis v Delaware Hardware Co, 2 A2d 114 (1938).*

In the absence of clear abuse of discretion by directors, amount of consideration received for no par common stock issue is usually of no moment, provided it meets constitutional requirements. *West v Sirian Lamp Co, 37 A2d 835 (1944), 42 A2d 883 (Ch Ct 1945), 44 A2d 658 (1945).*

Mere fact that corporation may have to expend money in the future to protect its interests in property rights acquired, and for which it has issued stock, does not necessarily make the consideration invalid. *West v Sirian Lamp Co, 37 A2d 835 (1944), 42 A2d 883 (Ch Ct 1945), 44 A2d 658 (1945).*

.6 Effect of issuance.—Issuance by corporation of certificate for its stock constitutes representation that person to whom certificate was issued is the holder of number of shares thereon indicated, upon truth of which bona fide purchaser for value can rely. *Delaware-New Jersey Ferry Co v Leeds, 186 A 913 (1936).* See *Diamond State Brewery, Inc v De Larigaudier, 17 A2d 313 (1941).*

4 [RESERVATION PROTECTIVE OF EXISTING CORPORATE RIGHTS].—The rights, privileges, immunities and estates of religious societies and corporate bodies, except as herein otherwise provided, shall remain as if the Constitution of this State had not been altered.

5 [FOREIGN CORPORATIONS, BEFORE DOING BUSINESS IN STATE, MUST APPOINT AGENT FOR SERVICE OF PROCESS].—No foreign corporation shall do any business in this State through or by branch offices, agents or representatives located in this State, without having an authorized agent or agents in the State upon whom legal process may be served.

.1 **Contract of sale by foreign corporation.**—Despite this section a contract of sale, by a foreign corporation not qualified under the laws of this state, through an agent located in the state, can be enforced against the purchaser who retains the benefits of the contract. *Model Heating Co v Magarity, 81 A 394 (1911).*

6 [SHARES OF NON-RESIDENTS SHALL NOT BE TAXED].—Shares of the capital stock of corporations created under the laws of this State, when owned by persons or corporations without this State, shall not be subject to taxation by any law now existing or hereafter to be made.

DELAWARE Secretary of State Certification

STATE OF DELAWARE
DEPARTMENT OF STATE

JEFFREY W. BULLOCK
SECRETARY OF STATE

I, JEFFREY W. BULLOCK, Secretary of State of the State of Delaware, **DO HEREBY CERTIFY** that the "General Corporation Law of the State of Delaware" may be published by Aspen Publishers under the authority granted me in accordance with the provisions of 8 *Del. C.* §396.

Dated this 4th day of April, in the Year of Our Lord Two-Thousand and Eleven.

Jeffrey W. Bullock

TOWNSEND BUILDING
401 FEDERAL STREET, SUITE 3
DOVER, DE 19901
(302) 739-4111
FAX: (302) 739-3811

CARVEL STATE OFFICE BUILDING
820 FRENCH STREET, FOURTH FLOOR
WILMINGTON, DE 19801
(302) 577-8767
FAX: (302) 577-2694

[The page following this is Corp.—101]

DELAWARE GENERAL CORPORATION LAW

(Delaware Code 1953 as amended)

(Extensive changes to the Delaware General Corporation Law were enacted by the 1973 and 1974 Legislatures, effective July 1, 1973 and July 11, 1974 respectively [Ch. 106, Laws of 1973 and Ch. 437, Laws of 1974].)

➺ Comments appearing herein relating to these amendments were prepared by the General Corporation Law Committee of the Delaware State Bar Association, and are used with its permission. ⇇

Editor's Note: Commentaries and synopses appearing at the end of some sections are taken from the legislation that amended those sections.

TITLE 8. CORPORATIONS

Chapter 1. General Corporation Law

SUBCHAPTER I. FORMATION

101 INCORPORATORS; HOW CORPORATION FORMED; PURPOSES.—
(a) Any person, partnership, association or corporation, singly or jointly with others, and without regard to [1]*such person's or entity's* residence, domicile or state of incorporation, may incorporate or organize a corporation under this chapter by filing with the Division of Corporations in the Department of State a certificate of incorporation which shall be executed, acknowledged and filed in accordance with §103 of this title.

(b) A corporation may be incorporated or organized under this chapter to conduct or promote any lawful business or purposes, except as may otherwise be provided by the Constitution or other law of this State.

(c) Corporations for constructing, maintaining and operating public utilities, whether in or outside of this State, may be organized under this chapter, but corporations for constructing, maintaining and operating public utilities within this State shall be subject to, in addition to this chapter, the special provisions and requirements of Title 26 applicable to such corporations. (Last amended by Ch. 339, L. '98, eff. 7-1-98.)

Ch. 339, L. '98, eff. 7-1-98, added matter in italic and deleted [1]"his or her or their".

Ch. 339, L. '98 Synopsis of Section 101

The amendments to these Sections eliminate masculine references in the statutes, and replace them with gender neutral references.

.1 **State law in federal courts.**—A state's statutes and decisions of its highest courts are binding on federal courts deciding questions of that state's law in diversity suits. *Erie R Co v Tompkins, 304 US 64 (1938).* So are decisions of a state's intermediate appellate courts, unless the federal court is convinced by other persuasive data that the state's highest court would decide otherwise. *West v Amer Tel & Tel Co, 311 US 223 (1940),* on remand, *121 F2d 142 (6th Cir),* cert denied, *314 US 672 (1941).*

.2 **Same—statutes of limitations.**—State statutes of limitations bind federal courts in diversity suits. *Guaranty Trust Co v York, 326 US 99 (1945).*

.3 **Same—uniform laws.**—State decisions construing uniform laws are authorities for federal courts to follow. If the federal court finds no decision in a particular state construing the section of the uniform law it is considering, it can use decisions of other states on the same section of the uniform law, *Burns Mortgage Co v Fried, 292 US 487 (1934).*

.4 **Service in diversity cases.**—Service in diversity case should be made as prescribed by federal rules of civil procedure, rather than by state law, so that service on defendant executor was properly made by leaving copies of summons and complaint with defendant's wife, as permitted by federal rules of civil procedure, rather than by "in hand" method prescribed by state law. *Hanna v Plumer, 380 US 460 (1965).*

.5 **Diversity jurisdiction.**—Derivative action cannot be brought in federal court of state on grounds of diversity of citizenship in state of which both suing stockholder and corporation are citizens. *Lavin v Lavin, 182 F2d 870 (2d Cir 1950).*

.6 **Promoters' contracts.**—Corporation can adopt contract made by promoters for its benefit, although such contract antedates corporation's existence. *Commissioners of Lewes v Breakwater Fisheries Co, 117 A 823 (Ch Ct 1922).*

Corporation is not bound by promoter's contract which it has not adopted. *Stringer v Electronics Supply Corp, 2 A2d 78 (Ch Ct 1938).*

.7 **Promoters' liabilities.**—Promoters must account to corporation for secret profit obtained at its expense and surrender for cancellation shares representing secret profit. *Birbeck v Am Toll Bridge Co of Cal, 2 A2d 158 (Ch Ct 1938).*

Corporation can maintain action against its promoters, who were also its financiers and managers, for accounting or to recover corporate property appropriated by them to their own use in breach of their fiduciary obligations as promoters. *Bovay v H*

M Byllesby & Co, 12 A2d 178 (Ch Ct 1940), demurrer to amended bill of complaint overruled *22 A2d 138 (Ch Ct 1941),* rev'd, *38 A2d 808 (1944).*
Court will approve derivative suit settlement that denies recovery from promoter for breach of fiduciary duty in underwriting transactions, when promoter bargained at arm's length with corporation and did not make any secret profits. *Gladstone v Bennett, 153 A2d 577 (Ch Ct 1959).*

.8 Internal affairs doctrine.—Delaware Supreme Court reaffirmed internal affairs doctrine, which holds that law of state of incorporation determines issues relating to corporation's internal affairs. Panama law governs issue of whether a Panamanian corporation's Delaware subsidiary may vote shares it holds in parent company under circumstances prohibited by Delaware law, but not Panamanian law. *McDermott Inc v Lewis, 531 A2d 206 (1987).*

102 CONTENTS OF CERTIFICATE OF INCORPORATION.—(a) The certificate of incorporation shall set forth:

(1) The name of the corporation, which (i) shall contain 1 of the words "association," "company," "corporation," "club," "foundation," "fund," "incorporated," "institute," "society," "union," "syndicate," or "limited," (or abbreviations thereof, with or without punctuation), or words (or abbreviations thereof, with or without punctuation) of like import of foreign countries or jurisdictions (provided they are written in roman characters or letters); provided, however, that the Division of Corporations in the Department of State may waive such requirement (unless it determines that such name is, or might otherwise appear to be, that of a natural person) if such corporation executes, acknowledges and files with the Secretary of State in accordance with §103 of this title a certificate stating that its total assets, as defined in subsection (i) of §503 of this title, are not less than $10,000,000, *or, in the sole discretion of the Division of Corporations in the Department of State, if the corporation is both a nonprofit nonstock corporation and an association of professionals,* (ii) shall be such as to distinguish it upon the records in the office of the Division of Corporations in the Department of State from the names that are reserved on such records and from the names on such records of each other corporation, partnership, limited partnership, limited liability company or statutory trust organized or registered as a domestic or foreign corporation, partnership, limited partnership, limited liability company or statutory trust under the laws of this State, except with the written consent of the person who has reserved such name or such other foreign corporation or domestic or foreign partnership, limited partnership, limited liability company or statutory trust, executed, acknowledged and filed with the Secretary of State in accordance with §103 of this title [1], *(iii) except as permitted by §395 of this title, shall not contain the word "trust," and (iv)* shall not contain the word "bank," or any variation thereof, except for the name of a bank reporting to and under the supervision of the State Bank Commissioner of this State or a subsidiary of a bank or savings association (as those terms are defined in the Federal Deposit Insurance Act, as amended, at 12 U.S.C. §1813), or a corporation regulated under the Bank Holding Company Act of 1956, as amended, 12 U.S.C. §1841 et seq.; or the Home Owners' Loan Act, as amended, 12 U.S.C. §1461 et seq.; provided, however, that this section shall not be construed to prevent the use of the word "bank," or any variation thereof, in a context clearly not purporting to refer to a banking business or otherwise likely to mislead the public about the nature of the business of the corporation or to lead to a pattern and practice of abuse that might cause harm to the interests of the public or the State as determined by the Division of Corporations in the Department of State;

(2) The address (which shall [2] *be stated in accordance with §131(c) of this title*) of the corporation's registered office in this State, and the name of its registered agent at such address;

(3) The nature of the business or purposes to be conducted or promoted. It shall be sufficient to state, either alone or with other businesses or purposes, that the purpose of the corporation is to engage in any lawful act or activity for which corporations may be organized under the General Corporation Law of Delaware, and by such statement all lawful acts and activities shall be within the purposes of the corporation, except for express limitations, if any;

(4) If the corporation is to be authorized to issue only 1 class of stock, the total number of shares of stock which the corporation shall have authority to issue and the par value of each of such shares, or a statement that all such shares are to be without par value. If the corporation is to be authorized to issue more than 1 class of stock, the certificate of incorporation shall set forth the total number of shares of all classes of stock which the corporation shall have authority to issue and the number of shares of each class and shall

specify each class the shares of which are to be without par value and each class the shares of which are to have par value and the par value of the shares of each such class. The certificate of incorporation shall also set forth a statement of the designations and the powers, preferences and rights, and the qualifications, limitations or restrictions thereof, which are permitted by §151 of this title in respect of any class or classes of stock or any series of any class of stock of the corporation and the fixing of which by the certificate of incorporation is desired, and an express grant of such authority as it may then be desired to grant to the board of directors to fix by resolution or resolutions any thereof that may be desired but which shall not be fixed by the certificate of incorporation. The foregoing provisions of this paragraph shall not apply to nonstock corporations. In the case of nonstock corporations, the fact that they are not authorized to issue capital stock shall be stated in the certificate of incorporation. The conditions of membership, or other criteria for identifying members, of nonstock corporations shall likewise be stated in the certificate of incorporation or the bylaws. Nonstock corporations shall have members, but failure to have members shall not affect otherwise valid corporate acts or work a forfeiture or dissolution of the corporation. Nonstock corporations may provide for classes or groups of members having relative rights, powers and duties, and may make provision for the future creation of additional classes or groups of members having such relative rights, powers and duties as may from time to time be established, including rights, powers and duties senior to existing classes and groups of members. Except as otherwise provided in this chapter, nonstock corporations may also provide that any member or class or group of members shall have full, limited, or no voting rights or powers, including that any member or class or group of members shall have the right to vote on a specified transaction even if that member or class or group of members does not have the right to vote for the election of the members of the governing body of the corporation. Voting by members of a nonstock corporation may be on a per capita, number, financial interest, class, group, or any other basis set forth. The provisions referred to in the 3 preceding sentences may be set forth in the certificate of incorporation or the bylaws. If neither the certificate of incorporation nor the bylaws of a nonstock corporation state the conditions of membership, or other criteria for identifying members, the members of the corporation shall be deemed to be those entitled to vote for the election of the members of the governing body pursuant to the certificate of incorporation or bylaws of such corporation or otherwise until thereafter otherwise provided by the certificate of incorporation or the bylaws;

(5) The name and mailing address of the incorporator or incorporators;

(6) If the powers of the incorporator or incorporators are to terminate upon the filing of the certificate of incorporation, the names and mailing addresses of the persons who are to serve as directors until the first annual meeting of stockholders or until their successors are elected and qualify.

(b) In addition to the matters required to be set forth in the certificate of incorporation by subsection (a) of this section, the certificate of incorporation may also contain any or all of the following matters:

(1) Any provision for the management of the business and for the conduct of the affairs of the corporation, and any provision creating, defining, limiting and regulating the powers of the corporation, the directors, and the stockholders, or any class of the stockholders, or the governing body, members, or any class or group of members of a nonstock corporation; if such provisions are not contrary to the laws of this State. Any provision which is required or permitted by any section of this chapter to be stated in the bylaws may instead be stated in the certificate of incorporation;

(2) The following provisions, in haec verba, viz:

(i), for a corporation other than a nonstock corporation,

"Whenever a compromise or arrangement is proposed between this corporation and its creditors or any class of them and/or between this corporation and its stockholders or any class of them, any court of equitable jurisdiction within the State of Delaware may, on the application in a summary way of this corporation or of any creditor or stockholder thereof or on the application of any receiver or receivers appointed for this corporation under §291 of Title 8 of the Delaware Code or on the application of trustees in dissolution or of any receiver or receivers appointed for this corporation under §279 of Title 8 of the Delaware Code order a meeting of the creditors or class of creditors, and/or of the stockholders or class of stockholders of this corporation, as the case may be, to be summoned in such manner as the said court directs. If a majority in number representing three fourths in value of the creditors or class of creditors, and/or of the stockholders or class of stockholders of this corporation, as the case may be, agree to any compromise or arrangement and to any reorganization of this corporation as consequence of such compromise or arrangement, the said compromise or arrangement and the said reorganization shall, if sanctioned by the court to which the said application has been made, be binding on all the creditors or class of creditors, and/or on all the stockholders or class of stockholders, of this corporation, as the case may be, and also on this corporation";

or (ii), for a nonstock corporation, viz:

"Whenever a compromise or arrangement is proposed between this corporation and its creditors or any class of them and/or between this corporation and its members or any class of them, any court of equitable jurisdiction within the State of Delaware may, on the application in a summary way of this corporation or of any creditor or member thereof or on the application of any receiver or receivers appointed for this corporation under §291 of Title 8 of the Delaware Code or on the application of trustees in dissolution or of any receiver or receivers appointed for this corporation under §279 of Title 8 of the Delaware Code order a meeting of the creditors or class of creditors, and/or of the members or class of members of this corporation, as the case may be, to be summoned in such manner as the said court directs. If a majority in number representing three fourths in value of the creditors or class of creditors, and/or of the members or class of members of this corporation, as the case may be, agree to any compromise or arrangement and to any reorganization of this corporation as consequence of such compromise or arrangement, the said compromise or arrangement and the said reorganization shall, if sanctioned by the court to which the said application has been made, be binding on all the creditors or class of creditors, and/or on all the members or class of members, of this corporation, as the case may be, and also on this corporation";

(3) Such provisions as may be desired granting to the holders of the stock of the corporation, or the holders of any class or series of a class thereof, the preemptive right to subscribe to any or all additional issues of stock of the corporation of any or all classes or series thereof, or to any securities of the corporation convertible into such stock. No stockholder shall have any preemptive right to subscribe to an additional issue of stock or to any security convertible into such stock unless, and except to the extent that, such right is expressly granted to such stockholder in the certificate of incorporation. All such rights in existence on July 3, 1967, shall remain in existence unaffected by this paragraph unless and until changed or terminated by appropriate action which expressly provides for the change or termination;

(4) Provisions requiring for any corporate action, the vote of a larger portion of the stock or of any class or series thereof, or of any other securities having voting power, or a larger number of the directors, than is required by this chapter;

(5) A provision limiting the duration of the corporation's existence to a specified date; otherwise, the corporation shall have perpetual existence;

(6) A provision imposing personal liability for the debts of the corporation on its stockholders to a specified extent and upon specified conditions; otherwise, the stockholders of a corporation shall not be personally liable for the payment of the corporation's debts except as they may be liable by reason of their own conduct or acts;

(7) A provision eliminating or limiting the personal liability of a director to the corporation or its stockholders for monetary damages for breach of fiduciary duty as a director, provided that such provision shall not eliminate or limit the liability of a director: (i) For any breach of the director's duty of loyalty to the corporation or its stockholders; (ii) for acts or omissions not in good faith or which involve intentional misconduct or a knowing violation of law; (iii) under §174 of this title; or (iv) for any transaction from which the director derived an improper personal benefit. No such provision shall eliminate or limit the liability of a director for any act or omission occurring prior to the date when such provision becomes effective. All references in this paragraph to a director shall also be deemed to refer to such other person or persons, if any, who, pursuant to a provision of the certificate of incorporation in accordance with §141(a) of this title, exercise or perform any of the powers or duties otherwise conferred or imposed upon the board of directors by this title.

(c) It shall not be necessary to set forth in the certificate of incorporation any of the powers conferred on corporations by this chapter.

(d) Except for provisions included pursuant to paragraphs (a)(1), (a)(2), (a)(5), (a)(6), (b)(2), (b)(5), (b)(7) of this section, and provisions included pursuant to paragraph (a)(4) of this section specifying the classes, number of shares, and par value of shares a corporation other than a nonstock corporation is authorized to issue, any provision of the certificate of incorporation may be made dependent upon facts ascertainable outside such instrument, provided that the manner in which such facts shall operate upon the provision is clearly and explicitly set forth therein. The term "facts," as used in this subsection, includes, but is not limited to, the occurrence of any event, including a determination or action by any person or body, including the corporation.

(e) The exclusive right to the use of a name that is available for use by a domestic or foreign corporation may be reserved by or on behalf of:

(1) Any person intending to incorporate or organize a corporation with that name under this chapter or contemplating such incorporation or organization;

(2) Any domestic corporation or any foreign corporation qualified to do business in the State of Delaware, in either case, intending to change its name or contemplating such a change;

(3) Any foreign corporation intending to qualify to do business in the State of Delaware and adopt that name or contemplating such qualification and adoption; and

(4) Any person intending to organize a foreign corporation and have it qualify to do business in the State of Delaware and adopt that name or contemplating such organization, qualification and adoption.

The reservation of a specified name may be made by filing with the Secretary of State an application, executed by the applicant, certifying that the reservation is made by or on behalf of a domestic corporation, foreign corporation or other person described in paragraphs (e)(1)-(4) of this section above, and specifying the name to be reserved and the name and address of the applicant. If the Secretary of State finds that the name is available for use by a domestic or foreign corporation, the Secretary shall reserve the name for the use of the applicant for a period of 120 days. The same applicant may renew for successive 120-day periods a reservation of a specified name by filing with the Secretary of State, prior to the expiration of such reservation (or renewal thereof), an application for renewal of such reservation, executed by the applicant, certifying that the reservation is renewed by or on behalf of a domestic corporation, foreign corporation or other person described in paragraphs (e)(1)-(4) of this section above and specifying the name reservation to be renewed and the name and address of the applicant. The right to the exclusive use of a reserved name may be transferred to any other person by filing in the office of the Secretary of State a notice of the transfer, executed by the applicant for whom the name was reserved, specifying the name reservation to be transferred and the name and address of the transferee. The reservation of a specified name may be cancelled by filing with the Secretary of State a notice of cancellation, executed by the applicant or transferee, specifying the name reservation to be cancelled and the name and address of the applicant or transferee. Unless the Secretary of State finds that any application, application for renewal, notice of transfer, or notice of cancellation filed with the Secretary of State as required by this subsection does not conform to law, upon receipt of all filing fees required by law the Secretary of State shall prepare and return to the person who filed such instrument a copy of the filed instrument with a notation thereon of the action taken by the Secretary of State. A fee as set forth in §391 of this title shall be paid at the time of the reservation of any name, at the time of the renewal of any such reservation and at the time of the filing of a notice of the transfer or cancellation of any such reservation. (Last amended by Ch. 96, L. '11, eff. 8-1-11.)

Ch. 96, L. '11, eff. 8-1-11, added matter in italic and deleted [1]"and (iii)" and [2]"include the street, number, city and county".

Ch. 96, L. '11 Synopsis of Section 102

This Section amends Section 102 to give the Division of Corporations the discretion to waive the requirement that a corporation's name contain certain words or abbreviations thereof (such as "incorporated"), if the corporation is both a nonprofit nonstock corporation and an association of professionals.

These sections amend Sections 102 and 395 to give the Director of the Division of Corporations and the State Bank Commissioner the discretion to waive certain requirements and restrictions that apply when a corporation has the word "trust" in its name, provided that the use of the word "trust" is clearly not purporting to refer to a trust business. Section 2 also includes in §102(a)(1) the restriction on the use of the word "trust" in a corporation's name so that all statutory name restrictions in Title 8 of the Code are referred to in that section. Sections 16, 17 and 18 also update the statutory reference to the Savings and Loan Holding Company Act, which was moved to section 10 of the Home Owners' Loan Act.

This Section amends Section 102 to clarify that, in a certificate of incorporation filed with the Secretary of State, the address of the registered office of the corporation in Delaware must be stated in accordance with Section 131(c).

Ch. 253, L. '10 Synopsis of Section 102

Section 1 amends §102(a)(4) of the DGCL to allow nonstock corporations to put the conditions of membership, or other criteria for identifying members, in their certificates of incorporation or in their bylaws. This Section further amends §102(a)(4) to clarify that nonstock corporations shall have members, but the failure to have members shall not affect otherwise valid corporate acts or work a forfeiture or dissolution of the corporation. This Section further amends §102(a)(4) to provide that, until provided otherwise in the corporation's certificate of incorporation or bylaws, the members of a nonstock corporation that fails to state the conditions of membership in its certificate of incorporation or bylaws shall be deemed to be those entitled to vote for the election of the members of the corporation's governing body under the corporation's certificate of incorporation or bylaws or otherwise. This Section further amends §102(a)(4) to clarify that nonstock corporations may provide for classes or groups of members; that nonstock corporations may provide for full, limited, or no voting rights and powers of members, including that members may be entitled to vote on certain transactions even if they are not entitled to vote for the election of members of the corporation's governing body; and that voting by members may be made on a per capita, number, financial interest, or any other basis. This Section further amends §102(a)(4) to provide that provisions regarding classes and voting rights of members may be set forth either in the corporation's certificate of incorporation or in its bylaws.

Section 2 amends §102(b)(1) of the DGCL to add language applying to nonstock corporations.

Sections 3 and 4 amend §102(b)(2) of the DGCL to provide language regarding compromises between the corporation and its creditors and/or between the corporation and its members appropriate for the certificate of incorporation of a nonstock corporation.

Sections 5, 6, 7, and 8 make technical changes to §102(b)(6), §102(b)(7), §102(d), and §109(a) of the DGCL consistent with the intent of the bill and with the translator provision in new §114(a).

Ch. 306, L. '06 Synopsis of Section 102

Section 1 amends §102(a)(1) to provide that the name of a Delaware corporation must be such as to distinguish it from the names (whether reserved or of record) of each other domestic or foreign corporation, partnership, limited partnership, limited liability company or statutory trust upon the records in the office of the Division of Corporations in the Department of State, except with the written consent of the person who has reserved such name or such other corporation, partnership, limited partnership, limited liability company or statutory trust.

Section 2 amends §102 to add new subsection (e), which clarifies who may reserve a name that is available for use by a domestic or foreign corporation and provides the procedures to be followed by the applicant and the Secretary of State to reserve such name.

Ch. 326, L. '04 Synopsis of Section 102(d)

New Section 102(d), which is consistent with changes previously made to Section 151, involving the terms of stock, and Subchapter IX, involving mergers and consolidations, confirms that a corporation's certificate of incorporation may, subject to certain exceptions, include provisions dependent on facts ascertainable outside the certificate of incorporation. The amendment is intended to negate any implication that the publicly filed nature of a certificate of incorporation precludes the inclusion of such provisions.

Ch. 329, L. '02 Synopsis of Section 102

The amendments set forth are made for the purpose of avoiding any implication that a trust formed under Chapter 38, Title 12 of the Delaware Code constitutes a " business trust" within the meaning of Title 11 of the United States Code. Such amendments are not intended to result in any substantive change in Delaware law. These amendments are made soley for the purpose of conforming the Delaware Code to the amendments set forth above.

Ch. 82, L. '01 Synopsis of Section 102

The Delaware Revised Uniform Partnership Act ("DRUPA") allows (and in some cases requires) partnerships to file various statements with the Secretary of State. Section 15-108 of DRUPA requires names of partnerships filing certificates to be distinguishable on the records of the Secretary of State from the names of other entities. The amendment to Section 102(a)(1) is the reciprocal of Section 15-108 of DRUPA.

Ch. 343, L. '00 Synopsis of Section 102

The amendment to Section 102(a)(1) adds the names of limited liability companies and business trusts to the names of business entities that may not, without consent, conflict with the name of a Delaware corporation.

Ch. 123, L. '99 Synopsis of Section 102

The amendment to Section 102(a)(1) provides that punctuation is optional in abbreviations of corporate names and that words (or abbreviations thereof) of foreign countries or jurisdictions, including, but not limited to, foreign countries or jurisdictions using the English language, designating corporate status are acceptable for purposes of Section 102(a)(1).

Ch. 339, L. '98 Synopsis of Section 102

The amendments to these Sections eliminate masculine references in the statutes, and replace them with gender neutral references.

Ch. 120, L. '97 Synopsis of Section 102

The amendment to Section 102(a)(1) codifies in the statute the established practice of the Secretary of State in regulating the use of "bank" in the name of a Delaware corporation.

Ch. 79, L. '95 Synopsis of Section 102

The amendments to Section 102(a)(1) permit the Division of Corporations to waive the requirement that the name of the corporation contain one of the listed terms that indicate the status of the entity (unless the Division determines that the name is or might otherwise appear to be that of a natural person) if the corporation files a certificate stating that its total assets are not less than 10 million dollars.

Ch. 61, L. '93 Synopsis of Section 102

The amendment to Section 102(b)(7) authorizes a corporation to include in its certificate of incorporation a provision limiting or eliminating the personal monetary liability of persons other than directors who exercise power of directors, pursuant to a provision in the certificate of incorporation authorized by Section 141(a), for certain breaches of fiduciary duty.

Commentary on Sections 102(a)(4), 170(a) and 256

In recent years various amendments to the General Corporation Law have been made to clarify that Delaware corporations can be set up as nonstock corporations for profit. Thus, in the 1974 amendment to Section 255(b) and (c), the words "nonprofit" were eliminated from the caption of the section, and in the 1987 amendment to Section 255(a) and (b), the words "nonprofit" were eliminated from subsection (a) and the words "whether or not organized for profit" were added. The Commentary to the 1987 amendment which accompanied the proposed amendment to Section 255 states: "In view of Section 257, there is no reason not to permit mergers of domestic nonstock corporations organized for profit." A similar amendment was not presented to Section 256. The 1987 amendment to Section 276 eliminated the word "nonprofit" at several places in the body of subsection (a). The Commentary to the 1987 amendment which accompanied the proposed amendment states that the purposes of these changes was "to make clear that Section 276 applies to all nonstock corporations." The proposed amendments will make the General Corporation Law more consistent in this regard.

.1 Classification of corporations.—"Corporations which are not organized for profit" are not synonymous with corporations for religious, literary, charitable, social or eleemosynary purposes; such classification does not necessarily exclude business, trading or commercial concerns. *Read v Tidewater Coal Exchange, 116 A 898 (Ch Ct 1922).*

.2 Certificate of incorporation as contract.—Certificate of incorporation is contract between state and corporation, between corporation and its stockholders, and between stockholders inter sese. *Morris v American Public Utilities Co, 122 A 696 (Ch Ct 1923).*

.3 Same—state's power to alter.—Buyers of stock in Delaware corporation become stockholders with actual or imputed knowledge that state's corporation law may be changed and corporate charter amended to conform to change, subject to limitation that stockholders' rights must be protected. *Weinberg v Baltimore Brick Co, 108 A2d 81 (Ch Ct 1954),* aff'd, *114 A2d 812 (1955).*

.4 Same—court's power to alter.—Court can order certificate of incorporation reformed to reflect stockholders' agreement regarding voting rights, when provision was omitted inadvertently, and its inclusion will not affect rights of third parties. *In re Farm Industries, Inc, 196 A2d 582 (Ch Ct 1963).*

.5 Same—court's power to cancel.—Court can cancel certificate of incorporation filed by Secretary of State in reliance on false representations therein that three persons had associated to form corporation. *State ex rel Southerland, Atty Gen v United States Realty Improvement Co, 132 A 138 (Ch Ct 1926).*

.6 Amended certificate of incorporation.—Amendment to articles of incorporation can raise percentage of stock required for shareholder approval to 80% in cases where directors do not favor merger even if, in cases where directors favor merger, only majority vote is required. *Seibert v Gulton Industries Inc, No. 5631 (Ch Ct 6-21-79).*

.7 Shareholders' agreement not included in certificate.—Shareholders' agreement that gave minority shareholder veto power over corporate business was enforceable even though agreement was not included in corporation's certificate of incorporation as required by Delaware statute, since agreement did not violate Delaware's public policy. *Zion v Kurtz, 50 NY2d 92 (1980).*

.8 Protection of name.—Court will enjoin use by corporation of name which causes confusion with name of another corporation. *Fox Fur Co v Fox Fur Co, 59 FSupp 701 (D Del 1945).*

Stockholder can sue derivatively to enjoin use of his corporation's name by competing corporation. *Taussig v Wellington Fund, Inc, 187 FSupp 179 (D Del 1960),* aff'd, *313 F2d 472 (3d Cir 1963).*

"American Plan Corporation" can enjoin use of same name by subsidiaries of another company engaged in closely related business, since (1) name is distinctive and so proof of secondary meaning is unnecessary, and (2) use of same name by other company will cause confusion among corporation's potential customers. *American Plan Corp v State Loan & Finance Corp, 365 F2d 635 (3d Cir 1966).*

Court will enjoin use of name "DuPont" for razor blades when original DuPont company was well-known as manufacturer of many kinds of consumer goods, including toiletries, even though it did not make razor blades. *El DuPont de Nemours & Co v DuPont Safety Razor Corp, 82 A2d 384 (Ch Ct 1951).*

.9 Use of family name.—Use of family name in corporate name by second user is permitted if second user makes clear to public it has no connection with first user. *Carl Springer, Inc v Carl Springer Supply Co, 104 A2d 637 (Ch Ct 1954).*

Individual has right to use his name in his business, even though his surname may have acquired secondary meaning, and this right includes right to transfer his business to corporation bearing his name. *Andrew Jergens Co v Woodbury, Inc, 273 F 952 (D Del 1921).*

.10 Prohibited name.—Corporation cannot be incorporated if its corporate name includes word "Trust," unless such corporation is authorized to engage in business as state bank, savings bank, safe deposit company, building and loan association, or trust company with trust powers and so is required to report to and be under supervision of State Bank Commissioner. *OAG to State Bank Comm'r (4-29-37).*

.11 Protection of assumed name.—Corporation generally known by name of "Philadelphia Trust instead of its full actual corporate name of "Philadelphia Trust, Safe Deposit & Insurance Co.," can enjoin use of name "Philadelphia Trust Co." by another corporation. *Philadelphia Trust, Safe Deposit & Ins Co v Philadelphia Trust Co, 123 F 534 (CC Del 1903).*

.12 Duty of Secretary of State.—Secretary of State fulfilled statutory duty in determining that name he was registering, Transamerica Airlines, Inc. was distinguishable from name already registered, Trans-Americas Airlines, Inc. on records of Division of Corporation. Secretary has no duty to determine whether similar corporate names already registered carry with them property rights on which other parties may not infringe. *Trans-Americas Airlines, Inc v Kenton, 491 A2d 1139 (1985).*

.13 Registered office distinguished from principal place of business.—Legal residence and domicile of Delaware corporation is in Delaware and it must maintain principal office or place of business in Delaware, and name of county, city, town or place within county in which principal office or place of business is located must be stated in certificate of incorporation; however, its principal place of business in sense of where corporation's actual business is conducted or transacted may be elsewhere. *Colorado Interstate Gas Co v Federal Power Commission, 142 F2d 943 (10th Cir 1944).*

.14 Purposes in general.—Corporation cannot be created and used as device for purpose of hindering and delaying creditors. *Shapiro v Wilgus,* 287 US 348 (1932).

Delaware corporation has valid existence, even though it is incorporated solely for purpose of acquiring, owning and operating building in Illinois. *Spivey v Spivey Bldg Corp,* 10 NE2d 385 (Ill 1937).

.15 Preferred stock.—If stockholders want to confer special rights upon given class of stock they must state that in certificate of incorporation, since statute designates certificate as place for recordation of stock preferences. *Gaskill v Gladys Belle Oil Co,* 146 A 337 (Ch Ct 1929).

Stock preferences so obscure as to be irreconcilably repugnant cannot be accorded recognition. *Holland v Nat Automotive Fibres, Inc,* 194 A 124 (Ch Ct 1937), reaff'd, 2 A2d 124 (Ch Ct 1938).

Neither general language in a certificate of incorporation concerning the powers of directors nor extrinsic evidence regarding the shareholders' intentions on that matter was sufficient under a state statute to give a corporation's board the power to create preferred stock voting rights. *Laster v Waggoner,* 581 A2d 1127 (Ch Ct 1989).

.16 Class voting.—Charter provision giving holders of common stock Series B right to elect minority directors means that majority in number of issued and outstanding Series B common stock must vote before Class B common directors can be elected, but successful nominees for Class B directors need receive only majority of shares voted. *Investment Associates, Inc v Standard Power & Light Corp,* 48 A2d 501 (Ch Ct 1946).

When certificate of incorporation provides that Class B stockholders elect majority of board of directors and Class A stockholders the remaining, Class B is entitled to elect only bare majority. *Young v Janas,* 103 A2d 299 (Ch Ct 1954).

.17 Shareholders' preemptive rights.—Amendment to certificate of incorporation can eliminate preemptive rights. *Gottlieb v Heyden Chemical Corp,* 83 A2d 595 (Ch Ct 1951), reversed on other grounds, 90 A2d 660 (1952), adhered to 92 A2d 594 (1952).

Stockholder can bring action against alleged fraudulent plan to increase number of shares to be issued for inadequate consideration, even though he has preemptive rights to subscribe to these shares, since if consideration is in fact inadequate, he must purchase additional shares to prevent dilution of his stock interest. *Bennett v Breuil Petroleum Corp,* 99 A2d 236 (Ch Ct 1953).

All that is required by rule on preemptive rights is that stockholder be accorded opportunity to subscribe for shares of new issue of stock; whether he takes such opportunity or not is immaterial. *Greenbaum v Keil,* 62 A2d 441 (Ch Ct 1948).

Court will enjoin sale of authorized but unissued stock when it is shown that primary reason for sale was to deprive majority stockholders of voting control. *Canada Southern Oils, Ltd v Manabi Exploration Co,* 96 A2d 810 (Ch Ct 1953).

When original corporation's stock was issued at intervals over considerable period of time, and block of shares went to promoter for services in selling this stock, no preemptive rights attached to that block of stock. *Yasik v Wachtel,* 17 A2d 309 (Ch Ct 1944). See, also, *Diamond State Brewery, Inc v De La Rigaudiere,* 17 A2d 313 (Ch Ct 1941).

Directors may, if they act in good faith and for best interests of corporation, offer no par value stock to one class of stockholders at lower price than to other classes of stockholder, since directors have large discretion in marketing no par value stock. *Bodell v General G & E Corp,* 140 A 264 (Ch Ct 1927).

.18 Certificate may contain bylaw provisions.—Provision in certificate of incorporation allowing majority of board to fix number of directors is not illegal. Under GCL §102(b)(1), any provision permitted to be stated in the bylaws may be stated in the certificate of incorporation. *The Henley Group, Inc v Santa Fe Southern Pacific Corp,* No. 9569 (Ch Ct 3-11-88).

.19 Provisions limiting director's liability.—After determining that a board of directors had breached their duty of disclosure by making only a "partial disclosure" in a Schedule 14D-9 that was disseminated by a corporation in connection with a tender offer, the Delaware Supreme Court found that the directors were nonetheless protected from liability under GCL §102(b)(7) and the amendment to their certificate of incorporation implementing the statutory provision. *Zirn v VLI Corp,* 681 A2d 1050 (1996)

Plaintiff stockholder sufficiently alleged that during a merger a controlling shareholder breached its fiduciary duties to the other shareholders, and that the merger process and price were an unfair, self-interested transaction. The court found that the complaint was sufficient and could not be dismissed under the exculpatory provisions in the certificate of incorporation. *O'Reilly v Transworld Healthcare, Inc,* C.A. No. 16507 (Ch Ct 8-20-99).

Where a corporation's former directors negotiated and approved a merger that uniquely benefitted one director and the son of another to the exclusion of the rest of the corporation's stockholders, plaintiffs stated claims for breach of the duties of loyalty and care, and therefore, an exculpatory clause in the corporation's charter barring damages for the breach of duty of care would not bar recovery for the breach of duty of loyalty. *Chaffin v GNI Group, Inc,* C.A. No. 16211-NC (Ch Ct 9-3-99).

Plaintiff's claim that a board failed to exercise due care in obtaining the best value for the shareholders in a sale of the corporation by allowing one bidder to acquire voting control which circumvented the board's ability to conduct a meaningful auction process was dismissed because (1) the corporation's articles of incorporation contained an exculpatory clause for directors' breaches of due care not motivated by bad faith or intentional misconduct, and (2) no breach of duty of loyalty was pleaded. *In re Frederick's of Hollywood, Inc Shareholders Litigation,* C.A. No. 15944 (Ch Ct 1-31-00).

A corporation's charter provision that bars director liability except in cases of bad faith and the breach of the duty of loyalty, will bar a claim of the breach of the duty of care where plaintiffs have, in addition, alleged a breach of the duty of loyalty and good

§102

faith, but cannot support such a claim, thus leaving only the duty of care claim. *Lu v Malpiede, 780 A2d 1075 (2001).*

.20 Shareholders' meeting to settle lawsuit.—GCL § 102(b)(2) may not be used as a procedural device to (i) enable a shareholder to propose a settlement of lawsuit, without any accompanying reorganization of the corporation's capital structure, and (ii) through the Court, force the corporation to present the proposed compromise directly to the shareholders, without obtaining the approval of (or even consulting with) the board of directors. *Siegman v Palomar Medical Technologies, Inc, No. 15894 (Ch Ct 2-2-98).*

.21 Exculpatory charter provisions.—A director's actions on a special committee in negotiating a merger between a parent corporation and its subsidiary, even if negligent or careless, are exculpated where the corporation's charter includes a provision that limits the personal liability of directors for all breaches of fiduciary duty, other than for breach of the duty of loyalty, failure to act in good faith, or intentional misconduct. *Gesoff v IIC Industries, Inc, 2006 Del. Ch. LEXIS (Ch Ct 2006).*

.22 Exculpation; demand excusal.—Even where demand is excused because sufficient particularized facts have been pleaded to show that a corporation's directors acted in a grossly negligent manner, a claim must be dismissed against the directors, but not the corporation's officers, where its certificate of incorporation provides for exculpation from liability to the full extent of Delaware law and it is not alleged that the directors acted in bad faith. *McPadden v Sidhu, 964 A2d 1262 (Ch Ct 2008).*

.23 Merger; fiduciary duties.—A decision of a board of directors to sell the corporation in a merger pursuant to a contractually mandated formula will not be subject to a breach of fiduciary claim for breach of the duty of loyalty where a majority of the board is independent and has no contractual flexibility to negotiate a higher price, and any duty of care claims based on the decision to sell will be dismissed where the corporation exculpates directors for negligence. *Hokanson v Petty, 2008 Del. Ch. LEXIS 182 (Ch Ct 2008).*

.24 Duty of loyalty.—Directors who use an adequate process and have a substantial basis to believe that a merger is fair do not breach their duty of loyalty by approving the merger and a termination fee that is a fraction of the merger consideration merely because the shareholders ultimately do not approve the merger. *In re Lear Corporation Shareholder Litigation, 967 A2d 640 (Ch Ct 2008).*

Directors' duty of loyalty to obtain the best price in a merger (*Revlon duty*) does not commence when a corporation is put "in play" but when the board embarks on a change of control transaction, so that directors do not breach their duty of loyalty where there is no evidence from which to infer that the directors knowingly ignored their responsibilities or utterly failed to attempt to obtain the best sale price. *Lyondell Chemical Corp v Ryan, 970 A2d 235 (2009).*

A plaintiff's allegations of directors' and officers' breach of the duty of loyalty must be dismissed where the allegations are insufficiently specific and conclusory, as great deference must be given to a board that is shown to be independent. Additionally, absent successful duty of loyalty claims, the *Revlon* standard will not be applied to breach of fiduciary claims in a change of control transaction involving merger consideration that is a mix of cash and stock where a corporation's certificate of incorporation contains an exculpatory clause that protects the directors from personal monetary liability for breaches of the duty of care. *In re Nymex Shareholder Litigation, 2009 Del. Ch. LEXIS 176 (Ch Ct 2009).*

.25 Fiduciary duties of officers; business judgment.—The Delaware Supreme Court, in a case of first impression, has made clear that officers owe the same fiduciary duties as owed by directors; those duties can be violated by delaying a due diligence process for self-interested motives. Moreover, the business judgment presumption may be overcome on a motion to dismiss by pleading sufficient facts to raise an inference that a majority of directors has breached their duty of loyalty. *Gantler v Stephens, 965 A2d 695 (2009).*

.26 Contractual waiver of duties.—A corporation charter provision that purports to treat interested directors as disinterested for purposes of immunizing interested transactions from entire fairness analysis is unenforceable; however, a similar provision in a limited liability company operating agreement would be enforceable. *Sutherland v Sutherland, 2009 Del. Ch. LEXIS 46 (Ch Ct 2009).*

103 EXECUTION, ACKNOWLEDGMENT, FILING, RECORDING AND EFFECTIVE DATE OF ORIGINAL CERTIFICATE OF INCORPORATION AND OTHER INSTRUMENTS; EXCEPTIONS.—(a) Whenever any instrument is to be filed with the Secretary of State or in accordance with this section or chapter, such instrument shall be executed as follows:

(1) The certificate of incorporation, and any other instrument to be filed before the election of the initial board of directors if the initial directors were not named in the certificate of incorporation, shall be signed by the incorporator or incorporators (or, in the case of any such other instrument, such incorporator's or incorporators' successors and assigns). If any incorporator is not available by reason of death, incapacity, unknown address, or refusal or neglect to act, then any such other instrument may be signed, with the same effect as if such incorporator had signed it, by any person for whom or on whose behalf such incorporator, in executing the certificate of incorporation, was acting directly or indirectly as employee or agent, provided that such other instrument shall state that such incorporator is not available

and the reason therefor, that such incorporator in executing the certificate of incorporation was acting directly or indirectly as employee or agent for or on behalf of such person, and that such person's signature on such instrument is otherwise authorized and not wrongful.

(2) All other instruments shall be signed:

a. By any authorized officer of the corporation; or

b. If it shall appear from the instrument that there are no such officers, then by a majority of the directors or by such directors as may be designated by the board; or

c. If it shall appear from the instrument that there are no such officers or directors, then by the holders of record, or such of them as may be designated by the holders of record, of a majority of all outstanding shares of stock; or

d. By the holders of record of all outstanding shares of stock.

(b) Whenever this chapter requires any instrument to be acknowledged, such requirement is satisfied by either:

(1) The formal acknowledgment by the person or 1 of the persons signing the instrument that it is such person's act and deed or the act and deed of the corporation, and that the facts stated therein are true. Such acknowledgment shall be made before a person who is authorized by the law of the place of execution to take acknowledgments of deeds. If such person has a seal of office such person shall affix it to the instrument.

(2) The signature, without more, of the person or persons signing the instrument, in which case such signature or signatures shall constitute the affirmation or acknowledgment of the signatory, under penalties of perjury, that the instrument is such person's act and deed or the act and deed of the corporation, and that the facts stated therein are true.

(c) Whenever any instrument is to be filed with the Secretary of State or in accordance with this section or chapter, such requirement means that:

(1) The signed instrument shall be delivered to the office of the Secretary of State;

(2) All taxes and fees authorized by law to be collected by the Secretary of State in connection with the filing of the instrument shall be tendered to the Secretary of State; and

(3) Upon delivery of the instrument, the Secretary of State shall record the date and time of its delivery. Upon such delivery and tender of the required taxes and fees, the Secretary of State shall certify that the instrument has been filed in the Secretary of State's office by endorsing upon the signed instrument the word "Filed," and the date and time of its filing. This endorsement is the "filing date" of the instrument, and is conclusive of the date and time of its filing in the absence of actual fraud. The Secretary of State shall file and index the endorsed instrument. Except as provided in paragraph (4) of this subsection and in subsection (i) of this section, such filing date of an instrument shall be the date and time of delivery of the instrument.

(4) Upon request made upon or prior to delivery, the Secretary of State may, to the extent deemed practicable, establish as the filing date of an instrument a date and time after its delivery. If the Secretary of State refuses to file any instrument due to an error, omission or other imperfection, the Secretary of State may hold such instrument in suspension, and in such event, upon delivery of a replacement instrument in proper form for filing and tender of the required taxes and fees within 5 business days after notice of such suspension is given to the filer, the Secretary of State shall establish as the filing date of such instrument the date and time that would have been the filing date of the rejected instrument had it been accepted for filing. The Secretary of State shall not issue a certificate of good standing with respect to any corporation with an instrument held in suspension pursuant to this subsection. The Secretary of State may establish as the filing date of an instrument the date and time at which information from such instrument is entered pursuant to subdivision (c)(7) of this section if such instrument is delivered on the same date and within 4 hours after such information is entered.

(5) The Secretary of State, acting as agent for the recorders of each of the counties, shall collect and deposit in a separate account established exclusively for that purpose a county assessment fee with respect to each filed instrument and shall thereafter weekly remit from such account to the recorder of each of the said counties the amount or amounts of such fees as provided for in subdivision (c)(5) of this section or as elsewhere provided by law. Said fees shall be for the purposes of defraying certain costs incurred by the counties in merging the information and images of such filed documents with the document information systems of each of the recorder's offices in the counties and in retrieving, maintaining and displaying

such information and images in the offices of the recorders and at remote locations in each of such counties. In consideration for its acting as the agent for the recorders with respect to the collection and payment of the county assessment fees, the Secretary of State shall retain and pay over to the General Fund of the State an administrative charge of 1 percent of the total fees collected.

(6) The assessment fee to the counties shall be $24 for each 1-page instrument filed with the Secretary of State in accordance with this section and $9 for each additional page for instruments with more than 1 page. The recorder's office to receive the assessment fee shall be the recorder's office in the county in which the corporation's registered office in this State is, or is to be, located, except that an assessment fee shall not be charged for either a certificate of dissolution qualifying for treatment under §391(a)(5)b. of this title or a document filed in accordance with Subchapter XV of this chapter.

(7) The Secretary of State, acting as agent, shall collect and deposit in a separate account established exclusively for that purpose a courthouse municipality fee with respect to each filed instrument and shall thereafter monthly remit funds from such account to the treasuries of the municipalities designated in §301 of Title 10. Said fees shall be for the purposes of defraying certain costs incurred by such municipalities in hosting the primary locations for the Delaware Courts. The fee to such municipalities shall be $20 for each instrument filed with the Secretary of State in accordance with this section. The municipality to receive the fee shall be the municipality designated in §301 of Title 10 in the county in which the corporation's registered office in this State is, or is to be, located, except that a fee shall not be charged for a certificate of dissolution qualifying for treatment under §391(a)(5)b. of this title, a resignation of agent without appointment of a successor under §136 of this title, or a document filed in accordance with Subchapter XV of this chapter.

(8) The Secretary of State shall cause to be entered such information from each instrument as the Secretary of State deems appropriate into the Delaware Corporation Information System or any system which is a successor thereto in the office of the Secretary of State, and such information and a copy of each such instrument shall be permanently maintained as a public record on a suitable medium. The Secretary of State is authorized to grant direct access to such system to registered agents subject to the execution of an operating agreement between the Secretary of State and such registered agent. Any registered agent granted such access shall demonstrate the existence of policies to ensure that information entered into the system accurately reflects the content of instruments in the possession of the registered agent at the time of entry.

(d) Any instrument filed in accordance with subsection (c) of this section shall be effective upon its filing date. Any instrument may provide that it is not to become effective until a specified time subsequent to the time it is filed, but such time shall not be later than a time on the 90th day after the date of its filing. If any instrument filed in accordance with subsection (c) of this section provides for a future effective date or time and if the transaction is terminated or its terms are amended to change the future effective date or time prior to the future effective date or time, the instrument shall be terminated or amended by the filing, prior to the future effective date or time set forth in such instrument, of a certificate of termination or amendment of the original instrument, executed in accordance with subsection (a) of this section, which shall identify the instrument which has been terminated or amended and shall state that the instrument has been terminated or the manner in which it has been amended.

(e) If another section of this chapter specifically prescribes a manner of executing, acknowledging or filing a specified instrument or a time when such instrument shall become effective which differs from the corresponding provisions of this section, then such other section shall govern.

(f) Whenever any instrument authorized to be filed with the Secretary of State under any provision of this title, has been so filed and is an inaccurate record of the corporate action therein referred to, or was defectively or erroneously executed, sealed or acknowledged, the instrument may be corrected by filing with the Secretary of State a certificate of correction of the instrument which shall be executed, acknowledged and filed in accordance with this section. The certificate of correction shall specify the inaccuracy or defect to be corrected and shall set forth the portion of the instrument in corrected form. In lieu of filing a certificate of correction the instrument may be corrected by filing with the Secretary of

State a corrected instrument which shall be executed, acknowledged and filed in accordance with this section. The corrected instrument shall be specifically designated as such in its heading, shall specify the inaccuracy or defect to be corrected, and shall set forth the entire instrument in corrected form. An instrument corrected in accordance with this section shall be effective as of the date the original instrument was filed, except as to those persons who are substantially and adversely affected by the correction and as to those persons the instrument as corrected shall be effective from the filing date.

(g) Notwithstanding that any instrument authorized to be filed with the Secretary of State under this title is when filed inaccurately, defectively or erroneously executed, sealed or acknowledged, or otherwise defective in any respect, the Secretary of State shall have no liability to any person for the preclearance for filing, the acceptance for filing or the filing and indexing of such instrument by the Secretary of State.

(h) Any signature on any instrument authorized to be filed with the Secretary of State under this title may be a facsimile, a conformed signature or an electronically transmitted signature.

(i)(1) If:

a. Together with the actual delivery of an instrument and tender of the required taxes and fees, there is delivered to the Secretary of State a separate affidavit (which in its heading shall be designated as an "affidavit of extraordinary condition") attesting, on the basis of personal knowledge of the affiant or a reliable source of knowledge identified in the affidavit, that an earlier effort to deliver such instrument and tender such taxes and fees was made in good faith, specifying the nature, date and time of such good faith effort and requesting that the Secretary of State establish such date and time as the filing date of such instrument; or

b. Upon the actual delivery of an instrument and tender of the required taxes and fees, the Secretary of State in the Secretary's discretion provides a written waiver of the requirement for such an affidavit stating that it appears to the Secretary of State that an earlier effort to deliver such instrument and tender such taxes and fees was made in good faith and specifying the date and time of such effort; and

c. The Secretary of State determines that an extraordinary condition existed at such date and time, that such earlier effort was unsuccessful as a result of the existence of such extraordinary condition, and that such actual delivery and tender were made within a reasonable period (not to exceed 2 business days) after the cessation of such extraordinary condition,

then the Secretary of State may establish such date and time as the filing date of such instrument. No fee shall be paid to the Secretary of State for receiving an affidavit of extraordinary condition.

(2) For purposes of this subsection, an "extraordinary condition" means: any emergency resulting from an attack on, invasion or occupation by foreign military forces of, or disaster, catastrophe, war or other armed conflict, revolution or insurrection, or rioting or civil commotion in, the United States or a locality in which the Secretary of State conducts its business or in which the good faith effort to deliver the instrument and tender the required taxes and fees is made, or the immediate threat of any of the foregoing; or any malfunction or outage of the electrical or telephone service to the Secretary of State's office, or weather or other condition in or about a locality in which the Secretary of State conducts its business, as a result of which the Secretary of State's office is not open for the purpose of the filing of instruments under this chapter or such filing cannot be effected without extraordinary effort. The Secretary of State may require such proof as it deems necessary to make the determination required under paragraph (1)c. of this subsection, and any such determination shall be conclusive in the absence of actual fraud.

(3) If the Secretary of State establishes the filing date of an instrument pursuant to this subsection, the date and time of delivery of the affidavit of extraordinary condition or the date and time of the Secretary of State's written waiver of such affidavit shall be endorsed on such affidavit or waiver and such affidavit or waiver, so endorsed, shall be attached to the filed instrument to which it relates. Such filed instrument shall be effective as of the date and time established as the filing date by the Secretary of State pursuant to this subsection, except as to those persons who are substantially and adversely affected by such establishment and, as to those persons, the instrument shall be effective from the

date and time endorsed on the affidavit of extraordinary condition or written waiver attached thereto.

(j) Notwithstanding any other provision of this chapter, it shall not be necessary for any corporation to amend its certificate of incorporation, or any other document, that has been filed prior to August 1, 2011, to comply with §131(c) of this title, provided that any certificate or other document filed under this chapter on or after August 1, 2011, and changing the address of a registered office shall comply with §131(c) of this title. (Last amended by Ch. 96, L. '11, eff. 8-1-11.)

Ch. 96, L. '11, eff. 8-1-11, added matter in italic.

.1 Certificate of merger.—A shareholder of a corporation loses its standing to bring a derivative action challenging the merger of the corporation when the Secretary of State certifies a certificate of merger so that the shareholder loses its status as a shareholder, notwithstanding that the shareholder's complaint alleges fraud in the merger. *Denver Area Meat Cutters and Employers Pension Plan v Clayton*, 120 SW3d 841 (Tenn Ct App 2003).

Ch. 96, L. '11 Synopsis of Section 103

This Section amends Section 103 to provide that it is not necessary for a Delaware corporation to amend its certificate of incorporation, or any other document, that has been filed with the Secretary of State prior to August 1, 2011, to comply with new Section 131(c), but that any certificate or other document filed on or after August 1, 2011 and changing the address of a registered office must comply with Section 131(c).

Ch. 118, L. '03 Synopsis of Section 103

This Bill establishes a $20 courthouse municipality fee to be assessed on corporate filings. The fee is expected to raise $1.5 million to be distributed to the municipalities designated as the places of holding the Court of Chancery. The fee will be distributed to the municipality in the county in which a business entity's registered office is located.

Ch. 9, L. '03 Synopsis of Section 103

These Amendments clarify the general rule that the filing date of an instrument filed with the Secretary of State is the date and time of delivery of the instrument and the limited exceptions to this rule.

To further enhance service to Delaware corporations, the amendment to Section 391(h)(1) also enables the Secretary of State to offer a new "1-hour" expedited service to complement the Secretary of State's existing "2-hour" service offering.

Ch. 298, L. '02 Synopsis of Section 103

The amendment to Section 103(c)(6) confirms that all instruments filed with the Secretary of State pursuant to Section 103 are permanently maintained as a public record.

Ch. 343, L. '00 Synopsis of Section 103

The amendment to Section 103(a)(1) clarifies that an instrument (other than the certificate of incorporation) to be filed before the election of the initial board of directors (if the initial directors were not named in the certificate of incorporation) may be signed by the incorporator's or incorporators' successors and assigns, and also provides that if any incorporator is not available by reason of death, unknown address, or refusal or neglect to act, any such instrument may be signed by any person for whom or on whose behalf such incorporator in executing the certificate of incorporation was acting as employee or agent, with the same effect as if such incorporator had signed it.

Ch. 339, L. '98 Synopsis of Section 103

The amendments to these Sections eliminate masculine references in the statutes, and replace them with gender neutral references.

Ch. 349, L. '96 Synopsis of Section 103

The 1995 amendments to Section 103(d) allowed a certificate of merger or consolidation to be terminated or amended before the future effective date or time stated therein by filing a Certificate of Termination or Amendment of a Certificate of Merger or Consolidation. This amendment specifies the procedures whereby corporations may terminate or amend filings which have future effective dates or times by the filing of a Certificate of Termination or Amendment of the original instrument before its future effective date or time.

Ch. 79, L. '95 Synopsis of Section 103

This amendment allows for a certificate of merger or consolidation to be terminated or amended before the effective date by filing a Certificate of Termination or amendment of a Certificate of Merger or Consolidation.

104 CERTIFICATE OF INCORPORATION; DEFINITION.—The term "certificate of incorporation," as used in this chapter, unless the context requires otherwise, includes not only the original certificate of incorporation filed to create a corporation but also all other certificates, agreements of merger or consolidation, plans of reorganization, or other instruments, howsoever designated, which are filed pursuant to §§102, 133-136, 151, 241-243, 245, 251-258, 263-264, *267,* 303, or any other section of this title, and which have the effect of amending or supplementing in some respect a corporation's original certificate of incorporation. (Last amended by Ch. 290, L. '10, eff. 8-2-10.)

Ch. 290, L. '10, eff. 8-2-10, added matter in italic.

Ch. 290, L. '10 Synopsis of Section 104

These sections amend Sections 104, 111(a)(6), 114(b)(2), 262(b)(3), and 262(d)(2), respectively, to reflect new Section 267.

Ch. 61, L. '93 Synopsis of Section 104

The amendment to Section 104 clarifies that an agreement of merger or consolidation or certificate of merger filed pursuant to Sections 263 or 264 are part of the certificate of incorporation of a Delaware corporation.

105 CERTIFICATE OF INCORPORATION AND OTHER CERTIFICATES; EVIDENCE.—[1]*A copy of a certificate of incorporation, or a restated certificate of incorporation, or of any other certificate which has been filed in the office of the Secretary of State as required by any provision of this title shall, when duly certified by the Secretary of State, be received in all courts, public offices and official bodies as prima facia evidence of:*

(1) Due execution, acknowledgment and filing of the instrument;

(2) Observance and performance of all acts and conditions necessary to have been observed and performed precedent to the instrument becoming effective; and

(3) Any other facts required or permitted by law to be stated in the instrument. (Last amended by Ch. 587, L. '96, eff. 11-24-97, date that Secretary of State certified installation and functioning of computer hardware and software in recorder's offices.)

Ch. 587, L. '96, eff. 11-24-97, added matter in italic and deleted [1]"*A copy of a certificate of incorporation, or of a composite or restated certificate of incorporation, or of any other certificate which has been filed in the office of the Secretary of State as required by any provision of this title shall, when duly certified by the Secretary of State and accompanied by the certificate of the recorder of the county in which it has been recorded under his hand and the seal of his office stating the fact and record of its recording in his office, be received in all courts, public offices and official bodies as prima facie evidence of:*

(1) Due execution, acknowledgment, filing and recording of the instrument;

(2) Observance and performance of all acts and conditions necessary to have been observed and performed precedent to the instrument becoming effective; and of

(3) Any other facts required or permitted by law to be stated in the instrument."

.1 Cancellation of certificate of Incorporation.— When certificate of incorporation was procured by fraud, attorney general can bring action to cancel it. *State v U.S. Realty Improvement Co, 132 A 138 (Ch Ct 1926).*

106 COMMENCEMENT OF CORPORATE EXISTENCE.—Upon the filing with the Secretary of State of the certificate of incorporation, executed and acknowledged in accordance with §103 of this title, the incorporator or incorporators who signed the certificate, and [1]*such incorporator's or incorporators'* successors and assigns, shall, from the date of such filing, be and constitute a body corporate, by the name set forth in the certificate, subject to subsection (d) of §103 of this title and subject to dissolution or other termination of its existence as provided in this chapter. (Last amended by Ch. 339, L. '98, eff. 7-1-98.)

Ch. 339, L. '98, eff. 7-1-98, added matter in italic and deleted "his or their".

Ch. 339, L. '98 Synopsis of Section 106

The amendments to these Sections eliminate masculine references in the statutes, and replace them with gender neutral references.

.1 De facto corporations.—De facto corporation cannot escape its obligations by raising question of its want of de jure existence; only state can question de jure existence of de facto corporation. *Mayor of Wilmington v Addicks, 43 A 297 (Ch Ct 1899).*

Corporation, which assumed to act as corporation and possessed every element of de facto existence, is estopped to deny its corporate existence when sued on obligation made in its corporate name. *Brady v Del Mut Life Ins Co, 45 A 345 (Ch Ct 1899).*

.2 Fiction of corporate entity.—A corporation is an artificial being created by and acting under authority of law. *Joseph Greenspon's Sons Iron and Steel Co v Pecos Valley Gas Co, 156 A 351 (1931); Southerland v Decimo Club, Inc, 142 A 786 (Ch Ct 1928).*

To prevent fraud or wrong doing, courts will disregard fiction of corporate entity. *Owl Fumigating Corp v Cal Cyanide Co, 24 F2d 718 (D Del 1928),* aff'd, *30 F2d 812 (3d Cir 1929); Martin v D B Martin Co, 88 A 612 (Ch Ct 1913).*

When corporation organized another corporation to carry on particular operation, court will refuse to disregard separate entity of subsidiary and will not permit parent to sue for wrongs done to subsidiary. *EM Fleishman Lumber Corp v Resources Corp International, 105 FSupp 681 (D Del 1952).*

Court will disregard corporate entity and will impose on parent corporation liability for unfair labor practices of subsidiary, when parent actively dealt with labor relations of subsidiary's employees. *NLRB v Condenser Corp of America, 128 F2d 67 (3d Cir 1942).*

When directors of corporation offered corporation's services to new company to be formed, which was to have same board of directors, and which would vote to compensate old corporation with all common stock of new corporation for its services in selling new corporation's preferred stock, court will order cancellation of common stock so issued and will ignore separate entity of corporations. *Blair v F H Smith Co, 156 A 207 (Ch Ct 1931).*

Domestic corporation cannot be forced to have its wholly owned foreign subsidiary discontinue lawsuit latter started in foreign jurisdiction, on ground that same issues are being litigated in domestic forum, when it is shown that foreign subsidiary's existence is for sound business reasons and there is no fraud or public wrong alleged; court will not disregard separate entities of the two corporations. *Pauley Petroleum, Inc v Continental Oil Co,* 239 A2d 629 (1968).

Delaware bank, which was attempting to pierce corporate veil to reach majority shareholder in order to hold him liable for corporation's bad checks, could not obtain materials relating to shareholder's personal account at Hawaii bank because these records were personal and protected by privilege against self incrimination. *Wilmington Savings Fund Society v Tucker,* No. 7977 (Ch Ct 3-13-86).

Parent corporations were not liable for government contract of wholly owned dissolved subsidiary even though there were some members common to boards of both parent and subsidiary, subsidiary's former president worked for parent, and parent dissolved and allegedly financed subsidiary, where (1) Subsidiary conducted and financed its own business operations, maintained its own accounting records, and contracted and subcontracted in its own name; (2) Parent did not guarantee and was not held responsible for subsidiary's performance of contract; (3) Subsidiary and government executed modifications to contract and there was no proof presented that subsidiary did not receive payment for them; (4) Subsidiary executed novations of other contracts in anticipation of its liquidation; and (5) There was inadequate evidence presented to support claims of undercapitalization and that parent made all decisions on contract after subsidiary's dissolution. *BLH, Inc v US,* 13 Cl Ct 265 (1987).

Companies were not responsible for subsidiaries' activities, even though parents wholly owned subsidiaries, there were officers and directors common to boards of both parent and subsidiary, and parent corporations were involved in substantial financial decisions of subsidiaries, where (1) Each subsidiary kept its books and records completely separate from parent corporation; (2) Each maintained its own bank accounts and paid its own taxes; and (3) Each subsidiary, although a Delaware corporation, had its principal place of business in Ecuador and was completely responsible for day to day operations in that country. *Phoenix Canada Oil Co v Texaco, Inc,* 658 FSupp 1061 (D Del 1987).

Creditor that involved itself in management of its troubled debtor did not thereby assume liability for debtor's contract obligations to third party. Court refused to pierce corporate veil to hold creditor liable because creditor's involvement did not constitute such domination and control so as to render debtor mere instrumentality of the creditor. *Irwin & Leighton, Inc v WM Anderson Co,* 532 A2d 983 (Ch Ct 1987).

Piercing corporate veil to hold parent liable might be proper when: (1) parent and sub shared same assets and liabilities; (2) they were operated by joint management; (3) parent's financial statements listed debentures as parent's long-term debt; and (4) Moody's and other credit rating services described the debentures as parent's obligations. *Mabon, Nugent & Co v Texas American Energy Corp,* No. 8578 (Ch Ct 1-27-88).

Doctrine of piercing the corporate veil is usually employed against a defendant corporation to hold its shareholders or its parent company liable; court ruled that plaintiff corporation could not invoke the doctrine in order to benefit from its own inattention to corporate formalities. *Johnson & Johnson v Coopervision,* 720 FSupp 1116 (D Del 1989).

Where acquired corporation had its own board of directors, executive officers, assets, and identity, the fact that parent corporation exercised the control incident to full ownership of subsidiary was not itself reason to ignore separate corporate identities under alter ego doctrine. *Holly Farms Corp v Taylor,* 722 FSupp 1152 (D Del 1989).

.3 Ownership of all stock of corporation.—Ownership of all stock by one person or corporation does not destroy corporation's corporate entity. *Eastern Industries v Traffic Controls, Inc,* 142 FSupp 381 (D Del 1956); *Frants v Templeman Oil Corp,* 134 A 47 (1926); *Francis v Medill,* 141 A 697 (Ch Ct 1928).

107 POWERS OF INCORPORATORS.—If the persons who are to serve as directors until the first annual meeting of stockholders have not been named in the certificate of incorporation, the incorporator or incorporators, until the directors are elected, shall manage the affairs of the corporation and may do whatever is necessary and proper to perfect the organization of the corporation, including the adoption of the original bylaws of the corporation and the election of directors.

.1 Acting by proxy.—Two of three incorporators may appoint third incorporator their proxy for organization meeting of corporation. *Lippman v Kehoe Stenograph Co,* 95 A 895 (Ch Ct 1915).

.2 Binding corporation.—Corporation can adopt contract made by promoters for its benefit, although such contract antedates corporation's existence. *Commissioners of Lewes v Breakwater Fisheries Co,* 117 A 823 (Ch Ct 1922).

Corporation is not bound by promoter's contract which it has not adopted. *Stringer v Electronics Supply Corp,* 2 A2d 78 (Ch Ct 1938).

.3 Liability to corporation.—Promoters must account to corporation for secret profits they obtained at its expense and surrender for cancellation shares representing secret profit. *Birbeck v Am Toll Bridge Co of Cal,* 2 A2d 158 (Ch Ct 1938).

Corporation can maintain action against its promoters, who were also its financiers and managers, for accounting or to recover corporate property appropriated by them to their own use in breach of their fiduciary obligations as promoters. *Bovay v H M Byllesby & Co,* 12 A2d 178 (Ch Ct 1940), demurrer to amended bill of complaint overruled 22 A2d 138 (Ch Ct 1941), rev'd, 38 A2d 808 (1944).

Court will approve derivative suit settlement that denies recovery from promoter for breach of fiduciary duty in underwriting transactions, when promoter bargained at arm's length with corporation and did not make any secret profits. *Gladstone v Bennett, 153 A2d 577 (Ch Ct 1959).*

.4 Directorial role.—Court of Chancery determined that the incorporator of a corporation was the sole director of corporation where no directors were named in the certificate of incorporation, no one held voting control of the corporation, and no shares of stock were lawfully issued. *The Brandner Corp v Stelnick, No. 14463 (Ch Ct 2-22-96).*

108 ORGANIZATION MEETING OF INCORPORATORS OR DIRECTORS NAMED IN CERTIFICATE OF INCORPORATION.—(a) After the filing of the certificate of incorporation an organization meeting of the incorporator or incorporators, or of the board of directors if the initial directors were named in the certificate of incorporation, shall be held, either within or without this State, at the call of a majority of the incorporators or directors, as the case may be, for the purposes of adopting bylaws, electing directors (if the meeting is of the incorporators) to serve or hold office until the first annual meeting of stockholders or until their successors are elected and qualify, electing officers if the meeting is of the directors, doing any other or further acts to perfect the organization of the corporation, and transacting such other business as may come before the meeting.

(b) The persons calling the meeting shall give to each other incorporator or director, as the case may be, at least 2 days' written notice thereof by any usual means of communication, which notice shall state the time, place and purposes of the meeting as fixed by the persons calling it. Notice of the meeting need not be given to anyone who attends the meeting or who signs a waiver of notice either before or after the meeting.

(c) Any action permitted to be taken at the organization meeting of the incorporators or directors, as the case may be, may be taken without a meeting if each incorporator or director, where there is more than 1, or the sole incorporator or director where there is only 1, signs an instrument which states the action so taken.

.1 Validity of first meeting.—Fact that only one of three incorporators, all of whom are subscribers to corporation's capital stock, is present in person at first meeting, other two being represented by proxy, does not affect meeting's validity, nor can its proceedings be impeached on that ground. *Lippman v Kehoe Stenograph Co, 95 A 895 (Ch Ct 1915).*

109 BYLAWS.—[1] *(a) The original or other bylaws of a corporation may be adopted, amended or repealed by the incorporators, by the initial directors of a corporation other than a nonstock corporation or initial members of the governing body of a nonstock corporation if they were named in the certificate of incorporation, or, before a corporation other than a nonstock corporation has received any payment for any of its stock, by its board of directors. After a corporation other than a nonstock corporation has received any payment for any of its stock, the power to adopt, amend or repeal bylaws shall be in the stockholders entitled to vote. In the case of a nonstock corporation, the power to adopt, amend or repeal bylaws shall be in its members entitled to vote. Notwithstanding the foregoing, any corporation may, in its certificate of incorporation, confer the power to adopt, amend or repeal bylaws upon the directors or, in the case of a nonstock corporation, upon its governing body. The fact that such power has been so conferred upon the directors or governing body, as the case may be, shall not divest the stockholders or members of the power, nor limit their power to adopt, amend or repeal bylaws.*

(b) The bylaws may contain any provision, not inconsistent with law or with the certificate of incorporation, relating to the business of the corporation, the conduct of its affairs, and its rights or powers or the rights or powers of its stockholders, directors, officers or employees. (Last amended by Ch. 253, L. '10, eff. 8-1-10.)

Ch. 253, L. '10, eff. 8-1-10, added matter in italic and deleted [1]"(a) The original or other bylaws of a corporation may be adopted, amended or repealed by the incorporators, by the initial directors if they were named in the certificate of incorporation, or, before a corporation has received any payment for any of its stock, by its board of directors. After a corporation has received any payment for any of its stock, the power to adopt, amend or repeal bylaws shall be in the stockholders entitled to vote, or, in the case of a nonstock corporation, in its members entitled to vote; provided, however, any corporation may, in its certificate of incorporation, confer the power to adopt, amend or repeal bylaws upon the directors or, in the case of a nonstock corporation, upon its governing body by whatever name designated. The fact that such power has been so conferred upon the directors or governing body, as the case may be, shall not divest the stockholders or members of the power, nor limit their power to adopt, amend or repeal bylaws."

Ch. 253, L. '10 Synopsis of Section 109

Sections 5, 6, 7, and 8 make technical changes to §102(b)(6), §102(b)(7), §102(d), and §109(a) of the DGCL consistent with the intent of the bill and with the translator provision in new §114(a).

Comment: This amendment to §109 makes it clear that stockholders always have the power to make, alter or repeal bylaws, even though the directors may also be delegated such power.

.1 Validity of.—Bylaw permitting removal of directors at any time by vote of majority of stockholders is in conflict with certificate of incorporation providing for staggered three-year terms for directors, and so bylaws is invalid and court will void stockholders' action that removed three of six directors at one time. *Essential Enterprise Corp v Automatic Steel Products, Inc, 159 A2d 288 (Ch Ct 1960).*

Voting trustee can enforce stockholders' agreement giving right to one class of stock to elect majority of board, when this right is set out in bylaws, even though it does not appear in certificate of incorporation. *In re Farm Industries, Inc, 196 A2d 582 (Ch Ct 1963).*

Stockholders can amend bylaws to give them right to create additional directors and then elect them without first amending certificate of incorporation. *Richman v DeVal Aerodynamics, Inc, 183 A2d 569 (Ch Ct 1962).*

Bylaw granting to stockholders power to fix number of directors, and election of directors without first fixing their number, is valid. *Ellin v Consolidated Caribou Silver Mines, Inc, 67 A2d 416 (Ch Ct 1949).*

Bylaw giving directors power to determining whether stockholder's request to inspect corporate records is for proper purpose, and denying him right to ask court to make this determination, is unreasonable and illegal. *State ex rel Brumley v Jessup & Moore Paper Co, 77 A 16 (1910).*

Bylaw cannot set one year term for directors if charter provides for staggered three-year terms; directors elected under such invalid bylaw serve only as de facto directors whose terms can be terminated at any time by stockholder action. *Prickett v American Steel and Pump Corp, 253 A2d 86 (Ch Ct 1969).*

Court granted injunction barring target from enforcing its interpretation of notice provision of new bylaws which would preclude tender offeror, even if it was successful in obtaining adjournment of annual meeting, from presenting any proposals at adjourned meeting. Notice bylaws did not expressly provide how they would operate in case of adjournment, and there is no settled Delaware law from which target's interpretation could have been determined with reasonable certainty. Therefore, target's failure to announce its interpretation of bylaws until after notice period had run was inequitable. *Mesa Petroleum v Unocal Corp, No. 7997 (Ch Ct 4-23-85).*

Supreme Court affirmed a Court of Chancery ruling that an article of defendant's charter requiring an 80 percent supermajority to amend the bylaws of defendant was clear and unambiguous. Consequently, plaintiffs could not enlarge the size of the board of directors without an 80 percent supermajority stockholder vote. *Centaur Partners, IV v National Intergroup, Inc, 582 A2d 923 (1990).*

Board's post-deadline agreement with and radical change of allegiance to third party represented a material change of circumstances such that considerations of fairness and the importance of the shareholder franchise required shareholders be able to nominate an opposing slate. Thus the duty to waive the bylaw requirement was imposed upon the board, even though board acted in good faith and bylaw was valid on its face and equitable at the time enacted. *Hubbard v Hollywood Park Realty Enterprises, Inc, No. 11779 (Ch Ct 1-14-91).*

Unless a corporation's articles of incorporation expressly authorize the board to amend the corporation's bylaws, a bylaw amendment purporting to confer such authority is void and ultra vires. *Lions Gate Entertainment Corp v Image Entertainment, Inc, 2006 Del. Ch. LEXIS 108 (Ch Ct 2006).*

.2 Amendment of bylaws.—Bylaw may be amended by implication without any formal action, when course of conduct relied on to effect change has continued for period of time to justify inference that stockholders had knowledge of change and consented to it; but one act inconsistent with bylaws is insufficient to consider bylaw amended, and so election of five directors, when bylaw provided, for three, is illegal, especially since it is not shown stockholders were aware of bylaw; fact corporation had only two stockholders and both voted for the five directors is immaterial. *In re Ivey & Ellington, Inc, 42 A2d 508 (Ch Ct 1945).*

One contending that bylaw has been amended by course of conduct inconsistent with it has burden of establishing existence of such custom and he does not sustain burden by showing mere inaction under bylaw. *Belle Isle Corp v MacBean, 49 A2d 5 (Ch Ct 1946).* See also, *In re Osteopathic Hospital Ass'n of Del, 195 A2d 759 (Ch Ct 1963),* on remand, *198 A2d 630 (Ch Ct 1964).*

When directors are empowered to amend bylaws only at regular meeting of board, amendment adopted at special board meeting from which two members were absent is invalid. *Moon v Moon Motor Car Co, 151 A 298 (Ch Ct 1930).*

Shareholder denied preliminary injunction restraining corporation and directors from issuing stock at stock sale because board had not breached fiduciary duty when it withdrew from stockholders, at stockholders' meeting, right to vote on bylaw amendment that repealed existing limitation on number of shares stockholders could own and then adopted amendment itself during meeting recess. *American International Rent A Car Inc v Cross, No. 7583 (Ch Ct 5-9-84).*

Delaware Supreme Court upheld a board of director's decision to amend corporation's bylaw, changing the notice requirement for a special stockholder meeting from 35 days to 60 days, where the special meeting was demanded by an unsolicited bidder who sought to interfere with the board's planned merger with another company by replacing the board of directors and implementing a takeover. *Kidsco, Inc v Dinsmore, Nos. 481, 1995, 482, 1995 (11-29-95).*

A bylaw amendment that provides for reimbursement of proxy expenses is a proper subject for shareholder action, but, unless the subject of the proposed bylaw is included in a corporation's certificate of incorporation, such a proposed bylaw violates state law that provides that the business and affairs of a corporation are to be managed by the board of directors. *CA, Inc v AFSCME Employees Pension Plan, 953 A2d 227 (2008).*

Votes based on voting rights purchased in violation of a restricted stock agreement are void and will not be counted. Moreover, a bylaw amendment that purports to shrink the number of board seats below the number of sitting directors is void, as is a bylaw that purports to establish qualifications for directorships that would disqualify a sitting director and terminate his service. *Crown EMAK Partners, LLC v Kurz, 2010 Del. LEXIS 182 (2010).*

A bylaw amendment providing that annual meetings will occur during a certain month other than a month in which they traditionally have been held, and which has the effect of reducing the amount of time served by a class of directors that is part of a staggered board, does not violate statutory law or a company's bylaws or charter where those are ambiguous as to what constitutes a director's "full term" and the meaning of "annual" and "year." *Airgas, Inc v Air Products and Chemicals, Inc, C.A. No. 5817 CC (Ch Ct Oct. 8, 2010).*

.3 Consistency with certificate.—Court issued preliminary injunction to enjoin acquiror from using Delaware consent procedure to amend bylaws to increase size of target's board and appoint its own directors to vacant slots. Under target's certificate of incorporation, only board may fill vacancies between meetings. *Homac, Inc v DSA Financial Corp, 661 FSupp 776 (ED Mich 1987).*

Certificate of incorporation of non-profit corporation contained provision that new members were to be elected by old members. Bylaws were amended to provide that only board of directors could constitute members of corporation. Court found that amended bylaw did not conflict with certificate of incorporation in violation of GCL §109(b). *Kirby v Kirby, No. 8604 (Ch Ct 7-29-87).*

.4 Modification of consent power.—Although GCL §228 allows stockholders to modify consent power through charter amendment, board of directors may not arrogate to itself through its power to amend the corporation's bylaws the right to substantially delay implementation of shareholder action taken by consent. Court issued preliminary injunction enjoining operation of bylaw that imposed 20-day period during which consent solicitation must stay open. *Prime Computer, Inc v Allen, No. 9557 (Ch 1-25-88).*

.5 Voting rights.—Votes based on voting rights purchased in violation of a restricted stock agreement are void and will not be counted. Moreover, a bylaw amendment that purports to shrink the number of board seats below the number of sitting directors is void, as is a bylaw that purports to establish qualifications for directorships that would disqualify a sitting director and terminate his service. *Crown EMAK Partners, LLC v Kurz, 2010 Del. LEXIS 182 (2010).*

.6 Advancement.—Advancement provisions in articles of incorporation may be limited by reasonable conditions in a corporation's bylaws where the articles and bylaws are executed at the same time, and such conditions may be imposed where a director has had the opportunity to examine both documents. *Xu Hong Bin v Heckmann Corp, 2010 Del. Ch. LEXIS 3 (Ch Ct 2010).*

110 EMERGENCY BYLAWS AND OTHER POWERS IN EMERGENCY.—
(a) The board of directors of any corporation may adopt emergency bylaws, subject to repeal or change by action of the stockholders, which shall notwithstanding any different provision elsewhere in this chapter or in Chapters 3 and 5 of Title 26, or in Chapter 7 of Title 5, or in the certificate of incorporation or bylaws, be operative during any emergency resulting from an attack on the United States or on a locality in which the corporation conducts its business or customarily holds meetings of its board of directors or its stockholders, or during any nuclear or atomic disaster, or during the existence of any catastrophe, or other similar emergency condition, as a result of which a quorum of the board of directors or a standing committee thereof cannot readily be convened for action. The emergency bylaws may make any provision that may be practical and necessary for the circumstances of the emergency, including provisions that:

(1) A meeting of the board of directors or a committee thereof may be called by any officer or director in such manner and under such conditions as shall be prescribed in the emergency bylaws;

(2) The director or directors in attendance at the meeting, or any greater number fixed by the emergency bylaws, shall constitute a quorum; and

(3) The officers or other persons designated on a list approved by the board of directors before the emergency, all in such order of priority and subject to such conditions and for such period of time (not longer than reasonably necessary after the termination of the emergency) as may be provided in the emergency bylaws or in the resolution approving the list, shall, to the extent required to provide a quorum at any meeting of the board of directors, be deemed directors for such meeting.

(b) The board of directors, either before or during any such emergency, may provide, and from time to time modify, lines of succession in the event that during such emergency any or all officers or agents of the corporation shall for any reason be rendered incapable of discharging their duties.

(c) The board of directors, either before or during any such emergency, may, effective in the emergency, change the head office or designate several alternative head offices or regional offices, or authorize the officers so to do.

(d) No officer, director or employee acting in accordance with any emergency bylaws shall be liable except for wilful misconduct.

(e) To the extent not inconsistent with any emergency bylaws so adopted, the bylaws of the corporation shall remain in effect during any emergency and upon its termination the emergency bylaws shall cease to be operative.

(f) Unless otherwise provided in emergency bylaws, notice of any meeting of the board of directors during such an emergency may be given only to such of the directors as it may be feasible to reach at the time and by such means as may be feasible at the time, including publication or radio.

(g) To the extent required to constitute a quorum at any meeting of the board of directors during such an emergency, the officers of the corporation who are present shall, unless otherwise provided in emergency bylaws, be deemed, in order of rank and within the same rank in order of seniority, directors for such meeting.

(h) Nothing contained in this section shall be deemed exclusive of any other provisions for emergency powers consistent with other sections of this title which have been or may be adopted by corporations created under this chapter.

111 JURISDICTION TO INTERPRET, APPLY, ENFORCE OR DETERMINE THE VALIDITY OF CORPORATE INSTRUMENTS AND PROVISIONS OF THIS TITLE.—(a) Any civil action to interpret, apply, enforce or determine the validity of the provisions of:

(1) The certificate of incorporation or the bylaws of a corporation;

(2) Any instrument, document or agreement by which a corporation creates or sells, or offers to create or sell, any of its stock, or any rights or options respecting its stock;

(3) Any written restrictions on the transfer, registration of transfer or ownership of securities under §202 of this title;

(4) Any proxy under §212 or 215 of this title;

(5) Any voting trust or other voting agreement under §218 of this title;

[1] *(6) Any agreement, certificate of merger or consolidation, or certificate of ownership and merger governed by §§251-253, §§255-258, §§263-264, or §267 of this title;*

(7) Any certificate of conversion under §265 or 266 of this title;

(8) Any certificate of domestication, transfer or continuance under §388, 389 or 390 of this title; or

(9) Any other instrument, document, agreement, or certificate required by any provision of this title;

May be brought in the Court of Chancery, except to the extent that a statute confers exclusive jurisdiction on a court, agency or tribunal other than the Court of Chancery.

(b) Any civil action to interpret, apply or enforce any provision of this title may be brought in the Court of Chancery. (Last amended by Ch. 290, L. '10, eff. 8-2-10.)

Ch. 290, L. '10, eff. 8-2-10, added matter in italic and deleted [1]"(6) Any agreement or certificate of merger or consolidation governed by §251-253, 255-258, 263 or 264 of this title;".

Ch. 290, L. '10 Synopsis of Section 111

These sections amend Sections 104, 111(a)(6), 114(b)(2), 262(b)(3), and 262(d)(2), respectively, to reflect new Section 267.

Ch. 84, L. '03 Synopsis of Section 111

This amendment expands the jurisdiction of the Court of Chancery with respect to a variety of matters pertaining to Delaware corporations.

Ch. 123, L. '99 Synopsis of Section 111

Section 111 is new. It clarifies that the Court of Chancery may entertain actions to interpret, apply or enforce any provision of the certificate of incorporation or bylaws of a corporation, regardless of whether there is some independent basis for subject matter jurisdiction in that court. Section 111 is not intended to limit in any way the subject matter jurisdiction of the Court of Chancery established under preexisting law.

112 ACCESS TO PROXY SOLICITATION MATERIALS.—The bylaws may provide that if the corporation solicits proxies with respect to an election of directors, it may be required, to the extent and subject to such procedures or conditions as may be provided in the bylaws, to include in its proxy solicitation materials (including any form of proxy it distributes), in addition to individuals nominated by the board of directors, 1 or more individuals nominated by a stockholder. Such procedures or conditions may include any of the following:

(1) A provision requiring a minimum record or beneficial ownership, or duration of ownership, of shares of the corporation's capital stock, by the nominating stockholder, and defining beneficial ownership to take into account options or other rights in respect of or related to such stock;

(2) A provision requiring the nominating stockholder to submit specified information concerning the stockholder and the stockholder's nominees, including information concerning ownership by such persons of shares of the corporation's capital stock, or options or other rights in respect of or related to such stock;

(3) A provision conditioning eligibility to require inclusion in the corporation's proxy solicitation materials upon the number or proportion of directors nominated by stockholders or whether the stockholder previously sought to require such inclusion;

(4) A provision precluding nominations by any person if such person, any nominee of such person, or any affiliate or associate of such person or nominee, has acquired or publicly proposed to acquire shares constituting a specified percentage of the voting power of the corporation's outstanding voting stock within a specified period before the election of directors;

(5) A provision requiring that the nominating stockholder undertake to indemnify the corporation in respect of any loss arising as a result of any false or misleading information or statement submitted by the nominating stockholder in connection with a nomination; and

(6) Any other lawful condition. (Added by Ch. 14, L. '09, eff. 8-1-09.)

Ch. 14, L. '09 Synopsis of Section 112

New Section 112 clarifies that the bylaws may require that if the corporation solicits proxies with respect to an election of directors, the corporation may be required to include in its proxy materials one or more nominees submitted by stockholders in addition to individuals nominated by the board of directors. Section 112 also identifies a non-exclusive list of conditions that the bylaws may impose on such a right of access to the corporation's proxy materials. In particular, and in the interest of avoiding election contests instituted by stockholders having little or no economic interest in the corporation, Section 112 authorizes the bylaws to prescribe a minimum level of stock ownership as a prerequisite to requiring inclusion of nominees in the corporation's proxy materials. In establishing such a minimum level of stock ownership, the bylaws may define beneficial ownership to take account of ownership of options or other rights in respect of or relating to stock (including rights that derive their value from the market price of the stock). Section 112 also permits the bylaws to limit a right of access according to whether or not a majority of board seats is to be contested, or whether nominations are related to an acquisition of a significant percentage of the corporation's stock. The bylaws may also prescribe any other lawful condition to the exercise of a right of access to the corporation's proxy materials.

.1 **SEC proxy rule invalidated.**—The Securities and Exchange Commission's (SEC's) proxy access regime, promulgated in Exchange Act Rule 14a-11, is invalid as arbitrary and capricious and not in accordance with law because the SEC failed to consider the regime's economic impact on efficiency, competition, and capital formation. *Business Roundtable v Securities and Exchange Commission, 2011 U.S. App. LEXIS 14988 (DC Cir 2011).*

113 PROXY EXPENSE REIMBURSEMENT.—(a) The bylaws may provide for the reimbursement by the corporation of expenses incurred by a stockholder in soliciting proxies in connection with an election of directors, subject to such procedures or conditions as the bylaws may prescribe, including:

(1) Conditioning eligibility for reimbursement upon the number or proportion of persons nominated by the stockholder seeking reimbursement or whether such stockholder previously sought reimbursement for similar expenses;

(2) Limitations on the amount of reimbursement based upon the proportion of votes cast in favor of one or more of the persons nominated by the stockholder seeking reimbursement,

or upon the amount spent by the corporation in soliciting proxies in connection with the election;

(3) Limitations concerning elections of directors by cumulative voting pursuant to §214 of this title; or

(4) Any other lawful condition.

(b) No bylaw so adopted shall apply to elections for which any record date precedes its adoption. (Added by Ch. 14, L. '09, eff. 8-1-09.)

Ch. 14, L. '09 Synopsis of Section 113

New Section 113 provides that a bylaw may require the corporation to reimburse proxy solicitation expenses incurred by a stockholder. Section 113 also identifies a non-exclusive list of conditions that the bylaws may impose on such a right to reimbursement.

114 APPLICATION OF CHAPTER TO NONSTOCK CORPORATIONS.—
(a) Except as otherwise provided in subsections (b) and (c) of this section, the provisions of this chapter shall apply to nonstock corporations in the manner specified in the following paragraphs (a)(1)-(4) of this section:

(1) All references to stockholders of the corporation shall be deemed to refer to members of the corporation;

(2) All references to the board of directors of the corporation shall be deemed to refer to the governing body of the corporation;

(3) All references to directors or to members of the board of directors of the corporation shall be deemed to refer to members of the governing body of the corporation; and

(4) All references to stock, capital stock, or shares thereof of a corporation authorized to issue capital stock shall be deemed to refer to memberships of a nonprofit nonstock corporation and to membership interests of any other nonstock corporation.

(b) Subsection (a) of this section shall not apply to:

(1) Sections 102(a)(4), (b)(1) and (2), 109(a), 114, 141, 154, 215, 228, 230(b), 241, 242, 253, 254, 255, 256, 257, 258, 271, 276, 311, 312, 313, and 390 of this title, which apply to nonstock corporations by their terms;

(2) Sections 151, 152, 153, 155, 156, 157(d), 158, 161, 162, 163, 164, 165, 166, 167, 168, 203, 211, 212, 213, 214, 216, 219, 222, 231, 243, 244, 251, 252, *267,* 274, 275, 324, and 391 of this title; and

(3) Subchapter XIV and subchapter XV of this chapter.

(c) In the case of a nonprofit nonstock corporation, subsection (a) of this section shall not apply to:

(1) The sections and subchapters listed in subsection (b) of this section;

(2) Sections 102(b)(3), 111(a)(2) and (a)(3), 144(a)(2), 217, 218(a) and (b), and 262 of this title; and

(3) Subchapter V and subchapter VI of this chapter.

(d) For purposes of this chapter:

(1) A "charitable nonstock corporation" is any non-profit nonstock corporation that is exempt from taxation under §501(c)(3) of the United States Internal Revenue Code, or any successor provisions.

(2) A "membership interest" is, unless otherwise provided in a nonstock corporation's certificate of incorporation, a member's share of the profits and losses of a nonstock corporation, or a member's right to receive distributions of the nonstock corporation's assets, or both;

(3) A "nonprofit nonstock corporation" is a nonstock corporation that does not have membership interests; and

(4) A "nonstock corporation" is any corporation organized under this chapter that is not authorized to issue capital stock. (Added by Ch. 253, L. '10, eff. 8-1-10; amended by Ch. 290, L. '10, eff. 8-2-10.)

Ch. 290, L. '10, eff. 8-2-10, added matter in italic.

Ch. 290, L. '10 Synopsis of Section 114

These sections amend Sections 104, 111(a)(6), 114(b)(2), 262(b)(3), and 262(d)(2), respectively, to reflect new Section 267.

Ch. 253, L. '10 Synopsis of Section 114

Section 9 amends the DGCL to add a new §114. Section 114 has four operative provisions. New §114(a) provides that, unless otherwise provided in §114(b) or §114(c), the provisions of the DGCL generally apply to nonstock corporations and that, for purposes of applying to nonstock corporations, the stock-corporation terms in each applicable section will be translated into nonstock-corporation terms. Section 114(a)(4) provides that members of non-profit nonstock corporations have memberships, while members of other nonstock corporations hold membership interests in the nonstock corporations. New §114(b) carves out certain provisions of the DGCL from the operation of §114(a), so the provisions listed in §114(b) are not translated by §114(a). Specifically, new §114(b)(1) lists provisions of the DGCL that apply to nonstock corporations by their terms and therefore require no translation; and §114(b)(2) and §114(b)(3) list sections and subchapters of the DGCL that do not apply to nonstock corporations by virtue of the translator provision in §114(a) (but which may be made otherwise applicable by a different provision). New §114(c) carves out provisions in addition to those listed in §114(b) to ensure that those provisions are not applied to non-profit nonstock corporations. New §114(d) defines the following terms relating to nonstock corporations: "nonstock corporation," "membership interest," "non-profit nonstock corporation," and "charitable nonstock corporation."

Section 144(a)(2) is listed in new §114(c)(2) in accordance with the concept noted in *Oberly v. Kirby*, 592 A.2d 445, 467 - 68 (Del. 1991), that the members of a non-profit nonstock corporation may not ratify such interested transactions because they have no financial interest in the corporation.

Because the translator provision in new §114(a) operates on §159 for nonstock corporations other than nonprofit nonstock corporations, membership interests in nonstock corporations are personal property.

SUBCHAPTER II. POWERS

121 GENERAL POWERS.—(a) In addition to the powers enumerated in §122 of this title, every corporation, its officers, directors and stockholders shall possess and may exercise all the powers and privileges granted by this chapter or by any other law or by its certificate of incorporation, together with any powers incidental thereto, so far as such powers and privileges are necessary or convenient to the conduct, promotion or attainment of the business or purposes set forth in its certificate of incorporation.

(b) Every corporation shall be governed by the provisions and be subject to the restrictions and liabilities contained in this chapter.

122 SPECIFIC POWERS.—Every corporation created under this chapter shall have power to:

(1) Have perpetual succession by its corporate name, unless a limited period of duration is stated in its certificate of incorporation;

(2) Sue and be sued in all courts and participate, as a party or otherwise, in any judicial, administrative, arbitrative or other proceeding, in its corporate name;

(3) Have a corporate seal, which may be altered at pleasure, and use the same by causing it or a facsimile thereof, to be impressed or affixed or in any other manner reproduced;

(4) Purchase, receive, take by grant, gift, devise, bequest or otherwise, lease, or otherwise acquire, own, hold, improve, employ, use and otherwise deal in and with real or personal property, or any interest therein, wherever situated, and to sell, convey, lease, exchange, transfer or otherwise dispose of, or mortgage or pledge, all or any of its property and assets, or any interest therein, wherever situated;

(5) Appoint such officers and agents as the business of the corporation requires and to pay or otherwise provide for them suitable compensation;

(6) Adopt, amend and repeal bylaws;

(7) Wind up and dissolve itself in the manner provided in this chapter;

(8) Conduct its business, carry on its operations and have offices and exercise its powers within or without this State;

(9) Make donations for the public welfare or for charitable, scientific or educational purposes, and in time of war or other national emergency in aid thereof;

(10) Be an incorporator, promoter, or manager of other corporations of any type or kind;

(11) Participate with others in any corporation, partnership, limited partnership, joint venture or other association of any kind, or in any transaction, undertaking or arrangement which the participating corporation would have power to conduct by itself, whether or not such participation involves sharing or delegation of control with or to others;

(12) Transact any lawful business which the corporation's board of directors shall find to be in aid of governmental authority;

(13) Make contracts, including contracts of guaranty and suretyship, incur liabilities, borrow money at such rates of interest as the corporation may determine, issue its notes, bonds and other obligations, and secure any of its obligations by mortgage, pledge or other encumbrance of all or any of its property, franchises and income, and make contracts of guaranty and suretyship which are necessary or convenient to the conduct, promotion or attainment of the business of (a) a corporation all of the outstanding stock of which is owned, directly or indirectly, by the contracting corporation, or (b) a corporation which owns, directly or indirectly, all of the outstanding stock of the contracting corporation, or (c) a corporation all of the outstanding stock of which is owned, directly or indirectly, by a corporation which owns, directly or indirectly, all of the outstanding stock of the contracting corporation, which contracts of guaranty and suretyship shall be deemed to be necessary or convenient to the conduct, promotion or attainment of the business of the contracting corporation, and make other contracts of guaranty and suretyship which are necessary or convenient to the conduct, promotion or attainment of the business of the contracting corporation;

(14) Lend money for its corporate purposes, invest and reinvest its funds, and take, hold and deal with real and personal property as security for the payment of funds so loaned or invested;

(15) Pay pensions and establish and carry out pension, profit sharing, stock option, stock purchase, stock bonus, retirement, benefit, incentive and compensation plans, trusts and provisions for any or all of its directors, officers, and employees, and for any or all of the directors, officers, and employees of its subsidiaries;

(16) Provide insurance for its benefit on the life of any of its directors, officers or employees, or on the life of any stockholder for the purpose of acquiring at such stockholder's death shares of its stock owned by such stockholder.

(17) Renounce, in its certificate of incorporation or by action of its board of directors, any interest or expectancy of the corporation in, or in being offered an opportunity to participate in, specified business opportunities or specified classes or categories of business opportunities that are presented to the corporation or 1 or more of its officers, directors or stockholders. (Last amended by Ch. 343, L. '00, eff. 7-1-00.)

Ch. 343, L. '00, eff. 7-1-00, added matter in italic.

Ch. 343, L. '00 Synopsis of Section 122

New subsection 122(17) clarifies that a corporation has the power to renounce in advance, in its certificate of incorporation or by action of its board of directors (including action approving an agreement to which the corporation is a party), the corporation's interest or expectancy in specified business opportunities or specified classes or categories of business opportunities. By way of example, the classes or categories of business opportunities may be specified by any manner of defining or delineating business opportunities or the corporation's or any other party's entitlement thereto or interest therein, including, without limitation, by line or type of business, identity of the originator of the business opportunity, identity of the party or parties to or having an interest in the business opportunity, identity of the recipient of the business opportunity, periods of time or geographical location. The subsection is intended to eliminate uncertainty regarding the power of a corporation to renounce corporate opportunities in advance raised in Siegman v. Tri-Star Pictures, Inc., C. A. No. 9477 (Del. Ch. May 5, 1989, revised May 30, 1989). It permits the corporation to determine in advance whether a specified business opportunity or class or category of business opportunities is a corporate opportunity of the corporation rather than to address such opportunities as they arise. The subsection does not change the level of judicial scrutiny that will apply to the renunciation of an interest or expectancy of the corporation in a business opportunity, which will be determined based on the common law of fiduciary duty, including the duty of loyalty.

Ch. 339, L. '98 Synopsis of Section 122

The amendments to these Sections eliminate masculine references in the statutes, and replace them with gender neutral references.

.1 Powers in general.—Delaware corporation, by appropriate language in its charter, may deny to itself action permitted by Delaware law. *Weinberg v Baltimore Brick Co, 108 A2d 81 (Ch Ct 1954),* aff'd, *114 A2d 812 (1955).*

Corporation possesses all powers conferred by its charter and statute creating it. *Davis v Louisville Gas & Electric Co, 142 A 654 (Ch Ct 1928).*

No power or authority can be conferred upon corporation by its charter which is not provided by

.2 Suits.—In absence of some special duty owing by corporation to persons injured, liability of corporation for malicious tort committed by its servant or agent rests upon authorization, direct or indirect, proceeding from nature of servant's or agent's employment, or upon adoption or ratification of agent's act. *MacDonough v A S Beck Shoe Corp, 10 A2d 510 (1939)*, reaffirmed on reargument, *16 A2d 219 (1940)*.

In action against corporation for trespass, it is not necessary to allege names of agents and officers of corporation through whom alleged trespass was committed. *Knight v Industrial Trust Co, 193 A 723 (1937)*.

Holder of corporate indenture notes has common law right to sue corporation to enforce payment of notes after maturity unless indenture provisions expressly or by necessary implication preclude such right. *Halle v Van Sweringen Corp, 185 A 236 (1936)*.

Corporation cannot appear in federal court in person to conduct its litigation. *Brandstein v White Lamps, Inc, 20 FSupp 369 (SDNY 1937)*.

Corporation may recover fines, penalties and litigation expenses from its employees arising out of state and federal antitrust violations for price fixing, when it is shown such violations were due solely to employees' unauthorized acts, in breach of their fiduciary duty to corporation. *Wilshire Oil Co of Texas v Riffe, 409 F2d 1277 (10th Cir 1969)*.

Note: Annotations on derivative suits appear under G.C.L. §327.

Corporation may also be vicariously or secondarily liable if the officer commits tort while acting on corporation's behalf, but officer remains personally liable. *Brandywine Mushroom Co v Hockession Mushroom Products, Inc, 682 FSupp 1307 (D Del 1988)*.

Corporation's preferred shareholders from People's Republic of China were entitled to participate on equal basis with other preferred shareholders in distribution of fund created by PRC's payment of reparations for confiscation of corporation's property. Fund was created by agreement between U.S. and PRC. Corporation's claims under Delaware law must yield when they are inconsistent with or impair U.S. foreign policy. *Judah v Shanghai Power Co, 546 A2d 981 (1988)*.

.3 Corporate seal.—Corporate seal implies that corporation, through its directors or those in power to conduct corporate business, authorize president or other officer acting in particular matter, to make contract evidenced by instrument on which seal is placed; and, in absence of opposing proof, instrument so sealed is to be regarded as binding act and deed of corporation. *Italo-Petroleum Corp of America v Hannigan, 14 A2d 401 (1940)*.

Corporation can contract without use of corporate seal, and so judgment on corporation's promissory note will not be refused because note did not bear corporate seal. *Peyton-DuPont Securities Co v Vesper Oil & Gas Co, 131 A 566 (1925)*.

.4 Property.—Corporation has power to hold property which it does as quasi trustee for its stockholders. *Southerland v Decimo Club Inc, 142 A 786 (Ch Ct 1928)*.

Delaware corporation can be organized solely for purpose of acquiring, owning and operating building on site in Illinois. *Spivey v Spivey Bldg Corp, 10 NE2d 385 (1937)*.

.5 Mortgages and bonds.—After-acquired property clause in corporate mortgage is valid, but holders of bonds secured by such mortgage take after-acquired property subject to any liens or equities with which it is impressed when acquired by corporation. *In re Frederica Water, Light & Power Co, 93 A 376 (Ch Ct 1915)*.

Holder of corporate bonds has common law right to sue corporation to enforce payment unless indenture provisions expressly or by necessary implication precludes such right, but such restrictions are strictly construed, and are effective only insofar as they are clear and reasonably free from doubt. *Japha v Delaware Valley Utilities Co, 15 A2d 432 (1940); Halle v Van Sweringen Corp, 185 A 236 (1936); Noble v European Mortgage & Investment Corp, 165 A 157 (Ch Ct 1933)*.

Unissued shares of capital stock of corporation may be pledged as collateral security for loan made to corporation. *In re International Radiator Co, 92 A 255 (Ch Ct 1914)*.

Court dismissed action by convertible debenture holders challenging merger of corporation for lack of entire fairness because debenture holders have to allege fraud in order to state claim other than contract claim based on indenture. Convertible debenture holders also could not maintain action for specific violations of indenture without complying with required "no-action" provisions of indenture because debenture holders were not asserting fraud in connection with alleged violations but, rather, breach of fiduciary duty. *Norte & Co v Manor Healthcare Corp, Nos. 6827 & 6831 (Ch Ct 11-21-85)*.

Court refused to dismiss complaint charging that parent was liable for payment of principal and interest due under debentures. "No recourse" clause, which waived any shareholders' liability for principal or interest, precluded recovery against parent under indenture. However, piercing corporate veil to hold parent liable might be proper when: (1) parent and sub shared same assets and liabilities; (2) they were operated by joint management; (3) parent's financial statements listed debentures as parent's long-term debt; and (4) Moody's and other credit rating services described the debentures as parent's obligations. *Mabon, Nugent & Co v Texas American Energy Corp, No. 8578 (Ch Ct 1-27-88)*.

Issuing corporation and directors do not owe fiduciary duty to holder of convertible debentures. Existing property right or equitable interest must be present to create a fiduciary duty. Holder of convertible debenture has no equitable interest until it is converted. He therefore remains a creditor of corporation whose interests are governed by indenture's contractual terms. *Simons v Cogan, 549 A2d 300 (1987)*.

.6 Agents.—When corporation receives and retains fruits of loan negotiated by its agent, it cannot deny agent's authority to borrow money, even though creditor made check out to agent personally, and

§122

after he deposited it in corporate account, book entries were made in corporation's records reflecting credit to agent's personal account in amount same as loan. *Mulco Products, Inc v Black, 127 A2d 851 (1956).*

.7 **Bylaws.**—Corporation has power to make reasonable bylaws which do not conflict with constitution, statutes or charter. *Gaskill v Gladys Belle Oil Co, 146 A 337 (Ch Ct 1929).*

Bylaws must be reasonable, and bylaw providing for five days' notice of special stockholders' meeting is reasonable. *Moon v Moon Motor Car Co, 151 A 298 (Ch Ct 1930).*

Directors, who authorized contract with president for term of five years and breached contract, cannot assert contract was invalid because executed in contravention of bylaw that president be chosen annually, since bylaws could be altered or amended by directors, and contract executed under their authority superseded and prevailed over inconsistent bylaws. *Realty Acceptance Corp v Montgomery, 51 F2d 636 (3d Cir 1930).*

President and sole stockholder of corporation signing contract on its behalf is unhampered by either absence of authorizing bylaws or by restraining force of existing by-laws. *Community Stores, Inc v Dean, 14 A2d 633 (1940).*

.8 **Dissolution and winding up.**—Corporation has power to dissolve. *Butler v New Keystone Copper Co, 93 A 380 (Ch Ct 1915).*

Corporation in dissolution must preserve assets for benefit of creditors, and cannot prefer stockholders. *Asmussen v Quaker City Corp, 156 A 180 (Ch Ct 1931).*

.9 **Profit-sharing plan.**—Officers are liable to their corporation for discount they gave its profit-sharing plan in selling corporation's own bonds to it, even though corporation acquired those bonds at same discount from public, when (1) officers were beneficiaries of plan, (2) sale was not approved by board, and (3) corporation did not need money so urgently that it could not have obtained it on more favorable terms elsewhere. *Schwartz v Miner, 146 A2d 801 (Ch Ct 1958).*

.10 **Business outside state.**—Corporation has power to do business in other states with their assent. *Magna Oil & Refining Co v White Star Refining Co, 280 F 52 (3d Cir 1922).*

While courts usually will not take jurisdiction of controversies involving internal management of foreign corporation, when all defendants are amenable to jurisdiction of court and its decrees can be effectually enforced, New York courts will take jurisdiction of causes regulating internal affairs of Delaware corporations. *Levy v Pacific Eastern Corp, 275 NY Supp 291 (NY 1934).*

When Delaware corporation holds its property and records and transacts all its business in New York, federal court in New York will take jurisdiction on grounds of diversity of citizenship, but it will construe the rights of different classes of stockholders of corporation under Delaware law. *Harr v Pioneer Mechanical Corp, 65 F2d 331 (2d Cir 1933).*

.11 **Attorney-client privilege.**—Corporation waives attorney-client privilege relating to communications with its attorney on bylaw and charter amendments when it has already voluntarily testified to specific discussions with him about same subject matter; absent waiver, corporation has same privilege as any other client *Lee National Corp v Deramus, 313 FSupp 224 (D Del 1970).*

Corporation that was majority stockholder could not use attorney-client privilege as defense to motion to compel production of documents in securities law suit by minority stockholders on ground that documents resulted from studies made by its counsel; majority stockholder owed fiduciary duty to minority and privilege could not be used to block required disclosure. *Valente v Pepsico, Inc, 68 FRD 361 (D Del 1975).*

.12 **Joint ventures.**—Corporation acted independently in joint ventures with companies that had nominees on its board and about 20% of its stock, since stock ownership alone, when less than majority, does not prove control. *Kaplan v Centex Corp, 284 A2d 119 (Ch Ct 1971).*

.13 **Self dealing.**—Parent company owning majority of stock of subsidiary commercial airline carrier parent was guilty of self-dealing when it delayed selling jet airplanes to subsidiary because latter would not agree to finance plan, thus forcing airline to lease jets from parent on day-to-day basis. *Trans World Airlines v Summa Corp, 374 A2d 5 (Ch Ct 1977).*

.14 **Blocking sale of stock.**—Corporation could not block sale of shareholders' stock because (1) shareholders were not privy to inside information making them ineligible to sell stock, (2) oral discussions with shareholders did not constitute agreement to become corporate employee or not to sell stock before product had been developed or marketed, and (3) any oral agreement that shareholders may have made was invalid if shares are to be deemed validly issued since future services are not legal consideration for issuance of stock. *Catherines v Copytele, Inc, 602 FSupp 1019 (ED NY 1985).*

.15 **Suit against alien corporation.**—Corporation's claims against People's Republic of China for expropriating its property in 1950 were extinguished by 1979 Executive Agreement between United States and PRC. Corporation could not assert that debt as counterclaim against PRC shareholders in their action to participate in settlement fund engendered by 1979 Executive Agreement. *Shanghai Power Co v Delaware Trust Co, 526 A2d 906 (Ch Ct 1987),* aff'd, *546 A2d 981 (1988).*

.16 **Attorney's fees, liability for.**—Corporation was not liable for attorney's fees incurred in minority shareholder's successful class action suit against corporation when (1) there was class recovery from which attorney's fees could be awarded, (2) although corporation violated its fiduciary duty to minority shareholders, there was no showing of corporation's bad faith or deliberate fraud, and (3) minority shareholders could not claim that corporation should pay attorney's fees because damage award was too low since this amounts to indirect reargument of damage award. *Weinberger v UOP, Inc, 517 A2d 653 (Ch Ct 1986).*

123 POWERS RESPECTING SECURITIES OF OTHER CORPORATIONS OR ENTITIES.—Any corporation organized under the laws of this State may guarantee, purchase, take, receive, subscribe for or otherwise acquire; own, hold, use or otherwise employ; sell, lease, exchange, transfer or otherwise dispose of; mortgage, lend, pledge or otherwise deal in and with, bonds and other obligations of, or shares or other securities or interests in, or issued by, and other domestic or foreign corporation, partnership, association, or individual, or by any government or agency or instrumentality thereof. A corporation while owner of any such securities may exercise all the rights, powers and privileges of ownership, including the right to vote.

.1 Purchase of stock in other corporations.—Delaware corporations may acquire securities of other corporations. *Leibert v Grinnell Corp, 194 A2d 846 (Ch Ct 1963); Butler v New Keystone Copper Co, 93 A 380 (Ch Ct 1915).*

Purchase by corporation of all stock of several corporations does not create de facto merger so as to give dissenting stockholder appraisal rights. *Orzeck v Englehart, 192 A2d 36 (Ch Ct), aff'd, 195 A2d 375 (1963).*

Officers can bind corporation to assume third party's guarantee of his business' obligations, even without prior specific board authorization or subsequent ratification, when assumption agreement is made in connection with corporation's continuing program of buying other businesses. *Harvard Industries, Inc v Wendel, 178 A2d 486 (Ch Ct 1962).*

.2 Voting of stock held by corporation.—If corporation has power to hold stock, it has incidental power to vote it, notwithstanding its certificate of incorporation confers no special power to that end. *Bouree v Trust Francais des Actions de la Franco-Wyoming Oil Co, 127 A 56 (Ch Ct 1924).*

Holding corporation owning controlling stock in another corporation can deposit stock in voting trust. *Adams v Clearance Corp, 116 A2d 893 (Ch Ct), aff'd, 121 A2d 302 (1955).*

.3 Parent and subsidiary.—Corporation has duty to share its allocation of quotas for importation of crude oil with subsidiary when government regulation states that parent and subsidiary are "one" crude oil importer; refiner who owns and controls another must deal with subsidiary on a fair and equitable basis in spite of contrary business judgment. *Getty Oil Co v Skelly Oil Co, 255 A2d 717 (Ch Ct 1969).*

124 EFFECT OF LACK OF CORPORATE CAPACITY OR POWER; ULTRA VIRES.—No act of a corporation and no conveyance or transfer of real or personal property to or by a corporation shall be invalid by reason of the fact that the corporation was without capacity or power to do such act or to make or receive such conveyance or transfer, but such lack of capacity or power may be asserted:

(1) In a proceeding by a stockholder against the corporation to enjoin the doing of any act or acts or the transfer of real or personal property by or to the corporation. If the unauthorized acts or transfer sought to be enjoined are being, or are to be, performed or made pursuant to any contract to which the corporation is a party, the court may, if all of the parties to the contract are parties to the proceeding and if it deems the same to be equitable, set aside and enjoin the performance of such contract, and in so doing may allow to the corporation or to the other parties to the contract, as the case may be, such compensation as may be equitable for the loss or damage sustained by any of them which may result from the action of the court in setting aside and enjoining the performance of such contract, but anticipated profits to be derived from the performance of the contract shall not be awarded by the court as a loss or damage sustained;

(2) In a proceeding by the corporation, whether acting directly or through a receiver, trustee or other legal representative, or through stockholders in a representative suit, against an incumbent or former officer or director of the corporation, for loss or damage due to [1]*such incumbent or former officer's or director's* unauthorized act;

(3) In a proceeding by the Attorney General to dissolve the corporation, or to enjoin the corporation from the transaction of unauthorized business. (Last amended by Ch. 339, L. '98, eff. 7-1-98.)

Ch. 339, L. '98, eff. 7-1-98, added matter in italic and deleted [1]"his".

Ch. 339, L. '98 Synopsis of Section 124

The amendments to these Sections eliminate masculine references in the statutes, and replace them with gender neutral references.

.1 No defense to tort liability.—Corporation cannot escape its tort liability by plea of ultra vires. *Northern Assurance Co v Rachlin Clothes Shop, Inc, 125 A 184 (1924).*

.2 Directors' ultra vires act.—When directors authorized transfer of life insurance policy on president's life, without consideration, to pay his debts, such transfer was ultra vires and void even though president used money he had borrowed to buy machinery for corporation. *Wolter v Johnston, 34 F2d 598 (3d Cir 1929).*

.3 Failure to show damage.—Corporation will not be enjoined from performing ultra vires act when complainant cannot show that it will be damaged thereby. *Philadelphia, W & B R Co v Wilmington City Ry Co, 38 A 1067 (Ch Ct 1897).*

125 CONFERRING ACADEMIC OR HONORARY DEGREES.—No corporation organized after April 18, 1945, shall have power to confer academic or honorary degrees unless the certificate of incorporation or an amendment thereof shall so provide and unless the certificate of incorporation or an amendment thereof prior to its being filed in the office of the Secretary of State shall have endorsed thereon the approval of the [1]*Department of Education* of this State. No corporation organized before April 18, 1945, any provision in its certificate of incorporation to the contrary notwithstanding, shall possess the power aforesaid without first filing in the office of the Secretary of State a certificate of amendment so providing, the filing of which certificate of amendment in the office of the Secretary of State shall be subject to prior approval of the [1]*Department of Education*, evidenced as hereinabove provided. Approval shall be granted only when it appears to the reasonable satisfaction of the [1]*Department of Education* that the corporation is engaged in conducting a bona fide institution of higher learning, giving instructions in arts and letters, science or the professions, or that the corporation proposes, in good faith, to engage in that field and has or will have the resources, including personnel, requisite for the conduct of an institution of higher learning. Upon dissolution, all such corporations shall comply with §8530 of Title 14. Notwithstanding any provision herein to the contrary, no corporation shall have the power to conduct a private business or trade school unless the certificate of incorporation or an amendment thereof, prior to its being filed in the office of the Secretary of State, shall have endorsed thereon the approval of the Department of Education pursuant to Chapter 85 of Title 14.

Notwithstanding the foregoing provisions, any corporation conducting a law school, which has its principal place of operation in Delaware, and which intends to meet the standards of approval of the American Bar Association, may, after it has been in actual operation for not less than 1 year, retain at its own expense a dean or dean emeritus of a law school fully approved by the American Bar Association to make an on-site inspection and report concerning the progress of the corporation toward meeting the standards for approval by the American Bar Association. Such dean or dean emeritus shall be chosen by the Attorney General from a panel of 3 deans whose names are presented to the Attorney General as being willing to serve. One such dean on this panel shall be nominated by the trustees of said law school corporation; another dean shall be nominated by a committee of the Student Bar Association of said law school; and the other dean shall be nominated by a committee of lawyers who are parents of students attending such law school. If any of the above-named groups cannot find a dean, it may substitute 2 full professors of accredited law schools for the dean it is entitled to nominate, and in such a case if the Attorney General chooses 1 of such professors, such professor shall serve the function of a dean as herein prescribed. If the dean so retained shall report in writing that, in such dean's professional judgment, the corporation is attempting, in good faith, to comply with the standards for approval of the American Bar Association and is making reasonable progress toward meeting such standards, the corporation may file a copy of the report with the Secretary of Education and with the Attorney General. Any corporation which complies with these provisions by filing such report shall be deemed to have temporary approval from the State and shall be entitled to amend its certificate of incorporation to authorize the granting of standard academic law degrees. Thereafter, until the law school operated by the corporation is approved by the American Bar Association, the corporation shall file once during each academic year a new report, in the same manner as the first report. If, at any time, the corporation fails to file such a report, or if the dean retained to render such report states that, in such dean's opinion, the corporation is not continuing to make reasonable progress toward accreditation, the Attorney General, at the request of the Secretary of Education, may file a complaint in the Court of Chancery to suspend said temporary approval and degree-granting power until a further report is filed by a dean or dean emeritus of an accredited law school that the school has resumed its progress towards meeting the standards for approval. Upon approval of the law school by the American Bar Association, temporary approval shall become final, and shall no longer be subject to suspension or vacation under this section. (Last amended by Ch. 249, L. '04, eff. 6-8-04.)

Ch. 249, L. '04, eff. 6-8-04, added matter in italic and deleted [1]"State Board of Education".

Ch. 249, L. '04 Synopsis of Section 125

This Act will transfer to the Department of Education the authority to approve certificates of incorporation or any amendment thereof, prior to filing of the same in the office of the Secretary of State, involving any corporation which desires to exercise the power to confer academic or honorary degrees. Section 2 of this Act will preserve the right of any corporation previously approved by the State Board of Education to continue to grant academic or honorary degrees.

Ch. 65, L. '01 Synopsis of Section 125

This Bill updates remaining references throughout the Delaware Code to the Department of Public Instruction and the Superintendent of Public Instruction, replacing them with the Department of Education and the Secretary of Education, respectively. It also corrects several references to the State Board of Education by replacing it with the Department of Education in those instances where the powers and duties have previously been transferred to the Department, preserving the State Board's approval authority where applicable.

Ch. 339, L. '98 Synopsis of Section 125

The amendments to these Sections eliminate masculine references in the statutes, and replace them with gender neutral references.

126 BANKING POWER DENIED.—(a) No corporation organized under this chapter shall possess the power of issuing bills, notes, or other evidences of debt for circulation as money, or the power of carrying on the business of receiving deposits of money.

(b) Corporations organized under this chapter to buy, sell and otherwise deal in notes, open accounts and other similar evidences of debt, or to loan money and to take notes, open accounts and other similar evidences of debt as collateral security therefor, shall not be deemed to be engaging in the business of banking. (Last amended by Ch. 148, L. '69, eff. 7-15-69.)

127 PRIVATE FOUNDATION; POWERS AND DUTIES.—A corporation of this State which is a private foundation under the United States internal revenue laws and whose certificate of incorporation does not expressly provide that this section shall not apply to it is required to act or to refrain from acting so as not to subject itself to the taxes imposed by 26 U.S.C. §4941 (relating to taxes on self-dealing), 4942 (relating to taxes on failure to distribute income), 4943 (relating to taxes on excess business holdings), 4944 (relating to taxes on investments which jeopardize charitable purpose), or 4945 (relating to taxable expenditures), or corresponding provisions of any subsequent United States internal revenue law. (Added by Ch. 87, L. '71, eff. 5-20-71.)

SUBCHAPTER III. REGISTERED OFFICE AND REGISTERED AGENT

131 REGISTERED OFFICE IN STATE; PRINCIPAL OFFICE OR PLACE OF BUSINESS IN STATE.—(a) Every corporation shall have and maintain in this State a registered office which may, but need not be, the same as its place of business.

(b) Whenever the term "corporation's principal office or place of business in this State" or "principal office or place of business of the corporation in this State," or other term of like import, is or has been used in a corporation's certificate of incorporation, or in any other document, or in any statute, it shall be deemed to mean and refer to, unless the context indicates otherwise, the corporation's registered office required by this section; and it shall not be necessary for any corporation to amend its certificate of incorporation or any other document to comply with this section.

(c) As contained in any certificate of incorporation or other document filed with the Secretary of State under this chapter, the address of a registered office shall include the street, number, city, county and postal code. (Last amended by Ch. 96, L. '11, eff. 8-1-11.)

Ch. 96, L. '11, eff. 8-1-11, added matter in italic.

Ch. 96, L. '11 Synopsis of Section 131

This Section adds a new subsection (c) to Section 131 providing that, in any certificate of incorporation or other document filed with the Secretary of State, the address of the registered office of the corporation must include the street, number, city, county and postal code.

.1 Principal office or place of business.—Federal court will not dismiss diversity action against corporation on its alleged ground that it had merged into corporation which was citizen of same state as complainant, when it is shown that corporation is Delaware citizen from fact of its incorporation there and that if maintained principal office and place of business in Delaware as required by that state's law. *Horner v Scott Bros, Inc, 200 FSupp 198 (ED Pa 1961).*

When it is shown that principal place of business of Delaware corporation is in Colorado, even though its principal [registered] office is in Delaware as required by that state's law, proper federal jurisdiction over corporation lies in Tenth Circuit (Colorado) rather than in Third Circuit (Delaware). *Colorado Interstate Gas Co v Federal Power Commission, 142 F2d 943 (10th Cir 1944).*

132 REGISTERED AGENT IN STATE; RESIDENT AGENT.—(a) Every corporation shall have and maintain in this State a registered agent, which agent may be any of:

(1) The corporation itself;

(2) An individual resident in this State;

(3) A domestic corporation (other than the corporation itself), a domestic partnership (whether general (including a limited liability partnership) or limited (including a limited liability limited partnership)), a domestic limited liability company or a domestic statutory trust; or

(4) A foreign corporation, a foreign partnership (whether general (including a limited liability partnership) or limited (including a limited liability limited partnership)), a foreign limited liability company or a foreign statutory trust.

(b) Every registered agent *for a domestic corporation or a foreign corporation* shall:

(1) If an entity, maintain a business office in this State which is generally open, or if an individual, be generally present at a designated location in this State, at sufficiently frequent times to accept service of process and otherwise perform the functions of a registered agent;

(2) If a foreign entity, be authorized to transact business in this State;

(3) Accept service of process and other communications directed to the corporations for which it serves as registered agent and forward same to the corporation to which the service or communication is directed; and

(4) Forward to the corporations for which it serves as registered agent the annual report required by §502 of this title or an electronic notification of same in a form satisfactory to the Secretary of State ("Secretary").

(c) Any registered agent who at any time serves as registered agent for more than 50 entities (a "commercial registered agent"), whether domestic or foreign, shall satisfy and comply with the following qualifications.

(1) A natural person serving as a commercial registered agent shall:

a. Maintain a principal residence or a principal place of business in this State;

b. Maintain a Delaware business license;

c. Be generally present at a designated location within this State during normal business hours to accept service of process and otherwise perform the functions of a registered agent as specified in subsection (b) of this section; and

d. Provide the Secretary upon request with such information identifying and enabling communication with such commercial registered agent as the Secretary shall require;

(2) A domestic or foreign corporation, a domestic or foreign partnership (whether general (including a limited liability partnership) or limited (including a limited liability limited partnership)), a domestic or foreign limited liability company, or a domestic or foreign statutory trust serving as a commercial registered agent shall:

a. Have a business office within this State which is generally open during normal business hours to accept service of process and otherwise perform the functions of a registered agent as specified in subsection (b) of this section;

b. Maintain a Delaware business license;

c. Have generally present at such office during normal business hours an officer, director or managing agent who is a natural person; and

d. Provide the Secretary upon request with such information identifying and enabling communication with such commercial registered agent as the Secretary shall require.

(3) For purposes of this subsection and paragraph (f)(2)a. of this section, a commercial registered agent shall also include any registered agent which has an officer, director or managing agent in common with any other registered agent or agents if such registered agents at any time during such common service as officer, director or managing agent collectively served as registered agents for more than 50 entities, whether domestic or foreign.

(d) Every corporation formed under the laws of this State or qualified to do business in this State shall provide to its registered agent and update from time to time as necessary the name, business address and business telephone number of a natural person who is an officer, director, employee, or designated agent of the corporation, who is then authorized to receive communications from the registered agent. Such person shall be deemed the communications contact for the corporation. Every registered agent shall retain (in paper or electronic form) the above information concerning the current communications contact for each corporation for which he, she or it serves as a registered agent. If the corporation

fails to provide the registered agent with a current communications contact, the registered agent may resign as the registered agent for such corporation pursuant to §136 of this title.

(e) The Secretary is authorized to issue such rules and regulations as may be necessary or appropriate to carry out the enforcement of subsections (b), (c) and (d) of this section, and to take actions reasonable and necessary to assure registered agents' compliance with subsections (b), (c) and (d) of this section. Such actions may include refusal to file documents submitted by a registered agent.

(f) Upon application of the Secretary, the Court of Chancery may enjoin any person or entity from serving as a registered agent or as an officer, director or managing agent of a registered agent.

(1) Upon the filing of a complaint by the Secretary pursuant to this section, the Court may make such orders respecting such proceeding as it deems appropriate, and may enter such orders granting interim or final relief as it deems proper under the circumstances.

(2) Any one or more of the following grounds shall be a sufficient basis to grant an injunction pursuant to this section:

a. With respect to any registered agent who at any time within 1 year immediately prior to the filing of the Secretary's complaint is a commercial registered agent, failure after notice and warning to comply with the qualifications set forth in subsection (b) of this section and/or the requirements of subsection (c) or (d) of this section above;

b. The person serving as a registered agent, or any person who is an officer, director or managing agent of an entity registered agent, has been convicted of a felony or any crime which includes an element of dishonesty or fraud or involves moral turpitude;

c. The registered agent has engaged in conduct in connection with acting as a registered agent that is intended to or likely to deceive or defraud the public.

(3) With respect to any order the court enters pursuant to this section with respect to an entity that has acted as a registered agent, the court may also direct such order to any person who has served as an officer, director, or managing agent of such registered agent. Any person who, on or after January 1, 2007, serves as an officer, director, or managing agent of an entity acting as a registered agent in this State shall be deemed thereby to have consented to the appointment of such registered agent as agent upon whom service of process may be made in any action brought pursuant to this section, and service as an officer, director, or managing agent of an entity acting as a registered agent in this State shall be a signification of the consent of such person that any process when so served shall be of the same legal force and validity as if served upon such person within this State, and such appointment of the registered agent shall be irrevocable.

(4) Upon the entry of an order by the Court enjoining any person or entity from acting as a registered agent, the Secretary shall mail or deliver notice of such order to each affected corporation at the address of its principal place of business as specified in its most recent franchise tax report or other record of the Secretary. If such corporation is a domestic corporation and fails to obtain and designate a new registered agent within 30 days after such notice is given, the Secretary shall declare the charter of such corporation forfeited. If such corporation is a foreign corporation, and fails to obtain and designate a new registered agent within 30 days after such notice is given, the Secretary shall forfeit its qualification to do business in this State. If the court enjoins a person or entity from acting as a registered agent as provided in this section and no new registered agent shall have been obtained and designated in the time and manner aforesaid, service of legal process against the corporation for which the registered agent had been acting shall thereafter be upon the Secretary in accordance with §321 of this title. The Court of Chancery may, upon application of the Secretary on notice to the former registered agent, enter such orders as it deems appropriate to give the Secretary access to information in the former registered agent's possession in order to facilitate communication with the corporations the former registered agent served.

(g) The Secretary is authorized to make a list of registered agents available to the public, and to establish such qualifications and issue such rules and regulations with respect to such listing as the Secretary deems necessary or appropriate.

(h) Whenever the term "resident agent" or "resident agent in charge of a corporation's principal office or place of business in this State," or other term of like import which refers to a corporation's agent required by statute to be located in this State, is or has been used in a corporation's certificate of incorporation, or in any other document, or in any statute, it shall be deemed to mean and refer to, unless the context indicates otherwise, the corporation's registered agent required by this section; and it shall not be necessary for any corporation to amend its certificate of incorporation or any other document to comply with this section. (Last amended by Ch. 290, L. '10, eff. 8-2-10.)

Ch. 290, L. '10, eff. 8-2-10, added matter in italic.

Ch. 290, L. '10 Synopsis of Section 132

This section amends Section 132(b) to clarify that such subsection applies to registered agents for both domestic corporations and foreign corporations.

Ch. 306, L. '06 (eff. 1-1-07) Synopsis of Section 132

Sections 9 and 10 amend §132 to expand the types of entities that may serve as registered agents; prescribe the duties of a registered agent; require that persons or entities serving as registered agent for more than 50 business entities be generally open during normal business hours and have a natural person present to operate such office and communicate with the Secretary of State on request; require Delaware corporations to provide registered agents with a designated natural person to receive communications from the registered agent and require the registered agent to maintain in its records the identity of such persons; authorize the Secretary of State to issue regulations to enforce these provisions; authorize the Secretary of State to bring a lawsuit in the Court of Chancery to enjoin from acting as a registered agent, or as an officer, or director, or managing agent of a registered agent, any person or entity who fails to comply with the statutory requirements, who has been convicted of a felony or any crime involving dishonesty, fraud or moral turpitude, or who has used the office of registered agent in a manner intended to defraud the public; and authorize the Secretary of State to make a list of registered agents available to the public.

Ch. 329, L. '02 Synopsis of Section 132

The amendments set forth are made for the purpose of avoiding any implication that a trust formed under Chapter 38, Title 12 of the Delaware Code constitutes a "business trust" within the meaning of Title 11 of the United States Code. Such amendments are not intended to result in any substantive change in Delaware law. These amendments are made solely for the purpose of conforming the Delaware Code to the amendments set forth above.

Ch. 339, L. '98 Synopsis of Section 132

The amendment to Section 132(a) provides that limited partnerships, limited liability companies and domestic business trusts may serve as registered agents for Delaware corporations.

Ch. 120, L. '97 Synopsis of Section 132

The amendment to Section 132(a) clarifies those entities which can serve as registered agents and further requires that a registered office generally be open during normal business hours to accept service of process and otherwise to perform the functions of a registered agent.

.1 Corporation as registered agent—When corporation's registered agent is itself, service of process may be made by any method authorized by statute for service either on corporations or on their registered agents. *Keith v Melvin I Joseph Constr Co, 451 A2d 842 (1982).*

133 CHANGE OF LOCATION OF REGISTERED OFFICE; CHANGE OF REGISTERED AGENT.—Any corporation may, by resolution of its board of directors, change the location of its registered office in this State to any other place in this State. By like resolution, the registered agent of a corporation may be changed to any other person or corporation including itself. In either such case, the resolution shall be as detailed in its statement as is required by §102(a)(2) of this title. Upon the adoption of such a resolution, a certificate certifying the change shall be executed, acknowledged, and filed in accordance with §103 of this title [1]. (Last amended by Ch. 587, L. '96, eff. 11-24-97, date that Secretary of State certified installation and functioning of computer hardware and software in recorder's offices.)

> Ch. 587, L. '96, eff. 11-24-97, deleted [1]"; and a certified copy shall be recorded in the office of the recorder for the county in which the new office is located".

134 CHANGE OF ADDRESS OR NAME OF REGISTERED AGENT.—(a) A registered agent may change the address of the registered office of the corporation or corporations for which the agent is a registered agent to another address in this State by filing with the Secretary of State a certificate, executed and acknowledged by such registered agent, setting forth the [1]address at which such registered agent has maintained the registered office for each of [2]*the corporations for which it is a registered agent,* and further certifying to the new address to which each such registered office will be changed on a given day, and at which new address such registered agent will thereafter maintain the registered office for each of the corporations [3]*for which it is a registered agent.* Thereafter, or until further change of address, as authorized by law, the registered office in this State of each of the corporations [3]*for which the agent is a registered agent* shall be located at the new address of the registered agent thereof as given in the certificate.

(b) In the event of a change of name of any person or corporation acting as registered agent in this State, such registered agent shall file with the Secretary of State a certificate, executed and acknowledged by such registered agent, setting forth the new name of such registered agent, the name of such registered agent before it was changed, [4]*and the address at which such registered agent has maintained the registered office for each of* [5]*the corporations for which it acts as a registered agent. A change of name of any person or corporation acting as a registered agent as a result of a merger or consolidation of the registered agent, with or into another person or corporation which succeeds to its assets by operation of law,* shall be deemed a change of name for purposes of this section. (Last amended by Ch. 82, L. '01, eff. 7-1-01.)

> Ch. 82, L. '01, eff. 7-1-01, added matter in italic and deleted [1]"names of all the corporations represented by such registered agent, and the"; [2]"such"; [3]"recited in the certificate"; [4]"the names of all the corporations represented by such registered agent"; and [5]"such corporations".

Ch. 82, L. '01 Synopsis of Section 134

The amendments to Section 134 clarify the procedures relating to changes in the address or name of a registered agent.

135 RESIGNATION OF REGISTERED AGENT COUPLED WITH APPOINTMENT OF SUCCESSOR.—[1]*The registered agent of 1 or more corporations may resign and appoint a successor registered agent by filing a certificate with the Secretary of State, stating the name and address of the successor agent, in accordance with §102(a)(2) of this title.* There shall be attached to such certificate a statement of each affected corporation ratifying and approving such change of registered agent. Each such statement shall be executed and acknowledged in accordance with §103 of this title. Upon such filing, the successor registered agent shall become the registered agent of such corporations as have ratified and approved such substitution and the successor registered agent's address, as stated in such certificate, shall become the address of each such corporation's registered office in this State. The Secretary of State shall then issue a certificate that the successor registered agent has become the registered agent of the corporations so ratifying and approving such change and setting out the names of such corporations. (Last amended by Ch. 587, L. '96, eff. 11-24-97, date that Secretary of State certified installation and functioning of computer hardware and software in recorder's offices.)

> Ch. 587, L. '96, eff. 11-24-97, added matter in italic and deleted [1]"The registered agent of 1 or more corporations may resign and appoint a successor registered agent by filing a certificate with the Secretary of State, stating the name and address of the successor agent, in accordance with paragraph (2) of subsection (a) of §102 of this title. There shall be attached to such certificate a statement of each affected corporation ratifying and approving such

change of registered agent. Each such statement shall be executed and acknowledged in accordance with §103 of this title. Upon such filing, the successor registered agent shall become the registered agent of such corporations as have ratified and approved such substitution and the successor registered agent's address, as stated in such certificate, shall become the address of each such corporation's registered office in this State. The Secretary of State shall then issue his certificate that the successor registered agent has become the registered agent of the corporations so ratifying and approving such change, and setting out the names of such corporations. The certificate of the Secretary of State shall be recorded in accordance with §103 of this title, and the recorder shall forthwith make a note of the change of registered office and registered agent on the margin of the record of the certificates of incorporation of those corporations which have ratified and approved such change. If the location of such office shall be changed from 1 county to another county, a certified copy of such certificate shall also be recorded in the office of the recorder for the county in which such office will thereafter be located."

136 RESIGNATION OF REGISTERED AGENT NOT COUPLED WITH APPOINTMENT OF SUCCESSOR.—[1](a) *The registered agent of 1 or more corporations may resign without appointing a successor by filing a certificate of resignation with the Secretary of State, but such resignation shall not become effective until 30 days after the certificate is filed. The certificate shall be executed and acknowledged by the registered agent, shall contain a statement that written notice of resignation was given to each affected corporation at least 30 days prior to the filing of the certificate by mailing or delivering such notice to the corporation at its address last known to the registered agent and shall set forth the date of such notice.*

(b) After receipt of the notice of the resignation of its registered agent, provided for in subsection (a) of this section, the corporation for which such registered agent was acting shall obtain and designate a new registered agent to take the place of the registered agent so resigning in the same manner as provided in §133 of this title for change of registered agent. If such corporation, being a corporation of this State, fails to obtain and designate a new registered agent as aforesaid prior to the expiration of the period of 30 days after the filing by the registered agent of the certificate of resignation, the Secretary of State shall declare the charter of such corporation forfeited. If such corporation, being a foreign corporation, fails to obtain and designate a new registered agent as aforesaid prior to the expiration of the period of 30 days after the filing by the registered agent of the certificate of resignation, the Secretary of State shall forfeit its authority to do business in this State.

(c) After the resignation of the registered agent shall have become effective as provided in this section and if no new registered agent shall have been obtained and designated in the time and manner aforesaid, service of legal process against the corporation for which the resigned registered agent had been acting shall thereafter be upon the Secretary of State in accordance with §321 of this title. (Last amended by Ch. 587, L. '96, eff. 11-24-97, date that Secretary of State certified installation and functioning of computer hardware and software in recorder's offices.)

Ch. 587, L. '96, eff. 11-24-97, added matter in italic and deleted [1] "(a) The registered agent of one or more corporations may resign without appointing a successor by filing a certificate with the Secretary of State; but such resignation shall not become effective until 30 days after the certificate is filed. The certificate shall be acknowledged by the registered agent, shall contain a statement that written notice of resignation was given to the corporation at least 30 days prior to the filing of the certificate by mailing or delivering such notice to the corporation at its address last known to the registered agent, and shall set forth the date of such notice.

(b) After receipt of the notice of the resignation of its registered agent, provided for in subsection (a) of this section, the corporation for which such registered agent was acting shall obtain and designate a new registered agent to take the place of the registered agent so resigning in the same manner as provided in §133 of this title for change of registered agent. If such corporation, being a corporation of this State, fails to obtain and designate a new registered agent as aforesaid prior to the expiration of the period of 30 days after the filing by the registered agent of the certificate of resignation, the Secretary of State shall declare the charter of such corporation forfeited. If such corporation, being a foreign corporation, fails to obtain and designate a new registered agent as aforesaid prior to the expiration of the period of 30 days after the filing by the registered agent of the certificate of resignation, the Secretary of State shall forfeit its authority to do business in this State.

(c) After the resignation of the registered agent shall have become effective as provided in this section and if no new registered agent shall have been obtained and designated in the time and manner aforesaid, service of legal process against the corporation for which the resigned registered agent had been acting shall thereafter be upon the Secretary of State in accordance with §321 of this title."

Ch. 79, L. '95 Synopsis of Section 136

This amendment allows registered agents to resign after notice is given to corporations by mailing or delivering such notice instead of by certified or registered mail. It also eliminates the requirement for an affidavit to be attached to the Certificate of Resignation.

SUBCHAPTER IV. DIRECTORS AND OFFICERS

141 BOARD OF DIRECTORS; POWERS; NUMBER, QUALIFICATIONS, TERMS AND QUORUM; COMMITTEES; CLASSES OF DIRECTORS; [1] *NONSTOCK CORPORATIONS; RELIANCE UPON BOOKS; ACTION WITHOUT MEETING; REMOVAL.*—(a) The business and affairs of every corporation organized under this chapter shall be managed by or under the direction of a board of directors, except as may be otherwise provided in this chapter or in its certificate of incorporation. If any such provision is made in the certificate of incorporation, the powers and duties conferred or imposed upon the board of directors by this chapter shall be exercised or performed to such extent and by such person or persons as shall be provided in the certificate of incorporation.

(b) The board of directors of a corporation shall consist of 1 or more members, each of whom shall be a natural person. The number of directors shall be fixed by, or in the manner provided in, the bylaws, unless the certificate of incorporation fixes the number of directors, in which case a change in the number of directors shall be made only by amendment of the certificate. Directors need not be stockholders unless so required by the certificate of incorporation or the bylaws. The certificate of incorporation or bylaws may prescribe other qualifications for directors. Each director shall hold office until such director's successor is elected and qualified or until such director's earlier resignation or removal. Any director may resign at any time upon notice given in writing or by electronic transmission to the corporation. A resignation is effective when the resignation is delivered unless the resignation specifies a later effective date or an effective date determined upon the happening of an event or events. A resignation which is conditioned upon the director failing to receive a specified vote for reelection as a director may provide that it is irrevocable. A majority of the total number of directors shall constitute a quorum for the transaction of business unless the certificate of incorporation or the bylaws require a greater number. Unless the certificate of incorporation provides otherwise, the bylaws may provide that a number less than a majority shall constitute a quorum which in no case shall be less than ⅓ of the total number of directors except that when a board of 1 director is authorized under the provisions of this section, then 1 director shall constitute a quorum. The vote of the majority of the directors present at a meeting at which a quorum is present shall be the act of the board of directors unless the certificate of incorporation or the bylaws shall require a vote of a greater number.

(c)(1) All corporations incorporated prior to July 1, 1996, shall be governed by paragraph (1) of this subsection, provided that any such corporation may by a resolution adopted by a majority of the whole board elect to be governed by paragraph (2) of this subsection, in which case paragraph (1) of this subsection shall not apply to such corporation. All corporations incorporated on or after July 1, 1996, shall be governed by paragraph (2) of this subsection. The board of directors may, by resolution passed by a majority of the whole board, designate 1 or more committees, each committee to consist of 1 or more of the directors of the corporation. The board may designate 1 or more directors as alternate members of any committee, who may replace any absent or disqualified member at any meeting of the committee. The bylaws may provide that in the absence or disqualification of a member of a committee, the member or members present at any meeting and not disqualified from voting, whether or not the member or members present constitute a quorum, may unanimously appoint another member of the board of directors to act at the meeting in the place of any such absent or disqualified member. Any such committee, to the extent provided in the resolution of the board of directors, or in the bylaws of the corporation, shall have and may exercise all the powers and authority of the board of directors in the management of the business and affairs of the corporation, and may authorize the seal of the corporation to be affixed to all papers which may require it; but no such committee shall have the power or authority in reference to amending the certificate of incorporation (except that a committee may, to the extent authorized in the resolution or resolutions providing for the issuance of shares of stock adopted by the board of directors as provided in subsection (a) of §151 of this title, fix the designations and any of the preferences or rights of such shares relating to dividends, redemption, dissolution, any distribution of assets of the corporation or the conversion into, or the exchange of such shares for, shares of any other class or classes or any other series of the same or any other class or classes of stock of the corporation or fix the number of shares of any series of stock or authorize the increase or decrease of the shares of any series), adopting an agreement of

§141

merger or consolidation under §251, §252, §254, §255, §256, §257, §258, §263, or §264 of this title, recommending to the stockholders the sale, lease or exchange of all or substantially all of the corporation's property and assets, recommending to the stockholders a dissolution of the corporation or a revocation of a dissolution, or amending the bylaws of the corporation; and, unless the resolution, bylaws or certificate of incorporation expressly so provides, no such committee shall have the power or authority to declare a dividend, to authorize the issuance of stock or to adopt a certificate of ownership and merger pursuant to §253 of this title.

(2) The board of directors may designate 1 or more committees, each committee to consist of 1 or more of the directors of the corporation. The board may designate 1 or more directors as alternate members of any committee, who may replace any absent or disqualified member at any meeting of the committee. The bylaws may provide that in the absence or disqualification of a member of a committee, the member or members present at any meeting and not disqualified from voting, whether or not such member or members constitute a quorum, may unanimously appoint another member of the board of directors to act at the meeting in the place of any such absent or disqualified member. Any such committee, to the extent provided in the resolution of the board of directors, or in the bylaws of the corporation, shall have and may exercise all the powers and authority of the board of directors in the management of the business and affairs of the corporation, and may authorize the seal of the corporation to be affixed to all papers which may require it; but no such committee shall have the power or authority in reference to the following matter: (i) approving or adopting, or recommending to the stockholders, any action or matter (other than the election or removal of directors) expressly required by this chapter to be submitted to stockholders for approval or (ii) adopting, amending or repealing any bylaw of the corporation.

(3) Unless otherwise provided in the certificate of incorporation, the bylaws or the resolution of the board of directors designating the committee, a committee may create 1 or more subcommittees, each subcommittee to consist of 1 or more members of the committee, and delegate to a subcommittee any or all of the powers and authority of the committee.

(d) The directors of any corporation organized under this chapter may, by the certificate of incorporation or by an initial bylaw, or by a bylaw adopted by a vote of the stockholders, be divided into 1, 2 or 3 classes; the term of office of those of the first class to expire at the first annual meeting held after such classification becomes effective; of the second class 1 year thereafter; of the third class 2 years thereafter; and at each annual election held after such classification becomes effective, directors shall be chosen for a full term, as the case may be, to succeed those whose terms expire. The certificate of incorporation or bylaw provision dividing the directors into classes may authorize the board of directors to assign members of the board already in office to such classes at the time such classification becomes effective. The certificate of incorporation may confer upon holders of any class or series of stock the right to elect 1 or more directors who shall serve for such term, and have such voting powers as shall be stated in the certificate of incorporation. The terms of office and voting powers of the directors elected separately by the holders of any class or series of stock may be greater than or less than those of any other director or class of directors. In addition, the certificate of incorporation may confer upon 1 or more directors, whether or not elected separately by the holders of any class or series of stock, voting powers greater than or less than those of other directors. Any such provision conferring greater or lesser voting power shall apply to voting in any committee or subcommittee, unless otherwise provided in the certificate of incorporation or bylaws. If the certificate of incorporation provides that 1 or more directors shall have more or less than 1 vote per director on any matter, every reference in this chapter to a majority or other proportion of the directors shall refer to a majority or other proportion of the votes of the directors.

(e) A member of the board of directors, or a member of any committee designated by the board of directors, shall, in the performance of such member's duties, be fully protected in relying in good faith upon the records of the corporation and upon such information, opinions, reports or statements presented to the corporation by any of the corporation's officers or employees, or committees of the board of directors, or by any other person as to matters the member reasonably believes are within such other person's professional or expert competence and who has been selected with reasonable care by or on behalf of the corporation.

(f) Unless otherwise restricted by the certificate of incorporation or bylaws, any action required or permitted to be taken at any meeting of the board of directors or of any committee thereof may be taken without a meeting if all members of the board or committee, as the case may be, consent thereto in writing, or by electronic transmission and the writing or writings or electronic transmission or transmissions are filed with the minutes of proceedings of the board, or committee. Such filing shall be in paper form if the minutes are maintained in paper form and shall be in electronic form if the minutes are maintained in electronic form.

(g) Unless otherwise restricted by the certificate of incorporation or bylaws, the board of directors of any corporation organized under this chapter may hold its meetings, and have an office or offices, outside of this State.

(h) Unless otherwise restricted by the certificate of incorporation or bylaws, the board of directors shall have the authority to fix the compensation of directors.

(i) Unless otherwise restricted by the certificate of incorporation or bylaws, members of the board of directors of any corporation, or any committee designated by the board, may participate in a meeting of such board, or committee by means of conference telephone or other communications equipment by means of which all persons participating in the meeting can hear each other, and participation in a meeting pursuant to this subsection shall constitute presence in person at the meeting.

[2] (j) *The certificate of incorporation of any nonstock corporation may provide that less than 1/3 of the members of the governing body may constitute a quorum thereof and may otherwise provide that the business and affairs of the corporation shall be managed in a manner different from that provided in this section. Except as may be otherwise provided by the certificate of incorporation, this section shall apply to such a corporation, and when so applied, all references to the board of directors, to members thereof, and to stockholders shall be deemed to refer to the governing body of the corporation, the members thereof and the members of the corporation, respectively; and all references to stock, capital stock, or shares thereof shall be deemed to refer to memberships of a nonprofit nonstock corporation and to membership interests of any other nonstock corporation.*

(k) Any director or the entire board of directors may be removed, with or without cause, by the holders of a majority of the shares then entitled to vote at an election of directors, except as follows:

(1) Unless the certificate of incorporation otherwise provides, in the case of a corporation whose board is classified as provided in subsection (d) of this section, [3] *stockholders* may effect such removal only for cause; or

(2) In the case of a corporation having cumulative voting, if less than the entire board is to be removed, no director may be removed without cause if the votes cast against such director's removal would be sufficient to elect such director if then cumulatively voted at an election of the entire board of directors, or, if there be classes of directors, at an election of the class of directors of which such director is a part.

Whenever the holders of any class or series are entitled to elect 1 or more directors by the certificate of incorporation, this subsection shall apply, in respect to the removal without cause of a director or directors so elected, to the vote of the holders of the outstanding shares of that class or series and not to the vote of the outstanding shares as a whole. (Last amended by Ch. 253, L. '10, eff. 8-1-10.)

Ch. 253, L. '10, eff. 8-1-10, added matter in italic and deleted [1]"NONPROFIT"; [2]"(j) The certificate of incorporation of any corporation organized under this chapter which is not authorized to issue capital stock may provide that less than ⅓ of the members of the governing body may constitute a quorum thereof and may otherwise provide that the business and affairs of the corporation shall be managed in a manner different from that provided in this section. Except as may be otherwise provided by the certificate of incorporation, this section shall apply to such a corporation, and when so applied, all references to the board of directors, to members thereof, and to stockholders shall be deemed to refer to the governing body of the corporation, the members thereof and the members of the corporation, respectively."; and [3]"shareholders".

Ch. 253, L. '10 Synopsis of Section 141

Sections 10, 11, 12, 13, and 14 make technical changes to §141 and §144 of the DGCL consistent with the intent of the bill and with the translator provision in new §114(a).

Ch. 145, L. '07 Synopsis of Section 141

The amendment to §141(d) clarifies that when a provision of the certificate of incorporation endows some directors with greater or lesser voting power than other directors, that differentiation of voting power applies both in voting by the board of directors and in voting by committees of the board and in subcommittees, unless otherwise provided in the certificate of incorporation or bylaws.

Ch. 306, L. '06 Synopsis of Section 141

Section 3 amends §141(b) to add a new provision that a resignation may be made effective upon the happening of a future event or events, coupled with authority granted in the same section to make certain resignations irrevocable. By permitting a corporation to enforce a director resignation conditioned upon the director failing to achieve a specified vote for reelection, e.g., more votes for than against, coupled with board acceptance of the resignation, these provisions permit corporations and individual directors to agree voluntarily, and give effect in a manner subsequently enforceable by the corporation, to voting standards for the election of directors which differ from the plurality default standard in Section 216. The new provisions of Section 141(b) do not, however, address whether resignations submitted in other contexts may be made irrevocable.

Section 4 amends the first sentence of §141(d) to clarify that the classified terms of directors commence after the classification of the board of directors becomes effective, thereby expressly permitting certificate of incorporation or bylaw provisions that provide for classification effective at a point in time after such provisions are adopted. The new sentence added to Section 141(d) permits the certificate of incorporation or bylaw provision that divides the directors into classes to include language authorizing the board of directors to assign members of the board already in office to the board classes at the time such classification becomes effective.

Ch. 30, L. '05 Synopsis of Section 141(d)

The amendments to Section 141(d) provide that the certificate of incorporation may confer greater or lesser voting powers on one or more directors, whether or not such director or directors is or are separately elected by the holders of any class or series of stock.

Ch. 326, L. '04 Synopsis of Section 141(c)(2)

The amendment to Section 141(c)(2) clarifies the authority to establish a committee with delegated power to recommend the nomination or removal of members of the board of directors.

Ch. 84, L. '03 Synopsis of Section 141

This section clarifies that a committee of the board of directors may create subcommittees unless the authority to create a subcommittee has been restricted by the certificate of incorporation, the bylaws or the resolution of the board of directors designating the committee.

Ch. 298, L. '02 Synopsis of Section 141

The amendment to Section 141(b) clarifies that directors must be natural persons.

Ch. 343, L. '00 Synopsis of Section 141

The amendments to subsections (b), (f) and (i) of Section 141(b) permit a corporation's directors to make use of available communication technologies. As amended, subsections 141(b) and (f) permit director resignations and actions by consent to be submitted or taken by electronic transmission, as defined in new Section 232(c).

Ch. 339, L. '98 Synopsis of Section 141

The amendments to these Sections eliminate masculine references in the statutes, and replace them with gender neutral references.

Ch. 349, L. '96 Synopsis of Section 141

This amendment is intended to simplify Section 141(c) and expand for corporations incorporated on or after July 1, 1996, the powers and authority that a board of directors may delegate to a committee of the board and to eliminate for such corporations the requirement that a committee of the board be formed by resolution passed by a majority of the whole board. Any corporation formed prior to July 1, 1996 will continue to be governed by the provisions of Section 141(c) in effect prior to this amendment, unless it elects to be governed by the new provisions.

Ch. 79, L. '95 Synopsis of Section 141

This section amends Section 141(c) of the Act to extend to mergers with non-stock corporations and other business entities the requirement that agreements of merger or consolidation be adopted by the entire board of directors, rather than a committee of the board. It does not affect parent-subsidiary mergers under Section 253.

.1 Directors acting as board.—Directors, when acting for corporation, must act as board; individual directors, acting as such, cannot bind board. *Bruch v National Credit Co, 116 A 738 (Ch Ct 1923).*

Verbal authority given by majority of board of directors, without any official action taken at directors' meeting, is insufficient action. *Mattoax Leather Co v Patzowsky, 80 A 241 (Ch Ct 1911).*

Directors who let dominant director manage corporation and negligently failed to supervise his conduct of corporation are equally liable with him for fees he collected from corporation for services he did not perform and for corporation's losses on illegal investments he caused it to make. *Lutz v Boas, 171 A2d 381 (Ch Ct 1961).*

Stock options are valid even though stock option committee was not appointed by majority of board, since committee only recommended options to board, and board gave its final approval. *Beard v Elster, 160 A2d 731 (1960)*, reversing, *Elster v American Airlines, Inc, 128 A2d 801 (Ch Ct 1960)*, followed on remand, *167 A2d 231 (Ch Ct 1961).*

Note: Under the law as it now reads, directors can act without formal meeting, if *all* of them approve in writing the action to be taken [§141(f)].

One director, who took different position from others, by arguing that his absence from two board meetings entitled him to be relieved of personal liability for failure of others to exercise due care at those meetings, did not have standing because his arguments were not timely asserted when (1) opportunity was afforded individual directors to present factual or legal reasons why they should be treated individually and (2) director could not now claim that another meeting, which he did attend, had no significance when he had been claiming that it was determinative of virtually all issues. *Smith v Van Gorkom, 488 A2d 858 (1985).*

Former shareholder challenging accomplished merger was denied preliminary injunction to bar acquirer from causing merged corporation to engage in any transaction outside of its ordinary course of business, *pendente lite,* except on 30 days' notice to court and plaintiff's counsel. Such restraint would impair directors' right to manage corporation and make plaintiff *ex officio* member of board. *Frazer v Worldwide Energy Corp, No. 8822 (Ch Ct 2-19-87).*

Provision in certificate of incorporation allowing majority of board to fix number of directors is not illegal. Under GCL §102(b)(1), any provision permitted to be stated in the bylaws may be stated in the certificate of incorporation. *The Henley Group, Inc v Santa Fe Southern Pacific Corp, No. 9569 (Ch Ct 3-11-88).*

Board of directors could not assert the attorney-client privilege against plaintiff's designated representative to the board with respect to legal advice furnished to the board during the representative's tenure. *Moore Business Forms, Inc v Cordant Holdings Corp, Nos. 13911 & 14595, 1996 (Ch Ct 6-4-96.)*

.2 Delegation of authority.—Directors cannot delegate their duty to manage corporate enterprise, but this does not prevent them from depositing in voting trust shares of stock owned by corporation, even though these shares represent sole substantial asset of corporation. *Adams v Clearance Corp, 121 A2d 302 (1956).*

To same effect on first point: *Clarke Memorial College v Minaghan Land Co, 257 A2d 234 (Ch Ct 1969).*

Corporation equally owned by two groups of stockholders can create new class of nonparticipating voting stock, and issue one share to odd numbered new director able to break deadlock; arrangement (1) is not voting trust subject to ten-year limit, since stockholders retained their voting rights; (2) does not violate any public policy by issuance of voting stock with no proprietary rights; and (3) is not unlawful delegation of directors' duties, since it was approved by unanimous vote of stockholders and effected through charter amendment, *Lehrman v Cohen, 222 A2d 800 (1966).*

Note: Under the present law, directors can delegate the management of the business and affairs of the corporation to a committee composed of one or more directors [§141(c)].

The Court of Chancery invalidated a merger agreement between two corporations based on statutory violations by directors of one of the corporations. GCL §251(b) does not permit directors to approve a merger agreement unless the agreement expressly states the consideration stockholders are to receive, and, GCL §141(c) does not allow the board to delegate its responsibilities under §251. In the present case the directors set a floor price for the merger consideration, but left the final decision as to any higher price to a third party; indeed, the outside advisors did ultimately set the merger price. *Jackson v Turnbull, No. 13042 (Ch Ct 2-8-94).*

.3 Directors as fiduciaries.—Directors in conduct of corporation are fiduciaries in relation to corporation and its stockholders. *Gottlieb v McKee, 107 A2d 240 (Ch Ct 1954); Bodell v General Gas & Electric Corp, 132 A 442 (1926).*

Generally, however, directors do not occupy fiduciary position as against individual stockholders in direct personal dealings as opposed to dealings with stockholders as class, and only when director is possessed of special knowledge of future plans or secret corporate resources and deliberately misleads stockholder who is ignorant of them will court impose fiduciary relationship upon director. *Kors v Carey, 158 A2d 136 (Ch Ct 1960).*

Director violates no fiduciary duty when he accepts option to buy stockholder's shares at book value, but does not mention outside offer to purchase

§141

corporate assets at higher price, since stockholder had previously voted to approve proposed sale of assets at that higher price and so knew book value was not shares' true worth when he gave option. *Lank v Steiner, 213 A2d 848 (Ch Ct 1965),* aff'd, *224 A2d 242 (1966).*

Court will dismiss stockholders' derivative suit against certain directors on claim they seized corporate opportunity by buying stock in company in which they were stockholders, and which company was 80% owned by their corporation, when it is shown corporation, while always interested in acquiring entire balance of stock interest did not want to acquire only part of it; further, stockholders' claim that board breached its fiduciary duty, by causing corporation to acquire remaining 20% at higher price per share than previously paid for by directors is unfounded, when board bought entire minority interest of 20% on stock exchange basis, whereas directors' transaction was for cash and only involved about one-fourth of those shares. *Kaplan v Fenton, 278 A2d 834 (1971).*

Shareholder's federal law claim that directors of Delaware corporation had deprived them of opportunity to sell shares at a premium by resisting takeover attempt was dismissed because the decision to resist a takeover is within scope of director's state law fiduciary duties, and there is no federal securities law duty to disclose one's motives in undertaking such resistance; state law claim of breach of fiduciary duty was also dismissed. *Panter v Marshall Field & Co, 646 F2d 271 (7th Cir 1981).*

Directors as corporate fiduciaries are denied benefit of statute of limitations when accused of fraud since they should be treated as trustees. *Laventhol Krekstein Horwarth & Horwarth v Tuckman, 372 A2d 168 (1976).*

Tender offer and subsequent cash-out merger were proper when group including two key officers/directors of target put together plan whereby they were able to acquire complete ownership of target by using target's assets to finance cost of acquisition because: (1) overall transaction did not amount to sale of substantially all of target's assets so it did not have to be approved by directors and stockholders and (2) officers did not breach fiduciary duty owed to target and its minority shareholders since they had not derived any special advantage from their fiduciary positions. *Field v Allyn, 457 A2d 1089 (Ch Ct),* aff'd, *467 A2d 1274 (1983).*

Absent a showing that corporation's directors engaged in unlawful conduct, directors did not breach fiduciary duty to preferred shareholders when they failed to structure spin-off, so preferred shareholders could keep their liquidation preference and redemption rights and still participate in subsidiary's stock dividend because directors owed fiduciary duty, not only to preferred shareholders, but also to common shareholders and corporation. *Robinson v T.I.M.E.—DC Inc, 566 FSupp 1077 (ND Tex 1983).*

Directors breached their fiduciary duty to shareholders when they approved corporation's merger after (1) failing to inform themselves of all relevant and reasonably available information and (2) failing to disclose all material information that reasonable shareholders would consider important in deciding whether to approve merger. Business judgment did not protect directors when failure to inform themselves constituted gross negligence. *Smith v Van Gorkom, 488 A2d 858 (1985).*

Shareholder denied preliminary injunction restraining corporation and directors from issuing stock at stock sale because board had not breached fiduciary duty when it withdrew from stockholders, at stockholders' meeting, right to vote on bylaw amendment that repealed existing limitation on number of shares stockholders could own and then adopted amendment itself during meeting recess; it was not *per se* breach of fiduciary duty for directors to act against majority shareholders' wishes because there were other factors that directors could consider when exercising business judgment. *American International Rent A Car Inc v Cross, No. 7583 (Ch Ct 5-9-84).*

Terms of merger which left preferred shareholders of pre-merger corporation as shareholders of post-merger corporation did not result from directors' breach of fiduciary duty. Although directors' actions in seeking merger partner based on what partner would offer common shareholders, without seeking anything specific for preferred shareholders, may have breached duty, merger partner's offer was not made in direct response to director's solicitations. *Dalton v American Investment Co, 490 A2d 574 (Ch Ct 1985).*

Target's directors violated fiduciary duty to shareholders by granting lock-up and no-shop guarantees to white knight in exchange for protection of rights of holders of notes that target had exchanged earlier for stock in order to deter takeover by hostile tender offeror. Lock-up and no-shop guarantees harmed shareholders because guarantees foreclosed further bidding in active bidding situation and were made in directors' self-interest because they promoted agreement that relieved directors of potentially damaging consequences (suit by noteholders) of their own defensive policies. *Revlon, Inc v MacAndrews & Forbes Holdings, Inc, 506 A2d 173 (1986).*

Majority shareholders/directors breached their fiduciary duties of fair dealing owed to minority shareholders when they approved cash-out merger because (1) merger had intended effect of terminating pending derivative litigation seeking recovery from majority shareholders/directors and (2) no independent agency, either board committee, special counsel or investment banker, provided basis to conclude that derivative claims were without value to corporation or that cash-out price was fair. *Merritt v Colonial Foods, Inc, 505 A2d 757 (Ch Ct 1986).*

Court refused to enjoin consummation of corporation's recapitalization plan that established ESOP controlling 25% interest in corporation because (1) Majority of directors who approved plan were disinterested. (2) ESOP was not entrenchment device, principally motivated for impermissible purpose. (3) ESOP was not fraud or waste of corporate assets because directors did not have obligation to sell stock to it only at fair market value. *In re Anderson, Clayton Shareholders' Litigation, 519 A2d 680 (Ch Ct 1986).*

Minority shareholders could not bring claim against directors of merged corporation for failing to exercise due care in responding to merger proposal when directors' special committee (1) consulted with independent legal and financial advisors, (2) considered merger proposal on at least four occasions over six week period, (3) consistent with advice of investment banker, concluded that offered price was fair, and (4) before accepting offered price, asked that it be raised. However, remaining directors' alleged failure to learn of parent's price commitment did state claim. *Rabkin v Philip A Hunt Chemical Corp, 547 A2d 963 (Ch Ct 1986).*

Court refused to dismiss the complaint in a class action attacking leveraged buy-out of corporation as breach of directors' fiduciary duty. However, court did dismiss suit against purchaser for aiding and abetting directors' alleged breach of fiduciary duty because granting of stock option was not inherently wrongful and purchaser was not aware of directors' alleged failure to properly inform themselves with respect to transaction. *Greenfield v National Medical Care, Inc, Nos. 7720 and 7765 Consolidated (Ch Ct 6-6-86).*

Court dismissed claim that target's directors should have disclosed in Schedule 14D-9 of Securities Exchange Act of 1934 *pro forma* financial projections that were filed with ICC as part of target's responsive application concerning merger of two of its competitors. Although court declined to adopt *per se* rule that would render nondisclosable all "soft" information and, instead, adopted balancing approach on case-by-case basis, information in projection was not reliable enough to necessitate disclosure. However, court refused to dismiss claim that target should have disclosed status of ICC proceedings concerning competitors' merger because materiality of information and whether omission of information in Schedule 14D-9 could be cured by target's prior public disclosures of same information must be determined at trial. Tender offerors are not liable for aiding and abetting directors' alleged breach of fiduciary duty because they played no role in directors' decision not to disclose existence of ICC proceedings or *pro forma* financial projections. *Weinberger v Rio Grande Industries, Inc, 519 A2d 116 (Ch Ct 1986).*

In action by takeover offeror charging target's directors with breaching their fiduciary duty when they refused to redeem certain stock purchase rights, target must provide offeror with (1) documents relating to directors' decision not to redeem rights, including information relating to directors' assessment of adequacy of offer's terms and to retention of and reliance on professional advisors in connection with offer and (2) materials considered by directors describing terms of prior proposed acquisitions, adequacy of proposals, and defensive measures in response to proposals. *Plaza Securities Co v Office, No. 8737 (Ch Ct 12-15-86).*

Proxy statement in connection with proposed merger did not omit material information when (1) deferred tax liability, which was reported in accordance with generally accepted accounting principles, did not have to be further explained to shareholders, (2) supplement adequately disclosed value of asset, and (3) information in undisclosed report was already adequately disclosed. Directors of corporation did not violate duty of due care when they did not have copy of report evaluating merger because they had access to source materials from which report was prepared. *Schlossberg v The First Artists Production Co, No. 6670 (Ch Ct 12-17-86).*

Court issued preliminary injunction to block corporation's self-tender, holding that challenger would likely prove that disclosures were inadequate and that offer was coercive. Corporation's directors and officers have stronger duty of disclosure in self-tender than in contested offer. That duty is to advise shareholders fully and impartially about advantages and disadvantages of tender.

Self-tender for preferred stock was coercive when it occurred when stock was at lowest level in five years, board had stated policy of not declaring dividends, and board advised shareholders that it intended to seek delisting of stock. *Eisenberg v Chicago Milwaukee Corp, 537 A2d 1051 (Ch Ct 1987).*

Parent did not breach its fiduciary duty to its wholly owned subsidiary, which was soon to be spun-off, when it caused subsidiary's directors to approve agreement arguably favorable to parent and unfavorable to subsidiary because purchasers of when-issued stock in subsidiary were owed no duties by subsidiary before spin-off, so parent was dealing with itself when it caused subsidiary to approve disputed agreement. *Anadarko Petroleum Corp v Panhandle Eastern Corp, 521 A2d 624 (Ch Ct 1987).*

Under Delaware law, directors considering poison pill have duty to inform themselves as to methods used to value corporation's stock for purposes of plan. Otherwise plan may be enjoined as "show-stopper," i.e., an overpriced plan that ultimately prevents shareholders from obtaining fair market price for stock. Court enjoined poison pill when directors never inquired into bases underlying $6 and $10 minimum prices for corporation's stock. *Buckhorn, Inc v Ropak Corp, 656 FSupp 209 (SD Ohio 1987).*

Court refused to dismiss complaint by minority shareholders challenging merger of corporation into wholly owned subsidiary of parent owning 93% of corporation's voting power. Suit challenged merger on grounds that price was unfair, material facts had been misrepresented, and merger terms had not been adequately considered by board that was dominated by parent. When parent corporation and sub's directors stand on both sides of a merger transaction, they have burden of establishing entire fairness of merger. *Sealy Mattress Co of New Jersey, Inc v Sealy, Inc, 532 A2d 1324 (Ch Ct 1987).*

In derivative action charging directors and their investment advisors with breach of fiduciary duty when they set up exchange offer to defeat takeover attempt, court denied preliminary injunction to require directors to notify plaintiffs prior to dismissing or settling California action against its investment advisors. Court found that there were no ongoing settlement negotiations between parties to the California action, and refused to assume that Unocal directors will breach their fiduciary duties by settling California action on unfavorable terms in order to protect themselves from potential liability. *Silverzweig v Unocal Corp, No. 9078 (Ch Ct 7-22-87).*

§141

Court dismissed suit charging three of target corporation's directors with violating their duty of care when they rejected friendly cash tender offer at 37% premium over market value. Complaint asserted cognizable legal theory when it sought to enforce shareholders' right to have corporation's directors make informed business judgment as to whether to accept offer or negotiate a transaction on different terms. However, plaintiff failed to allege sufficient nonconclusory facts to support theory that defendants were uninformed. *Lewis v Honeywell, Inc, No. 8651 (Ch Ct 7-28-87).*

Corporate board may take action designed to injure interests of specific shareholders only when such action is designed to promote corporate goal and is reasonable in relationship to end sought. Board improperly manipulated corporate machinery to remove supervisory power conferred on holders of Class B shares by certificate of incorporation, by postponement of annual meeting, issuance of shares to director to dilute B shareholders' voting power, and bylaw amendments that removed effective control of board from B shareholders. *Phillips v Instituform of North America, Inc, No. 9173 (Ch Ct 8-27-87).*

Court issued temporary restraining order barring target corporation from purchasing any of its own stock for 20-day period. Plaintiff tender offeror stated colorable claim of breach of duty. Target's purchase threatened legal injury to tender offeror in its capacity as shareholder seeking to increase ownership of firm, and injury may be irreparable. Purchases also threatened irreparable injury to shareholders who might desire to tender.

Court declined to restrain white knight from voting stock giving it 23% of target's voting power and also declined to require target to segregate proceeds of sale to white knight for purposes of possible rescission. *UIS, Inc v Walbro Corp, No. 9323 (Ch Ct 10-6-87).*

Court refused to enjoin corporation's implementation of stock reclassification plan which involved the distribution of a new issue of common stock, where plaintiff failed to show that: (1) restructuring was done only for purpose of perpetuating majority shareholders' voting control; (2) board of directors breached fiduciary duty by failing to seriously consider alternatives; (3) restructuring could only be used to thwart an imminent take-over threat; and (4) irreparable harm would result if preliminary injunction were denied. *Hahn v Carter-Wallace, Inc, No. 9097 (Ch Ct 10-19-87).*

Court denied preliminary injunction to require corporation to drop management-sponsored buyout and grant a lock-up option to competing hostile offeror, where corporation's board rejected competing offer and lock-up at recommendation of independent board committee. Under these circumstances, plaintiffs were unlikely to succeed in proving that directors had violated their duty to secure maximum return for shareholders in sale of company. *Freedman v Restaurant Associates Industries, Inc, No. 9212 (Ch Ct 10-16-87).*

Court refused to grant preliminary injunction to block street sweep of target corporation's stock executed by target's largest shareholder during hostile tender offer by outsider. Sweep was financed by target's declaration of $33 dividend in return for standstill agreement placing voting and transfer restrictions on sweeping shareholder.

Court ruled that tender offeror was unlikely to succeed in proving that transaction amounted to breach of fiduciary duty by target's board or that of sweeping shareholder where (1) declaration of dividend was protected by business judgment rule when there was no self-dealing or waste and it furthered several business objectives; (2) the transactions in question were not motivated by single entrenchment purpose when sweeping shareholder was potential bidder and transactions were negotiated at arm's-length; (3) street sweep was not coercive to sellers; market forces propelled the sale; (4) defensive measures were reasonable in relation to threat posed. *Ivanhoe Partners v Newmont Mining Corp, 533 A2d 585 (Ch Ct), aff'd, 535 A2d 1334 (1987).*

Court dismissed complaint charging issuer of convertible debentures with breaching fiduciary duties to holders by altering conversion rights following merger, allegedly to holders' detriment. Holder of convertible bond is creditor and is owed contractual but not fiduciary duties until he exercises power of conversion. *Simons v Cogan, 542 A2d 785 (Ch Ct 1987).*

Issuing corporation and directors do not owe fiduciary duty to holder of convertible debentures. Existing property right or equitable interest must be present to create a fiduciary duty. Holder of convertible debenture has no equitable interest until it is converted. He therefore remains a creditor of corporation whose interests are governed by indenture's contractual terms. *Simons v Cogan, 549 A2d 300 (1988), aff'g, 542 A2d 785 (Ch Ct 1987).*

Upon reargument, court persisted in refusal to dismiss complaint charging directors of merged corporation with breaching their fiduciary duties by failing to learn of price commitment that would have required acquiring corporation to pay $5 more per share if their corporation had been acquired earlier. One can conclude that in exercise of ordinary care, directors should have known of the price commitment. *Rabkin v Philip A Hunt Chemical Corp, No. 7547 (Ch Ct 12-17-87).*

Court refused to enjoin closing of white knight's tender offer for 90% of corporation's stock. Reliance on investment banker that owned 10% of white knight to negotiate tender offer by white knight was not grossly negligent when target's management retained important role in negotiations, and second investment banker indicated that transaction was fair one. *Solash v The Telex Corp, No. 9518 (Ch Ct 1-19-88).*

Controlling shareholder owed general fiduciary duty to corporation and minority shareholders even though certain specific transactions were immunized by governmental agency approval. Controlling shareholder breached this duty by taking actions for its own benefit that were materially detrimental to subsidiary's productivity and effectiveness. *Summa Corp v Trans World Airlines, Inc, 540 A2d 403 (1988).*

Court rejected argument that board violated duties under *Revlon, Inc v McAndrews & Forbes Holdings, Inc,* 506 A2d 173 (1986) by negotiating with only one bidder and not inviting further bids. Methods directors use to elicit bids from potential acquirors are normally a matter of director judgment. *Yanow v Scientific Leasing, Inc, Nos. 9536 and 9561 (Ch Ct 2-5-88).*

In auctioning company, board's decision to reject purportedly higher offer on terms in favor of all-cash offer with arguably lower value does not constitute breach of fiduciary duty when: (1) all-cash offer required no financing and deal could be closed quickly; and (2) other offer was in significant part paper, no specifics were given as to paper's terms, and deal could not be closed quickly. One who seeks to visit liability upon director for injury suffered by corporation as result of act of independent board must prove that action was grossly negligent or was not taken in honest attempt to foster corporation's welfare. *Citron v Fairchild Camera and Investment Corp, No. 6085 (Ch Ct 5-19-88).*

Court issued preliminary injunction to prevent target from restructuring to prevent takeover by outsider. Restructuring, which was not put to shareholder vote, was said to be worth $64.15 to shareholders. Outsider proposed either $73 per share cash tender offer or restructuring allegedly worth $5.65 more to shareholders than management's proposal. As fiduciaries, directors may not "cram down" transaction to protect shareholders from noncoercive, economically superior one. *Robert M Bass Group, Inc v Evans, 552 A2d 1227 (Ch Ct 1988).*

Corporation's board did not violate duty to auction under *Revlon, Inc v MacAndrews & Forbes Holdings, Inc,* 506 A2d 173 (1986), by permitting negotiations with management-affiliated buyout group to be completed before informing public that company was for sale. *In re Fort Howard Corp Shareholders Litigation, No. 9991 (Ch Ct 8-4-88).*

A position less than a majority stockholding may factually give rise to control which, in turn, gives rise to fiduciary duty. It is actual exercise of such control, however, not the simple potential for control, that creates the special duty. *Citron v Steego Corp, No. 10171 (Ch Ct 9-9-88).*

Absent improper purpose, corporation has right to buy back shares from dissident shareholders. No Delaware law exists to support plaintiffs' contention that directors had duty to extend buy-back to all shareholders. *In re General Motors Class E Stock Buyout Securities Litigation, 694 FSupp 1119 (D Del 1988).*

Court declined to enjoin preliminary leveraged buyout, where committee of directors who approved management's bid was fully informed when it knew that (1) corporation's financial adviser had solicited many possible bidders without success; (2) adviser did not think it could get bid higher than $19; and (3) adviser considered $19 to be fair price. *In re KDI Corp Shareholders Litigation, No. 10,278 (Ch Ct 11-1-88).*

Directors of target corporation did not violate their duty of loyalty to shareholders who had tendered their shares to hostile bidder by negotiating a substitute offer, open to all shareholders, that featured additional "back-end" procedural protections. Tendering shareholders have a protectible interest in their proration position, but that interest must yield to the paramount interests of the corporation or its shareholders as a whole. *Gilbert v The El Paso Co, Nos. 7075 and 7079 consolidated (Ch Ct 11-21-88).*

Court ordered target corporation to redeem poison pill rights in face of cash tender offer for all its shares by outsider, where target's decision to keep poison pill in place was not reasonable in relation to threat posed. *Grand Metropolitan Public Limited Co v The Pillsbury Co, 558 A2d 1049 (Ch Ct 1988).*

In a case where company was not being sold to a third party but was being acquired by its 42 percent stockholder, a *Revlon* situation did not arise; i.e., directors were not required to ensure that stockholders receive the maximum value possible for their shares. *Kleinhandler v Borgia, No. 8334 (Ch Ct 7-7-89).*

Court denied two applications for preliminary injunctive relief in connection with competing bidders' efforts to acquire target corporation. Court found that: (1) target did not establish any basis for an order barring bidders from entering into agreement to acquire target; and (2) bidder's application for injunction barring target and other bidder from proceeding with an auction of target failed to show irreparable harm and was not ripe. *In re Holly Farms Corp Shareholders Litigation, No. 10350 (Ch Ct 5-18-89).*

In a suit alleging that directors breached their fiduciary duties by failing to defend against an unsolicited cash tender offer, the board's failure to provide stockholders with the detailed advice about the offer from the company's financial adviser could have been material to the stockholder's determination of the adequacy of the price. *Day v Quotron Systems, No. 8502 (Ch Ct 11-20-89).*

The determination of whether directors breached their fiduciary duties of loyalty and due care when the directors did not conduct an active market survey, but instead relied on the advice of an investment bank to evaluate the fairness to shareholders of a change of control not involving outside bidders, is to be made on the basis of the adequacy of information available to the directors and in light of relevant circumstances. *Barkan v Amsted Industries, Inc, 567 A2d 1279 (Ch Ct 1989).*

The Court of Chancery refused to grant a motion to dismiss claims of breach of defendants' duty of candor for untimely and inaccurate supplemental proxies. The court questioned both the accuracy of defendants' characterization of consideration in that defendants gave two different values of the stock component in the litigated merger, and the defendants' timeliness in letting a supplemental proxy reach shareholders only one week before the shareholder meeting, when all information in the proxy was known to defendants well before that time. *Herd v Major Realty Corp, No. 10707 (Ch Ct 12-21-90).*

Plaintiffs' duty of care claim dismissed where defendants demonstrated that their action was ratified by a fully informed shareholder vote; plaintiffs' duty of loyalty claim dismissed where disinterested, independent board of directors, who engaged the corporation in an active bidding process, preferred a preexisting merger plan over a third party's unsolicited acquisition proposal. *In re Santa Fe Pacific Corporation Shareholder Litigation, No. 13587 (Ch Ct 5-31-95).*

§141

Plaintiffs failed to demonstrate that the board of directors breached its duty of care where the evidence showed that the board acted in good faith and that a majority of disinterested directors approved a transaction. Plaintiffs also failed to demonstrate the board breached its duty of candor by failing to disclose to the shareholders the details of a transaction where the board did not seek shareholder approval of the transaction. *Kahn, derivatively on behalf of Dekalb Genetics Corp v Roberts, No. 12324 (Ch Ct 12-6-95).*

A board of directors is not required by the law of fiduciary disclosure to articulate, in a proxy statement, the reasons why two directors of the corporation either opposed or abstained from commenting on a stock for stock merger with another corporation. *Newman v Warren, No. 15008 (Ch Ct 8-19-96).*

In determining that a proposed settlement of a derivative action for breach of duty to monitor corporate officers and employees was "fair and reasonable" in view of the fact that there was not much likelihood of plaintiff's prevailing, the Chancery Court articulated a good faith standard with which to judge directors on breach of monitoring duty claims. *In re Caremark International Inc Derivative Litigation, No. 133670 (Ch Ct 9-25-96).*

Plaintiffs failed to demonstrate that the board breached their duty of care, where the evidence revealed that the board, in deciding to approve a tender offer, relied on advice from financial advisors, adequately reviewed that advisors' findings, and considered other offers from potential acquirors. Plaintiffs also failed to show that the board breached the duty of disclosure, which requires a board to disclose "all material facts within its control that would have a significant effect upon a shareholder." *In re Cheyenne Software, Inc Shareholders Litigation, No. 14941 (Ch Ct 11-7-96).*

Where the issuance of stock would have the effect of eliminating a minority stockholder's call right on the majority stockholder's stock and a majority of the board of directors was comprised of representatives of the majority shareholder, the board may be blocked from such an issuance by a later determination that the stock issuance was in violation of the board's duty of loyalty, although the board has the legal authority to issue the stock. *Sicpa Holding S.A. v Optical Coating Laboratory, Inc., No. 15129 (Ch Ct 1-6-97).*

The fiduciary duties of directors and officers of a corporation may be imputed to a separate entity formed and controlled by those directors and officers where the allegations established that the directors and officers formed the separate entity for the purpose of engaging in a transaction with the corporation to whom they owed those duties. *Barbieri v Swing-N-Slide Corp, No. 14239 (Ch Ct 1-29-97).*

Where it is claimed that directors breached their duty of loyalty and care by granting the corporation's chairman a stock option agreement that constituted corporate waste, the independence of the corporation's directors is put into dispute where it is alleged that some of the directors were also executive officers who were beholden to the chairman; some of the directors received excessive compensation and were beholden to the chairman by virtue of fees paid to their firm; some of the directors, albeit outside directors, received excessive compensation; and some of the directors received valuable stock options. *Telxon Corp. v. Bogomolny, 792 A2d 964 (Ch Ct 2001).*

Bylaws amended by shareholder consent are invalid and will be struck down to the extent that they are used to further an inequitable purpose of the controlling shareholder. The Delaware Chancery Court first ruled that the Amendments were not inconsistent with the DGCL. The court found that by its own terms §141(c)(2) permits a board committee to exercise the power of the board only to the extent "provided in the resolution of the board ... or in the bylaws of the corporation." *Hollinger International, Inc v Black, 844 A2d 1022 (Ch Ct 2004).*

The Delaware Supreme Court affirmed opinions by the Chancery Court that imposed money damages on a CEO and his holding companies for self-dealing, that ruled invalid in equity bylaw amendments propounded by the CEO designated to assure his continuing control and self-dealing, and that upheld a shareholder rights plan designed to prevent the CEO from effecting his self-interested transactions. *Black v Hollinger International, Inc, 872 A2d 559 (2005).*

Directors of a corporation breach their fiduciary duty of loyalty where they act as mere "stooges" for the majority shareholder and let him do whatever he wants at the expense of the minority shareholders; in such a situation, the directors may be held jointly and severally liable with the majority shareholder for monetary damages, but will not be held liable for fee-shifting imposed on the majority shareholder. *ATR-Kim Eng Financial Corp v Araneta, 2006 Del. Ch. LEXIS 215 (Ch Ct 2006).*

Where a plaintiff alleges that directors issued stock options according to a shareholder-approved employee compensation plan and that the directors (a) possessed material non-public information soon to be released that would impact the company's share price, and (b) issued those options with the intent to circumvent otherwise valid shareholder-approved restrictions upon the exercise price of the options, the plaintiff successfully alleges that the directors' actions went beyond business judgment by being disloyal and in bad faith. *In re Tyson Foods, Inc. Consolidated Shareholder Litigation, 2007 Del. Ch. LEXIS 19 (Ch Ct 2007).*

A merger will not be preliminarily enjoined merely because management projections have not been disclosed in proxy materials; there is no per se rule that such projections are material. *In re CheckFree Corp Shareholders Litig, 2007 Del. Ch. LEXIS 148 (Ch Ct 2007).*

A challenge to a board's approval of a cash-out merger as being at an inadequate price will be dismissed where insufficient facts are alleged to rebut the presumptions of the business judgment rule. *Globis Partners, L.P. v Plumtree Software, Inc, 2007 Del. Ch. LEXIS 169 (Ch Ct 2007).*

If a corporate parent (or grandparent) of a fiduciary exercises dominion and control over the fiduciary in connection with a transaction that benefits the corporate parent at the expense of the underlying entity, the corporate parent may owe fiduciary duties directly to the underlying entity in connection with that transaction. *Cargill, Inc v JWH Special Circumstance LLC, 2008 Del. Ch. LEXIS 166 (Ch Ct 2008).*

Monetary or injunctive relief will not be granted for disclosure violations in a merger proxy solicitation where it has been three years since the merger's consummation and where there is no evidence of a breach of the duty of loyalty or good faith by the directors who authorized the disclosures; enthusiasm for a merger and engagement in the merger negotiations do not equate with disloyalty or bad faith.

The Chancery Court determined that it did not need to determine whether the purported misrepresented facts were material, whether the directors were protected by the exculpatory provision, or whether such disclosure would have amounted to "self-flagellation," because it held that all of the shareholders' disclosure claims were barred. In arriving at this holding, the court observed that a breach of the disclosure duty leads to irreparable harm, for which the court grants injunctive relief to prevent a vote from taking place where there is a credible threat that shareholders will be asked to vote without such complete and accurate information. The corollary to this point, however, is that once this irreparable harm has occurred—i.e., when shareholders have already voted without complete and accurate information—it is, by definition, too late to remedy the harm. Accordingly, the court concluded that because the solicitation of proxies for the shareholder vote approving the merger occurred over three years prior, and because the merger had been consummated, an injunctive order requiring supplemental, corrective disclosures at this stage would be an exercise in futility and frivolity. The court also concluded that there was no evidence of a breach of the duty of loyalty or good faith by the directors who authorized the disclosures. Instead, the court found that the evidence merely showed that the directors were engaged, active, and enthusiastic supporters and salesmen of the merger, but concluded that such conduct did not constitute disloyal behavior sufficient to defeat a motion for summary judgment. The court said that enthusiasm for a merger and engagement in the merger negotiations do not equate with disloyalty or bad faith. For these reasons, the court granted summary judgment to the director-defendants. *In re Transkaryotic Therapies, Inc, 954 A2d 346 (Ch Ct 2008).*

Directors do not breach their fiduciary duty of care in adopting a change-of-control trust indenture provision that permits noteholders to put their notes to the corporation at face value, thereby potentially posing a significant economic problem for the corporation and its shareholders, where the directors and its pricing committee have been advised on the indenture by highly-qualified counsel, management, and investment bankers; the provision has not been pointed out by these advisors as unusual; and the provision is a relatively very small portion of the entire indenture.

Applying New York law, the Delaware Chancery Court ruled that the board was entitled to approve the stockholder nominees if the board determined in good faith that the election of one or more of the dissident nominees would not be materially adverse to the interests of the corporation or its stockholders. As to the duty of care issue, applying Delaware law, the court ruled that the directors had not breached this fiduciary duty. Although it was shown that the pricing committee never discovered during its approval process that the proposed indenture contained a continuing directors provision, the court said that the directors' duty of care did not require them to review, discuss, and comprehend every word of the 98-page indenture, especially since they retained highly-qualified counsel and sought advice from company management and investment bankers as to the terms of the agreement. The board had asked its counsel if there was anything "unusual or not customary" in the terms of the notes, and it was told there was not. Only then did the board approve the issuance of the notes under the indenture. The court concluded that this was not the sort of conduct generally imagined when considering the concept of gross negligence, typically defined as a substantial deviation from the standard of care. However, the court admonished that in circumstances such as presented here, counsel advising a board should be especially mindful of the board's continuing duties to the stockholders to protect their interests. Specifically, terms which may affect the stockholders' range of discretion in exercising the franchise should, even if considered customary, be highlighted to the board. In this way, the board will be able to exercise its fully informed business judgment. *San Antonio Fire & Police Pension Fund v Amylin Pharmaceuticals, Inc, 2009 Del. Ch. LEXIS 83 (Ch Ct 2009).*

Directors owe fiduciary duties to preferred stockholders as well as common stockholders where the right claimed by the preferred is not to a preference as against the common stock but rather a right shared equally with the common. Thus, where parties agree on a price (or conversion equivalent) below which the issuance of stock will trigger anti-dilution provisions, the issuance of stock at a slightly higher price, which is above fair value, is neither a breach of fiduciary duties nor a breach of the implied covenant of good faith and fair dealing.

The Chancery Court found that the decision to issue stock at a price higher than its fair value simply did not satisfy the standard for breach of the duty of loyalty by an unconflicted board, such as the Company B board. The court also concluded that Company A failed to explain how a director who authorized the sale of company stock for more than its fair value could be said to have acted disloyally or otherwise not in the best interests of the corporation and its various shareholders. Putting aside the authority that preferred stockholders have no fiduciary duty claims against directors that are not also fiduciary duty claims of common stockholders, the court emphasized that the relationship between Company A and Company B was defined specifically in their agreement and included a specific understanding as to the minimum price at which stock would be issued; the anti-dilution provisions were not implicated. The court also observed that this was not a case where shares were issued for less than fair value and, thus, might have had a dilutive effect (but that would have been a claim shared with the common shareholders). Therefore, the court held there had been no breach of fiduciary duties. As to whether the issuance of stock at a price of $1.39 per share violated the covenant of good faith and fair dealing implicit in the parties' agreement, the court reasoned

§141

that simply because the applicable documents did not expressly address what would happen if shares were issued at a price equal to or greater than $1.36 per share, the only plausible inference was that the parties considered the issue and reached agreement as to what price would trigger anti-dilution protection. *Amazon.com, Inc v Hoffman, 2009 Del. Ch. LEXIS 119 (Ch Ct 2009).*

A claim for breach of the fiduciary duty of loyalty is made out where a board fails to take protective measures to prevent a majority shareholder from obtaining control through a creeping acquisition while the shareholder, who is also the corporation's CEO and chairman, is in merger negotiations to take the company private. A reasonable inference of the breach of the duty of loyalty also arises where that shareholder, with the board's acquiescence, negotiates a refinancing commitment on behalf of the company as part of an amended debt commitment letter, and where the board terminates the merger agreement, thus allowing the shareholder to avoid paying a $15 million reverse-termination fee. In such a situation, the shareholder exercises actual control and therefore owes fiduciary duties to the other stockholders and the corporation. Because the shareholder's knowledge is imputed to his 100%-owned shell corporations, which are used to effect the transaction, an aiding and abetting of fiduciary duties claim will not be dismissed against those corporations. Finally, because the situation raises a question as to whether the transaction was the product of a valid exercise of business judgment, presuit demand is excused as to a derivative waste claim, which will also not be dismissed. *Louisiana Municipal Police Employees' Ret Syst v Fertitta, 2009 Del. Ch. LEXIS 144 (Ch Ct 2009).*

.4 Same—regarding takeovers.—Until the conclusion of the tender offer, acquiror owed no fiduciary duty to target's shareholders, nor did target's board bear legal responsibility for alleged nondisclosures in acquiror's offer to purchase, absent some proof that the two boards engaged in joint conduct to mislead shareholders. *Citron v Fairchild Camera and Instrument Corp, 569 A2d 53 (1989).*

Mere allegation that fiduciaries benefitted from changed circumstances that favored directors over shareholders in a merger, but over which directors had no control, did not mandate a finding of selfdealing and, therefore, did not make the merger void or voidable. Special scrutiny given to a self-dealing transaction was not appropriate when merger price was fair, at least at the time it was agreed to, and the transaction was approved by stockholders after full disclosure. *Corwin v DeTrey, No. 6808 (Ch Ct 12-1-89).*

Despite a breach of fiduciary duties in considering a tender offer by a corporation's directors, the court refused to issue a preliminary injunction compelling the directors to redeem a "poison pill" where the tender offer price is negotiable and may not be the highest offer that will be made; where changes in circumstance dramatically alter the market for the stock; and where the terms of the offer are highly conditional and have not attracted a sufficiently high number of stocks tendered. *Sutton Holding Corp v DeSoto, Inc, Nos. 11221 and 11222 (Ch Ct 2-5-90).*

Delaware law foresees, generally, two circumstances that may implicate duties under *Revlon v MacAndrews & Forbes Holdings, Inc, 506 A2d 173 (Del 1986):* (1) when a corporation initiates a process to either sell itself or effect a reorganization involving a clear break-up of the company; and (2) when, "in response to a bidder's offer, a target abandons its long-term strategy and seeks an alternative transaction also involving the breakup of the company." Thus, if a board's reaction to a hostile offer is only a defensive response and not an abandonment of the company's continued existence, *Revlon* duties are not triggered although *Unocal* duties attach. *Paramount Communications, Inc v Time Inc, 571 A2d 1140 (1990).*

Derivative action upheld where it was alleged that controlling shareholder negligently sold control of the corporation to a buyer who allegedly looted the corporation. Where a sale of controlling interest in a corporation is coupled with an agreement for the seller to resign from the board of directors in such a way as to assure that the buyer's designees assume corporate office, the seller as a reasonably prudent person, owes a fiduciary duty to inquire as to the foreseeable harm to the corporation. *Harris v Carter, No. 8768 (Ch Ct 5-4-90).*

After noting that Delaware law does not require a board of directors to maximize short-term shareholder value or to abandon an existing corporate strategy in order to achieve short-term gain, court determined that a target corporation's board of directors acted reasonably when it refused to redeem its corporation's shareholder rights plan in response to an unsolicited tender offer where the board had demonstrated that it had conducted a reasonable investigation of the tender offer and had concluded, in good faith, that the unsolicited offer was both inadequate and posed a threat to the corporation and its shareholders. *Moore Corp Limited v Wallace Computer Services, Inc, 907 FSupp 1545 (D Del 1995).*

A going private transaction will be enjoined where the target's board has failed to fully disclose material information to shareholders. The target company will also be enjoined from using a standstill agreement to prevent a bidder from communicating with the target company's stockholder or presenting a bid that the stockholders could find materially more favorable than offered in the going private transaction. *In re the Topps Company Shareholders Litigation, 2007 Del. Ch. LEXIS 82 (Ch Ct 2007).*

.5 Exercise of good business judgment.—Directors who authorized corporation to purchase its own stock in order to resist takeover have burden of proving that such action was primarily in corporate interest and that change in control would threaten future business success of corporation. *Crane Co v Harsco Corp, 511 FSupp 294 (D Del 1981).*

Interlocking director is not personally liable for allegedly failing to have subsidiary demand timely payment of parent's debts, when there is no showing of bad faith, negligence or gross abuse of discretion. *Chasin v Gluck, 282 A2d 188 (Ch Ct 1971).*

Decision by board of directors to buy out founder and minority shareholder because of his extreme opposition to majority's plans for company was not waste of corporate assets; board exercised proper business judgment to eliminate clear threat to future of business. *Kaplan v Goldsamt, 380 A2d 556 (Ch Ct 1977).*

Minority shareholders who brought suit against directors for accepting allegedly inequitable tender offer and lock-up agreement could not enjoin tender offer and annual shareholders' meeting because directors' decision to accept tender offer and lock-up agreement one month before meeting at which other offers might have materialized was protected by business judgment rule. *Thompson v Enstar Corp, 509 A2d 578 (Ch Ct 1984).*

Directors had authority to adopt Rights Plan as preventive measure to ward off future advances by corporate raiders, where (1) action was not taken for entrenchment purposes, and (2) Plan was reasonable reaction by directors to perceived threat to corporation of coercive acquisition techniques. *Moran v Household International, Inc, 500 A2d 1346 (1985).*

Merger between parent and subsidiary was fair to subsidiary's minority shareholders when directors' decision to delegate subsidiary's asset valuation to engineering firm was proper exercise of business judgment. *Rosenblatt v Getty Oil Co, 493 A2d 929 (1985).*

Defendant-50% shareholder of corporation did not mismanage corporation or breach fiduciary duties to corporation or fellow shareholder, the plaintiff. Court found defendant's action after dissolution of the corporation, to pay back-pay to himself rather than paying outstanding debts was agreed to by both parties, and his failure to spend money to maintain a truck which plaintiff was to receive under the terms of the dissolution while investing sums in truck defendant was to receive, were within the realm of the business judgment rule, did not involve any injury to the corporation, and did not prove defendant intentionally or negligently dissipated the assets of the company. *Short v McNatt, No. 10077 (Ch Ct 5-17-91).*

Directors' funding of ESOP in response to shift of ownership was not valid because (1) directors had never considered funding ESOP as takeover defense that would increase number of outstanding shares to dilute majority status of consent holder, (2) directors were without power to ratify funding by less than unanimous vote after change in bylaws, and (3) corporate actions, which seek to undo takeover bids after control has passed, are not protected by business judgment rule. *Frantz Mfg Co v EAC Industry, 501 A2d 401 (1985).*

§141

Corporation's self tender for its shares which excluded participation of shareholder making hostile tender offer for corporation's stock, was valid because (1) selective stock repurchase plan was reasonable in relation to threat directors believed was posed by inadequate and coercive two-tier tender offer by corporate raider with reputation as "green-mailer" and (2) directors did not act in bad faith or to entrench themselves and therefore did not lose protection of business judgment rule when they tendered their shares in exchange offer since they were receiving benefits shared generally by all shareholders except raider. *Unocal Corp v Mesa Petroleum Co, 493 A2d 946 (1985).*

Court declined to require target corporation to redeem poison pill rights during auction for company's sale. Poison pill rights plan, if properly used, may provide directors with shield to fend off coercive offers and gavel to run an auction. Auction could produce bid superior to $27.50 being offered by tender offeror. Injunctive relief, however, could create significant risk that offeror could acquire target at $27.50 per share. *Facet Enterprises, Inc v The Prospect Group, Inc, No. 9746 (Ch Ct 4-11-88).*

Target's self-tender offer for 65% of its outstanding stock was not reasonable in relation to threat posed by takeover offer. Although target's directors could create option for shareholders permitting them to continue participation in target, they could not structure offer so that no rational shareholder would risk tendering into competing offer when to do so created risk of being frozen out of front end of self tender. *AC Acquisitions Corp v Anderson, Clayton & Co, 519 A2d 103 (Ch Ct 1986).*

Directors of corporation could not claim protection of business judgment rule in their decision to purchase company that was 80% owned by corporation's majority shareholder because directors voting in favor of acquisition were either (1) interested by virtue of having received personal financial benefit from sale of their stock in acquired company or (2) dominated by majority shareholder. *Gries Sports Enterprises, Inc v Cleveland Browns Football Co, 496 NE2d 959 (Ohio 1986).*

Court refused to enjoin leveraged buy-out whereby shareholders would receive $51 per share if majority approved transaction. Plaintiff failed to demonstrate reasonable probability of success on merits when there was no evidence to justify a conclusion that board acted improperly or that business judgment rule did not protect acts of board from further judicial scrutiny. Proxy statement was not materially misleading even though fairness opinion on which it was based was six months old, and statement neglected to point out that buy-out might mean loss of second quarter dividend. Plaintiffs failed to show irreparable harm because dissenting shareholders will still have right to seek appraisal. *Lewis v Leaseway Transportation Corp, No. 8720 (Ch Ct 6-12-87).*

Trial court erred in granting summary judgment against plaintiff on ground that corporation's decision to dismiss litigation was protected by business judgment rule. Defendant's proofs did not show business basis for the decision and left unresolved issue of whether it met reasonableness standard of *Zapata Corp v Maldonado, 430 A2d 779 (1981).*

Court upheld settlement agreement ending suit and counterclaim charging corporation and proxy contestants with violating §14(a) of '34 Securities Exchange Act, where (1) illegality of proxy solicitations did not deprive directors of power to reimburse contestants for proxy expenses as part of settlement nor make settlement unlawful; (2) settlement had business purpose—to preserve corporate policies believed to be in shareholders' best interests; (3) settlement was not illegal vote buying scheme; such schemes are not per se unlawful if they are intrinsically fair and the purpose is not to defraud or disenfranchise shareholders; here, purpose was not to disenfranchise shareholders, but to end threat to corporate policy. *Weinberger v Bankston, No. 6336 (Ch Ct 11-19-87).*

Board of directors' actions are protected by business judgment rule, and thus directors' decisions are ordinarily scrutinized according to standard of gross negligence. Rule does not apply to director inaction, however, so standard of ordinary care applies if directors abdicate their managerial responsibility. *Rabkin v Philip A Hunt Chemical Corp, No. 7547 (Ch Ct 12-17-87).*

Court refused to dismiss charges that directors violated Rule 10b-5 by failing to disclose greenmail negotiations. If proved, plaintiffs' theory would encompass attempt to manipulate stock prices by not disclosing negotiations that might lower stock values. *Fry v Trump, 681 FSupp 252 (D NJ 1988).*

Court refused to issue preliminary injunction to bar target corporation from issuing convertible preferred stock. Board had considered issuing stock as financing measure before start of tender offer and had tabled measure after its commencement. Target board was therefore entitled to protection of business judgment rule. Should board reconsider stock issue while tender offer is pending, it would have to satisfy test of *Unocal Corp v Mesa Petroleum Co, 493 A2d 946 (1985),* to qualify for protection of business judgment rule. *Doskocil Companies Inc v Griggy, No. 10,095 (Ch Ct 8-18-88).*

The Court of Chancery declined to enjoin corporation from implementing defensive measures, including poison pill plan, golden parachutes, or possible private placement of equity or debt securities with third party (white squire defense), where plaintiffs failed to establish reasonable probability that defensive measures were taken to entrench management or were unreasonable considering amount of plaintiff's offer. *Nomad Acquisition Corp v Damon Corp, No. 10173 (Ch Ct 9-16-88).*

The Court of Chancery refused to order target corporation to deactivate poison pill plan and supermajority vote provision to allow acquiror to complete tender offer, even though target's board had agreed to waive defenses with respect to lower competing offer. Stressing that third party was considering making offer, target took position that defenses must remain in place to preserve prospect of higher offer. Injunction would be inappropriate when there was evidence that target's directors intended to bring auction process to close on reasonable schedule. *Doskocil Companies Inc v Griggy, No. 10,095 (Ch Ct 10-7-88).*

Court refused to enjoin lock-up option, break-up fee, and expense reimbursement agreement between target and successful bidder in takeover contest. Break-up fees and expense reimbursement provisions are valid when they induce bidders to enter the contest and further an active auction. Fees and expenses worth 2.5% of transaction price not excessive. *Mills Acquisition Co v Macmillan, Inc, No. 10168 (Ch Ct 10-17-88).*

The Court of Chancery issued preliminary injunction to require target corporation to redeem poison pill rights in face of all-cash tender offer for $74 per share. Target was proceeding with restructuring said to be worth $76 per share to shareholders. Once target has chosen value-maximizing alternative to auction of company or negotiations with tender offeror, legitimate role of poison pill will have ended. At this stage, foreclosing shareholder choice is not reasonable in relation to threat posed. *City Capital Associates Limited Partnership v Interco Inc, 551 A2d 787 (Ch Ct 1988).*

Court refused to block going private merger despite serious questions as to effectiveness of special committee appointed to negotiate merger terms and the adequacy of disclosures to shareholders. These questions shifted burden of proof to defendants, who must show entire fairness of challenged transaction. *In re Trans World Airlines, Inc Shareholders Litigation, No. 9844 (Ch Ct 10-21-88).*

Court declined to preliminarily enjoin directors of target corporation from implementing poison pill, where (1) Evidence indicated that target's board adopted poison pill as a response to danger of unfair takeovers and to safeguard shareholders' interests; (2) Tender offeror did not claim that target's rights plan interfered with its ability to wage a proxy contest; (3) Evidence showed that target's board adopted plan pursuant to informed business judgment; (4) Poison pill did not preclude all hostile tender offers, and tender offer had been structured in such a way as to avoid pill's provisions; and (5) Evidence showed that directors did not adopt poison pill to entrench themselves in office. *Desert Partners, LP v USG Corp, 686 FSupp 1289 (ND Ill 1988).*

Court declined to set aside anti-takeover devices target adopted in response to tender offer. Of particular significance was short time tender offer had been pending and fact that in absence of takeover devices, plaintiff would not increase its offer. *MAI Basic Four, Inc v Prime Computer, Inc, No. 10428 (Ch Ct 12-20-88).*

Court enjoined preliminarily asset lock up in merger agreement between target and friendly bidder. However, court ruled that order requiring target to redeem poison pill rights would be premature when there was no evidence that board was using poison pill for any improper purpose, and pill might still have role in maximizing values. *In re Holly Farms Corp Shareholders Litigation, No. 10350 (Ch Ct 12-30-88).*

Target's ESOP was defensive device that is designed to add value to company and all of shareholder. Thus, plan adopted by shareholders, whether adequately considered or not, is fair and should not be invalidated. *Shamrock Holdings, Inc v Polaroid Corp, 559 A2d 257 (Ch Ct 1989).*

Directors did not violate duties of care and loyalty to shareholders when they approved takeover bid despite substantially equivalent bid from management group. When bidder imposes time restraints, board is forced to deal with that circumstance. If board exercises informed judgment, considers the risks imposed by deadline, and concludes it is prudent to act and acts with care, it has satisfied its duty. *In re RJR Nabisco, Inc, No. 10389, consolidated (Ch Ct 1-31-89).*

Target did not have duty to redeem poison pill rights even though more than 80% of its shareholders had accepted tender offer by hostile offeror. *Reason:* Closing of tender offer was conditioned on approval of offer and execution of merger agreement by target's board. Under the circumstances, board could decline merger proposal based on concern for long-term corporate values and without implicating duty to maximize current values for shareholders. *TW Services, Inc v SWT Acquisition Corp, No. 10427 (Ch Ct 3-2-89).*

Court refused to halt management leveraged buyout (LBO) because of market-test procedure that allowed directors to shop corporation for 30 business days to determine whether better deal was available. In denying preliminary injunction to stop buyout, court also found that shareholder-plaintiffs were unlikely to prove that directors had violated their fiduciary duties either by engaging in self-dealing or by not exercising due care. *In re Formica Corp Shareholders Litigation, No. 10598 consolidated (Ch Ct 3-22-89).*

Tender offeror could not prevent target's cash self-tender offer and repurchase plan by alleging violations of §13(e), §14(a) and §14(e) of the Securities Exchange Act of 1934. Court held that target's disclosures were adequate considering its pending patent infringement litigation, and therefore its recommendation that shareholders not accept tender offeror's bid did not indicate target was withholding information. Also, a reasonable shareholder could have discovered that self-tender offer was a defensive tactic. *Shamrock Holdings Inc v Polaroid Corp, 709 FSupp 1311 (D Del 1989).*

Court denied preliminary injunction to bar target corporation from making self-tender for 22% of its own shares or from selling $300 million in preferred stock to white squire. Target's directors were entitled to treat hostile offer as threat. There was evidence that $45 per share being offered was inadequate, and target's shareholders could not value their shares accurately because of uncertainty over size of target's recovery in patent infringement suit against competitor. *Shamrock Holdings, Inc v Polaroid Corp, 559 A2d 278 (Ch Ct 1989).*

Directors' approval of takeover offer, although quick, was nonetheless taken with due care when directors had rejected initial offers, consulted carefully with special outside financial advisers, and insisted on further negotiations. *Priddy v Edelman, 883 F2d 438 (6th Cir 1989).*

Acquiring corporation did not assume the role of a fiduciary to target company's shareholders when tender offer was made; no fiduciary duty of candor regarding the terms of the offer to purchase existed. *Zirn v VLI Corp, No. 9488 (Ch Ct 7-17-89).*

§141

Board's failure to repurchase all of corporation's outstanding 13 percent bonds at a 25 percent discount was protected by the business judgment rule, where (1) there was no board inaction because bond repurchase was precluded when board explicitly approved principal assets sale and thus, implicitly rejected repurchase opportunity; (2) shareholder failed to prove breach of loyalty claim since directors did not have conflicts of interest simply because investment advisors disfavored repurchase; and (3) gross negligence claim was foreclosed. *John Hancock Capital Growth Management, Inc v Aris Corp, No. 9920 (Ch Ct 8-24-90).*

Under "enhanced" review of directors' action where post-agreement market check procedure is used, court inquires into whether the circumstances afforded disinterested and well motivated director basis reasonably to conclude that the contemplated transaction was best available alternative for corporation and shareholders. Selling shareholders do not require same level of detail regarding financial projections required by purchasers of company, and offer to purchase need not include projections for each division of company. *Roberts v General Instrument Corp, No. 11639 (Ch Ct 8-13-90).*

The Supreme Court of Delaware affirmed a Court of Chancery's decision approving a settlement of a shareholder suit which challenged a decision by board of directors acting through a special committee of outside directors, to donate over $85 million to be used in the construction and funding of a museum and cultural center for art. The court concluded that, although the settlement was meager, it was adequate, considering all of the facts and the circumstances. *Kahn v Sullivan, 594 A2d 48 (1991).*

Plaintiff failed to state a claim for waste or neglect based on allegations that the directors had authorized excessive payments in settlement of two government investigations of corporate wrongdoing and had intentionally made a low bid for a contract to supply presidential jets to the government. Nothing suggested that the settlement amounts were so high in comparison to the company's potential liability that no one of sound mind would have agreed to them, and, as to the alleged low bid, there was no showing that the bid was submitted with the knowledge that it would result in a substantial loss, or that such losses were in fact incurred. *Boeing Co v Shrontz, No. 11,273 (Ch Ct 4-20-92).*

A board's decision not to pursue a shareholder's demand is protected by the business judgment rule unless the board's investigation of the shareholder's demand was not reasonable. Where a board chooses to entrust its investigation to a law firm, the directors must ensure that counsel is capable of independently evaluating the corporation's interests. Selection of a law firm that had actually represented the alleged wrongdoers in proceedings related to the same subject matter that the law firm was thereafter asked to neutrally investigate reached the level of gross negligence and was incompatible with the board's fiduciary duty to inform itself of all material information reasonably available prior to making a business decision. *Stepak v Addison, 20 F3d 398 (11th Cir 1994).*

The business judgment rule did not protect a board of directors who entered into an asset sale and merger that personally benefitted majority shareholders at the expense of minority shareholders. The Court found that the board, which failed to demonstrate that its actions met the entire fairness standard, breached its fiduciary duties by acting under a conflict of interest. *Ryan v Tads Enterprises, Inc, Nos. 10229, 11977 (Ch Ct 4-24-96).*

Board of directors' approval of asset sale and merger did not meet the "entire fairness" standard where the board did not provide independent representation for minority shareholders' interests; did not "offset or neutralize[ ]" the directors' conflict of interest; the shareholder vote approving of the transaction was dominated by the board; the conflicted board fixed the merger price without any independent, critical evaluation by an uninterested party; the board failed to institute any procedural safeguards to replicate an arms-length bargaining process; and the price fixed by the board favored majority shareholders. *Ryan v Tads Enterprises, Inc, Nos. 10229, 11977 (Ch Ct 4-24-96).*

Executive Committee's reliance on a Special Committee's fact-finding and recommendations when refusing plaintiff's pre-suit demand was a proper exercise of business judgment and did not constitute a lack of due care. *Scattered Corp v Chicago Stock Exchange, Inc, No. 14010 (Ch Ct 7-12-96).*

Business judgment rule protected board of directors from personal liability where plaintiff, in a derivative action, failed to allege: (1) that the board lacked independence or good faith in making decisions regarding the use of corporate funds; (2) that other business decisions were the product of improper motives or self-dealing; or (3) that certain losses suffered by the corporation were the result of a lack of good faith. *Gagliardi v Trifoods International, Inc, No. 14725 (Ch Ct 7-19-96).*

A controlling shareholder does not stand on both sides of a transaction, even though the shareholder remains in control after the transaction, where an unaffiliated third party initiated transaction negotiations with the shareholder and a Special Committee of the corporation's board completed those negotiations; therefore, entire fairness review of the transaction is not triggered ab initio. *Orman v Cullman, 794 A2d 5 (Ch Ct 2002).*

Demand futility is not satisfied where a plaintiff has not pled with particularity facts from which it can be reasonably concluded that the majority of the directors who were in office when the complaint was filed were disabled from impartially considering a demand due to a lack of disinterest or independence on their part, or that the challenged transactions were other than the product of a valid exercise of business judgment. *Highland Legacy Limited v Singer, 2006 Del. Ch. LEXIS 55 (Ch Ct 2006).*

In a sale of control transaction, the presumption of the business judgment rule is not rebutted by a mere allegation that a manager has pursued a corporate combination to increase his power. It is also not rebutted where the plaintiff cannot demonstrate that directors have acted to entrench themselves or that directors suffer from a conflict of interest or lack independence or disinterestedness. Finally, although the directors are under a duty to maximize the sale price, bad faith by directors cannot be shown if they have failed to do all they should have done under the circumstances; only if they have knowingly and completely failed to undertake their responsibilities would they breach their duty of loyalty.

The Chancery Court found that the plaintiff had failed to rebut the presumption of the business judgment rule that in making a business decision the directors of a corporation acted on an informed basis, in good faith and in the honest belief that the action taken is in the best interests of the company. In this regard, the court concluded that the complaint failed to state that the directors were interested in the transaction or otherwise violated their fiduciary duty of loyalty. The court also rejected the plaintiff's assertion that the two directors were attempting to entrench themselves, since it found that the directors' employment agreements were approved by the directors and had not been kept secret from the board. Additionally, the court said, "[a] mere allegation that a manager pursued a corporate combination out of a desire for a larger 'empire' is not sufficient to rebut the presumption of the business judgment rule. Indeed, to support such a claim a plaintiff would ultimately have to show that the manager's primary purpose for pursuing the transaction was a desire to increase the size of the company for the manager's benefit"—which would be very difficult to do. Moreover, the court determined that the plaintiff had not alleged facts to rebut the presumption that the members of the compensation committee exercised their independent and disinterested business judgment in approving the employment agreements.

As to the plaintiff's *Revlon* claim, the court noted that when a board of directors decides to sell control of the corporation, the "board must perform its fiduciary duties in the service of a specific objective: maximizing the sale price of the enterprise." In this regard, the court held that directors are not liable for failing to carry out a perfect process in a sale of control. The court said that "[b]ad faith cannot be shown by merely showing that the directors failed to do all they should have done under the circumstances. Rather, only if they knowingly and completely failed to undertake their responsibilities would they breach their duty of loyalty." The key question is whether the director defendants utterly failed to attempt to obtain the best sale price. Here, the court found that the board actively consulted with its advisors, regularly evaluated financial reports and analyses, and considered several facts and analyses in reaching a decision to approve the combination. Thus, even though the board did not "probe for alternatives" and did not obtain a control premium, the court concluded that it satisfied its *Revlon* duties. *Wayne County Employees' Retirement System v Corti*, 2009 Del. Ch. LEXIS 126 (Ch Ct 2009).

.6 Business judgment rule—defensive measures to takeover.—Where only two out of ten members of the board were inside directors, and neither dominated the remaining eight, and where a "prima facie showing of good faith and reasonable investigation" existed, the action to divest a lagging business segment after two years of discussion and analysis, and partially as a defensive measure to head off an approaching takeover, was "reasonable in relation to the threat posed" and thus protected from judicial scrutiny by the business judgment rule. *Tomczak v Thiokol*, No. 7861 (Ch Ct 4-5-90).

Where a takeover was inevitable and the heightened scrutiny of *Unocal Corp v Mesa Petroleum Co*, 493 A2d 946 (Del 1985) applied, the defensive measures employed by the board were "a balanced and reasonable response to the threat posed" and demonstrated the directors' "abiding concern" for shareholders who were otherwise subject to freezeout. The business judgment rule protected the board which: (1) rejected the tender offer; (2) diligently sought enhanced shareholder value through alternative opportunities; and (3) vigorously negotiated substantive improvements to shareholder protection. Summary judgment dismissing the stockholders' class action was affirmed where the directors "attempted and [were] able to negotiate a superior transaction for its shareholders than was available under the [earlier] offer." *Gilbert v The El Paso Co*, 575 A2d 1131 (1990).

District court for Eastern District of Pennsylvania, applying Delaware law, granted partial summary judgment and declared stock issuance by defendant corporation void. Court applied *Unocal* analysis and found defendant failed to meet its burden of proof showing that its response to a legitimately perceived threat to the corporation was rationally related to that threat. *Gregory v Correction Connection, Inc*, No. 88-7990 (ED Pa 3-27-91).

Precautionary adoption of defensive measures by the board of directors, that were not implemented in response to a specific takeover threat, were subjected to enhanced scrutiny and not protected by the business judgment rule. *In re Gaylord Container Corporation Shareholders Litigation*, No. 14616 (Ch Ct 12-19-96).

.7 Business judgment rule—backdated stock options.—Where a shareholder pleads in a derivative action that company stock options were backdated, the shareholder pleads a breach of the duty of loyalty sufficient to rebut the business judgment rule, since backdating option qualifies as one of those rare cases in which a transaction may be so egregious on its face that board approval cannot meet the test of business judgment. *Ryan v Gifford*, 2007 Del. Ch. LEXIS 22 (Ch Ct 2007).

A breach of fiduciary claim based on springloading of stock options will be allowed to proceed where a plaintiff can support an inference that directors engaged in self-dealing and attempted to hide their conduct from their stockholders. *In re Tyson Foods, Inc Consolidated Shareholder Litigation*, 2007 Del. Ch. LEXIS 120 (Ch Ct 2007).

.8 Corporate opportunity.—When real estate corporation sold lots to its president at less than fair market value, and he made profit on sale of homes he built there, he is liable to corporation for diverting corporate opportunity; liability is profit on sale of houses, not merely difference between price of lots and their fair value. *Maclary v Pleasant Hills, Inc*, 109 A2d 830 (Ch Ct 1954).

Director does not divert corporate opportunity, when he has his wholly owned subsidiary acquire options on corporation's shares, since (1) transaction is merely transfer of shares from one of his wholly owned subsidiaries to another, (2) shares were not essential to corporation's business, and (3) corporation had no policy for buying its own shares. *Equity Corp v Milton, 213 A2d 439 (Ch Ct 1965),* aff'd, *221 A2d 494 (1966).*

Dominant director of corporation which has funds to invest is not liable for diverting corporate opportunity when he takes for himself a business opportunity which (1) has no relation to any business in which corporation is engaged, (2) corporation has no interest or expectancy in it and (3) comes to director as individual; but he may not use corporation's resources to acquire business. *Johnson v Greene, 121 A2d 919 (1956),* rev'g, *Greene v Allen, 114 A2d 916 (Ch Ct 1955).*

Officers of mining corporation who took private advantage of new mining project and profited by its subsequent sale to corporation were not liable to stockholders for breach of fiduciary duty for appropriating corporate opportunity; corporation was not financially able to use opportunity, officers acted in good faith, and corporation benefited from officers' dealings. *Fliegler v Lawrence, 361 A2d 218 (1976).*

Where inventor of new product was unwilling to permit corporation to use his invention, and corporation was neither inclined nor financially able to develop new products, inventor's concept was not an opportunity available to corporation, and employee could legally seize it for himself and compete against employer. *Science Accessories Corp v Summagraphics Corp, 425 A2d 957 (1980).*

Court refused to accept recommendation of corporation's special litigation committee and dismiss shareholders' derivative suit alleging that directors and officers diverted corporate opportunity to themselves. *Reasons:* (1) Committee, consisting of one member, was not independent because member was director when challenged action took place and he had numerous political and financial dealings with corporation's chief executive officer/chairman of board who allegedly controlled board; (2) Committee did not establish reasonable basis for its conclusions that opportunity to purchase stock in another corporation was not corporate opportunity. *Lewis v Fuqua, 502 A2d 962 (Ch Ct 1985).*

In a case in which defendant was found to have usurped a corporate opportunity, the Court imposed, in favor of the corporation, a constructive trust on stock she had purchased from a deceased shareholder, where a stockholders' agreement granted corporation a right of first refusal to purchase any outstanding shares of the corporation that became available and also provided a mechanism for valuing shares in the event of a dispute. *Stephanis v Yiannatsis, No. 1508 (Ch Ct 10-4-93).*

President of a corporation did not breach any fiduciary duties by failing to present to the corporation's board of directors a corporate opportunity offered to him where the president rejected the offer and the plaintiff failed to demonstrate that the offer was available to any person or entity besides the president. *Brookside Enterprises v Baum, C.A. No. 92-4931 (D NJ 12-19-94).*

Director of corporation did not usurp a corporate opportunity to acquire a cellular phone license where the opportunity was presented to the director in his individual capacity, the corporation had been divesting itself of similar cellular holdings, the director had discussed the opportunity with other directors of the corporation who had expressed no interest in the opportunity, and at the time the opportunity was presented the corporation, the corporation was not financially able to purchase the license. *Broz v Cellular Information Systems, Inc, 673 A2d 148 (1996),* rev'g, *Cellular Information Systems, Inc v Broz, No. 14094 (Ch Ct 5-8-95).*

Directors of a corporation did not usurp corporate opportunities by diverting investment opportunities from the corporation to a limited partnership in which the directors were also partners where plaintiffs did not demonstrate: (1) the corporation was financially able to exploit the opportunity; (2) the opportunity was within the corporation's line of business; (3) the corporation had an interest or expectancy in the opportunity; and (4) by taking the opportunity for their own, the directors will be placed in a position inimicable to their duties to the corporation. *Balin v Amerimar Realty Co, No. 12896 (Ch Ct 11-15-96).*

Defendant directors' motion to dismiss plaintiffs' corporate opportunity claims on the ground that a shareholders' agreement required those claims to be governed by arbitration was denied by the Delaware Chancery Court where the court determined that the shareholders' agreement did not govern the resolution of plaintiffs' claims and merely provided guidance to the court for a resolution of the claims. *Havens v Attar, No. 15134 (Ch Ct 1-30-97).*

.9 Quorum.—Resolution authorizing issuance of stock at directors' meeting where no quorum was present is illegal and stock may be cancelled unless action is later ratified at meeting at which quorum is present, but mere approval of minutes of illegal meeting at subsequent meeting is not sufficient to be ratification of unauthorized act. *Belle Isle Corp v MacBean, 49 A2d 5 (Ch Ct 1946).*

Unfilled directorships are not counted for quorum purposes. *Belle Isle Corp v MacBean, 61 A2d 699 (Ch Ct 1948).*

When bylaws provide for board of from three to seven, and seven directors are elected but two decline to serve, any three of remaining five constitute quorum. *Bush v Thompson Automatic Arms Corp, 64 A2d 581 (1948).*

Directors who stayed away from meeting to prevent quorum are not estopped from questioning validity of action taken at meeting. *Tomlinson v Loew's, Inc, 134 A2d 518 (Ch Ct),* aff'd, *135 A2d 136 (1957).*

Directors' meeting with required quorum present of persons elected and qualified to act as directors is valid even though there were present other directors who were not qualified to act. *Lippman v Kehoe Stenograph Co, 98 A 943 (Ch Ct 1916),* aff'd, *102 A 988 (1918).*

Action taken at directors' meeting attended by only two of eight directors after four directors representing opposing faction had recently been elected was either ultra vires or illegal because action taken required authority of properly constituted board and participating directors had acted for personal reasons, not corporate reasons for benefit of shareholders or recently elected directors. *Whitman v Fuqua, 549 FSupp 351 (WD Pa 1982).*

.10 Election of directors.— Majority beneficiaries of trust, who were opposed to current management of corporation that was controlled by trust, were denied court order requiring trustee to vote majority's slate of director nominees at shareholders' meeting. *Reason:* The beneficiaries refused to identify the slate until the meeting. However, if, after trustee received instructions as to identify of slate and he determined that nominees would violate terms of trust, he could vote to adjourn meeting to seek instructions from court. *Wilmington Trust Co v Woodson, No. 7945 (Ch Ct 5-15-85).*

Corporation's board, even though acting in subjective good faith, could not validly act for primary purpose of preventing or impeding unaffiliated majority of shareholders from expanding board and electing new majority. However, citing inability to foresee all future settings in which board might seek to thwart shareholder vote, court refused to adopt per se rule invalidating every board action for such a purpose. *Blasius Industries, Inc v Atlas Corp, 564 A2d 651 (Ch Ct 1988).*

A technical defect in the authorization of a corporation's stock can be cured by a later, ratifying vote of a majority of the corporation's directors, thereby resolving a dispute over who constitutes the lawful board of directors and officers of the corporation *Kalageorgi v Victor Kamkin, Inc, C.A. No. 17111 (Ch Ct 9-10-99).*

Shareholders state direct claims for disclosure violations where they assert that a failure to disclose accurate information prevented them from making an informed decision when electing directors to the board. However, the shareholders lack standing to seek injunctive or monetary relief where the opportunity to avert or repair the harm has passed and where damages do not naturally arise from the violation.

The Chancery Court determined that the plaintiff shareholders had stated a direct claim for disclosure violations, noting that where it is claimed that a duty of disclosure violation impaired the stockholders' right to cast an informed vote, that claim is direct. Here, the court found that the shareholders were claiming that the failure to disclose accurate balance sheets and information related to stock option issuance prevented them from making an informed decision when electing the defendants to their positions on the board of directors, and, as a result, the company was mismanaged and descended into insolvency. The court also observed, however, that to the extent that the shareholders were complaining that bad things happened to the company (i.e., financial disaster) because they were induced into voting for allegedly inept directors, they "have done nothing more than painted derivative claims with a disclosure coating. To the extent that the Plaintiffs seek to recover for losses suffered by [the corporation], those claims are derivative in nature because any recovery would benefit the entity as a whole." *Thornton v Bernard Techs, Inc, 2009 Del. Ch. LEXIS 29 (Ch Ct 2009).*

"Stockholders of record" include the Depository Trust Company (DTC) participant banks and brokers listed on the "Cede & Co." (Cede) breakdown for purposes of determining the stockholders entitled to vote or act by written consent, thereby eliminating the need for a DTC omnibus proxy in such circumstances. Also, improper vote buying does not occur where the buyer does not use or receive corporate resources for the purchase (i.e., it is a third party purchase), no fraud or a disparity of information is involved, there is no misalignment between the voting interest and the economic interest of the shares, and no disenfranchisement occurs as a result. Finally, as a matter of first impression in Delaware, a bylaw amendment that purports to shrink the number of board seats below the number of sitting directors, is void, as is a bylaw that purports to a establish qualifications for directorships that would disqualify a sitting director and terminate his service.

The Chancery Court held for the insurgent faction on its claims, finding that the "street name" consents, which evidenced authority from the participating banks and brokers who appeared on the DTC participant listing, but omitted the omnibus proxy from DTC, had validly effected corporate action. In doing so, the court redefined "stockholders of record" to include the DTC participant banks and brokers listed on the Cede breakdown for purposes of determining the stockholders entitled to vote or act by written consent, thereby eliminating the need for a DTC omnibus proxy in such circumstances. The court also held that the Cede breakdown is part of a corporation's stock ledger for purposes of GCL §219(c), thus, aligning Delaware law's definition of record holders with federal regulations under which the participant banks and brokers are recognized as the record holders of the shares held by DTC.

The court rejected the preferred stockholder's claim that the insurgents had engaged in improper "vote buying" when their member-director purchased his shares to ensure that the insurgents' solicitation would have sufficient votes. The court found that the concept of vote buying is broad enough to encompass practices and techniques whereby voting rights are manipulated, including the decoupling of economic interests from voting rights, even in cases where corporate resources are not used to buy the stock. The Court stated that where such practices prove deleterious to stockholder voting, the "court can and should provide a remedy." Finding no evidence of fraud in the present case or disparity of information because, among other things, the seller was aware that the shares were the "swing votes," that in purchasing the shares Kurz had assumed the economic risks of ownership and that Kurz did not have any competing economic or personal interests that might create an overall negative economic ownership in EMAK, the Court concluded that the purchase by Kurz of the voting and economic rights to the EMAK shares was not a "legal wrong."

Finally, addressing the bylaw amendments that purported to reduce the number of directors on the board, the court found the amendments to be invalid, reasoning that the outcome would be either that

§141

the surplus directorships would terminate or would hold office without official seats, and that such outcomes conflicted with GCL §§141(b) and 141(k), so that the bylaw would be void. Similarly, the court reasoned that a bylaw provision that established qualifications for directorships that would disqualify a sitting director and terminate his service would likewise violate these statutory sections and thus be void.

Accordingly, the court held that the bylaw amendments adopted through the preferred stockholder's consents conflict were void and therefore ineffective to shrink the board or to require the calling of a special meeting. The court also held that the insurgents' consents validly effected corporate action and that the board therefore consisted of the three newly elected directors, the two incumbents, and one vacancy. *Kurz v Holbrook, 2010 Del. Ch. LEXIS 24 (Ch Ct 2010).*

A bylaw amendment providing that annual meetings will occur during a certain month other than a month in which they traditionally have been held, and which has the effect of reducing the amount of time served by a class of directors that is part of a staggered board, does not violate statutory law or a company's bylaws or charter where there are ambiguous as to what constitutes a director's "full term" and the meaning of "annual" and "year." *Airgas, Inc v Air Products and Chemicals, Inc, C.A. No. 5817-CC (Ch Ct Oct. 8, 2010).*

.11 Removal of directors.—Stockholders have power to remove director for cause, even though there is no statutory provision providing for removal of directors by stockholder action, and even though corporate bylaws provide for cumulative voting. *Campbell v Loew's, Inc, 134 A2d 852 (Ch Ct 1957).*

Directors and officers of first corporation were removable by resolution of board of second corporation that owned all stock of first corporation, on termination of their employment, even if it was shown their ouster was reprisal step taken by board of second corporation against ousted directors for instituting action, or that affairs of corporation had taken worse turn owing to ouster. *Beach v KDI Corp, 336 FSupp 229 (D Del 1971).*

Even though funds were available to pay preferred dividend arrearages, common stockholder could not have election of board of directors set aside for their wrongful refusal to pay such dividends without showing fraud and gross abuse of discretion by board in refusing to order such dividends; corporate charter gave preferred stockholders right to elect majority of board as long as payment of preferred dividends was in arrears. *Baron v Allied Artists Pictures Corp, 337 A2d 653 (Ch Ct 1975).*

Court enjoined corporation from removing shareholder from board of directors because shareholders' agreement gave her absolute right to elect two directors and she would suffer immediate, irreparable injury when her position on board was her only contact with corporation. *Prosser v Betty Brooks, Inc, No. 7938 (Ch Ct 7-25-85).*

Director, one of four directors elected by common shareholders on seven-person board, was not elected president, chairman of board, and chief executive officer of corporation by his vote combined with vote of three directors elected by preferred shareholder because there was no vacancy when term of current president, chairman of board, and chief executive officer was not over and no attempt (requiring threefourths vote) had been made to remove him. Director was not removed for cause by written consent executed by record holder of all common stock because, although there were adequate grounds to remove director for lack of loyalty to common shareholders' interests, director was not given specific charges, adequate notice, or full opportunity of meeting accusation. *Bossier v Connell, No. 8624 (Ch Ct 11-12-86).*

The right to remove directors is a fundamental element of stockholder authority, and therefore directors may not be removed for good cause unless clear evidence that a restriction on such stockholder authority is intended. *Rohe v Reliance Training Network, Inc, C.A. No. 17992 (Ch Ct 7-21-00).*

A shareholder consent purporting to remove a corporation's director for cause, even if no notice or opportunity to be heard was afforded the director, is not validated merely because the certificate of incorporation would have allowed removal of the director without cause. However, a plaintiff seeking to enforce such a consent is not obliged to include in its complaint factual allegations that it gave the director notice or an opportunity to be heard. *Superwire. Com, Inc v Hampton, 805 A2d 904 (Ch Ct 2002).*

Written consents may be used in lieu of a meeting to remove directors of a corporation that has cumulative voting, provided all requirements of the written consent procedures are met. The resolution of that question is governed by §141(k)(2), which governs removal voting. Finding that the minority had sufficient strength under §141(k)(2) to block the removal of the two targeted directors, the court held that the majority's attempt to use the written consent procedure to remove those directors and to reconstitute the board was not legally valid. *Crutcher v Tufts, 898 So2d 529 (La Ct App 2005).*

Where a shareholder agreement provides only that a shareholder shall be president of a corporation, the president serves at the board of directors' discretion; where such an agreement requires a unanimous shareholder vote to remove a director, and a director is removed temporarily without such vote, the removed director nonetheless suffers no compensable damages where the director does not lose income and where his absence does not otherwise cause him proximate damage. *Carlson v Hallinan, 2006 Del. Ch. LEXIS 58 (Ch Ct 2006).*

.12 Class—designated directors; removal. — Receivers holding majority of class of corporation's stock could execute consent to remove and replace four directors. Corporation could not assert voting agreement as defense to consent when neither corporation nor its board was signatory to agreement nor third party beneficiary of agreement. Receiver could vote stock in opposition to position of some beneficial owners.

Under GCL §141(d), corporation's certificate may give shareholder class right to elect certain directors. Certificate need not specify terms or voting rights of those directors. If not, one-year term and one vote per director is the rule.

Under GCL §141(k), class-designated directors may be removed by shareholders without cause. *Insituform of North America, Inc v Chandler*, 534 A2d 257 (Ch Ct 1987).

.13 Staggered term directors.—Bylaw permitting removal of directors at any time by vote of majority of stockholders is in conflict with certificate of incorporation proving for staggered three-year terms for directors, and so bylaw is invalid and court will void stockholders' action that removed three of six directors at one time. *Essential Enterprises Corp v Automatic Steel Products, Inc*, 159 A2d 288 (Ch Ct 1960).

Bylaw cannot set one year term for directors if charter provides for staggered three year terms; directors elected under such invalid bylaw serve only as de facto directors whose terms can be terminated at any time by stockholder action. *Prickett v American Steel and Pump Corp*, 251 A2d 576 (Ch Ct 1969).

Under GCL §141(k), shareholders may amend certificate of incorporation to eliminate bylaw setting up classified board so shareholders can remove director without cause. Directors of Delaware corporation have no vested right to hold office in defiance of properly expressed will of majority. *Roven v Cutter*, 547 A2d 603 (Ch Ct 1988).

A bylaw amendment providing that annual meetings will occur during a certain month other than a month in which they traditionally have been held, and which has the effect of reducing the amount of time served by a class of directors that is part of a staggered board, does not violate statutory law or a company's bylaws or charter where those are ambiguous as to what constitutes a director's "full term" and the meaning of "annual" and "year."*Airgas, Inc v Air Products and Chemicals, Inc*, C.A. No. 5817-CC (Ch. Ct. Oct. 8, 2010).

.14 Compensation.—Director who increased his own salary must justify increase as reasonable; factors include value of services, IRS allowance, salary range within corporation and within industry, and corporation's financial health. *Wilderman v Wilderman*, 315 A2d 610 (Ch Ct 1974).

Court issued preliminary injunction to bar operation of target corporation's trust that would fund several employee compensation plans that would make target less attractive as takeover candidate. All directors who approved trust's creation had a personal interest in one or another of compensation plans. Thus, plaintiffs had reasonable probability of showing that operation of trust was not protected by business judgment rule and that trust was not intrinsically fair. Irreparable harm flowed from irrevocability of trust's funding.

Court refused to interfere with target's poison pill, holding that rights plan serves useful purpose if it allows target board to seek more realistic offer. *Tate & Lyle PLC v Staley Continental, Inc*, No. 9813 (Ch Ct 5-9-88).

Limited partners alleged that the directors of the general partner, in an effort to conceal certain self-dealing activities, had converted the business entity from a corporation to a limited partnership, thereby enabling them to avoid disclosure obligations created by the federal securities laws and regulations. The court found that the limited partners failed to show that the business entity's conversion from a corporation to a limited partnership resulted in a situation in which a reasonably alert interest holder would not have been placed on notice of the conduct complained of. *In re USACafes, LP Litigation*, No. 11146 (Ch Ct 1-21-93).

.15 Golden parachutes.—Former shareholder could not bring derivative action attacking directors' and officers' golden parachutes as waste of corporate assets after corporation was merged into acquiror when (1) shareholder lost standing to pursue derivative action because he was no longer shareholder of corporation and (2) acquiror agreed to honor golden parachutes, so it must be assumed that it decided that golden parachute agreement did not give rise to cause of action. Former shareholder also could not bring class action attacking golden parachutes for reducing merger price paid by acquiror because claim is really derivative in nature and restatement of waste claim when shareholder failed to attach merger. *Bershad v Hartz*, No. 6960 (Ch Ct 1-29-87).

Directors of a corporation did not, as a matter of law, breach their duty of care in effecting a merger of the corporation, where plaintiffs asserted that the former corporation's chief negotiators were not independent because they had "golden parachutes" in their contracts, and thus knew that they would receive significant financial benefits if the merger was effected. The court stated that these employment contracts do not give rise to a *per se* breach of duty by the board, who reviewed the transaction after the negotiations were complete. *Rand v Western Air Lines, Inc*, No. 8632 (Ch Ct 2-25-94).

Golden parachute provisions that provide for change of control payments to a corporation's key employees if a majority of its board of directors ceases to be "Existing Directors"—defined as directors in office at the time of the golden parachute agreements and those new directors approved by Existing Directors—do not violate the rule that directors may not be granted distinctive voting powers unless they are authorized by the certificate of incorporation. *California Public Employees' Retirement System v Coulter*, 2005 Del. Ch. LEXIS 54 (Ch Ct 2005).

.16 Loans.—Loans by directors and their relatives to shore up staggering corporation were made in arms length dealing, so directors' claim could not be postponed to claims of subordinated lenders. *New York Stock Exchange v Pickard & Co*, 296 A2d 143 (Ch Ct 1972).

In action alleging defendants illegally obtained warrants and conversion rights that would give them voting control and windfall profits, court ruled that because the corporation was unable to raise funds elsewhere, any profits the directors would make from lending money to company were not causally connected to inside information the directors purportedly possessed about selling the firm. *Rosenberg v Oolie*, No. 11,134 (Ch Ct 10-16-89).

.17 Derivative actions—requirement of demand on board.—Disinterested directors of investment company can terminate stockholders' derivative suit brought against other directors under the Investment Company and Investment Advisers Acts. *Burks v Lasker, 441 US 471 (1979).*

Business judgment rule allowing disinterested independent directors to terminate derivative litigation if they decide such course is in best interests of corporation does not offend §10(b) or §14(a) of Securities Exchange Act of 1934. Court cannot apply own business judgment because Delaware business judgment rule bars judicial inquiry into such actions of directors when stockholder did not challenge good faith and independence of board. *Abramowitz v Posner, 672 F2d 1025 (2d Cir 1982).*

Under Delaware law, a corporation may, on direction of independent directors, terminate derivative action against other board members after reasonable good faith investigation of alleged wrongdoings; however, when the suing stockholder was excused from making demand that corporation sue directors on its own behalf due to futility (as in this case where all directors were named defendants) the court must also use its own independent business judgment to decide whether action should be terminated. *Maldonado v Flynn, 671 F2d 729 (2d Cir 1982).*

A demand by a stockholder to investigate and remedy alleged abuses is not voided because the demand was refused by the Executive Committee rather than the full board where the board of directors had passed a resolution, as authorized by GCL §141(c), appointing the committee and allowing it to review the investigation by the Special Committee and refuse plaintiff's pre-suit demand. To show reasonable doubt that her demand was properly refused, the plaintiff would have to make particularized allegations that the Executive Committee was biased, lacked independence or failed to conduct a reasonable investigation. *Scattered Corp v Chicago Stock Exchange, Inc, 701 A2d 70 (1997).*

Claims that a transaction precludes the pursuit of other value-maximizing transactions and transfers voting control without payment of a control premium are derivative and not direct where it cannot be shown that the corporation will not bear the consequences of the injuries affected by the transaction. *Agostino v Hicks, 845 A2d 1110 (Ch Ct 2004).*

Demand futility is not satisfied where a plaintiff has not pled with particularity facts from which it can be reasonably concluded that the majority of the directors who were in office when the complaint was filed were disabled from impartially considering a demand due to a lack of disinterest or independence on their part, or that the challenged transactions were other than the product of a valid exercise of business judgment. *Highland Legacy Limited v Singer, 2006 Del. Ch. LEXIS (Ch Ct 2006).*

A letter sent to a corporation's board by a terminated employee, who is also a corporate shareholder, that threatens litigation and requests reinstatement and to be placed on the corporation's board does not constitute demand for purposes of determining demand futility. *Khanna v McMinn, 2006 Del. Ch. LEXIS 86 (Ch Ct 2006).*

.18 Direct actions—special injury.—A common law claim for breach of fiduciary duty by a corporate director or officer can only be asserted by (a) the corporation or on the corporation's behalf in a derivative action or (b) individual shareholders when a "special injury" has occurred. Special injury is a wrong that either involves a "particular right" or is "distinct from that suffered by other shareholders" citing *Lipton v News Int'l, PLC, 514 A2d 1075 (1986).*

Shareholders sufficiently alleged "special injury" based on a theory of "distinct injury" when they claimed that the stock they had purchased had an artificially inflated price caused by the board of directors' mismanagement. *Zimmerman v Prime Medical Services, Inc, 729 FSupp 23 (SDNY 1990).*

A letter sent to a corporations board by a terminated employee, who is also a corporate shareholder, that threatens litigation and requests reinstatement and to be placed on the corporation's board does not constitute demand for purposes of determining demand futility. *Khanna v McMinn, 2006 Del. Ch LEXIS 86 (Ch Ct 2006).*

.19 Special litigation committee.— The use of a special litigation committee to investigate the circumstances surrounding an alleged improper acquisition of stock based on inside information immediately preceding the corporation's tender offer, did not constitute a waiver by the board of directors of its right to challenge the stockholder's allegation that demand was excused. *Spiegel v Buntrock, 571 A2d 767 (1990).*

Once a special litigation committee has entered into a proposed settlement with defendants, a derivative plaintiff is no longer entitled to engage in expansive discovery, but rather must limit its discovery requests to requests for information narrowly related to the independence and good faith of the special litigation committee. *Carlton Investments v TLC Beatrice International Holdings, Inc, No. 13950 (Ch Ct 1-28-97).*

.20 Independent negotiating committee.—Directors of a corporation did not, as a matter of law, breach their duty of care in effecting a merger of the corporation, where plaintiffs asserted that an independent negotiating committee was required by GCL §141 and case law. The court determined, however, that the statute is permissive and the case law merely recognizes the utility of independent committees in a variety of fact patterns; the court found no support for the proposition that boards of directors must delegate their responsibilities to special committees. *Rand v Western Air Lines, Inc, No. 8632 (Ch Ct 2-25-94).*

.21 Determination of merger price.—Majority shareholders breached their fiduciary duty of full disclosure of all material information regarding a merger, where defendants did not hire an independent investment advisor to value the company or employ an independent body to protect the interest of the minority, and failed to disclose to the minority share holders several material facts, namely, those relating to how they determined the merger price. While Delaware law did not require defendants to consult independent valuation experts or negotiate with minority shareholders during the course of the merger, defendants failed to provide any basis upon which defendants valued,monetarily, any of the considerations they took into account to reach the per share figure. *Wacht v Continental Hosts, Ltd, No. 7954 (Ch Ct 9-16-94).*

.22 Conflicts of interest.— There is no *per se* rule prohibiting a corporate officer from one corporation from sitting on the board of a competitor corporation. Because the stockholders have the power to elect directors and to remove them during the course of their term, there can be no director liability for "acquiescence " in the service of another director on the board, even one with a material conflict of interest. The question of the fitness of a person to serve as a director of a corporation is a question exclusively for the shareholders, not for the courts. *Bragger v Budacz, No. 13376 (Ch Ct 12-7-94).*

.23 Corporate waste doctrine.—Plaintiff's derivative action alleging waste of corporate assets was dismissed for failure to make demand or show why demand was futile where the Delaware Chancery Court found that a corporation's board of directors' grant of stock options to the Chief Executive Officer of the corporation for past services was protected by the business judgment rule.

In order for plaintiff to state his claim for waste where there was no allegation of director interest, plaintiff must establish that "no person of ordinary, sound business judgment would say that the consideration received for the options was a fair exchange for the options granted."

Court rejected plaintiff's claim that no reasonable director could have voted for the grant of options where the consideration for the options was past services. Consideration for stock options is often the reasonable prospect of obtaining the employee's valued future services. But that is not the only permissible from of consideration for a grant of stock options. Under certain limited circumstances, stock options may also be issued as a form of compensation for an employee's past services. *Zupnick v Goizueta, No. 148/4 (Ch Ct 1-21-97).*

.24 Notice to directors.—Plaintiff's allegations that he was a director of Instant Vision, Inc. at the time the amendment to the corporate charter to increase the authorized number of shares was considered, and voted upon, yet he was intentionally not given notice that this issue would be considered and that he therefore was deprived of the opportunity to join in the board's deliberations, stated a cognizable claim for relief. A director generally has a right of access to whatever corporate information was given to other directors during the director's tenure. *Cairns v Gelmon, C.A. 16062 (Ch Ct 5-21-98).*

.25 Classified board of directors.—Where a corporation's bylaws and articles of incorporation establishing a classified board of directors are unambiguous, they govern the establishment and timing of such a classified board. *Lions Gate Entertainment Corp v Image Entertainment, Inc, 2006 Del. Ch. LEXIS 108 (Ch Ct 2006).*

.26 Valid board meeting and action.—Where board members caucus among themselves, decide on a course of action, and communicate that action, but do not call a meeting or take a vote on the action, there has been no valid board action. *Fogel v U.S. Energy Systems, Inc, 2007 Del. Ch. LEXIS 178 (Ch Ct 2007).*

.27 Resignation of officers and directors.—To be effective, a resignation of an officer or director does not have to be in writing, and the resignation may be effective on the date oral notice or resignation is given, even if later confirmed in writing. *General Video Corp v Kertesz, 2008 Del. Ch. LEXIS 181 (Ch Ct 2008).*

.28 Bylaw amendments; expedited proceedings.—Where a bylaw proposal has been rejected on grounds that if adopted it would be inconsistent with state law and a corporation's governing documents, expedited proceedings may be avoided where the corporation's legal position is judicially preserved pending the outcome of a shareholder vote on the proposed bylaw. *Kistefos AS v Trico Marine Services, Inc, 2009 Del. Ch. LEXIS 58 (Ch Ct 2009).*

.29 Reformation of control transaction.—A court may reform a control transaction where directors standing on both sides of the transaction have breached their fiduciary duties by pushing through the self-interested control transaction and cannot demonstrate its entire fairness.

The Court of Chancery found that the transaction was unfair to the corporation and that the directors had breached their duty of loyalty by pushing through the self-interested control transaction. The court determined that the large stockholder had set in motion a process in which the only option that the special committee considered was a deal with the stockholder itself. Rather than acting as an effective agent for the public stockholders by aggressively demanding a market check or seeking out better-than-market terms from the large shareholder in exchange for no market check, the committee granted terms that were highly favorable to the shareholder, in comparison to the convertible preferred transactions its own advisor deemed advisable. These terms gave the shareholder a chokehold on the company's future and 63% of its equity. *In re Loral Space and Communications, Inc Consolidated Litigation, 2008 Del. Ch. LEXIS 136 (Ch Ct 2008).*

.30 Net operating loss (NOL) poison pill.—A board's decision to adopt and use a poison pill rights plan designed to protect the usability of the corporation's net operating losses (NOLs) is protected by the business judgment rule where such a plan meets legitimate corporate goals is not an unduly preclusive defensive measure, and is a proportionate measure. *Versata Enterprises, Inc v Selectica, Inc, 5 A3d 586 (2010).*

.31 Implied duty of good faith and fair dealing; breach of fiduciary duty.—Where directors are granted an absolute contractual right, they do not breach the implied duty of good faith and fair dealing where they have not acted arbitrarily or unreasonably in exercising that right, and a claim for breach of fiduciary duties based on the directors' exercise of the right will be barred as superfluous. *Nemec v Shrader, 991 A2d 1120 (2010).*

.32 Direct vs. derivative claims.—A claim is direct where directors purportedly allow unauthorized directors to participate in the management of the corporation and deny authorized directors the ability to participate in the management of the company, since these acts go against the structural relationship established by the shareholders, and it is consequently the shareholders who are directly harmed—not the company. *Grayson v Imagination Station, Inc, 2010 Del. Ch. LEXIS 169 (Ch Ct 2010).*

142 OFFICERS; TITLES, DUTIES, SELECTION, TERM; FAILURE TO ELECT; VACANCIES.—(a) Every corporation organized under this chapter shall have such officers with such titles and duties as shall be stated in the bylaws or in a resolution of the board of directors which is not inconsistent with the bylaws and as may be necessary to enable it to sign instruments and stock certificates which comply with §§103(a)(2) and 158 of this title. One of the officers shall have the duty to record the proceedings of the meetings of the stockholders and directors in a book to be kept for that purpose. Any number of offices may be held by the same person unless the certificate of incorporation or bylaws otherwise provide.

(b) Officers shall be chosen in such manner and shall hold their offices for such terms as are prescribed by the bylaws or determined by the board of directors or other governing body. [1]*Each officer shall hold office until such officer's successor is elected and qualified or until such officer's earlier resignation or removal.* Any officer may resign at any time upon written notice to the corporation.

(c) The corporation may secure the fidelity of any or all of its officers or agents by bond or otherwise.

(d) A failure to elect officers shall not dissolve or otherwise affect the corporation.

(e) Any vacancy occurring in any office of the corporation by death, resignation, removal or otherwise, shall be filled as the bylaws provide. In the absence of such provision, the vacancy shall be filled by the board of directors or other governing body. (Last amended by Ch. 339, L. '98, eff. 7-1-98.)

Ch. 339, L. '98, eff. 7-1-98, added matter in italic and deleted [1]"Each officer shall hold his office until his successor is elected and qualified or until his earlier resignation or removal."

Ch. 339, L. '98 Synopsis of Section 142

The amendments to these Sections eliminate masculine references in the statutes, and replace them with gender neutral references.

Comment: This amendment to §142 permits the designation and duties of officers to be in a resolution of the board, provided the resolution is not inconsistent with the by-laws. A minor wording change is made in the second sentence. The third sentence is unchanged.

.1 Election of officers.—Election of president was invalid because it preceded his election as director, even though both elections took place at same meeting. *Young v Janas, 103 A2d 299 (Ch Ct 1954).*

Illegally constituted board of directors is ineffectual to elect officers. *Gow v Consolidated Coppermines Corp, 165 A 137 (Ch Ct 1939).*

Director, one of four directors elected by common shareholders on seven person board was not elected president, chairman of board, and chief executive officer of corporation by his vote combined with vote of three directors elected by preferred shareholder because there was no vacancy when term of current president, chairman of board, and chief executive officer was not over and no attempt (requiring three-fourths vote) had been made to remove him. Director was not removed for cause by written consent executed by record holder of all common stock because, although there were adequate grounds to remove director for lack of loyalty to common shareholders' interests, director was not given specific charges, adequate notice, or full opportunity of meeting accusation. *Bossier v Connell, No. 8624 (Ch Ct 11-12-86).*

.2 Officers as corporate agents.—Corporation can only act through its agents; its officers are its agents. *Joseph Greenspon's Sons Iron & Steel Co v Pecos Valley Gas Co, 156 A 350 (Ch Ct 1931).*

General manager who is also executive vice president and treasurer and who is vested with entire control of corporation's business has implied power to borrow for corporate purposes from anyone willing to lend, notwithstanding existence of resolutions authorizing him to borrow from two specified banks, when those resolutions merely established borrowing procedure and did not limit his borrowing procedures and did not limit his borrowing powers. *Petition of Mulco Products, Inc, 123 A2d 95 (Super Ct),* aff'd, *Mulco Products, Inc v Black, 127 A2d 851 (1956).*

Two director-officers do not have implied authority to bind corporation to contract to hire architect for construction of race track, when such contract is not in ordinary course of corporation's business, nor do they have apparent authority to do so, when they never so acted in past and such powers as they did exercise did not justify reliance on their authority to bind corporation to so unusual contract. *Colish v Brandywine Raceway Assoc, 119 A2d 887 (Super Ct 1955).*

.3 Officers' duties.—When statutes use word "shall" as statutory direction to corporate officers it is to be given an imperative or mandatory meaning. *Gow v Consolidated Coppermines Corp, 165 A 137 (Ch Ct 1933).*

.4 Compensation of officers.—President who controlled 60% of corporation's stock and dominated its board must repay any salary he received above what his services were reasonably worth, together with all profits from options on company stock. *Teren v Howard, 322 F2d 949 (9th Cir 1963).*

Compensation of corporate officers should be fixed by clearly drawn contract, fairly negotiated and properly adopted before services are rendered. *Air Traffic Service Corp v Fay, 196 F2d 40 (DC Cir 1952).*

Deferred compensation plan is valid under which corporation may award to key employees (1) "units" whose value depends on increase, if any, in market value of corporation's stock between time they are awarded and time they are payable and (2) "dividend" credits equal to dividends employee would have received if he owned as many actual shares as "units," (3) when plan insures receipt by corporation of services it seeks. *Lieberman v Koppers Co, 149 A2d 756 (Ch Ct),* aff'd, *Lieberman v Becker, 155 A2d 597 (1959).*

Corporate officer cannot recover compensation for period during which he violated his fiduciary duty by participating in formation of competitive business while in corporation's employ. *Craig v Graphic Arts Studio, Inc, 166 A2d 444 (Ch Ct 1960).*

.5 Powers of president.—President has implied power to perform all acts of ordinary nature which by usage or necessity are incidents to his office, and he may enter contract and bind corporation in matters arising from and dealing with usual course of corporate business. *Joseph Greenspon's Sons Iron & Steel Co v Pecos Valley Gas Co, 156 A 350 (Ch Ct 1931); Canister Co v National Can Corp, 63 FSupp 361 (D Del 1945).*

President has no implied power or presumed authority to bind corporation by contract of guaranty in which it has no apparent interest. *Atlantic Refining Co v Ingallis & Co, 185 A 885 (1936).*

Presumption is that president has authority to bind corporation by execution and transfer of negotiable paper in ordinary course of corporation's business. *Italo-Petroleum Corp of America v Hannigan, 14 A2d 401 (1940).*

President cannot bind his corporation upon contract which corporation itself is powerless to make. *West Penn Chemical & Mfg Co v Prentice, 236 F 891 (3d Cir 1916); Acker v Girard Trust Co, 42 F2d 37 (3d Cir 1930).*

President has no implied or inherent power to consent to appointment of receiver for purpose of winding up corporate affairs. *Bruch v National Guarantee Credit Corp, 116 A 738 (Ch Ct 1922).*

President and sole stockholder of corporation signing contract on its behalf is unhampered by either absence of authorizing bylaws or by restraining force of existing bylaws. *Community Stores, Inc v Bean, 14 A2d 633 (1940).*

Employee cannot hold corporate president personally liable for unpaid bonus employee was promised, when it is shown that president's authority to authorize sale of machine such promise personally; but employee does have cause of action against corporation. *Brown v Colonial Chevrolet Co, 249 A2d 439 (1968).*

Corporation will be liable for employee's retirement benefits if, at trial, it is shown (1) president of corporation, who owned 80% of its stock, completely dominated and ran corporation's business without directors' action or approval, and (2) he repeatedly assured employee corporation will pay retirement benefits under such circumstances, president's promise need not be ratified by directors, nor does he need written authority from corporation to make promise. *Hessler, Inc v Farrell, 226 A2d 708 (1967).*

Court dismissed shareholders' class actions claiming that president and director breached their fiduciary duties to shareholders by rejecting tender offer in order to maintain their positions in corporation because (1) president did not control or dominate board or have power to accept or reject proposals on corporation's behalf, (2) press release issued by president was proper since he said he would submit matter to directors, and (3) president and directors did not extract stand-still agreement from tender offeror and then violate it by failing to provide confidential information to offeror. *Lewis v Straetz, No. 7859 (Ch Ct 2-12-86).*

Bank could obtain corporation's documents, even though corporation was not party to action to pierce its veil to reach majority shareholder, because shareholder, as president and sole director, had legal control over documents and could obtain possession of them. *Wilmington Savings Fund Society v Tucker, No. 7977 (Ch Ct 3-13-86).*

Court refused to enjoin exercise of stock options granted to two officers by target of leveraged buyout proposal because directors of target did not have to disclose, in connection with shareholders' meeting, that they adopted plan to sell corporation when (1) stock options were originally granted year before shareholders' meeting and (2) first manifestation of any real interest in target's acquisition came only day before meeting. *Kramer v Western Pacific Industries, Inc, No. 8675 (Ch Ct 11-13-86).*

.6 Same—estoppel to deny authority of.—Corporation that does not deny authority of its president to speak for it is estopped from repudiating representations made by him in its name. *Frazer v Couthy Land Co, 149 A 428 (Ch Ct 1929).*

.7 Vice-president.—Agency of vice-president cannot be proved by his statement that his authority has been enlarged and that he has been instructed by corporation's president to do certain things in connection with company's business. *Colvocoresses v W S Wasserman Co, 4 A2d 800 (Ch Ct 1939).*

.8 Secretary.—When corporation law provides for signing of certificate or paper by president and secretary, such officers only can sign; vice-president and/or assistant secretary cannot sign. *OAG to Sec'y of State (7-7-38).*

Failure of assistant secretary to attest corporation's bid for oil lease signed by president did not render bid invalid where it complied with all statutory requirements. *Stewart Capital Corp v Andrus, 468 FSupp 1261 (SDNY 1979).*

.9 Liability of officers.—Former officers of debtor corporation that exchanged stock for minority

§142

interest in second corporation as part of reorganization were not indebted to first corporation for withdrawals they made against accrued salaries, when salaries were part of first corporation's long term indebtedness of which second corporation was constructively aware; however, officers remained liable to second corporation for notes executed to first corporation in payment of key-man insurance policies on their lives. *Beach v KDI Corp, 344 FSupp 1230 (D Del 1972).*

Corporate officers who refused to market new gas-saving device because of corporation's failure to (1) obtain tax credits for use of device; (2) develop universal kit which made production of device commercial; and (3) obtain American Gas Association approval were not liable for breach of fiduciary duty under Delaware law absent showing of fraud, bad faith, gross overreaching, or abuse of discretion. *Massaro v Vernitron Corp, 559 FSupp 1068 (D Mass 1983).*

Corporate officer can be held personally liable for the torts he commits, including unfair competition, and cannot shield himself behind a corporation when he is an actual participant in the tort. Corporation may also be vicariously or secondarily liable if the officer commits tort while acting on corporation's behalf, but officer remains personally liable. *Brandywine Mushroom Co v Hockessin Mushroom Products, Inc, 682 FSupp 1307 (D Del 1988).*

.10 Covenant not to compete.—Film manufacturer could not enjoin former employee from working for competitor because (1) even if employee possessed some confidential information, he would have no occasion to use manufacturer's technology at competitor which made different film using different production process and machinery and (2) employee could not be prohibited from working with competitor simply because competitor might return to production of film that manufacturer makes. *American Hoechst Corp v Nuodex, Inc, No. 7950 (Ch Ct 4-23-85).*

Court refused to enforce covenant not to compete that former employee signed with personnel placement agency because (1) employee did not bring agency's customer lists or proprietary information to his current employer, (2) he is working exclusively in sector of placement business in which agency does little, if any, business, and (3) even in that sector, his activities are limited to geographical area beyond that covered by covenant. *LewMor, Inc v Fleming, No. 8355 (Ch Ct 1-29-86).*

Corporation's former employees who had breached covenant not to compete were enjoined from soliciting former employer's customers even though covenant did not contain any geographical restrictions, because the absence of geographical limitations did not automatically render covenant unenforceable. *Gas Oil Products, Inc of Delaware v Kabino, No. 9150 (Ch Ct 10-13-87).*

.11 Protection of trade secrets.—Employee who achieves technical expertise or general knowledge while in another's employ may thereafter use that knowledge in competition with the former employer so long as he does not use or disclose protected trade secrets in the process. Court refused to enjoin corporation's former employees from setting up company to market investment advisory service in competition with corporation's investment advisory service. *Wilmington Trust Co v Consistent Asset Management, No. 8867 (Ch Ct 3-25-87).*

.12 Fiduciary duty of acquiring corporation.—Acquiring corporation did not assume the role of a fiduciary to target company's shareholders when tender offer was made; no fiduciary duty of candor regarding the terms of the offer to purchase existed. *Zirn v VLI Corp, No. 9488 (Ch Ct 7-17-89).*

.13 Failure to comply with technical requirements—effect.—Lack of compliance with the technical requirements of Delaware corporate law in issuing new stock does not require a declaration that the stock is void and that no rights attach as a result of issuance of the stock. This lack of technical compliance also does not rob the court of power to grant plaintiffs what amounts to specific performance under §227. *Waggoner v STAAR Surgical Co, No. 11185 (Ch Ct 3-15-90).*

143 LOANS TO EMPLOYEES AND OFFICERS; GUARANTY OF OBLIGATIONS OF EMPLOYEES AND OFFICERS.—Any corporation may lend money to, or guaranty any obligation of, or otherwise assist any officer or other employee of the corporation or of its subsidiary, including any officer or employee who is a director of the corporation or its subsidiary, whenever, in the judgment of the directors, such loan, guaranty or assistance may reasonably be expected to benefit the corporation. The loan, guaranty or other assistance may be with or without interest, and may be unsecured, or secured in such manner as the board of directors shall approve, including, without limitation, a pledge of shares of stock of the corporation. Nothing in this section contained shall be deemed to deny, limit or restrict the powers of guaranty or warranty of any corporation at common law or under any statute.

.1 Corporate waste.—A board of director's decision to lend corporate funds to its CEO's for settlement of a lawsuit does not constitute corporate waste, and therefore is presumed to be a valid exercise of business judgment, where the CEO provides some collateral for the loan and there is no evidence that at the time of the transaction the transaction was not worthwhile. *White v Panic, 783 A2d 543 (2001).*

144 INTERESTED DIRECTORS; QUORUM.—(a) No contract or transaction between a corporation and 1 or more of its directors or officers, or between a corporation and any other corporation, partnership, association, or other organization in which 1 or more of its directors or officers, are directors or officers, or have a financial interest, shall be void or voidable solely for this reason, or solely because the director or officer is present at or participates in the meeting of the board or committee which authorizes the contract or transaction, or solely because any such director's or officer's votes are counted for such purpose, if:

(1) The material facts as to the director's or officer's relationship or interest and as to the contract or transaction are disclosed or are known to the board of directors or the committee, and the board or committee in good faith authorizes the contract or transaction by the affirmative votes of a majority of the disinterested directors, even though the disinterested directors be less than a quorum; or

(2) The material facts as to the director's or officer's relationship or interest and as to the contract or transaction are disclosed or are known to the [1] *stockholders* entitled to vote thereon, and the contract or transaction is specifically approved in good faith by vote of the [1] *stockholders*; or

(3) The contract or transaction is fair as to the corporation as of the time it is authorized, approved or ratified, by the board of directors, a committee or the [1] *stockholders*.

(b) Common or interested directors may be counted in determining the presence of a quorum at a meeting of the board of directors or of a committee which authorizes the contract or transaction. (Last amended by Ch. 253, L. '10, eff. 8-1-10.)

Ch. 253, L. '10, eff. 8-1-10, added matter in italic and deleted [1]"shareholders".

Ch. 253, L. '10 Synopsis of Section 144

Sections 10, 11, 12, 13, and 14 make technical changes to §141 and §144 of the DGCL consistent with the intent of the bill and with the translator provision in new §114(a).

Ch. 339, L. '98 Synopsis of Section 144

The amendments to these Sections eliminate masculine references in the statutes, and replace them with gender neutral references.

.1 Interested directors.—Dominant or management stockholders, directors and officers cannot disregard their fiduciary duty to corporation and its creditors so as to subordinate claims of latter to their own claims against company. *Pepper v Litton, 308 US 295 (1939).*

Directors are not liable for profits they make on interest in land they acquired, larger than that bought by corporation, when it is shown corporation was financially unable to invest more into project, they informed other directors what they were doing, and so they took no opportunity away from corporation. *Lipkin v Jacoby, 202 A2d 572 (Ch Ct 1964).*

Although adopted by votes of interested directors, profit sharing plan was legal when it was effectively ratified by majority stockholders. *Kerbs v California Eastern Airways, Inc, 94 A2d 217 (Ch Ct 1953).*

Directors' "adverse interest," not defined in charter, includes ownership of stock in other corporation. *The Martin Foundation, Inc v North American Rayon Corp, 68 A2d 313 (Ch Ct 1949).*

Charter provision is valid that permits counting of interested directors for quorum purposes to vote on any matter that will be later submitted for stockholder approval, such as merger. *Sterling v Mayflower Hotel Corp, 89 A2d 652 (Ch Ct), aff'd, 83 A2d 107 (1952).*

Contract between corporation and company controlled by former director of corporation was voidable because, although Delaware GCL §144 pertaining to interested director contracts is not exclusive method to validate these contracts, some sort of majority shareholder ratification is necessary, which did not occur. *Robert A Wachsler, Inc v Florafax International, Inc, 778 F2d 547 (10th Cir 1985).*

GCL §144 which allows ratification of interested director transactions is not only means of validation. Ratification process contemplated by statute presupposes functioning of corporate constituencies capable of providing approval. Just as statute cannot sanction unfairness neither can it invalidate fairness if, on judicial review, transaction withstands close scrutiny of its intrinsic elements. Lower court therefore properly applied intrinsic fairness test in determining validity of interested director transaction when steps afforded under statute were unavailable because of director-shareholder deadlock. *Marciano v Nakash, 535 A2d 400 (1987).*

A stockholder class action cannot be dismissed under Chancery Rule 12(b)(6) where the complaint adequately alleges that a majority of the directors recommending a merger to the stockholders had disabling conflicts of interest. *Krasner v Moffett, 826 A2d 277 (2003).*

.2 Certificate amendment.—No authority for claim that amendment to certificate of incorporation that shifted voting control from shareholders to a savings plan allegedly controlled by directors should be treated as a gift or waste of assets requiring unanimous shareholder ratification. Also, in light of the extensive proxy statement disclosure of critical features, purposes, and effects of this certificate amendment, that were omitted would not have significantly altered total mix of information available to stockholders. *Weiss v Rockwell International Corp, No. 8811 (Ch Ct 7-19-89).*

.3 Business judgment rule.—Where only two out of ten members of the board were inside directors, and neither dominated the remaining eight, and where a "prima facie showing of good faith and reasonable investigation" existed, the action to divest a lagging business segment after two years of discussion and analysis, and partially as a defensive measure to head off an approaching takeover, was "reasonable in relation

§144

to the threat posed" and thus protected from judicial scrutiny by the business judgment rule. *Tomczak v Thiokol, No. 7861 (Ch Ct 4-5-90).*

In an action alleging a board of directors breached the fiduciary duty of loyalty by approving merger terms despite the presence of a conflict of interest, the Court of Chancery determined that the business judgment rule and not the "entire fairness" test was the appropriate standard with which to review the board's actions. *In re Wheelabrator Technologies Inc Shareholders Litigation, No. 11495 (Ch Ct 5-16-95).*

Directors breached their fiduciary duties of loyalty and care to their corporation under both the business judgment rule and GCL §144 analysis by deliberately concealing their self-interests in transactions negotiated by one of the directors with the knowledge of the other director. *HMG/Courtland Properties, Inc v Gray, C.A. No. 15789 (Ch Ct 7-12-99).*

A board of director's decision to lend corporate funds to its CEO's for settlement of a lawsuit does not constitute corporate waste, and therefore is presumed to be a valid exercise of business judgment, where the CEO provides some collateral for the loan and there is no evidence that at the time of the transaction the transaction was not worthwhile. *White v Panic, 783 A2d 543 (2001).*

A board's decision to change terms of a settlement proposal to account for shareholders who may opt-out is protected by the business judgment rule where the directors are not interested in the transaction. *H-M Wexford, LLC v Encorp, Inc, 2003 Del. Ch. LEXIS 54 (Ch Ct 2003).*

Where disclosures in connection with a recapitalization plan are adequate, and where a plaintiff has failed to proffer sufficient evidence to overcome the business judgment rule or to demonstrate the unfairness of the plan, defendants are entitled to summary judgment. *Rosser v New Valley Corp, 2005 Del. Ch. LEXIS 81 (Ch Ct 2005).*

A settlement of a breach of fiduciary derivative or class action will not be approved where the consideration for the release of claims is of marginal value and confers little benefit on shareholders, and where the underlying claims of significant self-dealing are facially credible so that even where directors have complied with most of the requirements of the business judgment rule, that rule's protections are unavailable to them. *Off v Ross, 2008 Del. Ch. LEXIS 175 (Ch Ct 2008).*

.4 Futility of demand.—Demand on the board of an acquiring corporation in a merger is excused where plaintiff sufficiently demonstrates that the directors would have been unable to objectively consider a demand that the acquiring corporation's board sue the proponents of the merger. *Harbor Finance Partners v Huizenga, C.A. No. 14933 (Ch Ct 11-17-99).*

A stockholder is excused from making a demand in derivative litigation when one member of a two-member board of directors cannot impartially consider such demand. *Beneville v York, C.A. No. 17638 (Ch Ct 7-10-00).*

.5 Entire fairness standard.—Where a CEO's employment contract with a corporation automatically renews without the review of the corporation's board of directors and at the sole discretion of the CEO, and where the employment contract effectively insulates the CEO from board supervision, the CEO cannot meet his burden of proof of showing that the employment contract was entirely fair, especially where only the CEO and his former subordinate are the only ones who testify about the transaction's fairness. *Pereira v Cogan, 2001 U.S. Dist. LEXIS 15576 (SDNY 2001).*

Where a corporate bonus transaction is the result of a fatally flawed, entirely self-interested process dominated by management and bonus beneficiaries that results in grossly excessive bonuses, the recipients of the unfair bonuses must disgorge the entire bonus amount. *Valeant Pharmaceuticals International v Jerney, 2007 Del. Ch. LEXIS 31 (Ch Ct 2007).*

145 INDEMNIFICATION OF OFFICERS, DIRECTORS, EMPLOYEES AND AGENTS; INSURANCE.—(a) A corporation shall have power to indemnify any person who was or is a party or is threatened to be made a party to any threatened, pending or completed action, suit or proceeding, whether civil, criminal, administrative or investigative (other than an action by or in the right of the corporation) by reason of the fact that the person is or was a director, officer, employee or agent of the corporation, or is or was serving at the request of the corporation as a director, officer, employee or agent of another corporation, partnership, joint venture, trust or other enterprise, against expenses (including attorneys' fees), judgments, fines and amounts paid in settlement actually and reasonably incurred by the person in connection with such action, suit or proceeding if the person acted in good faith and in a manner the person reasonably believed to be in or not opposed to the best interests of the corporation, and, with respect to any criminal action or proceeding, had no reasonable cause to believe the person's conduct was unlawful. The termination of any action, suit or proceeding by judgment, order, settlement, conviction, or upon a plea of nolo contendere or its equivalent, shall not, of itself, create a presumption that the person did not act in good faith and in a manner which the person reasonably believed to be in or not opposed to the best interests of the corporation, and, with respect to any criminal action or proceeding, had reasonable cause to believe that the person's conduct was unlawful.

(b) A corporation shall have power to indemnify any person who was or is a party or is threatened to be made a party to any threatened, pending or completed action or suit by or in the right of the corporation to procure a judgment in its favor by reason of the fact that the person is or was a director, officer, employee or agent of the corporation, or is or was serving at the request of the corporation as a director, officer, employee or agent of another corporation, partnership, joint venture, trust or other enterprise against expenses (including attorneys' fees) actually and reasonably incurred by the person in connection with the defense or settlement of such action or suit if the person acted in good faith and in a manner the person reasonably believed to be in or not opposed to the best interests of the corporation and except that no indemnification shall be made in respect of any claim, issue or matter as to which such person shall have been adjudged to be liable to the corporation unless and only to the extent that the Court of Chancery or the court in which such action or suit was brought shall determine upon application that, despite the adjudication of liability but in view of all the circumstances of the case, such person is fairly and reasonably entitled to indemnity for such expenses which the Court of Chancery or such other court shall deem proper.

(c) To the extent that a present or former director or officer of a corporation has been successful on the merits or otherwise in defense of any action, suit or proceeding referred to in subsections (a) and (b) of this section, or in defense of any claim, issue or matter therein, such person shall be indemnified against expenses (including attorneys' fees) actually and reasonably incurred by such person in connection therewith.

(d) Any indemnification under subsections (a) and (b) of this section (unless ordered by a court) shall be made by the corporation only as authorized in the specific case upon a determination that indemnification of the present or former director, officer, employee or agent is proper in the circumstances because the person has met the applicable standard of conduct set forth in subsections (a) and (b) of this section. Such determination shall be made, with respect to a person who is a director or officer of the corporation at the time of such determination, (1) by a majority vote of the directors who are not parties to such action, suit or proceeding, even though less than a quorum, or (2) by a committee of such directors designated by majority vote of such directors, even though less than a quorum, or (3) if there are no such directors, or if such directors so direct, by independent legal counsel in a written opinion, or (4) by the stockholders.

(e) Expenses (including attorneys' fees) incurred by an officer or director of the corporation in defending any civil, criminal, administrative or investigative action, suit or proceeding may be paid by the corporation in advance of the final disposition of such action, suit or proceeding upon receipt of an undertaking by or on behalf of such director or officer to repay such amount if it shall ultimately be determined that such person is not entitled to be indemnified by the corporation as authorized in this section. Such expenses (including attorneys' fees) incurred by former directors and officers or other employees and agents of the corporation or by persons serving at the request of the corporation as directors, officers, employees or agents of another corporation, partnership, joint venture, trust or other enterprise may be so paid upon such terms and conditions, if any, as the corporation deems appropriate.

(f) The indemnification and advancement of expenses provided by, or granted pursuant to, the other subsections of this section shall not be deemed exclusive of any other rights to which those seeking indemnification or advancement of expenses may be entitled under any bylaw, agreement, vote of stockholders or disinterested directors or otherwise, both as to action in such person's official capacity and as to action in another capacity while holding such office. A right to indemnification or to advancement of expenses arising under a provision of the certificate of incorporation or a bylaw shall not be eliminated or impaired by an amendment to [1] *the certificate of incorporation or the bylaws* after the occurrence of the act or omission that is the subject of the civil, criminal, administrative or investigative action, suit or proceeding for which indemnification or advancement of expenses is sought, unless the provision in effect at the time of such act or omission explicitly authorizes such elimination or impairment after such action or omission has occurred.

(g) A corporation shall have power to purchase and maintain insurance on behalf of any person who is or was a director, officer, employee or agent of the corporation, or is or was serving at the request of the corporation as a director, officer, employee or agent of another corporation, partnership, joint venture, trust or other enterprise against any liability asserted against such person and incurred by such person in any such capacity, or arising out of such person's status as such, whether or not the corporation would have the power to indemnify such person against such liability under this section.

(h) For purposes of this section, references to "the corporation" shall include, in addition to the resulting corporation, any constituent corporation (including any constituent of a constituent) absorbed in a consolidation or merger which, if its separate existence had continued, would have had power and authority to indemnify its directors, officers, and employees or agents, so that any person who is or was a director, officer, employee or agent of such constituent corporation, or is or was serving at the request of such constituent corporation as a director, officer, employee or agent of another corporation, partnership, joint venture, trust or other enterprise, shall stand in the same position under this section with respect to the resulting or surviving corporation as such person would have with respect to such constituent corporation if its separate existence had continued.

(i) For purposes of this section, references to "other enterprises" shall include employee benefit plans; references to "fines" shall include any excise taxes assessed on a person with respect to any employee benefit plan; and references to "serving at the request of the corporation" shall include any service as a director, officer, employee or agent of the corporation which imposes duties on, or involves services by, such director, officer, employee, or agent with respect to an employee benefit plan, its participants or beneficiaries; and a person who acted in good faith and in a manner such person reasonably believed to be in the interest of the participants and beneficiaries of an employee benefit plan shall be deemed to have acted in a manner "not opposed to the best interests of the corporation" as referred to in this section.

(j) The indemnification and advancement of expenses provided by, or granted pursuant to, this section shall, unless otherwise provided when authorized or ratified, continue as to a person who has ceased to be a director, officer, employee or agent and shall inure to the benefit of the heirs, executors and administrators of such a person.

(k) The Court of Chancery is hereby vested with exclusive jurisdiction to hear and determine all actions for advancement of expenses or indemnification brought under this section or under any bylaw, agreement, vote of stockholders or disinterested directors, or otherwise. The Court of Chancery may summarily determine a corporation's obligation to advance expenses (including attorneys' fees). (Last amended by Ch. 96, L. '11, eff. 8-1-11.)

Ch. 96, L. '11, eff. 8-1-11, added matter in italic and deleted [1]"such provision".

Ch. 96, L. '11 Synopsis of Section 145

The amendment to Section 145(f) clarifies that a right to indemnification or advancement of expenses under a provision of a certificate of incorporation or bylaw cannot be eliminated or impaired by an amendment to the certificate of incorporation or the bylaws after the occurrence of the act or omission to which indemnification or advancement of expenses relates, unless the provision contains, at the time of the act or omission, an explicit authorization of such elimination or limitation.

Ch. 290, L. '10 Synopsis of Section 145

The amendment to Section 145(d) clarifies that the second sentence of the subsection, which requires that a determination that indemnification is proper be made by one of the specified decision-making bodies in certain circumstances, applies when the person requesting indemnification is a director or officer of the corporation at the time of such determination (as opposed to when a person requesting indemnification is not a director or officer of the corporation at such time but is serving at the request of the corporation as a director or officer of another corporation, partnership, joint venture, trust or other enterprise).

The amendment to Section 145(e) clarifies that the first sentence of Section 145(e) is intended to apply to advancement of expenses to present officers and directors of the corporation providing the advancement (and not to advancement to persons serving at the request of the corporation as officers and directors of another corporation, partnership, joint venture, trust or other enterprise) and further clarifies that expenses may be advanced to persons serving at the request of the corporation as directors, officers, employees or agents of another corporation, partnership, joint venture, trust or other enterprise upon such terms and conditions, if any, as the corporation deems appropriate.

Ch. 14, L. '09 Synopsis of Section 145

The amendment to Section 145(f) adopts a default rule different than the approach articulated in *Schoon v. Troy Corp.,* 948 A.2d 1157, 1165-1166 (Del. Ch. 2008). Under amended Section 145(f), a right to indemnification or advancement of expenses under a provision of a certificate of incorporation or bylaw cannot be eliminated or impaired by an amendment of the provision after the occurrence of the act or omission to which indemnification or advancement of expenses relates, unless the provision contains, at the time of the act or omission, an explicit authorization of such elimination or limitation.

Ch. 120, L. '97 Synopsis of Section 145

The amendment to Section 145(c) establishes that the Act does not prescribe mandatory indemnification with respect to employees and agents of the corporation who are neither officers nor directors of the corporation. Mandatory indemnification for such persons who satisfy the statutory standard of conduct will continue to be permissible under the Act. The amendments to Section 145(d) also clarify that the determination whether indemnification of a director or officer is proper in the circumstances may be made by a committee of directors who are not parties to the action, suit or proceeding as to which indemnification is sought, where that committee is designated by majority vote of all such directors even though less than a quorum of the full board of directors. The amendments also eliminate the requirement that indemnification of employees and agents who are not directors or officers be authorized by directors, independent counsel or the stockholders. Under this amendment and the amendment to Section 145(e), indemnification of and advancement of expenses to such employees and agent, as well as former directors and officers, may be made by any person or persons having corporate authority to act on the matter, including those persons who are authorized by statute to determine whether to indemnify directors and officers. The amendments to Section 145(e) are not intended to alter the procedure for authorizing advancement of expenses to directors and officers. The other amendments to Section 145 substitute gender neutral language for masculine terminology.

Ch. 261, L. '94 Synopsis of Section 145(d) and (k)

The amendment to Section 145(d) permits action on indemnification requests by a majority vote of those members of the board who are not parties to such action, suit or proceeding, whether or not they constitute a quorum of the board.

The amendment adding new subsection "(k)" provides the Court of Chancery with exclusive jurisdiction to hear and determine actions brought pursuant to Section 145, including but not limited to actions brought pursuant to charter and bylaw provisions, resolutions and contracts regarding indemnification and advancement. The provision is consistent with a number of other sections of the Delaware General Corporation Law that grant exclusive jurisdiction to the Court of Chancery. The amendment further provides for

summary treatment of actions brought pursuant to Section 145 seeking a determination as to whether a corporation is obligated to advance expenses prior to the final disposition of litigation.

Ch. 376, L. '90 Commentary on Section 145(e)

The amendments to Section 145(e) codify the decision in *Security America Corp. v. Walsh, Case, Coale, Brown & Burke*, No. 82-C-2953 (N.D. Ill. 1985) by making it clear that the expenses which a corporation may advance include attorneys' fees. The amendments also make Section 145(e) consistent with Section 145(a) by making clear that a corporation may advance expenses incurred in defending administrative or investigative proceedings as well as civil or criminal proceedings.

.1 No indemnification when misconduct shown.—Directors against whom misconduct was shown will not be allowed reimbursement of their expenses, even though they were successful in showing they had not paid themselves excessive salaries. *Teren v Howard*, 322 F2d 949 (9th Cir 1963).

Under bylaw that says director cannot be indemnified if he is adjudged "liable because of failure in the performance of his duties as a director, or to any compromise of any such liability," he is liable even if compromise was made before his liability was finally determined. *Essential Enterprises Corp v Dorsey Corp*, 182 A2d 647 (Ch Ct 1962).

Directors cannot be indemnified for legal fees they incurred in defending criminal action against them, when they are found guilty of overall charge of conspiracy, even though one aspect of charge, namely fraud, is withdrawn and dismissed; that is not vindication justifying indemnification within statute's intent. *Merritt-Chapman & Scott Corp v Wolfson*, 264 A2d 358 (1970).

In a case involving a claim for indemnity by the plaintiff from his former employer and its parent corporation for legal expenses arising out of litigation in connection with his activities in the silver market, the plaintiff was required to show either (i) that he acted in good faith and in a manner he reasonably believed was in the best interest of the corporation or (ii) that he had been successful on the merits or otherwise in the underlying actions. *Waltuch v Commodity Services, Inc*, No. 92 Civ. 0383 (MEL) (SDNY 9-17-93).

Officer of a corporation was not entitled to indemnification for unreimbursed legal expenses where the officer could not demonstrate he had acted in good faith, despite a provision in the corporation's articles of incorporation that requires the corporation to indemnify officers regardless of their good faith. *Waltuch v Conticommodity Services, Inc*, 88 F3d 87 (2d Cir 1996).

.2 Indemnity by reason of being director.—Corporation does not have to indemnify officer-director for his legal expenses in defending suits questioning stock options and employment contract he got before becoming director when by law indemnifies only expenses incurred by reason of his being or having been officer or director of corporation. *Sorensen v The Overland Corp*, 142 FSupp 354 (D Del 1956), aff'd, 242 F2d 70 (3d Cir 1957).

Corporation must pay litigation expenses of directors who successfully defend their right to hold office. *Essential Enterprises Corp v Automatic Steel Products, Inc*, 164 A2d 437 (1960). See also, *Hibbert v Hollywood Park, Inc*, 457 A2d 339 (1983).

Dismissal without prejudice of stockholder's action against director solely to avoid duplicity of actions did not entitle officer to indemnification, since dismissal was not vindication on merits nor did it result from technical defense that made it unnecessary to defend on merits. *Galdi v Berg*, 359 FSupp 698 (D Del 1973).

Company's failure to amend bylaws to reflect 1986 amendment of Delaware General Corporation Law was insignificant because the 1986 amendment impliedly amended the bylaws of company. Consequently board approval was not required for advance-ment of litigation expenses and, therefore, defendants were entitled to immediate indemnification benefits. *TBG, Inc v Bendis*, No. 89-2423-0 (D Kan 2-19-91).

Court found plaintiff's status as director was not a necessary element in suit that charged plaintiff had made material misrepresentations and omissions when selling his shares of stock even though his status may be relevant to his defense. Plaintiff was not being sued in his capacity as a director of defendant-corporation, but for actions he committed as an individual for personal gain. Therefore, plaintiff was not entitled to indemnification by defendantcompany. *Heffernan v Pacific Dunlop GNB Corp*, 767 FSupp 913 (ND Ill 1991).

A suit by a former corporate director seeking indemnification and legal expenses in connection with an action arising out of the acquisition of two corporations by another through the purchase of stock was wrongly dismissed, where the underlying complaint alleged that the director committed securities violations by selling his stock pursuant to a misleading prospectus (i.e., the stock purchase agreement) and repeatedly stated that, because of his status as a director, he knew or should have known about the liabilities that were omitted from the stock purchase agreement. Thus, it could not be stated as a matter of law that the director would not be able to show a right to indemnification, and summary dismissal was improper. *Heffernan v Pacific Dunlop GNB Corp*, 965 F2d 369 (7th Cir 1992).

An agreement between a corporation and one of its directors, which provided that the corporation would indemnify the director for expenses and liability incurred in connection with legal proceedings by reason of his service as a director and which further provided that such expenses would be paid in advance of the final disposition of the matter if the director agreed to repay the amounts advanced in the event that it was ultimately determined that he was not entitled to such indemnification, was applicable in a §16(b) action commenced by the corporation against the director in federal court. The Court disagreed with the corporation's contention that the expenses of defending the federal court action were not indemnifiable under the agreement because the action did not arise by reason of the director's services as a director and that therefore, since the expenses were not indemnifiable, there was no requirement to advance the money. The right to advances was not dependent upon the right to indemnity, held the Court, while noting that the parties retained their rights to an "ultimate determination" of their responsibilities under the indemnification provisions. *Citadel Holding Corp v Roven*, 603 A2d 818 (Super Ct 1992).

The former president of a corporation was not entitled to an advancement of his defense expenses in an action for breach of loyalty brought by the corporation. The court distinguished indemnification from advancement of expenses, and held that, while GCL §145(e) authorizes such advancements, it leaves to the business judgment of the board of directors the determination of whether the advancement is in the best interest of the corporation. *Advanced Mining Systems, Inc v Fricke*, No. 11823 (Ch Ct 8-4-92).

Officer was "successful on the merits or otherwise" and entitled to indemnification from the corporation pursuant to GCL §145(c) for unreimbursed legal fees where claims against the officer were dismissed with prejudice and without any payment or assumption of liability by him, although the corporation paid money to settle the action. *Waltuch v Conticommodity Services, Inc*, 88 F3d 87 (2d Cir 1996).

In a case of first impression, the Delaware Supreme Court held that the election of a director to the board of a wholly-owned subsidiary by the 100% stockholder parent constitutes a "request" that the director serve the subsidiary within the meaning of GCL §145(a); accordingly, the director was entitled to indemnification for legal fees incurred in settling third-party (nonderivative) actions. *VonFeldt v Stifel Financial Corp*, 714 A2d 79 (1998).

A corporation's bylaws that provide that a director is entitled to advancement when defending a lawsuit are inapplicable where a director initiates litigation. The court found that although the language in the bylaws defining the scope of indemnification arguably had broader application than the advancement clause, the advancement clause explicitly was limited to persons "defending" an action, and did not apply to a director merely "involved in any action, suit, or proceeding." *Brooks-McCollum v Emerald Ridge Service Corp*, 2004 Del. Ch. LEXIS 105 (Ch Ct 2004).

.3 Contract to indemnify.—Contract to indemnify officer or director for expenses incurred in defending suit is enforceable even though he never entered action and was never served with process, but was named in complaint; contract is also enforceable as long as he was involved in litigation by reason of his being or having been officer or director. *Mooney v Willys-Overland Motors, Inc*, 204 F2d 888 (3d Cir 1953).

Corporation must pay law firm for legal work done on behalf of chairman of board because corporation in settlement agreement with chairman indemnified him for acts and omissions while he was director of corporation. Chairman's lack of "good faith" under GCL §145(a) was of no consequence because under GCL §145(f) there may be indemnity agreement which is not founded in provisions of statute. Chairman did not breach his fiduciary duty to corporation or improperly benefit at corporation's expense. *Choate, Hall & Stewart v SCA Services, Inc*, 495 NE2d 562 (Mass Ct App 1986).

Defendant corporation was obligated to indemnify and advance plaintiff's costs and attorneys' fees in the underlying cause of action and the current action. The court stated that under §145, a corporation may provide for the advancement of expenses, including legal fees, and that the corporation can agree to make such advancements mandatory. The court determined that provisions of the merger agreement between defendant and its predecessor unambiguously provided for mandatory indemnification and advancement of expenses. *Kapoor v Fujisawa Pharmaceutical Co*, No. 93C-06-50 (Super Ct 5-10-94).

.4 Subpoena before federal grand jury.—Officer's expenses are indemnifiable. *Steward v Continental Copper & Steel Industries, Inc*, 414 NYS2d 910 (AD 1979).

.5 Stay.—Court would not dismiss or stay former corporate officer's indemnification suit for expenses involved in his successful defense of criminal charge that he used false corporate financial statements to obtain loan because, although officer was involved in Texas civil litigation involving common issues, (1) officer was not claiming indemnification for civil litigation and (2) requisites for recovery under GCL §145(a) and (b) are not requisites for recovery under relevant section, GCL §145(c). *Green v The Westcap Corp of Delaware*, 492 A2d 260 (1985).

A stay pending appeal will not be granted to a corporation required to pay its director's advancement fees and the costs of a special master's services where the corporation fails to demonstrate even the remotest likelihood of success on the merits or any evidence of irreparable harm. *Tafeen v Homestore, Inc*, 2005 Del. Ch. LEXIS 77 (Ch Ct 2005).

.6 Common law indemnification.—Statute providing for indemnification of officers, directors, and other employees by corporation is not exclusive means of indemnification. Director, therefore, could pursue a common law right for indemnification from other directors who were active wrongdoers. *Greenwald v American Medcare Corp*, 666 FSupp 489 (SDNY 1987).

.7 Refusal to accept corporation's attorney.—After being acquitted of criminal charges, a former corporate officer has a statutory right, under Delaware law, to the indemnification of legal expenses by former employer. This right is not considered waived by pretrial refusal to accept the corporation's offer of defense attorney. *McLean v International Harvester Co*, 817 F2d 1214 (5th Cir 1987).

.8 Advance indemnification.—The Court of Chancery granted plaintiff's motion to stay discovery pending a determination of his motion for partial summary judgment on the issue of whether he was entitled to advance indemnification, where purpose of advance indemnification statute is to promote the expedient resolution of disputes over indemnification and allowing discovery would create undue expense and delay. *Lipson v Supercuts, Inc, No. 15074-NCC (Ch Ct 9-6-96).*

The Court of Chancery granted plaintiffs' application for a preliminary injunction against defendant directors where plaintiffs demonstrated that (1) the directors were not contractually entitled to advanced indemnification; (2) plaintiffs overcame the business judgment rule by alleging sufficient facts that demonstrated defendants breached their duty of care in approving the advancement of expenses; and (3) defendants would be unable to show that their decision to advance expenses was entirely fair. *Havens v Attar, No. 15134 (Ch Ct 1-30-97).*

The Chancery Court held that in all but the most exceptional circumstances, claims under GCL §145(k) for advancement of expenses should not be stayed or dismissed in favor of prior pending foreign litigation that gives rise to them. *Fuisz v Biovail Technologies, Ltd, C.A. No. 18004 (Ch Ct 9-6-00).*

A stay pending appeal will not be granted to a corporation required to pay its director's advancement fees and the costs of a special master's services where the corporation fails to demonstrate even the remotest likelihood of success on the merits or any evidence of irreparable harm. *Tafeen v Homestore, Inc, 2005 Del. Ch. LEXIS 77 (Ch Ct 2005).*

An employee of a corporation who does not work for a sister corporation, but is not an employee of the sister corporation, and is not acting as an employee at the sister corporation's request, is not entitled to mandatory advancement from the sister company. *Flynn v CIBC World Markets Corp, 2005 Del. Ch. LEXIS 93 (Ch Ct 2005).*

A corporation's claims against a former officer and director for wrongful misappropriation of confidential information and use of the information to form a competing enterprise, regardless of whether the complaint contains references to wrongdoing arising out of the defendant's status as an officer or director, arise out of the defendant's former position as an officer and director, and, therefore, trigger advancement of attorneys' fees and expenses. *Brown v LiveOps, Inc, 2006 Del. Ch. LEXIS 113 (Ch Ct 2006).*

After the conversion of a limited liability company into a corporation, the corporation's bylaws providing a mandatory right of advancement to its officers and directors does not apply equally to the former managers of the LLC, even where the LLC's operating agreement provided for indemnification but not for mandatory advancement. *Bernstein v TractManager, Inc, 2007 Del. Ch. LEXIS 172 (Ch Ct 2007).*

Where "fees on fees" are awarded for expenses incurred in prosecuting an advancement action, they must be proportionate to the degree of success obtained. *Schoon v Troy Corp, 2008 Del. Ch. LEXIS 36 (Ch Ct 2008).*

Advancement by a corporation of legal fees incurred in "defense" of claims brought against the corporation's directors or officers is required as to counterclaims that are compulsory. *Reinhard v The Dow Chemical Company, 2008 Del. Ch. LEXIS 39 (Ch Ct 2008).*

A corporate employee who is neither an officer nor a director is entitled to advancement where the corporation's bylaws provide that nominal officers with management supervisory functions are entitled to advancement, and the employee fits within the definition of a nominal officer with such functions. *Sassano v CIBC World Markets Corp, 2008 Del. Ch. LEXIS 5 (Ch Ct 2008).*

A corporation's former outside litigation counsel is entitled to advancement as an "agent" when the corporation sues the former counsel not for malpractice but for claims arising out of a control contest. *Jackson Walker L.L.P. v Spira Footwear, Inc, 2008 Del. Ch. LEXIS 82 (Ch Ct 2008).*

For purposes of advancement, the "final disposition" of a criminal action is the final, nonappealable conclusion to that proceeding, as opposed to the time at which sentencing occurs at the trial court level. *Sun-Times Media Group, Inc v Black, 954 A2d 380 (Ch Ct 2008).*

.9 Recovery of expenses.—A corporate director, who was found to be entitled to indemnification fees and expenses incurred in his successful defense of a federal securities action, could not under GCL §145(c) recover the attorneys fees he incurred in the subsequent action in which he established his right to indemnification. *Mayer v Executive Telecard, Ltd, No. 14459 (Ch Ct 4-25-97).*

Advancement of litigation expenses is not mandatory under Delaware law absent a clearly worded bylaw or contract making it mandatory. *Havens v Attar, No. 15134 (Ch Ct 11-5-97).*

Estate of CEO is entitled to maintain action for breach of contract and breach of obligation of good faith against insurer that refused to reimburse estate for amount it paid to settle a shareholder derivative action; the insurer claimed that it did not have to pay because the policy excluded payments in connection with any claim for which the insureds may be indemnified by the corporation. *TLC Beatrice International Holdings, Inc v Cigna Insurance Co, 97 Civ 8589 (MBM) (SDNY 1-25-99).*

HealthTrust and Tenet, as voluntary, contractual indemnitors of plaintiff, were equally responsible for plaintiff's legal fees under the permissive provisions of GCL §145(b) in a case where the legal expenses incurred by plaintiff (in successfully defending himself in a derivative action brought against him and other directors of EPIC, HealthTrust's subsidiary) were paid by Tenet under his employment agreement with him. *Chamison v HealthTrust, Inc, C.A. No. 15904 (Ch Ct 1-12-99).*

Attorneys' fees and expenses incurred in prosecuting an indemnification action will not be awarded even where a corporation's bylaws permit indemnification to the "fullest extent" allowed by law, but do not specify that "fees for fees" are allowable. *Perconti v Thornton Oil Corp, 2002 Del Ch LEXIS 51 (Ch Ct 2002).*

The Delaware Supreme Court has held that indemnification for expenses incurred in successfully prosecuting an indemnification suit ("fees on fees") are permissible under GCL §145(a), and therefore are "authorized by law." *Stifel Financial Corp v Cochran, 809 A2d 555 (2002).*

© 2010 Aspen Publishers. All Rights Reserved.

§145

A "fees on fees" award for indemnification of litigation expenses incurred bringing an action pursuant to GCL §145 to enforce a contractual right to obtain an advancement of litigation expenses must be proportionate to the success achieved and to the efforts required to achieve that success. *Fasciana v Electronic Data Systems, Corp, 2003 Del. Ch. LEXIS 68 (Ch Ct 2003).*

.10 Statute of limitations.—A claim for indemnification brought by the officer or director of a Delaware corporation and based on its bylaws is governed by a three-year statute of limitations. *Cochran v Stifel Financial Corp, C.A. No. 17350 (Ch Ct 3-8-00).*

.11 Partial indemnification.—Where an officer or director of a corporation is partially successful in corporation-related litigation, an acceptable approach to determine partial indemnification of litigation expenses for that officer or director is to identify time and expenses to be excluded from the entire litigation, rather than to include only items that can be directly linked to successful issues. Also, subissues that are not addressed by the court are properly within the scope of partial indemnification, unless the court has expressly rejected them as insubstantial. *May v Bigmar, Inc, 2003 Del. Ch. LEXIS 134 (Ch Ct 2003).*

.12 Insurance and bankruptcy.—A creditor's committee that brings a breach of fiduciary action against directors of a bankrupt corporation is not acting for the corporate debtor-in-possession, but rather is bringing an action derivatively on behalf of the debtor's estate, so that an exclusion in a directors' and officers' insurance policy for "insured vs. insured" claims brought by or on behalf of the debtorin-possession is not triggered. *Cirka v National Union Fire Insurance Company of Pittsburgh, PA, 2004 Del. Ch. LEXIS 118 (Ch Ct 2004).*

.13 Cause of action.—Where a director or officer is indemnified by a third party, and incurs no out of pocket litigation costs, even where the corporation is obligated to concomitantly indemnify the director or officer, the director or officer does not have an indemnification cause of action against the corporation; instead, the third party has a contribution claim against the corporation. Also, as a matter of public policy and statutory interpretation, a contract will not be enforced to the extent that it allows "fees on fees" to be paid by a corporation for pursuing indemnification claims even if the claims are unsuccessful. *Levy v HLI Operating Co, 924 A2d 210 (Ch Ct 2007).*

.14 Validity of bylaws.—Bylaws adopted and amended by unanimous written consent are valid where prior bylaws provide for such amendment at a meeting of the board, but also provide for board action by unanimous written consent. *Underbrink v Warrior Energy Services Corp, 2008 Del. Ch. LEXIS 65 (Ch Ct 2008).*

Advancement provisions in articles of incorporation may be limited by reasonable conditions in a corporation's bylaws where the articles and bylaws are executed at the same time, and such conditions may be imposed where a director has had the opportunity to examine both documents.

The Chancery Court found that there was no precedent requiring that conditions on advancement have to be included in the same document that creates the advancement rights. The court held that the corporation was entitled to place reasonable conditions on the director's right to advancement, for two primary reasons. First, because the the articles and bylaws were executed at the same time and because under Delaware law, every effort should be made to reconcile the provisions of simultaneously enacted founding documents—which was possible here since the provisions were not contradictory. Second, because both the articles and the bylaws were in effect when the director began his directorship, so that he had every opportunity to read the articles and bylaws and become fully informed regarding the scope of his indemnification and advancement rights before agreeing to serve as a director. Accordingly, the court denied the director's motion for summary judgment for mandatory advancement. *Xu Hong Bin v Heckmann Corp, 2010 Del. Ch. LEXIS 3 (Ch Ct 2010).*

.15 Indemnification by third party.—Where a director or officer is indemnified by a third party, and incurs no out of pocket litigation costs, even where the corporation is obligated to concomitantly indemnify the director or officer, the director or officer does not have an indemnification cause of action against the corporation; instead, the third party has a contribution claim against the corporation. Also, as a matter of public policy and statutory interpretation, a contract will not be enforced to the extent that it allows "fees on fees" to be paid by a corporation for pursuing indemnification claims even if the claims are unsuccessful. *Levy v HLI Operating Co, 924 A2d 210 (Ch Ct 2007).*

146 SUBMISSION OF MATTERS FOR STOCKHOLDER VOTE.—A corporation may agree to submit a matter to a vote of its stockholders whether or not the board of directors determines at any time subsequent to approving such matter that such matter is no longer advisable and recommends that the stockholders reject or vote against the matter. (Added by Ch. 84, L. '03, eff. 8-1-03.)

Ch. 84, L. '03 Synopsis of Section 146

The deletion of the language from subsection (c) of Section 251 and the addition of new Section 146 clarify that the rule previously codified at Section 251(c) applies to any matter submitted to stockholders. Under this rule, directors may authorize the corporation to agree with another person to submit a matter to stockholders, but reserve the ability to change their recommendation.

SUBCHAPTER V. STOCK AND DIVIDENDS

151 CLASSES AND SERIES OF STOCK; REDEMPTION; RIGHTS.—
(a) Every corporation may issue 1 or more classes of stock or 1 or more series of stock within any class thereof, any or all of which classes may be of stock with par value or stock without par value and which classes or series may have such voting powers, full or limited, or no voting powers, and such designations, preferences and relative, participating, optional or other special rights, and qualifications, limitations or restrictions thereof, as shall be stated and expressed in the certificate of incorporation or of any amendment thereto, or in the resolution or resolutions providing for the issue of such stock adopted by the board of directors pursuant to authority expressly vested in it by the provisions of its certificate of incorporation. Any of the voting powers, designations, preferences, rights and qualifications, limitations or restrictions of any such class or series of stock may be made dependent upon facts ascertainable outside the certificate of incorporation or of any amendment thereto, or outside the resolution or resolutions providing for the issue of such stock adopted by the board of directors pursuant to authority expressly vested in it by its certificate of incorporation, provided that the manner in which such facts shall operate upon the voting powers, designations, preferences, rights and qualifications, limitations or restrictions of such class or series of stock is clearly and expressly set forth in the certificate of incorporation or in the resolution or resolutions providing for the issue of such stock adopted by the board of directors. The term "facts," as used in this subsection, includes, but is not limited to, the occurrence of any event, including a determination or action by any person or body, including the corporation. The power to increase or decrease or otherwise adjust the capital stock as provided in this chapter shall apply to all or any such classes of stock.

(b) [1]*Any stock of any class or series may be made subject to redemption by the corporation at its option or at the option of the holders of such stock or upon the happening of a specified event; provided, however, that immediately following any such redemption the corporation shall have outstanding 1 or more shares of 1 or more classes or series of stock, which share, or shares together, shall have full voting powers.* Notwithstanding the limitation stated in the foregoing proviso:

(1) Any stock of a regulated investment company registered under the Investment Company Act of 1940 [15 U.S.C. §80a-1 et seq.], as heretofore or hereafter amended, may be made subject to redemption by the corporation at its option or at the option of the holders of such stock.

(2) Any stock of a corporation which holds (directly or indirectly) a license or franchise from a governmental agency to conduct its business or is a member of a national securities exchange, which license, franchise or membership is conditioned upon some or all of the holders of its stock possessing prescribed qualifications, may be made subject to redemption by the corporation to the extent necessary to prevent the loss of such license, franchise or membership or to reinstate it.

Any stock which may be made redeemable under this section may be redeemed for cash, property or rights, including securities of the same or another corporation, at such time or times, price or prices, or rate or rates, and with such adjustments, as shall be stated in the certificate of incorporation or in the resolution or resolutions providing for the issue of such stock adopted by the board of directors pursuant to subsection (a) of this section.

(c) The holders of preferred or special stock of any class or of any series thereof shall be entitled to receive dividends at such rates, on such conditions and at such times as shall be stated in the certificate of incorporation or in the resolution or resolutions providing for the issue of such stock adopted by the board of directors as hereinabove provided, payable in preference to, or in such relation to, the dividends payable on any other class or classes or of any other series of stock, and cumulative or noncumulative as shall be so stated and expressed. When dividends upon the preferred and special stocks, if any, to the extent of the preference to which such stocks are entitled, shall have been paid or declared and set apart for payment, a dividend on the remaining class or classes or series of stock may then be paid out of the remaining assets of the corporation available for dividends as elsewhere in this chapter provided.

(d) The holders of the preferred or special stock of any class or of any series thereof shall be entitled to such rights upon the dissolution of, or upon any distribution of the assets of, the corporation as shall be stated in the certificate of incorporation or in the

§151

resolution or resolutions providing for the issue of such stock adopted by the board of directors as hereinabove provided.

(e) Any stock of any class or of any series thereof may be made convertible into, or exchangeable for, at the option of either the holder or the corporation or upon the happening of a specified event, shares of any other class or classes or any other series of the same or any other class or classes of stock of the corporation, at such price or prices or at such rate or rates of exchange and with such adjustments as shall be stated in the certificate of incorporation or in the resolution or resolutions providing for the issue of such stock adopted by the board of directors as hereinabove provided.

(f) If any corporation shall be authorized to issue more than 1 class of stock or more than 1 series of any class, the powers, designations, preferences and relative, participating, optional, or other special rights of each class of stock or series thereof and the qualifications, limitations, or restrictions of such preferences and/or rights shall be set forth in full or summarized on the face or back of the certificate which the corporation shall issue to represent such class or series of stock, provided that, except as otherwise provided in §202 of this title, in lieu of the foregoing requirements, there may be set forth on the face or back of the certificate which the corporation shall issue to represent such class or series of stock, a statement that the corporation will furnish without charge to each stockholder who so requests the powers, designations, preferences and relative, participating, optional, or other special rights of each class of stock or series thereof and the qualifications, limitations or restrictions of such preferences and/or rights. Within a reasonable time after the issuance or transfer of uncertificated stock, the corporation shall send to the registered owner thereof a written notice containing the information required to be set forth or stated on certificates pursuant to this section or §156, 202(a) or 218(a) of this title or with respect to this section a statement that the corporation will furnish without charge to each stockholder who so requests the powers, designations, preferences and relative participating, optional or other special rights of each class of stock or series thereof and the qualifications, limitations or restrictions of such preferences and/or rights. Except as otherwise expressly provided by law, the rights and obligations of the holders of uncertificated stock and the rights and obligations of the holders of certificates representing stock of the same class and series shall be identical.

(g) When any corporation desires to issue any shares of stock of any class or of any series of any class of which the powers, designations, preferences and relative, participating, optional or other rights, if any, or the qualifications, limitations or restrictions thereof, if any, shall not have been set forth in the certificate of incorporation or in any amendment thereto but shall be provided for in a resolution or resolutions adopted by the board of directors pursuant to authority expressly vested in it by the certificate of incorporation or any amendment thereto, a certificate of designations setting forth a copy of such resolution or resolutions and the number of shares of stock of such class or series as to which the resolution or resolutions apply shall be executed, acknowledged, filed and shall become effective, in accordance with §103 of this title. Unless otherwise provided in any such resolution or resolutions, the number of shares of stock of any such series to which such resolution or resolutions apply may be increased (but not above the total number of authorized shares of the class) or decreased (but not below the number of shares thereof then outstanding) by a certificate likewise executed, acknowledged and filed setting forth a statement that a specified increase or decrease therein had been authorized and directed by a resolution or resolutions likewise adopted by the board of directors. In case the number of such shares shall be decreased the number of shares so specified in the certificate shall resume the status which they had prior to the adoption of the first resolution or resolutions. When no shares of any such class or series are outstanding, either because none were issued or because no issued shares of any such class or series remain outstanding, a certificate setting forth a resolution or resolutions adopted by the board of directors that none of the authorized shares of such class or series are outstanding, and that none will be issued subject to the certificate of designations previously filed with respect to such class or series, may be executed, acknowledged and filed in accordance with §103 of this title and, when such certificate becomes effective, it shall have the effect of eliminating from the certificate of incorporation all matters set forth in the certificate of designations with respect to such class or series of stock. Unless otherwise provided in the certificate of incorporation, if no shares of stock have been issued of a class or series of stock established by a resolution of the board of directors, the voting powers, designations, preferences and relative, participating, optional or other rights, if any, or the qualifications, limitations or restrictions thereof, may be amended by a resolution or resolutions adopted by the board of directors. A certificate which (1) states that no shares of the class or series have been issued, (2) sets forth a copy of the resolution or resolutions and (3) if the designation of the class or series is being changed, indicates the original designation and the new designation, shall be executed, acknowledged and filed and shall become effective, in accordance with §103 of this title. When any certificate filed under this subsection becomes effective, it shall have the effect of amending the certificate of incorporation; except that neither the filing of such certificate nor the filing of a restated certificate of incorporation pursuant to §245 of this title shall prohibit the board of directors from subsequently adopting such resolutions as authorized by this subsection. (Last amended by Ch. 339, L. '98, eff. 7-1-98.)

Ch. 339, L. '98, eff. 7-1-98, added matter in italic and deleted [1]"The stock of any class or series may be made subject to redemption by the corporation at its option or at the option of the holders of such stock or upon the happening of a specified event; provided, however, that at the time of such redemption the corporation shall have outstanding shares of at least one class or series of stock with full voting powers which shall not be subject to redemption."

Ch. 339, L. '98 Synopsis of Section 151

The amendment to Section 151(b) clarifies that some, and not necessarily all, of the shares of a class or series of stock may be made subject to redemption. The amendment also eliminates the requirement that at the time of such redemption the corporation shall have outstanding shares of at least one class or series of stock with full voting powers which are not subject to redemption, and provides instead that it shall suffice if immediately following any such redemption the corporation has outstanding one or more shares of stock that together have full voting powers (whether or not such share or shares are redeemable).

Ch. 264, L. '94 Synopsis of Section 151(a)

The amendment to Section 151(a) is intended to make it clear that a "fact" can include an event or determination, including an event or determination within the control of the corporation or a person or body affiliated with the corporation, such as a decision by its board of directors or one of its officers or agents. This amendment is not intended to alter the fiduciary duties of a board of directors in authorizing the issuance of stock with rights

that turn on determinations or actions by any person or body, or in making any determination or taking any action constituting a fact under this section.

Ch. 376, L. '90 Commentary on Section 151(b)

Subject to two provisions already present in the statute, this subsection has been amended to permit the redemption of common, as well as preferred, stock so long as at least one class or series of stock with full voting powers is not redeemable. The two provisos are (i) with respect to regulated investment companies and (ii) corporations which hold government licenses or franchises or are members of national securities exchanges. The former proviso has been amended to provide that stock may be made redeemable at the option of the corporation as well as at the option of the holder, and to delete as surplusage limitations already imposed by Section 160. The latter proviso has been amended to provide for the possibility that the license, franchise or membership is held indirectly, rather than directly by the corporation.

.1 Value of stock.—Value of stock depends upon value of corporation's capital or assets; in case of par value stock it may be par or more or less than par. *Bodell v General Gas & Electric Corp, 132 A 442 (Ch Ct 1926).*

No par shares represent aliquot or proportionate parts of capital. *State v Benson, 128 A 107 (Ch Ct 1924).*

The value of shares that are to be repurchased under a mandatory buyback provision in a corporation's certificate of incorporation is to be based upon the consolidated, audited, annual financial statements of the corporation rather than a year end balance sheet prepared in conjunction with the corporation's annual tax return. *DiLoreto v Tiber Holding Corp, 804 A2d 1055 (2001).*

.2 Status of subscriber.—Subscriber to stock under employees' stock purchase plan is stockholder, not creditor, and is not entitled to file claim with receiver for amount he paid on his subscription. *Hegarty v American Commonwealth Power Corp, 174 A 273 (Ch Ct 1934).*

.3 Voting rights.—Corporation must have express authority in its charter before it can issue special kinds of stock restricting voting rights of certain shares. *Standard Scale & Supply Corp v Chappel, 141 A 191 (Ch Ct 1928).*

Voting trustee can enforce stockholders' agreement giving one class of stock right to elect majority of board, even though certificate of incorporation does not show those voting rights, when they are set out in bylaws. *In re Farm Industries, Inc, 196 A2d 582 (Ch Ct 1963).*

When voting power passes to preferred stockholder, he has right to challenge adjudication in bankruptcy made on petition of officers and directors elected at illegal meeting of stockholders. *In re Mississippi Valley Utilities Corp, 2 FSupp 995 (D Del 1933).*

Corporation equally owned by two groups of stockholders can create new class of non-participating voting stock, and issue one share to odd numbered new director able to break deadlock; arrangement (1) is not voting trust subject to ten-year limit, since stockholders retained their voting rights; (2) does not violate any public policy by issuance of voting stock with no proprietary rights; and (3) is not unlawful delegation of directors' duties, since it was approved by unanimous vote of stockholders and effected through charter amendment. *Lehrman v Cohen, 222 A2d 800 (1966).*

Amendment to articles of incorporation creating special class of stock equal in all respects to existing class of stock except that no person could be elected director if 40% of new stock was voted against him is not a voting right of stock, but was veto power, and not within law's intendment. *Aldridge v Franco Wyoming Oil Co, 14 A2d 380 (1940).*

Charter provision giving holders of common stock Series B right to elect minority directors means that majority in number of issued and outstanding Series B common stock must vote before Class B directors can be elected, but successful nominees need receive only majority in number of shares voted. *Investment Associates, Inc v Standard Power & Light Corp, 48 A2d 501 (Ch Ct 1946).*

Corporate charter provision for voting power based upon size of individual shareholder's holding rather than class differentiations was not invalid and corporation could gear its quorum definition to specified number of shares to be present rather than number of stockholders. *Providence and Worcester Co v Baker, 378 A2d 121 (1977).*

Preferred shareholders who were not paid dividends in 1975 and 1976, but were paid every year since 1978, are not entitled to vote at shareholders meetings of corporation, because certificate of preference gave preferred shareholders right to vote only when dividends were not paid for two consecutive years, but took right away when dividends were resumed for two consecutive years; two year gap in dividends ten years ago did not give shareholders permanent right to vote. *Flerlage v KDI Corp, No. 8007 (Ch Ct 4-10-86).*

Court enjoined implementation of recapitalization plan because shareholder vote approving issuance of supervoting common stock was fatally flawed when (1) principal shareholder/chief executive officer, for whose benefit stock had been fashioned, threatened to block transactions that may be in best interest of corporation, unless plan was approved and (2) proxy statement presents substantial risk of misleading shareholder on material point concerning principal shareholder's status as "restricted person." *Lacos Land Co v Arden Group, Inc, 517 A2d 271 (Ch Ct 1986).*

Court refused to enjoin corporation's implementation of stock reclassification plan which involved the distribution of a new issue of common stock. *Reasons:* Plaintiff failed to show that: (1) restructuring was done only for purpose of perpetuating majority shareholders' voting control; (2) board of directors breached fiduciary duty by failing to seriously consider alternatives; (3) restructuring could only be used to thwart an imminent take-over threat; and (4) irreparable harm would result if preliminary injunction were denied. *Hahn v Carter-Wallace, Inc, No. 9097 (Ch Ct 10-15-87).*

In an action brought by holders of a class of nonvoting preferred stock for a declaratory judgment that they were entitled to vote as a class on a proposed merger, the Court of Chancery held that the issue was determined by the wording of the corporation's certificate of incorporation, which should be narrowly construed. The certificate of incorporation provided that the holders of the preferred shares would be entitled to vote as a class if the corporation changed, by amendment to the certificate "or otherwise," the terms of the stock so as to adversely affect the rights and preferences of its holders. The court noted that mergers were not mentioned at all in the pertinent section of the certificate and that the certificate expressly conferred a class-vote right in the event of a merger upon the holders of a separate series of preferred stock (none of which was outstanding). The absence of any such provision in the certificate for the holders of the series of preferred stock held by the plaintiffs evidenced an intention of the drafters to not to confer such protection upon them. *Sullivan Money Management, Inc v FLS Holdings, Inc, No. 12731 (Ch Ct 11-20-92).*

A shareholder is not required to attend a shareholders meeting and record an objection in order to preserve its ability to challenge the propriety of a shareholder vote and challenge an adjournment of that vote as improper. *State of Wisconsin Investment Board v Peerless Systems Corp, C.A. No. 17637 (Ch Ct 12-4-00).*

.4 Capital stock and corporate solvency.—In determining corporation's solvency corporate liability to stockholders upon capital stock is not taken into consideration. *Central West Pub Service Co v Craig, 70 F2d 427 (8th Cir 1934).*

.5 Legality of issue.—Stockholder can maintain action for cancellation of another's stock for which corporation did not receive agreed consideration. *Bennett v Breuil Petroleum Corp, 99 A2d 236 (Ch Ct 1953); Ellis v Penn Beef Co, 80 A 666 (Ch Ct 1911).*

Action can be brought against majority stockholders who issue new shares mainly to freeze out minority, regardless whether price paid for stock is fair or not. *Bennett v Breuil Petroleum Corp, 99 A2d 236 (Ch Ct 1953).*

Stock issued solely for future services to be performed is without legal consideration. *In re Seminole Oil & Gas Corp, 150 A2d 20 (Ch Ct 1959),* appeal dismissed *159 A2d 276 (1959).*

No par stock issued under certificate of incorporation that failed to state number of shares issued is unauthorized and invalid. *Triplex Shoe Co v Rice & Hutchins, Inc, 152 A 242 (Ch Ct 1930).*

Void shares of stock have no voting rights. *Mau v Montana Pacific Oil Co, 141 A 828 (Ch Ct 1928).*

Lack of compliance with the technical requirements of Delaware corporate law in issuing new stock does not require a declaration that the stock is void and that no rights attach as a result of issuance of the stock. This lack of technical compliance also does not rob the court of power to grant plaintiffs what amounts to specific performance under §227. *Waggoner v STAAR Surgical Co, No. 11185 (Ch Ct 3-15-90).*

The Supreme Court of Delaware reversed lower court's award of common stock to plaintiff, defendant-company's former CEO and president. Based on trial court's findings, court held that preferred convertible shares originally issued to plaintiff were invalid and void under Delaware law, that legitimate common shares could not issue from invalid preferred shares and, consequently, lower court's grant to plaintiff of common stock as equitable relief for his personal guarantee Court in earlier case. *STAAR Surgical Co v Waggoner, 588 A2d 1130 (1991).*

The conversion of preferred shares, which had been invalidly issued, because of the failure of the corporation to adopt a certificate of incorporation provision or a resolution by the board of directors pursuant to an explicit grant of authority in the certificate of incorporation which fixed the powers, preferences, rights and other characteristics of a corporation's shares, as required pursuant to GCL §151, into common shares, according to the terms of the preferred shares, was a fortiori invalid. The board's failure to adopt a resolution and a certificate of designation which amended the fundamental document which imbued a corporation with its life and powers and defined the corporation's contract with its shareholders, could not be deemed a mere technical error. *Staar Surgical Co v Waggoner, 588 A2d 1130 (1991).*

.6 Description of preferences.—Mere designation of stock in charter as preferred is ineffectual without description of preferences. *Pennington v Com Hotel Const Co, 151 A 228 (Ch Ct 1930).*

Stock preferences will not be recognized when they are so obscurely expressed in certificate of incorporation as to be irreconcilably in conflict with each other. *Holland v National Automotive Fibres, Inc, 194 A 124 (Ch Ct 1937),* reaff'd, *2 A2d 124 (Ch Ct 1938).*

Unless certificate of incorporation provides for preferred stock, corporation cannot issue it, and so charter provisions relating to preferred stock cannot be altered or enlarged by bylaw enactment. *Gaskill v Gladys Belle Oil Co, 146 A 337 (Ch Ct 1929).*

Continued retention of preferred stock by finder created virtual veto power over those corporate matters that require consent of all classes, since it was only outstanding stock in its class, so stock was returnable, when stock acquisition agreement in connection with which stock was issued failed to close for lack of effective registration statement, and finder's fee was contemplated only upon successful stock acquisition. *Eckmar Corp v Malchin, 297 A2d 446 (Ch Ct 1972).*

Corporation's directors cannot pass resolution to issue preferred stock and to set up supermajority requirement for approving merger with "related person" (party owning 20% or more of stock) when holders of common stock are given right by applicable statutes to approve such transactions by simple majority vote. *Telvest, Inc v Olson,* No. 5798 (Ch Ct 3-8-79).

A corporation will be enjoined from issuing additional shares of its preferred stock or incurring additional debt where a protective provision in its certificate of incorporation prohibits the issuance of "any other equity security" without approval of a majority of the holders of the preferred stock, no such approval has been sought or obtained, and the corporation has violated other related protective provisions. *Telcom-SNI Investors, LLC v Sorrento Networks, Inc,* 2001 Del. Ch. LEXIS 114 (Ch Ct 2001).

.7 Rights and liabilities of preferred stockholders.—Holders of preferred stock are stockholders, not creditors. *In re Hawkeye Oil Co,* 19 F2d 151 (D Del 1927).

Holders of certificates of "contingent obligation" are treated as though they were stockholders instead of creditors of issuing corporation. *Moore v American Finance & Securities Co,* 73 A2d 47 (Ch Ct 1950).

Liquidation clause in charter providing only that preferred stockholders get the par value of their stock before common stockholders get anything is exhaustive, and so all assets remaining after paying preferred stockholders their stocks' par value must be paid to common stockholders. *Mohawk Carpet Mills, Inc v Delaware Rayon Co,* 110 A2d 305 (Ch Ct 1954).

Preferred stockholder cannot escape liability to creditors to pay par value of his stock on ground that corporation had no power to issue preferred stock and so issue is void and holder is immune from liability. *Cooney Co v Arlington Hotel Co,* 101 A 879 (Ch Ct 1917); *DuPont v Ball,* 106 A 39 (Ch Ct 1918).

Court refused to grant injunction against proposed class action settlement, which, in order to facilitate proposed merger, changed preferred shareholders' existing right to convert to common stock to right to convert to new adjusted rate preferred stock. Reasons: (1) arguments raised by preferred shareholders could be heard at future settlement hearings, (2) disputed right of preferred shareholders to vote on merger was subject to compromise, and (3) fairness of proposed settlement could only be addressed at settlement hearing. *Cohn v Crocker National Corp,* No. 7693 (Ch Ct 2-7-85).

Preferred shareholders' interest could be eliminated in tender offer-reverse cash-out merger at price less than liquidated value of preferred stock in corporate charter because (1) liquidation preference could only be paid in event of liquidation of assets, (2) merger was not a liquidation, (3) minority interest along with its preferential rights, can be eliminated by merger, and (4) payment was fair to preferred shareholders. *Rothschild International Corp v Liggett Group Inc,* 474 A2d 133 (1984).

Minority holder of preferred stock could not enjoin proposed merger as being unfair to preferred shareholders when they were offered less for their stock than offer to common shareholders because (1) preferred shares had no legal right to equivalent consideration in merger, (2) apportionment of consideration between preferred and common shareholders was fair, (3) majority shareholder did not have duty to include preferred shareholders in increased price he paid common shareholders out of his own funds, and (4) preferred shareholders were not injured by majority shareholder's timing of merger. *Jedwab v MGM Grand Hotels, Inc,* 509 A2d 584 (Ch Ct 1986).

Court enjoined voting of "supervoting" preferred stock issued to chairman/chief executive and allied investors, which gave them 44% of voting power, because, while raising capital may have been purpose for directors issuing stock, their primary purpose was to obstruct ability of shareholders to wage meaningful proxy contest in order to maintain their control when (1) "super-majority" voting provisions had never been used to help solve corporation's chronic cash problems and had only been considered as takeover defense, (2) provisions were only adopted after directors perceived proxy challenge, and (3) there were alternatives for financing. Challenging shareholders would be irreparably harmed if management were allowed to vote "super-majority" preferred stock because, at very least, vote would substantially influence directors' election and have chilling effect on shareholders' proxy solicitation. *Packer v Yampol,* No. 8432 (Ch Ct 4-18-86).

Court enjoined target's directors' attempt to employ anti-takeover measure of distribution of dividend of preferred stock. Each share of preferred stock entitled holder to cast 25 votes on all issues on which common stock could vote, but if transferred holders could only exercise five of those votes, which would make it impossible for tender offeror to acquire target. Change in corporate structure of this magnitude, reducing transferability of shareholders ability to vote and value of their assets, requires shareholder approval, which had not been obtained. *Unilever Acquisition Corp v Richardson-Vicks, Inc,* 618 FSupp 407 (SDNY 1985).

Corporations were not entitled to participate fund set up by settlement agreement to repay preferred shareholders for property confiscated by People's Republic of China because, although corporations had possession of preferred stock certificates delivered to them by their customers as security deposits, (1) they were not bona fide purchasers of stock, (2) their names do not appear as record owners of stock and they had no other proof of title, and (3) they did not have security interest in stock when debtor-creditor relation no longer existed with customers. *S A Judah v Shanghai Power Co,* 494 A2d 1244 (1985).

Acquiror did not breach stock purchase agreement when it merged with corporation at price below that which would have applied if merger had fallen within terms of agreement. Merger did not fall within terms of agreement because acquiror, at time of merger, had less than 40% of corporation's outstanding stock. Although acquiror did hold enough preferred stock and stock options to bring it above 40% threshold, acquiror was not owner of outstanding common stock until conversion of preferred or exercise of options. Preferred stock was not outstanding because it could not be voted. *Nerken v Standard Oil Co (Indiana),* 810 F2d 1230 (DC Cir 1987).

Preferred stockholders had no standing to sue even though they were not permitted to vote on a transaction in which the controlling stockholders sold a large portion of a corporation's assets and distributed the dividends to common stockholders. A corporation can limit the rights of certain classes of shares and the corporation's certificate of incorporation in this case expressly excluded preferred stockholders from the right to vote in any meeting. *Winston v Mandor, Nos. 14807, 15416 (Ch Ct 5-12-97).*

.8 Changing preferred stock by charter amendment.—Under prior law, corporation could not, by amending its certificate of incorporation, take away right to payment of past dividend preferences which had accrued. *Keller v Wilson & Co, 190 A 115 (1936).*

Now, corporation can eliminate accrued dividends by amending its charter, or through merger. See §242 and §251.

.9 Preferred stock, conversion as redemption.—Conversion of corporation's preferred stock to cash for $40 per share pursuant to merger agreement did not constitute redemption, thereby entitling each preferred shareholder to $100 per share under provision in corporation's certificate of incorporation. Under Delaware law, conversion of shares to cash in order to accomplish merger is legally distinct from redemption of shares by corporation. Action taken under one section of Delaware corporation law is legally independent and not to be tested by requirements of unrelated section. Thus, conversion of preferred stock to cash was protected by doctrine of independent legal significance. *Rauch v RCA Corp, 861 F2d 29 (2d Cir 1988).*

.10 Conversion of stock to trigger antidilution rights.—A corporation's offer to convert preferred shareholders into common stock did not trigger their antidilution rights resulting from a certificate of designation (COD) where, under the COD, conversions did not trigger the antidilution rights. The court rejected the preferred shareholders' argument that the transaction was more akin to a share exchange, which did trigger the antidilution rights. *Bernstein v Canet, No. 3924 (Ch Ct 6-11-96).*

.11 Stock repurchase.—A charter provision prohibiting a corporation from repurchasing its stock does not apply to the repurchases of the corporation's stock that are made by the corporation's subsidiaries. *In re Sunstates Corporation Shareholder Litigation, 2001 Del Ch LEXIS 63 (Ch. Ct. 2001).*

152 ISSUANCE OF STOCK; LAWFUL CONSIDERATION; FULLY PAID STOCK.—[1]*The consideration, as determined pursuant to subsections (a) and (b) of §153 of this title, for subscriptions to, or the purchase of, the capital stock to be issued by a corporation shall be paid in such form and in such manner as the board of directors shall determine. The board of directors may authorize capital stock to be issued for consideration consisting of cash, any tangible or intangible property or any benefit to the corporation, or any combination thereof. In the absence of actual fraud in the transaction, the judgment of the directors as to the value of such consideration shall be conclusive. The capital stock so issued shall be deemed to be fully paid and nonassessable stock upon receipt by the corporation of such consideration; provided, however, nothing contained herein shall prevent the board of directors from issuing partly paid shares under §156 of this title.* (Last amended by Ch. 326, L. '04, eff. 8-1-04.)

───

Ch. 326, L. '04, eff. 8-1-04, added matter in italic and deleted [1]"The consideration, as determined pursuant to subsections (a) and (b) of §153 of this title, for subscriptions to, or the purchase of, the capital stock to be issued by a corporation shall be paid in such form and in such manner as the board of directors shall determine. In the absence of actual fraud in the transaction, the judgment of the directors as to the value of such consideration shall be conclusive. The capital stock so issued shall be deemed to be fully paid and nonassessable stock; if: (1) The entire amount of such consideration has been received by the corporation in the form of cash, services rendered, personal property, real property, leases of real property, or a combination thereof; or (2) not less than the amount of the consideration determined to be capital pursuant to §154 of this title has been received by the corporation in such form and the corporation has received a binding obligation of the subscriber or purchaser to pay the balance of the subscription or purchase price; provided, however, nothing contained herein shall prevent the board of directors from issuing partly paid shares under §156 of this title."

Ch. 326, L. '04, Synopsis of Section 152

The amendment to Section 152 eliminates the requirement that the consideration paid for newly issued stock consist, either entirely or in part, of consideration in the form required by Section 263 of Article IX of the Constitution of the State of Delaware of 1897, as amended. That provision is being deleted from the Constitution of the State of Delaware of 1897, as amended, contemporaneously with the effective date of the amendment to Section 152.

Comment: This new §152 is completely rewritten, implementing the constitutional requirement regarding the quality of the consideration to be received for the valid issuance of fully paid and nonassessable stock. It expressly provides that the constitutional quality of consideration (*i.e.,* cash, services rendered, property) must be paid only to the extent of the par value or stated value of the fully paid stock, provided there is a binding obligation (such as a promissory note) for the balance.

The amendment makes explicit the fact that stock will be deemed to be fully paid and nonassessable if (1) the par value or stated value allocated to capital is paid in full by consideration of the quality required by the Constitution; (2) the balance or "surplus" consideration is supported by a binding obligation (*e.g.,* a promissory note) of the purchaser; and (3) the board of directors has not determined that the stock is to be issued as partly paid shares pursuant to Section 156.

The constitutional requirement is satisfied by this amendment since that provision was designed to be a "protection" for creditors by requiring that the *capital* need not be more than par value or stated value and would not be more than that allocated under §154; the "excess" would be surplus and need not be of constitutional quality unless the directors so require. See, *Lofland v Cahall,* 13 Del. Ch. 384, 118 A. 1 (1922); *Sohland v Baker,* 15 Del. Ch. 431, 141 A. 277 (1927); *Highlights for Children, Inc. v Crown,* 227 A2d 118 (Del. Ch. 1966). Even though the stock is not subject to call, the binding obligation is, in all events, enforceable by the corporation against the purchaser whether or not the purchaser has received (and perhaps sold) fully paid and nonassessable shares. Thus, §156 would not apply because the shares are fully paid and §§162 and 163 would not apply because the whole consideration (*e.g.,* the cash for "the capital" and the note for "the surplus") has been paid in.

.1 **Attorney's compensation.**—Stockholder's attorneys were entitled to reasonable compensation for their services in derivative action to prevent acquisition of another company's assets, even though transaction was later abandoned after filing of suit but before court action, since stockholder had cited fraud with reasonable hope of success. *Iroquois Industries Inc v Lewis, 318 A2d 134 (1974).*

Although a board of directors has legal authority to issue stock, the board may ultimately be blocked from such an issuance by a later determination that the stock issuance was in violation of the board's duty of loyalty. *Sipca Holding SA v Optical Coating Laboratory, Inc, No. 15129 (Ch Ct 1-6-97).*

.2 **Share ownership.**—Documentary evidence of the ownership of a corporation will be given greater weight than testimony where the documentary evidence is less contradictory and more coherent than the testimony. *Fonds de Regulation et de Controle Cafe Cacao v Lion Capital Management, LLC, 2007 Del. Ch. LEXIS 12 (Ch Ct 2007).*

153 CONSIDERATION FOR STOCK.—(a) Shares of stock with par value may be issued for such consideration, having a value not less than the par value thereof, as determined from time to time by the board of directors, or by the stockholders if the certificate of incorporation so provides.

(b) Shares of stock without par value may be issued for such consideration as is determined from time to time by the board of directors, or by the stockholders if the certificate of incorporation so provides.

(c) Treasury shares may be disposed of by the corporation for such consideration as may be determined from time to time by the board of directors, or by the stockholders if the certificate of incorporation so provides.

(d) If the certificate of incorporation reserves to the stockholders the right to determine the consideration for the issue of any shares, the stockholders shall, unless the certificate requires a greater vote, do so by a vote of a majority of the outstanding stock entitled to vote thereon. (Last amended by Ch. 148, L. '69, eff. 7-15-69.)

.1 **Subscription contract.**—Subscriber cannot compel corporation to issue to him shares of its authorized nonpar stock as contracted for, when he failed to advance working capital called for under subscription contract. *Riegel v The Only Package Pie, Inc, 128 A 110 (Ch Ct 1925).*

Subscriber to stock under employee stock purchase plan is stockholder, not creditor, and cannot make claim with receiver for amount paid on subscription. *Hegarty v American Commonwealth Power Corp, 174 A 273 (Ch Ct 1934).*

.2 **Consideration for stock.**—No par stock, as well as par stock, cannot be issued except for money paid, labor done, or personal property, real estate, or leases actually acquired by corporation. *Bodell v General Gas & Electric Corp, 132 A 442 (Ch Ct 1926).*

Fact that corporation may be required to expend money in future to protect its interests in property rights acquired, and for which it has issued stock, does not necessarily render consideration invalid. *West v Sirian Lamp Co, 37 A2d 835 (Ch Ct 1944).*

When stock is issued without legal consideration, but equities favor stockholder, court will grant him election to retain stock on payment of fair price. *Maclary v Pleasant Hills, Inc, 109 A2d 830 (Ch Ct 1954).*

Stockholder has burden of showing constructive fraud when he brings action to cancel increase in number of shares under alleged fraudulent plan for inadequate consideration. *Bennett v Breuil Petroleum Corp, 99 A2d 236 (Ch Ct 1953).*

Stock that promoters get is for inadequate consideration when (1) it is issued in return for patent license which promoters had acquired for no consideration, (2) and value of which lay in its successful exploitation which promoters were not equipped to do, and (3) initial capital was not raised by promoters. *Pipelife Corp v Bedford, 145 A2d 206 (Ch Ct 1958).*

Court rejected plaintiff's claim that no reasonable director could have voted for the grant of options where the consideration for the options was past services. Consideration for stock options is often the reasonable prospect of obtaining the employee's valued future services. But that is not the only permissible form of consideration for a grant of stock options. Under certain limited circumstances, stock options may also be issued as a form of compensation for an employee's past services. *Zupnick v Goizueta, No. 14874 (Ch Ct 1-21-97).*

In pressing its rights to receive consideration for its stock in a merger, a holder of preferred stock that fully negotiates a term sheet with the acquiring corporation must rely on the term sheet and not the rights it had as a preferred holder prior to executing the term sheet. *RGC International Investors LDC v Greka Energy Corp, C.A. No. 17674 (Ch Ct 11-6-00).*

.3 Valuation of consideration.—In absence of fraud, directors' valuation of labor done or property received for stock issue is conclusive. *Butler v New Keystone Copper Co, 93 A 380 (Ch Ct 1915).*

Prospective profits or future services do not constitute lawful consideration for stock. *Scully v Automobile Finance Co, 101 A 908, 109 A 49 (Ch Ct 1917).*

Directors cannot delegate, except in such manner as may be explicitly provided by statute, duty to determine value of property acquired as consideration for issuance of stock. *Field v Carlisle Corp, 68 A2d 817 (Ch Ct 1949).*

Directors cannot evaluate their own services as consideration for issuance of stock. *Maclary v Pleasant Hills, Inc, 109 A2d 830 (Ch Ct 1954).*

Par value stock issued for cash must be for full amount of par, and cannot be for promise to pay something less. *Bowen v Imperial Theatres, Inc, 115 A 918 (Ch Ct 1922).*

Treasury stock may be sold for less than par. *Belle Isle Corp v MacBean, 61 A2d 699 (Ch Ct 1948).*

Release of valid unliquidated claim against corporation is adequate consideration for stock issuance, and directors' judgment as to proper settlement amount is conclusive. *Blish v Thompson Automatic Arms Corp, 64 A2d 581 (1948); see also, Manacher v Reynolds, 165 A2d 741 (Ch Ct 1960).*

Sales of same stock issue at different prices to different people are lawful if not arbitrary, but based on business and commercial facts which, in exercise of fair business judgment, lead directors to adopt such course. *Atlantic Refining Co v Hodgman, 13 F2d 781 (3d Cir 1926),* rev'g, *Hodgman v Atlantic Refining Co, 300 F 590,* cert denied, *273 US 731 (1926).*

Corporation could not block sale of shareholders' stock because any oral agreement that shareholders may have made was invalid if shares are to be deemed validly issued since future services are not legal consideration for issuance of stock. *Catherines v Copytele, Inc, 602 FSupp 1019 (ED NY 1985).*

.4 Stock issued for notes.—Promissory note is not sufficient consideration for issuance of fully paid nonassessable stock. *Lofland v Cahall, 118 A 1 (Ch Ct 1922); Phillips v Slocomb, 167 A 698 (1933).*

Negotiable promissory note secured by proper collateral may be legal consideration for stock issue, but note secured by shares of corporation making note is not valid consideration when those shares are in fact valueless. *Sohland v Baker, 141 A 277 (Ch Ct 1927).*

Corporation cannot get summary judgment to cancel shares issued, with directors' and stockholders' approval, in consideration of ten-year promissory notes together with promise by recipient of shares that he will become corporation's employee, when he may show (1) he did become corporation's salaried employee, (2) he paid some of his notes in full and paid interest on others, (3) initial shares issued to him were treasury shares, that are not subject to same strict consideration restrictions as original shares, and (4) these treasury shares were deposited by him as collateral for issuance of original shares. *Highlights for Children, Inc v Crown, 227 A2d 118 (Ch Ct 1966).*

.5 Stock issued for organization services.—Pre-incorporation services (promotional or underwriting) are good consideration for stock issuance. *Blish v Thompson Automatic Arms Corp, 64 A2d 581 (1948).*

Services in selling shares is consideration for stock issuance, but directors selling par value stock have duty to authorize its issuance only for property equaling its full par value. *Bodell v General Gas & Electric Corp, 132 A 442 (Ch Ct 1926).* Also, payment of reasonable commissions to selling agents for marketing stock is lawful, provided it is not mere guise to conceal evasion of rule, even for purchases by agent himself as well as sales to others. *Yasik v Wachtel, 17 A2d 309 (Ch Ct 1941); see also, Diamond State Brewery, Inc v De La Rigaudiere, 17 A2d 313 (Ch Ct 1941).*

Issuance of stock by directors to themselves for services in organizing corporation and selling stock is unlawful unless authorized by charter, bylaws or stockholders. *Lofland v Cahall, 118 A 1 (1922); see also, Birbeck v American Toll Bridge Co, 2 A2d 158 (Ch Ct 1938).*

.6 Stock issued for property.—Unconditional license to use patent right is property for which, ordinarily, corporate stock can be issued. *West v Sirian Lamp Co, 37 A2d 835 (Ch Ct 1944).*

Corporation can issue its capital stock in exchange for proerty less in value than par, but agreement that such stock, so issued, shall be fully paid and nonassessable, is void against company and its creditors. *Peters v U.S. Mortgage Co, 114 A 598 (Ch Ct 1921).*

.7 Illegally issued stock.—Preferred stockholders have right to question legality of issuance of common stock. *Scully v Automobile Finance Co, 101 A 908 (Ch Ct 1917), 109 A 49 (Ch Ct 1920).*

Stockholder, or his personal representative, who has knowledge of and acquiesces in illegal issue of stock by corporation cannot maintain suit to declare issue void. *Topkis v Delaware Hardware Co, 2 A2d 114 (Ch Ct 1938).*

In suit to cancel illegally issued stock, court of equity has power to compel stockholder who has disposed illegally issued shares to surrender legally issued shares presently owned by him. *Belle Isle Corp v MacBean, 49 A2d 5 (Ch Ct 1946).*

When undisputed facts show stock was illegally issued, court will issue preliminary injunction to prevent exercise of prerogatives which otherwise attach to stock ownership. *Belle Isle Corp v MacBean, 49 A2d 5 (Ch Ct 1946).*

.8 Issuance.—When stock is issued without regard for corporate formalities, one who participates in or approves its issuance will be estopped from challenging defects in issuance. Stock is deemed issued when it actually or constructively comes into possession of owner by delivery to stockholder or some person acting as his agent. Resulting trust may be imposed on shares where circumstances indicate that party holding legal title was not intended to have beneficial interest in shares. *Danvir Corp v Wahl, No. 8386 (Ch Ct 9-8-87).*

.9 Share ownership.—Documentary evidence of the ownership of a corporation will be given greater weight than testimony where the documentary evidence is less contradictory and more coherent than the testimony. *Fonds de Regulation et de Controle Cafe Cacao v Lion Capital Management, LLC, 2007 Del. Ch. LEXIS 12 (Ch Ct 2007).*

.10 Stock cancellation and reissuance.—Where an attempt is made to cancel the common stock of a corporation without an amendment to the certificate of incorporation, such cancellation is invalid. Also, where an attempt is made to reissue the stock without consideration or benefit to the corporation, such issuance is also invalid. *MBKS Co Ltd v MBKS Inc, 2007 Del. Ch. LEXIS 52 (Ch Ct 2007).*

154 DETERMINATION OF AMOUNT OF CAPITAL; CAPITAL, SURPLUS AND NET ASSETS DEFINED.—Any corporation may, by resolution of its board of directors, determine that only a part of the consideration which shall be received by the corporation for any of the shares of its capital stock which it shall issue from time to time shall be capital; but, in case any of the shares issued shall be shares having a par value, the amount of the part of such consideration so determined to be capital shall be in excess of the aggregate par value of the shares issued for such consideration having a par value, unless all the shares issued shall be shares having a par value, in which case the amount of the part of such consideration so determined to be capital need be only equal to the aggregate par value of such shares. In each such case the board of directors shall specify in dollars the part of such consideration which shall be capital. If the board of directors shall not have determined (1) at the time of issue of any shares of the capital stock of the corporation issued for cash or (2) within 60 days after the issue of any shares of the capital stock of the corporation issued for consideration other than cash what part of the consideration for such shares shall be capital, the capital of the corporation in respect of such shares shall be an amount equal to the aggregate par value of such shares having a par value, plus the amount of the consideration for such shares without par value. The amount of the consideration so determined to be capital in respect of any shares without par value shall be the stated capital of such shares. The capital of the corporation may be increased from time to time by resolution of the board of directors directing that a portion of the net assets of the corporation in excess of the amount so determined to be capital be transferred to the capital account. The board of directors may direct that the portion of such net assets so transferred shall be treated as capital in respect of any shares of the corporation of any designated class or classes. The excess, if any, at any given time, of the net assets of the corporation over the amount so determined to be capital shall be surplus. Net assets means the amount by which total assets exceed total liabilities. Capital and surplus are not liabilities for this purpose. *Notwithstanding anything in this section to the contrary, for purposes of this section and §§160 and 170 of this title, the capital of any nonstock corporation shall be deemed to be zero.* (Last amended by Ch. 253, L. '10, eff. 8-1-10.)

Ch. 253, L. '10, eff. 8-1-10, added matter in italic.

Ch. 253, L. '10 Synopsis of Section 154

Section 15 amends §154 of the DGCL to make clear, for purposes of §154, §160, and §170, that capital in a nonstock corporation is zero.

Ch. 326, L. '04 Synopsis of Section 154

The amendment to Section 154 is consistent with the amendment to Section 152 and clarifies that the consideration paid for stock need not consist of property or cash.

Comment: This amendment to §154 simply gives the designation of stated capital to that amount of consideration determined by the board to be capital with respect to no par stock. The term "stated capital" is then used elsewhere in the General Corporation Law.

155 FRACTIONS OF SHARES.—A corporation may, but shall not be required to, issue fractions of a share. If it does not issue fractions of a share, it shall (1) arrange for the disposition of fractional interests by those entitled thereto, (2) pay in cash the fair value of fractions of a share as of the time when those entitled to receive such fractions are determined or (3) issue scrip or warrants in registered form (either represented by a certificate or uncertificated) or in bearer form (represented by a certificate) which shall entitle the holder to receive a full share upon the surrender of such scrip or warrants aggregating a full share. A certificate for a fractional share or an uncertificated fractional share shall, but scrip or warrants shall not unless otherwise provided therein, entitle the holder to exercise voting rights, to receive dividends thereon and to participate in any of the assets of the corporation in the event of liquidation. The board of directors may cause scrip or warrants to be issued subject to the conditions that they shall become void if not exchanged for certificates representing the full shares of uncertificated full shares before a specified date, or subject to the conditions that the shares for which scrip or warrants are exchangeable may be sold by the corporation and the proceeds thereof distributed to the holders of scrip or warrants, or subject to any other conditions which the board of directors may impose. (Last amended by Ch. 112, L. '83, eff. 7-1-83.)

.1 **Stock split.**—In a reverse/forward stock split designed to eliminate fractional shares of those holding less than a minimum number of shares, cashing out the holders of a small number of shares at fair market value is tantamount to providing those holders with fair value and is permitted by GCL §155. *Applebaum v Avaya, Inc, 805 A2d 209 (Ch Ct),* aff'd, *812 A2d 880 (2002).*

The Delaware Supreme Court has ruled that a corporation may validly initiate a reverse stock split and selectively dispose of the fractional interests held by stockholders who no longer own whole shares as part of a reverse/forward stock split, thus treating its shareholders unequally by cashing out the stockholders who own only fractional interests while opting not to dispose of fractional interests of stockholders who will end up holding whole shares of stock as well as fractional interests. *Applebaum v Avaya, Inc, 812 A2d 880 (2002).*

.2 **Business judgment rule.**—Shareholders challenging a reverse stock split overcome the presumptions of the business judgment rule where they adequately plead that a majority of the board is not independent, the board approved the reverse split and valued the shareholder's stock without adequate consideration, and the board did not act in good faith. *iXCore, S.A.S. v Triton Imaging, Inc, 2005 Del. Ch. LEXIS 102 (Ch Ct 2005).*

156 PARTLY PAID SHARES.—Any corporation may issue the whole or any part of its shares as partly paid and subject to call for the remainder of the consideration to be paid therefor. Upon the face or back of each stock certificate issued to represent any such partly paid shares, or upon the books and records of the corporation in the case of uncertificated partly paid shares, the total amount of the consideration to be paid therefor and the amount paid thereon shall be stated. Upon the declaration of any dividend on fully paid shares, the corporation shall declare a dividend upon partly paid shares of the same class, but only upon the basis of the percentage of the consideration actually paid thereon. (Last amended by Ch. 112, L. '83, eff. 7-1-83.)

157 RIGHTS AND OPTIONS RESPECTING STOCK.—(a) Subject to any provisions in the certificate of incorporation, every corporation may create and issue, whether or not in connection with the issue and sale of any shares of stock or other securities of the corporation, rights or options entitling the holders thereof to [1]*acquire* from the corporation any shares of its capital stock of any class or classes, such rights or options to be evidenced by or in such instrument or instruments as shall be approved by the board of directors.

(b) [2]*The terms upon which, including the time or times which may be limited or unlimited in duration, at or within which, and the consideration (including a formula by which such consideration may be determined) for which any such shares may be acquired from the corporation upon the exercise of any such right or option, shall be such as shall be stated in the certificate of incorporation, or in a resolution adopted by the board of directors providing for the creation and issue of such rights or options, and, in every case, shall be set forth or incorporated by reference in the instrument or instruments evidencing such rights or options.* In the absence of actual fraud in the transaction, the judgment of the directors as to the consideration for the issuance of such rights or options and the sufficiency thereof shall be conclusive.

(c) The board of directors may, by a resolution adopted by the board, authorize 1 or more officers of the corporation to do 1 or both of the following: (i) designate officers and employees of the corporation or of any of its subsidiaries to be recipients of such rights or options created by the corporation, and (ii) determine the number of such rights or options to be received by such officers and employees; provided, however, that the resolution so authorizing such officer or officers shall specify the total number of rights or options such officer or officers may so award. The board of directors may not authorize an officer to designate himself or herself as a recipient of any such rights or options.

(d) [3]*In case the shares of stock of the corporation to be issued upon the exercise of such rights or options shall be shares having a par value, the consideration so to be received therefor shall have a value not less than the par value thereof.* In case the shares of stock so to be issued shall be shares of stock without par value, the consideration therefor shall be determined in the manner provided in §153 of this title. (Last amended by Ch. 326, L. '04, eff. 8-1-04.)

Ch. 326, L. '04, eff. 8-1-04, added matter in italic and deleted [1]"purchase"; [2]"The terms upon which, including the time or times which may be limited or unlimited in duration, at or within which, and the price or prices (including a formula by which such price or prices may be determined) at which any such shares may be purchased from the corporation upon the exercise of any such right or option, shall be such as shall be stated in the certificate of incorporation, or in a resolution adopted by the board of directors providing for the creation and issue of such rights or options, and, in every case, shall be set forth or incorporated by reference in the instrument or instruments evidencing such rights or options."; and [3]"In case the shares of stock of the corporation to be issued upon the exercise of such rights or options shall be shares having a par value, the price or prices so to be received therefor shall not be less than the par value thereof."

Ch. 326, L. '04 Synopsis of Section 157

The amendments to Section 157 are consistent with the amendment to Section 152 and clarify that the consideration to be paid for stock issued upon the exercise of rights or options need not consist of property or cash.

Ch. 82, L. '01 Synopsis of Section 157

The amendments to Section 157 provide that the board of directors may authorize one or more officers to designate officers and employees of the corporation or of any of its subsidiaries to be issued rights or options of the corporation and to determine the number of rights or options to be issued to those officers and employees. The terms of the rights or options, including the exercise price (which may include a formula by which such price may be determined), must be established by the board of directors. The board of directors must specify the total number of rights or options that may be awarded by an officer, and an officer may not designate himself or herself as a recipient of a right or option.

.1 Stock options.—Stock options are internal corporate matter and governed by law of state of incorporation. *Beard v Elster, 160 A2d 731 (1960),* reversing *Elster v American Airlines, Inc, 128 A2d 801 (Ch Ct 1957);* on remand, *Elster v American Airlines, Inc, 167 A2d 231 (Ch Ct 1961).*

Stock options granted directors are valid when (1) they are exercisable only after five years' service with corporation, (2) option price is double market price, (3) stockholders have ratified them, and (4) they served as incentive to retain directors who successfully negotiated acquisition of several other companies to offset corporation's considerable tax loss. *Olson Brothers, Inc v Englehart, 245 A2d 166 (1968).*

Stockholder-ratified stock option plan proposed by disinterested board of directors is valid if directors believe it will benefit corporation by enabling it to retain services of valued employees, and if options cannot be exercised unless optionees are still employed by corporation. *Elster v American Airlines, Inc, 167 A2d 231 (Ch Ct 1961).*

Requirement of optionee's continued employment is legal consideration for restricted stock option plan, and burden is on one who is attacking plan's validity to show that this consideration in fact does not exist in plan. *Gottlieb v Hayden Chemical Corp, 99 A2d 507 (Ch Ct 1953).* But when the burden is met, and it is shown that plan does not require continued employment on optionee's part, since he could exercise his option immediately after it was issued and then resign, court will void the options. *Kerbs v California Eastern Airways, Inc, 90 A2d 652 (1952),* reargument denied, *91 A2d 62 (1952).*

Stock option may be granted for unlimited time, and if corporation, by voluntarily dissolving, renders itself powerless to honor option, optionee can recover on liquidation amount he would have received were he owner of the shares (less option price); but lapse of long time and great increase in stock's value may make enforcement of option inequitable, and corporation has burden to prove this inequity. *Gamble v Penn Valley Crude Oil Corp, 104 A2d 257 (Ch Ct 1954).*

When only possible consideration to corporation at time of granting options to its executives was a return to be derived by corporation from increased job satisfaction, such option is invalid for lack of consideration. *Frankel v Donovan, 120 A2d 311 (Ch Ct 1956).*

Provision that employee must remain with corporation for two years before he can exercise consecutive stock options means two years from time of the new stock option without "tacking on" time still remaining on previous options. *Stemerman v Ackerman, 184 A2d 28 (Ch Ct 1962).*

Directors cannot interpret stock option agreement to defeat employee's vested right even though plan says directors' interpretation is to be final; employee's executor can exercise any part of option employee has not exercised at his death. *Ellis v Elmhart Mfg Co, 191 A2d 546 (Conn 1963).*

Court will cancel stock options and shares issued under them, if optionees conspired with management to vote those shares for management. *Schwartz v Miner, 146 A2d 801 (Ch Ct 1958).*

Corporation can buy back shares optioned to discharged employee, when he signed stock option agreement allowing it to do so if his employment terminated in five years; that is so, even though employee claims he accepted position because of stock option opportunities mentioned in job description that did not disclose such options were subject to company's buyback provisions; job description is merely invitation to make offer or to negotiate terms of employment. *Keene Corp v Hoofe, 267 A2d 618 (Ch Ct 1970).*

Alleged option granted to consultants to acquire corporate stock was unenforceable when it was not shown corporation's board either considered or approved plan. *Scarpinato v National Patent Development Corp, 347 NYS2d 623 (1973).*

Stock options for employees of corporation's subsidiary ended when corporation sold that subsidiary; optionees then no longer came within express condition that they be employees for one year prior to exercise of options. *Liebler v Morton-Norwich Products Inc, 77 Civ 4956 (SDNY 9-30-78).*

Directors adopted Rights Plan as preventive measure to ward off future advances by corporate raiders. Adoption of Plan was appropriate exercise of directors' business judgment when (1) action was not taken for entrenchment purposes, and (2) Plan was reasonable reaction by directors to perceived threat to corporation of coercive acquisition techniques. *Moran v Household International, Inc, 500 A2d 1346 (1985).*

Acquiror was not owner of outstanding common stock until conversion of preferred or exercise of options. *Nerken v Standard Oil Co (Indiana), 810 F2d 1230 (DC Cir 1987).*

Board of directors breached its fiduciary duties by wasting corporate assets and interfering with plaintiffs' voting rights where it caused the corporation to issue stock options for board members at below market prices. *Byrne v Lord, Nos. 14040, 14215 (Ch Ct 11-9-95).*

Where the terms of an option to purchase stock in a corporation, allegedly granted by a corporation's board of directors for the benefit of a director's wife, were not stated separately in either the certificate of incorporation or in a resolution adopted by the board of directors, the option was void and unenforceable. *Niehenke v Right O Way Transportation, Inc, Nos. 14392, 14444 (Ch Ct 12-28-95).*

Court rejected plaintiff's claim that no reasonable director could have voted for the grant of options where the consideration for the options was past services. Consideration for stock options is often the reasonable prospect of obtaining the employee's valued future services. But that is not the only permissible from of consideration for a grant of stock options. Under certain limited circumstances, stock options may also be issued as a form of compensation for an employee's past services. *Zupnick v Goizueta, No. 14874 (Ch Ct 1-21-97).*

Plaintiff, who sought a declaratory judgment that the board breached its fiduciary duties in adopting a shareholder rights plan, demonstrated that the board's action caused present injury to plaintiff and presented evidence of strong likelihood of future harm, where the adoption of the rights plan depressed the value of plaintiff's current holdings in the corporation. *KLM Royal Dutch Airlines v Checchi, No. 14764 (Ch Ct 1-14-97).*

.2 Warrants.—Corporation is liable to holders of stock warrants that required notice of dissolution, and so corporation's failure to give such notice entitles holders to amount they would have received upon distribution had they exercised their warrants. *Tisch Family Foundations Inc, v Texas National Petroleum Co, 326 FSupp 1128 (D Del 1971).* On issue of damages for interest, see *336 FSupp 44.*

Undeliverable warrants are held in trust for unlocated stockholders; trustees cannot exercise warrants before expiration date and must deposit property or proceeds resulting therefrom into court to await claims of missing stockholders. *Pathe Industries Inc v Cadence Industries Corp, 425 A2d 952 (1981).*

.3 Injunction against issuance.—Court refused to enjoin issuance of stock pursuant to options granted to six of the seven directors of corporation because there was no showing of irreparable harm if injunction is not granted when (1) there was no showing that directors would not be able to satisfy money judgment, (2) there is no claim that additional stock will impact on voting control of corporation, (3) directors might not exercise their options and sell stock immediately when that might entail liability for short-swing profits under §16(b) of Securities Exchange Act of 1934, and (4) relief sought would not prevent any harm resulting from uninformed shareholders' vote to approve options. *Klein v Panic, No. 8721 (Ch Ct 11-20-86).*

.4 Injunction against exercise.—Court refused to enjoin exercise of stock options granted to two officers by target of leveraged buyout proposal because directors of target did not have to disclose, in connection with shareholders' meeting, that they adopted plan to sell corporation when (1) stock options were originally granted year before shareholders' meeting and (2) first manifestation of any real interest in target's acquisition came only day before meeting. *Kramer v Western Pacific Industries, Inc, No. 8675 (Ch Ct 11-7-86).*

158 STOCK CERTIFICATES; UNCERTIFICATED SHARES.—The shares of a corporation shall be represented by certificates, provided that the board of directors of the corporation may provide by resolution or resolutions that some or all of any or all classes or series of its stock shall be uncertificated shares. Any such resolution shall not apply to shares represented by a certificate until such certificate is surrendered to the corporation. [1]*Every* *holder of stock represented by certificates shall be entitled to have a certificate signed by, or in the name of the corporation by the chairperson or vice-chairperson of the board of directors, or the president or vice-president, and by the treasurer or an assistant treasurer, or the secretary or an assistant secretary of such corporation representing the number of shares registered in certificate form.* Any or all the signatures on the certificate may be a facsimile. In case any officer, transfer agent or registrar who has signed or whose facsimile signature has been placed upon a certificate shall have ceased to be such officer, transfer agent or registrar before such certificate is issued, it may be issued by the corporation with the same effect as if such person were such officer, transfer agent or registrar at the date of issue. A corporation shall not have power to issue a certificate in bearer form. (Last amended by Ch. 30, L. '05, eff. 7-1-05.)

Ch. 30, L. '05, eff. 7-1-05, added matter in italic and deleted [1]"Notwithstanding the adoption of such a resolution by the board of directors, every holder of stock represented by certificates and upon request every holder of uncertificated shares shall be entitled to have a certificate signed by, or in the name of the corporation by the chairperson or vice-chairperson of the board of directors, or the president or vice-president, and by the treasurer or an assistant treasurer, or the secretary or an assistant secretary of such corporation representing the number of shares registered in certificate form."

Ch. 30, L. '05 Synopsis of Section 158

The amendment to Section 158 eliminates the requirement that a corporation with uncertificated shares issue a certificate for such shares upon the request of the holder of such shares. Notwithstanding this amendment, a corporation with uncertificated shares still is permitted to issue a certificate upon the request of a holder, but the corporation is not obligated to do so.

Ch. 298, L. '02 Synopsis of Section 158

The amendment to Section 158 clarifies that a Delaware corporation may not issue stock certificates in bearer form.

Ch. 339, L. '98 Synopsis of Section 158

The amendments to these Sections eliminate masculine references in the statutes, and replace them with gender neutral references.

.1 Certificates as evidence of shares.—Issuance by corporation of certificate for its stock constitutes representation that person to whom certificate issued is holder of number of shares thereon indicated, upon which bona fide purchaser for value can rely. *Delaware-New Jersey Ferry Co v Leeds, 186 A 913 (Ch Ct 1936).*

Certificates of stock are only evidence of shares and not shares themselves. *Baker v Banker's Mortgage Co, 135 A 486 (Ch Ct 1926).* They are not essential to stockholding. *Mau v Montana Pacific Oil Co, 141 A 828 (Ch Ct 1928).*

If subscription to stock is made at premium above par value on part paid stock, the full amount including premium must be paid before fully paid and nonassessable certificate can be issued. *Grone v Economic Life Ins Co, 80 A 800 (Ch Ct 1911).*

When terms of respective rights and obligations of corporation and stockholders are set forth in certificate of stock it becomes also contract between corporation and stockholder. *Lehigh Structural Steel Co v CIR, 127 F2d 67 (3d Cir 1942).*

Certificates for shares of corporate stock are "securities" notwithstanding fact that they merely represent particular interest of owner in corporate capital and in its surplus assets on dissolution.

Equitable Trust Co v Marshall, 17 A2d 13 (Ch Ct 1940).

Provisions in stock certificate contrary to certificate of incorporation are void. *Delaware-New Jersey Ferry Co v Leeds, 186 A 913 (Ch Ct 1936); Standard Scale & Supply Corp v Chappel, 141 A 191 (Ch Ct 1928).*

Either actual or constructive delivery is essential before certificate of stock can be said to have been issued. *Smith v Universal Service Motors Co, 147 A 247 (Ch Ct 1929).*

.2 Reissuing certificate without restrictive legend.—Court ordered corporation to reissue to shareholder certificate for her stock without restrictive investment legend imprinted on her present certificate providing that stock could not be sold or transferred unless it was registered under Securities Act of 1933 or, in opinion of counsel, exempt from registration, where (1) Proposed transfer would be exempt under §4(1) of 1933 Act. (2) Corporation's reluctance to reissue certificate resulted, not from desire to protect its own legitimate interests, but to further individual interests of chief executive officer/ principal shareholder who had dispute with shareholder over payment for stock. *Bender v Memory Metals, Inc, 514 A2d 1109 (Ch Ct 1986).*

.3 Estoppel.—When stock is issued without regard for corporate formalities, one who participates in or approves its issuance will be estopped from challenging defects in issuance. Stock is deemed issued when it actually or constructively comes into possession of owner by delivery to stockholder or some person acting as his agent.

Resulting trust may be imposed on shares where circumstances indicate that party holding legal title was not intended to have beneficial interest in shares. *Danvir Corp v Wahl, No. 8386 (Ch Ct 9-8-87).*

159 SHARES OF STOCK; PERSONAL PROPERTY, TRANSFER AND TAXATION.—The shares of stock in every corporation shall be deemed personal property and transferable as provided in Article 8 of subtitle I of Title 6. No stock or bonds issued by any corporation organized under this chapter shall be taxed by this State when the same shall be owned by non-residents of this State, or by foreign corporations. Whenever any transfer of shares shall be made for collateral security, and not absolutely, it shall be so expressed in the entry of transfer if, when the certificates are presented to the corporation for transfer or uncertificated shares are requested to be transferred, both the transferor and transferee request the corporation to do so. (Last amended by Ch. 112, L. '83, eff. 7-1-83.)

.1 Shares as personal property.—Shares of stock are personal property and as such are subject to conversion, regardless whether certificate for them has been issued or not. *Haskell v Middle States Petroleum Corp, 165 A 562 (1933).*

.2 Transfer of shares.—It is not necessary to legal ownership of stock that it be transferred on corporation's books. *Drug, Inc v Hunt, 168 A 87 (1933); Lippman v Kehoe Sten Co, 98 A 943 (Ch Ct 1916),* aff'd, *102 A 988 (1918).*

Until transferor surrenders his certificate to corporation for transfer, transferee cannot compel corporation to issue certificate for share supposed to have been transferred. *Berl v Va Production Co, 163 A 641 (Ch Ct 1932),* reh'g denied, *164 A 402 (Ch Ct 1933).*

Transferee who purchased stock with full knowledge of infirmity in its issuance, and that corporation had cancelled it, cannot compel corporation to issue new certificate to him. *Bowen v Imperial Theatres, Inc, 115 A 918 (Ch Ct 1922).*

Bona fide transferees, who purchased stock from original subscriber and received certificates marked as fully paid, are not liable to corporate creditors when they had no knowledge or notice that there was unpaid balance due upon this stock. *Smith v Donges, 73 F2d 620 (3d Cir 1934).*

Stockholder who endorses his stock in blank for transfer, and delivers it to another, loses title to such other, even though that stock was not transferred on corporation's books. *Chadwick v Parkhill Corp, 141 A 823, 141 A 827 (Ch Ct 1928).*

.3 Pledged shares.—No record on corporation's books is needed to vest title in stock's pledgee, and such transfer of title is unaffected by later attachment in suit against record holder. *Banker's Mortgage Co v Sohland, 138 A 361 (1927).*

.4 Stock sale agreements.—Action may be brought to determine rights of parties to stock in accordance with pre-incorporation agreement. *Wightman v San Francisco Bay Toll-Bridge Co, 142 A 783 (Ch Ct 1928); Shore v Union Drug Co, 156 A 204 (Ch Ct 1931).*

Contract of sale of stock will be specifically enforced when no adequate remedy at law exists. *Francis v Medill, 141 A 697 (Ch Ct 1928); Baker Machine Co v U.S. Fire Apparatus Co, 97 A 613 (Ch Ct 1916).*

Parties did not enter into enforceable contract for sale of corporate stock and settlement of pending litigation, even though they had orally agreed to all of proposed contract's substantive terms and concluded negotiations. Reasons: (1) Defendants, acting through authorized agent, said that they were not consenting to be bound by contract until execution of writing evidencing agreement; and (2) Defendants withdrew from agreement before this was done. *Transamerican Steamship Corp v Murphy, No. 10511 (Ch Ct 2-14-89).*

160 CORPORATION'S POWERS RESPECTING OWNERSHIP, VOTING, ETC., OF ITS OWN STOCK; RIGHTS OF STOCK CALLED FOR REDEMPTION.—(a) Every corporation may purchase, redeem, receive, take or otherwise acquire, own and hold, sell, lend, exchange, transfer or otherwise dispose of, pledge, use and otherwise deal in and with its own shares; provided, however, that no corporation shall:

(1) Purchase or redeem its own shares of capital stock for cash or other property when the capital of the corporation is impaired or when such purchase or redemption would cause any impairment of the capital of the corporation, except that a corporation *other than a nonstock corporation* may purchase or redeem out of capital any of its own shares which are entitled upon any distribution of its assets, whether by dividend or in liquidation, to a preference over another class or series of its stock, or, if no shares entitled to such a preference are outstanding, any of its own shares, if such shares will be retired upon their acquisition and the capital of the corporation reduced in accordance with §§243 and 244 of this title. Nothing in this subsection shall invalidate or otherwise affect a note, debenture or other obligation of a corporation given by it as consideration for its acquisition by purchase, redemption or exchange of its shares of stock if at the time such note, debenture or

obligation was delivered by the corporation its capital was not then impaired or did not thereby become impaired;

(2) Purchase, for more than the price at which they may then be redeemed, any of its shares which are redeemable at the option of the corporation; or

[1] (3)(i) In the case of a corporation other than a nonstock corporation, redeem any of its shares, unless their redemption is authorized by §151(b) of this title and then only in accordance with such section and the certificate of incorporation, or (ii) in the case of a nonstock corporation, redeem any of its membership interests, unless their redemption is authorized by the certificate of incorporation and then only in accordance with the certificate of incorporation.

(b) Nothing in this section limits or affects a corporation's right to resell any of its shares theretofore purchased or redeemed out of surplus and which have not been retired, for such consideration as shall be fixed by the board of directors.

(c) Shares of its own capital stock belonging to the corporation or to another corporation, if a majority of the shares entitled to vote in the election of directors of such other corporation is held, directly or indirectly, by the corporation, shall neither be entitled to vote nor be counted for quorum purposes. Nothing in this section shall be construed as limiting the right of any corporation to vote stock, including but not limited to its own stock, held by it in a fiduciary capacity.

(d) Shares which have been called for redemption shall not be deemed to be outstanding shares for the purpose of voting or determining the total number of shares entitled to vote on any matter on and after the date on which written notice of redemption has been sent to holders thereof and a sum sufficient to redeem such shares has been irrevocably deposited or set aside to pay the redemption price to the holders of the shares upon surrender of certificates therefor. (Last amended by Ch. 253, L. '10, eff. 8-1-10.)

Ch. 253, L. '10, eff. 8-1-10, added matter in italic and deleted [1]"(3) Redeem any of its shares unless their redemption is authorized by subsection (b) of §151 of this title and then only in accordance with such section and the certificate of incorporation."

Ch. 253, L. '10 Synopsis of Section 160

Sections 16 and 17 amend §160 of the DGCL to ensure consistency with the amendment to §154 regarding the capital of a nonstock corporation, and to allow a nonstock corporation to redeem its membership interests if the redemption of such membership interests is authorized by the corporation's certificate of incorporation.

Ch. 349, L. '96 Synopsis of Section 160

This amendment permits a corporation to purchase shares of its common stock out of capital if no shares of preferred stock are outstanding and the shares will be retired upon their acquisition and the capital of the corporation will be reduced in accordance with §§243 and 244.

Comment: This amendment to §160 makes explicit the existing Delaware law that a Delaware corporation may exchange a debt security for its stock as long as its capital is not impaired.

.1 Purchase out of capital.—Corporation cannot buy its own stock when that would cause impairment of capital. *West Penn Chemical & Mfg Co v Prentice, 236 F 891 (3d Cir 1916); Acker v Girard Trust Co, 42 F2d 37 (3d Cir 1930); In re International Radiator Co, 92 A 255 (Ch Ct 1914); Pasotti v U.S. Guardian Corp, 156 A 255 (Ch Ct 1931).*

Former stockholders in bankrupt corporation liable to bankruptcy trustee for damages for impairment of corporate capital caused by their sale of shares back to corporation, even though they were not aware purchase by impaired corporation violated statute. *Matter of Kettle Fried Chicken of America, 513 F2d 807 (6th Cir 1975).*

Corporation was liable to shareholder when it only repurchased half of stock that shareholder offered to sell because (1) shareholder bought stock from corporation with option to sell it back to corporation at original purchase price and (2) corporation was adequately capitalized on day it obligated itself to repurchase its stock so it cannot rely on GCL §160 to invalidate obligation. *International Consolidated Industries, Inc v Norton & Co, 504 NYS2d 967 (1986).*

A corporation that has positive net assets and pays patronage dividends may nevertheless adopt a moratorium on the redemption of its stock when making such redemptions would impair its capital. Applying Delaware law, the Illinois Court of Appeals determined that the moratorium was valid because Delaware law contains a general prohibition against redeeming stock when doing so would impair the capital of the corporation. *TruServ Corp v Bess Hardware and Sports, Inc, 804 NE2d 611 (Ill App Ct 2004).*

.2 Permissible purchases.—Courts will not interfere with directors' decision to purchase corporation's own stock unless there is misconduct or fraud. *Bankers Securities Corp v Kresge Dept Stores, Inc, 54 FSupp 378 (D Del 1944).*

Directors can authorize their corporation to buy large block of its own stock to avoid possible battle for control by seller, who favored policies directors thought detrimental to corporation, if purchase did not impair capital, price paid (about 10% over market) and incidental expenses of purchase were not excessive, market price of stock rose substantially thereafter, and there was no mismanagement of corporation. *Kors v Carey, 158 A2d 136 (Ch Ct 1960).*

Directors are not liable for having corporation buy block of its shares at premium prices to fend off purchase by outsiders that they believed posed threat to corporation's continued existence; their belief was reasonable when based on personal investigation and competent professional advice. *Cheff v Mathes, 199 A2d 548 (1964),* rev'g, *190 A2d 524 (Ch Ct 1963).*

Corporation cannot purchase its own shares when its only purpose is to perpetuate control by dominant shareholder, when there is no showing that any real threat to corporate policy has occurred. *Propp v Sadacca, 175 A2d 33 (Ch Ct 1961),* reversed and affirmed in part, *Bennett v Propp, 187 A2d 405 (1962).*

Contract for purchase of its own stock at inadequate price by subsidiary from parent to give directors and officers common to both companies voting control of subsidiary can be rescinded by action of receiver of parent corporation. *Potter v Sanitary Co of Amer, 194 A 87 (Ch Ct 1937).*

Guarantee by corporation, which subsequently went bankrupt, to its former owners when they sold corporation was not illegal as a purchase of corporation's stock that impaired capital because capital was not impaired when guarantee was executed, though it was impaired when payments under agreement became due. *In re Reliable Mfg Corp, 703 F2d 996 (7th Cir 1983).*

Absent improper purpose, corporation has right to buy back shares from dissident shareholders. No Delaware law exists to support plaintiffs' contention that GM directors had duty to extend Perot buyback to all GM shareholders. *In re General Motors Class E Stock Buyout Securities Litigation, 694 FSupp 1119 (D Del 1988).*

The Court of Chancery denied an application for a temporary restraining order that would have precluded a corporation from expending corporate funds or credit for the purchase of its stock and was filed by plaintiff, a company which owned 11% of the corporation's stock that was committed to acquiring control of the corporation, where plaintiff did not establish irreparable injury. *Carson Pirie Scott & Co v Gould, No. 14359 (Ch Ct 7-12-95).*

.3 Capital defined.—Word "capital" does not mean just assets but is intended to mean that funds and property of corporation should not be used to purchase its own shares when value of its assets is less than aggregate amount of all shares of its issued capital stock. *In re International Radiator Co, 92 A 255 (Ch Ct 1914).*

.4 Pledge of unissued stock.—Corporation can pledge its unissued shares of capital stock as collateral security for loan made to it, and upon corporation's insolvency, pledgee must return stock held when he files claim as creditor. *Claude Banta, Inc v Wilmington Suburban Water Co, 46 A2d 876 (Ch Ct 1946); In re International Radiator Co,* above.

.5 Treasury stock.—Treasury stock should not be counted in determining quorum at stockholders' meeting. *Atterbury v Consolidated Copper Mines Corp, 20 A2d 743 (Ch Ct 1941).*

Stock of parent corporation registered in name of subsidiary corporation cannot be voted by subsidiary at stockholders' meeting of parent for election of parent's directors. *Italo Petroleum Corp of America v Producers' Oil Corp of America, 174 A 276 (Ch Ct 1934).*

.6 Redemption of common stock.—There is no authority for corporation to redeem its common stock, and fact that it is subject to specific restrictions, placed upon it in charter, does not bring it within category of "special shares"; special shares derive their status from favors and rights they enjoy, whereas common stock is under limitation of burdens and restrictions. *Starring v American Hair & Felt Co, 191 A 887 (Ch Ct 1937),* aff'd per curiam, *2 A2d 249 (1937).*

Charter provision authorizing directors at any time to call common stock of any stockholder, who was not employee, was unreasonable restraint of alienation. *Greene v E H Rollins & Sons, Inc, 2 A2d 249 (Ch Ct 1938).*

Redemption agreement of insolvent corporation was illegal because it violated statutory provisions prohibiting the redemption or purchase of insolvent corporation's stock in both Delaware, state of organization, and Maryland, state where law was to be applied according to agreement. Guaranty of payment under agreement, even if viewed as separate transaction, was unenforceable because agreement was illegal. *McGinley v Massey, 525 A2d 1076 (Md Ct Spec App 1987).*

.7 Redemption of preferred stock.—When corporation that has preferred stock with accumulated dividend arrearages is being reorganized, plan of reorganization can contemplate redemption of preferred shares and substitution of new low-interest bonds for them. *In re United Gas Corp, 58 FSupp 501 (D Del 1944).*

Selective redemption of preferred stock, prior to expiration of voting trust agreement giving control to certain directors and officers, was barred since it appeared that redemption would assure continued control of corporation by such directors and officers. *Petty v Penntech Papers, Inc, 347 A2d 140 (Ch Ct 1975).*

Creditors of insolvent post-merger corporation could not recover from former directors of premerger corporation amount of deposit of corporate funds made in connection with redemption of premerger corporation's preferred stock, allegedly in violation of GCL §160. *Reason:* Plaintiffs were not "creditors" of pre-merger corporation because they did not have claim against pre-merger corporation before it went out of existence. *Johnston v Wolf, 487 A2d 1132 (1985).*

.8 Reclassification of preferred stock.—Stockholder who acquiesces in change in capital structure which results in change of his preferred stock into shares of different character and extinguishes cumulated dividends cannot compel corporation to pay him those dividend arrearages, nor can he compel restoration of original capital stock structure on ground that change was illegal. *Trounstine v Remington Rand, Inc, 194 A 95 (Ch Ct 1937).*

.9 Voting subsidiary's stock.—Delaware subsidiary could not vote its Panamanian parent's stock because, although Panamanian law's restrictions on voting of parent's stock by subsidiary did not apply to Delaware corporation, Panama would refrain from applying its law to deny foreign minority shareholders protections it grants to Panamanian minority shareholders. Delaware prohibits subsidiaries from voting their parents' stock. *Lewis v McDermott Inc, Nos. 7034 & 7044 (Ch Ct 7-17-86).*

In a case of first impression, the Delaware Chancery Court decided that any shares of a corporation held by that corporation's direct (or indirect subsidiary) are "entitled to vote" for the purposes of GCL §160(c) in a cross-ownership structure in which two (or more) corporations each own a majority of the shares issued by the other, and, therefore, those shares are sterilized at all times from voting. *In re Best Lock Corp. Shareholder Litigation, 2001 Del. Ch. LEXIS 134 (Ch Ct 2001).*

.10 Self-tender.—Target's self-tender for 47% of its own shares in exchange offer did not constitute triggering event under rights plan it adopted to ward off tender offeror so as to give its shareholders contractual right to require issuance of notes. Target was not "acquiring person" whose acquisition of 30% or more of target's stock would trigger rights. *Edleman v Phillips Petroleum Co, Nos. 7899 & 7972 (Ch Ct 6-3-86).*

Court issued temporary restraining order barring target corporation from purchasing any of its own stock for 20-day period. Plaintiff tender offeror stated colorable claim of breach of duty. Target's purchase threatened legal injury to tender offeror in its capacity as shareholder seeking to increase ownership of firm, and injury may be irreparable. Purchases also threatened irreparable injury to shareholders who might desire to tender. *UIS, Inc v Walbro Corp, No. 9323 (Ch Ct 10-6-87).*

Corporation was guilty of affirmative misconduct in tender offer to repurchase shares from shareholders when: (1) disclosures in its Offer to Purchase were false, misleading, or incomplete, and (2) corporation withheld its Annual Report so that it could not be considered by offerees. Corporation's liability was not triggered by any fiduciary duty but by affirmative acts of misdisclosure. *Gaffin v Teledyne, Inc, No. 5786 (Ch Ct 10-9-87).*

Directors who do not have knowledge of a plan to take a corporation private after a self-tender do not breach their duty of disclosure during the self-tender. *Johnson v Shapiro, 2002 Del. Ch. LEXIS 122 (Ch Ct 2002).*

.11 Conflict of laws.—Delaware Supreme Court reaffirmed internal affairs doctrine, which holds that law of state of incorporation determines issues relating to corporation's internal affairs. Panama law governs issue of whether a Panamanian corporation's Delaware subsidiary may vote shares it holds in parent company under circumstances prohibited by Delaware law, but not Panamanian law. *McDermott Inc v Lewis, 531 A2d 206 (1987).*

.12 Circular ownership.—In some circumstances, circular ownership of stock may violate §160(c), which bars voting of stock belonging to issuer or another corporation controlled by issuer. Stock owned by subsidiary may "belong to" issuer and be barred from voting even if issuer does not hold majority of shares entitled to vote at election of subsidiary's directors. *Speiser v Baker, 525 A2d 1001 (Ch Ct 1987).*

161 ISSUANCE OF ADDITIONAL STOCK; WHEN AND BY WHOM.—The directors may, at any time and from time to time, if all of the shares of capital stock which the corporation is authorized by its certificate of incorporation to issue have not been issued, subscribed for, or otherwise committed to be issued, issue or take subscriptions for additional shares of its capital stock up to the amount authorized in its certificate of incorporation.

.1 Lack of formalities, effect.—When stock is issued without regard for corporate formalities, one who participates in or approves its issuance will be estopped from challenging defects in issuance. Stock is deemed issued when it actually or constructively comes into possession of owner by delivery to stockholder or some person acting as his agent. Resulting trust may be imposed on shares where circumstances indicate that party holding legal title was not intended to have beneficial interest in shares. *Danvir Corp v Wahl, No. 8386 (Ch Ct 9-8-87).*

162 LIABILITY OF STOCKHOLDER OR SUBSCRIBER FOR STOCK NOT PAID IN FULL.—(a) When the whole of the consideration payable for shares of a corporation has not been paid in, and the assets shall be insufficient to satisfy the claims of its creditors, each holder of or subscriber for such shares shall be bound to pay on each share held or subscribed for by [1]*such holder or subscriber* the sum necessary to complete the amount of the unpaid balance of the consideration for which such shares were issued or are to be issued by the corporation.

(b) The amounts which shall be payable as provided in subsection (a) of this section may be recovered as provided in §325 of this title, after a writ of execution against the corporation has been returned unsatisfied as provided in said §325.

(c) Any person becoming an assignee or transferee of shares or of a subscription for shares in good faith and without knowledge or notice that the full consideration therefor has not been paid shall not be personally liable for any unpaid portion of such consideration, but the transferor shall remain liable therefor.

(d) No person holding shares in any corporation as collateral security shall be personally liable as a stockholder but the person pledging such shares shall be considered the holder thereof and shall be so liable. No executor, administrator, guardian, trustee or other fiduciary shall be personally liable as a stockholder, but the estate or funds held by such executor, administrator, guardian, trustee or other fiduciary in such fiduciary capacity shall be liable.

(e) No liability under this section or under §325 of this title shall be asserted more than 6 years after the issuance of the stock or the date of the subscription upon which the assessment is sought.

(f) In any action by a receiver or trustee of an insolvent corporation or by a judgment creditor to obtain an assessment under this section, any stockholder or subscriber for stock of the insolvent corporation may appear and contest the claim or claims of such receiver or trustee. (Last amended by Ch. 339, L. '98, eff. 7-1-98.)

Ch. 339, L. '98, eff. 7-1-98, added matter in italic and deleted [1]"him".

Ch. 339, L. '98 Synopsis of Section 162

The amendments to these Sections eliminate masculine references in the statutes, and replace them with gender neutral references.

.1 Liability of stockholders.—Corporation cannot make subscription contracts which will free subscribers from liability to pay for their shares for benefit of creditors, since principle is that shares of stock in corporation are substitute for personal liability of partners. *John W Cooney Co v Arlington Hotel Co, 101 A 879 (Ch Ct 1917)*, aff'd, *Du Pont v Ball, 106 A 39 (1918)*; see also, *Finch v Warrior Cement Corp, 141 A 54 (Ch Ct 1928)*; *Wallace v Weinstein, 257 F 625 (3d Cir 1919)*; *Harman v Himes, 77 F2d 375 (DC Cir 1935)*.

As to creditors, there is no difference between liability of holders of stock and subscribers to stock, for both are liable. *John W Cooney Co v Arlington Hotel Co*, above; see also, *Harman v Himes*, above.

Assessment may be only for amount sufficient to pay outstanding claims of creditors, and not for entire balance due on stock. *Carpenter v Griffith Mortgage Corp, 172 A 447 (Ch Ct 1934)*.

Note: This decision was under old law. Present statute appears to impose a mandatory obligation to complete the full amount of the unpaid balance due on the shares, regardless whether this will result in an amount greater than creditors' claim.

When one takes shares in order to qualify to be director, he cannot subsequently escape liability for assessment by showing he never had any beneficial interest in stock but held it for another to whom he had delivered certificate with transfer endorsed on it. *Fell v Securities Co of North America, 100 A 788 (Ch Ct 1917)*; see also, *Taggart v Leo B Booker & Co, 20 A2d 690 (1942)*.

Holders of voting trust certificates received in exchange for part paid stock are liable for payment of balance due on subscription to stock. *John W Cooney Co v Arlington Hotel Co*, above.

.2 Liability of bona fide purchasers.—Transferee of stock from original subscriber is not liable to corporation's creditors for unpaid balance on stock issued and marked as paid for in full if transferee is bona fide purchaser without notice. *Smith v Donges, 73 F2d 620 (3d Cir 1934)*.

But innocent purchaser for value must bear burden of establishing his claim as such. *Blair v F H Smith Co, 156 A 207 (Ch Ct 1931)*.

.3 Enforcement of liability.—Liability to pay balance due on stock may be enforced by bill in chancery brought by receiver. *Cooper v Eastern Horse & Mule Co, 110 A 666 (Ch Ct 1920)*.

Court will grant petition of receiver of insolvent corporation that assessment be levied upon stockholders of corporation who have not paid par value for their stock to raise fund to pay corporate creditors. *Shaw v Lincoln Hotel Corp, 156 A 199 (Ch Ct 1931)*.

Receiver must show there is deficiency of corporate assets to meet outstanding claims of creditors before court will permit him to levy assessment on stockholders for unpaid portion of their stock. *Philips v Slocomb, 167 A 698 (1933)*; see also, *Cahall v Lofland, 108 A 732 (Ch Ct 1920)*.

Liability of stockholder, receiving stock at less than par, can be enforced by action in foreign state. *U.S. Rubber Co v Eagle Transp Co, 248 NW 729 (Minn 1933)*.

.4 Stock cancellation and reissuance.—Where an attempt is made to cancel the common stock of a corporation without an amendment to the certificate of incorporation, such cancellation is invalid. Also, where an attempt is made to reissue the stock without consideration or benefit to the corporation, such issuance is also invalid. *MBKS Company Ltd. v MBKS Inc, 2007 Del. Ch. LEXIS 52 (Ch Ct 2007)*.

163 PAYMENT FOR STOCK NOT PAID IN FULL.—The capital stock of a corporation shall be paid for in such amounts and at such times as the directors may require. The directors may, from time to time, demand payment, in respect of each share of stock not fully paid, of such sum of money as the necessities of the business may, in the judgment of the board of directors, require, not exceeding in the whole the balance remaining unpaid on said stock, and such sum so demanded shall be paid to the corporation at such times and by such installments as the directors shall direct. The directors shall give written notice of the time and place of such payments, which notice shall be mailed at least 30 days before the time for such payment, to each holder of or subscriber for stock which is not fully paid at [1]*such holder's or subscriber's* last known post-office address. (Last amended by Ch. 339, L. '98, eff. 7-1-98.)

Ch. 339, L. '98, eff. 7-1-98, added matter in italic and deleted [1]"his".

Ch. 339, L. '98 Synopsis of Section 163

The amendments to these Sections eliminate masculine references in the statutes, and replace them with gender neutral references.

.1 Applicability of section.—This section applies only to going corporations. *Philips v Slocomb, 167 A 698 (1933).*

.2 Subscribers.—In event of dissolution, employee-subscribers are stockholders and are subject to same liabilities as others; their motive in making subscription does not affect its validity. *Hegarty v Amer Commonwealth Power Corp, 174 A 273 (Ch Ct 1934).*

Subscribers who are delinquent in paying their subscriptions cannot be converted into creditors by issuance of "certificates of indebtedness" and cancellation of right to subscribe. *Pasotti v US Guardian Corp, 156 A 255 (Ch Ct 1931).*

Distinction between subscription to stock and purchase of stock is question of agreement's construction, but, generally, if transaction is with corporation and involves stock not previously issued, it is a subscription and not purchase. *Louisiana Oil Exploration Co v Raskob, 127 A 713 (1925).*

When corporation issues its stock to agent for resale to bona fide purchasers, who receive certificates marked "full-paid and non-assessable," such purchasers are not subscribers. *Smith v Donges, 73 F2d 620 (3d Cir 1934).*

Corporations cannot accept subscriptions on special terms which are fraudulent as to other stockholders; such subscriptions are void as to those special terms but otherwise valid. *Cahall v Lofland, 114 A 224 (Ch Ct 1921).*

.3 Necessity for assessment and call.—Before corporation can maintain action against alleged stockholder to recover unpaid subscription for stock, or unpaid purchase price for newly issued stock, it must show that assessment and call has been made upon alleged stockholder for amount required from

him. *Louisiana Oil Exploration Co v Raskob,* above; see also, *Cahill v Burbage, 119 A 574 (Ch Ct 1922); Philips v Slocomb, 167 A 698 (1933).*

.4 Liability as between principal and agent.—When shares of stock which stand on corporate books in name of one person are held as agent for another, either principal or agent is liable for unpaid subscription for such shares. *Fell v Securities Co of North America, 100 A 788 (Ch Ct 1917).*

.5 Fraud as defense to action for unpaid subscription.—If subscription contract is induced by fraud, subscriber may set it up as defense to action for balance due on subscription and amounts already paid in ignorance of fraud may be recovered. *Grone v Economic Life Ins Co, 80 A 809 (Ch Ct 1911).*

164 FAILURE TO PAY FOR STOCK; REMEDIES.—When any stockholder fails to pay any installment or call upon *¹such stockholder's* stock which may have been properly demanded by the directors, at the time when such payment is due, the directors may collect the amount of any such installment or call or any balance thereof remaining unpaid, from the said stockholder by an action at law, or they shall sell at public sale such part of the shares of such delinquent stockholder as will pay all demands then due from *²such stockholder* with interest and all incidental expenses, and shall transfer the shares so sold to the purchaser, who shall be entitled to a certificate therefor.

Notice of the time and place of such sale and of the sum due on each share shall be given by advertisement at least 1 week before the sale, in a newspaper of the county in this State where such corporation's registered office is located, and such notice shall be mailed by the corporation to such delinquent stockholder at *¹such stockholder's* last known post-office address, at least 20 days before such sale.

If no bidder can be had to pay the amount due on the stock, and if the amount is not collected by an action at law, which may be brought within the county where the corporation has its registered office, within 1 year from the date of the bringing of such action at law, the said stock and the amount previously paid in by the delinquent stockholder on the stock shall be forfeited to the corporation. (Last amended by Ch. 339, L. '98, eff. 7-1-98.)

Ch. 339, L. '98, eff. 7-1-98, added matter in italic and deleted ¹"his" and ²"him".

Ch. 339, L. '98 Synopsis of Section 164

The amendments to these Sections eliminate masculine references in the statutes, and replace them with gender neutral references.

Comment: This change in §164 is essentially a typographical correction. The original statute inadvertently omitted the word "stockholder" after the word "delinquent".

165 REVOCABILITY OF PREINCORPORATION SUBSCRIPTIONS.—Unless otherwise provided by the terms of the subscription, a subscription for stock of a corporation to be formed shall be irrevocable, except with the consent of all other subscribers or the corporation, for a period of 6 months from its date.

166 FORMALITIES REQUIRED OF STOCK SUBSCRIPTIONS.—A subscription for stock of a corporation, whether made before or after the formation of a corporation, shall not be enforceable against a subscriber, unless in writing and signed by the subscriber or by *¹such subscriber's* agent. (Last amended by Ch. 339, L. '98, eff. 7-1-98.)

Ch. 339, L. '98, eff. 7-1-98, added matter in italic and deleted ¹"his".

Ch. 339, L. '98 Synopsis of Section 166

The amendments to these Sections eliminate masculine references in the statutes, and replace them with gender neutral references.

167 LOST, STOLEN OR DESTROYED STOCK CERTIFICATES; ISSUANCE OF NEW CERTIFICATE OR UNCERTIFICATED SHARES.—A corporation may issue a new certificate of stock or uncertificated shares in place of any certificate theretofore issued by it, alleged to have been lost, stolen or destroyed, and the corporation may require the owner of the lost, stolen or destroyed certificate, or *¹such owner's* legal representative to give the corporation a bond sufficient to indemnify it against any claim that may be made against it on account of the alleged loss, theft or destruction of any such certificate or the issuance of such new certificate or uncertificated shares. (Last amended by Ch. 339, L. '98, eff. 7-1-98.)

Ch. 339, L. '98, eff. 7-1-98, added matter in italic and deleted ¹"his".

Ch. 339, L. '98 Synopsis of Section 167

The amendments to these Sections eliminate masculine references in the statutes, and replace them with gender neutral references.

.1 Proper delivery of certificate.—Acceptance by stockholder's mail of registered letter containing shares of stock was good delivery of shares to him; corporation can demand that he post indemnity bond for new certificates. *Graham v Commercial Credit Co*, 194 A2d 863 (Ch Ct 1963), aff'd, 200 A2d 828 (1964).

.2 Issuance of new certificate—bond.—New certificate must be issued for lost certificate on filing of bond. *In re Francis*, 108 A 31 (1919).

Corporation transferring stock, without receiving original certificate, becomes liable to any person holding such certificate in good faith whether or not it has notice of such third party's rights. *Drug, Inc v Hunt*, 168 A 87 (Super Ct 1933).

.3 False loss claim.—When stockholder of record sells his certificate and later obtains new one by claiming that original was lost, issuing corporation is liable for converting vendee's shares but may be protected by statute of limitations which begins to run when new certificate is issued, even if vendee does not know about it. *Mastellone v Argo Oil Corp*, 82 A2d 379 (1951).

.4 Certificate never issued.—If certificates have never been issued, this section of law does not apply. *Smith v Universal Service Motors Co*, 147 A 247 (Ch Ct 1929).

Before issuing replacement certificates for those lost, stolen or destroyed, trust could require brokerage houses to supply independent credible evidence that they were beneficial owners of stock registered in their names because brokerage houses had held stock in "street name" so there was no presumption that shareholder of record was also beneficial owner. *Merrill Lynch Pierce Fenner & Smith, Inc v North European Oil Royalty Trust*, 490 A2d 558 (1985).

168 JUDICIAL PROCEEDINGS TO COMPEL ISSUANCE OF NEW CERTIFICATE OR UNCERTIFICATED SHARES.—(a) If a corporation refuses to issue new uncertificated shares or a new certificate of stock in place of a certificate theretofore issued by it, or by any corporation of which it is the lawful successor, alleged to have been lost, stolen or destroyed, the owner of the lost, stolen or destroyed certificate or [1]*such owner's* legal representatives may apply to the Court of Chancery for an order requiring the corporation to show cause why it should not issue new uncertificated shares or a new certificate of stock in place of the certificate so lost, stolen or destroyed. Such application shall be by a complaint which shall state the name of the corporation, the number and date of the certificate, if known or ascertainable by the plaintiff, the number of shares of stock represented thereby and to whom issued, and a statement of the circumstances attending such loss, theft or destruction. Thereupon the court shall make an order requiring the corporation to show cause at a time and place therein designated, why it should not issue new uncertificated shares or a new certificate of stock in place of the one described in the complaint. A copy of the complaint and order shall be served upon the corporation at least 5 days before the time designated in the order.

(b) If, upon hearing, the court is satisfied that the plaintiff is the lawful owner of the number of shares of capital stock, or any part thereof, described in the complaint, and that the certificate therefor has been lost, stolen or destroyed, and no sufficient cause has been shown why new uncertificated shares or a new certificate should not be issued in place thereof, it shall make an order requiring the corporation to issue and deliver to the plaintiff new uncertificated shares or a new certificate for such shares. In its order the court shall direct that, prior to the issuance and delivery to the plaintiff of such new uncertificated shares or a new certificate, the plaintiff give the corporation a bond in such form and with such security as to the court appears sufficient to indemnify the corporation against any claim that may be made against it on account of the alleged loss, theft or destruction of any such certificate or the issuance of such new uncertificated shares or new certificate. No corporation which has issued uncertificated shares or a certificate pursuant to an order of the court entered hereunder shall be liable in an amount in excess of the amount specified in such bond. (Last amended by Ch. 339, L. '98, eff. 7-1-98.)

Ch. 339, L. '98, eff. 7-1-98, added matter in italic and deleted [1]"his".

Ch. 339, L. '98 Synopsis of Section 168

The amendments to these Sections eliminate masculine references in the statutes, and replace them with gender neutral references.

.1 Successor to assets.—Alleged successor to assets of former brokerage firm cannot compel corporation, some of whose stock is registered in firm's name, to declare him owner of stock, issue him new certificate, and pay him past unpaid dividends, when he cannot prove his claim with reasonable certainty. *Keech v Zenith Radio Corp*, 276 A2d 270 (Ch Ct 1971).

Petition for an order requiring defendant corporation to issue replacement stock certificates was denied where petitioner failed to establish with reasonable certainty that she was the beneficial owner of the stock and that the original shares were lost, stolen or destroyed. *In the Matter of North European Oil Corp, No. 753 (Ch Ct 8-9-95).*

.2 Loss of certificate.—Stockholder can make corporation issue new stock certificates to her, when these certificates were lost and she had never authorized their sale, even though corporation had transferred them to innocent purchaser for value. *Scott v Ametek Inc, 277 A2d 714 (Ch Ct 1971).*

169 SITUS OF OWNERSHIP OF STOCK.—For all purposes of title, action, attachment, garnishment and jurisdiction of all courts held in this State, but not for the purpose of taxation, the situs of the ownership of the capital stock of all corporations existing under the laws of this State, whether organized under this chapter or otherwise, shall be regarded as in this State.

.1 Situs of stock.—Shares of stock of Delaware corporation have their situs in Delaware. *Blumenthal v Blumenthal, 59 A2d 216 (Ch Ct 1944); Cantor v Sachs, 162 A 73 (Ch Ct 1932); Hodgman v Atlantic Refining Co, 274 F 104 (D Del 1921).*

No stockholder who accepts stock in Delaware corporation can be heard in court to deny its Delaware situs. *Bouree v Trust Francais des Actions de la Franco-Wyoming Oil Co, 127 A 56 (Ch Ct 1924).*

Transfer of stock of Delaware corporation is controlled by laws of Delaware since, for all purposes other than taxation, situs of its stock is there. *Drug, Inc v Hunt, 168 A 87 (Super Ct 1933); Pennington v Commonwealth Hotel Const Co, 156 A 259 (Ch Ct 1931).*

Statute determining Delaware to be fictional situs of stock could not be used to sequester stock and thus gain jurisdiction over out-of-state corporate directors since it was unconstitutional for not satisfying due process standards; directors' only contact with state was ownership of stock in Delaware corporation that had nothing to do with shareholder's cause of action. *Shaffer v Heitner, 433 US 186 (1977).*

.2 Power of court.—Court has power to order partition of shares of stock of Delaware corporation since they constitute res located in state. *Wightman v San Francisco Bay Toll-Bridge Co, 142 A 782 (Ch Ct 1928).*

Suit for cancellation or specific recovery of stock can be brought in federal court for district of Delaware and service on defendants residing elsewhere can be made under Judicial Code. *Myers v Occidental Oil Corp, 288 F 997 (D Del 1923).*

.3 Attachment.—Under provisions of this section and §324, it is not necessary that Delaware corporation be doing business in state before attachment is issued against shares of its capital stock, since corporation itself is not being summoned as garnishee. *Morgan v Ownbey, 100 A 411 (Ch Ct 1916),* aff'd, *105 A 838 (1919);* see also, *Cantor v Sachs, 162 A 73 (Ch Ct 1932).*

.4 Domicile in fact in another state.—Even though Delaware corporation executes trust whose entire corpus is stock in Delaware corporation, situs of trust is not in Delaware, since indenture was signed by corporation outside state, its provisions provided that trust be administered under another state's law, and in fact was so administered. *Baltimore Nat'l Bank v Central Public Utility Corp, 28 A2d 244 (Ch Ct 1942).*

.5 Subsidiary's stock.—Alien parent corporation that incorporated subsidiary in Delaware for purpose of purchasing another corporation's stock cannot claim that "mere" ownership of stock in subsidiary is insufficient contact between it and state to permit jurisdiction, since subsidiary was created to reap "benefits and protections" of state's laws and there existed significant contacts between state, parent and litigation. *Papendick v Robert Bosch GmbH, 389 A2d 1315 (1979).*

.6 Stock ownership; jurisdiction.—Ownership of stock in a Delaware corporation, on its own, is an insufficient basis for a court to exercise personal or in rem jurisdiction where the action does not relate directly to the legal existence, rights, characteristics, or attributes of the stock; does not allege a defect in the corporate process by which the stock was issued; and does not challenge transactions that substantially involve the stock. *OneScreen Inc v Hudgens, 2010 Del. Ch. LEXIS 62 (Ch Ct 2010).*

170 DIVIDENDS; PAYMENT; WASTING ASSET CORPORATIONS.—(a) The directors of every corporation, subject to any restrictions contained in its certificate of incorporation, may declare and pay dividends upon the shares of its capital stock [1] either (1) out of its surplus, as defined in and computed in accordance with §§154 and 244 of this title, or (2) in case there shall be no such surplus, out of its net profits for the fiscal year in which the dividend is declared and/or the preceding fiscal year. If the capital of the corporation, computed in accordance with §§154 and 244 of this title, shall have been diminished by depreciation in the value of its property, or by losses, or otherwise, to an amount less than the aggregate amount of the capital represented by the issued and outstanding stock of all classes having a preference upon the distribution of assets, the directors of such corporation shall not declare and pay out of such net profits any dividends upon any shares of any classes of its capital stock until the deficiency in the amount of capital represented by the issued and outstanding stock of all classes having a preference upon the distribution of assets shall have been repaired. Nothing in this subsection shall invalidate or otherwise affect a note, debenture or other obligation of the corporation paid by it as a dividend on shares of its stock, or any payment made thereon, if at the time such note, debenture or obligation was delivered by the corporation, the corporation had either surplus or net profits as provided in clause (1) or (2) of this subsection from which the dividend could lawfully have been paid.

(b) Subject to any restrictions contained in its certificate of incorporation, the directors of any corporation engaged in the exploitation of wasting assets (including but not limited to a corporation engaged in the exploitation of natural resources or other wasting assets, including patents, or engaged primarily in the liquidation of specific assets) may determine the net profits derived from the exploitation of such wasting assets or the net proceeds derived from such liquidation without taking into consideration the depletion of such assets resulting from lapse of time, consumption, liquidation or exploitation of such assets. (Last amended by Ch. 253, L. '10, eff. 8-1-10.)

Ch. 253, L. '10, eff. 8-1-10, deleted [1]", or to its members if the corporation is a nonstock corporation,".

Ch. 253, L. '10 Synopsis of Section 170

Section 18 amends §170 of the DGCL to ensure that the translator provision in new §114(a) operates properly on §170.

Ch. 123, L. '99 Synopsis of Section 170

The language of Section 170(a) has been revised to make clear that dividends may be declared and paid by nonstock nonprofit corporations as well as nonstock for profit corporations.

Commentary on Sections 102(a)(4), 170(a) and 256

In recent years various amendments to the General Corporation Law have been made to clarify that Delaware corporations can be set up as nonstock corporations for profit. Thus, in the 1974 amendment to Section 255(b) and (c), the words "nonprofit" were eliminated from the caption of the section, and in the 1987 amendment to Section 255(a) and (b), the words "nonprofit" were eliminated from subsection (a) and the words "whether or not organized for profit" were added. The Commentary to the 1987 amendment which accompanied the proposed amendment to Section 255 states: "In view of Section 257, there is no reason not to permit mergers of domestic nonstock corporations organized for profit." A similar amendment was not presented to Section 256. The 1987 amendment to Section 276 eliminated the word "nonprofit" at several places in the body of subsection (a). The Commentary to the 1987 amendment which accompanied the proposed amendment states that the purposes of these changes was "to make clear that Section 276 applies to all nonstock corporations." The proposed amendments will make the General Corporation Law more consistent in this regard.

The commentary to the 1993 amendment to Section 170(a) clarifies that the rule set forth in the last sentence of Section 160(a)(1), concerning the validity of notes, debentures or other obligations delivered by a corporation to acquire its own stock, also applies with respect to notes, debenture or other obligations issued by a corporation as a dividend.

.1 Nature of dividend.—Corporation's distribution to its stockholders of stock it owns in another corporation under compulsion of court divestiture order is not payment of dividend, but is return of capital to stockholders that diminishes corporation's asset value, so that stockholder husband, who is obligated by separation agreement to give to his wife any dividends he receives, does not have to turn over this stock distribution to her. *Fulweiler v Spruance, 222 A2d 555 (1966).*

Dividend is payment to stockholders as a return upon their investment. *Pennington v Commonwealth Hotel Const Corp, 155 A 514 (Ch Ct 1931).*

Directors and majority stockholders of corporation which, instead of paying dividends, provided stockholders with access to pool of railroad cars did not breach fiduciary duty to bankrupt minority stockholder that could no longer make use of this service. *Matter of Reading Co, 711 F2d 509 (3d Cir 1983).*

Court enjoined target's directors' attempt to employ anti-takeover measure of distribution of dividend of preferred stock. Each share of preferred stock entitled holder to cast 25 votes on all issues on which common stock could vote, but if transferred holders could only exercise five of those votes, which would make it impossible for tender offeror to acquire target. Change in corporate structure of this magnitude, reducing transferability of shareholders ability to vote and value of their assets, requires shareholder approval, which had not been obtained. *Unilever Ac-quisition Corp v Richardson-Vicks, Inc, 618 FSupp 407 (SDNY 1985).*

.2 When is dividend payable.—In ascertaining whether there are funds available for dividends, capital must be put down at its paid in and not at its par value. *Peters v US Mortgage Co, 114 A 598 (Ch Ct 1921).*

Net earnings retained for period of years as capital may be distributed as dividends and are then "profits" and not "capital." *Bryan v Aiken, 86 A 674 (1913).*

Assets for dividend purposes should be computed with allowance for depreciation; they cannot be counted at cost regardless of present worth. *Vogtman v Merchants Mtge & Credit Co, 178 A 99 (Ch Ct 1935).*

Dividends cannot be paid out of unrealized appreciated assets. *Kingston v Home Life Ins Co of America, 101 A 898 (Ch Ct 1917),* aff'd, *104 A 25 (1918).*

In absence of fraud or bad faith, directors' valuation of assets for dividend purposes on basis of acceptable data and by standards which directors are entitled to believe reasonably reflect present "values" is proper; court cannot substitute its view of valuation for that of directors. *Morris v Standard Gas & Electric Co, 63 A2d 577 (Ch Ct 1949).*

Charter provision permitting cumulative dividends out of "net earnings" means out of any earnings legally available; "net earnings" is not restricted to earned surplus, and includes current earnings. *Weinberg v Baltimore Brick Co, 114 A2d 812 (1955).*

.3 Right to dividends.—Stockholders cannot compel directors to declare dividends even though (1) there is large surplus and (2) corporation is holding company whose articles say its purpose is to receive and distribute dividends; directors' accumulation of surplus to buy out other companies is not abuse of discretion. *Leibert v Grinnell Corp, 194 A2d 846 (Ch Ct 1963).*

Directors need not pay arrearages to preferred stockholders from capital surplus realized out of sale of corporation's business assets if they are retaining it in good faith to buy new business and sale for that purpose has been approved by majority stockholders. *Treves v Menzies, 142 A2d 520 (Ch Ct 1958).*

Shareholder has no property interest in profits of business carried on by corporation until dividend has been declared out of such profits. *Pyle v Gallaker, 75 A 373 (1908); Carson v Allegheny Window Glass Co, 189 F 791 (D Del 1911).*

Dividends declared but unpaid can, if due, be recovered in action at law. *Jefferis v Wm D Mullen Co, 132 A 687 (Ch Ct 1926).*

Declaration of lawful dividend makes stockholder creditor of corporation and gives him right of action in contract against company. *Selly v Fleming Coal Co, 180 A 326 (1935).*

Money earned by corporation does not become property of its stockholders until it is distributed to them as dividends or on dissolution. *Managers Security Co v Mallery, 77 F2d 186 (3d Cir 1935); Bryan v Aiken, 86 A 674 (Ch Ct 1913).*

When parent corporation merged with subsidiary by buying out subsidiary's minority stockholders, minority could not compel parent to declare and pay dividend that would have been forthcoming for subsidiary had merger not taken place, because minority did not object to adequacy of price paid for their stock. *Gabelli & Co Profit Sharing Plan v Liggett Group Inc, 444 A2d 261 (Ch Ct 1982).*

Though funds were available to pay preferred dividend arrearages, common stockholder could not have election of board of directors set aside for their wrongful refusal to pay such dividends without showing fraud and gross abuse of discretion by board in refusing to order such dividends. *Baron v Allied Artists Pictures Corp, 337 A2d 653 (Ch Ct 1975).*

.4 Declaration as business judgment.—Minority shareholders could not compel corporation's board to pay quarterly dividend once corporation had merged and shareholders received cash for value of shares because board's failure to declare dividend was exercise of its business judgment. *Gabelli & Co Profit Sharing Plan v Ligget Group Inc, 479 A2d 276 (1984).*

Court refused to grant preliminary injunction to block street sweep of target corporation's stock executed by target's largest shareholder during hostile tender offer by outsider, where (1) Declaration of dividend was protected by business judgment rule when there was no self-dealing or waste and it furthered several business objectives; (2) the transactions in question were not motivated by single entrenchment purpose when sweeping shareholder was potential bidder and transactions were negotiated at arm's-length; (3) street sweep was not coercive to sellers; market forces propelled the sale; and (4) defensive measures were reasonable in relation to threat posed. *Ivanhoe Partners v Newmont Mining Corp, 533 A2d 585 (Ch Ct 1987).*

171 SPECIAL PURPOSE RESERVES.—The directors of a corporation may set apart out of any of the funds of the corporation available for dividends a reserve or reserves for any proper purpose and may abolish any such reserve.

172 LIABILITY OF DIRECTORS AND COMMITTEE MEMBERS AS TO DIVIDENDS OR STOCK REDEMPTION.—A member of the board of directors, or a member of any committee designated by the board of directors, shall be fully protected in relying in good faith upon the records of the corporation and upon such information, opinions, reports or statements presented to the corporation by any of its officers or employees, or committees of the board of directors, or by any other person as to matters the director reasonably believes are within such other person's professional or expert competence and who has been selected with reasonable care by or on behalf of the corporation as to the value and amount of the assets, liabilities and/or net profits of the corporation, or any other facts pertinent to the existence and amount of surplus or other funds from which dividends might properly be declared and paid, or with which the corporation's stock might properly be purchased or redeemed. (Last amended by Ch. 136, L. '87, eff. 7-1-87.)

173 DECLARATION AND PAYMENT OF DIVIDENDS.—No corporation shall pay dividends except in accordance with this chapter. Dividends may be paid in cash, in property, or in shares of the corporation's capital stock. If the dividend is to be paid in shares of the corporation's theretofore unissued capital stock the board of directors shall, by resolution, direct that there be designated as capital in respect of such shares an amount which is not less than the aggregate par value of par value being declared as a dividend and, in the case of shares without par value being declared as a dividend, such amount as shall be determined by the board of directors. No such designation as capital shall be necessary if shares are being distributed by a corporation pursuant to a split-up or division of its stock rather than as payment of a dividend declared payable in stock of the corporation. (Last amended by Ch. 127, L. '85, eff. 7-1-85.)

Comment: This amendment to §173 spells out clearly the procedure for handling stock dividends on the books of the corporation and distinguishes stock dividends from stock splits.

.1 To whom paid.—Dividends should be paid to party in whose name stock upon which they are declared is registered. *Wilmington Trust Co v Nye Odorless Incinerator Corp, 159 A 844 (Ch Ct 1932).*

All dividends which are unpaid on cumulative preferred stock at time of dissolution of corporation must be paid out of funds in receiver's hands before anything is paid on common stock. *Garrett v Edge Moor Iron Co, 194 A 15 (Ch Ct 1937),* aff'd, *199 A 671 (1938).*

Dividends on pledged stock belong to pledgee and cannot be attached in suit to another creditor of pledgor, and this is so regardless whether stock has been transferred into name of pledgee on corporation's books; pledgee is under duty to apply dividends to reduction of pledgor's debt. *Womack v De Witt, 10 A2d 504 (1939).*

Permitting class of stockholders to purchase with their dividends no par common stock at value considerably below market price does not amount to declaration of additional dividend to favored class even though stock so bought could be sold at profit, since such profit was not being taken out of corporation's earnings. *Bodell v General Gas & Electric Corp, 132 A 442 (Ch Ct 1926).*

Upon reclassification of stock by which preferred stock was changed into stock of different character and its dividend arrearages extinguished, stockholder, who acquiesced in change and accepted dividends on new stock, has no standing in court to complain against change and ask for dividend arrearages on his old shares. *Trounstine v Remington Rand, Inc, 194 A 95 (Ch Ct 1937).*

.2 Business judgment, dividend payment.—Minority shareholders could not compel corporation's board to pay quarterly dividend once corporation had merged and shareholders received cash for value of shares because board's failure to declare dividend was exercise of its business judgment. *Gabelli & Co Profit Sharing Plan v Liggett Group Inc, 479 A2d 276 (1984).*

Minority shareholder could not bring action alleging that payment to majority shareholder was actually de facto dividend resulting in debt to minority shareholder of undistributed dividends because directors may determine when to declare dividends and court has little leeway to decide whether directors have declared dividends in which all shareholders have right to share. *The Mann-Paller Foundation, Inc v Econometric Research, Inc, 644 FSupp 92 (DC DC 1986).*

174 LIABILITY OF DIRECTORS FOR UNLAWFUL PAYMENT OF DIVIDEND OR UNLAWFUL STOCK PURCHASE OR REDEMPTION; EXONERATION FROM LIABILITY; CONTRIBUTION AMONG DIRECTORS; SUBROGATION.—(a) In case of any wilful or negligent violation of §160 or 173 of this title, the directors under whose administration the same may happen shall be jointly and severally liable, at any time within 6 years after paying such unlawful dividend or after such unlawful stock purchase or redemption, to the corporation, and to its creditors in the event of its dissolution or insolvency, to the full amount of the dividend unlawfully paid, or to the full amount unlawfully paid for the purchase or redemption of the corporation's stock, with interest from the time such liability accrued. Any director who may have been absent when the same was done, or who may have dissented from the act or resolution by which the same was done, may [1]*be exonerated* from such liability by causing [2]*his or her* dissent to be entered on the books containing the minutes of the proceedings of the directors at the time the same was done, or immediately after [3]*such director* has notice of the same.

(b) Any director against whom a claim is successfully asserted under this section shall be entitled to contribution from the other directors who voted for or concurred in the unlawful dividend, stock purchase or stock redemption.

(c) Any director against whom a claim is successfully asserted under this section shall be entitled, to the extent of the amount paid by [4]*such director* as a result of such claim, to be subrogated to the rights of the corporation against stockholders who received the dividend on, or assets for the sale or redemption of, their stock with knowledge of facts indicating that such dividend, stock purchase or redemption was unlawful under this chapter, in proportion to the amounts received by such stockholders respectively. (Last amended by Ch. 339, L. '98, eff. 7-1-98.)

Ch. 339, L. '98, eff. 7-1-98, added matter in italic and deleted [1]"exonerate himself"; [2]"his"; [3]"he"; and [4]"him".

Ch. 339, L. '98 Synopsis of Section 174

The amendments to these Sections eliminate masculine references in the statutes, and replace them with gender neutral references.

Comment: Section 174 provides a penalty for the willful violation of §243, obviously in respect to the purchase or redemption of the corporation's own stock authorized by the existing §243. The authority to purchase or redeem stock will now be contained in §160 and the reference to that section is sufficient. Therefore, §174 should be amended by deletion of the reference to §243.

.1 Liability of directors.—Liability of directors under this section is not intended to be penal, but is aimed at making directors compensate creditors for wrongful dilution of corporation's capital, and courts of other states will enforce this liability. *Stratton v Bertles, 238 AD 87, 263 NY 466 (1933).*

Since statute permits it, directors can pay preferred stock dividends out of net profits for current or preceding year; charter provision that dividends could be paid only out of "net earnings" did not restrict directors' power when, at time charter provision was adopted, statute permitted dividends only out of "surplus or net profits." *Weinberg v Baltimore Brick Co, 108 A2d 81 (Ch Ct 1954).*

Parent corporation which dominates subsidiary's board of directors not liable to it in derivative action for dividends paid by subsidiary in excess of earnings when such payments were made out of surplus net profits in compliance with state statute since no showing that (1) dividend declaration resulted from fraud or overreaching by parent, or (2) parent received benefit to exclusion of subsidiary's minority stockholders. *Sinclair Oil Corp v Levien, 280 A2d 717 (1971).*

On remand, a court that is directed to apply an entire fairness standard to a transaction is not required to revisit all its previous factual findings and resolve all disputed inferences against the defendants when deciding contested issues of fact. *Emerald Partners v Berlin, 2003 Del. Ch. LEXIS 42 (Ch Ct),* aff'd, *840 A2d 641 (2003).*

.2 Liability of pre-merger directors.—Creditors of post-merger corporation that goes bankrupt cannot sue pre-merger corporation's board of directors for allegedly illegally impairing stated capital through redemption of corporate stock; only creditors who extended credit to pre-merger corporation based on that corporation's stated capital can sue. *Johnston v Wolfe, No. 6682 (Ch Ct 2-24-83).*

SUBCHAPTER VI. STOCK TRANSFERS

201 TRANSFER OF STOCK, STOCK CERTIFICATES AND UNCERTIFICATED STOCK.—[1]*Except as otherwise provided in this chapter, the transfer of stock and the certificates of stock which represent the stock or uncertificated stock shall be governed by Article 8 of subtitle I of Title 6. To the extent that any provision of this chapter is inconsistent with any provision of subtitle I of Title 6, this chapter shall be controlling.* (Last amended by Ch. 112, L. '83, eff. 7-1-83.)

Ch. 112, L. '83, eff. 7-1-83, added matter in italic and deleted [1]"Except as otherwise provided in this chapter, the transfer of stock and the certificates of stock which represent the stock shall be governed by Article 8 of Title 5A."

.1 Compelling transfer.—Court would not order transfer of stock certificates because stockholder failed to show that he had presented a certificate to corporation with request to register transfer as required under Delaware law. *Wanland v C E Thompson Co, 380 NE2d 1012 (Ill App Ct 1978).*

202 [1]***RESTRICTIONS ON TRANSFER AND OWNERSHIP OF SECURITIES.—***
(a) A written restriction or restrictions on the transfer or registration of transfer of a security of a corporation, or on the amount of the corporation's securities that may be owned by any person or group of persons, if permitted by this section and noted conspicuously on the certificate or certificates representing the security or securities so restricted or, in the case of uncertificated shares, contained in the notice or notices sent pursuant to §151(f) of this title, may be enforced against the holder of the restricted security or securities or any successor or transferee of the holder including an executor, administrator, trustee, guardian or other fiduciary entrusted with like responsibility for the person or estate of the holder. Unless noted conspicuously on the certificate or certificates representing the security or securities so restricted or, in the case of uncertificated shares, contained in the notice or notices sent pursuant to §151(f) of this title, a restriction, even though permitted by this section, is ineffective except against a person with actual knowledge of the restriction.

(b) A restriction on the transfer or registration of transfer of securities of a corporation, or on the amount of a corporation's securities that may be owned by any person or group of persons, may be imposed by the certificate of incorporation or by the bylaws or by an agreement among any number of security holders or among such holders and the corporation. No restrictions so imposed shall be binding with respect to securities issued prior to the adoption of the restriction unless the holders of the securities are parties to an agreement or voted in favor of the restriction.

(c) A restriction on the transfer or registration of transfer of securities of a corporation or on the amount of such securities that may be owned by any person or group of persons is permitted by this section if it:

(1) Obligates the holder of the restricted securities to offer to the corporation or to any other holders of securities of the corporation or to any other person or to any combination of the foregoing, a prior opportunity, to be exercised within a reasonable time, to acquire the restricted securities; or

(2) Obligates the corporation or any holder of securities of the corporation or any other person or any combination of the foregoing, to purchase the securities which are the subject of an agreement respecting the purchase and sale of the restricted securities; or

(3) Requires the corporation or the holders of any class or series of securities of the corporation to consent to any proposed transfer of the restricted securities or to approve the proposed transferee of the restricted securities, or to approve the amount of securities of the corporation that may be owned by an person or group of persons; or

(4) Obligates the holder of the restricted securities to sell or transfer an amount of restricted securities to the corporation or to any other holders of securities of the corporation or to any other person or to any combination of the foregoing, or causes or results in the automatic sale or transfer of an amount of restricted securities to the corporation or to any other holders of securities of the corporation or to any other person or to any combination of the foregoing; or

(5) Prohibits or restricts the transfer of the restricted securities to, or the ownership of restricted securities by, designated persons or classes of persons or groups of persons, and such designation is not manifestly unreasonable.

(d) Any restriction on the transfer or the registration of transfer of the securities of a corporation, or on the amount of securities of a corporation that may be owned by a person or group of persons, for any of the following purposes shall be conclusively presumed to be for a reasonable purpose:

(1) Maintaining any local, state, federal or foreign tax advantage to the corporation or its stockholders, including without limitation:

a. Maintaining the corporation's status as an electing small business corporation under subchapter S of the United States Internal Revenue Code [26 U.S.C. §1371 et seq.], or

b. Maintaining or preserving any tax attribute (including without limitation net operating losses), or

c. Qualifying or maintaining the qualification of the corporation as a real estate investment trust pursuant to the United States Internal Revenue Code or regulations adopted pursuant to the United States Internal Revenue Code, or

(2) Maintaining any statutory or regulatory advantage or complying with any statutory or regulatory requirements under applicable local, state, federal or foreign law.

(e) Any other lawful restriction on transfer or registration of transfer of securities, or on the amount of securities that may be owned by any person or group of persons, is permitted by this section. (Last amended by Ch. 123, L. '99, eff. 7-1-99.)

Ch. 123, L. '99, eff. 7-1-99, added matter in italic and deleted [1]"RESTRICTION ON TRANSFER OF SECURITIES. (a) A written restriction on the transfer or registration of transfer of a security of a corporation, if permitted by this section and noted conspicuously on the certificate representing the security or, in the case of uncertificated shares, contained in the notice sent pursuant to subsection (f) of §151 of this title, may be enforced against the holder of the restricted security or any successor or transferee of the holder including an executor, administrator, trustee, guardian or other fiduciary entrusted with like responsibility for the person or estate of the holder. Unless noted conspicuously on the certificate representing the security or, in the case of uncertificated shares, contained in the notice sent pursuant to subsection (f) of §151 of this title, a restriction, even though permitted by this section, is ineffective except against a person with actual knowledge of the restriction.

(b) A restriction on the transfer or registration of transfer of securities of a corporation may be imposed either by the certificate of incorporation or by the bylaws or by an agreement among any number of security holders or among such holders and the corporation. No restriction so imposed shall be binding with respect to securities issued prior to the adoption of the restriction unless the holders of the securities are parties to an agreement or voted in favor of the restriction.

(c) A restriction on the transfer of securities of a corporation is permitted by this section if it:

(1) Obligates the holder of the restricted securities to offer to the corporation or to any other holders of securities of the corporation or to any other person or to any combination of the foregoing, a prior opportunity, to be exercised within a reasonable time, to acquire the restricted securities; or

(2) Obligates the corporation or any holder of securities of the corporation or any other person or any combination of the foregoing, to purchase the securities which are the subject of an agreement respecting the purchase and sale of the restricted securities; or

(3) Requires the corporation or the holders of any class of securities of the corporation to consent to any proposed transfer of the restricted securities or to approve the proposed transferee of the restricted securities; or

(4) Prohibits the transfer of the restricted securities to designated persons or classes of persons, and such designation is not manifestly unreasonable.

(d) Any restriction on the transfer of the shares of a corporation for the purpose of maintaining its status as an electing small business corporation under subchapter S of the United States Internal Revenue Code [26 USCA §1371 et seq.] or of maintaining any other tax advantage to the corporation is conclusively presumed to be for a reasonable purpose.

(e) Any other lawful restriction on transfer or registration of transfer of securities is permitted by this section."

Ch. 123, L. '99 Synopsis of Section 202

The amendments to Section 202 clarify that reasonable written restrictions on the amount of a corporation's securities that may be owned by any person or group of persons are permitted under the General Corporation Law. Subsection (c) of Section 202 has been amended to provide that a restriction on transfer or ownership generally is permitted by Section 202 if it obligates the holder of restricted securities to sell or transfer restricted securities or if it causes or results in the automatic sale or transfer of restricted securities. The amendment to subsection (d) clarifies that maintaining or preserving tax attributes (including net operating losses) and qualifying a corporation as a real estate investment trust are among the tax advantages that are conclusively presumed to constitute a reasonable purpose for imposing restrictions on transfer or ownership. Subsection (d) also has been amended to provide that restrictions imposed for the purpose of maintaining any statutory or regulatory advantage or complying with any statutory or regulatory requirements under applicable law are conclusively presumed to be for a reasonable purpose.

The amendments to Section 202 regarding restrictions on the amounts of securities that may be owned by any person or group are not intended to impact existing law relating to other types of limitations or restrictions on the rights of security holders based on the amount of securities owned, such as limitations on voting rights, conversion rights, or redemption rights.

.1 Validity of transfer restrictions —Restrictions as to transfer placed upon stock certificates without authority in statute, articles of incorporation or bylaws are invalid. *Standard Scale and Supply Corp v Chappel, 141 A 191 (Ch Ct 1928).*

Compelling stockholder to sell his stock to corporation whenever directors see fit to require him to do so is unreasonable and invalid restraint upon alienation of stock. *Greene v E H Rollins & Sons, Inc, 2 A2d 249 (Ch Ct 1938).*

Restraint against sale of voting trust certificate holders' interest for ten years is unreasonable and so makes voting trust agreement itself invalid. *Tracey v Franklin, 61 A2d 780 (Ch Ct 1948),* aff'd, *67 A2d 56 (1949).*

Transfer restriction requiring stockholder first to offer his shares to corporation for fixed period of time before selling to outsiders is reasonable and valid. *Lawson v Household Finance Corp, 152 A 723 (1930).*

Restrictions placed on voting trust agreements subject to reasonableness test even though statute permits any "lawful" restrictions. *Grynberg v Burke, 378 A2d 139 (Ch Ct 1977).*

Bylaw restricting stock transfers to aliens in excess of "permitted percentage" to be determined by board of directors could not be imposed on shares issued and outstanding before bylaw's adoption unless shareholder was party to an agreement or voted in favor of bylaw, even though restriction notice was imprinted on all stock certificates transferred since bylaw's adoption. *Joseph E Seagram & Sons, Inc v Conoco, Inc, 519 FSupp 506 (D Del 1981).*

Employees' stock could be purchased by corporation at price set by directors because (1) employees were contractually bound to sell their stock back to corporation by terms of trust created to hold employee-owned stock, (2) employees had full notice of requirement, (3) trust agreement serves same ends as certificate of incorporation, and (4) trust agreement is not contrary to Delaware law. *Goldberg v United Parcel Service of America, 605 FSupp 588 (EDNY 1985).*

Court refused to issue a preliminary injunction to enforce terms of shareholders' agreement restricting transfer of corporation's stock conversion of shares effectuated by merger of old corporation and successor corporation did not constitute transfer or disposition of old corporation's shares that triggered right of first refusal under shareholders' agreement. *Shields v Shields, No. 7829 (Ch Ct 7-22-85).*

A corporation's compulsory stock transfer provision may be included in the corporation's by-law and does not have to be in the corporation's certificate of incorporation. *Capano v The Wilmington Country Club, 2001 Del Ch LEXIS 127 (Ch Ct 2001).*

203 BUSINESS COMBINATIONS WITH INTERESTED STOCKHOLDERS.—

(a) Notwithstanding any other provisions of this chapter, a corporation shall not engage in any business combination with any interested stockholder for a period of 3 years following the time that such stockholder became an interested stockholder, unless:

(1) Prior to such time the board of directors of the corporation approved either the business combination or the transaction which resulted in the stockholder becoming an interested stockholder;

(2) Upon consummation of the transaction which resulted in the stockholder becoming an interested stockholder, the interested stockholder owned at least 85% of the voting stock of the corporation outstanding at the time the transaction commenced, excluding for purposes of determining the voting stock outstanding (but not the outstanding voting stock owned by the interested stockholder) those shares owned (i) by persons who are directors and also officers and (ii) employee stock plans in which employee participants do not have the right to determine confidentially whether shares held subject to the plan will be tendered in a tender or exchange offer; or

(3) At or subsequent to such time the business combination is approved by the board of directors and authorized at an annual or special meeting of stockholders, and not by written consent, by the affirmative vote of at least 66 ⅔ % of the outstanding voting stock which is not owned by the interested stockholder.

(b) The restrictions contained in this section shall not apply if:

(1) The corporation's original certificate of incorporation contains a provision expressly electing not to be governed by this section;

(2) The corporation, by action of its board of directors, adopts an amendment to its bylaws within 90 days of February 2, 1988, expressly electing not to be governed by this section, which amendment shall not be further amended by the board of directors;

(3) The corporation, by action of its stockholders, adopts an amendment to its certificate of incorporation or bylaws expressly electing not to be governed by this section; provided that, in addition to any other vote required by law, such amendment to the certificate of incorporation or bylaws must be approved by the affirmative vote of a majority of the shares entitled to vote. An amendment adopted pursuant to this paragraph shall be effective immediately in the case of a corporation that both (i) has never had a class of voting stock that falls within any of the 3 categories set out in subsection (b)(4) hereof, and (ii) has not elected by a provision in its original certificate of incorporation or any amendment thereto to be governed by this section. In all other cases, an amendment adopted pursuant to this paragraph shall not be effective until 12 months after the adoption of such amendment and shall not apply to any business combination between such corporation and any person who became an interested stockholder of such corporation on or prior to such adoption. A bylaw amendment adopted pursuant to this paragraph shall not be further amended by the board of directors;

(4) The corporation does not have a class of voting stock that is: (i) Listed on a national securities exchange; (ii) [1]*or* held of record by more than 2,000 stockholders, unless any of the foregoing results from action taken, directly or indirectly, by an interested stockholder or from a transaction in which a person becomes an interested stockholder;

(5) A stockholder becomes an interested stockholder inadvertently and (i) as soon as practicable divests itself of ownership of sufficient shares so that the stockholder ceases to be an interested stockholder; and (ii) would not, at any time within the 3-year period immediately prior to a business combination between the corporation and such stockholder, have been an interested stockholder but for the inadvertent acquisition of ownership;

(6) The business combination is proposed prior to the consummation or abandonment of and subsequent to the earlier of the public announcement or the notice required hereunder of a proposed transaction which (i) constitutes one of the transactions described in the 2nd sentence of this paragraph; (ii) is with or by a person who either was not an interested stockholder during the previous 3 years or who became an interested stockholder with the approval of the corporation's board of directors or during the period described in paragraph (7) of this subsection (b); and (iii) is approved or not opposed by a majority of the members of the board of directors then in office (but not less than 1) who were directors prior to any person becoming an interested stockholder during the previous 3 years or were recommended for election or elected to succeed such directors by a majority of such directors. The proposed transactions referred to in the preceding sentence are limited to (x) a merger or consolidation of the corporation (except for a merger in respect of which, pursuant to §251(f) of the title, no vote of the stockholders of the corporation is required); (y) a sale, lease, exchange, mortgage, pledge, transfer or other disposition (in 1 transaction or a series of transactions), whether as part of a dissolution or otherwise, of assets of the corporation or of any direct or indirect majority-owned subsidiary of the corporation (other

than to any direct or indirect wholly-owned subsidiary or to the corporation) having an aggregate market value equal to 50% or more of either that aggregate market value of all of the assets of the corporation determined on a consolidated basis or the aggregate market value of all the outstanding stock of the corporation; or (z) a proposed tender or exchange offer for 50% or more of the outstanding voting stock of the corporation. The corporation shall give not less than 20 days' notice to all interested stockholders prior to the consummation of any of the transactions described in clause (x) or (y) of the 2nd sentence of this paragraph; or

(7) The business combination is with an interested stockholder who became an interested stockholder at a time when the restrictions contained in this section did not apply by reason of any of paragraphs (1) through (4) of this subsection (b), provided, however, that this paragraph (7) shall not apply if, at the time such interested stockholder became an interested stockholder, the corporation's certificate of incorporation contained a provision authorized by the last sentence of this subsection (b).

Notwithstanding paragraphs (1), (2), (3) and (4) of this subsection, a corporation may elect by a provision of its original certificate of incorporation or any amendment thereto to be governed by this section; provided that any such amendment to the certificate of incorporation shall not apply to restrict a business combination between the corporation and an interested stockholder of the corporation if the interested stockholder became such prior to the effective date of the amendment.

(c) As used in this section only, the term:

(1) "Affiliate" means a person that directly, or indirectly through 1 or more intermediaries, controls, or is controlled by, or is under common control with, another person.

(2) "Associate," when used to indicate a relationship with any person, means: (i) Any corporation, partnership, unincorporated association or other entity of which such person is a director, officer or partner or is, directly or indirectly, the owner of 20% or more of any class of voting stock; (ii) any trust or other estate in which such person has at least a 20% beneficial interest or as to which such person serves as trustee or in a similar fiduciary capacity; and (iii) any relative or spouse of such person, or any relative of such spouse, who has the same residence as such person.

(3) "Business combination," when used in reference to any corporation and any interested stockholder of such corporation, means:

(i) Any merger or consolidation of the corporation or any direct or indirect majority-owned subsidiary of the corporation with (A) the interested stockholder, or (B) with any other corporation, partnership, unincorporated association or other entity if the merger or consolidation is caused by the interested stockholder and as a result of such merger or consolidation subsection (a) of this section is not applicable to the surviving entity;

(ii) Any sale, lease, exchange, mortgage, pledge, transfer or other disposition (in 1 transaction or a series of transactions), except proportionately as a stockholder of such corporation, to or with the interested stockholder, whether as part of a dissolution or otherwise, of assets of the corporation or of any direct or indirect majority-owned subsidiary of the corporation which assets have an aggregate market value equal to 10% or more of either the aggregate market value of all the assets of the corporation determined on a consolidated basis or the aggregate market value of all the outstanding stock of the corporation;

(iii) Any transaction which results in the issuance or transfer by the corporation or by any direct or indirect majority-owned subsidiary of the corporation of any stock of the corporation or of such subsidiary to the interested stockholder, except: (A) Pursuant to the exercise, exchange or conversion of securities exercisable for, exchangeable for or convertible into stock of such corporation or any such subsidiary which securities were outstanding prior to the time that the interested stockholder became such; (B) pursuant to a merger under §251(g) of this title; (C) pursuant to a dividend or distribution paid or made, or the exercise, exchange or conversion of securities exercisable for, exchangeable for or convertible into stock of such corporation or any such subsidiary which security is distributed, pro rata to all holders of a class or series of stock of such corporation subsequent to the time the interested stockholder became such; (D) pursuant to an exchange offer by the corporation to purchase stock made on the same terms to all holders of said stock; or (E) any issuance or transfer of stock by the corporation; provided however, that in no case under

§203

items (C)-(E) of this subparagraph shall there be an increase in the interested stockholder's proportionate share of the stock of any class or series of the corporation or of the voting stock of the corporation;

(iv) Any transaction involving the corporation or any direct or indirect majority-owned subsidiary of the corporation which has the effect, directly or indirectly, of increasing the proportionate share of the stock of any class or series, or securities convertible into the stock of any class or series, of the corporation or of any such subsidiary which is owned by the interested stockholder, except as a result of immaterial changes due to fractional share adjustments or as a result of any purchase or redemption of any shares of stock not caused, directly or indirectly, by the interested stockholder; or

(v) Any receipt by the interested stockholder of the benefit, directly or indirectly (except proportionately as a stockholder of such corporation) of any loans, advances, guarantees, pledges, or other financial benefits (other than those expressly permitted in subparagraphs (i)-(iv) of this paragraph) provided by or through the corporation or any direct or indirect majority-owned subsidiary.

(4) "Control," including the terms "controlling," "controlled by" and "under common control with," means the possession, directly or indirectly, of the power to direct or cause the direction of the management and policies of a person, whether through the ownership of voting stock, by contract or otherwise. A person who is the owner of 20% or more of the outstanding voting stock of any corporation, partnership, unincorporated association or other entity shall be presumed to have control of such entity, in the absence of proof by a preponderance of the evidence to the contrary. Notwithstanding the foregoing, a presumption of control shall not apply where such person holds voting stock, in good faith and not for the purpose of circumventing this section, as an agent, bank, broker, nominee, custodian or trustee for 1 or more owners who do not individually or as a group have control of such entity.

(5) "Interested stockholder" means any person (other than the corporation and any direct or indirect majority-owned subsidiary of the corporation) that (i) is the owner of 15% or more of the outstanding voting stock of the corporation, or (ii) is an affiliate or associate of the corporation and was the owner of 15% or more of the outstanding voting stock of the corporation at any time within the 3-year period immediately prior to the date on which it is sought to be determined whether such person is an interested stockholder, and the affiliates and associates of such person; provided, however, that the term "interested stockholder" shall not include (x) any person who (A) owned shares in excess of the 15% limitation set forth herein as of, or acquired such shares pursuant to a tender offer commenced prior to, December 23, 1987, or pursuant to an exchange offer announced prior to the aforesaid date and commenced within 90 days thereafter and either (I) continued to own shares in excess of such 15% limitation or would have but for action by the corporation or (II) is an affiliate or associate of the corporation and so continued (or so would have continued but for action by the corporation) to be the owner of 15% or more of the outstanding voting stock of the corporation at any time within the 3-year period immediately prior to the date on which it is sought to be determined whether such a person is an interested stockholder or (B) acquired said shares from a person described in item (A) of this paragraph by gift, inheritance or in a transaction in which no consideration was exchanged; or (y) any person whose ownership of shares in excess of the 15% limitation set forth herein is the result of action taken solely by the corporation; provided that such person shall be an interested stockholder if thereafter such person acquires additional shares of voting stock of the corporation, except as a result of further corporate action not caused, directly or indirectly, by such person. For the purpose of determining whether a person is an interested stockholder, the voting stock of the corporation deemed to be outstanding shall include stock deemed to be owned by the person through application of paragraph (9) of this subsection but shall not include any other unissued stock of such corporation which may be issuable pursuant to any agreement, arrangement or understanding, or upon exercise of conversion rights, warrants or options, or otherwise.

(6) "Person" means any individual, corporation, partnership, unincorporated association or other entity.

(7) "Stock" means, with respect to any corporation, capital stock and, with respect to any other entity, any equity interest.

(8) "Voting stock" means, with respect to any corporation, stock of any class or series entitled to vote generally in the election of directors and, with respect to any entity that is not a corporation, any equity interest entitled to vote generally in the election of the governing body of such entity. Every reference to a percentage of voting stock shall refer to such percentage of the votes of such voting stock.

(9) "Owner" including the terms "own" and "owned" when used with respect to any stock means a person that individually or with or through any of its affiliates or associates:

(i) Beneficially owns such stock, directly or indirectly; or

(ii) Has (A) the right to acquire such stock (whether such right is exercisable immediately or only after the passage of time) pursuant to any agreement, arrangement or understanding, or upon the exercise of conversion rights, exchange rights, warrants or options, or otherwise; provided, however, that a person shall not be deemed the owner of stock tendered pursuant to a tender or exchange offer made by such person or any of such person's affiliates or associates until such tendered stock is accepted for purchase or exchange; or (B) the right to vote such stock pursuant to any agreement, arrangement or understanding; provided, however, that a person shall not be deemed the owner of any stock because of such person's right to vote such stock if the agreement, arrangement or understanding to vote such stock arises solely from a revocable proxy or consent given in response to a proxy or consent solicitation made to 10 or more persons; or

(iii) Has any agreement, arrangement or understanding for the purpose of acquiring, holding, voting (except voting pursuant to a revocable proxy or consent as described in item (B) of subparagraph (ii) of this paragraph), or disposing of such stock with any other person that beneficially owns, or whose affiliates or associates beneficially own, directly or indirectly, such stock.

(d) No provision of a certificate of incorporation or bylaw shall require, for any vote of stockholders required by this section, a greater vote of stockholders than that specified in this section.

(e) The Court of Chancery is hereby vested with exclusive jurisdiction to hear and determine all matters with respect to this section. (Last amended by Ch. 145, L. '07, eff. 8-1-07.)

Ch. 145, L. '07, eff. 8-1-07, added matter in italic and deleted [1]"authorized for quotation on the NASDAQ Stock Market; or (iii)".

Ch. 145, L. '07 Synopsis of Section 203

This amendment revises the specifications regarding the application of §203, in order to accommodate ongoing changes in the structure and identification of securities trading markets, including recent changes in the configuration and status of securities trading markets administered by The NASDAQ Stock Market, Inc.

Ch. 298, L. '02 Synopsis of Section 203

The amendments to Sections 203(a)(2), 203(c)(8), 212(a) and 223(c) clarify that references to "voting stock" or "shares" therein and elsewhere in the title, including in Sections 203, 223 and 253, are intended to adopt the voting power concept reflected in Section 212(a). The parenthetical phrase added to Section 203(a)(2) is intended to make it clear that while voting stock owned by persons who are directors and also officers and by certain employee stock plans would not be included in determining the total amount of voting stock outstanding to calculate the 85% exemption, that voting stock would be included in the determination of the amount of voting stock owned by the interested stockholder. The amendment to Section 203(c)(5) is intended to refer to the paragraph defining the term "owner". This reference should have been changed when the definition of "stock" was added in 1995.

Ch. 79, L. '95 Synopsis of Section 203

Section 203(a) has been altered to conform to recent case law interpreting the word "date" in that subsection to mean a specific time. Section 203(b)(3) of the statute has been amended to provide expressly that corporations that have never been subject to Section 203 may elect not to be governed by Section 203 without being subject to a waiting period. The change to Section 203(b)(4) reflects changes in the NASDAQ system. The amendment to Section 203(b)(5) clarifies that a person who becomes an interested stockholder inadvertently may divest itself of shares owned in any manner in order to avoid application of the restrictions contained in the statute. A new Section 203(b)(7) has been added to provide expressly that stockholders who become interested when the corporation is not covered by the statute will not be subject to the statutory restrictions if the corporation later becomes covered by the statute. The last sentence of Section 203(b)(6) has been moved to the end of the Section to clarify that it is intended to apply to all of Section 203(b).

A number of changes have been made to Section 203(c), which defines the terms used throughout the statute. The amendment to the definition of "business combination" in Section 203(c)(3)(i) makes to clear that mergers with non-corporate entities may not be used to evade the provisions of the statute. The change to Section 203(c)(3)(iii) makes it clear that holding company mergers, authorized by new Section 251(g), are not "business combinations" for the purposes of the statute. In addition, the definitions of "associate," "control" and "voting stock" have been amended and a definition of "stock" has been added to address equity interests in non-corporate entities. The definition of "interested stockholder" contained in Section 203(c)(5) has been amended by expanding a so- called "grandfather" provision (which prevents the statute from affecting negatively stockholders whose 15% or greater ownership interest predates the enactment of the statute) to make it clear that a grandfathered stockholder of the corporation who transfers stock so as to become a less than 15% stockholder, but continues to be an affiliate or associate of the corporation, will not thereby become an interested stockholder as a result of the so-called "look back" provisions of Section 203(c)(5)(ii).

Current Section 203

.1 Constitutionality.—Tender offeror's motion for preliminary injunction against target corporation to enjoin it from utilizing or enforcing the Delaware Business Combination Statute was denied when tender offeror failed to show irreparable injury, because (1) Section 203 could not stand as major roadblock to proposed merger when tender offeror could opt out of statute, and with or without Section 203, tender offeror's position would be exactly the same; and (2) tender offeror failed to show that Section 203's presence could affect its ability to complete tender offer because of a possible confusion in the marketplace about its constitutionality. *The Black and Decker Corp v American Standard Inc, 679 FSupp 1183 (D Del 1988).*

Court declined to issue preliminary injunction barring enforcement of Delaware's antitakeover statute, which restricts business transactions with interested shareholders. Plaintiff failed to establish reasonable probability of proving that statute is preempted by Williams Act [15 USC §78m(d)-(e); 78n(d)-(f)] or violates Commerce Clause. In addition, plaintiff failed to establish reasonable probability that target's directors violated fiduciary duties to shareholders by refusing to redeem poison pill rights. Refusal to redeem was reasonable in light of risk posed by plaintiff's offer. *BNS Inc v Koppers Co, 683 FSupp 458 (D Del 1988).*

Takeover law that protects shareholders will not contravene Williams Act even if it has some deterrent effect on hostile tender offers. Further, there was no violation of Commerce Clause because GCL §203 does not discriminate against interstate commerce by favoring resident offerors over nonresidents, it regulates only Delaware corporations, and it does not place burden on interstate commerce in excess of its local benefits. *RP Acquisition Corp v Staley Continental, Inc, No. 88-190-JRR (Ch Ct 5-9-88).*

Limited partnership making tender offer failed to convince federal court to enjoin enforcement of Delaware's antitakeover law as unconstitutional. Court rejected argument that law improperly delegates governmental authority to boards of private corporations in Delaware. *City Capital Associates Limited Partnership v Interco, Inc, 696 FSupp 1551 (D Del 1988).*

Tender offeror could not seek a declaratory judgment that Two-Thirds Residual Vote Requirement of GCL §203(a)(3) was unconstitutional as applied to potential all shares hostile tender offer. *Reason:* No justiciable case or controversy existed because the all shares tender offer had not been commenced. Court therefore dismissed plaintiff's complaint. *SWT Acquisition Corp v TW Services, Inc, 700 FSupp 1323 (D Del 1988).*

.2 Duty to auction.—Sale of control of company is equivalent to sale of company for purposes for directors' duty to auction company to obtain maximum value to shareholders under *Revlon, Inc v MacAndrews & Forbes Holdings, Inc,* 503 A2d 173 (1986). Target's recapitalization plan, which was adopted during tender offer, involved sale of control and therefore triggered director's *Revlon* duty to act as auctioneer for shareholders. Court issued preliminary injunction to bar target from implementing defensive measures, i.e., new severance plan plus early vesting provisions for benefit plans. *The Black & Decker Corp v American Standard, Inc, 682 FSupp 772 (D Del 1988).*

.3 Settlement.—Proposed settlement of several class action lawsuits arising from management sponsored ESOP leveraged buyout was fair and reasonable, where plaintiffs did not show that: (1) Corporation's board, acting through Special Committee of outside directors who were not ESOP beneficiaries, was grossly negligent in failing to negotiate for mechanism that permitted market check; or that (2) Board was not acting in good faith when negotiating approved transaction. *In re Amsted Industries Incorporated Litigation,* Cons. Civil Action No. 8224 (Ch Ct 8-24-88).

.4 Exemption; court ordered.—Court refused to compel target's board to exempt tender offer from Delaware's antitakeover law. To do so would be to usurp board's managerial powers by forcing it to approve offer board believed to be unfair.

Court upheld bylaw amendments requiring 60 days notice before submitting nomination for board. *Nomad Acquisition Corp v Damon Corp,* No. 10173 (Ch Ct 9-16-88).

.5 Poison pill.—Court declined to preliminarily enjoin directors of target corporation from implementing poison pill. *Reasons:* (1) Evidence indicated that target's board adopted poison pill as a response to danger of unfair takeovers and to safeguard shareholders' interests; (2) Tender offeror did not claim that target's rights plan interfered with its ability to wage a proxy contest; (3) Evidence showed that target's board adopted plan pursuant to informed business judgment; (4) Poison pill did not preclude all hostile tender offers, and tender offer had been structured in such a way as to avoid pill's provisions; and (5) Evidence showed that directors did not adopt poison pill to entrench themselves in office. *Desert Partners, LP v USG Corp,* 686 FSupp 1289 (ND Ill 1988).

A board's adoption of defensive measures in advance of the elimination of the company's dual class voting structure is not unreasonable where (1) the board was dominated by disinterested and independent directors, (2) the board acted in response to a legitimate threat that the corporation's stockholders could be susceptible to either an inadequate and/or structurally coercive tender offer, or a rapid proxy contest based on such an offer, and (3) the defensive measures were noncoercive and nonpreclusive and reasonably proportionate to that threat. *In re Gaylord Container Corporation Shareholders Litigation,* C.A. No. 14616 (Ch Ct 1-26-00).

Adoption by a board of directors of a poison pill without justification for its action does not necessarily invalidate the defensive measure where no legally cognizable harm is alleged to emanate from the adoption of the measure. *Coates v Netro Corp,* 2002 Del. Ch. LEXIS 107 (Ch Ct 2002).

.6 Attorney's fees, correction tender offer disclosures.—Representative shareholder was entitled to attorneys' fees of $300,000, plus expenses, for his counsel's successful efforts in correcting misleading and coercive disclosures in connection with corporation's self-tender offer. The corrections benefited the corporation and its shareholders, and the corporation was required to pay the fee and expenses.

The shareholder was also entitled to attorneys' fees of $200,000, plus expenses, for his counsel's successful efforts in causing a change in corporation's dividend policy. Change in policy benefited preferred shareholders and the fee and expenses were to come from their dividends. *Eisenberg v Chicago Milwaukee Corp,* No. 9374 (Ch Ct 10-25-88).

Until the conclusion of the tender offer, acquirer owed no fiduciary duty to target's shareholders, nor did target's board bear legal responsibility for alleged nondisclosures in acquirer's offer to purchase, absent some proof that the two boards engaged in joint conduct to mislead shareholders. *Citron v Fairchild Camera and Instrument Corp,* 569 A2d 53 (1989).

.7 ESOP.—Court upheld validity of employee stock ownership plan adopted by target partly in response to acquisition overtures by outsider. Given ESOP's confidential tendering provisions, its antitakeover effect did not make it less than fair. ESOPs with that feature are not suspect under GCL §203 because they do not necessarily interfere with bidder's ability to obtain 85% of target's voting stock. *Shamrock Holdings, Inc v Polaroid Corp,* 559 A2d 257 (Ch Ct 1989).

Court declined to grant corporate acquirer's motion for permanent injunction to invalidate target's defensive measures. It also dismissed as unripe the acquirer's motion for summary judgment declaring that certain ESOP and convertible preferred shares should not be included as outstanding stock under Delaware statute governing when interested shareholders may engage in business combinations with a target company. *Kingsbridge Capital Group v Dunkin' Donuts, Inc,* No. 10907 (Ch Ct 8-7-89).

.8 Option agreement.—In an action by a former shareholder challenging the legality of a merger, the Court of Chancery held that there was a material issue of fact, precluding summary judgment, as to whether the acquiring company became an "interested stockholder" in the acquired company for purposes of Delaware's takeover statute (GCL §203), where both the draft and later-signed option agreement expressly stated that they were conditioned on the approval of the parties respective boards. The court held that the mere existence of such language did not preclude it, after hearing all of the evidence, from finding that the language was a sham or mere window dressing. *Siegman v Columbia Pictures Entertainment Inc,* No. 11,252 (Ch Ct 1-12-93).

Former Section 203

.1 Constitutionality.—Court permanently bars officers of target company from enforcing provisions of Delaware Tender Offers Act against tender offeror because Act causes unnecessary burden on interstate commerce and is pre-empted by Williams Act (the Federal Business Take-Over Act). *Dart Industries, Inc v Conrad,* 462 FSupp 1 (SD Ind 1978).

Court refused to grant tender offeror temporary restraining order enjoining target and attorney general from attempting to enforce Delaware Tender Offer Act because (1) there is no likelihood that Act will be enforced against tender offeror when everyone concedes that Act is unconstitutional and (2) process is "meaningless charade" that is waste of time and energy to all involved. *Loral Corp v Sanders Associates, Inc,* 639 FSupp 639 (D Del 1986).

.2 Class action.—In class action for alleged fraudulent tender offer by defendants, stockholder is entitled to counsel fees and expenses, even though he was not defrauded seller and had not relied on deceptions charged; he can recover counsel fees and expenses from defendants by showing he created substantial benefits for others in same class, and that they "brazenly" settled such class action without consulting him in violation of Rule 23 of Federal Rules of Civil Procedure. *Kahan v Rosenstiel, 424 F2d 161 (3d Cir 1970).*

.3 Information required.—Statute calling for tender offeror to furnish its balance sheet and income statements prior to making of tender offer was complied with when offeror gave a consolidated balance sheet and consolidated income statements of parent and subsidiaries, since those actually gave offeree information statute desired. *Monogram Industries, Inc v Royal Industries, Inc, 367 A2d 650 (1976).*

Tender offer enjoined unless supplemented by disclosures of net worth of individuals and estimate of personal assets used to secure bank loan because these aspects bear on stock tender offering price. *Pabst Brewing Co v Kalmanovitz, 551 FSupp 882 (D Del 1982).*

.4 Antifraud rule actions.—Stockholder could bring antifraud suit when corporation announced tender offer to buy up shares of his company at stipulated price and upon obtaining over 90% of shares consummated short-form merger in accordance with state law, giving remaining stockholders same stipulated price, since stockholder became forced seller and failure to state that he could seek appraisal rights was material omission; however, there was no obligation to disclose pershare earnings in tender offer material since such data was readily available in financial reports. *Valente v Pepsico, Inc, 454 FSupp 1228 (D Del 1978).*

.5 Fiduciary duty.—Tender offeror, which acquired approximately 34.8% of target's stock, and its stockholders owed target no fiduciary duty because they did not exercise control over target's affairs. *Lewis v Knutson, 699 F2d 230 (5th Cir 1983).*

Tender offer by majority stockholder corporation to obtain stock held by minority in order to boost majority's holdings to 90% so it could effectuate short-form merger was enjoined because majority violated its fiduciary duty to offer fair price and make full disclosure to minority. *Joseph v Shell Oil Co, 482 A2d 335 (Ch Ct 1984).*

Tender offeror that terminated first tender offer in favor of second offer which denied participation to some shareholders was not liable to those shareholders after they sold their shares in open market at substantial discount under offer price. Offeror owed no duty to target's shareholders and had unqualified right to terminate first tender offer upon occurrence of events specified in tender offer. However, offeror could be liable for conspiracy with target if target breached its fiduciary duty to shareholders with offeror's knowing participation. *Gilbert v The El Paso Co, Nos. 7075 and 7079 (consolidated) (Ch Ct 1984).*

Shareholder denied preliminary injunction restraining corporation and directors from issuing stock at stock sale because board had not breached fiduciary duty when it withdrew from stockholders, at stockholders' meeting, right to vote on bylaw amendment that repealed existing limitation on number of shares stockholders could own and then adopted amendment itself during meeting recess; it was not *per se* breach of fiduciary duty for directors to act against majority shareholders' wishes because there were other factors that directors could consider when exercising business judgment. *American International Rent A Car Inc v Cross, No. 7583 (Ch Ct 1984).*

Target's directors violated fiduciary duty to shareholders by granting lock-up and no-shop guarantees to white knight in exchange for protection of rights of holders of notes that target had exchanged earlier for stock in order to deter takeover by hostile tender offeror. Lock-up and no-shop guarantees harmed shareholders because guarantees foreclosed further bidding in active bidding situation and were made in directors' self-interest because they promoted agreement that relieved directors of potentially damaging consequences (suit by noteholders) of their own defensive policies. *Revlon, Inc v MacAndrews & Forbes Holdings, Inc, 506 A2d 173 (1986).*

Corporation and directors breached fiduciary duty to minority shareholders because (1) disclosures made in leveraged cash tender offer failed to adequately show basis for book value of land, which was corporation's primary asset or adequately disclose method used to arrive at tender offer price and (2) method used to select tender offer price was not likely to assure that minority shareholders would receive true value for their shares. *Kahn v United States Sugar Corp, No. 7313 (Ch Ct 12-10-85).*

Court dismissed shareholders' class actions claiming that president and director breached their fiduciary duties to shareholders by rejecting tender offer in order to maintain their positions in corporation because (1) president did not control or dominate board or have power to accept or reject proposals on corporation's behalf, (2) press release issued by president was proper since he said he would submit matter to directors, and (3) president and directors did not extract stand-still agreement from tender offeror and then violate it by failing to provide confidential information to offeror. *Lewis v Straetz, No. 7859 (Ch Ct 1986).*

.6 Violation of federal securities laws.— Shareholder could not bring action under Williams Act after she lost opportunity to profit from hostile tender offer (offer was rescinded and tender offeror substituted friendly, less lucrative offer) because she alleged no injury resulting from deception. *Schreiber v Burlington Northern Inc, 731 F2d 163 (3d Cir 1984).*

Offeror did not violate Williams Act proration rules when it withdrew one offer and substituted another allowing target's officers and directors to tender shares because offers were separate and distinct with two separate proration pools; offeror did not improperly treat target or its officers differently than tendering shareholders because agreements to purchase target's stock and to recognize officer's golden parachutes were collateral to tender offer so Williams Act did not apply. *Brill v Burlington Northern Inc, 590 FSupp 893 (1984).*

Raider that eventually made hostile bid did not violate §§14(d) and (e) of Williams Act when it allegedly failed to disclose plans to use proceeds from public offering to acquire this particular target because (1) raider did not have duty to disclose acquisition strategy until it formulated terms for tender offer and (2) at time public offering took place, raider had not yet reached internal decision regarding price and structure of deal. Therefore, target was not entitled to preliminary injunction against raider. *Revlon, Inc v Pantry Pride, Inc 621 FSupp 804 (D Del 1985).*

Target that operates television and radio stations licensed by FCC could not obtain injunction against tender offer for violations of Williams Act, because (1) Failure of offer to purchase to disclose that tender offeror's sole shareholder was once officer of company that FCC had censured was not material because shareholder bore no responsibility for company's censure. (2) Failure to disclose extent of offeror's previous marketing of pornography was not material because activities violate no law and would have no voice in management after takeover. *MacFadden Holdings, Inc v John Blair & Co, Civil Action No. 86-161 MMS (D Del 1986).*

Court dismissed claim that target's directors should have disclosed in Schedule 14D-9 of Securities Exchange Act of 1934 *pro forma* financial projections that were filed with ICC as part of target's responsive application concerning merger of two of its competitors. Although court declined to adopt *per se* rule that would render nondisclosable all "soft" information and, instead, adopted balancing approach on case-by case basis, information in projection was not reliable enough to necessitate disclosure. *Weinberger v Rio Grande Industries, Inc, 519 A2d 116 (Ch Ct 1986).*

.7 Injunction barring tender offer.—"White knight" could not get injunction barring tender offeror from attempting to acquire it after offeror agreed to refrain from attempting to acquire control of target, which "white knight" later acquired and merged with. Reasons: (1) agreement only contemplated control of target not "white knight" and (2) "white knight" did not succeed to benefit of agreement after merger with target when that was not parties' intention. *Mesa Partners v Phillips Petroleum Co, 488 A2d 107 (Ch Ct 1984).*

.8 Business judgment.—Directors had authority to adopt Rights Plan as preventive measure to ward off future advances by corporate raiders. Adoption of Plan was appropriate exercise of directors' business judgment when (1) action was not taken for entrenchment purposes, and (2) Plan was reasonable reaction by directors to perceived threat to corporation of coercive acquisition techniques. *Moran v Household International, Inc, 500 A2d 1346 (1985).*

Target's self-tender offer for 65% of its outstanding stock was not reasonable in relation to threat posed by takeover offer. Although target's directors could create option for shareholders permitting them to continue participation in target, they could not structure offer so that no rational shareholder would risk tendering into competing offer when to do so created risk of being frozen out of front end of self tender. *AC Acquisitions Corp v Anderson, Clayton & Co, 519 A2d 103 (Ch Ct 1986).*

Shareholders could not enjoin sale of three subsidiaries because (1) subsidiaries' sale would not constitute sale of "substantially all" of corporation's assets, (2) sale of assets did not mandate liquidation of corporation, and (3) shareholders were guilty of

§203

laches. Shareholders also could not enjoin special meeting of shareholders to vote on planned liquidation of parent because (1) three separate votes on plan were not required and (2) proxy statement was not materially misleading. *Bacine v Scharffenberger, No. 7862 (Ch Ct 12-10-84).*

Minority shareholders who brought suit against directors for accepting allegedly inequitable tender offer and lock-up agreement could not enjoin tender offer and annual shareholders' meeting because directors' decision to accept tender offer and lock-up agreement one month before meeting at which other offers might have materialized was protected by business judgment rule. *Thompson v Enstar Corp, Nos. 7641 & 7643 (Ch Ct 6-20-84).*

Corporation's self tender for its shares which excluded participation of shareholder making hostile tender offer for corporation's stock was valid because (1) selective stock repurchase plan was reasonable in relation to threat directors believed was posed by inadequate and coercive two-tier tender offer by corporate raider with reputation as "green-mailer" and (2) directors did not act in bad faith or to entrench themselves and therefore did not lose protection of business judgment rule when they tendered their shares in exchange offer since they were receiving benefits shared generally by all shareholders except raider. *Unocal Corp v Mesa Petroleum Co, 493 A2d 946 (1985).*

Court refused to enjoin target from enforcing acquisition triggered flip-in shareholder rights plan to prevent partial tender offer and proxy fight because plan was adopted as means for insuring orderly auction of target so was reasonable when (1) tender offeror might have decided later to engage in second-step merger, (2) offeror's larger holding of stock would deter other potential bidders, and (3) plan maximized shareholder welfare. *Dynamics Corporation of America v CTS Corp, 635 FSupp 1174 (ND Ill 1986),* supplemented by *638 FSupp 802.*

.9 Identifying class members.—Although target shareholders challenging termination of tender offer are required to perform mechanical task of assembling and collating names and addresses of each class member in single document, tender offeror must bear cost of identifying name and addresses of class members because it failed to direct its agent to retain relevant records after it had notice of shareholder's action. *Gilbert v The El Paso Co, Consolidated Civil Action Nos. 7075 and 7079 (Ch Ct 6-17-86).*

.10 Voting trust.—Court refused to restrain target's implementation of voting trust established by merger agreement with tender offeror because competing tender offeror was not threatened by immediate irreparable injury when (1) implementation of voting trust had already occurred, (2) threatened harm, takedown of shares tendered to tender offeror, would not be prevented by restraining voting trust, (3) target's shareholders were not being coerced by tender offeror's timing advantage over competing offeror, and (4) timing advantage resulted from competing offeror's own actions. *Macfadden Holdings, Inc v John Blair & Co, Civil Action No. 8489 (Ch Ct 7-2-86).*

.11 Short-swing profits; indemnification.—Successor by merger of original issuer of securities can bring action alleging that unsuccessful tender offeror received illegal short-swing profits under §16(b) of Securities Exchange Act of 1934 when it sold original issuer's stock because cause of action survives merger. Unsuccessful tender offeror was not entitled to be indemnified by corporation that acquired issuer pursuant to their indemnification agreement because (1) agreement does not apply to purchase and sale of shares when purchase occurred prior to effective date of agreement and (2) enforcement of indemnification agreement would violate public policy under §16(b). *Bunker Ramo-Eltra Corp v Fairchild Industries, Inc, 639 FSupp 409 (D Md 1986).*

.12 Discovery.—Tender offeror was entitled to discovery into basis for target board's deliberations in connection with decision to recommend against acceptance of offer. Potential acquiror was also entitled to discovery relating to consideration of question whether or not to address issue of redemption of stock rights, and into any decision not to redeem such rights. Target corporation was not, however, precluded from asserting a white knight discovery privilege in future, even though it could not do so at present because assertions had been made on too broad a basis. *Computervision Corp v Prime Computer, Inc, No. 9513 (Ch Ct filed 1-27-88).*

SUBCHAPTER VII. MEETINGS, ELECTIONS, VOTING AND NOTICE

211 MEETINGS OF STOCKHOLDERS.—(a)(1) Meetings of stockholders may be held at such place, either within or without this State as may be designated by or in the manner provided in the certificate of incorporation or bylaws, or if not so designated, as determined by the board of directors. If, pursuant to this paragraph or the certificate of incorporation or the bylaws of the corporation, the board of directors is authorized to determine the place of a meeting of stockholders, the board of directors may, in its sole discretion, determine that the meeting shall not be held at any place, but may instead be held solely by means of remote communication as authorized by paragraph (a)(2) of this section.

(2) If authorized by the board of directors in its sole discretion, and subject to such guidelines and procedures as the board of directors may adopt, stockholders and proxyholders not physically present at a meeting of stockholders may, by means of remote communication:

a. Participate in a meeting of stockholders; and

b. Be deemed present in person and vote at a meeting of stockholders, whether such meeting is to be held at a designated place or solely by means of remote communication, provided that (i) the corporation shall implement reasonable measures to verify that each person deemed present and permitted to vote at the meeting by means of remote communication is a stockholder or proxyholder, (ii) the corporation shall implement reasonable measures to provide such stockholders and proxyholders a reasonable opportunity to participate in the meeting and to vote on matters submitted to the stockholders, including an opportunity to read or hear the proceedings of the meeting substantially concurrently with such proceedings, and (iii) if any stockholder or proxyholder votes or takes other action at the meeting by means of remote communication, a record of such vote or other action shall be maintained by the corporation.

(b) Unless directors are elected by written consent in lieu of an annual meeting as permitted by this subsection, an annual meeting of stockholders shall be held for the election of directors on a date and at a time designated by or in the manner provided in the bylaws. Stockholders may, unless the certificate of incorporation otherwise provides, act by written consent to elect directors; provided, however, that, if such consent is less than unanimous, such action by written consent may be in lieu of holding an annual meeting only if all of the directorships to which directors could be elected at an annual meeting held at the effective time of such action are vacant and are filled by such action. Any other proper business may be transacted at the annual meeting.

(c) A failure to hold the annual meeting at the designated time or to elect a sufficient number of directors to conduct the business of the corporation shall not affect otherwise valid corporate acts or work a forfeiture or dissolution of the corporation except as may be otherwise specifically provided in this chapter. If the annual meeting for election of directors is not held on the date designated therefor or action by written consent to elect directors in lieu of an annual meeting has not been taken, the directors shall cause the meeting to be held as soon as is convenient. If there be a failure to hold the annual meeting or to take action by written consent to elect directors in lieu of an annual meeting for a period of 30 days after the date designated for the annual meeting, or if no date has been designated, for a period of 13 months after the latest to occur of the organization of the corporation, its last annual meeting or the last action by written consent to elect directors in lieu of an annual meeting, the Court of Chancery may summarily order a meeting to be held upon the application of any stockholder or director. The shares of stock represented at such meeting, either in person or by proxy, and entitled to vote thereat, shall constitute a quorum for the purpose of such meeting, notwithstanding any provision of the certificate of incorporation or bylaws to the contrary. The Court of Chancery may issue such orders as may be appropriate, including, without limitation, orders designating the time and place of such meeting, [1]*the record date or dates for determination of stockholders entitled to notice of the meeting and to vote thereat,* and the form of notice of such meeting.

(d) Special meetings of the stockholders may be called by the board of directors or by such person or persons as may be authorized by the certificate of incorporation or by the bylaws.

(e) All elections of directors shall be by written ballot unless otherwise provided in the certificate of incorporation; if authorized by the board of directors, such requirement of a written ballot, shall be satisfied by a ballot submitted by electronic transmission, provided that any such electronic transmission must either set forth or be submitted with information from which it can be determined that the electronic transmission was authorized by the stockholder or proxy holder. (Last amended by Ch. 14, L. '09, eff. 8-1-09.)

Ch. 14, L. '09, eff. 8-1-09, added matter in italic and deleted [1]"the record date for determination of stockholders entitled to vote".

Ch. 14, L. '09 Synopsis of Section 211

This section amends Section 211(c) to reflect the changes in Section 213(a) providing for separate record dates for determining stockholders entitled to notice of and to vote at a meeting.

Ch. 343, L. '00 Synopsis of Section 211

The amendment to Subsection (a) expands the use companies may make of new technologies in the conduct of stockholder meetings. Paragraph (1) allows stockholder meetings to be held entirely by remote communication, without a venue for physical attendance, if so determined by the board of directors in its sole discretion. In addition, paragraph (a)(1) eliminates the former default provision that provided, absent a bylaw identifying the location, that stockholder meetings be held at the corporation's registered office in Delaware. Paragraph (2) of subsection (a) authorizes stockholder participation by remote communication, as well as presence and voting by remote communication, if so determined by the board of directors in its sole discretion. Such presence and voting is permitted only if the corporation implements (i) verification procedures, (ii) measures to ensure such stockholders have an opportunity to participate in the meeting and vote, and (iii) means to record the votes of such stockholders.

The amendment to Subsection (e) defines written ballot to include ballots submitted by electronic transmission, as defined by Section 232.

Ch. 120, L. '97 Synopsis of Section 211

The amendments to subsections (b) and 9(c) of Section 211 are intended to address issues relating to the relationship between Sections 228 and 211 that have arisen in recent decisions by the Court of Chancery. Subsection (b) has been amended to provide that action by written consent to elect directors pursuant to Section 228 can be a substitute for an annual meeting but that, unless such action is unanimous, it will fulfill the annual meeting requirement only if all directorships corresponding to those to which directors could have been elected if an annual meeting had been held at the effective time of the written consent are filled by such action and only if at such effective time all such directorships are vacant. Thus, the replacement of sitting directors by less than unanimous stockholder action will require their removal or resignation prior to the effectiveness of the consent action that substitutes for the election of directors at the annual meeting. Unanimous written consent (as that term is used in subsection (d) of Section 228) may be taken in lieu of an annual meeting whether or not the directorships to be filled are then vacant (*i.e.* without the prior removal or resignation of sitting directors). Subsection 9(c) has been amended to provide that the remedy provided for in that subsection will not be available if action by written consent in lieu of a meeting is taken within the required time periods and that the thirteen month time period provided for therein will begin to run from the later of the organization of the corporation, the last annual meeting or the last action by written consent in lieu of an annual meeting.

Comment: The amendment to §220 is designed to codify the common law right of a director of a Delaware corporation to examine the stock list, books and records and to permit the director to obtain summary relief in the Court of Chancery to enforce his right. Pursuant to the present case law, it is not clear whether the Court of Chancery has jurisdiction over such an action by a director. The amendment is not intended to effect any substantive changes in the directors' rights to inspect such corporate records.

The second and third amendments to Sections 211(c) and 225 are to permit a director as well as a stockholder to bring an action in the Delaware Court of Chancery to require the holding of an annual meeting, to determine the validity of any election and the right of a person to hold office. At the present time, the relevant case law does not permit a director to bring such an action in the Court of Chancery; it is limited to stockholders.

.1 Postponement of meeting.—Court will not postpone stockholders' meeting on ground stockholder needs more time to solicit proxies to oust present management, when he (1) made application to postpone meeting virtually on eve of meeting, (2) knew about corporation's annual meeting date about four months before he bought its stock, and (3) has not shown any wrong-doing on part of management. *Martin v Vitro Corp of America, NYLJ p. 16 (4-26-67).* Nor will court order postponement of stockholders' meeting called to consider proposed acquisition of certain assets, so as to enable stockholder to submit wholly unrelated proposal to other stockholders. *American Hardware Corp v Savage Arms Corp, 136 A2d 690 (Ch Ct 1957).*

However, court will postpone proposed stockholders' meeting to future date to enable court to pass on issues presented in stockholder's action against certain directors, who had allegedly caused corporation to pay for their solicitation of proxies in connection with such proposed meeting. *Campbell v Loew's Inc, 134 A2d 565 (Ch Ct 1957).* See also, *Lenahan v Nat'l Computer Analysis Corp, 310 A2d 661 (Ch Ct 1973).*

Corporate directors, faced with imminent proxy fight with dissident stockholders, cannot advance corporate meeting date by amending corporation's bylaws to provide for such earlier date, since newly set date handicaps dissident stockholders in their proxy fight, and it is inequitable and contrary to established principles of corporate democracy. *Schnell v Christ-Craft Industries, 285 A2d 437 (1971).*

Court refused to enjoin corporation's shareholders' meeting to allow shareholder more time to engage in proxy contest because a federal court enjoined voting of shareholder's proxies so that injunction, not conduct of corporate management, denied shareholder opportunity to participate in annual meeting through use of proxies. *Mount Vernon Corp v George Washington Corp, No. 8030 (Ch Ct 5-24-85).*

Court granted preliminary injunction barring directors from postponing meeting on evening before meeting was to be held. Postponement would cause irreparable harm to proxy contestants; postponement could defeat record date, thereby voiding plaintiffs' proxies, and this might thwart will of majority. *Aprahamiam v HBO & Co, 531 A2d 1204 (Ch Ct 1987).*

Court refused to postpone corporation's annual meeting at which 80% supermajority provision was proposed because proxy materials adequately disclosed all information about directors' holdings in corporation and there would not be irreparable harm if meeting is held. *Inition Partners v Tandycrafts, Inc, No. 38697 (Ch Ct 11-10-86).*

Court enjoined proposed recapitalization and merger not because these actions were themselves illegal but because board's actions to restrict B shareholders' power to interfere with proposals gave rise to "legitimate grievance." Those actions included postponement of annual meeting, issuance of shares to director to dilute B shareholders' voting power, and bylaw amendments that removed effective control of board from B shareholders. *Phillips v Insituform of North America, Inc, No. 9173 (Ch Ct 8-27-87).*

Preliminary injunction was properly denied to 30 percent shareholder asking that a corporation's board of directors be required to hold annual shareholders' meeting by certain date. Shareholder had made a tender offer and threatened proxy contest. However, since no meeting date had been set and no proxies solicited, there was no impairment of shareholders' franchise. The board's decision to postpone the meeting was a reasonable response to the perceived threat posed by shareholder's tender offer and therefore the action satisfied the proportionality under *Unocal Corp v Mesa Petroleum Co*, 493 A2d 946 (Del 1985). *Stahl v Apple Bancorp Inc, Nos. 11510-11248 (Ch Ct 5-17-90).*

.2 Cancellation of meeting.—A board and its "new" chairman may not cancel a special stockholders' meeting called by the corporation's "old" chairman without a compelling justification to do so. *Perlegos v Atmel Corp, 2007 Del. Ch. LEXIS 25 (Ch Ct 2007).*

.3 Special meetings.—In determining whether written request to call special meeting of stockholders complies with by-law, corporation must count signatures of those persons who were registered stockholders at date of delivery of such request; thus, though signatory to request was not registered stockholder at time of signing, but was such at date of delivery, his shares should be counted. *Richman v DeVal Aerodynamics Inc, 183 A2d 569 (Ch Ct 1962).*

Proxy to vote stock does not give proxy holder power to call special stockholders' meeting; where bylaw gives holders of ¼ of the outstanding voting stock power to call special stockholders' meeting, call by holders of less than the required amount of stock is invalid. *Josephson v Cosmo Color Corp, 64 A2d 35 (Ch Ct 1949).*

Court refused to enjoin special meeting of shareholders to vote on recapitalization plan after public announcement of offer by investment companies to buy corporation because, although offer is of enormous significance to shareholders in voting on recapitalization, they were not threatened with irreparable injury when (1) there was no indication that directors would fail to explore offer before committing to recapitalization, (2) directors prepared and distributed supplemental disclosure document describing offer and extended time in which proxies may be revoked or voted, and (3) vote for recapitalization does not commit directors to implement it. *In re Anderson, Clayton Shareholders Litigation, 519 A2d 694 (Ch Ct 1986).*

Court enjoined consummation of corporation's recapitalization plan that established ESOP controlling 25% interest in corporation because (1) proxy supplemental statement circulated on eve of shareholders' vote to approve recapitalization materially misled shareholders as to directors real attitude towards tender offer and (2) meaning and effect of shareholders' vote was further clouded by extremely short period shareholders had to receive, consider, and act upon significant new information contained in proxy statement. *In re Anderson, Clayton Shareholders' Litigation, 519 A2d 669 (Ch Ct 1986).*

.4 Court order to hold meeting.—Receiver can get court order convening stockholder meeting to elect directors even though majority stockholder opposes calling meeting, when it is shown there has not been stockholders' meeting for thirteen months. *Prickett v American Steel and Pump Corp, 251 A2d 576 (Ch Ct 1969).*

Court can summarily fix date of annual meeting on application of stockholder, when more than 15 months had elapsed since last meeting; however, though fact that more time was needed to clear directors' proxy statements with SEC does not justify failure to hold meeting, but court will consider it in mitigation in fixing of annual meeting date. *Tweedy, Browne & Knapp v The Cambridge Fund Inc, 318 A2d 635 (Ch Ct 1974).*

When corporation failed to hold shareholders' meeting for purpose of electing directors within 13 months, court could summarily act on shareholder's action and order meeting, even though action was pending in federal court among same parties on alleged federal securities violations as well as this election issue. *Coaxial Communications, Inc v CNA Financial Corp, 367 A2d 994 (1976).*

Corporate officers served with substituted process pursuant to statute calling for such service upon corporations only were improperly served; foreign corporation that held several auctions within state was doing sufficient business for suit against it to be maintained within jurisdiction. *Wier v Fairchild Galleries, 377 A2d 28 (Ch Ct 1977).*

Shareholder who rejected two previous annual meeting dates had no right to insist that third schedule date be advanced to prevent another shareholder from acquiring control of board of directors, despite fact statute permits court to order meeting on request of any shareholder where, as here, last meeting was more than 13 months earlier. *Savin Business Machines Corp v Rapifax Corp, No. 5331 (Ch Ct 7-1-77).*

Equity Committee made up of individuals and shareholders, some of whom acquired their interests in corporation after it filed bankruptcy petition, and shareholder who was member of Committee could not compel corporation to hold shareholders' meeting because (1) shareholder's dual status prevent him from pursuing private rights as shareholder when exercise of rights collides with his fiduciary obligation to Committee and (2) holding meeting would unfairly strengthen Equity Committee's bargaining position at expense of orderly reorganization and interests of all parties. *In re Johns-Manville Corp, 52 BR 879 (SDNY 1985).*

Court ordered shareholders' meeting for purpose of electing successor directors to be held when 50% shareholders petitioned that there had been no annual meeting for thirty days after date designated in corporate bylaws because second group of 50% shareholders refused to attend and defeated quorum. Fact that first group of shareholders wanted to end second group's control of corporation, although corporation was very profitable, does not indicate that they are attempting to destroy company and is not basis to deny petition. *Marciano v Nakash, No. 7910 (Ch Ct 6-19-85).*

Court ordered corporation to hold annual meeting at date earlier than date corporation desired to hold meeting, although dissident shareholders' consent solicitation and annual meeting proxy solicitation would, therefore, occur at same time, because (1) corporation had not held meeting for over year and (2) there is no reason to believe that shareholders would be unable to understand and appropriately respond to materials they receive. *Hecco Ventures v Texas American Energy Corp, No. 8520 (Ch Ct 7-3-86).*

Shareholders could bring action to compel holding annual meeting when it had not been held for over 13 months. Shareholders did not have to wait until 30 days after date of new annual meeting that corporation adopted in bylaws before bringing suit. *Seahawk Oil Management Corp v Discovery Oil Ltd, No. 8529 (Ch Ct 7-16-86).*

Bankruptcy court erred in granting summary judgment to bankrupt corporation and enjoining Equity Security Holders Committee from pursuing action to compel corporation to hold shareholders' meeting to replace directors so new directors might reconsider submitting plan earmarking billions to asbestos victims. *In re Johns-Manville Corp, 801 F2d 60 (2d Cir 1986).*

Once requirements of GCL §211 are met, right to order compelling annual meeting is virtually absolute. Plaintiff's acquiescence or connivance in failure to hold annual meeting is not affirmative defense in action to compel annual meeting. *Speiser v Baker, 525 A2d 1001 (Ch Ct 1987).*

Company's failure to provide audited financial statements was not an affirmative defense to an action to compel a shareholders' meeting. The Court of Chancery ordered the board of directors to hold a shareholder meeting after plaintiff established that he was a shareholder of the corporation and that the corporation had not held a shareholder meeting for over 13 months. *Byrne v Lord, Nos. 14040, 14215 (Ch Ct 11-9-95).*

A stockholder's suit to compel an annual stockholders' meeting under a statute that requires a corporation to set an annual meeting with 13 months from the date of the last meeting may be filed before the thirteen-month anniversary if, at the time the complaint is filed, it is legally impossible (1) for the corporation to convene an annual meeting by the date of the thirteen-month anniversary and (2) for the stockholders to act by written consent in lieu of an annual meeting by that same thirteen-month anniversary date. *MFC Bancorp Ltd v Equidyne Corp, 2003 Del. Ch. LEXIS 86 (Ch Ct 2003).*

.5 Annual meetings.—Action of corporation's board of directors in amending bylaws so as to leave date of annual meeting at board's discretion and requiring dissident shareholder to five names of nominees for the board, together with information concerning them, to corporation at least 70 days in advance of the date of annual meeting of shareholders, and then fixing date for meeting 63 days from time date was fixed, was invalid since it had inequitable effect of terminating shareholder opposition and perpetuating management in office. *Lerman v Diagnostic Data Inc, No. 6234 (Ch Ct 9-23-80).*

Delaware corporation doing business in California ordered to hold annual meeting in accord with own certificate of incorporation and bylaws, despite conflict with California statute purporting to impose cumulative voting and one-year directorships on foreign corporations doing majority of business in California. *Palmer v Arden-Mayfair Inc, No. 5549 (Ch Ct 7-6-78).*

Director/shareholder could compel annual meeting of shareholders though board had already scheduled later meeting and director had earlier acquiesced to meeting's postponement. *Shay v Morlan International Inc, No. 7243 (Ch Ct 7-29-83).*

Directors of merged corporation did not violate Rule 10b-5 when, in response to shareholders' informal requests, they failed to disclose information relating to corporation's financial status or hold annual meetings because corporation was "non-reporting company" under Securities Exchange Act of 1934 so directors had no duty to hold annual meetings or disclose information under Delaware law. *Polak v Continental Hosts, Ltd, 613 FSupp 153 (SDNY 1985).*

Court refused to enjoin target from holding its annual meeting or voting proxies. Even if bylaw amendments regarding nominations and notice of new business are invalid under GCL §211 in that they propose to limit business transacted at target's annual meeting, tender offerors would not be irreparably harmed because they had no proposals or nominations for meeting. *MacFadden Holdings, Inc v John Blair & Co, No. 86-161 MMS (D Del 5-16-86).*

Court refused to measure corporation's first year of organization by any time other than date of incorporation and held that corporation was organized for purpose and policy of GCL §211. *Walsh v Search Exploration, Inc, No. 11673 (Ch Ct 8-31-90).*

Board of director's holding of an annual meeting early to fulfill its objective of having one director's term expire and not reelecting him to the board was permissible and was not grounds for enjoining an otherwise properly and legally noticed shareholders' meeting. *Dolgoff v Projectavision, Inc, No. 14805 (Ch Ct 2-29-96).*

Written consent action taken pursuant to GCL §228 did not satisfy the mandatory requirement of GCL §211 that an annual meeting of shareholders be held. *Hoschett v TSI International Software, No. 14601 (Ch Ct 7-19-96).*

A shareholder may compel an annual stockholder meeting if such a meeting has not been held within a statutorily required period, regardless of the shareholder's goals in compelling such a meeting, provided the goals do not offend public policy. *Opportunity Partners L.P. v TransTech Service Partners, Inc, 2009 Del. Ch. LEXIS 49 (Ch Ct 2009).*

An annual meeting of a corporation with a staggered directorship scheduled to occur six months after the prior annual meeting will not be enjoined where the scheduling of the meeting is consistent with state law, the bylaws, and the company's earlier practices, and, where the company's poison pill is not being used defensively against shareholders or otherwise chilling shareholder communication and collaboration. *Goggin v Vermillion, Inc, 2011 Del. Ch. LEXIS 80 (Ch Ct 2011).*

.6 Trust beneficiaries, right to decide vote.—Majority beneficiaries of trust, who were opposed to current management of corporation that was controlled by trust, were denied court order requiring trustee to vote majority's slate of director nominees at shareholders' meeting, because the beneficiaries refused to identify the slate until the meeting. However, if, after trustee received instructions as to identity of slate and he determined that nominees would violate terms of trust, he could vote to adjourn meeting to seek instructions from court. *Wilmington Trust Co v Woodson, No. 7945 (Ch Ct 5-13-85).*

212 VOTING RIGHTS OF STOCKHOLDERS; PROXIES; LIMITATIONS.—(a) Unless otherwise provided in the certificate of incorporation and subject to §213 of this title, each stockholder shall be entitled to 1 vote for each share of capital stock held by such stockholder. If the certificate of incorporation provides for more or less than 1 vote for any share, on any matter, every reference in this chapter to a majority or other proportion of stock, *voting stock or shares* shall refer to such majority or other proportion of the votes of such stock, *voting stock or shares.*

(b) Each stockholder entitled to vote at a meeting of stockholders or to express consent or dissent to corporate action in writing without a meeting may authorize another person or persons to act for such stockholder by proxy, but no such proxy shall be voted or acted upon after 3 years from its date, unless the proxy provides for a longer period.

(c) Without limiting the manner in which a stockholder may authorize another person or persons to act for such stockholder as proxy pursuant to subsection (b) of this section, the following shall constitute a valid means by which a stockholder may grant such authority.

(1) A stockholder may execute a writing authorizing another person or persons to act for such stockholder as proxy. Execution may be accomplished by the stockholder or such stockholder's authorized officer, director, employee or agent signing such writing or causing such person's signature to be affixed to such writing by any reasonable means including, but not limited to, by facsimile signature.

(2) A stockholder may authorize another person or persons to act for such stockholder as proxy by transmitting or authorizing the transmission of a telegram, cablegram, or other means of electronic transmission to the person who will be the holder of the proxy or to a proxy solicitation firm, proxy support service organization or like agent duly authorized by the person who will be the holder of the proxy to receive such transmission, provided that any such telegram, cablegram or other means of electronic transmission must either set forth or be submitted with information from which it can be determined that the telegram, cablegram or other electronic transmission was authorized by the stockholder. If it is determined that such telegrams, cablegrams or other electronic transmissions are valid, the inspectors or, if there are no inspectors, such other persons making that determination shall specify the information upon which they relied.

(d) Any copy, facsimile telecommunication or other reliable reproduction of the writing or transmission created pursuant to subsection (c) of this section may be substituted or used in lieu of the original writing or transmission for any and all purposes for which the original writing or transmission could be used, provided that such copy, facsimile telecommunication or other reproduction shall be a complete reproduction of the entire original writing or transmission.

(e) A duly executed proxy shall be irrevocable if it states that it is irrevocable and if, and only as long as, it is coupled with an interest sufficient in law to support an irrevocable power. A proxy may be made irrevocable regardless of whether the interest with which it is coupled is an interest in the stock itself or an interest in the corporation generally. (Last amended by Ch. 298, L. '02, eff. 7-1-02.)

Ch. 298, L. '02, eff. 7-1-02, added matter in italic.

Ch. 298, L. '02 Synopsis of Section 212

The amendments to Sections 203(a)(2), 203(c)(8), 212(a) and 223(c) clarify that references to "voting stock" or "shares" therein and elsewhere in the title, including in Sections 203, 223 and 253, are intended to adopt the voting power concept reflected in Section 212(a). The parenthetical phrase added to Section 203(a)(2) is intended to make it clear that while voting stock owned by persons who are directors and also officers and by certain employee stock plans would not be included in determining the total amount of voting stock outstanding to calculate the 85% exemption, that voting stock would be included in the determination of the amount of voting stock owned by the interested stockholder. The amendment to Section 203(c)(5) is intended to refer to the paragraph defining the term "owner". This reference should have been changed when the definition of "stock" was added in 1995.

Ch. 339, L. '98 Synopsis of Section 212

The amendments to these Sections eliminate masculine references in the statutes, and replace them with gender neutral references.

Commentary on Sections 212 (c) and (d)

The amendment to Section 212 adds to that section two new subsections and renumbers pre-existing subsection (c) as subsection (e). New subsection (c) provides several nonexclusive means for a stockholder to validly grant the power of a proxy to another person. That subsection specifically authorizes the creation of a proxy relationship by telegram, cablegram or other means of electronic transmission provided that the telegram, cablegram or electronic transmission either sets forth or is submitted with information from which it can be determined that the telegram, cablegram or other electronic transmission was authorized by the stockholder. Also, if such proxies are determined to be valid, the person making that determination must specify the information establishing the proper authorization of such proxies.

New subsection (d) allows for the use of copies or reproductions of proxies for any purpose for which the original could be used provided that the entire proxy is reproduced. Included within this broad authorization is the use of "telecopied" proxies at meetings of the stockholders.

.1 Enforcement of voting agreement.—Voting trustee can enforce agreement that gives him the right to vote stock as trustee or as holder of an irrevocable proxy even though he never filed the agreement or had shares deposited as the statute called for, when failure to do so did not affect any parties outside the agreement. *In the Matter of Farm Industries, Inc, 196 A2d 582 (Ch Ct 1963).*

.2 Ratification of.—Stockholders cannot ratify corporation's gift of its assets to directors and officers. *Gottlieb v McKee, 107 A2d 240 (Ch Ct 1954).*

Sale of assets, approved by stockholders who have lost voting rights, will be set aside. *Macht v Merchants Mtge & Credit Co, 194 A 23 (Ch Ct 1937).*

Majority of stockholders cannot ratify their own acts, or acts of corporate officers, so as to cut off rights of minority stockholders, where such acts are a fraud on minority. *Hodgman v Atlantic Refining Co & Pierce Oil Co, 300 F 590 (D Del 1924).*

Unanimous ratification of a transaction by a close corporation's stockholders does not bar a later derivative suit attacking the transaction if the ratification was allegedly fraudulently obtained. *Brown v Dolese Bros Co, 154 A2d 233 (Ch Ct 1959),* aff'd, *Dolese Bros Co v Brown, 157 A2d 784 (1960).*

.3 Injunction.—Court will enjoin corporation's sale of authorized but unissued common stock, when evidence shows purpose was to deprive plaintiff of its voting control. *Canada Southern Oils Ltd v Manabi Exploration Co, 96 A2d 810 (Ch Ct 1953).*

Injunction seeking to stop target corporation from holding shareholder meeting and soliciting or voting proxies in favor of proposed charter amendment was denied because tender offeror and target's shareholders would not be irreparably harmed. *FMC Corp v R P Scherer Corp, 545 FSupp 318 (D Del 1982).*

Court refused to enjoin corporation's shareholders' meeting to allow shareholder more time to engage in proxy contest because a federal court enjoined voting of shareholder's proxies so that injunction, not conduct of corporate management, denied shareholder opportunity to participate in annual meeting through use of proxies. *Mount Vernon Corp v George Washington Corp, No. 8030 (Ch Ct 5-24-85).*

In shareholder's action to restrain corporation from exchanging 19% interest in its stock for 421/2% stock interest in wholly owned subsidiary, court denied temporary restraining order because (1) the "put" provisions of agreement were moot, and as such, did not act as deterrent to shareholder's intention to acquire controlling interest of corporation; (2) proposed transaction would not deprive shareholder of any present voting rights or positions; (3) threat of harm to shareholder was not irreparable; and (4) argument that value of corporate stock given up far exceeded value of stock to be received was not acceptable. *News International plc v Warner Communications Inc, No. 7420 (Ch Ct 1-12-84).*

Corporation could not get injunction preventing its former proxy solicitor from soliciting proxies on behalf of stockholders' committee that was challenging corporation's management. *Reasons:* (1) corporation had no written agreement with proxy solicitor prohibiting it from accepting employment after contract ended and (2) injunction would delay dissemination of committee's proxy materials. *Pantry Pride, Inc v Georgeson & Co, No. 7848 (Ch Ct 11-20-84).*

.4 Who may vote.—Only stockholder of record, voting trustee with whom stock has been deposited although not transferred on the books, a fiduciary, a pledgor whose shares have been transferred to the pledgee without power to vote, or holder of a valid and unrevoked proxy can vote at a corporate election. *In re Chilson, 168 A 82 (1933);* as to voting trustees, see *Smith v First Personal Bankers Corp, 171 A 839 (1934).* As to other trustees, see *Gans v Delaware Terminal Corp, 2 A2d 154 (Ch Ct 1938).*

Record holder of stock can vote it or give proxy although he has transferred it, transferee being unable to have it transferred on books because books have been closed or record date has been set prior to stockholders' meeting, but in appropriate case court of equity may control record holder's exercise of this right in favor of transferee's interests. *In re Giant Portland Cement Co, 21 A2d 697 (Ch Ct 1941).*

Stock of the parent corporation, registered in the name of subsidiary corporation, cannot be voted by

§212

subsidiary at stockholders' meeting of parent for the election of directors of parent corporation. *Italo Petroleum Corp of America v Producers' Oil Corp of America, 174 A 276 (1934).*

It is not necessary that stockholder shall have paid for his stock in full, in order to be entitled to vote. *Rice & Hutchins v Triplex Shoe Co, 147 A 317 (1929),* aff'd, *152 A 342 (1930).*

Registered, rather than real, owner of corporate stock has right to vote it at stockholders' meetings. *Tracy v Brentwood Village Corp, 59 A2d 708 (Ch Ct 1948).*

Partnership record holder can vote the stock without direction of beneficial owner in the absence of peculiar inequitable circumstances affecting the right of the real beneficial owner. *McLain v Lanova Corp, 39 A2d 209 (Ch Ct 1944).*

Right to vote stock by proxy will not be interfered with except for abuse of power even though it may be impossible to square his conduct with the rules of ethics. *McLain v Lanova Corp,* above. See also, *Schott v Climax Molybdenum Co, 154 A2d 221 (Ch Ct 1959).*

Holder of stock in escrow, or under agreement contingent on profits to be earned by issuer, was not legal owner, and so cannot vote stock at stockholders' meeting. *Norton v Digital Applications, Inc, 305 A2d 656 (Ch Ct 1973).*

Ownership of shares including right to vote did not pass on mere delivery to escrow agent so as to entitle purchaser to vote when purpose of escrow was to ensure full payment for shares before purchaser could assume control. *Kern v NCD Industries, Inc, 316 A2d 576 (Ch Ct 1937).*

Voting trustee can validly vote Class A voting stock that is converted from Class B non-voting stock for election of directors, when (1) Civil Aeronautics Board approved voting trust to liquidate corporation's stock by sale to non-affiliated person at specified date, meanwhile permitting trustee to vote that stock, and (2) corporation's charter permits Class B shares to be converted to Class A shares after beneficial ownership of those shares has been transferred to person not initial holder. *Sundlun v Executive Jet Aviation Inc, 273 A2d 282 (Ch Ct 1970).*

Preferred shareholders who were not paid dividends in 1975 and 1976, but were paid every year since 1978, are not entitled to vote at shareholders meetings of corporation, because certificate of preference gave preferred shareholders right to vote only when dividends were not paid for two consecutive years, but took right away when dividends were resumed for two consecutive years; two year gap in dividends ten years ago did not give shareholders permanent right to vote. However, plaintiff could not challenge adoption of amendment at 1984 shareholders meeting, even though preferred shareholders' votes were necessary for passage, because plaintiff was guilty of laches when he brought suit one year after meeting, a delay that is prejudicial to shareholders. *Flerlage v KDI Corp, No. 8007 (Ch Ct 4-10-86).*

A property settlement agreement between a divorced couple which gave ownership of a block of stock to the wife, but granted the husband voting rights for two years, constituted a valid proxy although the parties had not originally intended the agreement to be a proxy. *Lobato v Health Concepts IV, Inc, No. 12,203 (Ch Ct 10-29-91).*

.5 Right to change voting power.—Amendment of certificate of incorporation changing voting power of stock and having no further purpose is not conceived in fraud. *Topkis v Delaware Hardware Co, 2 A2d 114 (Ch Ct 1938).*

.6 Silence of stockholder.—Silence of stockholder at meeting estops him from later objecting to receipt of improper votes unless he did not know of infirmity in tendered votes or did not avail himself of available means of information in order to learn thereof. *Vogtman v Merchants Mtge & Credit Co, 194 A 19 (Ch Ct 1937).*

.7 Bylaw altering.—Bylaw that attempts to alter or restrict voting power of stock is void. *Brooks v State ex rel Richards, 79 A 790 (1911).*

.8 Compliance with conditions.—Conditions in charter giving preferred shareholders voting rights must be met before rights may be exercised; but once met, shareholders cannot be prevented from exercising these rights. *Petroleum Rights Corp v Midland Royalty Corp, 167 A 835 (Ch Ct 1933).* See also, *Bovrree v Trust Francais, 127 A 56 (1924); Ellingwood v Wolf's Head Oil Refining Co, 33 A2d 409 (Ch Ct 1943),* aff'd, *38 A2d 743 (1944).*

.9 Stockholder motives or interest.—Motive of stockholder in voting will not be inquired into by the court. *Gans v Delaware Terminal Corp, 2 A2d 154 (Ch Ct 1938).* Likewise, stockholder's right to vote is in no way vitiated by a personal interest. *Du Pont v Du Pont, 256 F 129 (3d Cir 1919),* modifying, *251 F 937 (D Del 1918); Heil v Standard Gas and Elec Co, 151 A 303 (Ch Ct 1930); Allied Chemical & Dye Corp v Sheet & Tube Co, 120 A 486 (Ch Ct 1923).*

Shareholder's vote is disqualified when given for a lucrative employment contract. *Hall v Isaacs, 146 A2d 602 (Ch Ct 1958).*

Registered holder of stock will not be recognized in equity as entitled to vote the same hostility to the wishes and desires of its owners who lack only the formality of a transfer on the books to make not only their title but as well the evidence thereof complete and absolute in all respects. *In re Canal Constr Co, 182 A 545 (Ch Ct 1936).*

.10 Rights of transferees.—Twenty days before meeting would have been March 17. Stockholders of record on the 25th were notified of the meeting. Court ruled that neither transferees nor transferors could vote stock transferred in the 20 day period. *Moon v Moon Motor Car Co, 151 A 298 (Ch Ct 1930).* This is contrary to opinion of same court in *In re Associated Automatic Sprinkler Co, 102 A 787 (Ch Ct 1917).*

Stock, registration of the transfer of which on the books of the corporation is deliberately and for an ulterior purpose prevented by the corporation or its transfer agent until the twenty days prior to the meeting, at which it is sought to vote the stock, have commenced to run, is entitled to be voted at the meeting. *Italo Petroleum Corp of America v Producers' Oil Corp of America, 174 A 276 (Ch Ct 1934).*

.11 Use of facsimile signature.—Inspectors of election can count proxies stamped with stockholders' facsimile signatures, unless those disputing the proxies show such signatures were unauthorized. *Schott v Climax Molybdenum Co, 154 A2d 221 (Ch Ct 1959).*

.12 Power of proxy holder.—Proxy to vote stock does not give proxy holder power to call special stockholders' meeting; where bylaw gives holders of ¼ of the outstanding voting stock power to call special stockholders' meeting, call by holders of less than the required amount of stock is invalid. *Josephson v Cosmo Color Corp, 64 A2d 35 (Ch Ct 1949).*

Unlimited proxy given to committee to vote shares at annual meeting and authorizing committee to attend and vote "with all powers the undersigned would possess if personally present" held to authorize proxy to vote on all matters that might come before meeting since stockholder is bound to know what might come before annual meeting. *Gow v Consolidated Coppermines Corp, 165 A 136 (Ch Ct 1933).*

Stockholder appointing directors as proxies held not bound by proxies' vote for resolution directing issuance to themselves of stock certificates. *Rice & Hutchins v Triplex Shoe Co, 147 A 317 (Ch Ct 1929),* aff'd, *152 A 342 (Ch Ct 1930); Blair v F H Smith Co, 156 A 207 (Ch Ct 1931).*

Attorney in fact given unrestricted proxy is presumed to act in accordance with will of stockholder in proper exercise of power. *Hexter v Columbia Baking Co, 145 A 115 (Ch Ct 1929); Chandler v Belanca Aircraft Corp, 162 A 63 (Ch Ct 1932).*

.13 False or misleading solicitation.—Annual meeting for election of directors would not be enjoined at suit of director on his complaint that stockholders who gave proxies to management did not know that after the proxy solicitation his name had been dropped from the slate and that they were thus misled. The authority of the proxy-holders (management) was unrestricted and it would be assumed that the stockholders expected that their proxies would be voted according to management's wishes. *Hauth v Giant Portland Cement Co, 95 A2d 233 (Ch Ct 1953).*

Proxy statement did not contain false or misleading statements where directors did, as stated therein, thoroughly consider facts relating to asset valuation. *Schiff v RKO Pictures Corp, 104 A2d 267 (Ch Ct 1954).*

Proxy material is not fraudulently misleading although it gives the impression that one director, rather than four, out of eleven opposed the plan to be voted on. *American Hardware Corp v Savage Arms Corp, 135 A2d 725 (Ch Ct 1957),* injunction pending appeal denied, *136 A2d 690 (1957).*

Corporation may maintain action to enjoin respondents from voting proxies which were procured by them after sending notices of meeting, proxy statements and proxies purportedly pursuant to authority given by incumbent board of directors but which were not in fact so authorized. *Empire Southern Gas Co v Gray, 46 A2d 741 (Ch Ct 1946).*

Proxies cannot be voted for removal of director for cause when director is not given opportunity to present his defense to stockholders, at corporation's expense, by statement accompanying or preceding solicitation of the proxies. *Campbell v Loew's Inc, 134 A2d 565 (Ch Ct 1957).*

Investors in company could get preliminary injunction barring wholly owned subsidiary from soliciting tender of company's shares in exchange for its stock when prospectus allegedly violated Exchange Act by not disclosing that major result of merger would be surrendering their one vote per share right and getting "scale voting." *Blanchette v Providence and Worcester Co, 428 FSupp 347 (D Del 1977).*

For opinions in Delaware courts concerning SEC's proxy rules, see *Dillon v Berg, 326 FSupp 1214 (D Del 1971); Gould v Amer Hawaiian SS Co, 331 FSupp 981 (D Del 1971),* aff'd, *351 FSupp 853 (D Del 1972); Puma v Mariott, 363 FSupp 751 (D Del 1973); Denison Mines Ltd v Fibreboard Corp, 388 FSupp 812 (D Del 1974); Nat'l Home Products, Inc v Gray, 416 FSupp 1293 (D Del 1976); Chris Craft Industries, Inc v Independent Stockholders Committee, 354 FSupp 895 (D Del 1973).*

Proxy statement seeking shareholders' approval of repurchase and creation of stock plan was not materially misleading when it neglected to disclose: (1) alternative methods of funding stock plan, (2) stock price included control premium, (3) stockholders' opposition to repurchase, and (4) lack of proper purpose for termination of old retirement plan. *Seibert v Harper & Row, Publishers, Inc, No. 6639 (Ch Ct 12-5-84).*

Court refused to enjoin target from holding its annual meeting or voting proxies. *Reasons:* (1) False proxy statement regarding vote to amend target's certificate of incorporation was not material under §14(a) of Securities Exchange Act of 1934 because it merely informed shareholders of voting procedure, not merits of proposed corporate action, and, in any case, statement was corrected by target by letter to shareholders who were informed that they could change their vote. (2) Alleged materially false and misleading statement in proxy materials about its intent in proposing amendments authorizing additional stock would not cause tender offerors irreparable harm. *MacFadden Holdings, Inc v John Blair & Co, 1986 U.S. Dist. LEXIS 30956 (D Del 5-5-86).*

Target's proxy material stating its interpretation of bylaw notice provision when annual meeting is adjourned was deficient because Delaware court found target's interpretation invalid so it should have anticipated legal challenge to its interpretation and disclosed that contingency in its proxy materials. *Unocal Corp v T Boone Pickens, Jr, 608 FSupp 1081 (CD Cal 1985).*

Court enjoined consummation of corporation's recapitalization plan that established ESOP controlling 25% interest in corporation because (1) proxy supplemental statement circulated on eve of shareholders' vote to approve recapitalization materially misled shareholders as to directors real attitude towards tender offer and (2) meaning and effect of shareholders' vote was further clouded by extremely short period shareholders had to receive, consider, and act upon significant new information contained in proxy statement. *In re Anderson, Clayton Shareholders' Litigation, 519 A2d 669 (Ch Ct 1986).*

Court enjoined implementation of recapitalization plan because shareholder vote approving issuance of supervoting common stock was fatally flawed when (1) principal shareholder/chief executive officer, for whose benefit stock had been fashioned,

§212

threatened to block transactions that may be in best interest of corporation, unless plan was approved and (2) proxy statement presents substantial risk of misleading shareholder on material point concerning principal shareholder's status as "restricted person." *Lacos Land Co v Arden Group, Inc, 517 A2d 271 (Ch Ct 1986).*

Court refused to postpone corporation's annual meeting at which 80% super majority provision was proposed because proxy materials adequately disclosed all information about directors' holdings in corporation and there would not be irreparable harm if meeting is held. *Initio Partners v Tandycrafts, Inc, No. 38697 (Ch Ct 11-10-86).*

Court refused to enjoin exercise of stock options granted to two officers by target of leveraged buyout proposal because directors of target did not have to disclose, in connection with shareholders' meeting, that they adopted plan to sell corporation when (1) stock options were originally granted year before shareholders' meeting and (2) first manifestation of any real interest in target's acquisition came only day before meeting. *Kramer v Western Pacific Industries, Inc, No. 8675 (Ch Ct 11-7-86).*

Proxy statement was not materially misleading even though fairness opinion on which it was based was six months old, and statement neglected to point out that buy-out might mean loss of 2nd quarter dividend. Plaintiffs failed to show irreparable harm because dissenting shareholders will still have right to seek appraisal. *Lewis v Leaseway Transportation Corp, No. 8720 (Ch Ct 6-12-87).*

Court upheld settlement agreement ending suit and counterclaim charging corporation and proxy contestants with violating §14(a) of '34 Securities Exchange Act, where (1) illegality of proxy solicitations did not deprive directors of power to reimburse contestants for proxy expenses as part of settlement nor make settlement unlawful; (2) settlement had business purpose—to preserve corporate policies believed to be in shareholders' best interests; (3) settlement was not illegal vote buying scheme; such schemes are not per se unlawful if they are intrinsically fair and the purpose is not to defraud or disenfranchise shareholders; here, purpose was not to disenfranchise shareholders, but to end threat to corporate policy. *Weinberger v Bankston, No. 6336 (Ch Ct 11-19-87).*

No authority for claim that amendment to certificate of incorporation that shifted voting control from shareholders to a savings plan allegedly controlled by directors should be treated as a gift or waste of assets requiring unanimous shareholder ratification. Also, in light of the extensive proxy statement disclosure of critical features, purposes, and effects of this certificate amendment, that were omitted would not have significantly altered total mix of information available to stockholders. *Weiss v Rockwell Int'l Corp, No. 8811 (Ch Ct 7-19-89).*

Injunction denied bank where minority shareholders, concerned with bank's financial health and eager to explore "maximization of shareholder value," sought proxy solicitation at upcoming annual meeting. The bank opposed and alleged fraud in proxy materials. Held: "the total mix of information conveyed...indicates...defendants seek an open analysis by the shareholders of the general receptivity of [the board] to overtures [of sale]." *D & N Financial Corp v RCM Partners Ltd, 735 FSupp 1242 (D Del 1990).*

Court denied motion for a preliminary injunction to enjoin the corporation from completing a merger where there was no breach of care, loyalty, or Revlon duties since, inter alia, an explanation in the proxy statement that advised shareholders that their opportunities to share in the company's future success would be limited, due to an option to redeem held by a purchasing company, was "remarkably clear" and the information that minority shareholders alleged should have been disclosed was either speculative and unreliable or did not require explanation for a reasonable shareholder to make an investment decision. *In re Genentech Inc Shareholders Litigation, No. 11377 (Ch Ct 6-6-90).*

A preliminary agreement on a subsidy rate reached between an airline and the Civil Aeronautics Board subsidy staff was correctly held immaterial for purposes of a proxy disclosure, where the result of the negotiations did not introduce a significant new fact into the mix of financial data that was already available to the shareholders and that the agreement was tentative in that it had been reached at the staff level and was subject to approval and possible modification by the Civil Aeronautics Board. *Kahn v Household Acquisition Corp and Household Finance Corp, 591 A2d 166 (1991).*

Monetary or injunctive relief will not be granted for disclosure violations in a merger proxy solicitation where it has been three years since the merger's consummation and where there is no evidence of a breach of the duty of loyalty or good faith by the directors who authorized the disclosures; enthusiasm for a merger and engagement in the merger negotiations do not equate with disloyalty or bad faith.

The Chancery Court determined that it did not need to determine whether the purported misrepresented facts were material, whether the directors were protected by the exculpatory provision, or whether such disclosure would have amounted to "self-flagellation," because it held that all of the shareholders' disclosure claims were barred. In arriving at this holding, the court observed that a breach of the disclosure duty leads to irreparable harm, for which the court grants injunctive relief to prevent a vote from taking place where there is a credible threat that shareholders will be asked to vote without such complete and accurate information. The corollary to this point, however, is that once this irreparable harm has occurred—i.e., when shareholders have already voted without complete and accurate information—it is, by definition, too late to remedy the harm. Accordingly, the court concluded that because the solicitation of proxies for the shareholder vote approving the merger occurred over three years prior, and because the merger had been consummated, an injunctive order requiring supplemental, corrective disclosures at this stage would be an exercise in futility and frivolity. The court also concluded that there was no evidence of a breach of the duty of loyalty or good faith by the directors who authorized the disclosures. Instead, the court found that the evidence merely showed that the directors were engaged, active, and enthusiastic supporters and salesmen of the merger, but concluded that such conduct did not constitute disloyal behavior sufficient to defeat a motion for summary judgment. The court said that enthusiasm for a merger and engagement in the merger negotiations do not equate with disloyalty or bad faith. For these reasons, the court granted summary judgment to the director-defendants. *In re Transkaryotic Therapies, Inc, 954 A2d 346 (Ch Ct 2008).*

.14 **Forged signature.**—Inspectors of election cannot pass upon possible forgeries in execution of proxies and cannot take cognizance of alleged variance in signatures on two proxies in name of single stockholder, but court will hear evidence as to alleged forgery in execution of corporate proxy and will require strict proof, i.e., nothing less than testimony of person whose signature was allegedly forged should be recognized unless such testimony is unavailable for reasons having substantial merit. *Investment Associates, Inc v Standard Power & Light Corp, 48 A2d 501 (Ch Ct 1946).*

.15 **Proxy expenses.**—In contest over corporate policy—as distinguished from contest purely over management personnel or for personal power or gain—directors can make reasonable and proper expenditures from corporate treasury for purpose of persuading stockholders of correctness of their position and to solicit their support. The stockholders, under same circumstances, can reimburse successful insurgents. *Rosenfeld v Fairchild Engine & Airplane Corp, 130 NE 610 (NY 1955).*

Solicitation of proxies through advertisement by directors was held to be legitimate corporate expense where information disseminated in advertisement related to management policies and proxies were not sought solely for retention of their offices by incumbent directors. *Hall v Trans-Lux Daylight Picture Screen Corp, 171 A 226 (1934).*

Expenses of successful insurgents in proxy contest may be reimbursed out of corporate funds. *Steinberg v Adams, 90 FSupp 604 (SDNY 1950).*

Court will not preliminarily enjoin management from expending corporate funds to hire professional proxy solicitors to solicit support for management in contest with stockholders where legality of management's course turned on sharp questions of fact which could only be determined after final hearing. *Hand v Missouri-Kansas Pipe Line Co, 54 FSupp 649 (D Del 1944).*

.16 **Filling in blanks.**—Proxies executed in France by French holders of stock in Delaware corporation before outbreak of World War II between United States and Germany, mailed to and received in this country after outbreak of War and thereafter filled in here by person to whom they were sent with his name and name of another as proxy holders, were valid and directors elected at the meeting in which they were voted were validly elected. *Aldridge v Franco-Wyoming Securities Corp, 39 A2d 246 (Ch Ct 1943).* See also, *42 A2d 879.*

.17 **Conflicting proxies.**—Where there are conflicting proxies given by same person, inspectors of election should consider post-mark in determining which proxy should be given effect. *Investment Associates, Inc v Standard Power & Light Corp, 48 A2d 501 (Ch Ct 1946).*

.18 **Who may sign.**—Stock in name of two persons who are in fact husband and wife, although certificate does not show that, is held in tenancy by entirety and stock could not be voted on proxy signed merely by one of the two. *In re Giant Portland Cement Co, 21 A2d 697 (Ch Ct 1941).*

Where proxy for stock recorded in partnership name, sent out by stockholder, purports to be signed in partnership name, it is prima facie evidence that signature thereto is authorized and it need not appear that person who signed partnership name was authorized to do so. *McLain v Lanova Corp, 39 A2d 209 (Ch Ct 1944).*

In absence of knowledge at time of proxy solicitation of facts contrary to those stated, there is no fraud in solicitation or use of proxies. As long as proxies have appearance of authenticity, differences between signatures and registered names are immaterial. *Atterbury v Consolidated Copper Mines Corp, 20 A2d 743 (Ch Ct 1941).* See also, *Kerbs v Calif Eastern Airways, 94 A2d 217 (Ch Ct 1952).*

.19 **Ballot.**—Any form of ballot that shows voters' intent may be used in election of directors, unless particular form is prescribed. *Chappel v Standard Scale & Supply Corp, 158 A 74 (Ch Ct 1927),* decree rev'd, *Standard Scale & Supply Corp v Chappel, 141 A 191 (Ch Ct 1928).*

.20 **Buying proxy.**—Stockholder cannot vote irrevocable proxies for election of his slate of directors, when he obtains such proxies from other stockholders by paying nominal price for them, since it is against public policy for any stockholder to sell his vote for consideration personal to himself, such sale being void; this is so even though price paid is nominal and stock itself is valueless. *Chew v Inverness Management Corp, 352 A2d 426 (Ch Ct 1976).*

.21 **Vote on exchange offer.**—Court refused to enjoin corporation's exchange offer for 50% of its outstanding common stock even though directors proposed exchange offer after recapitalization plan failed to receive required shareholder approval. *Reasons:* (1) exchange offer was not merely alternative recapitalization when recapitalization plan differed in many respects from offer, (2) nothing in Delaware GCL requires shareholder vote on exchange offer, even if it brings fundamental change in capital structure, and (3) shareholders indicated approval of exchange by tendering 90% of stock. *Lowenschuss v The Option Clearing Corp, No. 7972 (Ch Ct 3-27-85).*

.22 **Supermajorities.**—Court enjoined voting of "supervoting" preferred stock issued to chairman/chief executive and allied investors, which gave them 44% of voting power, because, while raising capital may have been purpose for directors issuing stock, their primary purpose was to obstruct ability of shareholders to wage meaningful proxy contest in order to maintain their control when (1) "supermajority" voting provisions had never been used to help solve corporation's chronic cash problems and had only been considered as takeover defense, (2) provisions were only adopted after directors perceived proxy challenge, and (3) there were alternatives for financing. Challenging shareholders would be irreparably harmed if management were allowed to vote "supermajority" preferred stock because, at very

§212

least, vote would substantially influence directors' election and have chilling effect on shareholders' proxy solicitation. *Packer v Yampol, No. 8432 (Ch Ct 4-18-86).*

Court of Chancery erred when it granted preliminary injunction to block merger. Provision in target's certificate requiring supermajority vote for business combinations did not apply after acquiror had reduced interest in target to less than 30%. *Berlin v Emerald Partners, 552 A2d 482 (1989).*

.23 Per capita voting.—Provisions in a corporation's bylaws and certificate of incorporation providing for per capita voting did not violate Delaware law and were valid. The provisions required approval of matters to be voted upon at shareholder meetings by both the majority of shares entitled to vote and a majority of the shareholders present in person or by proxy, and stated that when shares were held by persons or entities acting in concert or by virtue of an agreement, such persons were to be deemed to be one stockholder for purposes of calculating the required majority. *Sagusa, Inc v Magellan Petroleum Corp, 12,977 (Ch Ct 12-1-93).*

.24 Irrevocable proxies.—Defendant obtained an irrevocable proxy to vote shares of stock where the proxy stated it was irrevocable on its face and the defendant had a security interest in the shares of stock that were exchanged for the proxy. *Haft v Haft, No. 14425 (Ch Ct 11-14-95).*

Pledge agreement between defendant, a Delaware corporation, and plaintiff, a corporate shareholder of defendant, which entitled plaintiff to vote defendant's shares in the corporation by irrevocable proxy upon defendant's default on notes held by plaintiff, gave plaintiff the right, upon such default, to exercise the proxy and elect a new board of directors for defendant corporation by written consent. *Stone v Hungerford, No. 14494 (Ch Ct 2-9-96).*

.25 Defensive measure.—The dilutive voting mechanism of A Stock Employee Compensation Trust (SECT) will be analyzed on its own merits for reasonableness and proportionality where the SECT is adopted as a defensive measure in a proxy fight; where there is a tenuous relationship between the dilutive provision and the threat it putatively is supposed to address, the voting mechanism is unreasonable. *Aquila, Inc v Quanta Services, Inc, 805 A2d 196 (Ch Ct 2002).*

213 FIXING DATE FOR DETERMINATION OF STOCKHOLDERS OF RECORD.—[1] *(a) In order that the corporation may determine the stockholders entitled to notice of any meeting of stockholders or any adjournment thereof, the board of directors may fix a record date, which record date shall not precede the date upon which the resolution fixing the record date is adopted by the board of directors, and which record date shall not be more than 60 nor less than 10 days before the date of such meeting. If the board of directors so fixes a date, such date shall also be the record date for determining the stockholders entitled to vote at such meeting unless the board of directors determines, at the time it fixes such record date, that a later date on or before the date of the meeting shall be the date for making such determination. If no record date is fixed by the board of directors, the record date for determining stockholders entitled to notice of and to vote at a meeting of stockholders shall be at the close of business on the day next preceding the day on which notice is given, or, if notice is waived, at the close of business on the day next preceding the day on which the meeting is held. A determination of stockholders of record entitled to notice of or to vote at a meeting of stockholders shall apply to any adjournment of the meeting; provided, however, that the board of directors may fix a new record date for determination of stockholders entitled to vote at the adjourned meeting, and in such case shall also fix as the record date for stockholders entitled to notice of such adjourned meeting the same or an earlier date as that fixed for determination of stockholders entitled to vote in accordance with the foregoing provisions of this subsection (a) at the adjourned meeting.*

(b) In order that the corporation may determine the stockholders entitled to consent to corporate action in writing without a meeting, the board of directors may fix a record date, which record date shall not precede the date upon which the resolution fixing the record date is adopted by the board of directors, and which date shall not be more than 10 days after the date upon which the resolution fixing the record date is adopted by the board of directors. If no record date has been fixed by the board of directors, the record date for determining stockholders entitled to consent to corporate action in writing without a meeting, when no prior action by the board of directors is required by this chapter, shall be the first date on which a signed written consent setting forth the action taken or proposed to be taken is delivered to the corporation by delivery to its registered office in this State, its principal place of business or an officer or agent of the corporation having custody of the book in which proceedings of meetings of stockholders are recorded. Delivery made to a corporation's registered office shall be by hand or by certified or registered mail, return receipt requested. If no record date has been fixed by the board of directors and prior action by the board of directors is required by this chapter, the record date for determining stockholders entitled to

consent to corporate action in writing without a meeting shall be at the close of business on the day on which the board of directors adopts the resolution taking such prior action.

(c) In order that the corporation may determine the stockholders entitled to receive payment of any dividend or other distribution or allotment of any rights or the stockholders entitled to exercise any rights in respect of any change, conversion or exchange of stock, or for the purpose of any other lawful action, the board of directors may fix a record date, which record date shall not precede the date upon which the resolution fixing the record date is adopted, and which record date shall be not more than 60 days prior to such action. If no record date is fixed, the record date for determining stockholders for any such purpose shall be at the close of business on the day on which the board of directors adopts the resolution relating thereto. (Last amended by Ch. 14, L. '09, eff. 8-1-09.)

Ch. 14, L. '09, eff. 8-1-09, added matter in italic and deleted [1]"(a) In order that the corporation may determine the stockholders entitled to notice of or to vote at any meeting of stockholders or any adjournment thereof, the board of directors may fix a record date, which record date shall not precede the date upon which the resolution fixing the record date is adopted by the board of directors, and which record date shall not be more than 60 nor less than 10 days before the date of such meeting. If no record is fixed by the board of directors, the record date for determining stockholders entitled to notice of or to vote at a meeting of stockholders shall be at the close of business on the day next preceding the day on which notice is given, or, if notice is waived, at the close of business on the day next preceding the day on which the meeting is held. A determination of stockholders of record entitled to notice of or to vote at a meeting of stockholders shall apply to any adjournment of the meeting; providing, however, that the board of directors may fix a new record date for the adjourned meeting."

Editor's Note: This section is effective with respect to corporate actions taken by written consent, and to such written consent or consents, as to which the first written consent is executed or solicited after July 1, 1987.

Ch. 14, L. '09 Synopsis of Section 213

This amendment to Section 213(a) permits a board of directors to separate the record date for determining the stockholders entitled to vote at a meeting from the record date for determining those stockholders entitled to notice of the meeting. Under amended Section 213(a), the board of directors may chose a date later than the notice record date, on or before the meeting date, for determining those stockholders entitled to vote. This amendment is not intended to affect application of the doctrine expressed in *Schnell v. Chris-Craft Indus., Inc.*, 285 A.2d 437 (Del. 1971).

.1 Closing transfer books.—Record holder of stock is entitled to vote it or to give proxy although he has transferred it, transferee being unable to have it transferred on books because books have been closed or a record date has been set prior to the stockholders' meeting; but in appropriate case court of equity may control record holder's exercise of this right in favor of transferee's interests. *In re Giant Portland Cement Co, 21 A2d 697 (Ch Ct 1941).*

.2 Written consents.—Group of dissident shareholders could use statutory consent procedure to attempt to remove directors of widely held public corporation, even though they did not hold absolute majority of shares, since language of statute includes all Delaware corporations and does not limit shareholders who may exercise right; but written consents obtained were void because: (1) dissidents' consent statement that written consent would remain in force for 7 ½ months misstated GCL §213 which placed 60 day limit on consent; and (2) dissidents' consent statement that revocation of consent represented unsettled area of law was wrong. *Pabst Brewing Co v Jacobs, 549 FSupp 1068 (D Del 1982).*

Court refused to enjoin corporation's directors from setting on October 10, 1985 a stock record date of November 18, 1985 for shareholder's October 7, 1985 notice of solicitation of shareholder consents to remove and replace directors. *Reasons:* (1) Shareholder's notice in its October 7 demand letter that consents would be solicited did not establish October 7 as day on which first written consent was "expressed" when demand letter disclosed only in part full extent of action to be undertaken by shareholder consent so directors were not precluded from fixing different record date from date stated in demand letter. (2) Directors' designation of November 18 as record date did not violate GCL §228 because directors, in exercising business judgment, may set record date that would delay shareholder action by written consent. *Empire of Carolina, Inc v The Deltona Corp, 514 A2d 1091 (1986).*

Record date for determining which shareholders are entitled to vote in consent procedure initiated by group of shareholders seeking control of corporation was date on which first consent was expressed and corporation's directors did not have power to change date because it would (1) cause confusion and uncertainty among shareholders and (2) give unwarranted advantage to incumbent management in takeover struggle. *Midway Airlines, Inc v Carlson, 628 FSupp 244 (D Del 1985).*

Directors did not breach fiduciary duty or manipulate a record date for a shareholders meeting where the Board selected a record date only 12 days before a special shareholders meeting. *Wyser-Pratte v Smith, No. 15545-NC (Ch Ct 3-18-97).*

.3 Spin-off, status of future shareholders.—Individuals who were to receive stock in spin-off did not become good owners or beneficial owners of stock before spin-off; therefore, no fiduciary duties

§213

were owed to them. *Anadarko Petroleum Corp v Panhandle Eastern Corp, No. 8738 (Ch Ct 7-7-87).*

.4 Postponement of meeting to defeat record date.—Court granted preliminary injunction barring directors from postponing meeting on evening before meeting was to be held. Postponement would cause irreparable harm to proxy contestants; postponement could defeat record date, thereby voiding plaintiffs' proxies, and this might thwart will of majority. *Apra-hamian v HBO & Co, 531 A2d 1204 (Ch Ct 1987).*

.5 Invalid record date.—An invalid record date does not invalidate actions taken at an annual meeting to which the record date relates where the corporation's counsel relies on a judicial decision that through a typographical error increases the period for the record date by one day. *McKesson Corp v Derdiger, 793 A2d 385 (Ch Ct 2002).*

214 CUMULATIVE VOTING.—The certificate of incorporation of any corporation may provide that at all elections of directors of the corporation, or at elections held under specified circumstances, each holder of stock or of any class or classes or of a series or series thereof shall be entitled to as many votes as shall equal the number of votes which (except for such provision as to cumulative voting) [1]*such holder* would be entitled to cast for the election of directors with respect to [2]*such holder's* shares of stock multiplied by the number of directors to be elected by [3]*such holder,* and that [1]*such holder* may cast all of such votes for a single director or may distribute them among the number to be voted for, or for any 2 or more of them as [1]*such holder* may see fit. (Last amended by Ch. 339, L. '98, eff. 7-1-98.)

Ch. 339, L. '98, eff. 7-1-98, added matter in italic and deleted [1]"he"; [2]"his"; and [3]"him".

Ch. 339, L. '98 Synopsis of Section 214

The amendments to these Sections eliminate masculine references in the statutes, and replace them with gender neutral references.

.1 Removal of directors.—Directors elected by cumulative voting can be removed for cause. *Campbell v Loew's, Inc, 134 A2d 565 (Ch Ct 1957).*

.2 Straight voting.—Certificate of incorporation may be amended to provide for straight voting for directors instead of cumulative voting. *Maddock v Vorclone Corp, 147 A 255 (Ch Ct 1929).*

When votes were cumulated in mistaken belief that cumulative voting was permitted, but in fact had not been provided for in the certificate of incorporation, judges of election should have counted these votes as straight votes for the persons designated; that is, count the number of shares voted by each ballot for each individual voted for. *Standard Scale & Supply Corp v Chappel, 141 A 191 (1928).*

.3 Conflict with statute.—Delaware corporation doing business in California ordered to hold annual meeting in accord with own certificate of incorporation and bylaws, despite conflict with California statute purporting to impose cumulative voting and one-year directorships on foreign corporations doing majority of business in California. *Palmer v Arden-Mayfair Inc, No. 5549 (Ch Ct 7-6-78).*

215 [1] *VOTING RIGHTS OF MEMBERS OF NONSTOCK CORPORATIONS; QUORUM; PROXIES.*—(a) *Sections 211 through 214 and 216 of this title shall not apply to nonstock corporations, except that §211(a) and (d) of this title and §212(c), (d), and (e) of this title shall apply to such corporations, and, when so applied, all references therein to stockholders and to the board of directors shall be deemed to refer to the members and the governing body of a nonstock corporation, respectively; and all references to stock, capital stock, or shares thereof shall be deemed to refer to memberships of a nonprofit nonstock corporation and to membership interests of any other nonstock corporation.*

(b) Unless otherwise provided in the certificate of incorporation or the bylaws of a nonstock corporation, and subject to subsection (f) of this section, each member shall be entitled at every meeting of members to 1 vote on each matter submitted to a vote of members. A member may exercise such voting rights in person or by proxy, but no proxy shall be voted on after 3 years from its date, unless the proxy provides for a longer period.

(c) Unless otherwise provided in this chapter, the certificate of incorporation or bylaws of a nonstock corporation may specify the number of members having voting power who shall be present or represented by proxy at any meeting in order to constitute a quorum for, and the votes that shall be necessary for, the transaction of any business. In the absence of such specification in the certificate of incorporation or bylaws of a nonstock corporation:

(1) One-third of the members of such corporation shall constitute a quorum at a meeting of such members;

(2) In all matters other than the election of the governing body of such corporation, the affirmative vote of a majority of such members present in person or represented by proxy at

the meeting and entitled to vote on the subject matter shall be the act of the members, unless the vote of a greater number is required by this chapter;

(3) Members of the governing body shall be elected by a plurality of the votes of the members of the corporation present in person or represented by proxy at the meeting and entitled to vote thereon; and

(4) Where a separate vote by a class or group or classes or groups is required, a majority of the members of such class or group or classes or groups, present in person or represented by proxy, shall constitute a quorum entitled to take action with respect to that vote on that matter and, in all matters other than the election of members of the governing body, the affirmative vote of the majority of the members of such class or group or classes or groups present in person or represented by proxy at the meeting shall be the act of such class or group or classes or groups.

(d) If the election of the governing body of any nonstock corporation shall not be held on the day designated by the bylaws, the governing body shall cause the election to be held as soon thereafter as convenient. The failure to hold such an election at the designated time shall not work any forfeiture or dissolution of the corporation, but the Court of Chancery may summarily order such an election to be held upon the application of any member of the corporation. At any election pursuant to such order the persons entitled to vote in such election who shall be present at such meeting, either in person or by proxy, shall constitute a quorum for such meeting, notwithstanding any provision of the certificate of incorporation or the bylaws of the corporation to the contrary.

(e) If authorized by the governing body, any requirement of a written ballot shall be satisfied by a ballot submitted by electronic transmission, provided that any such electronic transmission must either set forth or be submitted with information from which it can be determined that the electronic transmission was authorized by the member or proxy holder.

(f) Except as otherwise provided in the certificate of incorporation, in the bylaws, or by resolution of the governing body, the record date for any meeting or corporate action shall be deemed to be the date of such meeting or corporate action; provided, however, that no record date may precede any action by the governing body fixing such record date. (Last amended by Ch. 253, L. '10, eff. 8-1-10.)

Ch. 253, L. '10, eff. 8-1-10, added matter in italic and deleted [1]"VOTING RIGHTS OF MEMBERS OF NONSTOCK CORPORATIONS; QUORUM; PROXIES.—(a) Sections 211 through 214 and 216 of this title shall not apply to corporations not authorized to issue stock, except that §211(a) of this title and §212(c) and (d) of this title shall apply to such corporations, and, when so applied, all references therein to stockholders and to the board of directors shall be deemed to refer to the members and the governing body of a nonstock corporation, respectively.

(b) Unless otherwise provided in the certificate of incorporation of a nonstock corporation, each member shall be entitled at every meeting of members to 1 vote in person or by proxy, but no proxy shall be voted on after 3 years from its date, unless the proxy provides for a longer period.

(c) Unless otherwise provided in this chapter, the certificate of incorporation or bylaws of a nonstock corporation may specify the number of members having voting power who shall be present or represented by proxy at any meeting in order to constitute a quorum for, and the votes that shall be necessary for, the transaction of any business. In the absence of such specification in the certificate of incorporation or bylaws of a nonstock corporation:

(1) One-third of the members of such corporation shall constitute a quorum at a meeting of such members;

(2) In all matters other than the election of the governing body of such corporation, the affirmative vote of a majority of such members present in person or represented by proxy at the meeting and entitled to vote on the subject matter shall be the act of the members, unless the vote of a greater number is required by this chapter; and

(3) Members of the governing body shall be elected by a plurality of the votes of the members of the corporation present in person or represented by proxy at the meeting and entitled to vote thereon.

(d) If the election of the governing body of any nonstock corporation shall not be held on the day designated by the bylaws, the governing body shall cause the election to be held as soon thereafter as convenient. The failure to hold such an election at the designated time shall not work any forfeiture or dissolution of the corporation, but the Court of Chancery may summarily order such an election to be held upon the application of any member of the corporation. At any election pursuant to such order the persons entitled to vote in such election who shall be present at such meeting, either in person or by proxy, shall constitute a quorum for such meeting, notwithstanding any provision of the certificate of incorporation or the bylaws of the corporation to the contrary.

(e) If authorized by the governing body, any requirement of a written ballot shall be satisfied by a ballot submitted by electronic transmission, provided that any such electronic transmission must either set forth or be submitted with information from which it can be determined that the electronic transmission was authorized by the member or proxy holder."

§215

Ch. 253, L. '10 Synopsis of Section 215

Section 19 amends §215(a) of the DGCL to apply §211(d) (regarding special meetings of members) and §212(e) (regarding irrevocable proxies) to nonstock corporations; this Section further amends §215(a) to ensure that it translates correctly the provisions to which it refers. This Section amends §215(b) of the DGCL to ensure consistency with the amendments to §102(a)(4) allowing the corporation's certificate of incorporation or bylaws to set forth the members' voting rights. This Section further amends §215(b) to provide that members' voting rights are subject to the record date for any particular meeting. This Section amends the DGCL to add new §215(c)(4). Consistent with the amendments to §102(a)(4), new §215(c)(4) defines the quorum and vote necessary to take action for separate votes of classes or groups of members. This Section also amends the DGCL to add new §215(f). New §215(f) provides that, except as otherwise provided in the corporation's certificate of incorporation, in the corporation's bylaws, or by resolution of the corporation's governing body, the record date for meetings of nonstock corporations shall be deemed to be the date of the meeting, so long as no record date precedes the action by the governing body fixing that record date.

Ch. 82, L. '01 Synopsis of Section 215

The amendment to Section 215(a) makes the provisions of Sections 211(a) and 212(c) and (d) applicable to nonstock corporations, with the references in such subsections to stockholders and the board of directors being deemed, when applied to a nonstock corporation, to be references to the members of such corporation and to the governing body of such corporation, respectively.

New subsection (e) of Section 215 provides that, in the specified circumstances, any requirement of a written ballot shall be satisfied by a ballot submitted by electronic transmission.

Ch. 339, L. '98 Synopsis of Section 215

The amendment to Section 215(c) effects a change in the required vote for the election of members of the governing body of a nonstock corporation, so that, absent a provision to the contrary in the certificate of incorporation or bylaws, the members of the governing body shall be elected by a plurality of the votes of the members of the corporation present in person or represented by proxy at the meeting and entitled to vote thereon, rather than a majority of such members present in person or represented by proxy at the meeting and entitled to vote thereon. This conforms Section 215(c) to the provisions of Section 216(c), applicable to the election of directors of a stock corporation.

Comment: This section has been amended to provide in subsection (a) that the provisions of §216 respecting the minimum for a quorum and other voting provisions for stock corporations shall not apply to a nonstock corporation. A new provision is added in subsection (c) to provide for quorum and voting rules for the meetings of members of a non-stock corporation.

216 QUORUM AND REQUIRED VOTE FOR STOCK CORPORATIONS.— Subject to this chapter in respect of the vote that shall be required for a specified action, the certificate of incorporation or bylaws of any corporation authorized to issue stock may specify the number of shares and/or the amount of other securities having voting power the holders of which shall be present or represented by proxy at any meeting in order to constitute a quorum for, and the votes that shall be necessary for, the transaction of any business, but in no event shall a quorum consist of less than one-third of the shares entitled to vote at the meeting, except that, where a separate vote by a class or series or classes or series is required, a quorum shall consist of no less than one-third of the shares of such class or series or classes or series. In the absence of such specification in the certificate of incorporation or bylaws of the corporation:

(1) A majority of the shares entitled to vote, present in person or represented by proxy, shall constitute a quorum at a meeting of stockholders;

(2) In all matters other than the election of directors, the affirmative vote of the majority of shares present in person or represented by proxy at the meeting and entitled to vote on the subject matter shall be the act of the stockholders;

(3) Directors shall be elected by a plurality of the votes of the shares present in person or represented by proxy at the meeting and entitled to vote on the election of directors; and

(4) Where a separate vote by a class or series or classes or series is required, a majority of the outstanding shares of such class or series or classes or series, present in person or represented by proxy, shall constitute a quorum entitled to take action with respect to that vote on that matter and, *in all matters other than the election of directors,* the affirmative vote of the majority of shares of such class or series or classes or series present in person or represented by proxy at the meeting shall be the act of such class or series or classes or series.

A bylaw amendment adopted by stockholders which specifies the votes that that shall be necessary for the election of directors shall not be further amended or repealed by the board of directors. (Last amended by Ch. 145, L. '07, eff. 8-1-07.)

Ch. 145, L. '07, eff. 8-1-07, added matter in italic.

Ch. 145, L. '07 Synopsis of Section 216

The amendment to §216(4) clarifies that, unless otherwise provided in the certificate of incorporation or the bylaws, a plurality vote (and not a majority of the quorum) is the vote required to elect directors where one or more classes or series of stock votes as a separate class or series on the election of directors.

Ch. 339, L. '98 Synopsis of Section 216

The amendments to Section 216 provide that, where a separate vote of a class or series or classes or series is required, a quorum shall be no less than one-third of the shares entitled to vote and clarify that the rules in that section that relate to class votes apply to any vote of a class or series or classes or series.

.1 Stockholder's withdrawal from meeting—effect on quorum.—All sessions of stockholders' meetings are but part of meeting and so quorum need not remain continuously throughout the meeting. *Atterbury v Consolidated Copper Mines Corp, 20 A2d 743 (Ch Ct 1941).*

Where there is a required quorum when meeting convenes, there is deemed to be a quorum for the entire meeting and the subsequent withdrawal before election of directors of holders of sufficient proxies to reduce voting shares below quorum needs will not invalidate such election. *Duffy v Loft, Inc, 151 A 223 (Ch Ct),* aff'd, *152 A 849 (1930).*

When a number of stockholders left the meeting before shares were counted to ascertain whether a quorum was present, such shares could not later be presumed to have been present in order to establish a quorum. *In re Gulia, 115 A 317 (Ch Ct 1921).*

Where two 50% shareholders constitute all shareholders of the corporation, and one leaves the meeting before official action is taken, no corporate action can be taken at the shareholders' meeting without the concurrence of both shareholders. *Testa v Jarvis, No. 12847 (Ch Ct 12-30-93).*

.2 No record of stockholders present.—When less than majority voted and no records of those present were kept, then there was no quorum present to hold the meeting. *Leamy v Sinaloa Exploration & Development Co, 130 A 282 (Ch Ct 1925).*

Where it is disputed that a meeting of a quorum of a board of directors occurred, the fact that the meeting occurred must be independently corroborated by evidence other than the testimony of the directors who purportedly attended the meeting. *In re Bigmar, Inc, Section 225 Litigation,* 2002 Del. Ch. LEXIS 45 *(Ch Ct 2002).*

.3 What shares may be counted.—Treasury stock should not be counted for quorum purposes. However, when stockholders appeared at annual meeting in their capacity as such and also owned shares registered in their names as nominees but had to authority to vote these shares, such nominee stock should be counted in determining whether a quorum is present. *Atterbury,* above.

Stockholder's shares cannot be counted for quorum purposes when he attended meeting solely to protest its legality and was ejected from the meeting before voting took place. *Leamy,* above.

Corporate charter provision for voting power based upon size of individual shareholder's holding rather than class differentiations was not invalid and corporation could gear its quorum definition to specified number of shares to be present rather than number of stockholders. *Providence and Worcester Co v Baker, 378 A2d 121 (1977).*

Shares of stock co-held in trust by two brothers could not be counted in determining a majority needed to amend close corporation's bylaws. Under a previous judicial order, neither brother could vote the trust shares unless they agreed how to vote; since they could not agree in the present dispute, no one was empowered to vote the shares—thus, the trust shares were not "entitled to vote on the subject matter" under GCL §216(2). *Hammersmith v Elmhurst-Chicago Stone Co, No. 10,837 (Ch Ct 1989).*

.4 "Shares present" v. "voting power present".—Court upheld distinction between shares present for quorum purposes and voting power present for voting purposes. Thus, shareholder represented by limited proxy may be present for quorum purposes, but if proxy does not empower holder to vote on particular proposal, shares represented by proxy cannot be considered as part of voting power present with respect to that proposal. *Berlin v Emerald Partners, 552 A2d 482 (1989).*

217 VOTING RIGHTS OF FIDUCIARIES, PLEDGORS AND JOINT OWNERS OF STOCK.—(a) Persons holding stock in a fiduciary capacity shall be entitled to vote the shares so held. Persons whose stock is pledged shall be entitled to vote, unless in the transfer by the pledgor on the books of the corporation [1]*such person* has expressly empowered the pledgee to vote thereon, in which case only the pledgee, or [2]*such pledgee's* proxy, may represent such stock and vote thereon.

(b) If shares or other securities having voting power stand of record in the names of 2 or more persons, whether fiduciaries, members of a partnership, joint tenants, tenants in common, tenants by the entirety or otherwise, or if 2 or more persons have the same fiduciary relationship respecting the same shares, unless the secretary of the corporation is given written notice to the contrary and is furnished with a copy of the instrument or order appointing them or creating the relationship wherein it is so provided, their acts with respect to voting shall have the following effect:

(1) If only 1 votes, [2]*such person's* act binds all;
(2) If more than 1 vote, the act of the majority so voting binds all;
(3) If more than 1 vote, but the vote is evenly split on any particular matter, each faction may vote the securities in question proportionally, or any person voting the shares, or a beneficiary, if any, may apply to the Court of Chancery or such other court as may have jurisdiction to appoint an additional person to act with the persons so voting the shares, which shall then be voted as determined by a majority of such persons and the person appointed by the Court. If the instrument so filed shows that any such tenancy is held in unequal interests, a majority or even split for the purpose of this subsection shall be a majority or even split in interest. (Last amended by Ch. 339, L. '98, eff. 7-1-98.)

Ch. 339, L. '98, eff. 7-1-98, added matter in italic and deleted [1]"he" and [2]"his".

Ch. 339, L. '98 Synopsis of Section 217

The amendments to these Sections eliminate masculine references in the statutes, and replace them with gender neutral references.

.1 Right of broker to vote.—Brokers' proxies covering shares in margin accounts are valid when beneficial owners have not objected, their beneficial interest does not appear on corporate stockbook, and there is no showing proxies are voted contrary to beneficial owners' instructions. *Schott v Climax Molybdenum Co, 154 A2d 221 (Ch Ct 1959).*

.2 Fiduciaries.—Stock registered in decedent's name may be voted by an executor or administrator. *Investment Associates v Standard Power & #38; Light Corp, 48 A2d 501 (Ch Ct 1947).*

Guardian's proxy for shares registered in ward's name (latter having been adjudged mentally incompetent) should be counted, since incompetency once established is presumed to continue until contrary is shown. *Gow v Consolidated Coppermines Corp, 165 A 136 (Ch Ct 1933).*

.3 Right of pledgor to vote.—Pledgor has right to vote stock registered in the name of pledgee unless in transfer on the books pledgor has expressly empowered pledgee to vote the shares. *Italo Petroleum Corp of America v Producers' Oil Corp of America, 174 A 276 (Ch Ct 1934).*

.4 Validity of vote.—Consent that purported to replace existing board of directors with new board was invalid because it was not signed by holders of 50% of outstanding shares of corporation entitled to vote. *Cook v Pumpelly, Nos. 7917 & #38; 7930 (Ch Ct 5-24-85).*

218 VOTING TRUSTS AND OTHER VOTING AGREEMENTS.—(a) One stockholder or 2 or more stockholders may by agreement in writing deposit capital stock of an original issue with or transfer capital stock to any person or persons, or [1]*entity or* *entities* authorized to act as trustee, for the purpose of vesting in such person or persons, [1]*entity or entities*, who may be designated voting trustee, or voting trustees, the right to vote thereon for any period of time determined by such agreement, upon the terms and conditions stated in such agreement. The agreement may contain any other lawful provisions not inconsistent with such purpose. After the filing of a copy of the agreement in the registered office of the corporation in this State, which copy shall be open to the inspection of any stockholder of the corporation or any beneficiary of the trust under the agreement daily during business hours, certificates of stock or uncertificated stock shall be issued to the voting trustee or trustees to represent any stock of an original issue so deposited with such voting trustee or trustees, and any certificates of stock or uncertificated stock so transferred to the voting trustee or trustees shall be surrendered and cancelled and new certificates or uncertificated stock shall be issued therefore to the voting trustee or trustees. In the certificate so issued, if any, it shall be stated that it is issued pursuant to such agreement, and that fact shall also be stated in the stock ledger of the corporation. The voting trustee or trustees may vote the stock so issued or transferred during the period specified in the agreement. Stock standing in the name of the voting trustee or trustees may be voted either in person or by proxy, and in voting the stock, the voting trustee or trustees shall incur no responsibility as stockholder, trustee or otherwise, except for their own individual malfeasance. In any case where 2 or more persons *or entities* are designated as voting trustees, and the right and method of voting any stock standing in their names at any meeting of the corporation are not fixed by the agreement appointing the trustees, the right to vote the stock and the manner of voting it at the meeting shall be determined by a majority of the trustees, or if they be equally divided as to the right and manner of voting the stock in any particular case, the vote of the stock in such case shall be divided equally among the trustees.

(b) Any amendment to a voting trust agreement shall be made by a written agreement, a copy of which shall be filed in the registered office of the corporation in this State.

(c) An agreement between 2 or more stockholders, if in writing and signed by the parties thereto, may provide that in exercising any voting rights, the shares held by them shall be voted as provided by the agreement, or as the parties may agree, or as determined in accordance with a procedure agreed upon by them.

(d) This section shall not be deemed to invalidate any voting or other agreement among stockholders or any irrevocable proxy which is not otherwise illegal. (Last amended by Ch. 82, L. '01, eff. 7-1-01.)

Ch. 82, L. '01, eff. 7-1-01, added matter in italic and deleted [1]"corporation or corporations".

Ch. 82, L. '01 Synopsis of Section 218

Under this amendment to Section 218(a), entities other than corporations may also become voting trustees.

Ch. 339, L. '98 Synopsis of Section 218

The amendments to these Sections eliminate masculine references in the statutes, and replace them with gender neutral references.

Ch. 263, L. '94 Synopsis of Section 218(a)

The agreement to the opening clause of Section 218(a) clarifies that a voting trust may be established by a single stockholder alone or by two or more stockholders together. The other amendments to Section 218 eliminate the 10-year limitation on the duration of voting trust agreements and voting agreements and the corresponding limitations on the extension of such agreements and make related conforming changes.

.1 **Construction.**—Agreement between two groups of stockholders, each owning equal amount of corporation's stock, to create new class of non-participating voting stock and issue one share to new director so he can break deadlock, is not voting trust subject to ten-year limit, since stockholders retained their voting rights; nor does issuance of voting stock with no proprietary rights violate public policy. *Lehrman v Cohen, 222 A2d 800 (1966).*

Nor is agreement to transfer stock to another, with transferor retaining right to surrender at any time certificate received in lieu of stock and receive back his stock or without so doing to receive blank proxy to vote his stock, a voting trust agreement. *Aldridge v Franco Wyoming Oil Co, 7 A2d 753 (Ch Ct 1939),* aff'd, *14 A2d 380 (1941).*

Creditor was holder of corporation's stock in voting trust it set up and voting trustees were its agents when (1) only practical effect of voting trust was to circumvent three-year limitation on proxy voting, (2) trustees were precluded from voting on corporation's structural changes, (3) trustees could not dispose of or encumber stock, (4) all dividends were paid to creditor, and (5) trust was terminable at creditor's will. Therefore, creditor never relinquished its status as holder of more than 10% of corporation's stock within purview of tax statute under review. *Genway Corp v Director, Division of Taxation, 8 NJ Tax 198 (Tax Ct 1986).*

.2 Definition.—Voting trust as commonly understood is device whereby two or more persons owning stock with voting powers divest voting right thereof from ownership. They retain ownership in themselves and transfer voting rights to trustees. *Peyton v Peyton Corp, 194 A2d 106 (Ch Ct 1937).*

.3 Enforceability.—Party to voting trust agreement may attack it or its renewal for failure of compliance with this section and may not be prevented from asserting such illegality because of existence of facts calling for application of doctrine of "clean hands" and estoppel. *Appon v Belle Isle Corp, 46 A2d 749 (Ch Ct),* aff'd, *49 A2d 1 (1946).* See also, *Belle Isle Corp v Mac Bean, 49 A2d 5 (Ch Ct 1946).*

When Delaware court had declared voting trust void and trustees began suit in Ohio to have trust declared valid, Delaware court lacked personal jurisdiction over trustees and so could not punish them for contempt, but it could consider quo warranto proceedings against corporation. *Smith v Biggs Boiler Works Co, 85 A2d 365 (Ch Ct 1951),* aff'd sub nom *Krizanek v Smith, 87 A2d 871 (1952).*

.4 Validity.—Restraint on alienation of voting trust certificates which is unreasonable makes voting trust agreement invalid; restraint against sale of voting trust certificate holder's interest for almost ten years is unreasonable. *Tracey v Franklin, 61 A2d 780 (Ch Ct 1948),* aff'd, *67 A2d 56 (1949).*

Stock-pooling agreement, which accomplishes purposes of voting trust by divorcing voting power from beneficiary ownership and giving it to "agents" who must vote as 7/8th of them decide, is void if it does not comply with statute dealing with voting trusts. *Abercrombie v Davies, 130 A2d 338 (1957),* rev'g, *123 A2d 893 (Ch Ct 1956).*

Court refused to restrain target's implementation of voting trust established by merger agreement with tender offeror because competing tender offeror was not threatened by immediate irreparable injury when (1) implementation of voting trust had already occurred, (2) threatened harm, takedown of shares tendered in tender offeror, would not be prevented by restraining voting trust, (3) target's shareholders were not being coerced by tender offeror's timing advantage over competing offeror, and (4) timing advantage resulted from competing offeror's own actions. *Macfadden Holdings, Inc v John Blair & Co, No. 8489 (Ch Ct 7-2-86).*

Where stock rights plan precluded 30 percent holder from forming joint slate with other shareholders or otherwise entering revocable stock voting agreements but plan was likely to have a minimal impact upon 30 percent holder's proxy campaign, court denied motion for partial summary judgment as to whether stock rights plan's definition of "beneficial ownership" caused plan to have inequitable effect on corporate franchise. Despite restrictions, plaintiff was able to put forth slate of candidates and communicate his position, and other shareholders were free to vote for slate without restriction. *Stahl v Apple Bancorp Inc, No. 11510 (Ch Ct 8-9-90).*

Restrictions on voting are read narrowly to disfavor the disenfranchisement of shares, and, therefore, unambiguous terms in a voting agreement will not, on a motion for summary judgment, be interpreted to have a meaning contrary to their plain meaning on the basis of extrinsic evidence that is less than clear and convincing. *Chandler v Ciccoricco, 2003 Del. Ch. LEXIS 47 (Ch Ct 2003).*

.5 Beneficial owner of stock has title.—Beneficial owner of stock has title as against one in whose name stock stands on corporation's books. *Chadwick v Parkhill Corp, 141 A 823 (Ch Ct 1928).*

.6 Rights of trustees other than voting trustees.—Validity of election of directors cannot be made to turn on (1) fact that directors were elected by shares voted by proxies of trustees of inter vivos trust who were not registered as owners of shares and on (2) fact that trust, although created by trustor having legal right to do so, was improperly motivated. *Gans v Delaware Terminal Corp, 2 A2d 154 (Ch Ct 1938).*

.7 Rights of voting trustees.—Trustees of stock in voting trust can, by proxy, delegate exercise of voting power to others, even in discretionary matters, under this section. The provision in this section that trustees may vote by proxy extends only to delegating to others ministerial act of voting after voting trustees have determined how vote shall be cast. *Chandler v Bellanca Aircraft Corp, 162 A 63 (Ch Ct 1932); Smith v First Personal Bankers' Corp, 171 A 839 (Ch Ct 1934).*

.8 Removal of voting trustees.—The court will remove voting trustees who are personally interested adversely to corporation in outcome of election of directors. *Lippard v Parish, 191 A 829 (Ch Ct 1937).*

.9 Rights of holders of voting trust certificates.—Fact that directors of holding company serve as voting trustees and can perpetuate themselves in office is not ground for preliminary injunction, in absence of fraud or overreaching. *Adams v Clearance Corp, 116 A2d 893 (Ch Ct 1955),* aff'd, *121 A2d 302 (1956).*

Restrictions on voting trust agreements must be reasonable. *Grynberg v Burke, 378 A2d 139 (Ch Ct 1977).*

.10 Termination of voting trust.—Corporation as sole settlor, depositing stockholder, and beneficiary of voting trust can terminate it against consent of voting trustees. *H M Byllesby & Co v Doriot, 12 A2d 603 (Ch Ct 1940).*

Irrevocable voting trust agreement may not be terminated by notice of depositing shareholder without consent of trustees, other voting trust certificate holders or banks holding outstanding loans to corporation. *Hearst v Consolidated Newspapers, 51 FSupp 171 (D Del 1943).*

Court may terminate voting trust agreement that does not comply strictly with requirements of this section. *Belle Isle Corp v Corcoran, 49 A2d 1 (1946).*

Stockholders who put control of corporation into voting trust were not able to regain control when (1) their amendatory agreement changing term of trust was invalid because it was not entered into within two years prior to expiration of original term (as required by statute), (2) amendatory agreement could not place stock pledged as security for corporate debts into voting trust, and (3) letter revoking voting trust was not binding on corporation that was not beneficiary of any such trust. *Grynberg v Burke,* above.

University cannot set aside extension of corporation's voting trust, since nominal stockholders of corporation formed for exclusive benefit of university are considered "beneficiaries" of voting trust, and so had power to extend it; however question of whether nominal stockholders were agents and fiduciaries acting in violation of their duty to university when they extended agreement is remanded for trial. *Foye v New York University, 269 A2d 63 (1970).*

.11 Right to deposit stock in voting trust.—Delaware holding corporation owning controlling stock in another corporation can deposit its stock in voting trust. *Adams v Clearance Corp, 116 A2d 893 (Ch Ct 1955),* aff'd, *121 A2d 302 (1956).*

.12 Fiduciary duties.—Voting trustees of a corporation's stock breach their fiduciary duties by executing agreements with some of the stockholder groups they represent, and not others, which purportedly bind the voting trustees to vote and act in a particular manner, and by concealing from certain shareholder the existence of the subsequent agreement that has affected the basic terms of the original voting trust agreement. *President and Fellows of Harvard College v Glancy, 2003 Del. Ch. LEXIS 25 (Ch Ct 2003).*

219 LIST OF STOCKHOLDERS ENTITLED TO VOTE; PENALTY FOR REFUSAL TO PRODUCE; STOCK LEDGER.—[1](a) *The officer who has charge of the stock ledger of a corporation shall prepare and make, at least 10 days before every meeting of stockholders, a complete list of the stockholders entitled to vote at the meeting; provided, however, if the record date for determining the stockholders entitled to vote is less than 10 days before the meeting date, the list shall reflect the stockholders entitled to vote as of the tenth day before the meeting date, arranged in alphabetical order, and showing the address of each stockholder and the number of shares registered in the name of each stockholder. Nothing contained in this section shall require the corporation to include electronic mail addresses or other electronic contact information on such list. Such list shall be open to the examination of any stockholder for any purpose germane to the meeting for a period of at least 10 days prior to the meeting: (i) on a reasonably accessible electronic network, provided that the information required to gain access to such list is provided with the notice of the meeting, or (ii) during ordinary business hours, at the principal place of business of the corporation. In the event that the corporation determines to make the list available on an electronic network, the corporation may take reasonable steps to ensure that such information is available only to stockholders of the corporation. If the meeting is to be held at a place, then a list of stockholders entitled to vote at the meeting shall be produced and kept at the time and place of the meeting during the whole time thereof and may be examined by any stockholder who is present. If the meeting is to be held solely by means of remote communication, then such list shall also be open to the examination of any stockholder during the whole time of the meeting on a reasonably accessible electronic network, and the information required to access such list shall be provided with the notice of the meeting.*

(b) If the corporation, or an officer or agent thereof, refuses to permit examination of the list by a stockholder, such stockholder may apply to the Court of Chancery for an order to compel the corporation to permit such examination. The burden of proof shall be on the

corporation to establish that the examination such stockholder seeks is for a purpose not germane to the meeting. The Court may summarily order the corporation to permit examination of the list upon such conditions as the Court may deem appropriate, and may make such additional orders as may be appropriate, including, without limitation, postponing the meeting or voiding the results of the meeting.

(c) The stock ledger shall be the only evidence as to who are the stockholders entitled by this section to examine the list required by this section or to vote in person or by proxy at any meeting of stockholders. (Last amended by Ch. 14, L. '09, eff. 8-1-09.)

Ch. 14, L. '09, eff. 8-1-09, added matter in italic and deleted [1]"(a) The officer who has charge of the stock ledger of a corporation shall prepare and make, at least 10 days before every meeting of stockholders, a complete list of the stockholders entitled to vote at the meeting, arranged in alphabetical order, and showing the address of each stockholder and the number of shares registered in the name of each stockholder. Nothing contained in this section shall require the corporation to include electronic mail addresses or other electronic contact information on such list. Such list shall be open to the examination of any stockholder for any purpose germane to the meeting for a period of at least 10 days prior to the meeting: (i) on a reasonably accessible electronic network, provided that the information required to gain access to such list is provided with the notice of the meeting, or (ii) during ordinary business hours, at the principal place of business of the corporation. In the event that the corporation determines to make the list available on an electronic network, the corporation may take reasonable steps to ensure that such information is available only to stockholders of the corporation. If the meeting is to be held at a place, then the list shall be produced and kept at the time and place of the meeting during the whole time thereof and may be examined by any stockholder who is present. If the meeting is to be held solely by means of remote communication, then the list shall also be open to the examination of any stockholder during the whole time of the meeting on a reasonably accessible electronic network, and the information required to access such list shall be provided with the notice of the meeting."

Ch. 14, L. '09 Synopsis of Section 219

This section amends Section 219(a) to clarify that, where the record date for determining stockholders entitled to vote is set less then ten days before the date of the meeting as provided for under Section 213(a), the corporation's obligation to provide a list of stockholders prior to the meeting is limited to preparing a list of those holders as of the tenth day before the meeting date. The amendment does not affect the list that must be provided at the meeting.

Ch. 252, L. '08 Synopsis of Section 219

The Amendment to Section 219(a), Title 8, of the Delaware Code, is to remove any suggestion that the words "examined" and "inspected" were intentionally distinct.

Section 219(b), Title 8, of the Delaware Code, has been substantially rewritten to eliminate the concept of "willful neglect" and to allocate and specify the burden of proof on an application to compel examination of a list. It replaces the single sanction of ineligibility to stand for election with a grant of broad authority to the Court of Chancery to fashion appropriate relief.

Ch. 84, L. '03 Synopsis of Section 219

This amendment will make Section 219(c) consistent with Section 220 as revised.

Ch. 343, L. '00 Synopsis of Section 219

The amendments to Section 219 delete from the existing statute provisions requiring that the list of stockholders be available either at a place within the city where the meeting is to be held or at the place of the meeting for 10 days prior to the meeting, and substitute in lieu thereof a requirement that the list either be made available on an electronic network or at the corporation's principal place of business. The amendments also provide that, in the case of a meeting of stockholders held without a physical location, the list shall be made available during the meeting on an electronic network.

.1 Who may inspect.—Record owner can inspect stock ledger, even though he is acting for beneficial owner. *Trans World Airlines, Inc v State, 183 A2d 174 (1962).*

.2 Failure to maintain proper stockholders' list.—Stockholders will not be deprived of their right to vote because corporation kept its stock ledger in such manner that stock list was deceptive. *In re Election of Directors of Associated Automatic Sprinkler Co, 102 A 787 (Ch Ct 1917).*

Corporation that did not maintain stock ledger and ignored other corporate formalities could not object to inspection of books and records on ground that shareholder seeking inspection was not shareholder of record, but wholly owned subsidiary of shareholder of record. Once court is forced to inquire into underlying facts concerning stock ownership because corporation has maintained no stock ledger, there is little continued utility in insisting that valid demand is one made by shareholder rather than wholly owned subsidiary of shareholder. *Pan Ocean Navigation, Inc v Rainbow Navigation, Inc, No. 8674 (Ch Ct 7-8-87),* aff'd, *535 A2d 1357 (1987).*

.3 Changing corporate record.—Group of shareholders was not entitled to damages when corporation delayed five months in changing name on its records from group's nominee account to names of individual shareholders, because they did not suffer any deprivation of their shareholder rights since they could have exercised rights at any time through nominee. *Loretto Literary & Benevolent Institution v Blue Diamond Coal Co, 444 A2d 256 (Ch Ct 1982).*

.4 Record owners.—Neither parent corporation nor directors of wholly owned subsidiary owe fiduciary duties to subsidiary's prospective shareholders after parent declares its intention to spin off subsidiary. Prior to distribution of assets in spinoff, prospective shareholders' interests in subsidiary are insufficient to impose fiduciary duties on parent or subsidiary's directors. Under GCL §219, stock ledger is only evidence as to stockholders of record. However, this only applies to listing of present stockholders of existing entities and not to prospective shareholders of subsidiary being spun off. *Anadarko Petroleum Corp v Panhandle Eastern Corp, 545 A2d 1171 (1988).*

In the face of no positive evidence of ownership to contradict the stock ledger, plaintiff failed to bear her burden of proof that she was a shareholder entitled to vote at a meeting or by consent. Because she was not a shareholder at the time of the shareholder meeting, that meeting was not invalid for want of notice to her. *Testa v Jarvis, No. 12847 (Ch Ct 12-30-93).*

Where plaintiff was terminated for cause from his position as chairman and chief executive officer of the corporation, which triggered a provision of a stockholders' agreement between plaintiff and the corporation requiring plaintiff to sell his stock back to the corporation, but remained a stockholder of record, the court held that a current stockholder of record has standing to seek inspection rights even though the possibility exists that he may later be divested of his stock in some other proceeding. *Holtzman v Gruen Holding Corp, No. 13500 (Ch Ct 8-5-94).*

A labor union which held stock in a Delaware corporation was entitled to a list of the corporation's shareholders following its properly made request. The union stated that it sought the list in order to contact other shareholders in connection with a resolution it wished to make concerning the corporation's purchase and resale of goods made in China, allegedly by forced labor, in violation of United States law. The corporation feared that the union sought the list in order to contact its employee-shareholders (who were not unionized) in order to further its organizing activities. However, the union had proposed measures that would have protected against this possibility, including deletion of the names of such employee-shareholders from the list and the court found this to be conclusive evidence that the union was not seeking to harm the corporation. Finally, the court held that the union's purpose in seeking the list in support of a resolution proposed solely for moral and political reasons was a permissible one under the inspection statute. *The Food and Allied Service Trades Department, AFL-CIO v Wal-Mart Stores, Inc, No. 12551 (Ch Ct 5-19-92).*

.5 Voting rights; bylaw amendments.—Votes based on voting rights purchased in violation of a restricted stock agreement are void and will not be counted. Moreover, a bylaw amendment that purports to shrink the number of board seats below the number of sitting directors is void, as is a bylaw that purports to establish qualifications for directorships that would disqualify a sitting director and terminate his service. *Crown EMAK Partners, LLC v Kurz, 2010 Del. LEXIS 182 (2010).*

220 INSPECTION OF BOOKS AND RECORDS.—(a) As used in this section:

[2] *(1)* "Stockholder" means a holder of record of stock in a stock corporation, or a person who is the beneficial owner of shares of such stock held either in a voting trust or by a nominee on behalf of such person [3].

[4] *(2)* "Subsidiary" means any entity directly or indirectly owned, in whole or in part, by the corporation of which the stockholder is a stockholder and over the affairs of which the corporation directly or indirectly exercises control, and includes, without limitation, corporations, partnerships, limited partnerships, limited liability partnerships, limited liability companies, statutory trusts and/or joint ventures.

[5] *(3)* "Under oath" includes statements the declarant affirms to be true under penalty of perjury under the laws of the United States or any state.

(b) Any stockholder, in person or by attorney or other agent, shall, upon written demand under oath stating the purpose thereof, have the right during the usual hours for business to inspect for any proper purpose, and to make copies and extracts from:

(1) The corporation's stock ledger, a list of its stockholders, and its other books and records; and

(2) A subsidiary's books and records, to the extent that:

a. The corporation has actual possession and control of such records of such subsidiary; or

b. The corporation could obtain such records through the exercise of control over such subsidiary, provided that as of the date of the making of the demand:

1. The stockholder inspection of such books and records of the subsidiary would not constitute a breach of an agreement between the corporation or the subsidiary and a person or persons not affiliated with the corporation; and

2. The subsidiary would not have the right under the law applicable to it to deny the corporation access to such books and records upon demand by the corporation.

In every instance where the stockholder is other than a record holder of stock in a stock corporation, or a member of a nonstock corporation, the demand under oath shall state the person's status as a stockholder, be accompanied by documentary evidence of beneficial ownership of the stock, and state that such documentary evidence is a true and correct copy of what it purports to be. A proper purpose shall mean a purpose reasonably related to such person's interest as a stockholder. In every instance where an attorney or other agent shall be the person who seeks the right to inspection, the demand under oath shall be accompanied by a power of attorney or such other writing which authorizes the attorney or other agent to so act on behalf of the stockholder. The demand under oath shall be directed to the corporation at its registered office in this State or at its principal place of business.

(c) If the corporation, or an officer or agent thereof, refuses to permit an inspection sought by a stockholder or attorney or other agent acting for the stockholder pursuant to subsection (b) of this section or does not reply to the demand within 5 business days after the demand has been made, the stockholder may apply to the Court of Chancery for an order to compel such inspection. The Court of Chancery is hereby vested with exclusive jurisdiction to determine whether or not the person seeking inspection is entitled to the inspection sought. The Court may summarily order the corporation to permit the stockholder to inspect the corporation's stock ledger, an existing list of stockholders, and its other books and records, and to make copies or extracts therefrom; or the Court may order the corporation to furnish to the stockholder a list of its stockholders as of a specific date on condition that the stockholder first pay to the corporation the reasonable cost of obtaining and furnishing such list and on such other conditions as the Court deems appropriate. Where the stockholder seeks to inspect the corporation's books and records, other than its stock ledger or list of stock-holders, such stockholder shall first establish that:

(1) Such stockholder is a stockholder;

(2) Such stockholder has complied with this section respecting the form and manner of making demand for inspection of such documents; and

(3) The inspection such stockholder seeks is for a proper purpose.

Where the stockholder seeks to inspect the corporation's stock ledger or list of stockholders and establishes that such stockholder is a stockholder and has complied with this section respecting the form and manner of making demand for inspection of such documents, the burden of proof shall be upon the corporation to establish that the inspection such stockholder seeks is for an improper purpose. The Court may, in its discretion, prescribe any limitations or conditions with reference to the inspection, or award such other or further relief as the Court may deem just and proper. The Court may order books, documents and records, pertinent extracts therefrom, or duly authenticated copies thereof, to be brought within this State and kept in this State upon such terms and conditions as the order may prescribe.

[6]*(d) Any director shall have the right to examine the corporation's stock ledger, a list of its stockholders and its other books and records for a purpose reasonably related to the director's position as a director. The Court of Chancery is hereby vested with the exclusive jurisdiction to determine whether a director is entitled to the inspection sought. The Court may summarily order the corporation to permit the director to inspect any and all books and records, the stock ledger and the list of stockholders and to make copies or extracts therefrom. The burden of proof shall be upon the corporation to establish that the inspection such director seeks is for an improper purpose. The Court may, in its discretion, prescribe any limitations or conditions with reference to the inspection, or award such other and further relief as the Court may deem just and proper.* (Last amended by Ch. 253, L. '10, eff. 8-1-10.)

Ch. 253, L. '10, eff. 8-1-10, added matter in italic and deleted [1]"(1) "List of stockholders" includes lists of members in a nonstock corporation."; [2]"(2)"; [3]", and also a member of a nonstick corporation as reflected on the records of the nonstock corporation"; [4]"(3)"; [5]"(4)"; and [6]"(d) Any director (including a member of the governing body of a nonstock corporation) shall have the right to examine the corporation's stock ledger, a list of its stockholders and its other books and records for a purpose reasonably related to the director's position as a director. The Court of Chancery is hereby vested with the exclusive jurisdiction to determine whether a director is entitled to the inspection sought. The Court may summarily order the corporation to permit the director to inspect any and all books and records, the stock ledger and the list of stockholder's and to make copies or extracts therefrom. The burden of proof shall be upon the corporation to establish that the inspection such director seeks is for an improper purpose. The Court may, in its discretion, prescribe any limitations or conditions with reference to the inspection, or award such other and further relief as the Court may deem just and proper."

Ch. 253, L. '10 Synopsis of Section 220

Sections 20, 21, 22, 23, 24, 25, and 26 make technical changes to §220, §223, and §225 of the DGCL consistent with the intent of the bill and with the translator provision in new §114(a).

Ch. 84, L. '03 Synopsis of Section 220

These sections amend Section 220 in four principal respects. First, inspection rights are extended to a person who beneficially owns stock through either a voting trustee or a nominee who holds the stock of record on behalf of such person. Second, the oath requirement is deemed satisfied by a declaration under penalty of perjury under the law of the United States or any state. Third, books and records subject to inspection include those of subsidiaries under certain conditions. Finally, a director's purpose for inspection is presumed to be proper. The amendment relating to inspection of books and records of subsidiaries is not intended to affect existing legal doctrine that, as a general matter, respects the separate legal existence of subsidiaries in relation to liability of stockholders to third parties, personal jurisdiction over subsidiaries of Delaware corporations, and discovery in litigation other than under Section 220.

Ch. 339, L. '98 Synopsis of Section 220

The amendments to these Sections eliminate masculine references in the statutes, and replace them with gender neutral references.

Ch. 79, L. '95 Synopsis of Section 220

These amendments to Section 220 are adopted in response to the decision of the Court of Chancery in *Scattered Corp. v. Chicago Stock Exchange, Inc.*, Del. Ch., C.A. No. 13703, Jacobs, V.C. (December 2, 1994) and expand the definitions of "stockholder" and "list of stockholders" to include members of nonstock corporations and lists of those members. The inspection rights of a member of the governing board of a nonstock corporation are included within those of directors under subsection (d).

Comment: The amendment to §220 is designed to codify the common law right of a director of a Delaware corporation to examine the stock list, books and records and to permit the director to obtain summary relief in the Court of Chancery to enforce his right. Pursuant to the present case law, it is not clear whether the Court of Chancery has jurisdiction over such an action by a director. The amendment is not intended to effect any substantive changes in the directors' rights to inspect such corporate records.

The second and third amendments to Sections 211(c) and 225 are to permit a director as well as a stockholder to bring an action in the Delaware Court of Chancery to require the holding of an annual meeting, to determine the validity of any election and the right of a person to hold office. At the present time, the relevant case law does not permit a director to bring such an action in the Court of Chancery; it is limited to stockholders.

.1 Scope of inspection.—Stockholder could not be denied access to corporate records on ground that they relate to class of stock other than that to which he belonged, since stockholder has right to inspect all corporate books that reasonably relate to his purpose if it is a proper one. *Western Pacific Industries Inc v Liggett & Myers, Inc, 310 A2d 669 (Ch Ct 1973).*

Stockholder with proper purpose may inspect and copy stockholder list even though no meeting of stockholders is imminent; stockholder is entitled to breakdown of Cede & Co. and similar listings that indicate stock held for brokerage firms and financial institutions; stockholder is entitled to daily transfer sheets, computer tapes, and similar data that is available to corporation regarding its lists of stockholders. *Hatleigh Corp v Lane Bryant Inc, 428 A2d 350 (Ch Ct 1981).*

Directors of merged corporation did not violate Rule 10b-5 when, in response to shareholders' informal requests, they failed to disclose information relating to corporation's financial status or hold annual meetings because (1) corporation was "non-reporting company" under Securities Exchange Act of 1934 so directors had no duty to hold annual meetings or disclose information under Delaware law and (2) shareholders did not make request to inspect books and records under GCL §220. *Polak v Continental Hosts, Ltd, 613 FSupp 153 (SDNY 1985).*

Shareholder was entitled to detailed information concerning vote on corporation's anti-takeover restructuring proposal and list of stockholders who elected to convert stock in order to ascertain if restructuring plan was adopted and implemented because shareholder's legitimate requests about adoption of plan were not answered by corporation. However, shareholder was not entitled to updated list of holders and beneficial owners of stock and copy of daily transfer sheets because shareholder did not show need for material when its only expressed aim was to learn whether reorganization was effective. *Nottingham Partners v Trans-Lux Corp, No. 8755 (Ch Ct 2-4-87).*

Shareholder made a written demand pursuant to GCL §220 to inspect certain books and records of corporation, only some of which were provided. Court found that shareholder was entitled to a review of corporate financial records, because (1) Corporation had disseminated only one financial statement to its public shareholders in ten years; (2) its last annual financial report was issued in 1975; and (3) there were apparently a number of self-dealing transactions involving corporation, its management, and management's family. Because shareholder was unqualified to conduct a meaningful review, further inspection was permitted on condition that inspection and written requests for information were conducted by a certified public accountant. *Orgel v Luna Industries, Inc, No. 8579 (Ch Ct 6-24-87).*

Court denied shareholders' motion to compel corporation to produce strike planning documents, balancing shareholders' need for discovering the information against corporation's need for its protection. A production of the documents was not necessary because: (1) corporation had already produced all documents that did not involve strike planning; (2) denying production of strike planning documents would not drastically impair prospect for accomplishing principal task for which discovery of documents was sought; and (3) documents could not be adequately protected by confidentiality order, and strike planning information was critically important to corporation. *Gioia v Texas Air Corp, No. 9500 (Ch Ct 3-4-88).*

Court held shareholder of 4,723 shares of privately held, high technology corporation was entitled to access to shareholder list where shareholder stated his sole purpose was to ascertain value of his shares and then offer a portion for sale. Shareholder was not, however, entitled to inspect a broad range of books and records and receive information about financial affairs beyond certain financial information he already received, where shareholder had previously indicated that he might disclose confidential information to competitors. *Eastlund v Fusion Systems Corp, No. 11574 (Ch Ct 8-29-90).*

Plaintiffs, two directors of a corporation, were granted leave to supplement their demand for inspection to include a list of shareholders' addresses for purposes of communicating with shareholders, despite the fact that their original demand only requested shareholders' names and numbers of shares owned, where the chairman of the board had contacted shareholders for purposes of criticizing plaintiffs, subsequent to plaintiffs' demand, thereby creating plaintiffs' need to contact shareholders and respond to the chairman's criticism. *Hall v Search Capital Group, Inc, No. 15264 (Ch Ct 11-12-96).*

Plaintiff-stockholder was entitled to inspect corporate books and records under GCL §220 to determine whether pre-suit demand he made was wrongfully refused. After the board of directors had refused his pre-suit demand without explanation, "or peremptorily" nearly one year after he had made it, plaintiff made a GCL §220 request for documents. *Grimes v DSC Communications Corp, C.A. No. 16145-NC (Ch Ct 8-5-98).*

A stockholder seeking to compel inspection of a corporation's books and records on the basis of suspected widespread mismanagement is entitled to a limited inspection of specific items of suspected mismanagement for which the stockholder can adduce sufficient evidence to meet its burden of proof, but is not entitled to a broader inspection where trial evidence does not show the likelihood of systemic mismanagement problems. *Sahagen Satellite Technology Group, LLC v Ellipso, Inc, C.A. No. 18020 NC (Ch Ct 9-27-00).*

The Delaware Supreme Court has held that a stockholder's request to inspect a corporation's books and records may not be denied solely because (1) the documents were prepared by third parties or (2) because the documents predate the stockholder's first investment in the corporation. *Saito v McKesson HBOC, Inc, 806 A2d 113 (2002).*

A corporation's decision to deregister its common stock, by itself, does not demonstrate a potential breach of duty sufficient to support a books and records inspection request, the purported purpose of which is to investigate probable mismanagement or wrongdoing. *Wynnefield Partners Small Cap Value L.P. v Niagara Corp, 2006 Del. Ch. LEXIS 119 (Ch Ct 2006).*

A books and records inspection will be permitted where a shareholder shows that even though each of several factors could individually be legitimate management decisions, taken as a whole they present some credible evidence of possible mismanagement. *Robotti & Company, LLC v Gulfport Energy Corp, 2007 Del. Ch. LEXIS 94 (Ch Ct 2007).*

.2 Purpose in demanding inspection.— Stockholder has statutory right to inspect stockholder's list for purpose of communicating with other stockholders regarding corporation's affairs; also, as director, he has common law right to inspect all other corporate books and records, even though he is hostile to management and possibly could violate his fiduciary duty by making information he gets available to persons not entitled to it; but he cannot appoint as his agent to do such inspecting law firm that represents other stockholders already involved in litigation with corporation. *Henshaw v American Cement Corp, 252 A2d 125 (Ch Ct 1969);* contra, *Weisman v Western Pacific Industries, Inc, 344 A2d 267 (Ch Ct 1975).*

Stockholder can inspect stockholders' list, when he wants to use same for proxy solicitation, even though he may have other purpose such as corporate takeover or merger. *General Time Corp v Talley Industries, Inc, 240 A2d 755 (1968),* cert denied, *393 US 1026 (1969).* To same effect, *Schnell v Chris-Craft Industries, Inc, 283 A2d 852 (Ch Ct 1971); Credit Bureau of St Paul, Inc v Credit Bureau Reports, Inc, 290 A2d 680 (Ch Ct 1972).*

Stockholder can inspect stockholders' list for purpose of communicating with them in proxy solicitation; provision in articles limiting inspection to holders of at least 25% of stock is invalid, and inspection need not wait till SEC approves proposed exchange offer to other stockholders. *Loew's Theatres, Inc v Commercial Credit Co, 243 A2d 78 (Ch Ct 1968).*

Civil Aeronautics Board action pending against stockholder for alleged illegal acquisition of stock in airline corporation is not ground for corporation to deny that stockholder right to inspect stockholders' list for purpose of proxy solicitation, since (1) stockholder meets all state statutory requirements to entitle him to inspect, (2) his purpose is proper even though expressed in general terms without any explanation of why he is seeking proxies, and (3) court has no authority to determine legality of his stock ownership, since federal statute gives that power exclu-

§220

sively to federal agency. *Kerkorian v Western Airlines, Inc, 253 A2d 221 (Ch Ct 1969).*

A shareholder was not entitled to inspect a corporation's books and records under GCL §220 in order to gather evidence for an administrative appeal of a Pension Benefit Guaranty Corporation's determination of the pension benefits to which the plaintiff was entitled as a long-time employee of the corporation's bankrupt successor. The court held that this purpose was not a "proper purpose" under Delaware law but noted that, while no facts were before the court as to procedures before the Pension Benefit Guaranty Corporation, the type of discovery which the plaintiff sought may be available through the Pension Benefit Guaranty Corporation. *Lynn v EnviroSource, Inc, No. 11770 (Ch Ct 5-10-91).*

Stockholder cannot inspect stockholders' list when he states that his purpose is to communicate with other stockholders with reference to special meeting of stockholders. *Northwest Industries, Inc v B F Goodrich Co, 260 A2d 428 (1969).*

Shareholders can examine stock list to solicit other shareholders' support in election contest; it is immaterial that examining shareholders control competing company. *E L Bruce Co v State, 144 A2d 533 (1958).*

Where stockholder, by class bill, seeks relief against corporate wrongdoing, and for purpose of communicating with other shareholders tries to assert his statutory right of examination of stock ledger, purpose of his examination is proper. *State v Standard Oil Co of Kansas, 18 A2d 235 (1941).*

It is not proper purpose, where stockholder seeks to obtain list of names and addresses of stockholders to sell to others. *State v Cities Service Co, 115 A 773 (1922);* nor where purpose is to institute annoying litigation and so compel corporation to purchase stockholder's shares, *State v United Brokerage Co, 101 A 433 (1917);* nor when it is to reverse corporation's policy of producing bombs, *State v Honeywell, Inc, 191 NW2d 406 (Minn 1971).*

Stockholder can inspect stockholders' list for purpose of buying additional shares of company's stock from other stockholders; his demand is not improper even though he bought his own shares originally in order to see list. *Mite Corp v Heli-Coil Corp, 256 A2d 855 (Ch Ct 1969).*

Shareholder cannot inspect list of dissenting shareholders to urge renewal of charter after majority has voted to reorganize; that is not proper purpose, since charter cannot be revived once its existence has been so terminated. *Willard v Harrworth Corp, 258 A2d 914 (Ch Ct 1969),* aff'd, *267 A2d 577 (1970).*

Director, removable at will by majority stockholder vote, cannot inspect corporation's records after his removal, even though he made his demand for inspection and started suit to enforce his demand while he was still director. *Everett v Transnation Development Corp, 267 A2d 627 (Ch Ct 1970).*

Stockholder cannot examine corporation's books and records for alleged purpose of informing himself about economics of proposed merger, when it is shown (1) his interest in merger is primarily as potential competitor, (2) certain records he demands to examine are subject to secrecy agreement signed by corporation, and (3) he can get enough information about merger from proxy statement to oppose it and get appraisal for his shares if he wishes. *State v Gulf Sulphur Corp, 233 A2d 457 (1967).*

Stockholder could inspect stockholder lists and corporate records for specific period of time in question when he had reasonable basis to suspect general corporate mismanagement after: (a) talks with former corporation president who resigned after discovering improprieties, (b) corporation's public disclosures and (c) business profit figures in relationship to industry standards; fact that stockholder was competitor or wanted to gain control of corporation does not bar his right of inspection. *Skoglund v Ormand Industries, Inc, 372 A2d 204 (Ch Ct 1976).*

Though shareholder had written letters and made threats that constituted harassment to corporation, he was allowed to inspect corporate books and records to investigate suspected corporate mismanagement because that was proper purpose. *Skouras v Admiralty Enterprises, Inc, 386 A2d 674 (Ch Ct 1978).*

Stockholder was entitled to inspection of corporate books and records to value his shares in order to negotiate sale of his stock, even though request could have been thinly veiled attempt to force corporation to buy stock at unfairly inflated price so it could keep its financial information secret, because stockholder's primary purpose for inspection was proper and once proper purpose had been established, any ulterior motives of stockholder became irrelevant; however, to protect corporation, any inspection by stockholder made contingent on requirements that: (1) stockholder not disclose any information to anyone who had not first made a written representation to stockholder that he was a bona fide prospective purchaser of stock and (2) prospective purchaser's name, address, and copy of his written representation had to be registered at least five days before disclosure. *CM&M Group Inc v Carroll, 453 A2d 788 (1982).*

Corporation need not provide shareholder with list of shareholders because shareholder only wanted list as means to communicate with other shareholders for unspecified reason without making reference to any impending event (meeting, tender offer, proxy solicitation, particular board activity) for which present access to list was needed. *Shamrock Associates v The Dorsey Corp, No. 7678 (Ch Ct 7-24-84).*

Shareholders who initiated consent procedure to gain control of corporation would not need to inspect list of holders of convertible bonds because bondholders who convert after record date were not entitled to vote in consent proceeding. *Midway Airlines, Inc v Carlson, 628 FSupp 244 (D Del 1985).*

Corporation could not deny shareholder opportunity to inspect shareholders list because (1) shareholder had proper purpose in seeking to support her position against recapitalization in upcoming vote, (2) shareholder could also properly encourage other shareholders to seek appraisal should recapitalization be approved, and (3) shareholder was not pawn of her attorneys to enlarge class that they may represent in forthcoming appraisal action. *Weiss v Anderson, Clayton & Co, No. 8488 (Ch Ct 5-22-86).*

Shareholder, which sought to communicate with other shareholders about alleged economic risks of corporation's business activity in Angola, is entitled to stockholder list. Desire to communicate with other stockholders about specific matter of corporate concern, especially in connection with pending stockholders' meeting, is proper purpose for obtaining stocklist. After plaintiff complied with form and manner of making demand for stockholder list, defendant had burden of establishing that inspection would be for improper purpose. Defendant failed to meet that burden. *The Conservative Caucus Research Analysis & Education Foundation, Inc v Chevron Corp, 525 A2d 569 (Ch Ct 1987).*

In order to inspect corporation's books and records, shareholder/contract creditor must be able to show purposes reasonably related to his interest as shareholder. Valid purposes for inspecting corporation's books and records were: (1) Shareholder's desire for valuation of minority interest in closely held corporation whose shares were not publicly traded and subject to restrictions that made their sale difficult; (2) Shareholder's desire to determine corporation's present and past ability to pay dividends; and (3) Shareholder's necessity to inform himself of corporate transactions about which he could have otherwise learned and voted upon if given proper notice. *Helmsman Management Services, Inc v A & S Consultants, Inc, 525 A2d 160 (Ch Ct 1987).*

Applying Delaware common law, court ruled that allegations of discriminatory treatment among members of non-stock profit corporation, reasonably related to requester's membership interest, set forth proper purpose to inspect corporate books and records. Requester is not required to come forward with proof of disparity in treatment or proof of wrongdoing by corporation, and scope of inspection may be limited to those documents relevant to proper purpose. *Fleisher Development Corp v Home Owners Warranty Corp, 856 F2d 1529 (DC Cir 1988).*

In litigation involving a shareholder's demand to inspect a corporation's books and records, court granted corporation's motion to dismiss because shareholder did not provide factual basis for suspicion of corporate mismanagement as required by Delaware law. Shareholder's reliance on apparent conflict between newspaper report of management imprudence and corporation's decision not to sue officers and directors was misplaced. Court found that no such conflict existed because report indicated that before plaintiff's demand, corporation had successfully sued the company responsible for disputed construction project. *Weiland v Central & South West Corp, No. 9769 (Ch Ct 5-9-89).*

Factual inconsistencies in shareholder's testimony were not sufficient to satisfy corporation's burden of proving that his request for stocklist was for improper purpose. *Weisman v Plains Resources, Inc, Nos. 10,814 & 10,840 (Ch Ct 5-30-89).*

A corporation formed to engage in real estate leasing, securities trading and arbitrage, had entered into a contract with another company to manage its portfolio. The contract provided that the portfolio management company would keep 25% of any profits, while the corporation remained totally liable for any losses. The corporation could cancel the contract at any time on notice. Both companies were controlled by the same individual shareholder. The corporation had suffered substantial losses on its investments. The court held that the directors of the corporation had not abdicated their managerial responsibilities and breached their duty of due care in failing to manage the company's portfolio themselves, since they could cancel the management contract at any time and thus retained ultimate control over the portfolio management company. Nor did the board's failure to cancel the contract as soon as the company suffered a loss constitute a breach of the duty of due care, since a loss in one year could very well be offset by gains in another. *Canal Capital Corp v French, No. 11,764 (Ch Ct 7-2-92).*

In an action brought against a corporation by one of its directors seeking access to the corporate books and records, the Court of Chancery held that the plaintiff's request to view the records was proper and should be granted, where the plaintiff requested access to the books and records of the defendant in his capacity as director, in order to verify the accuracy of information contained in a Form 10-K which was about to be filed. *Holdgriewe v The Nostalgia Network, Inc, No. 12914 (Ch Ct 4-29-93).*

Pursuant to §220, the Court of Chancery ordered a corporation's directors to provide shareholders of the corporation with prompt access to the corporation's books. Plaintiff shareholders advanced two purposes for their demand: (1) the valuation of their shares, especially in connection with their desire to exercise their put right; and (2) to investigate possible fraud or breach of duty by the president of the corporation. *Ostrow v Bonney Forge Corp, No. 13270 (Ch Ct 4-6-94).*

Court ordered a limited inspection of only those records that were essential and sufficient for the stockholder's purposes after the stockholder's demand to inspect for corporate waste or mismanagement was rejected and the stockholder introduced evidence of corporate mismanagement. The stockholder's evidence of mismanagement consisted of a director of the corporation who obtained a personal benefit from a transaction that was not conferred upon other shareholders and a derivative action filed by other shareholders against the board which also alleged mismanagement. *Everett v Hollywood Park, Inc, No. 14556 (Ch Ct 1-19-96).*

Plaintiff-stockholder's request to inspect a corporation's books and records (as they related to an unrealized merger between the corporation and another corporation) for possible corporate mismanagement stated a proper purpose. The Court of Chancery also determined that plaintiff's request to inspect for corporation mismanagement was not overly broad, where plaintiff's evidence of mismanagement, that the corporation paid $275,000 to the other corporation although it did not break the merger agreement, raised the plausibility of more than speculative, general mismanagement. *U.S. Die Casting and Development Co v Security First Corp, No. 14019 (Ch Ct 2-8-96).*

Corporate minority shareholder of a closely-held corporation that did not pay dividends was entitled to inspect a corporation's shareholder list in order to obtain a source of potential purchasers for the minority shareholder's stock. The minority shareholder was entitled to a limited inspection of the corporation's books and records for the purpose of valuing its investment. *Thomas & Betts Corp v Leviton Mfg Co, No. 14069 (Ch Ct 12-19-95),* aff'd, *Thomas & Betts Corp v Leviton Mfg Co, 681 A2d 1026 (1996).*

A shareholder fails to meet his burden of showing a proper purpose for a document inspection demand where the demand is sweepingly broad, the evidence presented by the shareholder does not support the breadth of the request, some of the information requested is publicly available, and the request is untimely. *Mattes v Checkers Drive-In Restaurants, Inc, 2001 Del. Ch. LEXIS 47 (Ch Ct 2001).*

Evaluating the non-payment of dividends can be a proper purpose for inspecting a corporation's books and records if it is combined, albeit in a separate demand, with the purpose of valuing minority shares. Investigation of corporate waste and mismanagement is also a proper purpose, provided sufficient evidence is adduced showing that there exists a credible basis to find probable corporate wrongdoing. *Dobler v Montgomery Cellular Holding Co, 2001 Del. Ch. LEXIS 126 (Ch Ct 2001).*

The stated purpose of inspecting waste and mismanagement is a proper purpose for demanding inspection of a corporation's books and records, and this purpose is supported by the corporation's financial restatements as well as by a formal SEC investigation of the same alleged conduct. Moreover, the fact that there are pending lawsuits against the corporation that challenge the same alleged conduct that forms the basis of the demand for inspection does not render the demand adverse to the corporation's interests. *Freund v Lucent Technologies, Inc, 2003 Del. Ch. LEXIS 3 (Ch Ct 2003).*

A shareholder's action to compel inspection of a corporation's books and records is not precluded by the shareholder's bringing a derivative action, based on allegations that the books and records are claimed to support, to prevent the derivative action from being time-barred. *Khanna v Covad Communications Group, Inc, 2004 Del. Ch. LEXIS 11 (Ch Ct 2004).*

A shareholder's demand to inspect corporate books and records for the purpose of investigating breaches of fiduciary duty are not automatically barred because there may be affirmative defenses to the transactions documented by the requested records. *Amalgamated Bank v UICI, 2005 Del. Ch. LEXIS 82 (Ch Ct 2005).*

A merger after commencement of a GCL §220 action for the inspection of a corporation's books and records does not nullify the plaintiff's standing to maintain the action where the plaintiff may continue to bring individual actions against the corporation or its agents. *Deephaven Risk Arb Trading Ltd v UnitedGlobalCom, Inc, 2005 Del. Ch. LEXIS 107 (Ch Ct 2005).*

A request to inspect a corporation's books and records for the purpose of discovering evidence of misrepresentations and breaches of trust by officers and directors related to federal securities law violations is made for a proper purpose and is not preempted by federal laws governing securities actions. *Romero v Career Education Corp, 2005 Del. Ch. LEXIS 112 (Ch Ct 2005).*

A shareholder's request to inspect a corporation's books and records for the purpose of investigating mismanagement, waste, or wrongdoing will be denied unless the shareholder presents some evidence suggesting a credible basis from which a court can infer that such mismanagement, waste, or wrongdoing may have occurred. *Seinfeld v Verizon Communications, Inc, 909 A2d 117 (2006).*

A shareholder's motion to compel inspection of a corporation's books and records will be denied where the corporation has already sufficiently complied with the shareholder's request and the additional requested documents are not essential to the satisfaction of the shareholder's stated purpose of conducting the inspection. *Kaufman v CA, Inc, 905 A2d 749 (Ch Ct 2006).*

A demand for a books and records inspection will be denied where the plaintiff cannot demonstrate any basis from which it can be inferred that a corporation's board of directors has engaged in any wrongdoing and cannot demonstrate any other proper purpose for the inspection. *City of Westland Police & Fire Retirement System v Axcelis Technologies, Inc, 2009 Del. Ch. LEXIS 173 (Ch Ct 2009).*

.3 Prerequisites for inspection.—Stockholder must make written demand under oath to get inspection. *Petrick v B-K Dynamics, Inc, 283 A2d 696 (Ch Ct 1971).*

The Court of Chancery dismissed a shareholder's complaint seeking inspection of the corporate defendant's stock ledger, list of shareholders and other books and records where the plaintiff failed to comply with the requirements of GCL §220. The plaintiff had originally demanded inspection in a letter to the corporation which, though notarized, did not state under oath that the contents were true and correct. *Frank v Libco Corp, No. 12412 (Ch Ct 12-8-92).*

Hearsay testimony may support a books and records inspection request where the testimony is found to be reliable as a credible basis to infer that waste and mismanagement have occurred. *Marmon v Arbinet-Thexchange, Inc, 2004 Del. Ch. LEXIS 44 (Ch Ct 2004).*

A demand for inspection of books and records will be denied where the only proof of beneficial ownership is a heavily redacted account statement that lacks the full name of the owner and the date of ownership. *Smith v Horizon Lines, Inc, 2009 Del. Ch. LEXIS 159 (Ch Ct 2009).*

.4 Who may inspect.—Director who was beneficial stockholder had no inspection right. *Lenahan v National Computer Analysis Corp, 310 A2d 661 (Ch Ct 1973).*

Executors of shareholder who died three days after making demand to inspect shareholders' list had right to inspect list. *Reasons:* (1) demand was for proper purpose: to solicit proxies, (2) executors had power to maintain action that could have been maintained by decedent, and (3) decedent's right to compel inspection survived his death. *Devon v Pantry Pride, Inc, No. 7843 (Ch Ct 11-21-84).*

Shareholders who were members of union that was striking corporation were not allowed to inspect shareholder list in connection with soliciting proxies for shareholder resolution at annual meeting because shareholders were not really interested in obtaining list to communicate about annual meeting. Instead they wanted to bring economic pressure on corporation to force it to accede to union's demands, an improper purpose for seeking list. *Carpenter v Texas Air Corp, No. 7976 (Ch Ct 4-18-85).*

Shareholder of parent corporation was entitled to inspect certain books and records of subsidiary even though he failed to make a demand on subsidiary. *Reasons:* Evidence of possible fraud existed when: (1) parent apparently transferred certain communication boards to subsidiary at artificially inflated price; and (2) funds withdrawn from subsidiary for purpose of paying executive payroll exceeded amount of that payroll. *Landgarten v York Research Corp, No. 8417 (Ch Ct 2-3-88).*

Shareholder who sought order under GCL §220 to compel production of stockholders' list was not sham plaintiff merely because he sought list for candidate who wanted to remove and replace directors. Shareholder believed increase in value of his stock could only be accomplished if candidate gained control of corporation. Therefore, he had proper economic purpose in seeking stock list. *Hirschfeld v Emery Air Freight Corp, No. 9806 (Ch Ct 4-22-88).*

Plaintiff shareholder was entitled to inspection of corporate books and records where plaintiff was the record owner, but not the beneficial owner, of 1.68 shares of the corporation and sent a demand letter to defendant seeking inspection of books and records, stating purposes for such inspection. *Macklowe v Planet Hollywood, Inc, No. 13450 (Ch Ct 9-29-94).*

Shareholder action to inspect a corporation's books and records does not have to be stayed or dismissed when, pursuant to federal law, discovery has been stayed in a suit involving the same defendant corporation and a shareholder class in which the plaintiff is a purported member where federal law is not in conflict with the state books and records action and the shareholder has alleged a proper purpose. *Cohen v El Paso Corp, 2004 Del. Ch. LEXIS 149 (Ch Ct 2004).*

The shareholder of a corporation is not entitled to inspect the books and records in the control and possession of a "subsidiary" corporation where the parent corporation cannot exercise actual control over the subsidiary. *Weinstein Enterprises, Inc v Orloff, 2005 Del. Ch. LEXIS 125 (2005).*

For purposes of books and records inspection, a short seller of stock that holds a net short position in that stock is a beneficial owner of the stock sales. *Deephaven Risk Arb Trading Ltd v UnitedGlobalCom, Inc, 2005 Del. Ch. LEXIS 107 (Ch Ct 2005).*

A stockholder may disclose to bona fide third-party prospective purchasers of its shares, who are also the corporation's competitors, information it obtains through a books and records inspection request, provided such disclosure is strictly restricted by a confidentiality agreement tailored to the degree of competition engaged in by the prospective purchaser. *Schoon v Troy Corp, 2006 Del. Ch. LEXIS 123 (Ch Ct 2006).*

A request to inspect a corporation's books and records will be denied where the only purpose for the request is to circumvent the mandates regarding discovery of federal legislation and to obtain, in an independent federal action, discovery that otherwise is barred. *Beiser v PMC-Sierra, Inc, 2009 Del. Ch. LEXIS 36 (Ch Ct 2009).*

.5 Common law right of inspection.—Court refused to apply either Delaware's or District of Columbia's inspection statute to request by members of Delaware nonstock profit corporation to inspect corporation's books and members' list because Delaware statute refers to "stockholders" and DC statute requires 5% ownership in corporation's stock, so both statutes are inapposite. Applying Delaware common law, court ruled that members had right to inspect corporation's books and records because purpose of inspection—to ascertain whether company was being prudently managed—was proper. However, members did not have right to inspect members' list because members did not indicate purpose of communication with other members. Members could inspect corporation's subsidiaries' books and records because (1) there was close relationship between parent and subsidiaries and (2) evidence of any corporate mismanagement will likely be found in subsidiaries' books and records. *Fleisher Development Corp v Home Owners Warranty Corp, 647 FSupp 661 (DC DC 1946).*

The Court of Chancery held that it did not have jurisdiction over inspection demands by nonstock corporations. Plaintiff was a member of defendant, a nonstock corporation. Plaintiff asserted that in adopting GCL §220, the legislature intended to transfer to the Court of Chancery the preexisting common law jurisdiction over inspection demands by members of nonstock corporations. The court rejected this argument, stating that §220, which expressly defines the class of persons entitled to enforce its provisions, does not include members of nonstock corporations. Accordingly, the court dismissed plaintiff's claim, holding that the Court of Chancery had exclusive jurisdiction to entertain inspection claims only by stockholders of record, and not members of nonstock corporations. *Scattered Corp v Chicago Stock Exchange, Inc, No. 13703 (Ch Ct 12-2-94).*

.6 Blank or nonexistent stock ledger.—Corporation that does not maintain stock ledger is estopped from arguing that shareholder may not inspect corporate books and records because he or she is not shareholder of record. When corporation maintains no stock ledger whatsoever, person with valid claim to either legal or equitable ownership of company's stock will be allowed inspection rights upon meeting his or her burden with respect to all other elements of claim under GCL §220. *Pan Ocean Navigation, Inc v Rainbow Navigation, Inc, No. 8674 (Ch Ct 2-18-87).*

Corporation that did not maintain stock ledger and ignored other corporate formalities could not object to inspection of books and records on gross that shareholder seeking inspection was not shareholder or record, but wholly owned subsidiary of shareholder of record. Once court is forced to inquire into underlying facts concerning stock ownership because corporation has maintained no stock ledger, there is little continued utility in insisting that valid demand is one made by shareholder rather than

§220

wholly owned subsidiary of shareholder. *Pan Ocean Navigation, Inc v Rainbow Navigation, No. 8874 (Ch Ct 7-8-87).*

Only stockholders of record are entitled to inspect corporate books and records. It is implicit in GCL §219 and GCL §220 that Delaware corporations have affirmative duty to maintain stock ledger. When stock ledger is blank or nonexistent, Court of Chancery has power to consider other evidence to ascertain and establish stockholder status. Because stockholder's status as record stockholder was supported by evidence, its right to inspect corporation's books will be enforced. *Rainbow Navigation, Inc v Pan Ocean Navigation, Inc, 535 A2d 1357 (1987).*

.7 NOBO list.—Corporation must provide information in its possession identifying certain beneficial owners of its stock (NOBO list) to shareholders soliciting proxies for election of opposition slate of directors because (1) shareholders should have same opportunity to solicit beneficial owners that directors have, (2) list is not confidential, and (3) Rule 14a-13(b)(2) of Securities Exchange Act does not preempt Delaware law and forbid release of NOBO list. Corporation may not, as general matter, condition its release of stocklist materials but must use NOBO list exclusively for corporate communications. *Shamrock Associates v Texas American Energy Corp, 517 A2d 658 (Ch Ct 1986).*

Once corporation has obtained NOBO list, i.e., list of beneficial owners of corporation's stock who do not object to disclosure of their name and address by registered owner of stock to corporation itself for purpose of facilitating direct communication on corporate matters, list must be made available to shareholder making inspection request under GCL §220. Otherwise, corporation has no duty to disclose list. *RB Assocs of New Jersey v The Gillette Co, No. 9711 (Ch Ct 3-22-88).*

.8 Discovery of corporate books; Family Court's right to order.—Family Court has authority to order non-party corporations to comply with reasonable discovery demands. Nowhere in GCL §220 is discovery of corporation's books and records by persons outside corporation barred. There is no support for assertion that GCL §220 is sole procedure for inspection of corporate books and records. Litigant's discovery was limited to those records needed to perform task, i.e., to those documents necessary and essential to valuation process. *In the Matter of B & F Towing and Salvage Co, 551 A2d 45 (1988).*

.9 Corporate bad faith.—A corporation acts in bad faith by not honoring repeated requests made by one of its directors to inspect corporate records and books that the corporation indicates will be forthcoming but in reality are not, and therefore attorneys' fees will be awarded to the director for litigation brought to compel production of the documents he had been requesting for months. *McGowan v Empress Entertainment, Inc, 2000 Del Ch LEXIS 177 (Ch Ct 2000).*

.10 Confidentiality.—A stockholder who obtains access to books and records under GCL §220 in order to investigate mismanagement or corporate waste is not free to publicly disseminate (for example, by placing the documents on a Web site) information found in those documents that the corporation regards as "confidential." *Disney v The Walt Disney Co, 857 A2d 444 (Ch Ct 2004).*

Confidential corporate information produced in the books and records context will be treated as confidential unless and until disclosed in the course of litigation (such as in a derivative action) or pursuant to some other legal requirement. *Stone v Ritter, 2005 Del. Ch. LEXIS 146 (Ch Ct 2005).*

Documents that are disclosed pursuant to a records inspection request that relate to communications among or deliberations of a corporation's board of directors, and the public release of which would harm the corporation more than benefit it, are subject to a confidentiality order. *Disney v The Walt Disney Co, 2005 Del. Ch. LEXIS 94 (Ch Ct 2005).*

A request to inspect letters written by a corporation's senior executives to its board, regarding non-public business and personnel matters, for the stated purposes of (1) communicating with stockholders regarding an ongoing proxy contest, (2) investigating the suitability of the current board of directors, and (3) investigating mismanagement and wrongdoing by the current board, will be denied where those letters are confidential and the true purpose of the request is to publicly broadcast otherwise improperly obtained and confidential information. *Pershing Square, L.P. v Ceridian Corp, 2007 Del. Ch. LEXIS 62 (Ch Ct 2007).*

.11 Demand futility.—Where a stockholder derivative plaintiff has had judgment entered against it for failure to plead demand futility in one court, but without prejudice to the claims asserted on behalf of the corporation, the plaintiff may not pursue a books and records inspection request to obtain information sufficient to adequately plead demand futility in a proposed derivative complaint brought in a second court. *West Coast Management & Capital, LLC v Carrier Access Corp, 2006 Del. Ch. LEXIS 195 (Ch Ct 2006).*

A shareholder may inspect books and records related to acts occurring prior to the time a shareholder owns shares where the purpose is to gather the details necessary to plead a sustained and systemic failure of oversight by the board that show demand futility (rather than to investigate potential claims that the shareholder has no standing to assert). *Melzer v CNET Networks, Inc, 934 A2d 912 (Ch Ct 2007).*

.12 Proper purpose.—A books and records inspection demand cannot be summarily dismissed merely because its stated purpose is to investigate mismanagement based on a discrepancy between management projections and results for a merger, and the failure of management to plan for the company's post-merger integration. *Shamrock Activist Value Fund, L.P. v iPass Inc, 2006 Del. Ch. LEXIS 212 (Ch Ct 2006).*

.13 Stock option backdating.—A suspicion of corporate misconduct based on a statistical correlation suggesting the possibility of stock option backdating or springloading presents the minimal quantum of evidence necessary to support a books and records inspection request—but just barely. *Louisiana Municipal Employees' Retirement System* *v Countrywide Financial Corp, 2007 Del. Ch. LEXIS 138 (Ch Ct 2007).*

.14 Special litigation committees.—The recommendation of a special litigation committee comprised of one individual will not be given weight where the committee fails to act in good faith or to conduct a reasonable investigation, and, specifically, fails to provide documentation to support its most important factual conclusions. *Sutherland v Sutherland, 958 A2d 235 (Ch Ct 2008).*

.15 Books and records inspection demand.—Where a books and records inspection demand is premised on the need to inspect possible wrongdoing, a shareholder's demand will be rejected where the shareholder fails to present evidence from which it can credibly be inferred that the board's actions were made pursuant to anything other than good faith business decisions. *City of Westland Police & Fire Retirement Sys v Axcelis Technologies, Inc, 1 A3d 281 (2010).*

A demand to inspect a corporation's books and records for the purpose of investigating whether the corporation's board wrongfully refused an earlier demand to pursue derivative litigation in reliance on recommendations of counsel and an audit committee will be granted where the board has otherwise provided no "substantive insight" into counsel's work or the committee's determinations. *Louisiana Municipal Police Employees Retirement System v Morgan Stanley & Co, 2011 Del. Ch. LEXIS 42 (Ch Ct 2011).*

A shareholder does not lack a proper inspection purpose where he has first filed a derivative suit that was dismissed without prejudice and with leave to amend, since bringing the inspection action to aid him in pleading demand futility in a to-be-amended derivative complaint constitutes a proper purpose. *King v VeriFone Holdings, Inc, 12 A3d 1140 (2011).*

221 VOTING, INSPECTION AND OTHER RIGHTS OF BONDHOLDERS AND DEBENTURE HOLDERS.—Every corporation may in its certificate of incorporation confer upon the holders of any bonds, debentures or other obligations issued or to be issued by the corporation the power to vote in respect to the corporate affairs and management of the corporation to the extent and in the manner provided in the certificate of incorporation and may confer upon such holders of bonds, debentures or other obligations the same right of inspection of its books, accounts and other records, and also any other rights, which the

stockholders of the corporation have or may have by reason of this chapter or of its certificate of incorporation. If the certificate of incorporation so provides, such holders of bonds, debentures or other obligations shall be deemed to be stockholders, and their bonds, debentures or other obligations shall be deemed to be shares of stock, for the purpose of any provision of this chapter which requires the vote of stockholders as a prerequisite to any corporate action and the certificate of incorporation may divest the holders of capital stock, in whole or in part, of their right to vote on any corporate matter whatsoever, except as set forth in paragraph (2) of subsection (b) of §242 of this title. (Last amended by Ch. 127, L. '85, eff. 7-1-85.)

.1 **Exchange offer to bondholders.**—Court refused to enjoin consummation of exchange offer and consent solicitation made by corporation to holders of its long-term debt securities because (1) nothing in indenture provisions granting bondholders power to veto modifications in indenture stops corporation from offering inducement to bondholders to consent to amendments, which was necessary before offer could go through, (2) consents will be granted or withheld only by those with financial interests in bonds and incentive to consent is available equally to all members of each class of bondholders, (3) offer is not functional equivalent of redemption, and (4) corporation would be irreparably harmed since it is in weak financial state and offer is integral part of major reorganization and recapitalization of corporation. *Katz v Oak Industries Inc, 508 A2d 873 (Ch Ct 1986).*

.2 **Inducement to amend debentures.**—Court refused to enjoin corporation from implementing proposed amendments to indenture governing debentures. Amendments would allow corporation to pay dividends to its shareholders in order to implement merger that corporation's directors recommended. Inducement that corporation offered debenture holders to get them to vote in amendments' favor was not illegal because (1) corporation has commercial relationship with debenture holders and offer was made to all debenture holders so no one was being disenfranchised and (2) consent payment mechanism does not constitute breach of implied contractual covenants of good faith and fair dealing between corporation and debenture holders. *Kass v Eastern Air Lines, Inc, Nos. 8700, 8701, 8711 (Ch Ct 11-14-86).*

.3 **Fiduciary duties to bondholders.**—Neither issuing corporation nor its directors owe fiduciary duties to holders of corporation debt instruments. An implied convenant of good faith and fair dealing cannot give debenture holders any rights inconsistent with those explicitly set out indenture. Court held that: (1) issuer that redeemed bond indentures did not owe any fiduciary duty to former holders; (2) issuer's redemption did not violate indenture's terms governing debentures; and (3) court's determination that explicit contractual provision involved was not breached, precluded finding of breach of implied covenant dealing with same subject. *Shenandoah Life Ins Co v Valero Energy Corp, No. 9032 (Ch Ct 6-21-88).*

222 NOTICE OF MEETINGS AND ADJOURNED MEETINGS.—[1](a) *Whenever stockholders are required or permitted to take any action at a meeting, a written notice of the meeting shall be given which shall state the place, if any, date and hour of the meeting, the means of remote communications, if any, by which stockholders and proxy holders may be deemed to be present in person and vote at such meeting, the record date for determining the stockholders entitled to vote at the meeting, if such date is different from the record date for determining stockholders entitled to notice of the meeting, and, in the case of a special meeting, the purpose or purposes for which the meeting is called.*

(b) Unless otherwise provided in this chapter, the written notice of any meeting shall be given not less than 10 nor more than 60 days before the date of the meeting to each stockholder entitled to vote at such meeting *as of the record date for determining the stockholders entitled to notice of the meeting.* If mailed, notice is given when deposited in the United States mail, postage prepaid, directed to the stockholder at such stockholder's address as it appears on the records of the corporation. An affidavit of the secretary or an assistant secretary or of the transfer agent or other agent of the corporation that the notice has been given shall, in the absence of fraud, be prima facie evidence of the facts stated therein.

(c) When a meeting is adjourned to another time or place, unless the bylaws otherwise require, notice need not be given of the adjourned meeting if the time, place, if any, thereof, and the means of remote communications, if any, by which stockholders and proxy holders may be deemed to be present in person and vote at such adjourned meeting are announced at the meeting at which the adjournment is taken. At the adjourned meeting the corporation may transact any business which might have been transacted at the original meeting. If the adjournment is for more than 30 days, [2]a notice of the adjourned meeting shall be given to each stockholder of record entitled to vote at the meeting. *If after the adjournment a new record date for stockholders entitled to vote is fixed for the adjourned meeting, the board of directors shall fix a new record date for notice of such adjourned meeting in accordance with §213(a) of this title, and shall give notice of the adjourned meeting to each stockholder of record entitled to vote at such adjourned meeting as of the record date fixed for notice of such adjourned meeting.* (Last amended by Ch. 14, L. '09, eff. 8-1-09.)

Ch. 14, L. '09, eff. 8-1-09, added matter in italic and deleted [1]"(a) Whenever stockholders are required or permitted to take any action at a meeting, a written notice of the meeting shall be given which shall state the place, if any, date and hour of the meeting, the means of remote communications, if any, by which stockholders and proxy holders may be deemed to be present in person and vote at such meeting, and, in the case of a special meeting, the purpose or purposes for which the meeting is called." and [2]"or if after the adjournment a new record date is fixed for the adjourned meeting,".

Ch. 14, L. '09 Synopsis of Section 222

These amendments to Section 222 reflect the changes in Section 213(a) permitting separate record dates for determining stockholders entitled to notice of and to vote at a meeting. The amended subsection (a) provides that where the board of directors fixes separate record dates, written notice under that subsection shall include the record date for determining stockholders entitled to vote. In addition, subsection (b) is amended to make clear that the timing requirements for providing written notice remain unchanged in that instance and that the corporation need only provide written notice to those stockholders entitled to vote as of the notice record date. Finally, the new sentence added to subsection (c) provides that where the board of directors sets a new record date for determining stockholders entitled to vote at an adjourned meeting, the board will be required to set a new notice record date in accordance with Section 213(a) and provide written notice to stockholders entitled to vote as of that date.

Ch. 343, L. '00 Synopsis of Section 222

The amendment to subsection (b) of Section 222 conforms to the corresponding provision in new Section 232. The amendments to subsections (a) and (c) conform the statutory notice requirements to the changes to Section 211, which permit stockholder meetings to be held by means of remote communication, if so determined by the board of directors in its sole discretion.

Ch. 339, L. '98 Synopsis of Section 222

The amendments to these Sections eliminate masculine references in the statutes, and replace them with gender neutral references.

.1 Effect of improper notice.—Stockholder who gave general proxy for annual meeting, which was voted in favor of resolutions ratifying certain acts of directors, was not estopped from later objecting to directors' acts where notice of the meeting did not state that resolutions—or any business other than stated matters—would be presented. *Gottlieb v McKee, 107 A2d 240 (Ch Ct 1954).*

Court denied the defendants' motion to dismiss plaintiffs' individual claims that the proposed notice of a reconvened shareholders' meeting had improper statements, finding that there were material defects in notice. *Stroud v Milliken Enterprises, Inc, 585 A2d 1306 (Ch Ct 1988).*

.2 Who may issue notice.—As a general rule actions of de facto officers are not binding on the corporation except as to third persons, but a more liberal rule has been applied when notices are given by de facto officers calling stockholders' meetings if they would have had that right as de jure officers. *Robert Drob v Nat'l Memorial Park, Inc, 41 A2d 589 (Ch Ct 1945).*

Request by voting trustee of controlling interest for further postponement of shareholders' meeting to allow time to resolve income beneficiaries' dispute over voting mandate was permissible under charter, and, even though charter requires fresh notices and agenda for reconvening meetings adjourned over 30 days, reconvened meetings would not be new meetings and would not involve delays prejudicial to income beneficiary's interest as to justify denying request for further adjournment. *Wilmington Trust Co v Lee, 298 A2d 358 (Ct Ch 1972).*

.3 Conflicting proxies.—Inspectors of election at stockholders' meeting must vote conflicting proxies submitted by broker-dealer holding shares in "street name" in such manner as broker-dealer's officer at meeting avers stock should be voted saying conflict was result of clerical error in broker's office; this is so, even though there is no showing beneficial owners instructed broker to vote shares the way he did, since corporation need not look beyond its stockholders of record to determine who can vote. *Williams v Sterling Oil of Oklahoma, Inc, 267 A2d 630 (Ch Ct 1970).*

.4 Bylaws.—Court granted injunction barring target from enforcing its interpretation of notice provision of new bylaws which would preclude tender offeror, even if it was successful in obtaining adjournment of annual meeting, from presenting any proposals at adjourned meeting. Notice bylaws did not expressly provide how they would operate in case of adjournment, and there is no settled Delaware law from which target's interpretation could have been determined with reasonable certainty. Therefore, target's failure to announce its interpretation of bylaws until after notice period had run was inequitable. *Mesa Petroleum v Unocal Corp, No. 7997 (Ch Ct 4-18-85).*

.5 Applicability.—GCL §222(c) deals with adjournment after a meeting has convened and is not relevant to issue of postponement before meeting is convened. *Aprahamian v HBO & Co, 531 A2d 1204 (Ch Ct 1987).*

.6 Ripeness.—Court refused to hear appeal in dispute as to whether proposed notice of shareholders' meeting called to consider charter and bylaw amendments met requirements of candor imposed by GCL §222 and GCL §242. Parties were seeking final judicial determination of management's statutory notice technique before putting process into effect. This would inappropriately draw courts into granting advisory opinion regarding significant question of corporation law that was not ripe for judicial intervention. *Stroud v Milliken Enterprises, Inc, 552 A2d 476 (1989).*

223 VACANCIES AND NEWLY CREATED DIRECTORSHIPS.—(a) Unless otherwise provided in the certificate of incorporation or bylaws:

(1) Vacancies and newly created directorships resulting from any increase in the authorized number of directors elected by all of the stockholders having the right to vote as a single class may be filled by a majority of the directors then in office, although less than a quorum, or by a sole remaining director;

(2) Whenever the holders of any class or classes of stock or series thereof are entitled to elect 1 or more directors by the certificate of incorporation, vacancies and newly created directorships of such class or classes or series may be filled by a majority of the directors elected by such class or classes or series thereof then in office, or by a sole remaining director so elected.

If at any time, by reason of death or resignation or other cause, a corporation should have no directors in office, then any officer or any stockholder or an executor, administrator, trustee or guardian of a stockholder, or other fiduciary entrusted with like responsibility for the person or estate of a stockholder, may call a special meeting of stockholders in accordance with the certificate of incorporation or the bylaws, or may apply to the Court of Chancery for a decree summarily ordering an election as provided in §211 *or §215* of this title.

(b) In the case of a corporation the directors of which are divided into classes, any directors chosen under subsection (a) of this section shall hold office until the next election of the class for which such directors shall have been chosen, and until their successors shall be elected and qualified.

(c) If, at the time of filling any vacancy or any newly created directorship, the directors then in office shall constitute less than a majority of the whole board (as constituted immediately prior to any such increase), the Court of Chancery may, upon application of any stockholder or stockholders holding at least 10 percent of the voting stock at the time outstanding having the right to vote for such directors, summarily order an election to be held to fill any such vacancies or newly created directorships, or to replace the directors chosen by the directors then in office as aforesaid, which election shall be governed by §211 *or §215* of this title as far as applicable.

(d) Unless otherwise provided in the certificate of incorporation of bylaws, when 1 or more directors shall resign from the board, effective at a future date, a majority of the directors then in office, including those who have so resigned, shall have power to fill such vacancy or vacancies, the vote thereon to take effect when such resignation or resignations shall become effective, and each director so chosen shall hold office as provided in this section in the filling of other vacancies. (Last amended by Ch. 253, L. '10, eff. 8-1-10.)

Ch. 253, L. '10, eff. 8-1-10, added matter in italic.

Ch. 253, L. '10 Synopsis of Section 223

Sections 20, 21, 22, 23, 24, 25, and 26 make technical changes to §220, §223, and §225 of the DGCL consistent with the intent of the bill and with the translator provision in new §114(a).

Ch. 298, L. '02 Synopsis of Section 223

The amendments to Sections 203(a)(2), 203(c)(8), 212(a) and 223(c) clarify that references to "voting stock" or "shares" therein and elsewhere in the title, including in Sections 203, 223 and 253, are intended to adopt the voting power concept reflected in Section 212(a). The parenthetical phrase added to Section 203(a)(2) is intended to make it clear that while voting stock owned by persons who are directors and also officers and by certain employee stock plans would not be included in determining the total amount of voting stock outstanding to calculate the 85% exemption, that voting stock would be included in the determination of the amount of voting stock owned by the interested stockholder. The amendment to Section 203(c)(5) is intended to refer to the paragraph defining the term "owner". This reference should have been changed when the definition of "stock" was added in 1995.

.1 Vacancies.—Where bylaw gives directors power to fill vacancies on the board, but bylaw "A" provided that board could act only through majority of directors "present at a meeting in the presence of a quorum (7)," while bylaw "B" provided that directors in office, although less than quorum could fill board vacancies, bylaw "A" controls when there is quorum of directors in office, and election of directors at meeting at which no quorum was present is invalid. *Tomlinson v Loew's, Inc, 134 A2d 518 (Ch Ct)*, aff'd, *135 A2d 136 (1957)*.

Three directors out of six-man board who are present at board meeting can elect fourth to replace one who resigned, when bylaw says that vacancies can be filed by majority of those in office; action taken by the four is then valid. *Continental Television Corp v Caster, 191 NE2d 607 (Ill App Ct 1963)*.

Where bylaw allows president to call special stockholders' meeting for any purpose, president can call meeting to (1) fill director vacancies, (2) increase number of directors, (3) fill new directorships, (4) increase quorum of directors, (5) remove directors for cause, and (6) fill vacancies created thereby. *Campbell v Loew's, Inc, 135 A2d 565 (Ch Ct 1957)*.

.2 Unfilled directorship.—Unfilled directorships are not vacancies which directors may fill; they must be filled by stockholders. *Belle Isle Corp v MacBean, 61 A2d 699 (Ch Ct 1948)*.

Bylaw amendment did not conflict with charter provision for electing directors at annual general meeting by permitting majority shareholders to elect directors to fill newly created directorships at special meeting, since charter provision related to regular election to replace incumbent directors; majority shareholders could elect directors to fill new directorships since positions were not vacancies required to be filled by board. *Burr v Burr Corp, 291 A2d 409 (Ch Ct 1972)*.

While appointment of new directors is reviewable instate even though challenged directors were non-residents and had not been elected by shareholders, their appointment by board to fill newly-created directorships was not void, since board's authority to appoint directors to fill newly-created directorships does not depend on prior incumbency; nor were appointments void as not having been made at special directors meeting, since attendance at directors meeting constitutes waiver of notice. *Grossman v Liberty Leasing Co, 295 A2d 749 (Ct Ch 1972)*.

.3 Term.—Bylaw cannot set one year term for directors if character provides for staggered three year terms; directors elected under such invalid bylaw serve only as de facto directors whose terms can be terminated at any time by stockholder action. *Prickett v American Steel and Pump Corp, 253 A2d 86 (Ch Ct 1969)*.

.4 Misleading proxy statement.—Management's proxy statement is materially misleading when it represents that its director nominees are "interim directors" when in fact their election was illegal under state law. *Dillon v Scotten, Dillon Co, 335 FSupp 566 (D Del 1971)*.

224 FORM OF RECORDS.—Any records maintained by a corporation in the regular course of its business, including its stock ledger, books of account, and minute books, may be kept on, *or by means of,* or be in the form of, [1]any [2]*information storage device, or method* provided that the records so kept can be converted into clearly legible [3]*paper* form within a reasonable time. Any corporation shall so convert any records so kept upon the request of any person entitled to inspect [4]*such records pursuant to any provision of this chapter.* When records are kept in such manner, a clearly legible [3]*paper* form produced from *or by means of* the [5]*information storage device or method* shall be admissible in evidence, and accepted for all other purposes, to the same extent as an original [3]*paper* record of the same information would have been, provided the [3]*paper* form accurately portrays the record. (Last amended by Ch. 343, L. '00, eff. 7-1-00.)

Ch. 343, L. '00, eff. 7-1-00, added matter in italic and deleted [1]"punch cards, magnetic tape, photographs, microphotographs, or"; [2]"other"; [3]"written"; [4]"the same"; and [5]"cards, tapes, photographs, microphotographs or other".

Ch. 343, L. '00 Synopsis of Section 224

The Amendments to Section 224 are intended to modernize and simplify the technical terminology describing non-paper forms of record storage that may be utilized by corporations. The amendments also relax existing requirements that the corporation must convert such records to clearly legible written form upon the request of any person entitled to inspection. As amended, the statute requires conversion only in respect to inspection rights arising under this chapter. The amendments are not intended to effect any changes of substance with respect to conversion requirements or inspection rights arising from other sources, including other statutes, regulations, and rules of procedure.

225 [1] *CONTESTED ELECTION OF DIRECTORS; PROCEEDINGS TO DETERMINE VALIDITY.*—(a) Upon application of any stockholder or director, or any officer whose title to office is contested, the Court of Chancery may hear and determine the validity of any election, appointment, removal or resignation of any director or officer of any corporation, and the right of any person to hold or continue to hold such office, and, in case any such office is claimed by more than 1 person, may determine the person entitled thereto; and to that end make such order or decree in any such case as may be just and proper, with power to enforce the production of any books, papers and records of the corporation relating to the issue. In case it should be determined that no valid election has been held, the Court of Chancery may order an election to be held in accordance with §211 or §215 of this title. In any such application, service of copies of the application upon the registered agent of the corporation shall be deemed to be service upon the corporation and upon the person whose title to office is contested and upon the person, if any, claiming such office; and the registered agent shall forward immediately a copy of the application to the corporation and to the person whose title to office is contested and to the person, if any, claiming such office, in a postpaid, sealed, registered letter addressed to such corporation and such person at their post-office addresses last known to the registered agent or furnished to the registered agent by the applicant stockholder. The Court may make such order respecting further or other notice of such application as it deems proper under the circumstances.

(b) Upon application of any stockholder or upon application of the corporation itself, the Court of Chancery may hear and determine the result of any vote of stockholders upon matters other than the election of directors or officers. Service of the application upon the registered agent of the corporation shall be deemed to be service upon the corporation, and no other party need be joined in order for the Court to adjudicate the result of the vote. The Court may make such order respecting notice of the application as it deems proper under the circumstances.

(c) If 1 or more directors has been convicted of a felony in connection with the duties of such director or directors to the corporation, or if there has been a prior judgment on the merits by a court of competent jurisdiction that 1 or more directors has committed a breach of the duty of loyalty in connection with the duties of such director or directors to that corporation, then, upon application by the corporation, or derivatively in the right of the corporation by any stockholder, in a subsequent action brought for such purpose, the Court of Chancery may remove from office such director or directors if the Court determines that the director or directors did not act in good faith in performing the acts resulting in the prior conviction or judgment and judicial removal is necessary to avoid irreparable harm to the corporation. In connection with such removal, the Court may make such orders as are necessary to effect such removal. In any such application, service of copies of the application upon the registered agent of the corporation shall be deemed to be service upon the corporation and upon the director or directors whose removal is sought; and the registered agent shall forward immediately a copy of the application to the corporation and to such director or directors, in a postpaid, sealed, registered letter addressed to such corporation and such director or directors at their post office addresses last known to the registered agent or furnished to the registered agent by the applicant. The Court may make such order respecting further or other notice of such application as it deems proper under the circumstances. (Last amended by Ch. 253, L. '10, eff. 8-1-10.)

Ch. 253, L. '10, eff. 8-1-10, added matter in italic and deleted [1]"CONTESTED ELECTION OF DIRECTORS; PROCEEDINGS TO DETERMINE VALIDITY.—(a) Upon application of any stockholder or director, or any officer whose title to office is contested, or any member of a corporation without capital stock, the Court of Chancery may hear and determine the validity of any election, appointment, removal or resignation of any director, member of the governing body, or officer of any corporation, and the right of any person to hold or continue to hold such office, and, in case any such office is claimed by more than 1 person, may determine the person entitled thereto; and to that end make such order or decree in any such case as may be just and proper, with power to enforce the production of any books, papers and records of the corporation relating to the issue. In case it should be determined that no valid election has been held, the Court of Chancery may order an election to be held in accordance with §211 or 215 of this title. In any such application, service of copies of the application upon the registered agent of the corporation shall be deemed to be service upon the corporation and upon the person whose title to office is contested and upon the person, if any, claiming such office; and the registered agent shall forward immediately a copy of the application to the corporation and to the person whose title to office is contested and to the person, if any, claiming such office, in a postpaid, sealed, registered letter addressed to such corporation and such person at their post-office addresses last known to the registered agent or furnished to the registered agent by the applicant stockholder. The Court may make such order respecting further or other notice of such application as it deems proper under the circumstances.

(b) Upon application of any stockholder or any member of a corporation without capital stock, or upon application of the corporation itself, the Court of Chancery may hear and determine the result of any vote of stockholders or members, as the case may be, upon matters other than the election of directors, officers or members of the governing body. Service of the application upon the registered agent of the corporation shall be deemed to be service upon the corporation, and no other party need be joined in order for the Court to adjudicate the result of the vote. The Court may make such order respecting notice of the application as it deems proper under the circumstances.

(c) If 1 or more directors has been convicted of a felony in connection with the duties of such director or directors to the corporation, or if there has been a prior judgment on the merits by a court of competent jurisdiction that 1 or more directors has committed a breach of the duty of loyalty in connection with the duties of such director or directors to that corporation, then, upon application by the corporation, or derivatively in the right of the corporation by any stockholder or any member of a nonstock corporation, in a subsequent action brought for such purpose, the Court of Chancery may remove from office such director or directors if the Court determines that the director or directors did not act in good faith in performing the acts resulting in the prior conviction or judgment and judicial removal is necessary to avoid irreparable harm to the corporation. In connection with such removal, the Court may make such orders as are necessary to effect such removal. In any such application, service of copies of the application upon the registered agent of the corporation shall be deemed to be service upon the corporation and upon the director or directors whose removal is sought; and the registered agent shall forward immediately a copy of the application to the corporation and to such director or directors, in a postpaid, sealed, registered letter addressed to such corporation and such director or directors at their post office addresses last known to the registered agent or furnished to the registered agent by the applicant. The Court may make such order respecting further or other notice of such application as it deems proper under the circumstances."

Ch. 253, L. '10 Synopsis of Section 225

Sections 20, 21, 22, 23, 24, 25, and 26 make technical changes to §220, §223, and §225 of the DGCL consistent with the intent of the bill and with the translator provision in new §114(a).

Ch. 14, L. '09 Synopsis of Section 225

This section, which adds a new subsection (c) to Section 225, changes existing law by granting to the Court of Chancery the power to remove directors under specified limited circumstances. An application for judicial removal of a director must be brought directly by or derivatively in the right of the corporation. Such an application must be preceded by either a felony conviction or a judgment of the sort specified in the new subsection. Removal of a director is permitted only when the Court determines that the director did not act in good faith and that judicial removal is necessary to avoid irreparable harm to the corporation.

Ch. 252, L. '08 Synopsis of Section 225

Section 3 amends §225(b) to include the corporation itself as a permissible applicant in an action brought under that subsection.

Ch. 84, L. '03 Synopsis of Section 225

This amendment clarifies that the Court of Chancery has jurisdiction to hear and determine controversies regarding the right of any person to hold or continue to hold office as a director, officer or member of the governing body of a Delaware corporation, irrespective of whether the controversy arose from the conduct of an election.

Comment: The amendment to §220 is designed to codify the common law right of a director of a Delaware corporation to examine the stock list, books and records and to permit the director to obtain summary relief in the Court of Chancery to enforce his right. Pursuant to the present case law, it is not clear whether the Court of Chancery has jurisdiction over such an action by a director. The amendment is not intended to effect any substantive changes in the directors' rights to inspect such corporate records.

The second and third amendments to Sections 211(c) and 225 are to permit a director as well as a stockholder to bring an action in the Delaware Court of Chancery to require the holding of an annual meeting, to determine the validity of any election and the right of a person to hold office. At the present time, the relevant case law does not permit a director to bring such an action in the Court of Chancery; it is limited to stockholders.

.1 Construction.—Chancery Court Rule 23(c) applies to dismissal and compromise of actions brought to review corporate elections. *Borer v Associated General Utilities Co, 111 A2d 707 (Ch Ct 1955).*

Court has discretion in determining whether even material misrepresentations in a proxy solicitation campaign warrant the ordering of a new election. It will deny a new election when the alleged misrepresentations were brought to the stockholders' attention, both sides made them and the contest was over personalities. *Matter of Seminole Oil & Gas Corp, 150 A2d 750 (Ch Ct 1959).*

In action to determine legal composition of board of directors, defendants could not assert as affirmative defense that plaintiffs, if they are declared to be in office so as to constitute board majority, intend to liquidate corporation to further their own interests, rather than corporation's. *Reason:* The issue in actions under §225 is validity of corporate election, not wisdom of permitting persons to act as directors, so affirmative defense was collateral matter not within contemplation of statute. *Bachman v Ontell, No. 7805 (Ch Ct 11-7-84).*

Purpose of GCL §225 is to allow quick review of corporate election process to prevent corporation from being immobilized by controversies as to identity of proper officers or directors. In order to rule on validity of election, court may go beyond mere determination of voting rights and adjudicate ownership of stock, invalidate stock found improperly issued, and set aside election at which invalid stock was voted. Once validity of election is established, however, such ancillary issues become moot and beyond scope of §225. *In the Matter of Hybrilonics, Inc, No. 8035 (Ch Ct 1-27-88).*

The scope of a proceeding under GCL §225 is narrow. Its purpose is to determine the validity of a corporate election to determine the right of a person to hold a corporate office in the event the office is claimed by more than one person. As such the statute is directed at the corporate election process and is in the nature of an in rem proceeding, the "res" being the corporate office or position in dispute. *Arbitrium (Cayman Islands) Handels AG v Johnston, No. 13506 (Ch Ct 9-17-97).*

Absent a board of directors' meeting, a director's removal and CEO's termination is ineffective where all board members do not consent thereto in writing, even where the directors who do not give consent are not disinterested. *Solstice Capital II, Ltd P'ship v Ritz, 2004 Del. Ch. LEXIS 39 (Ch Ct 2004).*

.2 Disputes as to result of election.—Where there is any dispute as to result of election, proper procedure is either by bill in equity, or by petition under GCL §225. *Ellingwood v Wolf's Head Oil Refining Co, 33 A2d 409 (Ch Ct 1943),* aff'd, *38 A2d 743 (S Ct 1944); Fleer v Frank H Fleer Corp, 125 A 411 (Ch Ct 1924); Standard Scale & Supply Co v Chappel, 141 A 191 (Ch Ct 1928); In re Canal Construction Co, 182 A 545 (Ch Ct 1936).*

In action to contest election of directors, respondent corporation will not be enjoined pendente lite from voting shares of a company which it controls where it is not shown that it will vote the stock to elect directors who will not properly represent interests of the controlled corporation. *Aldridge v Franco-Wyoming Securities Corp, 26 A2d 544 (Ch Ct 1942).*

Voting trustee can validly vote Class A voting stock that is converted from Class B non-voting stock for election of directors, when (1) Civil Aeronautics Board prior to divestiture of aviation corporation and railroad company for having interlocking directors approved voting trust to liquidate corporation's stock by sale to non-affiliated person at specified date, meanwhile permitting trustee to vote that stock, and (2) corporation's charter permits Class B shares to be converted to Class A shares after beneficial ownership of those shares has been transferred to person not initial holder; delivery of B shares to trustee made corporation no longer beneficial owner, so later conversion permitted under charter. *Sundlum v Executive Jet Aviation Inc, 273 A2d 282 (1970).*

Elections held at two special directors' meetings to replace opposing faction were both void, since as to first meeting, organizers failed to give required notice of special meeting to director and as to second meeting another director's absence was secured through misrepresenting date of meeting; thus, board was constituted by those that served prior to special meetings and compromise directors elected to fill vacancies on board after opposing factions enlarged number to provide continuity and regularity in corporation's management. *Schroder v Scotten, Dillon Co, 299 A2d 431 (Ch Ct 1972).*

Even though funds were available to pay preferred dividend arrearages, common stockholder could not have election of board of directors set aside for their wrongful refusal to pay such dividends without showing fraud and gross abuse of discretion by board in refusing to order such dividends. *Baron v Allied Artists Pictures Corp, 337 A2d 653 (Ch Ct 1975).*

Court confirmed election of first shareholder group's slate as directors. Agreement group made to acquire capital to finance its effort to gain control of corporation did not involve transfer of restricted shares over which competing shareholder group had right of first refusal under shareholder agreement. *Garrett v Brown, Nos. 8423, 8427 (Ch Ct 6-13-86).*

Shareholders, acting pursuant to consents, could not remove entire board of directors and replace them with new members because consents executed by brokerage houses were invalid when they were not executed by record holder and record holder had not given brokerage houses its proxy, so remaining consents represented less than 50% of corporation's voting shares. *Olson v Buffington, No. 8042 (Ch Ct 7-17-85).*

Neither of the actions taken by shareholder consent was effective to elect representatives of either of two opposing shareholder factions as directors because both sets of consents, after consents that court said could not be counted on behalf of either faction were thrown out, represented less than majority of outstanding shares. Therefore: (1) change of time and place of shareholders' meeting made by one director faction was ineffective, (2) board of directors continued to be constituted as it was before consents, and (3) court ordered shareholder meeting to be promptly held to properly elect directors. *Freeman v Fabiniak, No. 8035 (Ch Ct 8-15-85).*

A corporation adopted a profit sharing plan pursuant to ERISA under which a trust company serving as trustee of the plan was required to vote the plan shares as directed by the plan participants. The trust company voted the shares incorrectly. Although plan participants, who choose to hold their shares in the name of a nominee, have to accept the risk of that arrangement, including the risk that the nominee might vote their shares incorrectly. ERISA forbids

§225

the plan participants from holding their shares in their own name. Therefore, the court determined that they should not have been forced to bear the risk of a breach of duty by the trustee. *Allison v Preston, No. 13538 (Ch Ct 7-29-94).*

In an action for a determination of the de jure officers and directors of a corporation, the Court of Chancery found that it was not bound by the corporation's annotated stock list in order to determine the number of shares eligible to vote in a corporate election. *Viele v Devaney, No. 14729 (Ch Ct 5-9-96).*

A technical defect in the authorization of a corporation's stock can be cured by a later, ratifying vote of a majority of the corporation's directors, thereby resolving a dispute over who constitutes the lawful board of directors and officers of the corporation. *Kalageorgi v Victor Kamkin, Inc, C.A. No. 17111 (Ch Ct 9-10-99).*

In a case to determine whether a corporate director has been removed from the corporation's board and replaced, a party that advances a frivolous defense in bad faith is responsible for paying his opponent's attorneys' fees and costs. *Stavrou v Contogouris, 2002 Del. Ch. LEXIS 121 (Ch Ct 2002).*

.3 Election by preferred shareholders.—Election of majority directors by preferred stockholders at time of regular annual meeting is invalid, even though default in payment of dividends gave them right to elect, when they did not follow special election procedure set forth in charter. *Liese v Jupiter Corp, 241 A2d 492 (Ch Ct 1968).*

.4 Election of directors.—A non-shareholder may exercise written shareholder consents on behalf of his minor children pursuant to a court-approved stipulation, entered into in a divorce, that gives him the right to pursue his children's interest in a corporation. The non-shareholder may validly use the consents to elect himself and others as directors and officers of the corporation. *B.F. Rich Co v Gray, 2006 Del. Ch. LEXIS 193 (Ch Ct 2006).*

.5 Director's resignation.—Director who left director's meeting after being removed from position as Vice President—Research had not resigned as director when (1) directors were split about whether they heard him say that he was resigning, (2) minutes of meeting made no reference to resignation, and (3) member of faction opposed to director who was purporting to act as chairman acted as if he considered director to still be in office. *Bachmann v Ontell, No. 7805 (Ch Ct 11-27-84).*

.6 Improper vote.—Consent that purported to replace existing board of directors with new board was invalid because it was not signed by holders of 50% of outstanding shares of corporation entitled to vote, because (1) stock co-owner's consent was not effective as to all jointly owned stock because, although co-owner would be entitled to vote all shares, consent can only represent half shares in question since all shareholders are given notice of vote while consents are taken without notice or involvement of minority, (2) no consent could be given for stock in escrow because it could not be voted, and (3) president had no authority to release stock from escrow because release was not merely modification of employment contract but modification of consideration for issuance of shares so board approval was required. *Cook v Pumpelly, Nos. 7917 & 7930 (Ch Ct 5-24-85).*

Where a corporation's chief executive officer (CEO) conducted a consent solicitation to unseat the board of directors, and the corporation was not permitted by the Securities and Exchange Commission to send revocation of consent forms to stock-holders because its Form 10-K was overdue, the Court of Chancery held that the consents of 60% of the stockholders delivered to the CEO were valid and that the CEO and his nominees constituted the new board of directors. The CEO's solicitation sufficiently instructed the stockholders on how to revoke consent and the board also circulated information on how to revoke consent even though the board could not circulate the revocation forms. *Zaucha v Brody, No. 15638-NC (Ch Ct 5-8-97).*

The right to remove directors is a fundamental element of stockholder authority, and therefore directors may not be removed for good cause unless clear evidence that a restriction on such stockholder authority is intended. *Rohe v Reliance Training Network, Inc C.A. No. 17992 (Ch Ct 7-21-00).*

It is unfair for a majority of a corporation's board of directors to keep a director who is also a controlling shareholder in the dark about plans to wrest control from him at an upcoming board meeting, and, consequently, actions taken at the board meeting are invalid. *Adlerstein v Wertheimer, 2002 Del Ch LEXIS 13 (Ch Ct 2002).*

Where it is disputed that a meeting of a quorum of a board of directors occurred, the fact that the meeting occurred must be independently corroborated by evidence other than the testimony of the directors who purportedly attended the meeting. *In re Bigmar, Inc, Section 225 Litigation, 2002 Del. Ch. LEXIS 45 (Ch Ct 2002).*

A shareholder vote is invalid where the shareholders have been misled or misinformed by the board's president about the number of votes needed to approve a proposed transaction; nonetheless, the shareholders are entitled to vote on the transaction in accordance with the corporation's governing documents. *Baring v Watergate East, Inc, 2004 Del. Ch. LEXIS 17 (Ch Ct 2004).*

.7 Vacancy, election to fill.—Director, one of four directors elected by common shareholders on seven-person board, was not elected president, chairman of board, and chief executive officer of corporation by his vote combined with vote of three directors elected by preferred shareholder because there was no vacancy when term of current president, chairman of board, and chief executive officer was not over and no attempt (requiring three-fourths vote) had been made to remove him. *Bossier v Connell, No. 8624 (Ch Ct 11-12-86).*

Where a corporation's certificate of incorporation provides that a holdover board may only "determine the number" of directors who will serve on the first classified board and divide "such number" of directors into classes as nearly equal as possible, the holdover board itself is not empowered to elect the first classified board, and, therefore, all board members are up for election at the next shareholder's meeting. *Comac Partners, LP v Ghaznavi, 793 A2d 372 (Ch Ct 2001).*

.8 Newly created directorship, power to fill.—Bylaw providing that directors "shall" designate "successor director" in event "the office of any director becomes vacant" did not confer on director's exclusive power to designate persons to fill newly created directorships; shareholders, therefore, could consent to creation and filling of new directorships. *DiEleuterio v Cavaliers of Delaware, Inc, No. 8801 (Ch Ct 2-9-87).*

.9 Stay of action.—Summary Delaware action to determine rightfully elected directors of corporation should not be stayed pending outcome of previously filed but slower moving Texas action. *Reasons:* Texas action is not summary or expedited proceeding, no decision in the Texas action is expected in foreseeable future, and uncertainty created by stay might negatively affect corporation and those dealing with it. *Pulver v Stafford Holding Co, No. 8567 (Ch Ct 4-2-87).*

.10 Lawyer-client privilege; who may assert.—Shareholders of corporation do not have rights as individuals to suppress production of documents claimed to be subject to lawyer-client privilege when documents do not reflect a lawyer-client relationship with any person other than corporation itself.

In a suit for a judicial determination of a directors' election pursuant to GCL §225, it is not possible to know who is legally in position to assert corporation's claim of privilege. An appropriate balancing of interests requires that documents be made available to both sides of the litigation with an order requiring them not to disclose information learned only as a result of such production while lawsuit is pending. *Rainbow Navigation, Inc v Yonge, No. 9432 (Ch Ct 1-29-88).*

.11 Impeding shareholders' voting rights.—Corporation's board, even though acting in subjective good faith, could not validly act for primary purpose of preventing or impeding unaffiliated majority of shareholders from expanding board and electing new majority. However, citing inability to foresee all future settings in which board might seek to thwart shareholder vote, court refused to adopt per se rule invalidating every board action for such a purpose. *Blasius Industries, Inc v Atlas Corp, 564 A2d 651 (Ch Ct 1988).*

A member of a limited liability company who through fraud obtains a delegation of authority from another member to vote corporate shares cannot validly vote those shares (for example, as part of a written consent action) because the delegation of authority is not legally binding. *In re Bigmar, Inc, Section 225 Litigation, 2002 Del. Ch. LEXIS 45 (Ch Ct 2002).*

.12 Stay against trustee's vote, effect of.—Order by Michigan court, which stayed voting of shares held in trust, had effect of barring trustee from voting shares in favor of Delaware corporation's insurgent slate. In failing to withdraw vote for insurgents, trustee violated clearly deductible intent of order. Delaware court issued declaration that shares voted by trustee were not to be included in tabulation of votes. *Scherer v R P Scherer Corp, No. 10204 (Ch Ct 10-5-88).*

.13 Election pursuant to pledge agreement.—Defendants executed a promissory note in favor of plaintiff corporation, secured by pledge agreements in which defendants pledged all their shares in plaintiff corporation, and the voting power with respect to such shares, to the individual plaintiffs. When defendant defaulted on the note, pledge agreements were triggered, and plaintiffs exercised their rights. By unanimous written consent, plaintiffs voted their pledged shares to adopt resolutions removing defendants as the directors of the corporation, and electing a new board of directors. The court held that plaintiffs established, *prima facie*, a default under the note and their rights under the pledge agreements to vote the pledged shares. Accordingly, the court held that the election of the new board of directors was valid, and entered judgment in favor of plaintiffs. *Barra v Adams, No. 13482 (Ch Ct 7-1-94).*

.14 Res judicata.—The decision in an action brought under GCL §225 to determine the right of a person to hold corporate office has preclusive effect in a later action. Even though a GCL §225 action is an *in rem* proceeding (the res being the corporate office or position in dispute), a party who has appeared and litigated in that action may properly be precluded from relitigating that issue. An earlier Chancery decision, *Rosenfield v Standard Electric Equipment Corp,* 83 A2d 843 (1951), which declined to give a GCL §225 action the effect of collateral estoppel, "is no longer valid law." *Technicorp International II, Inc v Johnston, No. 5084 (Ch Ct 8-22-97).*

.15 Voluntary dismissal of action.—Directors (who were Maryland residents) of a Delaware corporation with its principal place of business in the Republic of the Philippines may not voluntarily dismiss their action under GCL §225 where they did not seek dismissal until after the defendants, one of whom was a resident of the Philippines, personally answered the complaint in Delaware. *Catibayan v Fischer Engineering & Maintenance Co, No. 14060 (Ch Ct 10-15-97).*

.16 Stockholder's agreement.—Where a stockholder's agreement, to which all stockholders and the corporation are parties, unambiguously does not vest the power to fill vacancies on the corporation's board of directors in a single director and the stockholders he claims to represent exclusively, the actions taken by a majority of the remaining directors to fill the vacancies are valid. *McIlquham v Feste,* 2002 Del. Ch. LEXIS 8 (Ch Ct 2002).

In order to prevail on a claim that, in a merger, management bought the votes of a shareholder that has a business relationship with the corporation, a plaintiff has the burden of presenting significant evidence that management coerced the shareholder into switching its votes in favor of the merger, and that the switch of those votes was not made for independent business reasons. *Hewlett v Hewlett-Packard Co,* 2002 Del. Ch. LEXIS 35 (Ch Ct 2002).

.17 Director nominations.—Where bylaw provisions relating to director nomination deadlines are subject to two interpretations, a claim that the bylaws are so confusing as to excuse compliance will be rejected where no compliance is attempted under either interpretation. *Openwave Systems, Inc v Harbinger Capital Partners Master Fund I, Ltd,* 924 A2d 228 (Ch Ct 2007).

§225

.18 Voting of shares owned by minors.—A parent's voting of his minor children's shares of stock constitutes a "use" of those shares within the meaning of a guardianship statute that requires the appointment of a guardian of a minor's estate where a parent receives or uses property of the minor child having a certain value. *B.F. Rich & Co v Gray, 933 A2d 1231 (2007).*

.19 Legal consents.—Where a putative written consent is exercised on an erroneous interpretation of an agreement that grants the consent, the consent is a nullity, as are any actions taken on the basis of the consent. *In re IAC/InterActive Corp, 948 A2d 471 (Ch Ct 2008).*

.20 Intervention by shareholder.—A shareholder whose stock is issued after a contested board is elected has standing to establish the legitimacy of the board in order to prove that its shares were validly issued by the board, and, accordingly, the shareholder may intervene in an action alleging that its stock is void for having been issued by an invalidly elected board. *Noe v Kropf, 2008 Del. Ch. LEXIS 148 (Ch Ct 2008).*

.21 Voting rights; bylaw amendments.—Votes based on voting rights purchased in violation of a restricted stock agreement are void and will not be counted. Moreover, a bylaw amendment that purports to shrink the number of board seats below the number of sitting directors is void, as is a bylaw that purports to establish qualifications for directorships that would disqualify a sitting director and terminate his service. *Crown EMAK Partners, LLC v Kurz, 2010 Del. LEXIS 182 (2010).*

.22 Stock splits.—A purported stock split is invalid where the formalities required to effect the split have not been strictly adhered to. *Blades v Wisehart, 2010 Del. Ch. LEXIS 227 (Ch Ct 2010).*

226 APPOINTMENT OF CUSTODIAN OR RECEIVER OF CORPORATION ON DEADLOCK OR FOR OTHER CAUSE.—(a) The Court of Chancery, upon application of any stockholder, may appoint 1 or more persons to be custodians, and, if the corporation is insolvent, to be receivers, of and for any corporation when:

(1) At any meeting held for the election of directors the stockholders are so divided that they have failed to elect successors to directors whose terms have expired or would have expired upon qualification of their successors; or

(2) The business of the corporation is suffering or is threatened with irreparable injury because the directors are so divided respecting the management of the affairs of the corporation that the required vote for action by the board of directors cannot be obtained and the stockholders are unable to terminate this division; or

(3) The corporation has abandoned its business and has failed within a reasonable time to take steps to dissolve, liquidate or distribute its assets.

(b) A custodian appointed under this section shall have all the powers and title of a receiver appointed under §291 of this title, but the authority of the custodian is to continue the business of the corporation and not to liquidate its affairs and distribute its assets, except when the Court shall otherwise order and except in cases arising under paragraph (3) of subsection (a) of this section or paragraph (2) of subsection (a) of §352 of this title.

(c) In the case of a charitable nonstock corporation, the applicant shall provide a copy of any application referred to in subsection (a) of this section to the Attorney General of the State of Delaware within 1 week of its filing with the Court of Chancery. (Last amended by Ch. 253, L. '10, eff. 8-1-10.)

Ch. 253, L. '10, eff. 8-1-10, added matter in italic.

Ch. 253, L. '10 Synopsis of Section 226

Section 27 amends the DGCL to add new §226(c) to provide that, in the case of a charitable nonstock corporation, the applicant must provide a copy of the application referred to in §226(a) to the Attorney General of the State of Delaware within one week of filing the application with the Court of Chancery.

.1 Construction.—Statutory provision that court "may" appoint receiver for a deadlocked corporation is discretionary; the court does not have to appoint a receiver. *Paulman v Kritzer Radiant Coils, Inc, 143 A2d 272 (Ch Ct 1958).*

Even though an equally divided stockholder vote has prevented the election of directors for four successive meetings, the court will not appoint a receiver when the corporation is not mismanaged, and is not being operated to benefit the controlling stockholders alone. *Paulman,* supra.

The Court of Chancery issued a preliminary injunction enjoining the voting of shares of stock of a corporation owned by another corporation, because of a deadlock between the latter corporation's two 50 percent shareholders and directors (Petrocelli and Hack) regarding how the latter corporation's shares should be voted. *Re: Hack v BMG Equities Corp, No. 12098 (Ch Ct 6-20-91).*

.2 When appointment is appropriate.—Action taken at directors' meeting attended by only two of eight directors after four directors representing opposing faction had recently been elected was either ultra vires or illegal; however, corporation was not dissolved because it was solvent and dissolution would have been harsh and precipitous so appointment of receiver would be appropriate to preserve its affairs for benefit of shareholders since deadlock existed. *Whitman v Fuqua, 549 FSupp 315 (WD Pa 1982).*

Custodian was appointed to resolve disputes of corporation's board of directors because shareholders were deadlocked and could not elect successor directors, thus perpetuating control of board by one 50% stockholder because legislature intended to create readily available remedy in shareholder deadlock situations to remedy injustices arising from deadlock that permits control to remain indefinitely in hands of self-perpetuating board of directors. *Giuricich v Emtrol Corp, 449 A2d 232 (1982).*

Court refused to declare deadlock in corporate activity and appoint custodian because corporation no longer had equal stock ownership after one 50% shareholder gave 10% of stock to wife of other 50% shareholder in exchange for her management services. *Modlin v Iselin, No. 8104 (Ch Ct 6-5-86).*

Court ordered shareholders' meeting for purpose of electing successor directors to be held when 50% shareholders petitioned that there had been no annual meeting for thirty days after date designated in corporate bylaws because second group of 50% shareholders refused to attend and defeated quorum. In event that successor directors are not elected at meeting or quorum is defeated again, court will appoint custodian because corporation will then be deadlocked. *Marciano v Nakash, No. 7910 (Ch Ct 6-19-85).*

Court granted board of director member's action which sought the appointment of a custodian for the corporation where the director demonstrated that he and the corporation's other director could not agree on necessary management decisions; the board could not resolve the deadlock; and the corporation was threatened with irreparable injury as a result of the deadlock. *Niehenke v Right O Way Transportation, Inc, Nos. 14392, 14444 (Ch Ct 12-28-95).*

Where plaintiff failed to prove that a corporation was unable to meet its debts as they fall due in the ordinary course of business, the Chancery Court denied plaintiff's petition for the appointment of a limited custodian under GCL §226(a)(2) in a case in which the legitimacy of plaintiff's claim depended on its allegation that the director deadlock arose from a capital call to cure the corporation's insolvency. *Francotyp-Postalia AG & Co v On Target Technology, Inc, C.A. 16330 (Ch Ct 12-24-98).*

A court may appoint a custodian where the shareholders of a corporation are deadlocked on the election of some, but not all, of the directors. *Bentas v Haseotes, C.A. No. 17223 (Ch Ct 3-6-00).*

An auction of a corporation is appropriate where the board of directors is deadlocked and there is no reliable information about whether there is a viable market for the corporation. *Haseotes v Haseotes, 2003 Del. Ch. LEXIS 24 (Ch Ct 2003).*

A custodian may be appointed for a limited time and with limited powers where co-equal shareholders are deadlocked so that directors cannot be appointed, but the impasse created by the deadlock does not threaten immediate irreparable harm to the corporation. *Miller v Miller, 2009 Del. Ch. LEXIS 16 (Ch Ct 2009).*

.3 Failure to comply with technical requirements—effect.—Lack of compliance with the technical requirements of Delaware corporate law in issuing new stock does not require a declaration that the stock is void and that no rights attach as a result of issuance of the stock. This lack of technical compliance also does not rob the court of power to great plaintiffs what amounts to specific performance under §227. *Waggoner v STARR Surgical Co, No. 11185 (Ch Ct 3-15-90).*

.4 Limited liability company dissolution.—A limited liability company will not be dissolved where its members are not in deadlock and it is not impracticable to carry on the limited liability company's business, even where the limited liability company is merely a passive investment vehicle. *In re Seneca Investments, LLC, 2008 Del. Ch. LEXIS 141 (Ch Ct 2008).*

227 POWERS OF COURT IN ELECTIONS OF DIRECTORS.—(a) The Court of Chancery, in any proceeding instituted under §211, 215 or 225 of this title may determine the right and power of persons claiming to own stock [1] to vote at any meeting of the stockholders [2].

(b) The Court of Chancery may appoint a Master to hold any election provided for in §211, 215 or 225 of this title under such orders and powers as it deems proper; and it may punish any officer or director for contempt in case of disobedience of any order made by the Court; and, in case of disobedience by a corporation of any order made by the Court, may enter a decree against such corporation for a penalty of not more than $5,000. (Last amended by Ch. 253, L. '10, eff. 8-1-10.)

Ch. 253, L. '10, eff. 8-1-10, deleted 1 ", or in the case of a corporation without capital stock, of the persons claiming to be members," and 2 "or members".

Ch. 253, L. '10 Synopsis of Section 227

Sections 28, 29, and 30 make technical changes to §227, §232, and §233 of the DGCL consistent with the intent of the bill and with the translator provision in new §114(a).

.1 Jurisdiction.—Where right of stockholder to vote in contested election is illegally denied, Chancellor may disregard stock records and determine true situation. *Italo Petroleum Corp of America v Producers' Oil Corp of America, 174 A 276 (1934).* See also, *Gans v Delaware Terminal Corp, 2 A2d 154 (Ch Ct 1938).*

Chancellor may appoint master to hold stockholder's meeting to elect new directors without first ordering directors to hold the meeting. *In re Gulla, 114 A 596 (1921); In re Jackson, 81 A 992 (1911).*

A quorum must be present at meeting called by master to elect directors. *In re Gulla, 115 A 317 (1921).*

Chancellor will determine stockholder's right to vote in election, even though stockholder is not party to the proceedings, but court will not determine status of stockholder or his right to his shares. *Chappel v Standard Scale & Supply Corp, 138 A 74, 141 A 191 (1927); Rosenfield v Standard Electric Equip Corp, 83 A2d 843 (Ch Ct 1951); No Amer Uranium and Oil Corp v So Texas Oil and Gas Co, 129 A2d 407 (Ch Ct 1957).*

.2 Jurisdiction of federal court.—Federal court cannot order election of directors of Delaware corporation. *Perrott v United States Banking Corp, 53 FSupp 953 (D Del 1944).*

.3 Intervention by shareholder.—A shareholder whose stock is issued after a contested board is elected has standing to establish the legitimacy of the board in order to prove that its shares were validly issued by the board, and, accordingly, the shareholder may intervene in an action alleging that its stock is void for having been issued by an invalidly elected board. *Noe v Kropf, 2008 Del. Ch. LEXIS 148 (Ch Ct 2008).*

228 CONSENT OF STOCKHOLDERS OR MEMBERS IN LIEU OF MEETING.—(a) Unless otherwise provided in the certificate of incorporation, any action required by this chapter to be taken at any annual or special meeting of stockholders of a corporation, or any action which may be taken at any annual or special meeting of such stockholders, may be taken without a meeting, without prior notice and without a vote, if a consent or consents in writing, setting forth the action so taken, shall be signed by the holders of outstanding stock having not less than the minimum number of votes that would be necessary to authorize or take such action at a meeting at which all shares entitled to vote thereon were present and voted and shall be delivered to the corporation by delivery to its registered office in this State, its principal place of business or an officer or agent of the corporation having custody of the book in which proceedings of meetings of stockholders are recorded. Delivery made to a corporation's registered office shall be by hand or by certified or registered mail, return receipt requested.

(b) Unless otherwise provided in the certificate of incorporation, any action required by this chapter to be taken at a meeting of the members of a nonstock corporation, or any action which may be taken at any meeting of the members of a nonstock corporation, may be taken without a meeting, without prior notice and without a vote, if a consent or consents in writing, setting forth the action so taken, shall be signed by members having not less than the minimum number of votes that would be necessary to authorize or take such action at a meeting at which all members having a right to vote thereon were present and voted and shall be delivered to the corporation by delivery to its registered office in this State, its principal place of business or an officer or agent of the corporation having custody of the book in which proceedings of meetings of members are recorded. Delivery made to a corporation's registered office shall be by hand or by certified or registered mail, return receipt requested.

(c) Every written consent shall bear the date of signature of each stockholder or member who signs the consent, and no written consent shall be effective to take the corporate action referred to therein unless, within 60 days of the earliest dated consent delivered in the manner required by this section to the corporation, written consents signed by a sufficient number of holders or members to take action are delivered to the corporation by delivery to its registered office in this State, its principal place of business or an officer or agent of the corporation having custody of the book in which proceedings of meetings of stockholders or members are recorded. Delivery made to a corporation's registered office shall be by hand or by certified or registered mail, return receipt requested.

(d)(1) A telegram, cablegram or other electronic transmission consenting to an action to be taken and transmitted by a stockholder, member or proxyholder, or by a person or persons authorized to act for a stockholder, member or proxyholder, shall be deemed to be written, signed and dated for the purposes of this section, provided that any such telegram, cablegram or other electronic transmission sets forth or is delivered with information from which the corporation can determine (A) that the telegram, cablegram or other electronic transmission was transmitted by the stockholder, member or proxyholder or by a person or persons authorized to act for the stockholder, member or proxyholder and (B) the date on which such stockholder, member or proxyholder or authorized person or persons transmitted such telegram, cablegram or electronic transmission. The date on which such telegram, cablegram or electronic transmission is transmitted shall be deemed to be the date on which such consent was signed. No consent given by telegram, cablegram or other electronic transmission shall be deemed to have been delivered until such consent is reproduced in paper form and until such paper form shall be delivered to the corporation by delivery to its registered office in this State, its principal place of business or an officer or agent of the corporation having custody of the book in which proceedings of meetings of stockholders or members are recorded. Delivery made to a corporation's registered office shall be made by hand or by certified or registered mail, return receipt requested. Notwithstanding the foregoing limitations on delivery, consents given by telegram, cablegram or other electronic transmission, may be otherwise delivered to the principal place of business of the corporation or to an officer or agent of the corporation having custody of the book in which proceedings of meetings of stockholders or members are recorded if, to the extent and in the manner provided by resolution of the board of directors or governing body of the corporation.

(2) Any copy, facsimile or other reliable reproduction of a consent in writing may be substituted or used in lieu of the original writing for any and all purposes for which the original writing could be used, provided that such copy, facsimile or other reproduction shall be a complete reproduction of the entire original writing.

(e) Prompt notice of the taking of the corporate action without a meeting by less than unanimous written consent shall be given to those stockholders or members who have not consented in writing and who, if the action had been taken at a meeting, would have been entitled to notice of the meeting if [1]*the record date for notice of such meeting* had been the date that written consents signed by a sufficient number of holders or members to take the action were delivered to the corporation as provided in subsection (c) of this section. In the event that the action which is consented to is such as would have required the filing of a certificate under any other section of this title, if such action had been voted on by stockholders or by members at a meeting thereof, the certificate filed under such other section shall state, in lieu of any statement required by such section concerning any vote of stockholders or members, that written consent has been given in accordance with this section. (Last amended by Ch. 14, L. '09, eff. 8-1-09.)

Ch. 14, L. '09, eff. 8-1-09, added matter in italic and deleted [1]"the record date for such meeting".

Ch. 14, L. '09 Synopsis of Section 228

This section is a technical amendment to Section 228(e) to make it consistent with the revisions to Section 213(a).

Ch. 82, L. '01 Synopsis of Section 228

The amendment to Section 228(d)(1) provides that such subsection applies to consents in lieu of a meeting by members of nonstock corporations.

Ch. 343, L. '00 Synopsis of Section 228

The amendments to Section 228 generally permit the use of electronically transmitted consents, and align Section 228 with Section 212(c), governing electronic proxies. The proposed amendments also address the circumstances in which an electronically transmitted consent is deemed to be in writing, dated, and signed by the stockholder, as well as delivery of such a consent.

Ch. 349, L. '96 Synopsis of Section 228

This amendment eliminates the requirement that, prior to the filing of a certificate under another section of the statute to effectuate an action by written consent, the notice of such action required by this subsection be given to stockholders who have not consented in writing (although the requirement that "prompt" notice be given remains unchanged). The amendment also clarifies that the stockholders entitled to receive such notice are the stockholders who would have been entitled to receive notice of a stockholders meeting if the action had been taken at a meeting.

Commentary on Sections 228(b) and (c)

The amendment to Section 228(b) replaces the reference to "stockholders" with a reference to "members" since Section 228(b) deals only with consents of members and not consents of stockholders. The amendment to Section 228(c) adds a reference to members to the existing reference to stockholders since Section 228(c) applies to consents of members as well as consents of stockholders. No substantive change of law is intended.

.1 Invalid consent.—Consent that purported to replace existing board of directors with new board was invalid because it was not signed by holders of 50% of outstanding shares of corporation entitled to vote, because (1) stock co-owner's consent was not effective as to all jointly owned stock because, although co-owner would be entitled to vote all shares, consent can only represent half shares in question since all shareholders are given notice of vote while consents are taken without notice or involvement of minority; (2) no consent could be given for stock in escrow because it could not be voted; and (3) president had no authority to release stock from escrow because release was not merely modification of employment contract but modification of consideration for issuance of shares so board approval was required. *Cook v Pumpelly, Nos. 7971&7930 (Ch Ct 5-24-85).*

Shareholders, acting pursuant to consents, could not remove entire board of directors and replace them with new members because consents executed by brokerage houses were invalid when they were not executed by record holder and record holder had not given brokerage houses its proxy, so remaining consents represented less than 50% of corporation's voting shares. *Olson v Buffington, No. 8042 (Ch Ct 7-17-85).*

Neither of the actions taken by shareholder consent was effective to elect representatives of either of two opposing shareholder factions as directors because both sets of consents, after consents that court said could not be counted on behalf of either faction were thrown out, represented less than majority of outstanding shares. *Freeman v Fabiniak, No. 8035 (Ch Ct 8-15-85).*

Although the consents executed constituted a majority of the voting stock in an action brought by shareholders pursuant to GCL §228 to unseat the director of a corporation, the action was not effective because the shares of one of the shareholders bringing the action—which were necessary to count in order for the consenting shares to constitute a majority—were subject to a call right which was effectively exercised before the consent action was brought. *Len v Fuller, No. 15352 (Ch Ct 5-30-97).*

A shareholder consent purporting to remove a corporation's director for cause, even if no notice or opportunity to be heard was afforded the director, is not validated merely because the certificate of incorporation would have allowed removal of the director without cause. However, a plaintiff seeking to enforce such a consent is not obliged to include in its complaint factual allegations that it gave the director notice or an opportunity to be heard. *Superwire. Com, Inc v Hampton, 2002 Del. Ch. LEXIS 32 (Ch Ct 2002).*

Written consents may be used in lieu of a meeting to remove directors of a corporation that has cumulative voting, provided all requirements of the written consent procedures are met. *Crutcher v Tufts, 898 So2d 529 (La Ct App 2005).*

.2 Bylaws.—Bylaw amendments properly enacted by shareholder consent procedure were valid, although they limited function of board of directors, because amendments were permissible part of consent holder's attempt to avoid disenfranchisement as majority shareholder. *Frantz Mfg Co v EAC Industries, 501 A2d 401 (1985).*

Court refused to enjoin target from holding its annual meeting or voting proxies. Even if bylaw amendments regarding target's shareholders' requests for corporate action by written consent are invalid under GCL §228 as deliberate attempts to thwart changes in control of target, tender offerors would not be irreparably harmed because they do not intend to solicit consents from shareholders for meeting. *MacFadden Holdings, Inc v John Blair & Co, No. 86-161 MMS (D Del 5-16-86).*

Bylaw providing that directors "shall" designate "successor director" in event "the office of any director becomes vacant" did not confer on directors exclusive power to designate persons to fill newly created directorships; shareholders, therefore, could consent to creation and filling of new directorships. *DiEleuterio v Cavaliers of Delaware, Inc, No. 8801 (Ch Ct 2-9-87).*

.3 Delay of consents, effect.—Corporation's bylaw, which imposed 60-day delay on shareholder action in lieu of meeting from time corporation received shareholder's notice of intent to solicit consents, was unenforceable because (1) consent action may not be lawfully deferred or thwarted on grounds not relating to legal sufficiency of consents obtained and (2) bylaw's intent to provide incumbent management with time to defeat consent action by soliciting its own proxies was unreasonable. *Datapoint Corp v Plaza Securities Co, 496 A2d 1031 (1985).*

Although GCL §228 allows stockholders to modify consent power through charter amendment, board of directors may not arrogate to itself through its power to amend the corporation's bylaws the right to substantially delay implementation of shareholder action taken by consent. Court issued preliminary injunction enjoining operation of bylaw that imposed 20-day period during which consent solicitation must stay open. However, bylaw imposing minimal provisions for ministerial review of action taken by consent might survive judicial scrutiny. *Prime Computer, Inc v Allen, No. 9557 (Ch Ct 1-22-88), rev 1-25-88.*

Court affirmed decision to issue preliminary injunction barring enforcement of bylaw placing 20-day delay on action by majority shareholder consent pending review of consents' validity. Exercise of right to act immediately by majority written consent may be modified or eliminated only by certificate of incorporation. Provisions for minimal, essential, ministerial review of action taken by consent may be contained in bylaws. Such provisions, however, must contain reasonable time periods and not be unduly elaborate. Bylaws that effectively abrogate exercise of shareholders' consent rights are invalid. *Allen v Prime Computer, Inc, 540 A2d 417 (1988).*

.4 Record date.—Court refused to enjoin corporation's directors from setting on October, 10, 1985 a stock record date of November 18, 1985 for shareholder's October 7, 1985 notice of solicitation of shareholder consents to remove and replace directors, because (1) Shareholder's notice in its October 7 demand letter that consents would be solicited did not establish October 7 as day on which first written consent was "expressed" when demand letter disclosed only in part full extent of action to be undertaken by shareholder consent so directors were not precluded from fixing different record date from date stated in demand letter. (2) Directors' designation of November 18 as record date did not violate GCL §228 because directors, in exercising business judgment, may set record date that would delay shareholder action by written consent. *Empire of Carolina, Inc v The Deltona Corp, 514 A2d 1091 (1986).*

Corporate bylaw giving board of directors the power to fix a record date in connection with a stockholder consent solicitation does not violate state statutes. *Edelman v Authorized Distribution Network, No. 11104 (Ch Ct 10-27-89).*

§228

.5 Receivers, right to execute consent.—Receivers holding majority of class of corporation's stock could execute consent to remove and replace four directors. Corporation could not assert voting agreement as defense to consent when neither corporation nor its board was signatory to agreement nor third party beneficiary of agreement. Receiver could vote stock in opposition to position of some beneficial owners. *Insituform of North America, Inc v Chandler,* 534 A2d 257 (Ch Ct 1987).

.6 Impeding shareholders' voting rights.—Corporation's board, even though acting in subjective good faith, could not validly act for primary purpose of preventing or impeding unaffiliated majority of shareholders from expanding board and electing new majority. However, citing inability to foresee all future settings in which board might seek to thwart shareholder vote, court refused to adopt per se rule invalidating every board action for such a purpose. *Blasius Industries, Inc v Atlas Corp,* 564 A2d 651 (Ch Ct 1988).

.7 Revocation of consent.—Where a corporation's chief executive officer (CEO) conducted a consent solicitation pursuant to GCL §228 to unseat the board of directors, and the corporation was not permitted by the Securities and Exchange Commission to send revocation of consent forms to stockholders because its Form 10-K was overdue, the Court of Chancery held that the consents of 60% of the stockholders delivered to the CEO were valid and that the CEO and his nominees constituted the new board of directors. The CEO's solicitation sufficiently instructed the stockholders on how to revoke consent and the board also circulated information on how to revoke consent even though the board could not circulate the revocation forms. *Zaucha v Brody,* No. 15638-NC (Ch Ct 5-8-97).

.8 Prompt notice.—Minority shareholders, who held Class B common shares in a closely-held family corporation, were entitled to specific performance of a mandatory buyback provision contained in the corporation's bylaws and authorized in its certificate of incorporation where the majority shareholders secretly deleted the transfer restriction and failed to file the amended certificate or serve notice to its minority shareholders of the deletion. *Di Loreto v Tiber Holding Corp, C.A.* No. 16564 (Ch Ct 5-12-99).

Under Delaware law, corporate action, such as adopting a reverse stock split, may be conducted by written consent that does not require notice to minority shareholders. *Ahlberg v Timm Medical Technologies, Inc,* 2003 Minn. App. LEXIS 1370 (Minn Ct App 2003).

.9 Class certification.—A claim alleging inadequate disclosure of a corporate action approved by written consent of less than all the shareholders of the corporation will not be certified as a class action absent shareholder action based on the allegedly inadequate disclosure. *Dubroff v Wren Holdings, LLC,* 2010 Del. Ch. LEXIS 178 (Ch Ct 2010).

229 WAIVER OF NOTICE.—Whenever notice is required to be given under any provision of this chapter or the certificate of incorporation or bylaws, a written waiver, signed by the person entitled to notice, *or a waiver by electronic transmission by the person entitled to notice,* whether before or after the time stated therein, shall be deemed equivalent to notice. Attendance of a person at a meeting shall constitute a waiver of notice of such meeting, except when the person attends a meeting for the express purpose of objecting at the beginning of the meeting, to the transaction of any business because the meeting is not lawfully called or convened. Neither the business to be transacted at, nor the purpose of, any regular or special meeting of the stockholders, directors or members of a committee of directors need be specified in any written waiver of notice *or any waiver by electronic transmission* unless so required by the certificate of incorporation or the bylaws. (Last amended by Ch. 343, L. '00, eff. 7-1-00.)

Ch. 343, L. '00, eff. 7-1-00, added matter in italic.

Ch. 343, L. '00 Synopsis of Section 229

The amendment to Section 229 provides that a waiver of notice may be given by electronic transmission (as defined in Section 232 of Title 8), and that neither the business to be transacted at, nor the purpose of, a meeting need be specified in a waiver by electronic transmission, unless the certificate of incorporation or bylaws so require.

.1 Application.—Director, who had bylaw declared invalid because he did not receive notice of directors' meeting at which it was adopted, could not thereafter, to suit his current purpose, restore bylaw's effectiveness by waiving notice of that meeting. *In re Seminole Oil & Gas Corp,* 155 A2d 887 (Ch Ct 1959). Appointments of new directors was void as not having been made at special directors' meeting, since attendance at directors' meeting constitutes waiver of notice. *Grossman v Liberty Leasing Co,* 295 A2d 749 (Ch Ct 1972).

230 EXCEPTION TO REQUIREMENTS OF NOTICE.—(a) Whenever notice is required to be given, under any provision of this chapter or of the certificate of incorporation or bylaws of any corporation, to any person with whom communication is unlawful, the giving of such notice to such person shall not be required and there shall be no duty to apply to any governmental authority or agency for a license or permit to give such notice to such person. Any action or meeting which shall be taken or held without notice to any such person with whom communication is unlawful shall have the same force and effect as if such notice had been duly given. In the event that the action taken by the corporation is such as to require the filing of a certificate under any of the other sections of this title, the certificate shall state, if such is the fact and if notice is required, that notice was given to all persons entitled to receive notice except such persons with whom communication is unlawful.

(b) Whenever notice is required to be given, under any provision of this title or the certificate of incorporation or bylaws of any corporation, to any stockholder or, if the corporation is a nonstock corporation, to any member, to whom (1) notice of 2 consecutive annual meetings, and all notices of meetings or of the taking of action by written consent without a meeting to such person during the period between such 2 consecutive annual meetings, or (2) all, and at least 2, payments (if sent by first-class mail) of dividends or interest on securities during a 12-month period, have been mailed addressed to such person at such person's address as shown on the records of the corporation and have been returned undeliverable, the giving of such notice to such person shall not be required. Any action or meeting which shall be taken or held without notice to such person shall have the same force and effect as if such notice had been duly given. If any such person shall deliver to the corporation a written notice setting forth such person's then current address, the requirement that notice be given to such person shall be reinstated. In the event that the action taken by the corporation is such as to require the filing of a certificate under any of the other sections of this title, the certificate need not state that notice was not given to persons to whom notice was not required to be given pursuant to this subsection.

(c) *The exception in paragraph (b)(1) of this section to the requirement that notice be given shall not be applicable to any notice returned as undeliverable if the notice was given by electronic transmission.* (Last amended by Ch. 343, L. '00, eff. 7-1-00.)

Ch. 343, L. '00, eff. 7-1-00, added matter in italic.

Ch. 343, L. '00, Synopsis of Section 230

New subsection (c) of Section 230 provides that the exception to requirements of notice under subsection 230(b)(1) does not apply to a notice that has been given by electronic transmission.

Ch. 339, L. '98 Synopsis of Section 230

The amendments to these Sections eliminate masculine references in the statutes, and replace them with gender neutral references.

231 VOTING PROCEDURES AND INSPECTORS OF ELECTIONS.—(a) The corporation shall, in advance of any meeting of stockholders, appoint 1 or more inspectors to act at the meeting and make a written report thereof. The corporation may designate 1 or more persons as alternate inspectors to replace any inspector who fails to act. If no inspector or alternate is able to act at a meeting of stockholders, the person presiding at the meeting shall appoint 1 or more inspectors to act at the meeting. Each inspector, before entering upon the discharge of the duties of inspector, shall take and sign an oath faithfully to execute the duties of inspector with strict impartiality and according to the best of such inspector's ability.

(b) The inspectors shall:

(1) Ascertain the number of shares outstanding and the voting power of each;

(2) Determine the shares represented at a meeting and the validity of proxies and ballots;

(3) Count all votes and ballots;

(4) Determine and retain for a reasonable period a record of the disposition of any challenges made to any determination by the inspectors; and

(5) Certify their determination of the number of shares represented at the meeting, and their count of all votes and ballots.

The inspectors may appoint or retain other persons or entities to assist the inspectors in the performance of the duties of the inspectors.

(c) The date and time of the opening and the closing of the polls for each matter upon which the stockholders will vote at a meeting shall be announced at the meeting. No ballot, proxies or votes, nor any revocations thereof or changes thereto, shall be accepted by the inspectors after the closing of the polls unless the Court of Chancery upon application by a stockholder shall determine otherwise.

(d) In determining the validity and counting of proxies and ballots, the inspectors shall be limited to an examination of the proxies, any envelopes submitted with those proxies, any information provided in accordance with [1]*§211(e) or §212(c)(2) of this title, or any information provided pursuant to §211(a)(2)(B)(i) or (iii) of this title,* ballots and the regular books and records of the corporation, except that the inspectors may consider other reliable information for the limited purpose of reconciling proxies and ballots submitted by or on behalf of banks, brokers, their nominees or similar persons which represent more votes than the holder of a proxy is authorized by the record owner to cast or more votes than the stockholder holds of record. If the inspectors consider other reliable information for the limited purpose permitted herein, the inspectors at the time they make their certification pursuant to subsection (b)(5) of this section shall specify the precise information considered by them including the person or persons from whom they obtained the information, when the information was obtained, the means by which the information was obtained and the basis for the inspectors' belief that such information is accurate and reliable.

(e) Unless otherwise provided in the certificate of incorporation or bylaws, this section shall not apply to a corporation that does not have a class of voting stock that is:

(1) Listed on a national securities exchange;

(2) Authorized for quotation on an interdealer quotation system of a registered national securities association; or

(3) Held of record by more than 2,000 stockholders. (Last amended by Ch. 343, L. '00, eff. 7-1-00.)

Ch. 343, L. '00, eff. 7-1-00, added matter in italic and deleted [1]"§212(c)(2)".

Ch. 343, L. '00 Synopsis of Section 231

The amendment to subsection (d) of Section 231 of Title 8 expands the types of material that inspectors of election may rely on to include any verification information required of stockholders voting electronically, whether by electronic transmission in lieu of a written ballot or otherwise.

Ch. 339, L. '98 Synopsis of Section 231

The amendments to these Sections eliminate masculine references in the statutes, and replace them with gender neutral references.

Commentary on Section 231

Section 231 is an entirely new section which sets forth certain provisions relating to voting procedures at meetings of the stockholders. The section is only applicable to corporations which are listed on a national securities exchange, authorized for quotation on an interdealer quotation system or which have shares held of record by more than 2,000 shareholders.

Subsection (a) requires that the corporation appoint inspectors of election for each meeting of the shareholders, and subsection (b) specifies the duties of the inspectors. Subsection (c) requires the announcement at each stockholder meeting of the date and time for the opening and closing of the polls for each matter upon which the stockholders will vote at that meeting. After the polls are closed, the inspectors may not accept any new votes, ballots or proxies and may not accept any revocations or changes to any ballots, proxies or votes.

Subsection (d) specifies the information the inspectors may consider in determining the validity and counting proxies and ballots. This subsection is intended to be a codification of pre-existing common law with two exceptions. One change from the pre-existing common law is that inspectors are permitted to examine "reliable information" other than the proxies, ballots and books and records of the corporation, but only for the limited purpose of reconciling bank and broker "over votes" *viz.,* proxies and ballots which represent more votes than the holder of the proxy is authorized by the record owner to cast or more votes than the stockholder holds of record. If the inspectors consider other reliable information for that limited purpose, the inspectors must specify the precise information considered by them. The second change is that the inspectors are permitted to consider information submitted with "telegraphic" or "electronic" proxies as authorized by Section 212(c)(2).

.1 Application.—In a case arising from a control fight, a property settlement agreement between a divorced couple which gave ownership of a block of stock to the wife, but granted the husband voting rights for two years, constituted a valid proxy. The court held that, even if the parties had not originally intended the agreement to be a proxy, it met the requirements of Delaware law for such use, in that it appointed someone to vote the shares and was signed. *Lobato v Health Concepts IV, Inc, 606 A2d 1343 (Ch Ct 1991).*

.2 Mistake on face of proxy.—The Court of Chancery determined that ERISA plan participants intended to vote plaintiffs as the directors of a corporation despite fact that the nominee for plan participants under an ERISA plan incorrectly voted the plan shares intended to be in favor of plaintiffs for defendants. The court rejected defendant's argument that plan participants ran the risk of the nominee voting incorrectly, stating that the rule did not apply under an ERISA plan where participants are forbidden from holding their shares in their own name and must place the shares with a nominee. *Allison v Preston, 651 A2d 772 (Ch Ct 1994).*

.3 "Overvote".—A proxy inspector properly discharges its duties in defining an "overvote" in a way that disqualifies some, but not all, proxies given by one bank or broker. *Seidman and Associates, LLC v GA Financial, Inc, 837 A2d 21 (Ch Ct 2003).*

232 NOTICE BY ELECTRONIC TRANSMISSION.—(a) Without limiting the manner by which notice otherwise may be given effectively to stockholders, any notice to stockholders given by the corporation under any provision of this chapter, the certificate of incorporation, or the bylaws shall be effective if given by a form of electronic transmission consented to by the stockholder to whom the notice is given. Any such consent shall be revocable by the stockholder by written notice to the corporation. Any such consent shall be deemed revoked if (1) the corporation is unable to deliver by electronic transmission 2 consecutive notices given by the corporation in accordance with such consent and (2) such inability becomes known to the secretary or an assistant secretary of the corporation or to the transfer agent, or other person responsible for the giving of notice; provided, however, the inadvertent failure to treat such inability as a revocation shall not invalidate any meeting or other action.

(b) Notice given pursuant to subsection (a) of this section shall be deemed given: (1) if by facsimile telecommunication, when directed to a number at which the stockholder has consented to receive notice; (2) if by electronic mail, when directed to an electronic mail address at which the stockholder has consented to receive notice; (3) if by a posting on an electronic network together with separate notice to the stockholder of such specific posting, upon the later of (A) such posting and (B) the giving of such separate notice; and (4) if by any other form of electronic transmission, when directed to the stockholder. An affidavit of the secretary or an assistant secretary or of the transfer agent or other agent of the corporation that the notice has been given by a form of electronic transmission shall, in the absence of fraud, be prima facie evidence of the facts stated therein.

(c) For purposes of this chapter, "electronic transmission" means any form of communication, not directly involving the physical transmission of paper, that creates a record that may be retained, retrieved and reviewed by a recipient thereof, and that may be directly reproduced in paper form by such a recipient through an automated process.

(d) [1] *[Repealed.]*

(e) This section shall not apply to §164, 296, 311, 312, or 324 of this title. (Last amended by Ch. 253, L. '10, eff. 8-1-10.)

Ch. 253, L. '10, eff. 8-1-10, added matter in italic and deleted [1]"This section shall apply to a corporation organized under this chapter that is not authorized to issue capital stock, and when so applied, all references to stockholders shall be deemed to refer to members of such a corporation."

Ch. 253, L. '10 Synopsis of Section 232

Sections 28, 29, and 30 make technical changes to §227, §232, and §233 of the DGCL consistent with the intent of the bill and with the translator provision in new §114(a).

Ch. 82, L. '01 Synopsis of Section 232

The amendment to Section 232 makes the title of such section "Notice by electronic transmission."

Ch. 343, L. '00 Synopsis of Section 232

Section 232 is new. Subsection (a) provides that any notice by the corporation to a stockholder by a form of electronic transmission is effective if the stockholder has consented to the corporation giving notice by that particular form of electronic transmission. It also provides that a stockholder may revoke such consent by written notice to the corporation. Subsection (a) is not intended to suggest that a notice given by a form of electronic transmission and actually received is ineffective solely because the recipient has not consented to the giving of notice by such form of electronic transmission. Subsection (a) further provides that a stockholder's consent to notice by electronic transmission is revoked if the corporation is unable to deliver two consecutive electronic transmission notices, and such inability becomes known to the secretary, assistant secretary, the transfer agent, or other person responsible for giving notice. Subsection (a) also makes clear, however, that the inadvertent failure to treat such inability as a revocation of consent shall not invalidate any meeting or other action. Subsection (b) of Section 232 specifies when notice by a form of electronic transmission is deemed to have been given. Subsection (c) provides a definition of the term "electronic transmission." Subsection (e) specifies that Section 232 does not apply to certain enumerated Sections of the DGCL.

233 NOTICE TO STOCKHOLDERS SHARING AN ADDRESS.—(a) Without limiting the manner by which notice otherwise may be given effectively to stockholders, any notice to stockholders given by the corporation under any provision of this chapter, the certificate of incorporation, or the bylaws shall be effective if given by a single written notice to stockholders who share an address if consented to by the stockholders at that address to whom such notice is given. Any such consent shall be revocable by the stockholder by written notice to the corporation.

(b) Any stockholder who fails to object in writing to the corporation, within 60 days of having been given written notice by the corporation of its intention to send the single notice permitted under subsection (a) of this section, shall be deemed to have consented to receiving such single written notice.

(c) [1] *[Repealed.]*

(d) This section shall not apply to §164, 296, 311, 312 or 324 of this chapter. (Last amended by Ch. 253, L. '10, eff. 8-1-10.)

Ch. 253, L. '10, eff. 8-1-10, added matter in italic and deleted [1]"This section shall apply to a corporation organized under this chapter that is not authorized to issue capital stock, and when so applied, all references to stockholders shall be deemed to refer to members of such a corporation."

Ch. 253, L. '10 Synopsis of Section 233

Sections 28, 29, and 30 make technical changes to §227, §232, and §233 of the DGCL consistent with the intent of the bill and with the translator provision in new §114(a).

Ch. 298, L. '02 Synopsis of Section 233

Certain amendments to the proxy rules promulgated under the Securities Exchange Act of 1934 permit "householding" of certain documents, such as proxy statements and information statements, sent to stockholders. These householding rules permit corporations to satisfy the requirements for sending proxy statements, information statements and certain other materials with respect to two or more stockholders sharing the same address by sending a single document to those stockholders. This amendment provides that sending non-objecting stockholders such a "householded" document that includes a notice required to be given under this chapter, the certificate of incorporation or the bylaws shall satisfy the requirement that such notice be given to each stockholder.

SUBCHAPTER VIII. AMENDMENT OF CERTIFICATE OF INCORPORATION; CHANGES IN CAPITAL AND CAPITAL STOCK

241 AMENDMENT OF CERTIFICATE OF INCORPORATION BEFORE RECEIPT OF PAYMENT FOR STOCK.—(a) Before a corporation has received any payment for any of its stock, it may amend its certificate of incorporation at any time or times, in any and as many respects as may be desired, so long as its certificate of incorporation as amended would contain only such provisions as it would be lawful and proper to insert in an original certificate of incorporation filed at the time of filing the amendment.

(b) The amendment of a certificate of incorporation authorized by this section shall be adopted by a majority of the incorporators, if directors were not named in the original certificate of incorporation or have not yet been elected, or, if directors were named in the original certificate of incorporation or have been elected and have qualified, by a majority of the directors. A certificate setting forth the amendment and certifying that the corporation has not received any payment for any of its stock, *or that the corporation has no members, as applicable,* and that the amendment has been duly adopted in accordance with this section shall be executed, acknowledged and filed in accordance with §103 of this title. Upon such filing, the corporation's certificate of incorporation shall be deemed to be amended accordingly as of the date on which the original certificate of incorporation became effective, except as to those persons who are substantially and adversely affected by the amendment and as to those persons the amendment shall be effective from the filing date.

(c) This section will apply to a nonstock corporation before such a corporation has any members; provided, however, that all references to directors shall be deemed to be references to members of the governing body of the corporation. (Last amended by Ch. 253, L. '10, eff. 8-1-10.)

Ch. 253, L. '10, eff. 8-1-10, added matter in italic.

Ch. 253, L. '10 Synopsis of Section 241

Section 31 and 32 amend §241 of the DGCL, amending §241(b) to ensure that §241 properly applies to nonstock corporations, and adding new §241(c) to provide that §241 applies to nonstock corporations before such corporations have any members.

242 AMENDMENT OF CERTIFICATE OF INCORPORATION AFTER RECEIPT OF PAYMENT FOR STOCK; NONSTOCK CORPORATIONS.—(a) After a corporation has received payment for any of its capital stock, *or after a nonstock corporation has members,* it may amend its certificate of incorporation, from time to time, in any and as many respects as may be desired, so long as its certificate of incorporation as amended would contain only such provisions as it would be lawful and proper to insert in an original certificate of incorporation filed at the time of the filing of the amendment; and, if a change in stock or the rights of stockholders, or an exchange, reclassification, subdivision, combination or cancellation of stock or rights of stockholders is to be made, such provisions as may be necessary to effect such change, exchange, reclassification, subdivision, combination or cancellation. In particular, and without limitation upon such general power of amendment, a corporation may amend its certificate of incorporation, from time to time, so as:

(1) To change its corporate name; or

(2) To change, substitute, enlarge or diminish the nature of its business or its corporate powers and purposes; or

(3) To increase or decrease its authorized capital stock or to reclassify the same, by changing the number, par value, designations, preferences, or relative, participating, optional, or other special rights of the shares, or the qualifications, limitations or restrictions of such rights, or by changing shares with par value into shares without par value, or shares without par value into shares with par value either with or without increasing or decreasing the number of shares, or by subdividing or combining the outstanding shares of any class or series of a class of shares into a greater or lesser number of outstanding shares; or

(4) To cancel or otherwise affect the right of the holders of the shares of any class to receive dividends which have accrued but have not been declared; or

(5) To create new classes of stock having rights and preferences either prior and superior or subordinate and inferior to the stock of any class then authorized, whether issued or unissued; or

(6) To change the period of its duration.

Any or all such changes or alterations may be effected by 1 certificate of amendment.

(b) Every amendment authorized by subsection (a) of this section shall be made and effected in the following manner:

(1) If the corporation has capital stock, its board of directors shall adopt a resolution setting forth the amendment proposed, declaring its advisability, and either calling a special meeting of the stockholders entitled to vote in respect thereof for the consideration of such amendment or directing that the amendment proposed be considered at the next annual meeting of the stockholders. Such special or annual meeting shall be called and held upon notice in accordance with §222 of this title. The notice shall set forth such amendment in full

or a brief summary of the changes to be effected thereby [1]. At the meeting a vote of the stockholders entitled to vote thereon shall be taken for and against the proposed amendment. If a majority of the outstanding stock entitled to vote thereon, and a majority of the outstanding stock of each class entitled to vote thereon as a class has been voted in favor of the amendment, a certificate setting forth the amendment and certifying that such amendment has been duly adopted in accordance with this section shall be executed, acknowledged and filed and shall become effective in accordance with §103 of this title.

(2) The holders of the outstanding shares of a class shall be entitled to vote as a class upon a proposed amendment, whether or not entitled to vote thereon by the certificate of incorporation, if the amendment would increase or decrease the aggregate number of authorized shares of such class, increase or decrease the par value of the shares of such class, or alter or change the powers, preferences, or special rights of the shares of such class so as to affect them adversely. If any proposed amendment would alter or change the powers, preferences, or special rights of 1 or more series of any class so as to affect them adversely, but shall not so affect the entire class, then only the shares of the series so affected by the amendment shall be considered a separate class for the purposes of this paragraph. The number of authorized shares of any such class or classes of stock may be increased or decreased (but not below the number of shares thereof then outstanding) by the affirmative vote of the holders of a majority of the stock of the corporation entitled to vote irrespective of this subsection, if so provided in the original certificate of incorporation, in any amendment thereto which created such class or classes of stock or which was adopted prior to the issuance of any shares of such class or classes of stock, or in any amendment thereto which was authorized by a resolution or resolutions adopted by the affirmative vote of the holders of a majority of such class or classes of stock.

[2] *(3) If the corporation is a nonstock corporation, then the governing body thereof shall adopt a resolution setting forth the amendment proposed and declaring its advisability. If a majority of all the members of the governing body shall vote in favor of such amendment, a certificate thereof shall be executed, acknowledged and filed and shall become effective in accordance with §103 of this title. The certificate of incorporation of any nonstock corporation may contain a provision requiring any amendment thereto to be approved by a specified number or percentage of the members or of any specified class of members of such corporation in which event such proposed amendment shall be submitted to the members or to any specified class of members of such corporation in the same manner, so far as applicable, as is provided in this section for an amendment to the certificate of incorporation of a stock corporation; and in the event of the adoption thereof by such members, a certificate evidencing such amendment shall be executed, acknowledged and filed and shall become effective in accordance with §103 of this title.*

[3] *(4) Whenever the certificate of incorporation shall require for action by the board of directors of a corporation other than a nonstock corporation or by the governing body of a nonstock corporation, by the holders of any class or series of shares or by the members, or by the holders of any other securities having voting power the vote of a greater number or proportion than is required by any section of this title, the provision of the certificate of incorporation requiring such greater vote shall not be altered, amended or repealed except by such greater vote.*

(c) The resolution authorizing a proposed amendment to the certificate of incorporation may provide that at any time prior to the effectiveness of the filing of the amendment with the Secretary of State, notwithstanding authorization of the proposed amendment by the stockholders of the corporation or by the members of a nonstock corporation, the board of directors or governing body may abandon such proposed amendment without further action by the stockholders or members. (Last amended by Ch. 253, L. '10, eff. 8-1-10 and Ch. 290, L. '10, eff. 8-2-10.)

Ch. 253, L. '10, eff. 8-1-10, added matter in italic and deleted [2]"(3) If the corporation has no capital stock, then the governing body thereof shall adopt a resolution setting forth the amendment proposed and declaring its advisability. If a majority of all the members of the governing body shall vote in favor of such amendment, a certificate thereof shall be executed, acknowledged and filed and shall become effective in accordance with §103 of this title. The certificate of incorporation of any such corporation without capital stock may contain a provision requiring any amendment thereto to be approved by a specified number or percentage of the members or of any specified class of members of such corporation in which event such proposed amendment shall be submitted to the members or to any specified class of members of such corporation without capital stock in the same manner, so far as applicable, as is provided in this section for an amendment to the certificate of incorporation of a stock corporation; and in the event of the adoption thereof by such members, a certificate evidencing such amendment shall be executed, acknowledged and filed and shall become effective in accordance with §103 of this title." and [3]"(4) Whenever the certificate of incorporation shall require for action by the board of directors, by the holders of any class or series of shares or by the holders of any other securities having voting power the vote of a greater number or proportion than is required by any section of this title, the provision of the certificate of incorporation requiring such greater vote shall not be altered, amended or repealed except by such greater vote." Ch. 290, L. '10, eff. 8-2-10, deleted [1]", as the directors shall deem advisable".

Ch. 290, L. '10 Synopsis of Section 242

This amendment to Section 242(b) clarifies that the decision to include either a copy or a summary of a proposed amendment to the certificate of corporation in a notice of a stockholder meeting need not be approved by a specific act of the board of directors. The amendment is not intended to define or limit any duty of directors relating to disclosure to stockholders in connection with the transaction.

Ch. 253, L. '10 Synopsis of Section 242

Sections 33, 34, and 35 amend §242 of the DGCL to ensure that §242 is consistent with the terms used in the translator provision in new §114(a), and to clarify that §242(b)(4) applies to nonstock corporations.

Ch. 123, L. '99 Synopsis of Section 242

The amendments to Section 242(b)(3) are intended to delete as redundant the requirement for a second meeting of the governing body of a nonstock corporation in connection with the amendment of its certificate of incorporation and to clarify the procedures for adopting such an amendment where a vote of the members of such corporation is required by the certificate of incorporation.

Ch. 349, L. '96 Synopsis of Section 242

These amendments (§§242(a) and 242(a)(3)) make clear that an amendment to the certificate of incorporation is necessary in connection with a forward or reverse stock split. A stock dividend, sometimes referred to as a "stock split in the nature of a dividend," is unaffected by these amendments.

This amendment (§242(c)) is intended to conform with the 1996 amendment to Section 103(d) which enables corporations to terminate or amend all filings which have future effective dates or times by the filing of a Certificate of Termination or Amendment of the original instrument before its future effective date or time.

Commentary on Section 242

The amendment to Section 242 would add a new subsection (c) permitting the board of directors of a stock corporation or governing body of a nonstock corporation to abandon a proposed amendment to the certificate of incorporation, notwithstanding prior stockholder or member approval, provided that such authority was contained in the resolution adopted by the stockholders or members. Similar provisions are found in Sections 251, 271 and 275 of the General Corporation Law.

.1 Right to amend.—Right of controlling stockholders to amend in matters covered by this section must be exercised with fair and impartial regard for rights and interests of all stockholders of every class; any other action would be fiduciary relation of majority stockholders toward minority and would constitute fraud. *Hartford Acc & Ind Co v Dickey Clay Mfg Co, 21 A2d 178 (Ch Ct 1941),* aff'd, *24 A2d 315 (1942).*

.2 Amendment affecting preferred stock.—When charter requires vote of holders of 75% of preferred shares to change voting rights of that stock, charter cannot be amended by mere majority vote to reduce percentage requirement from 75% to 60%. *Sellers v Joseph Bancroft & Sons Co, 2 A2d 108 (1938).* To the same effect, see also, *Sellers v Joseph Bancroft & Sons Co, 17 A2d 831 (Ch Ct 1941).*

Stockholder who acquiesces in change of capital stock structure, which results in change of his preferred shares into shares of different character and in extinguishment of dividends accumulated on his old shares cannot compel corporation to pay him dividends on his old shares. *Trounstine v Remington Rand, Inc, 194 A 95 (Ch Ct 1937).*

Charter amendment which creates class of prior preference stock ahead of existing preference stock, but does not affect priority of preference stock over common stock, is valid, even though it may reduce probability of actual payment to preferred stockholders of their accrued but unpaid dividends. *Shanik v White Sewing Mach Corp, 15 A2d 169 (Ch Ct 1940),* aff'd, *19 A2d 831 (1941).*

When charter provided for preferred stock, for Class A stock, and for common stock, and gave voting rights to preferred stock and common stock, in voting on charter amendment affecting Class A stock, votes of preferred and common shares were properly voted as one class, and counting of majority of these two classes together was proper, even though majority of common stock alone did not approve amendment. *Hartford Accident & Indem Co v WS Dickey Mfg Co, 21 A2d 178 (Ch Ct),* aff'd, *24 A2d 315 (1942).*

Corporation can, with requisite consent of stockholders, alter rights of preferred stockholders by creating new prior preference shares with rights to ordinary or liquidating dividends ahead of right of standing preferred stock to receive past due cumulative dividends. *Harr v Pioneer Mechanical Corp, 65 F2d 332 (2d Cir),* cert denied, *290 US 673 (1933).*

.3 Amendment causing no injury to minority stockholder.—Court will not enjoin corporation from putting charter amendment into effect when minority shareholder showed no immediate and irreparable injury though deciding votes were cast by (1) corporate proxy executed by vice president without accompanying certified copy of directors' resolution showing his authority to sign proxy, and (2) later dated proxies, even if they conflict with earlier ones and there was no proof of later postmark dates; these proxies are prima facie authentic. *Levin v Metro-Goldwyn-Mayer, Inc, 221 A2d 499 (Ch Ct 1966).*

Having satisfied the requirements of GCL §§242(b)(1) and 222(a) in its notice, and, since it was not soliciting proxies in connection with the meeting, a board was not required (as the plaintiffs had alleged) to include additional statements explaining the differences between proposed amendments to the charter and bylaws to be voted on at the meeting and earlier proposed amendments that had been withdrawn without being put to a vote. *Stroud v Grace, 606 A2d 75 (1992).*

.4 Amendment withdrawing right to retire stock.—Charter may be amended to withdraw right to retire stock and to readjust participation in future dividends. *Davis v Louisville Gas & Electric Co, 142 A 654 (Ch Ct 1928).*

.5 Cumulative voting.—Right of common stockholder to cumulative voting is one which may be altered by amendment. *Maddock v Vorclone Corp, 147 A 255 (Ch Ct 1931).*

.6 Construction of amendment.—Charter amendment changing capital stock structure is to be construed by rules applicable to construction of statute rather than contracts, and so stock preference so obscurely expressed as to be irreconcilably repugnant cannot be given recognition. *Holland v National Automotive Fibres, Inc, 2 A2d 124 (Ch Ct 1938),* reaff'd, *194 A 124 (Ch Ct 1937).*

Despite not being shareholders of record, plaintiffs have the right by virtue of their claimed equitable interest in the disputed shares to challenge the amendment to Instant Vision Inc.'s corporate charter increasing its authorized stock from 3,000 to 10,000,000 shares. *Cairns v Gelmon, C.A. 16462 (Ch Ct 5-21-98).*

.7 Ineffectual amendment.—Corporation cannot, by amendment of its charter, validate original issue of non-par stock which was void because of omission in charter. *Rice & Hutchins, Inc v Triplex Shoe Co, 16 Del Ch 298 (Ch Ct 1929),* aff'd, *152 A 342 (1930).*

Court refused to enjoin target from holding its annual meeting or voting proxies. Target did not violate provisions of GCL §242 by its erroneous proxy statement about voting procedure because its correction of letter demonstrated that vote would be consistent with Delaware law. *MacFadden Holdings, Inc v John Blair & Co, 1986 U.S. Dist. LEXIS 30956 (D Del 5-5-86).*

Where directors unilaterally approved a substantial amendment to the poison pill provision of the stockholder rights plan so that: (1) the "flip-in" trigger was reduced from 20 to 10 percent and an exception for current holders of 10 percent or more was created; (2) the amendment effectively destroyed the plan's "flip-over" protection that was triggered in the event of a merger or if more than 50 percent of the assets of the corporation was sold; and (3) included an exchange feature that conferred a right on the board to exchange one share for each right in the event that the plan was triggered, the change was "such a radical and material alternation of the plan as to constitute a new plan" and the amendment was held invalid for lack of shareholder approval. *In re National Intergroup Inc, Nos. 11484 & 11511 (Ch Ct 7-3-90).*

.8 Challenge by derivative action.—Court granted corporation's and directors' motion to dismiss shareholders' derivative claims challenging validity of proposed amendments to Articles of Incorporation and bylaws when shareholders: (1) failed to make a pre-suit demand for relief on board; and (2) did not show that a pre-suit demand would have been futile.

Shareholders' individual claims that the proposed amendments were part of an entrenchment scheme were also dismissed. Entrenchment claim did not involve the individual contractual rights of shareholders, but affected corporation as a whole, and should have been brought as derivative action.

Shareholders' individual claims that the proposed amendments impermissibly required a supermajority vote were dismissed as well. The court, however, denied the defendants' motion to dismiss plaintiffs' individual claims that the proposed notice of a reconvened shareholders' meeting had improper statements, finding that there were material defects in notice. *Stroud v Milliken Enterprises, Inc, 585 A2d 1306 (Ch Ct 1988).*

.9 Justiciability.—Court refused to hear appeal in dispute as to whether proposed notice of shareholders' meeting called to consider charter and bylaw amendments met requirements of candor imposed by GCL §222 and GCL §242. Parties were seeking final judicial determination of management's statutory notice technique before putting process into effect. This would inappropriately draw courts into granting advisory opinion regarding significant question of corporation law that was not ripe for judicial intervention. *Stroud v Milliken Enterprises, Inc, 552 A2d 476 (1989).*

.10 Right to class vote.—The Court of Chancery determined that under §242 common stockholders did not have the right to a class vote on an amendment to the certificate of incorporation that would allow the corporation to issue a new series of preferred stock as part of the corporation's recapitalization plan. *Orban v Field, No. 12820 (Ch Ct 12-30-93).*

.11 Stock cancellation.—Where an attempt is made to cancel the common stock of a corporation without an amendment to the certificate of incorporation, such cancellation is invalid. Also, where an attempt is made to reissue the stock without consideration or benefit to the corporation, such issuance is also invalid. *MBKS Company Ltd. v MBKS Inc, 2007 Del. Ch. LEXIS 52 (Ch Ct 2007).*

An attempt to cancel shares is legally ineffective where a corporation's charter is not amended to authorize such an alteration to its capital structure. *Reddy v MKBS Co, 945 A2d 1080 (2008).*

.12 Appraisal; valuation of preferred stock.—Preferred stock is validly issued where a corporation's board properly adopts resolutions authorizing the issuance of the preferred stock and files certificates of designation with the state's secretary of state, and a court in an appraisal proceeding has discretion to value the stock on an as-if-converted basis. *Hildreth v Castle Dental Centers, Inc, 939 A2d 1281 (2007).*

.13 Stock splits.—A purported stock split is invalid where the formalities required to effect the split have not been strictly adhered to. *Blades v Wisehart, 2010 Del. Ch. LEXIS 227 (Ch Ct 2010).*

243 RETIREMENT OF STOCK.—(a) A corporation, by resolution of its board of directors, may retire any shares of its capital stock that are issued but are not outstanding.[1]

(b) *Whenever any shares of the capital stock of a corporation are retired, they shall resume the status of authorized and unissued shares of the class or series to which they belong unless the certificate of incorporation otherwise provides. If the certificate of incorporation prohibits the reissuance of such shares, or prohibits the reissuance of such shares as a part of a specific series only, a certificate stating that reissuance of the shares (as part of the class or series) is prohibited identifying the shares and reciting their retirement shall be executed, acknowledged and filed and shall become effective in accordance with §103 of this title. When such certificate becomes effective, it shall have the effect of amending the certificate of incorporation so as to reduce accordingly the number of authorized shares of the class or series to which such shares belong or, if such retired shares constitute all of the authorized shares of the class or series to which they belong, of eliminating from the certificate of incorporation all reference to such class or series of stock.*

(c) If the capital of the corporation shall be reduced by or in connection with the retirement of shares, the reduction of capital shall be effected pursuant to §244 of this title. (Last amended by Ch. 136, L. '87, eff. 7-1-87.)

Ch. 136, L. '87, eff. 7-1-87, added matter in italic and deleted [1]"If a corporation acquires any of its shares, whether by purchase or redemption or by their having become converted into or exchanged for other shares of the corporation, and capital, as computed in accordance with §§154, 242 and 244 of this title, is applied in connection with such acquisition, the shares so acquired, upon their acquisition and without other action by the corporation, shall have the status of retired shares. (b) Whenever any shares of the capital stock of a corporation are retired, they shall resume the status of authorized and unissued shares of the class to which they belong unless the certificate of incorporation prohibits their reissuance. If the certificate of incorporation prohibits the reissuance of such shares, a certificate, so stating, identifying the shares and reciting their retirement shall be executed, acknowledged and filed and shall become effective in accordance with §103 of this title. When such certificate becomes effective, it shall have the effect of amending the certificate of incorporation so as to reduce accordingly the number of authorized shares of the class to which such shares belong or, if such retired shares constitute all of the authorized shares of the class or series to which they belong, of eliminating from the certificate of incorporation all reference to such class or series of stock."

244 REDUCTION OF CAPITAL.—(a) A corporation, by resolution of its board of directors, may reduce its capital in any of the following ways:

(1) By reducing or eliminating the capital represented by shares of capital stock which have been retired;

(2) By applying to an otherwise authorized purchase or redemption of outstanding shares of its capital stock some or all of the capital represented by the shares being purchased or redeemed, or any capital that has not been allocated to any particular class of its capital stock;

(3) By applying to an otherwise authorized conversion or exchange of outstanding shares of its capital stock some or all of the capital represented by the shares being converted or exchanged, or some or all of any capital that has not been allocated to any particular class of its capital stock, or both, to the extent that such capital in the aggregate exceeds the total aggregate par value or the stated capital of any previously unissued shares issuable upon such conversion or exchange; or

(4) By transferring to surplus (i) some or all of the capital not represented by any particular class of its capital stock; (ii) some or all of the capital represented by issued shares of its par value capital stock, which capital is in excess of the aggregate par value of such shares; or (iii) some of the capital represented by issued shares of its capital stock without par value.

(b) Notwithstanding the other provisions of this section, no reduction of capital shall be made or effected unless the assets of the corporation remaining after such reduction shall be sufficient to pay any debts of the corporation for which payment has not been otherwise provided. [1]No reduction of capital shall release any liability of any stockholder whose shares have not been fully paid. [2](Last amended by Ch. 112, L. '83, eff. 7-1-83.)

Ch. 112, L. '83, eff. 7-1-83, deleted [1]"and the certificate required by subsection (c) of this section shall so state" and [2]"(c) Whenever capital of a corporation is to be reduced, such reduction shall not become effective until a certificate has been executed, acknowledged and filed and has become effective in accordance with section 103 of this title. Such certificate shall set forth the manner in and the extent to which the capital is to be reduced, including an identification of any shares of capital stock retired in connection with such reduction."

245 RESTATED CERTIFICATE OF INCORPORATION.—(a) A corporation may, whenever desired, integrate into a single instrument all of the provisions of its certificate of incorporation which are then in effect and operative as a result of there having theretofore been filed with the Secretary of State 1 or more certificates or other instruments pursuant to any of the sections referred to in §104 of this title, and it may at the same time also further amend its certificate of incorporation by adopting a restated certificate of incorporation.

(b) If the restated certificate of incorporation merely restates and integrates but does not further amend the certificate of incorporation, as theretofore amended or supplemented by any instrument that was filed pursuant to any of the sections mentioned in §104 of this title, it may be adopted by the board of directors without a vote of the stockholders, or it may be proposed by the directors and submitted by them to the stockholders for adoption, in which case the procedure and vote required, *if any,* by §242 of this title for amendment of the certificate of incorporation shall be applicable. If the restated certificate of incorporation restates and integrates and also further amends in any respect the certificate of incorporation, as theretofore amended or supplemented, it shall be proposed by the directors and adopted by the stockholders in the manner and by the vote prescribed by §242 of this title or, if the corporation has not received any payment for any of its stock, in the manner and by the vote prescribed by §241 of this title.

(c) A restated certificate of incorporation shall be specifically designated as such in its heading. It shall state, either in its heading or in an introductory paragraph, the corporation's present name, and, if it has been changed, the name under which it was originally incorporated, and the date of filing of its original certificate of incorporation with the Secretary of State. A restated certificate shall also state that it was duly adopted in accordance with this section. If it was adopted by the board of directors without a vote of the stockholders (unless it was adopted pursuant to §241 *of this title or without a vote of members pursuant to §242(b)(3)* of this title), it shall state that it only restates and integrates and does not further amend the provisions of the corporation's certificate of incorporation as theretofore amended or supplemented, and that there is no discrepancy between those provisions and the provisions of the restated certificate. A restated certificate of incorporation may omit (a) such provisions of the original certificate of incorporation which named the incorporator or incorporators, the initial board of directors and the original subscribers for shares, and (b) such provisions contained in any amendment to the certificate of incorporation as were necessary to effect a change, exchange, reclassification, subdivision, combination or cancellation of stock, if such change, exchange, reclassification, subdivision, combination or cancellation has become effective. Any such omissions shall not be deemed a further amendment.

(d) A restated certificate of incorporation shall be executed, acknowledged and filed in accordance with §103 of this title. Upon its filing with the Secretary of State, the original certificate of incorporation, as theretofore amended or supplemented, shall be superseded; thenceforth, the restated certificate of incorporation, including any further amendments or changes made thereby, shall be the certificate of incorporation of the corporation, but the original date of incorporation shall remain unchanged.

(e) Any amendment or change effected in connection with the restatement and integration of the certificate of incorporation shall be subject to any other provision of this chapter, not inconsistent with this section, which would apply if a separate certificate of amendment were filed to effect such amendment or change. (Last amended by Ch. 253, L. '10, eff. 8-1-10.)

<small>Ch. 253, L. '10, eff. 8-1-10, added matter in italic.</small>

Ch. 253, L. '10 Synopsis of Section 245

Sections 36 and 37 amend §245 of the DGCL to clarify that §245 applies to a nonstock corporation even if no vote of the members of the corporation is required to amend the corporation's certificate of incorporation.

Ch. 82, L. '01 Synopsis of Section 245

The amendment to Section 245(c) brings that section into conformity with Section 242(a) as amended in 1996. See 72 Del. Laws, C.123, §5.

246 COMPOSITE CERTIFICATE OF INCORPORATION.—(Repealed by Ch. 352, L. '88, eff. 7-12-88.)

<small>Prior to its repeal by Ch. 352, L. '88, eff. 7-12-88, this section read as follows: "The Secretary of State shall prepare and furnish upon request a certified composite certificate of incorporation which shall contain only such provisions of a corporation's certificate of incorporation which are then in effect and operative as a result of there having theretofore been filed with the Secretary of State 1 or more certificates or other instruments pursuant to any of the sections referred to in §104 of this title. The Secretary of State shall make in each case such reasonable charge therefore as he deems proper. A composite certificate of incorporation shall not be filed by the Secretary of State as a corporate instrument, nor shall it be recorded in the office of any recorder in this State, unless it is accompanied by a certificate of the corporation, executed and acknowledged in accordance with §103 of this title, stating that the filing and recording of the composite certificate have been duly authorized by the corporation's board of directors. The filing by a corporation of a composite certificate of incorporation shall not have the effect of superseding its original certificate of incorporation, as theretofore amended or supplemented."</small>

SUBCHAPTER IX. MERGER, CONSOLIDATION OR CONVERSION

251 MERGER OR CONSOLIDATION OF DOMESTIC CORPORATIONS.—(a) Any 2 or more corporations existing under the laws of this State may merge into a single corporation, which may be any 1 of the constituent corporations or may consolidate into a new corporation formed by the consolidation, pursuant to an agreement of merger or consolidation, as the case may be, complying and approved in accordance with this section.

(b) The board of directors of each corporation which desires to merge or consolidate shall adopt a resolution approving an agreement of merger or consolidation and declaring its advisability. The agreement shall state: (1) The terms and conditions of the merger or consolidation; (2) the mode of carrying the same into effect; (3) in the case of a merger, such amendments or changes in the certificate of incorporation of the surviving corporation as are desired to be effected by the merger *(which amendments or changes may amend and restate the certificate of incorporation of the surviving corporation in its entirety)*, or, if no such amendments or changes are desired, a statement that the certificate of incorporation of the surviving corporation shall be its certificate of incorporation; (4) in the case of a consolidation, that the certificate of incorporation of the resulting corporation shall be as is set forth in an attachment to the agreement; (5) the manner, if any, of converting the shares of each of the constituent corporations into shares or other securities of the corporation surviving or resulting from the merger or consolidation, or of cancelling some or all of such shares, and, if any shares of any of the constituent corporations are not to remain outstanding, to be converted solely into shares or other securities of the surviving or resulting corporation or to be cancelled, the cash, property, rights or securities of any other corporation or entity which the holders of such shares are to receive in exchange for, or upon conversion of such shares and the surrender of any certificates evidencing them, which cash, property, rights or securities of any other corporation or entity may be in addition to or in lieu of shares or other securities of the surviving or resulting corporation; and (6) such other details or provisions as are deemed desirable, including, without limiting the generality of the foregoing, a provision for the payment of cash in lieu of the issuance or recognition of fractional shares, interests or rights, or for any other arrangement with respect thereto, consistent with §155 of this title. The agreement so adopted shall be executed and acknowledged in accordance with §103 of this title. Any of the terms of the agreement of merger or consolidation may be made dependent upon facts ascertainable outside of such agreement, provided that the manner in which such facts shall operate upon the terms of the agreement is clearly and expressly set forth in the agreement of merger or consolidation. The term "facts," as used in the preceding sentence, includes, but is not limited to, the occurrence of any event, including a determination or action by any person or body, including the corporation.

(c) The agreement required by subsection (b) of this section shall be submitted to the stockholders of each constituent corporation at an annual or special meeting for the purpose of acting on the agreement. Due notice of the time, place and purpose of the meeting shall be mailed to each holder of stock, whether voting or nonvoting, of the corporation at the stockholder's address as it appears on the records of the corporation, at least 20 days prior to the date of the meeting. The notice shall contain a copy of the agreement or a brief summary thereof [1]. At the meeting, the agreement shall be considered and a vote taken for its adoption or rejection. If a majority of the outstanding stock of the corporation entitled to vote thereon shall be voted for the adoption of the agreement, that fact shall be certified on the agreement by the secretary or assistant secretary of the corporation, provided that such certification on the agreement shall not be required if a certificate of merger or consolidation is filed in lieu of filing the agreement. If the agreement shall be so adopted and certified by each constituent corporation, it shall then be filed and shall become effective, in accordance with §103 of this title. In lieu of filing the agreement of merger or consolidation required by this section, the surviving or resulting corporation may file a certificate of merger or consolidation, executed in accordance with §103 of this title, which states:

(1) The name and state of incorporation of each of the constituent corporations;

(2) That an agreement of merger or consolidation has been approved, adopted, executed and acknowledged by each of the constituent corporations in accordance with this section;

(3) The name of the surviving or resulting corporation;

(4) In the case of a merger, such amendments or changes in the certificate of incorporation of the surviving corporation as are desired to be effected by the merger *(which amendments or changes may amend and restate the certificate of incorporation of the surviving corporation in its entirety)*, or, if no such amendments or changes are desired, a statement that the certificate of incorporation of the surviving corporation shall be its certificate of incorporation;

(5) In the case of a consolidation, that the certificate of incorporation of the resulting corporation shall be as set forth in an attachment to the certificate;

(6) That the executed agreement of consolidation or merger is on file at an office of the surviving corporation, stating the address thereof; and

(7) That a copy of the agreement of consolidation or merger will be furnished by the surviving corporation, on request and without cost, to any stockholder of any constituent corporation.

(d) Any agreement of merger or consolidation may contain a provision that at any time prior to the time that the agreement (or a certificate in lieu thereof) filed with the Secretary of State becomes effective in accordance with §103 of this title, the agreement may be terminated by the board of directors of any constituent corporation notwithstanding approval of the agreement by the stockholders of all or any of the constituent corporations; in the event the agreement of merger or consolidation is terminated after the filing of the agreement (or a certificate in lieu thereof) with the Secretary of State but before the agreement (or a certificate in lieu thereof) has become effective, a certificate of termination or merger or consolidation shall be filed in accordance with §103 of this title. Any agreement of merger or consolidation may contain a provision that the boards of directors of the constituent corporations may amend the agreement at any time prior to the time that the agreement (or a certificate in lieu thereof) filed with the Secretary of State becomes effective in accordance with §103 of this title, provided that an amendment made subsequent to the adoption of the agreement by the stockholders of any constituent corporation shall not (1) alter or change the amount or kind of shares, securities, cash, property and/or rights to be received in exchange for or on conversion of all or any of the shares of any class or series thereof of such constituent corporation, (2) alter or change any term of the certificate of incorporation of the surviving corporation to be effected by the merger or consolidation, or (3) alter or change any of the terms and conditions of the agreement if such alteration or change would adversely affect the holders of any class or series thereof of such constituent corporation; in the event the agreement of merger or consolidation is amended after the filing thereof with the Secretary of State but before the agreement has become effective, a certificate of amendment of merger or consolidation shall be filed in accordance with §103 of this title.

(e) In the case of a merger, the certificate of incorporation of the surviving corporation shall automatically be amended to the extent, if any, that changes in the certificate of incorporation are set forth in the agreement of merger.

(f) Notwithstanding the requirements of subsection (c) of this section, unless required by its certificate of incorporation, no vote of stockholders of a constituent corporation surviving a merger shall be necessary to authorize a merger if (1) the agreement of merger does not amend in any respect the certificate of incorporation of such constituent corporation, (2) each share of stock of such constituent corporation outstanding immediately prior to the effective date of the merger is to be an identical outstanding or treasury share of the surviving corporation after the effective date of the merger, and (3) either no shares of common stock of the surviving corporation and no shares, securities or obligations convertible into such stock are to be issued or delivered under the plan of merger, or the authorized unissued shares or the treasury shares of common stock of the surviving corporation to be issued or delivered under the plan of merger plus those initially issuable upon conversion of any other shares, securities or obligations to be issued or delivered under such plan do not exceed 20% of the shares of common stock of such constituent corporation outstanding immediately prior to the effective date of the merger. No vote of stockholders of a constituent corporation shall be necessary to authorize a merger or consolidation if no shares of the stock of such corporation shall have been issued prior to the adoption by the board of directors of the resolution approving the agreement of merger or consolidation. If an agreement of merger is adopted by the constituent corporation surviving the merger, by action of its board of directors and without any vote of its stockholders pursuant to this subsection, the secretary or assistant secretary of that corporation shall certify on the agreement that the agreement has been adopted pursuant to this subsection and, (1) if it has been adopted pursuant to the first sentence of this subsection, that the conditions specified in that sentence have been satisfied, or (2) if it has been adopted pursuant to the second sentence of this subsection, that no shares of stock of such corporation were issued prior to the adoption by the board of directors of the resolution approving the agreement of merger or consolidation, provided that such certification on the agreement shall not be required if a certificate of merger or consolidation is filed in lieu of filing the agreement. The agreement so adopted and certified shall then be filed and shall become effective, in accordance with §103 of this title. Such filing shall constitute a representation by the person who executes the agreement that the facts stated in the certificate remain true immediately prior to such filing.

(g) Notwithstanding the requirements of subsection (c) of this section, unless expressly required by its certificate of incorporation, no vote of stockholders of a constituent corporation shall be necessary to authorize a merger with or into a single direct or indirect wholly-owned subsidiary of such constituent corporation if: (1) such constituent corporation and the direct or indirect wholly-owned subsidiary of such constituent corporation are the only constituent entities to the merger; (2) each share or fraction of a share of the capital stock of the constituent corporation outstanding immediately prior to the effective time of the merger is converted in the merger into a share or equal fraction of share of capital stock of a holding company having the same designations, rights, powers and preferences, and the qualifications, limitations and restrictions thereof, as the share of stock of the constituent corporation being converted in the merger; (3) the holding company and the constituent corporation are corporations of this State and the direct or indirect wholly-owned subsidiary that is the other constituent entity to the merger is a corporation or limited liability company of this State; (4) the certificate of incorporation and by-laws of the holding company immediately following the effective time of the merger contain provisions identical to the certificate of incorporation and by-laws of the constituent corporation immediately prior to the effective time of the merger (other than provisions, if any, regarding the incorporator or incorporators, the corporate name, the registered office and agent, the initial board of directors and the initial subscribers for shares and such provisions contained in any amendment to the certificate of incorporation as were necessary to effect a change, exchange, reclassification, subdivision, combination or cancellation of stock, if such change, exchange, reclassification, subdivision, combination or cancellation has become effective); (5) as

§251

a result of the merger the constituent corporation or its successor becomes or remains a direct or indirect wholly-owned subsidiary of the holding company; (6) the directors of the constituent corporation become or remain the directors of the holding company upon the effective time of the merger; (7) the organizational documents of the surviving entity immediately following the effective time of the merger contain provisions identical to the certificate of incorporation of the constituent corporation immediately prior to the effective time of the merger (other than provisions, if any, regarding the incorporator or incorporators, the corporate or entity name, the registered office and agent, the initial board of directors and the initial subscribers for shares, references to members rather than stockholders or shareholders, references to interests, units or the like rather than stock or shares, references to managers, managing members or other members of the governing body rather than directors and such provisions contained in any amendment to the certificate of incorporation as were necessary to effect a change, exchange, reclassification, subdivision, combination or cancellation of stock, if such change, exchange, reclassification, subdivision, combination or cancellation has become effective); provided, however, that (i) if the organizational documents of the surviving entity do not contain the following provisions, they shall be amended in the merger to contain provisions requiring that (A) any act or transaction by or involving the surviving entity, other than the election or removal of directors or managers, managing members or other members of the governing body of the surviving entity, that requires for its adoption under this chapter or its organizational documents the approval of the stockholders or members of the surviving entity shall, by specific reference to this subsection, require, in addition, the approval of the stockholders of the holding company (or any successor by merger), by the same vote as is required by this chapter and/or by the organizational documents of the surviving entity; provided, however, that for purposes of this clause (i)(A), any surviving entity that is not a corporation shall include in such amendment a requirement that the approval of the stockholders of the holding company be obtained for any act or transaction by or involving the surviving entity, other than the election or removal of directors or managers, managing members or other members of the governing body of the surviving entity, which would require the approval of the stockholders of the surviving entity if the surviving entity were a corporation subject to this chapter; (B) any amendment of the organizational documents of a surviving entity that is not a corporation, which amendment would, if adopted by a corporation subject to this chapter, be required to be included in the certificate of incorporation of such corporation, shall, by specific reference to this subsection, require, in addition, the approval of the stockholders of the holding company (or any successor by merger), by the same vote as is required by this chapter and/or by the organizational documents of the surviving entity; and (C) the business and affairs of a surviving entity that is not a corporation shall be managed by or under the direction of a board of directors, board of managers or other governing body consisting of individuals who are subject to the same fiduciary duties applicable to, and who are liable for breach of such duties to the same extent as, directors of a corporation subject to this chapter; and (ii) the organizational documents of the surviving entity may be amended in the merger (A) to reduce the number of classes and shares of capital stock or other equity interests or units that the surviving entity is authorized to issue and (B) to eliminate any provision authorized by subsection (d) of §141 of this title; and (8) the stockholders of the constituent corporation do not recognize gain or loss for United States federal income tax purposes as determined by the board of directors of the constituent corporation. Neither subsection (g)(7)(i) of this section nor any provision of a surviving entity's organizational documents required by subsection (g)(7)(i) shall be deemed or con-strued to require approval of the stockholders of the holding company to elect or remove directors or managers, managing members or other members of the governing body of the surviving entity. The term "organizational documents", as used in subsection (g)(7) and in the preceding sentence, shall, when used in reference to a corporation, mean the certificate of incorporation of such corporation, and when used in reference to a limited liability company, mean the limited liability company agreement of such limited liability company.

As used in this subsection only, the term "holding company" means a corporation which, from its incorporation until consummation of a merger governed by this subsection, was at all times a direct or indirect wholly-owned subsidiary of the constituent corporation and whose capital stock is issued in such merger. From and after the effective time of a merger adopted by a constituent corporation by action of its board of directors and without any vote of stockholders pursuant to this subsection: (i) to the extent the restrictions of §203 of this title applied to the constituent corporation and its stockholders at the effective time of the merger, such restrictions shall apply to the holding company and its stockholders immediately after the effective time of the merger as though it were the constituent corporation, and all shares of stock of the holding company acquired in the merger shall for purposes of §203 of this title be deemed to have been acquired at the time that the shares of stock of the constituent corporation converted in the merger were acquired, and provided further that any stockholder who immediately prior to the effective time of the merger was not an interested stockholder within the meaning of §203 of this title shall not solely by reason of the merger become an interested stockholder of the holding company, (ii) if the corporate name of the holding company immediately following the effective time of the merger is the same as the corporate name of the constituent corporation immediately prior to the effective time of the merger, the shares of capital stock of the holding company into which the shares of capital stock of the constituent corporation are converted in the merger shall be represented by the stock certificates that previously represented shares of capital stock of the constituent corporation capital stock of the constituent corporation and (iii) to the extent a stockholder of the constituent corporation immediately prior to the merger had standing to institute or maintain derivative litigation on behalf of the constituent corporation, nothing in this section shall be deemed to limit or extinguish such standing. If an agreement of merger is adopted by a constituent corporation by action of its board of directors and without any vote of stockholders pursuant to this subsection, the secretary or assistant secretary of the constituent corporation shall certify on the agreement that the agreement has been adopted pursuant to this subsection and that the conditions specified in the first sentence of this subsection have been satisfied, provided that such certification on the agreement shall not be required if a certificate of merger or consolidation is filed in lieu of filing the agreement. The agreement so adopted and certified shall then be filed and become effective, in accordance with §103 of this title. Such filing shall constitute a representation by the person who executes the agreement that the facts stated in the certificate remain true immediately prior to such filing. (Last amended by Ch. 290, L. '10, eff. 8-2-10.)

Ch. 290, L. '10, eff. 8-2-10, added matter in italic and deleted [1]", as the directors shall deem advisable."

Ch. 290, L. '10 Synopsis of Section 251

These sections amend Sections 251(b)(3), 251(c)(4), 252(c)(4), 254(d)(4), 263(c)(4), and 264(c)(4), respectively, to clarify that in a merger the certificate of incorporation of the surviving corporation may be amended and restated in its entirety.

This amendment to Section 251(c) clarifies that the decision to include either a copy or a summary of an agreement of merger or consolidation in a notice of a stockholder meeting need not be approved by a specific act of the board of directors. The amendment is not intended to define or limit any duty of directors relating to disclosure to stockholders in connection with the transaction.

Ch. 145, L. '07 Synopsis of Section 251

The amendments to §251 and §255 eliminate the requirement that an agreement of merger or consolidation include a certification by the secretary or assistant secretary of the corporation that the agreement has been adopted by the requisite vote of the stockholders or members, as applicable, or otherwise approved in accordance with §251 without a vote of the stockholders, if a certificate of merger or consolidation is filed in lieu of filing the agreement. The certification requirement for a Delaware corporation is also eliminated from §§252, 254, 256, 257, 258, 263 and 264 by virtue of the cross-references to §251 and §255. Any certification required under other applicable law is not affected by the amendments to §251 and §255.

Ch. 30, L. '05 Synopsis of Section 251(g)(7)(ii)

The amendment to Section 251(g)(7)(ii) now permits the organizational documents of the surviving entity to be amended to eliminate a classified board provision or any other provision authorized by subsection (d) of Section 141 of Title 8.

Ch. 84, L. '03 Synopsis of Section 251

The deletion of the language from subsection (c) of Section 251 and the addition of new Section 146 clarify that the rule previously codified at Section 251(c) applies to any matter submitted to stockholders. Under this rule, directors may authorize the corporation to agree with another person to submit a matter to stockholders, but reserve the ability to change their recommendation.

The amendments to Sections 251, 252, 253, 254, 255, 256, 257, 263 and 264 clarify that shares or other interests of a constituent corporation or other entity to a merger or consolidation may be converted, cancelled or unaffected by the merger.

Ch. 82, L. '01 Synopsis of Section 251

These amendments to Section 251(g) expand the types of entities that may be used in a holding company reorganization to include limited liability companies of this State. In order to protect the rights of the former corporation's stockholders, the limited liability company will be required to adopt provisions in its organizational documents which impose on the limited liability company and its managers certain duties and requirements applicable to corporations and directors of corporations of this State.

The amendment to Section 251(g)(4) brings that subsection into conformity with Section 242(a) as amended in 1996. See 72 Del. Laws, C.123, §5.

The amendment to the second paragraph of Section 251(g) is intended to ensure that a holding company reorganization involving a limited liability company of this State does not affect, limit or extinguish the prior standing of a stockholder to institute or maintain derivative litigation on behalf of the constituent corporation, consistent with decisions of the courts of this State preserving such rights in holding company reorganizations involving corporations of this State.

Ch. 123, L. '99 Synopsis of Section 251

The amendment to Section 251(g) clarifies that a vote of the holding company's stockholders is not required to elect or remove directors of a subsidiary (surviving) corporation and that the certificate of incorporation of a subsidiary (surviving) corporation need not be amended to so provide.

Ch. 339, L. '98 Synopsis of Section 251

The amendment to subsection (b) of Section 251 requiring a determination by the board of directors that a merger agreement is advisable conforms the board approval requirement in that subsection to the requirement in subsection (b)(1) of Section 242 that the board of directors declare a charter amendment advisable prior to submitting it to stockholders. The amendment to subsection (c) provides that a merger agreement may require that it be submitted to the stockholders even if the board, subsequent to its initial approval thereof, determines that the agreement is no longer advisable and recommends that the stockholders reject it. *Compare Smith v. Van Gorkom,* 488 A.2d 858, 887-88 (Del. Supr. 1985). The amendments are not intended to address the question whether such a submission requirement is appropriate in any particular set of factual circumstances.

Ch. 349, L. '96 Synopsis of Section 251

The amendments to Sections 251(b), 252(b), 254(c), 255(b), 256(b), 257(b), 263(b), and 264(b) are intended to conform these sections with the 1994 amendment to Section 151(a). The amendments make clear that a "fact" can include an event or a determination or action by any person or body, including an event or determination within the control of the corporation or a person or body affiliated with the corporation, such as a decision by its board of directors or one of its officers or agents. These amendments are not intended to alter the fiduciary duties of a board of directors in authorizing a merger agreement with terms that turn on determinations or actions made by any person or body, or in making any determination or taking any action constituting a fact under these sections.

The amendments to Sections 251(c)(6), 252(c)(6), 254(d)(6), 263(c)(6) and 264(c)(6) eliminate the requirement that the executed agreement of consolidation or merger be on file at the principal place of business of the surviving corporation or entity in cases where a certificate of merger or consolidation is filed with the Secretary of State in lieu of the agreement of consolidation or merger. The amendment permits the executed agreement of consolidation or merger to be on file at any office of the surviving corporation or entity, whether or not its principal place of business.

Ch. 79, L. '95 Synopsis of Section 251

These sections amend Section 251(d) of the Act to permit the termination or amendment of an agreement of merger or consolidation prior to the effective time of the merger or consolidation rather than the time of filing the agreement with the Secretary of State, and to reference the requirement in Section 103(d) that a certificate of termination be filed if an agreement of merger or consolidation is terminated after the filing of the agreement (or a certificate in lieu thereof) with the Secretary of State but prior to its effective date.

New Section 251(g) permits a Delaware corporation to reorganize by merging with or into a direct or indirect wholly-owned subsidiary of a holding company (as defined) without stockholder approval, unless the corporation's certificate of incorporation, by explicit reference to a holding company reorganization of the type provided for in this subsection, requires such a vote. The provisions of the new statute are intended to insure that the rights of the stockholders of the corporation are not changed by or as a result of such a reorganization, except and to the same extent that such rights could be changed without stockholder approval under existing law. Thus, stockholders of the corporation must receive in the merger the same number of shares of the holding company as they owned in the corporation prior to the reorganization, which stock must have the same voting powers, designations, preferences and rights, and the qualifications, restrictions and limitations thereof, with respect to the holding company as such stock had with respect to the corporation prior to

the reorganization. The resulting holding company must be a Delaware corporation with the same certificate of incorporation (except for provisions that could have been amended or deleted without stockholder approval) and bylaws that the corporation had prior to the reorganization. As a result of the reorganization the corporation or its successor must become a direct or indirect wholly-owned subsidiary of the holding company. The directors of the corporation immediately prior to the reorganization must be the same as the directors of the holding company after the merger. To ensure that the rights of the stockholders of the constituent corporation to vote on certain acts and transactions under the General Corporation Law are not changed by the fact that they become stockholders of the holding company as a result of a reorganization, the certificate of incorporation of the surviving corporation must provide that any act or transaction by or involving the surviving corporation that requires for its adoption under the General Corporation Law or the certificate of incorporation of the surviving corporation the approval of the stockholders of the surviving corporation shall require, in addition, the approval of the stockholders of the holding company by such vote as is required under the General Corporation Law and/or by the surviving corporation's certificate of incorporation. Otherwise, the certificate of incorporation of the surviving corporation immediately after the merger must be the same as the certificate of incorporation of the constituent corporation immediately prior to the merger, except for provisions that could have been amended or deleted without stockholder approval, and except that the certificate of incorporation of the surviving corporation may be amended in the merger to reduce the number of classes and shares of capital stock that the surviving corporation is authorized to issue. In order that any restrictions on stockholders of the corporation imposed by Section 203, or any exemption from such restrictions, apply with equal force and effect to the stockholders of the holding company after the reorganization, the statute provides that, with respect to persons who are stockholders of the holding company immediately after the effectiveness of the reorganization, the provisions of Section 203 will apply to such persons to the same extent that they applied to stockholders of the corporation. To avoid the burden of issuing certificates for shares of the holding company to the former stockholders of the corporation, the outstanding stock certificates of the corporation would, after the reorganization, constitute stock certificates of the holding company so long as the name of the holding company after the reorganization is the same as the name of the corporation prior to the reorganization. Finally, the reorganization must be tax-free for federal income tax purposes to stockholders of the corporation. Appraisal rights are not available in the event of such a reorganization.

Commentary on Section 251 (d) and (f)

The amendment to Section 251(d) will make the first sentence of Section 251(d) consistent with the second sentence of that subsection, which permits the amendment of a merger agreement by the board of directors of any constituent corporation, notwithstanding prior stockholder approval, at any time prior to the filing of the "agreement with the Secretary of State" or a certificate in lieu thereof. The amendment to Section 251(f) will clarify what must be set forth in a certification accompanying a merger agreement authorized without stockholder vote.

Ed. Note: This section is effective only with respect to mergers and consolidations for which the notice of the stockholders meeting to vote thereon has been mailed after July 1, 1987.

.1 Application of section.—Specific section that permits merger of subsidiary into parent does not bar such merger under general section providing for merger of any two domestic corporations. *Federal United Corp v Havender, 11 A2d 331 (1940),* rev'g, *Havender v Federal United Corp, 6 A2d 618 (Ch Ct 1939).*

.2 De facto merger.—Stockholders cannot set aside purchase by their corporation of assets of another corporation in exchange for stock on ground that this is de facto merger carried through without 2/3rds approval statute calls for; it is not merger, but simply acquisition of corporate property, even though effect may be same as if merger. *Heilbrunn v Sun Chemical Corp, 146 A2d 757 (Ch Ct 1958),* aff'd, *150 A2d 755 (1959).*

There is not even colorable compliance with merger statute when one corporation (a home for the aged) transferred its property and moved its inmates to another home and then went out of existence, so second home cannot take bequest made to first on ground it was successor by merger. *Blackstone v Chandler, 130 A 34 (Ch Ct 1925).*

Purchase by corporation of all the stock of several other corporations does not create a de facto merger so as to give dissenting stockholder of purchasing corporation appraisal rights. *Orzeck v Englehart, 192 A2d 36 (Ch Ct),* aff'd, *195 A2d 375 (1963).*

§251

.3 Effect of merger.—Creditor of constituent corporation cannot bar its consolidation with another corporation, since he may pursue his remedy against consolidated corporation. *Cole v National Cash Credit Ass'n, 156 A 183 (Ch Ct 1931).*

Shares of stock that were sequestered in aid of derivative suit were released from that sequestration when they lost their situs in Delaware as result of corporation's merger with an out-of-state corporation. *Union Chemical & Materials Corp v Cannon, 148 A2d 348 (1959),* rev'g, *144 A2d 142 (Ch Ct 1958).*

.4 Enjoining merger.—Preferred stockholders cannot bar merger merely on claim that it advantaged common stockholders more than it did preferred, when plan is not grossly inequitable. *MacFarlane v North American Cement Corp, 157 A 396 (Ch Ct 1928).*

Nor will mere allegations of fraud suffice, when not supported by substantial evidence. *Rankin v Interstate Equities Corp, 180 A 541 (Ch Ct 1935).*

New York court will not enjoin stockholders' meeting of Delaware corporation called to consider recapitalization and merger, even though preferred stockholders and directors residents of New York, particularly since same matter is at issue in litigation in Delaware court. *Newman v United Profit-Sharing Corp, 178 NYS2d 990 (1958).*

Minority shareholders of subsidiary, 84% owned by parent, cannot bar parent's vote to merge subsidiary into another subsidiary on alleged grounds merger is unfair, since no fraud or blatant overreaching is demonstrated and minority shareholders have recourse to appraisal. *David J Greene & Co v Schenley Inc, 281 A2d 30 (Ch Ct 1971).*

Charge that exchange ratio of one share for one share between companies proposing to merge would result in slight loss of earnings per share and substantial loss in book value is not enough to enjoin merger, when controlling stockholder in both companies demonstrates fairness of merger by showing that advantages far outweigh such loss in earnings and book value. *Bastian v Bourns, Inc, 256 A2d 680 (Ch Ct),* aff'd, *278 A2d 467 (1969).*

Dissenting minority stockholders could not enjoin merger of their corporation into subsidiary of corporate majority stockholder formed solely for purpose of merger, since merger had valid business purpose and minority had adequate remedy of appraisal. *Grimes v Donaldson Lufkin & Jenrette, Inc, 392 FSupp 1393 (ND Fla 1975).*

Long-form cash-out merger between interested parties is void when only purpose is to freeze out minority interest. Use of corporate power to eliminate minority in this manner absent valid business purpose breaches fiduciary obligation of majority to minority. *Singer v Magnavox Co, 367 A2d 1349 (1977).*

Shareholder could not enjoin shareholder meeting to vote on merger because it was unlikely he could prevail on the merits, substantial premium over market price was offered to shareholders electing to participate in merger, and dissenters were entitled to full hearing and to appraisal rights. *Weinberger v United Financial Corp of California, 405 A2d 134 (Ch Ct 1979).*

Court refused to grant injunction against proposed class action settlement, which, in order to facilitate proposed merger, changed preferred shareholders' existing right to convert to common stock into right to convert to new adjusted rate preferred stock. Reasons: (1) arguments raised by preferred shareholders could be heard at future settlement hearings, (2) disputed right of preferred shareholders to vote on merger was subject to compromise, and (3) fairness of proposed settlement could only be addressed at settlement hearing. *Cohn v Crocker National Corp, No. 7693 (Ch Ct 2-7-85).*

Court refused to issue a preliminary injunction to enforce terms of shareholder's agreement restricting transfer of corporation's stock, enjoin voting of stock in successor corporation, and set aside successor corporation's incorporation because (1) conversion of shares effectuated by merger of old corporation and successor corporation did not constitute transfer or disposition of old corporation's shares that triggered right of first refusal under shareholder's agreement and (2) merger for sole purpose of nullifying effect of agreement was proper when majority shareholders would not benefit from merger in way different from other shareholders or to detriment of corporation. *Shields v Shields, No. 7829 (Ch Ct 7-22-85).*

Court refused to enjoin merger of corporation and company it controlled because merger would cause no irreparable harm to shareholders of controlled company. If shareholders show that exchange ratio was unfair, corporation could pay damages or issue additional stock plus company would continue to exist as corporation's subsidiary. Enjoining merger would harm corporations because they would lose $39 million federal tax benefit. Shareholders also did not show reasonable probability of proving that (1) proxy materials were fatally flawed, (2) procedures followed by company and its special committee considering merger were unfair, or (3) exchange ratio was unfair. *In re Chromalloy Stockholders Litigation, No. 8537 (Ch Ct 12-17-86).*

Court refused to enjoin going private merger whereby majority shareholder sought to cash out minority shareholders of airline corporation allegedly to deny them opportunity to realize profit on investment because (1) adequate remedy can be provided by upward adjustment of cash-out price, (2) majority shareholder did not usurp corporate opportunity when it acquired other airlines instead of allowing corporation to do so, and (3) apparent breach of one minority shareholder's contractual rights in warrants to purchase corporation's stock can be remedied by appropriate relief such as specific performance. *American General Corp v Texas Air Corp, Nos. 8390, 8406, 8650, 8805 (Ch Ct 2-5-87).*

Court issued preliminary injunction to prevent corporation that owned 93% of second corporation from proceeding with a cash-out merger of second corporation into a wholly owned subsidiary. Second corporation's minority shareholders challenged merger on ground that price was unfair, material facts had been misrepresented, and merger terms had not been adequately considered by a board that was dominated by parent. Plaintiffs would likely succeed in proving that parent and the directors had violated their fiduciary duty of fair dealing to second corporation's minority shareholders. When parent corporation and sub's directors stand on both sides of a merger transaction, they have burden of establishing entire fairness of merger. *Sealy Mattress Co of New Jersey, Inc v Sealy, Inc, 532 A2d 1324 (Ch Ct 1987).*

Application to enjoin the merger of two corporations was granted in an action brought by shareholders of one corporation to challenge the merger, where the merger agreement failed to provide for the approval of 80% of all stockholders as was required by one corporation's Restated Certificate of Incorporation. *Pasternak v Glazer, No. 15026 (Ch Ct 9-24-96).*

A merger will not be enjoined where the board of the acquired corporation, while negotiating only with a single bidder, bargained hard and made sure that the transaction was subject to a post-agreement market check unobstructed by onerous deal protection measures that would impede a topping bid. *In re Pennaco Energy, Inc. Shareholder Litigation, 2001 Del. Ch. LEXIS 19 (Ch Ct 2001).*

A merger will not be preliminarily enjoined merely because management projections have not been disclosed in proxy materials; there is no per se rule that such projections are material. *In re CheckFree Corp. Shareholders Litig, 2007 Del. Ch. LEXIS 148 (Ch Ct 2007).*

A merger will not be preliminarily enjoined where a board's reliance on information and its approval of deal protection measures, including a poison pill carve out, is reasonable under the circumstances, and where information and projections disclosed to shareholders by the board during the tender offer are accurate and sufficient. *In re Orchid Cellmark Inc. Shareholder Litigation, 2011 Del. Ch. LEXIS 75 (Ch Ct 2011).*

.5 Exchange of stock.—No merger occurs when one corporation acquires stock of another in exchange for its own stock, and both continue in operation. *Fidanque v American Maracaibo Co, 92 A2d 311 (Ch Ct 1952).*

.6 Exchange of stock in merger—taxability.—Transfer of stock of absorbed corporation to surviving corporation is subject to federal tax on transfer, since merger is result of voluntary acts of parties, and not merely result of "operation of law." *Koppers Coal & Transportation Co v United States, 107 F2d 706 (3d Cir 1930); Niagara Hudson Power Corp v Hoey, 117 F2d 414 (2d Cir 1941).* [Ed: Federal stamp tax no longer imposed.]

.7 Interested directors.—Charter provision does not contravene any public policy when it permits interested directors to be counted toward quorum, so merger approved at such meeting is not thereby invalidated. *Sterling v Mayflower Hotel Corp, 89 A2d 862 (Ch Ct), aff'd, 93 A2d 107 (1952).*

.8 Purchase and sale of assets.—Creditor of corporation cannot hold second corporation liable as "successor" of first when "succession" was result merely of acquiring first corporation's assets without consideration; there was no de facto merger. *Hart v Miller, 119 A2d 751 (1955).*

Creditor of transferror corporation can secure judgment against transferee of all transferror's assets in exchange for stock when that stock is not issued to transferror corporation, but instead is given directly to its stockholders; that is a de facto merger. *Drug v Hunt, 168 A 87 (1933).*

Transfer of corporation's assets to second corporation in exchange for latter's stock does not amount to merger that would make latter liable for former's debts. *Cleveland Worsted Mills Co v Consolidated Textile Corp, 292 F 129 (3d Cir 1923).*

Stockholder cannot enjoin directors from submitting to stockholders a plan to exchange assets for stock of another corporation; it is not merger or consolidation when each corporation continues its own corporate existence. *Butler v New Keystone Copper Co, 93 A 380 (Ch Ct 1915).*

.9 Percentage of vote to approve merger.—Amendment to articles of incorporation can raise percentage of stock required for shareholder approval to 80% in cases where directors do not favor merger even if, in cases where directors favor merger, only majority vote is required. *Seibert v Gulton Industries, Inc, No. 5631 (Ch Ct 6-21-79).*

Court enjoined merger between corporation and several other corporations owned by its majority shareholder. Under corporation's certificate, supermajority vote was required when board authorized merger unless authorization occurred prior to acquiring entity's gaining 30% or more of corporation's common stock. In this case, board authorized merger long after majority shareholder/acquiring entity obtained 30% of corporation's stock. *Emerald Partners v Berlin, No. 9700 (Ch Ct 3-18-88).*

.10 Proxy statement.—Proxy statement was upheld as not materially false and misleading although it allegedly omitted some aspects because statement gave "total mix" of information so that minority stockholders' vote on merger proposal was informed vote and therefore was no breach of fiduciary duty to minority. *Bershad v Curtiss-Wright Corp, Nos. 5827 and 5830 (Ch Ct 3-21-83).*

Proxy statement in connection with proposed merger did not omit material information when (1) deferred tax liability, which was reported in accordance with generally accepted accounting principles, did not have to be further explained to shareholders, (2) supplement adequately disclosed value of asset, and (3) information in undisclosed report was already adequately disclosed. Directors of corporation did not violate duty of due care when they did not have copy of report evaluating merger because they had access to source materials from which report was prepared. *Schlossberg v The First Artists Production Co, No. 6670 (Ch Ct 12-17-86).*

Court refused to preliminarily enjoin proposed cash out merger when plaintiff failed to show reasonable probability of success on claim that there had been an inadequate disclosure of information in proxy materials sent to shareholders of corporation to be merged and that he and other shareholders would suffer irreparable harm if there were no injunction, where (1) Certain future financial projections prepared by management did not have to be disclosed because they were only concocted for bargaining purposes; (2) proxy's failure to disclose fact that acquiror sold stock purchase warrants for corporation's stock to corporation's financial advisor before negotiations was not fatal since proxy did set forth acquiror's stock holdings and ownership; (3) proxy materials adequately disclosed acquiror's prior financial relationships with advisor; and (4) financial advisor's purchase of acquiror's commercial paper in normal course of business did not have to be disclosed. *Snyder v Convergent, Inc, No. 10236 (Ch Ct 12-21-88).*

§251

Summary judgment was inappropriate where highly intricate disclosure issues were heavily disputed in case brought by stockholders challenging the validity of corporate merger that resulted in corporation's subsidiary status. Plaintiffs alleged material misrepresentations or omissions in a joint proxy statement that defendant corporations together prepared. *Frazer v Worldwide Energy Corp, No. 8822 (Ch Ct 5-3-90).*

A merger will not be preliminarily enjoined merely because management projections have not been disclosed in proxy materials; there is no per se rule that such projections are material. *In re Check-Free Corp. Shareholders Litig, 2007 Del. Ch. LEXIS 148 (Ch Ct 2007).*

.11 Fiduciary duty.—Direct fiduciary duty to shareholders when they approved corporation's merger after (1) failing to inform themselves of all relevant and reasonably available information and (2) failing to disclose all material information that reasonable shareholders would consider important in deciding whether to approve merger. Business judgment did not protect directors when failure to inform themselves constituted gross negligence. Directors were liable for damages to shareholders to extent fair value of shares exceeded merger price. *Smith v Van Gorkom, 488 A2d 858 (1985).*

Terms of merger which left preferred shareholders of pre-merger corporation as shareholders of post-merger corporation did not result from directors' breach of fiduciary duty. Although directors' actions in seeking merger partner based on what partner would offer common shareholders, without seeking anything specific for preferred shareholders, may have breached duty, merger partner's offer was not made in direct response to directors' solicitations. Preferred shareholders were not entitled to vote as class on proposed merger because sinking fund for mandatory redemption of their stock did not alter prior redemption preferences adversely when shareholders were not deprived of redemption rights they possessed before merger. *Dalton v American Investment Co, 490 A2d 574 (Ch Ct), aff'd, 501 A2d 1238 (1985).*

In parent-subsidiary merger, parent's directors have no duty to auction subsidiary to highest bidder pursuant to *Revlon, Inc v MacAndrews & Forbes Holdings, Inc,* 506 A2d 173 (1986). Real issues are price and fairness. *Bershad v Curtiss-Wright Corp, 535 A2d 840 (1987).*

Target corporation's board that is engaged in auction of company does not necessarily violate its duty under *Revlon, Inc v MacAndrews & Forbes Holdings, Inc,* 506 A2d 173 (1986) to obtain maximum value for shareholders if it takes actions that favor one competitive bidder over another. Board owes shareholders duty of fairness, not persons seeking to acquire company. Thus, board may tilt playing field in bidder's favor, but only if it is in shareholder's interest to do so.

Court refused to enjoin offer for target by bidder granted expense reimbursement provision and topping fee, holding that those advantages granted to bidder likely furthered bidding process and thus benefited shareholders as well. *West Point-Pepperell, Inc v J P Stevens & Co,* 542 A2d 770 (Ch Ct 1988).

Minority shareholder, who sold shares in target corporation to acquiror for a premium, did not violate fiduciary duties to target's remaining shareholders. *Reason:* Minority shareholder did not dominate or control target, so it owed no fiduciary duties to target's shareholders. Therefore, court dismissed complaint charging shareholder with breach of duty.

Court also dismissed complaint charging minority shareholder with aiding and abetting breach of fiduciary duty by target board. Complaint alleged no facts indicating that shareholder actually knew or was fairly chargeable with knowledge that target directors were breaching fiduciary duty by approving premium for shareholder. *In re Sea-Land Shareholders Litigation, No. 8453 (Ch Ct 5-13-88).*

Target did not have duty to redeem poison pill rights even though more than 80% of its shareholders had accepted tender offer by hostile offeror. *Reason:* Closing of tender offer was conditioned on approval of offer and execution of merger agreement by target's board. Under the circumstances, board could decline merger proposal based on concern for long-term corporate values and without implicating duty to maximize current values for shareholders. *TW Services, Inc v SWT Acquisition Corp, No. 10427 (Ch Ct 1989).*

Court invalidated lockup option that target had granted to favored bidder to purchase some of target's core businesses. *Reason:* Lockup served only to end bidding for target, and board's actions did not meet rigorous standard of entire fairness. *Mills Acquisition Co v Macmillan, Inc, 559 A2d 1261 (1989).*

Defendant's board of directors had the power to forgo immediate cash sale to plaintiff in favor of potential long-term benefits from a merger with another party. *Paramount Communications Inc v Time Inc, No. 10866; In re Time Inc Shareholder Litigation, No. 10670 (Ch Ct 6-9-89).*

Directors of a corporation did not, as a matter of law, breach their duty of care in effecting a merger of the corporation, although the former corporation's chief negotiators had "golden parachutes" in their contracts, and thus knew that they would receive significant financial benefits if the merger was effected. The court stated that these employment contracts do not give rise to a *per se* breach of duty by the board, who reviewed the transaction after the negotiations were complete.

The court further upheld a "no-shop" provision and a "lock-up" agreement in the member agreements. By the time the directors agreed to these provisions, the "market of potential acquirors had been fully canvassed." Thus, the court determined that the corporation gained a substantial benefit for its stockholders by maintaining negotiations with the only party expressing any interest in a merger, while assuring itself that the transaction would be consummated. *Rand v Western Air Lines, Inc, No. 8632 (Ch Ct 2-25-94).*

A board of directors is not required by the law of fiduciary disclosure to articulate, in a proxy statement, the reasons why two directors of the corporation either opposed or abstained from commenting on a stock for stock merger with another corporation. *Newman v Warren, No. 15008 (Ch Ct 8-19-96).*

Corporate merger was not void and corporate defendants were not liable for conversion of a shareholder's stocks where the defendants complied with all the statutory requirements for merger but made a good faith violation of the common law duty of disclosure in the merger proxy statement. *Arnold v Society for Savings Bancorp, Inc, 678 A2d 533 (1996).*

Defendant directors were given fair notice of plaintiff's entire fairness and best price claims concerning a merger, where the complaint alleged facts about the negotiation of the merger and defendant directors' breach of their fiduciary duties. *Emerald Partners v Berlin, 726 A2d 1215 (1999).*

The Delaware Supreme Court held that a board of directors, in the context of evaluating a proposal for a sale of its entire corporation to a third party at the behest of the majority shareholder, owes a duty of due care to make an independent, informed and deliberate judgment, in good faith, about whether the sale to the third party that was proposed by the majority shareholder would result in a maximization of value for the minority shareholders. *McMullin v Beran, 765 A2d 910 (2000).*

A corporation breaches in bad faith in a merger transaction where following the signing of the term sheet and the closing of a profitable merger, the corporation attempts not only to renegotiate a critical issue that has been addressed by the term sheet, but also conditions the transaction contemplated by the term sheet on this renegotiation. *RGC International Investors, LDC v Greka Energy Corp, 2001 Del Ch LEXIS 107 (Ch Ct 2001).*

An acquiring corporation in a merger does not aid or abet a breach of fiduciary duty by directors of the target corporation where the acquiring corporation does not conspire with the directors, the collateral agreements granted by the non-fiduciary acquiror to the fiduciary directors are not excessive, and no *specific facts* are pled from which a court can reasonably infer knowledge of the breach. *McGowan v Ferro, 2002 Del Ch LEXIS 3 (Ch Ct 2002).*

Where directors of an insolvent corporation owe a fiduciary duty to the corporation's creditors, the business judgment rule nevertheless applies to the directors' approval of a merger, and to overcome the business judgment rule's presumption, the creditors must show that the directors did not act in good faith after a reasonable investigation. *Angelo, Gordon & Co, LP v Allied Riser Communications Corp, 805 A2d 221 (Ch Ct 2002).*

The Delaware Supreme Court, in a case of first impression, has made clear that officers owe the same fiduciary duties as owed by directors; those duties can be violated by delaying a due diligence process for self-interested motives. Moreover, the business judgment presumption may be overcome on a motion to dismiss by pleading sufficient facts to raise an inference that a majority of directors has breached their duty of loyalty. *Gantler v Stephens, 965 A2d 695 (2009).*

.12 Interference with merger agreement.—Target and tender offeror were not liable to corporation for breach of merger agreement or tortious interference with merger agreement between target and corporation when tender offeror acquired target after target recommended that shareholders accept tender offeror's offer. Target board's recommendation of tender offer was not breach of merger agreement because (1) board was without statutory power to bind corporation to proposed merger absent shareholder approval and (2) board's fiduciary duties obligated it to withdraw its recommendation of merger proposal and recommend tender offer since tender offer was superior to merger proposal. *ConAgra, Inc v Cargill, Inc, 388 NW2d 458 (Neb 1986).*

.13 Obtaining corporate documents.—Preferred shareholder, who brought suit to enjoin merger of her corporation, could obtain documents reflecting communications to lawyers of her corporation from lawyers of corporation contemplating merger with her corporation because (1) lawyer-client privilege does not extend to these documents since they were not confidential and (2) communication did not relate to development of factual record or strategies with respect to preferred shareholder's litigation. *Jedwab v MGM Grand Hotels, Inc, No. 8077 (Ch Ct 3-20-86).*

.14 Derivative standing; former shareholder.—Former shareholder could not bring derivative action attacking directors' and officers' golden parachutes as waste of corporate assets after corporation was merged into acquiror when (1) shareholder lost standing to pursue derivative action because he was no longer shareholder of corporation and (2) acquiror agreed to honor golden parachutes, so it must be assumed that it decided that golden parachute agreement did not give rise to cause of action. Former shareholder also could not bring class action attacking golden parachutes for reducing merger price paid by acquiror because claim is really derivative in nature and restatement of waste claim when shareholder failed to attach merger. *Bershad v Hartz, No. 6960 (Ch Ct 1-29-87).*

.15 "Best efforts" clause.—Court refused to issue an injunction specifically enforcing best efforts clause of agreement promoting merger when complaint did not state an anticipatory breach of contract nor breach of obligation to use best efforts to promote merger transaction. Specific enforcement of contractual obligation to proceed in good faith is unavailable when contract sued on relates to future transaction. *Carteret Bancorp, Inc v The Home Group, Inc, Nos. 9380 and 9836 (Ch Ct 1-13-88).*

.16 Settlement.—Court approved settlement of public shareholders' class action challenging merger of corporations having common controlling shareholders and directors.

In approving the settlement, the court stressed that plaintiffs' claims were weak and that the transaction was negotiated by independent negotiating committee with advice of investment banker. Settlement provided modest benefits to public shareholders—an improved exchange ratio and contingent right to receive more stock in surviving corporation if its common does not reach certain target prices in four years. Therefore, settlement represented fair and reasonable consideration for release of plaintiffs' claims. *In re MAXXAM Group, Inc Stockholders Litigation, No. 8636 (Ch Ct 4-16-87).*

Short sellers of stock that is the subject of a settlement of a class action may not intervene in the action, or have the settlement order modified, where they had received notice of the settlement and its terms and did not challenge the settlement at the time of the settlement hearing. *In re Digex, Inc Shareholders Litigation, 2002 Del. Ch. LEXIS 40 (Ch Ct 2002).*

.17 **Waiver of claim.**—By failing to oppose merger, shareholders waived any claim that they were injured by acquiror's alleged bad faith in inducing merger at distress price. Shareholders could not bring action alleging that acquiror breached its fiduciary duty by weakening corporation to force premature merger because action had to be brought derivatively and they were no longer shareholders after agreeing to merge and selling their stock. *Nerken v Standard Oil Co (Indiana), 810 F2d 1230 (DC Cir 1987).*

.18 **Accomplished merger, relief pending challenge to.**—Former shareholder challenging accomplished merger was denied preliminary injunction to bar acquiror from causing merged corporation to engage in any transaction outside of its ordinary course of business, *pendente lite,* except on 30 days' notice to court and plaintiff's counsel. Threat that acquiror would cause merged corporation to take action to impair plaintiff's rescission remedy did not justify such relief. Injunctive relief on facts presented would do violence to requirement that there be threat of imminent irreparable harm. Such restraint would impair directors' right to manage corporation and make plaintiff *ex officio* member of board. *Frazer v Worldwide Energy Corp, No. 8822 (Ch Ct 2-19-87).*

.19 **Merger; stock conversion as redemption.**—Conversion of corporation's preferred stock to cash for $40 per share pursuant to merger agreement did not constitute redemption, thereby entitling each preferred shareholder to $100 per share under provision in corporation's certificate of incorporation. Under Delaware law, conversion of shares to cash in order to accomplish merger is legally distinct from redemption of shares by corporation. Action taken under one section of Delaware corporation law is legally independent and not to be tested by requirements of unrelated section. Thus, conversion of preferred stock to cash was protected by doctrine of independent legal significance. *Rauch v RCA Corp, 861 F2d 29 (2d Cir 1988).*

.20 **Successor in interest, standing of.**—Corporation's successor in interest may have standing to litigate breach of contract claim against corporation's former investment banker. *Kidder, Peabody & Co v Maxus Energy Corp, No. 9424 (Ch Ct 12-27-88).*

.21 **Supermajority vote.**—Chancery Court erred when it granted preliminary injunction to block merger. Provision in target's certificate requiring supermajority vote for business combinations did not apply after acquiror had reduced interest in target to less than 30%. *Berlin v Emerald Partners, 552 A2d 482 (1989).*

.22 **Fraudulent concealment—effect.**—A fiduciary relationship existed between parties that prevented charging shareholder in family corporation with constructive notice of a fifteen-year-old merger that shareholder now challenged. Suit is not time barred, nor will laches be applied to defeat complaint since fraudulent concealment was an issue in the case. *Dunleavy v Dugan, No. 88-57 (D Del 4-20-90).*

.23 **Notice requirement.**—In action by minority shareholder challenging cash-out merger, court granted defendant's motion to dismiss allegation that defendant breached its duty of loyalty by timing a merger announcement to give plaintiff less than the statutory minimum time to determine whether minority shareholder would consent to freeze-out merger. Court stated that the time of mailing and not the time of receipt is determinative under Delaware law, that defendants mailed announcement 23 days prior to merger consummation; therefore, defendants complied with 20 day statutory minimum. *Ince & Co v Silgan Corp, No. 10941 (Ch Ct 1-7-91).*

.24 **Director's duty to disclose.**—In a class action in which the stockholders alleged that the directors breached their duty of disclosure and committed equitable fraud in connection with the corporation's merger, the lower court's focus upon the information the directors subjectively considered important to shareholders in tendering their stock, rather than the information a reasonable investor would consider important, erroneously placed upon the stockholders the burden of proving that a precipitous decline in the stock market was the primary factor in the directors' renegotiation of a merger agreement, resulting in the stockholders receiving less money for their shares than they would have otherwise received. Under an objective analysis of what the directors might consider relevant to the stockholders from an investor's standpoint, the directors should have disclosed not only their primary reason for renegotiating the merger agreement, but any other reasons, including whatever consideration they had given to the stock market decline in reaching their decision. *Zirn v VLI Corp, 621 A2d 773 (1993).*

GM's board of directors did not breach its duty of disclosure to shareholders of GMH stock (a "tracking stock" tied to the performance of Hughes Electronics (Hughes), a wholly-owned subsidiary, which itself consisted of several subsidiaries including Hughes Defense, Hughes Telecom, and Delco,) where the GMH shareholders had a choice of voting either for the status quo or for the restructuring transactions and obtaining the potential benefits of a merger with Raytheon, among other upside advantages, by simultaneously waiving application of a favorable recapitalization charter provision giving GMH shareholders the right to receive GM $1 2/3 stock (one of several GM trading stocks) worth 120% of the market value of their GMH stock upon sale, transfer, assignment or other disposition by GM of "substantially all" of the Hughes business. *In re General Motors Class H Shareholders Litigation, CA No 15517-NC (Ch Ct 3-22-99).*

.25 **Right to class vote.**—The Court of Chancery determined that under §242 common stockholders did not have the right to a class vote on a merger. *Orban v Field, No. 12820 (Ch Ct 12-30-93).*

Preferred stockholder protective provisions that do not expressly provide for class voting rights in the face of a merger do not protect the preferred stockholders even where a merger will effect changes in capital structure for which the protective provisions require a class vote. *Benchmark Capital Partners IV, LP v Vague, 2002 Del Ch LEXIS 90 (Ch Ct 2002).*

.26 **Copy of merger agreement.**—The Court of Chancery, after finding other violations in the way two corporations handled their merger, invalidated the merger agreement between two corporations where, after the certificate of merger was filed and recorded in the counties in which each of the merging corporations was registered, the surviving corporation failed to furnish copies of the merger agreement to stockholders upon request. The court emphasized that the provision in the GCL allowing merging corporations to file a certificate of merger was not designed to permit the corporations to avoid disclosure of all merger terms to the stockholders. *Jackson v Turnbull, No. 13042 (Ch Ct 2-8-94).*

.27 **Fiduciary out provisions.**—A merger agreement entered into after a market search, before any prospect of a topping bid has emerged, which locks up stockholder approval and does not contain a "fiduciary out" provision, is per se invalid when a later significant topping bid emerges. *Omnicare, Inc v NCS Healthcare, Inc, 818 A2d 914 (2003).*

.28 **Freeze-out; injunction of.**—A freeze-out of minority shareholders by a controlling shareholder, structured as a first-step tender offer to be followed by a second-step short-form merger, will not be enjoined, even though the proposed transaction is subject to entire fairness review, because any harm to the putative class can be remedied through a post-closing damages action. *In re CNX Gas Corporation Shareholders Litigation, 2010 Del. Ch. LEXIS 119 (Ch Ct 2010).*

252 MERGER OR CONSOLIDATION OF DOMESTIC AND FOREIGN CORPORATIONS; SERVICE OF PROCESS UPON SURVIVING OR RESULTING CORPORATION.—(a) Any 1 or more corporations of this State may merge or consolidate with 1 or more other corporations of any other state or states of the United States, or of the District of Columbia if the laws of the other state or states, or of the District permit a corporation of such jurisdiction to merge or consolidate with a corporation of another jurisdiction. The constituent corporations may merge into a single corporation, which may be any 1 of the constituent corporations, or they may consolidate into a new corporation formed by the consolidation, which may be a corporation of the state of incorporation of any 1 of the constituent corporations, pursuant to an agreement of merger or consolidation, as the case may be, complying and approved in accordance with this section. In addition, any 1 or more corporations existing under the laws of this State may merge or consolidate with 1 or more corporations organized under the laws of any jurisdiction other than 1 of the United States if the laws under which the other corporation or corporations are organized permit a corporation of such jurisdiction to merge or consolidate with a corporation of another jurisdiction.

(b) All the constituent corporations shall enter into an agreement of merger or consolidation. The agreement shall state: (1) The terms and conditions of the merger or consolidation; (2) the mode of carrying the same into effect; (3) the manner, if any, of converting the shares of each of the constituent corporations into shares or other securities of the corporation surviving or resulting from the merger or consolidation, or of cancelling some or all of such shares, and, if any shares of any of the constituent corporations are not to remain outstanding, to be converted solely into shares or other securities of the surviving or resulting corporation or to be cancelled, the cash, property, rights or securities of any other corporation or entity which the holders of such shares are to receive in exchange for, or upon conversion of, such shares and the surrender of any certificates evidencing them, which cash, property, rights or securities of any other corporation or entity may be in addition to or in lieu of the shares or other securities of the surviving or resulting corporation; (4) such other details or provisions as are deemed desirable, including, without limiting the generality of the foregoing, a provision for the payment of cash in lieu of the issuance or recognition of fractional shares of the surviving or resulting corporation or of any other corporation the securities of which are to be received in the merger or consolidation, or for some other arrangement with respect thereto consistent with §155 of this title; and (5) such other provisions or facts as shall be required to be set forth in certificates of incorporation by the laws of the state of which are stated in the agreement to be the laws that shall govern the surviving or resulting corporation and that can be stated in the case of a merger or consolidation. Any of the terms of the agreement of merger or consolidation may be made dependent upon facts ascertainable outside of such agreement, provided that the manner in which such facts shall operate upon the terms of the agreement is clearly and expressly set forth in the agreement of merger or consolidation. The term "facts," as used in the preceding sentence, includes, but is not limited to, the occurrence of any event, including a determination or action by any person or body, including the corporation.

(c) The agreement shall be adopted, approved, certified, executed and acknowledged by each of the constituent corporations in accordance with the laws under which it is formed, and, in the case of a Delaware corporation, in the same manner as is provided in §251 of this title. The agreement shall be filed and shall become effective for all purposes of the laws of this State when and as provided in §251 of this title with respect to the merger or consolidation of corporations of this State. In lieu of filing the agreement of merger or consolidation, the surviving or resulting corporation may file a certificate of merger or consolidation, executed in accordance with §103 of this title, which states:

(1) The name and state or jurisdiction of incorporation of each of the constituent corporations;

(2) That an agreement of merger or consolidation has been approved, adopted, certified, executed and acknowledged by each of the constituent corporations in accordance with this subsection;

(3) The name of the surviving or resulting corporation;

(4) In the case of a merger, such amendments or changes in the certificate of incorporation of the surviving corporation as are desired to be effected by the merger *(which amendments or changes may amend and restate the certificate of incorporation of the surviving corporation in its entirety)*, or, if no such amendments or changes are desired, a statement that the certificate of incorporation of the surviving corporation shall be its certificate of incorporation;

(5) In the case of a consolidation, that the certificate of incorporation of the resulting corporation shall be as is set forth in an attachment to the certificate;

(6) That the executed agreement of consolidation or merger is on file at an office of the surviving corporation and the address thereof;

(7) That a copy of the agreement of consolidation or merger will be furnished by the surviving corporation, on request and without cost, to any stockholder of any constituent corporation;

(8) If the corporation surviving or resulting from the merger or consolidation is to be a corporation of this State, the authorized capital stock of each constituent corporation which is not a corporation of this State; and

(9) The agreement, if any, required by subsection (d) of this section.

(d) [1] *If the corporation surviving or resulting from the merger or consolidation is to be governed by the laws of the District of Columbia or any state or jurisdiction other than this State, it shall agree that it may be served with process in this State in any proceeding for enforcement of any obligation of any constituent corporation of this State, as well as for enforcement of any obligation of the surviving or resulting corporation arising from the merger or consolidation, including any suit or other proceeding to enforce the right of any stockholders as determined in appraisal proceedings pursuant to §262 of this title, and shall irrevocably appoint the Secretary of State as its agent to accept service of process in any such suit or other proceedings and shall specify the address to which a copy of such process shall be mailed by the Secretary of State. Process may be served upon the Secretary of State under this subsection by means of electronic transmission but only as prescribed by the Secretary of State. The Secretary of State is authorized to issue such rules and regulations with respect to such service as the Secretary of State deems necessary or appropriate. In the event of such service upon the Secretary of State in accordance with this subsection, the Secretary of State shall forthwith notify such surviving or resulting corporation thereof by letter, directed to such surviving or resulting corporation at its address so specified, unless such surviving or resulting corporation shall have designated in writing to the Secretary of State a different address for such purpose, in which case it shall be mailed to the last address so designated. Such letter shall be sent by a mail or courier service that includes a record of mailing or deposit with the courier and a record of delivery evidenced by the signature of the recipient.* Such letter shall enclose a copy of the process and any other papers served on the Secretary of State pursuant to this subsection. It shall be the duty of the plaintiff in the event of such service to serve process and any other papers in duplicate, to notify the Secretary of State that service is being effected pursuant to this subsection and to pay the Secretary of State the sum of $50 for the use of the State, which sum shall be taxed as part of the costs in the proceeding, if the plaintiff shall prevail therein. The Secretary of State shall maintain an alphabetical record of any such service setting forth the name of the plaintiff and the defendant, the title, docket number and nature of the proceeding in which process has been served, the fact that service has been effected pursuant to this subsection, the return date thereof, and the day and hour service was made. The Secretary of State shall not be required to retain such information longer than 5 years from receipt of the service of process.

(e) Subsection (d) and the second sentence of subsection (c) of §251 of this title shall apply to any merger or consolidation under this section; subsection (e) of §251 of this title shall apply to a merger under this section in which the surviving corporation is a corporation of this State; subsection (f) of §251 of this title shall apply to any merger under this section. (Last amended by Ch. 290, L. '10, eff. 8-2-10.)

> Ch. 290, L. '10, eff. 8-2-10, added matter in italic and deleted [1]"If the corporation surviving or resulting from the merger or consolidation is to be governed by the laws of the District of Columbia or any state or jurisdiction other than this State, it shall agree that it may be served with process in this State in any proceeding for enforcement of any obligation of any constituent corporation of this State, as well as for enforcement of any obligation of the surviving or resulting corporation arising from the merger or consolidation, including any suit or other proceeding to enforce the right of any stockholders as determined in appraisal proceedings pursuant to §262 of this title, and shall irrevocably appoint the Secretary of State as its agent to accept service of process in any such suit or other proceedings and shall specify the address to which a copy of such process shall be mailed by the Secretary of State. In the event of such service upon the Secretary of State in accordance with this subsection, the Secretary of State shall forthwith notify such surviving or resulting corporation thereof by letter, certified mail, return receipt requested, directed to such surviving or resulting corporation at its address so specified, unless such surviving or resulting corporation shall have designated in writing to the Secretary of State a different address for such purpose, in which case it shall be mailed to the last address so designated."

Ch. 290, L. '10 Synopsis of Section 252

These sections amend Sections 251(b)(3), 251(c)(4), 252(c)(4), 254(d)(4), 263(c)(4), and 264(c)(4), respectively, to clarify that in a merger the certificate of incorporation of the surviving corporation may be amended and restated in its entirety.

These sections amend Sections 252(d), 256(d), 263(d), 264(d), 266(c)(6), 321(b), 376(b), 381(c), 381(d), 382(a), 382(c), and 390(h)(5), respectively, to allow for service of process upon the Secretary of State thereunder by means of electronic transmission but only as prescribed by the Secretary of State, to authorize the Secretary of State to issue such rules and regulations with respect to such service as the Secretary of State deems necessary or appropriate, and to enable the Secretary of State, in the event that service is effected through the Secretary of State in accordance therewith, to provide notice of service by letter sent by a mail or courier service that includes a record of mailing or deposit with the courier and a record of delivery evidenced by the signature of the recipient.

Ch. 84, L. '03 Synopsis of Section 252

The amendments to Sections 251, 252, 253, 254, 255, 256, 257, 263 and 264 clarify that shares or other interests of a constituent corporation or other entity to a merger or consolidation may be converted, cancelled or unaffected by the merger.

Ch. 339, L. '98 Synopsis of Section 252

The amendment to subsection (e) of Section 252 provides that the contemporaneous amendment to Section 251(c) shall be applicable to mergers and consolidations under this section.

Ch. 349, L. '96 Synopsis of Section 252

The amendments to Sections 251(b), 252(b), 254(c), 255(b), 256(b), 257(b), 263(b), and 264(b) are intended to conform these sections with the 1994 amendment to Section 151(a). The amendments make clear that a "fact" can include an event or a determination or action by any person or body, including an event or determination within the control of the corporation or a person or body affiliated with the corporation, such as a decision by its board of directors or one of its officers or agents. These amendments are not intended to alter the fiduciary duties of a board of directors in authorizing a merger agreement with terms that turn on determinations or actions made by any person or body, or in making any determination or taking any action constituting a fact under these sections.

The amendments to Sections 251(c)(6), 252(c)(6), 254(d)(6), 263(c)(6) and 264(c)(6) eliminate the requirement that the executed agreement of consolidation or merger be on file at the principal place of business of the surviving corporation or entity in cases where a certificate of merger or consolidation is filed with the Secretary of State in lieu of the agreement of consolidation or merger. The amendment permits the executed agreement of consolidation or merger to be on file at any office of the surviving corporation or entity, whether or not its principal place of business.

Commentary on Section 252

The amendments to Sections 252 and 253 by Ch. 61, L. '93, eff. 7-1-93, authorize a Delaware corporation to merge directly into a non-U.S. corporation if the laws under which the non-U.S. corporation is organized permits a corporation of such jurisdiction to merge or consolidate with a corporation of another jurisdiction.

.1 Enjoining merger.—Stockholder opposing merger of his Delaware corporation with foreign corporation has appraisal rights, so he cannot set it aside unless he can show actual or constructive fraud. *Krantman v Liberty Loan Corp, 152 FSupp 705 (ND Ill 1956),* aff'd, *246 F2d 581 (7th Cir),* cert denied, *355 US 905 (1957).*

Charge that exchange ratio of stock in merger is disproportionate is not enough to bar it; there must be showing of such gross undervaluation as to amount to fraud. *Bruce v E L Bruce Co, 174 A2d 29 (Ch Ct 1961).*

New York court will not enjoin stockholders' meeting of Delaware corporation called to consider recapitalization and merger, even though preferred stockholders and directors residents of New York, particularly since same matter is at issue in litigation in Delaware court. *Newman v United Profit-Sharing Corp, 178 NYS2d 990 (NY SCt 1958).*

Minority shareholder could not enjoin short-form merger of her corporation with parent because her sole remedy was appraisal when (1) she did not demonstrate inadequacy of appraisal, (2) parent did not deal unfairly with minority, (3) parent properly disclosed to minority its intentions and options concerning acquisition of shares not tendered pursuant to tender offer it made prior to its short-form merger. *Stepak v Scharffenberger, No. 6530 (Ch Ct 8-9-85).*

For preliminary injunction purposes, the possibility that a higher takeover bid would materialize did not constitute irreparable harm; even if irreparable harm to the plaintiff could be shown, a greater risk existed to the corporation that its business suppliers would react adversely to the enjoining of the merger in that uncertainty surrounding the firm's control and management would be extended. *Norberg v Young's Market Co, No. 11208 (Ch Ct 12-19-89).*

.2 Purchase and sale of assets.—Purchase by foreign corporation of assets of Delaware corporation in exchange for stock is not merger giving stockholder of Delaware corporation any right of appraisal. *Hariton v Arco Electronics, Inc, 182 A2d 22,* aff'd, *188 A2d 123 (1963).*

Stockholders of Delaware corporation cannot set aside its sale of its assets to Minnesota corporation in exchange for latter's stock, on ground Delaware corporation had not honored its alleged obligation to purchase stockholders' shares; especially when stockholders waited more than three years after transaction consummated. *Peterson v New England Furniture & Carpet Co, 299 NW 208 (1941).*

.3 Sequestration.—Shares of stock that were sequestered in aid of derivative suit were released from that sequestration when they lost their situs in Delaware as result of corporation's merger with an out of state corporation. *Union Chemical & Materials Corp v Cannon, 148 A2d 348 (1959),* rev'g, *144 A2d 142 (Ch Ct 1958).*

253 MERGER OF PARENT CORPORATION AND SUBSIDIARY OR SUBSIDIARIES.—(a) In any case in which at least 90% of the outstanding shares of each class of the stock of a corporation or corporations (other than a corporation which has in its certificate of incorporation the provision required by §251(g)(7)(i) of this title), of which class there are outstanding shares that, absent this subsection, would be entitled to vote on such merger, is owned by another corporation and 1 of the corporations is a corporation of this State and the other or others are corporations of this State, or any other state or states, or the District of Columbia and the laws of the other state or states, or the District permit a corporation of such jurisdiction to merge with a corporation of another jurisdiction, the corporation having such stock ownership may either merge the other corporation or corporations into itself and assume all of its or their obligations, or merge itself, or itself and 1 or more of such other corporations, into 1 of the other corporations by executing, acknowledging and filing, in accordance with §103 of this title, a certificate of such ownership and merger setting forth a copy of the resolution of its board of directors to so merge and the date of the adoption; provided, however, that in case the parent corporation shall not own all the outstanding stock of all the subsidiary corporations, parties to a merger as aforesaid, the resolution of the board of directors of the parent corporation shall state the terms and conditions of the merger, including the securities, cash, property, or rights to be issued, paid, delivered or granted by the surviving corporation upon surrender of each share of the subsidiary corporation or corporations not owned by the parent corporation, or the cancellation of some or all of such shares. Any of the terms of the resolution of the board of directors to so merge may be made dependent upon facts ascertainable outside of such resolution, provided that the manner in which such facts

shall operate upon the terms of the resolution is clearly and expressly set forth in the resolution. The term "facts," as used in the preceding sentence, includes, but is not limited to, the occurrence of any event, including a determination or action by any person or body, including the corporation. If the parent corporation be not the surviving corporation, the resolution shall include provision for the pro rata issuance of stock of the surviving corporation to the holders of the stock of the parent corporation on surrender of any certificates therefor, and the certificate of ownership and merger shall state that the proposed merger has been approved by a majority of the outstanding stock of the parent corporation entitled to vote thereon at a meeting duly called and held after 20 days' notice of the purpose of the meeting mailed to each such stockholder at the stockholder's address as it appears on the records of the corporation if the parent corporation is a corporation of this State or state that the proposed merger has been adopted, approved, certified, executed and acknowledged by the parent corporation in accordance with the laws under which it is organized if the parent corporation is not a corporation of this State. [1] *If the surviving corporation exists under the laws of the District of Columbia or any state or jurisdiction other than this State,*
    (1) Section 252(d) of this title or §258(c) of this title, as applicable, shall also apply to a merger under this section; and
    (2) The terms and conditions of the merger shall obligate the surviving corporation to provide the agreement, and take the actions, required by §252(d) of this title or §258(c) of this title, as applicable.
    (b) If the surviving corporation is a Delaware corporation, it may change its corporate name by the inclusion of a provision to that effect in the resolution of merger adopted by the directors of the parent corporation and set forth in the certificate of ownership and merger, and upon the effective date of the merger, the name of the corporation shall be so changed.
    (c) Subsection (d) of §251 of this title shall apply to a merger under this section, and subsection (e) of §251 of this title shall apply to a merger under this section in which the surviving corporation is the subsidiary corporation and is a corporation of this State. References to "agreement of merger" in subsections (d) and (e) of §251 of this title shall mean for purposes of this subsection the resolution of merger adopted by the board of directors of the parent corporation. Any merger which effects any changes other than those authorized by this section or made applicable by this subsection shall be accomplished under [2] §251, §252, §257, or §258 of this title. Section 262 of this title shall not apply to any merger effected under this section, except as provided in subsection (d) of this section.
    (d) In the event all of the stock of a subsidiary Delaware corporation party to a merger effected under this section is not owned by the parent corporation immediately prior to the merger, the stockholders of the subsidiary Delaware corporation party to the merger shall have appraisal rights as set forth in §262 of this title.
    (e) A merger may be effected under this section although 1 or more of the corporations parties to the merger is a corporation organized under the laws of a jurisdiction other than 1 of the United States; provided that the laws of such jurisdiction permit a corporation of such jurisdiction to merge with a corporation of another jurisdiction.
    (f) This section shall apply to nonstock corporations if the parent corporation is such a corporation and is the surviving corporation of the merger; provided, however, that references to the directors of the parent corporation shall be deemed to be references to members of the governing body of the parent corporation, and references to the board of directors of the parent corporation shall be deemed to be references to the governing body of the parent corporation.
    (g) Nothing in this section shall be deemed to authorize the merger of a corporation with a charitable nonstock corporation, if the charitable status of such charitable nonstock corporation would thereby be lost or impaired. (Last amended by Ch. 253, L. '10, eff. 8-1-10 and Ch. 290, L. 10, eff. 8-2-10.)

Ch. 253, L. '10, eff. 8-1-10, added matter in italic and deleted [2]"§251 or §252" in paragraph (c). Ch. 290, L. '10, eff. 8-2-10, added matter in italic and deleted [1]"If the surviving corporation exists under the laws of the District of Columbia or any state or jurisdiction other than this State, subsection (d) of §252 of this title or subsection (c) of §258 of this title, as applicable, shall also apply to a merger under this section." in paragraph (a).

Ch. 290, L. '10 Synopsis of Section 253

This section amends Section 253(a) solely to conform text in Section 253(a) to text in new Section 267(a).

Ch. 253, L. '10 Synopsis of Section 253

Sections 38, 39, and 40 amend the DGCL to add new §253(f) and amend §253 of the DGCL to allow a nonstock corporation that owns 90% of the outstanding shares of each class of stock of a subsidiary otherwise entitled to vote on a merger to effect a short-form merger, so long as the nonstock corporation is the surviving corporation. These Sections also amend the DCGL to add new §253(g) to provide that nothing in §253 shall be deemed to authorize the merger of a corporation with a charitable nonstock corporation, if the charitable status of such charitable nonstock corporation would thereby be lost or impaired.

Ch. 84, L. '03 Synopsis of Section 253

The amendments to Sections 251, 252, 253, 254, 255, 256, 257, 263 and 264 clarify that shares or other interests of a constituent corporation or other entity to a merger or consolidation may be converted, cancelled or unaffected by the merger.

Ch. 123, L. '99 Synopsis of Section 253

The amendment to Section 253(a) provides that the 90% ownership requirement applies only to a class of stock of which there are outstanding shares that would otherwise be entitled to vote on the merger, so that, if the only outstanding shares of a class of stock are shares that would otherwise not be entitled to vote on the merger, then the 90% ownership requirement for effecting a short form merger would not apply to such class of stock.

Ch. 349, L. '96 Synopsis of Section 253

The amendment to Section 253(a) is meant to conform Section 253(a) with the 1974 amendment to Section 251(b) and the 1994 amendment to Section 151(a). The amendment makes clear that the terms of the merger may be made dependent upon facts ascertainable outside of the resolution of the board of directors to so merge, so long that it is made clear in the resolution the precise way that these facts will affect the terms of the resolution. The amendment to Section 253(a) also makes clear that a "fact" can include an event or a determination or action by any person or body, including an event or determination within the control of the corporation or a person or body affiliated with the corporation, such as a decision by its board of directors or one of its officers or agents. This amendment is not intended to alter the fiduciary duties of a board of directors in adopting such a merger resolution with terms that turn on determinations or actions made by any person or body, or in making any determination or taking any action constituting a fact under this section.

Ch. 299, L. '95 Synopsis of Section 253

Section 251(g), enacted in 1995, authorizes a corporation to engage in a holding company reorganization, without stockholder approval, subject to compliance with the conditions specified in Section 251(g). The amendment to Section 253(a) prevents circumvention of the protections accorded by subsection (g)(7)(i) of Section 251 through a short-form merger with an intermediate parent corporation.

Commentary on Section 253

The amendments to Sections 252 and 253 by Ch. 61, L. '93, eff. 7-1-93, authorize a Delaware corporation to merge directly into a non-U.S. corporation if the laws under which the non-U.S. corporation is organized permits a corporation of such jurisdiction to merge or consolidate with a corporation of another jurisdiction.

.1 Application of section.—Specific section that permits merger of subsidiary into parent does not bar such merger under general section providing for merger of any two domestic corporations. *Federal United Corp v Havender, 11 A2d 331 (1940),* rev'g, *Havender v Federal United Corp, 6 A2d 618 (Ch Ct 1939).*

Short-form cash-out merger by 97.6% stockholders with corporation they set up was void when only purpose was to freeze out minority interest and terms of merger were grossly inadequate and unfair to minority; use of corporate power, absent valid business purpose and fair transaction, breached fiduciary duty of majority to minority. *Roland International Corp v Najjar, 407 A2d 1032 (1979).*

Tender offer and subsequent cash-out merger were proper when group including two key officers/directors of target put together plan whereby they were able to acquire complete ownership of target by using target's assets to finance cost of acquisition. *Field v Allyn, 457 A2d 1089 (Ch Ct),* aff'd, *467 A2d 1274 (1983).*

Minority stockholders' positive vote on proposed merger was uninformed because material information was withheld by majority stockholder under circumstances amounting to breach of fiduciary duty so merger did not meet test of fair dealing or fair price and minority was entitled to appraisal. Requirement that merger be for business purpose is no longer necessary in view of fairness test required in parent-subsidiary mergers, expanded appraisal remedy now available to shareholders, and broad discretion Chancellor has to fashion relief. *Weinberger v UOP Inc, 457 A2d 701 (1983).*

Short-form merger that complies with statutory procedures and does not violate fiduciary duty of fairness and good faith owed by majority to minority stockholders may be lawful even though it is freeze-out merger; so when minority stockholder had contracted to sell his stock back to corporation upon termination of employment, that special contractual relationship rendered freeze-out merger not necessarily improper; cashed-out minority stockholder was not entitled to summary judgment granting relief. *Coleman v Taub, 638 F2d 628 (3d Cir 1981).*

Merger between parent and subsidiary was fair to subsidiary's minority shareholders when (1) merger negotiations were conducted at arms length and parent did not dictate terms of merger, (2) price paid for minority's share was fair, (3) directors' decision to delegate subsidiary's asset valuation to engineering firm was proper exercise of business judgment, and (4) subsidiary met its duty of complete candor in proxy statement. *Rosenblatt v Getty Oil Co, 493 A2d 929 (1985).*

The entire fairness standard of review for a merger is triggered where a 50% unit-holder in an limited liability company that is also represented by a majority of the board of managers approves a merger of the limited liability company into its wholly-owned subsidiary in a transaction that will reduce the other unit-holder's interest from 50% to 5% and no advance notice of the merger is given to the other unit-holder. *Solar Cells, Inc v True North Partners, LLC, 2002 Del Ch LEXIS 38 (Ch Ct 2002).*

Directors breached their fiduciary duty of loyalty to minority shareholders of a corporation by allowing its wholly-owned subsidiary to become the corporation's parent, leaving the former parent with no assets other than its now-minority interest in the former subsidiary. *Grace Brothers, Ltd v UniHolding Corp, C.A. No. 17612 (Ch Ct 7-12-00).*

.2 Duty of complete candor—breach.—Failure to disclose oil and gas reserves of approximately $1 billion ($3.00—$3.45 per share) prior to a cash-out merger constituted a breach of the corporation's duty of complete candor. The minority shareholders were denied material information since understatement of the reserves "significantly alter[ed] the total mix of information available" to the reasonable shareholder's decision whether to accept consideration from the short-form merger or to alternatively elect the remedy of appraisal. *Smith v Shell Petroleum, Inc, No. 8395 (Ch Ct 6-19-90).*

Facts showed that parent-subsidiary merger negotiations were conducted in a fair and appropriately deliberative manner; proxy statement was extensive and fully informed the minority shareholders who overwhelmingly approved merger; and minority shareholders received their substantial, fair equivalent in value for their surrendered shares. Thus, minority shareholder failed to prove either unfair dealings or unfair price and court dismissed ten year old class action. *Citron v DuPont de Nemours & Co, No. 6219 (Ch Ct 6-29-90).*

A majority shareholder making a tender offer for all of a corporation's stock does not make inequitably coercive disclosures where its disclosures are made in good faith and merely relay truthful facts about the corporation and its situation. *Next Level Communications, Inc v Motorola, Inc., 2003 Del. Ch. LEXIS 13 (Ch Ct 2003).*

In a short-form merger, a single number purporting to encompass the value of a corporation that is not supported with any financial information whatsoever is insufficient, as a matter of law, to satisfy the duty of disclosure. *Erickson v Centennial Beauregard Cellular, 2003 Del. Ch. LEXIS 38 (Ch Ct 2003).*

.3 Alien corporation.—Statute that prohibits "short merger" between an alien corporation and a domestic one permits merger between two domestic corporations, even though they are wholly owned subsidiaries of domestic corporation. *Braasch v Goldschmidt, 199 A2d 760 (Ch Ct 1964).*

.4 Accumulated dividends.—Delaware corporation can eliminate accumulated dividends on preferred stock by merging with wholly owned subsidiary. *Hottenstein v York Ice Mach Corp, 136 F2d 944 (3d Cir 1943).*

.5 Appraisal rights.—In fixing value of share of stockholders' dissenting from "short-merger," court will use (1) earnings and dividends for five-year period before merger, (2) premium prices offered for shares as factor in market value, and (3) exclusive distribution agreement as part of assets value; earnings and assets should each be weighed 25%, market value at 50%. *In re Olivetti Underwood Corp, 246 A2d 800 (Ch Ct 1968).*

Stockholders dissenting from short merger are not entitled to liquidating value, but only to same "going-concern" value as in regular merger, since they have opportunity to remain as stockholders in surviving corporation. *Application of Delaware Racing Ass'n, 213 A2d 203 (1965).*

Stockholders dissenting from short merger do not get appraisal rights when, though they file written objections, they fail also to demand payment for their shares; also, corporation cannot look behind registered owner's right to seek appraisal, when it has no proof any beneficial owner objects. *Abraham & Co v Olivetti Underwood Corp, 204 A2d 740 (Ch Ct 1964).*

In short form merger, dissenting stockholder of subsidiary corporation cannot get appraisal for his shares when he does not specifically make written demand for payment of their value, even though he could not object to merger itself and he did make written objection to cash amount he was being offered as "unrealistic"—that is not enough to meet statute's mandatory demand requirements. *Carl Marks & Co v Universal City Studios, Inc, 233 A2d 63 (1967).*

A dissenter's demand for payment for his shares on the merger of a subsidiary into its parent must be postmarked within 20 days after the postmark date on the notice of merger. *Coyne v Schenley Industries, Inc, 147 A2d 647 (Ch Ct 1958),* aff'd, *Schenley Industries, Inc v Curtis, 152 A2d 300 (1959).* See also, *Stauffer v Standard Brands, Inc, 178 A2d 311 (Ch Ct),* aff'd, *187 A2d 78 (1962).*

Minority stockholder of subsidiary can seek damages from parent for violation of federal securities acts, when parent allegedly used false and misleading statements to buy up enough shares to enable it to effect merger with subsidiary, since merger statute would obligate stockholder to sell her shares at appraised value. *Voege v American Sumatra Tobacco Corp, 241 FSupp 369 (D Del 1965).*

Majority stockholder is not liable to minority stockholders when he causes corporation to distribute shares it owns in another corporation as stock dividend, and then makes tender offer for these shares at price allegedly below another offer, since other offer is for purchase of net assets for liquidation purposes, not for going concern value of shares, even though majority stockholder did become owner of 90% of other corporation's stock, and can, if he wishes, effect short form merger of liquidation. *Eps-tein v The Celotex Corp, 238 A2d 843 (Ch Ct 1968).*

Corporate directors that effected short merger to freeze out minority stockholders did not violate antifraud rule; minority could have their shares appraised, so allegedly low valuation placed on them did not, in itself, constitute actionable fraud. *Green v Santa Fe Industries Inc, 391 FSupp 849 (SDNY 1975).*

Court will approve appraiser's final report that fixed merger price of $28 per share for stockholders of corporation who refused to accept price of $28 originally offered for their stock for merger of corporation's 92% subsidiary into it, since appraiser's price was properly weighted 25% on assets, 40% on market value and 35% on earnings. *Lebman v National Union Electric Corp, 414 A2d 824 (Ch Ct 1980).*

Preferred shareholders' interest could be eliminated in tender offer-reverse cash-out merger at price less than liquidated value of preferred stock in corporate charter because (1) liquidation preference could only be paid in event of liquidation of assets, (2) merger was not a liquidation, (3) minority interest along with its preferential rights, can be eliminated by merger, and (4) payment was fair to preferred shareholders. *Rothschild International Corp v Liggett Group Inc, 474 A2d 133 (1984).*

Minority shareholders who were "cashed out" pursuant to Delaware short-form merger could not bring action under New York's Martin Act because merger was not fraudulent or unfair so their sole remedy was to seek appraisal. *Loengard v Santa Fe Industries, Inc, 639 FSupp 673 (SDNY 1986).*

Shareholder who elected to pursue appraisal remedy is not foreclosed from thereafter bringing action to rescind merger, when at time of making election it did not know facts upon which right to rescission allegedly rests. However, shareholder may not simultaneously litigate to judgment statutory action for fair value of stock and action for fraud or breach of fiduciary duty seeking rescission of merger because forms of relief—appraisal relief and either rescissory relief or damages—are inconsistent and shareholder must choose between them at some time. Shareholders must make election no later than time at which either of two actions is set for trial, this gives them fullest opportunity to discover facts relating to election. *Cede & Co v Technicolor, Inc, Nos. 7129 and 8358 (Ch Ct 1-13-87).*

A non-tendering stockholder with appraisal rights who is squeezed out in a back-end, cash-out merger after a tender offer may not challenge the disclosures issued in connection with that tender offer when the tender offer was effected by a majority stockholder who already possessed the voting power to force the merger. *Andra v Blount, C.A. No. 17154 (Ch Ct 3-29-00).*

Minority shareholders who waived their appraisal rights are not entitled to expedited proceedings to determine the value of their investment in a squeeze out merger where they waited five months after the initiation of the merger process to request the expedited proceedings and where monetary damages could compensate them for any injury they suffered. *Wand Equity Portfolio II LP v AMFM Internet Holding Inc, 2001 Del. Ch. LEXIS 17 (Ch Ct 2001).*

A modified quasi-appraisal remedy, requiring opt-in and repayment of consideration received by minority shareholders, is an appropriate remedy for a breach of the duty to disclose in connection with a short-form merger where full disclosure is no longer necessary. *Gilliland v Motorola, Inc, 2005 Del. Ch. LEXIS 33 (Ch Ct 2005).*

The discounted cash flow (DCF) method of valuation is preferred in an appraisal action where management projections are reliable. *Andaloro v. PFPC Worldwide, Inc, 2005 Del. Ch. LEXIS 125(Ch Ct 2005).*

.6 Effect of merger.—Delaware parent that merges with its wholly owned Delaware subsidiary can take over unemployment insurance merit rating earned by subsidiary while qualified and doing business in Florida. *Texas Co v Florida Industrial Comm'n, 20 So2d 680 (Fla 1945).*

.7 Enjoining merger.—Minority stockholders of subsidiary cannot set aside its merger into parent unless it affirmatively shows terms are unfair to them; they are not unfair merely because there is disparity between value of subsidiary's transferred assets and that of parent's stock received in exchange. *Sterling v Mayflower Hotel Corp, 89 A2d 862 (Ch Ct), aff'd, 93 A2d 107 (1952).*

Preferred stockholders of New York corporation cannot bar its merger with its wholly owned New York and Delaware subsidiaries merely because plan would eliminate accrued arrears of dividends and would make them majority rather then minority stockholders, unless they can show such unfairness as to amount to fraud. *Zobel v American Locomotive Co, 44 NYS2d 33 (SCt 1943).*

Preferred stockholders cannot bar merger of their corporation with its wholly owned subsidiary when they do not proffer substantial evidence that the merger would unduly advance interests of common stockholders as against preferred; they must show unfairness tantamount to fraud. *Porges v Vadsco Sales Corp, 32 A2d 148 (Ch Ct 1943).* To same effect, *MacCrone v American Capital Corp, 51 FSupp 462 (D Del 1943).* Same test applies to any plan of reclassification of stock interests, even when merger is not involved. *Barrett v Denver Tramway Corp, 146 F2d 701 (3d Cir 1944).*

When reorganization is to give stockholders of old company interest in new one, transfer of corporate assets to new corporation will be set aside as fraudulent, unless all stockholders of same class can participate on equally favorable terms. *Eagleson v Pacific Timber Co, 270 F 1008 (D Del 1920).*

Short-form merger enjoinable under antifraud rule. *Green v Santa Fe Industries, Inc, 533 F2d 1283 (2d Cir 1976).* United States Supreme Court reversed at *Santa Fe Industries v Green, 430 US 462 (1977).*

When parent corporation tried to get around provision in charter of its subsidiary requiring 80% vote for merger with corporation that held more than 5% of its shares, by causing subsidiary to merge into newly formed subsidiary wholly owned by first subsidiary under another charter provision that allowed merger with nonoperating corporation by majority vote, court said basic purpose of merger was to eliminate minority shares in first subsidiary and granted injunction without passing on fairness of price offered per share of alleged benefits of merger with parent. *Young v Valhi, Inc, 382 A2d 1372 (Ch Ct 1978).*

Stockholder claiming sole purpose of merger was to eliminate minority stockholders at inadequate price must establish that no valid business purpose existed for merger when corporation's notice of merger gave several reasons that might constitute valid purpose. *Temple v Combined Properties Corp, 410 A2d 1375 (Ch Ct 1979).*

Court issued preliminary injunction to prevent corporation that owned 93% of second corporation from proceeding with a cash-out merger of second corporation into a wholly owned subsidiary.

Merger will cause irreparable harm when shareholders have not received sufficient information to make informed decision whether to accept merger price or elect appraisal or other judicial remedy. Irreparable harm warranting injunctive relief may be found when damages will be difficult to prove. *Sealy Mattress Co of New Jersey, Inc v Sealy, Inc, 532 A2d 1324 (Ch Ct 1987).*

A noncoercive tender offer made by a corporation's majority shareholder will not be enjoined even though the corporation's board is not independent and has not offered an opinion as to the fairness of the transaction. *In re Aquila, Inc Shareholders Litigation, 805 A2d 184 (Ch Ct 2002).*

A tender offer by a controlling shareholder for all shares of a corporation that it does not already own is coercive where it includes within the definition of the "minority" those stockholders that are affiliated

§253

with the controlling shareholder and those members of the corporation's management whose incentives are skewed by various agreements. *In re Pure Resources, Inc, Shareholders Litigation,* 2002 Del. Ch. LEXIS 112 (Ch Ct 2002).

.8 Challenge to merger.—Defeated tender offeror could not challenge merger between target and competing tender offeror. *Reason:* defeated tender offeror had bid to control target which removed him from status of shareholder confronted with ordinary shareholder decisions to that of competing tender offeror without standing to sue. *Kalmanovitz v G Heileman Brewing Co,* 595 FSupp 1385 (D Del 1984).

In suit challenging cash-out merger, plaintiff must allege specified acts of fraud, misrepresentation, or other items of misconduct to demonstrate unfairness of merger terms to minority. Court dismissed complaint in suit challenging cash-out merger because allegations in complaint did not support entire fairness claim predicated upon unfair price and purported failure to obtain highest possible price for company. Delaware no longer requires business purpose for cash-out mergers. *Kleinhandler v Borgia,* No. 8334 (Ch Ct 3-31-87).

Minority shareholders of a bank holding company, challenging a short-form merger of their corporation into the majority shareholder (another corporation) on substantive (un)fairness grounds, stated cognizable claims of unfair dealing and unfair price where they alleged that defendants, directors of the majority shareholder corporation, did not utilize a special committee of disinterested directors or provide for appraisal by a vote of a majority of the minority stockholders and used a legally improper valuation method to determine the merger price. *Nebel v Southwest Bancorp, Inc, C.A.* No. 13618 (Ch Ct 3-9-99).

.9 Equitable remedies.—Complaint by minority shareholder alleging breach of fiduciary duty by majority shareholder in approving merger allegedly fraudulent to minority stated cause of action in equity when monetary relief was only practical remedy available and majority established that minority had overwhelmingly approved merger. *Harman v Masoneilan International Inc,* 442 A2d 487 (1982).

Rescissory damages were inappropriate as remedy for minority shareholders who sold stock after receiving misleading proxy statement outlining proposed merger. Rescissory damages are appropriate even when majority's breach of fiduciary duty was arguably unintended. But they were inappropriate in this case because of speculative nature of their proof. Court fixed minority's damages at $1 per share because price was in range that would have been fair to minority. *Weinberger v UOP, Inc,* No. 5642 (Ch Ct 1-30-85).

The only appropriate remedy, absent illegality or fraud, for a minority shareholder challenging a statutory short-form merger is appraisal; and where a minority shareholder challenged the entire fairness of a merger without seeking appraisal, that shareholder was left without a remedy. *In re Unocal Exploration Corp Shareholders Litigation, C.A.* No. 12453 (Ch Ct 6-13-00).

.10 Surviving corporation as successor.—Surviving corporation can enforce an agreement with the absorbed corporation's vice-president that he would not divulge its trade secrets nor work for a competitor anywhere in the United States for five years after leaving its employ. *Alabama Binder & Chem Corp v Pa Ind Chem Corp,* 189 A2d 180 (Pa Com Pls 1963).

.11 Derivative standing; former shareholder.—Controlling shareholders were not liable for any alleged misstatements or fraud in connection with freeze-out merger because misstatements caused no injury to shareholder who was frozen out. Shareholder did not have standing to bring derivative suit for breach of fiduciary duty because he was no longer shareholder and remedies available to minority shareholders facing short-form merger are limited to injunctive relief if merger is unfair and appraisal rights if merger is fair. *Harnett v Billman,* 800 F2d 1308 (4th Cir 1986).

.12 Warrants.—A standard anti-destruction clause in a warrant does not entitle the warrantholder to a quasi-appraisal remedy when the corporation, the stock of which is represented by the warrant, merges with another corporation—warrantholders who are entitled to receive the same merger consideration as common stockholders are not thereby guaranteed all the rights (contractual, statutory, or common law) that would have belonged to them had they actually converted their warrants into common stock before the merger. *Aspen Advisors LLC v United Artists Theatre Co,* 843 A2d 697 (Ch Ct), aff'd, 861 A2d 1251 (2004).

.13 Tender offer disclosures.—The omission of management projections in tender offer disclosures are not material where they constitute minutiae that do not alter the total mix of information available to a reasonable investor. *Abrons v Maree,* 2006 Del. Ch. LEXIS 170 (Ch Ct 2006).

.14 Short form merger; number of shares needed.—A minority shareholder does not state a claim, in an attempt to challenge a short form merger, by claiming that preferred shareholders' right to approve and consent to the merger is equivalent to the right to vote on the merger where the certificate of designation provides that the preferred shareholders may approve a merger, but have no voting rights. *Matulich v Aegis Comm'ns Group, Inc,* 2007 Del. Ch. LEXIS 80 (Ch Ct 2007).

.15 Statutory short-form merger; fiduciary duties.—The appropriate remedy in a "short form" merger, where the corporation's minority stockholders are involuntarily cashed out without being furnished the factual information material to an informed shareholder decision whether or not to seek appraisal, is a quasi-appraisal class action to recover the difference between fair value and the merger price without having to opt in to that proceeding or to escrow any merger proceeds that they received. *Berger v Pubco Corp,* 2009 Del. LEXIS 345 (2009).

254 MERGER OR CONSOLIDATION OF DOMESTIC CORPORATION AND JOINT-STOCK OR OTHER ASSOCIATION.—(a) The term "joint-stock association" as used in this section, includes any association of the kind commonly known as a joint-stock association or joint-stock company and any unincorporated association, trust or enterprise having members or having outstanding shares of stock or other evidences of financial or beneficial interest therein, whether formed by agreement or under statutory authority or otherwise, but does not include a corporation, partnership or limited liability company. The term "stockholder" as used in this section, includes every member of such joint-stock association or holder of a share of stock or other evidence of financial or beneficial interest therein.

(b) Any 1 or more corporations of this State may merge or consolidate with 1 or more joint-stock associations, except a joint-stock association formed under the laws of a state which forbids such merger or consolidation. Such corporation or corporations and such 1 or more joint-stock associations may merge into a single corporation, or joint-stock association, which may be any 1 of such corporations or joint-stock associations, or they may consolidate into a new corporation or joint-stock association of this State, pursuant to an agreement of merger or consolidation, as the case may be, complying and approved in accordance with this section. The surviving or resulting entity may be organized for profit or not organized for profit, and if the surviving or resulting entity is a corporation, it may be a stock corporation or a nonstock corporation.

(c) Each such corporation and joint-stock association shall enter into a written agreement of merger or consolidation. The agreement shall state: (1) The terms and conditions of the merger or consolidation; (2) the mode of carrying the same into effect; (3) the manner, if any, of converting the shares of stock of each stock corporation, the interest of members of each nonstock corporation, and the shares, membership or financial or beneficial interests in each of the joint-stock associations into shares or other securities of a stock corporation or membership interests of a nonstock corporation or into shares, memberships or financial or beneficial interests of the joint-stock association surviving or resulting from such merger or consolidation, or of cancelling some or all of such shares, memberships or financial or beneficial interests, and, if any shares of any such stock corporation, any membership interests of any such nonstock corporation or any shares, memberships or financial or beneficial interests in any such joint-stock association are not to remain outstanding, to be converted solely into shares or other securities of the stock corporation or membership interests of the nonstock corporation or into shares, memberships or financial or beneficial interests of the joint-stock association surviving or resulting from such merger or consolidation or to be cancelled, the cash, property, rights or securities of any other corporation or entity which the holders of shares of any such stock corporation, membership interests of any such nonstock corporation, or shares, memberships or financial or beneficial interests of any such joint-stock association are to receive in exchange for, or upon conversion of such shares, membership interests or shares, memberships or financial or beneficial interests, and the surrender of any certificates evidencing them, which cash, property, rights or securities of any other corporation or entity may be in addition to or in lieu of shares or other securities of the stock corporation or membership interests of the nonstock corporation or shares, memberships or financial or beneficial interests of the joint-stock association surviving or resulting from such merger or consolidation; and (4) such other details or provisions as are deemed desirable, including, without limiting the generality of the foregoing, a provision for the payment of cash in lieu of the issuance of fractional shares where the surviving or resulting entity is a corporation. There shall also be set forth in the agreement such other matters or provisions as shall then be required to be set forth in certificates of incorporation or documents required to establish and maintain a joint-stock association by the laws of this State and that can be stated in the case of such merger or consolidation. Any of the terms of the agreement of merger or consolidation may be made dependent upon facts ascertainable outside of such agreement, provided that the manner in which such facts shall operate upon the terms of the agreement is clearly and expressly set forth in the agreement of merger or consolidation. The term "facts," as used in the preceding sentence, includes, but is not limited to, the occurrence of any event, including a determination or action by any person or body, including the corporation.

(d) The agreement required by subsection (c) of this section shall be adopted, approved, certified, executed and acknowledged by each of the stock or nonstock corporations in the same manner as is provided in §251 or §255 of this title, respectively, and in the case of the joint-stock associations in accordance with their articles of association or other instrument containing the provisions by which they are organized or regulated or in accordance with the laws of the state under which they are formed, as the case may be. Where the surviving or resulting entity is a corporation, the agreement shall be filed and shall become effective for all purposes of the laws of this State when and as provided in §251 of this title with respect to the merger or consolidation of corporations of this State. In lieu of filing the agreement of merger or consolidation, where the surviving or resulting entity is a corporation it may file a certificate of merger or consolidation, executed in accordance with §103 of this title, which states:

(1) The name and state of domicile of each of the constituent entities;

(2) That an agreement of merger or consolidation has been approved, adopted, certified, executed and acknowledged by each of the constituent entities in accordance with this subsection;

(3) The name of the surviving or resulting corporation;

(4) In the case of a merger, such amendments or changes in the certificate of incorporation of the surviving corporation as are desired to be effected by the merger *(which amendments or changes may amend and restate the certificate of incorporation of the surviving corporation in its entirety)*, or, if no such amendments or changes are desired, a statement that the certificate of incorporation of the surviving corporation shall be its certificate of incorporation;

(5) In the case of a consolidation, that the certificate of incorporation of the resulting corporation shall be as is set forth in an attachment to the certificate;

(6) That the executed agreement of consolidation or merger is on file at an office of the surviving corporation and the address thereof; and

(7) That a copy of the agreement of consolidation or merger will be furnished by the surviving corporation, on request and without cost, to any stockholder of any constituent entity.

Where the surviving or resulting entity is a joint-stock association, the agreement shall be filed and shall be effective for all purposes when filed in accordance with the laws regulating the creation of joint-stock associations.

(e) Sections 251(d), 251(e), 251(f), 252(d), 259 through 262 and 328 of this title shall, insofar as they are applicable, apply to mergers or consolidations between corporations and joint-stock associations; the word "corporation" where applicable, as used in those sections, being deemed to include joint-stock associations as defined herein. The second sentence of §251(c) of this title shall be applicable to any merger or consolidation under this section. Where the surviving or resulting entity is a corporation, the personal liability, if any, of any stockholder of a joint-stock association existing at the time of such merger or consolidation shall not thereby be extinguished, shall remain personal to such stockholder and shall not become the liability of any subsequent transferee of any share of stock in such surviving or resulting corporation or of any other stockholder of such surviving or resulting corporation.

(f) Nothing in this section shall be deemed to authorize the merger of a charitable nonstock corporation or charitable joint-stock association into a stock corporation or joint-stock association if the charitable status of such nonstock corporation or joint-stock association would be thereby lost or impaired, but a stock corporation or joint-stock association may be merged into a charitable nonstock corporation or charitable joint-stock association which shall continue as the surviving corporation or joint-stock association. (Last amended by Ch. 290, L. '10, eff. 8-2-10.)

Ch. 290, L. '10, eff. 8-2-10, added matter in italic.

Ch. 290, L. '10 Synopsis of Section 254

These sections amend Sections 251(b)(3), 251(c)(4), 252(c)(4), 254(d)(4), 263(c)(4), and 264(c)(4), respectively, to clarify that in a merger the certificate of incorporation of the surviving corporation may be amended and restated in its entirety.

Ch. 84, L. '03 Synopsis of Section 254

The amendments to Sections 251, 252, 253, 254, 255, 256, 257, 263 and 264 clarify that shares or other interests of a constituent corporation or other entity to a merger or consolidation may be converted, cancelled or unaffected by the merger.

Ch. 339, L. '98 Synopsis of Section 254

The amendments to Sections 251, 252, 253, 254, 255, 256, 257, 263 and 264 clarify that shares or other interests of a constituent corporation or other entity to a merger or consolidation may be converted, cancelled or unaffected by the merger.

The amendment to subsection (e) of Section 254 provides that the contemporaneous amendment to Section 251(c) shall be applicable to mergers and consolidations under this section.

Ch. 120, L. '97 Synopsis of Section 254

The amendment to Section 254(e) is meant to conform Section 254 to other sections relating to mergers and consolidations by requiring a non-Delaware joint-stock or other association surviving a merger or consolidation to appoint the Secretary of State as agent for service of process following the merger or consolidation.

Ch. 349, L. '96 Synopsis of Section 254

The amendments to Sections 251(b), 252(b), 254(c), 255(b), 256(b), 257(b), 263(b), and 264(b) are intended to conform these sections with the 1994 amendment to Section 151(a). The amendments make clear that a "fact" can include an event or a determination or action by any person or body, including an event or determination within the control of the corporation or a person or body affiliated with the corporation, such as a decision by its board of directors or one of its officers or agents. These amendments are not intended to alter the fiduciary duties of a board of directors in authorizing a merger agreement with terms that turn on determinations or actions made by any person or body, or in making any determination or taking any action constituting a fact under these sections.

The amendments to Sections 251(c)(6), 252(c)(6), 254(d)(6), 263(c)(6) and 264(c)(6) eliminate the requirement that the executed agreement of consolidation or merger be on file at the principal place of business of the surviving corporation or entity in cases where a certificate of merger or consolidation is filed with the Secretary of State in lieu of the agreement of consolidation or merger. The amendment permits the executed agreement of consolidation or merger to be on file at any office of the surviving corporation or entity, whether or not its principal place of business.

Commentary on Section 254(b), (c), (d), (e) and (f)

The amendments to Section 254(b) permit an existing corporation to be merged into an existing corporation to consolidate with an existing joint-stock association into a new joint-stock association.

Section 254(c) has been revised to explain what requirements must be in the written agreement of merger or consolidation where the surviving or new entity is a joint-stock association.

Section 254(d) has been amended to provide that where the surviving or resulting entity is a joint-stock association, the agreement created pursuant to subsection (c) need only be filed as required by the laws governing joint-stock associations.

Section 254(e) has been amended to provide that where the surviving or resulting entity is a corporation, the liability of a stockholder to the corporation will continue to not become the liability of a subsequent transferee.

Section 254(f) has been redrafted to insure that the current restrictions and benefits involved in a merger between a charitable nonstock corporation and a stock corporation, are extended to include the same restrictions and benefits where the particular entities may be joint-stock associations or charitable joint-stock associations.

255 [1] **MERGER OR CONSOLIDATION OF DOMESTIC NONSTOCK CORPORATIONS.**—(a) Any 2 or more nonstock corporations of this State, whether or not organized for profit, may merge into a single corporation, which may be any 1 of the constituent corporations, or they may consolidate into a new nonstock corporation, whether or not organized for profit, formed by the consolidation, pursuant to an agreement of merger or consolidation, as the case may be, complying and approved in accordance with this section.

(b) Subject to subsection (d) of this section, the governing body of each corporation which desires to merge or consolidate shall adopt a resolution approving an agreement of merger or consolidation. The agreement shall state:
(1) The terms and conditions of the merger or consolidation;
(2) The mode of carrying the same into effect;
(3) Such other provisions or facts required or permitted by this chapter to be stated in a certificate of incorporation for nonstock corporations as can be stated in the case of a merger or consolidation, stated in such altered form as the circumstances of the case require;
(4) The manner, if any, of converting the memberships or membership interests of each of the constituent corporations into memberships or membership interests of the corporation surviving or resulting from the merger or consolidation, or of cancelling some or all of such memberships or membership interests; and
(5) Such other details or provisions as are deemed desirable.
The agreement so adopted shall be executed and acknowledged in accordance with §103 of this title. Any of the terms of the agreement of merger or consolidation may be made dependent upon facts ascertainable outside of such agreement, provided that the manner in which such facts shall operate upon the terms of the agreement is clearly and expressly set forth in the agreement of merger or consolidation. The term "facts," as used in the preceding sentence, includes, but is not limited to, the occurrence of any event, including a determination or action by any person or body, including the corporation.

(c) Subject to subsection (d) of this section, the agreement shall be submitted to the members of each constituent corporation, at an annual or special meeting thereof for the purpose of acting on the agreement. Due notice of the time, place and purpose of the meeting shall be mailed to each member of each such corporation who has the right to vote for the election of the members of the governing body of the corporation and to each other member who is entitled to vote on the merger under the certificate of incorporation or the bylaws of such corporation, at the member's address as it appears on the records of the corporation, at least 20 days prior to the date of the meeting. The notice shall contain a copy of the agreement or a brief summary thereof. At the meeting the agreement shall be considered and a vote, in person or by proxy, taken for the adoption or rejection of the agreement. If the agreement is adopted by a majority of the members of each such corporation entitled to vote for the election of the members of the governing body of the corporation and any other members entitled to vote on the merger under the certificate of incorporation or the bylaws of such corporation, then that fact shall be certified on the agreement by the officer of each such corporation performing the duties ordinarily performed by the secretary or assistant secretary of a corporation, provided that such certification on the agreement shall not be required if a certificate of merger or consolidation is filed in lieu of filing the agreement. If the agreement shall be adopted and certified by each constituent corporation in accordance with this section, it shall be filed and shall become effective in accordance with §103 of this title. The provisions set forth in the last sentence of §251(c) of this title shall apply to a merger under this section, and the reference therein to "stockholder" shall be deemed to include "member" hereunder.

(d) Notwithstanding subsections (b) or (c) of this section, if, under the certificate of incorporation or the bylaws of any 1 or more of the constituent corporations, there shall be no members who have the right to vote for the election of the members of the governing body of the corporation, or for the merger, other than the members of the governing body themselves, no further action by the governing body or the members of such corporation shall be necessary if the resolution approving an agreement of merger or consolidation has been adopted by a majority of all the members of the governing body thereof, and that fact shall be certified on the agreement in the same manner as is provided in the case of the adoption of the agreement by the vote of the members of a corporation, provided that such certification on the agreement shall not be required if a certificate of merger or consolidation is filed in lieu of filing the agreement, and thereafter the same procedure shall be followed to consummate the merger or consolidation.

(e) Section 251(d) of this title shall apply to a merger under this section; provided, however, that references to the board of directors, to stockholders, and to shares of a constituent corporation shall be deemed to be references to the governing body of the corporation, to members of the corporation, and to memberships or membership interests, as applicable, respectively.

(f) Section 251(e) of this title shall apply to a merger under this section.

(g) Nothing in this section shall be deemed to authorize the merger of a charitable nonstock corporation into a nonstock corporation if such charitable nonstock corporation would thereby have its charitable status lost or impaired; but a nonstock corporation may be merged into a charitable nonstock corporation which shall continue as the surviving corporation. (Last amended by Ch. 253, L. '10, eff. 8-1-10.)

Ch. 253, L. '10, eff. 8-1-10, added matter in italic and deleted [1]"MERGER OR CONSOLIDATION OF DOMESTIC NONSTOCK CORPORATIONS.—(a) Any 2 or more nonstock corporations of this State, whether or not organized for profit, may merge into a single corporation, which may be any 1 of the constituent corporations, or they may consolidate into a new nonstock corporation, whether or not organized for profit, formed by the consolidation, pursuant to an agreement of merger or consolidation, as the case may be, complying and approved in accordance with this section.

(b) The governing body of each corporation which desires to merge or consolidate shall adopt a resolution approving an agreement of merger or consolidation. The agreement shall state: (1) The terms and conditions of the merger or consolidation; (2) the mode of carrying the same into effect; (3) such other provisions or facts required or permitted by this chapter to be stated in a certificate of incorporation for nonstock corporations as can be stated in the case of a merger or consolidation, stated in such altered form as the circumstances of the case require; (4) the manner, if any, of converting the memberships of each of the constituent corporations into memberships of the corporation surviving or resulting from the merger or consolidation, or of cancelling some or all of such membership interests; and (5) such other details or provisions as are deemed desirable. Any of the terms of the agreement of merger or consolidation may be made dependent upon facts ascertainable outside of such agreement, provided that the manner in which such facts shall operate upon the terms of the agreement is clearly and expressly set forth in the agreement of merger or consolidation. The term "facts," as used in the preceding sentence, includes, but is not limited to, the occurrence of any event, including a determination or action by any person or body, including the corporation.

(c) The agreement shall be submitted to the members of each constituent corporation who have the right to vote for the election of the members of the governing body of their corporation, at an annual or special meeting thereof for the purpose of acting on the agreement. Due notice of the time, place and purpose of the meeting shall be mailed to each member of each such corporation who has the right to vote for the election of the members of the governing body of the corporation, at the member's address as it appears on the records of the corporation, at least 20 days prior to the date of the meeting. The notice shall contain a copy of the agreement or a brief summary thereof, as the governing body shall deem advisable. At the meeting the agreement shall be considered and a vote by ballot, in person or by proxy, taken for the adoption or rejection of the agreement. If a majority of the voting power of members of each such corporation who have the voting power above mentioned shall be for the adoption of the agreement, then that fact shall be certified on the agreement by the officer of each such corporation performing the duties ordinarily performed by the secretary or assistant secretary of a corporation, provided that such certification on the agreement shall not be required if a certificate of merger or consolidation is filed in lieu of filing the agreement. The agreement so adopted and certified shall be executed, acknowledged and filed, and shall become effective, in accordance with §103 of this title. The provisions set forth in the last sentence of subsection (c) of §251 shall apply to a merger under this section, and the reference therein to "stockholder" shall be deemed to include "member" hereunder.

(d) If, under the certificate of incorporation of any 1 or more of the constituent corporations, there shall be no members who have the right to vote for the election of the members of the governing body of the corporation other than the members of that body themselves, the agreement duly entered into as provided in subsection (b) of this section shall be submitted to the members of the governing body of such corporation or corporations, at a meeting thereof. Notice of the meeting shall be mailed to the members of the governing body in the same manner as is provided in the case of a meeting of the members of a corporation. If at the meeting two thirds of the total number of members of the governing body shall vote by ballot, in person, for the adoption of the agreement, that fact shall be certified on the agreement in the same manner as is provided in the case of the adoption of the agreement by the vote of the members of a corporation, provided that such certification on the agreement shall not be required if a certificate of merger or consolidation is filed in lieu of filing the agreement, and thereafter the same procedure shall be followed to consummate the merger or consolidation.

(e) Subsection (e) of §251 shall apply to a merger under this section.

(f) Nothing in this section shall be deemed to authorize the merger of a charitable nonstock corporation into a nonstock corporation if such charitable nonstock corporation would thereby have its charitable status lost or impaired; but a nonstock corporation may be merged into a charitable nonstock corporation which shall continue as the surviving corporation."

Ch. 253, L. '10 Synopsis of Section 255

Section 41 amends §255 of the DGCL to ensure that §255 is consistent with the terms used in the translator provision in new §114(a) and to clarify procedures regarding the execution, acknowledgment, adoption, and certification of the merger agreement. This Section also amends §255(c) to clarify that members may vote on a merger if, under the corporation's certificate or incorporation or bylaws, they are entitled to vote on the merger or for the election of the members of the governing body. The amendment to §255(c) further clarifies that the decision to include either a copy or a summary of an agreement of merger or consolidation in a notice of a meeting of the members of a constituent nonstock corporation need not be approved by a specific act of the governing body of the nonstock corporation. The amendment is not intended to define or limit any duty of members of the governing body relating to disclosure to members in connection with the transaction. This Section further amends §255 to provide that, if no members of the corporation are entitled to vote on the merger other those who are members of the governing body, only a single vote is required to approve the agreement of merger or consolidation, so long as the resolution approving that agreement of merger or consolidation is approved by a majority of all the members of the governing body. This amendment dispenses with the need for a second vote authorizing a merger and decreases the necessary vote from two-thirds of the members of the governing body to a majority of the members of the governing body. This Section also amends the DCGL to add new §255(e), which provides that §251(d), as translated for application to nonstock corporations, shall apply to mergers under §255.

Ch. 145, L. '07 Synopsis of Section 255

The amendments to §251 and §255 eliminate the requirement that an agreement of merger or consolidation include a certification by the secretary or assistant secretary of the corporation that the agreement has been adopted by the requisite vote of the stockholders or members, as applicable, or otherwise approved in accordance with §251 without a vote of the stockholders, if a certificate of merger or consolidation is filed in lieu of filing the agreement. The certification requirement for a Delaware corporation is also eliminated from §§252, 254, 256, 257, 258, 263 and 264 by virtue of the cross-references to §251 and §255. Any certification required under other applicable law is not affected by the amendments to §251 and §255.

Ch. 84, L. '03 Synopsis of Section 255

The amendments to Sections 251, 252, 253, 254, 255, 256, 257, 263 and 264 clarify that shares or other interests of a constituent corporation or other entity to a merger or consolidation may be converted, cancelled or unaffected by the merger.

Ed. Note: This section is effective only with respect to mergers and consolidations for which the notice of the stockholders meeting to vote thereon has been mailed after July 1, 1987.

Ch. 123, L. '99 Synopsis of Section 255

The amendment to Section 255(c) conforms the vote of the members required to approve a merger of a nonstock corporation to the vote required to approve a merger of a stock corporation by changing the required vote from a two-thirds vote to a majority vote of the members.

Ch. 349, L. '96 Synopsis of Section 255

The amendments to Sections 251(b), 252(b), 254(c), 255(b), 256(b), 257(b), 263(b), and 264(b) are intended to conform these sections with the 1994 amendment to Section 151(a). The amendments make clear that a "fact" can include an event or a determination or action by any person or body, including an event or determination within the control of the corporation or a person or body affiliated with the corporation, such as a decision by its board of directors or one of its officers or agents. These amendments are not intended to alter the fiduciary duties of a board of directors in authorizing a merger agreement with terms that turn on determinations or actions made by any person or body, or in making any determination or taking any action constituting a fact under these sections.

256 MERGER OR CONSOLIDATION OF DOMESTIC AND FOREIGN NONSTOCK CORPORATIONS; SERVICE OF PROCESS UPON SURVIVING OR RESULTING CORPORATION.—(a) Any 1 or more nonstock corporations of this State may merge or consolidate with 1 or more other nonstock corporations of any other state or states of the United States, or of the District of Columbia if the laws of such other state or states or of the District permit a corporation of such jurisdiction to merge with a corporation of another jurisdiction. The constituent corporations may merge into a single corporation, which may be any 1 of the constituent corporations, or they may consolidate into a new nonstock corporation formed by the consolidation, which may be a corporation of the state of incorporation of any 1 of the constituent corporations, pursuant to an agreement of merger or consolidation, as the case may be, complying and approved in accordance with this section. In addition, any 1 or more nonstock corporations organized under the laws of any jurisdiction other than 1 of the United States may merge or consolidate with 1 or more nonstock corporations of this State if the surviving or resulting corporation will be a corporation of this State, and if the laws under which the other corporation or corporations are formed permit a corporation of such jurisdiction to merge with a corporation of another jurisdiction.

(b) All the constituent corporations shall enter into an agreement of merger or consolidation.[1] *The agreement shall state:*
 (1) *The terms and conditions of the merger or consolidation;*
 (2) *The mode of carrying the same into effect;*
 (3) *The manner, if any, of converting the memberships or membership interests of each of the constituent corporations into memberships or membership interests of the corporation surviving or resulting from such merger or consolidation or of cancelling some or all of such memberships or membership interests;*
 (4) *Such other details and provisions as shall be deemed desirable; and*
 (5) *Such other provisions or facts as shall then be required to be stated in a certificate of incorporation by the laws of the state which are stated in the agreement to be the laws that shall govern the surviving or resulting corporation and that can be stated in the case of a merger or consolidation.*

Any of the terms of the agreement of merger or consolidation may be made dependent upon facts ascertainable outside of such agreement, provided that the manner in which such facts shall operate upon the terms of the agreement is clearly and expressly set forth in the agreement of merger or consolidation. The term "facts," as used in the preceding sentence, includes, but is not limited to, the occurrence of any event, including a determination or action by any person or body, including the corporation.

(c) The agreement shall be adopted, approved, certified, executed and acknowledged by each of the constituent corporations in accordance with the laws under which it is formed and, in the case of a Delaware corporation, in the same manner as is provided in §255 of this title. The agreement shall be filed and shall become effective for all purposes of the laws of this State when and as provided in §255 of this title with respect to the merger of nonstock corporations of this State. Insofar as they may be applicable, the provisions set forth in the last sentence of subsection (c) of §252 of this title shall apply to a merger under this section, and the reference therein to "stockholder" shall be deemed to include "member" hereunder.

(d) [2] *If the corporation surviving or resulting from the merger or consolidation is to be governed by the laws of any state other than this State, it shall agree that it may be served with process in this State in any proceeding for enforcement of any obligation of any constituent corporation of this State, as well as for enforcement of any obligation of the surviving or resulting corporation arising from the merger or consolidation and shall irrevocably appoint the Secretary of State as its agent to accept service of process in any suit or other proceedings and shall specify the address to which a copy of such process shall be mailed by the Secretary of State.* Process may be served upon the Secretary of State under this subsection by means of electronic transmission but only as prescribed by the Secretary of State. The Secretary of State is authorized to issue such rules and regulations with respect to such service as the Secretary of State deems necessary or appropriate. In the event of such service upon the Secretary of State in accordance with this subsection, the Secretary of State shall forthwith notify such surviving or resulting corporation thereof by letter, directed to such corporation at its address so specified, unless such surviving or resulting corporation shall have designated in writing to the Secretary of State a different address for such purpose, in which case it shall be mailed to the last address so designated. Such letter shall be sent by a mail or courier service that includes a record of mailing or deposit with the courier and a record of delivery evidenced by the signature of the recipient. Such letter shall enclose a copy of the process and any other papers served upon the Secretary of State. It shall be the duty of the plaintiff in the event of such service to serve process and any other papers in duplicate, to notify the Secretary of State that service is being made pursuant to this subsection, and to pay the Secretary of State the sum of $50 for the use of the State, which sum shall be taxed as a part of the costs in the proceeding if the plaintiff shall prevail therein. The Secretary of State shall maintain an alphabetical record of any such service setting forth

§256

the name of the plaintiff and defendant, the title, docket number and nature of the proceeding in which process has been served upon the Secretary of State, the fact that service has been effected pursuant to this subsection, the return date thereof, and the day and hour when the service was made. The Secretary of State shall not be required to retain such information for a period longer than 5 years from receipt of the service of process.

(e) Subsection (e) of §251 of this title shall apply to a merger under this section if the corporation surviving the merger is a corporation of this State.

(f) Section 251(d) of this title shall apply to a merger under this section; provided, however, that references to the board of directors, to stockholders, and to shares of a constituent corporation shall be deemed to be references to the governing body of the corporation, to members of the corporation, and to memberships or membership interests, as applicable, respectively.

(g) Nothing in this section shall be deemed to authorize the merger of a charitable nonstock corporation into a nonstock corporation, if the charitable status of such charitable nonstock corporation would thereby be lost or impaired; but a nonstock corporation may be merged into a charitable nonstock corporation which shall continue as the surviving corporation. (Last amended by Ch. 253, L. '10, eff. 8-1-10 and Ch. 290, L. '10, eff. 8-2-10.)

Ch. 253, L. '10, eff. 8-1-10, added matter in italic and deleted [1]"The agreement shall state: (1) The terms and conditions of the merger or consolidation; (2) the mode of carrying the same into effect; (3) the manner, if any, of converting the memberships of each of the constituent corporations into memberships of the corporation surviving or resulting from such merger or consolidation or of cancelling some or all of such memberships; (4) such other details and provisions as shall be deemed desirable; and (5) such other provisions or facts as shall then be required to be stated in a certificate of incorporation by the laws of the state which are stated in the agreement to be the laws that shall govern the surviving or resulting corporation and that can be stated in the case of a merger or consolidation." in paragraph (b). Ch. 290, L. '10, eff. 8-2-10, added matter in italic and deleted [2]"If the corporation surviving or resulting from the merger or consolidation is to be governed by the laws of any state other than this State, it shall agree that it may be served with process in this State in any proceeding for enforcement of any obligation of any constituent corporation of this State, as well as for enforcement of any obligation of the surviving or resulting corporation arising from the merger or consolidation and shall irrevocably appoint the Secretary of State as its agent to accept service of process in any suit or other proceedings and shall specify the address to which a copy of such process shall be mailed by the Secretary of State. In the event of such service upon the Secretary of State in accordance with this subsection, the Secretary of State shall forthwith notify such surviving or resulting corporation thereof by letter, certified mail, return receipt requested, directed to such corporation at its address so specified, unless such surviving or resulting corporation shall have designated in writing to the Secretary of State a different address for such purpose, in which case it shall be mailed to the last address so designated. Such letter shall enclose a copy of the process and any other papers served upon the Secretary of State." in paragraph (d).

Ch. 290, L. '10 Synopsis of Section 256

These sections amend Sections 252(d), 256(d), 263(d), 264(d), 266(c)(6), 321(b), 376(b), 381(c), 382(a), 382(c), and 390(b)(5), respectively, to allow for service of process upon the Secretary of State thereunder by means of electronic transmission but only as prescribed by the Secretary of State, to authorize the Secretary of State to issue such rules and regulations with respect to such service as the Secretary of State deems necessary or appropriate, and to enable the Secretary of State, in the event that service is effected through the Secretary of State in accordance therewith, to provide notice of service by letter sent by a mail or courier service that includes a record of mailing or deposit with the courier and a record of delivery evidenced by the signature of the recipient.

Ch. 253, L. '10 Synopsis of Section 256

Sections 42 and 43 amend §256 of the DGCL to ensure that §256 is consistent with the terms used in the translator provision in new §114(a); to add new §256(f), which provides that §251(d), as translated for application to nonstock corporations, shall apply to mergers under §256; and to add new §256(g) to clarify that nothing in §256 shall be deemed to authorize the merger of a charitable nonstock corporation into a nonstock corporation, if the charitable status of such charitable nonstock corporation would thereby be lost or impaired.

Ch. 84, L. '03 Synopsis of Section 256

The amendments to Sections 251, 252, 253, 254, 255, 256, 257, 263 and 264 clarify that shares or other interests of a constituent corporation or other entity to a merger or consolidation may be converted, cancelled or unaffected by the merger.

Ch. 339, L. '98 Synopsis of Section 256

The amendment to this Section eliminates masculine references in the statutes, and replaces them with gender neutral references.

Ch. 349, L. '96 Synopsis of Section 256

The amendments to Sections 251(b), 252(b), 254(c), 255(b), 256(b), 257(b), 263(b), and 264(b) are intended to conform these sections with the 1994 amendment to Section 151(a). The amendments make clear that a "fact" can include an event or a determination or action by any person or body, including an event or determination within the control of the corporation or a person or body affiliated with the corporation, such as a decision by its board of directors or one of its officers or agents. These amendments are not intended to alter the fiduciary duties of a board of directors in authorizing a merger agreement with terms that turn on determinations or actions made by any person or body, or in making any determination or taking any action constituting a fact under these sections.

Commentary on Sections 102(a)(4), 170(a) and 256

In recent years various amendments to the General Corporation Law have been made to clarify that Delaware corporations can be set up as nonstock corporations for profit. Thus, in the 1974 amendment to Section 255(b) and (c), the words "nonprofit" were eliminated from the caption of the section, and in the 1987 amendment to Section 255(a) and (b), the words "nonprofit" were eliminated from subsection (a) and the words "whether or not organized for profit" were added. The Commentary to the 1987 amendment which accompanied the proposed amendment to Section 255 states: "In view of Section 257, there is no reason not to permit mergers of domestic nonstock corporations organized for profit." A similar amendment was not presented to Section 256. The 1987 amendment to Section 276 eliminated the word "nonprofit" at several places in the body of subsection (a). The Commentary to the 1987 amendment which accompanied the proposed amendment states that the purposes of these changes was "to make clear that Section 276 applies to all nonstock corporations." The proposed amendments will make the General Corporation Law more consistent in this regard.

.1 **Procedure—notice.**—When statute requires giving of notice by registered mail, written notice actually given and received by ordinary mail will be sufficient, at least under Miller Act, which court said was highly remedial. *Fleisher Engineering & Constr Co v U.S., 311 US 15 (1940)*.

257 [1] *MERGER OR CONSOLIDATION OF DOMESTIC STOCK AND NONSTOCK CORPORATIONS.*—(a) *Any 1 or more nonstock corporations of this State, whether or not organized for profit, may merge or consolidate with 1 or more stock corporations of this State, whether or not organized for profit. The constituent corporations may merge into a single corporation, which may be any 1 of the constituent corporations, or they may consolidate into a new corporation formed by the consolidation, pursuant to an agreement of merger or consolidation, as the case may be, complying and approved in accordance with this section. The surviving constituent corporation or the new corporation may be organized for profit or not organized for profit and may be a stock corporation or a nonstock corporation.*

(b) The board of directors of each stock corporation which desires to merge or consolidate and the governing body of each nonstock corporation which desires to merge or consolidate shall adopt a resolution approving an agreement of merger or consolidation. The agreement shall state:

(1) The terms and conditions of the merger or consolidation;

(2) The mode of carrying the same into effect;

(3) Such other provisions or facts required or permitted by this chapter to be stated in a certificate of incorporation as can be stated in the case of a merger or consolidation, stated in such altered form as the circumstances of the case require;

(4) The manner, if any, of converting the shares of stock of a stock corporation and the memberships or membership interests of a nonstock corporation into shares or other securities of a stock corporation or memberships or membership interests of a nonstock corporation surviving or resulting from such merger or consolidation or of cancelling some or all of such shares or memberships or membership interests, and, if any shares of any such stock corporation or memberships or membership interests of any such nonstock corporation are not to remain outstanding, to be converted solely into shares or other securities of the stock corporation or memberships or membership interests of the nonstock corporation surviving or resulting from such merger or consolidation or to be cancelled, the cash, property, rights or securities of any other corporation or entity which the holders of shares of any such stock corporation or memberships or membership interests of any such nonstock

corporation are to receive in exchange for, or upon conversion of such shares or memberships or membership interests, and the surrender of any certificates evidencing them, which cash, property, rights or securities of any other corporation or entity may be in addition to or in lieu of shares or other securities of any stock corporation or memberships or membership interests of any nonstock corporation surviving or resulting from such merger or consolidation; and

(5) Such other details or provisions as are deemed desirable.

In such merger or consolidation the memberships or membership interests of a constituent nonstock corporation may be treated in various ways so as to convert such memberships or membership interests into interests of value, other than shares of stock, in the surviving or resulting stock corporation or into shares of stock in the surviving or resulting stock corporation, voting or nonvoting, or into creditor interests or any other interests of value equivalent to their memberships or membership interests in their nonstock corporation. The voting rights of members of a constituent nonstock corporation need not be considered an element of value in measuring the reasonable equivalence of the value of the interests received in the surviving or resulting stock corporation by members of a constituent nonstock corporation, nor need the voting rights of shares of stock in a constituent stock corporation be considered as an element of value in measuring the reasonable equivalence of the value of the interests in the surviving or resulting nonstock corporations received by stockholders of a constituent stock corporation, and the voting or nonvoting shares of a stock corporation may be converted into any type of membership or membership interest, however designated, creditor interests or participating interests, in the nonstock corporation surviving or resulting from such merger or consolidation of a stock corporation and a nonstock corporation. Any of the terms of the agreement of merger or consolidation may be made dependent upon facts ascertainable outside of such agreement, provided that the manner in which such facts shall operate upon the terms of the agreement is clearly and expressly set forth in the agreement of merger or consolidation. The term "facts," as used in the preceding sentence, includes, but is not limited to, the occurrence of any event, including a determination or action by any person or body, including the corporation.

(c) The agreement required by subsection (b) of this section, in the case of each constituent stock corporation, shall be adopted, approved, certified, executed and acknowledged by each constituent corporation in the same manner as is provided in §251 of this title and, in the case of each constituent nonstock corporation, shall be adopted, approved, certified, executed and acknowledged by each of said constituent corporations in the same manner as is provided in §255 of this title. The agreement shall be filed and shall become effective for all purposes of the laws of this State when and as provided in §251 of this title with respect to the merger of stock corporations of this State. Insofar as they may be applicable, the provisions set forth in the last sentence of §251(c) of this title shall apply to a merger under this section, and the reference therein to "stockholder" shall be deemed to include "member" hereunder.

(d) Section 251(e) of this title shall apply to a merger under this section, if the surviving corporation is a corporation of this State; §251(d) of this title and the second sentence of §251(c) of this title shall apply to any constituent stock corporation participating in a merger or consolidation under this section; and §251(f) of this title shall apply to any constituent stock corporation participating in a merger under this section.

(e) Section 251(d) of this title shall apply to a merger under this section; provided, however, that, for purposes of a constituent nonstock corporation, references to the board of directors, to stockholders, and to shares of a constituent corporation shall be deemed to be references to the governing body of the corporation, to members of the corporation, and to memberships or membership interests, as applicable, respectively.

(f) Nothing in this section shall be deemed to authorize the merger of a charitable nonstock corporation into a stock corporation, if the charitable status of such nonstock corporation would thereby be lost or impaired; but a stock corporation may be merged into a charitable nonstock corporation which shall continue as the surviving corporation. (Last amended by Ch. 253, L. '10, eff. 8-1-10.)

Ch. 253, L. '10, eff. 8-1-10, added matter in italic and deleted [1]"MERGER OR CONSOLIDATION OF DOMESTIC STOCK AND NONSTOCK CORPORATIONS.—(a) Any 1 or more nonstock corporations of this State, whether or not organized for profit, may merge or consolidate with 1 or more stock corporations of this State, whether or not organized for profit. The constituent corporations may merge into a single corporation, which may be any 1 of the constituent corporations, or they may consolidate into a new corporation formed by the consolidation, pursuant to an agreement of merger or consolidation, as the case may be, complying and approved in accordance with this section. The surviving constituent corporation or the new corporation may be organized for profit or not organized for profit and may be a stock corporation or a nonstock corporation.

(b) The board of directors of each stock corporation which desires to merge or consolidate and the governing body of each nonstock corporation which desires to merge or consolidate shall adopt a resolution approving an agreement of merger or consolidation. The agreement shall state: (1) The terms and conditions of the merger or consolidation; (2) the mode of carrying the same into effect; (3) such other provisions or facts required or permitted by this chapter to be stated in a certificate of incorporation as can be stated in the case of a merger or consolidation, stated in such altered form as the circumstances of the case require; (4) the manner, if any, of converting the shares of stock of a stock corporation and the interests of the members of a nonstock corporation into shares or other securities of a stock corporation or membership interests of a nonstock corporation surviving or resulting from such merger or consolidation or of cancelling some or all of such shares or interests, and, if any shares of any such stock corporation or membership interests of any such nonstock corporation are not to remain outstanding, to be converted solely into shares or other securities of the stock corporation or membership interests of the nonstock corporation surviving or resulting from such merger or consolidation or to be cancelled, the cash, property, rights or securities of any other corporation or entity which the holders of shares of any such stock corporation or membership interests of any such nonstock corporation are to receive in exchange for, or upon conversion of such shares or membership interests, and the surrender of any certificates evidencing them, which cash, property, rights or securities of any other corporation or entity may be in addition to or in lieu of shares or other securities of any stock corporation or membership interests of any nonstock corporation surviving or resulting from such merger or consolidation; and (5) such other details or provisions as are deemed desirable. In such merger or consolidation the interests of members of a constituent nonstock corporation may be treated in various ways so as to convert such interests into interests of value, other than shares of stock, in the surviving or resulting stock corporation or into shares of stock in the surviving or resulting stock corporation, voting or nonvoting, or into creditor interests or any other interests of value equivalent to their membership interests in their nonstock corporation. The voting rights of members of a constituent nonstock corporation need not be considered an element of value in measuring the reasonable equivalence of the value of the interests received in the surviving or resulting stock corporation by members of a constituent nonstock corporation, nor need the voting rights of shares of stock in a constituent stock corporation be considered as an element of value in measuring the reasonable equivalence of the value of the interests in the surviving or resulting nonstock corporations received by stockholders of a constituent stock corporation, and the voting or nonvoting shares of a stock corporation may be converted into voting or nonvoting regular, life, general, special or other type of membership, however designated, creditor interests or participating interests, in the nonstock corporation surviving or resulting from such merger or consolidation of a stock corporation and a nonstock corporation. Any of the terms of the agreement of merger or consolidation may be made dependent upon facts ascertainable outside of such agreement, provided that the manner in which such facts shall operate upon the terms of the agreement is clearly and expressly set forth in the agreement of merger or consolidation. The term "facts," as used in the preceding sentence, includes, but is not limited to, the occurrence of any event, including a determination or action by any person or body, including the corporation.

(c) The agreement required by subsection (b) of this section, in the case of each constituent stock corporation, shall be adopted, approved, certified, executed and acknowledged by each constituent corporation in the same manner as is provided in §251 of this title and, in the case of each constituent nonstock corporation, shall be adopted, approved, certified, executed and acknowledged by each of said constituent corporations in the same manner as is provided in §255 of this title. The agreement shall be filed and shall become effective for all purposes of the laws of this State when and as provided in §251 of this title with respect to the merger of stock corporations of this State. Insofar as they may be applicable, the provisions set forth in the last sentence of subsection (c) of §251 of this title shall apply to a merger under this section, and the reference therein to "stockholder" shall be deemed to include "member" hereunder.

(d) Subsection (e) of §251 of this title shall apply to a merger under this section, if the surviving corporation is a corporation of this State; subsection (d) and the second sentence of subsection (c) of §251 of this title shall apply to any constituent stock corporation participating in a merger or consolidation under this section; and subsection (f) of §251 of this title shall apply to any constituent stock corporation participating in a merger under this section.

(e) Nothing in this section shall be deemed to authorize the merger of a charitable nonstock corporation into a stock corporation, if the charitable status of such nonstock corporation would thereby be lost or impaired; but a stock corporation may be merged into a charitable nonstock corporation which shall continue as the surviving corporation."

Ch. 253, L. '10 Synopsis of Section 257

Section 44 amends §257 of the DGCL consistent with the intent of the bill and with the translator provision in new §114(a). This Section also amends the DGCL to add new §257(e), which provides that §251(d), as translated for application to nonstock corporations, shall apply to mergers under §257.

Ch. 84, L. '03 Synopsis of Section 257

The amendments to Sections 251, 252, 253, 254, 255, 256, 257, 263 and 264 clarify that shares or other interests of a constituent corporation or other entity to a merger or consolidation may be converted, cancelled or unaffected by the merger.

Ch. 339, L. '98 Synopsis of Section 257

The amendment to subsection (d) of Section 257 provides that the contemporaneous amendment to Section 251(c) shall be applicable to mergers and consolidations under this section.

Ch. 349, L. '96 Synopsis of Section 257

The amendments to Sections 251(b), 252(b), 254(c), 255(b), 256(b), 257(b), 263(b), and 264(b) are intended to conform these sections with the 1994 amendment to Section 151(a). The amendments make clear that a "fact" can include an event or a determination or action by any person or body, including an event or determination within the control of the corporation or a person or body affiliated with the corporation, such as a decision by its board of directors or one of its officers or agents. These amendments are not intended to alter the fiduciary duties of a board of directors in authorizing a merger agreement with terms that turn on determinations or actions made by any person or body, or in making any determination or taking any action constituting a fact under these sections.

.1 Merger with charitable corporation.— Business corporation cannot merge with charitable corporation, even though statute permits merger of stock and nonstock corporations. *Stevens Bros Foundation, Inc v Commissioner,* 324 F2d 633 (8th Cir 1963).

258 MERGER OR CONSOLIDATION OF DOMESTIC AND FOREIGN STOCK AND NONSTOCK CORPORATIONS.—(a) Any 1 or more corporations of this State, whether stock or nonstock corporations and whether or not organized for profit, may merge or consolidate with 1 or more other corporations of any other state or states of the United States or of the District of Columbia whether stock or nonstock corporations and whether or not organized for profit, if the laws under which the other corporation or corporations are formed shall permit such a corporation of such jurisdiction to merge with a corporation of another jurisdiction. The constituent corporations may merge into a single corporation, which may be any 1 of the constituent corporations, or they may consolidate into a new corporation formed by the consolidation, which may be a corporation of the place of incorporation of any 1 of the constituent corporations, pursuant to an agreement of merger or consolidation, as the case may be, complying and approved in accordance with this section. The surviving or new corporation may be either a stock corporation or a [1] *nonstock* corporation, as shall be specified in the agreement of merger required by subsection (b) of this section.

(b) The method and procedure to be followed by the constituent corporations so merging or consolidating shall be as prescribed in §257 of this title in the case of Delaware corporations. The agreement of merger or consolidation shall also set forth such other matters or provisions as shall then be required to be set forth in certificates of incorporation by the laws of the state which are stated in the agreement to be the laws which shall govern the surviving or resulting corporation and that can be stated in the case of a merger or consolidation. The agreement, in the case of foreign corporations, shall be adopted, approved, certified, executed and acknowledged by each of the constituent foreign corporations in accordance with the laws under which each is formed.

[1] *(c) The requirements of §252(d) of this title as to the appointment of the Secretary of State to receive process and the manner of serving the same in the event the surviving or new corporation is to be governed by the laws of any other state shall also apply to mergers or consolidations effected under this section. Section 251(e) of this title shall apply to mergers effected under this section if the surviving corporation is a corporation of this State; §251(d) of this title shall apply to any constituent corporation participating in a merger or consolidation under this section (provided, however, that for purposes of a constituent nonstock corporation, references to the board of directors, to stockholders, and to shares shall be deemed to be references to the governing body of the corporation, to members of the corporation, and to memberships or membership interests of the corporation, as applicable, respectively); and §251(f) of this title shall apply to any constituent stock corporation participating in a merger under this section.*

(d) Nothing in this section shall be deemed to authorize the merger of a charitable nonstock corporation into a stock corporation, if the charitable status of such nonstock corporation would thereby be lost or impaired; but a stock corporation may be merged into a charitable nonstock corporation which shall continue as the surviving corporation. (Last amended by Ch. 253, L. '10, eff. 8-1-10.)

Ch. 253, L. '10, eff. 8-1-10, added matter in italic and deleted [1]"membership" and [2]"(c) The requirements of subsection (d) of §252 of this title as to the appointment of the Secretary of State to receive process and the manner of serving the same in the event the surviving or new corporation is to be governed by the laws of any other state shall also apply to mergers or consolidations effected under this section. Subsection (e) of §251 of this title shall apply to mergers effected under this section if the surviving corporation is a corporation of this State; subsection (d) of §251 of this title shall apply to any constituent stock corporation participating in a merger or consolidation under this section; and subsection (f) of §251 of this title shall apply to any constituent stock corporation participating in a merger under this section."

Ch. 253, L. '10 Synopsis of Section 258

Sections 45 and 46 amend §258 of the DGCL consistent with the intent of the bill and with the translator provision in new §114(a) and to clarify that §251(d), as translated for application to nonstock corporations, shall apply to mergers under §258.

Ch. 145, L. '07 Synopsis of Section 258

The amendment to §258(b) clarifies that the agreement of merger or consolidation must also be certified by each of the constituent foreign corporations in accordance with the laws under which each was formed.

259 STATUS, RIGHTS, LIABILITIES, OF CONSTITUENT AND SURVIVING OR RESULTING CORPORATIONS FOLLOWING MERGER OR CONSOLIDATION.—(a) When any merger or consolidation shall have become effective under this chapter, for all purposes of the laws of this State the separate existence of all the constituent corporations, or of all such constituent corporations except the one into which the other or others of such constituent corporations have been merged, as the case may be, shall cease and the constituent corporations shall become a new corporation, or be merged into 1 of such corporations, as the case may be, possessing all the rights, privileges, powers and franchises as well of a public as of a private nature, and being subject to all the restrictions, disabilities and duties of each of such corporations so merged or consolidated; and all and singular, the rights, privileges, powers and franchises of each of said corporations, and all property, real, personal and mixed, and all debts due to any of said constituent corporations on whatever account, as well for stock subscriptions as all other things in action or belonging to each of such corporations shall be vested in the corporation surviving or resulting from such merger or consolidation; and all property, rights, privileges, powers and franchises, and all and every other interest shall be thereafter as effectually the property of the surviving or resulting corporation as they were of the several and respective constituent corporations, and the title to any real estate vested by deed or otherwise, under the laws of this State, in any of such constituent corporations, shall not revert or be in any way impaired by reason of this chapter; but all rights of creditors and all liens upon any property of any of said constituent corporations shall be preserved unimpaired, and all debts, liabilities and duties of the respective constituent corporations shall thenceforth attach to said surviving or resulting corporation, and may be enforced against it to the same extent as if said debts, liabilities and duties had been incurred or contracted by it.

(b) In the case of a merger of banks or trust companies, without any order or action on the part of any court or otherwise, all appointments, designations, and nominations, and all other rights and interests as trustee, executor, administrator, registrar of stocks and bonds, guardian of estates, assignee, receiver, trustee of estates of persons mentally ill and in every other fiduciary capacity, shall be automatically vested in the corporation resulting from or surviving such merger; provided, however, that any party in interest shall have the right to apply to an appropriate court or tribunal for a determination as to whether the surviving corporation shall continue to serve in the same fiduciary capacity as the merged corporation, or whether a new and different fiduciary should be appointed. (Last amended by Ch. 186, L. '67, eff. 1-2-68.)

.1 Effect of section.—Separate existence of all constituent merging corporations terminates except the one into which they are merged. Under it the existence of the merging corporations is terminated on the date of the merger. *U.S. v Borden Co, 23 FSupp 177 (ND Ill 1939),* appeal dismissed in part, and judgment reversed and cause remanded in part, *308 US 188 (1939),*

Jones v Noble Drilling Co, 135 F2d 721 (10th Cir 1943).

Shareholder of acquired corporation cannot maintain derivative suit against surviving corporation after merger is effective; such suit is asset of acquired corporation and passes to surviving company when merger is completed. *Bokat v Getty Oil Co, 262 A2d 246 (1970).* See also, *Heit v Tenneco Inc, 319 FSupp 884 (D Del 1970); Lewis v Anderson, 453 A2d 474 (Ch Ct 1982),* aff'd, *477 A2d 1040 (1984).*

.2 Enjoining merger.—New York court will not enjoin stockholders meeting of Delaware corporation called to consider recapitalization and merger, even though preferred stockholders and directors residents of New York, particularly since same matter is at issue in litigation in Delaware court. *Newman v United Profit-Sharing Corp, 178 NYS 2d 990 (1958).*

Creditor of constituent corporation cannot bar its consolidation with another corporation, since he may pursue his remedy against consolidated corporation. *Cole v National Cash Credit Ass'n, 156 A 183 (Ch Ct 1931).*

Board's decision to acquire target company at relatively high premium with resulting dilution in corporate stock prices, and refusal to back out of merger after stockholder challenge when merger agreement provided for this, were both sound business decisions, since (1) decision to merge was made after long exhaustive study and price was well within authorized range; (2) refusal to back out did not indicate any fraud; and (3) issuance of control stock to allegedly friendly shareholders was not done in order to perpetuate present management. *Muschel v Western Union Corp, 310 A2d 904 (Ch Ct 1973).*

Once merger is accomplished merged corporation ceases to exist for all purposes and former shareholder who wants to challenge validity of merger can only serve surviving corporation even though trial on merits could result in resurrection of merged corporation. *Beals v Washington International, Inc, 386 A2d 1156 (Ch Ct 1978).*

Minority shareholders of subsidiary, 84% owned by parent, cannot bar parent's vote to merge subsidiary into another subsidiary on alleged grounds merger is unfair, since no fraud or blatant overreaching is demonstrated and minority shareholders have recourse to appraisal. *David J Greene & Co v Schenley Industries Inc, 281 A2d 30 (Ch Ct 1971).*

"White knight" could not get injunction barring tender offeror from attempting to acquire it after offeror agreed to refrain from attempting to acquire control of target, which "white knight" later acquired and merged with. *Reasons:* (1) agreement only contemplated control of target not "white knight" and (2) "white knight" did not succeed to benefit of agreement after merger with target when that was not parties' intention. *Mesa Partners v Phillips Petroleum Co, 488 A2d 107 (Ch Ct 1984).*

.3 Short-swing profits.—Corporation surviving merger has right to bring action for short-swing profits under federal securities acts against insider for profits on purchase and sale of stock of merged corporation. *Western Auto Supply Co v Gamble-Skogmo, Inc, 348 F2d 736 (8th Cir 1965),* cert denied, *382 US 987 (1966).*

Successor by merger of original issuer of securities can bring action alleging that unsuccessful tender offeror received illegal short-swing profits under §16(b) of Securities Exchange Act of 1934 when it sold original issuer's stock because cause of action survives merger. *Bunker Ramo-Eltra Corp v Fairchild Industries, Inc, 639 FSupp 409 (D Md 1986).*

.4 Sequestration.—Shares of stock that were sequestered in aid of derivative suit were released from that sequestration when they lost their situs in Delaware as result of corporation's merger with an out of state corporation. *Union Chemical & Materials Corp v Cannon, 148 A2d 348 (1959)* rev'g, *144 A2d 142 (Ch Ct 1958).*

.5 Unemployment insurance.—Delaware parent that mergers with its wholly owned Delaware subsidiary can take over unemployment insurance merit rating earned by subsidiary while qualified and doing business in Florida. *Texas Co v Florida Industrial Comm'n, 20 So2d 680 (Fla 1945).*

.6 Collective bargaining.—While legal requirement that surviving corporation to merger constituent's obligations includes obligations created in favor of employees under collective bargaining agreement, state court cannot enforce rights and duties under agreement until appropriate federal agencies have declared or failed to declare them. *Fitzsimmons v Western Airlines, Inc, 290 A2d 682 (Ch Ct 1972).*

.7 Mutual aid fund agreement.—Surviving corporation in merger assumed constituent's obligations under mutual aid fund agreement, even though agreement had no "successors and assigns" clause, since, on merging, constituent's obligations attach to, and are enforceable against survivor. *Western Airlines, Inc v Allegheny Airlines, Inc, 313 A2d 145 (Ch Ct 1973).*

.8 Liability of successor.—Corporation that merged with manufacturer of insulating materials containing asbestos may be held liable as successor for punitive damages for asbestos injuries because corporation did not simply buy manufacturer's assets, but merged with it, so corporation assumed all manufacturer's liabilities as if it had incurred them itself. *Krull v Celotex Corp, 611 FSupp 146 (ND Ill 1985).*

.9 Agreement governing lender's rights.—Lender corporation, which challenged going-private merger between debtor corporation and debtor's principal shareholder, was entitled to same option to purchase shares of surviving corporation as shareholder-employees of constituent corporation received. *Reason:* Lending corporation had obtained those option rights pursuant to merger provision in its loan agreement with debtor corporation. Corporation was not, however, entitled to any rights or benefits not set forth in loan agreement. Going-private merger also did not breach loan agreement's anti-dilution option when no new shares were being issued; defendants were therefore awarded summary judgment on that part of claim. *American General Corp v Continental Airlines Corp, No. 8390 (Ch Ct 1-26-88).*

.10 Merger, effect on shareholder's standing.—In order to be permitted to maintain a stockholder derivative suit, a plaintiff must be a stockholder at the time of filing of the suit and must remain a shareholder throughout the litigation. A plaintiff who loses his shareholder status by being merged out may attack the validity of allegedly excessive termination payments, provided that he concomitantly challenges the fairness of the merger. A former shareholder who fails to attack merger's fairness is therefore without standing to pursue derivative claims. *Kramer v Western Pacific Industries, Inc, No. 8675 (Ch Ct 9-11-87).*

.11 Derivative claims.—The Delaware Supreme Court declined to overrule *Lewis v. Anderson* so that stock-for-stock mergers between unaffiliated corporations would not preclude continuing stockholders of the parent corporation from pursuing derivative litigation on behalf of a subsidiary corporation. *Lewis v Ward, 852 A2d 896 (2004).*

.12 Double derivative actions.—To maintain a double derivative action, a shareholder who was a pre-merger shareholder in the acquired company and who is a current shareholder, by virtue of a stock-for-stock merger, in the post-merger parent company, is not required to demonstrate that, at the time of the alleged wrongdoing at the acquired company, the shareholder owned stock in the acquiring company, and the acquiring company owned stock in the acquired company. *Lambrecht v O'Neal, 3 A3d 277 (2010).*

260 POWERS OF CORPORATION SURVIVING OR RESULTING FROM MERGER OR CONSOLIDATION; ISSUANCE OF STOCK, BONDS OR OTHER INDEBTEDNESS.—When 2 or more corporations are merged or consolidated, the corporation surviving or resulting from the merger may issue bonds or other obligations, negotiable or otherwise, and with or without coupons or interest certificates thereto attached, to an amount sufficient with its capital stock to provide for all the payments it will be required to make, or obligations it will be required to assume, in order to effect the merger or consolidation. For the purpose of securing the payment of any such bonds and obligations, it shall be lawful for the surviving or resulting corporation to mortgage its corporate franchise, rights, privileges and property, real, personal or mixed. The surviving or resulting corporation may issue certificates of its capital stock *or uncertificated stock if authorized to do so* and other securities to the stockholders of the constituent corporations in exchange or payment for the original shares, in such amount as shall be necessary in accordance with the terms of the agreement of merger or consolidation in order to effect such merger or consolidation in the manner and on the terms specified in the agreement. (Last amended by Ch. 112, L. '83, eff. 7-1-83.)

Ch. 112, L. '83, eff. 7-1-83, added matter in italic.

.1 Corporate separateness—proof of control.—Cross motions for summary judgment were denied in a suit to pierce corporate veil and hold parent corporation liable for payment of interest and principal due on debentures issued by subsidiary prior to merger where there existed triable issues as to (1) the reasonableness of plaintiffs' reliance on rating agencies' reports to prove parent company's control of subsidiaries and (2) whether parent company's use of subsidiaries' assets amounted to lack of corporate separateness. *Mabon, Nugent & Co v Texas American Energy Corp, No. 8578 (Ch Ct 4-12-90).*

261 EFFECT OF MERGER UPON PENDING ACTIONS.—Any action or proceeding, whether civil, criminal or administrative, pending by or against any corporation which is a party to a merger or consolidation shall be prosecuted as if such merger or consolidation had not taken place, or the corporation surviving or resulting from such merger or consolidation may be substituted in such action or proceeding.

.1 Effect of merger on criminal prosecution.—Good faith merger under Delaware law abates criminal prosecution against constituent corporation for violation of Sherman Act. *U.S. v Line Material Co*, 202 F2d 929 (6th Cir 1953). To same effect: *United States v Union Carbide and Carbide Corp*, 132 FSupp 388 (D Colo 1955).

Merger of Delaware corporation into another does not abate indictment for antitrust violations that is pending against first corporation when merger takes place. *United States v Maryland & Virginia Milk Producers, Inc*, 145 FSupp 374 (DC DC 1956).

.2 Effect of merger on stockholder suit.—Corporation had to pay attorney fees for stockholder who had sued corporation and lost by summary judgment, but whose appeal was rendered moot when corporation merged; there was no final decision on merits at time merger made further proceedings unnecessary. *Baron v Allied Artists Pictures Corp*, 395 A2d 375 (Ch Ct 1978).

Majority shareholders/directors breached their fiduciary duties of fair dealing owed to minority shareholders when they approved cash-out merger because (1) merger had intended effect of terminating pending derivative litigation seeking recovery from majority shareholders/directors and (2) no independent agency, either board committee, special counsel or investment banker, provided basis to conclude that derivative claims were without value to corporation or that cash-out price was fair. *Merritt v Colonial Foods, Inc, No. 6078 (Ch Ct 1986).*

262 APPRAISAL RIGHTS.—(a) Any stockholder of a corporation of this State who holds shares of stock on the date of the making of a demand pursuant to subsection (d) of this section with respect to such shares, who continuously holds such shares through the effective date of the merger or consolidation, who has otherwise complied with subsection (d) of this section and who has neither voted in favor of the merger or consolidation nor consented thereto in writing pursuant to §228 of this title shall be entitled to an appraisal by the Court of Chancery of the fair value of the stockholder's shares of stock under the circumstances described in subsections (b) and (c) of this section. [1] *As used in this section, the word "stockholder" means a holder of record of stock in a corporation; the words "stock" and "share" mean and include what is ordinarily meant by those words; and the words "depository receipt" mean a receipt or other instrument issued by a depositary representing an interest in 1 or more shares, or fractions thereof, solely of stock of a corporation, which stock is deposited with the depositary.*

(b) Appraisal rights shall be available for the shares of any class or series of stock of a constituent corporation in a merger or consolidation to be effected pursuant to §251 (other than a merger effected pursuant to §251(g) of this title), §252, §254, *§255, §256,* §257, §258, §263 or §264 of this title:

(1) Provided, however, that no appraisal rights under this section shall be available for the shares of any class or series of stock, which stock, or depository receipts in respect thereof, at the record date fixed to determine the stockholders entitled to receive notice of the meeting of stockholders to act upon the agreement of merger or consolidation, were either (i) listed on a national securities exchange or (ii) held of record by more than 2,000 holders; and further provided that no appraisal rights shall be available for any shares of stock of the constituent corporation surviving a merger if the merger did not require for its approval the vote of the stockholders of the surviving corporation as provided in §251(f) of this title.

(2) Notwithstanding paragraph (1) of this subsection, appraisal rights under this section shall be available for the shares of any class or series of stock of a constituent corporation if the holders thereof are required by the terms of an agreement of merger or consolidation pursuant to §§251, 252, 254, *255, 256,* 257, 258, 263 and 264 of this title to accept for such stock anything except:

a. Shares of stock of the corporation surviving or resulting from such merger or consolidation, or depository receipts in respect thereof;

b. Shares of stock of any other corporation, or depository receipts in respect thereof, which shares of stock (or depository receipts in respect thereof) or depository receipts at the effective date of the merger or consolidation will be either listed on a national securities exchange or held of record by more than 2,000 holders;

c. Cash in lieu of fractional shares or fractional depository receipts described in the foregoing subparagraphs a. and b. of this paragraph; or

d. Any combination of the shares of stock, depository receipts and cash in lieu of fractional shares or fractional depository receipts described in the foregoing subparagraphs a., b. and c. of this paragraph.

[2] *(3) In the event all of the stock of a subsidiary Delaware corporation party to a merger effected under §253 or §267 of this title is not owned by the parent immediately prior to the merger, appraisal rights shall be available for the shares of the subsidiary Delaware corporation.*

(c) Any corporation may provide in its certificate of incorporation that appraisal rights under this section shall be available for the shares of any class or series of its stock as a result of an amendment to its certificate of incorporation, any merger or consolidation in which the corporation is a constituent corporation or the sale of all or substantially all of the assets of the corporation. If the certificate of incorporation contains such a provision, the procedures of this section, including those set forth in subsections (d) and (e) of this section, shall apply as nearly as is practicable.

(d) Appraisal rights shall be perfected as follows:

[3] *(1) If a proposed merger or consolidation for which appraisal rights are provided under this section is to be submitted for approval at a meeting of stockholders, the corporation, not less than 20 days prior to the meeting, shall notify each of its stockholders who was such on the record date for notice of such meeting (or such members who received notice in accordance with §255(c) of this title) with respect to shares for which appraisal rights are available pursuant to subsection (b) or (c) of this section that appraisal rights are available for any or all of the shares of the constituent corporations, and shall include in such notice a copy of this section and, if 1 of the constituent corporations is a nonstock corporation, a copy of §114 of this title. Each stockholder electing to demand the appraisal*

of such stockholder's shares shall deliver to the corporation, before the taking of the vote on the merger or consolidation, a written demand for appraisal of such stockholder's shares. Such demand will be sufficient if it reasonably informs the corporation of the identity of the stockholder and that the stockholder intends thereby to demand the appraisal of such stockholder's shares. A proxy or vote against the merger or consolidation shall not constitute such a demand. A stockholder electing to take such action must do so by a separate written demand as herein provided. Within 10 days after the effective date of such merger or consolidation, the surviving or resulting corporation shall notify each stockholder of each constituent corporation who has complied with this subsection and has not voted in favor of or consented to the merger or consolidation of the date that the merger or consolidation has become effective; or

(2) If the merger or consolidation was approved pursuant to [4] §228, §253, or §267 of this title, then either a constituent corporation before the effective date of the merger or consolidation or the surviving or resulting corporation within 10 days thereafter shall notify each of the holders of any class or series of stock of such constituent corporation who are entitled to appraisal rights of the approval of the merger or consolidation and that appraisal rights are available for any or all shares of such class or series of stock of such constituent corporation, and shall include in such notice a copy of this section *and, if 1 of the constituent corporations is a nonstock corporation, a copy of §114 of this title.* Such notice may, and, if given on or after the effective date of the merger or consolidation, shall, also notify such stockholders of the effective date of the merger or consolidation. Any stockholder entitled to appraisal rights may, within 20 days after the date of mailing of such notice, demand in writing from the surviving or resulting corporation the appraisal of such holder's shares. Such demand will be sufficient if it reasonably informs the corporation of the identity of the stockholder and that the stockholder intends thereby to demand the appraisal of such holder's shares. If such notice did not notify stockholders of the effective date of the merger or consolidation, either (i) each such constituent corporation shall send a second notice before the effective date of the merger or consolidation notifying each of the holders of any class or series of stock of such constituent corporation that are entitled to appraisal rights of the effective date of the merger or consolidation or (ii) the surviving or resulting corporation shall send such a second notice to all such holders on or within 10 days after such effective date; provided, however, that if such second notice is sent more than 20 days following the sending of the first notice, such second notice need only be sent to each stockholder who is entitled to appraisal rights and who has demanded appraisal of such holder's shares in accordance with this subsection. An affidavit of the secretary or assistant secretary or of the transfer agent of the corporation that is required to give either notice that such notice has been given shall, in the absence of fraud, be prima facie evidence of the facts stated therein. For purposes of determining the stockholders entitled to receive either notice, each constituent corporation may fix, in advance, a record date that shall be not more than 10 days prior to the date the notice is given, provided, that if the notice is given on or after the effective date of the merger or consolidation, the record date shall be such effective date. If no record date is fixed and the notice is given prior to the effective date, the record date shall be the close of business on the day next preceding the day on which the notice is given.

(e) Within 120 days after the effective date of the merger or consolidation, the surviving or resulting corporation or any stockholder who has complied with subsections (a) and (d) of this section hereof and who is otherwise entitled to appraisal rights, may commence an appraisal proceeding by filing a petition in the Court of Chancery demanding a determination of the value of the stock of all such stockholders. Notwithstanding the foregoing, at any time within 60 days after the effective date of the merger or consolidation, any stockholder who has not commenced an appraisal proceeding or joined that proceeding as a named party shall have the right to withdraw such stockholder's demand for appraisal and to accept the terms offered upon the merger or consolidation. Within 120 days after the effective date of the merger or consolidation, any stockholder who has complied with the requirements of subsections (a) and (d) of this section hereof, upon written request, shall be entitled to receive from the corporation surviving the merger or resulting from the consolidation a statement setting forth the aggregate number of shares not voted in favor of the merger or consolidation and with respect to which demands for appraisal have been received and the aggregate number of holders of such shares. Such written statement shall be mailed to the stockholder within 10 days after such stockholder's written request for such a statement is received by the surviving or resulting corporation or within 10 days after expiration of the period for delivery of demands for appraisal under subsection (d) of this section hereof, whichever is later. Notwithstanding subsection (a) of this section, a person who is the beneficial owner of shares of such stock held either in a voting trust or by a nominee on behalf of such person may, in such person's own name, file a petition or request from the corporation the statement described in this subsection.

(f) Upon the filing of any such petition by a stockholder, service of a copy thereof shall be made upon the surviving or resulting corporation, which shall within 20 days after such service file in the office of the Register in Chancery in which the petition was filed a duly verified list containing the names and addresses of all stockholders who have demanded payment for their shares and with whom agreements as to the value of their shares have not been reached by the surviving or resulting corporation. If the petition shall be filed by the surviving or resulting corporation, the petition shall be accompanied by such a duly verified list. The Register in Chancery, if so ordered by the Court, shall give notice of the time and place fixed for the hearing of such petition by registered or certified mail to the surviving or resulting corporation and to the stockholders shown on the list at the addresses therein stated. Such notice shall also be given by 1 or more publications at least 1 week before the day of the hearing, in a newspaper of general circulation published in the City of Wilmington, Delaware or such publication as the Court deems advisable. The forms of the notices by mail and by publication shall be approved by the Court, and the costs thereof shall be borne by the surviving or resulting corporation.

(g) At the hearing on such petition, the Court shall determine the stockholders who have complied with this section and who have become entitled to appraisal rights. The Court may require the stockholders who have demanded an appraisal for their shares and who hold stock represented by certificates to submit their certificates of stock to the Register in Chancery for notation thereon of the pendency of the appraisal proceedings; and if any stockholder fails to comply with such direction, the Court may dismiss the proceedings as to such stockholder.

(h) After the Court determines the stockholders entitled to an appraisal, the appraisal proceeding shall be conducted in accordance with the rules of the Court of Chancery, including any rules specifically governing appraisal proceedings. Through such proceeding the Court shall determine the fair value of the shares exclusive of any element of value arising from the accomplishment or expectation of the merger or consolidation, together with interest, if any, to be paid upon the amount determined to be the fair value. In determining such fair value, the Court shall take into account all relevant factors. Unless the Court in its discretion determines otherwise for good cause shown, interest from the effective date of the merger through the date of payment of the judgment shall be compounded quarterly and shall accrue at 5% over the Federal Reserve discount rate (including any surcharge) as established from time to time during the period between the effective date of the merger and the date of payment of the judgment. Upon application by the surviving or resulting corporation or by any stockholder entitled to participate in the appraisal proceeding, the Court may, in its discretion, proceed to trial upon the appraisal prior to the final determination of the stockholders entitled to an appraisal. Any stockholder whose name appears on the list filed by the surviving or resulting corporation pursuant to subsection (f) of this section and who has submitted such stockholder's certificates of stock to the Register in Chancery, if such is required, may participate fully in all proceedings until it is finally determined that such stockholder is not entitled to appraisal rights under this section.

(i) The Court shall direct the payment of the fair value of the shares, together with interest, if any, by the surviving or resulting corporation to the stockholders entitled thereto. Payment shall be so made to each such stockholder, in the case of holders of uncertificated stock forthwith, and the case of holders of shares represented by certificates upon the surrender to the corporation of the certificates representing such stock. The Court's decree may be enforced as other decrees in the Court of Chancery may be enforced, whether such surviving or resulting corporation be a corporation of this State or of any state.

(j) The costs of the proceeding may be determined by the Court and taxed upon the parties as the Court deems equitable in the circumstances. Upon application of a stockholder, the Court may order all or a portion of the expenses incurred by any stockholder in connection with the appraisal proceeding, including, without limitation, reasonable attorney's fees and the fees and expenses of experts, to be charged pro rata against the value of all the shares entitled to an appraisal.

(k) From and after the effective date of the merger or consolidation, no stockholder who has demanded appraisal rights as provided in subsection (d) of this section shall be entitled to vote such stock for any purpose or to receive payment of dividends or other distributions on the stock (except dividends or other distributions payable to stockholders of record at a date which is prior to the effective date of the merger or consolidation); provided, however, that if no petition for an appraisal shall be filed within the time provided in subsection (e) of this section, or if such stockholder shall deliver to the surviving or resulting corporation a written withdrawal of such stockholder's demand for an appraisal and an acceptance of the merger or consolidation, either within 60 days after the effective date of the merger or consolidation as provided in subsection (e) of this section or thereafter with the written approval of the corporation, then the right of such stockholder to an appraisal shall cease. Notwithstanding the foregoing, no appraisal proceeding in the Court of Chancery shall be dismissed as to any stockholder without the approval of the Court, and such approval may be conditioned upon such terms as the Court deems just; provided, however that this provision shall not affect the right of any stockholder who has not commenced an appraisal proceeding or joined that proceeding as a named party to withdraw such stockholder's demand for appraisal and to accept the terms offered upon the merger or consolidation within 60 days after the effective date of the merger or consolidation, as set forth in subsection (e) of this section.

(l) The shares of the surviving or resulting corporation to which the shares of such objecting stockholders would have been converted had they assented to the merger or consolidation shall have the status of authorized and unissued shares of the surviving or resulting corporation. (Last amended by Ch. 253, L. '10, eff. only with respect to transactions consummated pursuant to agreements entered into after August 1, 2010 (or, in the case of mergers pursuant to Section 253, resolutions of the board of directors adopted after August 1, 2010), and appraisal proceedings arising out of such transactions and Ch. 290, L. '10, eff. only with respect to transactions consummated pursuant to agreements entered into after August 1, 2010 (or, in the case of mergers pursuant to Section 253, resolutions of the board of directors adopted after August 1, 2010 and in the case of mergers pursuant to Section 267, mergers authorized after August 1, 2010), and appraisal proceedings arising out of such transactions.)

Ch. 253, L. '10, eff. as stated above, added matter in italic and deleted [1]"As used in this section, the word "stockholder" means a holder of record of stock in a stock corporation and also a member of record of a nonstock corporation; the words "stock" and "share" mean and include what is ordinarily meant by those words and also membership or membership interest of a member of a nonstock corporation; and the words "depository receipt" mean a receipt or other instrument issued by a depository representing an interest in one or more shares, or fractions thereof, solely of stock of a corporation, which stock is deposited with the depository." and [3]"(1) If a proposed merger or consolidation for which appraisal rights are provided under this section is to be submitted for approval at a meeting of stockholders, the corporation, not less than 20 days prior to the meeting, shall notify each of its stockholders who was such on the record date for notice of such meeting with respect to shares for which appraisal rights are available pursuant to subsection (b) or (c) hereof that appraisal rights are available for any or all of the shares of the constituent corporations, and shall include in such notice a copy of this section. Each stockholder electing to demand the appraisal of such stockholder's shares shall deliver to the corporation, before the taking of the vote on the merger or consolidation, a written demand for appraisal of such stockholder's shares. Such demand will be sufficient if it reasonably informs the corporation of the identity of the stockholder and that the stockholder intends thereby to demand the appraisal of such stockholder's shares. A proxy or vote against the merger or consolidation shall not constitute such a demand. A stockholder electing to take such action must do so by a separate written demand as herein provided. Within 10 days after the effective date of such merger or consolidation, the surviving or resulting corporation shall notify each stockholder of each constituent corporation who has complied with this subsection and has not voted in favor of or consented to the merger or consolidation of the date that the merger or consolidation has become effective; or" in paragraphs (a), (b), (b)(2), (d)(1), and (d)(2). Ch. 290, L. '10, eff. as stated above, added matter in italic and deleted [2]"(3) In the event all of the stock of a subsidiary Delaware corporation party to a merger effected under §253 of this title is not owned by the parent corporation immediately prior to the merger, appraisal rights shall be available for the shares of the subsidiary Delaware corporation." in paragraph (b)(3) and [4]"§228 or §253" in paragraph (d)(2).

Ch. 290, L. '10 Synopsis of Section 262

These sections amend Sections 104, 111(a)(6), 114(b)(2), 262(b)(3), and 262(d)(2), respectively, to reflect new Section 267.

Ch. 253, L. '10 Synopsis of Section 262

Sections 47, 48, 49, and 50 amend §262 of the DGCL to ensure that the translator provision in new §114(a) operates properly on §262, to clarify that §262 applies to mergers under §255 and §256, and to amend §262(d) to provide notice procedures appropriate for nonstock corporations, including requiring that a copy of new §114 be provided if one of the constituent corporations is a nonstock corporation. These amendments shall be effective only with respect to transactions consummated pursuant to agreements entered into after August 1, 2010 (or, in the case of mergers pursuant to Section 253, resolutions of the board of directors adopted after August 1, 2010), and appraisal proceedings arising out of such transactions.

Ch. 14, L. '09 Synopsis of Section 262

These sections are technical amendments to Section 262 to make it consistent with the revisions to Section 213(a).

Ch. 145, L. '07 Synopsis of Section 262

These amendments revise the specifications regarding the application of §262 and the availability of appraisal rights, in order to accommodate ongoing changes in the structure and identification of securities trading markets, including recent changes in the configuration and status of securities trading markets administered by The National Association of Securities Dealers, Inc.

The amendment to §262(k) and an amendment to §262(e) clarify the right of a stockholder who has demanded appraisal to withdraw that demand and receive the merger consideration at any time within 60 days after the effective date of the merger, even if a petition for appraisal has been filed, as long as that stockholder has not filed such a petition or otherwise joined the proceeding as a named party. Another amendment to §262(e) enables beneficial holders of shares of stock held in street name to (i) file petitions for appraisal, and (ii) request a statement of shares with respect to which demands for appraisal have been received, in their own name rather than in the name of the stockholder of record.

These Sections amend the approach to awarding interest in appraisal proceedings, principally by establishing a presumption that interest is to be awarded for the period from the effective date of the merger until the date of payment of judgment, compounded quarterly and accruing at the rate of 5% over the Federal Reserve discount rate, giving effect to any variation in that rate during that period. The Court of Chancery may depart from this presumptive approach for good cause, in order, for example, to avoid an inequitable result such as rewarding, or insufficiently compensating for, improper delay of the proceeding or unreasonable or bad faith assertion of valuation claims. The amendments to §262(h) also clarify that the Court of Chancery in appraisal proceedings does not determine the fair value of shares on its own initiative, and that appraisal proceedings are adversary proceedings to be litigated in accordance with generally applicable rules of the Court of Chancery.

Ch. 82, L. '01 Synopsis of Section 262

The amendment to Section 262(d)(2) clarifies that notice of appraisal rights given after a merger or consolidation is to be given by the surviving or resulting corporation.

Ch. 339, L. '98 Synopsis of Section 262

The amendments to these Sections eliminate masculine references in the statutes, and replace them with gender neutral references.

Ed. Note: This section is effective only with respect to mergers or consolidations consummated pursuant to an agreement of merger or consolidation entered into after July 1, 1987.

Ch. 120, L. '97 Synopsis of Section 262

The amendment to Section 262(b)(2)b clarifies that, assuming the requirements of Section 262(b)(1) are satisfied, appraisal rights are not available for shares held by a depository if in the merger such shares are to be converted into or exchanged for shares of another corporation (whether or not widely-held or publicly traded) in respect of which depository receipts will be widely-held or publicly traded at the effective time.

Ch. 349, L. '96 Synopsis of Section 262

The amendment to Section 262(d) provides a mechanism for sending separate notices with respect to (a) the approval and (b) the effective date of a merger or consolidation approved pursuant to Section 228 or Section 253, in order to permit the start of the twenty day period for appraisal demands where the effective date is not known at the time the notice of the approval of the merger is sent. The amendment also (1) provides for the fixing of a record date for determining the stockholders to whom the notices provided for in this subsection shall be sent (and provides that notices given prior to the effective date shall be given by the appropriate constituent corporation rather than by the surviving corporation, as previously provided), and (2) eliminates the requirement that notices be sent by certified or registered mail, return receipt requested (and provides that, as in Section 222(b), an affidavit of the Secretary, Assistant Secretary or Transfer Agent shall constitute evidence of the giving of such notice).

Ch. 299, L. '95 Synopsis of Section 262

The amendments to Section 262(b) and Section 262(b)(1) correct certain oversights in the 1995 amendment to Section 262(b)(1) and implement the stated objective of the 1995 amendment that appraisal rights not be available for the shares of a constituent corporation to a merger effected in accordance with Section 251(g).

Ch. 79, L. '95 Synopsis of Section 262

New Section 251(g) permits a Delaware corporation to reorganize by merging with or into a direct or indirect wholly-owned subsidiary of a holding company (as defined) without stockholder approval, unless the corporation's certificate of incorporation, by explicit reference to a holding company reorganization of the type provided for in this subsection, requires such a vote. The provisions of the new statute are intended to insure that the rights of the stockholders of the corporation are not changed by or as a result of such a reorganization, except and to the same extent that such rights could be changed without stockholder approval under existing law. Thus, stockholders of the corporation must receive in the merger the same number of shares of the holding company as they owned in the corporation prior to the reorganization, which stock must have the same voting powers, designations, preferences and rights, and the qualifications, restrictions and limitations thereof, with respect to the holding company as such stock had with respect to the corporation prior to the reorganization. The resulting holding company must be a Delaware corporation with the same certificate of incorporation (except for provisions that could have been amended or deleted without stockholder approval) and bylaws that the corporation had prior to the reorganization. As a result of the reorganization the corporation or its successor must become a direct or indirect wholly-owned subsidiary of the holding company. The directors of the corporation immediately prior to the reorganization must be the same as the directors of the holding company after the merger. To ensure that the rights of the stockholders of the constituent corporation to vote on certain acts and transactions under the General Corporation Law are not changed by the fact that they become stockholders of the holding company as a result of a reorganization, the certificate of incorporation of the surviving corporation must provide that any act or transaction by or involving the surviving corporation that requires for its adoption under the General Corporation Law or the certificate of incorporation of the surviving corporation the approval of the stockholders of the surviving corporation shall require, in addition, the approval of the stockholders of the holding company by such vote as is required under the General Corporation Law and/or by the surviving corporation's certificate of incorporation. Otherwise, the certificate of incorporation of the surviving corporation immediately after the merger must be the same as the certificate of incorporation of the constituent corporation immediately prior to the merger, except for provisions that could have been amended or deleted without stockholder approval, and except that the certificate of incorporation of the surviving corporation may be amended in the merger to reduce the number of classes and shares of capital stock that the surviving corporation is authorized to issue. In order that any restrictions on stockholders of the corporation imposed by Section 203, or any exemption from such restrictions, apply with equal force and effect to the stockholders of the holding company after the reorganization, the statute provides that, with respect to persons who are stockholders of the holding company immediately after the effectiveness of the reorganization, the provisions of Section 203 will apply to such persons to the same extent that they applied to stockholders of the corporation. To avoid the burden of issuing certificates for shares of the holding company to the former stockholders of the corporation, the outstanding stock certificates of the corporation would, after the reorganization, constitute stock certificates of the holding company so long as the name of the holding company after the reorganization is the same as the name of the corporation prior to the reorganization. Finally, the reorganization must be tax-free for federal income tax purposes to stockholders of the corporation. Appraisal rights are not available in the event of such a reorganization.

Ch. 262, L. '94 Synopsis of Section 262

The amendments to Section 262 are intended to broaden the existing "market out" exception to the availability of appraisal rights to include, under comparable circumstances, shares of stock represented by depository receipts that are widely held or publicly traded.

Ch. 61, L. '93 Synopsis of Section 262(d)

The amendment to Section 262(d)(1) clarifies the notice requirement of that subsection in view of the 1987 amendments to Section 262(a) regarding the stockholders entitled to seek appraisal. The amendment to Section 262(d)(2) makes Section 262(d)(2) consistent with Section 262(d)(1) and clarifies that it is the written demand itself which effectuates the stockholder demand and no further action is necessary to complete the demand for appraisal.

.1 Appraisal value.—Measure of damages in suit by minority stockholder against majority for inducing him to sell his stock by alleged fraudulent misrepresentations is difference between stock's actual value and price paid; actual value is that used in statutory stock appraisal proceedings, and so must include earnings, dividends, market price, assets and any other pertinent "going concern" factors. *Poole v N V Deli Maatschappij*, 224 A2d 260 (1966).

Stockholders dissenting from merger of real estate investment company are entitled to have earnings capitalized by higher multiplier than ordinarily used, to reflect company's investment policy of capital appreciation rather than acquiring ordinary income; stockholders excepting to appraiser's report are entitled to 5% interest from date of that exception. *Swanton v State Guaranty Corp*, 215 A2d 242 (Ch Ct 1965).

Appraisal value of stock in merger may include not only market price but 11 independent elements, such as asset value and value derived from earnings and dividends which will give a dollar and cents appraisal. *Jacques Coe & Co v Minneapolis-Moline Co*, 75 A2d 244 (Ch Ct 1950).

Dissenting stockholders are to receive actual rather than market value of stock. *Chicago Corp v Munds*, 172 A 452 (1934).

Appraisal determines the intrinsic value of the stock must be determined by treat-including all factors and elements which might reasonably enter into the fixing of value. Thus market value, asset value, dividends, earning prospects, the nature of the enterprise and any other facts which are known or can be ascertained as of the date of the merger or which throw any light on future prospects must be considered by the appraiser. However, the value of the stock must be determined by treating the merged corporation as a "going concern" and not as one being liquidated. *Tri-Continental Corp v Battye*, 74 A2d 71 (Ch Ct 1950). See also, *Levin v Midland-Ross Corp*, 194 A2d 50 (Ch Ct 1963).

In appraising dissenters' shares, market value should be given no weight where the surviving corporation had maintained the market in the constituent's stock for two years. *Sporborg v City Specialty Stores, Inc*, 123 A2d 121 (Ch Ct 1956). Compare, *Adams v R C Williams & Co*, 158 A2d 797 (Ch Ct 1960), and *Heller v Munsingwear, Inc*, 98 A2d 774 (Ch Ct 1953).

Earnings and assets are the factors to weigh in appraising the shares of dissenters to a merger where there is no market value; if the best measure of fixed assets is their replacement cost less depreciation and that value is greater than their going concern value it must still be given independent weight; however, greater weight may be given to earnings. *Felder v Anderson, Clayton & Co*, 158 A2d 278 (Ch Ct 1960).

Merger of 90% owned subsidiary into its parent, in compliance with "short-merger" statute, cannot be set aside for fraud by subsidiary's minority stockholders, even though the merger makes them take cash for their stock; they cannot get more than the parent offered for their stock unless they make a timely demand for appraisal. *Stauffer v Standard Brands, Inc*, 178 A2d 311 (Ch Ct), aff'd, 187 A2d 78 (1962).

Averaging past earnings over five-year period to determine multiplier for capitalizing earnings in appraising dissidents' stock was proper, since five-year period was representative of motion picture company's earnings experience in broader context of industry and none of those years was shown to be so extraordinary as to justify exclusion from span to be averaged. *Francis I duPont & Co v Universal City Studios*, 312 A2d 344 (Ch Ct 1973).

Court decreased appraisal value of dissenter's shares from about $44, as set by court's own appraiser, to about $54 although former majority stockholder got $53 a share for his controlling block of stock; court's new appraisal formula excluded value of isolated, unusually profitable sale of merged corporation's subsidiary and value of merged corporation's assets, and included only stock's market value at time of merger, earnings average for previous five years and interest. *Gibbons v Schenley Industries, Inc*, 339 A2d 460 (Ch Ct 1975).

Appraisal of dissenting shares based 60% on earnings and 40% on assets was proper, even though shareholders in natural resource (lumber) company had urged that assets be given 90% weight because of basic differences from typical manufacturing corporation. *Bell v Kirby Lumber Corp*, 395 A2d 730 (Ch Ct 1978).

Minority stockholders of subsidiary corporation can temporarily enjoin merger with parent, when (1) they show parent breached its fiduciary duties to subsidiary and its minority stockholders by diverting subsidiary's corporate opportunity, and (2) parent failed to show that conversion ratio of stock to be exchanged in merger was fair and reasonable. *Greene v Dunhill International, Inc*, No. 2894 (Ch Ct 12-24-69).

Twenty percent premium for listed stock is fair. *Tanzer v International Gen Industries*, 402 A2d 382 (Ch Ct 1979).

Stockholder that dissented to merger and demanded appraisal could not seek payment for lost option rights; sole issue in appraisal is value of merged corporation's stock; nor could he seek appraisal of only portion of his stock, since dissent to merger amounted to irrevocable election to withdraw from corporate enterprise. *Lichtman v Recognition Equipment Inc*, 295 A2d 771 (Ch Ct 1972).

Surviving corporation could not, by settling at premium with handful of dissenting stockholders that filed appraisal petition, defeat rights of those other dissenting shareholders who had perfected right to appraisal but did not file individual petitions, since only one petition was necessary to require hearing for valuation of dissenters' stock. *Raynor v LTV Aerospace Corp*, 317 A2d 43 (Ch Ct 1974).

In determining which stockholders dissenting to merger are entitled to appraisal rights, court held pre-vote objection notice signed by one spouse of a pair of joint tenants sufficient notice for corporation and entitles holders to appraisal; but pre-vote payment demand by dissenting joint tenants must be signed by both. *Raab v Villager Industries, Inc*, 355 A2d 888 (1976).

Dissenting stockholder who sought to have value of his stock appraised has absolute right to such action; corporation cannot interpose counterclaim al-

§262

leging stockholder's bad faith. *Kaye v Pantone, Inc, 395 A2d 369 (Ch Ct 1978).*

Shareholder could not enjoin shareholder meeting to vote on merger because it was unlikely he could prevail on the merits, substantial premium over market price was offered to shareholders electing to participate in merger, and dissenters were entitled to full hearing and to appraisal rights. *Weinberger v United Financial Corp of California, No. 5915 (Ch Ct 7-30-79).*

Shareholder who does not accept terms of merger may petition for court appraisal of his stock, but is then foreclosed (60 days after merger) from withdrawing his request for appraisal and resuming his rights as a stockholder unless he first obtains corporate consent. *Dofflemyer v W F Hall Printing Co, 432 A2d 1198 (1981).*

When parent corporation merged with subsidiary by buying out subsidiary's minority stockholders, minority could not compel parent to declare and pay dividend that would have been forthcoming for subsidiary had merger not taken place, because minority did not object to adequacy of price paid for their stock. *Gabelli & Co Profit Sharing Plan v Liggett Group Inc, No. 6225/1980 (Ch Ct 4-8-82).*

Shareholder was entitled to appraisal of shares because, although its demand letter did not expressly brand merger price inadequate, letter implied that shareholder was dissatisfied and was seeking appraisal. *Tabbi v Pollution Control Industries, Inc, 508 A2d 867 (Ch Ct 1986).*

Courts are no longer limited to "prudent investor" standard in fixing appropriate rate of interest on amount due shareholder in appraisal action but may consider "all relevant factors" including what the surviving corporation had to pay to borrow money while proceeding was pending. Appraisal award cannot be increased to reflect effect of inflation because it would be inconsistent to award interest as if funds were invested and at same time restore spending power of funds by means of inflation adjustment. Compound interest cannot be awarded in appraisal proceeding absent specific statutory authority. *Charlip v Lear Singer, Inc, No. 5178 (Ch Ct 7-2-85).*

Delaware appraisal law does not permit appraised value of corporation to be discounted to reflect fact that dissenting shareholder's stock represents a minority interest and is not readily marketable. Objective of appraisal under GCL §262 is to value corporation itself as distinguished from a specific fraction of its shares as they may exist in hands of particular shareholder. Under GCL §262, dissenting shareholder is entitled to his proportionate interest in overall fair value of corporation appraised as going concern. *Cavalier Oil Corp v Harnett, Nos. 7959, 7960, 7967, 7968 (Ch Ct 1988).*

On June 19, 1990, the Court of Chancery found disclosure documents by SPNV Holdings, Inc., now Shell Petroleum Inc., in connection with its 1985 cash-out merger, violated defendant's duty of complete candor; the appropriate relief to be awarded to plaintiff Class was not decided at that time. Subsequently, the court rejected the proposals of both parties and, relying on the facts that the primary disclosure violation was inadvertent, that the disputed short-term merger was completed over five years ago, and that the existence of other minor disclosure violations were "indicative of a conscious decision of the defendant to be less than candid," entered an order awarding $2 per share to the plaintiff Class. *Smith v Shell Petroleum, Inc, No. 8395 (Ch Ct 11-26-90).*

The Court of Chancery erred by appraising dissenting shareholders' shares using a segmented valuation technique which valued the corporation's three operating subsidiaries as going concerns and therefore did not value the corporation on a liquidation basis. *Rapid-American Corp v Harris, 603 A2d 796 (1992).*

The Court of Chancery determined the fair value of dissenting shareholders' stock to reflect capital expenditures equaling depreciation, rejecting elements from both the shareholders' and the corporation's experts' analysis. *Saloman Brothers Inc v Interstate Bakeries Corp, No. 10,054 (Ch Ct 5-1-92).*

In an appraisal action arising from a cash-out merger, the Court of Chancery held that the expert retained by the corporation to value the shares had improperly included a discount for lack of marketability. The determination of fair value in an appraisal may not include any stockholder level discount for lack of marketability. The expert had stated in her valuation report that the size of the holding being valued and the number of restrictions attached to the stock were factors in determining an appropriate lack of marketability discount. The court held that both of these factors may affect the value of particular shares, but have no impact on the value of the company as a going concern and thus constituted a stockholder level discount. *Hodas v Spectrum Technology, Inc, No. 11,265 (Ch Ct 12-7-92).*

Court of Chancery's pretrial announced decision that the Chancellor intended to accept the methodology and valuation factors of one expert (even though the Chancellor did not indicate which side he would favor) to the exclusion of other relevant evidence and his implementation of that mind-set in the appraisal process was error as a matter of law. Where the Court of Chancery is faced with opinion evidence of absurdly differing values, it has the inherent authority to appoint neutral witnesses in order to better sift through a welter of complex and often contradictory evidence. *Gonsalves v Straight Arrow Publishers, Inc, 701 A2d 357 (1997),* rev'g, *No. 8474 (Ch Ct 8-22-96).*

Although the merger price was $41 per share, the Chancery Court concluded that the fair value of the shares of a subsidiary corporation that was merged into its corporate parent was $85 per share, using the comparative acquisition approach (in which a control premium is inherent). *Le Beau v MG Bancorporation, Inc, No. 13414 (Ch Ct 1-29-98).*

In a statutory appraisal proceeding to value a bank holding company, where the comparative acquisition approach to valuation is used, it is appropriate to include a control premium for majority ownership of subsidiaries as an element of the fair value of the holding company's majority-owned subsidiaries, regardless of whether those subsidiaries engaged in different businesses and then to add the value of the holding company's remaining assets to his valuation of the two subsidiaries. *M.G. Bancorporation, Inc v Le Beau, 737 A2d 513 (1999).*

In a statutory appraisal action under GCL §262, arising from a merger, a court may use its own independent appraisal method, and need not apply an appraisal analysis that gives weight to the terms of the merger or to prior offers for equity stakes in the subject corporation. *M.P.M. Enterprises, Inc v Gilbert, 731 A2d 790 (1999).*

Where illicit conduct makes it impossible to determine the price a corporation's stock warrants would have been sold for in a market untainted by the illicit conduct, traditional valuation methods must be used to ascertain the warrants' fair market value. *Agranoff v Miller, 2001 Del Ch LEXIS 71 (Ch Ct 2001).*

In an appraisal action, a valuation that is not litigation-driven and that is prepared by a disinterested party shortly before a merger will carry significantly more weight than litigation-driven valuations so long as the pre-merger valuation is not prepared merely as a comparative valuation and is not otherwise flawed. *Gray v Cytokine Pharma Sciences, Inc, 2002 Del Ch 48 (Ch Ct 2002).*

Holders of options do not have a right of appraisal to receive the fair value of the options they are forced to give up in a merger in exchange for other consideration. *Andaloro v PFPC Worldwide, Inc, 2003 Del. Ch. LEXIS 90 (Ch Ct 2003).*

In an appraisal proceeding, the fair value of shares of a bank holding company that has been deemed a troubled financial institution is the merger price less synergies. *In re Speedway Motorsports, Inc Derivative Litigation, 2003 Del. Ch. LEXIS 115 (Ch Ct 2003).*

In a dissenter's rights appraisal case requiring a determination of fair value, it is inappropriate to ignore management projections made during the regular course of business, and an expert who replaces those projections with his own, runs the risk of having his valuation rejected. *Cede & Co v Technicolor, Inc, 2003 Del. Ch. LEXIS 146 (Ch Ct 2003).*

A liquidation valuation based on "net asset value" may be used in a dissenter's rights action to determine fair value where it is used in conjunction with other valuation methods. *Ng v Heng Sang Realty Corp, 2004 Del. Ch. LEXIS 54 (Ch Ct 2004).*

A discounted cash flow method of determining fair value in an appraisal action is the preferred method for valuing a niche corporation that has contracts with affiliated entities, that has a very short track record, and that is uniquely positioned in a unique market. *Acker v Transurgical, Inc, 2004 Del. Ch. LEXIS 49 (Ch Ct 2004).*

A discounted cash flow (DCF) method of valuation will be rejected where the assumptions and projections used to support it are speculative and not based in fact or are "untethered to reality." *Finkelstein v Liberty Digital, Inc, 2005 Del. Ch. LEXIS 53 (Ch Ct 2005).*

A trial court in an appraisal action errs neither in rejecting a valuation that is based on legally and factually flawed inputs and that improperly incorporates deal-making synergies instead of only business-related synergies, nor in accepting a valuation that is based on corrected reports and supported by third-party authorities. *Montgomery Cellular Holding Co v Dobler, 880 A2d 206 (2005).*

In an appraisal action where the parties' experts valuation opinions are unreliable, the court will exercise its independent judgment and conclude its own opinion of value. *Highfields Capital, Ltd v AXA Financial, Inc, 2007 Del. Ch. LEXIS 126 (Ch Ct 2007).*

In an appraisal proceeding, the court need not defer, either conclusively or presumptively, to the merger price as indicative of fair value, and companies subject to an appraisal proceeding are not bound by the data in their proxy materials. *Golden Telecom, Inc v Global GT LP, 11 A3d 214 (2010).*

.2 Duty of complete candor—breach.—Failure to disclose oil and gas reserves of approximately $1 billion ($3.00—$3.45 per share) prior to a cashout merger constituted a breach of the corporation's duty of complete candor. The minority shareholders were denied material information since understatement of the reserves "significantly alter[ed] the total mix of information available" to the reasonable shareholder's decision whether to accept consideration from the short-form merger or to alternatively elect the remedy of appraisal. *Smith v Shell Petroleum, Inc, No. 8395 (Ch Ct 11-26-90).*

Where two corporations merge, the directors of the acquired corporation, and not those of the surviving corporation, have a fiduciary duty to disclose material information about the corporation being acquired in order for shareholders of the acquired corporation to be able to determine whether to approve the merger or demand appraisal. *Turner v Bernstein, C.A. No. 16190 (Ch Ct 2-9-99).*

In a short-form merger, a single number purporting to encompass the value of a corporation that is not supported with any financial information whatsoever is insufficient, as a matter of law, to satisfy the duty of disclosure. *Erickson v Centennial Beauregard Cellular, 2003 Del. Ch. LEXIS 38 (Ch Ct 2003).*

A director, CEO, and majority shareholder of a corporation does not breach his fiduciary duties to minority shareholders in a merger where he is informed and reasonably believes the projections he provides that form the basis of a supporting fairness opinion and that are included in proxy materials. *Crescent/Mach I Partnership, L.P. v Turner, 2007 Del. Ch. LEXIS 63 (Ch Ct 2007).*

.3 Interest on appraised value.—Stockholder dissenting from merger is not entitled to interest on appraised value of shares from effective date of merger, but from the time the corporation is obliged to pay the award. *Meade v Pacific Gamble Robinson Co, 58 A2d 415 (1948).* But see, *Sporborg v City Specialty Stores, Inc, 123 A2d 121 (Ch Ct 1956),* wherein it was held that interest is allowable from the effective date of the merger.

The Court of Chancery was asked to determine the appropriate interest rate to be applied to the agreed upon valuation of a corporation's stock pursuant to merger. The court decided to employ a sliding scale that altered the relevance of the prudent investor rate and the cost of borrowing rate according to the relative fault of the parties in causing the delay. The court determined that both parties sought a prompt resolution of the dispute, but their inability to agree despite good faith bargaining caused the long delay in determining the fair value of plaintiff's shares. Accordingly, the court gave equal values to the prudent

§262

investor and cost of borrowing rates. The court gave no weight to the legal interest rate as a relevant factor. *Chang's Holdings, S.A. v Universal Chemicals and Coatings, Inc, No. 10856 (Ch Ct 11-22-94).*

Even though the Chancery Court has broad discretion under the appraisal statute to award either simple or compound interest, the Court must explain its selection of one type of interest over another and cannot choose one type of interest as a matter of course; the option provided by GCL §262(i) precludes, ips facto, the routine application of a standard which may have no relation to the record evidence or the merits of the appraisal proceeding. *Gonsalves v Straight Arrow Publishers, Inc, 725 A2d 442 (1999).*

.4 Assessability of costs and expenses.—Litigation expenses of proceeding pursuant to this section other than costs are not assessable; costs are assessable against the corporation but may be apportioned between the parties. *Meade v Pacific Gamble Robinson Co, 58 A2d 415 (1948).*

Court will not order an appraiser to employ an expert, as requested by the dissenting stockholders to a merger, when the appraiser does not feel an expert is necessary. *Adams v Williams & Co, 152 A2d 112 (Ch Ct 1959).*

Stockholders dissenting from merger cannot recover proportionate share of their counsel fees and other expenses of the valuation proceeding from other dissenters who did not join with them. *Levin v Midland-Ross Corp, 194 A2d 853 (Ch Ct 1963).*

In appraisal proceeding, shareholders who had received $75.60 per share pursuant to an August 1985 cash-out merger were awarded $180.60 per share and an interest rate of 12½ percent based on the fair value of shares. They did not recover expert witness and attorney fees under the appraisal statute, GCL §262, since valuation methods—not unfair dealings—caused price discrepancy. By alleging unfair dealings under appraisal statute, shareholders sought "hybrid" action that required erroneous broadening of §262, which provides limited legislative remedy of judicial determination of fair value to shareholders dissenting from a merger on the grounds of inadequacy of the offering price. *Neal v Alabama By-Products Corp, No. 8282 (Ch Ct 8-1-90).*

.5 Beneficial owner.—Corporation can disregard letter objecting to merger sent by beneficial owner of stock registered in street name, since letter did not identify them as agents for registered owner; objection by registered owner filed too late when received one-half hour after meeting, though mailed two days prior thereto. *Carl M Loeb, Rhoades & Co v Hilton Hotels Corp, 222 A2d 789 (1966).* To same effect, *Raynor v LTV Aerospace Corp, 331 A2d 393 (Ch Ct 1975).*

Brokers holding stock of merged corporation in street name can get stock appraised without having to identify beneficial owners, since under merger appraisal statute only registered owners are "stockholders"; further, in short merger of subsidiary into parent, stockholder can elect to accept offered price for portion of his stock and demand appraisal as to rest. *Olivetti Underwood Corp v Jacques Coe & Co, 217 A2d 683 (1966),* aff'g, *Abraham & Co v Olivetti Underwood Corp, 204 A2d 704 (Ch Ct 1964).*

Holder of certificate under voting trust agreement which gives voting trustees power to vote for and to take other necessary steps to effect merger of corporation is not stockholder entitled to appraisal of stock pursuant to this section. *Scott v Arden Farms Co, 23 A2d 81 (Ch Ct 1942).*

Beneficial owner of stock is not "stockholder" within this section for the purpose of objecting to a consolidation or merger and obtaining payment for his stock as a dissatisfied stockholder. *Schenck v Salt Dome Oil Corp, 41 A2d 583 (1945),* rev'g, *34 A2d 249 (Ch Ct 1943),* followed in *Coyne v Schenley Industries, Inc, 155 A2d 238 (1959).*

Stockholder who ceases to be registered holder of stock after the record date for determination of stockholders entitled to vote on merger and filing of petition under this section is not entitled to appraisal as to his shares. *In re Application of General Realty & Utilities Corp, 42 A2d 24 (Ch Ct 1945).*

Registered holders of stock are the only "share holders" entitled to object to proposed merger of corporation. *Schwartz v The Olympic Inc, 119 Phila L Intelligencer p. 1 7-8-48 (3d Cir 1943).*

Dissenting stockholder's right to payment is lost for want of written dissent when a brokerage firm, as the record owner of the stock, sends in a proxy but its letter of transmittal says only that (1) the proxy is a dissenting one and (2) it reflects the customer's instructions. *F S Moseley & Co v Midland-Ross Corp, 179 A2d 295 (1962).*

Stockholder who votes some of the shares registered in his name in favor of a merger may dissent as to the other shares and receive the appraised value of those shares. *Colonial Realty Corp v Reynolds Metals Co, 185 A2d 754 (Ch Ct 1962),* aff'd, *Reynolds Metals Co v Colonial Realty Corp, 190 A2d 752 (1963).*

Beneficial owner was not entitled to appraisal of shares pursuant to merger because record owner of shares had tendered them for payment and was paid merger consideration. Owner's letter demanding appraisal did not make him party to appraisal proceeding before tender and payment and even if it did, order is not controlling. *LeCompte v Oakbrook Consolidated, Inc, No. 8028 (Ch Ct 3-17-86).*

Demands for appraisal by beneficial owners that were not made in name of record shareholders were adequate because (1) corporation's proxy statement contained inadequate instructions concerning compliance with appraisal statute and (2) although beneficial owners knew that demand had to be submitted by or for record shareholders, they did not know how to comply. *Tabbi v Pollution Control Industries, Inc, 508 A2d 867 (Ch Ct 1986).*

Beneficial owners of stock were entitled to appraisal and to receive settlement consideration, although their pre-merger demands for appraisal were not submitted by record owner, nominee of central security depository that held shareholders' stock, because corporation did not instruct shareholders how exercise of appraisal rights was to be accomplished when stock was held in name of nominee of central security depository. *Matter of Appraisal of ENSTAR Corp, No. 7802 (consolidated) (Ch Ct 7-17-86).*

Under GCL §262, only stockholder of record has right to appraisal. Persons whose shares are held in "street" or nominee names do not qualify as shareholders of record for appraisal purposes. *In the Matter of the Appraisal of Enstar Corp v Senouf, 535 A2d 1351 (1987).*

A beneficial owner of stock is not entitled to appraisal where the "holder of record" of the stock has not demanded appraisal. The corporation may wait until a petition is filed to begin analyzing and objecting to insufficient appraisal demands so long as the company makes no express or implied waiver in its correspondence with stockholders that it will not later object to their demands, and the obligation to comply with the record holder requirement is not relieved by alleged disclosure violations of the corporation or its management. *DiRienzo v Steel Partners Holdings L.P., 2009 Del. Ch. LEXIS 205 (Ch Ct 2009).*

.6 De facto merger.—Purchase by corporation of all the stock of several other corporations does not create a de facto merger so as to give dissenting stockholder of purchasing corporation appraisal rights. *Orzeck v Englehart, 192 A2d 36 (Ch Ct), aff'd, 195 A2d 375 (1963).*

.7 Designation of third appraiser by court.— If stockholder objecting to merger fails to designate "disinterested" person as appraiser, as required by this section, and corporation has not waived its right to object to the person designated for lack of disinterestedness, there is no occasion for the court to designate a third appraiser, and stockholder's bill for that purpose will be dismissed. *Scott v Arden Farms Co, 28 A2d 81 (Ch Ct 1942).*

Courts of Washington have no power to appoint a third appraiser under this section. *Meade v Pacific Gamble Robinson Co, 153 P2d 686 (1944).* To same effect, *Grant v Pacific Gamble Robinson Co, 154 P2d 301 (1944).*

.8 Enjoining merger.—Preferred stockholders cannot bar merger of their corporation with its wholly owned subsidiary when they do not proffer substantial evidence that the merger would unduly advance interests of common stockholders as against preferred; they must show unfairness amounting to fraud. *Porges v Vadsco Sales Corp, 32 A2d 148 (Ch Ct 1943),* principle applied in *MacCrone v Am Capital Corp, 51 FSupp 462 (D Del 1943).*

In examining a plan of reclassification, altering rights of preferred stock, federal District Court may not leave the limits of the "gross unfairness" test of the Delaware cases and look independently at the facts of each plan in arriving at conclusion on questions of unfairness. *Barrett v Denver Tramway Corp, 53 FSupp 198 (D Del 1944).*

Recapitalization plan effected by amendment of charter will not be condemned at suit of dissenting minority preferred stockholder unless it is so unfair as to amount to constructive fraud, the reasons for the amendment were the business necessity behind it not being matters for judicial determination. *Bailey v Tubize Rayon Corp, 56 FSupp 418 (D Del 1944).*

Dissenting minority stockholders could not bar merging of their corporation into subsidiary majority stockholders formed solely for purpose of merger, even though there was no showing of valid business purpose, since merger of corporation designed primarily to "freeze-out" minority and benefit parent company was not improper in absence of fraud or blatant overreaching and minority stockholders still had appraisal rights. *Singer v Magnavox Co, 367 A2d 1349 (Ch Ct 1976).*

Shareholder dissenting from corporation's merger was not foreclosed from asserting misrepresentation and fraudulent proxy statement after he petitioned for court appraisal of stock because valid issues of fraud may have existed under federal law. *Dofflemyer v W F Hall Printing Co, 558 FSupp 372 (D Del 1983).*

Court dismissed action by convertible debenture holders challenging merger of corporation for lack of entire fairness because debenture holders have to allege fraud in order to state claim other than contract claim based on indenture. Convertible debenture holders also could not maintain action for specific violations of indenture without complying with required "no-action" provision of indenture because debenture holders were not asserting fraud in connection with alleged violations but, rather, breach of fiduciary duty. *Norte & Co v Manor Healthcare Corp, Nos. 6827 and 6831 (Ch Ct 11-21-85).*

Minority holder of preferred stock could not enjoin proposed merger as being unfair to preferred shareholders when they were offered less for their stock than offer to common shareholders because (1) preferred shares had no legal right to equivalent consideration in merger, (2) apportionment of consideration between preferred and common shareholders was fair, (3) majority shareholder did not have duty to include preferred shareholders in increased price he paid common shareholders out of his own funds, and (4) preferred shareholders were not injured by majority shareholder's timing of merger. *Jedwab v MGM Grand Hotels, Inc, 509 A2d 584 (Ch Ct 1986).*

Former shareholders of merged corporation who tendered stock were adequate representatives of class of tendering shareholders and merged out shareholders because (1) shareholders' claim challenged tender offer and merger on grounds that go beyond allegedly inadequate disclosures so reliance on disclosures and unique defense based on reliance are not material and (2) alleged unfair dealing effected both tendering and merged out shareholders in same way and their interests are not antagonistic. *Rosen v Juniper Petroleum Corp, No. 7016 (Ch Ct 4-11-86).*

Minority shareholder could not enjoin short-form merger of her corporation with parent because her sole remedy was appraisal when (1) she did not demonstrate inadequacy of appraisal, (2) parent did not deal unfairly with minority, (3) parent properly disclosed to minority its intentions and options concerning acquisition of shares not tendered pursuant to tender offer it made prior to its short-form merger. *Stepak v Scharffenberger, No. 6530 (Ch Ct 8-9-85).*

Court refused to enjoin going private merger whereby majority shareholder sought to cash out minority shareholders of airline corporation allegedly to deny them opportunity to realize profit on investment because (1) adequate remedy can be provided by upward adjustment of cash-out price, (2) majority shareholder did not usurp corporate opportunity when it acquired other airlines instead of allowing corporation to do so, and (3) apparent breach of one minority shareholder's contractual rights in warrants to purchase corporation's stock can be remedied by appropriate relief such as specific performance. *American General Corp v Texas Air Corp, Nos. 8390, 8406, 8650, 8805 (Ch Ct 2-5-87).*

In order to be permitted to maintain a stockholder derivative suit, a plaintiff must be a stockholder at the time of filing of the suit and must remain a shareholder throughout the litigation. A plaintiff who loses his shareholder status by being merged out may attack the validity of allegedly excessive termination payments, provided that he concomitantly challenges the fairness of the merger. A former shareholder who fails to attack merger's fairness is therefore without standing to pursue derivative claims. *Kramer v Western Pacific Industries, No. 8675 (Ch Ct 9-11-87).*

.9 Interested directors.—Charter provisions permits counting of interested directors for quorum purposes to vote on merger (or any matter that will later be submitted for stockholder approval). *Sterling v Mayflower Hotel Corp, 89 A2d 652 (Ch Ct),* aff'd, *83 A2d 107 (1952).*

.10 Remedy in federal courts.—Dissenting stockholders' remedies are available in state courts only. *McGhee v General Finance Corp, 84 FSupp 24 (WD Va 1949); Sheridan v American Motors Corp, 132 FSupp 121 (ED Pa 1955).*

.11 Right to appeal.—Stockholders demanding payment for their shares are not thereby barred from prosecuting appeal from denial of their motion to enjoin contemplated merger. *Ramsberg v American Investment Co of Illinois, 231 F2d 333 (7th Cir 1956).*

§262

Shareholders could not have appraisal proceeding reopened so that asset and market values of stock could be considered, because (1) At original appraisal proceedings, shareholders stipulated that neither market nor asset values would be part of case, and that stipulation was binding; (2) Decision in *Weinberger v UOP, Inc.*, which requires that determination of fair value be based on all "relevant factors," does not require consideration of factors to which parties failed to present evidence. *Charlip v Lear Siegler, Inc, No. 5178 (Ch Ct 11-27-84).*

.12 Rights of objecting stockholders.—Dissenting stockholders of absorbed corporations cannot sue derivatively, since that right passed to surviving corporation; they cannot sue representatively on behalf of other stockholders who (1) sold their shares pursuant to an offer to buy, (2) surrendered their shares on merge, or (3) retained their shares following merger and asked appraisal. *Braasch v Goldschmidt, 199 A2d 760 (Ch Ct 1964).*

Unless the merger is subject to nullification for fraud, dissenting stockholder is put to an election by the statute: either to become stockholder in consolidated enterprise, or secure valuation of his stock in money and collect the same as debt due. *Cole v National Cash Credit Ass'n, 156 A 183 (Ch Ct 1931).*

Petition by surviving corporation to compel stockholders of constituent corporation who objected to the merger, to assign and transfer to the surviving corporation their stock certificates upon payment of the appraised value of the stock is incident to and a continuation of the original proceedings under the section. Motion to dismiss the petition will be denied. *Root v York Corp, 39 A2d 780 (Ch Ct 1944).*

In determining whether written communication constitutes sufficient objection to merger, the communication will be liberally construed. *Wiswall v General Water Works Corp, 66 A2d 424 (Ch Ct 1949).*

Majority stockholder breached fiduciary duty to minority who tendered their stock for $12 per share in response to offer that constituted less than full and frank disclosure because it failed to reveal two critical facts: (1) "highly qualified petroleum geologist" who was member of target company's management had calculated its net asset value to be significantly more than minimum amount disclosed in offer, and (2) offeror's management had authorized open market purchases of target's stock for bids up to $15 per share. *Lynch v Vickers Energy Corp, 383 A2d 278 (1977).* Even so, the minority could not recover damages when the value of the stock at the time of the tender offer was under $12 a share and the amount $12 would have grown too if prudently invested by the minority from the time they turned in their stock to the time of the second trial in this action was more than the market value of the stock in question at the time of the second trial. On remand, *402 A2d 5 (Ch Ct 1979).*

Measure of damages in suit by minority who were induced to sell their stock by majority's "breach of fiduciary duty" (failure to disclose critical facts concerning tender offer) is difference between price paid and value of stock on date of court judgment, when it is impractical to return stock. *Lynch v Vickers Energy Corp, 429 A2d 497 (1981).*

Stockholder could bring antifraud suit when corporation announced tender offer to buy up shares of his company at stipulated price and upon obtaining over 90% of shares consummated short-form merger in accordance with state law, giving remaining stockholders same stipulated price, since stockholder became forced seller and failure to state that he could seek appraisal rights was material omission. *Valente v Pepsico Inc, 454 FSupp 1228 (D Del 1978).*

Minority stockholders' positive vote on proposed merger was uninformed because material information was withheld by majority stockholder under circumstances amounting to breach of fiduciary duty so merger did not meet test of fair dealing or fair price and minority was entitled to appraisal. *Weinberger v UOP Inc, 457 A2d 701 (1983).*

Court refused to dismiss shareholder's derivative action seeking to enjoin proposed short form merger. Although remedy would ordinarily be confined to appraisal, when appraisals may be inadequate, as in this case involving allegations of overreaching by board, other relief may be granted. *Joseph v Shell Oil Co, 498 A2d 1117 (Ch Ct 1985).*

Appraisal was not exclusive remedy when subsidiary's minority shareholders brought suit alleging that parent breached its fiduciary duty of fair dealing by purposely timing cash-out merger to avoid its one-year price commitment with subsidiary's former majority shareholder because (1) mandate in *Weinberger v UOP, Inc* of fair dealing does not turn solely on issue of deception and (2) shareholders are not arguing questions of valuation, which are traditional subjects of appraisal, but are seeking to enforce contractual right, which they claim was unfairly destroyed by parent's manipulative conduct. *Rabkin v Philip A Hunt Chemical Corp, 498 A2d 1099 (1985).*

Former minority shareholder of corporation could bring suit attacking reverse stock split that cashed-out minority shareholders because shareholder's exclusive remedy was not appraisal when shareholder alleged, not only unfair price, but also unfair dealing in form of material omissions in corporation's information statements. *Edick v Contran Corp, No. 7662 (Ch Ct 3-18-86).*

Minority shareholder challenging cash-out merger of corporation was entitled to quasi-appraisal remedy established in *Weinberger v UOP, Inc,* notwithstanding shareholder's failure, even after date of *Weinberger* decision, to follow statutory requirements for perfecting appraisal. However, court dismissed shareholder's claims of unfair dealing because (1) shareholders were given sufficient time to review proxy materials when they were mailed 31 days before meeting and (2) proxy adequately informed shareholders of their appraisal rights, future prospects of corporation, and details of merger transaction. *Patents Management Corp v O'Connor, No. 7110 (Ch Ct 6-10-85).*

Former shareholder of merged corporation could not bring class action alleging that directors and successful tender offeror wrongfully manipulated tender offer battle and improperly expended corporate funds to favor successful tender offeror because (1) former shareholder's breach of fiduciary duty could only be brought as derivative action which he could no longer do and (2) appraisal was adequate remedy. *Shapiro v Pabst Brewing Co, No. 7339 (Ch Ct 7-30-85).*

Former shareholder did not have standing to bring derivative suit for breach of fiduciary duty because he was no longer shareholder and remedies available to minority shareholders facing short-form merger are limited to injunctive relief if merger is unfair and appraisal rights if merger is fair. *Harnett v Billman, 800 F2d 1308 (4th Cir 1986).*

Minority shareholders who were "cashed out" pursuant to Delaware short-form merger could not bring action under New York's Martin Act because merger was not fraudulent or unfair so their sole remedy was to seek appraisal. *Loengard v Santa Fe Industries, Inc, 639 FSupp 673 (SDNY 1986).*

Appraisal is not exclusive remedy in cases involving breach of duty of fair dealing. *Sealy Mattress Co of New Jersey, Inc v Sealy, Inc, 532 A2d 1324 (Ch Ct 1987).*

When informed minority shareholder either votes in merger's favor or accepts its benefits, he or she cannot thereafter attack its fairness. However, shareholders who neither vote in merger's favor nor tender their shares might be entitled to quasi appraisal remedy under *Weinberger v UOP, 457 A2d 701 (1983),* if events occurred before February 1, 1983. *Bershad v Curtiss-Wright Corp, 535 A2d 840 (1987).*

Shareholder who elected to pursue appraisal remedy is not foreclosed from thereafter bringing action to rescind merger, when at time of making election it did not know facts upon which right to rescission allegedly rests. However, shareholder may not simultaneously litigate to judgment statutory action for fair value of stock and action for fraud or breach of fiduciary duty seeking rescission of merger because forms of relief—appraisal relief and either rescissory relief or damages—are inconsistent and shareholder must choose between them at some time. Shareholders must make election no later than time at which either of two actions is set for trial, this gives them fullest opportunity to discover facts relating to election. *Cede & Co v Technicolor, Inc, Nos. 7129 and 8358 (Ch Ct 1-13-87).*

Minority shareholder who has dissented from cash-out merger and begun appraisal proceeding under GCL §262 may pursue later-discovered claim of fraud in merger through action for rescissory damages against participants for breach of fiduciary duty to shareholder. Appraisal action may not be enlarged to include fraud claim since fair value of shares is only issue. Claims may be consolidated for trial, however. If fraud is found, appraisal action will be rendered moot. If not, plaintiff may still obtain appraisal. But plaintiff may not recover duplicative judgments or obtain double recovery. *Cede & Co v Technicolor, Inc, 542 A2d 1182 (1988).*

Appraisal was not exclusive remedy of minority shareholder challenging cash-out merger when complaint charged majority shareholder with manipulating timing of merger and failing to disclose material facts relating to merger's fairness. However, $6.00 per share cash out price was not fair value of corporation. Investment banker that opined that this was fair price relied on corporation's financial results during period when strike was under way. Court found that $7.27 was fair value of corporation's stock at time of merger. *Kahn v Household Acquisition Corp, No. 6293 (Ch Ct 5-6-88).*

In a stock valuation case, a corporate opportunity unlawfully diverted to another company has a direct bearing on the fair value of the stock, but not on the validity of the merger itself. Thus, the minority shareholder's claim is more personal than derivative and properly belongs to a GCL §262 proceeding. *Cavalier Oil Corp v Harnett, 564 A2d 1137 (1989).*

Plaintiff failed to make a prima facie case for negligent misrepresentation where the prospectus stated clearly that plaintiff's shares were subject to a cash-out merger at any time. *Sanders v Devine, No. 14679 (Ch Ct 9-24-97).*

Minority shareholders of a bank holding company, challenging a short-form merger of their corporation into the majority shareholder (another corporation) on substantive (un)fairness grounds, stated cognizable claims of unfair dealing and unfair price where they alleged that defendants, directors of the majority shareholder corporation, did not utilize a special committee of disinterested directors or provide for appraisal by a vote of a majority of the minority stockholders and used a legally improper valuation method to determine the merger price. *Nebel v Southwest Bancorp, Inc, C.A. No. 13618 (Ch Ct 3-9-99).*

The Delaware Supreme Court refused to create a new disclosure standard in merger cases where appraisal was an option and where stockholders were given all the financial data they would need as if the stockholders were making an independent determination of fair value. *Skeen v Jo-ann Stores, Inc, 750 A2d 1170 (2000).*

A shareholder who has accepted merger consideration is not barred by the doctrine of acquiescence from challenging the fairness of the consideration unless the shareholder knew all, and not merely some, of the material facts regarding the merger at the time the merger consideration was accepted. *Clements v Rogers, 790 A2d 1222 (Ch Ct 2001).*

A modified quasi-appraisal remedy, requiring opt-in and repayment of consideration received by minority shareholders, is an appropriate remedy for a breach of the duty to disclose in connection with a short-form merger where full disclosure is no longer necessary. *Gilliland v Motorola, Inc, 2005 Del. Ch. LEXIS 33 (Ch Ct 2005).*

A discounted cash flow analysis is the preferred valuation method in Delaware for dissenters' rights actions, provided the assumptions and projections used are reliable. *Henke v Trilithic, Inc, 2005 Del. Ch. LEXIS 170 (Ch Ct 2005).*

.13 Time to object.—Twenty-day period for stockholder objecting to merger to make demand runs from time notice is posted, not when it is received by corporation. *Schenley Industries, Inc v Curtis, 152 A2d 300 (1959).*

Stockholder dissenting from merger cannot have appraisal; when he does not file timely objections, even though corporation did not reject his objections till after suit begun. *In re Hilton Hotels Corp, 210 A2d 185 (Ch Ct 1965).*

Stockholder's objection to consolidation must be made before consolidation vote is taken by consolidating corporations. *Stephenson v Commonwealth & Southern Corp, 156 A 215 (Ch Ct 1931),* aff'd, *168 A 211 (1933).*

§262

Stockholder's agent need not submit evidence of his authority to object to consolidation; however, corporation may request such evidence. *Zeeb v Atlas Powder Co, 87 A2d 123 (1952).*

To be entitled to an appraisal under this section, stockholder dissenting from merger need not be a registered stockholder at the record date set by the Board of Directors for determining those entitled to vote on the proposed merger, but only by time he must file his written objection. *Lewis v Corroon & Reynolds Corp, 57 A2d 632 (1948).* See also, *Nickles v United Nuclear Corp, 192 A2d 628 (Ch Ct 1963).*

Dissenting stockholder cannot claim that he failed to make timely demand for cash value of his stock because the directors, in soliciting his approval to the plan of consolidation had not advised him that under Delaware law he had a certain prescribed time to dissent and demand full value of his stock, when stockholder had been sent full literature about the plan and that literature contained in four places direct and unmistakable references to the legal right of withdrawal and payment. *Leland Stanford Junior University v National Supply Co, 134 F2d 689 (9th Cir), cert denied, 320 US 773 (1943).*

While surviving corporation's delay in notifying shareholders about merger should be taken into account in reckoning time available for perfecting petition for appraisal, that did not excuse dissenting shareholder for filing late appraisal petition, since it did not automatically extend time for petition and delay was not in bad faith. *Schneyer v Shenandoah Oil Corp, 316 A2d 570 (Ch Ct 1974).*

Former shareholder lost standing to bring derivative suit against corporation's officers and directors for waste after corporation merged into surviving corporation because shareholder's claim became exclusive property right of surviving corporation and its sole shareholder. *Lewis v Anderson, 477 A2d 1040 (1984).*

Shareholders could not enjoin sale of three subsidiaries because (1) subsidiaries' sale would not constitute sale of "substantially all" of corporation's assets, (2) sale of assets did not mandate liquidation of corporation, and (3) shareholders were guilty of laches. Shareholders also could not enjoin special meeting of shareholders to vote on planned liquidation of parent because (1) three separate votes on plan were not required and (2) proxy statement was not materially misleading. *Bacine v Scharffenberger, No. 7862 (Ch Ct 12-11-84).*

Shareholder was not entitled to appraisal of shares pursuant to merger because its demand was untimely when demand was delivered after merger vote and shareholder had reasonable alternatives to assure timely delivery. *Tabbi v Pollution Control Industries, Inc, 508 A2d 867 (Ch Ct 1986).*

.14 Accelerating payment.—Dissenting shareholders to merger cannot ask Court to set minimum value for shares and to order payment for same, pending formal appraisal, on basis of (a) mere conjecture that surviving corporation will not be able ultimately to satisfy appraisal interest or (b) that they are being forced to subsidize corporation during period required to complete appraisal procedure. *Loeb v Schenley Industries, Inc, 285 A2d 829 (Ch Ct 1971).*

.15 Removing action to another jurisdiction.—Corporation could have dissenting stockholder's suit for breach of implied contract in connection with appraisal proceedings transferred from state of stockholder's residence to its state of incorporation on ground that trial instate was inconvenient to corporation; other jurisdiction was more appropriate since action was based on its appraisal statute. *Hammerman v Schenley Industries, Inc, NYLJ, p. 6 (11-3-75).*

.16 Settlement.—Court rejected shareholder's proposed modification of settlement agreement which provided $2 per share to all shareholders who tender but stopped non-tendering shareholders from including any claim for breach of fiduciary duty in their appraisal actions. Settlement was fair to non-tendering shareholders who exercised their rights to appraisal because they benefitted by opportunity to tender shares at higher price. *Selfe v Joseph, 501 A2d 409 (1985).*

Dissenters from merger were not entitled to summary judgment enforcing settlement of statutory ap-praisal claim, even though evidence showed that settlement was agreed to by parties' attorneys. There were material facts in dispute going to question of corporation's defenses of mistake, fraud, or unclean hands involving: (1) circumstances surrounding dissenters' alleged receipt of original merger consideration and subsequent dividends; (2) extent of parties' knowledge of record owner's prior tender of dissenters' shares; and (3) intention of dissenters whether or not to tender. *Matter of Enstar Corp, No. 7802 (Ch Ct 1-31-89).*

.17 Preemption.—Shareholders could not bring appraisal action following cash-out merger between two railroad corporations because appraisal remedy was preempted when Interstate Commerce Commission approved merger as "just and reasonable." *Bruno v Western Pacific Railroad Co, 498 A2d 171 (Ch Ct 1985).*

.18 Stay due to out-of-state action.—Discovery was not stayed in appraisal action filed by shareholders in Delaware, even though another action arising out of same transaction had been filed in Ohio. *Reasons:* (1) appraisal issue was not part of Ohio action; and (2) it was likely that corporation would have to pay interest on shares' value as a result of appraisal. Court also declined to direct shareholders to elect between Delaware appraisal claim and Ohio litigation pending a ruling by Delaware Supreme Court. *Van Gorp v Hepar Industries, Inc, No. 9163 (Ch Ct 1-5-88).*

Plaintiff's motion to stay defendant corporation's appraisal action was granted where: (1) plaintiff filed a breach of fiduciary duty action against defendant in California prior to defendant's filing the appraisal action in Delaware; (2) the determination of the California action in favor of plaintiff will result in plaintiff's recovery of fair value for its shares, rendering defendant's appraisal action moot; (3) proceeding first with the California action will not unduly prejudice defendant; and (4) because plaintiff is the potentially aggrieved party in both actions, courts generally do not permit a defendant to defeat a plaintiff's choice of forum. *In the Matter of Application of Advanced*

Drivers Education Products and Training, Inc, No. 14905 (Ch Ct 8-16-96).

.19 Broker's right to demand appraisal.—Under Delaware law, only a shareholder of record may demand an appraisal. Broker was not entitled to demand appraisal, even though its demand letters identified record holder, referred to record holder as its nominee, named beneficial owners, and stated that it was authorized to act on beneficial owners' behalf. *Reasons:* (1) Broker's demand letters were internally inconsistent; and (2) Delaware Supreme Court has rejected idea that corporation must interpret ambiguous demand letters to determine whether they were made on record shareholders' behalf. *Neal v Alabama By-Products Corp, No. 8282 (Ch Ct 10-11-88).*

.20 Burden of proof.—Burden of proof in appraisal action under GCL §262 should be same as in ordinary civil action, i.e., proof by preponderance of evidence. There is no need to engraft "entire fairness" concept upon appraisal actions. If, however, corporate fiduciaries engage in self dealing and fix merger price by procedures not calculated to yield fair price (by not obtaining independent appraisal by disinterested party or not establishing independent negotiating committee, for example), court will consider those facts in assessing credibility of corporation's valuation contention.

By its own terms, GCL §262(j) does not authorize court to tax plaintiff's attorneys' fees and other litigation expenses against surviving corporation. Those expenses are recoverable only by a *pro rata* apportionment against value of shares entitled to appraisal. *Pinson v Campbell-Taggart, Inc, No. 7499 (Ch Ct 2-28-89)* (opinion revised 4-21, 8-11, and 11-8).

A beneficial owner, who acquires shares after the record date, does not have to prove that each of its specific shares for which it seeks appraisal was not voted in favor of the merger by the previous beneficial owner. *In re: Appraisal of Transkaryotic Therapies, Inc, 2007 Del. Ch. LEXIS 57 (Ch Ct 2007).*

.21 Conspiracy with breaching fiduciary.—Court granted a motion to dismiss complaint that third party conspired with a breaching fiduciary in a merger agreement. While it is not clear at what point a third party must refrain from dealing with a suspected breaching fiduciary, a charge of "knowledge" of such a breach requires more than mere conclusory allegations of conspiracy. *Greenfield v Tele-Communications, Inc, No. 9814 (Ch Ct 5-10-89).*

.22 Entire fairness doctrine.—Where there were no allegations that a leveraged buyout (LBO) involved influence by either a majority stockholder or directors with divided loyalties, no freeze-out merger occurred and an "entire fairness" suit, brought by shareholders cashed out after the LBO, was dismissed. The "entire fairness" standard requires that special scrutiny be given to transactions effectuated by controlling stockholders or directors with divided loyalties. *Lewis v Leaseway Transportation Corp, No. 8720 (Ch Ct 5-16-90).*

Where defendant corporation did not deliberately time merger to avoid a one year price commitment and "entire fairness" (i.e., fair dealing and fair price) characterized corporation's dealings with plaintiffs, no breach of loyalty occurred when plaintiffs purchased the corporation. *Rabkin v Olin Corp, No. 7547 (Ch Ct 4-17-90).*

A freeze-out merger intended to eliminate a minority shareholder does not meet the entire fairness standard of fair dealing and fair price where there are no procedural protections designed to ensure arm's-length bargaining or to approximate a fair valuation procedure.

The Chancery Court applied an entire fairness standard, as the defendants had not used any procedural devices that could temper its application, such as a special negotiating committee of disinterested and independent directors or a majority-of-the-minority stockholder vote provision. Under this standard, the court found that the goal of the merger was to eliminate the minority shareholder and obtain her stock at the formula price for use in the stock swap. The court also found that in their totality, the defendants' tactics and approaches were nothing short of strong-armed and that the process was anything but fair. Instead, it concluded that the defendants had employed a process that was jerryrigged every step of the way. The ultimate step in the process, the merger, included no procedural protections designed to ensure arm's-length bargaining or to approximate a fair valuation procedure. There was no special committee, no opportunity for genuine negotiations regarding the merger consideration, and no dissemination of material information that would level the playing field and prevent the minority shareholder from becoming a drastically disadvantaged minority shareholder. The court also found that the fairness opinion itself was highly suspect. Accordingly, the court concluded that the "fairness opinion" was a mere afterthought, pure window dressing intended by defendants to justify the preordained result of a merger at the formula price. The court, after reviewing valuation evidence, concluded that the fair price for the stock at the time of the merger was $114 per share. It also awarded the minority shareholder all of her court costs and her experts' fees, but not her attorneys' fees. *In re Sunbelt Beverage Corp Shareholder Litigation, 2010 Del. Ch. LEXIS 1 (Ch Ct 2010).*

.23 Termination of appraisal rights.—The Court of Chancery granted a motion to compel the payment of appraisal consideration for shares that had been redeemed after a short-term merger for $75.60 per share prior to the Court of Chancery's determination that their value was $180.60 per share. GCL §262(k) sets forth the steps that must be followed in order to cease appraisal rights, the three most important of which—for purposes of this action—are: (1) a written request by the withdrawing party; (2) written approval by the corporation; and (3) approval by the Court of Chancery. In this case, the transactions did not meet the requirements of this section. The stockholders did not provide a written request to withdraw from the appraisal proceeding, but simply cashed in their shares. In addition, the successor corporation did not properly approve the transaction. Its act of paying merger consideration cannot be construed as implicit approval because the statute unambiguously requires written approval. Finally, the Court of Chancery did not approve a settlement or dismissal of the appraisal proceeding as to the shareholders. *Neal v Alabama By-Products and Drummond Co, No. 8282 (Ch Ct 9-22-93).*

.24 Demand requirement.—Minority shareholder's appraisal action dismissed for failure to make a demand on the corporation where the corporation's secretary, by sworn statement, asserted that the corporation never received the shareholder's demand. Because the shareholder failed to establish that the demand was received by the corporation, the corporation's motion to dismiss was granted. *In the Matter of the Application of Vision Hardware Group Inc, No. 13385 (Ch Ct 4-4-95).*

Demand letter that contained a typographical error nonetheless put the corporation on notice that petitioners were demanding an appraisal. *Sapala v Forest Health Service Corp, No. 14260, 1996 (Ch Ct 1-26-96).*

An appraisal demand that does not strictly comply with statutory requirements governing the timeframes within which demand must be made, or with other statutory requirements, is insufficient; however, where there is a factual dispute over whether a demand is in compliance, and a reasonable inference can be drawn that it is, the demand will be deemed sufficient. *Konfirst v Willow CSN Inc, 2006 Del. Ch. LEXIS 211 (Ch Ct 2006).*

.25 Rights of preferred stockholders.—A dissenting, preferred stockholder's right to a §262 appraisal action may be modified by its accompanying certificate of designation, a document that describes the specific terms of the stock. *In the Matter of the Appraisal of Ford Holdings, Inc Preferred Stock, No. 14852 (Ch Ct 3-20-97).*

Preferred stock is validly issued where a corporation's board properly adopts resolutions authorizing the issuance of the preferred stock and files certificates of designation with the state's secretary of state, and a court in an appraisal proceeding has discretion to value the stock on an as-if-converted basis. *Hildreth v Castle Dental Centers, Inc, 939 A2d 1281 (2007).*

.26 Loss of share certificates.—Petitioner, a minority shareholder, is entitled to proceed with his appraisal action under GCL §262 despite respondent's allegation that he (petitioner) does not possess the certificates representing his shares of stock. *Gilbert v MPM Enterprises, Inc, No. 14416 (Ch Ct 9-2-97).*

.27 Tolling.—The strict filing requirements of an appraisal statute may be equitably tolled where the shareholder seeking appraisal abides by all the statute's technical requirements, does not sleep on its rights, and the corporation has actual and timely notice of the appraisal action at all times and is not prejudiced by such tolling. *Encompass Services Holding Corp v Prosero Inc, 2005 Del. Ch. LEXIS 17 (Ch Ct 2005).*

.28 Entitlement to appraisal rights.—A special dividend and a stock-for-stock merger constitute an integrated transaction entitling dissenting shareholders to appraisal rights. *Louisiana Municipal Police Employee Retirement System v Crawford, 2007 Del. Ch. LEXIS 27 (Ch Ct 2007).*

.29 Statutory short-form merger; fiduciary duties.—The directors of a corporation seeking to effect a statutory short-form merger breach their fiduciary duties of disclosure by failing to attach to the notice of minority shareholders' appraisal rights a copy of the state's current appraisal statute and by failing to disclose all material information. A remedy for such breach is a "quasi-appraisal" remedy. *Berger v Pubco Corp, 2008 Del. Ch. LEXIS 63 (Ch Ct 2008).*

Where after a short-form merger a minority shareholder demands appraisal within the statutorily prescribed period provided, the appraisal demand is valid notwithstanding that the minority shareholder initially waived its statutory right and revoked its tender but then returned an uncashed check for the merger consideration. *Roam-Tel Partners v AT&T Mobility Wireless Operations Holdings, Inc, 2010 Del. Ch. LEXIS 247 (Ch Ct 2010).*

263 MERGER OR CONSOLIDATION OF DOMESTIC CORPORATIONS AND PARTNERSHIPS.—(a) Any 1 or more corporations of this State may merge or consolidate with 1 or more partnerships (whether general (including a limited liability partnership) or limited (including a limited liability limited partnership)), of this State or of any other state or states of the United States, or of the District of Columbia, unless the laws of such other state or states or the District of Columbia forbid such merger or consolidation. Such corporation or corporations and such 1 or more partnerships may merge with or into a corporation, which may be any 1 of such corporations, or they may merge with or into a partnership, which may be any 1 of such partnerships, or they may consolidate into a new corporation or partnership formed by the consolidation, which shall be a corporation or partnership of this State or any other state of the United States, or the District of Columbia, which permits such merger or consolidation, pursuant to an agreement of merger or consolidation, as the case may be, complying and approved in accordance with this section.

(b) Each such corporation and partnership shall enter into a written agreement of merger or consolidation. The agreement shall state: (1) The terms and conditions of the merger or consolidation; (2) the mode of carrying the same into effect; (3) the manner, if any, of converting the shares of stock of each such corporation and the partnership interests of each such partnership into shares, partnership interests or other securities of the entity surviving or resulting from such merger or consolidation or of cancelling some or all of such shares or interests, and if any shares of any such corporation or any partnership interests of any such partnership are not to remain outstanding, to be converted solely into shares, partnership interests or other securities of the entity surviving or resulting from such merger or consolidation or to be cancelled, the cash, property, rights or securities of any other corporation or entity which the holders of such shares or partnership interests are to receive in exchange for, or upon conversion of such shares or partnership interests and the surrender of any certificates evidencing them, which cash, property, rights or securities of any other corporation or entity may be in addition to or in lieu of shares, partnership interests or other securities of the entity surviving or resulting from such merger or consolidation; and (4) such other details or provisions as are deemed desirable, including, without limiting the generality of the foregoing, a provision for the payment of cash in lieu of the issuance of fractional shares or interests of the surviving or resulting corporation or partnership. Any of the terms of the agreement of merger or consolidation may be made dependent upon facts ascertainable outside of such agreement, provided that the manner in which such facts shall operate upon the terms of the agreement is clearly and expressly set forth in the agreement of merger or consolidation. The term "facts," as used in the preceding sentence, includes, but is not limited to, the occurrence of any event, including a determination or action by any person or body, including the corporation.

(c) [1] *The agreement required by subsection (b) of this section shall be adopted, approved, certified, executed and acknowledged by each of the corporations in the same manner as is provided in §251 or §255 of this title and, in the case of the partnerships, in accordance with their partnership agreements and in accordance with the laws of the state under which they are formed, as the case may be. If the surviving or resulting entity is a partnership, in addition to any other approvals, each stockholder of a merging corporation who will become a general partner of the surviving or resulting partnership must approve the agreement of merger or consolidation. The agreement shall be filed and shall become effective for all purposes of the laws of this State when and as provided in §251 or §255 of this title with respect to the merger or consolidation of corporations of this State.* In lieu of filing the agreement of merger or consolidation, the surviving or resulting corporation or partnership may file a certificate of merger or consolidation, executed in accordance with §103 of this title, if the surviving or resulting entity is a corporation, or by a general partner, if the surviving or resulting entity is a partnership, which states: (1) The name and state of domicile of each of the constituent entities; (2) that an agreement of merger or consolidation has been approved, adopted, certified, executed and acknowledged by each of the constituent entities in accordance with this subsection; (3) the name of the surviving or resulting corporation or partnership; (4) in the case of a merger in which a corporation is the surviving entity, such amendments or changes in the certificate of incorporation of the surviving corporation as are desired to be effected by the merger *(which amendments or changes may amend and restate the certificate of incorporation of the surviving corporation in its entirety)*, or, if no such amendments or changes are desired, a statement that the certificate of incorporation of the surviving corporation shall be its certificate of incorporation; (5) in the case of a consolidation in which a corporation is the resulting entity, that the certificate of incorporation of the resulting corporation shall be as is set forth in an attachment to the certificate; (6) that the executed agreement of consolidation or merger is on file at an office of the surviving corporation or partnership and the address thereof; (7) that a copy of the agreement of consolidation or merger will be furnished by the surviving or resulting entity, on request and without cost, to any stockholder of any constituent corporation or any partner of any constituent partnership; and (8) the agreement, if any, required by subsection (d) of this section.

(d) [2] *If the entity surviving or resulting from the merger or consolidation is to be governed by the laws of the District of Columbia or any state other than this State, it shall agree that it may be served with process in this State in any proceeding for enforcement of any obligation of any constituent corporation or partnership of this State, as well as for enforcement of any obligation of the surviving or resulting corporation or partnership arising from the merger or consolidation, including any suit or other proceeding to enforce the right of any stockholders as determined in appraisal proceedings pursuant to §262 of this title, and shall irrevocably appoint the Secretary of State as its agent to accept service of process in any such suit or other proceedings and shall specify the address to which a copy of such process shall be mailed by the Secretary of State. Process may be served upon the Secretary of State under this subsection by means of electronic transmission but only as prescribed by the Secretary of State.* The Secretary of State is authorized to issue such rules and regulations with respect to such service as the Secretary of State deems necessary or appropriate. In the event of such service upon the Secretary of State in accordance with this subsection, the Secretary of State shall forthwith notify such surviving or resulting corporation or partnership thereof by letter, directed to such surviving or resulting corporation or partnership at its address so specified, unless such surviving or resulting corporation or partnership shall have designated in writing to the Secretary of State a different address for such purpose, in which case it shall be mailed to the last address so designated. Such letter shall be sent by a mail or courier service that includes a record of mailing or deposit with the courier and a record of delivery evidenced by the signature of the recipient. Such letter shall enclose a copy of the process and any other papers served on the Secretary of State pursuant to this subsection. It shall be the duty of the plaintiff in the event of such service to serve process and any other papers in duplicate, to notify the Secretary of State that service is being effected pursuant to this subsection and to pay the Secretary of State the sum of $50 for the use of the State, which sum shall be taxed as part of the costs in the proceeding, if the plaintiff shall prevail therein. The Secretary of State shall maintain an alphabetical record of any such service setting forth the name of the plaintiff and the defendant, the title, docket number and nature of the proceeding in which process has been served upon the Secretary of State, the fact that service has been effected pursuant to this subsection, the return date thereof, and the day and hour service was made. The Secretary of State shall not be required to retain such information longer than 5 years from receipt of the service of process.

[3] *(e) Sections 251(c) (second sentence) and (d)-(f), 255(c) (second sentence) and (d)-(f), 259-261 and 328 of this title shall, insofar as they are applicable, apply to mergers or consolidations between corporations and partnerships.*

(f) Nothing in this section shall be deemed to authorize the merger of a charitable nonstock corporation into a partnership, if the charitable status of such nonstock corporation would thereby be lost or impaired; but a partnership may be merged into a charitable nonstock corporation which shall continue as the surviving corporation. (Last amended by Ch. 253, L. '10, eff. 8-1-10 and Ch. 290, L. '10, eff. 8-2-10.)

Ch. 253, L. '10, eff. 8-1-10, added matter in italic and deleted [1]"The agreement required by subsection (b) of this section shall be adopted, approved, certified, executed and acknowledged by each of the corporations in the same manner as is provided in §251 of this title and, in the case of the partnerships, in accordance with their partnership agreements and in accordance with the laws of the state under which they are formed, as the case may be. If the surviving or resulting entity is a partnership, in addition to any other approvals, each stockholder of a merging corporation who will become a general partner of the surviving or resulting partnership must approve the agreement of merger or consolidation. The agreement shall be filed and shall become effective for all purposes of the laws of this State when and as provided in §251 of this title with respect to the merger or consolidation of corporations of this State." and [3]"(e) Sections 251(c) (second sentence) and (d)-(f), 259-261 and 328 of this title shall, insofar as they are applicable, apply to mergers or consolidations between corporations and partnerships." in paragraphs (c) and (e). Ch. 290, L. '10, eff. 8-2-10, added matter in italic in paragraph (c)(4) and (d) and deleted [2]"If the entity surviving or resulting from the merger or consolidation is to be governed by the laws of the District of Columbia or any state other than this State, it shall agree that it may be served with process in this State in any proceeding for enforcement of any obligation of any constituent corporation or partnership of this State, as well as for enforcement of any obligation of the surviving or resulting corporation or partnership arising from the merger or consolidation, including any suit or other proceeding to enforce the right of any stockholders as determined in appraisal proceedings pursuant to §262 of this title, and shall irrevocably appoint the Secretary of State as its agent to accept service of process in any such suit or other proceedings and shall specify the address to which a copy of such process shall be mailed by the Secretary of State. In the event of such service upon the Secretary of State in accordance with this subsection, the Secretary of State shall forthwith notify such surviving or resulting corporation or partnership thereof by letter, certified mail, return receipt requested, directed to such surviving or resulting corporation or partnership at its address so specified, unless such surviving or resulting corporation or partnership shall have designated in writing to the Secretary of State a different address for such purpose, in which case it shall be mailed to the last address so designated."

Ch. 290, L. '10 Synopsis of Section 263

These sections amend Sections 251(b)(3), 251(c)(4), 252(c)(4), 254(d)(4), 263(c)(4), and 264(c)(4), respectively, to clarify that in a merger the certificate of incorporation of the surviving corporation may be amended and restated in its entirety.

These sections amend Sections 252(d), 256(d), 263(d), 264(d), 266(c)(6), 321(b), 376(b), 381(c), 382(a), 382(c), and 390(b)(5), respectively, to allow for service of process upon the Secretary of State thereunder by means of electronic transmission but only as prescribed by the Secretary of State, to authorize the Secretary of State to issue such rules and regulations with respect to such service as the Secretary of State deems necessary or appropriate, and to enable the Secretary of State, in the event that service is effected through the Secretary of State in accordance therewith, to provide notice of service by letter sent by a mail or courier service that includes a record of mailing or deposit with the courier and a record of delivery evidenced by the signature of the recipient.

Ch. 253, L. '10 Synopsis of Section 263

Sections 51, 52, and 53 amend §263 of the DGCL to ensure that the translator provision in new §114(a) operates properly on §263 and to clarify that §263 applies to nonstock corporations, and add new §263(f) to clarify that nothing in §263 shall be deemed to authorize the merger of a charitable nonstock corporation into a partnership, if the charitable status of such charitable nonstock corporation would thereby be lost or impaired.

Ch. 84, L. '03 Synopsis of Section 263

The amendments to Sections 251, 252, 253, 254, 255, 256, 257, 263 and 264 clarify that shares or other interests of a constituent corporation or other entity to a merger or consolidation may be converted, cancelled or unaffected by the merger.

Ch. 298, L. '02 Synopsis of Section 263

The purpose of the amendment to Section 263(b) is to correct the inadvertent deletion of the word "limited" from the last sentence of Section 263(b) that resulted from the former amendment.

Ch. 82, L. '01 Synopsis of Section 263

The amendments to Section 263 permit Delaware corporations to merge with general partnerships, as well as limited partnerships. The amendment to Section 263(c) protects any stockholder of a merging corporation who would become a general partner of a surviving or resulting partnership by requiring that the stockholder approve the agreement of merger or consolidation.

Ch. 339, L. '98 Synopsis of Section 263(d) and (e)

The amendments to these Sections eliminate masculine references in the statutes, and replace them with gender neutral references.

The amendment to subsection (e) of Section 263 provides that the contemporaneous amendment to Section 251(c) shall be applicable to mergers and consolidations under this section.

Ch. 349, L. '96 Synopsis of Section 263

The amendments to Sections 251(b), 252(b), 254(c), 255(b), 256(b), 257(b), 263(b), and 264(b) are intended to conform these sections with the 1994 amendment to Section 151(a). The amendments make clear that a "fact" can include an event or a determination or action by any person or body, including an event or determination within the control of the corporation or a person or body affiliated with the corporation, such as a decision by its board of directors or one of its officers or agents. These amendments are not intended to alter the fiduciary duties of a board of directors in authorizing a merger agreement with terms that turn on determinations or actions made by any person or body, or in making any determination or taking any action constituting a fact under these sections.

The amendments to Sections 251(c)(6), 252(c)(6), 254(d)(6), 263(c)(6) and 264(c)(6) eliminate the requirement that the executed agreement of consolidation or merger be on file at the principal place of business of the surviving corporation or entity in cases where a certificate of merger or consolidation is filed with the Secretary of State in lieu of the agreement of consolidation or merger. The amendment permits the executed agreement of consolidation or merger to be on file at any office of the surviving corporation or entity, whether or not its principal place of business.

264 MERGER OR CONSOLIDATION OF DOMESTIC CORPORATION AND LIMITED LIABILITY COMPANY.—(a) Any 1 or more corporations of this State may merge or consolidate with 1 or more limited liability companies, of this State or of any other state or states of the United States, or of the District of Columbia, unless the laws of such other state or states or the District of Columbia forbid such merger or consolidation. Such corporation or corporations and such 1 or more limited liability companies may merge with or into a corporation, which may be any 1 of such corporations, or they may merge with or into a limited liability company, which may be any 1 of such limited liability companies, or they may consolidate into a new corporation or limited liability company formed by the consolidation, which shall be a corporation or limited liability company of this State or any other state of the United States, or the District of Columbia, which permits such merger or consolidation, pursuant to an agreement of merger or consolidation, as the case may be, complying and approved in accordance with this section.

(b) Each such corporation and limited liability company shall enter into a written agreement of merger or consolidation. The agreement shall state:
 (1) The terms and conditions of the merger or consolidation;
 (2) The mode of carrying the same into effect;
 (3) The manner, if any, of converting the shares of stock of each such corporation and the limited liability company interests of each such limited liability company into shares, limited liability company interests or other securities of the entity surviving or resulting from such merger or consolidation or of cancelling some or all of such shares or interests, and if any shares of any such corporation or any limited liability company interests of any such limited liability company are not to remain outstanding, to be converted solely into shares, limited liability company interests or other securities of the entity surviving or resulting from such merger or consolidation or to be cancelled, the cash, property, rights or securities of any other corporation or entity which the holders of such shares or limited liability company interests are to receive in exchange for, or upon conversion of such shares or limited liability company interests and the surrender of any certificates evidencing them, which cash, property, rights or securities of any other corporation or entity may be in addition to or in lieu of shares, limited liability company interests or other securities of the entity surviving or resulting from such merger or consolidation; and
 (4) Such other details or provisions as are deemed desirable, including, without limiting the generality of the foregoing, a provision for the payment of cash in lieu of the issuance of fractional shares or interests of the surviving or resulting corporation or limited liability company. Any of the terms of the agreement of merger or consolidation may be made dependent upon facts ascertainable outside of such agreement, provided that the manner in which such facts shall operate upon the terms of the agreement is clearly and expressly set forth in the agreement of merger or consolidation. The term "facts," as used in the preceding sentence, includes, but is not limited to, the occurrence of any event, including a determination or action by any person or body, including the corporation.

(c) [1] *The agreement required by subsection (b) of this section shall be adopted, approved, certified, executed and acknowledged by each of the corporations in the same manner as is provided in §251 or §255 of this title and, in the case of the limited liability companies, in accordance with their limited liability company agreements and in accordance with the laws of the state under which they are formed, as the case may be. The agreement shall be filed and shall become effective for all purposes of the laws of this State when and as provided in §251 or §255 of this title with respect to the merger or consolidation of corporations of this State.* In lieu of filing the agreement of merger or consolidation, the surviving or resulting corporation or limited liability company may file a certificate of merger or consolidation, executed in accordance with §103 of this title, if the surviving or resulting entity is a corporation, or by an authorized person, if the surviving or resulting entity is a limited liability company, which states:
 (1) The name and state of domicile of each of the constituent entities;
 (2) That an agreement of merger or consolidation has been approved, adopted, certified, executed and acknowledged by each of the constituent entities in accordance with this subsection;
 (3) The name of the surviving or resulting corporation or limited liability company;
 (4) In the case of a merger in which a corporation is the surviving entity, such amendments or changes in the certificate of incorporation of the surviving corporation as are desired to be effected by the merger *(which amendments or changes may amend and restate the certificate of incorporation of the surviving corporation in its entirety)*, or, if no such amendments or changes are desired, a statement that the certificate of incorporation of the surviving corporation shall be its certificate of incorporation;
 (5) In the case of a consolidation in which a corporation is the resulting entity, that the certificate of incorporation of the resulting corporation shall be as is set forth in an attachment to the certificate;
 (6) That the executed agreement of consolidation or merger is on file at an office of the surviving corporation or limited liability company and the address thereof;

(7) That a copy of the agreement of consolidation or merger will be furnished by the surviving or resulting entity, on request and without cost, to any stockholder of any constituent corporation or any member of any constituent limited liability company; and

(8) The agreement, if any, required by subsection (d) of this section.

(d) [2] *If the entity surviving or resulting from the merger or consolidation is to be governed by the laws of the District of Columbia or any state other than this State, it shall agree that it may be served with process in this State in any proceeding for enforcement of any obligation of any constituent corporation or limited liability company of this State, as well as for enforcement of any obligation of the surviving or resulting corporation or limited liability company arising from the merger or consolidation, including any suit or other proceeding to enforce the right of any stockholders as determined in appraisal proceedings pursuant to the provisions of §262 of this title, and shall irrevocably appoint the Secretary of State as its agent to accept service of process in any such suit or other proceedings and shall specify the address to which a copy of such process shall be mailed by the Secretary of State. Process may be served upon the Secretary of State under this subsection by means of electronic transmission but only as prescribed by the Secretary of State. The Secretary of State is authorized to issue such rules and regulations with respect to such service as the Secretary of State deems necessary or appropriate. In the event of such service upon the Secretary of State in accordance with this subsection, the Secretary of State shall forthwith notify such surviving or resulting corporation or limited liability company thereof by letter, directed to such surviving or resulting corporation or limited liability company at its address so specified, unless such surviving or resulting corporation or limited liability company shall have designated in writing to the Secretary of State a different address for such purpose, in which case it shall be mailed to the last address so designated. Such letter shall be sent by a mail or courier service that includes a record of mailing or deposit with the courier and a record of delivery evidenced by the signature of the recipient.* Such letter shall enclose a copy of the process and any other papers served on the Secretary of State pursuant to this subsection. It shall be the duty of the plaintiff in the event of such service to serve process and any other papers in duplicate, to notify the Secretary of State that service is being effected pursuant to this subsection and to pay the Secretary of State the sum of $50 for the use of the State, which sum shall be taxed as part of the costs in the proceeding, if the plaintiff shall prevail therein. The Secretary of State shall maintain an alphabetical record of any such service setting forth the name of the plaintiff and the defendant, the title, docket number and nature of the proceeding in which process has been served upon the Secretary of State, the fact that service has been effected pursuant to this subsection, the return date thereof, and the day and hour service was made. The Secretary of State shall not be required to retain such information longer than 5 years from receipt of the service of process.

[3] *(e) Sections 251(c) (second sentence) and (d)-(f), 255(c) (second sentence) and (d)-(f), 259-261 and 328 of this title shall, insofar as they are applicable, apply to mergers or consolidations between corporations and limited liability companies.*

(f) Nothing in this section shall be deemed to authorize the merger of a charitable nonstock corporation into a limited liability company, if the charitable status of such nonstock corporation would thereby be lost or impaired; but a limited liability company may be merged into a charitable nonstock corporation which shall continue as the surviving corporation. (Last amended by Ch. 253, L. '10, eff. 8-1-10 and Ch. 290, L. '10, eff. 8-2-10.)

Ch. 253, L. '10, eff. 8-1-10, added matter in italic and deleted [1]"The agreement required by subsection (b) shall be adopted, approved, certified, executed and acknowledged by each of the corporations in the same manner as is provided in §251 of this title and, in the case of the limited liability companies, in accordance with their limited liability company agreements and in accordance with the laws of the state under which they are formed, as the case may be. The agreement shall be filed and shall become effective for all purposes of the laws of this State when and as provided in §251 of this title with respect to the merger or consolidation of corporations of this State." and [3]"(e) Sections 251(c) (second sentence) and (d)—(f), 259—261 and 328 of this title shall, insofar as they are applicable, apply to mergers or consolidations between corporations and limited liability companies." in paragraphs (c), (e), and (f). Ch. 290, L. '10, eff. 8-2-10, added matter in italic in paragraph (c)(4) and (d) and deleted [2]"If the entity surviving or resulting from the merger or consolidation is to be governed by the laws of the District of Columbia or any state other than this State, it shall agree that it may be served with process in this State in any proceeding for enforcement of any obligation of any constituent corporation or limited liability company of this State, as well as for enforcement of any obligation of the surviving or resulting corporation or limited liability company arising from the merger or consolidation, including any suit or other proceeding to enforce the right of any stockholders as determined in appraisal proceedings pursuant to the provisions of §262 of this title, and shall irrevocably appoint the Secretary of State as its agent to accept service of process in any such suit or other proceedings and shall specify the address to which a copy of such process shall be mailed by the Secretary of State. In the event of such service upon the Secretary of State in accordance with this subsection, the Secretary of State shall forthwith notify such surviving or resulting corporation or limited liability company thereof by letter, certified mail, return receipt requested, directed to such surviving or resulting corporation or limited liability company at its address so specified, unless such surviving or resulting corporation or limited liability company shall have designated in writing to the Secretary of State a different address for such purpose, in which case it shall be mailed to the last address so designated."

Ch. 290, L. '10 Synopsis of Section 264

These sections amend Sections 251(b)(3), 251(c)(4), 252(c)(4), 254(d)(4), 263(c)(4), and 264(c)(4), respectively, to clarify that in a merger the certificate of incorporation of the surviving corporation may be amended and restated in its entirety.

These sections amend Sections 252(d), 256(d), 263(d), 264(d), 266(c)(6), 321(b), 376(b), 381(c), 381(d), 382(a), 382(c), and 390(b)(5), respectively, to allow for service of process upon the Secretary of State thereunder by means of electronic transmission but only as prescribed by the Secretary of State, to authorize the Secretary of State to issue such rules and regulations with respect to such service as the Secretary of State deems necessary or appropriate, and to enable the Secretary of State, in the event that service is effected through the Secretary of State in accordance therewith, to provide notice of service by letter sent by a mail or courier service that includes a record of mailing or deposit with the courier and a record of delivery evidenced by the signature of the recipient.

Ch. 253, L. '10 Synopsis of Section 264

Sections 54, 55, and 56 amend §264 of the DGCL to ensure that the translator provision in new §114(a) operates properly on §264 and to clarify that §264 applies to nonstock corporations, and add new §264(f) to clarify that nothing in §264 shall be deemed to authorize the merger of a charitable nonstock corporation into a limited liability company, if the charitable status of such charitable nonstock corporation would thereby be lost or impaired.

Ch. 84, L. '03 Synopsis of Section 264(d)

The amendments to Sections 251, 252, 253, 254, 255, 256, 257, 263 and 264 clarify that shares or other interests of a constituent corporation or other entity to a merger or consolidation may be converted, cancelled or unaffected by the merger.

Ch. 339, L. '98 Synopsis of Section 264(d) and (e)

The amendment to this Section eliminates masculine references in the statutes, and replaces them with gender neutral references.

The amendment to subsection (e) of Section 264 provides that the contemporaneous amendment to Section 251(c) shall be applicable to mergers and consolidations under this section.

Ch. 349, L. '96 Synopsis of Section 264

The amendments to Sections 251(b), 252(b), 254(c), 255(b), 256(b), 257(b), 263(b), and 264(b) are intended to conform these sections with the 1994 amendment to Section 151(a). The amendments make clear that a "fact" can include an event or a determination or action by any person or body, including an event or determination within the control of the corporation or a person or body affiliated with the corporation, such as a decision by its board of directors or one of its officers or agents. These amendments are not intended to alter the fiduciary duties of a board of directors in authorizing a merger agreement with terms that turn on determinations or actions made by any person or body, or in making any determination or taking any action constituting a fact under these sections.

The amendments to Sections 251(c)(6), 252(c)(6), 254(d)(6), 263(c)(6) and 264(c)(6) eliminate the requirement that the executed agreement of consolidation or merger be on file at the principal place of business of the surviving corporation or entity in cases where a certificate of merger or consolidation is filed with the Secretary of State in lieu of the agreement of consolidation or merger. The amendment permits the executed agreement of consolidation or merger to be on file at any office of the surviving corporation or entity, whether or not its principal place of business.

Commentary on Section 264

New Section 264 added by Ch. 61, L. '93, eff. 7-1-93, authorizes the merger of corporations and limited liability companies. The amendments to Sections 254 and 262 reflect the adoption of Section 264.

265 CONVERSION OF OTHER ENTITIES TO A DOMESTIC CORPORATION.—(a) As used in this section, the term "other entity" means a limited liability company, statutory trust, business trust or association, real estate investment trust, common-law trust or any other unincorporated business including a partnership (whether general (including a limited liability partnership) or limited (including a limited liability limited partnership)), or a foreign corporation.

(b) Any other entity may convert to a corporation of this State by complying with subsection (h) of this section and filing in the office of the Secretary of State:

(1) A certificate of conversion to corporation that has been executed in accordance with subsection (i) of this section and filed in accordance with §103 of this title; and

(2) A certificate of incorporation that has been executed, acknowledged and filed in accordance with §103 of this title.

Each of the certificates required by this subsection (b) shall be filed simultaneously in the office of the Secretary of State and, if such certificates are not to become effective upon their filing as permitted by §103(d) of this title, then each such certificate shall provide for the same effective date or time in accordance with §103(d) of this title.

(c) The certificate of conversion to corporation shall state:

(1) The date on which and jurisdiction where the other entity was first created, incorporated, formed or otherwise came into being and, if it has changed, its jurisdiction immediately prior to its conversion to a domestic corporation;

(2) The name of the other entity immediately prior to the filing of the certificate of conversion to corporation; and

(3) The name of the corporation as set forth in its certificate of incorporation filed in accordance with subsection (b) of this section.

(d) Upon the effective time of the certificate of conversion to corporation and the certificate of incorporation, the other entity shall be converted to a corporation of this State and the corporation shall thereafter be subject to all of the provisions of this title, except that notwithstanding §106 of this title, the existence of the corporation shall be deemed to have commenced on the date the other entity commenced its existence in the jurisdiction in which the other entity was first created, formed, incorporated or otherwise came into being.

(e) The conversion of any other entity to a corporation of this State shall not be deemed to affect any obligations or liabilities of the other entity incurred prior to its conversion to a corporation of this State or the personal liability of any person incurred prior to such conversion.

(f) When an other entity has been converted to a corporation of this State pursuant to this section, the corporation of this State shall, for all purposes of the laws of the State of Delaware, be deemed to be the same entity as the converting other entity. When any conversion shall have become effective under this section, for all purposes of the laws of the State of Delaware, all of the rights, privileges and powers of the other entity that has converted, and all property, real, personal and mixed, and all debts due to such other entity, as well as all other things and causes of action belonging to such other entity, shall remain vested in the domestic corporation to which such other entity has converted and shall be the property of such domestic corporation and the title to any real property vested by deed or otherwise in such other entity shall not revert or be in any way impaired by reason of this chapter; but all rights of creditors and all liens upon any property of such other entity shall be preserved unimpaired, and all debts, liabilities and duties of the other entity that has converted shall remain attached to the corporation of this State to which such other entity has converted, and may be enforced against it to the same extent as if said debts, liabilities and duties had originally been incurred or contracted by it in its capacity as a corporation of this State. The rights, privileges, powers and interests in property of the other entity, as well as the debts, liabilities and duties of the other entity, shall not be deemed, as a consequence of the conversion, to have been transferred to the domestic corporation to which such other entity has converted for any purpose of the laws of the State of Delaware.

(g) Unless otherwise agreed for all purposes of the laws of the State of Delaware or as required under applicable non-Delaware law, the converting other entity shall not be required to wind up its affairs or pay its liabilities and distribute its assets, and the conversion shall not be deemed to constitute a dissolution of such other entity and shall constitute a continuation of the existence of the converting other entity in the form of a corporation of this State.

(h) Prior to filing a certificate of conversion to corporation with the office of the Secretary of State, the conversion shall be approved in the manner provided for by the document, instrument, agreement or other writing, as the case may be, governing the internal affairs of the other entity and the conduct of its business or by applicable law, as appropriate, and a certificate of incorporation shall be approved by the same authorization required to approve the conversion.

(i) The certificate of conversion to corporation shall be signed by any person who is authorized to sign the certificate of conversion to corporation on behalf of the other entity.

(j) In connection with a conversion hereunder, rights or securities of, or interests in, the other entity which is to be converted to a corporation of this State may be exchanged for or converted into cash, property, or shares of stock, rights or securities of such corporation of this State or, in addition to or in lieu thereof, may be exchanged for or converted into cash, property, or shares of stock, rights or securities of or interests in another domestic corporation or other entity or may be cancelled. (Last amended by Ch. 96, L. '11, eff. 8-1-11.)

Ch. 96, L. '11, eff. 8-1-11, added matter in italic.

Ch. 96, L. '11 Synopsis of Section 265

This Section amends Section 265 to clarify that the certificate of conversion to corporation and the certificate of incorporation of another entity converting to a Delaware corporation must be filed simultaneously in the office of the Secretary of State and, to the extent such certificates are to have a post-filing effective date or time, such certificates must provide for the same effective date or time.

Ch. 30, L. '05 Synopsis of Section 265

The amendments to Section 265 provide for the conversion of an other entity, including a non-Delaware other entity, to a Delaware corporation. The addition of subsection (f) makes it clear that upon conversion to a corporation, the corporation is a continuation of the existence of the converting other entity. The addition of subsection (j) confirms the flexibility permitted in the Code regarding a conversion to a domestic corporation.

Ch. 329, L. '02 Synopsis of Section 265

The amendments set forth are made for the purpose of avoiding any implication that a trust formed under Chapter 38, Title 12 of the Delaware Code constitutes a "business trust" within the meaning of Title 11 of the United States Code. Such amendments are not intended to result in any substantive change in Delaware law. These amendments are made solely for the purpose of conforming the Delaware Code to the amendments set forth above.

Ch. 82, L. '01 Synopsis of Section 265

The amendments to Section 265 permit a Delaware general partnership to convert to a Delaware corporation.

Ch. 123, L. '99 Synopsis of Section 265

This section adds a new §265 of the Act which provides that any limited liability company, limited partnership or business trust of this State may convert to a corporation of this State upon obtaining the requisite approval of a certificate of conversion and a certificate of incorporation by such converting entity, and the filing of such certificate of conversion and certificate of incorporation with the Secretary of State. Such conversion shall not affect any obligations or liabilities of the converting entity incurred prior to its conversion or the personal liability of any person incurred prior to such conversion.

266 CONVERSION OF A DOMESTIC CORPORATION TO OTHER ENTITIES.—(a) A corporation of this State may, upon the authorization of such conversion in accordance with this section, convert to a limited liability company, statutory trust, business trust or association, real estate investment trust, common-law trust or any other unincorporated business including a partnership (whether general (including a limited liability partnership) or limited (including a limited liability limited partnership)) or a foreign corporation.

(b) The board of directors of the corporation which desires to convert under this section shall adopt a resolution approving such conversion, specifying the type of entity into which the corporation shall be converted and recommending the approval of such conversion by the stockholders of the corporation. Such resolution shall be submitted to the stockholders of the corporation at an annual or special meeting. Due notice of the time, and purpose of the meeting shall be mailed to each holder of stock, whether voting or nonvoting, of the corporation at the address of the stockholder as it appears on the records of the corporation, at least 20 days prior to the date of the meeting. At the meeting, the resolution shall be considered and a vote taken for its adoption or rejection. If all outstanding shares of stock of the corporation, whether voting or nonvoting, shall be voted for the adoption of the resolution, the conversion shall be authorized.

(c) If a corporation shall convert in accordance with this section to another entity organized, formed or created under the laws of a jurisdiction other than the State of Delaware, the corporation shall file with the Secretary of State a certificate of conversion executed in accordance with §103 of this title, which certifies:

(1) The name of the corporation, and if it has been changed, the name under which it was originally incorporated;

(2) The date of filing of its original certificate of incorporation with the Secretary of State;

(3) The name and jurisdiction of the entity to which the corporation shall be converted;

(4) That the conversion has been approved in accordance with the provisions of this section;

(5) The agreement of the corporation that it may be served with process in the State of Delaware in any action, suit or proceeding for enforcement of any obligation of the corporation arising while it was a corporation of this State, and that it irrevocably appoints the Secretary of State as its agent to accept service of process in any such action, suit or proceeding; and

(6) [1] *The address to which a copy of the process referred to in paragraph (c)(5) of this section shall be mailed to it by the Secretary of State. Process may be served upon the Secretary of State in accordance with paragraph (c)(5) of this section by means of electronic transmission but only as prescribed by the Secretary of State. The Secretary of State is authorized to issue such rules and regulations with respect to such service as the Secretary of State deems necessary or appropriate. In the event of such service upon the Secretary of State in accordance with paragraph (c)(5) of this section, the Secretary of State shall forthwith notify such corporation that has converted out of the State of Delaware by letter, directed to such corporation that has converted out of the State of Delaware at the address so specified, unless such corporation shall have designated in writing to the Secretary of State a different address for such purpose, in which case it shall be mailed to the last address designated. Such letter shall be sent by a mail or courier service that includes a record of mailing or deposit with the courier and a record of delivery evidenced by the signature of the recipient.* Such letter shall enclose a copy of the process and any other papers served on the Secretary of State pursuant to this subsection. It shall be the duty of the plaintiff in the event of such service to serve process and any other papers in duplicate, to notify the Secretary of State that service is being effected pursuant to this subsection and to pay the Secretary of State the sum of $50 for the use of the State, which sum shall be taxed as part of the costs in the proceeding, if the plaintiff shall prevail therein. The Secretary of State shall maintain an alphabetical record of any such service setting forth the name of the plaintiff and the defendant, the title, docket number and nature of the proceeding in which process has been served, the fact that service has been effected pursuant to this subsection, the return date thereof, and the day and hour service was made. The Secretary of State shall not be required to retain such information longer than 5 years from receipt of the service of process.

(d) Upon the filing in the Office of the Secretary of State of a certificate of conversion to non-Delaware entity in accordance with subsection (c) of this section or upon the future effective date or time of the certificate of conversion to non-Delaware entity and payment to the Secretary of State of all fees prescribed under this title, the Secretary of State shall certify that the corporation has filed all documents and paid all fees required by this title, and thereupon the corporation shall cease to exist as a corporation of this State at the time the certificate of conversion becomes effective in accordance with §103 of this title. Such certificate of the Secretary of State shall be prima facie evidence of the conversion by such corporation out of the State of Delaware.

§266

(e) The conversion of a corporation out of the State of Delaware in accordance with this section and the resulting cessation of its existence as a corporation of this State pursuant to a certificate of conversion to non-Delaware entity shall not be deemed to affect any obligations or liabilities of the corporation incurred prior to such conversion or the personal liability of any person incurred prior to such conversion, nor shall it be deemed to affect the choice of law applicable to the corporation with respect to matters arising prior to such conversion.

(f) Unless otherwise provided in a resolution of conversion adopted in accordance with this section, the converting corporation shall not be required to wind up its affairs or pay its liabilities and distribute its assets, and the conversion shall not constitute a dissolution of such corporation.

(g) In connection with a conversion of a domestic corporation to another entity pursuant to this section, shares of stock, of the corporation of this State which is to be converted may be exchanged for or converted into cash, property, rights or securities of, or interests in, the entity to which the corporation of this State is being converted or, in addition to or in lieu thereof, may be exchanged for or converted into cash, property, shares of stock, rights or securities of, or interests in, another domestic corporation or other entity or may be cancelled.

(h) When a corporation has been converted to another entity or business form pursuant to this section, the other entity or business form shall, for all purposes of the laws of the State of Delaware, be deemed to be the same entity as the corporation. When any conversion shall have become effective under this section, for all purposes of the laws of the State of Delaware, all of the rights, privileges and powers of the corporation that has converted, and all property, real, personal and mixed, and all debts due to such corporation, as well as all other things and causes of action belonging to such corporation, shall remain vested in the other entity or business form to which such corporation has converted and shall be the property of such other entity or business form, and the title to any real property vested by deed or otherwise in such corporation shall not revert or be in any way impaired by reason of this chapter; but all rights of creditors and all liens upon any property of such corporation shall be preserved unimpaired, and all debts, liabilities and duties of the corporation that has converted shall remain attached to the other entity or business form to which such corporation has converted, and may be enforced against it to the same extent as if said debts, liabilities and duties had originally been incurred or contracted by it in its capacity as such other entity or business form. The rights, privileges, powers and interest in property of the corporation that has converted, as well as the debts, liabilities and duties of such corporation, shall not be deemed, as a consequence of the conversion, to have been transferred to the other entity or business form to which such corporation has converted for any purpose of the laws of the State of Delaware.

(i) No vote of stockholders of a corporation shall be necessary to authorize a conversion if no shares of the stock of such corporation shall have been issued prior to the adoption by the board of directors of the resolution approving the conversion.

(j) *Nothing in this section shall be deemed to authorize the conversion of a charitable nonstock corporation into another entity, if the charitable status of such charitable nonstock corporation would thereby be lost or impaired.* (Last amended by Ch. 253, L. '10, eff. 8-1-10 and Ch. 290, L. '10, eff. 8-2-10.)

Ch. 253, L. '10, eff. 8-1-10, added matter in italic in paragraph (j). Ch. 290, L. '10, eff. 8-2-10, added matter in italic and deleted [1]"The address to which a copy of the process referred to in subsection (c)(5) of this section shall be mailed to it by the Secretary of State. In the event of such service upon the Secretary of State in accordance with subsection (c)(5) of this section, the Secretary of State shall forthwith notify such corporation that has converted out of the State of Delaware by letter, certified mail, return receipt requested, directed to such corporation that has converted out of the State of Delaware at the address so specified, unless such corporation shall have designated in writing to the Secretary of State a different address for such purpose, in which case it shall be mailed to the last address designated." in paragraph (c)(6).

Ch. 290, L. '10 Synopsis of Section 266

These sections amend Sections 252(d), 256(d), 263(d), 264(d), 266(c)(6), 321(b), 376(b), 381(c), 381(d), 382(a), 382(c), and 390(b)(5), respectively, to allow for service of process upon the Secretary of State thereunder by means of electronic transmission but only as prescribed by the Secretary of State, to authorize the Secretary of State to issue such rules and regulations with respect to such service as the Secretary of State deems necessary or appropriate, and to enable the Secretary of State, in the event that service is effected through the Secretary of State in accordance therewith, to provide notice of service by letter sent by a mail or courier service that includes a record of mailing or deposit with the courier and a record of delivery evidenced by the signature of the recipient.

Ch. 253, L. '10 Synopsis of Section 266

Section 57 amends the DGCL to add new §266(j) to clarify that nothing in §266 shall be deemed to authorize the conversion of a charitable nonstock corporation into another entity, if the charitable status of such charitable nonstock corporation would thereby be lost or impaired.

Ch. 30, L. '05 Synopsis of Section 266

The amendments to Section 266 provide for the conversion of a Delaware corporation to an other entity, including a non-Delaware other entity. The amendments to subsections (e) and (f) and the addition of subsection (h) clarify the effects of a conversion of a Delaware corporation to an other entity. New subsection (g) confirms the flexibility permitted in this section regarding a conversion of a domestic corporation. New subsection (i) provides that if a converting Delaware corporation has no outstanding capital stock, no vote of stockholders is required to authorize the conversion.

Ch. 84, L. '03 Synopsis of Section 266

This amendment to Section 266 confirms that Delaware corporations which desire to convert to Delaware limited liability companies, general partnerships, limited partnerships or statutory trusts must also comply with the applicable requirements of the statutes governing the formation of those entities to complete the conversion.

Ch. 329, L. '02 Synopsis of Section 266

The amendments set forth are made for the purpose of avoiding any implication that a trust formed under Chapter 38, Title 12 of the Delaware Code constitutes a "business trust" within the meaning of Title 11 of the United States Code. Such amendments are not intended to result in any substantive change in Delaware law. These amendments are made solely for the purpose of conforming the Delaware Code to the amendments set forth above.

Ch. 82, L. '01 Synopsis of Section 266

The amendments to Section 266 permit a Delaware corporation to convert to a Delaware general partnership.

Ch. 123, L. '99 Synopsis of Section 266

This section adds a new §266 of the Act which provides that any corporation of this State may convert to a limited liability company, limited partnership or business trust of this State upon obtaining the requisite approval, including the approval of the holders of all outstanding shares of stock of the corporation, whether voting or nonvoting, and the filing of a certificate of conversion with the Secretary of State. Such conversion shall not affect any obligations or liabilities of the converting corporation incurred prior to its conversion or the personal liability of any person incurred prior to such conversion.

267 MERGER OF PARENT ENTITY AND SUBSIDIARY CORPORATION OR CORPORATIONS.—(a) In any case in which: (1) at least 90% of the outstanding shares of each class of the stock of a corporation or corporations (other than a corporation which has in its certificate of incorporation the provision required by §251(g)(7)(i) of this title), of which class there are outstanding shares that, absent this subsection, would be entitled to vote on such merger, is owned by an entity, (2) 1 or more of such corporations is a corporation of this State, and (3) any entity or corporation that is not an entity or corporation of this State is an entity or corporation of any other state or the District of Columbia, the laws of which do not forbid such merger, the entity having stock ownership may either merge the corporation or corporations into itself and assume all of its or their obligations, or merge itself, or itself and 1 or more of such corporations, into 1 of the other corporations by (a) authorizing such merger in accordance with such entity's governing documents and the laws of the jurisdiction under which such entity is formed or organized and (b) acknowledging and filing with the Secretary of State, in accordance with §103 of this title, a certificate of such ownership and merger certifying that such merger was authorized in accordance with such entity's governing documents and the laws of the jurisdiction under which such entity is formed or organized, such certificate executed in accordance with such entity's governing documents and in accordance with the laws of the jurisdiction under which such entity is formed or organized; provided, however, that in case the entity shall not own all the outstanding stock of all the corporations, parties to a merger as aforesaid, (A) the certificate of ownership and merger shall state the terms and conditions of the merger, including the securities, cash, property, or rights to be issued, paid, delivered or granted by the surviving constituent party upon surrender of each share of the corporation or corporations not owned by the entity, or the cancellation of some or all of such shares and (B) such terms and conditions of the merger may not result in a holder of stock in a corporation becoming a general partner in a surviving entity that is a partnership (other than a limited liability partnership or a limited liability limited partnership). Any of the terms of the merger may be made dependent upon facts ascertainable outside of the certificate of ownership and merger, provided that the manner in which such facts shall operate upon the terms of the merger is clearly and expressly set forth in the certificate of ownership and merger. The term "facts," as used in the preceding sentence, includes, but is not limited to, the occurrence of any event, including a determination or action by any person or body, including the entity. If the surviving constituent party exists under the laws of the District of Columbia or any state or jurisdiction other than this State, (1) §252(d) of this title shall also apply to a merger under this section; if the surviving constituent party is the entity, the word "corporation" where applicable, as used in §252(d) of this title, shall be deemed to include an entity as defined herein; and (2) the terms and conditions of the merger shall obligate the surviving constituent party to provide the agreement, and take the actions, required by §252(d) of this title.

(b) Sections 259, 261, and 328 of this title shall, insofar as they are applicable, apply to a merger under this section, and §260 and §251(e) of this title shall apply to a merger under this section in which the surviving constituent party is a corporation of this State. For purposes of this subsection, references to "agreement of merger" in §251(e) of this title shall mean the terms and conditions of the merger set forth in the certificate of ownership and merger, and references to "corporation" in §§259-261 of this title, and §328 of this title shall be deemed to include the entity, as applicable. Section 262 of this title shall not apply to any merger effected under this section, except as provided in subsection (c) of this section.

(c) In the event all of the stock of a Delaware corporation party to a merger effected under this section is not owned by the entity immediately prior to the merger, the stockholders of such Delaware corporation party to the merger shall have appraisal rights as set forth in §262 of this title.

(d) A merger may be effected under this section although 1 or more of the constituent parties is a corporation organized under the laws of a jurisdiction other than 1 of the United States; provided that the laws of such jurisdiction do not forbid such merger.

(e) As used in this section only, the term:

(1) "Constituent party" means an entity or corporation to be merged pursuant to this section;

(2) "Entity" means a partnership (whether general (including a limited liability partnership) or limited (including a limited liability limited partnership)), limited liability company, any association of the kind commonly known as a joint-stock association or joint-stock company and any unincorporated association, trust or enterprise having members or having outstanding shares of stock or other evidences of financial or beneficial interest therein, whether formed by agreement or under statutory authority or otherwise; and

(3) "Governing documents" means a partnership agreement, limited liability company agreement, articles of association or any other instrument containing the provisions by which an entity is formed or organized. (Added by Ch. 290, L. '10, eff. 8-2-10.)

Ch. 290, L. '10 Synopsis of Section 267

Section 267 is new. Section 267 provides a mechanism for a short form merger of a subsidiary corporation or corporations and a parent non-corporate entity.

SUBCHAPTER X. SALE OF ASSETS, DISSOLUTION AND WINDING UP

271 SALE, LEASE OR EXCHANGE OF ASSETS; CONSIDERATION; PROCEDURE.—(a) Every corporation may at any meeting of its board of directors or governing body sell, lease or exchange all or substantially all of its property and assets, including its goodwill and its corporate franchises, upon such terms and conditions and for such consideration, which may consist in whole or in part of money or other property, including shares of stock in, and/or other securities of, any other corporation or corporations, as its board of directors or governing body deems expedient and for the best interests of the corporation, when and as authorized by a resolution adopted by the holders of a majority of the outstanding stock of the corporation entitled to vote thereon or, if the corporation is a nonstock corporation, by a majority of the members having the right to vote for the election of the members of the governing body *and any other members entitled to vote thereon under the certificate of incorporation or the bylaws of such corporation*, at a meeting duly called upon at least 20 days' notice. The notice of the meeting shall state that such a resolution will be considered.

(b) Notwithstanding authorization or consent to a proposed sale, lease or exchange of a corporation's property and assets by the stockholders or members, the board of directors or governing body may abandon such proposed sale, lease or exchange without further action by the stockholders or members, subject to the rights, if any, of third parties under any contract relating thereto.

(c) For purposes of this section only, the property and assets of the corporation include the property and assets of any subsidiary of the corporation. As used in this subsection, "subsidiary" means any entity wholly-owned and controlled, directly or indirectly, by the corporation and includes, without limitation, corporations, partnerships, limited partnerships, limited liability partnerships, limited liability companies, and/or statutory trusts. Notwithstanding subsection (a) of this section, except to the extent the certificate of incorporation otherwise provides, no resolution by stockholders or members shall be required for a sale, lease or exchange of property and assets of the corporation to a subsidiary. (Last amended by Ch. 253, L. '10, eff. 8-1-10.)

Ch. 253, L. '10, eff. 8-1-10, added matter in italic.

Ch. 253, L. '10 Synopsis of Section 271

Section 58 amends §271(a) of the DGCL to clarify that members may vote on a sale, lease or exchange of all or substantially all of its property and assets if, under the corporation's certificate or incorporation or bylaws, they are entitled to vote thereon or for the election of the members of the governing body.

Ch. 30, L. '05, Synopsis of Section 271

Section 271 has been amended to add new subsection (c). The purpose of subsection (c) is to provide that (i) no stockholder vote is required for a sale, lease or exchange of assets to or with a direct or indirect wholly-owned and controlled subsidiary, and (ii) the assets of such a subsidiary are to be treated as assets of its ultimate parent for purposes of applying, at the parent level, the requirements set forth in subsection (a). The amendment is not intended to address the application of subsection (a) to a sale, lease or exchange of assets by, or to or with, a subsidiary that is not wholly-owned and controlled, directly or indirectly, by the ultimate parent.

.1 Sale of assets.—If power is given in charter to sell substantially all the property of the company with the assent of holders of 3/4 of the stock everyone taking shares is bound by that provision. *Butler v New Keystone Copper Co, 93 A 380 (Ch Ct 1915).*

Transfer of assets to new corporation organized by officers of insolvent corporation without compliance with Bulk Sales Act is void as to creditors. *Keedy v Sterling Electric Appliance Co, 115 A 359 (Ch Ct 1921).*

Sale of assets by one corporation to another contingent on pending suit for injunction by minority stockholders cannot be set aside by court without bringing buying corporation into court. *Allied Chemical & Dye Corp v Steel & Tube Corp, 122 A 142 (Ch Ct 1923).*

By selling entire corporate assets as voted by stockholders for purpose of dissolving, directors are presumed to act in good faith for best interests of corporation. *Robinson v Pittsburgh Oil Refining Corp, 126 A 46 (Ch Ct 1924)*, followed in *Mitchell v Highland-Western Glass Co, 167 A 831 (Ch Ct 1933).* See also, *Finch v Warrior Cement Corp, 141 A 54 (Ch Ct 1928); Hellier v Bausch Machine Tool Co, 21 F2d 705 (1st Cir 1927); Karasik v Pacific Eastern Corp, 180 A 604 (Ch Ct 1935).*

Affirmative vote of 2/3 of common stock is sufficient to authorize sale of whole of corporate property where bylaw provides that preferred stock has no voting power, and another bylaw provide that affirmative vote of ⅔ of "capital stock issued and out-standing" is necessary to authorize such sale. *Morrell v Geo Brooks & Son Co, 164 F 501 (D Del 1908).*

Sale of corporate assets which has been approved by stockholders who have lost voting rights will be set aside. *Macht v Merchants Mtge & Credit Co, 194 A 23 (Ch Ct 1937).*

Sale of assets under this section, while voidable for fraud, cannot be attacked for failure to comply with merger and consolidation statutes, or to secure unanimous consent of stockholders on the ground that transaction constitutes statutory or common-law consolidation or merger. *Argenbright v Phoenix Finance Corp, 187 A 124 (Ch Ct 1936).*

Preliminary injunction against sale of assets and liquidation will be denied, when (1) stockholders were adequately informed about plan of sale and part played by alleged interested directors, (2) proxy statement adequately appraised corporation's assets, and (3) corporation's adoption of buyer's appraisal was justified and independent appraisal was not necessary. *Gropper v The North Central Texas Oil Co, 114 A2d 231 (Ch Ct 1955).*

Sale of corporation's entire assets is valid although a 50% stockholder-director whose vote is necessary for sale's approval is given a lucrative employment contract by buying corporation, when selling corporation receives fair value for its assets and buying corporation would not make the deal without securing that director's services and agreement not to compete. *Smith v The Good Music Station, Inc, 129 A2d 242 (Ch Ct 1957).*

Board breached its duty in rejecting offer to buy corporation's only asset, a large tract of land, at highest bid; it should again ask for bids on corporate lands and submit them for stockholders' vote. *Thomas v Kempner, No. 4138 (Ch Ct 3-22-73).*

Board's decision to sell conglomerate's oil and gas holdings did not amount to sale of substantially all of corporation's assets so as to require shareholder approval, even though oil and gas business continued to be listed as corporation's principal purpose, and even though oil and gas assets were quantitatively substantial within conglomerate. *Gimbel III v The Signal Companies, Inc, 316 A2d 599 (Ch Ct), aff'd, 316 A2d 619 (1974).*

Proposed sale of corporation's Canadian operations, which constituted 51% of corporation's assets and which generated approximately 45% of corporation's 1980 net sales, would, if consummated, constitute a sale of substantially all of corporation's assets requiring approval by a majority of stockholders at a stockholders' meeting. *Katz v Bregman, 431 A2d 1274 (Ch Ct 1981).*

Although corporate sale of property to officer shareholders for less than adequate consideration is generally voidable at corporation's option, in this case, to avoid "windfall" to shareholder who treated corporate assets as his own, officers/shareholders who bought the property had to pay the difference between property's purchase price and market value corporation. *Warren v Warren, 460 A2d 526 (1983).*

A sale of corporate assets that occurred pursuant to a special board of directors' meeting that was neither called by the proper director nor voted upon by the full board was invalid since the meeting took place in violation of the corporate bylaws; defendants' contention that the relevant statute did not apply in emergency situations was not decided since no emergency was present. *Russell v Morris, No. 10009 (Ch Ct 2-14-90).*

A corporation registered under the Exchange Act that is considering an asset sale that, as a matter of law and the company's certificate of incorporation, requires the affirmative vote of a majority of the common stockholders, must await such a vote before proceeding with the sale, even though it is prohibited from calling a stockholder meeting because it has not filed its required annual 10-K report. *Esopus Creek Value LP v Hauf, 2006 Del. Ch. LEXIS 200 (Ch Ct 2006).*

A corporation's proposal to split off certain business as a new company does not violate its indenture's successor obligation clause—pursuant to which the corporation has agreed not to transfer substantially all of its assets unless the successor entity assumes its obligations under the indenture—where, under the step-transaction doctrine, its prior transfers of corporate assets are not aggregated with its proposed transfer because they are not sufficiently related. *Liberty Media Corp v The Bank of New York Mellon Trust Co, N.A., 2011 Del. Ch. LEXIS 66 (Ch Ct 2011).*

.2 Same—consideration.—Agreement to take shares in another company for assets is valid. *Butler v New Keystone Copper Co, 93 A 380 (Ch Ct 1915).*

A legally inadequate price for corporate assets is an inadequacy "so gross as to display itself as a badge of fraud." *Mitchell v Highland-Western Glass Co, 167 A 831 (Ch Ct 1933).*

Sale of corporate assets, where buying corporation issues stock and notes in exchange for assets bought, cannot be attacked on ground that notes are void for lack of consideration absent proof of overvaluation of assets of selling corporation. *Gott v Live Poultry Transit Co, 156 A 292 (Ch Ct), aff'd, 161 A 150 (1932).*

Absent showing that directors and majority stockholders are in some manner to share in profits arising from sale of assets, the requisite vote of stockholders authorizing the sale normally prevents court review of such sale. If, however, plaintiff can successfully carry the burden of showing that disparity between value of the property to be sold and money to be received is so unreasonable as to be attributable to bad faith, court will infer some improper motive on part of the sellers, or will assume that sellers are recklessly indifferent to the interests of whole body of stockholders. *Allied Chemical & Dye Corp v Steel & Tube Co, 120 A 486 (Ch Ct 1923); Shiff v RKO Pictures Corp, 104 A2d 267 (Ch Ct 1954).*

The value in sale of corporate assets is not cost or replacement value but value in connection with sale. Such sale presupposes willing buyer and willing seller; buyer can be expected to anticipate profit, and majority stockholders of selling corporation are not guilty of improper motives in wanting to make speculative profit. *Allaun v Consolidated Oil Co, 147 A 257 (Ch Ct 1929).*

When agreement for sale of a business obligates buying corporation to issue additional shares of its stock to sellers if the business makes a given amount of profit, sellers cannot get that additional stock when buying corporation terminates business after good faith determination that it cannot operate it profitably. *Harvard Industries, Inc v Wendel, 178 A2d 486 (Ch Ct 1962).*

Though consideration offered on sale of assets was much less than book value, disparity was not so great as to be violation of fiduciary duty by directors and majority stockholders when earnings per share had dropped about 80% in four years and outlook for further profitable operation was dim. *Baron v Pressed Metals of America, Inc, 117 A2d 357 (Ch Ct 1955),* rearg denied, *188 A2d 360,* aff'd, *123 A2d 848 (1956).*

Although not all the directors were conversant with the value factors involved in fixing consideration for sale of assets, the board's approval is never-theless valid; capitalization rate of seven or eight times normal earnings was reasonable for a family corporation in heavy industry. *Cottrell v The Pawcatuck Co, 116 A2d 787 (Ch Ct 1955),* aff'd, *128 A2d 225 (1956).*

Minority stockholders in 95%-owned subsidiary that sold its assets to parent and liquidated cannot get additional compensation for their surrendered shares when the sale price is supported by an uncontradicted expert appraisal, even though their corporation could have gotten a higher price by sale to a third party, or by an exchange of its stock with a third corporation that controlled both buyer and seller. *Abelow v Symonds, 184 A2d 173 (Ch Ct 1962),* aff'd, *Abelow v Mid-States Oil Corp, 189 A2d 675 (1963).*

Derivatively suing stockholders cannot set aside a sale of all their corporation's assets unless they show fraud or a price so low it amounts to fraud; they do not show fraud when (1) the price was arrived at by arm's-length bargaining, and (2) the price was the same at which bids had been invited for the assets, with no offers received. *Marks v Wolfson, 188 A2d 680 (Ch Ct 1963); Amsterdam v Baker, 188 A2d 680 (Ch Ct 1963).*

Court will not review adequacy of purchase price of corporate assets unless disparity is so great as to shock the conscience of the court or warrant the conclusion that the majority was actuated by improper motives, thereby working injury to the minority; mistakes of judgment do not justify interference in corporate transactions otherwise valid. *Massaro v Fisk Rubber Corp, 36 FSupp 382 (D Mass 1941).*

.3 Same—validity.—A sale of corporate assets that occurred pursuant to a special board of directors' meeting that was neither called by the proper director nor voted upon by the full board, was invalid since the meeting took place in violation of the corporate bylaws; defendants' contention that the relevant statute did not apply in emergency situations was not decided since no emergency was present. *Russell v Morris, No. 10009 (Ch Ct 2-14-90).*

.4 Power of president to dispose of corporate assets.—President cannot make contract which divests the corporation of all its assets, absent corporate authorization or ratification. *Andrew Jergens Co v Woodbury, Inc, 273 F 952 (D Del 1921).*

.5 Buyer's liability.—That California corporation succeeded to business of Delaware corporation would not, in itself, make California company responsible for certain alleged fraudulent acts previously committed by Delaware corporation in the sale of the Delaware company's stock. *Braren v Reliable Carpet Works, Inc, 13 P2d 972 (Cal Ct App 1932).*

Corporate transferee of assets of corporate transferor assuming obligations and liabilities of transferor, includes therein torts and liabilities of all kinds that might come to light, as well as those known to the party at the time. *Marlin v Texas Co, 26 FSupp 611 (ND Tex 1939).*

Transferee corporation generally is not liable for debts of transferor. *West Texas Refining & Development Co v Comm of Int Rev, 68 F2d 77 (10th Cir 1933); Bryant Griffith&Brunson, Inc v Gen Newspapers, Inc, 178 A 645 (1935).*

Corporation that purchased manufacturer's industrial products division was not independently liable for failing to warn manufacturer's customers of asbestos danger when (1) Delaware law would apply because it was place of tort and Delaware does not require warning by successor and (2) even if Pennsylvania law applies, corporation had no contractual obligations regarding manufacturer's allegedly defective asbestos products. *In re Asbestos Litigation (Bell), 517 A2d 697 (1986).*

.6 Preferred stockholders.—Sale of assets under a plan of reorganization manifestly unfair to preferred stockholders should be set aside. *Eagleson v Pacific Timber Co, 270 F 1008 (D Del 1920).*

Directors need not pay arrearages to preferred stockholders from capital surplus realized out of sale of corporation's business assets if they are keeping it in good faith to buy new business and sale for that purpose has been approved by majority stockholders. *Treves v Menzies, 142 A2d 520 (Ch Ct 1958).*

Spin-off transfer of Delaware trucking corporation's real estate to subsidiary did not constitute "liquidation," entitling corporation's preferred shareholders to receive liquidation preference, because (1) corporation continued in trucking operation with remaining assets totalling more than $45 million and (2) there were valid business reasons for spin-off; absent a showing that corporation's directors engaged in unlawful conduct, directors did not breach fiduciary duty to preferred shareholders when they failed to structure spin-off, so preferred shareholders could keep their liquidation preference and redemption rights and still participate in subsidiary's stock dividend because directors owed fiduciary duty, not only to preferred shareholders, but also to common shareholders and corporation. *Robinson v T.I.M.E.—DC Inc, 566 FSupp 1077 (ND Tex 1983).*

.7 Rights of minority stockholders.—Aggrieved minority stockholder may petition in equity for relief. *Allied Chemical & Dye Corp v Steel & Tube Co, 120 A 486 (Ch Ct 1923); Churchill v Frontier Mtg Co, 220 NYS 68 (AD 1927).*

Minority stockholder, seeking rescission of sale of all assets of his corporation to another, is barred by laches when he does not attack sale until 5 months after its consummation. *Union Financial Corp of Amer v United Investors' Securities Corp, 156 A 220 (Ch Ct 1931).* Cf, *Peterson v New England Furniture & Carpet Co, 299 NW 208 (Minn 1941).*

Minority stockholders are entitled to have all the proceeds of a sale of corporate assets distributed ratably among all the stockholders. Majority stockholders must account for any secret profit made out of a corporate transaction. *Dunnett v Arn, 71 F2d 913 (10th Cir 1934).*

Stockholders can exercise wide judgment in voting and admit personal profit or even caprice into making their choice so long as they get no advantage at expense of fellow stockholders. *Heil v Standard Gas and Elec Co, 151 A 303 (Ch Ct 1930).*

Sale of corporate assets, properly approved by the directors and stockholders, can be attacked by

§271

the minority stockholders only on ground of fraud. *Hill v St Louis Coke & Iron Corp, 9 FSupp 69 (D Del 1934).* See also, *Schiff v RKO Pictures Corp, 104 A2d 267 (Ch Ct 1954).*

Majority shareholders did not breach fiduciary duty to corporation by benefiting themselves at the expense of minority shareholders when corporation was dissolved and assets sold, because: (1) noncompetition and consulting agreements negotiated by majority shareholders with a purchaser of some of company's assets did not come at the expense of corporation since agreements were desired by purchaser and freely negotiated and (2) price paid by majority shareholders on their purchase of remaining corporate assets was fair. *Jacobs v Hanson, 525 FSupp 292 (D Del 1981).*

Rescissory damages were inappropriate as remedy for minority shareholders who sold stock after receiving misleading proxy statement outlining proposed merger. Rescissory damages are appropriate even when majority's breach of fiduciary duty was arguably unintended, but they were inappropriate in this case because of speculative nature of their proof. *Weinberger v UOP, Inc, No. 5642 (Ch Ct 1-30-85).*

Derivative action upheld where it was alleged that controlling shareholder negligently sold control of the corporation to a buyer who allegedly looted the corporation. Where a sale of controlling interest in a corporation is coupled with an agreement for the seller to resign from the board of directors in such a way as to assure that the buyer's designees assume corporate office, the seller as a reasonably prudent person, owes a fiduciary duty to inquire as to the foreseeable harm to the corporation. *Harris v Carter, No. 8768 (Ch Ct 5-4-90).*

.8 De facto merger.—Transaction is valid in which Ecks Corporation buys Wye Corporation's stock from Wye's stockholders, then exchanges the Wye stock for substantially all Wye's assets; this is not a de facto merger giving right of appraisal to dissenting stockholders in Wye; price for Wye's stock, and thus for its assets, is adequate when it was reached after arm's-length bargaining. *Alcott v Hyman, 202 A2d 501 (1965).*

As to the distinctions between a merger and a sale of assets, see *Drug Inc v Hunt, 168 A 87 (1933); Moy v Colonial Finance Corp, 129 A 115 (Pa. 1925); Colonial Ice Cream Co v Southland Ice Utilities Corp, 53 F2d 932 (DC Cir 1931).*

.9 Rights of creditors.—If all of a corporation's assets are disposed of without consideration or distributed among its stockholders, a creditor of the corporation is entitled to pursue those assets. *Berwick v Associated Gas & Elec Co, 174 A 122 (Ch Ct 1934); Unemployment Comp Comm v Geo W McCaulley & Son, Inc, 22 A2d 862 (Ch Ct 1941).*

Creditors may pursue the corporate assets into the hands of the transferee corporation when, on the sale of corporate assets, no provision is made for the payment of corporate debts. *McKee v Standard Minerals Corp, 156 A 193 (Ch Ct 1931); Colonial Ice Cream Co v Southland Ice Utilities Corp, 53 F2d 932 (DC Cir 1931).*

.10 Liquidation plan.—Stockholders' meeting to approve plan of liquidation of corporation following sale of all its assets would not be preliminarily enjoined, where ultimate remedy plaintiff sought was return of corporation to status quo; the sale and the facts made that impossible. *Cottrell v The Pawcatuck Co, 106 A2d 709 (Ch Ct 1954).*

.11 Spin off.—Parent did not breach its fiduciary duty to its wholly owned subsidiary, which was soon to be spun-off, when it caused subsidiary's directors to approve agreement arguably favorable to parent and unfavorable to subsidiary because purchasers of when-issued stock in subsidiary were owed no duties by subsidiary before spin-off, so parent was dealing with itself when it caused subsidiary to approve disputed agreement. *Anadarko Petroleum Corp v Panhandle Eastern Corp, 521 A2d 624 (Ch Ct 1987).*

.12 Continuation theory of successor liability.—Court, applying Delaware law, found that buyer could not be held liable under continuation theory of successor liability for seller's allegedly defective product, even though buyer used seller's officers and employees, and maintained some of seller's business. Reasons: (1) Sale of business was arms-length transaction; (2) Successor had different owners than predecessor; and (3) Portion of business pertaining to product's manufacture was not continued. *Elmer v Tenneco Resins, Inc, 698 FSupp 535 (D Del 1988).*

.13 Liability of controlling shareholders.—Controlling shareholders of a corporation who signed a letter of intent to sell their stock in another company, which constituted the principal asset of the corporation, without disclosing the opportunity to the corporation's board of directors, were liable in damages for money they had received for signing a letter of intent and for expenses the corporation incurred to accommodate the majority shareholders' pursuit of their own interests. The controlling shareholders were liable despite the fact that they could have vetoed the action, which constituted the sale of substantially all of the corporation's assets, if it had been undertaken by the corporation. *Thorpe v CERBCO, Inc, 676 A2d 436 (1996),* rev'g, *Thorpe v CERBCO, Inc, No. 11713 (Ch Ct 8-9-95).*

A controlling stockholder whose own involvement in misconduct has resulted in legal inhibitions on its exercise of control does not nonetheless have a non-statutory, "natural right" in equity to veto the good faith business decisions of the independent board it has elected. *Hollinger Inc v Hollinger International, Inc, 858 A2d 342 (Ch Ct 2004).*

272 MORTGAGE OR PLEDGE OF ASSETS.—The authorization or consent of stockholders to the mortgage or pledge of a corporation's property and assets shall not be necessary, except to the extent that the certificate of incorporation otherwise provides.

.1 Mortgage of all assets.—Purpose of law section on sale of assets is protection of stockholders only, not protection of corporation or of its creditors. Hence, corporation's trustee in bankruptcy, who represents creditors, cannot attack validity of mortgage on ground it was not authorized by majority of stockholders. *Greene v RFC, 100 F2d 34 (1st Cir 1938).*

273 DISSOLUTION OF JOINT VENTURE CORPORATION HAVING 2 STOCKHOLDERS.—(a) If the stockholders of a corporation of this State, having only 2 stockholders each of which own 50% of the stock therein, shall be engaged in the prosecution of a joint venture and if such stockholders shall be unable to agree upon the desirability of discontinuing such joint venture and disposing of the assets used in such venture, either stockholder may, unless otherwise provided in the certificate of incorporation of the corporation or in a written agreement between the stockholders, file with the Court of Chancery a petition stating that it desires to discontinue such joint venture and to dispose of the assets used in such venture in accordance with a plan to be agreed upon by both stockholders or that, if no such plan shall be agreed upon by both stockholders, the corporation be dissolved. Such petition shall have attached thereto a copy of the proposed plan of discontinuance and distribution and a certificate stating that copies of such petition and plan have been transmitted in writing to the other stockholder and to the directors and officers of such corporation. The petition and certificate shall be executed and acknowledged in accordance with §103 of this title.

(b) Unless both stockholders file with the Court of Chancery (1) within 3 months of the date of the filing of such petition, a certificate similarly executed and acknowledged stating that they have agreed on such plan, or a modification thereof, and (2) within 1 year from the date of the filing of such petition, a certificate similarly executed and acknowledged stating that the distribution provided by such plan had been completed, the Court of Chancery may dissolve such corporation and may by appointment of 1 or more trustees or receivers with all the powers and title of a trustee or receiver appointed under §279 of this title, administer and wind up its affairs. Either or both of the above periods may be extended by agreement of the stockholders, evidenced by a certificate similarly executed, acknowledged and filed with the Court of Chancery prior to the expiration of such period.

(c) *In the case of a charitable nonstock corporation, the petitioner shall provide a copy of any petition referred to in subsection (a) of this section to the Attorney General of the State of Delaware within 1 week of its filing with the Court of Chancery.* (Last amended by Ch. 253, L. '10, eff. 8-1-10.)

Ch. 253, L. '10, eff. 8-1-10, added matter in italic.

Ch. 253, L. '10 Synopsis of Section 273

Section 59 amends the DGCL to add new §273(c) to provide that, in the case of a charitable nonstock corporation, the petitioner must provide a copy of the petition referred to in §273(a) to the Attorney General of the State of Delaware within one week of filing the petition with the Court of Chancery.

Ch. 349, L. '96 Synopsis of Section 273

This amendment provides that stockholders of joint venture corporations may, by provision in the certificate of incorporation or written agreement, opt out of the dissolution procedure otherwise afforded by Section 273.

.1 Purpose; evidence permitted.—Purpose of GCL §273 is to provide mechanism for dissolving joint venture that obviates a deadlocked vote of two equal shareholders. A shareholder seeking dissolution under this provision may use any competent evidence to prove that the shareholders cannot agree on the desirability of discontinuing the joint venture and disposing of assets. *In re Venture Advisers, Inc, No. 9439 (Ch Ct 12-1-88).*

.2 Liability for federal tax.—After husband's death, shareholder was sole owner of 50% stock interest issued in both their names, which shareholder held free and clear of U.S. tax liens against husband, and was entitled to 50% of distributable proceeds from corporation's dissolution because (1) shareholder and husband were tenants by the entireties, so when husband died, stock devolved upon shareholder by operation of law, (2) husband was not bankrupt when replacement certificates were issued jointly to husband and shareholder, and (3) tax liens did not become effective until two years after tenancy by the entireties was created. *In re Tidal Equipment Co, 623 FSupp 933 (D Del 1985).*

.3 Limitations on remedy.—Actions that are adversarial in nature—actions for breach of fiduciary duty or misappropriation of corporate opportunity—cannot be raised in dissolution proceeding. Issues in dissolution proceeding are narrowly limited to those concerns directly related to dissolution. *In re Cambridge Financial Group, Ltd, No. 9279 (Ch Ct 11-9-87).*

In action for dissolution of corporation, court denied first 50% shareholder's motion to compel production of documents controlled by principals of second 50% shareholder relating to second 50% shareholder's alleged diversion of corporate opportunity because (1) first 50% shareholder did not claim in petition that second 50% shareholder diverted corporate opportunity and (2) diversion of corporate opportunity claim cannot be asserted in dissolution proceeding. *In re Southern One-Stop, Inc, 623 FSupp 933 (D Del 1985).*

.4 Elements of a joint venture corporation.—In an action to dissolve a corporation under §273, the Court of Chancery determined that the subject corporation was a joint venture corporation where the facts demonstrated that the two corporate investors each owned a half interest in the performance of the third corporation; shared profits and losses of the third corporation; maintained equal control in the subject corporation; and impliedly agreed to engage in business for each one's mutual benefit. *Wah Chang Smelting and Refining Co of America, Inc v Cleveland Tungsten Inc, No. 1324-K (Ch Ct 8-19-96).*

.5 Asset distributions upon dissolution.—Once assets are contributed to a corporation, its shareholders hold those assets in proportion to their ownership interests, regardless of whether the shareholders contributed equity or labor, and, upon dissolution, the corporate assets will be distributed in proportion to the shareholders' interests, rather than in proportion to their capital contributions. *Grimm v Beach Fries, Inc, 2010 Del. Ch. LEXIS 147 (Ch Ct 2010).*

.6 Third-party intervenors.—A third party's attempt to intervene in a dissolution action will be denied where the third party does not assert an interest in the corporation being dissolved, but, rather, in the corporation's alleged subsidiary. *In re Food Ingredients International, Inc, 2010 Del. Ch. LEXIS 233 (Ch Ct 2010).*

274 DISSOLUTION BEFORE ISSUANCE OF SHARES OR BEGINNING OF BUSINESS; PROCEDURE.—If a corporation has not issued shares or has not commenced the business for which the corporation was organized, a majority of the incorporators, or, if directors were named in the certificate of incorporation or have been elected, a majority of the directors, may surrender all of the corporation's rights and franchises by filing in the office of the Secretary of State a certificate, executed and acknowledged by a majority of the incorporators or directors, stating: that no shares of stock have been issued or that the business or activity for which the corporation was organized has not been begun; *the date of filing of the corporation's original certificate of incorporation with the Secretary of State;* that no part of the capital of the corporation has been paid, or, if some capital has been paid, that the amount actually paid in for the corporation's shares, less any part thereof disbursed for necessary expenses, has been returned to those entitled thereto; that if the corporation has begun business but it has not issued shares, all debts of the corporation have been paid; that if the corporation has not begun business but has issued stock certificates, all issued stock certificates, if any, have been surrendered and cancelled; and that all rights and franchises of the corporation are surrendered. Upon such certificate becoming effective in accordance with §103 of this title, the corporation shall be dissolved. (Last amended by Ch. 290, L. '10, eff. 8-2-10.)

Ch. 290, L. '10, eff. 8-2-10, added matter in italic.

Ch. 290, L. '10 Synopsis of Section 274

These sections amend Sections 274 and 275(d), respectively, to require that a certificate of dissolution filed thereunder must set forth the date of filing of the corporation's original certificate of incorporation with the Secretary of State.

275 DISSOLUTION GENERALLY; PROCEDURE.—(a) If it should be deemed advisable in the judgment of the board of directors of any corporation that it should be dissolved, the board, after the adoption of a resolution to that effect by a majority of the whole board at any meeting called for that purpose, shall cause notice of the adoption of the resolution and of a meeting of stockholders to take action upon the resolution to be mailed to each stockholder entitled to vote thereon as of the record date for determining the stockholders entitled to notice of the meeting.

(b) At the meeting a vote shall be taken upon the proposed dissolution. If a majority of the outstanding stock of the corporation entitled to vote thereon shall vote for the proposed dissolution, a certification of dissolution shall be filed with the Secretary of State pursuant to subsection (d) of this section.

(c) Dissolution of a corporation may also be authorized without action of the directors if all the stockholders entitled to vote thereon shall consent in writing and a certificate of dissolution shall be filed with the Secretary of State pursuant to subsection (d) of this section.

(d) If dissolution is authorized in accordance with this section, a certificate of dissolution shall be executed, acknowledged and filed, and shall become effective, in accordance with §103 of this title. Such certificate of dissolution shall set forth:
(1) The name of the corporation;
(2) The date dissolution was authorized;
(3) That the dissolution has been authorized by the board of directors and stockholders of the corporation, in accordance with subsections (a) and (b) of this section, or that the dissolution has been authorized by all of the stockholders of the corporation entitled to vote on a dissolution, in accordance with subsection (c) of this section; [1]
(4) The names and addresses of the directors and officers of the corporation; *and*
(5) *The date of filing of the corporation's original certificate of incorporation with the Secretary of State.*
(e) The resolution authorizing a proposed dissolution may provide that notwithstanding authorization or consent to the proposed dissolution by the stockholders, or the members of a nonstock corporation pursuant to §276 of this title, the board of directors or governing body may abandon such proposed dissolution without further action by the stockholders or members.
(f) Upon a certificate of dissolution becoming effective in accordance with §103 of this title, the corporation shall be dissolved. (Last amended by Ch. 290, L. '10, eff. 8-2-10.)

Ch. 290, L. '10, eff. 8-2-10, added matter in italic and deleted [1]"and".

Ch. 290, L. '10 Synopsis of Section 275

These sections amend Sections 274 and 275(d), respectively, to require that a certificate of dissolution filed thereunder must set forth the date of filing of the corporation's original certificate of incorporation with the Secretary of State.

Ch. 14, L. '09 Synopsis of Section 275

This section amends Section 275(a) to make it consistent with the revisions to Sections 213(a) and 222 by requiring notice only be mailed to those stockholders entitled to vote as of the notice record date.

.1 Bankruptcy reorganization.—Dissolution of Delaware corporation in Bankruptcy Act reorganization is under GCL §303. *OAG, 2-28-38.*

.2 When effected.—Dissolution is not accomplished until the affidavit of publication is filed in the Secretary of State's office. A deed executed before this date is therefore valid though it is executed two days after consent to dissolution. *Pure Oil Co v The Franklin Real Estate Co, 138 A 602 (Ch Ct 1926).* See also, *Washington Fire Co v Yates, 115 A 365 (1921).*

Corporation is not dissolved upon filing voluntary petition in bankruptcy. *In re De Camp Glass Casket Co, 272 F 558 (6th Cir),* cert denied, *256 US 703 (1921).*

.3 Corporate acts and dissolution.—As to whether or not the transfer of assets of one corporation in return for the issuance to its stockholders of the stock of another corporation constitutes a dissolution of the former, see *Cleveland Worsted Mills Co v Consolidated Textile Corp, 292 F 129 (3d Cir 1923).*

.4 Compelling dissolution.—Court will not compel dissolution of corporation which has not failed in its object. *Graham-Newman Corp v Franklin Co Distilling Co, 27 A2d 142 (Ch Ct 1942).*

Minority stockholder in personal holding company cannot compel dissolution because (1) company's shares sell at substantial discount from asset value when stockholder knew this at time he bought share, or (2) its status as holding company compels it to pay substantial taxes and expenses, or (3) it lost opportunities to buy additional shares of affiliated company's stock, when it could not do that due to its need to distribute most of its income. *Warshaw v Calhoun, 221 A2d 487 (1966).*

.5 Appointment of receiver to dissolve corporation.—Court of equity will not appoint receiver to dissolve corporation absent acts of fraud on part of officers and directors, or failure of primary corporate purposes. *Lewis v Commonwealth Securities, Inc, 51 FSupp 33 (D Del 1943).*

.6 What law governs.—The state which creates a corporation alone has power to wind up its affairs and dissolve it. *Ward v Foulkrod, 264 F 627 (3d Cir 1920); Meehl v Barr Transfer Co, 9 NW2d 540 (Mich 1943).*

.7 Rights of subscribers to assets on dissolution.—Subscribers to stock are deemed stockholders and not creditors with reference to the assets on dissolution: some of their rights as stockholders merely having been restricted until full payment of the par value and premiums. *Grone v Economic Life Ins Co, 80 A 809 (Ch Ct 1911).*

.8 Rights of stockholders.—Where the decision to dissolve a corporation was unanimous, and all stockholders were informed thereof and none of them objected, all stockholders were held bound by the action taken at the meeting. *Mallery v Manager's Securities Corp, 1 FSupp 942 (D Del 1932).*

Carrying out of dissolution plan will not be temporarily enjoined at suit of minority stockholders if the plan is fair to all the stockholders. *Shrage v Bridgeport Oil Co, 68 A2d 317 (Ch Ct 1949);* plan disapproved, *71 A2d 882 (Ch Ct 1950).*

Shareholder could not enjoin sale of three subsidiaries because (1) subsidiaries' sale would not

§275

constitute sale of "substantially all" of corporation's assets, (2) sale of assets did not mandate liquidation of corporation, and (3) shareholders were guilty of laches. Shareholders also could not enjoin special meeting of shareholders to vote on planned liquidation of parent because (1) three separate votes on plan were not required and (2) proxy statement was not materially misleading. *Bacine v Scharffenberger, Nos. 7862, 7866 (Ch Ct 12-11-84).*

.9 Appointment of receiver does not effect dissolution.—The appointment of receivers and the administration of an insolvent corporation's assets for the benefit of creditors does not effect the company's dissolution. *Hirschfield v Reading Finance & Securities Co, 82 A 690 (Ch Ct 1912); Du Pont v Standard Arms Co, 82 A 692 (Ch Ct 1912).*

.10 Expenditures.—Court issued injunction restraining directors from spending corporate funds or assets other than for purposes of liquidation and winding up of corporation's affairs because shareholder agreement stated that corporation had to be dissolved if it was unable to obtain required FCC approvals by certain date. However, court authorized reasonable expenditures incurred in connection with corporation's efforts to obtain FCC approval, if corporation provided security bond, because harm of lost opportunity to participate in possible lucrative business was greater than harm to plaintiffs of diminution of corporate assets if injunction were denied. *Brinati v TeleSTAR, Inc, No. 8118 (Ch Ct 9-3-85).*

.11 Limitations on recovery.—Actions that are adversarial in nature—actions for breach of fiduciary duty or misappropriation of corporate opportunity—cannot be raised in dissolution proceeding. Issues in dissolution proceeding are narrowly limited to those concerns directly related to dissolution. *In re Cambridge Financial Group, Ltd, No. 9279 (Ch Ct 11-9-87).*

.12 Constructive dissolution.—A Delaware corporation's board does not create a constructive or *de facto* liquidation when it (1) approves shutting down primary operations, (2) embarks upon a sale of most of its assets, (3) grants its CEO a lavish severance allowance while continuing to employ him, and (4) takes no action to block the CEO's purchase of the corporation's common stock, because all of these actions were a good faith response to potential insolvency. *Quadrangle Offshore (Cayman) LLC v Kenetech Corp, C.A. No. 16362 (Ch Ct 10-13-99),* aff'd, *2000 Del. LEXIS 147 (4-6-00).*

276 [1] ***DISSOLUTION OF NONSTOCK CORPORATION; PROCEDURE.***—*(a) Whenever it shall be desired to dissolve any nonstock corporation, the governing body shall perform all the acts necessary for dissolution which are required by §275 of this title to be performed by the board of directors of a corporation having capital stock. If any members of a nonstock corporation are entitled to vote for the election of members of its governing body or are entitled to vote for dissolution under the certificate of incorporation or the bylaws of such corporation, such members shall perform all the acts necessary for dissolution which are contemplated by §275 of this title to be performed by the stockholders of a corporation having capital stock, including dissolution without action of the members of the governing body if all the members of the corporation entitled to vote thereon shall consent in writing and a certificate of dissolution shall be filed with the Secretary of State pursuant to §275(d) of this title. If there is no member entitled to vote thereon, the dissolution of the corporation shall be authorized at a meeting of the governing body, upon the adoption of a resolution to dissolve by the vote of a majority of members of its governing body then in office. In all other respects, the method and proceedings for the dissolution of a nonstock corporation shall conform as nearly as may be to the proceedings prescribed by §275 of this title for the dissolution of corporations having capital stock.*

(b) If a nonstock corporation has not commenced the business for which the corporation was organized, a majority of the governing body or, if none, a majority of the incorporators may surrender all of the corporation rights and franchises by filing in the office of the Secretary of State a certificate, executed and acknowledged by a majority of the incorporators or governing body, conforming as nearly as may be to the certificate prescribed by §274 of this title. (Last amended by Ch. 253, L. '10, eff. 8-1-10.)

Ch. 253, L. '10, eff. 8-1-10, added matter in italic and deleted [1]"DISSOLUTION OF NONSTOCK CORPORATION; PROCEDURE.—(a) Whenever it shall be desired to dissolve any corporation having no capital stock, the governing body shall perform all the acts necessary for dissolution which are required by §275 of this title to be performed by the board of directors of a corporation having capital stock. If the members of a corporation having no capital stock are entitled to vote for the election of members of its governing body, they shall perform all the acts necessary for dissolution which are required by §275 of this title to be performed by the stockholders of a corporation having capital stock. If there is no member entitled to vote thereon, the dissolution of the corporation shall be authorized at a meeting of the governing body, upon the adoption of a resolution to dissolve by the vote of a majority of members of its governing body then in office. In all other respects, the method and proceedings for the dissolution of a corporation having no capital stock shall conform as nearly as may be to the proceedings prescribed by §275 of this title for the dissolution of corporations having capital stock.

(b) If a corporation having no capital stock has not commenced the business for which the corporation was organized, a majority of the governing body or, if none, a majority of the incorporators may surrender all of the corporation rights and franchises by filing in the office of the Secretary of State a certificate, executed and acknowledged by a majority of the incorporators or governing body, conforming as nearly as may be to the certificate prescribed by §274 of this title."

Ch. 253, L. '10 Synopsis of Section 276

Section 60 amends §276 of the DGCL to ensure that the translator provision in new §114(a) operates properly on §276; to clarify that members may vote for dissolution if, under the corporation's certificate of incorporation or bylaws, they are entitled to vote thereon or for the election of the members of the governing body; and to clarify that members of the corporation may authorize dissolution without action of the members of the governing body if all the members of the corporation entitled to vote thereon shall consent in writing and a certificate of dissolution shall be properly filed with the Secretary of State.

277 PAYMENT OF FRANCHISE TAXES BEFORE [1] *DISSOLUTION, MERGER, TRANSFER OR CONVERSION*.—[2] *No corporation shall be dissolved, merged, transferred (without continuing its existence as a corporation of this State) or converted under this chapter until:*

(1) All franchise taxes due to or assessable by the State including all franchise taxes due or which would be due or assessable for the entire calendar month during which such dissolution, merger, transfer or conversion becomes effective have been paid by the corporation; and

(2) All annual franchise tax reports including a final annual franchise tax report for the year in which such dissolution, merger, transfer or conversion becomes effective have been filed by the corporation;

notwithstanding the foregoing, if the Secretary of State certifies that an instrument to effect a dissolution, merger, transfer or conversion has been filed in the Secretary of State's office, such corporation shall be dissolved, merged, transferred or converted at the effective time of such instrument. (Last amended by Ch. 96, L. '11, eff. 8-1-11.)

Ch. 96, L. '11, eff. 8-1-11, added matter in italic and deleted [1]"DISSOLUTION OR MERGER" and [2]"No corporation shall be dissolved or merged under this chapter until all franchise taxes due to or assessable by the State including all franchise taxes due or which would be due or assessable for the entire calendar month during which the dissolution or merger becomes effective have been paid by the corporation."

Ch. 96, L. '11 Synopsis of Section 277

These Sections amend Section 277 to clarify that before a corporation is dissolved, merged, transferred (without continuing its existence as a Delaware corporation) or converted under Title 8 of the Delaware Code, such corporation must pay all franchise taxes due to or assessable by the State including all franchise taxes due or which would be due or assessable for the entire calendar month during which such dissolution, merger, transfer or conversion becomes effective and such corporation must file all annual franchise tax reports including a final annual franchise tax report for the year in which such dissolution, merger, transfer or conversion becomes effective. Notwithstanding the foregoing, if the Secretary of State certifies that an instrument to affect a dissolution, merger, transfer or conversion has been filed in the Secretary of State's office, such corporation shall be dissolved, merged, transferred or converted at the effective time of such instrument.

Ch. 120, L. '97 Synopsis of Section 277

The amendment to Section 277 clarifies that upon a dissolution or merger the franchise tax for the entire calender month during which the dissolution or merger takes place becomes due and payable at the time of dissolution or merger.

Ch. 79, L. '95 Synopsis of Section 277

This amendment confirms that franchise taxes are due when a corporation merges out of existence.

278 CONTINUATION OF CORPORATION AFTER DISSOLUTION FOR PURPOSES OF SUIT AND WINDING UP AFFAIRS.—All corporations, whether they expire by their own limitation or are otherwise dissolved, shall nevertheless be continued, for the term of 3 years from such expiration or dissolution or for such longer period as the Court of Chancery shall in its discretion direct, bodies corporate for the purpose of prosecuting and defending suits, whether civil, criminal or administrative, by or against them, and of enabling them gradually to settle and close their business, to dispose of and convey their property, to discharge their liabilities and to distribute to their stockholders any remaining assets, but not for the purpose of continuing the business for which the corporation was organized. With respect to any action, suit or proceeding begun by or against the corporation either prior to or within 3 years after the date of its expiration or dissolution, the action shall not abate by reason of the dissolution of the corporation; the corporation shall, solely for the purpose of such action, suit or proceeding, be continued as a body corporate beyond the 3-year period and until any judgments, orders or decrees therein shall be fully executed, without the necessity for any special direction to that effect by the Court of Chancery.

Sections 279 through 282 of this title shall apply to any corporation that has expired by its own limitation, and when so applied, all references in those sections to a dissolved corporation or dissolution shall include a corporation that has expired by its own limitation and to such expiration, respectively. (Last amended by Ch. 290, L. '10, eff. 8-2-10.)

Ch. 290, L. '10, eff. 8-2-10, added matter in italic.

Ch. 290, L. '10 Synopsis of Section 278

This amendment to Section 278 confirms that the provisions of Section 279 through Section 282, including those provisions dealing with winding up of a corporation, apply to a corporation that has expired by its own limitation.

.1 Nonpayment of franchise taxes.—Any corporation whose charter had been proclaimed as forfeited for non-payment of taxes may, upon compliance with certain provisions, and upon payment of the taxes due, obtain the restoration or revival of its charter with all the rights, franchises, privileges and immunities it formerly held. The tax itself does not accrue during the period the charter is inoperative. *State v Surety Corp of America, 162 A 852 (Ch Ct 1932).* See also, *Fortinberry Co v Blundell, 242 P2d 427 (Okla 1952).*

Dissolved corporation is continued beyond three-year period for purpose of redemption of its property from tax sale. *Stensvad v Ottman, 208 P2d 507 (Mont 1949).*

.2 Purpose of continuing corporate existence.—The continuance of corporate existence is for the purposes expressed in this section only. Thus during the three year period a corporation cannot take by devise but if the charter is renewed a legacy vested during the period before renewal can be taken. *McBride v Murphy, 124 A 798 (Ch Ct 1914); Blackstone v Chandler, 130 A 34 (Ch Ct 1925).* Neither dissolution nor the expiration of the three-year winding-up extinguishes the possibility of reverter held by a corporation. *Addy v Short, 89 A2d 136 (1952).*

.3 Same—collection of debts.—Debts of a corporation whose charter has been forfeited by the state may be collected by three years later by suits against the corporation as the sole defendant. *Townsend v Del Glue Co, 103 A 576 (Ch Ct 1918).* See, *Slaughter v Moore, 82 A 963 (Ch Ct 1912).*

.4 Method of liquidating corporation.—Although the manner in winding up the affairs of this corporation was without warrant in law, the court would not appoint a liquidating receiver since no rights of creditors were involved and no fraud charged or intimated. The court said that since the complaining stockholder differed with the directors and other stockholders solely upon the method of liquidating, and since all that a receiver could accomplish was to secure the return of the assets to the corporation at heavy expense, the court was of the opinion that if complainant had any right to a remedy it should be in some other form. *Salembier v Great Neck Bond & Mortgage Corp, 194 A 35 (Ch Ct 1937).*

Dissolved corporation could not liquidate by creating liquidating trust because liquidation of a dissolved corporation can only be achieved by (1) corporation's existing officers and directors and (2) court appointed trustee under court supervision. *Products Engineering Co v OKC Corp, 590 FSupp 547 (ED La 1984).*

.5 Suits.—During the three-year period specified in the above section, a corporation can sue and/or be sued. *Kelly v International Clay Products Co, 140 A 143 (Pa 1928); Lyman v Knickerbocker Theatre Co, 5 F2d 538 (DC Cir 1925); Meehl v Barr Transfer Co, 9 NW2d 540 (Mich 1943).*

Delaware corporation qualified in New York cannot be sued in New York over three years after dissolution in Delaware and after filing of certificate of withdrawal in New York, on cause of action which arose in New York before that filing. *Trimble v Bauer, Pogue & Co, 51 NYS2d 754 (AD 1944).*

After expiration of three-year period, dissolved corporation may file counterclaim in suit started before. *U.S. v Cummins Distilleries Corp, 166 F2d 17 (6th Cir 1948).* On the other hand, counterclaim against corporation is barred after that period in action the corporation began during it. *Smith-Johnson SS Corp v U.S., 231 FSupp 184 (D Del 1964).*

Dissolved corporation is continued beyond three-year term by the commencement of an administrative proceeding against it for the collection of additional federal income taxes; but even if the corporation is not continued under the state law, its existence is recognized for tax purposes and it may invoke the jurisdiction of the Tax Court. *Bahen & Wright, Inc v Commr of Int Rev, 176 F2d 538 (4th Cir 1949).*

Stockholders of dissolved Delaware corporation cannot, in derivative action, hold directors personally liable for loss resulting from judicial sale of corporate property where directors did not misuse their position to bring about the result and did not personally obtain the property of their company. *Arn v Bradshaw Oil & Gas Co, 108 F2d 125 (5th Cir 1939),* cert denied, *310 US 646 (1940).*

Stockholder of dissolved corporation may, when no receiver or trustee has been appointed, maintain a derivative action against company and its directors and officers. Such suit, started within, may be continued beyond the three-year period. *Arn v Bradshaw Oil & Gas Co, 93 F2d 728 (5th Cir 1938).* See, also, *Arn v Dunnett, 93 F2d 634 (10th Cir 1938),* and *Arn v Bradshaw Oil and Gas Co, 108 F2d 125 (5th Cir 1939),* cert denied, *310 US 646 (1940).*

Receiver appointed in a dissolution proceeding is a statutory receiver, an official liquidator of the corporation, not a mere chancery receiver, and as such has title to a cause of action belonging to the company, which title is entitled to constitutional full faith and credit in other states so that a receiver appointed in another state cannot sue on such cause of action. *Hirson v United Stores Corp, 34 NYS2d 122 (AD 1942).*

Attorneys can recover judgment against dissolved corporation for services rendered though action begun three years after corporation's dissolution, when they were employed within three-year period. *Ross v Venezuelan-American Independent Oil Producers Ass'n, Inc, 230 FSupp 701 (D Del 1964).*

Even though forum state's corporate dissolution statute contained time period during which dissolved corporation remained subject to suit, it was not statute of limitations; dissolution is substantive matter so law of state of incorporation controls and dissolved corporation could be sued. *Casselman v Denver Tramway Corp, 577 P2d 293 (Colo 1978).*

Delaware corporation that was dissolved in 1961 could not bring suit to recover damages for Syria's alleged nationalization of its assets when (1) according to Delaware law, dissolved corporations continue to exist for only three years for purpose of prosecuting and defending suits and (2) action commenced in Syria did not operate to extend corporation's existence even if two suits were brought to enforce same cause of action. *Syrian Arabian Oil Co v Syrian Arab Republic, 791 F2d 602 (7th Cir 1986).*

.6 Abatement of suit.—Suits pending at the dissolution of corporations do not abate at expiration of three-year period. Suits begun by a corporation within the three year period do not abate at the expiration thereof. However, suits begun against the corporation after its dissolution abate at the end of the three year period except when the Court of Chancery appoints a receiver to represent the corporation. *Atkins v Harriman & Co, 69 F2d 66 (2d Cir 1934).*

After a suit has abated the question of revivor, being wholly one of procedure, is determined by the forum. *Amer Transportation Co v Swift & Co, 24 F2d 310 (2d Cir 1928).*

Dissolution does not abate suit against corporation for damages for personal injury. *Eastman, Gardiner & Co v Warren, 109 F2d 193 (5th Cir 1940).*

Phrase "suits by or against" means civil actions, not criminal prosecutions. Hence, after dissolution, corporation cannot be criminally prosecuted for Sherman Anti-Trust Act violation. *U.S. v Safeway Stores, Inc, 140 F2d 834 (1st Cir 1944),* followed in *U.S. v U.S. Vanadium Corp, 230 F2d 646 (10th Cir 1956).*

Dissolution of Delaware and Maryland corporations does not extinguish their liability in criminal proceedings pending against them. *Melrose Distilleries, Inc v U.S., 258 F2d 726 (4th Cir 1958).*

Good faith merger under Delaware law abates criminal prosecution against constituent corporation for violation of Sherman Act. *U.S. v Line Material Co, 202 F2d 929 (6th Cir 1953).*

Corporation may be criminally prosecuted though dissolved eight months before the criminal information was filed where its incorporating state (Delaware) continues the existence of dissolved corporations for the purpose of prosecuting or defending proceedings by or against them. *U.S. v P F Collier & Son Corp, 208 F2d 936 (7th Cir 1953).*

.7 Effect of dissolution.—Corporation dissolved for non-payment of taxes could not thereafter conduct any business, other than winding up its affairs. Therefore, an agreement that, should it discontinue the manufacture of a certain article, all rights to certain trade-marks, formulae and patent applications would vest in plaintiff as absolute owner was held operative since the voiding of the corporate charter was taken as an intention on the part of the corporation to discontinue manufacturing. *Broza v Aluminum Cleaner Corp, 159 A 430 (Ch Ct 1932).*

Corporation whose charter is declared void for non-payment of taxes is permitted to continue for the purpose of winding up its affairs. *Big Sespe Oil Co v Cochran, 272 F 216 (9th Cir 1921).*

Where corporation, by voluntarily dissolving, renders itself powerless to honor a stock option it granted, optionee can recover on liquidation the amount he would have received were he the owner of the shares (less the option price). *Gamble v Penn Valley Crude Oil Corp, 104 A2d 257 (Ch Ct 1954).*

Corporation which voluntarily dissolves must perform obligation to pay for services to be rendered over a specified period though that period extends beyond the dissolution date. *Martin v Star Publishing Co, 126 A2d 238 (1956).*

A dissolved foreign corporation can continue to remove standing timber it had bought, when a statute of its state of incorporation permits it to exist for three years after dissolution to wind up its affairs. *Elk River Mill & Lumber Co v Georgia-Pacific Corp, 164 Cal App2d 459, 330 P2d 404 (1958).*

Dissolved corporation could not be sued after three-year statutory wind-up period; it was not doing business subject to long-arm statute although it retained directors, held meetings and invested assets, since these activities were solely for wind-up purposes. *Johnson v Helicopter & Airplane Services Corp, 404 FSupp 726 (D Md 1975).*

Court had no power to "continue" corporation for winding up purposes after corporation ceased to exist when statutory three-year period expired. *In re Citadel Industries Inc, No. 6066 (Ch Ct 11-21-80).*

Corporation dissolved more than three years prior to action's institution was improperly named as defendant; Delaware law bars commencement of actions against dissolved corporation more than three years after dissolution. *Behunin v Dow Chemical Co, 650 FSupp 1387 (DC DC 1987).*

.8 Service on dissolved corporation's officer.—Officer of a dissolved corporation retains sufficient authority to receive service of process for the corporation. Unlike Minnesota, Delaware law provides that the authority of Delaware corporate officers continues after dissolution unless a trustee or receiver is appointed, and service on such officers is therefore sufficient to obtain jurisdiction over the corporation. *Benchmark Computer Systems v London, 417 NW2d 714 (Minn Ct App 1988).*

§278

.9 Parent, liability on contract of dissolved subsidiary.—Parent corporations were not liable for government contract of wholly owned dissolved subsidiary even though there were some members common to boards of both parent and subsidiary, subsidiary's former president worked for parent, and parent dissolved and allegedly financed subsidiary, because (1) Subsidiary conducted and financed its own business operations, maintained its own accounting records, and contracted and subcontracted in its own name; (2) Parent did not guarantee and was not held responsible for subsidiary's performance of contract; (3) Subsidiary and government executed modifications to contract and there was no proof presented that subsidiary did not receive payment for them; (4) Subsidiary executed novations of other contracts in anticipation of its liquidation; and (5) There was inadequate evidence presented to support claims of undercapitalization and that parent made all decisions on contract after subsidiary's dissolution. *BLH, Inc v U.S., 13 Cl Ct 265 (1987).*

.10 Receiver, effect of appointment.—Delaware corporation that had been dissolved by gubernatorial proclamation ceased to exist legally after expiration of three year continuation period of GCL §278 even though a receiver had been appointed to protect rights of certain former shareholders. Reasons: (1) Court of Chancery refused to extend corporate existence; (2) Receiver had been appointed after three year period; and (3) Corporation had distributed all its assets and ceased doing business. The defunct corporation, therefore, was not required to file returns or pay taxes. *U.S. v McDonald & Eide, Inc, 670 FSupp 1226 (D Del 1987).*

.11 Liquidating trust.—The Delaware Supreme Court determined that because a liquidating trust that was the successor to a dissolved corporation and was established to hold assets for both the shareholders and creditors of the corporation was a separate entity, it was not subject to the three year period imposed by §278 and as such was liable for payment of a creditor's claim asserted after the three year period. *City Investing Company Liquidating Trust v Continental Casualty Co, 624 A2d 1191 (1993).*

The Delaware Supreme Court held that the Court of Chancery acted within its authority in establishing a successor trust to succeed a liquidating trust that was about to expire on its own terms and to replace on the grounds of conflict of interest the trustees of the liquidating trust upon creation of the successor trust. *Rosenbloom v Esso Virgin Islands, Inc, 766 A2d 451 (2000).*

.12 Appointment of receiver.—Where a corporation has been dissolved for longer than the period during which suits may be brought against it, and has no undistributed assets, a receiver will not be appointed to enable the pursuit of an after-discovered claim. *In the Matter of Dow Chemical Int'l Inc. of Delaware, 2008 Del. Ch. LEXIS 147 (Ch Ct 2008).*

.13 Winding up.—A corporation's certificate of dissolution will not be nullified, nor its full corporate existence restored or a receiver appointed, where, although the dissolved corporation is a party to ongoing litigation, its management is actively winding up its affairs, and, the company's existence as a body corporate will not end before the conclusion of the litigation. *LeCrenier v Central Oil Asphalt Corp, 2010 Del. Ch. LEXIS 246 (Ch Ct 2010).*

279 TRUSTEES OR RECEIVERS FOR DISSOLVED CORPORATIONS; APPOINTMENT; POWERS; DUTIES.

—When any corporation organized under this chapter shall be dissolved in any manner whatever, the Court of Chancery, on application of any creditor, stockholder or director of the corporation, or any other person who shows good cause therefor, at any time, may either appoint 1 or more of the directors of the corporation to be trustees, or appoint 1 or more persons to be receivers, of and for the corporation, to take charge of the corporation's property, and to collect the debts and property due and belonging to the corporation, with power to prosecute and defend, in the name of the corporation, or otherwise, all such suits as may be necessary or proper for the purposes aforesaid, and to appoint an agent or agents under them, and to do all other acts which might be done by the corporation, if in being, that may be necessary for the final settlement of the unfinished business of the corporation. The powers of the trustees or receivers may be continued as long as the Court of Chancery shall think necessary for the purposes aforesaid. (Last amended by Ch. 136, L. '87, eff. 7-1-87.)

.1 Title of receiver.—Receiver has title of the corporation to all property wherever situated, except real estate outside the state. *Adler v Campeche Laguna Corp, 257 F 789 (D Del 1919).*

.2 Appointment of receiver—does not dissolve corporation, or cut short its legal existence. *Du Pont v Standard Arms Co, 81 A 1089 (1912).*

Appointment of receiver is not mandatory. *Eastman, Gardiner & Co v Warren, 109 F2d 193 (5th Cir 1940).*

Where the Court of Chancery, under this section, appoints a receiver to represent the corporation, suits begun against the corporation after dissolution do not abate at the end of the three-year period. *Atkins v Harriman & Co, 69 F2d 66 (2d Cir 1934).*

Court of Chancery, upon application of minority stockholder, can wind up affairs of solvent corporation and appoint receiver for that purpose because of fraud and gross mismanagement by its officers, but it will do so only when there is real imminent danger of material loss that cannot be prevented otherwise; mere errors of judgment in business management, mere apprehension of future misconduct or failure of officers to furnish stockholder with reasonable information relating to activities and financial condition of corporation will not suffice. *Lichens Co v Standard Commercial Tobacco Co*, 40 A2d 447 (Ch Ct 1944).

Court will appoint a receiver to wind up a solvent corporation on the ground of directors' fraud and mismanagement only when the misconduct of the directors is current and danger of loss to the corporation is imminent. *Campbell v Pa Industries, Inc*, 99 FSupp 199 (D Del 1951). See also, *Tansey v Oil Producing Royalties, Inc*, 133 A2d 141 (Ch Ct 1957).

When there has been a revivor of the corporate charter under §312 the court will not appoint a receiver under the above section. *McKee v Standard Minerals Corp*, 156 A 193 (1931).

Corporation, charter of which is void and powers of which are inoperative for failure to pay franchise taxes, is dissolved for purpose of appointment of receiver, such dissolution not being dependent upon proclamation of governor, and court may proceed to appointment of receiver although there is pending in another court an application for the appointment of a receiver to protect the property of the corporation and to enforce alleged rights claimed against persons not parties to either proceeding, since purpose of appointment of a receiver under this section, is fundamentally the final settlement of the corporation's affairs. *Wuerfel v F H Smith Co*, 13 A2d 601 (Ch Ct 1940), cited in *United Automatic Rifles Corp v Johnson*, 41 FSupp 86 (D Mass 1941).

Court will not appoint a liquidating receiver for a solvent well-managed, close corporation on the ground that the directors (1) keep inadequate books and records, if the records meet Internal Revenue Service requirements and, (2) deny minority stockholders the right to make an independent audit, and (3) refuse to declare dividends. *Hall v John S Isaacs & Sons Farms, Inc*, 163 A2d 288 (1960).

Dissolved corporation could not liquidate by creating liquidating trust because liquidation of a dissolved corporation can only be achieved by (1) corporation's existing officers and directors and (2) court appointed trustee under court supervision. *Products Engineering Co v OKC Corp*, 590 FSupp 547 (ED La 1984).

.3 Same—effect of.—A receiver is an agent appointed by the court to take charge of, conserve, and, in most cases, to administer the assets of a corporation; his appointment is for the benefit of all interested parties, including those who may ultimately establish rights in the case. *Jersawit v Banning*, 118 A 727 (1922).

The effect of filing a claim with a receiver is, however, merely to give notice of such claim, and it is not equivalent to a pleading in the case in which he is appointed. Nor is it equivalent to an intervention in the receivership action. *International Banking Corp v Lynch*, 269 F 242 (9th Cir 1920); *Lucey Mfg Corp v Morlan*, 14 F2d 920 (9th Cir 1926); *Hannigan v Italo Petroleum Corp of America*, 181 A 4 (1935).

.4 Powers of corporation suspended.—Corporation in receivership is deprived of all management of its property and affairs except, perhaps, the doing of acts necessary to the perpetuation of its corporate existence. *Du Pont v Standard Arms Co*, 81 A 1089 (1912).

.5 Power to appoint receiver.—A corporation declared void by Governor for failure to pay franchise taxes may have receiver appointed by Chancellor for it. *Harned v Beacon Hill Real Estate Co*, 80 A 805 (1911), aff'd, 84 A 229 (1912); *Cahall v Lofland*, 107 A 769 (1919).

However, the court will not appoint a receiver where there are no assets available for distribution. *Asmussen v Quaker City Corp*, 156 A 180 (1931).

Power to appoint receiver for a dissolved corporation "at any time" is not limited to the three years from expiration or dissolution. *Slaughter v Moore*, 82 A 963 (1912); *Harned v Beacon Hill Real Estate Co*, 80 A 805 (1911), aff'd, 84 A 229 (1912).

.6 Receiver can sue outside Delaware.—*Wachsman v Tobacco Products Corp*, 129 F2d 815 (3d Cir 1942).

.7 Administration—court control.—In pending receivership of corporation, court need not, either because it lacks jurisdiction or because it exercises its discretion not to exercise it if it has it, order receiver to sell enough authorized but unissued stock to stockholder to pay corporate indebtedness and discharge receivership. *In re Public Service Holding Corp*, 24 A2d 584 (1942).

.8 Directors as trustees after dissolution.—After dissolution directors of corporation continue as directors for a period of three years, and not as trustees, to close up the corporate business. They will not be removed except for cause shown. *Carlo v International Clay Products Co*, 132 A 892 (1926); *Cahall v Lofland*, 107 A 769 (1919).

Court may appoint a receiver to displace the directors acting as trustees at any time. *Townsend v Delaware Glue Co*, 103 A 576 (1918).

.9 Claims of creditors.—The claims of a creditor, in a liquidation receivership proceeding under this section, cannot be answered by a counterclaim filed by the receiver or by a stockholder in behalf of the corporation. *Gen Elec Co v Penn Heat Control Co*, 178 A 587 (1935).

.10 Claims of preferred stockholders.—All dividends which are unpaid on the cumulative preferred stock at the time of the dissolution of the corporation must be paid out of the funds in the hands of the receiver before anything is paid on the common stock. *Garrett v Edge Moor Iron Co*, 194 A 15 (Ch Ct 1937), aff'd, 199 A 671 (1938).

.11 Claims for taxes.—Claim of U.S. for unpaid withholding and Social Security taxes is held entitled to priority, in voluntary dissolution and receivership of corporation in a proceeding in the Chancery Court, over the claim of the State Unemployment Compensation Commission for unpaid contributions. *In re Receivership of Mitchell's Restaurant, Inc*, 67 A2d 64 (Ch Ct 1949).

.12 Trustees' duties.—Trustees of dissolved corporation were negligent in relying only on one broker for sale of corporate assets, a large tract of land, but could not be surcharged, absent loss to trust corpus or showing of self-dealing, since cash terms of sale were reasonable and consistent with principal purpose of trust. *Lockwood v OFB Corp*, 305 A2d 636 (Ch Ct 1973).

§279

.13 Removal.—Court refused to approve agreement whereby corporation's liquidating trust would sell stock held by trust for less than book value. Stock was worth more than book value, so agreement was unfair to trust beneficiaries.

Court refused to remove trustee who proposed agreement and refused to follow plan favored by corporation's directors. Trustee acted in good faith on advice of counsel. However, court ordered trustee to consider plan favored by directors or come up with better alternative and to report monthly on his progress. *In the Matter of Heizer Corp, No. 7949 (Ch Ct 6-6-88).*

.14 Effect on three-year continuation period.—Delaware corporation that had been dissolved by gubernatorial proclamation ceased to legally exist after expiration of three year continuation period of GCL §278 even though a receiver had been appointed to protect rights of certain former shareholders. *Reasons:* (1) Court of Chancery refused to extend corporate existence; (2) Receiver had been appointed after three year period; and (3) Corporation had distributed all its assets and ceased doing business. The defunct corporation, therefore, was not required to file returns or pay taxes. *U.S. v McDonald & Eide, Inc, 670 FSupp 1226 (D Del 1987).*

.15 Appointment of receiver.—Where a corporation has been dissolved for longer than the period during which suits may be brought against it, and has no undistributed assets, a receiver will not be appointed to enable the pursuit of an after-discovered claim. *In the Matter of Dow Chemical Int'l Inc. of Delaware, 2008 Del. Ch. LEXIS 147 (Ch Ct 2008).*

.16 Asset distributions.—Once assets are contributed to a corporation, its shareholders hold those assets in proportion to their ownership interests, regardless of whether the shareholders contributed equity or labor, and, upon dissolution, the corporate assets will be distributed in proportion to the shareholders' interests, rather than in proportion to their capital contributions. *Grimm v Beach Fries, Inc, 2010 Del. Ch. LEXIS 147 (Ch Ct 2010).*

280 NOTICE TO CLAIMANTS; FILING OF CLAIMS.—(a)(1) After a corporation has been dissolved in accordance with the procedures set forth in this chapter, the corporation or any successor entity may give notice of the dissolution, requiring all persons having a claim against the corporation other than a claim against the corporation in a pending action, suit or proceeding to which the corporation is a party to present their claims against the corporation in accordance with such notice. Such notice shall state:

a. That all such claims must be presented in writing and must contain sufficient information reasonably to inform the corporation or successor entity of the identity of the claimant and the substance of the claim;

b. The mailing address to which such a claim must be sent;

c. The date by which such a claim must be received by the corporation or successor entity, which date shall be no earlier than 60 days from the date thereof; and

d. That such claim will be barred if not received by the date referred to in subparagraph c. of this subsection; and

e. That the corporation or a successor entity may make distributions to other claimants and the corporation's stockholders or persons interested as having been such without further notice to the claimant; and

f. The aggregate amount, on an annual basis, of all distributions made by the corporation to its stockholders for each of the 3 years prior to the date the corporation dissolved.

Such notice shall also be published at least once a week for 2 consecutive weeks in a newspaper of general circulation in the county in which the office of the corporation's last registered agent in this State is located and in the corporation's principal place of business and, in the case of a corporation having $10,000,000 or more in total assets at the time of its dissolution, at least once in all editions of a daily newspaper with a national circulation. On or before the date of the first publication of such notice, the corporation or successor entity shall mail a copy of such notice by certified or registered mail, return receipt requested, to each known claimant of the corporation including persons with claims asserted against the corporation in a pending action, suit or proceeding to which the corporation is a party.

(2) Any claim against the corporation required to be presented pursuant to this subsection is barred if a claimant who was given actual notice under this subsection does not present the claim to the dissolved corporation or successor entity by the date referred to in subparagraph (1)c. of this subsection.

(3) A corporation or successor entity may reject, in whole or in part, any claim made by a claimant pursuant to this subsection by mailing notice of such rejection by certified or registered mail, return receipt requested, to the claimant within 90 days after receipt of such claim and, in all events, at least 150 days before the expiration of the period described in §278 of this title; provided however, that in the case of a claim filed pursuant to §295 of this title against a corporation or successor entity for which a receiver or trustee has been appointed by the Court of Chancery the time period shall be as provided in §296 of

this title, and the 30-day appeal period provided for in §296 of this title shall be applicable. A notice sent by a corporation or successor entity pursuant to this subsection shall state that any claim rejected therein will be barred if an action, suit or proceeding with respect to the claim is not commenced within 120 days of the date thereof, and shall be accompanied by a copy of §§278-283 of this title and, in the case of a notice sent by a court-appointed receiver or trustee and as to which a claim has been filed pursuant to §295 of this title, copies of §§295 and 296 of this title.

(4) A claim against a corporation is barred if a claimant whose claim is rejected pursuant to paragraph (3) of this subsection does not commence an action, suit or proceeding with respect to the claim no later than 120 days after the mailing of the rejection notice.

(b)(1) A corporation or successor entity electing to follow the procedures described in subsection (a) of this section shall also give notice of the dissolution of the corporation to persons with contractual claims contingent upon the occurrence or nonoccurrence of future events or otherwise conditional or unmatured, and request that such persons present such claims in accordance with the terms of such notice. Provided however, that as used in this section and in §281 of this title, the term "contractual claims" shall not include any implied warranty as to any product manufactured, sold, distributed or handled by the dissolved corporation. Such notice shall be in substantially the form, and sent and published in the same manner, as described in subsection (a)(1) of this section.

(2) The corporation or successor entity shall offer any claimant on a contract whose claim is contingent, conditional or unmatured such security as the corporation or successor entity determines is sufficient to provide compensation to the claimant if the claim matures. The corporation or successor entity shall mail such offer to the claimant by certified or registered mail, return receipt requested, within 90 days of receipt of such claim and, in all events, at least 150 days before the expiration of the period described in §278 of this title. If the claimant offered such security does not deliver in writing to the corporation or successor entity a notice rejecting the offer within 120 days after receipt of such offer for security, the claimant shall be deemed to have accepted such security as the sole source from which to satisfy the claim against the corporation.

(c)(1) A corporation or successor entity which has given notice in accordance with subsection (a) of this section shall petition the Court of Chancery to determine the amount and form of security that will be reasonably likely to be sufficient to provide compensation for any claim against the corporation which is the subject of a pending action, suit or proceeding to which the corporation is a party other than a claim barred pursuant to subsection (a) of this section.

(2) A corporation or successor entity which has given notice in accordance with subsections (a) and (b) of this section shall petition the Court of Chancery to determine the amount and form of security that will be sufficient to provide compensation to any claimant who has rejected the offer for security made pursuant to subsection (b)(2) of this section.

(3) A corporation or successor entity which has given notice in accordance with subsection (a) of this section shall petition the Court of Chancery to determine the amount and form of security which will be reasonably likely to be sufficient to provide compensation for claims that have not been made known to the corporation or that have not arisen but that, based on facts known to the corporation or successor entity, are likely to arise or to become known to the corporation or successor entity within 5 years after the date of dissolution or such longer period of time as the Court of Chancery may determine not to exceed 10 years after the date of dissolution. The Court of Chancery may appoint a guardian ad litem in respect of any such proceeding brought under this subsection. The reasonable fees and expenses of such guardian, including all reasonable expert witness fees, shall be paid by the petitioner in such proceeding.

(d) The giving of any notice or making of any offer pursuant to this section shall not revive any claim then barred or constitute acknowledgment by the corporation or successor entity that any person to whom such notice is sent is a proper claimant and shall not operate as a waiver of any defense or counterclaim in respect of any claim asserted by any person to whom such notice is sent.

(e) As used in this section, the term "successor entity" shall include any trust, receivership or other legal entity governed by the laws of this State to which the remaining assets and liabilities of a dissolved corporation are transferred and which exists solely for the purposes of prosecuting and defending suits, by or against the dissolved corporation, enabling the dissolved corporation to settle and close the business of the dissolved corporation to dispose of and convey the property of the dissolved corporation, to discharge the liabilities of the dissolved corporation and to distribute to the dissolved corporation's stockholders any remaining assets, but not for the purpose of continuing the business for which the dissolved corporation was organized.

(f) The time periods and notice requirements of this section shall, in the case of a corporation or successor entity for which a receiver or trustee has been appointed by the Court of Chancery, be subject to variation by, or in the manner provided in, the Rules of the Court of Chancery.

(g) *In the case of a nonstock corporation, any notice referred to in the last sentence of paragraph (a)(3) of this section shall include a copy of §114 of this title. In the case of a non-profit nonstock corporation, provisions of this section regarding distributions to members shall not apply to the extent that those provisions conflict with any other applicable law or with that corporation's certificate of incorporation or bylaws.* (Last amended by Ch. 253, L. '10, eff. only with respect to dissolutions made effective after August 1, 2010, and the filing of claims arising out of such dissolutions.)

Ch. 253, L. '10, eff. as stated above, added matter in italic.

Ch. 253, L. '10 Synopsis of Section 280

Section 61 amends the DGCL to add new §280(g) to provide that, in the case of a nonstock corporation, any notice referred to in the last sentence of §280(a)(3) shall include a copy of new §114 and to provide that, in the case of a non-profit nonstock corporation, provisions of §280 regarding distributions to members shall not apply to the extent that those provisions conflict with any other applicable law or with that corporation's certificate of incorporation or bylaws. This amendment shall be effective only with respect to dissolutions made effective after August 1, 2010, and the filing of claims arising out of such dissolutions.

Ch. 266, L. '94 Synopsis of Section 280

The amendments of §280(a) provide that the claim of any claimant who receives actual notice under the subsection is barred if the claim is not presented to the corporation or its successor entity within the specified time period or if the claim is rejected by the corporation or successor entity and the claimant does not commence an action, suit or proceeding to enforce the claim within 120 days. The amendments also modify the information that must be included in the notice sent pursuant to the subsection.

The amendments to §280(b) permit the required mailing to be made by registered as well as certified mail, return receipt requested.

The amendments to §280(c) place a temporal limitation on the claims for which a dissolved corporation or successor entity must post security and require the dissolved corporation or successor entity to petition the Court of Chancery for a determination as to the amount and form of security that will be reasonably likely to be sufficient to provide compensation for claims that are the subject of a pending action, suit or proceeding.

Ch. 376, L. '90 Commentary on Sections 280 and 281

The amendments to Section 280(a) and new subsection (f) harmonize Section 280 with Sections 295 and 296 and the Rules of the Court of Chancery in cases where a receiver or trustee is appointed by the Court of Chancery. The amendments to Section 280(b) provide that the subsection is intended only to cover contingent contractual claims that are not based on implied product warranties. The amendments to Section 280(c) provide that corporations or successor entities are required to petition the Court of Chancery to determine the amount which will be reasonably likely to be sufficient to provide compensation for claims that have not been made known to the corporation or that have not arisen only when the corporation is aware of facts demonstrating that such claims are likely to arise or to become known to the corporations prior to the expiration of applicable statutes of limitation. The amendments also provide that the Court of Chancery has discretion with respect to the appointment of a guardian ad litem. The amendment to Section 281(a) specifies the nature of those obligations not enumerated in Section 281(1)-(3), which a dissolved corporation which has elected to follow the procedures set forth in Section 280 is required to satisfy. Section 281(b) has been changed to require that corporations that do not choose to follow the procedures set forth in Section 281(a) are required to pay or make reasonable provision for the same classes of claims described in the first sentence of Section 280(c)(2), as amended.

281 PAYMENT AND DISTRIBUTION TO CLAIMANTS AND STOCKHOLDERS.—(a) A dissolved corporation or successor entity which has followed the procedures described in §280 of this title:

(1) Shall pay the claims made and not rejected in accordance with §280(a) of this title,

(2) Shall post the security offered and not rejected pursuant to §280(b)(2) of this title,

(3) Shall post any security ordered by the Court of Chancery in any proceeding under §280(c) of this title, and

(4) Shall pay or make provision for all other claims that are mature, known and uncontested or that have been finally determined to be owing by the corporation or such successor entity.

Such claims or obligations shall be paid in full and any such provision for payment shall be made in full if there are sufficient assets. If there are insufficient assets, such claims and obligations shall be paid or provided for according to their priority, and, among claims of equal priority, ratably to the extent of assets legally available therefor. Any remaining assets shall be distributed to the stockholders of the dissolved corporation; provided, however, that such distribution shall not be made before the expiration of 150 days from the date of the last notice of rejections given pursuant to §280(a)(3) of this title. In the absence of actual fraud, the judgment of the directors of the dissolved corporation or the governing persons of such successor entity as to the provision made for the payment of all obligations under paragraph (4) of this subsection shall be conclusive.

(b) A dissolved corporation or successor entity which has not followed the procedures described in §280 of this title shall, prior to the expiration of the period described in §278 of this title, adopt a plan of distribution pursuant to which the dissolved corporation or successor entity (i) shall pay or make reasonable provision to pay all claims and obligations, including all contingent, conditional or unmatured contractual claims known to the corporation or such successor entity, (ii) shall make such provision as will be reasonably likely to be sufficient to provide compensation for any claim against the corporation which is the subject of a pending action, suit or proceeding to which the corporation is a party and (iii) shall make such provision as will be reasonably likely to be sufficient to provide compensation for claims that have not been made known to the corporation or that have not arisen but that, based on facts known to the corporation or successor entity, are likely to arise or to become known to the corporation or successor entity within 10 years after the date of dissolution. The plan of distribution shall provide that such claims shall be paid in full and any such provision for payment made shall be made in full if there are sufficient assets. If there are insufficient assets, such plan shall provide that such claims and obligations shall be paid or provided for according to their priority and, among claims of equal priority, ratably to the extent of assets legally available therefor. Any remaining assets shall be distributed to the stockholders of the dissolved corporation.

(c) Directors of a dissolved corporation or governing persons of a successor entity which has complied with subsection (a) or (b) of this section shall not be personally liable to the claimants of the dissolved corporation.

(d) As used in this section, the term "successor entity" has the meaning set forth in §280(e) of this title.

(e) The term "priority," as used in this section, does not refer either to the order of payments set forth in subsection (a)(1)-(4) of this section or to the relative times at which any claims mature or are reduced to judgment.

(f) In the case of a nonprofit nonstock corporation, provisions of this section regarding distributions to members shall not apply to the extent that those provisions conflict with any other applicable law or with that corporation's certificate of incorporation or bylaws. (Last amended by Ch. 253, L. '10, eff. only with respect to dissolutions made effective after August 1, 2010, and the filing of claims arising out of such dissolutions.)

Ch. 253, L. '10, eff. as stated above, added matter in italic.

Ch. 253, L. '10 Synopsis of Section 281

Section 62 amends the DGCL to add new §281(f) to provide that, in the case of a nonprofit nonstock corporation, provisions of §281 regarding distributions to members shall not apply to the extent that those provisions conflict with any other applicable law or with that corporation's certificate of incorporation or bylaws. This amendment shall be effective only with respect to dissolutions made effective after August 1, 2010, and the filing of claims arising out of such dissolutions.

Ch. 120, L. '97 Synopsis of Section 281

The amendments to Section 281(a) and 281(b), respectively, conform the terminology of Section 281 to that of Sections 278, 280 and 282. The word "funds" created an unintended ambiguity concerning whether Section 281 altered existing law by prohibiting in kind distributions of property to stockholders following dissolution. The amendments eliminate that ambiguity.

Ch. 299, L. '95 Synopsis of Section 281

The amendment to Section 281(a) corrects the subsection cross reference in light of the 1994 amendments to Section 280.

Ch. 266, L. '94 Synopsis of Section 281

The amendments to §281(b) provide that a dissolved corporation or successor entity that does not elect to follow the procedures in §280 shall adopt a plan of distribution prior to the expiration of the period described in §278 of this title, provide a temporal limitation on the claims for which a dissolved corporation or successor entity must make provision and provide that a dissolved corporation or successor entity must make provision for claims that are the subject of a pending action, suit or proceeding.

Ch. 163, L. '91 Commentary on Sections 280 and 281

The amendments to Section 280(a) and new subsection (f) harmonize Section 280 with Sections 295 and 296 and the Rules of the Court of Chancery in cases where a receiver or trustee is appointed by the Court of Chancery. The amendments to Section 280(b) provide that the subsection is intended only to cover contingent contractual claims that are not based on implied product warranties. The amendments to Section 280(c) provide that corporations or successor entities are required to petition the Court of Chancery to determine the amount which will be reasonably likely to be sufficient to provide compensation for claims that have not been made known to the corporation or that have not arisen only when the corporation is aware of facts demonstrating that such claims are likely to arise or to become known to the corporations prior to the expiration of applicable statutes of limitation. The amendments also provide that the Court of Chancery has discretion with respect to the appointment of a guardian ad litem. The amendment to Section 281(a) specifies the nature of those obligations not enumerated in Section 281(1)-(3), which a dissolved corporation which has elected to follow the procedures set forth in Section 280 is required to satisfy. Section 281(b) has been changed to require that corporations that do not choose to follow the procedures set forth in Section 281(a) are required to pay or make reasonable provision for the same classes of claims described in the first sentence of Section 280(c)(2), as amended.

.1 Officer as creditor.—An officer may be a creditor and prove a claim. *Grone v Economic Life Ins Co,* 80 A 809 (Ch Ct 1911).

While an insolvent corporation can prefer one creditor to another it cannot prefer a director-creditor. In applying this rule the court will disregard the fiction of corporate entity to reach the real parties and real situation in issue. *Pennsylvania Co v South Broad St Theatre Co,* 174 A 112 (1934).

.2 Medium of distribution to creditors.—Distribution does not have to be in cash. It may take the form of stock in another corporation. *Robinson v Pittsburgh Oil Ref Corp,* 126 A 46 (1924); *Frich v Warrior Cement Corp,* 141 A 54 (1928). See, *Diamond State Iron Co v Husbands,* 68 A 240 (1898).

Debentures and preferred stock issued by domestic corporation could not participate in distribution of lump sum settlement made by foreign government that confiscated all of corporation's property, since currency to which securities were tied had lost all value through devaluation as to make it impossible to set dollar equivalent for those securities. *Shanghai Power Co v Delaware Trust Co,* 316 A2d 589 (Ch Ct 1974).

.3 Preferred creditors.—Corporation can prefer one creditor to another as long as it does not prefer director- or officer-creditors. Such preference is not affected by the solvency or insolvency of the corporation if its affairs are not being administered by a court. *Asmussen v Quaker City Corp,* 156 A 180 (Ch Ct 1931).

Creditors of dissolved corporation that were left unsatisfied after distribution of assets to stockholders could recover directly from distributees, since assets were impressed with lien in their favor. *John Julian Constr Co v Monarch Builders Inc, 306 A2d 29 (1973).*

In an action against corporation and its directors for breach of fiduciary duty by defendants' failure to make reasonable provisions to pay all claims and obligations known to defendants at time corporation was dissolved pursuant to GCL §281, court found directors owed plaintiffs, as creditors, a fiduciary duty upon corporation's dissolution and placement of its assets in trust for the benefit of the corporation's creditors and stockholders. *Kidde Indus, Inc v Weaver Corp, 593 A2d 563 (1991).*

.4 Status of stockholders.—Subscribers to the capital stock who defaulted on the payment of their shares and were given certificates of indebtedness by the corporation instead of stock certificates did not thereby become creditors of the corporation. On dissolution the holders of certificates of indebtedness are to be considered as holders of partly paid shares. *Pasotti v U.S. Guardian Corp, 156 A 255 (Ch Ct 1931).*

After the claims of corporate creditors have been settled, and there are insufficient assets to make full distribution to the stockholders the partly paid stock was required to equalize itself with the fully paid stock of the same class before participating with it on a pro tanto basis in the distribution of the corporate assets. *Penington v Commonwealth Hotel Const Corp, 151 A 228,* modified, *155 A 514 (Ch Ct 1931).*

In the distribution of corporate assets all outstanding stock is entitled to share ratably unless the statute or charter provides otherwise. *Gaskill v Gladys Belle Oil Co, 146 A 337 (Ch Ct 1929).*

.5 Same—preferred stockholders.—On dissolution of the corporation unpaid cumulative dividends on the preferred stock must be paid out of the funds in the receiver's hands before anything is paid on the common stock. *Garrett v Edge Moor Iron Co, 194 A 15 (Ch Ct 1937),* aff'd, *199 A 671 (1938).*

.6 Liability of receiver.—Receiver is liable for conducting business of corporations at a loss without express authorization of appointing court. *U.S. v Johnson, 98 F2d 462 (8th Cir 1938).*

National Labor Relations Board collective bargaining and reinstatement order may be enforced against receiver for corporation in state receivership. *NLRB v Bachelder, 120 F2d 574 (7th Cir 1941).*

.7 Reasonableness of fees of guardian ad litem.—Over the objection of the trustee of a claimant's trust, the Court of Chancery approved the fee application of a guardian ad litem appointed pursuant to GCL §280. The court held that, though a monetary benefit to the trust could not be shown, the guardian's work was important to the resolution of the matter and assisted in the development of a plan of security that more nearly achieved the goals of §§280-282 than had the company's original proposal. The court noted that (1) The hours expended by the guardian were not unreasonable. (2) The hourly rates were those customarily charged by the firm with which the guardian was associated; the trustee's argument that the guardian's work was a quasi-public service that deserved to be paid at a discount was without legal authority. *In re RegO, No. 11651 (Ch Ct 10-8-93).*

282 LIABILITY OF STOCKHOLDERS OF DISSOLVED CORPORATIONS.—
(a) A stockholder of a dissolved corporation the assets of which were distributed pursuant to §281(a) or (b) of this title shall not be liable for any claim against the corporation in an amount in excess of such stockholder's pro rata share of the claim or the amount so distributed to [1]*such stockholder,* whichever is less.

(b) A stockholder of a dissolved corporation the assets of which were distributed pursuant to §281(a) of this title shall not be liable for any claim against the corporation on which an action, suit or proceeding is not begun prior to the expiration of the period described in §278 of this title.

(c) The aggregate liability of any stockholder of a dissolved corporation for claims against the dissolved corporation shall not exceed the amount distributed to [1]*such stockholder* in dissolution. (Last amended by Ch. 339, L. '98, eff. 7-1-98.)

Ch. 339, L. '98, eff. 7-1-98, added matter in italic and deleted [1]"him".

Ch. 339, L. '98 Synopsis of Section 282

The amendments to these Section eliminate masculine references in the statutes, and replace them with gender neutral references.

.1 Application of section.—This section has reference only to suits pending at the time of dissolution. *Townsend v Delaware Glue Co, 103 A 576 (1918).*

.2 Effect of dissolution—abatement of suit.—Dissolution does not cause the abatement of any action pending on the date of the dissolution of any corporation. Statutes prolonging the existence of a dissolved corporation are remedial and should be given a liberal construction. They apply even where the corporation, before dissolution, has disposed of all of its assets to its creditors. Such dissolution does not abate a suit against the dissolved corporation for damages for personal injury. *Eastman, Gardiner & Co v Warren, 109 F2d 193 (5th Cir 1940).*

283 JURISDICTION.—The Court of Chancery shall have jurisdiction of any application prescribed in this subchapter and of all questions arising in the proceedings thereon, and may make such orders and decrees and issue injunctions therein as justice and equity shall require. (Added by Ch. 136, L. '87, eff. 7-1-87.)

284 REVOCATION OR FORFEITURE OF CHARTER; PROCEEDINGS.— (a) The Court of Chancery shall have jurisdiction to revoke or forfeit the charter of any corporation for abuse, misuse or nonuse of its corporate powers, privileges or franchises. The Attorney General shall, upon [1]*the Attorney General's* own motion or upon the relation of a proper party, proceed for this purpose by complaint in the county in which the registered office of the corporation is located.

(b) The Court of Chancery shall have power, by appointment of receivers or otherwise, to administer and wind up the affairs of any corporation whose charter shall be revoked or forfeited by any court under any section of this title or otherwise, and to make such orders and decrees with respect thereto as shall be just and equitable respecting its affairs and assets and the rights of its stockholders and creditors.

(c) No proceeding shall be instituted under this section for nonuse of any corporation's powers, privileges or franchises during the first 2 years after its incorporation. (Last amended by Ch. 339, L. '98, eff. 7-1-98.)

Ch. 339, L. '98, eff. 7-1-98, added matter in italic and deleted [1]"his".

Ch. 339, L. '98 Synopsis of Section 284

The amendments to these Sections eliminate masculine references in the statutes, and replace them with gender neutral references.

.1 **Proceedings under section.**—The section applies to an action to dissolve a non-profit corporation for abuse of franchises by seeking to operate as a profit corporation. *Southerland v Decimo Club, Inc, 142 A 736 (Ch Ct 1928)*.

Upon the repeal of the corporate charter, the corporation becomes dissolved by operation of law. *Berl v Crutcher, 60 F2d 440 (8th Cir 1932)*.

Concerning the appointment of a receiver *pendente lite,* see *Satterthwaite v Eastern Bankers' Corp, 154 A 475 (Ch Ct 1931)*.

[1]**285 DISSOLUTION OR FORFEITURE OF CHARTER BY DECREE OF COURT; FILING.**—Whenever any corporation is dissolved or its charter forfeited by decree or judgment of the Court of Chancery, the decree or judgment shall be forthwith filed by the Register in Chancery of the county in which the decree or judgment was entered, in the office of the Secretary of State, and a note thereof shall be made by the Secretary of State on the corporation's charter or certificate of incorporation and on the index thereof. (Last amended by Ch. 136, L. '87, eff. 7-1-87.)

Ch. 136, L. '87, eff. 7-1-87, added matter in italic and deleted [1]"284".

SUBCHAPTER XI. INSOLVENCY; RECEIVERS AND TRUSTEES

291 RECEIVERS FOR INSOLVENT CORPORATIONS; APPOINTMENT AND POWERS.—Whenever a corporation shall be insolvent, the Court of Chancery, on the application of any creditor or stockholder thereof, may, at any time, appoint 1 or more persons to be receivers of and for the corporation, to take charge of its assets, estate, effects, business and affairs, and to collect the outstanding debts, claims, and property due and belonging to the corporation, with power to prosecute and defend, in the name of the corporation or otherwise, all claims or suits, to appoint an agent or agents under them, and to do all other acts which might be done by the corporation and which may be necessary or proper. The powers of the receivers shall be such and shall continue so long as the Court shall deem necessary.

.1 **Application for receivership.**—Only stockholders or creditors of the corporation can seek a receiver on the ground of insolvency. *Frantz v Templeman Oil Co, 134 A 100 (Ch Ct 1926)*.

A federal court sitting in equity has not, by reason of this section jurisdiction to appoint a receiver of an insolvent Delaware corporation on application of an unsecured simple contract creditor, as the statute confers a remedy available in the state court, rather than a substantive right available in either a state or federal court. *Pusey & Jones Co v Hanssen, 261 US 491 (1923).* But see, *Myers v Occidental Oil Corp, 288 F 997 (D Del 1923)*.

Creditor who has assented to readjustment plan for liquidating of corporation cannot ask for the appointment of a receiver under this section. Chancellor will not exercise discretion conferred by this section to appoint a receiver where the corporation is being impartially and equitably liquidated pursuant to a voluntary plan in the state where the corporation has its principal office and place of business. *Wright v Mtge Guarantee Co, 174 A 271 (1934).*

Court will delay appointing a receiver for an insolvent corporation to give creditors and majority stockholders, who wished to continue corporation, time to show that they could put corporation's operations on a current basis; upon such showing, the court in the exercise of its discretion will dismiss the petition. *Foster v Del Drug Co, 114 A2d 228 (Ch Ct 1955).*

Bondholders may not pursue statutory claim seeking appointment of receiver for insolvent corporation when indenture expressly denies such a claim without first following specified procedure relating to trustee. *Elliott Associates, LP v Bio-Response, Inc, No. 10,624 (Ch Ct 5-23-89).*

.2 Receiver pendente lite and injunction.—Receiver pendente lite should not be appointed or injunction issued in case of active and prosperous corporation simply because of dissensions among its owners over questions of business policy. *Salnita Corp v Walter Holding Corp, 168 A 74 (1933).*

.3 Grounds for receivership.—Stockholder cannot get receivership only for fraud and breaches of trust by officers. *Myers v Occidental Oil Corp, 288 F 997 (D Del 1923).*

Court will appoint a receiver of a solvent corporation which is run by its majority stockholder for his own convenience and in disregard of the rights of the minority as evidenced by the majority stockholder's misuse of the corporation's credit and his ignoring corporate law formalities. *Tansey v Oil Producing Royalties, Inc, 133 A2d 141 (Ch Ct 1957).*

Court will not appoint a receiver for a solvent, close corporation whose controlling directors (1) concealed financial data from a minority stockholders, if they did not issue false reports' or dissipate assets and the corporation's books met Internal Revenue requirements and (2) paid themselves salaries not authorized by a disinterested board of directors or ratified by independent stockholder vote, if the salaries might be justifiable. *Hall v Isaacs, 146 A2d 602 (Ch Ct 1958).*

Mismanagement is not a necessary requisite for the appointment of a receiver. *Sill v Kentucky Coal & Timber Development Co, 97 A 617 (1916).*

.4 Determination of insolvency.—That general receiver has been appointed elsewhere is immaterial on question of corporation's insolvency. In suit for receiver on that ground, it must be shown by clear and convincing evidence. *Manning v Middle States Oil Corp, 137 A 79 (1927).*

Because its assets were in the hands of temporary receivers appointed in another state it was held that the corporation was not necessarily insolvent, although its officers were no longer able to pay obligations as they matured. Ample funds were in hands of receiver who was appointed because of fraud and mismanagement. The receiver paid all obligations he knew of as they matured. *Bruch v Nat'l Guarantee Credit Corp, 116 A 738 (1922).*

While a Delaware corporation may be insolvent under Delaware law, because unable to meet its obligations in due course of business, it is not insolvent under Pennsylvania law, its principal office and most of its property being located in Pennsylvania, it having assets largely exceeding its liabilities. A federal court for Pennsylvania, in a suit of creditors, appointed a receiver to conserve its assets and conduct its business. Held, the court would not revoke its appointment, in favor of receivers appointed by a court of Delaware at suit of a single stockholder, comity not requiring it, and the creditors opposing it. *Wheeler v Badenhausen Co, 360 F 991 (ED Pa 1919).*

Insolvency is either inability to pay debts as they mature * * * in the ordinary course of business or an excess of liabilities over assets. Neither definition is to be adopted to the exclusion of the other. *Sill v Ky Coal & Timber Development Co, 97 A 617 (1916).* See, also, *Hobson v Consol Management Ass'n, 163 A 621 (1932).*

If corporation, charged to be insolvent only in sense that it cannot pay its current bills can borrow enough to meet them, court ought not generally to appoint a receiver for it. *Shaten v Volco Cement Corp, 2 A2d 152 (Ch Ct 1938),* followed in *Banks v Christina Copper Mines, Inc, 99 A2d 504 (Ch Ct 1953).*

Corporation without enough liquid assets to pay obligations is not insolvent for receivership purposes when it has enough property to finance liabilities. *McKee v Standard Minerals Corp, 156 A 193 (1931).*

In suit for receiver for foreign holding company, foreign receiver having been appointed without admission of insolvency, insolvency must be proved independently, unaided by adjudication or admission of its existence. *Rogers v Bancokentucky Co, 156 A 217 (1931).*

.5 Powers of receiver.—A receiver of an insolvent corporation is not bound by its executory contracts and may repudiate burdensome lease without paying year's rent. *Conover v Sterling Stores Corp, 120 A 740 (1923).*

A receiver cannot assert claim in behalf of general creditors which corporation could not have asserted as against special creditors claiming lien on corporation assets. *Denny v Wilmington Ice & Coal Co, 128 A 123 (1925).*

.6 Receiver-duties.—State receiver of corporation subsequently adjudicated bankrupt must turn over property of corporation to trustee in bankruptcy. If he has received compensation out of assets of the estate by state court order he must include same in property turned over to receiver and have any allowance he may be entitled to fixed by bankruptcy court. *Taylor v Sternberg, 293 US 470 (1935).*

.7 Power of court to appoint receiver.—Under this section allegations that defendant is heavily indebted is without credit and is threatened with several suits are insufficient without showing of immediate danger of irreparable loss to require appointment of receiver pendente lite. *Moore v Associated Producing & Refining Corp, 121 A 655 (1923).*

Power of the chancellor to appoint a receiver is discretionary. *Noble v European Mortgage & Investment Corp, 165 A 157 (1933).*

Except in extreme cases, the appointment of a receiver for a domestic corporation should be made whenever a foreign court has appointed a receiver, if the jurisdictional facts exist. *Stone v The Jewett Bigelow & Brooks Coal Co, 125 A 340 (1924).*

Where assets of corporation have been collected and sold by receiver in another state, court can refuse to appoint receiver even though funds realized have not been distributed to stockholders. *Jones v Maxwell Motor Corp, 15 A 312 (1921).*

President has no implied or inherent power to consent to the appointment of a receiver to wind up corporation's affairs. *Bruch v National Guarantee Credit Corp, 116 A 738 (1922).*

A Delaware court can appoint a general receiver for a Delaware corporation after a foreign court has taken charge of the assets within its jurisdiction and appointed a purported general receiver for the company. *Frankland v Remington Phonograph Corp, 119 A 127 (1922).*

Court may appoint receiver to run corporation and when it can meet its obligations in the usual course of business, or there is reasonable prospect its business can be successfully continued despite deficiency of assets, court may discharge the receiver. *Bradenhausen Co v Kidwell, 107 A 297 (1919).*

In a receivership suit against a corporation, where there were no direct averments of threats to sell, remove or conceal securities owned by the company pending hearing of the rule for preliminary injunction or of facts from which danger of disposition of the securities could be inferred and the company's answer denied its insolvency, held a restraining order, dissolved unless suitable security be given by complainant. *Whitmer v William Whitmer & Sons, 98 A 940 (1916).*

Where two courts have concurrent jurisdiction of actions involving different issues and seeking different relief, but affecting the same res, that court which first gains actual possession of the res will retain jurisdiction though action was first brought in the other court. *Ward v Foulkrod, 264 F 627 (3d Cir 1920).*

Court of the domicile of a corporation may appoint a receiver and authorize him to take possession of its property in a foreign jurisdiction. He must, however, apply for ancillary receivership in the jurisdiction where the property is found. *Ward v Foulkrod,* above.

.8 Title of receiver to corporate property.—Transfer of title of property to the receiver takes place as of the beginning of the day he qualifies. Hence a judgment filed at 4:30 P.M. on the same day was not a lien against the property of the corporation as it had already passed to the receivers. *Ferris v Chic-Mint Gum Co, 125 A 343 (1924).*

.9 Claims.—Where claim against an insolvent corporation is improperly verified under Chancery Rule 156 leave will be granted to amend the verification notwithstanding time for filing claims has passed. *Hawkins v Lewes Journal Co, 119 A 243 (1922).*

As against stockholders, the assets of an insolvent corporation are regarded as a trust fund for creditors. *Asmussen v Quaker City Corp, 156 A 180 (1931).*

While insolvent corporation can prefer one creditor over another, it cannot prefer a director-creditor. In applying this rule the court will disregard fiction of corporate entity to reach the real parties and real situation in issue. *Pennsylvania Co v South Broad St Theatre Co, 174 A 112 (1934).*

Subscriber to stock under employees' stock purchase plan is stockholder and not creditor and is not entitled to file claim with receiver for amount paid on subscription. *Hegarty v American Commonwealths Power Corp, 174 A 273 (1934).*

Rejection, by federal district court in California of a claim filed against an insolvent Delaware corporation in equity receivership proceeding, does not necessarily bar creditor from later suing the corporation on the claim. *Hannigan v Italo Petroleum Corp, 181 A 660 (1935).*

.10 Same—tax claim-property.—Unpaid federal income taxes get priority over state franchise and license taxes in liquidation of insolvent corporation. *Churchill v SW Straus Investment Corp, 25 FSupp 316 (D Del 1938),* aff'd, *NY v US, 106 F2d 210 (3d Cir 1939).*

.11 Foreclosure of mortgage on property in receivership.—Granting of leave to foreclose mortgage on property of corporation in receivership under this section is discretionary and will be withheld for a reasonable time in the best interest of all concerned. *McGlinn v Wilson Line, Inc, 174 A 365 (1934).*

.12 Reorganization—legal fees.—State courts cannot hear suit for extra pay for legal services rendered to a stockholders' committee in a Chapter X proceeding. *Leiman v Guttman, 336 US 1 (1949).*

.13 Expedited hearing.—Court refused to set matters for expedited hearing to consider whether receiver should be appointed for corporation because appointment of receiver is ultimate sanction, which must not be done precipitously without giving corporation adequate opportunity to respond. *Greenfield v Caporella, No. 8710 (Ch Ct 12-3-86).*

.14 Appointment of receiver.—A receiver for a debtor corporation will not be appointed at a creditor's request where the creditor fails to provide clear and convincing evidence that the corporation's liabilities exceed its assets or that it cannot pay its current obligations in the ordinary course of business. *Banet v Fonds de Regulation et de Controle Café Cacao, 2009 Del. Ch. LEXIS 24 (Ch Ct 2009).*

Notwithstanding that a limited liability company is insolvent, a receiver will not be appointed where the requesting party cannot demonstrate the existence of special circumstances of great exigency or that the appointment of a receiver will produce a benefit or avoid a harm. *Pope Investments LLC v Benda Pharmaceutical, Inc, 2010 Del. Ch. LEXIS 239 (Ch Ct 2010).*

292 TITLE TO PROPERTY; FILING ORDER OF APPOINTMENT; EXCEPTION.—(a) Trustees or receivers appointed by the Court of Chancery of and for any corporation, and their respective survivors and successors, shall, upon their appointment and qualification or upon the death, resignation or discharge of any cotrustee or coreceiver, be vested by operation of law and without any act or deed, with the title of the corporation to all of its property, real, personal or mixed of whatsoever nature, kind, class or description, and wheresoever situate, except real estate situate outside this State.

(b) Trustees or receivers appointed by the Court or Chancery shall, within 20 days from the date of their qualification, file in the office of the recorder in each county in this State, in which any real estate belonging to the corporation may be situated, a certified copy of the order of their appointment and evidence of their qualification.

(c) This section shall not apply to receivers appointed pendente lite.

.1 Protection of name and business of old corporation as against new corporation.—A preliminary injunction lies to restrain advertisements giving impression that new corporation is continuation of old, and use of address of old corporation operated by receiver, where name of former owners appear in names of both corporations. *Sellers v McCormick, 165 A 569 (1933).*

293 NOTICES TO STOCKHOLDERS AND CREDITORS.—All notices required to be given to stockholders and creditors in any action in which a receiver or trustee for

a corporation was appointed shall be given by the Register in Chancery, unless otherwise ordered by the Court of Chancery.

294 RECEIVERS OR TRUSTEES; INVENTORY; LIST OF DEBTS AND REPORT.—Trustees or receivers shall, as soon as convenient, file in the office of the Register in Chancery of the county in which the proceeding is pending, a full and complete itemized inventory of all the assets of the corporation which shall show their nature and probable value, and an account of all debts due from and to it, as nearly as the same can be ascertained. They shall make a report to the Court of their proceedings, whenever and as often as the Court shall direct.

295 CREDITORS' PROOFS OF CLAIMS; WHEN BARRED; NOTICE.—All creditors shall make proof under oath of their respective claims against the corporation, and cause the same to be filed in the office of the Register in Chancery of the county in which the proceeding is pending within the time fixed by and in accordance with the procedure established by the Rules of the Court of Chancery. All creditors and claimants failing to do so, within the time limited by this section, or the time prescribed by the order of the Court, may, by direction of the Court, be barred from participating in the distribution of the assets of the corporation. The Court may also prescribe what notice, by publication or otherwise, shall be given to the creditors of the time fixed for the filing and making proof of claims. (Last amended by Ch. 106, L. '73, eff. 7-1-73.)

Comment: The purpose of the amendment to §295 is to resolve the apparent conflict between the statute and the Rules of the Court of Chancery concerning the procedure for the filing of proofs of claim for corporations where a receiver or trustee has been appointed.

296 ADJUDICATION OF CLAIMS; APPEAL.—(a) The Register in Chancery, immediately upon the expiration of the time fixed for the filing of claims, in compliance with the provisions of §295 of this title, shall notify the trustee or receiver of the filing of the claims, and the trustee or receiver, within 30 days after receiving the notice, shall inspect the claims, and if the trustee or receiver or any creditor shall not be satisfied with the validity or correctness of the same, or any of them, the trustee or receiver shall forthwith notify the creditors whose claims are disputed of [1]*such trustee's or receiver's* decision. The trustee or receiver shall require all creditors whose claims are disputed to submit themselves to such examination in relation to their claims as the trustee or receiver shall direct, and the creditors shall produce such books and papers relating to their claims as shall be required. The trustee or receiver shall have power to examine, under oath or affirmation, all witnesses produced before [2]*such trustee or receiver* touching the claims, and shall pass upon and allow or disallow the claims, or any part thereof, and notify the claimants of [1]*such trustee's or receiver's* determination.

(b) Every creditor or claimant who shall have received notice from the receiver or trustee that [1]*such creditor's or claimant's* claim has been disallowed in whole or in part may appeal to the Court of Chancery within 30 days thereafter. The Court, after hearing, shall determine the rights of the parties. (Last amended by Ch. 339, L. '98, eff. 7-1-98.)

Ch. 339, L. '98, eff. 7-1-98, added matter in italic and deleted [1]"his" and [2]"him".

Ch. 339, L. '98 Synopsis of Section 296

The amendments to these Sections eliminate masculine references in the statutes, and replace them with gender neutral references.

297 SALE OF PERISHABLE OR DETERIORATING PROPERTY.—Whenever the property of a corporation is at the time of the appointment of a receiver or trustee encumbered with liens of any character, and the validity, extent or legality of any lien is disputed or brought in question, and the property of the corporation is of a character which will deteriorate in value pending the litigation respecting the lien, the Court of Chancery may order the receiver or trustee to sell the property of the corporation, clear of all encumbrances, at public or private sale, for the best price that can be obtained therefor, and pay the net proceeds arising from the sale thereof after deducting the costs of the sale into the Court, there to remain subject to the order of the Court, and to be disposed of as the Court shall direct.

298 COMPENSATION, COSTS AND EXPENSES OF RECEIVER OR TRUSTEE.—The Court of Chancery, before making distribution of the assets of a corporation among the creditors or stockholders thereof, shall allow a reasonable compensation to the receiver or trustee for [1]*such receiver's or trustee's* services, and the costs and expenses incurred in and about the execution of [1]*such receiver's or trustee's* trust, and the costs of the proceedings in the Court, to be first paid out of the assets. (Last amended by Ch. 339, L. '98, eff. 7-1-98.)

Ch. 339, L. '98, eff. 7-1-98, added matter in italic and deleted [1]"his".

Ch. 339, L. '98 Synopsis of Section 298

The amendments to these Sections eliminate masculine references in the statutes, and replace them with gender neutral references.

.1 Allowances.—Allowances may be made to the receiver and his counsel for their services and out-of-pocket expenses. Allowances may also be made for services of others, such as appraisers. Ordinarily, they may not be made to stockholders' committees and their counsel unless they render very helpful services either in adding to or preserving the receivership estate. *Veeder v Public Service Holding Corp, 70 F2d 22 (5th Cir 1949).* Thus, expenses of committee in watching the progress of the administration, conferring with the receivers, gratuitously advising and assuming to act as overseers of the receivers are not compensable unless those activities create or preserve the fund. *R. A. McWilliams, Tr. Co. v Mo.-Kan. Pipe Line Co, 190 A 569 (Ch Ct 1936).* See, also, *Boggs v Bellevue, Inc, 156 A 202 (Ch Ct 1931); Shaw v Lincoln Hotel Corp, 156 A 99 (Ch Ct 1931).*

.2 Recovery of allowances.—In receivership of corporation allowances to receiver and counsel for services and expenses are, if there are no assets of receivership estate available for their payment, recoverable from complainant and surety on cost bond. *Brill v Southerland, 14 A2d 408 (1940).*

299 SUBSTITUTION OF TRUSTEE OR RECEIVER AS PARTY; ABATEMENT OF ACTIONS.—A trustee or receiver, upon application by [1]*such receiver or trustee* in the court in which any suit is pending, shall be substituted as party plaintiff in the place of the corporation in any suit or proceeding which was so pending at the time of [2]*such receiver's or trustee's* appointment. No action against a trustee or receiver of a corporation shall abate by reason of [2]*such receiver's or trustee's* death, but, upon suggestion of the facts on the record, shall be continued against [2]*such receiver's or trustee's* successor or against the corporation in case no new trustee or receiver is appointed. (Last amended by Ch. 339, L. '98, eff. 7-1-98.)

Ch. 339, L. '98, eff. 7-1-98, added matter in italic and deleted [1]"him" and [2]"his".

Ch. 339, L. '98 Synopsis of Section 299

The amendments to these Sections eliminate masculine references in the statutes, and replace them with gender neutral references.

300 EMPLOYEE'S LIEN FOR WAGES WHEN CORPORATION INSOLVENT.—Whenever any corporation of this State, or any foreign corporation doing business in this State, shall become insolvent, the employees doing labor or service of whatever character in the regular employ of the corporation, shall have a lien upon the assets thereof for the amount of the wages due to them, not exceeding 2 months' wages respectively, which shall be paid prior to any other debt or debts of the corporation. The word "employee" shall not be construed to include any of the officers of the corporation.

.1 Service must be regular employment.—One employed to procure band of musicians for advertising by parades cannot get priority of claim for services. *Garretson v Del. State Fair Inc, 123 A 919 (Ch Ct 1925).*

.2 Priority to mortgage debt.—Where the realty proceeds of insolvent corporation were insufficient to discharge a mortgage debt, wage claimants could not claim preference thereto. *Clough v Superior Equipment Corp, 156 A 249 (Ch Ct 1931).*

.3 Effect of preference under a local law.—Extent to which a wage claimant received payment under a local law would abate his claim under this section. *Di Angelo v McCormick Bros Inc, 168 A 79 (Ch Ct 1933).*

.4 "Officer" construed.—Word "officer" includes directors even though director may be a foreman and in that sense an employee. *In re Peninsula Cut Stone Co, 82 A 689 (Ch Ct 1912).*

301 DISCONTINUANCE OF LIQUIDATION.—The liquidation of the assets and business of an insolvent corporation may be discontinued at any time during the liquidation proceedings when it is established that cause for liquidation no longer exists. In such event the Court of Chancery in its discretion, and subject to such condition as it may deem appropriate, may dismiss the proceedings and direct the receiver or trustee to redeliver to the corporation all of its remaining property and assets.

302 COMPROMISE OR ARRANGEMENT BETWEEN CORPORATION AND CREDITORS OR STOCKHOLDERS.—(a) Whenever the provision permitted by paragraph (2) of subsection (b) of §102 of this title is included in the original certificate of incorporation of any corporation, all persons who become creditors or stockholders thereof shall be deemed to have become such creditors or stockholders subject in all respects to that provision and the same shall be absolutely binding upon them. Whenever that provision is inserted in the certificate of incorporation of any such corporation by an amendment of its certificate all persons who become creditors or stockholders of such corporation after such amendment shall be deemed to have become such creditors or stockholders subject in all respects to that provision and the same shall be absolutely binding upon them.

(b) The Court of Chancery may administer and enforce any compromise or arrangement made pursuant to the provision contained in paragraph (2) of subsection (b) of §102 of this title and may restrain, pendente lite, all actions and proceedings against any corporation with respect to which the Court shall have begun the administration and enforcement of that provision and may appoint a temporary receiver for such corporation and may grant the receiver such powers as it deems proper, and may make and enforce such rules as it deems necessary for the exercise of such jurisdiction.

.1 Reorganization of solvent corporation.—Court will reorganize solvent corporation that cannot locate majority of its stockholders, and will make missing stockholders' stock non-voting until they appear to claim their stock, and will appoint corporation trustee for its missing stockholders. *In re North European Oil Corp*, 129 A2d 259 (Ch Ct 1957).

Plaintiff was not entitled to convene a special meeting of stockholders to vote on a compromise proposal he submitted to settle an action he had brought, without obtaining the approval of (or even consulting with) the board of directors. *Siegman v Palomar Medical Technologies, Inc*, No. 15894 (Ch Ct 2-25-98).

303 [1]PROCEEDING UNDER THE FEDERAL BANKRUPTCY CODE OF THE UNITED STATES; EFFECTUATION.—(a) Any corporation of this State, an order for relief with respect to which has been entered pursuant to the Federal Bankruptcy Code, 11 U.S.C. §101 et seq., or any successor statute, may put into effect and carry out any decrees and orders of the court or judge in such bankruptcy proceeding and may take any corporate action provided or directed by such decrees and orders, without further action by its directors or stockholders. Such power and authority may be exercised, and such corporate action may be taken, as may be directed by such decrees or orders, by the trustee or trustees of such corporation appointed or elected in the bankruptcy proceeding (or a majority thereof), or if none be appointed or elected and acting, by designated officers of the corporation, or by a representative appointed by the court or judge, with like effect as if exercised and taken by unanimous action of the directors and stockholders of the corporation.

(b) Such corporation may, in the manner provided in subsection (a) of this section, but without limiting the generality or effect of the foregoing, alter, amend or repeal its bylaws; constitute or reconstitute and classify or reclassify its board of directors, and name, constitute or appoint directors and officers in place of or in addition to all or some of the directors or officers then in office; amend its certificate of incorporation, and make any change in its capital or capital stock, or any other amendment, change, or alteration, or provision, authorized by this chapter; be dissolved, transfer all or part of its assets, merge or consolidate as permitted by this chapter, in which case, however, no stockholder shall have any statutory right of appraisal of such stockholder's stock; change the location of its registered office, change its registered agent, and remove or appoint any agent to receive service of process; authorize and fix the terms, manner and conditions of, the issuance of bonds, debentures or other obligations, whether or not convertible into stock of any class, or bearing warrants or other evidences of optional rights to purchase or subscribe for stock of any class; or lease its property and franchises to any corporation, if permitted by law.

(c) A certificate of any amendment, change or alteration, or of dissolution, or any agreement of merger or consolidation, made by such corporation pursuant to the foregoing provisions, shall be filed with the Secretary of State in accordance with §103 of this title, *and, subject to subsection (d) of said §103 of this title, shall thereupon become effective in accordance with its terms and the provisions hereof. Such certificate, agreement of merger or other instrument shall be made, executed and acknowledged, as may be directed by such decrees or orders, by the trustee or trustees appointed or elected in the bankruptcy proceeding (or a majority thereof), or, if none be appointed or elected and acting, by the officers of the corporation, or by a representative appointed by the court or judge, and shall certify that provision for the making of such certificate, agreement or instrument is contained in a decree or order of a court or judge having jurisdiction of a proceeding under such Federal Bankruptcy Code or successor statute.*

(d) This section shall cease to apply to such corporation upon the entry of a final decree in the bankruptcy proceeding closing the case and discharging the trustee or trustees, if any; provided however, that the closing of a case and discharge of trustee or trustees, if any, will not affect the validity of any act previously performed pursuant to subsections (a) through (c) of this section.

(e) On filing any certificate, agreement, report or other paper made or executed pursuant to this section, there shall be paid to the Secretary of State for the use of the State the same fees as are payable by corporations not in bankruptcy upon the filing of like certificates, agreements, reports or other papers. (Last amended by Ch. 326, L. '04, eff. 8-1-04.)

Ch. 326, L. '04, eff. 8-1-04, added matter in italic and deleted [1]"**REORGANIZATION UNDER A STATUTE OF THE UNITED STATES; EFFECTUATION.**—(a) Any corporation of this State, a plan of reorganization of which, pursuant to any applicable statute of the United States relating to reorganizations of corporations, has been or shall be confirmed by the decree or order of a court of competent jurisdiction, may put into effect and carry out the plan and the decrees and orders of the court judge relative thereto and may take any proceeding and do any act provided in the plan or directed by such decrees and orders, without further action by its directors or stockholders. Such power and authority may be exercised, and such proceedings and acts may be taken, as may be directed by such decrees or orders, by the trustee or trustees of such corporation appointed in the reorganization proceedings (or a majority thereof), or if none be appointed and acting, by designated officers of the corporation, or by a Master or other representative appointed by the court or judge, with like effect as if exercised and taken by unanimous action of the directors and stockholders of the corporation.

(b) Such corporation may, in the manner provided in subsection (a) of this section, but without limiting the generality or effect of the foregoing, alter, amend or repeal its bylaws; constitute or reconstitute and classify or reclassify its board of directors, and name, constitute or appoint directors and officers in place of or in addition to all or some of the directors or officers then in office; amend its certificate of incorporation, and make any change in its capital or capital stock, or any other amendment, change, or alteration, or provision, authorized by this chapter; be dissolved, transfer all or part of its assets, merge or consolidate as permitted by this chapter, in which case, however, no stockholder shall have any statutory right of appraisal of such shareholder's stock; change the location of its registered office, change its registered agent, and remove or appoint any agent to receive service of process; authorize and fix the terms, manner and conditions of, the issuance of bonds, debentures or other obligations, whether or not convertible into stock of any class, or bearing warrants or other evidences of optional rights to purchase or subscribe for stock of any class; or lease its property and franchises to any corporation, if permitted by law.

(c) A certificate of any amendment, change or alteration, or of dissolution, or any agreement of merger or consolidation, made by such corporation pursuant to the foregoing provisions, shall be filed with the Secretary of State in accordance with §103 of this title, and, subject to subsection (d) of said §103, shall thereupon become effective in accordance with its terms and the provisions thereof. Such certificate, agreement of merger or other instrument shall be made, executed and acknowledged, as may be directed by such decrees or orders, by the trustee or trustees appointed in the reorganization proceedings (or a majority thereof), or, if none be appointed and acting, by the officers of the corporation, or by a Master or other representative appointed by the court or judge, and shall certify that provision for the making of such certificate, agreement or instrument is contained in a decree or order of a court or judge having jurisdiction of a proceeding under such applicable statute of the United States for the reorganization of such corporation.

(d) This section shall cease to apply to such corporation upon the entry of a final decree in the reorganization proceedings closing the case and discharging the trustee or trustees, if any.

(e) On filing any certificate, agreement, report or other paper made or executed pursuant to this section, there shall be paid to the Secretary of State for the use of the State the same fees as are payable by corporations not in reorganization upon the filing of like certificates, agreements, reports or other papers."

Ch. 326, L. '04 Synopsis of Section 303

The amendments to Section 303 are intended to clarify that the provisions of the statute apply to any type of federal bankruptcy proceeding, whether liquidation or reorganization, and that the validity of corporate action undertaken pursuant to the statute is not dependent upon the existence or pendency of a confirmed plan of reorganization.

Ch. 339, L. '98 Synopsis of Section 303

The amendments to these Sections eliminate masculine references in the statutes, and replace them with gender neutral references.

SUBCHAPTER XII. RENEWAL, REVIVAL, EXTENSION AND RESTORATION OF CERTIFICATE OF INCORPORATION OR CHARTER

311 REVOCATION OF VOLUNTARY DISSOLUTION.—(a) At any time prior to the expiration of 3 years following the dissolution of a corporation pursuant to §275 of this title, or, at any time prior to the expiration of such longer period as the Court of Chancery may have directed pursuant to §278 of this title, a corporation may revoke the dissolution theretofore effected by it in the following manner:

(1) For purposes of this section, the term "stockholders" shall mean the stockholders of record on the date the dissolution became effective.

(2) The board of directors shall adopt a resolution recommending that the dissolution be revoked and directing that the question of the revocation be submitted to a vote at a special meeting of stockholders;

(3) Notice of the special meeting of stockholders shall be given in accordance with §222 of this title to each of the stockholders;

(4) At the meeting a vote of the stockholders shall be taken on a resolution to revoke the dissolution. If a majority of the stock of the corporation which was outstanding and entitled to vote upon a dissolution at the time of its dissolution shall be voted for the resolution, a certificate of revocation of dissolution shall be executed, and acknowledged in accordance with §103 of this title, which shall state:

a. The name of the corporation;
b. The names and respective addresses of its officers;
c. The names and respective addresses of its directors;
d. That a majority of the stock of the corporation which was outstanding and entitled to vote upon a dissolution at the time of its dissolution have voted in favor of a resolution to revoke the dissolution; or, if it be the fact, that, in lieu of a meeting and vote of stockholders, the stockholders have given their written consent to the revocation in accordance with §228 of this title.

(b) Upon the filing in the office of the Secretary of State of the certificate of revocation of dissolution, the Secretary of State, upon being satisfied that the requirements of this section have been complied with, shall issue a certificate that the dissolution has been revoked. Upon the issuance of such certificate by the Secretary of the State, the revocation of the dissolution shall become effective and the corporation may again carry on its business.

(c) Upon the issuance of the certificate by the Secretary of State to which subsection (b) of this section refers, the provisions of §211(c) of this title shall govern, and the period of time the corporation was in dissolution shall be included within the calculation of the 30- day and 13-month periods to which §211(c) of this title refers. An election of directors, however, may be held at the special meeting of stockholders to which subsection (a) of this section refers and, in that event, that meeting of stockholders shall be deemed an annual meeting of stockholders for purposes of §211(c) of this title.

(d) If after the dissolution became effective any other corporation organized under the laws of this State shall have adopted the same name as the corporation, or shall have adopted a name so nearly similar thereto as not to distinguish it from the corporation, or any foreign corporation shall have qualified to do business in this State under the same name as the corporation or under a name so nearly similar thereto as not to distinguish it from the corporation, then, in such case, the corporation shall not be reinstated under the same name which it bore when its dissolution becomes effective, but shall adopt and be reinstated under some other name, and in such case the certificate to be filed under this section shall set forth the name borne by the corporation at the time its dissolution became effective and the new name under which the corporation is to be reinstated.

(e) Nothing in this section shall be construed to affect the jurisdiction or power of the Court of Chancery under §279 or 280 of this title.

(f) At any time prior to the expiration of 3 years following the dissolution of a nonstock corporation pursuant to §276 of this title, or, at any time prior to the expiration of such longer period as the Court of Chancery may have directed pursuant to §278 of this title, a nonstock corporation may revoke the dissolution theretofore effected by it in a manner *analogous to that by which the dissolution was authorized, including (i) if applicable, a vote of the members entitled to vote, if any, on the dissolution and (ii) the filing of a certificate of revocation of dissolution containing information comparable to that required by paragraph (a)(4) of this section. Notwithstanding the foregoing, only subsections (b), (d), and (e) of this section shall apply to nonstock corporations.* (Last amended by Ch. 253, L. '10, eff. 8-1-10.)

Ch. 253, L. '10, eff. 8-1-10, added matter in italic.

Ch. 253, L. '10 Synopsis of Section 311

Section 63 amends the DGCL to add new §311(f) to provide that, in a procedure analogous to that for a stock corporation, a nonstock corporation can revoke a dissolution effected by it. New §311(f) provides that the revocation of dissolution will include, if applicable, a vote of the members entitled to vote (if any) on the dissolution and the filing of a certificate of revocation of dissolution containing information comparable to that described in §311(a)(4).

Ch. 298, L. '02 Synopsis of Section 311

The amendment to Section 311, which applies to revocation of voluntary dissolution, adds a new subsection (c) which is comparable to subsection (i) of Section 312, which applies to renewal, revival, extension and restoration of the certificate of incorporation, thereby conforming the two sections with respect to the application of Section 211 following the revocation or the renewal, revival, extension or restoration, as the case may be.

Ch. 82, L. '01 Synopsis of Section 311

The amendments to Section 311(a) clarify which stockholders are entitled to vote on revocation of dissolution. The intent of the statute is to confer such a vote on those who were the stockholders at the time of dissolution. The current language of the statute, however, could be read to permit a vote by transferees subsequent to dissolution. This amendment removes that potential ambiguity.

312 RENEWAL, REVIVAL, EXTENSION AND RESTORATION OF CERTIFICATE OF INCORPORATION.—(a) As used in this section, the term "certificate of incorporation" includes the charter of a corporation organized under any special act or any law of this State.

(b) Any corporation may, at any time before the expiration of the time limited for its existence and any corporation whose certificate of incorporation has become forfeited or void pursuant to this title and any corporation whose certificate of incorporation has expired by reason of failure to renew it or whose certificate of incorporation has been renewed, but, through failure to comply strictly with the provisions of this chapter, the validity of whose renewal has been brought into question, may at any time procure an extension, restoration, renewal or revival of its certificate of incorporation, together with all the rights, franchises, privileges and immunities and subject to all of its duties, debts and liabilities which had been secured or imposed by its original certificate of incorporation and all amendments thereto.

(c) The extension, restoration, renewal or revival of the certificate of incorporation may be procured by executing, acknowledging and filing a certificate in accordance with §103 of this title.

(d) The certificate required by subsection (c) of this section shall state:

(1) The name of the corporation, which shall be the existing name of the corporation or the name it bore when its certificate of incorporation expired, except as provided in subsection (f) of this section, and the date of filing of its original certificate of incorporation with the Secretary of State;

(2) The address (which shall include the street, city and county) of the corporation's registered office in this State and the name of its registered agent at such address;

(3) Whether or not the renewal, restoration or revival is to be perpetual and if not perpetual the time for which the renewal, restoration or revival is to continue and, in case of renewal before the expiration of the time limited for its existence, the date when the renewal is to commence, which shall be prior to the date of the expiration of the old certificate of incorporation which it is desired to renew;

(4) That the corporation desiring to be renewed or revived and so renewing or reviving its certificate of incorporation was organized under the laws of this State;

(5) The date when the certificate of incorporation would expire, if such is the case, or such other facts as may show that the certificate of incorporation has become forfeited or void pursuant to this title, or that the validity of any renewal has been brought into question;

(6) That the certificate for renewal or revival is filed by authority of those who were directors or members of the governing body of the corporation at the time its certificate of incorporation expired or who were elected directors or members of the governing body of the corporation as provided in subsection (h) of this section.

(e) Upon the filing of the certificate in accordance with §103 of this title the corporation shall be renewed and revived with the same force and effect as if its certificate of incorporation had not been forfeited or void pursuant to this title, or had not expired by limitation. Such reinstatement shall validate all contracts, acts, matters and things made, done and performed within the scope of its certificate of incorporation by the corporation, its officers and agents during the time when its certificate of incorporation was forfeited or void pursuant to this title, or after its expiration by limitation, with the same force and effect and to all intents and purposes as if the certificate of incorporation had at all times remained in full force and effect. All real and personal property, rights and credits, which belonged to the corporation at the time its certificate of incorporation became forfeited or void pursuant to this title, or expired by limitation and which were not disposed of prior to the time of its revival or renewal shall be vested in the corporation, after its revival and renewal, as fully and amply as they were held by the corporation at and before the time its certificate of incorporation became forfeited or void pursuant to this title, or expired by limitation, and the corporation after its renewal and revival shall be as exclusively liable for all contracts, acts, matters and things made, done or performed in its name and on its behalf by its officers and agents prior to its reinstatement, as if its certificate of incorporation had at all times remained in full force and effect.

(f) If, since the certificate of incorporation became forfeited or void pursuant to this title, or expired by limitation, any other corporation organized under the laws of this State shall have adopted the same name as the corporation sought to be renewed or revived or shall have adopted a name so nearly similar thereto as not to distinguish it from the corporation to be renewed or revived or any foreign corporation qualified in accordance with §371 of this title shall have adopted the same name as the corporation sought to be renewed or revived or shall have adopted a name so nearly similar thereto as not to distinguish it from the corporation to be renewed or revived, then in such case the corporation to be renewed or revived shall not be renewed under the same name which it bore when its certificate of incorporation became forfeited or void pursuant to this title, or expired but shall adopt or be renewed under some other name and in such case the certificate to be filed under the provisions of this section shall set forth the name borne by the corporation at the time its certificate of incorporation became forfeited or void pursuant to this title, or expired and the new name under which the corporation is to be renewed or revived.

(g) Any corporation that renews or revives its certificate of incorporation under this chapter shall pay to this State a sum equal to all franchise taxes, penalties and interest thereon due at the time its certificate of incorporation became forfeited or void pursuant to this title, or expired by limitation or otherwise; provided, however, that any corporation that renews or revives its certificate of incorporation under this chapter whose certificate of incorporation has been forfeited, void or expired for more than 5 years shall, in lieu of the payment of the franchise taxes and penalties otherwise required by this subsection, pay a sum equal to 3 times the amount of the annual franchise tax that would be due and payable by such corporation for the year in which the renewal or revival is effected, computed at the then current rate of taxation. No payment made pursuant to this subsection shall reduce the amount of franchise tax due under Chapter 5 of this title for the year in which the renewal or revival is effected.

(h) If a sufficient number of the last acting officers of any corporation desiring to renew or revive its certificate of incorporation are not available by reason of death, unknown address or refusal or neglect to act, the directors of the corporation or those remaining on the board, even if only 1, may elect successors to such officers. In any case where there shall be no directors of the corporation available for the purposes aforesaid, the stockholders may elect a full board of directors, as provided by the bylaws of the corporation, and the board shall then elect such officers as are provided by law, by the certificate of incorporation

§312

or by the bylaws to carry on the business and affairs of the corporation. A special meeting of the stockholders for the purposes of electing directors may be called by any officer, director or stockholder upon notice given in accordance with §222 of this title.

(i) After a renewal or revival of the certificate of incorporation of the corporation shall have been effected, the provisions of §211(c) of this title shall govern and the period of time the certificate of incorporation of the corporation was forfeited pursuant to this title, or after its expiration by limitation, shall be included within the calculation of the 30-day and 13-month periods to which §211(c) of this title refers. A special meeting of stockholders held in accordance with subsection (h) of this section shall be deemed an annual meeting of stockholders for purposes of §211(c) of this title.

[1] *(j) Except as otherwise provided in §313, whenever it shall be desired to renew or revive the certificate of incorporation of any nonstock corporation, the governing body shall perform all the acts necessary for the renewal or revival of the charter of the corporation which are performed by the board of directors in the case of a corporation having capital stock, and the members of any nonstock corporation who are entitled to vote for the election of members of its governing body and any other members entitled to vote for dissolution under the certificate of incorporation or the bylaws of such corporation, shall perform all the acts necessary for the renewal or revival of the certificate of incorporation of the corporation which are performed by the stockholders in the case of a corporation having capital stock. Except as otherwise provided in §313 of this title, in all other respects, the procedure for the renewal or revival of the certificate of incorporation of nonstock corporation shall conform, as nearly as may be applicable, to the procedure prescribed in this section for the renewal or revival of the certificate of incorporation of a corporation having capital stock; provided, however, that subsection (i) of this section shall not apply to nonstock corporations.* (Last amended by Ch. 253, L. '10, eff. 8-1-10.)

Ch. 253, L. '10, eff. 8-1-10, added matter in italic and deleted [1]"(j) Whenever it shall be desired to renew or revive the certificate of incorporation of any corporation organized under this chapter not for profit and having no capital stock, the governing body shall perform all the acts necessary for the renewal or revival of the charter of the corporation which are performed by the board of directors in the case of a corporation having capital stock. The members of any corporation not for profit and having no capital stock who are entitled to vote for the election of members of its governing body, shall perform all the acts necessary for the renewal or revival of the certificate of incorporation of the corporation which are performed by the stockholders in the case of a corporation having capital stock. In all other respects, the procedure for the renewal or revival of the certificate of incorporation of a corporation not for profit or having no capital stock shall conform, as nearly as may be applicable, to the procedure prescribed in this section for the renewal or revival of the certificate of incorporation of a corporation having capital stock."

Ch. 253, L. '10 Synopsis of Section 312

Section 64 amends §312(j) of the DGCL to ensure that §312(j) is consistent with the terms used in the translator provision in new §114(a); to clarify that members may vote for renewal or revival if, under the corporation's certificate of incorporation or bylaws, they are entitled to vote for dissolution or for the election of the members of the governing body; to clarify that §312(j) is subject to the provisions of §313; and to clarify that §312(i) does not apply to nonstock corporations.

Ch. 306, L. '06 Synopsis of Section 312

Sections 11 through 16 are technical Amendments to §312 to make it consistent with revisions to §§ 132, 502, 503, 510, 511, 514, and 517.

Ch. 298, L. '02 Synopsis of Section 312

The amendment to Section 312(i) clarifies that the measurement of the time period after which a stockholder may demand that an annual meeting be held includes the period during which the corporate charter was forfeited, inoperative, void or expired.

Ch. 82, L. '01 Synopsis of Section 312

The amendment to Section 312(i) eliminates the requirement of calling a meeting of stockholders immediately after renewal or revival of the certificate of incorporation. A meeting of stockholders could be ordered to be held under Section 211(c) if the periods for which Section 211(c) provides have passed while the corporation was in dissolution.

.1 Name.—If name used in revival proceeding unmistakably identifies original corporation which it is sought to revive, it meets statutory requirement. *Pippin v McMahon Bros, Inc*, 130 A 37 (1925).

.2 Franchise tax.—Corporation whose existence was limited to 20 years filed its renewal certificate making its existence perpetual. Such renewal was exempt from franchise tax. *Burris v Jessup & Moore Co*, 59 A 860 (1904). See also, *Ozan Lumber Co v Davis Sewing Machine Co*, 284 F 161 (D Del 1922).

Franchise tax on renewal assessable only for year of voiding and prior year. *OAG, 3-9-78*.

.3 Forfeiture of revived charter.—Once a forfeited charter has been revived, only the State can void it on the ground that the parties applying for renewal were not so authorized. *Engstrum v Paul Engstrum Associates, Inc*, 124 A2d 722 (Ch Ct 1956).

Where certificate for renewal of dissolved corporation is issued by secretary of state and duly recorded, only state can question finality of record. *McKee v Standard Minerals Corp*, 156 A 193 (Ch Ct 1931).

.4 Expiration before renewal.—As to the vesting of title to property where there has been an interval between the expiration of the period of duration and the renewal thereof, see *Washington Fire Co v Yates*, 115 A 365 (Ch Ct 1921); *Diamond State Iron Co v Husbands*, 68 A 240 (Ch Ct 1898); *Blackstone v Chandler*, 130 A 34 (Ch Ct 1925); *McBride v Murphy*, 124 A 798 (Ch Ct), aff'd, 130 A 283 (Ch Ct 1925).

As to the validity of acts performed during the interval between expiration and renewal of corporate existence, see *Schoen v Lipkin*, 159 A 198 (Pa Super 1932).

.5 Effect of revivor.—President is not personally liable on contract he signed on behalf of corporation during period its charter was forfeited for nonpayment of taxes, when charter subsequently was reinstated; reinstatement validates all acts of officers during that forfeiture period and makes them binding on corporation. *Frederic G Krapf & Son, Inc v Gorson*, 243 A2d 713 (1968).

.6 Annual meeting.—A court will not order an annual meeting for reviving a publicly traded corporation, where the ulterior purpose of such revival is to transform a private company into a public company while avoiding federal securities laws and expenses. *Clabault v Caribbean Select, Inc*, 805 A2d 913 (Ch Ct 2002).

313 RENEWAL OF CERTIFICATE OF INCORPORATION OR CHARTER OF [1] **EXEMPT CORPORATIONS.**—(a) [2] *Every exempt corporation* whose certificate of incorporation or charter has become inoperative and void, by operation of §510 of this title for failure to file annual franchise tax reports required, and for failure to pay taxes or penalties from which it would have been exempt if the reports had been filed, shall be deemed to have filed all the reports and be relieved of all the taxes and penalties, upon satisfactory proof submitted to the Secretary of State of its right to be classified [3] *as an exempt corporation pursuant to §501(b) of this title*, and upon filing with the Secretary of State a certificate of renewal and revival in manner and form as required by §312 of this title.

(b) Upon the filing by the corporation of the proof of classification as required by subsection (a) of this section, the filing of the certificate of renewal and revival and payment of the required filing fees, the Secretary of State shall issue a certificate that the corporation's certificate of incorporation or charter has been renewed and revived as of the date of the certificate and the corporation shall be renewed and revived with the same force and effect as provided in §312(e) of this title for other corporations.

(c) *As used in this section, the term "exempt corporation" shall have the meaning given to it in §501(b) of this title.* Nothing contained in this section relieves any *exempt* corporation [4] from filing the annual report required by §502 of this title. (Last amended by Ch. 96, L. '11, eff. 8-1-11.)

Ch. 96, L. '11, eff. 8-1-11, added matter in italic and deleted [1]"RELIGIOUS, CHARITABLE, EDUCATIONAL, ETC.,"; [2]"Every religious corporation, and every purely charitable or educational association, and every company, association or society, which by its certificate of incorporation, had, at the time its certificate of incorporation or charter became void by operation of law, for its object the assistance of sick, needy or disabled members, or the defraying of funeral expenses of deceased members, or to provide for the wants of the widows and families after death of its members, and any other exempt corporation as defined in §501(b) of this title,"; [3]"under any of the classifications set out in this subsection"; and [4]"of the classifications set out in subsection (a) of this section".

Ch. 96, L. '11 Synopsis of Section 313

The amendments to Section 313 are intended to conform Section 313 to Section 501(b) which was amended in 2010 to adopt the definition of "exempt corporation" for those corporations not subject to paying franchise taxes.

Ch. 253, L. '10 Synopsis of Section 313

Section 65 amends §313(a) of the DGCL to provide that §313 applies to all exempt corporations, as defined under new §501(b) of Title 8.

314 STATUS OF CORPORATION.—Any corporation desiring to renew, extend and continue its corporate existence, shall upon complying with applicable constitutional provisions of this State, continue for the time stated in its certificate of renewal, a corporation and shall, in addition to the rights, privileges and immunities conferred by its charter, possess and enjoy all the benefits of this chapter, which are applicable to the nature of its business, and shall be subject to the restrictions and liabilities by this chapter imposed on such corporations.

.1 Effect of renewal.—Corporation renewing charter does not become new corporation. *Burris v Jessup & Moore Paper Co, 59 A 860 (1904).*

SUBCHAPTER XIII. SUITS AGAINST CORPORATIONS, DIRECTORS, OFFICERS OR STOCKHOLDERS

321 SERVICE OF PROCESS ON CORPORATIONS.—(a) Service of legal process upon any corporation of this State shall be made by delivering a copy personally to any officer or director of the corporation in this State, or the registered agent of the corporation in this State, or by leaving it at the dwelling house or usual place of abode in this State of any officer, director or registered agent (if the registered agent be an individual), or at the registered office or other place of business of the corporation in this State. If the registered agent be a corporation, service of process upon it as such agent may be made by serving, in this State, a copy thereof on the president, vice-president, secretary, assistant secretary or any director of the corporate registered agent. Service by copy left at the dwelling house or usual place of abode of any officer, director or registered agent, or at the registered office or other place of business of the corporation in this State, to be effective must be delivered thereat at least 6 days before the return date of the process, and in the presence of an adult person, and the officer serving the process shall distinctly state the manner of service in such person's return thereto. Process returnable forthwith must be delivered personally to the officer, director or registered agent.

(b) [1] *In case the officer whose duty it is to serve legal process cannot by due diligence serve the process in any manner provided for by subsection (a) of this section, it shall be lawful to serve the process against the corporation upon the Secretary of State, and such service shall be as effectual for all intents and purposes as if made in any of the ways provided for in subsection (a) of this section. Process may be served upon the Secretary of State under this subsection by means of electronic transmission but only as prescribed by the Secretary of State. The Secretary of State is authorized to issue such rules and regulations with respect to such service as the Secretary of State deems necessary or appropriate. In the event that service is effected through the Secretary of State in accordance with this subsection, the Secretary of State shall forthwith notify the corporation by letter, directed to the corporation at its principal place of business as it appears on the records relating to such corporation on file with the Secretary of State or, if no such address appears, at its last registered office. Such letter shall be sent by a mail or courier service that includes a record of mailing or deposit with the courier and a record of delivery evidenced by the signature of the recipient.* Such letter shall enclose a copy of the process and any other papers served on the Secretary of State pursuant to this subsection. It shall be the duty of the plaintiff in the event of such service to serve process and any other papers in duplicate, to notify the Secretary of State that service is being effected pursuant to this subsection, and to pay the Secretary of State the sum of $50 for the use of the State, which sum shall be taxed as part of the costs in the proceeding if the plaintiff shall prevail therein. The Secretary of State shall maintain an alphabetical record of any such service setting forth the name of the plaintiff and defendant, the title, docket number and nature of the proceeding in which process has been served upon the Secretary of State, the fact that service has been effected pursuant to this subsection, the return date thereof, and the day and hour when the service was made. The Secretary of State shall not be required to retain such information for a period longer than 5 years from receipt of the service of process.

(c) Service upon corporations may also be made in accordance with §3111 of Title 10 or any other statute or rule of court. (Last amended by Ch. 290, L. '10, eff. 8-2-10.)

Ch. 290, L. '10, eff. 8-2-10, added matter in italic and deleted [1]"In case the officer whose duty it is to serve legal process cannot by due diligence serve the process in any manner provided for by subsection (a) of this section, it shall be lawful to serve the process against the corporation upon the Secretary of State, and such service shall be as effectual for all intents and purposes as if made in any of the ways provided for in subsection (a) hereof. In the event that service is effected through the Secretary of State in accordance with this subsection, the Secretary of State shall forthwith notify the corporation by letter, certified mail, return receipt requested, directed to the corporation at its principal place of business as it appears on the records relating to such corporation on file with the Secretary of State or, if no such address appears, at its last registered office. Such letter shall enclose a copy of the process and any other papers served on the Secretary of State pursuant to this subsection."

Ch. 290, L. '98 Synopsis of Section 321

These sections amend Sections 252(d), 256(d), 263(d), 264(d), 266(c)(6), 321(b), 376(b), 381(c), 381(d), 382(a), 382(c), and 390(b)(5), respectively, to allow for service of process upon the Secretary of State thereunder by means of electronic transmission but only as prescribed by the Secretary of State, to authorize the Secretary of State to issue such rules and regulations with respect to such service as the Secretary of State deems necessary or appropriate, and to enable the Secretary of State, in the event that service is effected through the Secretary of State in accordance therewith, to provide notice of service by letter sent by a mail or courier service that includes a record of mailing or deposit with the courier and a record of delivery evidenced by the signature of the recipient.

Ch. 339, L. '98 Synopsis of Section 321

The amendments to these Sections eliminate masculine references in the statutes, and replace them with gender neutral references.

.1 Corporations to which section applies.—Law applies to corporations organized before law was passed even if president was not in state for service of process. *Bay State Gas Co v State,* 57 A 291 (1904), opinions in 57 A 291; 57 A 1120.

.2 Same—dissolved corporations.—Resident agent's power to accept service of process on domestic corporation is ended by dissolution of corporation; thereafter, service must be on Secretary of State. *International Pulp Equipment Co v St Regis Kraft Co,* 54 FSupp 745 (D Del 1944).

.3 Invalid service.—Service is invalid if a copy of the process is not left with the person served. *Clough v Superior Equipment Corp,* 157 A 306 (1931).

.4 Garnishment proceedings.—Service on a corporation under this section is not sufficient in garnishment proceedings to attach stock of corporation. *Fowler v Dickson,* 74 A 601 (1909).

.5 Procedure not exclusive.—This section does not present an exclusive method of procedure. *Wax v Riverview Cemetery Co,* 24 A2d 431 (1942).

.6 President.—Notice to president is valid notice of foreclosure, when, because of consolidation, corporation had no principal office. *Real Estate Trust Co v Wilmington & NCRR Co,* 77 A 828 (1910).

Corporation can open default judgment based on service on corporate secretary under statute that permits such service if president resides out of state; here president had died. *Richards v Hammon,* 178 A2d 140 (1962).

.7 Resident agent.—Absent fraud, service on registered agent binds corporation. *Crites v Photometric Products Corp,* 169 A 164 (1933).

.8 Motion to vacate service.—A motion to vacate service on a person as president on the ground that the person served is not president should show who the president is or show some other officer on whom service may be had or show there is no such officer. *Arnold v Sentinel Printing Co,* 77 A 966 (1910).

322 FAILURE OF CORPORATION TO OBEY ORDER OF COURT; APPOINTMENT OF RECEIVER.—Whenever any corporation shall refuse, fail or neglect to obey any order or decree of any court of this State within the time fixed by the court for its observance, such refusal, failure or neglect shall be a sufficient ground for the appointment of a receiver of the corporation by the Court of Chancery. If the corporation be a foreign corporation, such refusal, failure or neglect shall be a sufficient ground for the appointment of a receiver of the assets of the corporation within this State.

323 FAILURE OF CORPORATION TO OBEY WRIT OF MANDAMUS; QUO WARRANTO PROCEEDINGS FOR FORFEITURE OF CHARTER.—If any corporation fails to obey the mandate of any peremptory writ of mandamus issued by a court of competent jurisdiction of this State for a period of 30 days after the serving of the writ upon the corporation in any manner as provided by the laws of this State for the service of writs, any party in interest in the proceeding in which the writ of mandamus issued may [1]*file a statement of such fact prepared by such party or such party's attorney* with the Attorney General of this State, and it shall thereupon be the duty of the Attorney General to forthwith commence proceedings of quo warranto against the corporation in a court of competent jurisdiction, and the court, upon competent proof of such state of facts and proper proceedings had in such proceeding in quo warranto, shall decree the charter of the corporation forfeited. (Last amended by Ch. 339, L. '98, eff. 7-1-98.)

Ch. 339, L. '98, eff. 7-1-98, added matter in italic and deleted [1]"either himself or through his or its attorney file a statement of such fact".

Ch. 339, L. '98 Synopsis of Section 323

The amendments to these Sections eliminate masculine references in the statutes, and replace them with gender neutral references.

.1 Quo warranto.—When Delaware Court had declared voting trust void and trustees started action in Ohio to have the trust declared valid, the Delaware Court, lacking personal jurisdiction over the trustees and thus unable to punish them for contempt, would consider quo warranto proceedings against the corporation. *Smith v The Biggs Boiler Works Co, 85 A2d 365 (Ch Ct 1951),* aff'd sub nom, *Krizanek v Smith, 87 A2d 871 (1952).*

324 ATTACHMENT OF SHARES OF STOCK OR ANY OPTION, RIGHT OR INTEREST THEREIN; PROCEDURE; SALE; TITLE UPON SALE; PROCEEDS.— [1]*(a) The shares of any person in any corporation with all the rights thereto belonging, or any person's option to acquire the shares, or such person's right or interest in the shares, may be attached under this section for debt, or other demands, if such person appears on the books of the corporation to hold or own such shares, option, right or interest. So many of the shares, or so much of the option, right or interest therein may be sold at public sale to the highest bidder, as shall be sufficient to satisfy the debt, or other demand, interest and costs, upon an order issued therefor by the court from which the attachment process issued, and after such notice as is required for sales upon execution process. Except as to an uncertificated security as defined in §8-102 of Title 6, the attachment is not laid and no order of sale shall issue unless §8-112 of Title 6 has been satisfied. No order of sale shall be issued until after final judgment shall have been rendered in any case. If the debtor lives out of the county, a copy of the order shall be sent by registered or certified mail, return receipt requested, to such debtor's last known address, and shall also be published in a newspaper published in the county of such debtor's last known residence, if there be any, 10 days before the sale; and if the debtor be a nonresident of this State shall be mailed as aforesaid and published at least twice for 2 successive weeks, the last publication to be at least 10 days before the sale, in a newspaper published in the county where the attachment process issued. If the shares of stock or any of them or the option to acquire shares or any such right or interest in shares, or any part of them, be so sold, any assignment, or transfer thereof, by the debtor, after attachment, shall be void.*

(b) When *attachment process issues for* shares of stock, or any option to acquire such or any right or interest in such, [2] a certified copy of the process shall be left in this State with any officer or director, or with the registered agent of the corporation. Within 20 days after service of the process, the corporation shall serve upon the plaintiff a certificate of the number of shares held or owned by the debtor in the corporation, with the number or other marks distinguishing the same, or in the case the debtor appears on the books of the corporation to have an option to acquire shares of stock or any right or interest in any shares of stock of the corporation, there shall be served upon the plaintiff within 20 days after service of the process a certificate setting forth any such option, right or interest in the shares of the corporation in the language and form in which the option, right or interest appears on the books of the corporation, anything in the certificate of incorporation or bylaws of the corporation to the contrary notwithstanding. Service upon a corporate registered agent may be made in the manner provided in §321 of this title.

(c) [3] If, after sale made and confirmed, a certified copy of the order of sale and return *and the stock certificate, if any,* be left with any officer or director or with the registered agent of the corporation, the purchaser shall be thereby entitled to the shares or any option to acquire shares or any right or interest in shares so purchased, and all income, or dividends which may have been declared, or become payable thereon since the attachment laid. Such sale, returned and confirmed, shall transfer the shares or the option to acquire shares or any right or interest in shares sold to the purchaser, as fully as if the debtor, or defendant, had transferred the same to [4] *such purchaser* according to the certificate of incorporation or bylaws of the corporation, anything in the certificate of incorporation or bylaws to the contrary notwithstanding. [5] The court which issued the levy and confirmed the sale shall have the power to make an order compelling the corporation, the shares of which were sold, to issue new certificates or uncertificated shares to the purchaser at the sale and to cancel the registration of the shares attached on the books of the corporation upon the giving of an open end bond by such purchaser adequate to protect such corporation.

(d) The money arising from the sale of the shares or from the sale of the option or right or interest shall be applied and paid, by the public official receiving the same, as by law is directed as to the sale of personal property in cases of attachment. (Last amended by Ch. 339, L. '98, eff. 7-1-98.)

Ch. 339, L. '98, eff. 7-1-98, added matter in italic and deleted [1]"(a) The shares of any person in any corporation with all the rights thereto belonging, or any person's option to acquire the shares, or his right or interest in the shares, may be attached for debt, or other demands. So many of the shares, or so much of the option, right or interest therein may be sold at public sale to the highest bidder, as shall be sufficient to satisfy the debt, or other demand, interest and costs, upon an order issued therefor by the court from which the attachment process issued, and after such notice as is required for sales upon execution process. If the debtor lives out of the county, a copy of the order shall be sent by registered or certified mail, return receipt requested, to his last known address, and shall also be published in a newspaper published in the county of his last known residence, if there be any, 10 days before the sale; and if the debtor be a nonresident of this State shall be mailed as aforesaid and published at least twice for 2 successive weeks, the last publication to be at least 10 days before the sale, in a newspaper published in the county where the attachment process issued."; [2]"shall be so attached,"; [3]"If the shares of stock or any of them or the option to acquire shares or any such right or interest in shares, or any part of them, be sold as provided in subsection (a) of this section, any assignment, or transfer thereof, by the debtor, after attachment so laid, shall be void."; [4]"him"; and [5]"No order of sale shall be issued until after final judgment shall have been rendered in any case."

Ch. 339, L. '98 Synopsis of Section 324

The amendments to Section 324 establish that the execution process it provides is available only for securities of a debtor identified on the books of the corporation and, as to certificated securities, only upon satisfaction of the requirements of section 8-112 of Title 6, including presentation of the stock certificate(s). The amendment is intended to enhance the utility of stock of a Delaware corporation as collateral.

.1 Constitutionality.—This section held unconstitutional insofar as it authorized seizure of stock or rights or interests therein since it denied due process as against a person who was not registered as the owner of the stock on the corporate books and whose only notice of the pendency of the suit was such as might go to him from seizure or constructive seizure of the stock or rights or interests therein under writ of attachment. *Sportuno v Woods, 192 A 689 (1937);* followed in *Womack v De Witt, 10 A2d 504 (1939);* (shares of stock standing on books of corporation in name of another for debtor cannot be subjected to attachment at the suit of the creditor although the corporation has notice or knowledge that the stock is so held).

.2 Shares subject to attachment.—Under this and the following sections, shares of Delaware corporations in names of non-residents are subject to attachment. *Haskell v Middle States Petroleum Corp, 165 A 562 (1933).* This and the following sections are constitutional. They do not deprive of property without due process of law contrary to U.S. Const. *McLaughlin v Bahre, 166 A 800 (1933).*

Where corporation has illegally loaned money to stockholder on the security of his shares in the corporation, it still has greater rights in shares than subsequently attaching creditor. *Graham v Young, 167 A 906 (1933).*

.3 Nature of attachment.—An attachment looking toward the sale of stock is in the nature of an ex parte proceeding, not a garnishment, and the company in whose hands the attachment is laid need only give a certificate showing the number of shares standing in the debtor's name on its books. *State v NY-Mexican Oil Co, 122 A 55 (1923).*

A writ of injunction in equity cannot be employed as an attachment at law. *Cities Service Co v McDowell, 116 A 4 (Ch Ct 1922).*

.4 Power of court.—A court of equity has no power to proceed against non-residents after the manner of foreign attachments at law, and cannot acquire jurisdiction over a non-resident defendant by such seizure of defendant's stock in a domestic corporation. *Skinner v Educational Pictures Securities Corp, 129 A 857 (1925).* See however, Title 10, §366. See also, *Ozan Lumber Co v Davis Sewing Machine Co, 284 F 161, 285 F 395 (D Del 1922).*

A monetary judgment in a divorce suit can be enforced by attaching and selling stock under this section and the purchaser of the stock can compel the corporation to issue new certificates to her where certificates for attached stock cannot be produced. *Bartlett v General Motors Corp, 127 A2d 470 (Ch Ct 1956).*

For cases on attachment and levy of corporate stock, see *Morgan v Ownbey, 100 A 411 (1916),* aff'd, *105 A 835 (1919); Fowler v Dickson, 74 A 601 (1909); Allen v Stewart, 44 A 786 (Ch Ct 1895); Nye Odorless Incinerator Corp v Nye Odorless Crematory Co, 156 A 176 (Ch Ct 1931).*

.5 Same—right to intervene.—In an attachment suit, the right to intervene is within the discretion of the court. *Banker's Mtge Co v Sohland, 138 A 364 (1927).*

.6 Same—appearance.—In a suit instituted by foreign attachment, entry of appearance without giv-

ing security for costs will be permitted in some circumstances but terms will be imposed when stock attached has been pledged. *Hutchison & Hoey, Inc v Tobin, 138 A 638 (1927).*

.7 Corporations to which section applies.—Domestic corporations and foreign corporations doing business in Delaware are subject to its attachment laws. *Ryan v Galliher, 168 A 77 (1933).*

.8 Attachment.—The statute contemplates the attachment of shares of stock and it is complied with when a certificate is obtained from proper corporate officer. Garnishee answers when it gives certificate provided for by law. *Mann v Perr, 55 A 335 (1903).*

When copy of process was left with company, all of the stock of the defendant in that company was attached. *Gibson v Gillispie, 138 A 600 (1927).*

A duplicate original of a writ on foreign attachment may be served in lieu of a certified copy. *Brainard v Canaday, 112 A2d 862 (1955).*

Corporation may get leave to file an amended or supplemental certificate of number of shares owned by debtor. *Morgan v Nailor, 69 A 1067 (1909).*

.9 Right to dividends as between attaching creditor and pledgee.—Dividends on pledged stock belong to the pledgee, whether the stock has been transferred into the name of the pledgee or not, and cannot be attached at the suit of the pledgor's creditor, the pledgee being under the duty to apply the dividends in reduction of the debt. *Womack v De Witt, 10 A2d 504 (1939).*

325 ACTIONS AGAINST OFFIAERS, DIRECTORS OR STOCKHOLDERS TO ENFORCE LIABILITY OF CORPORATION; UNSATISFIED JUDGMENT AGAINST CORPORATION.—(a) When the officers, directors or stockholders of any corporation shall be liable by the provisions of this chapter to pay the debts of the corporation, or any part thereof, any person to whom they are liable may have an action, at law or in equity, against any 1 or more of them, and the complaint shall state the claim against the corporation, and the ground on which the plaintiff expects to charge the defendants personally.

(b) No suit shall be brought against any officer, director or stockholder for any debt of a corporation of which [1]*such person* is an officer, director or stockholder, until judgment be obtained therefor against the corporation and execution thereon returned unsatisfied. (Last amended by Ch. 339, L. '98, eff. 7-1-98.)

Ch. 339, L. '98, eff. 7-1-98, added matter in italic and deleted [1]"he".

Ch. 339, L. '98 Synopsis of Section 325

The amendments to these Sections eliminate masculine references in the statutes, and replace them with gender neutral references.

.1 Enforcement of liability.—Provision in §161, above, providing enforcement of that section as provided in this section does not mean that these provisions are exclusive, as such liability may be enforced by receivers in insolvency. *DuPont v Ball, 106 A 39 (Ch Ct 1918).* See also, *Roebling's Sons Co v Mode, 43 A 480 (1899).*

However, a receiver cannot maintain a suit to collect a note given for an unpaid stock subscription unless he shows that such collection is necessary to pay the corporate debts or for purposes of equalization among stockholders. *Philips v Slocomb, 167 A 698 (1933).*

Louisiana law governs transactions between directors or majority stockholders of Delaware corporation and its minority stockholders when neither the corporate charter nor Delaware statutory law apply and when the corporation's only contact with Delaware is its incorporation there. *Mansfield Hardwood Lumber Co v Johnson, 263 F2d 748 (5th Cir 1959),* reh'g denied, *268 F2d 317 (5th Cir 1959),* cert denied, *361 US 885 (1959).*

Stockholders do not have to be joined as defendants, in a representative suit against the corporation. *Mansfield, above.*

.2 Nature of bill.—Creditor's remedy by " bill in chancery" against a stockholder of a corporate debtor given by this section must be a creditors' bill. *DuPont v Ball, 106 A 39 (Ch Ct 1918).*

.3 Defense.—This section applies to domestic corporations and failure to comply therewith cannot be brought up as a defense when a stockholder in a foreign corporation residing in Delaware is sued by an assignee of the foreign corporation for liability as a stockholder. *Love v Pusey & Jones Co, 52 A 542 (1902).*

.4 Section applies to collection of corporate debts.—This section applies only where an attempt is made to collect corporate debts from directors or stockholders individually. It does not apply where a receiver is attempting to enforce directors' liability for illegal payment of dividends. *Cochran v Shetler, 133 A 232 (Pa 1926).*

This section does not apply where receiver sues stockholders for unpaid balances on subscriptions. Such suit may be maintained although creditors have not obtained judgment against corporation. *Cooney Co v Arlington Hotel Co, 101 A 879 (Ch Ct 1917); DuPont v Ball, 106 A 39 (Ch Ct 1918).*

.5 Access to records.—In Delaware, where a judgment creditor of a corporation seeks access to the corporation's records, for the purpose of piercing the corporate veil on the theory that a fraud has been perpetrated, the creditor must allege with specificity facts sufficient to support such a claim and must do so first in the Superior Court, not in the Chancery Court. *Gillen v 397 Properties LLC, 2002 Del Ch LEXIS 10 (Ch Ct 2002).*

326 ACTION BY OFFICER, DIRECTOR OR STOCKHOLDER AGAINST CORPORATION FOR CORPORATE DEBT PAID.—When any officer, director or stockholder shall pay any debt of a corporation for which [1]*such person* is made liable by the provisions of this chapter, [1]*such person* may recover the amount so paid in an action against the corporation for money paid for its use, and in such action only the property of the corporation shall be liable to be taken, and not the property of any stockholder. (Last amended by Ch. 339, L. '98, eff. 7-1-98.)

Ch. 339, L. '98, eff. 7-1-98, added matter in italic and deleted [1]"he".

Ch. 339, L. '98 Synopsis of Section 326

The amendments to these Sections eliminate masculine references in the statutes, and replace them with gender neutral references.

327 STOCKHOLDER'S DERIVATIVE ACTION; ALLEGATION OF STOCK OWNERSHIP.—In any derivative suit instituted by a stockholder of a corporation, it shall be averred in the complaint that the plaintiff was a stockholder of the corporation at the time of the transaction of which [1]*such stockholder* complains or that [2]*such stockholder's* stock thereafter devolved upon [3]*such stockholder* by operation of law. (Last amended by Ch. 339, L. '98, eff. 7-1-98.)

Ch. 339, L. '98, eff. 7-1-98, added matter in italic and deleted [1]"he"; [2]"his"; and [3]"him".

Ch. 339, L. '98 Synopsis of Section 327

The amendments to these Sections eliminate masculine references in the statutes, and replace them with gender neutral references.

.1 Nature of derivative action.—Stockholders who bring derivative action against corporation's management are asserting claim belonging to corporation, and so such action is equivalent to (1) suit to compel corporation to sue, and (2) suit by corporation asserted by stockholders in its behalf against those liable to it. *Cantor v Sachs, 162 A 73 (Ch Ct 1932).*

Stockholder has no right to sue derivatively unless he first makes demand on corporation that it bring suit and that such demand has been refused, unless it is shown such demand would have been futile. *Sohland v Baker, 141 A 277 (Ch Ct 1928); Dann v Chrysler Corp, 166 A2d 431 (Ch Ct 1960).*

Derivative suit to redress alleged frauds committed by directors on corporation does not require prior demand that suit be brought. *Mayer v Adams, 141 A2d 458 (1958),* rev'g, *135 A2d 119 (Ch Ct 1957).*

Unanimous ratification of transaction by close corporation's stockholders does not bar later derivative suit attacking transaction if ratification was allegedly fraudulently obtained. *Brown v Dolese Bros Co, 154 A2d 233 (Ch Ct 1959),* aff'd, *Dolese Bros Co v Brown, 157 A2d 784 (1960).*

Derivative action lies by executrix of only stockholder of corporation which was defrauded when all other stockholders turned over corporate assets to another company for inadequate consideration. *Taormina v Taormina Corp, 82 A2d 102 (1951).*

Even though derivative action seeks distribution of any recovery directly to stockholders, corporation is still indispensable party, and suit will be dismissed when (1) it has not appeared and cannot be made to appear, since sequestration to compel appearance does not apply to corporations, and (2) corporation's state or country of incorporation does not permit derivative suits. *Levine v Milton, 219 A2d 145 (Ch Ct 1966).*

State court has no jurisdiction to hear stockholder's derivative action against directors for mismanagement when ultimate basis of action is inquiry into certain rates as fixed by Federal Power Commission. *Glassberg v Boyd, 116 A2d 711 (Ch Ct 1955).*

Derivative action may be brought in federal court when there is necessary diversity of citizenship to confer jurisdiction, and stockholder can sue derivatively for declaratory judgment under federal Declaratory Judgment Act. *Motor Terminal, Inc v National Car Co, 92 FSupp 155 (D Del 1949).*

Minority stockholder does not show grounds for derivative suit against his corporation, second corporation, and jointly owned subsidiary of both, when he claims second corporation (1) illegally diverted profits from subsidiary for its own benefit, and (2) owned 12% of his corporation's stock and so dominated its directors, since he does not show actual control by second corporation, nor that directors' refusal to sue second corporation constituted failure to exercise their business judgment in good faith. *Issner v Aldrich, 254 FSupp 696 (D Del 1966).*

Stockholder who has started derivative suit can appeal judgment in it, even though corporation has merged after entry of judgment. *Teren v Howard, 322 F2d 949 (9th Cir 1963).*

Prayer for "accounting" in stockholder's derivative action against parent did not turn action essentially for breach of contract into equitable action for accounting so as to compel court to follow traditional accounting procedure. *Levien v Sinclair Oil Corp, 300 A2d 28 (Ch Ct 1972).*

Stockholder could not maintain derivative action against directors merely because they delayed transferring her restricted stock into unrestricted status, and while she was waiting, transferred and issued unrestricted stock to another stockholder. *Reeves v Transport Data Communications, Inc, 318 A2d 147 (Ch Ct 1974).*

Individual shareholders could not assert counterclaim against creditor of corporation for allegedly causing injury to their corporation since: (1) injury to corporation fell equally on all stockholders and (2) injury to individuals was not caused by breach of duty owed specifically to them but was merely incidental to injury to corporation. *The Continental Group Inc v Justice, 536 FSupp 658 (D Del 1982).*

Target's shareholder who also owned stock in company interested in acquiring target was allowed to bring derivative action charging target's directors with improper actions and waste of corporate assets in response to incomplete takeover attempt by acquiring company because his conflict of interest was not so serious that he could not be expected to adequately and fairly represent stockholders and prosecute derivative action. *Youngman v Tahmoush, No. 6611 (Ch Ct 1-5-83).*

Shareholders' derivative action was dismissed when it attempted to recover compensation paid officers and directors who had been criminally prosecuted since forfeiture of compensation requires more than charges of disloyalty and unfaithfulness. *Citron v Merritt Chapman & Scott, 409 A2d 607 (Ch Ct 1977).*

Stockholder who acquired his shares after parent corporation amended its management contract and tax allocation agreement with subsidiary corporation had no standing to bring derivative action but could sue on allegations of subsequent diversion of corporate opportunity and waste of corporate assets which were non-unanimously ratified by stockholders. *Schreiber v Bryan, No. 4250 (Ch Ct 9-6-78).*

Ratification by majority of stockholders barred stockholder's derivative action based on claim directors lacked authority to modify stock option plan and to grant new options but, since ratification was not unanimous, it did not bar stockholder's right to trial on claim of waste of corporate assets. *Michelson v Duncan, 407 A2d 211 (1979).*

Minority stockholders in subsidiary corporation that had voted 96% in favor of paying management fee to parent corporation could not sue derivatively for waste of corporate assets and unsound business judgment since they were fully informed in proxy materials of all germane facts and management contract itself was intrinsically fair. *Schreiber v Pennzoil Co, 419 A2d 952 (Ch Ct 1980).*

Individual stockholder could not sue corporate directors for entering compensation agreements with corporate executives, which provided for payment of $9.4 million if board control changed, because board's action amounted to alleged waste of corporate assets, which could only be challenged by derivative lawsuit. *Colonial Securities Corp v Allen, No. 6778 (Ch Ct 4-18-83).*

Minority shareholder could not bring individual action charging that majority shareholders had manipulated corporate business for personal profit because claim had to be brought derivatively when shareholder did not suffer harm independent of harm to corporation or other shareholders. *Cowin v Bresler, 741 F2d 410 (DC Cir 1984).*

Shareholders did not have to bring derivative suit because their claim that they were wrongfully obstructed in proxy contest was individual. *Packer v Yampol, No. 8432 (Ch Ct 4-18-86).*

Stipulation of dismissal of shareholder's action was not improper because, although shareholder pleaded claims that support both individual and derivative causes of action, shareholder proceeded with suit individually so parties to stipulation did not have to comply with required notice and court approval procedures for dismissal of derivative suit. *Lipton v News International, Plc, 514 A2d 1075 (1986).*

Minority shareholders could bring direct claim against parent's nominees on merged corporation's board of directors for breaching their duty of loyalty because claim was not derivative when injury was only suffered by minority shareholders. Minority shareholders could not bring claim against remaining directors of merged corporation for failing to exercise due care in responding to merger proposal when director's special committee (1) consulted with independent legal and financial advisors, (2) considered merger proposal on at least four occasions over six week period, (3) consistent with advice of investment banker, concluded that offered price was fair, and (4) before accepting offered price, asked that it be raised. However, remaining directors' alleged failure to learn of parent's price commitment did state claim. *Rabkin v Philip A Hunt Chemical Corp, 547 A2d 963 (Ch Ct 1986).*

Court dismissed complaint in shareholder's class action against corporation and directors. Complaint did not state any claim of breach of shareholders' contractual rights, nor any fact, which, if true, would allow shareholders to pursue special or individual claims in a class action. Plaintiffs' injury, if any, was the same as injury to all other shareholders; action was, therefore, derivative one, and shareholder should have made a pre-suit demand on board for relief or have shown that a demand would have been futile. *Sumers v Beneficial Corp, No. 8788 (Ch Ct 3-9-88).*

Shareholders' demand letter was adequate even though it only requested suit against corporate president and not the other wrongdoers named in the complaint. *Reason:* The letter identified the alleged wrongdoers and described the factual basis of the wrongful acts.

Derivative suit was not filed prematurely after demand, even though complaint was only filed one month after demand letter was mailed. No complex technological issues were involved, and board could have responded to shareholders' demand instead of taking no action at all. *Rubin v Posner, 701 FSupp 1041 (D Del 1988).*

General and conclusory allegations made about directors' lack of disinterest, independence, and proper business judgment were not sufficient to create a reasonable doubt about the board fulfilling its fiduciary duties that would excuse the failure of the plaintiffs in a derivative action to make pre-suit demand. *Decker v Clausen, Nos. 10,684 & 10,685 (Ch Ct 11-6-89).*

In evaluating whether demand on a board of directors should have been made before filing a suit challenging the board's decision at an emergency meeting to sell the corporation's major asset, a reasonable doubt existed about whether the board's interest was divided between the interest of the corporation and the interest of the board's chairman, and a reasonable doubt existed as to whether the board validly exercised its business judgment in hastily approving a stock sale under supposedly "emergency" conditions. *In re NVF Co Litigation, No. 9050 (Ch Ct 11-21-89).*

A member of a class seeking injunctive relief from alleged "entrenchment" measures taken by a board of directors had no constitutional right to opt

§327

out of the class. *Nottingham Partners v Dana No. 9755 (Ch Ct 8-29-89).*

Although court found benefits received by the corporation and its shareholders to be meager, court approved negotiated settlement of derivative suit that alleged waste of corporate assets, disclosure violations, and breach of duty of care by individual directors in relation to board's approval of proposal to fund construction of museum adjacent to corporate headquarters. *Sullivan v Hammer, No. 10823 (Ch Ct 8-7-90).*

Shareholder alleged that directors breached fiduciary duties to corporation through series of decisions over 16 year period involving construction of nuclear power plant and storage facility. Court affirmed trial court's rejection of committee's recommendation to dismiss where it lacked good faith: committee relied on summarized information prepared by counsel. Committee's conclusions were not reasonable where it rejected without adequate explanation, findings by Georgia Public Service Commission that certain decisions were imprudent and cost corporation several hundred million dollars. Court also affirmed that under Delaware law shareholder was excused from demand requirement because directors effectively conceded that demand was excused when they appointed special litigation committee with sole authority to determine merits of suit. *Peller v Southern Co, 911 F2d 1532 (11th Cir 1990).*

Claims brought under Delaware law were properly brought as a class action, in that they concerned a specific group of shareholders alleging a specific type of harm (the purchase of shares at inflated prices) which could not have been suffered by the corporation and therefore, the action was not derivative in nature and no showing of a demand on the defendant's board, or excusal of the demand requirement, was necessary. *Weiner v The Southern Co, No. 10525 (Ch Ct 1-24-92).*

A claim of proxy non-disclosure was itself not a derivative claim, since the right to vote stock is the individual right of the owner of the stock and any interference with that right violates individual rights of shareholders. *Thorpe v CERBCO, Inc, No. 11713 (Ch Ct 1-26-93).*

Minority shareholders of a Delaware corporation filed a direct action in Alabama against majority shareholders alleging breach of fiduciary duties. Minority shareholders may bring a direct action under Delaware law against majority shareholders who interfere with their voting rights because interference with the minority stockholders' right to participation does no injury to the corporation. Where relief to the corporation would not cure the wrong, a direct action lies. *In re Chalk Line Mfg, No. 93-42773 (Bankr ND Ala 7-26-94).*

A class action and not a derivative action was appropriate where plaintiffs demonstrated special harm by showing that directors and controlling shareholders of the corporation benefitted from informa-tion in connection with the corporation's self-tender offer which was not available to shareholders generally. *Barbieri v Swing-N-Slide Corp, No. 14239 (Ch Ct 5-7-96).*

Plaintiff's abdication claim against a corporation's board of directors based on a newly awarded employment contract to the corporation's CEO failed where plaintiff failed to establish that the employment contract amounted to a "de facto" abdication of directorial authority. *Grimes v Donald, 673 A2d 1207 (1996).*

The Delaware Supreme Court dismissed plaintiff shareholders' derivative suit for failure to set forth facts rebutting the presumption that a corporation's board of directors exercised proper business judgment when it approved the CEO's employment and termination agreements, and for failure to rebut the presumption that the board members were independent and disinterested when doing so. *Brehm v Eisner, 746 A2d 244 (2000).*

A breach of fiduciary claim based on knowing misrepresentation is derivative in nature and will be dismissed with prejudice where the plaintiff has disavowed any intention of bringing a derivative action. *Manzo v Rite Aid Corp, 2002 Del. Ch. LEXIS 147 (Ch Ct 2002).*

Allegedly misleading partial disclosures in a proxy statement soliciting shareholder votes for the election of directors is not an injury to the individual voting rights of the shareholders, and, therefore, an action based on those misleading disclosures must be brought derivatively. *Paskowitz v Wohlstadter, 822 A2d 1272 (Md Ct Spec App 2003).*

.2 Grounds—injury to corporation—mismanagement depressing value of stock.—Where stockholder brought class action alleging chief officer's failure to communicate to the board of directors an offer to acquire the corporation and sought damages for alleged loss of takeover premium, the suit was derivative in nature and the motion to dismiss was proper, since an allegation of mismanagement that depresses the value of stock is a wrong to the corporation and injury, if any, falls equally upon all stockholders. *Lewis v Spencer, 577 A2d 753 (1990).*

A claim against a corporation based on alleged nondisclosures in tender offer-merger documents was not maintainable by the shareholders. The corporation, stated the court, was not a fiduciary of the shareholders and, thus, could not owe them a fiduciary duty. A corporation's fiduciary duty could arise only under a theory of legal or equitable fraud, noted the court; and the shareholders could not establish equitable fraud against the corporation since they did not plead justifiable reliance on the claimed misinformation. *In re Dataproducts Corp Shareholders Litigation, No. 11164 (Ch Ct 8-22-91).*

When there is no evidence that directors are interested or motivated to act other than in the best interests of all of the stockholders, the business judgment rule may still not be the proper method of review where issues of corporate control are at stake. The court, in so holding, applied the enhanced *Unocal* (entire fairness) standard to actions by directors in a corporate combination to determine whether there was disparate treatment of the bidders and whether the board's actions were reasonable in relation to the advantage that the board sought to achieve. The court concluded that the board adopted best possible procedures in these circumstances. *Yanow and Mandlebaum v Scientific Leasing, Inc, Nos. 9536, 9561 (Ch Ct 7-31-91).*

The Illinois Appellate Court (applying Delaware law) held that the lower court erred in failing to dismiss a shareholder's individual claims against a corporation for devaluation of stock and corporate waste, since these claims accrue to the corporation and must be brought derivatively on behalf of the corporation and its shareholders. *Seinfeld v Bays, Nos. 1-90-3414, 1-90-3415, 1-90-3416 consolidated (Ill App Ct 5-22-92).*

.3 **Demand on directors.**—Individual stockholder can initiate derivative lawsuit on corporation's behalf but has no absolute right under Delaware law to continue suit if board of directors, acting on recommendation of independent committee that has proved its independence, good faith and reasonableness of investigation, seeks to dismiss it; court must then apply its own "business judgment" in deciding whether corporate interest and public policy is best served by dismissing suit. *Zapata Corp v Maldonado, 430 A2d 779 (1981).* See also, *Maldonado v Flynn, 671 F2d 729 (2d Cir 1982).*

In order to be allowed to maintain derivative action, plaintiff who has not made demand on board of directors must state with particularity reasons for

not having done so. Excuse that demand would have required directors to sue themselves was not valid since at time of commencing action only one director was individual defendant. *Stepak v Dean, 434 A2d 388 (Ch Ct 1981).*

Shareholders did not have to make demand on directors before they brought derivative suit alleging abuses in connection with stock appreciation rights granted to some directors since none of the directors were truly disinterested when all either voted for stock plan that benefitted them or allegedly made false or misleading statements in recommending that shareholders ratify plan. *Bergstein v Texas International Co, 453 A2d 467 (Ch Ct 1982).* See also, *Weiss v Temporary Investment Fund Inc, 730 F2d 939 (3d Cir 1984).*

After board of directors received report from independent committee recommending that further legal proceedings were not in corporation's best interest, unanimous decision by board (with defendant directors not voting) to refuse stockholder's demand that corporation pursue suit against defendant directors, was not disturbed by court applying Delaware law; under such circumstances, court cannot apply own business judgment because Delaware business judgment rule bars judicial inquiry into such actions of directors when stockholder did not challenge good faith and independence of board. *Abramowitz v Posner, 672 F2d 1025 (2d Cir 1982).*

Shareholder's derivative action must await recommendation of litigation committee created by board of directors; motion by corporate counsel to dismiss now because shareholder lacked standing to initiate lawsuit is inconsistent with appointment of committee to investigate. *Abbey v Computer & Communications Technology Corp, 457 A2d 368 (Ch Ct 1983).*

Shareholder derivative suit dismissed for failure to make demand on directors or to demonstrate futility of demand could not be appealed once demand was made since board had not yet acted and it would be premature to assume directors would take action detrimental to shareholders; however, trial court retained jurisdiction pending action by board. *Stotland v GAF Corp, 469 A2d 421 (1983).*

Shareholders' demand on directors prior to filing of derivative suit alleging that certain transactions between corporation and 47% shareholder constituted waste of corporate assets, was not excused as futile because shareholders had failed to allege facts with particularity indicating that directors were tainted by interest, lacked independence, or took action contrary to corporation's best interests in order to create reasonable doubt about applicability of business judgment rule. *Aronson v Lewis, 473 A2d 805 (1984).* But see, *Kaufman v Beal, Nos. 6485 & 6526 (Ch Ct 2-25-83).*

Derivative suit alleging board of directors' invalidly modified stock option plan was dismissed after shareholders did not make demand on board as required under business judgment rule, because: (1) majority of board was not financially interested in option plan; (2) board did not breach its fiduciary duty by amending plan without shareholder approval since plan provided for modification; (3) approval of option plan and its amendments were within discretion of board; and (4) Delaware law did not require shareholder approval of stock option plans. *Haber v Bell, 465 A2d 353 (Ch Ct 1983).*

Shareholder's derivative suit was properly dismissed because shareholder failed to: (1) provide corporation with reasonable demand for corporate action prior to suit, (2) sufficiently identify shareholders so corporation could answer complaint, and (3) verify complaint to insure reasonableness of suit. *Smachlo v Birkelo, 576 FSupp 1439 (D Del 1983).*

Derivative suit, charging that directors wrongly rejected tender offer and that officer-directors received excessive payments under compensation plan keyed to market price for shares that had increased due to tender offer, was dismissed when shareholders failed to make demand that was necessary because shareholders failed to support claim that (1) directors breached fiduciary duty by rejecting tender offer solely to retain control; (2) plan, which was administered by committee of outside directors, was devoid of legitimate corporate purpose and was waste of corporate assets; (3) four officer-directors who benefitted from plan controlled other ten outside directors who had no interest in plan. *Pogostin v Rice, 480 A2d 619 (1984).*

When shareholders did not make demand on directors to sue, shareholder's derivative suit alleging that directors acted unlawfully by allowing officers who held stock options to gain profits at corporate expense was dismissed because (1) majority of directors were disinterested and (2) decision by directors to cancel officers' stock option to allow them to benefit from tender offer premium was protected by business judgment rule. *Kaufman v Belmont, 479 A2d 282 (Ch Ct 1984).*

Shareholder who brought derivative suit against six directors for breach of their fiduciary duties arising from their permitting production and sale of defective autos was not excused from making demand on board of directors because six directors neither constituted majority of board nor dominated it. Suit was dismissed because directors' exercise of business judgment was not wrongful when board of directors (1) was not tainted by self interest, (2) did not act in bad faith or fraudulently, or (3) through gross negligence, failed to reach informed decision. *Allison v General Motors Corp, 604 FSupp 1106 (D Del 1985).*

Shareholders did not have to make demand on directors before bringing derivative suit alleging that directors breached their fiduciary duties when they approved corporation's purchase of 1/3 of its outstanding stock to fund new employee stock plan, because directors were interested in the transaction because repurchase enabled them to obtain voting control over repurchased stock. *Seibert v Harper & Row, Publishers, Inc, No. 6639 (Ch Ct 12-5-84).*

Court ruled that demand on directors was not excused in shareholder's derivative action challenging certain transactions as waste of corporate assets, because (1) directors were independent and not controlled by large stockholder or chairman of board, (2) directors had not acted in grossly negligent manner, (3) allegations that compensation granted large stockholder's family constituted waste since it was not related to their experience in managing corporation were unsupported, and (4) sale of two corporate divisions was not waste, even if another offer was

§327

lower, when difference in terms could have accounted for acceptance of lower price. However, court concluded that demand was excused for allegations that waste occurred when directors, many of whom held options, reduced option price of previously granted options without any consideration paid for reduction. *Stein v Orloff, No. 7276 (Ch Ct 5-30-85).*

Court did not dismiss shareholders' derivative action alleging that directors wasted corporate assets when they purchased stock from former president/chairman of board of premium, even though shareholders made no demand on directors, because corporation did not have to purchase stock at premium or otherwise when president was required to divest pursuant to order of New Jersey Casino Control Commission. *Tabas v Mullane, 608 FSupp 759 (D NJ 1985).*

Court dismissed consolidated derivative suit charging that corporation's directors and officers violated Racketeer Influenced and Corrupt Organizations act and their fiduciary duties to corporation after corporation pled guilty to mail and wire fraud because shareholders did not make necessary demand on directors. Demand was not excused when (1) shareholders had not made particularized allegations of conflict of interest with respect to majority of board, (2) receipt of directors' fees does not suggest conflict of interest, (3) director/officers acceptance of bonuses tied to corporation's profitability does not substantiate claim of self-dealing unless voting or calculation of bonuses involved self-dealing, (4) directors' ratification of corporation's conduct does not mean directors would refuse to take up derivative suit, and (5) corporation's plea bargain agreement does not show that demand would be futile. *In re E F Hutton Banking Practices Litigation, 634 FSupp 265 (SDNY 1986).*

Shareholder could not bring derivative suit charging that Delaware corporation's officers and directors breached their fiduciary duty and wasted corporate assets when they failed to get New Jersey casino license and sold casino project because they did not make demand on directors. Demand was not excused because (1) directors decision to pursue and then abandon casino project was not motivated by personal interest and (2) there was nothing to suggest that casino transaction was product of anything besides valid business judgment. *Cottle v Hilton Hotels Corp, 635 FSupp 1094 (ND Ill 1986).*

Shareholders who brought derivative suit challenging directors' decision to sell division in response to perceived takeover threat did not have to make demand on directors because shareholders' allegations raised reasonable doubts as to whether directors' decision to approve sale was valid exercise of their business judgment. Shareholders' allegations include that: (1) only two directors knew of proposed transaction when meeting at which sale was approved was convened, (2) despite lack of emergency, directors approved sale immediately, (3) outside directors had only two short oral presentations to guide them when they voted to approve sale, (4) directors were not informed of basis for valuations of division or corporation's stock controlled by purchaser, and (5) directors ignored opportunities to obtain higher price for division. *Tomczak v Morton Thiokol, Inc, No. 7861 (Ch Ct 5-7-86).*

Court dismissed acquiror's shareholders' derivative action against target to set aside acquiror's indemnity undertaking in target's favor and to recover damages it owed to competing acquiror because shareholders' lack of demand on directors was not excused when (1) directors did not personally benefit from wrongful transaction, (2) indemnification as adjunct to business transaction is not illegal or necessarily imprudent, and (3) judgment against acquiror for interfering with competing acquiror's agreement with target does not show directors' wrongdoing when judgment is being appealed and does not determine directors' knowledge of wrongdoing. *Good v Getty Oil Co, 514 A2d 1104 (Ch Ct 1986).*

Court dismissed shareholder's derivative claims attacking alleged unlawful restructuring of corporation because he made no pre-suit demand and made no effort to show why demand would have been futile. However, shareholder's claims alleging violation of federal securities law and diminution of voting rights can be brought individually so there is no requirement for pre-suit demand. *Margolies v Pope & Talbot, Inc, No. 8244 (Ch Ct 12-23-86).*

The Court of Chancery dismissed derivative action that charged corporation's directors with wasting corporate assets when they approved repurchase of stock and notes issued to stockholder/director who had been criticizing company publicly. Plaintiffs failed to make a demand on board or plead with particularity facts that would establish that demand would be futile. Facts pleaded did not support plaintiffs' contentions that (1) directors were interested; (2) directors were controlled and dominated by management; (3) primary purpose of transaction was to silence shareholder/director's criticism. *Grobow v Perot, 526 A2d 914 (Ch Ct 1987).*

Suit could proceed derivatively despite lack of demand. Pre-suit demand is excused where under particularized facts alleged, reasonable doubt is created that directors are disinterested and independent and challenged transaction was otherwise the product of valid exercise of business judgment. *Sealy Mattress Co of New Jersey, Inc v Sealy, Inc, 532 A2d 1324 (Ch Ct 1987).*

Court dismissed shareholder's derivative suit alleging that directors breached their fiduciary duty to corporation and wasted assets by their handling of proposed casino/hotel project because shareholder did not plead with particularity why directors' refusal of his demand was not entitled to deference under business judgment rule. *Lewis v Hilton, 648 FSupp 725 (ND Ill 1986).*

In derivative suit challenging note agreement as entrenchment device, shareholders were excused from demand requirement when complaint's allegations created a reasonable doubt that directors were disinterested. The complaint alleged that: (1) There was no business purpose for the agreement: (2) note agreement was designed to avoid hostile takeover and was implemented quickly so its protective features would be in place before a tender offer was made; and (3) Corporation had no need for the borrowed funds, and had altered plans in order to obtain note agreement. *L A Partners, L P v Allegis Corp, No. 9033 (Ch Ct 10-22-87).*

When corporation's board refuses derivative plaintiff's demand and moves to dismiss action, plaintiff is not entitled to discovery to establish that directors acted wrongfully in refusing demand. Motion to dismiss in demand-refused case is like motion to dismiss complaint, sole issue being sufficiency of complaint's allegations. In demand-excused case, however, limited discovery is available. *Levine v Smith, No. 8833 (Ch Ct 12-22-87).*

Test for demand futility should be whether well pleaded facts of particular complaint support reasonable doubt of business judgment judgment protection, not whether facts support judicial finding that directors' actions are not protected by business judgment rule. Trial court erred in adhering to latter view. It also erred in ruling that fairness is pivotal question in demand excused cases. Fairness becomes issue only if presumption of business judgment rule is defeated.

Lower court's errors did not require reversal, however, because applying reasonable double standard, claim of demand futility was not established. Therefore, court affirmed dismissal of derivative action that charged corporation's directors with wasting corporate assets when they approved repurchase of dissident shareholder's stock and notes. *Grobow v Perot, 539 A2d 180 (1988).*

Court granted corporation's and directors' motion to dismiss shareholder's derivative claims challenging validity of proposed amendments to Articles of Incorporation and bylaws when shareholders: (1) failed to make a pre-suit demand for relief on board; and (2) did not show that a pre-suit demand would have been futile. *Stroud v Milliken Enterprises, Inc, No. 8969 (Ch Ct 3-22-88).*

Plaintiff's failure to make demand in derivative suit may be asserted as defense by "outside" defendant—one who is stranger to corporation on whose behalf suit is brought. Therefore, corporation's auditors could block derivative suit against them on ground that plaintiff had failed to make demand on corporation.

Corporation's posture of neutrality with respect to derivative action did not constitute acquiescence by its directors in its continuation. Their referral of prior stockholder demands to special litigation committee did not operate as a concession that demand was excused with respect to "outside" defendant. *Kaplan v Peat, Marwick, Mitchell & Co, 529 A2d 254 (Ch Ct 1987).*

Plaintiff's failure to make demand in derivative suit may be raised as defense by "outside" defendants—those who are strangers to corporation on whose behalf suit is brought. When corporation chooses to take position regarding derivative action asserted on its behalf, it must affirmatively object to or support continuation of litigation. Neutrality as to suit constitutes tacit approval and excuses demand. *Kaplan v Peat, Marwick, Mitchell & Co, 540 A2d 726 (1988).*

Refusal of plaintiff's demand not protected by business judgment rule when board's decision to reject demand was not informed one in that board allegedly never reviewed initial decision to approve transaction nor made any inquiry in response to demand letter. *In re General Motors Class E Stock Buyout Securities Litigation, 694 FSupp 1119 (D Del 1988).*

Conclusory allegations that target board opposed tender offer out of desire to entrench themselves are not sufficient to excuse derivative suit demand on basis of futility. Opposition to unsolicited tender offer does not, of itself, indicate primary purpose to retain control.

Costliness of exchange offer designed to defeat tender offer does not create presumption that decision to adopt it was not product of valid business judgment. Fact that there are costs, even great costs, associated with business decisions does not take that decision outside protection of business judgment rule. *Silverzweig v Unocal Corp, No. 9078 (Ch Ct 1-19-89).*

Court, applying Delaware law, has ruled that shareholder could not maintain derivative action against corporation's directors when she failed to make a pre-suit demand and did not allege with particularity sufficient facts to establish demand futility. Court found that shareholder's allegations, that directors' actions were not product of proper business judgment, were conclusory and did not excuse demand requirement. *Starrels v First National Bank of Chicago, 870 F2d 1168 (7th Cir 1989).*

Court, applying Delaware law, found that shareholder who failed to make pre-suit demand could not maintain action against corporation's directors even though he contended that he had pleaded both individual and derivative claims. *Reasons:* (1) Shareholder's allegations of mismanagement affected all shareholders equally; (2) His claim that potential buyers were deterred from acquiring corporation's stock on open market because of directors' adoption of poison pill did not allege a direct restriction on share transferability; and (3) Shareholder's allegation of a restriction on his voting rights was based on complaint of mismanagement rather than an actual restriction on voting. *Seidel v Allegis Corp, 702 FSupp 1409 (ND Ill 1989).*

In evaluating whether a board properly rejected a shareholder's demand that the board rescind an allegedly improper repurchase of stock and contingent notes, no evidence existed that the board rejected the demand in order to defend itself from a raider's threat, and no particularized facts existed to support an allegation that the board was not adequately informed about the repurchase plan it approved. *Levine v Smith, No. 8833 (Ch Ct 11-27-89).*

Court of Chancery granted defendants' motion to dismiss complaint because no demand was made and no basis existed to excuse demand and found plaintiffs' allegations that defendant company failed to consider alternative bids for purchase of company, wasted corporate assets, mismanaged corporate affairs and breached fiduciary duties of care and loyalty were unsubstantiated, conclusory and failed to establish demand futility. *Carvara v Saligman, No. 11135 (Ch Ct 12-21-90).*

State law governed the issue of demand in an action with state and federal claims and that federal rules regarding the adequacy of a derivative plaintiff's efforts to secure director action was not a source of a demand requirement but was only a procedural requirement empowering federal courts to determine from the pleadings whether the demand requirement

§327

had been met. Therefore, plaintiffs, having established futility under Delaware law, were entitled to proceed with action. *RCM Securities Fund, Inc v Stanton, 928 F2d 1318 (2d Cir 1991).*

Minority shareholders alleged that the sale of a controlling block of shares of a holding company by the majority shareholders to a competitor of the corporation constituted usurpation of a corporate opportunity. Although by demanding that the board act to prevent the sale the plaintiffs tacitly conceded that the board was independent enough to deal with the issue, the subsequent actions of the board as alleged in the complaint raised a reasonable doubt as to its good faith and led the court to conclude that Rule 23.1, pertaining to the demand requirement in derivative suits, had been complied with. *Thorpe v CERBCO, Inc, No. 11713 (Ch Ct 11-15-91).*

The Court of Chancery held that the plaintiffs in a derivative suit were excused from making a pre-suit demand on the corporation where their allegations, if true, raised a reasonable doubt that the decision of the corporation's board to sell the corporation's assets at one-half the premium originally offered (with the other half allegedly going directly to the controlling shareholder) could have been the product of a valid exercise of business judgment. *Andreae v Andreae, No. 11905 (Ch Ct 3-5-92).*

Plaintiff in a "first cousin to a double derivative suit" was excused from the demand requirement. The focus of the complaint was the alleged misuse of funds raised in a sale of corporate notes by the board of a corporation of which the plaintiff was a shareholder and which soon after the sale became a wholly-owned subsidiary of another corporation. Thus, the board of the parent corporation never approved the transaction at issue. The court held that where there is no conscious decision by the directors to act or to refrain from acting, the business judgment rule has no application. Instead, it is appropriate in such situations to examine whether the board that would be addressing the demand can impartially consider its merits without being influenced by improper calculations. In the case at bar, the court found that there were three common directors on the boards of the two corporations who must be considered to be interested in any decision relating to the suit, and that the allegations in the complaint raised a reasonable doubt as to the independence of several other directors, so that demand on the board would be excused. *Rales v Blasband, 634 A2d 927 (1993).*

Plaintiff complained of six transactions and events that he alleged amounted to self-dealing, waste of corporate assets, corporate mismanagement, and usurpation of a corporate opportunity by the defendant directors. The court found that plaintiff had established that the alleged self-dealing created a reasonable doubt that a majority of the directors were disinterested, and demand with regard to those claims would have been futile. *Yaw v Talley, No. 12882 (Ch Ct 3-2-94).*

Shareholder's attempt to demonstrate demand futility by alleging that the risk of liability for failure to oversee subordinates would have disabled the board from responding to the demand fairly failed where the certificate of incorporation exempted directors from liability for the conduct alleged in the complaint. *In re Baxter International Inc Shareholders Litigation, No. 13130 (Ch Ct 3-7-95).*

Plaintiff was excused from the requirement of making a pre-suit demand upon the board of directors where the complaint created a reasonable doubt as to whether the directors validly exercised their business judgment. *Rothenberg v Santa Fe Pacific Corp, No. 11749 (Ch Ct 9-5-95).*

Where plaintiff alleged facts that demonstrated that two of the three directors on a corporation's board of directors either dominated the board or lacked independence, plaintiff met the burden of proving demand futility and was excused from making a pre-suit demand on the board. *Friedman v Beningson, No. 12232 (Ch Ct 12-4-95).*

Plaintiff's claims against a corporation for improper redemption of shares and dilution of voting and earning power of public shareholders were derivative in nature and were dismissed where plaintiff failed to make a pre-suit demand upon the board of directors and failed to establish demand futility. *Katz v Halperin, No. 13811 (Ch Ct 2-5-96).*

Plaintiff waived the right to claim demand was excused in a derivative action alleging waste, excessive compensation and breach of duty of care where plaintiff had made an initial demand on the board with respect to related claims. *Grimes v Donald, 673 A2d 1207 (1996).*

Pre-suit demand on a board of directors in a derivative action alleging corporate waste was not required where plaintiff's complaint alleged that the agreement between the board and the CEO lacked consideration.

Plaintiffs established demand futility in a derivative action for corporate waste where they created a reasonable doubt that the agreement between a corporation and its CEO, in which the CEO received certain benefits while the corporation did not receive consideration, was the result of a valid exercise of business judgment. *Green v Philips, No. 14436 (Ch Ct 6-19-96).*

Plaintiffs' derivative action challenging a board of directors' decision to terminate merger negotiations was dismissed for failure to make demand or demonstrate why demand was excused where: (1) plaintiffs failed to establish that the directors, who were also shareholders of the corporation, terminated sale negotiations because of personal financial motivation, where plaintiffs could not establish that the directors' actions would have accorded them a financial benefit different from that which was accorded other shareholders; (2) plaintiffs could not demonstrate that the directors rejected the proposed sale for entrenchment purposes where the evidence did not show that the sale posed an actual threat to the directors' employment; and (3) plaintiffs failed to establish that the board as a whole was interested in terminating the sale negotiations where plaintiffs did not demonstrate that certain board members, who plaintiffs claimed dominated the other board members, were interested. *Bodkin v Mercantile Stores Co, No. 13770 (Ch Ct 11-1-96).*

Plaintiff, a 40% shareholder, adequately plead demand futility in a derivative action to recover funds allegedly misappropriated by sole director and 60% shareholder and her ex-husband, the former sole director and 60% shareholder. She had received her shares pursuant to a property settlement with her ex-husband. After finding that plaintiff had alleged sufficient facts that, if true, would support his claims, the court determined that demand would be excused as futile since the factual allegations of the complaint raised a reasonable doubt that the sole director could have exercised disinterested business judgment. *Smith v Smitty McGee's, Inc, No. 15668 (Ch Ct 5-8-98).*

An action for breach of fiduciary duty that is brought derivatively will be dismissed for demand failure where all directors of the corporation are named, but a majority of them have no management positions and no evidence is adduced to suggest that the non-management directors were not independent or disinterested. *Akins v Cobb, 2001 Del Ch LEXIS 135 (Ch Ct 2001).*

Where a subsidiary's board is comprised of a majority of directors who are affiliated with the parent corporation—some as full-time managerial employees of the parent—or are otherwise beholden to the parent, demand is excused in a derivative action that alleges that the subsidiary was managed in a way that benefited the parent at the expense of the subsidiary. *In re The Student Loan Corp Derivative Litigation, 2002 Del Ch LEXIS 7 (Ch Ct 2002).*

Shareholders meet their burden of showing demand futility where they show that half the directors of a corporation's board, which has an even number of directors, are directly interested or are subject to a reasonable doubt about their independence. *In re The Limited, Inc Shareholders Litigation, 2002 Del Ch LEXIS 28 (Ch Ct 2002).*

In a derivative action involving a closely-held corporation, demand is excused where there are two opposing director factions and a director whose independence is at issue is consistently allied with the faction that opposes the faction that is bringing the derivative action. *Haseotes v Bentas, 2002 Del Ch LEXIS 106 (Ch Ct 2002).*

Pre-suit demand is excused for a derivative claim that a corporation's board granted key executives severance packages for the purpose of entrenchment where doubt is cast about the disinterest and independence of a majority of the directors. *California Public Employees' Retirement System v Coulter, 2002 Del. Ch. LEXIS 144 (Ch Ct 2002).*

In a case that sends a strong message that in a derivative action demand excusal must be supported by particularized facts, the Chancery Court dismissed a complaint alleging breach of fiduciary duty where the court found that the plaintiffs did not "come close" to meeting their burden of showing that directors were interested, and admonished the plaintiffs for having failed to seek books and records that could have provided the basis for particularized fact pleading. *Guttman v Jen-Hsun-Huang, 2003 Del. Ch. LEXIS 48 (Ch Ct 2003).*

A corporation's director is not interested for purposes of demand futility where, absent conflicted loyalties, the director simultaneously serves as an officer of the corporation's debtor and has a relationship with the corporation's CEO and Chairman. *Litt v Wycoff, 2003 Del. Ch. LEXIS 23 (Ch Ct 2003).*

A derivative action must be dismissed where the plaintiffs have not made pre-suit demand on the board, and where no directors are interested or dependent, the directors were adequately informed of the challenged transaction, and the directors do not face a substantial likelihood of personal liability.

Shareholders brought a derivative suit against the corporation's directors and officers, alleging various breaches of fiduciary duties based on their approval of the merger as well as on failure to supervise claims based on allegations of bribery related to the venture transaction. They took issue with the board's decision to enter a merger agreement without a financing condition and asserted that the directors placed the corporation in a precarious position, facing potential financial ruin if specific performance of the merger transaction was ordered. The plaintiffs did not make pre-suit demand before bringing their action, and the defendants moved to dismiss the action. The shareholder-plaintiffs claimed demand futility.

The Court of Chancery applied the two-pronged *Aronson* test to determine if demand would have been futile as to the directors' affirmative actions. The first prong of the test is whether a majority of the directors who approved the transaction in question were disinterested and independent. The second prong is whether the transaction was the product of the board's good faith, informed business judgment. According to the plaintiffs, at least half of the board members, or six of the board's twelve directors, failed the test of being disinterested and independent because of their relationships with one of the directors who was a director of one of the banks that was slated to provide bridge financing for the transaction. The court, however, found that this director was not himself interested, so that even if he dominated the other six, or they were beholden to him, such beholdenness or dominance was irrelevant since there was no director that would do anything contrary to the best interest of the company and its stockholders. As to the second prong, the court found that nothing in the complaint indicated the board was not adequately informed about the transaction, and that in light of its financial condition at the time it entered the merger agreement, the plaintiffs could not rebut or address the accepted facts that the board was negotiating in a seller's market. The court also observed that by focusing on the substantive content of the directors' decision, as opposed to their process, the plaintiffs were engaging in precisely the kind of inquiry that the business judgment rule prohibits. Finally, the court was unable to find that the directors had acted in any way other than honestly and in good faith.

As to the plaintiffs' failure to supervise claims, and other *Caremark*-type claims, the court adopted the *Rales* test for demand futility, under which demand will be excused based on a possibility of personal director liability only in the rare case when a plaintiff is able to show director conduct that is so egregious on its face that board approval cannot meet the test of business judgment, and a substantial likelihood of director liability therefore exists. Here, the court determined that there was insufficient evidence that the directors had "utterly failed" in their supervision duty, and concluded that the plaintiffs had failed to plead with particularity that there were "red flags" that would have alerted the board to possible bribery or other wrongdoing. Thus, the directors could not

§327

have consciously disregarded their duty to supervise and, therefore, passed the *Rales* test. Accordingly, because the plaintiffs were unable to show that demand would have been futile, the court dismissed all the claims. *In re the Dow Chemical Co Derivative Litigation, 2010 Del. Ch. LEXIS 2 (Ch Ct 2010).*

.4 **Ownership of shares.**—Owner of margined stock was beneficial owner who could sue derivatively when various brokers at all times held shares for her account; two-week delay by one broker in making physical delivery of certificate to new broker on transfer of stockholder's account was not "break" in ownership. *Rosen v Allegany Corp, 133 FSupp 858 (SDNY 1955).*

When corporate agreement is made subject to stockholder approval, one who became stockholder after agreement was entered into, but before stockholder approval, could sue derivatively on agreement. *Lavine v Gulf Coast Leaseholds, Inc, 122 A2d 550 (Ch Ct 1956).*

When predecessor corporation was compelled to split its business between two new corporations, stockholder who had owned stock in predecessor could sue directors of one of the new corporations derivatively for alleged wrongs antedating split up. *Helfand v Gambee, 136 A2d 558 (Ch Ct 1957).*

Stockholder suing derivatively need not own same stock he owned at time of transaction complained of. *Dann v Chrysler Corp, 174 A2d 696 (Ch Ct 1961).*

When issuance of stock is derivatively attacked, transaction is not complete for purposes of determining whether plaintiffs were stockholders at time of transaction until certificates for stock are issued; plaintiffs can sue if they are by then at least equitable stockholders. *Maclary v Pleasant Hills, Inc, 109 A2d 830 (Ch Ct 1954).*

In derivative action, stockholder must allege he was stockholder at time of transaction of which he complains, so that allegation that directors authorized corporation to buy bonds at inflated price two years before he became stockholder bars him from bringing suit, even though he also alleges that after he became stockholder directors harmed corporation by holding on to such bonds. *Nickson v Filtrol Corp, 262 A2d 267 (Ch Ct 1970).*

Holders of 5% convertible subordinated debentures could not bring derivative action for payment of improper dividend because they were not "stockholders." *Harff v Kerkorian, 324 A2d 215 (Ch Ct 1974).*

Stockholder had standing to bring derivative suit against directors for alleged official misconduct even though she was not legal owner of stock at time of activity complained of; stockholder had sufficient equitable interest based on contract with nowdeceased stockholder to make will leaving stock to her. *Jones v Taylor, 348 A2d 188 (Ch Ct 1975).*

Stockholder who acquired his shares after parent corporation amended its management contract and tax allocation agreement with subsidiary corporation had no standing to bring derivative action but could sue on allegations of subsequent diversion of corporate opportunity and waste of corporate assets which were non-unanimously ratified by stockholders. *Schreiber v Bryan, 396 A2d 522 (Ch Ct 1978).*

Stockholder had equitable standing to bring derivative suit challenging propriety of loan from corporation A to corporation B, even though he was not stockholder at time of suit after corporate reorganization, because reorganization was involuntary and had no meaningful effect on stockholder's ownership of the business enterprise. *Schreiber v Carney, 447 A2d 17 (Ch Ct 1982).*

Former shareholder of Conoco Inc. lost standing to continue to prosecute derivative action when, after his action was filed, DuPont Holding Inc. merged with Conoco, becoming its sole shareholder, and shareholder was given interest in DuPont in exchange for interest in Conoco because, although cause of action may not have been rendered moot by merger, beneficiary of claim was now DuPont and not shareholder of original Conoco. *Lewis v Anderson, No. 6505 (Ch Ct 10-8-82).*

Former shareholder of merged corporation could not bring class action alleging that directors and successful tender offeror wrongfully manipulated tender offer battle and improperly expended corporate funds to favor successful tender offeror because (1) former shareholder's breach of fiduciary duty could only be brought as derivative action which he could no longer do and (2) appraisal was adequate remedy. *Shapiro v Pabst Brewing Co, No. 7339 (Ch Ct 7-30-85).*

Shareholder did not have standing to bring derivative suit for breach of fiduciary duty because he was no longer shareholder and remedies available to minority shareholders facing short-term merger are limited to injunctive relief if merger is unfair and appraisal rights if merger is fair. *Harnett v Billman, 800 F2d 1308 (4th Cir 1986).*

Former shareholder could not bring derivative action attacking directors' and officers' golden parachutes as waste of corporate assets after corporation was merged into acquiror when (1) shareholder lost standing to pursue derivative action because he was no longer shareholder of corporation and (2) acquiror agreed to honor golden parachutes, so it must be assumed that it decided that golden parachute agreement did not give rise to cause of action. Former shareholder also could not bring class action attacking golden parachutes for reducing merger price paid by acquiror because claim is really derivative in nature and restatement of waste claim when shareholder failed to attach merger. *Bershad v Hartz, No. 6960 (Ch Ct 1-29-87).*

Shareholders could not bring action alleging that acquiror breached its fiduciary duty by weakening corporation to force premature merger because action had to be brought derivatively and they were no longer shareholders after agreeing to merge and selling their stock. *Nerken v Standard Oil Co (Indiana), 810 F2d 1230 (DC Cir 1987).*

Shareholder lacked standing to pursue derivative action to challenge allegedly excessive severance payments after it was cashed out as shareholder pursuant to two-step merger. To maintain derivative action, plaintiff must be stockholder of corporation at time suit is filed and must remain stockholder throughout litigation. *Penn Mart Realty Co v Perelman, No. 8349 (Ch Ct 4-15-87).*

Stockholder's derivative action dismissed for lack of standing where stockholder's complaint contained merely conclusory allegations of contemporaneous ownership and defendant corporation contended that the stockholder did not purchase his stock until after the commission of the wrongs alleged. *7547 Partners v Beck, No. 13252 (Ch Ct 2-24-95).*

Where plaintiff (1) currently owns shares in two independent corporations that used to stand in a parent/wholly-owned subsidiary relationship, and (2) once had legal standing as a shareholder of the parent to bring a double derivative action on behalf of the former subsidiary for its directors' alleged breach of fiduciary duty, but (3) lost that legal standing when the parent spun off the subsidiary, he nonetheless has equitable standing to bring a derivative action on behalf of the former subsidiary to recover for the alleged breach of fiduciary duty, even though the challenged actions occurred before plaintiff could have owned shares in the subsidiary. *Shaev v Wyly, No. 15559-NC (Ch Ct 1-6-98).*

A shareholder who brings a derivative action challenging a corporate transaction does not satisfy the contemporaneous ownership requirement where he owns stock at the time of the challenged transaction and at the time of bringing suit, but sells his shares—owning only warrants in the corporation's stock—and subsequently reacquires stock in the corporation. *In re New Valley Corporation Derivative Litigation, 2004 Del. Ch. LEXIS 107 (Ch Ct 2004).*

Demand will be excused as futile where a majority of a corporation's board of directors is either interested or not independent. *Zimmerman v Braddock, 2005 Del. Ch. LEXIS 135 (Ch Ct 2005).*

.5 Continuing wrongs.—When wrong complained of is continuing one, transferee of stock may sue, even though wrong began before transfer; but when wrong complained of was diversion by corporate officer of opportunity to buy stock in other corporations and last stock purchase took place before suing stockholder acquired his stock, he is barred from suing derivatively. *Newkirk v W J Rainey, Inc, 76 A2d 121 (Ch Ct 1950).*

Illegal grant of stock options is not continuing wrong; complaining stockholder must have been such on date of grant. *Elster v American Airlines, Inc, 100 A2d 219 (Ch Ct 1953).*

.6 Settlement of derivative suit.—Court will not approve voluntary settlement of stockholder's derivative suit that would make it dismiss suit without prejudice, when settlement provides only for divestiture of control of corporation, but does not provide for repayment of moneys allegedly fraudulently obtained, when the complaint alleges (1) control of corporation by one stockholder, (2) frauds accomplished through that control, (3) losses to corporation through excessive salaries, bonuses and stock options, and (4) issuance of false prospectuses. *Steigman v Beery, 203 A2d 463 (Ch Ct 1964).*

Court will approve settlement of derivative action that lets corporation continue to buy all its products from partnership owned by corporation's majority shareholders, when (1) settlement reduced partnership's profits and (2) granted corporation option to purchase partnership at price substantially less than its then market value. *Goodman v Futrovsky, 213 A2d 899 (1965).*

Minority stockholders cannot block settlement of derivative suit merely because it does not give corporation money, when (1) stockholders overwhelmingly approve it, (2) corporation gains advantages by ending litigation and improving executive incentive plan, and (3) provable facts would not sustain big money award. *Hoffman v Dann, 205 A2d 343 (1964).*

Derivative suit charging that president dominated business to his personal benefit was reasonably settled by agreement in which corporation cancelled its lease on theatre owned by him, and terminated his employment contract and his stock option. *Krinsky v Helfand, 157 A2d 90 (1959).*

Court will not approve voluntary settlement of derivative suit when it is shown (1) challenged attempt to acquire stock of another corporation was discontinued (2) new board was appointed and made changes in corporate structure, and (3) severance allowances, salaries and legal expenses were paid; all this was done before settlement hearing and so petition for settlement is moot. *Chickering v Giles, 270 A2d 373 (Ch Ct 1970).*

Stockholder's derivative action charging parent, with mismanagement of subsidiary's demand account was barred by settlement in previous derivative action, and so could not be reopened without showing of fraud. *Singer v Creole Petroleum Corp, 297 A2d 440 (Ch Ct 1972).*

Twenty percent shareholder who brought derivative class action against corporation and its directors and then, without approval of trial court or notice to shareholders, settled for stock redemption did not breach fiduciary duty to other shareholders because (1) redemption was not secret; (2) other shareholders were not left without recourse; (3) shareholder did not prejudice other shareholders' claims; (4) profit was not at expense of other shareholders; and (5) trial court had determined shareholder's actions were fair. *Wied v Valhi Inc, 466 A2d 9 (1983).*

Notice to corporate shareholders of settlement agreement of three separate derivative suits adequately informed shareholders of settlement, and probability that settlement approval would preclude further shareholder claims. *Maher v Zapata Corp, 714 F2d 436 (5th Cir 1983).*

Settlement of shareholder's derivative suit seeking rescission of premium price stock repurchase agreement was approved by court. *Reasons:* (1) business judgment rule would be substantial impediment to getting to merits of shareholder's challenge; (2) seller of stock had reputation as corporate raider, and (3) corporation benefited because new mechanism, approval by outside directors, was grafted upon corporation's block repurchase procedure. *Citron v Burns, No. 7647 (Ch Ct 2-4-85).*

Court ruled settlement of consolidated derivative actions challenging bank merger was fair to holders of preferred convertible stock because (1) only cure for bank's financial problems was merger and (2) preferred shareholders benefited from merger since probability was that bank's stock would never have traded high

§327

enough to make conversion worthwhile and value of shares in new merged corporation was significantly higher than pre-merger bank shares. *In re Crocker Shareholders Litigation, No. 7405 (Ch Ct 5-21-85).*

Proposed settlement of minority shareholders' action challenging stock for stock merger of their corporation, which modified exchange ratio of stock, was fair because (1) mere existence of another lawsuit challenging same transaction on different theory was not enough to warrant disapproval of settlement when minority shareholders' counsel had access to all discovery obtained in other suit and (2) auditor's evaluation of merger proposal, on which original exchange ratio was based, was thorough and fair. *Goldstone v Texas International Co, Nos. 6651, 6652, 6665 (Ch Ct 7-10-85).*

Court rejected shareholder's proposed modification of settlement agreement which provided $2 per share to all shareholders who tender but stopped non-tendering shareholders from including any claim for breach of fiduciary duty in their appraisal actions. Settlement was fair to non-tendering shareholders who exercised their rights to appraisal because they benefitted by opportunity to tender shares at higher price. *Selfe v Joseph, 501 A2d 409 (1985).*

Settlement of consolidated derivative actions challenging bank merger was fair to holders of preferred convertible stock because (1) preferred shareholders' right to vote as separate class on proposed merger was subject to good-faith dispute, so it could be compromised during settlement negotiations and (2) preferred shareholders benefited from merger since, without settlement and merger, outlook for bank's securities would have been bleak and value of shares in new merged corporation was significantly higher than value of pre-merger bank shares. *Cohn v Zarowitz, 501 A2d 1235 (1985).*

Common shareholders had standing to bring derivative suit challenging preferred shareholders' right to vote at annual meetings. *Reasons:* (1) First shareholder was not sham plaintiff, even though second shareholder was paying his legal fees, because he had substantial interest in litigation and was active participant. (2) Second shareholder, who only became shareholder after record date of 1985 meeting, could challenge enfranchisement of preferred shareholders because, based on corporation's interpretation of Certificate of Preference, enfranchisement could continue indefinitely. *Flerlage v KDI Corp, No. 8007 (Ch Ct 1-29-86).*

Court did not have to approve settlement of dispute over attorney's fees that arose when attorneys were dissatisfied with amount of fees court awarded them after settlement of derivative action because, after settlement of derivative action and award of attorneys' fees, directors were no longer disabled by conflicts of interest since any prospect of their liability on derivative claims had been eliminated. *Fox v Chase Manhattan Corp, No. 8192-85 (Ch Ct 2-6-86).*

Court approved settlement of class action suit challenging merger as coercive when merger agreement called for $300 million liquidated damages from one corporation if its shareholders did not approve merger. Settlement benefited corporation because it stretched out period over which $300 million would be payable and granted corporation license to distribute product. There were also substantial obstacles for plaintiffs to overcome in order to prevail on claim that liquidated damages clause infringed on shareholders' right to freely vote their shares. *Friedman v Baxter Travenol Laboratories, Inc, No. 8209 (Ch Ct 2-19-86).*

Court approved settlement of shareholders' derivative action challenging corporation's purchase at premium of block of shares because (1) directors lacked self-interest when 10 of 13 were outside directors, (2) directors made reasonable investigation relying on advice by corporation's investment banker and counsel, (3) greenmail is permitted when hostile takeover attempt would have disruptive effect on corporation in light of administrative complexities generated by litigation, and (4) modification of repurchased stock's voting rights was sufficient consideration for settlement. *Polk v Good, 507 A2d 531 (1986).*

Settlement of shareholders' class and derivative actions seeking to enjoin takeover was fair to shareholders and corporation because they received real benefits from settlement: (1) termination of tender offeror's option in target's assets, (2) rescission of target's no shopping provision, (3) reduction of target's termination payment to tender offeror, (4) increase in interest paid on shareholders' preferred stock, (5) payment of target's March dividend which could have been resisted by tender offeror, (6) additional payment of $5,000,000 to target's shareholders at closing, and (7) reduction in target's executives' compensation (golden parachutes). *In re Beatrice Companies, Inc Litigation, No. 8248 (consolidated) (Ch Ct 4-16-86).*

Court approved settlement agreement resolving derivative action charging directors with breaching fiduciary duties and wasting assets because (1) Delaware law had been properly applied when corporation was Delaware corporation and directors' alleged improper acts were performed while acting in official capacities, (2) even if Iowa law were to apply, objecting shareholder's prospects for prevailing on merits were weak, and (3) expense of trial and appeal might outweigh any damages. *Wiener v Roth, 791 F2d 661 (8th Cir 1986).*

Settlement of derivative action attacking proposed exchange offer, which would have transferred voting control from common shareholders to chief executive officer, was proper, even though representative plaintiffs, in buy-out negotiated in settlement, received $5 per share more than other shareholders who elect to sell their stock in self-tender. Representatives did not violate duty of loyalty to corporation by negotiating more favorable terms for themselves because (1) their large stockholdings represented attractive springboard for potential acquirors, and (2) representatives gave up option available to other shareholders of remaining in corporation. *Lacos Land Co v Arden Group, Inc, No. 8519 (Ch Ct 12-24-86).*

The Court of Chancery refused to approve a settlement of a shareholder action on the ground that the proposed settlement would, in return for no real monetary benefit, release both, at best, extremely weak state law claims in the Delaware action and also release the federal securities law claims appearing to have at least arguable merit in a California federal action. The court noted that, if the settlement had offered class members sufficient consideration, the settlement could have been approved despite the absence of a provision which allowed class members to opt out of the settlement since, at the time that the settlement agreement was entered into, the acquisition had not been completed and the actions, therefore, still asserted primarily equitable claims. *In re MCA, Inc Shareholders Litigation, No. 11,740 (Ch Ct 4-22-91).*

The six factors to be examined by a court in determining whether to approve a proposed settlement consist of: "(i) the probable validity of the claims; (ii) the apparent difficulties in enforcing the claims through the courts; (iii) the collectibility of any judgment recovered; (iv) the delay, expense and trouble of litigation; (v) the amount of compromise as compared with the amount and collectibility of a judgment; and (vi) the views of the parties involved, pro and con." *Needham v Cruver, Nos. 12428, 12430 (Ch Ct 8-16-95).*

Where shareholders bring a derivative suit and the case is pressed as a class action, the shareholders may not disqualify their counsel for entering into a settlement to which the shareholders object. *In re M&F Worldwide Corp Shareholders Litigation, 799 A2d 1164 (Ch Ct 2002).*

.7 Allowance of counsel fees.—Stockholders bringing derivative action are entitled to fees for their attorneys when institution of suit caused corporation to adopt new employees' incentive plan that enabled it to attract higher quality personnel, even though plan more costly; however, they are not entitled to fees for achieving change in composition of management, when no showing that suit was actual cause of that change. *Dann v Chrysler Corp, 215 A2d 709 (Ch Ct 1965),* aff'd, *223 A2d 384 (1966).*

Attorney for stockholder can recover his fees from corporation when stockholder's suit to enjoin if from buying equipment and giving its key employees stock options and employment contracts is successful. *Richman v DeVal Aero-Dynamics, Inc, 185 A2d 884 (Ch Ct 1962).*

Stockholders can recover their attorney's fees when they successfully sue to cancel illegally issued stock. *Mencher v Sachs, 164 A2d 320 (1960).*

Attorneys' fee of $100,000 is reasonable when their work resulted in $500,000 benefit to corporation. *Krinsky v Helfand, 157 A2d 90 (1959).*

Mere filing of stockholder's derivative suit, which induces court-approved settlement, entitles stockholder to compensation for his attorney's services, but not measured by amount of settlement. *Aaron v Parsons, 139 A2d 365 (Ch Ct 1958).*

Losing stockholder in derivative action was not entitled to disbursements and counsel fees on ground litigation benefited corporation in that it resulted in exposition of law relating to stock options. *Gottlieb v Heyden Chemical Corp, 99 A2d 507 (Ch Ct 1953).*

Corporation that cancels option plan after stockholder sued derivatively to make it do so must pay stockholder's attorney's fees, unless it can show that (1) suit did not cause cancellation of plan and (2) management could have defeated suit. *Rosenthal v Burry Biscuit Corp, 60 A2d 106 (Ch Ct 1948).*

Stockholder of former subsidiary could recover attorneys' fees in derivative suit from surviving corporation, when suit showed likelihood of success prior to mootness caused by subsequent merger that was largely induced by suit. *McDonnell Douglas Corp v Palley, 310 A2d 635 (1973).*

Shareholders who brought derivative action challenging loan made by corporation were not entitled to award of attorney fees after loan was repaid because (1) shareholder did not have reasonable likelihood of success when suit was filed and (2) repayment of loan occurred because subsidiary sold its one substantial asset, not because shareholders instituted suit. *Monheit v Chalk, No. 6433 (Ch Ct 4-16-85).*

Shareholder who intervened in derivative action brought by tender offeror was entitled to allowance for counsel fees and expenses after corporation settled suit. Tender offeror's derivative suit was stratagem in private battle for control of corporation, while shareholder's suit was to assure that battle did not result in possible misuse of corporate machinery by board which would detrimentally affect all shareholders. *Burlington Northern Inc v Sterman, No. 7050 (Ch Ct 12-7-84).*

Shareholders who brought derivative suit to enjoin proposed merger that would take corporation private were entitled to counsel fees and litigation expenses after suit was rendered moot when directors abandoned merger and, instead, sought shares of public shareholders through tender offer. *Reasons:* (1) there was causal connection between derivative suit and abandonment of merger and (2) suit was meritorious when filed. *Brennan v Automated Marketing Systems, Inc, No. 6745 (Ch Ct 12-19-84).*

Shareholder who brought derivative suit against directors for wasting corporate assets was not entitled to attorneys' fees after his action was mooted by settlement of other shareholders' derivative suit because, although shareholder's claim was meritorious when filed and directors took action benefitting corporation, actions benefitting corporation were taken in response to second derivative suit, not shareholder's suit. *Maldonado v Flynn, 413 A2d 1251 (Ch Ct 1985).*

Shareholder who, after derivative suit challenging restructure of corporation's stock was settled, intervened in suit was entitled to attorneys' fees when she reached modified settlement that was more favorable to shareholders than original settlement. *Rosen v Smith, No. 7863 (Ch Ct 9-18-85).*

Corporation was not liable for attorney's fees incurred in minority shareholder's successful class action suit against corporation when (1) there was class recovery from which attorney's fees could be awarded, (2) although corporation violated its fiduciary duty to minority shareholders, there was no showing of corporation's bad faith or deliberate fraud, and (3) minority shareholders could not claim that corporation should pay attorney's fees because damage award was too low since this amounts to indirect reargument of damage award. *Weinberger v UOP, Inc, 517 A2d 653 (Ch Ct 1986).*

Attorney's fees worth 25% of $8 million class action judgment plus $164,601 in expenses were awarded to attorneys in shareholders' suit. Counsel's services were rendered with persistence, skill, and

§327

expertise. Case was unusually demanding, and services were rendered entirely on a contingency basis. *Weinberger v UOP, Inc, No. 5642 (Ch Ct 3-10-87).*

Shareholder who filed suit challenging adequacy of statement in management's proxy solicitation involving proposed reorganization was not entitled to award of counsel fees. Reasons: (1) shareholder's question concerning adequacy of disclosure became moot when board resolved to exercise its contractual right to abandon deal; and (2) defendants established that action mooting litigation was not causally related to filing of shareholder's complaint. *Sun Equities Corp v Computer Memories, Inc, No. 9353 (Ch Ct 2-16-88).*

Representative shareholder was entitled to attorneys' fees of $300,000, plus expenses, for his counsel's successful efforts in correcting misleading and coercive disclosures in connection with corporation's self-tender offer. The corrections benefited the corporation and its shareholders, and the corporation was required to pay the fee and expenses.

The shareholder was also entitled to attorney's fees of $200,000, plus expenses, for his counsel's successful efforts in causing a change in corporation's dividend policy. Change in policy benefited preferred shareholders and the fee and expenses were to come from their dividends. *Eisenberg v Chicago Milwaukee Corp, No. 9374 (Ch Ct 10-25-88).*

In corporate class action litigation, a court may order the payment of attorney fees and expenses to a plaintiff whose efforts result in the creation of a fund for the benefit of the class or the conferring of a corporate benefit on the class. *Zlotnick v Metex, No. 9781 (Ch Ct 11-14-89).*

Generally, each party in litigation bears its own attorneys' fees and expenses, but in corporate litigation where a common fund is created or a corporate benefit is conferred by the litigation, fees may be awarded if the lawsuit was meritorious when filed and there is a causal connection between the suit and the benefit. *Stern v Day, Nos. 9411,* 9480, and *9701 (Ch Ct 1989).*

The Court of Chancery approved partial settlement of class action pursuant to which a fund would be created; however, fund would not be distributed to shareholders until after completion of action against defendants who were not settling in class action and only upon condition that attorneys' fees would not be paid from settlement fund to attorneys for plaintiffs until fund itself was distributed to shareholders. Court noted that precise amount of benefit to class was not able to be ascertained because of possibility of indemnification and/or contribution claims and further noted that there was no reason why counsel should receive fees from fund while class was required to await its benefits. Court, however, did permit attorneys for plaintiffs to collect their out-of-pocket costs of action and settlement notice expenses. *Frazer v Worldwide Energy Corp, No. 8822 (Ch Ct 5-6-91).*

In a case determining the appropriate amount to be awarded for attorney's fees, the Court of Chancery discounted plaintiffs' attorney's requested fees, determining that they failed to prove that the entire benefit conferred on plaintiffs was caused by the previous litigation. *Croyden Associates v Tesoro Petroleum Corp, No. 13162 (Ch Ct 4-13-94).*

The Appellate Court of Illinois held that, under Delaware law, shareholders could not recover costs and fees allegedly associated with their having inured a benefit to the defendant corporation where there was no corporate approval for the reimbursement and no underlying lawsuit had been filed. *Foley v Santa Fe Pacific Corp, 641 NE2d 992 (Ill App Ct 1994).*

Motion to dismiss a shareholder's complaint seeking attorney's fees for costs incurred in making demand upon a corporation that resulted in corrective action by the corporation's board of directors was granted by the Court of Chancery where plaintiff's reimbursement claim failed to present a meritorious legal claim. *Bird v Lida, Inc, No. 14486 (Ch Ct 4-5-96).*

The Delaware Supreme Court approved the Chancery Court's award of attorney's fees in connection with the settlement of a class action in the amount of "one-third of the gross amount paid out to claimants not to exceed $515,000." The Delaware Supreme Court found that "[b]y conditioning the award of attorney's fees upon the claims actually submitted, the Court of Chancery exercised its discretion equitably, to correlate the attorneys' compensation with the structure of the settlement benefits the attorneys had negotiated for the class." *Goodrich v E F Hutton Group, Inc, 681 A2d 1039 (1996).*

Class action plaintiffs' counsel were awarded fees and expenses for their participation in merger negotiations where the class claims were meritorious when filed, the [corporation's] public shareholders received a benefit, and that there exists a causal link between the claims filed and some benefit received. In determining the amount of the award, the court considered: (1) the results achieved, (2) the time and effort of counsel, (3) the relative complexity of the issues involved, (4) the skill evidenced by counsel in their efforts, and (5) the degree of financial risk assumed by counsel. *In re QVC, Inc Shareholders Litigation Consolidated, No. 13590-NC (Ch Ct 2-5-97.)*

The amount of attorney's fees and expenses awarded to derivative action plaintiffs' counsel was limited to a percentage of the common fund generated by the litigation where the court determined that the common fund constituted the only substantial benefit to the corporation's shareholders that was not highly speculative. *Thorpe v Cerbco, Inc, No. 11713 (Ch Ct 2-6-97).*

.8 Participation in wrong.—Stockholder-director could not bring derivative suit against former president for alleged misuse of lessee corporation's funds paid to partnership-lessor dominated by former president and his father, since stockholder did not originally object to lease's terms or president's acts and stockholder himself benefited from alleged misconduct as member of partnership. *Courtland Manor, Inc v Leeds, 347 A2d 144 (Ch Ct 1975).*

A derivative action asserting that directors have breached their duty of loyalty will be dismissed where their actions are not self-interested, they have not bowed to the will of a controlling shareholder or consciously disregarded their duties in bad faith, and their actions are otherwise protected by the business judgment rule.

The Chancery Court dismissed the action for failure to state a claim, finding that the anti-dilution provisions simply maintained unchallenged, pre-existing contractual rights of the defendant directors, which left them in substantially the same position they were in before the rights offering. The court found dismissal was appropriate also because the shareholder had not otherwise sufficiently alleged that the directors engaged in disloyal conduct. Because the defendants did not receive a personal gain by way of the collateral consequences of the offering or consciously disregarded their duties, their decision to consummate the offering was protected by the business judgment rule. Regarding allegations of bad faith within the context of a duty of loyalty claim, the court indicated that mere gross negligence, which includes the failure to inform oneself of available material facts, cannot constitute bad faith. Bad faith, and thus a breach of the duty of loyalty, can arise only when a fiduciary consciously disregards his or her responsibilities. Here, the court found that the shareholder never claimed that the defendant directors "knowingly and completely" failed to undertake their responsibilities, nor could it draw such an inference from the complaint. Instead, the shareholder argued that the directors failed to consider certain aspects of the offering, including the effect that the low price would have on the anti-dilution provisions, alternative methods of financing, and even the need for the transaction. Lastly, the court ruled that the derivative claims were barred because the shareholder failed to plead that the directors were either interested or under the control or domination of an interested party as of the time the derivative claims were asserted. *Robotti & Co LLC v Liddell*, 2010 Del. Ch. LEXIS 4 (Ch Ct 2010).

.9 Standing.—Former shareholder lost standing to bring derivative suit against corporation's officers and directors for waste after corporation merged into surviving corporation because shareholder's claim became exclusive property right of surviving corporation and its sole shareholder. *Lewis v Anderson*, 453 A2d 474 (1984).

Shareholder of target had no standing to bring derivative action against its officers and directors because, prior to suit, shareholder was deemed to have sold his interest by failing to respond to notice of stock split sent to his address appearing on target's shareholders' list because, under Delaware law, target could rely on shareholders' list when notifying shareholders of significant corporate matters such as stock split and when target's bylaws placed duty on shareholder to notify target of his address. *Lewis v Knutson*, 699 F2d 230 (5th Cir 1983).

After railroad merged with another corporation and its shareholders received stock in new corporation in exchange for their railroad corporation stock, shareholders lacked standing to maintain derivative action because claim now belonged to new corporation when (1) merger was not fraudulent device to eliminate derivative claim and (2) merger did not simply effect reorganization that left shareholders' relationship with railroad unaltered. *Bonime v Biaggini*, Nos. 6925 and 6980 (Ch Ct 12-7-84).

Shareholders who brought derivative suits against corporation's director and second corporation for violations of Clayton Anti-Trust Act lost standing to assert claims when, pursuant to terms of combination agreement, their corporation became wholly owned subsidiary of new holding company whose stock they received in exchange for corporation's. Right to continue suits passed to holding company, and its directors must have opportunity to decide whether or not to take over action. *Fischer v CF&I Steel Corp*, 599 FSupp 340 (SDNY 1984).

To the extent that claims alleging officers' breach of the duty of candor were derivative, plaintiffs, who were no longer shareholders by virtue of a merger, did not have standing to maintain the suit and claims were therefore dismissed. The court upheld another claim that alleged wrongful deprivation of shareholders' right to cast an informed vote because the allegation was both an individual and class claim rather than a derivative claim. *In re Tri-Star Pictures, Inc*, No. 9477 (Ch Ct 6-14-90).

Tender offeror lacked standing to bring suit under §14(e) of Securities Exchange Act of 1934 because (1) offerors do not have standing to bring suit under §14(e) and (2) offeror, although nominal shareholder of target, may be considered only as offeror for purpose of judging his standing. *Kalmanovitz v G Heileman Brewing Co*, 769 F2d 152 (3d Cir 1985).

Cash-out merger will extinguish former shareholder's ability to sue corporation for mismanagement leading to corporate waste. Mismanagement that depresses stock values is wrong to corporation that must be asserted in derivative action, and former shareholder can challenge merger derivatively only when (1) merger is fraudulent in that it was made merely to deprive shareholders of standing to bring derivative action; or (2) merger is really reorganization that does not affect plaintiff's ownership in business enterprise. *Kramer v Western Pacific Industries, Inc*, 546 A2d 348 (1988).

In a case to determine whether a plaintiff who exchanged his shares in a corporation for those of a new corporation pursuant to a stock-for-stock merger had standing to maintain a derivative action on behalf of the new corporation, the Appeals Court of Massachusetts held in the affirmative. Pursuant to a stock-for-stock merger, a shareholder has a continuity of interest in the derivative claim, satisfying the policies of Delaware law. The court further asserted that the fact that the original corporation ceased to exist did not change the result: the original corporation's claim passed to and was absorbed by the surviving corporation and plaintiff owned stock of the surviving corporation as a result of the merger. Accordingly, plaintiff had standing to maintain the derivative action on behalf of the surviving corporation. *Kessler v Sinclair*, 641 NE2d 135 (Mass App Ct 1994).

The Delaware Supreme Court found that the Court of Chancery, in dismissing plaintiffs' derivative action for lack of standing, correctly relied on a prospectus issued by a corporation's board of directors in connection with an IPO to determine that plaintiffs were not contemporaneous owners of stock in the corporation at the time that the wrongs alleged by plaintiffs occurred. *7547 Partners v Beck*, 682 A2d 160 (1996).

A plaintiff has standing to maintain his derivative claims where an insider sale that was part of a merger was authorized when the plaintiff was not a stockholder, was consummated when the shares were issued to the insiders, which occurred after plaintiff became a shareholder. *Leung v Schuler, C.A. No. 17089 (Ch Ct 2-29-00).*

An underwriting agreement that provides for mandatory arbitration for any dispute, controversy, or claim that is "connected to" the agreement, covers well-pled claims for breach of fiduciary duty that do not depend on proof of a breach of the underwriting agreement. *Parfi Holding AB v Mirror Image Internet, Inc, 794 A2d 1211 (Ch Ct 2001).*

A third-party corporation has standing to challenge the effect of voting agreements entered into by a target corporation's directors in connection with a proposed merger, even though the third-party corporation acquires its shares in the target only after public disclosure of the merger agreement and the voting agreements, where judgment on the effect of the voting agreements may affect the outcome of the vote on the merger, and the third-party corporation is a bona fide competing bidder for the target. *Omnicare, Inc v NCS Healthcare, Inc, 2002 Del. Ch. LEXIS 120 (Ch Ct 2002).*

.10 Adequate representative.—Shareholder could not bring derivative suit against directors for wasting corporate assets and breaching their fiduciary duties. *Reasons:* (1) he was not adequate representative of corporation's shareholders because he had other litigation pending against corporation and was hostile to corporation and (2) he did not make proper pre-suit demand on directors. *The Scopas Technology Co v Lord, No. 7559 (Ch Ct 1984).*

Raider who, as shareholder, brought derivative suit seeking to invalidate poison pill plan adopted by target's directors was adequate representative of target's shareholders because (1) although raider's long-term goals may differ from other shareholder's goals, in short term, raider wanted to remove restriction on market activity so all shareholders can volun-tarily participate in tender offer and (2) raider's tender offer is not two tiered so it lacks inherent coerciveness and potential for creating unfairness between groups of shareholders that characterize two-tiered offers. *MacAndrews & Forbes Holdings, Inc v Revlon, Inc, No. 8126 (Ch Ct 10-9-85).*

.11 Recommendation of special litigation committee.—Shareholder's derivative action that chairman of board/chief executive officer usurped corporate opportunities and received excessive compensation was dismissed on recommendation of corporation's special litigation committee because (1) committee acted independently of corporation and other influences, (2) it conducted, in good faith, reasonable investigation upon which it based its conclu-sions, and (3) court, in its discretion, refused to overrule recommendation of committee. *Kaplan v Wyatt, 499 A2d 1184 (1985).*

Court refused to accept recommendation of corporation's special litigation committee and dismiss shareholders' derivative suit alleging that directors and officers diverted corporate opportunity to themselves. *Reasons:* (1) Committee, consisting of one member, was not independent because member was director when challenged action took place and he had numerous political and financial dealings with corporation's chief executive officer/chairman of board who allegedly controlled board; (2) Committee did not establish reasonable basis for its conclusions that opportunity to purchase stock in another corporation was not corporate opportunity. *Lewis v Fuqua, 502 A2d 962 (Ch Ct 1985).*

Majority shareholders/directors breached their fiduciary duties of fair dealing owed to minority shareholders when they approved cash-out merger because (1) merger had intended effect of terminating pending derivative litigation seeking recovery from majority shareholders/directors and (2) no independent agency, either board committee, special counsel or investment banker, provided basis to conclude that derivative claims were without value to corporation or that cash-out price was fair. *Merritt v Colonial Foods, Inc, 505 A2d 757 (Ch Ct 1986).*

Decision of special litigation committee not to pursue derivative suit was protected by business judgment rule. When complaint does not allege facts excusing demand or when such facts cannot be proven, court is under no duty to take second-step inquiry into substance of committee's decision. Complaint did not allege facts that raise reasonable doubt that board was disabled from passing on question whether it was in corporation's interest to press claim. *Spiegel v Buntrock, No. 8936 (Ch Ct 11-17-88).*

A Special Litigation Committee's settlement agreement between a corporation and one of its board members is not satisfactory where the Special Litigation Committee, while solving the most egregious abuses by the director, glossed over the significance of some of the alleged abuses claimed against the director without engaging in a reasonably thorough investigation of the facts underlying those allegations. *Electra Investment Trust PLC v Crews, C.A. No. 15890 (Ch Ct 2-24-99).*

Derivative plaintiffs may not voluntarily dismiss their derivative action over the objections of the corporation's Special Litigation Committee, which has primacy in controlling the litigation on behalf of the corporation. *In re Oracle Corp Derivative Litigation, 808 A2d 1206 (Ch Ct 2002).*

.12 Statute of limitations.—Shareholder's derivative action was not time barred because cause of action for money damages from unjustifiable use of proxies begins when injury occurs, not when plaintiff has knowledge of possible wrongdoing. *Baron v Allied Artists Pictures Corp, 717 F2d 105 (3d Cir 1983).*

.13 Realignment of defendant as plaintiff.—Corporation named as defendant in derivative suit may be realigned as plaintiff so long as there is no hint of collusion between corporation and defendants to suit or evidence that corporation may not prosecute action in good faith. If realignment were motivated by directors' self-interest or other improper motives, stockholders could seek redress for alleged waste of corporate assets. *Bluth v Bellow, No. 6823 (Ch Ct 4-9-87).*

.14 Declaratory Judgment Act as bar to derivative suit.—Corporation could not use Declaratory Judgment Act, 10 Del C. §6512, to head off a derivative suit before it was filed, because (1) Purpose of declaratory judgment procedure is to provide a technique for early resolution of disputes when a party is suffering practical consequences from uncertainty arising from assertion by another of a legal claim. Demand letter filed under Rule 23.1 mentioning a future derivative suit was the only action taken by shareholders at time board filed complaint for declaratory judgment; and (2) Assertions in demand letter did not impose any practical or imminent injury on corporation. *Schick Incorporated v Amalgamated Clothing and Textile Workers Union,* 533 A2d 1235 (Ch Ct 1987).

.15 Vexatious litigant.—Court refused to enjoin allegedly vexatious litigant from participating in derivative action against corporation despite individual's long history of *pro se* involvement in corporate litigation. Application for injunction was premature when litigant had not pursued repetitive or frivolous motions in that particular case, and possible sanctions in another case might temper his conduct in Delaware actions. *In re American Brands, Inc Shareholders Litigation,* Nos. 9586, 9616 (Ch Ct 9-13-88.)

.16 Majority shareholder duty.—In an action by a minority, non-tendering shareholder against defendants, the target of a tender offer and the tender offeror, the court held that the tender offeror, upon becoming a majority shareholder, owed a fiduciary duty to plaintiff. Therefore, plaintiff's assertion of breach of fiduciary duty by defendant stated a claim upon which relief could be granted to the extent such breach occurred after defendant became majority shareholder. Plaintiff also challenged the fairness and level of candor throughout the entire transaction and deficiencies in the Notice of Merger, Offer to Purchase and defendant's 14D-9 statement. The court held such claims related not just to the merger but to other aspects of the transaction as well and therefore a viable claim had been stated. *Zirn v VLI Corp,* No. 9488 (Ch Ct 2-15-91).

.17 Intervention in a derivative suit.—The Court of Chancery granted motion to intervene to a corporate shareholder that sought—two years after the shareholders' derivative action commenced—to replace the original plaintiff, an individual who no longer was a shareholder in the defendant corporation. *Steiner v Meyerson,* No. 13139 (Ch Ct 6-13-97).

.18 Choice of forum.—The Chancery Court denied plaintiffs' motion to stay or dismiss their derivative action until an identical action they filed in California was litigated where the court determined that: plaintiffs deliberately chose Delaware as the forum for the derivative action; defendants already appeared in the Delaware action; defendants filed a potentially dispositive motion to dismiss plaintiffs' action prior to plaintiffs' filing of the motion to stay or dismiss; and plaintiffs conceded that they filed the Delaware action for tactical reasons, which, according to defendants, were to "monopolize the Delaware forum against other plaintiffs." *In re The Walt Disney Company Derivative Litigation,* No. 15452 (Ch Ct 3-13-97).

.19 Backdated stock options.—Where a shareholder pleads in a derivative action that company stock options were backdated, the shareholder pleads a breach of the duty of loyalty sufficient to rebut the business judgment rule, since backdating option qualifies as one of those rare cases in which a transaction may be so egregious on its face that board approval cannot meet the test of business judgment. *Ryan v Gifford,* 2007 Del. Ch. LEXIS 22 (Ch Ct 2007).

.20 Stock option claims; direct vs. derivative.—A claim that a shareholder failed to receive adequate merger consideration because of previously issued stock options to which merger consideration was allocated is a derivative claim. *Feldman v Cutaia,* 951 A2d 727 (2008).

.21 Class and derivative actions.—Where the facts support both class and derivative claims, shareholders are not limited to pursuing only the derivative claims, and both types of claims may be litigated at the same time. *Loral Space & Communications Inc v Highland Crusader & Offshore Partners, L.P.,* 977 A2d 867 (2009).

.22 Double derivative actions.—To maintain a double derivative action, a shareholder who was a pre-merger shareholder in the acquired company and who is a current shareholder, by virtue of a stock-for-stock merger, in the post-merger parent company, is not required to demonstrate that, at the time of the alleged wrongdoing at the acquired company, the shareholder owned stock in the acquiring company, and the acquiring company owned stock in the acquired company. *Lambrecht v O'Neal,* 3 A3d 277 (2010).

328 EFFECT OF LIABILITY OF CORPORATION ON IMPAIRMENT OF CERTAIN TRANSACTIONS.—The liability of a corporation of this State, or the stockholders, directors or officers thereof, or the rights or remedies of the creditors thereof, or of persons doing or transacting business with the corporation, shall not in any way be lessened or impaired by the sale of its assets, or by the increase or decrease in the capital stock of the corporation, or by its merger or consolidation with 1 or more corporations or by any change or amendment in its certificate of incorporation.

.1 Successor corporation liability.—Successor corporation that transported hazardous substances from automobile plant site used by two manufacturers held liable for environmental cleanup under CERCLA, where an agreement existed that expressly stated that corporation assumed liability for any cause of action based upon conduct that occurred before date of agreement. Hauler was not liable under continuation of business theory since original company remained in existence and both corporations engaged in separate and distinct lines of business. One automobile manufacturer entered agreement with EPA and court refused to release second manufacturer charged as person who arranged for disposal when it challenged joint and several liability but failed to demonstrate that environmental harm was divisible. *United States v Chrysler Corp,* No. 88-341—88-534 Consolidated (D Del 8-28-90).

329 DEFECTIVE ORGANIZATION OF CORPORATION AS DEFENSE.—(a) No corporation of this State and no person sued by any such corporation shall be permitted to assert the want of legal organization as a defense to any claim.

(b) This section shall not be construed to prevent judicial inquiry into the regularity or validity of the organization of a corporation, or its lawful possession of any corporate power it may assert in any other suit or proceeding where its corporate existence or the power to exercise the corporate rights it asserts is challenged, and evidence tending to sustain the challenge shall be admissible in any such suit or proceeding.

.1 Corporate existence attacked.—Corporate existence cannot be attacked collaterally. *McKee v Standard Minerals Corp, 156 A 193 (Ch Ct 1931); St Nicholas Ruthenian Greek Catholic Church v Bilanski, 162 A 60 (Ch Ct 1932); Read v Tidewater Coal Exchange, Inc, 116 A 898 (Ch Ct 1922); Standard Sewing Machine Co v Frame, 48 A 188 (1900); Mayor of Wilmington v Addicks, 43 A 297 (Ch Ct 1899).*

330 USURY; PLEADING BY CORPORATION.—No corporation shall plead any statute against usury in any court of law or equity in any suit instituted to enforce the payment of any bond, note or other evidence of indebtedness issued or assumed by it.

.1 Application.—The disability of a corporation to plead usury does not obtain in suits instituted against it outside the state. *E C Warner Co v W B Foshay Co, 57 F2d 656 (7th Cir 1932).* Receiver may plead usury. *Bradford Co v United Leather Co, 95 A 308 (Ch Ct 1914).*

SUBCHAPTER XIV. CLOSE CORPORATIONS; SPECIAL PROVISIONS

341 LAW APPLICABLE TO CLOSE CORPORATION.—(a) This subchapter applies to all close corporations, as defined in §342 of this title. Unless a corporation elects to become a close corporation under this subchapter in the manner prescribed in this subchapter, it shall be subject in all respects to this chapter, except this subchapter.

(b) This chapter shall be applicable to all close corporations, as defined in §342 of this title, except insofar as this subchapter otherwise provides.

.1 Corporation law—state statutes and decisions in other states' courts.—Courts of states other than Delaware passing upon question concerning financing of Delaware company will apply Delaware law. *People v Graves, 18 NYS2d 340 (1940).*

.2 Status of Delaware corporation in other state.—A Delaware corporation has a valid existence although incorporated solely to acquire, own and operate Illinois building. *Spivey v Spivey Bldg Corp, 10 NE2d 385 (Ill 1937).*

When Delaware issues a charter to a corporation in compliance with the statutory requirements of the state, the corporation's right to exist cannot be challenged, for irregularities in its formation, in another state's courts. *Home Inv Co v Fidelty Petroleum Co, 249 SW 1109 (Tex Civ App 1923).*

342 CLOSE CORPORATION DEFINED; CONTENTS OF CERTIFICATE OF INCORPORATION.—(a) A close corporation is a corporation organized under this chapter whose certificate of incorporation contains the provisions required by §102 of this title and, in addition, provides that:

(1) All of the corporation's issued stock of all classes, exclusive of treasury shares, shall be represented by certificates and shall be held of record by not more than a specified number of persons, not exceeding 30; and

(2) All of the issued stock of all classes shall be subject to 1 or more of the restrictions on transfer permitted by §202 of this title; and

(3) The corporation shall make no offering of any of its stock of any class which would constitute a "public offering" within the meaning of the United States Securities Act of 1933 [15 U.S.C. §77a et seq.] as it may be amended from time to time.

(b) The certificate of incorporation of a close corporation may set forth the qualifications of stockholders, either by specifying classes of persons who shall be entitled to be holders of record of stock of any class, or by specifying classes of persons who shall not be entitled to be holders of stock of any class or both.

(c) For purposes of determining the number of holders of record of the stock of a close corporation, stock which is held in joint or common tenancy or by the entireties shall be treated as held by 1 stockholder. (Last amended by Ch. 112, L. '83, cff. 7 1-83.)

.1 Ownership of shares.—Incorporating attorney for three stockholders in close corporation cannot resolve dispute among them over ownership of the stock by buying the stock of the majority; he must give the minority first chance to buy. *Opdyke v Kent Liquor Mart, Inc, 181 A2d 579 (1962).*

343 FORMATION OF A CLOSE CORPORATION.—A close corporation shall be formed in accordance with §§101, 102 and 103 of this title, except that:

(1) Its certificate of incorporation shall contain a heading stating the name of the corporation and that it is a close corporation; and

(2) Its certificate of incorporation shall contain the provisions required by §342 of this title.

344 ELECTION OF EXISTING CORPORATION TO BECOME A CLOSE CORPORATION.—Any corporation organized under this chapter may become a close corporation under this subchapter by executing, acknowledging [1]*and filing,* in accordance with §103 of this title, a certificate of amendment of its certificate of incorporation which shall contain a statement that it elects to become a close corporation, the provisions required by §342 of this title to appear in the certificate of incorporation of a close corporation, and a heading stating the name of the corporation and that it is a close corporation. Such amendment shall be adopted in accordance with the requirements of §241 or 242 of this title, except that it must be approved by a vote of the holders of record of at least two thirds of the shares of each class of stock of the corporation which are outstanding. (Last amended by Ch. 587, L. '96, eff. 11-24-97, date that Secretary of State certified installation and functioning of computer hardware and software in recorder's offices.)

Ch. 587, L. '96, eff. 11-24-97, added matter in italic and deleted [1]", filing and recording".

345 LIMITATIONS ON CONTINUATION OF CLOSE CORPORATION STATUS.—A close corporation continues to be such and to be subject to this subchapter until:

(1) It files with the Secretary of State a certificate of amendment deleting from its certificate of incorporation the provisions required or permitted by §342 of this title to be stated in the certificate of incorporation to qualify it as a close corporation; or

(2) Any 1 of the provisions or conditions required or permitted by §342 of this title to be stated in a certificate of incorporation to qualify a corporation as a close corporation has in fact been breached and neither the corporation nor any of its stockholders takes the steps required by §348 of this title to prevent such loss of status or to remedy such breach.

346 VOLUNTARY TERMINATION OF CLOSE CORPORATION STATUS BY AMENDMENT OF CERTIFICATE OF INCORPORATION; VOTE REQUIRED.—
(a) A corporation may voluntarily terminate its status as a close corporation and cease to be subject to this subchapter by amending its certificate of incorporation to delete therefrom the additional provisions required or permitted by §342 of this title to be stated in the certificate of incorporation of a close corporation. Any such amendment shall be adopted and shall become effective in accordance with §242 of this title, except that it must be approved by a vote of the holders of record or at least two-thirds of the shares of each class of stock of the corporation which are outstanding.

(b) The certificate of incorporation of a close corporation may provide that on any amendment to terminate its status as a close corporation, a vote greater than two-thirds or a vote of all shares of any class shall be required; and if the certificate of incorporation contains such a provision, that provision shall not be amended, repealed or modified by any vote less than that required to terminate the corporation's status as a close corporation.

347 ISSUANCE OR TRANSFER OF STOCK OF A CLOSE CORPORATION IN BREACH OF QUALIFYING CONDITIONS.—(a) If stock of a close corporation is issued or transferred to any person who is not entitled under any provision of the certificate of incorporation permitted by subsection (b) of §342 of this title to be a holder of record of stock of such corporation, and if the certificate for such stock conspicuously notes the qualifications of the persons entitled to be holders of record thereof, such person is conclusively presumed to have notice of the fact of [1]*such person's* ineligibility to be a stockholder.

(b) If the certificate of incorporation of a close corporation states the number of persons, not in excess of 30, who are entitled to be holders of record of its stock, and if the certificate for such stock conspicuously states such number, and if the issuance or transfer of stock to any person would cause the stock to be held by more than such number of persons, the person to whom such stock is issued or transferred is conclusively presumed to have notice of this fact.

(c) If a stock certificate of any close corporation conspicuously notes the fact of a restriction on transfer of stock of the corporation, and the restriction is one which is permitted by §202 of this title, the transferee of the stock is conclusively presumed to have notice of the fact that [2]*such person* has acquired stock in violation of the restriction, if such acquisition violates the restriction.

(d) Whenever any person to whom stock of a close corporation has been issued or transferred has, or is conclusively presumed under this section to have, notice either (1) that [2]*such person* is a person not eligible to be a holder of stock of the corporation, or (2) that transfer of stock to [3]*such person* would cause the stock of the corporation to be held by more than the number of persons permitted by its certificate of incorporation to hold stock of the corporation, or (3) that the transfer of stock is in violation of a restriction on transfer of stock, the corporation may, at its option, refuse to register transfer of the stock into the name of the transferee.

(e) Subsection (d) of this section shall not be applicable if the transfer of stock, even though otherwise contrary to subsections (a), (b) or (c), of this section has been consented to by all the stockholders of the close corporation, or if the close corporation has amended its certificate of incorporation in accordance with §346 of this title.

(f) The term "transfer", as used in this section, is not limited to a transfer for value.

(g) The provisions of this section do not in any way impair any rights of a transferee regarding any right to rescind the transaction or to recover under any applicable warranty express or implied. (Last amended by Ch. 339, L. '98, eff. 7-1-98.)

Ch. 339, L. '98, eff. 7-1-98, added matter in italic and deleted [1]"his"; [2]"he"; and [3]"him".

Ch. 339, L. '98 Synopsis of Section 347

The amendments to these Sections eliminate masculine references in the statutes, and replace them with gender neutral references.

.1 Illegally issued stock.—A transferee who takes with notice that stock was illegally issued cannot compel a transfer. *Bowen v Imperial Theatres, Inc*, 115 A 918 (Ch Ct 1922).

.2 Redemption of shares.—Corporation can enforce agreement with its officers to buy back their stock at small fraction of its value upon their discharge for cause; failure to achieve the results for which they were hired, whatever the reason, is good cause for discharge. *Georesearch, Inc v Morriss*, 193 FSupp 163 (WD La 1961).

348 INVOLUNTARY TERMINATION OF CLOSE CORPORATION STATUS; PROCEEDING TO PREVENT LOSS OF STATUS.—(a) If any event occurs as a result of which 1 or more of the provisions or conditions included in a close corporation's certificate of incorporation pursuant to §342 of this title to qualify it as a close corporation has been breached, the corporation's status as a close corporation under this subchapter shall terminate unless:

(1) Within 30 days after the occurrence of the event, or within 30 days after the event has been discovered, whichever is later, the corporation files with the Secretary of State a certificate, executed and acknowledged in accordance with §103 of this title, stating that a specified provision or condition included in its certificate of incorporation pursuant to §342 of this title to qualify it as a close corporation has ceased to be applicable, and furnishes a copy of such certificate to each stockholder; and

(2) The corporation concurrently with the filing of such certificate takes such steps as are necessary to correct the situation which threatens its status as a close corporation, including, without limitation, the refusal to register the transfer of stock which has been wrongfully transferred as provided by §347 of this title, or a proceeding under subsection (b) of this section.

(b) The Court of Chancery, upon the suit of the corporation or any stockholder, shall have jurisdiction to issue all orders necessary to prevent the corporation from losing its status as a close corporation, or to restore its status as a close corporation by enjoining or setting aside any act or threatened act on the part of the corporation or a stockholder which would be inconsistent with any of the provisions or conditions required or permitted by §342 of this title to be stated in the certificate of incorporation of a close corporation, unless it is an act approved in accordance with §346 of this title. The Court of Chancery may enjoin or set aside any transfer or threatened transfer of stock of a close corporation which is contrary to the terms of its certificate of incorporation or of any transfer restriction permitted by §202 of this title, and may enjoin any public offering, as defined in §342 of this title, or threatened public offering of stock of the close corporation.

349 CORPORATE OPTION WHERE A RESTRICTION ON TRANSFER OF A SECURITY IS HELD INVALID.—If a restriction on transfer of a security of a close corporation is held not to be authorized by §202 of this title, the corporation shall nevertheless have an option, for a period of 30 days after the judgment setting aside the restriction becomes final, to acquire the restricted security at a price which is agreed upon by the parties, or if no agreement is reached as to price, then at the fair value as determined by the Court of Chancery. In order to determine fair value, the Court may appoint an appraiser to receive evidence and report to the Court [1]*such appraiser's* findings and recommendation as to fair value. (Last amended by Ch. 339, L. '98, eff. 7-1-98.)

Ch. 339, L. '98, eff. 7-1-98, added matter in italic and deleted [1]"his".

Ch. 339, L. '98 Synopsis of Section 349

The amendments to these Sections eliminate masculine references in the statutes, and replace them with gender neutral references.

350 AGREEMENTS RESTRICTING DISCRETION OF DIRECTORS.—A written agreement among the stockholders of a close corporation holding a majority of the outstanding stock entitled to vote, whether solely among themselves or with a party not a stockholder, is not invalid, as between the parties to the agreement, on the ground that it so relates to the conduct of the business and affairs of the corporation as to restrict or interfere with the discretion or powers of the board of directors. The effect of any such agreement shall be to relieve the directors and impose upon the stockholders who are parties to the agreement the liability for managerial acts or omissions which is imposed on directors to the extent and so long as the discretion or powers of the board in its management of corporate affairs is controlled by such agreement.

.1 **Liability of management stockholders.**—Management stockholders cannot so far disregard their fiduciary duty to the corporation and its creditors as to subordinate the claims of the latter to their own doubtful claims against the company. *Pepper v Litton, 308 US 295 (1939)*.

351 MANAGEMENT BY STOCKHOLDERS.—The certificate of incorporation of a close corporation may provide that the business of the corporation shall be managed by the stockholders of the corporation rather than by a board of directors. So long as this provision continues in effect:

(1) No meeting of stockholders need be called to elect directors;
(2) Unless the context clearly requires otherwise, the stockholders of the corporation shall be deemed to be directors for purposes of applying provisions of this chapter; and
(3) The stockholders of the corporation shall be subject to all liabilities of directors.

Such a provision may be inserted in the certificate of incorporation by amendment if all incorporators and subscribers or all holders of record of all of the outstanding stock, whether or not having voting power, authorize such a provision. An amendment to the certificate of incorporation to delete such a provision shall be adopted by a vote of the holders of a majority of all outstanding stock of the corporation, whether or not otherwise entitled to vote. If the certificate of incorporation contains a provision authorized by this section, the existence of such provision shall be noted conspicuously on the face or back of every stock certificate issued by such corporation.

.1 **Effect of unanimous stockholder ratification.**—Unanimous ratification of a transaction by a close corporation's stockholders does not bar a later derivative suit attacking the transaction if the ratification was fraudulently obtained. *Brown v Dolese Bros Co, 154 A2d 233 (Ch Ct 1959)*, aff'd, *157 A2d 784 (1960)*.

.2 **Corporate opportunity.**—Sole stockholders of close corporation did not breach fiduciary duty to later stockholders when they bought with their own funds a partnership that was the corporation's sole produce supplier. *Goodman v Futrovsky, 213 A2d 899 (1965)*.

352 APPOINTMENT OF CUSTODIAN FOR CLOSE CORPORATION.—(a) In addition to §226 of this title respecting the appointment of a custodian for any corporation, the Court of Chancery, upon application of any stockholder, may appoint 1 or more persons to be custodians, and, if the corporation is insolvent, to be receivers, of any close corporation when:

(1) Pursuant to §351 of this title the business and affairs of the corporation are managed by the stockholders and they are so divided that the business of the corporation is suffering or is threatened with irreparable injury and any remedy with respect to such deadlock provided in the certificate of incorporation or bylaws or in any written agreement of the stockholders has failed; or

(2) The petitioning stockholder has the right to the dissolution of the corporation under a provision of the certificate of incorporation permitted by §355 of this title.

(b) In lieu of appointing a custodian for a close corporation under this section or §226 of this title the Court of Chancery may appoint a provisional director, whose powers and status shall be as provided in §353 of this title if the Court determines that it would be in the best interest of the corporation. Such appointment shall not preclude any subsequent order of the Court appointing a custodian for such corporation.

.1 **Attempt to veto custodian.**—One group of 50% shareholders of deadlocked corporation attempted to effectively veto court's selection of custodian by refusing to give him personal indemnities and guarantees without which he refused to continue to serve. To prevent this, if deadlocked shareholders refused to agree on replacement custodian or satisfactory protections for current custodian, court was prepared to order (1) corporation to obtain letter of credit and (2) 10-day moratorium following any deadlock-breaking vote by custodian. During that time, either group of shareholders could apply to court for relief. After that actions against custodian arising from this matter would be barred. *Marciano v Nakash, No. 7910 (Ch Ct 4-2-86).*

353 APPOINTMENT OF A PROVISIONAL DIRECTOR IN CERTAIN CASES.—(a) Notwithstanding any contrary provision of the certificate of incorporation or the bylaws or agreement of the stockholders, the Court of Chancery may appoint a provisional director for a close corporation if the directors are so divided respecting the management of the corporation's business and affairs that the votes required for action by the board of directors cannot be obtained with the consequence that the business and affairs of the corporation can no longer be conducted to the advantage of the stockholders generally.

(b) An application for relief under this section must be filed (1) by at least one half of the number of directors then in office, (2) by the holders of at least one third of all stock then entitled to elect directors, or, (3) if there be more than 1 class of stock then entitled to elect 1 or more directors, by the holders of two thirds of the stock of any such class; but the certificate of incorporation of a close corporation may provide that a lesser proportion of the directors or of the stockholders or of a class of stockholders may apply for relief under this section.

(c) A provisional director shall be an impartial person who is neither a stockholder nor a creditor of the corporation or of any subsidiary or affiliate of the corporation, and whose further qualifications, if any, may be determined by the Court of Chancery. A provisional director is not a receiver of the corporation and does not have the title and powers of a custodian or receiver appointed under §§226 and 291 of this title. A provisional director shall have all the rights and powers of a duly elected director of the corporation, including the right to notice of and to vote at meetings of directors, until such time as [1]*such person* shall be removed by order of the Court of Chancery or by the holders of a majority of all shares then entitled to vote to elect directors or by the holders of two thirds of the shares of that class of voting shares which filed the application for appointment of a provisional director. [2]*A provisional director's* compensation shall be determined by agreement between [3]*such person* and the corporation subject to approval of the Court of Chancery, which may fix [4]*such person's* compensation in the absence of agreement or in the event of disagreement between the provisional director and the corporation.

(d) Even though the requirements of subsection (b) of this section relating to the number of directors or stockholders who may petition for appointment of a provisional director are not satisfied, the Court of Chancery may nevertheless appoint a provisional director if permitted by subsection (b) of §352 of this title. (Last amended by Ch. 339, L. '98, eff. 7-1-98.)

Ch. 339, L. '98, eff. 7-1-98, added matter in italic and deleted [1]"he"; [2]"His"; [3]"him"; and [4]"his".

Ch. 339, L. '98 Synopsis of Section 353

The amendments to these Sections eliminate masculine references in the statutes, and replace them with gender neutral references.

.1 Difference between receiver and provisional director.—Receiver takes possession of all corporate property and assets and exercises complete control over all affairs of corporation including management of its everyday business, whereas provisional director is merely a director who is entitled to notice of board meetings and may vote at such meetings until existing deadlock of board is broken or until he is removed by court order or by vote or written consent of holders of majority of voting shares; he is merely a director and has none of those plenary powers which are granted to receiver. *In re Jamison Steel Corp, 322 P2d 246 (Calif Ct App 1958).*

.2 Non-participating voting stock.—Before the enactment of this section, it was held that a corporation equally owned by two groups of stockholders could create new class of non-participating voting stock, and issue one share to odd numbered new director able to break deadlock; arrangement was approved by unanimous vote of stockholders and effected through charter amendment. *Lehrman v Cohen, 222 A2d 800 (1966).*

354 OPERATING CORPORATION AS PARTNERSHIP.—No written agreement among stockholders of a close corporation, nor any provision of the certificate of incorporation or of the bylaws of the corporation, which agreement or provision relates to any phase of the affairs of such corporation, including but not limited to the management of its business or declaration and payment of dividends or other division of profits or the election of directors or officers or the employment of stockholders by the corporation or the arbitration of disputes, shall be invalid on the ground that it is an attempt by the parties to the agreement or by the stockholders of the corporation to treat the corporation as if it were a partnership or to arrange relations among the stockholders or between the stockholders and the corporation in a manner that would be appropriate only among partners.

.1 **Voting rights.**—Voting trustee can enforce a stockholder's agreement giving one class of stock the right to elect a majority of the board even though the certificate of incorporation is silent, when those voting rights are in bylaw. *In re Farm Industries, Inc, 196 A2d 582 (Ch Ct 1963).*

.2 **Voting agreement.**—Prior to the adoption of this section, an agreement between stockholders "to agree" as to how they would vote their stock, providing that they would be bound by the decision of an arbitrator if they were unable to agree, was an enforceable contract and not contrary to public policy as an attempted delegation of irrevocable control over voting rights. *Ringling v Ringling Bros-Barnum & Bailey Combined Shows, Inc, 49 A2d 603,* mod, *53 A2d 441 (Ch Ct 1946).*

355 STOCKHOLDERS' OPTION TO DISSOLVE CORPORATION.—(a) The certificate of incorporation of any close corporation may include a provision granting to any stockholder, or to the holders of any specified number or percentage of shares of any class of stock, an option to have the corporation dissolved at will or upon the occurrence of any specified event or contingency. Whenever any such option to dissolve is exercised, the stockholders exercising such option shall give written notice thereof to all other stockholders. After the expiration of 30 days following the sending of such notice, the dissolution of the corporation shall proceed as if the required number of stockholders having voting power had consented in writing to dissolution of the corporation as provided by §228 of this title.

(b) If the certificate of incorporation as originally filed does not contain a provision authorized by subsection (a) of this section, the certificate may be amended to include such provision if adopted by the affirmative vote of the holders of all the outstanding stock, whether or not entitled to vote, unless the certificate of incorporation specifically authorizes such an amendment by a vote which shall be not less than two thirds of all the outstanding stock whether or not entitled to vote.

(c) Each stock certificate in any corporation whose certificate of incorporation authorizes dissolution as permitted by this section shall conspicuously note on the face thereof the existence of the provision. Unless noted conspicuously on the face of the stock certificate, the provision is ineffective. (Last amended by Ch. 186, L. '67, eff. 1-2-68.)

.1 **Compelling dissolution.**—Court will not appoint a liquidating receiver for a solvent, well-managed close corporation on the ground that the directors (1) keep inadequate books and records, if the records meet IRS requirements, (2) deny minority stockholders the right to make an independent audit, and (3) refuse to declare dividends. *Hall v John S Isaacs & Sons Farms, Inc, 163 A2d 288 (1960).*

Court will delay appointing a receiver for an insolvent corporation to give creditors and majority stockholders, who wish to continue corporation, time to show that they could put business on current basis; upon such showing, court will exercise its discretion to dismiss petition. *Foster v Del Drug Co, 114 A2d 228 (Ch Ct 1955).*

Court will appoint receiver of solvent corporation which is run by its majority stockholder for his own convenience and in disregard of the rights of the minority as evidenced by the majority stockholder's misuse of the corporation's credit and his ignoring corporate law formalities. *Tansey v Oil Producing Royalties, Inc, 133 A2d 141 (Ch Ct 1957).*

356 EFFECT OF THIS SUBCHAPTER ON OTHER LAWS.—This subchapter shall not be deemed to repeal any statute or rule of law which is or would be applicable to any corporation which is organized under this chapter but is not a close corporation.

SUBCHAPTER XV. FOREIGN CORPORATIONS

371 DEFINITION; QUALIFICATION TO DO BUSINESS IN STATE; PROCEDURE.—(a) As used in this chapter, the words "foreign corporation" mean a corporation organized under the laws of any jurisdiction other than this State.

(b) No foreign corporation shall do any business in this State, through or by branch offices, agents or representatives located in this State, until it shall have paid to the Secretary of State of this State for the use of this State, $80, and shall have filed in the Office of the Secretary of State:

(1) A certificate, *as of a date not earlier than 6 months prior to the filing date,* issued by an authorized officer of the jurisdiction of its incorporation evidencing its corporate existence. If such certificate is in a foreign language, a translation thereof, under oath of the translator, shall be attached thereto;

(2) A statement executed by an authorized officer of each corporation setting forth (i) the name and address of its registered agent in this State, [1] *which agent may be any of the foreign corporation itself, an individual resident in this State, a domestic corporation, a domestic partnership (whether general (including a limited liability partnership) or limited (including a limited liability limited partnership)), a domestic limited liability company, a domestic statutory trust, a foreign corporation (other than the foreign corporation itself), a foreign partnership (whether general (including a limited liability partnership) or limited (including a limited liability limited partnership)), a foreign limited liability company or a foreign statutory trust,* (ii) a statement, as of a date not earlier than 6 months prior to the filing date, of the assets and liabilities of the corporation, and (iii) the business it proposes to do in this State, and a statement that it is authorized to do that business in the jurisdiction of its incorporation. The statement shall be acknowledged in accordance with §103 of this title.

(c) The certificate of the Secretary of State, under seal of office, of the filing of the certificates required by subsection (b) of this section, shall be delivered to the registered agent upon the payment to the Secretary of State of the fee prescribed for such certificates, and the certificate shall be prima facie evidence of the right of the corporation to do business in this State; provided, that the Secretary of State shall not issue such certificate unless the name of the corporation is such as to distinguish it upon the records in the office of the Division of Corporations in the Department of State from the names that are reserved on such records and from the names on such records of each other corporation, partnership, limited partnership, limited liability company or statutory trust organized or registered as a domestic or foreign corporation, partnership, limited partnership, limited liability company or statutory trust under the laws of this State, except with the written consent of the person who has reserved such name or such other corporation, partnership, limited partnership, limited liability company or statutory trust, executed, acknowledged and filed with the Secretary of State in accordance with §103 of this title. If the name of the foreign corporation conflicts with the name of a corporation, partnership, limited partnership, limited liability company or statutory trust organized under the laws of this State, or a name reserved for a corporation, partnership, limited partnership, limited liability company or statutory trust to be organized under the laws of this State, or a name reserved or registered as that of a foreign corporation, partnership, limited partnership, limited liability company or statutory trust under the laws of this State, the foreign corporation may qualify to do business if it adopts an assumed name which shall be used when doing business in this State as long as the assumed name is authorized for use by this section. (Last amended by Ch. 290, L. '10, eff. 8-2-10.)

Ch. 290, L. '10, eff. 8-2-10, added matter in italic and deleted [1]"which agent shall be either an individual resident in this State when appointed or another corporation authorized to transact business in this State,".

Ch. 290, L. '10 Synopsis of Section 371

This section amends Section 371(b)(1) to require that the certificate from the jurisdiction of the foreign corporation's incorporation to be filed thereunder must be as of a date not earlier than 6 months prior to the filing date.

This section amends Section 371(b)(2) to expand the types of entities that may serve as registered agents for foreign corporations that are qualified to do business in Delaware.

Ch. 306, L. '06 Synopsis of Section 371

Section 6 amends §371 to provide that before a foreign corporation shall have the right to do business in Delaware, the name of such foreign corporation must be such as to distinguish it from the names (whether reserved or of record) of each other domestic or foreign corporation, partnership, limited partnership, limited liability company or statutory trust upon the records in the office of the Division of Corporations in the Department of State, except with the written consent of the person who has reserved such name or such other corporation, partnership, limited partnership, limited liability company or statutory trust.

Ch. 329, L. '02 Synopsis of Section 371

The amendments set forth are made for the purpose of avoiding any implication that a trust formed under Chapter 38, Title 12 of the Delaware Code constitutes a "business trust" within the meaning of Title 11 of the United States Code. Such amendments are not intended to result in any substantive change in Delaware law. These amendments are made solely for the purpose of conforming the Delaware Code to the amendments set forth above.

.1 Power of state over foreign corporations.—Courts of Delaware will not control internal affairs of foreign corporations. *Hanssen v Pusey & Jones Co, 276 F 296 (D Del 1921).*

Courts of foreign corporation's home state must give full faith and credit to judgment rendered against foreign corporation in suit in which jurisdiction of it was obtained by service under state statutes. *Adam v Saenger, 303 US 59,* reh'g denied, *303 US 666 (1938).*

Judgment based on implied contractual obligation of Illinois corporation qualifying to do business in Wisconsin for failure to pay taxes assessed against it upon income received from business transacted in Wisconsin can be enforced by suit against corporation in Illinois federal court. *Milwaukee County v M E White Co, 296 US 268 (1935).*

A state is free to choose whether it will hear an in personam suit against an amply notified foreign corporation on a claim arising outside the state and not related to the activities of the corporation in state. *Perkins v Benguet Cons Min Co, 342 US 437 (1952).*

Supreme Court will require federal district court to hear diversity suit for money judgment, possibly involving the internal affairs of a foreign corporation. *Williams v G B & W R Co, 326 US 549 (1946).*

Federal court has discretionary jurisdiction of minority stockholder's derivative suit against foreign corporation and its directors, whether or not it is bound to follow the law of the state, and it should take jurisdiction where the suit does not involve the internal affairs of the foreign corporation and where, although a similar suit is pending in a court of the foreign corporation's home state, that court could not afford adequate relief because personal service could not be effected on defendant directors within its jurisdiction. *Overfield v Pennroad Corp, 113 F2d 6 (3d Cir 1940).*

When foreign corporation registers to do business in Delaware and appoints agent there to receive service of process, corporation consents to general jurisdiction of Delaware courts. Also, foreign corporation's ownership of Delaware subsidiary is minimum contact that may allow Delaware courts to exercise specific jurisdiction over foreign parent in double derivative action against parent and subsidiary. *Sternberg v O'Neil, No. 377, 1987 (11-18-88),* rev'g, *532 A2d 993 (Ch Ct 1987).*

.2 Doing business—in general.—To be subject to service of process in Delaware a foreign corporation must (1) be doing business in the state (2) of a nature and to an extent (3) to warrant the inference that by the business done the corporation has subjected itself to the jurisdiction of the state and is present by its officers or agents. *Bell v Viavi Co, 143 A 255 (1928).*

Mere solicitation by an agent is not doing business for service of process purpose. *Atlas Mutual Benefit Ass'n v Portscheller, 46 A2d 643 (1945).* Must obey laws of state where it does business. *Warner Co v Foshey Co, 57 F2d 656 (3d Cir 1932).*

Person who contracted with a corporation is estopped to deny its right to do business in the state. *Standard Sewing-Machine Co v Frame, 48 A 188 (Pa 1900).*

Foreign corporation qualifying under a special statute does not necessarily become citizen of the state. *Magna Oil & Refining Co v White Star Refining Co, 280 F 52 (3d Cir 1922).*

Creditor may attach any property of a foreign corporation which he finds within the jurisdiction, whether or not the corporation has qualified. *Albright v United Clay Production Co, 117 A 726 (Pa 1904).*

Unqualified corporation that solicits business and performs heating and air conditioning job instate is subject to service of process under state's long-arm statute, even though that job was only its second job instate in 14 years. *Crowell Corp v Topkis Constr Co, 267 A2d 613 (1970).*

Unqualified corporation cannot bring action instate when it (1) advertised in local newspapers; (2) engaged in credit transactions instate; (3) maintained local bank account; and (4) provided transportation to its out-of-state lodge; statute required qualification for transaction of "any business" instate and barred maintenance of "any action" as penalty for failure to qualify. Sinwellan Corporation v Farmers Bank of the State of Delaware reversed. See also *Farmers Bank of the State of Delaware v Sinwellan Corp, 367 A2d 180 (1976).*

.3 Solicitation.—Regular and systematic solicitation of orders in a state by foreign corporation's salesmen, including display of samples, sometimes in permanent display rooms, and resulting in a large volume of interstate business, constitutes sufficient activity to establish corporation's presence within the state, making corporation amenable to process and subject to suit by state for tax laid upon the exercise of the privilege of employing salesmen within the state. The activities which establish the corporation's presence in the state subject it alike to taxation and make it reasonable and just according to our traditional conception of fair play and substantial justice to permit the state to enforce the obligations which it has incurred there. *International Shoe Co v Washington, 326 US 310 (1945).*

.4 Filling orders.—Foreign corporation that fills orders from stock on hand within state and continuously polices its dealers in regard to its Fair Trade contracts is "doing business" for service of process purpose. *Klein v Sunbeam Corp, 94 A2d 385 (1952).*

.5 Doing business for tax purposes.—A state can include, in the computation of the business receipts fraction of its franchise tax, proceeds from goods manufactured in the state, no matter where sold or delivered. *International Harvester Co v Evatt, 329 US 416 (1947).*

Shipment of scales into state under contract made in state by agent is not doing business for license tax purpose. *Wilmington Dry Goods Co v Nat Automatic Mach Co, 190 A2d 735 (1937).*

.6 **Attachment against foreign corporation.**—Property of foreign corporation can be attached in suit in federal court where it is not amenable to personal service of process whether suit was commenced in the federal court or removed there from state court prior to perfecting of lien of attachment. *Rorick v Devon Syndicate Ltd, 307 US 299 (1939).*

.7 **Registration and default judgments.**—A default judgment against a foreign corporation will be upheld where the foreign corporation has failed to register with the state, and the plaintiff's efforts to serve the corporation are not unreasonable. *Centralia Mining Co v Crawford, 14 A3d 519 (2011).*

372 ADDITIONAL REQUIREMENTS IN CASE OF CHANGE OF NAME, CHANGE OF BUSINESS PURPOSE OR MERGER OR CONSOLIDATION.—(a) Every foreign corporation admitted to do business in this State which shall change its corporate name, or enlarge, limit or otherwise change the business which it proposes to do in this State, shall, within 30 days after the time said change becomes effective, file with the Secretary of State a certificate, which shall set forth:

(1) The name of the foreign corporation as it appears on the records of the Secretary of State of this State;

(2) The jurisdiction of its incorporation;

(3) The date it was authorized to do business in this State;

(4) If the name of the foreign corporation has been changed, a statement of the name relinquished, a statement of the new name and a statement that the change of name has been effected under the laws of the jurisdiction of its incorporation and the date the change was effected;

(5) If the business it proposes to do in this State is to be enlarged, limited or otherwise changed, a statement reflecting such change and a statement that it is authorized to do in the jurisdiction of its incorporation the business which it proposes to do in this State.

(b) Whenever a foreign corporation authorized to transact business in this State shall be the survivor of a merger permitted by the laws of the state or country in which it is incorporated, it shall, within 30 days after the merger becomes effective, file a certificate, issued by the proper officer of the state or country of its incorporation, attesting to the occurrence of such event. If the merger has changed the corporate name of such foreign corporation or has enlarged, limited or otherwise changed the business it proposes to do in this State, it shall also comply with subsection (a) of this section.

(c) Whenever a foreign corporation authorized to transact business in this State ceases to exist because of a statutory merger or consolidation, it shall comply with §381 of this title.

(d) The Secretary of State shall be paid, for the use of the State, $50 for filing and indexing each certificate required by subsection (a) or (b) of this section, and in the event of a change of name an additional [1]*$50* shall be paid for a certificate to be issued as evidence of filing the change of name. (Last amended by Ch. 78, L. '09, eff. 8-1-09.)

Ch. 78, L. '09, eff. 8-1-09, added matter in italic and deleted [1]"$20".

Ch. 78 L. '09 Synopsis of Section 372

This Act increases various fees and taxes assessed by the Delaware Secretary of State.

.1 **Registration and default judgments.**—A default judgment against a foreign corporation will be upheld where the foreign corporation has failed to register with the state, and the plaintiff's efforts to serve the corporation are not unreasonable. *Centralia Mining Co v Crawford, 14 A3d 519 (2011).*

373 EXCEPTIONS TO REQUIREMENTS.—(a) No foreign corporation shall be required to comply with §§371 and 372 of this title, under any of the following conditions:

(1) If it is in the mail order or a similar business, merely receiving orders by mail or otherwise in pursuance of letters, circulars, catalogs or other forms of advertising, or solicitation, accepting the orders outside this State, and filling them with goods shipped into this State;

(2) If it employs [1]*salespersons,* either resident or traveling, to solicit orders in this State, either by display of samples or otherwise (whether or not maintaining sales offices in this State), all orders being subject to approval at the offices of the corporation without this State, and all goods applicable to the orders being shipped in pursuance thereof from without this State to the vendee or to the seller or [2]*such seller's* agent for delivery to the vendee, and if any samples kept within this State are for display or advertising purposes only, and no sales, repairs or replacements are made from stock on hand in this State;

(3) If it sells, by contract consummated outside this State, and agrees, by the contract, to deliver into this State, machinery, plants or equipment, the construction, erection or installation of which within this State requires the supervision of technical engineers or skilled employees performing services not generally available, and as a part of the contract of sale agrees to furnish such services, and such services only, to the vendee at the time of construction, erection or installation;

(4) If its business operations within this State, although not falling within the terms of paragraphs (1), (2) and (3) of this subsection or any of them, are nevertheless wholly interstate in character;

(5) If it is an insurance company doing business in this State;

(6) If it creates, as borrower or lender, or acquires, evidences of debt, mortgages or liens on real or personal property;

(7) If it secures or collects debts or enforces any rights in property securing the same.

(b) This section shall have no application to the question of whether any foreign corporation is subject to service of process and suit in this State under §382 of this title or any other law of this State. (Last amended by Ch. 339, L. '98, eff. 7-1-98.)

Ch. 339, L. '98, eff. 7-1-98, added matter in italic and deleted [1]"salesmen" and [2]"his".

Ch. 339, L. '98 Synopsis of Section 373

The amendments to these Sections eliminate masculine references in the statutes, and replace them with gender neutral references.

.1 Bonding activities—of foreign company were interstate in nature even though local real estate was used as security for loans it arranged for residents, since with one exception, all lenders were nonresidents; thus company could sue to collect commission for procuring loan even though neither company nor its principal operator was licensed to do business locally. *Bond Associates, Inc v Continental Arms, Inc, 310 A2d 875 (1973).*

374 ANNUAL REPORT.—On or before June 30 in each year, a foreign corporation doing business in this State shall file a report with the Secretary of State. The report shall be made on behalf of the corporation by its president, secretary, treasurer or other officer duly authorized so to act, or by any 2 of its directors, or by any incorporator in the event its board of directors shall not have been elected. The fact that an individual's name is signed on a certification attached to a corporate report shall be prima facie evidence that such individual is authorized to certify the report on behalf of the corporation; however the official title or position of the individual signing the corporate report shall be designated. The report shall be on a calendar year basis and shall state the address ([1] *in accordance with §131(c) of this title*) of its registered office in this State; the name of its registered agent at such address upon whom service of process against the corporation may be served; the address (which shall include the street, number, city, state or foreign country) of the main or headquarters place of business of the corporation without this State; the names and addresses of all the directors and officers of the corporation and when the term of each expires; the date appointed for the next annual meeting of the stockholders for the election of directors; the number of shares of each class of its capital stock which it is authorized to issue, if any, and the par value thereof when applicable; and the number of shares of each class of the capital stock actually issued, if any; the amount of capital invested in real estate and other property in this State, and the tax paid thereon; and, if exempt from taxation in this State for any cause, the specific facts entitling the corporation to such exemption from taxation. (Last amended by Ch. 96, L. '11, eff. 8-1-11.)

Ch. 96, L. '11, eff. 8-1-11, added matter in italic and deleted [1]"which shall include the street, number, city and county".

Ch. 96, L. '11 Synopsis of Section 374

This Section amends Section 374 to clarify that, in an annual report of a foreign corporation filed with the Secretary of State, the address of the registered office of the foreign corporation in Delaware must be stated in accordance with new Section 131(c).

375 FAILURE TO FILE REPORT.—Upon the failure, neglect or refusal of any foreign corporation to file an annual report as required by §374 of this title, the Secretary of State may, in [1]*the Secretary of State's* discretion, investigate the reasons therefor and shall terminate the right of the foreign corporation to do business within this State upon failure of the corporation to file an annual report within any 2-year period. *(Last amended by Ch. 339, L. '98, eff. 7-1-98.)*

_{Ch. 339, L. '98, eff. 7-1-98, added matter in italic and deleted [1]"his".}

Ch. 339, L. '98 Synopsis of Section 375

The amendments to these Sections eliminate masculine references in the statutes, and replace them with gender neutral references.

376 SERVICE OF PROCESS UPON QUALIFIED FOREIGN CORPORATIONS.—(a) All process issued out of any court of this State, all orders made by any court of this State, all rules and notices of any kind required to be served on any foreign corporation which has qualified to do business in this State may be served on the registered

agent of the corporation designated in accordance with §371 of this title, or, if there be no such agent, then on any officer, director or other agent of the corporation then in this State.

(b) [1] *In case the officer whose duty it is to serve legal process cannot by due diligence serve the process in any manner provided for by subsection (a) of this section, it shall be lawful to serve the process against the corporation upon the Secretary of State, and such service shall be as effectual for all intents and purposes as if made in any of the ways provided for in subsection (a) of this section. Process may be served upon the Secretary of State under this subsection by means of electronic transmission but only as prescribed by the Secretary of State. The Secretary of State is authorized to issue such rules and regulations with respect to such service as the Secretary of State deems necessary or appropriate. In the event that service is effected through the Secretary of State in accordance with this subsection, the Secretary of State shall forthwith notify the corporation by letter, directed to the corporation at its principal place of business as it appears on the last annual report filed pursuant to §374 of this title or, if no such address appears, at its last registered office. Such letter shall be sent by a mail or courier service that includes a record of mailing or deposit with the courier and a record of delivery evidenced by the signature of the recipient.* Such letter shall enclose a copy of the process and any other papers served upon the Secretary of State pursuant to this subsection. It shall be the duty of the plaintiff in the event of such service to serve process and any other papers in duplicate, to notify the Secretary of State that service is being effected pursuant to this subsection, and to pay the Secretary of State the sum of $50 for the use of the State, which sum shall be taxed as a part of the costs in the proceeding if the plaintiff shall prevail therein. The Secretary of State shall maintain an alphabetical record of any such service setting forth the name of the plaintiff and the defendant, the title, docket number and nature of the proceeding in which process has been served upon the Secretary of State, the fact that service has been effected pursuant to this subsection, the return date thereof, and the day and hour when the service was made. The Secretary of State shall not be required to retain such information for a period longer than 5 years from receipt of such service. (Last amended by Ch. 290, L. '10, eff. 8-2-10.)

Ch. 290, L. '10, eff. 8-2-10, added matter in italic and deleted [1]"In case the officer whose duty it is to serve legal process cannot by due diligence serve the process in any manner provided for by subsection (a) of this section, it shall be lawful to serve the process against the corporation upon the Secretary of State and such service shall be as effectual for all intents and purposes as if made in any of the ways provided for in subsection (a) of this section. In the event of service upon the Secretary of State pursuant to this subsection, the Secretary of State shall forthwith notify the corporation by letter, certified mail, return receipt requested, directed to the corporation at its principal place of business as it appears on the last annual report filed pursuant to §374 of this title or, if no such address appears, at its last registered office."

Ch. 290, L. '10 Synopsis of Section 376

These sections amend Sections 252(d), 256(d), 263(d), 264(d), 266(c)(6), 321(b), 376(b), 381(c), 381(d), 382(a), 382(c), and 390(b)(5), respectively, to allow for service of process upon the Secretary of State thereunder by means of electronic transmission but only as prescribed by the Secretary of State, to authorize the Secretary of State to issue such rules and regulations with respect to such service as the Secretary of State deems necessary or appropriate, and to enable the Secretary of State, in the event that service is effected through the Secretary of State in accordance therewith, to provide notice of service by letter sent by a mail or courier service that includes a record of mailing or deposit with the courier and a record of delivery evidenced by the signature of the recipient.

Ch. 339, L. '98 Synopsis of Section 376

The amendments to these Sections eliminate masculine references in the statutes, and replace them with gender neutral references.

.1 Effect of designation of agent.—Foreign corporation which designates an agent for service of process in a state in which it qualifies to do business thereby consents to be sued there under the "diversity of citizenship" clause of the U.S. Constitution. It also consents to be sued in a federal court there even though the suit is not solely a diversity suit. *Beard v Continental Oil Co, 42 FSupp 310 (ED La 1941).*

When foreign corporation registers to do business in Delaware and appoints agent there to receive service of process, corporation consents to general jurisdiction of Delaware courts. Also, foreign corporation's ownership of Delaware subsidiary is minimum contact that may allow Delaware courts to exercise specific jurisdiction over foreign parent in double derivative action against parent and subsidiary. *Sternberg v O'Neil, 550 A2d 1105 (1988),* rev'g, *532 A2d 993 (Ch Ct 1987).*

377 CHANGE OF REGISTERED AGENT.—(a) Any foreign corporation, which has qualified to do business in this State, may change its registered agent and substitute another registered agent by filing a certificate with the Secretary of State, acknowledged in accordance with §103 of this title, setting forth: (1) The name and address of its registered agent designated in this State upon whom process directed to said corporation may be served; and (2) a revocation of all previous appointments of agent for such purposes. Such registered agent shall be either an individual residing in this State when appointed or a corporation authorized to transact business in this State.

[1]*(b) Any individual or corporation designated by a foreign corporation as its registered agent for service of process may resign by filing with the Secretary of State a signed statement that the registered agent is unwilling to continue to act as the registered agent of the corporation for service of process, including in the statement the post-office address of the main or headquarters office of the foreign corporation, but such resignation shall not become effective until 30 days after the statement is filed. The statement shall be acknowledged by the registered agent and shall contain a representation that written notice of resignation was given to the corporation at least 30 days prior to the filing of the statement by mailing or delivering such notice to the corporation at its address given in the statement.*

(c) If any agent designated and certified as required by §371 of this title shall die or remove from this State, or resign, then the foreign corporation for which the agent had been so designated and certified shall, within 10 days after the death, removal or resignation of its agent, substitute, designate and certify to the Secretary of State, the name of another registered agent for the purposes of this subchapter, and all process, orders, rules and notices mentioned in §376 of this title may be served on or given to the substituted agent with like effect as is prescribed in that section. (Last amended by Ch. 120, L. '97, eff. 7-1-97.)

Ch. 120, L. '97, eff. 7-1-97, added matter in italic and deleted [1]"(b) Any individual or corporation designated by a foreign corporation as its registered agent for service of process may resign by filing with the Secretary of State a signed statement that he or it is unwilling to continue to act as the registered agent of the corporation for service of process, including in the statement the post-office address of the main or headquarters office of the foreign corporation. Upon the expiration of 30 days after the filing of the statement with the Secretary of State, the capacity of the individual or corporation, as registered agent, shall terminate. Upon the filing of the statement, the Secretary of State forthwith shall give written notice to the corporation by mail of the filing of the statement, which notice shall be addressed to the corporation at the post-office address given in the statement and also, if different, to the corporation at its post-office address given in the corporation's last annual report filed pursuant to §374 of this title."

Ch. 120, L. '97 Synopsis of Section 377

The amendment to Section 377(b) revises the procedure for resignation of a registered agent for a foreign corporation by adding a requirement that the registered agent give thirty days prior notice to the foreign corporation and eliminating the previous requirement that the Secretary of State give such notice upon receipt of the registered agent's resignation.

Comment: This change in subsection (a) makes clear what must be set forth in the certificate which must be filed by a foreign corporation to change its registered agent. The provision as it presently stands makes a reference to §371 which does not clearly define what such a certificate for a change of registered agent must contain.

378 PENALTIES FOR NONCOMPLIANCE.—Any foreign corporation doing business of any kind in this State without first having complied with any section of this subchapter applicable to it, shall be fined not less than $200 nor more than $500 for each such offense. Any agent of any foreign corporation that shall do any business in this State for any foreign corporation before the foreign corporation has complied with any section of this subchapter applicable to it, shall be fined not less than $100 nor more than $500 for each such offense.

379 BANKING POWERS DENIED.—(a) No foreign corporation shall, within the limits of this State, by any implication or construction, be deemed to possess the power of discounting bills, notes or other evidence of debt, of receiving deposits, of buying and selling bills of exchange, or of issuing bills, notes or other evidences of debt upon loan for circulation as money, anything in its charter or articles of incorporation to the contrary notwithstanding, except as otherwise provided in subchapter VII of Chapter 7 *or in Chapter 14 of Title 5.*

(b) All certificates issued by the Secretary of State under §371 of this title shall expressly set forth the limitations and restrictions contained in this section. (Last amended by Ch. 254, L. '98, eff. 3-30-98.)

Ch. 112, L. '95, eff. 9-29-95, added matter in italic.

380 FOREIGN CORPORATION AS FIDUCIARY IN THIS STATE.—A corporation organized and doing business under the laws of the District of Columbia or of any state of the United States other than Delaware, duly authorized by its certificate of incorporation or bylaws so to act, may be appointed by any last will and testament or other testamentary writing, probated within this State, or by a deed of trust, mortgage or other agreement, as executor, guardian, trustee or other fiduciary, and may act as such within this State, when and to the extent that the laws of the District of Columbia or of the state in which the foreign corporation is organized confer like powers upon corporations organized and doing business under the laws of this State. (Last amended by Ch. 84-353, L. '84, eff. 7-17-84.)

381 WITHDRAWAL OF FOREIGN CORPORATION FROM STATE; PROCEDURE; SERVICE OF PROCESS ON SECRETARY OF STATE.—(a) Any foreign corporation which shall have qualified to do business in this State under §371 of this title, may surrender its authority to do business in this State and may withdraw therefrom by filing with the Secretary of State:

(1) A certificate executed in accordance with §103 of this title, stating that it surrenders its authority to transact business in the state and withdraws therefrom; and stating the address to which the Secretary of State may mail any process against the corporation that may be served upon the Secretary of State, or

(2) A copy of a certificate of dissolution issued by the proper official of the State or other jurisdiction of its incorporation, certified to be a true copy under the hand and official seal of the official, together with a certificate, which shall be executed in accordance with paragraph (1) of this subsection, stating the address to which the Secretary of State may mail any process against the corporation that may be served upon the Secretary of State; or

(3) A copy of an order or decree of dissolution made by any court of competent jurisdiction or other competent authority of the State or other jurisdiction of its incorporation, certified to be a true copy under the hand of the clerk of the court or other official body, and the official seal of the court or official body or clerk thereof, together with a certificate executed in accordance with paragraph (1) of this subsection, stating the address to which the Secretary of State may mail any process against the corporation that may be served upon the Secretary of State.

(b) The Secretary of State shall, upon payment to the Secretary of State of the fees prescribed in §391 of this title, issue a sufficient number of certificates, under the Secretary of State's hand and official seal, evidencing the surrender of the authority of the corporation to do business in this State and its withdrawal therefrom. One of the certificates shall be furnished to the corporation withdrawing and surrendering its right to do business in this State; 1 certificate shall be delivered to the agent of the corporation designated as such immediately prior to the withdrawal.

(c) Upon the issuance of the certificates by the Secretary of State, the appointment of the registered agent of the corporation in this State, upon whom process against the corporation may be served, shall be revoked, and the corporation shall be deemed to have consented that service of process in any action, suit or proceeding based upon any cause of action arising in this State, during the time the corporation was authorized to transact business in this State, may thereafter be made by service upon the Secretary of State. *Process may be served upon the Secretary of State under this subsection by means of electronic transmission but only as prescribed by the Secretary of State. The Secretary of State is authorized to issue such rules and regulations with respect to such service as the Secretary of State deems necessary or appropriate.*

(d) In the event of service upon the Secretary of State in accordance with subsection (c) of this section, the Secretary of State shall forthwith notify the corporation by letter, [1] directed to the corporation at the address stated in the certificate which was filed by the corporation with the Secretary of State pursuant to subsection (a) of this section. *Such letter shall be sent by a mail or courier service that includes a record of mailing or deposit with the courier and a record of delivery evidenced by the signature of the recipient.* Such letter shall enclose a copy of the process and any other papers served upon the Secretary of State. It shall be the duty of the plaintiff in the event of such service to serve process and any other papers in duplicate, to notify the Secretary of State that service is being made pursuant to this subsection, and to pay the Secretary of State the sum of $50 for the use of the State, which sum shall be taxed as part of the cost of the action, suit or proceeding if the plaintiff shall prevail therein. The Secretary of State shall maintain an alphabetical record of such service setting forth the name of the plaintiff and defendant, the title, docket number and nature of the proceeding in which the process has been served upon the Secretary of State, the fact that service has been effected pursuant to this subsection, the return date thereof, and the day and hour when the service was made. The Secretary of State shall not be required to retain such information for a period longer than 5 years from receipt of the service of process. (Last amended by Ch. 290, L. '10, eff. 8-2-10.)

Ch. 290, L. '10, eff. 8-2-10, added matter in italic and deleted [1]"certified mail, return receipt requested,".

Ch. 290, L. '10 Synopsis of Section 381

These sections amend Sections 252(d), 256(d), 263(d), 264(d), 266(c)(6), 321(b), 376(b), 381(c), 381(d), 382(a), 382(c), and 390(b)(5), respectively, to allow for service of process upon the Secretary of State thereunder by means of electronic transmission but only as prescribed by the Secretary of State, to authorize the Secretary of State to issue such rules and regulations with respect to such service as the Secretary of State deems necessary or appropriate, and to enable the Secretary of State, in the event that service is effected through the Secretary of State in accordance therewith, to provide notice of service by letter sent by a mail or courier service that includes a record of mailing or deposit with the courier and a record of delivery evidenced by the signature of the recipient.

Ch. 339, L. '98 Synopsis of Section 381

The amendments to these Sections eliminate masculine references in the statutes, and replace them with gender neutral references.

Ch. 79, L. '95 Synopsis of Section 381

This amendment eliminates the requirement for a Certificate of Withdrawal of a foreign corporation to be signed by the president or a vice president. The execution will be in accordance with Section 103 the same as other documents filed in accordance with the General Corporation Law.

382 SERVICE OF PROCESS ON NONQUALIFYING FOREIGN CORPORATIONS.—(a) Any foreign corporation which shall transact business in this State without having qualified to do business under §371 of this title shall be deemed to have thereby appointed and constituted the Secretary of State of this State its agent for the acceptance of legal process in any civil action, suit or proceeding against it in any state or federal court in this State arising or growing out of any business transacted by it within this State. The transaction of business in this State by such corporation shall be a signification of the agreement of such corporation that any such process when so served shall be of the same legal force and validity as if served upon an authorized officer or agent personally within this State. *Process may be served upon the Secretary of State under this subsection by means of electronic transmission but only as prescribed by the Secretary of State. The Secretary of State is authorized to issue such rules and regulations with respect to such service as the Secretary of State deems necessary or appropriate.*

(b) Section 373 of this title shall not apply in determining whether any foreign corporation is transacting business in this State within the meaning of this section; and "the transaction of business" or "business transacted in this State," by any such foreign corporation, whenever those words are used in this section, shall mean the course or practice of carrying on any business activities in this State, including, without limiting the generality of the foregoing, the solicitation of business or orders in this State. This section shall not apply to any insurance company doing business in this State.

(c) In the event of service upon the Secretary of State in accordance with subsection (a) of this section, the Secretary of State shall forthwith notify the corporation thereof by letter, [1] directed to the corporation at the address furnished to the Secretary of State by the plaintiff in such action, suit or proceeding. *Such letter shall be sent by a mail or courier service that includes a record of mailing or deposit with the courier and a record of delivery evidenced by the signature of the recipient.* Such letter shall enclose a copy of the process and any other papers served upon the Secretary of State. It shall be the duty of the plaintiff in the event of such service to serve process and any other papers in duplicate, to notify the Secretary of State that service is being made pursuant to this subsection, and to pay the Secretary of State the sum of $50 for the use of the State, which sum shall be taxed as a part of the costs in the proceeding if the plaintiff shall prevail therein. The Secretary of State shall maintain an alphabetical record of any such process setting forth the name of the plaintiff and defendant, the title, docket number and nature of the proceeding in which process has been served upon the Secretary of State, the fact that service has been effected pursuant to this subsection, the return date thereof, and the day and hour when the service was made. The Secretary of State shall not be required to retain such information for a period longer than 5 years from receipt of the service of process. (Last amended by Ch. 290, L. '10, eff. 8-2-10.)

Ch. 290, L. '10, eff. 8-2-10, added matter in italic and deleted [1]"certified mail, return receipt requested,".

Ch. 290, L. '10 Synopsis of Section 382

These sections amend Sections 252(d), 256(d), 263(d), 264(d), 266(c)(6), 321(b), 376(b), 381(c), 381(d), 382(a), 382(c), and 390(b)(5), respectively, to allow for service of process upon the Secretary of State thereunder by means of electronic transmission but only as prescribed by the Secretary of State, to authorize the Secretary of State to issue such rules and regulations with respect to such service as the Secretary of State deems necessary or appropriate, and to enable the Secretary of State, in the event that service is effected through the Secretary of State in accordance therewith, to provide notice of service by letter sent by a mail or courier service that includes a record of mailing or deposit with the courier and a record of delivery evidenced by the signature of the recipient.

Ch. 339, L. '98 Synopsis of Section 382

The amendments to these Sections eliminate masculine references in the statutes, and replace them with gender neutral references.

.1 Solicitation.—Out-of-state heating units manufacturer can be sued under state's long-arm statute, when it solicited orders, sold products through independent manufacturer's agents, and visited customers instate. *County Plumbing and Heating Co v Strine, 272 A2d 340 (1970).*

Unqualified corporation can be sued instate for personal injuries under state's long-arm statute, when its representative though independent contractor (1) systematically solicits customers instate, (2) forwards orders to corporation, and (3) occasionally displays corporation's products instate. *Gentry v Wilmington Trust Co, 321 FSupp 1379 (1971).*

.2 Not doing business.—Domestic corporation could not sue unqualified corporations instate for breach of agreement to install equipment in different state, when unqualified corporations did not transact business generally instate and breach of agreement did not arise out of particular business done instate.

Delaware Lead Construction Co v Young Industries, Inc, 360 FSupp 1244 (D Del 1973).

Unqualified parent corporation that guaranteed payment of purchases of its unqualified subsidiary could move to quash service of process on Secretary of State and dismiss complaint for lack of personal jurisdiction, when activities of its subsidiary in telephoning and mailing orders for merchandise to seller's instate office and accepting four F.O.B. deliveries there, were insufficient to constitute transaction of business instate. *General Foods Corp v Haines and Company, Inc, 458 FSupp 1167 (D Del 1978).*

.3 Service of process was improper.—Corporate officers served with substituted process pursuant to statute calling for such service upon corporations only were improperly served; foreign corporation that held several auctions within state was doing sufficient business for suit against it to be maintained within jurisdiction. *Wier v Fairchild Galleries, No. 5221 (Ch Ct 7-18-77).*

383 ACTIONS BY AND AGAINST UNQUALIFIED FOREIGN CORPORATIONS.—(a) A foreign corporation which is required to comply with §§371 and 372 of this title and which has done business in this State without authority shall not maintain any action or special proceeding in this State unless and until such corporation has been authorized to do business in this State and has paid to the State all fees, penalties and franchise taxes for the years or parts thereof during which it did business in this State without authority. This prohibition shall not apply to any successor in interest of such foreign corporation.

(b) The failure of a foreign corporation to obtain authority to do business in this State shall not impair the validity of any contract or act of the foreign corporation or the right of any other party to the contract to maintain any action or special proceeding thereon, and shall not prevent the foreign corporation from defending any action or special proceeding in this State.

.1 Enforcing contract.—Unqualified corporation can enforce contract of sale against buyer who retained its benefits. *Model Heating Co v Magarity, 81 A 394 (1911); Lehigh Structural Steel Co v Atlantic Smelting & Refining Works, 111 A 376 (NJ 1920).*

.2 Suit in federal court.—Foreign corporation, barred from suing in state court, because "doing business" without authority, cannot sue in federal court. *Woods v Interstate Realty Co, 337 US 535 (1949).*

.3 Bringing suit while unqualified.—Unqualified corporation cannot bring action instate when it (1) advertised in local newspapers; (2) engaged in credit transactions instate; (3) maintained local bank account; and (4) provided transportation to its out of state lodge; statute required qualification to do business instate and barred maintenance of "any action" as penalty for failure to qualify. *Farmers Bank of Delaware v Sinwellan Corp, 367 A2d 180 (1976).*

One transaction does not constitute "doing business"; hence, this section not operate to bar suit on the grounds that the corporation was not qualified. *Coyle v Peoples, 349 A2d 870 (1975).*

384 FOREIGN CORPORATIONS DOING BUSINESS WITHOUT HAVING QUALIFIED; INJUNCTIONS.—The Court of Chancery shall have jurisdiction to enjoin any foreign corporation, or any agent thereof, from transacting any business in this State if such corporation has failed to comply with any section of this subchapter applicable to it or if such corporation has secured a certificate of the Secretary of State under §371 of this title on the basis of false or misleading representations. The Attorney General shall, upon [1]*the Attorney General's* own motion or upon the relation of proper parties, proceed for this purpose by complaint in any county in which such corporation is doing business. (Last amended by Ch. 339, L. '98, eff. 7-1-98.)

Ch. 339, L. '98, eff. 7-1-98, added matter in italic and deleted [1]"his".

Ch. 339, L. '98 Synopsis of Section 384

The amendments to these Sections eliminate masculine references in the statutes, and replace them with gender neutral references.

385 FILING OF CERTAIN INSTRUMENTS WITH RECORDER OF DEEDS NOT REQUIRED.—No instrument that is required to be filed with the Secretary of State of this State by this subchapter need be filed with the Recorder of Deeds of any county of this State in order to comply with this subchapter. (Added by Ch. 112, L. '83, eff. 7-1-83.)

SUBCHAPTER XVI. DOMESTICATION AND TRANSFER

388 DOMESTICATION OF NON-UNITED STATES ENTITIES.—(a) As used in this section, the term:

(1) "Foreign jurisdiction" means any foreign country or other foreign jurisdiction (other than the United States, any state, the District of Columbia, or any possession or territory of the United States); and

(2) "Non-United States entity" means a corporation, a limited liability company, a statutory trust, a business trust or association, a real estate investment trust, a common-law trust, or any other unincorporated business or entity, including a partnership (whether general (including a limited liability partnership) or limited (including a limited liability limited partnership)), formed, incorporated, created or that otherwise came into being under the laws of any foreign jurisdiction.

(b) Any non-United States entity may become domesticated as a corporation in this State by complying with subsection (h) of this section and filing with the Secretary of State:

(1) A certificate of corporate domestication which shall be executed in accordance with subsection (g) of this section and filed in accordance with §103 of this title; and

(2) A certificate of incorporation, which shall be executed, acknowledged and filed in accordance with §103 of this title.

Each of the certificates required by this subsection (b) shall be filed simultaneously with the Secretary of State and, if such certificates are not to become effective upon their filing as permitted by §103(d) of this title, then each such certificate shall provide for the same effective date or time in accordance with §103(d) of this title.

(c) The certificate of corporate domestication shall certify:

(1) The date on which and jurisdiction where the non-United States entity was first formed, incorporated, created or otherwise came into being;

(2) The name of the non-United States entity immediately prior to the filing of the certificate of corporate domestication;

(3) The name of the corporation as set forth in its certificate of incorporation filed in accordance with subsection (b) of this section; and

(4) The jurisdiction that constituted the seat, siege social, or principal place of business or central administration of the non-United States entity or any other equivalent thereto under applicable law, immediately prior to the filing of the certificate of corporate domestication; and

(5) That the domestication has been approved in the manner provided for by the document, instrument, agreement or other writing, as the case may be, governing the internal affairs of the non-United States entity and the conduct of its business or by applicable non-Delaware law, as appropriate.

(d) Upon the certificate of corporate domestication and the certificate of incorporation becoming effective in accordance with §103 of this title, the non-United States entity shall be domesticated as a corporation in this State and the corporation shall thereafter be subject to all of the provisions of this title, except that notwithstanding §106 of this title, the existence of the corporation shall be deemed to have commenced on the date the non-United States entity commenced its existence in the jurisdiction in which the non-United States entity was first formed, incorporated, created or otherwise came into being.

(e) The domestication of any non-United States entity as a corporation in this State shall not be deemed to affect any obligations or liabilities of the non-United States entity incurred prior to its domestication as a corporation in this State, or the personal liability of any person therefor.

(f) The filing of a certificate of corporate domestication shall not affect the choice of law applicable to the non-United States entity, except that, from the effective time of the domestication, the law of the State of Delaware, including this title, shall apply to the non-United States entity to the same extent as if the non-United States entity had been incorporated as a corporation of this State on that date.

(g) The certificate of corporate domestication shall be signed by any person who is authorized to sign the certificate of corporate domestication on behalf of the non-United States entity.

(h) Prior to the filing of a certificate of corporate domestication with the Secretary of State, the domestication shall be approved in the manner provided for by the document, instrument, agreement or other writing, as the case may be, governing the internal affairs of the non-United States entity and the conduct of its business or by applicable non-Delaware law, as appropriate, and the certificate of incorporation shall be approved by the same authorization required to approve the domestication.

(i) When a non-United States entity has become domesticated as a corporation pursuant to this section, for all purposes of the laws of the State of Delaware, the corporation shall be deemed to be the same entity as the domesticating non-United States entity and the domestication shall constitute a continuation of the existence of the domesticating non-United States entity in the form of a corporation of this State. When any domestication shall have become effective under this section, for all purposes of the laws of the State of Delaware, all of the rights, privileges and powers of the non-United States entity that has been domesticated, and all property, real, personal and mixed, and all debts due to such non-United States entity, as well as all other things and causes of action belonging to such non-United States entity, shall remain vested in the corporation to which such non-United States entity has been domesticated (and also in the non-United States entity, if and for so long as the non-United States entity continues its existence in the foreign jurisdiction in which it was existing immediately prior to the domestication) and shall be the property of such corporation (and also of the non-United States entity, if and for so long as the non-United States entity continues its existence in the foreign jurisdiction in which it was existing immediately prior to the domestication), and the title to any real property vested by deed or otherwise in such non-United States entity shall not revert or be in any way impaired by reason of this title; but all rights of creditors and all liens upon any property of such non-United States entity shall be preserved unimpaired, and all debts, liabilities and duties of the non-United States entity that has been domesticated shall remain attached to the corporation to which such non-United States entity has been domesticated (and also to the non-United States entity, if and for so long as the non-United States entity continues its existence in the foreign jurisdiction in which it was existing immediately prior to the domestication), and may be enforced against it to the same extent as if said debts, liabilities and duties had originally been incurred or contracted by it in its capacity as such corporation. The rights, privileges, powers and interests in property of the non-United States entity, as well as the debts, liabilities and duties of the non-United States entity, shall not be deemed, as a consequence of the domestication, to have been transferred to the corporation to which such non-United States entity has domesticated for any purpose of the laws of the State of Delaware.

(j) Unless otherwise agreed or otherwise required under applicable non-Delaware law, the domesticating non-United States entity shall not be required to wind up its affairs or pay its liabilities and distribute its assets, and the domestication shall not be deemed to constitute a dissolution of such non-United States entity. If, following domestication, a non-United States entity that has become domesticated as a corporation of this State continues its existence in the foreign jurisdiction in which it was existing immediately prior to domestication, the corporation and such non-United States entity shall, for all purposes of the laws of the State of Delaware, constitute a single entity formed, incorporated, created or otherwise having come into being, as applicable, and existing under the laws of the State of Delaware and the laws of such foreign jurisdiction.

(k) In connection with a domestication under this section, shares of stock, rights or securities of, or interests in, the non-United States entity that is to be domesticated as a corporation of this State may be exchanged for or converted into cash, property, or shares of stock, rights or securities of such corporation or, in addition to or in lieu thereof, may be exchanged for or converted into cash, property, or shares of stock, rights or securities of, or interests in, another corporation or other entity or may be cancelled. (Last amended by Ch. 96, L. '11, eff. 8-1-11.)

Ch. 96, L. '11, eff. 8-1-11, added matter in italic.

Ch. 96, L. '11 Synopsis of Section 388

This Section amends Section 388 to clarify that the certificate of corporate domestication and the certificate of incorporation of a non-United States entity domesticating to Delaware as a Delaware corporation must be filed simultaneously with the Secretary of State and, to the extent such certificates are to have a post-filing effective date or time, such certificates must provide for the same effective date or time.

Ch. 30, L. '05 Synopsis of Section 388

The amendments to Section 388 provide that any non-United States entity may domesticate in Delaware. New subsections (i) and (j) clarify the effects of a domestication of a non-United States entity as a Delaware corporation. New subsection (k) confirms the flexibility permitted in the Code regarding a domestication as a Delaware corporation.

389 TEMPORARY TRANSFER OF DOMICILE INTO THIS STATE.—(a) As used in this section:

[1]*(1) The term "foreign jurisdiction" and the term "non-United States entity" shall have the same meanings as set forth in §388(a) of this title.*

(2) The terms "officers" and "directors" include, in addition to such persons, trustees, managers, partners and all other persons performing functions equivalent to those of officers and directors, however named or described in any relevant instrument.

(3) The term "emergency condition" shall be deemed to include but not be limited to any of the following:
    a. War or other armed conflict;
    b. Revolution or insurrection;

c. Invasion or occupation by foreign military forces;
d. Rioting or civil commotion of an extended nature;
e. Domination by a foreign power;
f. Expropriation, nationalization or confiscation of a material part of the assets or property of the [2]*non-United States entity*;
g. Impairment of the institution of private property (including private property held abroad);
h. The taking of any action under the laws of the United States whereby persons resident in the jurisdiction, the law of which governs the internal affairs of the [2]*non-United States entity*, might be treated as "enemies" or otherwise restricted under laws of the United States relating to trading with enemies of the United States;
i. The immediate threat of any of the foregoing; and
[3]*j. Such other event which, under the law of the jurisdiction governing the internal affairs of the non-United States entity, permits the non-United States entity to transfer its domicile.*
[4]*(b) Any non-United States entity may, subject to and upon compliance with this section, transfer its domicile (which term, as used in this section, shall be deemed to refer in addition to the seat, siège social or principal place of business or central administration of such entity, or any other equivalent thereto under applicable law) into this State, and may perform the acts described in this section, so long as the law by which the internal affairs of such entity are governed does not expressly prohibit such transfer.*
(c) Any [2]*non-United States entity* that shall propose to transfer its domicile into this State shall submit to the Secretary of State for the Secretary of State's review, at least 30 days prior to the proposed transfer of domicile, the following:
(1) A copy of its certificate of incorporation and bylaws (or the equivalent thereof under applicable law), certified as true and correct by the appropriate director, officer or government official;
[5]*(2) A certificate issued by an authorized official of the jurisdiction the law of which governs the internal affairs of the non-United States entity evidencing its existence;*
(3) A list indicating the person or persons who, in the event of a transfer pursuant to this section, shall be the authorized officers and directors of the [2]*non-United States entity*, together with evidence of their authority to act and their respective executed agreements in writing regarding service of process as set out in subsection (j) of this section;
(4) A certificate executed by the appropriate officer or director of the [2]*non-United States entity*, setting forth:
a. The name and address of its registered agent in this State;
b. A general description of the business in which it is engaged;
c. That the filing of such certificate has been duly authorized by any necessary action and does not violate the certificate of incorporation or bylaws (or equivalent thereof under applicable law) or any material agreement or instrument binding on such entity;
d. A list indicating the person or persons authorized to sign the written communications required by subsection (e) of this section;
e. An affirmation that such transfer is not expressly prohibited under the law by which the internal affairs of the [2]*non-United States entity* are governed; and
f. An undertaking that any transfer of domicile into this State will take place only in the event of an emergency condition in the jurisdiction the law of which governs the internal affairs of the [2]*non-United States entity* and that such transfer shall continue only so long as such emergency condition, in the judgment of the [2]*non-United States entity's* management, so requires; and
(5) The examination fee prescribed under §391 of this title.
[6]*If any of the documents referred to in paragraphs (1)-(5) of this subsection are not in English, a translation thereof, under oath of the translator, shall be attached thereto. If such documents satisfy the requirements of this section, and if the name of the non-United States entity meets the requirements of §102(a)(1) of this title, the Secretary of State shall notify the non-United States entity that such documents have been accepted for filing, and the records of the Secretary of State shall reflect such acceptance and such notification. In addition, the Secretary of State shall enter the name of the non-United States entity on the Secretary of State's reserved list to remain there so long as the non-United States entity*

§389

is in compliance with this section. No document submitted under this subsection shall be available for public inspection pursuant to Chapter 100 of Title 29 until, and unless, such entity effects a transfer of its domicile as provided in this section. The Secretary of State may waive the 30-day period and translation requirement provided for in this subsection upon request by such entity, supported by facts (including, without limitation, the existence of an emergency condition) justifying such waiver.

[7]*(d) On or before the March 1 in each year, prior to the transfer of its domicile as provided for in subsection (e) of this section, during any such transfer and, in the event that it desires to continue to be subject to a transfer of domicile under this section, after its domicile has ceased to be in this State, the non-United States entity shall file a certificate executed by an appropriate officer or director of the non-United States entity, certifying that the documents submitted pursuant to this section remain in full force and effect or attaching any amendments or supplements thereto and translated as required in subsection (c) of this section, together with the filing fee prescribed under §391 of this title. In the event that any non-United States entity fails to file the required certificate on or before March 1 in each year, all certificates and filings made pursuant to this section shall become null and void on March 2 in such year, and any proposed transfer thereafter shall be subject to all of the required submissions and the examination fee set forth in subsection (c) of this section.*

[8]*(e) If the Secretary of State accepts the documents submitted pursuant to subsection (c) of this section for filing, such entity may transfer its domicile to this State at any time by means of a written communication to such effect addressed to the Secretary of State, signed by 1 of the persons named on the list filed pursuant to subparagraph d. of paragraph (4) of subsection (c) of this section, and confirming that the statements made pursuant to paragraph (4) of subsection (c) of this section remain true and correct; provided, that if emergency conditions have affected ordinary means of communication, such notification may be made by telegram, telex, telecopy or other form of writing so long as a duly signed duplicate is received by the Secretary of State within 30 days thereafter. The records of the Secretary of State shall reflect the fact of such transfer. Upon the payment to the Secretary of State of the fee prescribed under §391 of this title, the Secretary of State shall certify that the non-United States entity has filed all documents and paid all fees required by this title. Such certificate of the Secretary of State shall be prima facie evidence of transfer by such non-United States entity of its domicile into this State.*

[9]*(f) Except to the extent expressly prohibited by the laws of this State, from and after the time that a non-United States entity transfers its domicile to this State pursuant to this section, the non-United States entity shall have all of the powers which it had immediately prior to such transfer under the law of the jurisdiction governing its internal affairs and the directors and officers designated pursuant to paragraph (3) of subsection (c) of this section, and their successors, may manage the business and affairs of the non-United States entity in accordance with the laws of such jurisdiction. Any such activity conducted pursuant to this section shall not be deemed to be doing business within this State for purposes of §371 of this title. Any reference in this section to the law of the jurisdiction governing the internal affairs of a non-United States entity which has transferred its domicile into this State shall be deemed to be a reference to such law as in effect immediately prior to the transfer of domicile.*

(g) For purposes of any action in the courts of this State, no [2]*non-United States entity which has obtained the certificate of the Secretary of State referred to in subsection (e) of this section shall be deemed to be an "enemy" person or entity for any purpose, including, without limitation, in relation to any claim of title to its assets, wherever located, or to its ability to institute suit in said courts.*

[10]*(h) The transfer by any non-United States entity of its domicile into this State shall not be deemed to affect any obligations or liabilities of such non-United States entity incurred prior to such transfer.*

[11]*(i) The directors of any non-United States entity which has transferred its domicile into this State may withhold from any holder of equity interests in such entity any amounts payable to such holder on account of dividends or other distributions, if the directors shall determine that such holder will not have the full benefit of such payment, so long as the*

directors shall make provision for the retention of such withheld payment in escrow or under some similar arrangement for the benefit of such holder.

[12](j) All process issued out of any court of this State, all orders made by any court of this State and all rules and notices of any kind required to be served on any non-United States entity which has transferred its domicile into this State may be served on the non-United States entity pursuant to §321 of this title in the same manner as if such entity were a corporation of this State. The directors of a non-United States entity which has transferred its domicile into this State shall agree in writing that they will be amenable to service of process by the same means as, and subject to the jurisdiction of the courts of this State to the same extent as are directors of corporations of this State, and such agreements shall be submitted to the Secretary of State for filing before the respective directors take office.

[13](k) Any non-United States entity which has transferred its domicile into this State may voluntarily return to the jurisdiction the law of which governs its internal affairs by filing with the Secretary of State an application to withdraw from this State. Such application shall be accompanied by a resolution of the directors of the non-United States entity authorizing such withdrawal and by a certificate of the highest diplomatic or consular official of such jurisdiction accredited to the United States indicating the consent of such jurisdiction to such withdrawal. The application shall also contain, or be accompanied by, the agreement of the non-United States entity that it may be served with process in this State in any proceeding for enforcement of any obligation of the non-United States entity arising prior to its withdrawal from this State, which agreement shall include the appointment of the Secretary of State as the agent of the non-United States entity to accept service of process in any such proceeding and shall specify the address to which a copy of process served upon the Secretary of State shall be mailed. Upon the payment of any fees and taxes owed to this State, the Secretary of State shall file the application and the non-United States entity's domicile shall, as of the time of filing, cease to be in this State. (Last amended by Ch. 30, L. '05, eff. 8-1-05.)

Ch. 30, L. '05, eff. 8-1-05, added matter in italic and deleted [1]"(1) The term "corporation" and the term "non-United States corporation" shall have the same meanings as set forth in §388(a) of this title."; [2]"corporation"; [3]"j. Such other event which, under the law of the jurisdiction governing the internal affairs of the corporation, permits the corporation to transfer its domicile."; [4]"(b) Any non-United States corporation may, subject to and upon compliance with this section, transfer its domicile (which term, as used in this section, shall be deemed to refer in addition to the seat, siege social, or principal place of business or central administration of such corporation, or any other equivalent thereto under applicable law) into this State, and may perform the acts described in this section, so long as the law by which the internal affairs of such corporation are governed does not expressly prohibit such transfer."; [5]"(2) A certificate issued by an authorized officer of the jurisdiction the law of which governs the internal affairs of the corporation evidencing its corporate existence;"; [6]"If any of the documents referred to in paragraphs (1)-(5) of this subsection are not in English, a translation thereof, under oath of the translator, shall be attached thereto. If such documents satisfy the requirements of this section, and if the name of the corporation meets the requirements of §102(a)(1) of this title, the Secretary of State shall notify the corporation that such documents have been accepted for filing, and the records of the Secretary of State shall reflect such acceptance and such notification. In addition, the Secretary of State shall enter the name of the corporation on the Secretary of State's reserved list to remain there so long as the corporation is in compliance with this section. No document submitted under this subsection shall be available for public inspection pursuant to Chapter 100 of Title 29 until, and unless, such corporation effects a transfer of its domicile as provided in this section. The Secretary of State may waive the 30-day period and translation requirement provided for in this subsection upon request by such corporation, supported by facts (including, without limitation, the existence of an emergency condition) justifying such waiver."; [7]"(d) On or before the 1st day of March in each year, prior to the transfer of its domicile as provided for in subsection (e) of this section, during any such transfer and, in the event that it desires to continue to be subject to a transfer of domicile under this section, after its domicile has ceased to be in this State, the corporation shall file a certificate executed by an appropriate officer or director of the corporation, certifying that the documents submitted pursuant to this section remain in full force and effect or attaching any amendments or supplements thereto and translated as required in subsection (c) of this section, together with the filing fee prescribed under §391 of this title. In the event that any corporation fails to file the required certificate on or before the 1st day of March in each year, all certificates and filings made pursuant to this section shall become null and void on the 2nd day of March in such year, and any proposed transfer thereafter shall be subject to all of the required submissions and the examination fee set forth in subsection (c) of this section."; [8]"(e) If the Secretary of State accepts the documents submitted pursuant to subsection (c) of this section for filing, such corporation may transfer its domicile to this State at any time by means of a written communication to such effect addressed to the Secretary of State, signed by one of the persons named on the list filed pursuant to subparagraph d. of paragraph (4) of subsection (c) of this section, and confirming that the statements made pursuant to paragraph (4) of subsection (c) of this section remain true and correct; provided, that if emergency conditions have affected ordinary means of communication, such notification may be made by telegram, telex, telecopy or other form of writing so long as a duly

§389

signed duplicate is received by the Secretary of State within 30 days thereafter. The records of the Secretary of State shall reflect the fact of such transfer. Upon the payment to the Secretary of State of the fee prescribed under §391 of this title, the Secretary of State shall certify that the corporation has filed all documents and paid all fees required by this title. Such certificate of the Secretary of State shall be prima facie evidence of transfer by such corporation of its domicile into this State."; [9]"(f) Except to the extent expressly prohibited by the laws of this State, from and after the time that a non-United States corporation transfers its domicile to this State pursuant to the provisions of this section, the corporation shall have all of the powers which it had immediately prior to such transfer under the law of the jurisdiction governing its internal affairs and the directors and officers designated pursuant to paragraph (3) of subsection (c) of this section, and their successors, may manage the business and affairs of the corporation in accordance with the laws of such jurisdiction. Any such activity conducted pursuant to this section shall not be deemed to be doing business within this State for purposes of §371 of this title. Any reference in this section to the law of the jurisdiction governing the internal affairs of a corporation which has transferred its domicile into this State shall be deemed to be a reference to such law as in effect immediately prior to the transfer of domicile."; [10]"(h) The transfer by any corporation of its domicile into this State shall not be deemed to affect any obligations or liabilities of such corporation incurred prior to such transfer."; [11]"(i) The directors of any corporation which has transferred its domicile into this State may withhold from any stockholder any amounts payable to such stockholder on account of dividends or other distributions, if the directors shall determine that such stockholder will not have the full benefit of such payment, so long as the directors shall make provision for the retention of such withheld payment in escrow or under some similar arrangement for the benefit of such stockholder."; [12]"(j) All process issued out of any court of this State, all orders made by any court of this State, and all rules and notices of any kind required to be served on any corporation which has transferred its domicile into this State may be served on the corporation pursuant to §321 of this title in the same manner as if such corporation were a corporation of this State. The directors of a corporation which has transferred its domicile into this State shall agree in writing that they will be amenable to service of process by the same means as, and subject to the jurisdiction of the courts of this State to the same extent as are directors of corporations of this State, and such agreements shall be submitted to the Secretary of State for filing before the respective directors take office."; and [13]"(k) Any corporation which has transferred its domicile into this State may voluntarily return to the jurisdiction the law of which governs its internal affairs by filing with the Secretary of State an application to withdraw from this State. Such application shall be accompanied by a resolution of the directors of the corporation authorizing such withdrawal and by a certificate of the highest diplomatic or consular officer of such jurisdiction accredited to the United States indicating the consent of such jurisdiction to such withdrawal. The application shall also contain, or be accompanied by, the agreement of the corporation that it may be served with process in this State in any proceeding for enforcement of any obligation of the corporation arising prior to its withdrawal from this State, which agreement shall include the appointment of the Secretary of State as the agent of the corporation to accept service of process in any such proceeding and shall specify the address to which a copy of process served upon the Secretary of State shall be mailed. Upon the payment of any fees and taxes owed to this State, the Secretary of State shall file the application and the corporation's domicile shall, as of the time of filing, cease to be in this State."

Ch. 30, L. '05 Synopsis of Section 389

The amendments to Section 389 reflect the newly defined terms "non-United States entity" and "foreign jurisdiction" in Section 388, Title 8, Delaware Code.

Ch. 339, L. '98 Synopsis of Section 389

The amendments to these Sections eliminate masculine references in the statutes, and replace them with gender neutral references.

390 TRANSFER, DOMESTICATION OR CONTINUANCE OF DOMESTIC CORPORATIONS.—(a) Upon compliance with the provisions of this section, any corporation existing under the laws of this State may transfer to or domesticate or continue in any foreign jurisdiction and, in connection therewith, may elect to continue its existence as a corporation of this State. As used in this section, the term:

(1) "Foreign jurisdiction" means any foreign country, or other foreign jurisdiction (other than the United States, any state, the District of Columbia, or any possession or territory of the United States); and

(2) "Resulting entity" means the entity formed, incorporated, created or otherwise coming into being as a consequence of the transfer of the corporation to, or its domestication or continuance in, a foreign jurisdiction pursuant to this section.

(b) The board of directors of the corporation which desires to transfer to or domesticate or continue in a foreign jurisdiction shall adopt a resolution approving such transfer, domestication or continuance specifying the foreign jurisdiction to which the corporation shall be transferred or in which the corporation shall be domesticated or continued and, if applicable, that in connection with such transfer, domestication or continuance the corporation's existence as a corporation of this State is to continue and recommending the approval of such transfer or domestication or continuance by the stockholders of the corporation. Such resolution shall be submitted to the stockholders of the corporation at an annual or special meeting. Due notice of the time, place and purpose of the meeting shall be mailed to each holder of stock, whether voting or nonvoting, of the corporation at the address of the stockholder as it appears on the records of the corporation, at least 20 days prior to the date of the meeting. At the meeting, the resolution shall be considered and a vote taken for its adoption or rejection. If all outstanding shares of stock of the corporation, whether voting or nonvoting, shall be voted for the adoption of the resolution, the corporation shall file with the Secretary of State a certificate of transfer if its existence as a corporation of this State is to cease or a certificate of transfer and domestic continuance if its existence as a corporation of this State is to continue, executed in accordance with §103 of this title, which certifies:

(1) The name of the corporation, and if it has been changed, the name under which it was originally incorporated.

(2) The date of filing of its original certificate of incorporation with the Secretary of State.

(3) The foreign jurisdiction to which the corporation shall be transferred or in which it shall be domesticated or continued and the name of the resulting entity.

(4) That the transfer, domestication or continuance of the corporation has been approved in accordance with the provisions of this section.

(5) In the case of a certificate of transfer, (i) that the existence of the corporation as a corporation of this State shall cease when the certificate of transfer becomes effective, and (ii) the agreement of the corporation that it may be served with process in this State in any proceeding for enforcement of any obligation of the corporation arising while it was a corporation of this State which shall also irrevocably appoint the Secretary of State as its agent to accept service of process in any such proceeding and specify the address to which a copy of such process shall be mailed by the Secretary of State. *Process may be served upon the Secretary of State under this subsection by means of electronic transmission but only as prescribed by the Secretary of State. The Secretary of State is authorized to issue such rules and regulations with respect to such service as the Secretary of State deems necessary or appropriate. In the event of service upon the Secretary of State in accordance with this subsection, the Secretary of State shall forthwith notify such corporation that has transferred out of the State of Delaware by letter, directed to such corporation that has transferred out of the State of Delaware at the address so specified, unless such corporation shall have designated in writing to the Secretary of State a different address for such purpose, in which case it shall be mailed to the last address designated. Such letter shall be sent by a mail or courier service that includes a record of mailing or deposit with the courier and a record of delivery evidenced by the signature of the recipient. Such letter shall enclose a copy of the process and any other papers served on the Secretary of State pursuant to this subsection. It shall be the duty of the plaintiff in the event of such service to serve process and any other papers in duplicate, to notify the Secretary of State that service is being effected pursuant to this subsection and to pay the Secretary of State the sum of $50 for the use of the State, which sum shall be taxed as part of the costs in the proceeding, if the plaintiff shall prevail therein. The Secretary of State shall maintain an alphabetical record of any such service setting forth the name of the plaintiff and the defendant, the title, docket number and nature of the proceeding in which process has been served, the fact that service has been effected pursuant to this subsection, the return date thereof, and the day and hour service was made. The Secretary of State shall not be required to retain such information longer than 5 years from receipt of the service of process.*

(6) In the case of a certificate of transfer and domestic continuance, that the corporation will continue to exist as a corporation of this State after the certificate of transfer and domestic continuance becomes effective.

(c) Upon the filing of a certificate of transfer in accordance with subsection (b) of this section and payment to the Secretary of State of all fees prescribed under this title, the Secretary of State shall certify that the corporation has filed all documents and paid all fees required by this title, and thereupon the corporation shall cease to exist as a corporation of this State at the time the certificate of transfer becomes effective in accordance with §103 of this title. Such certificate of the Secretary of State shall be prima facie evidence of the transfer, domestication or continuance by such corporation out of this State.

§390

(d) The transfer, domestication or continuance of a corporation out of this State in accordance with this section and the resulting cessation of its existence as a corporation of this State pursuant to a certificate of transfer shall not be deemed to affect any obligations or liabilities of the corporation incurred prior to such transfer, domestication or continuance, the personal liability of any person incurred prior to such transfer, domestication or continuance, or the choice of law applicable to the corporation with respect to matters arising prior to such transfer, domestication or continuance. Unless otherwise agreed or otherwise provided in the certificate of incorporation, the transfer, domestication or continuance of a corporation out of the State of Delaware in accordance with this section shall not require such corporation to wind up its affairs or pay its liabilities and distribute its assets under this title and shall not be deemed to constitute a dissolution of such corporation.

(e) If a corporation files a certificate of transfer and domestic continuance, after the time the certificate of transfer and domestic continuance becomes effective, the corporation shall continue to exist as a corporation of this State, and the law of the State of Delaware, including this title, shall apply to the corporation to the same extent as prior to such time. So long as a corporation continues to exist as a corporation of the State of Delaware following the filing of a certificate of transfer and domestic continuance, the continuing corporation and the resulting entity shall, for all purposes of the laws of the State of Delaware, constitute a single entity formed, incorporated, created or otherwise having come into being, as applicable, and existing under the laws of the State of Delaware and the laws of the foreign jurisdiction.

(f) When a corporation has transferred, domesticated or continued pursuant to this section, for all purposes of the laws of the State of Delaware, the resulting entity shall be deemed to be the same entity as the transferring, domesticating or continuing corporation and shall constitute a continuation of the existence of such corporation in the form of the resulting entity. When any transfer, domestication or continuance shall have become effective under this section, for all purposes of the laws of the State of Delaware, all of the rights, privileges and powers of the corporation that has transferred, domesticated or continued, and all property, real, personal and mixed, and all debts due to such corporation, as well as all other things and causes of action belonging to such corporation, shall remain vested in the resulting entity (and also in the corporation that has transferred, domesticated or continued, if and for so long as such corporation continues its existence as a corporation of this State) and shall be the property of such resulting entity (and also of the corporation that has transferred, domesticated or continued, if and for so long as such corporation continues its existence as a corporation of this State), and the title to any real property vested by deed or otherwise in such corporation shall not revert or be in any way impaired by reason of this title; but all rights of creditors and all liens upon any property of such corporation shall be preserved unimpaired, and all debts, liabilities and duties of such corporation shall remain attached to the resulting entity (and also to the corporation that has transferred, domesticated or continued, if and for so long as such corporation continues its existence as a corporation of this State), and may be enforced against it to the same extent as if said debts, liabilities and duties had originally been incurred or contracted by it in its capacity as such resulting entity. The rights, privileges, powers and interests in property of the corporation, as well as the debts, liabilities and duties of the corporation, shall not be deemed, as a consequence of the transfer, domestication or continuance, to have been transferred to the resulting entity for any purpose of the laws of the State of Delaware.

(g) In connection with a transfer, domestication or continuance under this section, shares of stock of the transferring, domesticating or continuing corporation may be exchanged for or converted into cash, property, or shares of stock, rights or securities of, or interests in, the resulting entity or, in addition to or in lieu thereof, may be exchanged for or converted into cash, property, or shares of stock, rights or securities of, or interests in, another corporation or other entity or may be cancelled.

(h) No vote of the stockholders of a corporation shall be necessary to authorize a transfer, domestication or continuance if no shares of the stock of such corporation shall have been issued prior to the adoption by the board of directors of the resolution approving the transfer, domestication or continuance.

(i) *Whenever it shall be desired to transfer to or domesticate or continue in any foreign jurisdiction any nonstock corporation, the governing body shall perform all the acts necessary to effect a transfer, domestication or continuance which are required by* this section to be performed by the board of directors of a corporation having capital stock. *If the members of a nonstock corporation are entitled to vote for the election of members of its governing body or are entitled under the certificate of incorporation or the bylaws of such corporation to vote on such transfer, domestication or continuance or on a merger, consolidation, or dissolution of the corporation, they, and any other holder of any membership interest in the corporation, shall perform all the acts necessary to effect a transfer, domestication or continuance which are required by this section to be performed by the stockholders of a corporation having capital stock. If there is no member entitled to vote thereon, nor any other holder of any membership interest in the corporation, the transfer, domestication or continuance of the corporation shall be authorized at a meeting of the governing body, upon the adoption of a resolution to transfer or domesticate or continue by the vote of a majority of members of its governing body then in office.* In all other respects, the method and proceedings for the transfer, domestication or continuance of a nonstock corporation shall conform as nearly as may be to the proceedings prescribed by this section for the transfer, domestication or continuance of corporations having capital stock. *In the case of a charitable nonstock corporation, due notice of the corporation's intent to effect a transfer, domestication or continuance shall be mailed to the Attorney General of the State of Delaware 10 days prior to the date of the proposed transfer, domestication or continuance.* (Last amended by Ch. 253, L. '10, eff. 8-1-10 and Ch. 290, L. '10, eff. 8-2-10.)

Ch. 253, L. '10, eff. 8-1-10, added matter in italic in paragraph (i). Ch. 290, L. '10, eff. 8-2-10, added matter in italic in paragraph (b)(5).

Ch. 290, L. '10 Synopsis of Section 390

These sections amend Sections 252(d), 256(d), 263(d), 264(d), 266(c)(6), 321(b), 376(b), 381(c), 381(d), 382(a), 382(c), and 390(b)(5), respectively, to allow for service of process upon the Secretary of State thereunder by means of electronic transmission but only as prescribed by the Secretary of State, to authorize the Secretary of State to issue such rules and regulations with respect to such service as the Secretary of State deems necessary or appropriate, and to enable the Secretary of State, in the event that service is effected through the Secretary of State in accordance therewith, to provide notice of service by letter sent by a mail or courier service that includes a record of mailing or deposit with the courier and a record of delivery evidenced by the signature of the recipient.

Ch. 253, L. '10 Synopsis of Section 390

Section 66 amends the DGCL to add new §390(i) to provide that nonstock corporations may transfer to or domesticate or continue in any foreign jurisdiction in a manner analogous to that of a stock corporation and, in the case of a charitable nonstock corporation, that the Attorney General of the State of Delaware must be provided with notice of the corporation's intent to effect a transfer, domestication or continuance 10 days prior to the date of the proposed transfer, domestication or continuance.

Ch. 30, L. '05 Synopsis of Section 390

The amendments to Section 390 create two types of filings under Section 390: a certificate of transfer when the Delaware corporation is not to continue its existence in Delaware and a certificate of transfer and domestic continuance when the Delaware corporation elects to continue its existence as a Delaware corporation. The amendments confirm that so long as a corporation continues to exist as a corporation of the State of Delaware the resulting entity is the same entity as existed prior to transfer. The amendments to subsections (d) and (e) and new subsection (f) clarify the effects of a transfer of a Delaware corporation. New subsection (g) confirms the flexibility permitted in the Code regarding a transfer of a Delaware corporation. New subsection (h) provides that if a transferring Delaware corporation has no outstanding capital stock, no vote of stockholders is required to authorize the transfer.

Ch. 120, L. '97 Synopsis of Section 390

As originally enacted in 1995, Section 390 prescribed a procedure by which a Delaware corporation could transfer to a jurisdiction outside the United States, whereupon its existence as a Delaware corporation would terminate. That procedure remains available.

The amendments to Section 390 add a new procedure by which a Delaware corporation may domesticate or continue in a jurisdiction outside the United States and also preserve its existence and status as a Delaware corporation. These amendments do not affect the validity of any action taken under other applicable law to incorporate, or domesticate or continue, in another jurisdiction and continue to exist as a Delaware corporation.

Ch. 79, L. '95 Synopsis of Section 390

New section 390 is intended to facilitate and simplify reincorporation of Delaware corporations in jurisdictions outside the United States upon the fulfilling of three requirements: a vote by 100% of the Delaware corporation's stockholders in favor of the transfer, the payment of all fees required by the General Corporation Law and the filing of a certificate of transfer with the Secretary of State. The transfer of the corporation out of Delaware is deemed not to affect any of the obligations or liabilities of the corporation incurred prior to the transfer. Upon the issuance of the certification by the Secretary of State that the certificate of transfer and required fees have been paid, the corporation no longer exists as a Delaware corporation.

SUBCHAPTER XVII. MISCELLANEOUS PROVISIONS

391 TAXES AND FEES PAYABLE TO SECRETARY OF STATE UPON FILING CERTIFICATE OR OTHER PAPER.—(a) The following taxes and fees shall be collected by and paid to the Secretary of State, for the use of the State:

(1) Upon the receipt for filing of an original certificate of incorporation, the tax shall be computed on the basis of 2 cents for each share of authorized capital stock having par value up to and including 20,000 shares, 1 cent for each share in excess of 20,000 shares up to and including 200,000 shares, and two-fifths of a cent for each share in excess of 200,000 shares; 1 cent for each share of authorized capital stock without par value up to and including 20,000 shares, one-half of a cent for each share in excess of 20,000 shares up to and including 2,000,000 shares, and two-fifths of a cent for each share in excess of 2,000,000 shares. In no case shall the amount paid be less than $15. For the purpose of computing the tax on par value stock each $100 unit of the authorized capital stock shall be counted as 1 taxable share.

(2) Upon the receipt for filing of a certificate of amendment of certificate of incorporation, or a certificate of amendment of certificate of incorporation before payment of capital, or a restated certificate of incorporation, increasing the authorized capital stock of a corporation, the tax shall be an amount equal to the difference between the tax computed at the foregoing rates upon the total authorized capital stock of the corporation including the proposed increase, and the tax computed at the foregoing rates upon the total authorized capital stock excluding the proposed increase. In no case shall the amount paid be less than $30.

(3) Upon the receipt for filing of a certificate of amendment of certificate of incorporation before payment of capital and not involving an increase of authorized capital stock, or an amendment to the certificate of incorporation not involving an increase of authorized capital stock, or a restated certificate of incorporation not involving an increase of authorized capital stock, or a certificate of retirement of stock, the tax to be paid shall be $30. For all other certificates relating to corporations, not otherwise provided for, the tax to be paid shall be $5.00. In *the* case of *exempt* corporations [1] no tax shall be paid.

(4) Upon the receipt for filing of a certificate of merger or consolidation of 2 or more corporations, the tax shall be an amount equal to the difference between the tax computed at the foregoing rates upon the total authorized capital stock of the corporation created by the merger or consolidation, and the tax so computed upon the aggregate amount of the total authorized capital stock of the constituent corporations. In no case shall the amount paid be less than $75. The foregoing tax shall be in addition to any tax or fee required under any other law of this State to be paid by any constituent entity that is not a corporation in connection with the filing of the certificate of merger or consolidation.

(5) Upon the receipt for filing of a certificate of dissolution, there shall be paid to and collected by the Secretary of State a tax of:

    a. Forty dollars ($40); or

b. Ten dollars ($10) in the case of a certificate of dissolution which certifies that:
1. The corporation has no assets and has ceased transacting business; and
2. The corporation, for each year since its incorporation in this State, has been required to pay only the minimum franchise tax then prescribed by §503 of this title; and
3. The corporation has paid all franchise taxes and fees due to or assessable by this State through the end of the year in which said certificate of dissolution is filed.

(6) Upon the receipt for filing of a certificate or other paper of surrender and withdrawal from the State by a foreign corporation, there shall be collected by and paid to the Secretary of State a tax of $10.

(7) For receiving and filing and/or indexing any certificate, affidavit, agreement or any other paper provided for by this chapter, for which no different fee is specifically prescribed, a fee of $115 in each case shall be paid to the Secretary of State. The fee in the case of a certificate of incorporation filed as required by §102 of this title shall be $25. For entering information from each instrument into the Delaware Corporation Information System in accordance with §103(c)(8) of this title, the fee shall be $5.
a. A certificate of dissolution which meets the criteria stated in paragraph (5)b. of this subsection shall not be subject to such fee; and
b. A certificate of incorporation filed in accordance with §102 of this title shall be subject to a fee of $25.

(8) For receiving and filing and/or indexing the annual report of a foreign corporation doing business in this State, a fee of $125 shall be paid. In the event of neglect, refusal or failure on the part of any foreign corporation to file the annual report with the Secretary of State on or before June 30 each year, the corporation shall pay a penalty of $125.

(9) For recording and indexing articles of association and other papers required by this chapter to be recorded by the Secretary of State, a fee computed on the basis of 1 cent a line shall be paid.

(10) For certifying copies of any paper on file provided by this chapter, a fee of $50 shall be paid for each copy certified. In addition, a fee of $2 per page shall be paid in each instance where the Secretary of State provides the copies of the document to be certified.

(11) For issuing any certificate of the Secretary of State other than a certification of a copy under paragraph (10) of this subsection, or a certificate that recites all of a corporation's filings with the Secretary of State, a fee of $50 shall be paid for each certificate. For issuing any certificate of the Secretary of State that recites all of a corporation's filings with the Secretary of State, a fee of $175 shall be paid for each certificate.

(12) For filing in the office of the Secretary of State any certificate of change of location or change of registered agent, as provided in §133 of this title, there shall be collected by and paid to the Secretary of State a fee of $50, provided that no fee shall be charged pursuant to §103(c)(6) and §103(c)(7) of this title.

(13) For filing in the office of the Secretary of State any certificate of change of address or change of name of registered agent, as provided in §134 of this title, there shall be collected by and paid to the Secretary of State a fee of $50, plus the same fees for receiving, filing, indexing, copying and certifying the same as are charged in the case of filing a certificate of incorporation.

(14) For filing in the office of the Secretary of State any certificate of resignation of a registered agent and appointment of a successor, as provided in §135 of this title, there shall be collected by and paid to the Secretary of State a fee of $50.

(15) For filing in the office of the Secretary of State, any certificate of resignation of a registered agent without appointment of a successor, as provided in §§136 and 377 of this title, there shall be collected by and paid to the Secretary of State a fee of $2 for each corporation whose registered agent has resigned by such certificate.

(16) For preparing and providing a written report of a record search, a fee of $50 shall be paid.

(17) For preclearance of any document for filing, a fee of $250 shall be paid.

(18) For receiving and filing and/or indexing an annual franchise tax report of a corporation provided for by §502 of this title, a fee of $25 shall be paid by exempt corporations and a fee of $50 shall be paid by all other corporations.

(19) For receiving and filing and/or indexing by the Secretary of State of a certificate of domestication and certificate of incorporation prescribed in §388(d) of this title, a fee of

$165, plus the tax and fee payable upon the receipt for filing of an original certificate of incorporation, shall be paid.

(20) For receiving, reviewing and filing and/or indexing by the Secretary of State of the documents prescribed in §389(c) of this title, a fee of $10,000 shall be paid.

(21) For receiving, reviewing and filing and/or indexing by the Secretary of State of the documents prescribed in §389(d) of this title, an annual fee of $2,500 shall be paid.

(22) Except as provided in this section, the fees of the Secretary of State shall be as provided for in §2315 of Title 29.

(23) In the case of exempt corporations, the total fees payable to the Secretary of State upon the filing of a Certificate of Change of Registered Agent and/or Registered Office or a Certificate of Revival shall be $5 and such filings shall be exempt from any fees or assessments pursuant to the requirements of §103(c)(6) and (c)(7) of this title.

(24) For accepting a corporate name reservation application, an application for renewal of a corporate name reservation, or a notice of transfer or cancellation of a corporate name reservation, there shall be collected by and paid to the Secretary of State a fee of up to $75.

(25) For receiving and filing and/or indexing by the Secretary of State of a certificate of transfer or a certificate of continuance prescribed in §390 of this title, a fee of $1,000 shall be paid.

(26) For receiving and filing and/or indexing by the Secretary of State of a certificate of conversion and certificate of incorporation prescribed in §265 of this title, a fee of $115, plus the tax and fee payable upon the receipt for filing of an original certificate of incorporation, shall be paid.

(27) For receiving and filing and/or indexing by the Secretary of State of a certificate of conversion prescribed in §266 of this title, a fee of $165 shall be paid.

(b)(1) For the purpose of computing the taxes prescribed in paragraphs (1), (2) and (4) of subsection (a) of this section the authorized capital stock of a corporation shall be considered to be the total number of shares which the corporation is authorized to issue, whether or not the total number of shares that may be outstanding at any one time be limited to a less number.

(2) For the purpose of computing the taxes prescribed in paragraphs (2) and (3) of subsection (a) of this section, a certificate of amendment of certificate of incorporation, or an amended certificate of incorporation before payment of capital, or a restated certificate of incorporation, shall be considered as increasing the authorized capital stock of a corporation provided it involves an increase in the number of shares, or an increase in the par value of shares, or a change of shares with par value into shares without par value, or a change of shares without par value into shares with par value, or any combination of 2 or more of the above changes, and provided further that the tax computed at the rates set forth in paragraph (1) of subsection (a) of this section upon the total authorized capital stock of the corporation including the proposed change or changes exceeds the tax so computed upon the total authorized stock of the corporation excluding such change or changes.

(c) The Secretary of State may issue photocopies or electronic image copies of instruments on file, as well as instruments, documents and other papers not on file, and for all such photocopies or electronic image copies which are not certified by the Secretary of State, a fee of $10 shall be paid for the first page and $2 for each additional page. The Secretary of State may also issue microfiche copies of instruments on file as well as instruments, documents and other papers not on file, and for each such microfiche a fee of $2 shall be paid therefor. Notwithstanding Delaware's Freedom of Information Act or other provision of this Code granting access to public records, the Secretary of State shall issue only photocopies, microfiche or electronic image copies of records in exchange for the fees described above.

(d) No fees for the use of the State shall be charged or collected from any corporation incorporated for the drainage and reclamation of lowlands or for the amendment or renewal of the charter of such corporation.

(e) The Secretary of State may in the Secretary of State's discretion permit the extension of credit for the taxes or fees required by this section upon such terms as the Secretary of State shall deem to be appropriate.

(f) The Secretary of State shall retain from the revenue collected from the taxes or fees required by this section a sum sufficient to provide at all times a fund of at least $500, but not more than $1,500, from which the Secretary of State may refund any payment made pursuant to this section to the extent that it exceeds the taxes or fees required by this section. The fund shall be deposited in the financial institution which is the legal depository of state moneys to the credit of the Secretary of State and shall be disbursable on order of the Secretary of State.

(g) The Secretary of State may in the Secretary of State's discretion charge a fee of $60 for each check received for payment of any fee or tax under Chapter 1 or Chapter 6 of this title that is returned due to insufficient funds or as the result of a stop payment order.

(h) In addition to those fees charged under subsections (a) and (c) of this section, there shall be collected by and paid to the Secretary of State the following:

(1) For all services described in subsection (a) of this section that are requested to be completed within 30 minutes on the same day as the day of the request, an additional sum of up to $7,500 and for all services described in subsections (a) and (c) of this section that are requested to be completed within 1 hour on the same day as the day of the request, an additional sum of up to $1,000 and for all services described in subsections (a) and (c) of this section that are requested to be completed within 2 hours on the same day as the day of the request, an additional sum of up to $500; and

(2) For all services described in subsections (a) and (c) of this section that are requested to be completed within the same day as the day of the request, an additional sum of up to $300; and

(3) For all services described in subsections (a) and (c) of this section that are requested to be completed within a 24-hour period from the time of the request, an additional sum of up to $150.

The Secretary of State shall establish (and may from time to time alter or amend) a schedule of specific fees payable pursuant to this subsection.

(i) A domestic corporation or a foreign corporation registered to do business in this State that files with the Secretary of State any instrument or certificate, and in connection therewith, neglects, refuses or fails to pay any fee or tax under Chapter 1 or Chapter 6 of this title shall, after written demand therefor by the Secretary of State by mail addressed to such domestic corporation or foreign corporation in care of its registered agent in this State, cease to be in good standing as a domestic corporation or registered as a foreign corporation in this State on the 90th day following the date of mailing of such demand, unless such fee or tax and, if applicable, the fee provided for in subsection (g) of this section are paid in full prior to the 90th day following the date of mailing of such demand. A domestic corporation that has ceased to be in good standing or a foreign corporation that has ceased to be registered by reason of the neglect, refusal or failure to pay any such fee or tax shall be restored to and have the status of a domestic corporation in good standing or a foreign corporation that is registered in this State upon the payment of the fee or tax which such domestic corporation or foreign corporation neglected, refused or failed to pay together with the fee provided for in subsection (g) of this section, if applicable. The Secretary of State shall not accept for filing any instrument authorized to be filed with the Secretary of State under this title in respect of any domestic corporation that is not in good standing or any foreign corporation that has ceased to be registered by reason of the neglect, refusal or failure to pay any such fee or tax, and shall not issue any certificate of good standing with respect to such domestic corporation or foreign corporation, unless and until such domestic corporation or foreign corporation shall have been restored to and have the status of a domestic corporation in good standing or a foreign corporation duly registered in this State.

(j) As used in this section, the term "exempt corporation" shall have the meaning given to it in §501(b) of this title. (Last amended by Ch. 96, L. '11, eff. 8-1-11.)

Ch. 96, L. '11, eff. 8-1-11, added matter in italic and deleted [1]"created solely for religious or charitable purposes".

Ch. 96, L. '11 Synopsis of Section 391

. The amendments to Section 391 are intended to conform Section 391 to Section 501(b) which was amended in 2010 to adopt the definition of "exempt corporation" for those corporations not subject to paying franchise taxes.

Ch. 253, L. '10 Synopsis of Section 391

Section 67 amends §391(j) of the DGCL to refer to the definition of "exempt corporation" in new §501(b) of Title 8.

Ch. 78, L. '09 Synopsis of Section 391

This Act increases various fees and taxes assessed by the Delaware Secretary of State.

Ch. 286, L. '08 Synopsis of Section 391

This Act increases the annual report fee for foreign corporations from $60 to $100 and increases the rates for computation of the annual franchise tax.

Ch. 306, L. '06 Synopsis of Section 391

Section 7 amends §391 to provide that a fee of up to $75 shall be collected by and paid to the Secretary of State for accepting a corporate name reservation application as well as an application for renewal of a corporate name reservation or a notice of transfer or cancellation of a corporate name reservation.

Ch. 51, L. '03 Synopsis of Section 391

Increases the fee for entering information from each instrument into the Delaware Corporation Information System from $20 to $25 and eliminates the exception that provides a lower fee for entering such information for a certificate of incorporation.

Increases the annual report fee for foreign corporations from $50 to $60 and increases the penalty for neglect, refusal, or failure to file the annual report from $50 to $100.

Increases the fee for certifying copies from $20 and $1 per page to $30 and $2 per page.

Increases the fee for a short form certificate of good standing from $20 to $30 and increases the fee for a long form certificate of good standing from $100 to $125.

Clarifies the fees for receiving, filing, indexing, copying and certifying an instrument filed with the Secretary of State to change the location of a corporation's registered office or to change a corporation's registered agent.

Increases the annual franchise tax report fee from $20 to $25.

Increases the fee for receiving and filing and/or indexing a certificate of conversion from a domestic corporation to another entity from $50 to $100.

Increases the fee for uncertified copies of instruments, documents and other papers from $5 for the first page and $1 for each additional page to $10 for the first page and $2 for each additional page.

Increases the amount the Secretary of State may charge for each check received for payment of fees that is returned for insufficient funds or as the result of a stop payment order from $25 to $60.

Ch. 118, L. '03 Synopsis of Section 391

This Bill establishes a $20 courthouse municipality fee to be assessed on limited liability company (LLC) filings. The fee is expected to raise $1.6 million to be disturbed to the municipalities designated as the places of holding the Court of Chancery. The fee will be distributed to the municipality in the county in which a business entity's registered office is located. To ensure that Delaware's LLC filing fees remain competitive, the Bill maintains the State's aggregate formation fee of $90 and the aggregate amending filing fee of $100.

Ch. 9, L. '03 Synopsis of Section 391

These Amendments clarify the general rule that the filing date of an instrument filed with the Secretary of State is the date and time of delivery of the instrument and the limited exceptions to this rule.

To further enhance service to Delaware corporations, the amendment to Section 391(h)(1) also enables the Secretary of State to offer a new "1-hour" expedited service to complement the Secretary of State's existing "2-hour" service offering.

Ch. 123, L. '99 Synopsis of Section 391

The additions of subsections (a)(25) and (a)(26) to §391 provide the applicable fees in connection with filings under §§265 and 266.

Ch. 339, L. '98 Synopsis of Section 391

The amendments to these Sections eliminate masculine references in the statutes, and replace them with gender neutral references.

Ch. 120, L. '97 Synopsis of Section 391

The amendment to Section 391(a)(23) adds corporate name reservations made by hand delivery or mail to telephone reservations subject to a fee of $10.

Section 391(a)(24) is amended to reflect the new procedure created by the amendment to Section 390.

Ch. 79, L. '95 Synopsis of Section 391

New section 390 is intended to facilitate and simplify reincorporation of Delaware corporations in jurisdictions outside the United States upon the fulfilling of three requirements: a vote by 100% of the Delaware corporation's stockholders in favor of the transfer, the payment of all fees required by the General Corporation Law and the filing of a certificate of transfer with the Secretary of State. The transfer of the corporation out of Delaware is deemed not to affect any of the obligations or liabilities of the corporation incurred prior to the transfer. Upon the issuance of the certification by the Secretary of State that the certificate of transfer and required fees have been paid, the corporation no longer exists as a Delaware corporation.

Ch. 245, L. '94 Synopsis of Section 391

This Amendment reflects the enhancements to Delaware's corporate information system and the ability to offer electronic image copies upon request. The Amendment confirms that all requests for information under Delaware's Freedom of Information Act or similar provisions shall comply with the established statutory fee structure and shall seek information in photocopy, microfiche, or electronic image format. Requests for information in other formats including computer diskettes or magnetic media shall not be honored. This Amendment confirms the legislative intent and the current practice to obtain established fees for corporate information furnished by the Division of Corporations.

Commentary to Section 391

The amendment to Section 391 by Ch. 52, L. '93, eff. 6-25-93, allows the Division of Corporations to charge a fee of up to $500 for two-hour same day processing of corporate documents.

.1 **Redesignation.**—Corporation that adopted single resolution to amend charter to (1) increase number of authorized shares of common stock and (2) redesignate all common stock as no par shares and then filed two separate certificates of amendment covering each aspect was obligated to pay tax of $10 rather than $318,050 upon second filing because redesignation was separate transaction that did not increase authorized capital stock. *Chrysler Corp v State of Delaware, 457 A2d 345 (1983).*

392 IMPROPERLY RECORDED CERTIFICATES OR OTHER DOCUMENTS; EFFECT.—(Repealed by Ch. 587, L. '96, eff. 11-24-97, date that Secretary of State certified installation and functioning of computer hardware and software in recorder's offices.)

Prior to its repeal by Ch. 587, L. '96, eff. 11-24-97, this section read as follows: "In case any certificate or other document of any kind required by any of the provisions of this chapter to be recorded in the office of any of the recorders of the several counties of this State shall have heretofore been, or shall hereafter be, recorded in the office of the recorder of a county of this State other than the county in which the certificate or other document is required to be recorded, the subsequent recording of the document in the recorder's office in which the certificate or other document should have been recorded shall validate and confirm all acts done under or pursuant to the certificate or document, with like force and effect as if the certificate or document had been originally recorded as required by this chapter."

393 RIGHTS, LIABILITIES AND DUTIES UNDER PRIOR STATUTES.—All rights, privileges and immunities vested or accrued by and under any laws enacted prior to the adoption or amendment of this chapter, all suits pending, all rights of action conferred, and all duties, restrictions, liabilities and penalties imposed or required by and under laws enacted prior to the adoption or amendment of this chapter, shall not be impaired, diminished or affected by this chapter.

394 RESERVED POWER OF STATE TO AMEND OR REPEAL CHAPTER; CHAPTER PART OF CORPORATION'S CHARTER OR CERTIFICATE OF INCORPORATION.—This chapter may be amended or repealed, at the pleasure of the General Assembly, but any amendment or repeal shall not take away or impair any remedy under this chapter against any corporation or its officers for any liability which shall have been previously incurred. This chapter and all amendments thereof shall be a part of the charter or certificate of incorporation of every corporation except so far as the same are inapplicable and inappropriate to the objects of the corporation.

.1 **Legislative powers.**—Stock is held subject to power of legislature to amend law so as to enlarge power of amending provisions of certificate of incorporation relating to classification and relative rights of stock. *Davis v Louisville Gas & Elec Co, 142 A 654 (Ch Ct 1928).*

Under reserved power, the corporate charter may be repealed or amended, and, within limits, the interrelations of state, corporation, and stockholders may be changed; but neither vested property rights nor the obligations of contracts of third persons may be destroyed or impaired. *Combes v Getz, 285 US 434 (1932).*

Accrued, unpaid, cumulative dividends on preferred stock became a vested interest, which, absent prior consent, could not be extinguished by charter amendment. A sinking fund provision in the charter was a contractual commitment and an amendment that abolished such provision was invalid. *Yoakam v Providence Biltmore Hotel Co, 34 F2d 533 (D RI 1929).*

Charter amendment could not wipe out past dividend preferences that had accrued. *Keller v Wilson & Co, 190 A 115 (1936).*

GCL amendments govern all corporations including those whose creation antedated them. *Gow v Consolidated Coppermines Corp, 165 A 136 (Ch Ct 1933).*

.2 **Amendatory powers.**—A corporate charter may be amended to increase an authorized capital stock issue by appropriate vote of stockholders. Validity of amendment depends on construction of charter, including GCL provisions that are impliedly written into it. *Hartford Acc & Ind Co v W S Dickey Clay Mfg Co, 21 A2d 178 (Ch Ct 1941),* aff'd, *24 A2d 315 (1942).*

395 CORPORATIONS USING "TRUST" IN NAME, ADVERTISEMENTS AND OTHERWISE; RESTRICTIONS; VIOLATIONS AND PENALTIES; EXCEPTIONS.—(a) [1] *Except as provided below in subsection (d) of this section, every corporation of this State using the word "trust" as part of its name, except a corporation regulated under the Bank Holding Company Act of 1956, 12 U.S.C. §1841 et seq., or* [2] *section 10 of the Home Owners' Loan Act, 12 U.S.C. §1467a et seq., as those statutes shall from time to time be amended, shall be under the supervision of the State Bank Commissioner of this State and shall make not less than 2 reports during each year to the Commissioner, according to the form which shall be prescribed by the Commissioner, verified by the oaths or affirmations of the president or vice-president, and the treasurer or secretary of the corporation, and attested by the signatures of at least 3 directors.

(b) [3] *Except as provided below in subsection (d) of this section, no* corporation of this State shall use the word "trust" as part of its name, except a corporation reporting to and under the supervision of the State Bank Commissioner of this State or a corporation regulated under the Bank Holding Company Act of 1956, 12 U.S.C. §1841 et seq., [2] *§10 of the Home Owners' Loan Act, 12 U.S.C. §1467a et seq., as those statutes shall from time to time be amended.* [4] *Except as provided below in subsection (d) of this section, the* name of any such corporation shall not be amended so as to include the word "trust" unless such corporation shall report to and be under the supervision of the Commissioner, or unless it is regulated under the Bank Holding Company Act of 1956 or the Savings and Loan Holding Company Act.

(c) No corporation of this State, except corporations reporting to and under the supervision of the State Bank Commissioner of this State or corporations regulated under the Bank Holding Company Act of 1956, 12 U.S.C. §1841 et seq., or [2] *§10 of the Home Owners' Loan Act, 12 U.S.C. §1467a et seq., as those statutes shall from time to time be amended,* shall advertise or put forth any sign as a trust company, or in any way solicit or receive deposits or transact business as a trust company [5].

(d) The requirements and restrictions set forth above in subsections (a) and (b) of this section shall not apply to, and shall not be construed to prevent the use of the word "trust" as part of the name of, a corporation that is not subject to the supervision of the State Bank Commissioner of this State and that is not regulated under the Bank Holding Company Act of 1956, 12 U.S.C. §1841 et seq., or §10 of the Home Owners' Loan Act, 12 U.S.C. §1467a et seq., where use of the word "trust" as part of such corporation's name clearly:

(1) Does not refer to a trust business;

(2) Is not likely to mislead the public into believing that the nature of the business of the corporation includes activities that fall under the supervision of the State Bank Commissioner of this State or that are regulated under the Bank Holding Company Act of 1956,

12 U.S.C. §1841 et seq., or §10 of the Home Owners' Loan Act, 12 U.S.C. §1467a et seq., and

(3) Will not otherwise lead to a pattern and practice of abuse that might cause harm to the interests of the public or the State, as determined by the Director of the Division of Corporations and the State Bank Commissioner. (Last amended by Ch. 96, L. '11, eff. 8-1-11.)

> Ch. 96, L. '11, eff. 8-1-11, added matter in italic and deleted [1]"Every"; [2]"the Savings and Loan Holding Company Act, 12 U.S.C. §1730a et seq."; [3]"No"; [4]"The"; and [5]", or use the word "trust" as a part of such corporation's name".

Ch. 96, L. '11 Synopsis of Section 395

These sections amend Sections 102 and 395 to give the Director of the Division of Corporations and the State Bank Commissioner the discretion to waive certain requirements and restrictions that apply when a corporation has the word "trust" in its name, provided that the use of the word "trust" is clearly not purporting to refer to a trust business. Section 2 also includes in §102(a)(1) the restriction on the use of the word "trust" in a corporation's name so that all statutory name restrictions in Title 8 of the Code are referred to in that section. Sections 16, 17 and 18 also update the statutory reference to the Savings and Loan Holding Company Act, which was moved to section 10 of the Home Owners' Loan Act.

Ch. 298, L. '02 Synopsis of Section 395

The amendments to Section 395 correct the reference to the Savings and Loan Holding Company Act in subsection (b) and limit the application of subsection (c) exclusively to corporations (and not other persons and entities).

Ch. 339, L. '98 Synopsis of Section 395

The amendments to these Sections eliminate masculine references in the statutes, and replace them with gender neutral references.

396 PUBLICATION OF CHAPTER BY SECRETARY OF STATE; DISTRIBUTION.—The Secretary of State may have printed, from time to time as [1]*the Secretary of State* deems necessary, pamphlet copies of this chapter, and [1]*the Secretary of State* shall dispose of the copies to persons and corporations desiring the same for a sum not exceeding the cost of printing. The money received from the sale of the copies shall be disposed of as are other fees of the office of the Secretary of State. Nothing in this section shall prevent the free distribution of single pamphlet copies of this chapter by the Secretary of State, for the printing of which provision is made from time to time by joint resolution of the General Assembly. (Last amended by Ch. 339, L. '98, eff. 7-1-98.)

> Ch. 339, L. '98, eff. 7-1-98, added matter in italic and deleted [1]"he".

Ch. 339, L. '98 Synopsis of Section 396

The amendments to these Sections eliminate masculine references in the statutes, and replace them with gender neutral references.

397 PENALTY FOR UNAUTHORIZED PUBLICATION OF CHAPTER.—Whoever prints or publishes the provisions of this chapter without the authority of the Secretary of State of this State, shall be fined not more than $500 or imprisoned not more than 3 months, or both.

398 SHORT TITLE.—This chapter shall be known and may be identified and referred to as the "General Corporation Law of the State of Delaware."

[The page following this is Corp.—501]

CHAPTER 5. CORPORATION FRANCHISE TAX

501 CORPORATIONS SUBJECT TO AND EXEMPT FROM FRANCHISE TAX.—(a) Every telegraph, telephone or cable company, every electric company organized for the production and/or distribution of light, heat or power, every company organized for the purpose of producing and/or distributing steam, heat or power, every company organized for the purpose of the production and/or distribution and/or sale of gas, every parlor, palace or sleeping car company, every express company, every pipeline company, every life insurance company, every other insurance company of whatever kind *(other than a captive insurance company licensed under Chapter 69 of Title 18)* and every corporation now existing or hereafter to be incorporated under the laws of this State, shall pay an annual tax, for the use of the State, by way of license for the corporate franchise as prescribed in this chapter. No such tax shall be paid by any exempt corporation, any banking corporation, savings bank [1], *building and loan association or any captive insurance company licensed under Chapter 69 of Title 18*, or any corporation for drainage and reclamation of lowlands [2].

(b) As used in this chapter, the term "exempt corporation" shall be defined as any corporation organized under Chapter 1 of this title that:

(1) Is exempt from taxation under §501(c) of the United States Internal Revenue Code (26 U.S.C. §501(c)) or any similar provisions of the Internal Revenue Code, or any successor provisions;

(2) Qualifies as a civic organization under §8110(a)(1) of Title 9 or §6840(4) of Title 16;

(3) Qualifies as a charitable/fraternal organization under §2593(1) of Title 6;

(4) Is listed in §8106(a) of Title 9;

(5) Is organized primarily or exclusively for religious or charitable purposes, *or is a religious corporation or purely charitable or educational association, or is a company, association or society, which, by its certificate of incorporation, has for its object the assistance of sick, needy or disabled members, or the defraying of funeral expenses of deceased members, or to provide for the wants of the widows or widowers and families after death of its members;* or

(6)a. Is organized not for profit; and

b. No part of its net earnings inures to the benefit of any member or individual. (Last amended by Ch. 96, L. '11, eff. 8-1-11.)

Ch. 96, L. '11, eff. 8-1-11, added matter in italic and deleted [1]"or building and loan association" and [2]", or religious corporation, or purely charitable or educational association, or any company, association or society, which, by its certificate of incorporation, shall have for its object the assistance of sick, needy or disabled members, or the defraying of funeral expenses of deceased members, or to provide for the wants of the widows and families after death of its members".

Ch. 96, L. '11 Synopsis of Section 501

These Sections amend Section 501 to clarify that captive insurance companies licensed under chapter 69 of Title 18 are not required to pay annual franchise taxes and to clarify that the definition of "exempt corporation" includes a religious corporation or purely charitable or educational association, and a company, association or society, which, by its certificate of incorporation, has for its object the assistance of sick, needy or disabled members, or the defraying of funeral expenses of deceased members, or to provide for the wants of the widows and families after death of its members.

Ch. 253, L. '10 Synopsis of Section 501

Section 68 amends §501 of Chapter 5 of Title 8 to incorporate the definition of "exempt corporation," which has been expanded to include stock corporations, and to clarify that exempt corporations are exempt from the franchise tax.

502 ANNUAL FRANCHISE TAX REPORT; CONTENTS; FAILURE TO FILE AND PAY TAX; DUTIES OF SECRETARY OF STATE.—(a) Annually on or before March 1, every corporation now existing or hereafter incorporated under Chapter 1 of this title or which has accepted the Constitution of this State, shall make an annual franchise tax report to the Secretary of State. The report shall be made on a form designated by the Secretary of State and shall be signed by the corporation's president, secretary, treasurer or other proper officer duly authorized so to act, or by any of its directors, or by any incorporator in the event its board of directors shall not have been elected. The fact that an individual's name is signed on the report shall be prima facie evidence that such individual is authorized to certify the report on behalf of the corporation; however, the official title or position of the individual signing the corporate report shall be designated. The report shall contain the following information:

(1) The location of its registered office in this State, stated with the degree of particularity required by paragraph (2) of subsection (a) of §102 of this title;

(2) The name of the agent upon whom service of process against the corporation may be served;

(3) The location (city, town, street and number of same, if number there be) of the principal place of business of the corporation;

(4) The names and addresses of all the directors as of the filing date of the report and the name and address of the officer who signs the report;

(5) The number of shares and the par value per share of each class of capital stock having a par value and the number of shares of each class of stock without par value which the corporation is authorized to issue;

(6) If exempt from taxation for any cause, the specific facts entitling the corporation to exemption from taxation; and

(7) Such additional information, schedules and attachments as the Secretary shall require to ascertain the franchise tax due to the State.

(b) If any officer or director of a corporation required to make an annual franchise tax report to the Secretary of State shall knowingly make any false statement in the report, such officer or director shall be guilty of perjury.

(c) If the annual franchise tax report and the franchise tax due are not filed or paid by the corporation as required by this chapter, the Secretary of State shall ascertain and fix the amount of the franchise tax as determined in the manner prescribed by §503(a) of this title and the amount so fixed by the Secretary of State shall stand as the basis of taxation under the provisions of this chapter unless the corporation shall thereafter elect to compute the franchise tax in the manner prescribed by §503(a)(2) of this title by filing the annual franchise tax report and complying with the provisions of §503(b) of this title. In the event of neglect, refusal or failure on the part of any corporation to file a complete annual franchise tax report with the Secretary of State on or before March 1, the corporation shall pay the sum of [1] *$125* to be recovered by adding that amount to the franchise tax as herein determined and fixed, and such additional sum shall become a part of the franchise tax as so determined and fixed, and shall be collected in the same manner and subject to the same penalties.

(d) In case any corporation shall fail to file its annual franchise tax report and the franchise tax due within the time required by this chapter, and in case the agent in charge of the registered office of any corporation upon whom process against the corporation may be served shall die, resign, refuse to act as such, remove from this State or cannot with due diligence be found, it shall be lawful while default continues to serve process against the corporation upon the Secretary of State. Such service upon the Secretary of State shall be made in the manner and shall have the effect stated in subsection (b) of §321 of this title and shall be governed in all respects by said subsection.

(e) The Secretary of State shall safely keep all reports returned in such manner as they may be open to the inspection of all persons pursuant to the provisions set forth in Chapter 100 of Title 29. Any tax information provided pursuant to paragraph (a)(7) of this section, contained on annual franchise tax reports filed after tax year 2006 shall not be deemed public.

(f) The Secretary of State shall not issue certificates of good standing that pertain to any corporation that has an unpaid franchise tax balance due to the State or does not have on file a completed annual franchise tax report for the relevant time period. (Last amended by Ch. 78, L. '09, eff. for the tax year beginning on 1-1-10.)

Ch. 78, L. '09, eff. for the tax year beginning on 1-1-10, added matter in italic and deleted [1]"$100".

Ch. 78, L. '09 Synopsis of Section 502

This Act increases various fees and taxes assessed by the Delaware Secretary of State.

Ch. 306, L. '06 Synopsis of Section 502

Sections 18 through 26 amend §§502, 503, 510, 511, 514, and 517 to require Delaware corporations to file a complete annual franchise tax report including, among other things, the names and addresses of all of the corporation's directors as of the filing date of the report and the name and address of the officer who signs the report, and require the Secretary of State to declare void the charter of any corporation that fails to file a complete annual franchise tax report.

Ch. 51, L. '03 Synopsis of Section 502

Increases the tax for neglect, refusal, or failure to file an annual franchise tax report from $50 to $100.

Ch. 339, L. '98 Synopsis of Section 502

The amendments to these Sections eliminate masculine references in the statutes, and replace them with gender neutral references.

Commentary to Section 502

The amendment to Section 502(a) by Ch. 53, L. '93, eff. 6-30-93, reduces the number of officers which corporations must name on their annual franchise tax reports to no more than two, but requires that any officer who signs the report be one of those two. The amendment also eliminates the need to state the next annual meeting date on the reports. The annual franchise tax report issued by the Division of Corporations only has limited space. These changes should reduce the use of attachments to the reports which become burdensome and hamper the timely processing of these documents.

The amendment to Section 502(f) by Ch. 54, L. '93, eff. 6-30-93, corrects an error which currently appears in the Delaware Code by removing the term "blank" annual franchise tax reports. The Delaware Division of Corporations does not forward blank annual franchise tax reports.

503 [Eff. until January 1, 2014] RATES AND COMPUTATION OF FRANCHISE TAX.—(a) All corporations accepting the provisions of the Constitution of this State and coming under Chapter 1 of this title, and all corporations which have heretofore filed or may hereafter file a certificate of incorporation under said chapter, shall pay to the Secretary of State as an annual franchise tax whichever of the applicable amounts prescribed by paragraphs (a)(1) and (a)(2) of this section is the lesser:

(1) Where a corporation that is not authorized to issue capital stock is not an exempt corporation under §501(b) of this title, $75; where the authorized capital stock does not exceed 5,000 shares, $75; where the authorized capital stock exceeds 5,000 shares, but is not more than 10,000 shares, $150; and the further sum of $75 on each 10,000 shares or part thereof.

(2) Seventy-five dollars where the assumed no-par capital of the corporation, found in the manner provided in this paragraph, does not exceed $500,000; $150 where the assumed no-par capital exceeds $500,000 but is not more than $1,000,000; and the further sum of $75 for each $1,000,000 or part thereof of such additional assumed no-par capital.

For the purpose of computing the tax in accordance with paragraph (a)(2) of this section, the corporation's assumed no-par capital, whenever the phrase "assumed no-par capital" is used in paragraph (a)(2) of this section, shall be found by multiplying the number of authorized shares of capital stock without par value by $100.

To the amount of tax attributable to the corporation's assumed no-par capital, computed as above prescribed, add $350 for each $1,000,000 or fraction thereof in excess of $1,000,000 of an assumed par value capital, found by multiplying the number of authorized shares of capital stock having par value by the quotient resulting from dividing the amount of the total assets of the corporation, as shown in the manner hereinafter provided, by the total number of issued shares of all denominations and classes. If the quotient shall be less than the par value of any denomination or class of authorized shares having par value, the number of the shares of each class shall be multiplied by their par value for the purpose of ascertaining the assumed par value capital in respect of the shares and the number of authorized shares having a par value to be multiplied by the quotient, as aforesaid, shall be reduced by the number of the shares whose par value exceeds the quotient; and where, to determine the assumed par value capital, it is necessary to multiply a class or classes of shares by the quotient and also to multiply a class or classes of shares by the par value of the shares, the assumed par value capital of the corporation shall be the sum of the products of the multiplications. Whenever the amount of the assumed par value capital, computed as above prescribed, is less than $1,000,000, the amount of the tax attributable thereto shall be the amount that bears the same relation to $350 that the amount of the assumed par value capital bears to $1,000,000.

(b) Unless a corporation shall submit to the Secretary of State, at the time of filing its annual franchise tax report, a statement setting forth the number of shares of each class of stock actually issued, if any, and the amount of the total gross assets of the corporation, as of the nearest date on which the amount is obtainable, including in the statement its goodwill valued at the same amount at which it is valued in the books of account of the corporation, it shall pay a franchise tax for such year computed in the manner prescribed by paragraph (a)(1) of this section.

(c) In no case shall the tax on any corporation for a full taxable year, computed by paragraph (a)(1) of this section be more than $180,000 nor less than $75; or computed by paragraph (a)(2) of this section be more than $180,000 nor less than $350.

(d) In case the corporation has not been in existence during the whole year, the amount of tax due, at the foregoing rates and as above provided, shall be prorated for the portion of the year during which the corporation was in existence.

(e) In case a corporation shall have changed during the taxable year the amount of its authorized capital stock, the total annual franchise tax payable at the foregoing rates shall be arrived at by adding together the franchise taxes calculated as above set forth as prorated for the several periods of the year during which each distinct authorized amount of capital stock was in effect.

(f) Every corporation which shall show on its annual franchise tax report that it has not been engaged in any of the business activities for which it was granted a certificate of incorporation, shall pay only at the rate of one half of the amount of taxes scheduled above for the portion of the year as it shall not have been so engaged and at the full rate for the remainder of the year. The Secretary of State may require the filing of a supplemental affidavit stating fully the pertinent facts upon which the claim for one-half rate is based.

(g) For the purpose of computing the taxes imposed by this section, the authorized capital stock of a corporation shall be considered to be the total number of shares which the corporation is authorized to issue, whether or not the number of shares that may be outstanding at any one time be limited to a less number.

(h) All corporations as defined in this section which are regulated investment companies as defined by §851 of the federal Internal Revenue Code [26 U.S.C. §851], shall pay to the Secretary of State as an annual franchise tax, a tax computed either under paragraph (a)(1) or (a)(2) of this section, or a tax at the rate of $350 per annum for each $1,000,000, or fraction thereof in excess of $1,000,000, of the average gross assets thereof during the taxable year, whichever be the least, provided that in no case shall the tax on any corporation for a full taxable year under this subsection be more than $90,000. The average assets for the purposes of this section shall be taken to be the mean of the gross assets on January 1 and December 31 of the taxable year. Any corporation electing to pay a tax under this subsection shall show on its annual franchise tax report that the corporation is a regulated investment company as above defined, and the amount of its assets on January 1 and December 31 of the taxable year, and the mean thereof. The Secretary of State may investigate the facts set forth in the report and if it should be found that the corporation so electing to pay under this subsection shall not be a regulated investment company, as above defined, shall assess upon the corporation a tax under paragraphs (a)(1) and (a)(2) of this section, whichever be the lesser.

(i) As used in subsections (a) and (b) of this section, the term "total assets" and the term "total gross assets" are identical terms and mean all assets of the corporation, net only of allowances for bad debts, accumulated depreciation, accumulated depletion, accumulated amortization of land and accumulated amortization of intangible assets.

Such total assets and total gross assets shall be those "total assets" reported to the United States on U.S. Form 1120 Schedule L, relative to the company's fiscal year ending in the calendar year prior to filing with the Secretary of State pursuant to this section. If such schedule is no longer in use, the Secretary of State shall designate a replacement. The Secretary of State may at any time require a true and correct copy of such schedule to be filed with the Secretary of State's office. *If such schedule or its replacement reports on a consolidated basis, the reporting corporation shall submit to the Secretary of State the consolidating ending balance sheets which accompany such schedule as a reconciliation of its reported total assets or total gross assets to the consolidated total assets reported on the schedule.*[2]

Interests in entities which are consolidated with the reporting company shall be included within "total assets" and "total gross assets" at a value determined in accordance with generally accepted accounting principles. (Last amended by Ch. 216, L. '10, eff. retroactively to 1-1-06 and Ch. 253, L. '10, eff. 8-1-10.)

Ch. 253, L. '10, eff. 8-1-10, added matter in italic in paragraph (a)(1) and deleted [1]"(1) Where the authorized capital stock does not exceed 5,000 shares, $75; where the authorized capital stock exceeds 5,000 shares, but is not more than 10,000 shares, $150; and the further sum of $75 on each 10,000 shares or part thereof."

Ch. 216, L. '10, eff. retroactively to 1-1-06, added matter in italic and deleted [2]"No corporation shall consolidate with its assets the assets of another entity for purposes of this section. If such schedule or its replacement reports on a consolidated basis, the reporting corporation shall submit to the Secretary of State a reconciliation of its reported total assets or total gross assets to the consolidated total assets reported on the schedule."

503 [Eff. January 1, 2014] RATES AND COMPUTATION OF FRANCHISE TAX.—(a) All corporations accepting the provisions of the Constitution of this State and coming under Chapter 1 of this title, and all corporations which have heretofore filed or may hereafter file a certificate of incorporation under said chapter, shall pay to the Secretary of State as an annual franchise tax whichever of the applicable amounts prescribed by paragraphs (a)(1) and (a)(2) of this section is the lesser:

[1] *(1) Where a corporation that is not authorized to issue capital stock is not an exempt corporation under §501(b) of this title, $75; where the authorized capital stock does not exceed 5,000 shares, $75; where the authorized capital stock exceeds 5,000 shares, but is not more than 10,000 shares, $150; and the further sum of $75 on each 10,000 shares or part thereof.*

(2) Seventy-five dollars where the assumed no-par capital of the corporation, found in the manner provided in this paragraph, does not exceed $500,000; $150 where the assumed no-par capital exceeds $500,000 but is not more than $1,000,000; and the further sum of $75 for each $1,000,000 or part thereof of such additional assumed no-par capital.

For the purpose of computing the tax in accordance with paragraph (a)(2) of this section, the corporation's assumed no-par capital, whenever the phrase "assumed no-par capital" is used in paragraph (a)(2) of this section, shall be found by multiplying the number of authorized shares of capital stock without par value by $100.

To the amount of tax attributable to the corporation's assumed no-par capital, computed as above prescribed, add $250 for each $1,000,000 or fraction thereof in excess of $1,000,000 of an assumed par value capital, found by multiplying the number of authorized shares of capital stock having par value by the quotient resulting from dividing the amount of the total assets of the corporation, as shown in the manner hereinafter provided, by the total number of issued shares of all denominations and classes. If the quotient shall be less than the par value of any denomination or class of authorized shares having par value, the number of the shares of each class shall be multiplied by their par value for the purpose of ascertaining the assumed par value capital in respect of the shares and the number of authorized shares having a par value to be multiplied by the quotient, as aforesaid, shall be reduced by the number of the shares whose par value exceeds the quotient; and where, to determine the assumed par value capital, it is necessary to multiply a class or classes of shares by the quotient and also to multiply a class or classes of shares by the par value of the shares, the assumed par value capital of the corporation shall be the sum of the products of the multiplications. Whenever the amount of the assumed par value capital, computed as above prescribed, is less than $1,000,000, the amount of the tax attributable thereto shall be the amount that bears the same relation to $250 that the amount of the assumed par value capital bears to $1,000,000.

(b) Unless a corporation shall submit to the Secretary of State, at the time of filing its annual franchise tax report, a statement setting forth the number of shares of each class of stock actually issued, if any, and the amount of the total gross assets of the corporation, as of the nearest date on which the amount is obtainable, including in the statement its goodwill valued at the same amount at which it is valued in the books of account of the corporation, it shall pay a franchise tax for such year computed in the manner prescribed by paragraph (a)(1) of this section.

(c) In no case shall the tax on any corporation for a full taxable year, by whichever of paragraphs (a)(1) and (a)(2) of this section the same is computed, be more than $165,000 nor less than $75.

(d) In case the corporation has not been in existence during the whole year, the amount of tax due, at the foregoing rates and as above provided, shall be prorated for the portion of the year during which the corporation was in existence.

(e) In case a corporation shall have changed during the taxable year the amount of its authorized capital stock, the total annual franchise tax payable at the foregoing rates shall be arrived at by adding together the franchise taxes calculated as above set forth as prorated for the several periods of the year during which each distinct authorized amount of capital stock was in effect.

(f) Every corporation which shall show on its annual franchise tax report that it has not been engaged in any of the business activities for which it was granted a certificate of incorporation, shall pay only at the rate of one half of the amount of taxes scheduled above for the portion of the year as it shall not have been so engaged and at the full rate for the remainder of the year. The Secretary of State may require the filing of a supplemental affidavit stating fully the pertinent facts upon which the claim for one-half rate is based.

(g) For the purpose of computing the taxes imposed by this section, the authorized capital stock of a corporation shall be considered to be the total number of shares which the corporation is authorized to issue, whether or not the number of shares that may be outstanding at any one time be limited to a less number.

(h) All corporations as defined in this section which are regulated investment companies as defined by §851 of the federal Internal Revenue Code [26 U.S.C. §851], shall pay to the Secretary of State as an annual franchise tax, a tax computed either under paragraph (a)(1) or (a)(2) of this section, or a tax at the rate of $250 per annum for each $1,000,000, or fraction thereof in excess of $1,000,000, of the average gross assets thereof during the taxable year, whichever be the least, provided that in no case shall the tax on any corporation for a full taxable year under this subsection be more than $75,000. The average assets for the purposes of this section shall be taken to be the mean of the gross assets on January 1 and December 31 of the taxable year. Any corporation electing to pay a tax under this subsection shall show on its annual franchise tax report that the corporation is a regulated investment company as above defined, and the amount of its assets on January 1 and December 31 of the taxable year, and the mean thereof. The Secretary of State may investigate the facts set forth in the report and if it should be found that the corporation so electing to pay under this subsection shall not be a regulated investment company, as above defined, shall assess upon the corporation a tax under paragraphs (a)(1) and (a)(2) of this section, whichever be the lesser.

(i) As used in subsections (a) and (b) of this section, the term "total assets" and the term "total gross assets" are identical terms and mean all assets of the corporation, net only of allowances for bad debts, accumulated depreciation, accumulated depletion, accumulated amortization of land and accumulated amortization of intangible assets.

Such total assets and total gross assets shall be those "total assets" reported to the United States on U.S. Form 1120 Schedule L, relative to the company's fiscal year ending in the calendar year prior to filing with the Secretary of State pursuant to this section. If such schedule is no longer in use, the Secretary of State shall designate a replacement. The Secretary of State may at any time require a true and correct copy of such schedule to be filed with the Secretary of State's office. *If such schedule or its replacement reports on a consolidated basis, the reporting corporation shall submit to the Secretary of State the consolidating ending balance sheets which accompany such schedule as a reconciliation of its reported total assets or total gross assets to the consolidated total assets reported on the schedule.*[2]

Interests in entities which are consolidated with the reporting company shall be included within "total assets" and "total gross assets" at a value determined in accordance with generally accepted accounting principles. (Last amended by Ch. 216, L. '10, eff. retroactively to 1-1-06 and Ch. 253, L. '10, eff. 8-1-10.)

Ch. 253, L. '10, eff. 8-1-10, added matter in italic in paragraph (a)(1) and deleted [1]"(1) Where the authorized capital stock does not exceed 5,000 shares, $75; where the authorized capital stock exceeds 5,000 shares, but is not more than 10,000 shares, $150; and the further sum of $75 on each 10,000 shares or part thereof."

Ch. 216, L. '10, eff. retroactively to 1-1-06, added matter in italic and deleted [2]"No corporation shall consolidate with its assets the assets of another entity for purposes of this section. If such schedule or its replacement reports on a consolidated basis, the reporting corporation shall submit to the Secretary of State a reconciliation of its reported total assets or total gross assets to the consolidated total assets reported on the schedule."

Ch. 253, L. '10 Synopsis of Section 503

Section 69 amends §503(a)(1) of Chapter 5 of Title 8 to provide that the franchise tax applicable to nonstock corporations (except exempt corporations, which are exempt from the franchise tax) is $75.

Ch. 216, L. '10 Synopsis of Section 503

This bill confirms existing statutes and practices related to the administration of the corporation franchise tax.

Ch. 78, L. '09 Synopsis of Section 503

This Act increases various fees and taxes assessed by the Delaware Secretary of State.

Ch. 286, L. '08 Synopsis of Section 503

This Act increases the annual report fee for foreign corporations from $60 to $100 and increases the rates for computation of the annual franchise tax.

Ch. 306, L. '06 Synopsis of Section 503

Sections 18 through 26 amend §§502, 503, 510, 511, 514, and 517 to require Delaware corporations to file a complete annual franchise tax report including, among other things, the names and addresses of all of the corporation's directors as of the filing date of the report and the name and address of the officer who signs the report, and require the Secretary of State to declare void the charter of any corporation that fails to file a complete annual franchise tax report.

Ch. 51, L. '03 Synopsis of Section 503

Increases the rates for computation of the annual franchise tax.

Ch. 339, L. '98 Synopsis of Section 503

The amendments to these Sections eliminate masculine references in the statutes, and replace them with gender neutral references.

504 COLLECTION AND DISPOSITION OF TAX; TENTATIVE RETURN AND TAX; PENALTY INTEREST; INVESTIGATION OF ANNUAL FRANCHISE TAX REPORT; NOTICE OF ADDITIONAL TAX DUE.—(a) The franchise tax shall be due and payable on March 1 following the close of the calendar year, except that with respect to a corporation whose franchise tax liability for the current calendar year is estimated to be $5,000 or more, a tentative return and tax shall be due and payable as follows:

(1) Forty percent of the estimated tax on June 1 of the current year;
(2) Twenty percent of the estimated tax on September 1 of the current year;
(3) Twenty percent of the estimated tax on December 1 of the current year; and
(4) The remainder of the tax as finally determined together with the annual franchise tax report on March 1 following the close of the calendar year.

(b) The Department of State shall receive the franchise tax and pay over all taxes collected to the Department of Finance, except as provided in §506 of this title.

(c) If the tax of any corporation remains unpaid after the due dates established by this section, the tax shall bear interest at the rate of 1 percent for each month or portion thereof until fully paid.

(d) The Secretary of State has power to inquire into the truth or falsity or accuracy of every report required to be filed to carry out this chapter. The Secretary of State may require the production of the books of any corporation referred to in this chapter and may swear or affirm and examine witnesses in relation thereto. Where the Secretary of State shall determine the amount of franchise tax which has been paid is less than the franchise tax due, the Secretary of State shall notify the taxpayer of the additional tax and any interest thereon which is due. Such additional tax and interest thereon shall be paid, or a petition for review thereof shall be filed, within 60 days after the notification to the taxpayer.

(e) The tentative return and tax paid thereon under subsection (a) of this section shall be based on the annual franchise tax of the preceding year.

(f) The penalties for nonpayment of the tentative franchise tax as set forth in subsection (a) of this section shall be the same as those applied for any nonpayment of franchise tax in this title.

(g) The Secretary of State may in the Secretary of State's discretion charge a fee of [1]$60 for each check received for payment of franchise taxes, penalties or interest thereon that is returned due to insufficient funds or as the result of a stop payment order to be recovered by adding the amount of that fee to the franchise tax, and such sum shall become a part of the franchise tax and shall be collected in the same manner and subject to the same penalties. (Last amended by Ch. 51, L. '03, eff. 8-1-03.)

Ch. 51, L. '03, eff. 8-1-03, added matter in italic and deleted [1]"$25".

Ch. 51, L. '03 Synopsis of Section 504

Increases the amount the Secretary of State may add to a corporation's franchise tax for each check received for payment of franchise taxes, penalties or interest that is returned for insufficient funds or as the result of a stop payment order from $25 to $60.

Ch. 339, L. '98 Synopsis of Section 504

The amendments to these Sections eliminate masculine references in the statutes, and replace them with gender neutral references.

Commentary to Section 504

The amendment to Section 504 by Ch. 54, L. '93, eff. 6-30-93, corrects an error which currently appears in the Delaware Code by amending the Delaware Code to clarify the section regarding quarterly franchise tax payments. The intent of the original law was that those companies owing $5,000 or more annually would be required to pay in quarterly installments. Because of the way the language in the Delaware Code is written, those owing exactly $5,000 are not required to pay quarterly. This amendment corrects that error.

505 REVIEW AND REFUND; JURISDICTION AND POWER OF THE SECRETARY OF STATE; APPEAL.—(a) If any corporation claims that the annual franchise tax or any penalties or interest were erroneously or illegally fixed or paid with respect to a calendar year, the corporation may, not later than March 1 of the 2nd calendar year following the close of such calendar year, petition the Secretary of State for a reduction or refund of such tax, penalties or interest.

(b) Prior to the filing of a certificate required by subsection (c) of §312 of this title, a corporation may petition the Secretary of State for a reduction of taxes, penalties or interest which the State claims are due it pursuant to subsection (g) of §312 of this title and which the corporation claims have been erroneously or illegally fixed.

(c) If the Secretary of State determines the tax, interest and/or penalties fixed by the Secretary or taxes paid are excessive or incorrect, in whole or in part, the Secretary shall resettle the same and adjust the assessment of tax, interest or penalties accordingly and shall refund to the corporation any amount paid in excess of the proper amount of tax, interest and/or penalties so determined to be due. In the case of any corporation which is not required to pay an annual tax under [1] *§501(a)* of this title, the Secretary of State may remit all or part of the penalties and interest provided in this chapter. Any refund due to a corporation which has merged into another Delaware domestic corporation shall be credited to the surviving Delaware corporation.

(d) Any corporation, within a period of 60 days after the determination by the Secretary of State on a petition filed pursuant to subsections (a) and (b) of this section, may petition the Court of Chancery, in and for the county where the registered office or place of business of the corporation is located, for a review de novo of the determination of the Secretary of State. The petition shall set forth the facts upon which the petitioner relies. The Secretary of State shall be named as respondent in any such petition and be served therewith in the same manner as if the Secretary of State were a defendant in a civil suit.

(e) If the Court of Chancery determines that the tax, interest and/or penalties determined by the Secretary of State pursuant to subsections (a) and (b) of this section are excessive or incorrect, in whole or in part, it shall resettle the same and adjust the assessment of tax, interest or penalties accordingly, and notify the corporation and the Secretary of State of its determination and direct the Secretary of State to refund to the corporation any amount paid in excess of the proper amount of tax, interest and/or penalties so determined to be due. The Court of Chancery may remit all or part of the penalties and interest provided in §502 of this title. (Last amended by Ch. 253, L. '10, eff. 8-1-10.)

Ch. 253, L. '10, eff. 8-1-10, added matter in italic and deleted [1]"§501".

Ch. 253, L. '10 Synopsis of Section 505

Section 70 amends §505(c) of Chapter 5 of Title 8 to ensure that it is consistent with the amendment of §501 of Chapter 5 of Title 8.

Ch. 339, L. '98 Synopsis of Section 505

The amendments to these Sections eliminate masculine references in the statutes, and replace them with gender neutral references.

Ch. 79, L. '95 Synopsis of Section 505

This amendment requires the Secretary of State to apply any refund due a merged corporation to the credit of the surviving corporation.

506 FUND FOR PAYMENT OF REFUNDS.—(Repealed by Ch. 216, L. '10, eff. retroactively to 1-1-06.)

Prior to its repeal by Ch. 216, L. '10, eff. retroactively to 1-1-06, this section read as follows: "The Secretary of State shall retain in the Secretary of State's hands out of the revenue collected from the taxes imposed by this chapter a sum sufficient to provide at all times a fund of at least $5,000, but not more than $70,000, out of which the Secretary of State shall pay any refunds to which corporations shall become entitled under this chapter. The fund shall be deposited in the financial institution which is legal depository of state moneys to the credit of the Secretary of State and shall be disbursable on order of the Secretary of State."

Ch. 216, L. '10 Synopsis of Section 503

This bill confirms existing statutes and practices related to the administration of the corporation franchise tax.

Ch. 339, L. '98 Synopsis of Section 506

The amendments to these Sections eliminate masculine references in the statutes, and replace them with gender neutral references.

507 COLLECTION OF TAX; PREFERRED DEBT.—The franchise tax [1]shall be a debt due from the corporation to the State, for which an action at law may be maintained after the same shall have been in arrears for a period of 1 month. The tax shall also be a preferred debt in case of insolvency. (Last amended by Ch. 450, L. '71, eff. 1-1-73.)

Ch. 450, L. '71, eff. 1-1-73, deleted [1]"as assessed and levied in accordance with the provisions of this chapter".

508 INJUNCTION AGAINST EXERCISE OF FRANCHISE OR TRANSACTING BUSINESS.—The Attorney General, either of [1]*the Attorney General's* own motion or upon request of the Secretary of State, whenever any franchise tax due under this chapter from any corporation shall have remained in arrears for a period of 3 months after the tax shall have become payable, may apply to the Court of Chancery, by petition in the name of the State, on 5 days' notice to the corporation, which notice may be served in such manner as the Court may direct, for an injunction to restrain the corporation from the exercise of any franchise or the transaction of any business within the State, until the payment of the tax, interest due thereon and the cost of the application, which shall be fixed by the Court. The Court of Chancery may grant the injunction, if a proper case appears, and upon granting and service of the injunction, the corporation thereafter shall not exercise any franchise or transact any business within this State until the injunction shall be dissolved. (Last amended by Ch. 339, L. '98, eff. 7-1-98.)

Ch. 339, L. '98, eff. 7-1-98, added matter in italic and deleted [1]"his".

Ch. 339, L. '98 Synopsis of Section 508

The amendments to these Sections eliminate masculine references in the statutes, and replace them with gender neutral references.

509 FURTHER REMEDY IN COURT OF CHANCERY; APPOINTMENT OF RECEIVER OR TRUSTEE; SALE OF PROPERTY.—(a) After any corporation, now existing or hereafter incorporated under [1] Chapter 1 of this title, has failed or neglected for the period of [2]*1 year* to pay the franchise taxes imposed by law, and the Secretary of State shall have reported such corporation to the Governor of the State, as provided in §511 of this title, then the Attorney General of this State may proceed against the corporation in the Court of Chancery of this State for the appointment of a receiver, or otherwise.

(b) The Court of Chancery in the proceeding shall ascertain the amount of the taxes remaining due and unpaid by the corporation to this State, and shall enter a final decree for the amount so ascertained. Thereupon a fieri facias or other process shall issue for the collection of the same as other debts are collected. If no property which may be seized and sold on fieri facias shall be found within this State sufficient to pay the decree, the Court shall further order and decree that the corporation, within 10 days from and after the service of notice of the decree upon any officer of the corporation upon whom service of process may be lawfully made, or such notice as the Court shall direct, shall assign and transfer to the trustee or receiver appointed by the Court, any chose in action, or any patent or patents, or any assignments of or license under any patented invention or inventions owned by, leased or licensed to or controlled in whole or in part by the corporation, to be sold by the receiver or trustee for the satisfaction of the decree. No injunction theretofore issued nor any forfeiture of the charter of any corporation shall be held to exempt the corporation from compliance with the order of the Court.

(c) If the corporation neglects or refuses within 10 days from and after the service of the notice of the decree to assign and transfer the same to the receiver or trustee for sale as aforesaid, the Court shall appoint a trustee to make the assignment of the same, in the name and on behalf of the corporation, to the receiver or trustee appointed to make the sale. The receiver or trustee shall thereupon, after such notice and in such manner as required for the sale under fieri facias of personal property, sell the same to the highest bidder. The receiver or trustee, upon the payment of the purchase money, shall execute and deliver to the purchaser an assignment and transfer of all the patents and interests of the corporation so sold, which assignment or transfer shall vest in the purchaser a valid title to all right, title and interest whatsoever of the corporation therein, and the proceeds of the sale shall be applied to the payment of the unpaid taxes, together with the costs of the proceedings. (Last amended by Ch. 712, L. '69, eff. 7-15-70.)

Ch. 712. L. '69, eff. 7-15-70, added matter in italic and deleted [1]"the provisions of" and [2]"2 consecutive years".

510 [1]*FAILURE TO PAY TAX OR FILE A COMPLETE ANNUAL REPORT FOR 1 YEAR; CHARTER VOID; EXTENSION OF TIME.*—*If any corporation, accepting the Constitution of this State and coming under Chapter 1 of this title, or any corporation which has heretofore filed or may hereafter file a certificate of incorporation under said chapter, neglects or refuses for 1 year to pay the State any franchise tax or taxes, which has or have been, or shall be assessed against it, or which it is required to pay under this chapter, or shall neglect or refuse to file a complete annual franchise tax report, the charter of the corporation shall be void, and all powers conferred by law upon the corporation are declared inoperative, unless the Secretary of State, for good cause shown, shall have given further time for payment of the tax or taxes or the completion of an annual franchise tax report, in which case a certificate thereof shall be filed in the office of the Secretary of State stating the reason therefor. On or before November 30 in each year, the Secretary of State shall notify each corporation which has neglected or refused to pay the franchise tax or taxes assessed against it or becoming due during the year or has refused or neglected to file a complete annual franchise tax report, that the charter of the corporation shall become void unless such taxes are paid and such complete annual franchise tax report is filed on or before March 1 of the following year.* (Last amended by Ch. 306, L. '06, eff. 1-1-08.)

Ch. 306, L. '06, eff. 1-1-08, added matter in italic and deleted [1]"FAILURE TO PAY TAX FOR 1 YEAR; CHARTER VOID; EXTENSION OF TIME.—If any corporation, accepting the Constitution of this State and coming under Chapter 1 of this title, or any corporation which as heretofore filed or may hereafter file a certificate of incorporation under said chapter, neglects or refuses for 1 year to pay the State any franchise tax or taxes, which has or have been, or shall be assessed against it, or which it is required to pay under this chapter, the charter of the corporation shall be void, and all powers conferred by law upon the corporation are declared inoperative, unless the Secretary of State, for good cause shown, shall have given further time for the payment of the tax or taxes, in which case a certificate thereof shall be filed in the office of the Secretary of State stating the reason therefor. On or before the last day of November in each year, the Secretary of State shall notify each corporation which has neglected or refused to pay the franchise tax or taxes assessed against it or becoming due during the year that the charter of the corporation shall become void unless such taxes are paid on or before March 1 of the following year."

Ch. 306, L. '06 Synopsis of Section 510

Sections 18 through 26 amend §§502, 503, 510, 511, 514, and 517 to require Delaware corporations to file a complete annual franchise tax report including, among other things, the names and addresses of all of the corporation's directors as of the filing date of the report and the name and address of the officer who signs the report, and require the Secretary of State to declare void the charter of any corporation that fails to file a complete annual franchise tax report.

Ch. 339, L. '98 Synopsis of Section 510

The amendments to these Sections eliminate masculine references in the statutes, and replace them with gender neutral references.

511 REPEAL OF CHARTERS OF DELINQUENT CORPORATIONS; REPORT TO GOVERNOR AND PROCLAMATION.—On or before June 30 in each year, the Secretary of State shall report to the Governor a list of all the corporations, which for 1 year next preceding such report, have failed, neglected or refused to pay the franchise taxes assessed against them or due by them *or to file a complete annual franchise tax report,* under the laws of this State, and the Governor shall forthwith issue a proclamation declaring that the charters of these corporations are repealed. (Last amended by Ch. 306, L. '06, eff. 1-1-08.)

Ch. 306, L. '06, eff. 1-1-08, added matter in italic.

Ch. 306, L. '06 Synopsis of Section 510

Sections 18 through 26 amend §§502, 503, 510, 511, 514, and 517 to require Delaware corporations to file a complete annual franchise tax report including, among other things, the names and addresses of all of the corporation's directors as of the filing date of the report and the name and address of the officer who signs the report, and require the Secretary of State to declare void the charter of any corporation that fails to file a complete annual franchise tax report.

Ch. 339, L. '98 Synopsis of Section 511

The amendments to these Sections eliminate masculine references in the statutes, and replace them with gender neutral references.

512 FILING AND PUBLICATION OF PROCLAMATION.—[1]*A list of those corporations whose charters were repealed by gubernatorial proclamation pursuant to §511 of this title shall be filed in the office of the Secretary of State. On or before October 31 of each calendar year, the Secretary of State shall publish such proclamation on the Internet or on a similar medium for a period of 1 week and shall advertise the website or other address where such proclamation can be accessed in at least 1 newspaper of general circulation in the State of Delaware.* (Last amended by Ch. 298, L. '02, eff. 7-1-02.)

Ch. 298, L. '02, eff. 7-1-02, added matter in italic and deleted [1]"The proclamation of the Governor shall be filed in the office of the Secretary of State and advertised in at least 1, and not more than 3, newspapers published within this State."

Ch. 298, L. '02 Synopsis of Section 512

This amendment permits the Secretary of State to carry out its obligation to provide notice of corporations proclaimed void by giving notice through the use of electronic communication.

513 ACTING UNDER PROCLAIMED CHARTER; PENALTY.—Whoever exercises or attempts to exercise any powers under the certificate of incorporation of any corporation which has been proclaimed by the Governor, after the issuance of the proclamation, shall be fined not more than $1,000 or imprisoned not more than 1 year, or both.

514 MISTAKES IN PROCLAMATION; CORRECTION.—Whenever it is established to the satisfaction of the Governor that any corporation named in the proclamation has not neglected or refused to pay the franchise tax *or file a completed annual franchise tax report* within 1 year, or has been inadvertently reported to the Governor by the Secretary of State as refusing or neglecting to pay the taxes *or file a completed annual franchise tax report,* the Governor may correct the mistake and may make the same known by filing a proclamation to that effect in the office of the Secretary of State, who shall restore to the corporation its charter, together with all the rights, privileges and immunities and subject to all its duties, debts and liabilities which had been secured or imposed by its original charter and all amendments thereto. (Last amended by Ch. 306, L. '06, eff. 1-1-08.)

Ch. 306, L. '06, eff. 1-1-08, added matter in italic.

Ch. 306, L. '06 Synopsis of Section 514

Sections 18 through 26 amend §§502, 503, 510, 511, 514, and 517 to require Delaware corporations to file a complete annual franchise tax report including, among other things, the names and addresses of all of the corporation's directors as of the filing date of the report and the name and address of the officer who signs the report, and require the Secretary of State to declare void the charter of any corporation that fails to file a complete annual franchise tax report.

Ch. 339, L. '98 Synopsis of Section 514

The amendments to these Sections eliminate masculine references in the statutes, and replace them with gender neutral references.

515 ANNUAL REPORT OF SECRETARY OF STATE.—The Secretary of State shall prepare and publish an annual report containing such statistics as may be available with respect to the operation of this chapter, including the amounts collected and amounts unpaid for each year for which the tax is assessed, and such other facts as are pertinent and desirable.

516 RETALIATORY TAXATION AND REGULATION; IMPOSITION.—When, by the laws of any other state or nation, any other or greater taxes, fines, penalties, licenses, fees, or other obligations or requirements are imposed upon corporations chartered under Chapter 1 of this title, doing business in the other state or nation, or upon their agents therein, than the law of this State imposes upon their corporations or agents doing business in this State, so long as the laws continue in force in the other state or nation, the same taxes, fines, penalties, licenses, fees, obligations and requirements of whatever kind shall be imposed upon all corporations of the other state or nations doing business within this State or upon their agents here. Nothing in this section shall be held to repeal any duty, condition or requirement now imposed by law upon the corporations of other states or nations transacting business in this State.

517 DUTIES OF ATTORNEY GENERAL.—The Attorney General shall have all the powers and authorities in conjunction with the Secretary of State to collect franchise taxes and penalties due from proclaimed corporations and corporations whose charter has become void by operation of law [1]. (Last amended by Ch. 306, L. '06, eff. 1-1-08.)

Ch. 306, L. '06, eff. 1-1-08, deleted [1]"for nonpayment of taxes".

Ch. 306, L. '06 Synopsis of Section 517

Sections 18 through 26 amend §§502, 503, 510, 511, 514, and 517 to require Delaware corporations to file a complete annual franchise tax report including, among other things, the names and addresses of all of the corporation's directors as of the filing date of the report and the name and address of the officer who signs the report, and require the Secretary of State to declare void the charter of any corporation that fails to file a complete annual franchise tax report.

518 RELIEF FOR CORPORATIONS WITH ASSETS IN CERTAIN UNFRIENDLY NATIONS.—All corporations incorporated and existing under the laws of this State, all of whose assets are located in any country from which it is impossible to remove such assets or withdraw income, or whose assets are located at any place where it is made unlawful by any law of the United States of America now or hereafter enacted or by any rule, regulation or proclamation or executive order issued under any such law, to send any communications, may, in the discretion of the Secretary of State, be relieved and freed from any and all assessment of franchise taxes provided for by this chapter and such corporations may further be relieved by the Secretary of State of the necessity of filing any state reports due or required.

The Secretary of State shall administer this section and may require such evidence, submitted by any officer or agent, as in [1]*the Secretary of State's* judgment may be necessary or desirable to determine whether or not a corporation deserves such relief from taxes and the filing of reports, and may make such regulations in relation thereto as [2]*the Secretary of State* may deem desirable or necessary. (Last amended by Ch. 339, L. '98, eff. 7-1-98.)

Ch. 339, L. '98, eff. 7-1-98, added matter in italic and deleted [1]"his" and [2]"he".

Ch. 339, L. '98 Synopsis of Section 518

The amendments to these Sections eliminate masculine references in the statutes, and replace them with gender neutral references.

[The page following this is Corp.—551]

CHAPTER 6. PROFESSIONAL SERVICE CORPORATIONS

601 LEGISLATIVE INTENT.—It is the legislative intent to provide for the incorporation of an individual, or group of individuals to render the same professional service to the public, for which such individuals are required by law to be licensed or to obtain other legal authorization.

602 SHORT TITLE.—This chapter may be cited as "The Professional Service Corporation Act."

.1 Federal income tax treatment of professional corporations.—Professional corporations that possess corporate characteristics such as limited liability, transferability, continuity and central management will be treated for federal tax purposes as corporations and not partnerships. *Empey v U.S.,* 272 FSupp 851 (D Colo 1967), aff'd, 406 F2d 157 (10th Cir 1969); *O'Neill v U.S.,* 410 F2d 888 (6th Cir 1969), aff'g, 281 FSupp 359 (ND Ohio 1968); *Holder v US,* 22 AFTR2d 5203 (ND Ga 1968); *Kurzner v U.S.,* 413 F2d 97 (5th Cir 1969).

603 DEFINITIONS.—As used in this chapter the following words shall have the meaning indicated:

(1) The term, "professional service" shall mean any type of personal service to the public which requires as a condition precedent to the rendering of such service the obtaining of a license or other legal authorization, and which, by reason of law, prior to June 7, 1969, could not be performed by a corporation. In addition, and by way of example without limiting the generality thereof, the personal services which come within the provisions of this chapter are the personal services rendered by architects, certified or other public accountants, chiropodists, chiropractors, doctors of dentistry, doctors of medicine, optometrists, osteopaths, professional engineers, veterinarians and, subject to the Rules of the Supreme Court, attorneys at law.

(2) The term "professional corporation" means a corporation which is organized, under this chapter, for the sole and specific purpose of rendering professional service, and which has as its shareholders only individuals who themselves are duly licensed or otherwise legally authorized within this State to render the same professional service as the corporation.

604 EXEMPTIONS.—This chapter shall not apply to any individual or groups of individuals within this State, who prior to June 7, 1969, were permitted to organize a corporation and perform personal services to the public by the means of a corporation, and this chapter shall not apply to any corporations organized by any individual or group of individuals prior to June 7, 1969, unless, any such individual, or group of individuals, or any such corporation bring themselves and such corporation within this chapter by amending the certificate of incorporation, in a manner so as to be consistent with all the provisions of this chapter, and by affirmatively stating in the amended certificate of incorporation that the shareholders have elected to bring the corporation within this chapter, or be incorporated initially under this chapter.

605 AUTHORITY TO ORGANIZE; LAW GOVERNING.—One or more persons, each of whom is duly licensed or otherwise legally authorized to render the same professional services within this State, may organize and become a shareholder or shareholders of a professional corporation for pecuniary profit, under this title, for the sole and specific purpose of rendering the same professional services.

606 NUMBER OF DIRECTORS; OFFICERS.—A professional corporation which has only 1 shareholder need have only 1 director, who shall be such shareholder. The 1 shareholder shall also serve as the president of the corporation. The other officers of the corporation, in such a case, need not be licensed or otherwise legally authorized to render the same professional service within this State, as such 1 shareholder. A professional corporation which has only 2 shareholders need have only 2 directors who shall be such shareholders. The 2 shareholders shall, between them, fill all the offices of the professional corporation.

607 RENDITION OF PROFESSIONAL SERVICES THROUGH LICENSED OFFICERS, EMPLOYEES AND AGENTS.—No corporation organized and incorporated under this chapter, may render professional services except through its officers, employees and agents who are duly licensed or otherwise legally authorized to render such professional services within this State; provided, however, this provision shall not be interpreted to include in the term "employee" as used in this chapter, clerks, secretaries, nurses, administrators, bookkeepers, technicians and other assistants who are not usually and ordinarily considered by law, custom and practice to be rendering professional services to the public for which a license, or other legal authorization, is required in connection with the profession to be practiced, nor does the term "employee" include any other person who performs all [1]*of such person's* employment under the direct supervision and control of an officer, employee or agent who [2]*renders* professional service to the public on behalf of the professional corporation; provided that, no person shall, under the guise of employment, practice a profession unless duly licensed to practice that profession under the laws of this State. Notwithstanding any other or contrary provisions of the laws of this State, a professional corporation, organized under this chapter, may charge for the services of its officers, employees and agents, may collect such charges, and may compensate those who render such professional services. (Last amended by Ch. 339, L. '98, eff. 7-1-98.)

Ch. 339, L. '98, eff. 7-1-98, added matter in italic and deleted [1]"his" and [2]"is himself rendering".

Ch. 339, L. '98 Synopsis of Section 607

The amendments to these Sections eliminate masculine references in the statutes, and replace them with gender neutral references.

608 CHAPTER NOT TO AFFECT PROFESSIONAL RELATIONSHIP; LEGAL LIABILITIES AND STANDARDS FOR PROFESSIONAL CONDUCT; NEGLIGENCE; ATTACHMENT OF ASSETS.—Nothing contained in this chapter shall be interpreted to abolish, repeal, modify, restrict or limit the law now in effect in this State, applicable to the professional relationship and the contract, tort and other legal liabilities between the person furnishing the professional services and the person receiving the professional service, and to the standards for professional conduct, including the confidential relationship between the person rendering the professional services and the person receiving such professional service, if any; and all confidential relationships previously enjoyed under the laws of this State or hereafter enacted shall remain inviolate. Any officer, employee, agent or shareholder of a corporation, organized under this chapter, shall remain personally and fully liable and accountable for any negligent, wrongful acts, or misconduct committed by [1]*such person,* or by any person under [2]*such person's* direct supervision and control, while rendering professional service on behalf of the corporation to the person for whom such professional services were being rendered. The corporation shall be liable up to the full value of its property for any negligent, wrongful acts, or misconduct committed by any of its officers, employees, agents or shareholders while they are engaged in behalf of the corporation in the rendering of professional services. The assets of a professional corporation shall not be liable to attachment for the individual debts of its shareholders. Notwithstanding the foregoing, the relationship of an individual to a professional corporation, organized under this chapter, with which such individual is or may be associated, whether as officer, employee, agent, or shareholder director, shall be in no way modify, extend, or diminish the jurisdiction over such individual, of and by whatever state agency, or office which licensed or otherwise legally authorized [1]*such person* for or to render service in a particular field of endeavor. (Last amended by Ch. 339, L. '98, eff. 7-1-98.)

Ch. 339, L. '98, eff. 7-1-98, added matter in italic and deleted [1]"him" and [2]"his".

Ch. 339, L. '98 Synopsis of Section 608

The amendments to these Sections eliminate masculine references in the statutes, and replace them with gender neutral references.

609 ENGAGING IN OTHER BUSINESS PROHIBITED.—No corporation organized under this chapter shall engage in any business other than the rendering of the professional services for which it was specifically incorporated provided, however, nothing in this chapter or in any other provisions of existing law applicable to corporations shall be interpreted to prohibit such corporation from investing its funds in real estate, mortgages, stocks, bonds, or any other type of investments, or from owning real or personal property necessary for, or appropriate or desirable in, the fulfillment or rendering of its professional services.

610 ISSUANCE OF CAPITAL STOCK TO LICENSED INDIVIDUALS; VOTING TRUST AGREEMENTS PROHIBITED; HOLDING OF STOCK BY SHAREHOLDER'S ESTATE.—No corporation, organized under this chapter, may issue any of its capital stock to anyone other than an individual who is duly licensed or otherwise legally authorized to render the same specific professional services as those for which the corporation was incorporated. No shareholder of a corporation, organized under this chapter, shall enter into a voting trust agreement, proxy, or any other type of agreement vesting another person with the authority to exercise the voting power of any or all of [1]*such shareholder's* stock. Subject to the corporation's certificate of incorporation, the estate of a shareholder who was a person duly licensed or otherwise legally authorized to render the same professional service as that for which the professional corporation was organized may continue to hold stock pursuant to the certificate of incorporation for a reasonable period of administration of the estate, but shall not be authorized to participate in any decisions concerning the rendering of professional service. (Last amended by Ch. 339, L. '98, eff. 7-1-98.)

Ch. 339, L. '98, eff. 7-1-98, added matter in italic and deleted [1]"his".

Ch. 339, L. '98 Synopsis of Section 610

The amendments to these Sections eliminate masculine references in the statutes, and replace them with gender neutral references.

611 DISQUALIFICATION OF OFFICER, SHAREHOLDER, AGENT OR EMPLOYEE.—If any officer, employee, agent or shareholder of a corporation, organized under this chapter, becomes legally disqualified to render such professional services within this State, or either (a) is elected to a public office that, or (b) accepts employment that, pursuant to existing law, places restrictions or limitations upon [1]*such person's* continued rendering of such professional services, [2]*such person* shall sever all employment with, and financial interests in, the corporation, forthwith. A corporation's failure to require compliance with this provision shall constitute a ground for the forfeiture of its charter and its dissolution. When a corporation's failure to comply with this provision is brought to the attention of the office of the Secretary of State, the Secretary of State shall forthwith certify that fact to the Attorney General for appropriate action to dissolve the corporation. (Last amended by Ch. 339, L. '98, eff. 7-1-98.)

Ch. 339, L. '98, eff. 7-1-98, added matter in italic and deleted [1]"his" and [2]"he".

Ch. 339, L. '98 Synopsis of Section 611

The amendments to these Sections eliminate masculine references in the statutes, and replace them with gender neutral references.

612 SALE OR TRANSFER OF SHARES.—Except as provided in §616 of this title, no shareholder of a corporation, organized under this chapter, may sell or transfer [1]*such shareholder's* shares in the corporation, except to the corporation, or to another individual who is eligible to be a shareholder of such corporation, and such sale or transfer may be made only after the same shall have been approved, at a stockholders' meeting specially called for such purpose, or at an annual meeting with 10 days notice of such additional purpose, by such proportion, not less than a majority, of the outstanding stock entitled to be voted on that question as may be provided in the certificate of incorporation or in the bylaws. At such shareholders' meeting the shares of stock held by the shareholder proposing to sell or transfer [1]*such shareholder's* shares may not be voted or counted for any purpose. The certificate of incorporation may provide specifically for additional restraints on the alienation of shares, and may require the redemption or purchase of such shares by the corporation at prices and in a specific manner, or authorize the corporation's board of directors or its shareholders to adopt bylaws restraining the alienation of shares and providing for the purchase or redemption by the corporation of its shares; provided, however, such provisions, dealing with the purchase or redemption by the corporation of its shares, may not be invoked at a time or in a manner that would impair the capital of the corporation. (Last amended by Ch. 339, L. '98, eff. 7-1-98.)

Ch. 339, L. '98, eff. 7-1-98, added matter in italic and deleted [1]"his".

Ch. 339, L. '98 Synopsis of Section 612

The amendments to these Sections eliminate masculine references in the statutes, and replace them with gender neutral references.

613 PRICE FOR SHARES.—If the certificate of incorporation or bylaws of a professional corporation fail to fix a price at which a professional corporation or its shareholders may purchase the shares of a deceased, retired, expelled or disqualified shareholder, and if the certificate of incorporation or bylaws do not otherwise provide, then the price for such share or shares shall be the book value at the end of the month immediately preceding the death or disqualification of the shareholder. Book value shall be determined by an independent certified public accountant employed by the professional corporation. The determination by the certified public accountant of book value shall be conclusive on the professional corporation and its shareholders.

614 PERPETUAL CORPORATE EXISTENCE.—A corporation under this chapter shall have perpetual existence until dissolved in accordance with other provisions of this chapter.

615 CONVERSION INTO BUSINESS CORPORATION.—Whenever all shareholders of a corporation, licensed under this chapter, cease at any time, and for any reason, to be licensed, certified or registered in the particular field of endeavor for which such corporation was organized, the corporation shall thereupon be treated as converted into and shall operate henceforth solely as a business corporation under applicable provisions of Chapter 1 of this title, exclusive of this chapter.

616 TIME FOR TRANSFER OF SHARES UPON DEATH OR DISQUALIFICATION.—Within 375 days following the date of death of a shareholder, or within 30 days following [1]*such shareholder's* disqualification to own shares in the corporation, as provided in this chapter, all of the shares of such shareholder shall be transferred to, and acquired by, the corporation or persons qualified to own such shares. If no other provision to accomplish such transfer and acquisition is in effect and carried out within said period, the corporation shall thereafter purchase and redeem all of[1] *such shareholder's* shares of its stock at the book value thereof, determined as of the end of the month immediately preceding death or disqualification. For this purpose, the book value shall be determined from the books and records of the corporation in accordance with the regular methods of accounting used by it for the purposes of determining its net taxable income for federal income tax purposes; and no subsequent adjustment of such income, whether by the corporation itself, by federal income tax audit made and agreed to, or by a court decision which has become final, shall alter the redemption price. Nothing contained in this section shall prevent the parties involved from making any other arrangement or provision in the certificate of incorporation, bylaws, or by contract to transfer the shares of a deceased or disqualified shareholder to the corporation or to persons qualified to own the same, whether made before or after the death or disqualification of the shareholder, provided that within the period specified by this section, all the stock involved shall have been so transferred. (Last amended by Ch. 339, L. '98, eff. 7-1-98.)

Ch. 339, L. '98, eff. 7-1-98, added matter in italic and deleted[1] "his".

Ch. 339, L. '98 Synopsis of Section 616

The amendments to these Sections eliminate masculine references in the statutes, and replace them with gender neutral references.

617 CORPORATE NAME.—The corporate name of a corporation organized under this chapter shall contain either a word or words descriptive of the professional service to be rendered by the corporation or shall contain the last names of 1 or more of its present, prospective or former shareholders or of persons who were associated with a predecessor person, partnership, corporation or other organization or whose name or names appeared in the name of such predecessor organization. The corporate name shall also contain the words "chartered" or "professional association" or abbreviation "P.A." The use of the word "company," "corporation" or "incorporated" or any other word, words, abbreviations, affix or prefix indicating that it is a corporation, in the corporate name of a corporation organized under this chapter, is specifically prohibited. However, it shall be permissible for the professional service corporation and its shareholders to render professional services and to exercise the corporation's authorized powers under a name which is identical to its corporate name except for the omission of the words "chartered" or "professional association" or the omission of the abbreviation "P.A."

618 APPLICABILITY OF GENERAL CORPORATION LAW; CONSOLIDATION OR MERGER OF CORPORATIONS; ANNUAL REPORT.—This title shall be applicable to a corporation organized pursuant to this chapter, except to the extent that any of the provisions of this chapter are interpreted to be in conflict with the provisions of this title, and in such event the provisions and sections of this chapter shall take precedence with respect to a corporation organized pursuant to this chapter. A professional corporation, organized under this chapter, may consolidate or merge only with another professional corporation organized under this chapter, empowered to render the same specific professional service; and a merger or consolidation with any foreign corporation is prohibited. Sections 501—518 of this title shall be applicable to a corporation organized pursuant to this chapter; but in addition to the information called for on the annual report of all corporations by those provisions, the annual report of a corporation organized pursuant to this chapter shall certify that its shareholders, directors and officers listed on such report are duly licensed, certified, registered or otherwise legally authorized to render the same professional or other personal service in this State. (Last amended by Ch. 421, L. '70, eff. 7-1-70.)

619 CONSTRUCTION OF CHAPTER.—This chapter shall not be construed as repealing, modifying or restricting the applicable provisions of law relating to incorporations, sales of securities, or regulating the several professions enumerated in this chapter, except insofar as such laws conflict with this chapter. (Added by Ch. 127, L. '69, eff. 6-7-69.)

[The page following this is LLC-i]

2011 AMENDMENTS TO THE DELAWARE LIMITED LIABILITY COMPANY ACT—ANALYSIS

By Mark V. Purpura
Richards, Layton & Finger, P.A.
Wilmington, Delaware

I. Introduction

Consistent with Delaware's commitment to maintaining statutes that are state-of-the-art with respect to limited liability companies, the Delaware Limited Liability Company Act, 6 *Del. C.* § 18-101, *et seq.* (the "Act"), was amended in 2011. The 2011 amendments to the Act (the "2011 Amendments") became effective on August 1, 2011. Some of the 2011 Amendments are technical in nature, but the more substantive aspects of the 2011 Amendments are discussed below.

II. Address of Registered Office and Registered Agent [6 Del. C. §§ 18-104(k) and 18-206(g)]

The 2011 Amendments add a new subsection (k) to Section 18-104 of the Act, which requires the address of the registered agent or the registered office of a limited liability company listed in any certificate or other document filed with the Secretary of State to include the street, number, city and postal code. The 2011 Amendments also amend Section 18-206 of the Act by adding a new subsection (g), which provides that such requirement in Section 18-104(k) does not apply to any document filed with the Secretary of State prior to August 1, 2011, unless a filing is being made to change the address of a registered agent or registered office.

III. Certificate of Correction of Certificate of Cancellation [6 Del. C. § 18-203]

The 2011 Amendments amend Section 18-203 of the Act to confirm that a certificate of cancellation that has been filed prior to the dissolution or the completion of the winding up of a limited liability company may be corrected as an erroneously executed certificate by filing a certificate of correction of such certificate of cancellation. The amendment thus permits the termination of a limited liability to be negated in certain situations, such as when assets of a terminated limited liability company are later discovered, liabilities or potential liabilities of a terminated limited liability company are threatened or discovered before the statute of limitations has expired, or a certificate of cancellation was inadvertently filed or not duly authorized.

IV. Future Effective Dates [6 Del. C. § 18-206(b)]

The 2011 Amendments amend Section 18-206(b) of the Act to provide that a future effective date or time specified in any certificate filed under the Act on or after January 1, 2012 shall not be later than a time on the 180th day after the date such certificate has been filed with the Secretary of State.

V. Simultaneous Filings for Domestications or Conversions [6 Del. C. §§ 18-212(b) and 18-214 (b)]

The 2011 Amendments amend Section 18-212 of the Act to clarify that a certificate of domestication and a certificate of formation for a non-United States entity domesticating to Delaware as a limited liability company must be filed simultaneously in the office of the Secretary of State and, to the extent such certificates have a future effective date or time, such certificates must provide for the same effective date or time. The 2011 Amendments also amend Section 18-214 of the Act to clarify that a certificate of conversion to limited liability company and a certificate of formation for an entity converting to a limited liability company must be filed simultaneously in the office of the Secretary of State and, to the extent such certificates have a future effective date or time, such certificates must provide for the same effective date or time.

VI. Amendments to Limited Liability Company Agreements [6 Del. C. §§ 18-302(e) and 18-302(f)]

The 2011 Amendments amend Section 18-302(e) of the Act to provide that supermajority amendment provisions in a limited liability company agreement apply only to provisions expressly included in such agreement and do not apply to default voting provisions of the Act unless otherwise provided in the limited liability company agreement. In a 2004 case, *In re LJM2 Co-Investment, L.P. Limited Partners Litigation*, 866 A.2d 762 (Del. Ch. 2004) ("*LJM2*"), the Delaware Court of Chancery considered an amendment provision in a limited partnership agreement prohibiting amendments to any provision of the agreement that affected the vote required in such provision unless the proposed amendment was approved by at least the vote originally required in such provision. The Court of Chancery held that the amendment section of the agreement applied to amendments to default voting provisions of the Delaware Revised Uniform Limited Partnership Act that became part of the limited partnership agreement in the absence of any specific contractual provision to the contrary. Thus, the amendment to Section 18-302(e) adopts a rule different from the analysis articulated by the Court of Chancery in *LJM2*.

In addition, the 2011 Amendments add a new subsection (f) to Section 18-302 of the Act to confirm that a limited liability company agreement that does not provide for the manner in which it may be amended may be amended with the approval of all of the limited liability company's members, or as otherwise permitted by law (including as permitted by Section 18-209(f) of the Act in a merger agreement). This default approach parallels the approach already contained in the Delaware Uniform Limited Partnership Act. Section 18-302(f) will only apply to a limited liability company whose original certificate of formation is filed with the Secretary of State on or after January 1, 2012.

VII. Written and Electronically Transmitted Consents [6 Del. C. §§ 18-302(d) and 18-404(d)]

The 2011 Amendments amend Section 18-302(d) of the Act to clarify that actions by members of a limited liability company without a meeting may take the form of a written consent or an electronic transmission. Similarly, the 2011 Amendments amend Section 18-404(d) of the Act to clarify that managers of a limited liability company may take action without a meeting in the form of a written consent or an electronic transmission. The amendments to Sections 18-302(d) and 18-404(d) make the Act consistent with Section 141(f) of the General Corporation Law of the State of Delaware, which authorizes board action by written consent or electronic transmission.

[The page following this is Corp.—601]

DELAWARE LIMITED LIABILITY COMPANY ACT
TITLE 6. COMMERCE AND TRADE
Limited Liability Company Act
(Added by Ch. 434, L. '92, eff. 10-1-92.)
Subchapter I. General Provisions

18-101 DEFINITIONS.—As used in this chapter unless the context otherwise requires:

(1) "Bankruptcy" means an event that causes a person to cease to be a member as provided in §18-304 of this title.

(2) "Certificate of formation" means the certificate referred to in §18-201 of this title, and the certificate as amended.

(3) "Contribution" means any cash, property, services rendered or a promissory note or other obligation to contribute cash or property or to perform services, which a person contributes to a limited liability company in the person's capacity as a member.

(4) "Foreign limited liability company" means a limited liability company formed under the laws of any state or under the laws of any foreign country or other foreign jurisdiction and denominated as such under the laws of such state or foreign country or other foreign jurisdiction.

(5) "Knowledge" means a person's actual knowledge of a fact, rather than the person's constructive knowledge of the fact.

(6) "Limited liability company" and "domestic limited liability company" means a limited liability company formed under the laws of the State of Delaware and having 1 or more members.

(7) "Limited liability company agreement" means any agreement (whether referred to as a limited liability company agreement, operating agreement or otherwise), written, oral or implied, of the member or members as to the affairs of a limited liability company and the conduct of its business. A member or manager of a limited liability company or an assignee of a limited liability company interest is bound by the limited liability company agreement whether or not the member or manager or assignee executes the limited liability company agreement. A limited liability company is not required to execute its limited liability company agreement. A limited liability company is bound by its limited liability company agreement whether or not the limited liability company executes the limited liability company agreement. A limited liability company agreement of a limited liability company having only 1 member shall not be unenforceable by reason of there being only 1 person who is a party to the limited liability company agreement. *A limited liability company agreement is not subject to any statute of frauds (including §2714 of this title).* A limited liability company agreement may provide rights to any person, including a person who is not a party to the limited liability company agreement, to the extent set forth therein. A written limited liability company agreement or another written agreement or writing:

a. May provide that a person shall be admitted as a member of a limited liability company, or shall become an assignee of a limited liability company interest or other rights or powers of a member to the extent assigned:

1. If such person (or a representative authorized by such person orally, in writing or by other action such as payment for a limited liability company interest) executes the limited liability company agreement or any other writing evidencing the intent of such person to become a member or assignee; or

2. Without such execution, if such person (or a representative authorized by such person orally, in writing or by other action such as payment for a limited liability company interest) complies with the conditions for becoming a member or assignee as set forth in the limited liability company agreement or any other writing; and

b. Shall not be unenforceable by reason of its not having been signed by a person being admitted as a member or becoming an assignee as provided in subparagraph a. of this paragraph, or by reason of its having been signed by a representative as provided in this chapter.

(8) "Limited liability company interest" means a member's share of the profits and losses of a limited liability company and a member's right to receive distributions of the limited liability company's assets.

(9) "Liquidating trustee" means a person carrying out the winding up of a limited liability company.

(10) "Manager" means a person who is named as a manager of a limited liability company in, or designated as a manager of a limited liability company pursuant to, a limited liability company agreement or similar instrument under which the limited liability company is formed.

(11) "Member" means a person who is admitted to a limited liability company as a member as provided in §18-301 of this title or, in the case of a foreign limited liability company, in accordance with the laws of the state or foreign country or other foreign jurisdiction under which the foreign limited liability company is formed.

(12) "Person" means a natural person, partnership (whether general or limited), limited liability company, trust (including a common law trust, business trust, statutory trust, voting trust or any other form of trust), estate, association (including any group, organization, co-tenancy, plan, board, council or committee), corporation, government (including a country, state, county or any other governmental subdivision, agency or instrumentality), custodian, nominee or any other individual or entity (or series thereof) in its own or any representative capacity, in each case, whether domestic or foreign.

(13) "Personal representative" means, as to a natural person, the executor, administrator, guardian, conservator or other legal representative thereof and, as to a person other than a natural person, the legal representative or successor thereof.

(14) "State" means the District of Columbia or the Commonwealth of Puerto Rico or any state, territory, possession or other jurisdiction of the United States other than the State of Delaware. (Last amended by Ch. 287, L. '10, eff. 8-2-10.)

Ch. 287, L. '10, eff. 8-2-10, added matter in italic.

Ch. 287, L. '10 Synopsis of Section 18-101

This section amends §18-101(7) of the Act to provide, in light of the decision of the Delaware Supreme Court in *Olson v. Halvorsen,* C.A. No. 1884 (Del. Supr. Dec. 15, 2009), that a limited liability company agreement is not subject to any statute of frauds.

Ch. 387, L. '08 Synopsis of Section 18-101

This section amends §18-101(12) of the Act to confirm the intended broad scope of the term "trust" as used in the definition of "Person".

Ch. 105, L. '07 Synopsis of Section 18-101(7) and 18-101(11)

This section amends §18-101(7) of the Act to conform the definition of limited liability company agreement to the definition of partnership agreement under the Delaware Revised Uniform Partnership Act to include implied agreements.

This section amends §18-101(11) of the Act to clarify the intended meaning of such subsection.

Ch. 317, L. '06 Synopsis of Section 18-101(12)

This Section amends §18-101(12) of the Act to confirm the broad scope of the defined term "person".

Ch. 51, L. '05 Synopsis of Section 18-101(7)

This section amends §18-101(7) of the Act to confirm that a member and manager of a limited liability company and an assignee of a limited liability company interest are bound by the limited liability company agreement.

Ch. 275, L. '04 Synopsis of Section 18-101

This amendment confirms the flexibility permitted in drafting a limited liability company agreement, including providing for the manner in which it may be amended.

Ch. 295, L. '02 Synopsis of Section 18-101

This section amends §18-101(7) of the Act to confirm the flexibility permitted by this section.

This section amends §18-101(7) of the Act to confirm that a limited liability company is bound by its limited liability company agreement.

Ch. 83, L. '01 Synopsis of Section 18-101

This section amends §18-101(12) of the Act to confirm the broad scope of the defined term "person."

Ch. 129, L. '99 Synopsis of Section 18-101

This section amends §18-101(7) of the Act to confirm the enforceability of a single member limited liability company agreement.

Ch. 341, L. '98 Synopsis of Section 18-101

This section amends §18-101(7)(a)(ii) of the Act to delete unnecessary words so as to facilitate the admission of members to a limited liability company.

Ch. 77, L. '97 Synopsis of Section 18-101

This Section amends §18-101(7) of the Act to add words dealing with a one member limited liability company.

This Section amends §18-101 of the Act to add a new defined term for use in other Sections of the Act

Ch. 75, L. '95 Synopsis of Section 18-101

This Section eliminates a definition from the Act which is no longer used in the Act.
This Section permits a one member limited liability company.
This Section permits the use of an oral limited liability company agreement.

.1 Operating agreements; statute of frauds.—The statute of frauds applies to limited liability company operating agreements. *Olson v Halvorsen*, 986 A2d 1150 (2009).

18-102 NAME SET FORTH IN CERTIFICATE.—The name of each limited liability company as set forth in its certificate of formation:

(1) Shall contain the words "Limited Liability Company" or the abbreviation "L.L.C." or the designation "LLC";

(2) May contain the name of a member or manager;

(3) Must be such as to distinguish it upon the records in the office of the Secretary of State from the name on such records of any corporation, partnership, limited partnership, statutory trust or limited liability company reserved, registered, formed or organized under the laws of the State of Delaware or qualified to do business or registered as a foreign corporation, foreign limited partnership, foreign statutory trust, foreign partnership, or foreign limited liability company in the State of Delaware; provided however, that a limited liability company may register under any name which is not such as to distinguish it upon the records in the office of the Secretary of State from the name on such records of any domestic or foreign corporation, partnership, limited partnership, *or* statutory trust or *foreign* limited liability company reserved, registered, formed or organized under the laws of the State of Delaware with the written consent of the other corporation, partnership, limited partnership, statutory trust or *foreign* limited liability company, which written consent shall be filed with the Secretary of State; *provided further, that, if on July 31, 2011, a limited liability company is registered (with the consent of another limited liability company) under a name which is not such as to distinguish it upon the records in the office of the Secretary of State from the name on such records of such other domestic limited liability company, it shall not be necessary for any such limited liability company to amend its certificate of formation to comply with this subsection;* and

(4) May contain the following words: "Company", "Association", "Club", "Foundation", "Fund", "Institute", "Society", "Union", "Syndicate", "Limited" or "Trust" (or abbreviations of like import). (Last amended by Ch. 95, L. '11, eff. 8-1-11.)

Ch. 95, L. '11, eff. 8-1-11, added matter in italic.

Ch. 95, L. '11 Synopsis of Section 18-102

This section amends §18-102(3) of the Act to provide that a limited liability company may not register under a name that is not such as to distinguish it upon the records in the office of the Secretary of State from the name on such records of another domestic limited liability company, provided that a limited liability company registered as of July 31, 2011 under such a name need not amend its certificate of formation to comply with this subsection.

Ch. 329, L. '02 Synopsis of Section 18-102

The amendments set forth are made for the purpose of avoiding any implication that a trust formed under Chapter 38, Title 12 of the Delaware Code constitutes a "business trust" within the meaning of Title 11 of the United States Code. Such amendments are not intended to result in any substantive change in Delaware law. These amendments are made solely for the purpose of conforming the Delaware Code to the amendments set forth above.

Ch. 83, L. '01 Synopsis of Section 18-102

This section amends §18-102(3) of the Act to clarify the intended meaning of the section.

Ch. 389, L. '00 Synopsis of Section 18-102

These sections amend §18-102(3), §18-209(a), §18-212(a), §18-214(a) and §18-216 of the Act to eliminate an unnecessary word.

Ch. 75, L. '95 Synopsis of Section 18-102

This Section permits the use of the designation "LLC" without periods as part of the name of a limited liability company.

Ch. 95, L. '11 Synopsis of Section 18-102

This sections amends §18-102(3) of the Act to provide that a limited liability company may not register under a name that is not such as to distinguish it upon the records in the office of the Secretary of State from the name on such records of another domestic limited liability company, provided that a limited liability company registered as of July 31, 2011 under such a name need not amend its certificate of formation to comply with this subsection.

18-103 RESERVATION OF NAME.—(a) The exclusive right to the use of a name may be reserved by:

(1) Any person intending to organize a limited liability company under this chapter and to adopt that name;

(2) Any domestic limited liability company or any foreign limited liability company registered in the State of Delaware which, in either case, proposes to change its name;

(3) Any foreign limited liability company intending to register in the State of Delaware and adopt that name; and

(4) Any person intending to organize a foreign limited liability company and intending to have it register in the State of Delaware and adopt that name.

(b) The reservation of a specified name shall be made by filing with the Secretary of State an application, executed by the applicant, specifying the name to be reserved and the name and address of the applicant. If the Secretary of State finds that the name is available for use by a domestic or foreign limited liability company, [1]*the Secretary* shall reserve the name for the exclusive use of the applicant for a period of 120 days. Once having so reserved a name, the same applicant may again reserve the same name for successive 120-day periods. The right to the exclusive use of a reserved name may be transferred to any other person by filing in the office of the Secretary of State a notice of the transfer, executed by the applicant for whom the name was reserved, specifying the name to be transferred and the name and address of the transferee. The reservation of a specified name may be cancelled by filing with the Secretary of State a notice of cancellation, executed by the applicant or transferee, specifying the name reservation to be cancelled and the name and address of the applicant or transferee. Unless the Secretary of State finds that any application, notice of transfer, or notice of cancellation filed with the Secretary of State as required by this subsection does not conform to law, upon receipt of all filing fees required by law [1]*the Secretary* shall prepare and return to the person who filed such instrument a copy of the filed instrument with a notation thereon of the action taken by the Secretary of State.

(c) A fee as set forth in §18-1105(a)(1) of this title shall be paid at the time of the initial reservation of any name, at the time of the renewal of any such reservation and at the time of the filing of a notice of the transfer or cancellation of any such reservation. (Last amended by Ch. 186, L. '95, eff. 7-10-95.)

Ch. 186, L. '95, eff. 7-10-95, added matter in italic and deleted [1]"he".

18-104 REGISTERED OFFICE; REGISTERED AGENT.—(a) Each limited liability company shall have and maintain in the State of Delaware:

(1) A registered office, which may but need not be a place of its business in the State of Delaware; and

(2) A registered agent for service of process on the limited liability company, having a business office identical with such registered office, which agent may be any of:
  a. The limited liability company itself,
  b. An individual resident in the State of Delaware,
  c. A domestic limited liability company (other than the limited liability company itself), a domestic corporation, a domestic partnership (whether general (including a limited liability partnership) or limited (including a limited liability limited partnership)), or a domestic statutory trust, or
  d. A foreign corporation, a foreign partnership (whether general (including a limited liability partnership) or limited (including a limited liability limited partnership)), a foreign limited liability company, or a foreign statutory trust.

(b) A registered agent may change the address of the registered office of the limited liability company(ies) for which it is registered agent to another address in the State of Delaware by paying a fee as set forth in §18-1105(a)(2) of this title and filing with the Secretary of State a certificate, executed by such registered agent, setting forth the address at which such registered agent has maintained the registered office for each of the limited liability companies for which it is a registered agent, and further certifying to the new address to which each such registered office will be changed on a given day, and at which new address such registered agent will thereafter maintain the registered office for each of the limited liability companies for which it is a registered agent. Upon the filing of such certificate, the Secretary of State shall furnish to the registered agent a certified copy of the same under the Secretary's hand and seal of office, and thereafter, or until further change of address, as authorized by law, the registered office in the State of Delaware of each of the limited liability companies for which the agent is a registered agent shall be located at the new address of the registered agent thereof as given in the certificate. In the event of a change of name of any person acting as a registered agent of a limited liability company, such registered agent shall file with the Secretary of State a certificate executed by such registered agent setting forth the new name of such registered agent, the name of such registered agent before it was changed, and the address at which such registered agent has maintained the registered office for each of the limited liability companies for which it is a registered agent, and shall pay a fee as set forth in §18-1105(a)(2) of this title. Upon the filing of such certificate, the Secretary of State shall furnish to the registered agent a certified copy of the certificate under the Secretary of State's own hand and seal of office. A change of name of any person acting as a registered agent of a limited liability company as a result of a merger or consolidation of the registered agent with or into another person which succeeds to its assets and liabilities by operation of law shall be deemed a change of name for purposes of this section. Filing a certificate under this section shall be deemed to be an amendment of the certificate of formation of each limited liability company affected thereby, and each such limited liability company shall not be required to take any further action with respect thereto to amend its certificate of formation under §18-202 of this title. Any registered agent filing a certificate under this section shall promptly, upon such filing, deliver a copy of any such certificate to each limited liability company affected thereby.

(c) The registered agent of 1 or more limited liability companies may resign and appoint a successor registered agent by paying a fee as set forth in §18-1105(a)(2) of this title and filing a certificate with the Secretary of State stating that it resigns and the name and address of the successor registered agent. There shall be attached to such certificate a statement of each affected limited liability company ratifying and approving such change of registered agent. Upon such filing, the successor registered agent shall become the registered agent of such limited liability companies as have ratified and approved such substitution, and the successor registered agent's address, as stated in such certificate, shall become the address of each such limited liability company's registered office in the State of Delaware. The Secretary of State shall then issue a certificate that the successor registered agent has become the registered agent of the limited liability companies so ratifying and approving such change and setting out the names of such limited liability companies. Filing of such certificate of resignation shall be deemed to be an amendment of the certificate of formation of each limited liability company affected thereby, and each such limited liability company shall not be required to take any further action with respect thereto to amend its certificate of formation under §18-202 of this title.

(d) The registered agent of 1 or more limited liability companies may resign without appointing a successor registered agent by paying a fee as set forth in §18-1105(a)(2) of this title and filing a certificate of resignation with the Secretary of State, but such resignation shall not become effective until 30 days after the certificate is filed. The certificate shall contain a statement that written notice of resignation was given to each affected limited liability company at least 30 days prior to the filing of the certificate by mailing or delivering such notice to the limited liability company at its address last known to the registered agent and shall set forth the date of such notice. After receipt of the notice of the resignation of its registered agent, the limited liability company for which such registered agent was acting shall obtain and designate a new registered agent, to take the place of the registered agent so resigning. If such limited liability company fails to obtain and designate a new registered agent as aforesaid prior to the expiration of the period of 30 days after the filing by the registered agent of the certificate of resignation, the certificate of formation of such limited liability company shall be canceled. After the resignation of the registered agent shall have become effective as provided in this section and if no new registered agent shall have been obtained and designated in the time and manner aforesaid, service of legal process against each limited liability company for which the resigned registered agent had been acting shall thereafter be upon the Secretary of State in accordance with §18-105 of this title.

(e) Every registered agent shall:

(1) If an entity, maintain a business office in the State of Delaware which is generally open, or if an individual, be generally present at a designated location in the State of Delaware, at sufficiently frequent times to accept service of process and otherwise perform the functions of a registered agent;

(2) If a foreign entity, be authorized to transact business in the State of Delaware;

(3) Accept service of process and other communications directed to the limited liability companies and foreign limited liability companies for which it serves as registered agent and forward same to the limited liability company or foreign limited liability company to which the service or communication is directed; and

(4) Forward to the limited liability companies and foreign limited liability companies for which it serves as registered agent the statement for the annual tax described in §18-1107 of this title or an electronic notification of same in a form satisfactory to the Secretary of State.

(f) Any registered agent who at any time serves as registered agent for more than 50 entities (a "commercial registered agent"), whether domestic or foreign, shall satisfy and comply with the following qualifications:

(1) A natural person serving as a commercial registered agent shall:

a. Maintain a principal residence or a principal place of business in the State of Delaware;

b. Maintain a Delaware business license;

c. Be generally present at a designated location within the State of Delaware during normal business hours to accept service of process and otherwise perform the functions of a registered agent as specified in subsection (e) of this section; and

d. Provide the Secretary of State upon request with such information identifying and enabling communication with such commercial registered agent as the Secretary of State shall require.

(2) A domestic or foreign corporation, a domestic or foreign partnership (whether general (including a limited liability partnership) or limited (including a limited liability limited partnership)), a domestic or foreign limited liability company, or a domestic or foreign statutory trust serving as a commercial registered agent shall:

a. Have a business office within the State of Delaware which is generally open during normal business hours to accept service of process and otherwise perform the functions of a registered agent as specified in subsection (e) of this section;

b. Maintain a Delaware business license;

c. Have generally present at such office during normal business hours an officer, director or managing agent who is a natural person; and

d. Provide the Secretary of State upon request with such information identifying and enabling communication with such commercial registered agent as the Secretary of State shall require.

(3) For purposes of this subsection and subsection (i)(2)a., a commercial registered agent shall also include any registered agent which has an officer, director or managing agent in common with any other registered agent or agents if such registered agents at any time during such common service as officer, director or managing agent collectively served as registered agents for more than 50 entities, whether domestic or foreign.

(g) Every limited liability company formed under the laws of the State of Delaware or qualified to do business in the State of Delaware shall provide to its registered agent and update from time to time as necessary the name, business address and business telephone number of a natural person who is a member, manager, officer, employee or designated agent of the limited liability company, who is then authorized to receive communications from the registered agent. Such person shall be deemed the communications contact for the limited liability company. Every registered agent shall retain (in paper or electronic form) the above information concerning the current communications contact for each limited liability company and each foreign limited liability company for which that registered agent serves as registered agent. If the limited liability company fails to provide the registered agent with a current communications contact, the registered agent may resign as the registered agent for such limited liability company pursuant to this section.

(h) The Secretary of State is authorized to issue such rules and regulations as may be necessary or appropriate to carry out the enforcement of subsections (e), (f) and (g) of this section, and to take actions reasonable and necessary to assure registered agents' compliance with subsections (e), (f) and (g) of this section. Such actions may include refusal to file documents submitted by a registered agent.

(i) Upon application of the Secretary of State, the Court of Chancery may enjoin any person or entity from serving as a registered agent or as an officer, director or managing agent of a registered agent.

(1) Upon the filing of a complaint by the Secretary of State pursuant to this section, the court may make such orders respecting such proceeding as it deems appropriate, and may enter such orders granting interim or final relief as it deems proper under the circumstances.

(2) Any 1 or more of the following grounds shall be a sufficient basis to grant an injunction pursuant to this section:

a. With respect to any registered agent who at any time within 1 year immediately prior to the filing of the Secretary of State's complaint is a commercial registered agent, failure after notice and warning to comply with the qualifications set forth in subsection (e) of this section and/or the requirements of subsections (f) or (g) of this section above;

b. The person serving as a registered agent, or any person who is an officer, director or managing agent of an entity registered agent, has been convicted of a felony or any crime which includes an element of dishonesty or fraud or involves moral turpitude; or

c. The registered agent has engaged in conduct in connection with acting as a registered agent that is intended to or likely to deceive or defraud the public.

(3) With respect to any order the court enters pursuant to this section with respect to an entity that has acted as a registered agent, the court may also direct such order to any person who has served as an officer, director or managing agent of such registered agent. Any person who, on or after January 1, 2007, serves as an officer, director or managing agent of an entity acting as a registered agent in the State of Delaware shall be deemed thereby to have consented to the appointment of such registered agent as agent upon whom service of process may be made in any action brought pursuant to this section, and service as an officer, director or managing agent of an entity acting as a registered agent in the State of Delaware shall be a signification of the consent of such person that any process when so served shall be of the same legal force and validity as if served upon such person within the State of Delaware, and such appointment of the registered agent shall be irrevocable.

(4) Upon the entry of an order by the court enjoining any person or entity from acting as a registered agent, the Secretary of State shall mail or deliver notice of such order to each affected limited liability company:

a. That has specified the address of a place of business in a record of the Secretary of State, to the address specified, or

b. An address of which the Secretary of State has obtained from the limited liability company's former registered agent, to the address obtained.

§18-104

If such a limited liability company is a domestic limited liability company and fails to obtain and designate a new registered agent within 30 days after such notice is given, the certificate of formation of such limited liability company shall be cancelled. If such a limited liability company is a foreign limited liability company and fails to obtain and designate a new registered agent within 30 days after such notice is given, such foreign limited liability company shall not be permitted to do business in the State of Delaware and its registration shall be cancelled. If any other affected limited liability company is a domestic limited liability company and fails to obtain and designate a new registered agent within 60 days after entry of an order by the court enjoining such limited liability company's registered agent from acting as a registered agent, the certificate of formation of such limited liability company shall be cancelled. If any other affected limited liability company is a foreign limited liability company and fails to obtain and designate a new registered agent within 60 days after entry of an order by court enjoining such limited liability company's registered agent from acting as a registered agent, such foreign limited liability company shall not be permitted to do business in the State of Delaware and its registration shall be cancelled. If the court enjoins a person or entity from acting as a registered agent as provided in this section and no new registered agent shall have been obtained and designated in the time and manner aforesaid, service of legal process against the limited liability company for which the registered agent had been acting shall thereafter be upon the Secretary of State in accordance with §18-105 or §18-911 of this title. The Court of Chancery may, upon application of the Secretary of State on notice to the former registered agent, enter such orders as it deems appropriate to give the Secretary of State access to information in the former registered agent's possession in order to facilitate communication with the limited liability companies the former registered agent served.

(j) The Secretary of State is authorized to make a list of registered agents available to the public, and to establish such qualifications and issue such rules and regulations with respect to such listing as the Secretary of State deems necessary or appropriate.

(k) *As contained in any certificate of formation, application for registration as a foreign limited liability company, or other document filed in the office of the Secretary of State under this chapter, the address of a registered agent or registered office shall include the street, number, city and postal code.* (Last amended by Ch. 95, L. '11, eff. 8-1-11.)

Ch. 95, L. '11, eff. 8-1-11, added matter in italic.

Ch. 95, L. '11 Synopsis of Section 18-104

This section adds a new subsection (k) to §18-104 of the Act providing that, in any certificate or other document filed with the Secretary of State, the address of the registered agent or registered office of the limited liability company must include the street, number, city and postal code.

Ch. 105, L. '07 Synopsis of Section 18-104

This section amends §18-104(a)(2) of the Act to confirm that the business office of a limited liability company's registered agent shall be identical to the registered office of the limited liability company in the State of Delaware.

This section amends §18-104(d) of the Act to make a technical change.

This section amends §18-104(e)(3) of the Act to confirm that such subsection also applies to a foreign limited liability company.

This section amends §18-104(e)(4) of the Act to confirm that such subsection also applies to a foreign limited liability company.

This section amends §18-104(g) of the Act to confirm that such subsection also applies to a foreign limited liability company.

This section amends §18-104(i)(4)b. of the Act to make technical changes.

Ch. 317, L. '06 Synopsis of Section 18-104

These Sections amend §18-104 of the Act to expand the types of entities that may serve as registered agents; prescribe the duties of a registered agent; require that persons or entities serving as registered agent for more than fifty entities (a "Commercial Registered Agent") be generally open during normal business hours and have a natural person present to operate such office and communicate with the Secretary of State on request; require Delaware limited liability companies to provide registered agents with a designated natural person to receive communications from the registered agent and require the registered agent to maintain in its records the identity of such persons; authorize the Secretary of State to issue regulations to enforce these provisions; authorize the Secretary of State to bring a lawsuit in the Court of Chancery to enjoin any person or entity from acting as a registered agent, or as an officer, or director or managing agent of a registered agent, any person or entity who fails to comply with the statutory requirements, who has been convicted of a felony or any crime involving dishonesty, fraud or moral turpitude, or who has used the office of registered agent in a manner intended to defraud the public; provide that the certificate of formation or registration of a domestic or foreign limited liability company will be cancelled if it fails, within a prescribed period, to obtain and designate a new registered agent if the Court of Chancery enjoins any person or entity from acting as a registered agent for such limited liability company; and authorize the Secretary of State to make a list of registered agents available to the public.

Ch. 329, L. '02 Synopsis of Section 18-104

The amendments set forth are made for the purpose of avoiding any implication that a trust formed under Chapter 38, Title 12 of the Delaware Code constitutes a "business trust" within the meaning of Title 11 of the United States Code. Such amendments are not intended to result in any substantive change in Delaware law. These amendments are made solely for the purpose of conforming the Delaware Code to the amendments set forth above.

Ch. 83, L. '01 Synopsis of Section 18-104

This section amends §18-104(b), §18-104(c) and §18-104(d) of the Act to clarify the procedures relating to the change in the address of a registered office, the change in the name of a registered agent and the resignation of a registered agent.

Ch. 77, L. '97 Synopsis of Section 18-104

This Section amends §18-104(a)(2) of the Act to expand the types of entities that may act as a registered agent.

This Section amends §18-104(a)(2) of the Act to add a requirement that a registered agent must be generally open during normal business hours to perform its functions as a registered agent.

18-105 SERVICE OF PROCESS ON DOMESTIC LIMITED LIABILITY COMPANIES.—(a) Service of legal process upon any domestic limited liability company shall be made by delivering a copy personally to any manager of the limited liability company in the State of Delaware or the registered agent of the limited liability company in the State of Delaware, or by leaving it at the dwelling house or usual place of abode in the State of Delaware of any such manager or registered agent (if the registered agent be an individual), or at the registered office or other place of business of the limited liability company in the State of Delaware. If the registered agent be a corporation, service of process upon it as such may be made by serving, in the State of Delaware, a copy thereof on the president, vice-president, secretary, assistant secretary or any director of the corporate registered agent. Service by copy left at the dwelling house or usual place of abode of a manager or registered agent, or at the registered office or other place of business of the limited liability company in the State of Delaware, to be effective, must be delivered thereat at least 6 days before the return date of the process, and in the presence of an adult person, and the officer serving the process shall distinctly state the manner of service in the officer's return thereto. Process returnable forthwith must be delivered personally to the manager or registered agent.

(b) [1] *In case the officer whose duty it is to serve legal process cannot by due diligence serve the process in any manner provided for by subsection (a) of this section, it shall be lawful to serve the process against the limited liability company upon the Secretary of State, and such service shall be as effectual for all intents and purposes as if made in any of the ways provided for in subsection (a) of this section. Process may be served upon the Secretary of State under this subsection by means of electronic transmission but only as prescribed by the Secretary of State. The Secretary of State is authorized to issue such rules and regulations with respect to such service as the Secretary of State deems necessary or appropriate. In the event that service is effected through the Secretary of State in accordance with this subsection, the Secretary of State shall forthwith notify the limited liability company by letter, directed to the limited liability company at its address as it appears on the records relating to such limited liability company on file with the Secretary of State or, if no such address appears, at its last registered office.* Such letter shall enclose a copy of the process and any other papers served on the Secretary of State pursuant to this subsection. It shall be the duty of the plaintiff in the event of such service to serve process and any other papers in duplicate, to notify the Secretary of State that service is being effected pursuant to this subsection, and to pay the Secretary of State the sum of $50 for the use of the State of Delaware, which sum shall be taxed as part of the costs in the proceeding if the plaintiff shall prevail therein. The Secretary of State shall maintain an alphabetical record of any such service setting forth the name of the plaintiff and defendant, the title, docket number and nature of the proceeding in which process has been served upon the Secretary, the fact that service has been effected pursuant to this subsection, the return date thereof, and the day and hour when the service was made. The Secretary of State shall not be required to retain such information for a period longer than 5 years from the Secretary's receipt of the service of process. (Last amended by Ch. 287, L. '10, eff. 8-2-10.)

Ch. 287, L. '10, eff. 8-2-10, added matter in italic and deleted [1] "In case the officer whose duty it is to serve legal process cannot by due diligence serve the process in any manner provided for by subsection (a) of this section, it shall be lawful to serve the process against the limited liability company upon the Secretary of State, and such service shall be as effectual for all intents and purposes as if made in any of the ways provided for in subsection (a) of this section. In the event that service is effected through the Secretary of State in accordance with this subsection, the Secretary of State shall forthwith notify the limited liability company by letter, certified mail, return receipt requested, directed to the limited liability company at its address as it appears on the records relating to such limited liability company on file with the Secretary of State or, if no such address appears, at its last registered office."

Ch. 287, L. '10 Synopsis of Section 18-105

Sections 2, 26, 27 and 28 amend §§18-105(b), 18-910(b), 18-911(a) and 18-911(c) of the Act to allow for service of process upon the Secretary of State thereunder by means of electronic transmission but only as prescribed by the Secretary of State, to authorize the Secretary of State to issue such rules and regulations with respect to such service as the Secretary of State deems necessary or appropriate, and to enable the Secretary of State, in the event that service is effected through the Secretary of State in accordance therewith, to provide notice of service by letter sent by a mail or courier service that includes a record of mailing or deposit with the courier and a record of delivery evidenced by the signature of the recipient.

18-106 NATURE OF BUSINESS PERMITTED; POWERS.—(a) A limited liability company may carry on any lawful business, purpose or activity, whether or not for profit, with the exception of the business of banking as defined in §126 of Title 8.

(b) A limited liability company shall possess and may exercise all the powers and privileges granted by this chapter or by any other law or by its limited liability company agreement, together with any powers incidental thereto, including such powers and privileges as are necessary or convenient to the conduct, promotion or attainment of the business, purposes or activities of the limited liability company.

(c) Notwithstanding any provision of this chapter to the contrary, without limiting the general powers enumerated in subsection (b) of this section, a limited liability company shall, subject to such standards and restrictions, if any, as are set forth in its limited liability company agreement, have the power and authority to make contracts of guaranty and suretyship, and enter into interest rate, basis, currency, hedge or other swap agreements, or cap, floor, put, call, option, exchange or collar agreements, derivative agreements or other agreements similar to any of the foregoing.

(d) *Unless otherwise provided in a limited liability company agreement, a limited liability company has the power and authority to grant, hold or exercise a power of attorney, including an irrevocable power of attorney.* (Last amended by Ch. 287, L. '10, eff. 8-2-10.)

Ch. 287, L. '10, eff. 8-2-10, added matter in italic.

Ch. 287, L. '10 Synopsis of Section 18-106

This section amends §18-106 of the Act to confirm the broad powers of a limited liability company.

Ch. 51, L. '05 Synopsis of Section 18-106 (a)

This section amends §18-106(a) of the Act to expand the permitted purposes of a limited liability company.

Ch. 295, L. '02 Synopsis of Section 18-106

This section amends §18-106 of the Act to confirm and clarify the broad powers of a limited liability company.

Ch. 129, L. '99 Synopsis of Section 18-106

This section amends §18-106(b) of the Act to clarify the intended meaning of the section concerning incidental powers.

Ch. 77, L. '97 Synopsis of Section 18-106

This Section amends §18-106(a) of the Act to clarify the activities for which a limited liability company may be used.

18-107 BUSINESS TRANSACTIONS OF MEMBER OR MANAGER WITH THE LIMITED LIABILITY COMPANY.—Except as provided in a limited liability company agreement, a member or manager may lend money to, borrow money from, act as a surety, guarantor or endorser for, guarantee or assume 1 or more obligations of, provide collateral for, and transact other business with, a limited liability company and, subject to other applicable law, has the same rights and obligations with respect to any such matter as a person who is not a member or manager. (Last amended by Ch. 260, L. '94, eff. 8-1-94.)

18-108 INDEMNIFICATION.—Subject to such standards and restrictions, if any, as are set forth in its limited liability company agreement, a limited liability company may, and shall have the power to, indemnify and hold harmless any member or manager or other person from and against any and all claims and demands whatsoever.

18-109 SERVICE OF PROCESS ON MANAGERS AND LIQUIDATING TRUSTEES.—(a) A manager or a liquidating trustee of a limited liability company may be served with process in the manner prescribed in this section in all civil actions or proceedings brought in the State of Delaware involving or relating to the business of the limited liability company or a violation by the manager or the liquidating trustee of a duty to the limited liability company, or any member of the limited liability company, whether or not the manager or the liquidating trustee is a manager or a liquidating trustee at the time suit is commenced. A manager's or a liquidating trustee's serving as such constitutes such person's consent to the appointment of the registered agent of the limited liability company (or, if there is none, the Secretary of State) as such person's agent upon whom service of process may be made as provided in this section. Such service as a manager or a liquidating trustee shall signify the consent of such manager or liquidating trustee that any process when so served shall be of the same legal force and validity as if served upon such manager or liquidating trustee within the State of Delaware and such appointment of the registered agent (or, if there is none, the Secretary of State) shall be irrevocable. As used in this subsection (a) and in [1]*subsections (b), (c) and (d)* of this section, the term "manager" refers (i) to a person who is a manager as defined in §18-101(10) of this title and (ii) [2]*to a person, whether or not a member of a limited liability company, who,* although not a manager as defined in §18-101(10) of this title, participates materially in the management of the limited liability company; provided, however, that the power to elect or otherwise select or to participate in the election or selection of a person to be a manager as defined in §18-101(10) of this title shall not, by itself, constitute participation in the management of the limited liability company.

(b) Service of process shall be effected by serving the registered agent (or, if there is none, the Secretary of State) with 1 copy of such process in the manner provided by law for service of writs of summons. In the event service is made under this subsection upon the Secretary of State, the plaintiff shall pay to the Secretary of State the sum of $50 for the use of the State of Delaware, which sum shall be taxed as part of the costs of the proceeding if the plaintiff shall prevail therein. In addition, the Prothonotary or the Register in Chancery of the court in which the civil action or proceeding is pending shall, within 7 days of such service, deposit in the United States mails, by registered mail, postage prepaid, true and attested copies of the process, together with a statement that service is being made pursuant to this section, addressed to such manager or liquidating trustee at the registered office of the limited liability company and at the manager's or liquidating trustee's address last known to the party desiring to make such service.

(c) In any action in which any such manager or liquidating trustee has been served with process as hereinabove provided, the time in which a defendant shall be required to appear and file a responsive pleading shall be computed from the date of mailing by the Prothonotary or the Register in Chancery as provided in subsection (b) of this section; however, the court in which such action has been commenced may order such continuance or continuances as may be necessary to afford such manager or liquidating trustee reasonable opportunity to defend the action.

(d) In a written limited liability company agreement or other writing, a manager or member may consent to be subject to the nonexclusive jurisdiction of the courts of, or arbitration in, a specified jurisdiction, or the exclusive jurisdiction of the courts of the State of Delaware, or the exclusivity of arbitration in a specified jurisdiction or the State of Delaware, and to be served with legal process in the manner prescribed in such limited liability company agreement or other writing. Except by agreeing to arbitrate any arbitrable matter in a specified jurisdiction or in the State of Delaware, a member who is not a manager may not waive its right to maintain a legal action or proceeding in the courts of the State of Delaware with respect to matters relating to the organization or internal affairs of a limited liability company.

(e) Nothing herein contained limits or affects the right to serve process in any other manner now or hereafter provided by law. This section is an extension of and not a limitation upon the right otherwise existing of service of legal process upon nonresidents.

(f) The Court of Chancery and the Superior Court may make all necessary rules respecting the form of process, the manner of issuance and return thereof and such other rules which may be necessary to implement this section and are not inconsistent with this section. (Last amended by Ch. 389, L. '00, eff. 8-1-00.)

Ch. 389, L. '00, eff. 8-1-00, added matter in italic and deleted [1]"subsections (b) and (c)" and [2]"to a person who is a member of a limited liability company and who".

Ch. 389, L. '00 Synopsis of Section 18-109

This section amends §18-109(a) of the Act to clarify who is deemed to have consented to service of process in Delaware.

This section amends §18-109(d) of the Act to provide that, except by agreeing to arbitrate any arbitrable matter in a specified jurisdiction or in the State of Delaware, a member who is not a manager may not waive its right to maintain a legal action or proceeding in the courts of the State of Delaware with respect to matters relating to the organization or internal affairs of a limited liability company.

Ch. 129, L. '99 Synopsis of Section 18-109

This section amends §18-109(a) of the Act to clarify who is deemed to have consented to service of process in Delaware.

Ch. 77, L. '97 Synopsis of Section 18-109

This Section amends §18-109(d) of the Act to clarify that arbitration outside of the State of Delaware is permitted.

.1 **Jurisdiction over foreign manager.**—A court may exercise personal jurisdiction over a limited liability company manager who resides in a foreign country and has no other contacts with the forum state where breach of fiduciary claims, as well as contract claims that "involve or relate" to the manager's rights, duties, and obligations as manager of the limited liability company, are asserted against the manager. *PT China LLC v PT Korea LLC, 2010 Del. Ch. LEXIS 38 (Ch Ct 2010).*

.2 **Implied consent.**—Neither merely conferring with members of management on occasion and being involved in a single issue before a company's board nor having a direct role in the formation of a limited liability company and executing documents on its behalf constitutes material participation and management for purposes of implied consent. *Ross Holding and Management Co v Advance Realty Group LLC, 2010 Del. Ch. LEXIS 86 (Ch Ct 2010).*

18-110 CONTESTED MATTERS RELATING TO MANAGERS; CONTESTED VOTES.—(a) Upon application of any member or manager, the Court of Chancery may hear and determine the validity of any admission, election, appointment, removal or resignation of a manager of a limited liability company, and the right of any person to become or continue to be a manager of a limited liability company, and, in case the right to serve as a manager is claimed by more than 1 person, may determine the person or persons entitled to serve as managers; and to that end make such order or decree in any such case as may be just and proper, with power to enforce the production of any books, papers and records of the limited liability company relating to the issue. In any such application, the limited liability company shall be named as a party and service of copies of the application upon the registered agent of the limited liability company shall be deemed to be service upon the limited liability company and upon the person or persons whose right to serve as a manager is contested and upon the person or persons, if any, claiming to be a manager or claiming the right to be a manager; and the registered agent shall forward immediately a copy of the application to the limited liability company and to the person or persons whose right to serve as a manager is contested and to the person or persons, if any, claiming to be a manager or the right to be a manager, in a postpaid, sealed, registered letter addressed to such limited liability company and such person or persons at their post-office addresses last known to the registered agent or furnished to the registered agent by the applicant member or manager. The Court may make such order respecting further or other notice of such application as it deems proper under these circumstances.

(b) Upon application of any member or manager, the Court of Chancery may hear and determine the result of any vote of members or managers upon matters as to which the members or managers of the limited liability company, or any class or group of members or managers, have the right to vote pursuant to the limited liability company agreement or other agreement or this chapter (other than the admission, election, appointment, removal or resignation of managers). In any such application, the limited liability company shall be named as a party and service of the application upon the registered agent of the limited liability company shall be deemed to be service upon the limited liability company, and no other party need be joined in order for the Court to adjudicate the result of the vote. The Court may make such order respecting further or other notice of such application as it deems proper under these circumstances.

(c) As used in this section, the term "manager" refers to a person:
a. Who is a manager as defined in §18-101(10) of this title; and
b. Whether or not a member of a limited liability company, who, although not a manager as defined in §18-101(10) of this title, participates materially in the management of the limited liability company;

provided however, that the power to elect or otherwise select or to participate in the election or selection of a person to be a manager as defined in §18-101(10) of this title shall not, by itself, constitute participation in the management of the limited liability company.

[1](d) Nothing herein contained limits or affects the right to serve process in any other manner now or hereafter provided by law. This section is an extension of and not a limitation upon the right otherwise existing of service of legal process upon nonresidents. (Last amended by Ch. 387, L. '08, eff. 8-1-08.)

Ch. 387, L. '08, eff. 8-1-08, added matter in italic and deleted [1]"(c)".

Ch. 387, L. '08 Synopsis of Section 18-110

These sections amend §§18-110 and 18-111 of the Act to provide that the term "manager" as used in those sections is defined consistently with the manner in which the term "manager" is defined in §18-109(a) of the Act (Service of process on managers and liquidating trustees).

Ch. 77, L. '97 Synopsis of Section 18-110

This Section amends §18-110 of the Act to clarify the jurisdiction of the Court of Chancery in connection with certain matters relating to limited liability companies.

.1 **Advancement rights.**—Where a limited liability company agreement is clear that advancement is available only for the defense or other defensive disposition of an actual or threatened proceeding, a managing member is not entitled to advancement where the non-managing members have not brought or threatened any proceedings against him. *Donohue v Corning, 949 A2d 574 (Ch Ct 2008).*

18-111 INTERPRETATION AND ENFORCEMENT OF LIMITED LIABILITY COMPANY AGREEMENT.—Any action to interpret, apply or enforce the provisions of a limited liability company agreement, or the duties, obligations or liabilities of a limited liability company to the members or managers of the limited liability company, or the duties, obligations or liabilities among members or managers and of members or managers to the limited liability company, or the rights or powers of, or restrictions on, the limited liability company, members or managers, *or any provision of this chapter, or any other instrument, document, agreement or certificate contemplated by any provision of this chapter,* may be brought in the Court of Chancery.

As used in this section, the term "manager" refers to a person:

(1) Who is a manager as defined in §18-101(10) of this title; and

(2) Whether or not a member of a limited liability company, who, although not a manager as defined in §18-101(10) of this title, participates materially in the management of the limited liability company; provided however, that the power to elect or otherwise select or to participate in the election or selection of a person to be a manager as defined in §18-101(10) of this title shall not, by itself, constitute participation in the management of the limited liability company. (Last amended by Ch. 58, L. '09, eff. 8-1-09.)

Ch. 58, L. '09, eff. 8-1-09, added matter in italic.

Ch. 58, L. '09 Synopsis of Section 18-111

This section amends §18-111 of the Act to clarify the jurisdiction of the Court of Chancery with respect to matters pertaining to Delaware limited liability companies.

Ch. 387, L. '08 Synopsis of Section 18-111

These sections amend §§18-110 and 18-111 of the Act to provide that the term "manager" as used in those sections is defined consistently with the manner in which the term "manager" is defined in §18-109(a) of the Act (Service of process on managers and liquidating trustees).

.1 Legal fees.—A limited liability company must advance legal fees to its members where its operating agreement provides that "to the fullest extent permitted by applicable law" expenses incurred by a member in defending any claim, demand, action, suit, or proceeding shall be advanced prior to disposition of such claim, demand, action, suit, or proceeding. *Morgan v Grace, 2003 Del. Ch. LEXIS 113 (Ch Ct 2003).*

.2 Advancement rights.—Where a limited liability company agreement is clear that advancement is available only for the defense or other defensive disposition of an actual or threatened proceeding, a managing member is not entitled to advancement where the non-managing members have not brought or threatened any proceedings against him. *Donohue v Corning, 949 A2d 574 (Ch Ct 2008).*

Subchapter II. Formation; Certificate of Formation

18-201 CERTIFICATE OF FORMATION.—(a) In order to form a limited liability company, 1 or more authorized persons must execute a certificate of formation. The certificate of formation shall be filed in the office of the Secretary of State and set forth:

(1) The name of the limited liability company;

(2) The address of the registered office and the name and address of the registered agent for service of process required to be maintained by §18-104 of this title; and

(3) Any other matters the members determine to include therein.

(b) A limited liability company is formed at the time of the filing of the initial certificate of formation in the office of the Secretary of State or at any later date or time specified in the certificate of formation if, in either case, there has been substantial compliance with the requirements of this section. A limited liability company formed under this chapter shall be a separate legal entity, the existence of which as a separate legal entity shall continue until cancellation of the limited liability company's certificate of formation.

(c) The filing of the certificate of formation in the office of the Secretary of State shall make it unnecessary to file any other documents under Chapter 31 of this title.

(d) A limited liability company agreement [1]*shall be entered into or otherwise existing* either before, after or at the time of the filing of a certificate of formation and, whether entered into *or otherwise existing* before, after or at the time of such filing, may be made effective as of the formation of the limited liability company or at such other time or date as provided in *or reflected by* the limited liability company agreement. (Last amended by Ch. 105, L. '07, eff. 8-1-07.)

Ch. 105, L. '07, eff. 8-1-07, added matter in italic and deleted [1]"may".

Ch. 105, L. '07 Synopsis of Section 18-201

This section amends §18-201(d) of the Act to confirm that a limited liability company agreement is required by the Act and to make changes conforming to the amendments to §18-101(7).

Ch. 75, L. '95 Synopsis of Section 18-201

This Section deals with the timing of the entering into of a limited liability company agreement.

.1 Representation of a limited liability company.—A limited liability company, like a corporation, requires representation by legal counsel in court and neither a member nor a manager of a limited liability company who is not an attorney can appear in court to represent the limited liability company. *Poore v Fox Hollow Enterprises, No. 93A-09-005 (Super Ct 3-29-94).*

18-202 AMENDMENT TO CERTIFICATE OF FORMATION.—(a) A certificate of formation is amended by filing a certificate of amendment thereto in the office of the Secretary of State. The certificate of amendment shall set forth:

(1) The name of the limited liability company; and
(2) The amendment to the certificate of formation.

(b) A manager or, if there is no manager, then any member who becomes aware that any statement in a certificate of formation was false when made, or that any matter described has changed making the certificate of formation false in any material respect, shall promptly amend the certificate of formation.

(c) A certificate of formation may be amended at any time for any other proper purpose.

(d) Unless otherwise provided in this chapter or unless a later effective date or time (which shall be a date or time certain) is provided for in the certificate of amendment, a certificate of amendment shall be effective at the time of its filing with the Secretary of State.

.1 Certificate of formation; operating agreement.—For the purpose of determining the membership of a limited liability company, the certificate of formation is superseded by the operating agreement. *In re Grupo Dos Chiles, LLC, 2006 Del. Ch. LEXIS 54 (Ch Ct 2006).*

18-203 CANCELLATION OF CERTIFICATE.—*(a)* A certificate of formation shall be canceled upon the dissolution and the completion of winding up of a limited liability company, or as provided in §18-104(d) or §18-104(i)(4) or §18-1108 of this title, or upon the filing of a certificate of merger or consolidation or a certificate of ownership and merger if the limited liability company is not the surviving or resulting entity in a merger or consolidation or upon the future effective date or time of a certificate of merger or consolidation or a certificate of ownership and merger if the limited liability company is not the surviving or resulting entity in a merger or consolidation, or upon the filing of a certificate of transfer or upon the future effective date or time of a certificate of transfer, or upon the filing of a certificate of conversion to non-Delaware entity or upon the future effective date or time of a certificate of conversion to non-Delaware entity. A certificate of cancellation shall be filed in the office of the Secretary of State to accomplish the cancellation of a certificate of formation upon the dissolution and the completion of winding up of a limited liability company and shall set forth:

(1) The name of the limited liability company;
(2) The date of filing of its certificate of formation;
(3) The future effective date or time (which shall be a date or time certain) of cancellation if it is not to be effective upon the filing of the certificate; and
(4) Any other information the person filing the certificate of cancellation determines.

(b) A certificate of cancellation that is filed in the office of the Secretary of State prior to the dissolution or the completion of winding up of a limited liability company may be corrected as an erroneously executed certificate of cancellation by filing with the office of the Secretary of State a certificate of correction of such certificate of cancellation in accordance with §18-211 of this title.

(c) The Secretary of State shall not issue a certificate of good standing with respect to a limited liability company if its certificate of formation is canceled. (Last amended by Ch. 95, L. '11, eff. 8-1-11.)

Ch. 95, L. '11, eff. 8-1-11, added matter in italic.

Ch. 95, L. '11 Synopsis of Section 18-203

This section designates all but the final sentence of §18-203 of the Act as a new subsection (a), designates the final sentence of §18-203 of the Act as a new subsection (c), and adds a new subsection (b) confirming that a certificate of correction may be filed to correct a certificate of cancellation that has been filed prior to the dissolution or the completion of winding up of a limited liability company.

Ch. 287, L. '10 Synopsis of Section 18-203

Sections 4, 6, 7, 8, 9, 10, 11, 13, 14, 15, 16, 17, 20 and 30 amend §§18-203, 18-206(a), 18-206(b), 18-206(d), 18-209(a), 18-209(b), 18-209(c), 18-209(d), 18-209(e), 18-209(f), 18-209, 18-210, 18-301(b) and 18-1105(a) of the Act to provide a mechanism to implement a short form merger under new Section 267 of Title 8 where a domestic limited liability company is the parent Entity (as defined in new Section 267(e)(2) of Title 8).

Ch. 105, L. '07 Synopsis of Section 18-203

This section amends §18-203 of the Act to make technical changes, and to confirm that a certificate of good standing shall not be issued for a limited liability company if its certificate of formation is cancelled.

Ch. 317, L. '06 Synopsis of Section 18-203

This Section amends §18-203 of the Act to conform to new §18-104(i)(4) of the Act which provides for the cancellation of a certificate of formation in the circumstances therein provided.

Ch. 85, L. '03 Synopsis of Section 18-203

These amendments permit conversion of a Delaware limited liability company to a non-Delaware entity.

Ch. 295, L. '02 Synopsis of Section 18-203

This section amends §18-203 of the Act to delete the requirement of setting forth the reason for filing a certificate of cancellation in the certificate of cancellation.

Ch. 389, L. '00 Synopsis of Section 18-203

These sections amend §18-203 of the Act to delete the requirement of the filing of a certificate of cancellation upon the conversion of a limited liability company.

Ch. 341, L. '98 Synopsis of Section 18-203

This section amends §18-203 of the Act to add a requirement that, when a limited liability company is converting to another form of entity, the certificate of cancellation of the converting entity state the name of the entity to which the limited liability company has been converted.

Ch. 77, L. '97 Synopsis of Section 18-203

This Section amends §18-203 of the Act to conform the section, which deals with the filing of a certificate of cancellation for a limited liability company, to other changes being made in the Act.

Ch. 75, L. '95 Synopsis of Section 18-203

This Section modifies the cancellation provisions of the Act to reflect the certificate of revival authorized by new §18-1109 and to reflect the possibility of having a one member limited liability company.

18-204 EXECUTION.—(a) Each certificate required by this subchapter to be filed in the office of the Secretary of State shall be executed by 1 or more authorized persons or, in the case of a certificate of conversion to limited liability company or certificate of limited liability company domestication, by any person authorized to execute such certificate on behalf of the other entity or non-United States entity, respectively, except that a certificate of merger or consolidation filed by a surviving or resulting other business entity shall be executed by any person authorized to execute such certificate on behalf of such other business entity.

(b) Unless otherwise provided in a limited liability company agreement, any person may sign any certificate or amendment thereof or enter into a limited liability company agreement or amendment thereof by an agent, including an attorney-in-fact. An authorization, including a power of attorney, to sign any certificate or amendment thereof or to enter into a limited liability company agreement or amendment thereof need not be in writing, need not be sworn to, verified or acknowledged, and need not be filed in the office of the Secretary of State, but if in writing, must be retained by the limited liability company.

(c) *For all purposes of the laws of the State of Delaware, a power of attorney with respect to matters relating to the organization, internal affairs or termination of a limited liability company or granted by a person as a member or assignee of a limited liability company interest or by a person seeking to become a member or an assignee of a limited* liability company interest shall be irrevocable if it states that it is irrevocable and it is coupled with an interest sufficient in law to support an irrevocable power. Such irrevocable power of attorney, unless otherwise provided therein, shall not be affected by subsequent death, disability, incapacity, dissolution, termination of existence or bankruptcy of, or any other event concerning, the principal. A power of attorney with respect to matters relating to the organization, internal affairs or termination of a limited liability company or granted by a person as a member or an assignee of a limited liability company interest or by a person seeking to become a member or an assignee of a limited liability company interest and, in either case, granted to the limited liability company, a manager or member thereof, or any of their respective officers, directors, managers, members, partners, trustees, employees or agents shall be deemed coupled with an interest sufficient in law to support an irrevocable power.

[1] *(d)* The execution of a certificate by a person who is authorized by this chapter to execute such certificate constitutes an oath or affirmation, under the penalties of perjury in the third degree, that, to the best of such person's knowledge and belief, the facts stated therein are true. (Last amended by Ch. 287, L. '10, eff. 8-2-10.)

Ch. 287, L. '10, eff. 8-2-10, added matter in italic and deleted [1]"(c)".

Ch. 287, L. '10 Synopsis of Section 18-204

This section amends §18-204 of the Act to clarify, for purposes of the laws of the State of Delaware, when a power of attorney will be irrevocable, and the effects of such irrevocability.

Ch. 58, L. '09 Synopsis of Section 18-204

This section amends §18-204(a) of the Act to clarify that a certificate of merger or consolidation filed by a surviving or resulting other business entity must be executed by any person authorized to execute such certificate on behalf of such other business entity

Ch. 387, L. '08 Synopsis of Section 18-204

This section amends §18-204(a) of the Act to clarify that a certificate of conversion to limited liability company or certificate of limited liability company domestication may be executed either by an authorized person of the limited liability company or by any person authorized to execute such certificate on behalf of the other entity or non-United States entity, respectively.

This section amends §18-204(c) of the Act to make changes conforming to the amendment to §18-204(a) of the Act.

18-205 EXECUTION, AMENDMENT OR CANCELLATION BY JUDICIAL ORDER.—(a) If a person required to execute a certificate required by this subchapter fails or refuses to do so, any other person who is adversely affected by the failure or refusal may petition the Court of Chancery to direct the execution of the certificate. If the Court finds that the execution of the certificate is proper and that any person so designated has failed or refused to execute the certificate, it shall order the Secretary of State to record an appropriate certificate.

(b) If a person required to execute a limited liability company agreement or amendment thereof fails or refuses to do so, any other person who is adversely affected by the failure or refusal may petition the Court of Chancery to direct the execution of the limited liability company agreement or amendment thereof. If the Court finds that the limited liability company agreement or amendment thereof should be executed and that any person required to execute the limited liability company agreement or amendment thereof has failed or refused to do so, it shall enter an order granting appropriate relief.

18-206 FILING.—(a) The signed copy of the certificate of formation and of any certificates of amendment, correction, amendment of a certificate with a future effective date or time, termination of a certificate with a future effective date or time or cancellation (or of any judicial decree of amendment or cancellation), and of any certificate of merger or consolidation, any certificate of ownership and merger, any restated certificate, any corrected certificate, any certificate of conversion to limited liability company, any certificate of conversion to a non-Delaware entity, any certificate of transfer, any certificate of transfer and domestic continuance, any certificate of limited liability company domestication, and of any certificate of revival shall be delivered to the Secretary of State. A person who executes a certificate as an agent or fiduciary need not exhibit evidence of that person's authority as a prerequisite to filing. Any signature on any certificate authorized to be filed with the Secretary of State under any provision of this chapter may be a facsimile, a conformed signature or an electronically transmitted signature. Upon delivery of any certificate, the Secretary of State shall record the date and time of its delivery. Unless the Secretary of State finds that any certificate does not conform to law, upon receipt of all filing fees required by law the Secretary of State shall:

(1) Certify that the certificate of formation, the certificate of amendment, the certificate of correction, the certificate of amendment of a certificate with a future effective date or time, the certificate of termination of a certificate with a future effective date or time, the certificate of cancellation (or of any judicial decree of amendment or cancellation), the certificate of merger or consolidation, the certificate of ownership and merger, the restated certificate, the corrected certificate, the certificate of conversion to limited liability company, the certificate of conversion to a non-Delaware entity, the certificate of transfer, the certificate of transfer and domestic continuance, the certificate of limited liability company domestication or the certificate of revival has been filed in the Secretary of State's office by endorsing upon the signed certificate the word "Filed," and the date and time of the filing. This endorsement is conclusive of the date and time of its filing in the absence of actual fraud. Except as provided in subdivision (a)(5) or (a)(6) of this section, such date and time of filing of a certificate shall be the date and time of delivery of the certificate;

(2) File and index the endorsed certificate;

(3) Prepare and return to the person who filed it or that person's representative a copy of the signed certificate, similarly endorsed, and shall certify such copy as a true copy of the signed certificate; and

(4) Cause to be entered such information from the certificate as the Secretary of State deems appropriate into the Delaware Corporation Information System or any system which is a successor thereto in the office of the Secretary of State, and such information and a copy of such certificate shall be permanently maintained as a public record on a suitable medium. The Secretary of State is authorized to grant direct access to such system to registered agents subject to the execution of an operating agreement between the Secretary of State and such registered agent. Any registered agent granted such access shall demonstrate the existence of policies to ensure that information entered into the system accurately reflects the content of certificates in the possession of the registered agent at the time of entry.

(5) Upon request made upon or prior to delivery, the Secretary of State may, to the extent deemed practicable, establish as the date and time of filing of a certificate a date and time after its delivery. If the Secretary of State refuses to file any certificate due to an error, omission or other imperfection, the Secretary of State may hold such certificate in suspension, and in such event, upon delivery of a replacement certificate in proper form for filing and tender of the required fees within 5 business days after notice of such suspension is given to the filer, the Secretary of State shall establish as the date and time of filing of such certificate the date and time that would have been the date and time of filing of the rejected certificate had it been accepted for filing. The Secretary of State shall not issue a certificate of good standing with respect to any limited liability company with a certificate held in suspension pursuant to this subsection. The Secretary of State may establish as the date and time of filing of a certificate the date and time at which information from such certificate is entered pursuant to subdivision (a)(4) of this section if such certificate is delivered on the same date and within 4 hours after such information is entered.

(6) If:

a. Together with the actual delivery of a certificate and tender of the required fees, there is delivered to the Secretary of State a separate affidavit (which in its heading shall be designated as an affidavit of extraordinary condition) attesting, on the basis of personal knowledge of the affiant or a reliable source of knowledge identified in the affidavit, that an earlier effort to deliver such certificate and tender such fees was made in good faith, specifying the nature, date and time of such good faith effort and requesting that the Secretary of State establish such date and time as the date and time of filing of such certificate; or

b. Upon the actual delivery of a certificate and tender of the required fees, the Secretary of State in the Secretary of State's own discretion provides a written waiver of the requirement for such an affidavit stating that it appears to the Secretary of State that an earlier effort to deliver such certificate and tender such fees was made in good faith and specifying the date and time of such effort; and

c. The Secretary of State determines that an extraordinary condition existed at such date and time, that such earlier effort was unsuccessful as a result of the existence of such extraordinary condition, and that such actual delivery and tender were made within a reasonable period (not to exceed 2 business days) after the cessation of such extraordinary condition, then the Secretary of State may establish such date and time as the date and time of filing of such certificate. No fee shall be paid to the Secretary of State for receiving an affidavit of extraordinary condition. For purposes of this subsection, an extraordinary condition means: any emergency resulting from an attack on, invasion or occupation by foreign military forces of, or disaster, catastrophe, war or other armed conflict, revolution or insurrection or rioting or civil commotion in, the United States or a locality in which the Secretary of State conducts its business or in which the good faith effort to deliver the certificate and tender the required fees is made, or the immediate threat of any of the foregoing; or any malfunction or outage of the electrical or telephone service to the Secretary of State's office, or weather or other condition in or about a locality in which the Secretary of State conducts its business, as a result of which the Secretary of State's office is not open for the purpose of the filing of certificates under this chapter or such filing cannot be effected without extraordinary effort. The Secretary of State may require such proof as it deems necessary to make the determination required under this subparagraph of subdivision (a)(6), and any such determination shall be conclusive in the absence of actual fraud. If the Secretary of State establishes the date and time of filing of a certificate pursuant to this subsection, the date and time of delivery of the affidavit of extraordinary condition or the date and time of the Secretary of State's written waiver of such affidavit shall be endorsed on such affidavit or waiver and such affidavit or waiver, so endorsed, shall be attached to the filed certificate to which it relates. Such filed certificate shall be effective as of the date and time established as the date and time of filing by the Secretary of State pursuant to this subsection, except as to those persons who are substantially and adversely affected by such establishment and, as to those persons, the certificate shall be effective from the date and time endorsed on the affidavit of extraordinary condition or written waiver attached thereto.

(b) *Notwithstanding any other provision of this chapter, any certificate filed under this chapter shall be effective at the time of its filing with the Secretary of State or at any later date or time (not later than a time on the one hundred and eightieth day after the date of its filing if such date of filing is on or after January 1, 2012) specified in the certificate.* Upon the filing of a certificate of amendment (or judicial decree of amendment), certificate of correction, corrected certificate or restated certificate in the office of the Secretary of State, or upon the future effective date or time of a certificate of amendment (or judicial decree thereof) or restated certificate, as provided for therein, the certificate of formation shall be amended, corrected or restated as set forth therein. Upon the filing of a certificate of cancellation (or a judicial decree thereof), or a certificate of merger or consolidation or certificate of ownership and merger which acts as a certificate of cancellation or a certificate of transfer, or a certificate of conversion to a non-Delaware entity, or upon the future effective date or time of a certificate of cancellation (or a judicial decree thereof) or of a certificate of merger or consolidation or certificate of ownership and merger which acts as a certificate of cancellation or a certificate of transfer, or a certificate of conversion to a non-Delaware entity, as provided for therein, or as specified in §18-104(d), §18-104(i)(4) or §18-1108(a) of this title, the certificate of formation is canceled. Upon the filing of a certificate of limited liability company domestication or upon the future effective date or time of a certificate of limited liability company domestication, the entity filing the certificate of limited liability company domestication is domesticated as a limited liability company with the effect provided in §18-212 of this title. Upon the filing of a certificate of conversion to limited liability company or upon the future effective date or time of a certificate of conversion to limited liability company, the entity filing the certificate of conversion to limited liability company is converted to a limited liability company with the effect provided in §18-214 of this title. Upon the filing of a certificate of revival, the limited liability company is revived with the effect provided in §18-1109 of this title. Upon the filing of a certificate of transfer and domestic continuance, or upon the future effective date or time of a certificate of transfer and domestic continuance, as provided for therein, the limited liability company filing the

§18-206

certificate of transfer and domestic continuance shall continue to exist as a limited liability company of the State of Delaware with the effect provided in §18-213 of this title.

(c) If any certificate filed in accordance with this chapter provides for a future effective date or time and if, prior to such future effective date or time set forth in such certificate, the transaction is terminated or its terms are amended to change the future effective date or time or any other matter described in such certificate so as to make such certificate false or inaccurate in any respect, such certificate shall, prior to the future effective date or time set forth in such certificate, be terminated or amended by the filing of a certificate of termination or certificate of amendment of such certificate, executed in accordance with §18-204 of this title, which shall identify the certificate which has been terminated or amended and shall state that the certificate has been terminated or the manner in which it has been amended. Upon the filing of a certificate of amendment of a certificate with a future effective date or time, the certificate identified in such certificate of amendment is amended. Upon the filing of a certificate of termination of a certificate with a future effective date or time, the certificate identified in such certificate of termination is terminated.

(d) A fee as set forth in §18-1105(a)(3) of this title shall be paid at the time of the filing of a certificate of formation, a certificate of amendment, a certificate of correction, a certificate of amendment of a certificate with a future effective date or time, a certificate of termination of a certificate with a future effective date or time, a certificate of cancellation, a certificate of merger or consolidation, a certificate of ownership and merger, a restated certificate, a corrected certificate, a certificate of conversion to limited liability company, a certificate of conversion to a non-Delaware entity, a certificate of transfer, a certificate of transfer and domestic continuance, a certificate of limited liability company domestication or a certificate of revival.

(e) The Secretary of State, acting as agent, shall collect and deposit in a separate account established exclusively for that purpose, a courthouse municipality fee with respect to each filed instrument and shall thereafter monthly remit funds from such account to the treasuries of the municipalities designated in §301 of Title 10. Said fees shall be for the purposes of defraying certain costs incurred by such municipalities in hosting the primary locations for the Delaware Courts. The fee to such municipalities shall be $20 for each instrument filed with the Secretary of State in accordance with this section. The municipality to receive the fee shall be the municipality designated in §301 of Title 10 in the county in which the limited liability company's registered office in this State is, or is to be, located, except that a fee shall not be charged for a document filed in accordance with subchapter IX of this chapter.

(f) A fee as set forth in §18-1105(a)(4) of this title shall be paid for a certified copy of any paper on file as provided for by this chapter, and a fee as set forth in §18-1105(a)(5) of this title shall be paid for each page copied.

(g) *Notwithstanding any other provision of this chapter, it shall not be necessary for any limited liability company or foreign limited liability company to amend its certificate of formation, its application for registration as a foreign limited liability company, or any other document that has been filed in the office of the Secretary of State prior to August 1, 2011, to comply with §§18-104(k) of this title; notwithstanding the foregoing, any certificate or other document filed under this chapter on or after August 1, 2011, and changing the address of a registered agent or registered office shall comply with §18-104(k) of this title.* (Last amended by Ch. 95, L. '11, eff. 8-1-11.)

Ch. 95, L. '11, eff. 8-1-11, added matter in italic.

Ch. 95, L. '11 Synopsis of Section 18-206

This section amends §18-206(b) of the Act to confirm that a certificate may be made effective at a date or time later than its filing as specified in the certificate and to provide, for filings made on or after January 1, 2012, that such later date or time shall not be later than a time on the 180th day after the filing date.

This section amends §18-206 of the Act by adding a new subsection (g) to provide that there is no need for an amendment to a certificate of formation or any other document on file with the Secretary of State before August 1, 2011, to comply with new §18-104(k) of the Act, but that any certificate or other document filed on or after August 1, 2011 and changing the address of a registered agent or registered office must comply with §18-104(k) of the Act.

Ch. 287, L. '10 Synopsis of Section 18-206

Sections 4, 6, 7, 8, 9, 10, 11, 13, 14, 15, 16, 17, 20 and 30 amend §§18-203, 18-206(a), 18-206(b), 18-206(d), 18-209(a), 18-209(b), 18-209(c), 18-209(d), 18-209(e), 18-209(f),

18-209, 18-210, 18-301(b) and 18-1105(a) of the Act to provide a mechanism to implement a short form merger under new Section 267 of Title 8 where a domestic limited liability company is the parent Entity (as defined in new Section 267(e)(2) of Title 8).

Ch. 105, L. '07 Synopsis of Section 18-206

Sections 11, 12, 13, 14, and 35 amend §§18-206 and 18-1105 of the Act to make technical changes.

Ch. 317, L. '06 Synopsis of Section 18-206(b)

This Section amends §18-206(b) of the Act to conform to new §18-104(i)(4) of the Act which provides for the cancellation of a certificate of formation in the circumstances therein provided.

Ch. 85, L. '03 Synopsis of Section 18-206

These amendments permit conversion of a Delaware limited liability company to a non-Delaware entity.

These amendments clarify the general rule that the date and time of filing of a certificate filed with the Secretary of State is the date and time of delivery of the certificate and the limited exceptions to this rule.

Ch. 119, L. '03 Synopsis of Section 18-206

This Bill establishes a $20 courthouse municipality fee to be assessed on limited liability company (LLC) filings. The fee is expected to raise $1.6 million to be distributed to the municipalities designated as the places of holding the Court of Chancery. The fee will be distributed to the municipality in the county in which a business entity's registered office is located. To ensure that Delaware's LLC filing fees remain competitive, the Bill maintains the State's aggregate formation fee of $90 and the aggregate amending filing fee of $100.

Ch. 295, L. '02 Synopsis of Section 18-206

This section amends §18-206 of the Act to confirm that all certificates filed with the Secretary of State pursuant to this chapter are permanently maintained as a public record.

Ch. 83, L. '01 Synopsis of Section 18-206

These sections amend §18-206 of the Act to expressly refer to corrected certificates.

These sections amend §18-206, §18-209 and §18-1105(a)(3) of the Act to provide for the amendment or termination, prior to an effective time or date, of any certificate with a future effective date or time (including a certificate of merger or consolidation) that may be filed pursuant to the Act.

Ch. 77, L. '97 Synopsis of Section 18-206

These Sections amend §18-206 of the Act to deal with the filing and related matters involved in connection with a certificate of transfer and continuance being adopted in connection with §18-213 of the Act.

Ch. 360, L. '96 Synopsis of Section 18-206

These Sections amend §18-206 of the Act to refer to the certificate of limited liability company domestication authorized by new §18-212 of the Act, the certificate of transfer authorized by new §18-213 of the Act, and the certificate of conversion to limited liability company authorized by new §18-214 of the Act.

Ch. 75, L. '95 Synopsis of Section 18-206

These Sections amend §18-206 of the Act to refer to the certificate of revival authorized by new §18-1109, to provide for the use of conformed and electronically transmitted signatures and to provide for the amendment, prior to an effective time or date, of a certificate of merger or consolidation.

18-207 NOTICE.—The fact that a certificate of formation is on file in the office of the Secretary of State is notice that the entity formed in connection with the filing of the certificate of formation is a limited liability company formed under the laws of the State of Delaware and is notice of all other facts set forth therein which are required to be set forth in a certificate of formation by §18-201(a)(1) and (2) of this title *and which are* permitted to be set forth in a certificate of formation by §18-215(b) of this title. (Last amended by Ch. 360, L. '96, eff. 8-1-96.)

Ch. 360, L. '96, eff. 8-1-96, added matter in italic.

Ch. 360, L. '96 Synopsis of Section 18-207

This section amends §18-207 of the Act to provide that the certificate of formation shall provide notice of the limitation on liabilities of a series that is set forth therein in accordance with new §18-215(b) of the Act.

18-208 RESTATED CERTIFICATE.—(a) A limited liability company may, whenever desired, integrate into a single instrument all of the provisions of its certificate of formation which are then in effect and operative as a result of there having theretofore been filed with the Secretary of State 1 or more certificates or other instruments pursuant to any of the sections referred to in this subchapter, and it may at the same time also further amend its certificate of formation by adopting a restated certificate of formation.

(b) If a restated certificate of formation merely restates and integrates but does not further amend the initial certificate of formation, as theretofore amended or supplemented by any instrument that was executed and filed pursuant to any of the sections in this subchapter, it shall be specifically designated in its heading as a "Restated Certificate of Formation" together with such other words as the limited liability company may deem appropriate and shall be executed by an authorized person and filed as provided in §18-206 of this title in the office of the Secretary of State. If a restated certificate restates and integrates and also further amends in any respect the certificate of formation, as theretofore amended or supplemented, it shall be specifically designated in its heading as an "Amended and Restated Certificate of Formation" together with such other words as the limited liability company may deem appropriate and shall be executed by at least 1 authorized person, and filed as provided in §18-206 of this title in the office of the Secretary of State.

(c) A restated certificate of formation shall state, either in its heading or in an introductory paragraph, the limited liability company's present name, and, if it has been changed, the name under which it was originally filed, and the date of filing of its original certificate of formation with the Secretary of State, and the future effective date or time (which shall be a date or time certain) of the restated certificate if it is not to be effective upon the filing of the restated certificate. A restated certificate shall also state that it was duly executed and is being filed in accordance with this section. If a restated certificate only restates and integrates and does not further amend a limited liability company's certificate of formation as theretofore amended or supplemented and there is no discrepancy between those provisions and the restated certificate, it shall state that fact as well.

(d) Upon the filing of a restated certificate of formation with the Secretary of State, or upon the future effective date or time of a restated certificate of formation as provided for therein, the initial certificate of formation, as theretofore amended or supplemented, shall be superseded; thenceforth, the restated certificate of formation, including any further amendment or changes made thereby, shall be the certificate of formation of the limited liability company, but the original effective date of formation shall remain unchanged.

(e) Any amendment or change effected in connection with the restatement and integration of the certificate of formation shall be subject to any other provision of this chapter, not inconsistent with this section, which would apply if a separate certificate of amendment were filed to effect such amendment or change.

18-209 MERGER AND CONSOLIDATION.—(a) As used in this section and in §18-204 of this title, "other business entity" means a corporation, a statutory trust, a business trust, an association, a real estate investment trust, a common-law trust, or any other unincorporated business or entity, including a partnership (whether general (including a limited liability partnership) or limited (including a limited liability limited partnership)), and a foreign limited liability company, but excluding a domestic limited liability company. *As used in this section and in §§18-210 and 18-301 of this title, "plan of merger" means a writing approved by a domestic limited liability company, in the form of resolutions or otherwise, that states the terms and conditions of a merger under subsection (i) of this section.*

(b) Pursuant to an agreement of merger or consolidation, 1 or more domestic limited liability companies may merge or consolidate with or into 1 or more domestic limited liability companies or 1 or more other business entities formed or organized under the laws of the State of Delaware or any other state or the United States or any foreign country or other foreign jurisdiction, or any combination thereof, with such domestic limited liability company or other business entity as the agreement shall provide being the surviving or resulting domestic limited liability company or other business entity. Unless otherwise provided in the limited liability company agreement, [1] *an agreement of* merger or consolidation *or a plan of merger* shall be approved by each domestic limited liability company which is to merge or consolidate by the members or, if there is more than one class or group of members, then by each class or group of members, in either case, by members who own more than 50 percent of the then current percentage or other interest in the profits of the domestic limited liability company owned by all of the members or by the members in each class or group, as appropriate. In connection with a merger or consolidation hereunder, rights or securities of, or interests in, a domestic limited liability company or other business entity which is a constituent party to the merger or consolidation may be exchanged for or converted into cash, property, rights or securities of, or interests in, the surviving or resulting domestic limited liability company or other business entity or, in addition to or in lieu thereof, may be exchanged for or converted into cash, property, rights or securities of, or interests in, a domestic limited liability company or other business entity which is not the surviving or resulting limited liability company or other business entity in the merger or consolidation or may be cancelled. Notwithstanding prior approval, an agreement of merger or consolidation *or a plan of merger* may be terminated or amended pursuant to a provision for such termination or amendment contained in the agreement of merger or consolidation *or plan of merger.*

(c) [2] *Except in the case of a merger under subsection (i) of this section, if* a domestic limited liability company is merging or consolidating under this section, the domestic limited liability company or other business entity surviving or resulting in or from the merger or consolidation shall file a certificate of merger or consolidation executed by 1 or more authorized persons on behalf of the domestic limited liability company when it is the surviving or resulting entity in the office of the Secretary of State. The certificate of merger or consolidation shall state:

(1) The name and jurisdiction of formation or organization of each of the domestic limited liability companies and other business entities which is to merge or consolidate;

(2) That an agreement of merger or consolidation has been approved and executed by each of the domestic limited liability companies and other business entities which is to merge or consolidate;

(3) The name of the surviving or resulting domestic limited liability company or other business entity;

(4) In the case of a merger in which a domestic limited liability company is the surviving entity, such amendments, if any, to the certificate of formation of the surviving domestic limited liability company to change its name, registered office or registered agent as are desired to be effected by the merger;

(5) The future effective date or time (which shall be a date or time certain) of the merger or consolidation if it is not to be effective upon the filing of the certificate of merger or consolidation;

(6) That the agreement of merger or consolidation is on file at a place of business of the surviving or resulting domestic limited liability company or other business entity, and shall state the address thereof;

(7) That a copy of the agreement of merger or consolidation will be furnished by the surviving or resulting domestic limited liability company or other business entity, on request and without cost, to any member of any domestic limited liability company or any person holding an interest in any other business entity which is to merge or consolidate; and

(8) If the surviving or resulting entity is not a domestic limited liability company, or a corporation, partnership (whether general (including a limited liability partnership) or limited (including a limited liability limited partnership)) or statutory trust organized under the laws of the State of Delaware, a statement that such surviving or resulting other business entity agrees that it may be served with process in the State of Delaware in any action, suit or proceeding for the enforcement of any obligation of any domestic limited liability company which is to merge or consolidate, irrevocably appointing the Secretary of State as its agent to accept service of process in any such action, suit or proceeding and specifying the address to which a

copy of such process shall be mailed to it by the Secretary of State. *Process may be served upon the Secretary of State under this subsection by means of electronic transmission but only as prescribed by the Secretary of State. The Secretary of State is authorized to issue such rules and regulations with respect to such service as the Secretary of State deems necessary or appropriate.* In the event of service hereunder upon the Secretary of State, the procedures set forth in § 18-911(c) of this title shall be applicable, except that the plaintiff in any such action, suit or proceeding shall furnish the Secretary of State with the address specified in the certificate of merger or consolidation provided for in this section and any other address which the plaintiff may elect to furnish, together with copies of such process as required by the Secretary of State, and the Secretary of State shall notify such surviving or resulting other business entity at all such addresses furnished by the plaintiff in accordance with the procedures set forth in § 18-911(c) of this title.

(d) Unless a future effective date or time is provided in a certificate of merger or consolidation, *or in the case of a merger under subsection (i) of this section in a certificate of ownership and merger,* in which event a merger or consolidation shall be effective at any such future effective date or time, a merger or consolidation shall be effective upon the filing in the office of the Secretary of State of a certificate of merger or consolidation *or a certificate of ownership and merger.*

(e) A certificate of merger or consolidation *or a certificate of ownership and merger* shall act as a certificate of cancellation for a domestic limited liability company which is not the surviving or resulting entity in the merger or consolidation. A certificate of merger that sets forth any amendment in accordance with subsection (c)(4) of this section shall be deemed to be an amendment to the certificate of formation of the limited liability company, and the limited liability company shall not be required to take any further action to amend its certificate of formation under § 18-202 of this title with respect to such amendments set forth in the certificate of merger. Whenever this section requires the filing of a certificate of merger or consolidation, such requirement shall be deemed satisfied by the filing of an agreement of merger or consolidation containing the information required by this section to be set forth in the certificate of merger or consolidation.

(f) An agreement of merger or consolidation *or a plan of merger* approved in accordance with subsection (b) of this section may:

(1) Effect any amendment to the limited liability company agreement; or

(2) Effect the adoption of a new limited liability company agreement, for a limited liability company if it is the surviving or resulting limited liability company in the merger or consolidation.

Any amendment to a limited liability company agreement or adoption of a new limited liability company agreement made pursuant to the foregoing sentence shall be effective at the effective time or date of the merger or consolidation and shall be effective notwithstanding any provision of the limited liability company agreement relating to amendment or adoption of a new limited liability company agreement, other than a provision that by its terms applies to an amendment to the limited liability company agreement or the adoption of a new limited liability company agreement, in either case, in connection with a merger or consolidation. The provisions of this subsection shall not be construed to limit the accomplishment of a merger or of any of the matters referred to herein by any other means provided for in a limited liability company agreement or other agreement or as otherwise permitted by law, including that the limited liability company agreement of any constituent limited liability company to the merger or consolidation (including a limited liability company formed for the purpose of consummating a merger or consolidation) shall be the limited liability company agreement of the surviving or resulting limited liability company.

(g) When any merger or consolidation shall have become effective under this section, for all purposes of the laws of the State of Delaware, all of the rights, privileges and powers of each of the domestic limited liability companies and other business entities that have merged or consolidated, and all property, real, personal and mixed, and all debts due to any of said domestic limited liability companies and other business entities, as well as all other things and causes of action belonging to each of such domestic limited liability companies and other business entities, shall be vested in the surviving or resulting domestic limited liability company or other business entity, and shall thereafter be the property of the surviving or resulting domestic limited liability company or other business entity as they were of each of the domestic limited liability companies and other business entities that have merged or consolidated, and the title to any real property vested by deed or otherwise, under the laws of the State of Delaware, in any of such domestic limited liability companies and other business entities, shall not revert or be in any way impaired by reason of this chapter; but all rights of creditors and all liens upon any property of any of said domestic limited liability companies and other business entities shall be preserved unimpaired, and all debts, liabilities and duties of each of the said domestic limited liability companies and other business entities that have merged or consolidated shall thenceforth attach to the surviving or resulting domestic limited liability company or other business entity, and may be enforced against it to the same extent as if said debts, liabilities and duties had been incurred or contracted by it. Unless otherwise agreed, a merger or consolidation of a domestic limited liability company, including a domestic limited liability company which is not the surviving or resulting entity in the merger or consolidation, shall not require such domestic limited liability company to wind up its affairs under §18-803 of this title or pay its liabilities and distribute its assets under §18-804 of this title, and the merger or consolidation shall not constitute a dissolution of such limited liability company.

(h) A limited liability company agreement may provide that a domestic limited liability company shall not have the power to merge or consolidate as set forth in this section.

(i) In any case in which (i) at least 90% of the outstanding shares of each class of the stock of a corporation or corporations (other than a corporation which has in its certificate of incorporation the provision required by §251(g)(7)(i) of Title 8), of which class there are outstanding shares that, absent §267(a) of Title 8, would be entitled to vote on such merger, is owned by a domestic limited liability company, (ii) 1 or more of such corporations is a corporation of the State of Delaware, and (iii) any corporation that is not a corporation of the State of Delaware is a corporation of any other state or the District of Columbia or another jurisdiction, the laws of which do not forbid such merger, the domestic limited liability company having such stock ownership may either merge the corporation or corporations into itself and assume all of its or their obligations, or merge itself, or itself and 1 or more of such corporations, into 1 of the other corporations, pursuant to a plan of merger. If a domestic limited liability company is causing a merger under this subsection, the domestic limited liability company shall file a certificate of ownership and merger executed by 1 or more authorized persons on behalf of the domestic limited liability company in the office of the Secretary of State. The certificate of ownership and merger shall certify that such merger was authorized in accordance with the domestic limited liability company's limited liability company agreement and this chapter, and if the domestic limited liability company shall not own all the outstanding stock of all the corporations that are parties to the merger, shall state the terms and conditions of the merger, including the securities, cash, property, or rights to be issued, paid, delivered or granted by the surviving domestic limited liability company or corporation upon surrender of each share of the corporation or corporations not owned by the domestic limited liability company, or the cancellation of some or all of such shares. If a corporation surviving a merger under this subsection is not a corporation organized under the laws of the State of Delaware, then the terms and conditions of the merger shall obligate such corporation to agree that it may be served with process in the State of Delaware in any proceeding for enforcement of any obligation of the domestic limited liability company or any obligation of any constituent corporation of the State of Delaware, as well as for enforcement of any obligation of the surviving corporation, including any suit or other proceeding to enforce the right of any stockholders as determined in appraisal proceedings pursuant to §262 of Title 8, and to irrevocably appoint the Secretary of State as its agent to accept service of process in any such suit or other proceedings, and to specify the address to which a copy of such process shall be mailed by the Secretary of State. Process may be served upon the Secretary of State under this subsection by means of electronic transmission but only as prescribed by the Secretary of State. The Secretary of State is authorized to issue such rules and regulations with respect to such service as the Secretary of State deems necessary or appropriate. In the event of such service upon the Secretary of State in accordance with this subsection, the Secretary of State shall forthwith notify such surviving corporation thereof by letter, directed to such surviving corporation at its address so specified, unless such surviving corporation shall have designated in writing to the Secretary of State a different address for such purpose, in which case it shall be mailed to the last address so designated. Such letter shall be sent by a mail or courier

service that includes a record of mailing or deposit with the courier and a record of delivery evidenced by the signature of the recipient. Such letter shall enclose a copy of the process and any other papers served on the Secretary of State pursuant to this subsection. It shall be the duty of the plaintiff in the event of such service to serve process and any other papers in duplicate, to notify the Secretary of State that service is being effected pursuant to this subsection and to pay the Secretary of State the sum of $50 for the use of the State of Delaware, which sum shall be taxed as part of the costs in the proceeding, if the plaintiff shall prevail therein. The Secretary of State shall maintain an alphabetical record of any such service setting forth the name of the plaintiff and the defendant, the title, docket number and nature of the proceeding in which process has been served, the fact that service has been effected pursuant to this subsection, the return date thereof, and the day and hour service was made. The Secretary of State shall not be required to retain such information longer than 5 years from receipt of the service of process. (Last amended by Ch. 287, L. '10, eff. 8-2-10.)

Ch. 287, L. '10, eff. 8-2-10, added matter in italic and deleted [1]"a" and [2]"If".

Ch. 287, L. '10 Synopsis of Section 18-209

Sections 4, 6, 7, 8, 9, 10, 11, 13, 14, 15, 16, 17, 20 and 30 amend §§18-203, 18-206(a), 18-206(b), 18-206(d), 18-209(a), 18-209(b), 18-209(c), 18-209(d), 18-209(e), 18-209(f), 18-209, 18-210, 18-301(b) and 18-1105(a) of the Act to provide a mechanism to implement a short form merger under new Section 267 of Title 8 where a domestic limited liability company is the parent Entity (as defined in new Section 267(e)(2) of Title 8).

Sections 12, 18 and 19 amend §§18-209(c)(8), 18-213(b)(7), and 18-216(e)(7) of the Act to allow for service of process upon the Secretary of State thereunder by means of electronic transmission but only as prescribed by the Secretary of State, and to authorize the Secretary of State to issue such rules and regulations with respect to such service as the Secretary of State deems necessary or appropriate.

Ch. 58, L. '09 Synopsis of Section 18-209

This section amends §18-209(a) of the Act to make changes conforming to the amendment to §18-204(a) of the Act.

This section amends §18-209(c)(4) of the Act to permit a change of the registered office or registered agent to be set forth in a certificate of merger filed by a surviving domestic limited liability company.

This section amends §18-209(f) of the Act to confirm the ability by merger or consolidation to amend a limited liability company agreement or adopt a new limited liability company agreement for a limited liability company that is the surviving or resulting limited liability company in a merger or consolidation by obtaining the approval required by §18-209(b) of the Act, unless the limited liability company agreement by its terms limits such amendment or adoption.

Ch. 105, L. '07 Synopsis of Section 18-209

This section amends §18-209(a) of the Act to confirm the flexibility that exists under §18-209.

This section amends §18-209(c)(8) of the Act to provide that a certificate of merger need not contain a consent to jurisdiction where the surviving or resulting entity is a Delaware general partnership, and to simplify the wording of such subsection.

This section amends §18-209(g) of the Act to confirm that a merger or consolidation of a domestic limited liability company does not constitute a dissolution of such limited liability company unless otherwise agreed.

Sections 18, 21 and 30 amend §§18-209, 18-213 and 18-216 of the Act by adding new subsections that confirm the ability to provide in the limited liability company agreement that a limited liability company does not have power to merge or consolidate under §18-209 of the Act, transfer, domesticate or continue under §18-213 of the Act, or convert under §18-216 of the Act. These amendments are not intended to imply that the limited liability company agreement may not deny other powers to the limited liability company.

Ch. 317, L. '06 Synopsis of Section 18-209(b)

This Section amends §18-209(b) of the Act to correct words used in the subsection.

Ch. 275, L. '04 Synopsis of Section 18-209

This amendment confirms the flexibility permitted in the Act regarding a merger or consolidation.

These amendments permit a change of the name of a surviving domestic limited liability company to be set forth in a certificate of merger.

Ch. 329, L. '02 Synopsis of Section 18-209

The amendments set forth are made for the purpose of avoiding any implication that a trust formed under Chapter 38, Title 12 of the Delaware Code constitutes a "business trust" within the meaning of Title 11 of the United States Code. Such amendments are not intended to result in any substantive change in Delaware law. These amendments are made solely for the purpose of conforming the Delaware Code to the amendments set forth above.

Ch. 83, L. '01 Synopsis of Section 18-209

These sections amend §18-206, §18-209(d) and §18-1105(a)(3) of the Act to provide for the amendment or termination, prior to an effective time or date, of any certificate with a future effective date or time (including a certificate of merger or consolidation) that may be filed pursuant to the Act.

Ch. 389, L. '00 Synopsis of Section 18-209

These sections amend §18-102(3), §18-209(a), §18-212(a), §18-214(a) and §18-216 of the Act to eliminate an unnecessary word.

Ch. 341, L. '98 Synopsis of Section 18-209

These sections amend §18-209(b) and §§18-209(c)(1) and (c)(2) of the Act to confirm that mergers and consolidations involving more than one entity can be done.

This section amends §18-209(c) of the Act to confirm who must execute a certificate of merger or consolidation.

This section amends §18-209(d) of the Act to provide that if authorized by an agreement of merger or consolidation, a certificate of merger or consolidation may be amended to change the future effective date or time of a merger or consolidation without the amendment of an agreement of merger or consolidation.

This section amends §18-209(e) of the Act to provide that an agreement of merger or consolidation which satisfies the requirements for a certificate of merger or consolidation may be filed in place of the filing of a certificate of merger or consolidation.

Ch. 75, L. '95 Synopsis of Section 18-209

This Section confirms that a definition includes a registered limited liability limited partnership.

This Section provides for the amendment, prior to an effective time or date, of a certificate of merger or consolidation.

.1 Fee shifting.—Prelitigation conduct that constitutes a breach of fiduciary duty is not so egregious as to require fee shifting where that conduct, though not minor, is less than unusually deplorable behavior and is not undertaken in bad faith. *VGS, Inc v Castiel, 2001 Del. Ch. LEXIS 117 (Ch Ct 2001).*

.2 Managers' and members' duties during merger; derivative actions.—Where an LLC agreement authorizes mergers, and a merger complies with the requirements of the agreement, a member whose interest is eliminated by the merger does not have standing to bring derivative claims arising out of the merger. The former member may, however, maintain direct claims, such as for breach of fiduciary duty. In the absence of a provision explicitly altering fiduciary duties owed by managers to the LLC and its members and by members to each other, an LLC's managers and controlling members in a manager-managed LLC owe the traditional fiduciary duties that directors and controlling shareholders in a corporation would. Consequently, where managers willfully violate their duty of loyalty or care, the former member may bring a direct claim for such a breach, as well as for the aiding and abetting of such breach.

After reviewing a former member's direct claims, the court found that he had alleged facts that, if proven, could support a finding that the LLC's managers and controlling members breached their fiduciary duties by willfully engaging in a non-arm's length, unfair, self-dealing transaction aimed at squeezing the member out of his interest in the LLC, and that the acquiring LLC aided and abetted that breach. Accordingly, the court permitted those claims, as well as the defamation claim, to proceed. *Kelly v Blum, 2010 Del. Ch. LEXIS 31 (Ch Ct 2010).*

18-210 CONTRACTUAL APPRAISAL RIGHTS.—A limited liability company agreement or an agreement of merger or consolidation *or a plan of merger* may provide that contractual appraisal rights with respect to a limited liability company interest or another interest in a limited liability company shall be available for any class or group or series of members or limited liability company interests in connection with any amendment of a limited liability company agreement, any merger or consolidation in which the limited liability company is a constituent party to the merger or consolidation, any conversion of the limited liability company to another business form, any transfer to or domestication or continuance in any jurisdiction by the limited liability company, or the sale of all or substantially all of the limited liability company's assets. The Court of Chancery shall have jurisdiction to hear and determine any matter relating to any such appraisal rights. (Last amended by Ch. 287, L. '10, eff. 8-2-10.)

Ch. 287, L. '10, eff. 8-2-10, added matter in italic.

Ch. 287, L. '10 Synopsis of Section 18-210

Sections 4, 6, 7, 8, 9, 10, 11, 13, 14, 15, 16, 17, 20 and 30 amend §§18-203, 18-206(a), 18-206(b), 18-206(d), 18-209(a), 18-209(b), 18-209(c), 18-209(d), 18-209(e), 18-209(f), 18-209, 18-210, 18-301(b) and 18-1105(a) of the Act to provide a mechanism to implement a short form merger under new Section 267 of Title 8 where a domestic limited liability company is the parent Entity (as defined in new Section 267(e)(2) of Title 8).

Ch. 105, L. '07 Synopsis of Section 18-210

This section amends §18-210 of the Act to make technical changes and to confirm the flexibility that exists under §18-210.

Ch. 295, L. '02 Synopsis of Section 18-210

This section amends §18-210 of the Act to confirm the ability to provide for contractual appraisal rights in certain circumstances.

18-211 CERTIFICATE OF CORRECTION.—(a) Whenever any certificate authorized to be filed with the office of the Secretary of State under any provision of this chapter has been so filed and is an inaccurate record of the action therein referred to, or was defectively or erroneously executed, such certificate may be corrected by filing with the office of the Secretary of State a certificate of correction of such certificate. The certificate of correction shall specify the inaccuracy or defect to be corrected, shall set forth the portion of the certificate in corrected form, and shall be executed and filed as required by this chapter. The [1]*certificate of correction* shall be effective as of the date the original certificate was filed, except as to those persons who are substantially and adversely affected by the correction, and as to those persons the [1]*certificate of correction* shall be effective from the filing date.

(b) *In lieu of filing a certificate of correction, a certificate may be corrected by filing with the Secretary of State a corrected certificate which shall be executed and filed as if the corrected certificate were the certificate being corrected, and a fee equal to the fee payable to the Secretary of State if the certificate being corrected were then being filed shall be paid and collected by the Secretary of State for the use of the State of Delaware in connection with the filing of the corrected certificate. The corrected certificate shall be specifically designated as such in its heading, shall specify the inaccuracy or defect to be corrected and shall set forth the entire certificate in corrected form. A certificate corrected in accordance with this section shall be effective as of the date the original certificate was filed, except as to those persons who are substantially and adversely affected by the correction and as to those persons the certificate as corrected shall be effective from the filing date.* (Last amended by Ch. 77, L. '97, eff. 8-1-97.)

Ch. 77, L. '97, eff. 8-1-97, added matter in italic and deleted [1]"corrected certificate".

Ch. 77, L. '97 Synopsis of Section 18-211

This section amends §18-211 of the Act to provide for the use of a corrected certificate.

18-212 DOMESTICATION OF NON-UNITED STATES ENTITIES.—(a) As used in this section and in §18-204 of this title, "non-United States entity" means a foreign limited liability company (other than one formed under the laws of a state) or a corporation, a statutory trust, a business trust, an association, a real estate investment trust, a common-law trust or any other unincorporated business or entity, including a partnership (whether general (including a limited liability partnership) or limited (including a limited liability limited partnership)) formed, incorporated, created or that otherwise came into being under the laws of any foreign country or other foreign jurisdiction (other than any state).

(b) Any non-United States entity may become domesticated as a limited liability company in the State of Delaware by complying with subsection (g) of this section and filing in the office of the Secretary of State in accordance with §18-206 of this title:

(1) A certificate of limited liability company domestication that has been executed in accordance with §18-204 of this title; and

(2) A certificate of formation that complies with §18-201 of this title and has been executed by 1 or more authorized persons in accordance with §18-204 of this title.

Each of the certificates required by this subsection (b) shall be filed simultaneously in the office of the Secretary of State and, if such certificates are not to become effective upon their filing as permitted by §18-206(b) of this title, then each such certificate shall provide for the same effective date or time in accordance with §18-206(b) of this title.

(c) The certificate of limited liability company domestication shall state:

(1) The date on which and jurisdiction where the non-United States entity was first formed, incorporated, created or otherwise came into being;

(2) The name of the non-United States entity immediately prior to the filing of the certificate of limited liability company domestication;

(3) The name of the limited liability company as set forth in the certificate of formation filed in accordance with subsection (b) of this section;

(4) The future effective date or time (which shall be a date or time certain) of the domestication as a limited liability company if it is not to be effective upon the filing of the certificate of limited liability company domestication and the certificate of formation;

(5) The jurisdiction that constituted the seat, siege social, or principal place of business or central administration of the non-United States entity, or any other equivalent thereto under applicable law, immediately prior to the filing of the certificate of limited liability company domestication; and

(6) That the domestication has been approved in the manner provided for by the document, instrument, agreement or other writing, as the case may be, governing the internal affairs of the non-United States entity and the conduct of its business or by applicable non-Delaware law, as appropriate.

(d) Upon the filing in the office of the Secretary of State of the certificate of limited liability company domestication and the certificate of formation or upon the future effective date or time of the certificate of limited liability company domestication and the certificate of formation, the non-United States entity shall be domesticated as a limited liability company in the State of Delaware and the limited liability company shall thereafter be subject to all of the provisions of this chapter, except that notwithstanding §18-201 of this title, the existence of the limited liability company shall be deemed to have commenced on the date the non-United States entity commenced its existence in the jurisdiction in which the non-United States entity was first formed, incorporated, created or otherwise came into being.

(e) The domestication of any non-United States entity as a limited liability company in the State of Delaware shall not be deemed to affect any obligations or liabilities of the non-United States entity incurred prior to its domestication as a limited liability company in the State of Delaware, or the personal liability of any person therefor.

(f) The filing of a certificate of limited liability company domestication shall not affect the choice of law applicable to the non-United States entity, except that from the effective date or time of the domestication, the law of the State of Delaware, including the provisions of this chapter, shall apply to the non-United States entity to the same extent as if the non-United States entity had been formed as a limited liability company on that date.

(g) Prior to the filing of a certificate of limited liability company domestication with the office of the Secretary of State, the domestication shall be approved in the manner provided for by the document, instrument, agreement or other writing, as the case may be, governing the internal affairs of the non-United States entity and the conduct of its business or by applicable non-Delaware law, as appropriate, and a limited liability company agreement shall be approved by the same authorization required to approve the domestication.

(h) When any domestication shall have become effective under this section, for all purposes of the laws of the State of Delaware, all of the rights, privileges and powers of the non-United States entity that has been domesticated, and all property, real, personal and mixed, and all debts due to such non-United States entity, as well as all other things and causes of action belonging to such non-United States entity, shall remain vested in the domestic limited liability company to which such non-United States entity has been domesticated (and also in the non-United States entity, if and for so long as the non-United States entity continues its existence in the foreign jurisdiction in which it was existing immediately prior to the domestication) and shall be the property of such domestic limited liability company (and also of the non-United States entity, if and for so long as the non-United States entity continues its existence in the foreign jurisdiction in which it was existing immediately prior to the domestication), and the title to any real property vested by deed or otherwise in such non-United States entity shall not revert or be in any way impaired by reason of this chapter; but all rights of creditors and all liens upon any property of such non-United States entity shall be preserved unimpaired, and all debts, liabilities and duties of the non-United States entity that has been domesticated shall remain attached to the domestic limited liability company to which such non-United States entity has been domesticated (and also to the non-United States entity, if and for so long as the non-United States entity continues its existence in the foreign jurisdiction in which it was existing immediately prior to the domestication), and may be enforced against it to the same extent as if said debts, liabilities and duties had originally been incurred or contracted by it in its capacity as a domestic limited liability company. The rights, privileges, powers and interests in property of the non-United States entity, as well as the debts, liabilities and duties of the non-United States entity, shall not be deemed, as a consequence of the domestication, to have been transferred to the domestic limited liability company to which such non-United States entity has domesticated for any purpose of the laws of the State of Delaware.

(i) When a non-United States entity has become domesticated as a limited liability company pursuant to this section, for all purposes of the laws of the State of Delaware, the limited liability company shall be deemed to be the same entity as the domesticating non-United States entity and the domestication shall constitute a continuation of the existence of the domesticating non-United States entity in the form of a domestic limited liability company. Unless otherwise agreed, for all purposes of the laws of the State of Delaware, the domesticating non-United States entity shall not be required to wind up its affairs or pay its liabilities and distribute its assets, and the domestication shall not be deemed to constitute a dissolution of such non-United States entity. If, following domestication, a non-United States entity that has become domesticated as a limited liability company continues its existence in the foreign country or other foreign jurisdiction in which it was existing immediately prior to domestication, the limited liability company and such non-United States entity shall, for all purposes of the laws of the State of Delaware, constitute a single entity formed, incorporated, created or otherwise having come into being, as applicable, and existing under the laws of the State of Delaware and the laws of such foreign country or other foreign jurisdiction.

(j) In connection with a domestication hereunder, rights or securities of, or interests in, the non-United States entity that is to be domesticated as a domestic limited liability company may be exchanged for or converted into cash, property, rights or securities of, or interests in, such domestic limited liability company or, in addition to or in lieu thereof, may be exchanged for or converted into cash, property, rights or securities of, or interests in, another domestic limited liability company or other entity or may be cancelled. (Last amended by Ch. 95, L. '11, eff. 8-1-11.)

Ch. 95, L. '11, eff. 8-1-11, added matter in italic.

Ch. 95, L. '11 Synopsis of Section 18-212

This section amends §18-212 of the Act to clarify that the certificate of limited liability company domestication and the certificate of formation of a non-United States entity domesticating to Delaware as a Delaware limited liability company must be filed simultaneously in the office of the Secretary of State and, to the extent such certificates are to have a post-filing effective date or time, such certificates must provide for the same effective date or time.

Ch. 387, L. '08 Synopsis of Section 18-212

This section amends §18-212(a) of the Act to make changes conforming to the amendment to §18-204 of the Act.

This section amends §18-212(b)(1) of the Act to make changes conforming to the amendment to §18-204 of the Act.

Ch. 317, L. '06 Synopsis of Section 18-212

Sections 7 through 32 of the Bill make technical changes to §18-212 (domestication of non-US entities), §18-213 (transfer or continuance of domestic limited liability companies), §18-214 (conversion of certain entities to a limited liability company) and §18-216 (approval of conversion of a limited liability company) of the Act to conform these Sections to the parallel provisions in the Delaware General Corporation Law adopted in 2005.

Ch. 51, L. '05 Synopsis of Section 18-212(i)

These sections amend §18-212(i) and §18-214(g) of the Act to confirm that these sections of the Act address the effect of domestication and conversion, respectively, as a matter of Delaware law.

Ch. 275, L. '04 Synopsis of Section 18-212(j)

This amendment confirms the flexibility permitted in the Act regarding domestication as a domestic limited liability company.

Ch. 83, L. '01 Synopsis of Section 18-212

This section amends §18-212 of the Act to confirm the flexibility permitted in connection with a domestication of a non-United States entity as a domestic limited liability company.

Ch. 389, L. '00 Synopsis of Section 18-212

These sections amend §18-102(3), §18-209(a), §18-212(a), §18-214(a) and §18-216 of the Act to eliminate an unnecessary word.

This section amends §18-212 of the Act to confirm that no transfer occurs as a consequence of a domestication.

Ch. 129, L. '99 Synopsis of Section 18-212

These sections amend §18-212 and §18-213 of the Act dealing with domestication into Delaware of non-United States entities and the transfer or continuance to foreign jurisdictions of Delaware limited liability companies and confirm that a domesticated or transferred entity is the same entity as existed prior to domestication or transfer.

Ch. 77, L. '97 Synopsis of Section 18-212

This section amends §18-212(g) of the Act to clarify mechanics relating to domestication into Delaware of a non-United States entity as a Delaware limited liability company.

Ch. 360, L. '96 Synopsis of Section 18-212

This section adds a new §18-212 to the Act which provides that any entity governed by a jurisdiction other than the United States or any part thereof may be domesticated as a limited liability company in the State of Delaware upon the obtaining of the requisite approval of a limited liability company agreement by such entity and the filing of a certificate of limited liability company domestication and a certificate of formation with the Secretary of State. Upon and after such domestication, Delaware law, including the Act, shall apply to the domesticated limited liability company. However, such domestication shall not otherwise affect the choice of law available to such entity or any obligations or liabilities incurred prior to its domestication as a limited liability company in the State of Delaware.

18-213 TRANSFER OR CONTINUANCE OF DOMESTIC LIMITED LIABILITY COMPANIES.—(a) Upon compliance with this section, any limited liability company may transfer to or domesticate *or continue* in any jurisdiction, other than any state, and, in connection therewith, may elect to continue its existence as a limited liability company in the State of Delaware.

(b) If the limited liability company agreement specifies the manner of authorizing a transfer or domestication or continuance described in subsection (a) of this section, the transfer or domestication or continuance shall be authorized as specified in the limited liability company agreement. If the limited liability company agreement does not specify the manner of authorizing a transfer or domestication or continuance described in subsection (a) of this section and does not prohibit such a transfer or domestication or continuance, the transfer or domestication or continuance shall be authorized in the same manner as is specified in the limited liability company agreement for authorizing a merger or consolidation that involves the limited liability company as a constituent party to the merger or consolidation. If the limited liability company agreement does not specify the manner of authorizing a transfer or domestication or continuance described in subsection (a) of this section or a merger or consolidation that involves the limited liability company as a constituent party and does not prohibit such a transfer or domestication or continuance, the transfer or domestication or continuance shall be authorized by the approval by the members or, if there is more than 1 class or group of members, then by each class or group of members, in either case, by the members who own more than 50% of the then current percentage or other interest in the profits of the domestic limited liability company owned by all of the members or by the members in each class or group, as appropriate. If a transfer or domestication or continuance described in subsection (a) of this section shall be authorized as provided in this subsection (b), a certificate of transfer if the limited liability company's existence as a limited liability company of the State of Delaware is to cease, or a certificate of transfer and domestic continuance if the limited liability company's existence as a limited liability company in the State of Delaware is to continue, executed in accordance with §18-204 of this title, shall be filed in the office of the Secretary of State in accordance with §18-206 of this title. The certificate of transfer or the certificate of transfer and domestic continuance shall state:

(1) The name of the limited liability company and, if it has been changed, the name under which its certificate of formation was originally filed;

(2) The date of the filing of its original certificate of formation with the Secretary of State;

(3) The jurisdiction to which the limited liability company shall be transferred or in which it shall be domesticated or continued and the name of the entity or business form formed, incorporated, created or that otherwise comes into being as a consequence of the transfer of the limited liability company to, or its domestication or continuance in, such foreign jurisdiction;

(4) The future effective date or time (which shall be a date or time certain) of the transfer to or domestication or continuance in the jurisdiction specified in subsection (b)(3) of this section if it is not to be effective upon the filing of the certificate of transfer or the certificate of transfer and domestic continuance;

(5) That the transfer or domestication or continuance of the limited liability company has been approved in accordance with this section;

(6) In the case of a certificate of transfer, (i) that the existence of the limited liability company as a limited liability company of the State of Delaware shall cease when the certificate of transfer becomes effective, and (ii) the agreement of the limited liability company that it may be served with process in the State of Delaware in any action, suit or proceeding for enforcement of any obligation of the limited liability company arising while it was a limited liability company of the State of Delaware, and that it irrevocably appoints the Secretary of State as its agent to accept service of process in any such action, suit or proceeding;

(7) The address to which a copy of the process referred to in subsection (b)(6) of this section shall be mailed to it by the Secretary of State. *Process may be served upon the Secretary of State under paragraph (b)(6) of this section by means of electronic transmission but only as prescribed by the Secretary of State. The Secretary of State is authorized to issue such rules and regulations with respect to such service as the Secretary of State deems necessary or appropriate.* In the event of service hereunder upon the Secretary of State, the procedures set forth in §18-911(c) of this title shall be applicable, except that the plaintiff in any such action, suit or proceeding shall furnish the Secretary of State with the address specified in this subsection and any other address that the plaintiff may elect to furnish, together with copies of such process as required by the Secretary of State, and the Secretary of State shall notify the limited liability company that has transferred or domesticated or continued out of the State of Delaware at all such addresses furnished by the plaintiff in accordance with the procedures set forth in §18-911(c) of this title; and

(8) In the case of a certificate of transfer and domestic continuance, that the limited liability company will continue to exist as a limited liability company of the State of Delaware after the certificate of transfer and domestic continuance becomes effective.

(c) Upon the filing in the office of the Secretary of State of the certificate of transfer or upon the future effective date or time of the certificate of transfer and payment to the Secretary of State of all fees prescribed in this chapter, the Secretary of State shall certify that the limited liability company has filed all documents and paid all fees required by this chapter, and thereupon the limited liability company shall cease to exist as a limited liability company of the State of Delaware. Such certificate of the Secretary of State shall be prima facie evidence of the transfer or domestication or continuance by such limited liability company out of the State of Delaware.

(d) The transfer or domestication or continuance of a limited liability company out of the State of Delaware in accordance with this section and the resulting cessation of its existence as a limited liability company of the State of Delaware pursuant to a certificate of transfer shall not be deemed to affect any obligations or liabilities of the limited liability company incurred prior to such transfer or domestication or continuance or the personal liability of any person incurred prior to such transfer or domestication or continuance, nor shall it be deemed to affect the choice of law applicable to the limited liability company with respect to matters arising prior to such transfer or domestication or continuance. Unless otherwise agreed, the transfer or domestication or continuance of a limited liability company out of the State of Delaware in accordance with this section shall not require such limited liability company to wind up its affairs under §18-803 of this title or pay its liabilities and distribute its assets under §18-804 of this title and shall not be deemed to constitute a dissolution of such limited liability company.

(e) If a limited liability company files a certificate of transfer and domestic continuance, after the time the certificate of transfer and domestic continuance becomes effective, the limited liability company shall continue to exist as a limited liability company of the State of Delaware, and the laws of the State of Delaware, including this chapter, shall apply to the limited liability company to the same extent as prior to such time. So long as a limited liability company continues to exist as a limited liability company of the State of Delaware following the filing of a certificate of transfer and domestic continuance, the continuing domestic limited liability company and the entity or business form formed, incorporated, created or that otherwise came into being as a consequence of the transfer of the limited liability company to, or its domestication or continuance in, a foreign country or other foreign jurisdiction shall, for all purposes of the laws of the State of Delaware, constitute a single entity formed, incorporated, created or otherwise having come into being, as applicable, and existing under the laws of the State and the laws of such foreign country or other foreign jurisdiction.

(f) In connection with a transfer or domestication or continuance of a domestic limited liability company to or in another jurisdiction pursuant to subsection (a) of this section, rights or securities of, or interests in, such limited liability company may be exchanged for or converted into cash, property, rights or securities of, or interests in, the entity or business form in which the limited liability company will exist in such other jurisdiction as a consequence of the transfer or domestication or continuance or, in addition to or in lieu thereof, may be exchanged for or converted into cash, property, rights or securities of, or interests in, another entity or business form or may be cancelled.

(g) When a limited liability company has transferred or domesticated or continued out of the State of Delaware pursuant to this section, the transferred or domesticated or continued entity or business form shall, for all purposes of the laws of the State of Delaware, be deemed to be the same entity as the limited liability company and shall constitute a continuation of the existence of such limited liability company in the form of the transferred or domesticated or continued entity or business form. When any transfer or domestication or continuance of a limited liability company out of the State of Delaware shall have become effective under this section, for all purposes of the laws of the State of Delaware, all of the rights, privileges and powers of the limited liability company that has transferred or domesticated or continued, and all property, real, personal and mixed, and all debts due to such limited liability company, as well as all other things and causes of action belonging to such limited liability company, shall remain vested in the transferred or domesticated or continued entity or business form (and also is the limited liability company that has transferred, domesticated or continued, if and for so long as such limited liability company continues its existence as a domestic limited liability company) and shall be the property of such transferred or domesticated or continued entity or business form (and also of the limited liability company that has transferred, domesticated or continued, if and for so long as such limited liability company continues its existence as a domestic limited liability company), and the title to any real property vested by deed or otherwise in such limited liability company shall not revert or be in any way impaired by reason of this chapter; but all rights of creditors and all liens upon any property of such limited liability company shall be preserved unimpaired, and all debts, liabilities and duties of the limited liability company that has transferred or domesticated or continued shall remain attached to the transferred or domesticated or continued entity or business form (and also to the limited liability company that has transferred, domesticated or continued, if and for so long as such limited liability company continues its existence as a domestic limited liability company), and may be enforced against it to the same extent as if said debts, liabilities and duties had originally been incurred or contracted by it in its capacity as the transferred or domesticated or continued entity or business form. The rights, privileges, powers and interests in property of the limited liability company that has transferred or domesticated or continued, as well as the debts, liabilities and duties of such limited liability company, shall not be deemed, as a consequence of the transfer or domestication or continuance out of the State of Delaware, to have been transferred to the transferred or domesticated or continued entity or business form for any purpose of the laws of the State of Delaware.

(h) A limited liability company agreement may provide that a domestic limited liability company shall not have the power to transfer, domesticate or continue as set forth in this section. (Last amended by Ch. 287, L. '10, eff. 8-2-10.)

Ch. 287, L. '10, eff. 8-2-10, added matter in italic.

Ch. 287, L. '10 Synopsis of Section 18-213

Sections 12, 18 and 19 amend §§18-209(c)(8), 18-213(b)(7), and 18-216(e)(7) of the Act to allow for service of process upon the Secretary of State thereunder by means of electronic transmission but only as prescribed by the Secretary of State, and to authorize the Secretary of State to issue such rules and regulations with respect to such service as the Secretary of State deems necessary or appropriate.

Ch. 105, L. '07 Synopsis of Section 18-213

This section amends §18-213(g) of the Act to make a technical change.

Ch. 317, L. '06 Synopsis of Section 18-213

Sections 7 through 32 of the Bill make technical changes to §18-212 (domestication of non-US entities), §18-213 (transfer or continuance of domestic limited liability companies), §18-214 (conversion of certain entities to a limited liability company) and §18-216 (approval of conversion of a limited liability company) of the Act to conform these Sections to the parallel provisions in the Delaware General Corporation Law adopted in 2005.

Ch. 51, L. '05 Synopsis of Section 18-213(b)

This section amends §18-213(b) to conform the approval requirements for the transfer of a domestic limited liability company to the requirements for the conversion of a domestic limited liability company.

Ch. 275, L. '04 Synopsis of Section 18-213(f) and (g)

This amendent confirms the flexibility permitted in a Act regarding a transfer or domestication of a domestic limited liability company.

This amendent confirms the treatment under Delaware law of limited liability companies that have transferred or domesticated out of the State of Delaware.

Ch. 85, L. '03 Synopsis of Section 18-213

This amendment clarifies the language of §18-213(a) of the Act to be consistent with language used in other analogous sections of the Act.

Ch. 83, L. '01 Synopsis of Section 18-213

This section amends §18-213 of the Act to confirm the flexibility permitted in connection with a transfer or domestication of a domestic limited liability company.

Ch. 389, L. '00 Synopsis of Section 18-213

This section amends §18-213 of the Act to confirm that a Delaware limited liability company that transfers or domesticates to a non-United States jurisdiction is not required to wind up its affairs or pay its liabilities and distribute its assets.

Ch. 129, L. '99 Synopsis of Section 18-213

These sections amend §18-212 and §18-213 of the Act dealing with domestication into Delaware of non-United States entities and the transfer or continuance to foreign jurisdictions of Delaware limited liability companies and confirm that a domesticated or transferred entity is the same entity as existed prior to domestication or transfer.

Ch. 341, L. '98 Synopsis of Section 18-213

This section amends §18-213 of the Act to provide that, if permitted under a limited liability agreement, a limited liability company may be transferred or domesticated or continued to a jurisdication, other than any state, without the apporval of all of the members of the limited liability company.

Ch. 77, L. '97 Synopsis of Section 18-213

This Section amends §18-213 of the Act concerning the transfer out of the State of Delaware to a foreign jurisdiction and the possible continuance in the State of Delaware of a transferring Delaware limited liability company. The existing section has been modified to permit, as an option, in connection with a transfer, continuance in the State of Delaware. In a situation in which a limited liability company is to transfer out of the State of Delaware to a foreign country and continue in the State of Delaware, provision is made for a certificate of transfer and continuance.

Ch. 360, L. '96 Synopsis of Section 18-213

This Section adds a new §18-213 to the Act which provides that a limited liability company may transfer to or domesticate or continue in any jurisdiction other than the United States or any part thereof that permits such action upon the approval of all of the members and managers of the limited liability company and the filing of a certificate of transfer with the Secretary of State. Upon such transfer, the limited liability company will cease to exist as a domestic limited liability company, but such transfer will not affect the liabilities of the limited liability company incurred prior to the transfer or the choice of law applicable to matters arising prior to the transfer.

18-214 CONVERSION OF CERTAIN ENTITIES TO A LIMITED LIABILITY COMPANY.—(a) As used in this section and in §18-204 of this title, the term "other entity" means a corporation, a statutory trust, a business trust, an association, a real estate investment trust, a common-law trust or any other unincorporated business or entity, including a partnership (whether general (including a limited liability partnership) or limited (including a limited liability limited partnership)) or a foreign limited liability company.

(b) Any other entity may convert to a domestic limited liability company by complying with subsection (h) of this section and filing in the office of the Secretary of State in accordance with §18-206 of this title:

(1) A certificate of conversion to limited liability company that has been executed [1]in accordance with §18-204 of this title; and

(2) A certificate of formation that complies with §18-201 of this title and has been executed by 1 or more authorized persons in accordance with §18-204 of this title.

Each of the certificates required by this subsection (b) shall be filed simultaneously in the office of the Secretary of State and, if such certificates are not to become effective upon their filing as permitted by §18-206(b) of this title, then each such certificate shall provide for the same effective date or time in accordance with §18-206(b) of this title.

(c) The certificate of conversion to limited liability company shall state:

(1) The date on which and jurisdiction where the other entity was first created, incorporated, formed or otherwise came into being and, if it has changed, its jurisdiction immediately prior to its conversion to a domestic limited liability company;

(2) The name of the other entity immediately prior to the filing of the certificate of conversion to limited liability company;

(3) The name of the limited liability company as set forth in its certificate of formation filed in accordance with subsection (b) of this section; and

(4) The future effective date or time (which shall be a date or time certain) of the conversion to a limited liability company if it is not to be effective upon the filing of the certificate of conversion to limited liability company and the certificate of formation.

(d) Upon the filing in the office of the Secretary of State of the certificate of conversion to limited liability company and the certificate of formation or upon the future effective date or time of the certificate of conversion to limited liability company and the certificate of formation, the other entity shall be converted into a domestic limited liability company and the limited liability company shall thereafter be subject to all of the provisions of this chapter, except that notwithstanding §18-201 of this title, the existence of the limited liability company shall be deemed to have commenced on the date the other entity commenced its existence in the jurisdiction in which the other entity was first created, formed, incorporated or otherwise came into being.

(e) The conversion of any other entity into a domestic limited liability company shall not be deemed to affect any obligations or liabilities of the other entity incurred prior to its conversion to a domestic limited liability company or the personal liability of any person incurred prior to such conversion.

(f) When any conversion shall have become effective under this section, for all purposes of the laws of the State of Delaware, all of the rights, privileges and powers of the other entity that has converted, and all property, real, personal and mixed, and all debts due to such other entity, as well as all other things and causes of action belonging to such other entity, shall remain vested in the domestic limited liability company to which such other entity has converted and shall be the property of such domestic limited liability company, and the title to any real property vested by deed or otherwise in such other entity shall not revert or be in any way impaired by reason of this chapter; but all rights of creditors and all liens upon any property of such other entity shall be preserved unimpaired, and all debts, liabilities and duties of the other entity that has converted shall remain attached to the domestic limited liability company to which such other entity has converted, and may be enforced against it to the same extent as if said debts, liabilities and duties had originally been incurred or contracted by it in its capacity as a domestic limited liability company. The rights, privileges, powers and interests in property of the other entity, as well as the debts, liabilities and duties of the other entity, shall not be deemed, as a consequence of the conversion, to have been transferred to the domestic limited liability company to which such other entity has converted for any purpose of the laws of the State of Delaware.

(g) Unless otherwise agreed, for all purposes of the laws of the State of Delaware, the converting other entity shall not be required to wind up its affairs or pay its liabilities and distribute its assets, and the conversion shall not be deemed to constitute a dissolution of such other entity. When an other entity has been converted to a limited liability company pursuant to this section, for all purposes of the laws of the State of Delaware, the limited liability company shall be deemed to be the same entity as the converting other entity and the conversion shall constitute a continuation of the existence of the converting other entity in the form of a domestic limited liability company.

(h) Prior to filing a certificate of conversion to limited liability company with the office of the Secretary of State, the conversion shall be approved in the manner provided for by the document, instrument, agreement or other writing, as the case may be, governing the internal affairs of the other entity and the conduct of its business or by applicable law, as appropriate and a limited liability company agreement shall be approved by the same authorization required to approve the conversion.

(i) In connection with a conversion hereunder, rights or securities of or interests in the other entity which is to be converted to a domestic limited liability company may be exchanged for or converted into cash, property, rights or securities of or interests in such domestic limited liability company or, in addition to or in lieu thereof, may be exchanged for or converted into cash, property, rights or securities of or interests in another domestic limited liability company or other entity or may be cancelled.

(j) The provisions of this section shall not be construed to limit the accomplishment of a change in the law governing, or the domicile of, an other entity to the State of Delaware by any other means provided for in a limited liability company agreement or other agreement or as otherwise permitted by law, including by the amendment of a limited liability company agreement or other agreement. (Last amended by Ch. 95, L. '11, eff. 8-1-11.)

Ch. 95, L. '11, eff. 8-1-11, added matter in italic.

Ch. 95, L. '11 Synopsis of Section 18-214

This section amends §18-214 of the Act to clarify that the certificate of conversion to limited liability company and the certificate of formation of an other entity converting to a Delaware limited liability company must be filed simultaneously in the office of the Secretary of State and, to the extent such certificates are to have a post-filing effective date or time, such certificates must provide for the same effective date or time.

Ch. 387, L. '08 Synopsis of Section 18-214

This section amends §18-214(a) of the Act to make changes conforming to the amendment to §18-204 of the Act.

This section amends §18-214(b)(1) of the Act to make changes conforming to the amendment to §18-204 of the Act.

Ch. 317, L. '06 Synopsis of Section 18-214

Sections 7 through 32 of the Bill make technical changes to §18-212 (domestication of non-US entities), §18-213 (transfer or continuance of domestic limited liability companies), §18-214 (conversion of certain entities to a limited liability company) and §18-216 (approval of conversion of a limited liability company) of the Act to conform these Sections to the parallel provisions in the Delaware General Corporation Law adopted in 2005.

Ch. 51, L. '05 Synopsis of Section 18-214(g)

These sections amend §18-212(i) and §18-214(g) of the Act to confirm that these sections of the Act address the effect of domestication and conversion, respectively, as a matter of Delaware law.

Ch. 275, L. '04 Synopsis of Section 18-214(i)

This amendment confirms the flexibility permitted in the Act regarding a conversion to a domestic limited liability company.

Ch. 329, L. '02 Synopsis of Section 18-214

The amendments set forth are made for the purpose of avoiding any implication that a trust formed under Chapter 38, Title 12 of the Delaware Code constitutes a "business trust" within the meaning of Title 11 of the United States Code. Such amendments are not intended to result in any substantive change in Delaware law. These amendments are made solely for the purpose of conforming the Delaware Code to the amendments set forth above.

Ch. 389, L. '00 Synopsis of Section 18-214

These sections amend §18-102(3), §18-209(a), §18-212(a), §18-214(a) and §18-216 of the Act to eliminate an unnecessary word.

This section amends §18-214 of the Act to confirm that no transfer occurs as a consequence of a conversion.

This section amends §18-214 of the Act to confirm the flexibility permitted by the Act in connection with a conversion to a Delaware limited liability company.

Ch. 129, L. '99 Synopsis of Section 18-214

These sections amend §18-214 and §18-216 of the Act and provide for the conversion of a corporation to a limited liability company and the conversion of a limited liability company to a corporation and confirm that a limited liability company that has been converted continues as the same entity.

Ch. 77, L. '97 Synopsis of Section 18-214

This Section amends §18-214(c)(1) of the Act to eliminate an unnecessary word.

This Section amends §18-214(g) of the Act to make it clear that upon conversion to a limited liability company, the limited liability company is a continuation of the existence of the converting other entity.

This Section amends §18-214(h) of the Act to clarify mechanics relating to the conversion of other entities to a limited liability company.

Ch. 360, L. '96 Synopsis of Section 18-214

This section adds a new §18-214 to the Act which provides that any business trust, partnership or foreign limited liability company or other entity (except for a corporation) may convert to a limited liability company in the State of Delaware upon the obtaining of the requisite approval of a limited liability company agreement by such converting entity and the filing of a certificate of conversion to limited liability company and a certificate of formation with the Secretary of State. Such conversion shall not affect the ownership of property owned, the liabilities incurred, or any actions pending, prior to the conversion.

18-215 SERIES OF MEMBERS, MANAGERS [1], LIMITED LIABILITY COMPANY INTERESTS *OR ASSETS.*—(a) A limited liability company agreement may establish or provide for the establishment of 1 or more designated series of members, managers [2], limited liability company interests [3]*or assets. Any such series may have* separate rights, powers or duties with respect to specified property or obligations of the limited liability company or profits and losses associated with specified property or obligations, and any such series may have a separate business purpose or investment objective.

(b) Notwithstanding anything to the contrary set forth in this chapter or under other applicable law, in the event that a limited liability company agreement establishes or provides for the establishment of 1 or more series, and if [4]*the* records [5]maintained for any such series [6]*account for* the assets associated with [7]*such series* separately from the other assets of the limited liability company, or any other series thereof, and if the limited liability company agreement so provides, and if notice of the limitation on liabilities of a series as referenced in this subsection is set forth in the certificate of formation of the limited liability company, then the debts, liabilities, and obligations and expenses incurred, contracted for or otherwise existing with respect to a particular series shall be enforceable against the assets of such series only, and not against the assets of the limited liability company generally or any other series thereof, and, unless otherwise provided in the limited liability company agreement, none of the debts, liabilities, obligations and expenses incurred, contracted for or otherwise existing with respect to the limited liability company generally or any other series thereof shall be enforceable against the assets of such series. *Assets associated with a series may be held directly or indirectly, including in the name of such series, in the name of the limited liability company, through a nominee or otherwise. Records maintained for a series that reasonably identify its assets, including by specific listing, category, type, quantity, computational or allocational formula or procedure (including a percentage or share of any asset or assets) or by any other method where the identity of such assets is objectively determinable, will be deemed to account for the assets associated with such series separately from the other assets of the limited liability company, or any other series thereof.* Notice in a certificate of formation of the limitation on liabilities of a series as referenced in this subsection shall be sufficient for all purposes of this subsection whether or not the limited liability company has established any series when such notice is included in the certificate of formation, and there shall be no requirement that any specific series of the limited liability company be referenced in such notice. The fact that a certificate of formation that contains the foregoing notice of the limitation on liabilities of a series is on file in the office of the Secretary of State shall constitute notice of such limitation on liabilities of a series.

(c) A series established in accordance with subsection (b) of this section may carry on any lawful business, purpose or activity, whether or not for profit, with the exception of the business of banking as defined in §126 of Title 8. Unless otherwise provided in a limited liability company agreement, a series established in accordance with subsection (b) of this section shall have the power and capacity to, in its own name, contract, hold title to assets (including real, personal and intangible property), grant liens and security interests, and sue and be sued.

[8]*(d)* Notwithstanding §18-303(a) of this title, under a limited liability company agreement or under another agreement, a member or manager may agree to be obligated personally for any or all of the debts, obligations and liabilities of one or more series.

[9]*(e)* A limited liability company agreement may provide for classes or groups of members or managers associated with a series having such relative rights, powers and duties as the limited liability company agreement may provide, and may make provision for the future creation in the manner provided in the limited liability company agreement of additional classes or groups of members or managers associated with the series having such relative rights, powers and duties as may from time to time be established, including rights, powers and duties senior to existing classes and groups of members or managers

associated with the series. A limited liability company agreement may provide for the taking of an action, including the amendment of the limited liability company agreement, without the vote or approval of any member or manager or class or group of members or managers, including an action to create under the provisions of the limited liability company agreement a class or group of the series of limited liability company interests that was not previously outstanding. A limited liability company agreement may provide that any member or class or group of members associated with a series shall have no voting rights.

[10]*(f)* A limited liability company agreement may grant to all or certain identified members or managers or a specified class or group of the members or managers associated with a series the right to vote separately or with all or any class or group of the members or managers associated with the series, on any matter. Voting by members or managers associated with a series may be on a per capita, number, financial interest, class, group or any other basis.

[11]*(g)* Unless otherwise provided in a limited liability company agreement, the management of a series shall be vested in the members associated with such series in proportion to the then current percentage or other interest of members in the profits of the series owned by all of the members associated with such series, the decision of members owning more than 50 percent of the said percentage or other interest in the profits controlling; provided, however, that if a limited liability company agreement provides for the management of the series, in whole or in part, by a manager, the management of the series, to the extent so provided, shall be vested in the manager who shall be chosen in the manner provided in the limited liability company agreement. The manager of the series shall also hold the offices and have the responsibilities accorded to the manager as set forth in a limited liability company agreement. A series may have more than 1 manager. Subject to §18-602 of this title, a manager shall cease to be a manager with respect to a series as provided in a limited liability company agreement. Except as otherwise provided in a limited liability company agreement, any event under this chapter or in a limited liability company agreement that causes a manager to cease to be a manager with respect to a series shall not, in itself, cause such manager to cease to be a manager of the limited liability company or with respect to any other series thereof.

[12]*(h)* Notwithstanding §18-606 of this title, but subject to subsections [13]*(i) and (l)* of this section, and unless otherwise provided in a limited liability company agreement, at the time a member associated with a series that has been established in accordance with subsection (b) of this section becomes entitled to receive a distribution with respect to such series, the member has the status of, and is entitled to all remedies available to, a creditor of the series, with respect to the distribution. A limited liability company agreement may provide for the establishment of a record date with respect to allocations and distributions with respect to a series.

[14]*(i)* Notwithstanding §18-607(a) of this title, a limited liability company may make a distribution with respect to a series that has been established in accordance with subsection (b) of this section. A limited liability company shall not make a distribution with respect to a series that has been established in accordance with subsection (b) of this section to a member to the extent that at the time of the distribution, after giving effect to the distribution, all liabilities of such series, other than liabilities to members on account of their limited liability company interests with respect to such series and liabilities for which the recourse of creditors is limited to specified property of such series, exceed the fair value of the assets associated with such series, except that the fair value of property of the series that is subject to a liability for which the recourse of creditors is limited shall be included in the assets associated with such series only to the extent that the fair value of that property exceeds that liability. For purposes of the immediately preceding sentence, the term "distribution" shall not include amounts constituting reasonable compensation for present or past services or reasonable payments made in the ordinary course of business pursuant to a bona fide retirement plan or other benefits program. A member who receives a distribution in violation of this subsection, and who knew at the time of the distribution that the distribution violated this subsection, shall be liable to a series for the amount of the distribution. A member who receives a distribution in violation of this subsection, and who did not know at the time of the distribution that the distribution violated this subsection, shall not be liable for the amount of the distribution. Subject to §18-607(c) of this title, which shall apply to any distribution made with respect to a

§18-215

series under this subsection, this subsection shall not affect any obligation or liability of a member under an agreement or other applicable law for the amount of a distribution.

[15]*(j)* Unless otherwise provided in the limited liability company agreement, a member shall cease to be associated with a series and to have the power to exercise any rights or powers of a member with respect to such series upon the assignment of all of the member's limited liability company interest with respect to such series. Except as otherwise provided in a limited liability company agreement, any event under this chapter or a limited liability company agreement that causes a member to cease to be associated with a series shall not, in itself, cause such member to cease to be associated with any other series or terminate the continued membership of a member in the limited liability company or cause the termination of the series, regardless of whether such member was the last remaining member associated with such series.

[16]*(k)* Subject to §18-801 of this title, except to the extent otherwise provided in the limited liability company agreement, a series may be terminated and its affairs wound up without causing the dissolution of the limited liability company. The termination of a series established in accordance with subsection (b) of this section shall not affect the limitation on liabilities of such series provided by subsection (b) of this section. A series is terminated and its affairs shall be wound up upon the dissolution of the limited liability company under §18-801 of this title or otherwise upon the first to occur of the following:

(1) At the time specified in the limited liability company agreement;

(2) Upon the happening of events specified in the limited liability company agreement;

(3) Unless otherwise provided in the limited liability company agreement, upon the affirmative vote or written consent of the members of the limited liability company associated with such series or, if there is more than 1 class or group of members associated with such series, then by each class or group of members associated with such series, in either case, by members associated with such series who own more than two-thirds of the then-current percentage or other interest in the profits of the series of the limited liability company owned by all of the members associated with such series or by the members in each class or group of such series, as appropriate; or

(4) The termination of such series under subsection [17]*(m)* of this section.

[18]*(l)* Notwithstanding §18-803(a) of this title, unless otherwise provided in the limited liability company agreement, a manager associated with a series who has not wrongfully terminated the series or, if none, the members associated with the series or a person approved by the members associated with the series or, if there is more than 1 class or group of members associated with the series, then by each class or group of members associated with the series, in either case, by members who own more than 50 percent of the then current percentage or other interest in the profits of the series owned by all of the members associated with the series or by the members in each class or group associated with the series, as appropriate, may wind up the affairs of the series; but, if the series has been established in accordance with subsection (b) of this section, the Court of Chancery, upon cause shown, may wind up the affairs of the series upon application of any member associated with the series, the member's personal representative or assignee, and in connection therewith, may appoint a liquidating trustee. The persons winding up the affairs of a series may, in the name of the limited liability company and for and on behalf of the limited liability company and such series, take all actions with respect to the series as are permitted under §18-803(b) of this title. The persons winding up the affairs of a series shall provide for the claims and obligations of the series and distribute the assets of the series as provided in §18-804 of this title, which section shall apply to the winding up and distribution of assets of a series. Actions taken in accordance with this subsection shall not affect the liability of members and shall not impose liability on a liquidating trustee.

[17]*(m)* On application by or for a member or manager associated with a series established in accordance with subsection (b) of this section, the Court of Chancery may decree termination of such series whenever it is not reasonably practicable to carry on the business of the series in conformity with a limited liability company agreement.

[19]*(n)* If a foreign limited liability company that is registering to do business in the State of Delaware in accordance with §18-902 of this title is governed by a limited liability company agreement that establishes or provides for the establishment of designated series of members, managers [2], limited liability company interests *or assets* having separate rights,

powers or duties with respect to specified property or obligations of the foreign limited liability company or profits and losses associated with specified property or obligations, that fact shall be so stated on the application for registration as a foreign limited liability company. In addition, the foreign limited liability company shall state on such application whether the debts, liabilities and obligations incurred, contracted for or otherwise existing with respect to a particular series, if any, shall be enforceable against the assets of such series only, and not against the assets of the foreign limited liability company generally or any other series thereof, and [2]*whether any* of the debts, liabilities, obligations and expenses incurred, contracted for or otherwise existing with respect to the foreign limited liability company generally or any other series thereof shall be enforceable against the assets of such series. (Last amended by Ch. 105, L. '07, eff. 8-1-07.)

Ch. 105, L. '07, eff. 8-1-07, added matter in italic and deleted [1]"OR"; [2]"or"; [3]"having"; [4]"separate and distinct"; [5]"are"; [6]"and"; [7]"any such series are held in such separate and distinct records (directly or indirectly, including through a nominee or otherwise) and accounted for in such separate and distinct records"; [8]"(c)"; [9]"(d)"; [10]"(e)"; [11]"(f)"; [12]"(g)"; [13]"(h) and (k)"; [14]"(h)"; [15]"(i)"; [16]"(j)"; [17]"(l)"; [18]"(k)"; [19]"(m)"; and [20]", unless otherwise provided in the limited liability company agreement, none".

Ch. 105, L. '07 Synopsis of Section 18-215

These sections amend §18-215 of the Act to provide that a limited liability company agreement may establish a series of assets.

This section amends §18-215(b) of the Act to clarify the requirements regarding the manner in which assets must be accounted for pursuant to such subsection and to confirm the flexibility that exists thereunder.

This section redesignates existing subsections and adds a new subsection (c) to §18-215 of the Act to confirm the broad purposes and powers permitted of a series established under subsection 18-215(b) of the Act.

This section amends newly designated §18-215(h) to make conforming changes

This section amends newly designated §18-215(k)(4) to make a conforming change.

This section amends newly designated §18-215(n) of the Act to make conforming changes and to make technical changes.

Ch. 275, L. '03 Synopsis of Section 18-215(b)

This amendment confirms the manner in which assets may be held and accounted for pursuant to such section.

Ch. 85, L. '03 Synopsis of Section 18-215

These sections amend §18-215 of the Act to confirm the ability to provide for the establishment of 1 or more series and the sufficiency of a general notice of the limitation on liabilities of a series without referring to any specific series.

Ch. 389, L. '00 Synopsis of Section 18-215

This section amends §18-215(b) of the Act to confirm the flexibility regarding the way in which assets associated with a series may be held.

This section amends §18-215(h) of the Act to clarify the limitations on distributions with respect to a series.

This section amends §18-215(j) of the Act to confirm that termination of a series may be approved by a vote in addition to a consent.

This section amends §18-215(j) of the Act to eliminate an inconsistency in the Act relating to series.

This section amends §18-215(k) of the Act to clarify existing provisions of the Act relating to series.

Ch. 341, L. '98 Synopsis of Section 18-215

These sections amend §18-215 of the Act to clarify the series concept contained in the Act.

Ch. 77, L. '97 Synopsis of Section 18-215

These Sections amend §18-215 of the Act to clarify existing provisions of the Act relating to the use of the series concept contained in the Act.

This Section amends §18-215(l) of the Act to correct a word used in the Section.

Ch. 360, L. '96 Synopsis of Section 18-215

This Section adds a new §18-215 to the Act which provides that a limited liability company may have designated series of members, managers and limited liability company interests with separate purposes, and separate rights, powers and duties with respect to specified assets and liabilities of the limited liability company, and the profits and losses associated therewith. Further, upon compliance with the requirements of new §18-215(b), a limited liability company may provide that such series shall be treated in many important respects as if the series were a separate limited liability company, including limiting the recourse of creditors with respect to liabilities of the series to the assets associated with the series, and not the assets of the limited liability company generally or the assets of any other series.

18-216 APPROVAL OF CONVERSION OF A LIMITED LIABILITY COMPANY.—(a) Upon compliance with this section, a domestic limited liability company may convert to a corporation, a statutory trust, a business trust, an association, a real estate investment trust, a common-law trust or any other unincorporated business or entity, including a partnership (whether general (including a limited liability partnership) or limited (including a limited liability limited partnership)) or a foreign limited liability company.

(b) If the limited liability company agreement specifies the manner of authorizing a conversion of the limited liability company, the conversion shall be authorized as specified in the limited liability company agreement. If the limited liability company agreement does not specify the manner of authorizing a conversion of the limited liability company and does not prohibit a conversion of the limited liability company, the conversion shall be authorized in the same manner as is specified in the limited liability company agreement for authorizing a merger or consolidation that involves the limited liability company as a constituent party to the merger or consolidation. If the limited liability company agreement does not specify the manner of authorizing a conversion of the limited liability company or a merger or consolidation that involves the limited liability company as a constituent party and does not prohibit a conversion of the limited liability company, the conversion shall be authorized by the approval by the members or, if there is more than 1 class or group of members, then by each class or group of members, in either case, by members who own more than 50 percent of the then current percentage or other interest in the profits of the domestic limited liability company owned by all of the members or by the members in each class or group, as appropriate.

(c) Unless otherwise agreed, the conversion of a domestic limited liability company to another entity or business form pursuant to this section shall not require such limited liability company to wind up its affairs under §18-803 of this title or pay its liabilities and distribute its assets under §18-804 of this title, and the conversion shall not constitute a dissolution of such limited liability company. When a limited liability company has converted to another entity or business form pursuant to this section, for all purposes of the laws of the State of Delaware, the other entity or business form shall be deemed to be the same entity as the converting limited liability company and the conversion shall constitute a continuation of the existence of the limited liability company in the form of such other entity or business form.

(d) In connection with a conversion of a domestic limited liability company to another entity or business form pursuant to this section, rights or securities of or interests in the domestic limited liability company which is to be converted may be exchanged for or converted into cash, property, rights or securities of or interests in the entity or business form into which the domestic limited liability company is being converted or, in addition to or in lieu thereof, may be exchanged for or converted into cash, property, rights or securities of or interests in another entity or business form or may be cancelled.

(e) If a limited liability company shall convert in accordance with this section to another entity or business form organized, formed or created under the laws of a jurisdiction other than the State of Delaware, a certificate of conversion to non-Delaware entity executed in accordance with §18-204 of this title, shall be filed in the office of the Secretary of State in accordance with §18-206 of this title. The certificate of conversion to non-Delaware entity shall state:

(1) The name of the limited liability company and, if it has been changed, the name under which its certificate of formation was originally filed;

(2) The date of filing of its original certificate of formation with the Secretary of State;

(3) The jurisdiction in which the entity or business form, to which the limited liability company shall be converted, is organized, formed or created, and the name of such entity or business form;

(4) The future effective date or time (which shall be a date or time certain) of the conversion if it is not to be effective upon the filing of the certificate of conversion to non-Delaware entity;

(5) That the conversion has been approved in accordance with this section;

(6) The agreement of the limited liability company that it may be served with process in the State of Delaware in any action, suit or proceeding for enforcement of any obligation of the limited liability company arising while it was a limited liability company of the State of Delaware, and that it irrevocably appoints the Secretary of State as its agent to accept service of process in any such action, suit or proceeding;

(7) The address to which a copy of the process referred to in paragraph (6) of this section shall be mailed to it by the Secretary of State. *Process may be served upon the Secretary of State under paragraph (e)(6) of this section by means of electronic transmission but only as prescribed by the Secretary of State. The Secretary of State is authorized to issue such rules and regulations with respect to such service as the Secretary of State deems necessary or appropriate.* In the event of service hereunder upon the Secretary of State, the procedures set forth in §18-911(c) of this title shall be applicable, except that the plaintiff in any such action, suit or proceeding shall furnish the Secretary of State with the address specified in this subdivision and any other address that the plaintiff may elect to furnish, together with copies of such process as required by the Secretary of State, and the Secretary of State shall notify the limited liability company that has converted out of the State of Delaware at all such addresses furnished by the plaintiff in accordance with the procedures set forth in §18-911(c) of this title.

(f) Upon the filing in the office of the Secretary of State of the certificate of conversion to non-Delaware entity or upon the future effective date or time of the certificate of conversion to non-Delaware entity and payment to the Secretary of State of all fees prescribed in this chapter, the Secretary of State shall certify that the limited liability company has filed all documents and paid all fees required by this chapter, and thereupon the limited liability company shall cease to exist as a limited liability company of the State of Delaware. Such certificate of the Secretary of State shall be prima facie evidence of the conversion by such limited liability company out of the State of Delaware.

(g) The conversion of a limited liability company out of the State of Delaware in accordance with this section and the resulting cessation of its existence as a limited liability company of the State of Delaware pursuant to a certificate of conversion to non-Delaware entity shall not be deemed to affect any obligations or liabilities of the limited liability company incurred prior to such conversion or the personal liability of any person incurred prior to such conversion, nor shall it be deemed to affect the choice of law applicable to the limited liability company with respect to matters arising prior to such conversion.

(h) When any conversion shall have become effective under this section, for all purposes of the laws of the State of Delaware, all of the rights, privileges and powers of the limited liability company that has converted, and all property, real, personal and mixed, and all debts due to such limited liability company, as well as all other things and causes of action belonging to such limited liability company, shall remain vested in the other entity or business form to which such limited liability company has converted and shall be the property of such other entity or business form, and the title to any real property vested by deed or otherwise in such limited liability company shall not revert or be in any way impaired by reason of this chapter; but all rights of creditors and all liens upon any property of such limited liability company shall be preserved unimpaired, and all debts, liabilities and duties of the limited liability company that has converted shall remain attached to the other entity or business form to which such limited liability company has converted, and may be enforced against it to the same extent as if said debts, liabilities and duties had originally been incurred or contracted by it in its capacity as such other entity or business form. The rights, privileges, powers and interests in property of the limited liability company that has converted, as well as the debts, liabilities and duties of such limited liability company, shall not be deemed, as a consequence of the conversion, to have been transferred to the other entity or business form to which such limited liability company has converted for any purpose of the laws of the State of Delaware.

(i) A limited liability company agreement may provide that a domestic limited liability company shall not have the power to convert as set forth in this section. (Last amended by Ch. 287, L. '10, eff. 8-2-10.)

Ch. 287, L. '10, eff. 8-2-10, added matter in italic.

Ch. 287, L. '10 Synopsis of Section 18-216

Sections 12, 18 and 19 amend §§18-209(c)(8), 18-213(b)(7), and 18-216(e)(7) of the Act to allow for service of process upon the Secretary of State thereunder by means of electronic transmission but only as prescribed by the Secretary of State, and to authorize the Secretary of State to issue such rules and regulations with respect to such service as the Secretary of State deems necessary or appropriate.

Ch. 105, L. '07 Synopsis of Section 18-216

This section amends §18-216(h) of the Act to make a technical change.

Ch. 317, L. '06 Synopsis of Section 18-216

Sections 7 through 32 of the Bill make technical changes to §18-212 (domestication of non-US entities), §18-213 (transfer or continuance of domestic limited liability companies), §18-214 (conversion of certain entities to a limited liability company) and §18-216 (approval of conversion of a limited liability company) of the Act to conform these Sections to the parallel provisions in the Delaware General Corporation Law adopted in 2005.

Ch. 275, L. '04 Synopsis of Section 18-216(d) and (h)

This amendment confirms the flexibility permitted in the Act regarding a conversion of a domestic limited liability company.

This amendment confirms the treatment under Delaware law of limited liability companies that have converted to another business form.

Ch. 85, L. '03 Synopsis of Section 18-216

These amendments permit conversion of a Delaware limited liability company to a non-Delaware entity.

Ch. 329, L. '02 Synopsis of Section 18-216

The amendments set forth are made for the purpose of avoiding any implication that a trust formed under Chapter 38, Title 12 of the Delaware Code constitutes a "business trust" within the meaning of Title 11 of the United States Code. Such amendments are not intended to result in any substantive change in Delaware law. These amendments are made solely for the purpose of conforming the Delaware Code to the amendments set forth above.

Ch. 389, L. '00 Synopsis of Section 18-216

These sections amend §18-102(3), §18-209(a), §18-212(a), §18-214(a) and §18-216 of the Act to eliminate an unnecessary word.

This section amends §18-216 of the Act to confirm (i) that a Delaware limited liability company that converts to another business form is not required to wind up its affairs or pay its liabilities and distribute its assets and (ii) the flexibility permitted in connection with a conversion of a Delaware limited liability company.

Ch. 129, L. '99 Synopsis of Section 18-216

These sections amend §18-214 and §18-216 of the Act and provide for the conversion of a corporation to a limited liability company and the conversion of a limited liability company to a corporation and confirm that a limited liability company that has been converted continues as the same entity.

Ch. 360, L. '96 Synopsis of Section 18-216

This section adds a new §18-216 of the Act which provides for the manner in which a conversion of a limited liability company to another type of Delaware entity (except for a corporation) shall be authorized by the members.

Subchapter III. Members

18-301 ADMISSION OF MEMBERS.—(a) In connection with the formation of a limited liability company, a person is admitted as a member of the limited liability company upon the later to occur of:

(1) The formation of the limited liability company; or

(2) The time provided in and upon compliance with the limited liability company agreement or, if the limited liability company agreement does not so provide, when the person's admission is reflected in the records of the limited liability company.

(b) After the formation of a limited liability company, a person is admitted as a member of the limited liability company:

(1) In the case of a person who is not an assignee of a limited liability company interest, including a person acquiring a limited liability company interest directly from the limited liability company and a person to be admitted as a member of the limited liability company without acquiring a limited liability company interest in the limited liability company at the time provided in and upon compliance with the limited liability company agreement or, if the limited liability company agreement does not so provide, upon the consent of all members and when the person's admission is reflected in the records of the limited liability company;

(2) In the case of an assignee of a limited liability company interest, as provided in §18-704(a) of this title and at the time provided in and upon compliance with the limited liability company agreement or, if the limited liability company agreement does not so provide, when any such person's permitted admission is reflected in the records of the limited liability company; or

(3) In the case of a person being admitted as a member of a surviving or resulting limited liability company pursuant to a merger or consolidation approved in accordance with §18-209(b) of this title, as provided in the limited liability company agreement of the surviving or resulting limited liability company or in the agreement of merger or consolidation *or plan of merger*, and in the event of any inconsistency, the terms of the agreement of merger or consolidation *or plan of merger* shall control; and in the case of a person being admitted as a member of a limited liability company pursuant to a merger or consolidation in which such limited liability company is not the surviving or resulting limited liability company in the merger or consolidation, as provided in the limited liability company agreement of such limited liability company.

(c) In connection with the domestication of a non-United States entity (as defined in §18-212 of this title) as a limited liability company in the State of Delaware in accordance with §18-212 of this title or the conversion of an other entity (as defined in §18-214 of this title) to a domestic limited liability company in accordance with §18-214 of this title, a person is admitted as a member of the limited liability company as provided in the limited liability company agreement.

(d) A person may be admitted to a limited liability company as a member of the limited liability company and may receive a limited liability company interest in the limited liability company without making a contribution or being obligated to make a contribution to the limited liability company. Unless otherwise provided in a limited liability company agreement, a person may be admitted to a limited liability company as a member of the limited liability company without acquiring a limited liability company interest in the limited liability company. Unless otherwise provided in a limited liability company agreement, a person may be admitted as the sole member of a limited liability company without making a contribution or being obligated to make a contribution to the limited liability company or without acquiring a limited liability company interest in the limited liability company.

(e) Unless otherwise provided in a limited liability company agreement or another agreement, a member shall have no preemptive right to subscribe to any additional issue of limited liability company interests or another interest in a limited liability company. (Last amended by Ch. 287, L. '10, eff. 8-2-10.)

Ch. 287, L. '10, eff. 8-2-10, added matter in italic.

Ch. 287, L. '10 Synopsis of Section 18-301

Sections 4, 6, 7, 8, 9, 10, 11, 13, 14, 15, 16, 17, 20 and 30 amend §§18-203, 18-206(a), 18-206(b), 18-206(d), 18-209(a), 18-209(b), 18-209(c), 18-209(d), 18-209(e), 18-209(f),

18-209, 18-210, 18-301(b) and 18-1105(a) of the Act to provide a mechanism to implement a short form merger under new Section 267 of Title 8 where a domestic limited liability company is the parent Entity (as defined in new Section 267(e)(2) of Title 8).

Ch. 51, L. '05 Synopsis of Section 18-301(b)(3) and (c)

This section amends §18-301(b)(3) of the Act to clarify the way in which a person is admitted as a member of a limited liability company pursuant to a merger or consolidation.

This section amends §18-301(c) of the Act to confirm that a person is admitted as a member of a limited liability company in connection with a domestication or a conversion as provided in the limited liability company agreement.

Ch. 295, L. '02 Synopsis of Section 18-301

This section amends §18-301 of the Act to confirm that a member has no preemptive rights unless otherwise provided in a limited liability company agreement or another agreement.

Ch. 77, L. '97 Synopsis of Section 18-301

This Section amends §18-301 of the Act to clarify the mechanics for the admission of a member in connection with the domestication of a non-United States entity as a Delaware limited liability company and in connection with the conversion of another entity to a Delaware limited liability company.

This Section amends §18-301 of the Act to confirm that a person may be admitted as the sole member of a limited liability company without making a contribution or being obligated to make a contribution to, or without acquiring an interest in, a limited liability company.

Ch. 75, L. '95 Synopsis of Section 18-301

This Section eliminates unnecessary words from the Act.

18-302 CLASSES AND VOTING.—(a) A limited liability company agreement may provide for classes or groups of members having such relative rights, powers and duties as the limited liability company agreement may provide, and may make provision for the future creation in the manner provided in the limited liability company agreement of additional classes or groups of members having such relative rights, powers and duties as may from time to time be established, including rights, powers and duties senior to existing classes and groups of members. A limited liability company agreement may provide for the taking of an action, including the amendment of the limited liability company agreement, without the vote or approval of any member or class or group of members, including an action to create under the provisions of the limited liability company agreement a class or group of limited liability company interests that was not previously outstanding. A limited liability company agreement may provide that any member or class or group of members shall have no voting rights.

(b) A limited liability company agreement may grant to all or certain identified members or a specified class or group of the members the right to vote separately or with all or any class or group of the members or managers, on any matter. Voting by members may be on a per capita, number, financial interest, class, group or any other basis.

(c) A limited liability company agreement may set forth provisions relating to notice of the time, place or purpose of any meeting at which any matter is to be voted on by any members, waiver of any such notice, action by consent without a meeting, the establishment of a record date, quorum requirements, voting in person or by proxy, or any other matter with respect to the exercise of any such right to vote.

(d) Unless otherwise provided in a limited liability company agreement, meetings of members may be held by means of conference telephone or other communications equipment by means of which all persons participating in the meeting can hear each other, and participation in a meeting pursuant to this subsection shall constitute presence in person at the meeting. Unless otherwise provided in a limited liability company agreement, on any matter that is to be voted on, consented to or approved by members, the members may take such action without a meeting, without prior notice and without a vote if [1] *consented to, in writing or by eletronic transmission, by* members having not less than the minimum number of votes that would be necessary to authorize or take such action at a meeting at which all members entitled to vote thereon were present and voted. Unless otherwise provided in a limited liability company agreement, on any matter that is to be voted on by members, the members may vote in person or by proxy, and such proxy may be granted in writing, by means of electronic transmission or as otherwise permitted by applicable law. Unless otherwise provided in a limited liability company agreement, a consent transmitted by electronic transmission by a member or by a person or persons authorized to act for a member shall be deemed to be written and signed for purposes of this subsection. For purposes of this subsection, the term "electronic transmission" means any form of communication not directly involving the physical transmission of paper that creates a record that may be retained, retrieved and reviewed by a recipient thereof and that may be directly reproduced in paper form by such a recipient through an automated process.

(e) If a limited liability company agreement provides for the manner in which it may be amended, including by requiring the approval of a person who is not a party to the limited liability company agreement or the satisfaction of conditions, it may be amended only in that manner or as otherwise permitted by law, including as permitted by §18-209(f) of this title (provided that the approval of any person may be waived by such person and that any such conditions may be waived by all persons for whose benefit such conditions were intended). *Unless otherwise provided in a limited liability company agreement, a supermajority amendment provision shall only apply to provisions of the limited liability company agreement that are expressly included in the limited liability company agreement. As used in this section, "supermajority amendment provision" means any amendment provision set forth in a limited liability company agreement requiring that an amendment to a provision of the limited liability company agreement be adopted by no less than the vote or consent required to take action under such latter provision.*

(f) If a limited liability company agreement does not provide for the manner in which it may be amended, the limited liability company agreement may be amended with the approval of all of the members or as otherwise permitted by law, including as permitted by §18-209(f) of this title. This subsection shall only apply to a limited liability company whose original certificate of formation was filed with the Secretary of State on or after January 1, 2012. (Last amended by Ch. 95, L. '11, eff. 8-1-11.)

Ch. 95, L. '11, eff. 8-1-11, added matter in italic and deleted [1] "if a consent or consents in writing, setting forth the action so taken, shall be signed by the".

Ch. 95, L. '11 Synopsis of Section 18-302

This section amends §18-302(d) of the Act to clarify the manner in which members of a limited liability company may take action without a meeting.

This section amends §18-302(e) of the Act to adopt a rule different from the approach articulated in In re LJM2 Co-Investment, L.P. Limited Partners Litigation, 866 A.2d 762 (Del. Ch. 2004) with respect to the application of the type of amendment provision contained in the partnership agreement at issue in that case. This amendment provides that such amendment provisions only apply to provisions expressly included in the limited liability company agreement and do not apply to default voting provisions of the statute unless otherwise provided in the limited liability company agreement. This amendment is not intended to affect the interpretation of such amendment provisions as applied to provisions expressly included in the limited liability company agreement.

This section adds a new subsection (f) to §18-302 of the Act to provide a default rule for the manner of amending a limited liability company agreement where the limited liability company agreement does not provide for the manner in which it may be amended. This subsection shall only apply to a limited liability company whose original certificate of formation was filed with the Secretary of State on or after January 1, 2012.

Ch. 58, L. '09 Synopsis of Section 18-302

This section amends §18-302(e) of the Act to confirm that the reference in such section to "as otherwise permitted by law" includes an amendment made as permitted by §18-209(f) of the Act.

Ch. 317, L. '06 Synopsis of Section 18-302(d)

This Section amends §18-302(d) of the Act to clarify that meetings of members of a Delaware limited liability company may be held by conference telephone or similar communications equipment unless otherwise provided in a limited liability company agreement.

Ch. 275, L. '04 Synopsis of Section 18-302(e)

This amendment confirms the flexibility permitted in drafting a limited liability company agreement, including providing for the manner in which it may be amended.

Ch. 83, L. '01 Synopsis of Section 18-302

These sections amend §18-302(d) and §18-404(d) of the Act to clarify the ability to act by written consent, to clarify that proxies may be granted by any legally permissible means, including by electronic transmission, and to provide that written consents may be delivered by electronic transmission. These sections also provide a definition for the term "electronic transmission."

Ch. 389, L. '00 Synopsis of Section 18-302

This section amends §18-302(d) of the Act to deal with a quorum requirement.

Ch. 129, L. '99 Synopsis of Section 18-302

This section amends §18-302(d) of the Act to deal with a quorum requirement.

Ch. 341, L. '98 Synopsis of Section 18-302

These sections amend §18-302(c) and §18-404(c) of the Act to clarify that the limited liability company agreement may deal with matters relating to voting regardless of whether a right to vote is established under a limited liability company agreement, the Act or otherwise.

Ch. 77, L. '97 Synopsis of Section 18-302

This Section amends §18-302 of the Act to confirm the ability of members to take action by written consent and to act by proxy.

Ch. 75, L. '95 Synopsis of Section 18-302

This Section adds a new sentence to §18-302(a) of the Act to confirm that a limited liability company agreement may deny members the right to vote.

18-303 LIABILITY TO THIRD PARTIES.—(a) Except as otherwise provided by this chapter, the debts, obligations and liabilities of a limited liability company, whether arising in contract, tort or otherwise, shall be solely the debts, obligations and liabilities of the limited liability company, and no member or manager of a limited liability company shall be obligated personally for any such debt, obligation or liability of the limited liability company solely by reason of being a member or acting as a manager of the limited liability company.

(b) Notwithstanding the provisions of §18-303(a) of this chapter, under a limited liability company agreement or under another agreement, a member or manager may agree to be obligated personally for any or all of the debts, obligations and liabilities of the limited liability company. (Last amended by Ch. 260, L. '94, eff. 8-1-94.)

.1 Requirement of legal representation.—For a limited liability company to appear or conduct business in a Delaware court, it must be represented by a member of the Delaware bar. A member or manager of the limited liability company cannot represent the limited liability company. The court reasoned that a limited liability company mor closely resembles a corporation, which requires legal representation, than a partnership, which does not. *Poore v Fox Hollow Enterprises, No. 93A-09-005 (Super Ct 3-29-94).*

.2 Piercing the corporate veil.—Defendant members or managers of a limited liability company are not shielded by its corporate veil where liability arises from defendants' participation in acts or events not engaged in solely by reason of being, or acting as, limited liability company members or managers. *The Pepsi-Cola Bottling Company of Salisbury, Maryland v Handy, C.A. No. 1973-S (Ch Ct 3-15-00).*

.3 Breach of fiduciary duties.—Breach of fiduciaries claims based on knowledge of bribery by a limited liability company's managers must be plead asserting scienter. *Metro Communication Corp BVI v Advanced MobileComm Technologies, Inc, 854 A2d 121 (Ch Ct 2004).*

A claim for aiding and abetting a breach of fiduciary duty by a limited liability company's manager is made where another member has either not objected to, or has enjoyed the benefit of, actions taken by the manager that constitute a breach of fiduciary duty.

Three brothers controlled a multitude of LLCs. Eventually, significant disputes arose between brother #1 and the other two. Brother #1 alleged, among other things, that Brother #2, with the consent of Brother #3, retaliated against Brother #1 by dramatically increasing the fees his management company charged the LLCs. Even though no additional services were provided, the management fees allegedly increased by 400% were not approved by any disinterested party, reviewed for fairness by any outside consultant, or presented to Brother #1 for his approval before they took effect. He claimed, that this constituted, inter alia, a claim for aiding and abetting the breach of fiduciary duties against Brother #3, and sought the recovery of excess management fees. Brother #3 contended that he was not a fiduciary of at least one of the entities on whose behalf Brother #1 was bringing suit, and sought dismissal.

The Court of Chancery ruled that under the plaintiff-friendly motion to dismiss standard, the allegations that Brother #3 consented to the increase in fees, which benefited a company controlled by the other brothers, were sufficient to support a reasonable inference that Brother #3 participated in the alleged wrongdoing. The court reasoned that the fact that Brother #2 could have taken that action on his own as a manager did not negate a reasonable inference that Brother #3 may have been involved in the decision. The evidence conceivably could show that Brother #3 knew about the increase and supported it, even though he also knew that a fee increase of 400% would have been suspect, especially in light of the family feud he and Brother #2 had with Brother #1 and the fact that he and Brother #2 stood to benefit from the increased fees. Accordingly, the court denied the motion to dismiss the claim. *Julian v Julian, 2009 Del. Ch. LEXIS 164 (Ch Ct 2009).*

18-304 EVENTS OF BANKRUPTCY.—A person ceases to be a member of a limited liability company upon the happening of any of the following events:

(1) Unless otherwise provided in a limited liability company agreement, or with the written consent of all members, a member:

a. Makes an assignment for the benefit of creditors;

b. Files a voluntary petition in bankruptcy;

c. Is adjudged a bankrupt or insolvent, or has entered against [1]*the member* an order for relief, in any bankruptcy or insolvency proceeding;

d. Files a petition or answer seeking for [2]*the member* any reorganization, arrangement, composition, readjustment, liquidation, dissolution or similar relief under any statute, law or regulation;

e. Files an answer or other pleading admitting or failing to contest the material allegations of a petition filed against [1]*the member* in any proceeding of this nature;

f. Seeks, consents to or acquiesces in the appointment of a trustee, receiver or liquidator of the member or of all or any substantial part of [3]*the member's* properties; or

(2) Unless otherwise provided in a limited liability company agreement, or with the written consent of all members, 120 days after the commencement of any proceeding against the member seeking reorganization, arrangement, composition, readjustment, liquidation, dissolution or similar relief under any statute, law or regulation, if the proceeding has not been dismissed, or if within 90 days after the appointment without [3]*the member's* consent or acquiescence of a trustee, receiver or liquidator of the member or of all or any substantial part of [3]*the member's* properties, the appointment is not vacated or stayed, or within 90 days after the expiration of any such stay, the appointment is not vacated. (Last amended by Ch. 186, L. '95, eff. 7-10-95.)

Ch. 186, L. '95, eff. 7-10-95, added matter in italic and deleted [1]"him"; [2]"himself"; and [3]"his".

18-305 ACCESS TO AND CONFIDENTIALITY OF INFORMATION; RECORDS.—(a) Each member of a limited liability company has the right, subject to such reasonable standards (including standards governing what information and documents are to be furnished at what time and location and at whose expense) as may be set forth in a limited liability company agreement or otherwise established by the manager or, if there is no manager, then by the members, to obtain from the limited liability company from time to time upon reasonable demand for any purpose reasonably related to the member's interest as a member of the limited liability company:

(1) True and full information regarding the status of the business and financial condition of the limited liability company;

(2) Promptly after becoming available, a copy of the limited liability company's federal, state and local income tax returns for each year;

(3) A current list of the name and last known business, residence or mailing address of each member and manager;

(4) A copy of any written limited liability company agreement and certificate of formation and all amendments thereto, together with executed copies of any written powers of attorney pursuant to which the limited liability company agreement and any certificate and all amendments thereto have been executed;

(5) True and full information regarding the amount of cash and a description and statement of the agreed value of any other property or services contributed by each member

and which each member has agreed to contribute in the future, and the date on which each became a member; and

(6) Other information regarding the affairs of the limited liability company as is just and reasonable.

(b) Each manager shall have the right to examine all of the information described in subsection (a) of this chapter for a purpose reasonably related to the position of manager.

(c) The manager of a limited liability company shall have the right to keep confidential from the members, for such period of time as the manager deems reasonable, any information which the manager reasonably believes to be in the nature of trade secrets or other information the disclosure of which the manager in good faith believes is not in the best interest of the limited liability company or could damage the limited liability company or its business or which the limited liability company is required by law or by agreement with a 3rd party to keep confidential.

(d) A limited liability company may maintain its records in other than a written form if such form is capable of conversion into written form within a reasonable time.

(e) Any demand by a member under this section shall be in writing and shall state the purpose of such demand.

(f) Any action to enforce any right arising under this section shall be brought in the Court of Chancery. If the limited liability company refuses to permit a member to obtain or a manager to examine the information described in subsection (a) [1] of this section or does not reply to the demand that has been made within 5 business days *(or such shorter or longer period of time as is provided for in a limited liability company agreement but not longer than 30 business days)* after the demand has been made, the demanding member or manager may apply to the Court of Chancery for an order to compel such disclosure. The Court of Chancery is hereby vested with exclusive jurisdiction to determine whether or not the person seeking such information is entitled to the information sought. The Court of Chancery may summarily order the limited liability company to permit the demanding member to obtain or manager to examine the information described in subsection (a) [1] of this section and to make copies or abstracts therefrom, or the Court of Chancery may summarily order the limited liability company to furnish to the demanding member or manager the information described in subsection (a) [1] of this section on the condition that the demanding member or manager first pay to the limited liability company the reasonable cost of obtaining and furnishing such information and on such other conditions as the Court of Chancery deems appropriate. When a demanding member seeks to obtain or a manager seeks to examine the information described in subsection (a) [1] of this section, the demanding member or manager shall first establish (1) that the demanding member or manager has complied with the provisions of this section respecting the form and manner of making demand for obtaining or examining of such information, and (2) that the information the demanding member or manager seeks is reasonably related to the member's interest as a member or the manager's position as a manager, as the case may be. The Court of Chancery may, in its discretion, prescribe any limitations or conditions with reference to the obtaining or examining of information, or award such other or further relief as the Court of Chancery may deem just and proper. The Court of Chancery may order books, documents and records, pertinent extracts therefrom, or duly authenticated copies thereof, to be brought within the State of Delaware and kept in the State of Delaware upon such terms and conditions as the order may prescribe.

(g) The rights of a member or manager to obtain information as provided in this section may be restricted in an original limited liability company agreement or in any subsequent amendment approved or adopted by all of the members [2] *or in compliance with any applicable requirements of the limited liability company agreement. The provisions of this subsection shall not be construed to limit the ability to impose restrictions on the rights of a member or manager to obtain information by any other means permitted under this* [3] *chapter.*
(Last amended by Ch. 287 L. '10, eff. 8-2-10.)

Ch. 287, L. '10, eff. 8-2-10, added matter in italic and deleted [1]"(3)"; [2]"and"; and [3]"section".

Ch. 287, L. '10 Synopsis of Section 18-305

This section amends §18-305(f) of the Act to clarify both the categories of information that are within its scope and that the prescribed time period for responding to an information demand may be varied by a limited liability company agreement.

This section amends §18-305(g) of the Act to make it consistent with other sections of the Act and to clarify and confirm that all amendments are valid if adopted in the manner provided for in the limited liability company agreement.

Ch. 83, L. '01 Synopsis of Section 18-305

This section amends §18-305 of the Act to permit a limited liability company agreement to further restrict the rights of a member or manager to obtain information.

Ch. 360, L. '96 Synopsis of Section 18-305

This section amends §18-305(f) of the Act to set forth procedures for the enforcement by the Court of Chancery of certain of a member's or manager's information rights under the Act, including the procedures for how the Court of Chancery may deal with matters relating to certain information requests on a summary proceeding basis.

.1 Right of inspection.—A books and records inspection demand made by a member of a limited liability company will be granted where the member is seeking to investigate wrongdoing and mismanagement, as well as to value its membership interest in the limited liability company. *Somerville S Trust v USV Partners, LLC, 2002 Del. Ch. LEXIS 103 (Ch Ct 2002).*

A member of a limited liability company has the right to inspect its books and records, and such inspection rights are not strictly limited to persons named as members in the operating agreement. *Mickman v American International Processing, LLC, 2009 Del. Ch. LEXIS 43 (Ch Ct 2009).*

.2 Appointment of receiver.—Notwithstanding that a limited liability company operating agreement or the Limited Liability Company Act does not provide for appointment of a receiver for an insolvent limited liability company, members of a limited liability company may seek such appointment where they have made sufficient allegations that, if true, would support the appointment of a receiver, because a court may appoint a receiver in the exercise of its general equity powers, but the members must prove that they are entitled to the requested relief. *Ross Holding and Management Co v Advance Realty Group LLC, 2010 Del. Ch. LEXIS 184 (Ch Ct 2010).*

18-306 REMEDIES FOR BREACH OF LIMITED LIABILITY COMPANY AGREEMENT BY MEMBER.—A limited liability company agreement may provide that:

(1) A member who fails to perform in accordance with, or to comply with the terms and conditions of, the limited liability company agreement shall be subject to specified penalties or specified consequences, and

(2) At the time or upon the happening of events specified in the limited liability company agreement, a member shall be subject to specified penalties or specified consequences.

Such specified penalties or specified consequences may include and take the form of any penalty or consequence set forth in §18-502(c) of this title. (Last amended by Ch. 83, L. '01, eff. 8-1-01.)

Ch. 83, L. '01, eff. 8-1-01, added matter in italic.

Ch. 83, L. '01 Synopsis of Section 18-306

This section amends §18-306 of the Act to clarify the flexibility permitted in connection with providing for specified penalties or specified consequences in a limited liability company agreement.

Subchapter IV. Managers

18-401 ADMISSION OF MANAGERS.—A person may be named or designated as a manager of the limited liability company as provided in §18-101(10) of this title. (Last amended by Ch. 260, L. '94, eff. 8-1-94.)

18-402 MANAGEMENT OF LIMITED LIABILITY COMPANY.—Unless otherwise provided in a limited liability company agreement, the management of a limited liability company shall be vested in its members in proportion to the then current percentage or other interest of members in the profits of the limited liability company owned by all of the members, the decision of members owning more than 50 percent of the said percentage or other interest in the profits controlling; provided however, that if a limited liability company agreement provides for the management, in whole or in part, of a limited liability company by a manager, the management of the limited liability company, to the extent so provided, shall be vested in the manager who shall be chosen in the manner provided in the limited liability company agreement. The manager shall also hold the offices and have the *responsibilities accorded to the manager by or in the manner provided in a limited liability company agreement.* Subject to §18-602 of this title, a manager shall cease to be a manager as provided in a limited liability company agreement. A limited liability company may have more than 1 manager. Unless otherwise provided in a limited liability company agreement, each member and manager has the authority to bind the limited liability company. (Last amended by Ch. 129, L. '99, eff. 8-1-99.)

Ch. 129, L. '99, eff. 8-1-99, added matter in italic and deleted [1]"The manager shall also hold the offices and have the responsibilities accorded to the manager by the members and set forth in a limited liability company agreement. Subject to §18-602 of this title, a manager shall cease to be a manager as provided in a limited liability company agreement."

Ch. 129, L. '99 Synopsis of Section 18-402

This section amends §18-402 of the Act so as to confirm mechanics relating to managers of limited liability companies.

Ch. 341, L. '98 Synopsis of Section 18-402

This section amends §18-402 of the Act to eliminate words of limitation which are unnecessary.

Ch. 75, L. '95 Synopsis of Section 18-402

This Section confirms that a limited liability company may have more than one manager.

18-403 CONTRIBUTIONS BY A MANAGER.—A manager of a limited liability company may make contributions to the limited liability company and share in the profits and losses of, and in distributions from, the limited liability company as a member. A person who is both a manager and a member has the rights and powers, and is subject to the restrictions and liabilities, of a manager and, except as provided in a limited liability company agreement, also has the rights and powers, and is subject to the restrictions and liabilities, of a member to the extent of [1]*the manager's* participation in the limited liability company as a member. (Last amended by Ch. 186, L. '95, eff. 7-10-95.)

Ch. 186, L. '95, eff. 7-10-95, added matter in italic and deleted [1]"his".

18-404 CLASSES AND VOTING.—(a) A limited liability company agreement may provide for classes or groups of managers having such relative rights, powers and duties as the limited liability company agreement may provide, and may make provision for the future creation in the manner provided in the limited liability company agreement of additional classes or groups of managers having such relative rights, powers and duties as may from time to time be established, including rights, powers and duties senior to existing classes and groups of managers. A limited liability company agreement may provide for the taking of an action, including the amendment of the limited liability company agreement, without the vote or approval of any manager or class or group of managers, including an action to create under the provisions of the limited liability company agreement a class or group of limited liability company interests that was not previously outstanding.

(b) A limited liability company agreement may grant to all or certain identified managers or a specified class or group of the managers the right to vote, separately or with all or any class or group of managers or members, on any matter. Voting by managers may be on a per capita, number, financial interest, class, group or any other basis.

(c) A limited liability company agreement may set forth provisions relating to notice of the time, place or purpose of any meeting at which any matter is to be voted on by any manager or class or group of managers, waiver of any such notice, action by consent without a meeting, the establishment of a record date, quorum requirements, voting in person or by proxy, or any other matter with respect to the exercise of any such right to vote.

(d) Unless otherwise provided in a limited liability company agreement, meetings of managers may be held by means of conference telephone or other communications equipment by means of which all persons participating in the meeting can hear each other, and participation in a meeting pursuant to this subsection shall constitute presence in person at the meeting. Unless otherwise provided in a limited liability company agreement, on any matter that is to be voted on, consented to or approved by managers, the managers may take such action without a meeting, without prior notice and without a vote if [1] *consented to, in writing or by electronic transmission, by* managers having not less than the minimum number of votes that would be necessary to authorize or take such action at a meeting at which all managers entitled to vote thereon were present and voted. Unless otherwise provided in a limited liability company agreement, on any matter that is to be voted on by managers, the managers may vote in person or by proxy, and such proxy may be granted in writing, by means of electronic transmission or as otherwise permitted by applicable law. Unless otherwise provided in a limited liability company agreement, a consent transmitted by electronic transmission by a manager or by a person or persons authorized to act for a manager shall be deemed to be written and signed for purposes of this subsection. For purposes of this subsection, the term "electronic transmission" means any form of communication not directly involving the physical transmission of paper that creates a record that may be retained, retrieved and reviewed by a recipient thereof and that may be directly reproduced in paper form by such a recipient through an automated process. (Last amended by Ch. 95, L. '11, eff. 8-1-11.)

Ch. 95, L. '11, eff. 8-1-11, added matter in italic and deleted [1]"a consent or consents in writing, setting forth the action so taken, shall be signed by".

Ch. 95, L. '11 Synopsis of Section 18-404

This section amends §18-404(d) of the Act to clarify the manner in which managers of a limited liability company may take action without a meeting..

Ch. 317, L. '06 Synopsis of Section 18-404(d)

This Section amends §18-404(d) of the Act to clarify that meetings of managers of a Delaware limited liability company may be held by conference telephone or similar communications equipment unless otherwise provided in a limited liability company agreement.

Ch. 83, L. '01 Synopsis of Section 18-404

These sections amend §18-302(d) and §18-404(d) of the Act to clarify the ability to act by written consent, to clarify that proxies may be granted by any legally permissible means, including by electronic transmission, and to provide that written consents may be delivered by electronic transmission. These sections also provide a definition for the term "electronic transmission."

Ch. 389, L. '00 Synopsis of Section 18-404

This section amends §18-404(d) of the Act to deal with a quorum requirement.

Ch. 341, L. '98 Synopsis of Section 18-404

These sections amend §18-302(c) and §18-404(c) of the Act to clarify that the limited liability company agreement may deal with matters relating to voting regardless of whether a right to vote is established under a limited liability company agreement, the Act or otherwise.

Ch. 77, L. '97 Synopsis of Section 18-404

This section amends §18-404 of the Act to confirm the ability of managers to take action by written consent and to act by proxy.

.1 LLC merger invalidated because of board member's breach of duty of loyalty.—There is a breach of the duty of loyalty and an invalid merger where two of three board members of a limited liability company clandestinely act, without notice to the third member (the majority owner of the LLC), to merge the LLC into another corporation, whereby the majority owner becomes a minority owner. *VGS, Inc v Castiel, C.A. No. 17995 (Ch Ct 8-31-00).*

18-405 REMEDIES FOR BREACH OF LIMITED LIABILITY COMPANY AGREEMENT BY MANAGER.—A limited liability company agreement may provide that:

(1) A manager who fails to perform in accordance with, or to comply with the terms and conditions of, the limited liability company agreement shall be subject to specified penalties or specified consequences; and

(2) At the time or upon the happening of events specified in the limited liability company agreement, a manager shall be subject to specified penalties or specified consequences.

18-406 RELIANCE ON REPORTS AND INFORMATION BY MEMBER, MANAGER OR LIQUIDATION TRUSTEE.—A member, [1]manager *or liquidation trustee* of a limited liability company shall be fully protected in relying in good faith upon the records of the limited liability company and upon [2]information, opinions, reports or statements presented ³*by another manager, member or liquidating trustee, an officer or employee of* the limited liability company ⁴, or committees of the limited liability company, *members or managers,* or by any other person ⁵as to matters the member ¹, manager *or liquidating trustees* reasonably believes are within such other person's professional or expert competence ⁶, including information, opinions, reports or statements as to the value and amount of the assets, liabilities, profits or losses of the limited liability company, *or the value and amount of assets or reserves or contracts, agreements or other undertakings that would be sufficient to pay claims and obligations of the limited liability company or to make reasonable provision to pay such claims and obligations,* or any other facts pertinent to the existence and amount of assets from which distributions to members *or creditors* might properly be paid. (Last amended by Ch. 51, L. '05, eff. 8-1-05.)

Ch. 51, L. '05, eff. 8-1-05, added matter in italic and deleted ¹"or"; ²"such"; ³"to"; ⁴"by any of its other managers, members, officers, employees,"; ⁵",", and ⁶"and who has been selected with reasonable care by or on behalf of the limited liability company".

Ch. 51, L. '05 Synopsis of Section 18-406

This section amends §18-406 of the Act to clarify the circumstances under which members, managers and liquidating trustees of a limited liability company may rely on the records of, or information relating to, the limited liability company.

18-407 DELEGATION OF RIGHTS AND POWERS TO MANAGE.—Unless otherwise provided in the limited liability company agreement, a member or manager of a limited liability company has the power and authority to delegate to 1 or more other persons the member's or manager's, as the case may be, rights and powers to manage and control the business and affairs of the limited liability company, including to delegate to agents, officers and employees of a member or manager or the limited liability company, and to delegate by a management agreement or another agreement with, or otherwise to, other persons. Unless otherwise provided in the limited liability company agreement, such delegation by a member or manager of a limited liability company shall not cause the member or manager to cease to be a member or manager, as the case may be, of the limited liability company *or cause the person to whom any such rights and powers have been delegated to be a member or manager, as the case may be, of the limited liability company.* (Last amended by Ch. 295, L. '02, eff. 8-1-02.)

Ch. 295, L. '02, eff. 8-1-02, added matter in italic.

Ch. 295, L. '02 Synopsis of Section 18-407

This section amends §18-407 of the Act to confirm that delegation of any rights or powers by a member or manager will not cause the delegatee to be a member or manager.

Ch. 77, L. '97 Synopsis of Section 18-407

This Section amends §18-407 of the Act to confirm that a limited liability company may have agents and employees who are denominated as officers.

Subchapter V. Finance

18-501 FORM OF CONTRIBUTION.—The contribution of a member to a limited liability company may be in cash, property or services rendered, or a promissory note or other obligation to contribute cash or property or to perform services.

18-502 LIABILITY FOR CONTRIBUTION.—(a) Except as provided in a limited liability company agreement, a member is obligated to a limited liability company to perform any promise to contribute cash or property or to perform services, even if ¹*the member* is unable to perform because of death, disability or any other reason. If a member does not make the required contribution of property or services, ¹*the member* is obligated at the option of the limited liability company to contribute cash equal to that portion of the agreed value (as stated in the records of the limited liability company) of the contribution that has not been made. The foregoing option shall be in addition to, and not in lieu of, any other rights, including the right to specific performance, that the limited liability company may have against such member under the limited liability company agreement or applicable law.

(b) Unless otherwise provided in a limited liability company agreement, the obligation of a member to make a contribution or return money or other property paid or distributed in violation of this chapter may be compromised only by consent of all the members. Notwithstanding the compromise, a creditor of a limited liability company who extends credit, after the entering into of a limited liability company agreement or an amendment thereto which, in either case, reflects the obligation, and before the amendment thereof to reflect the compromise, may enforce the original obligation to the extent that, in extending credit, the creditor reasonably relied on the obligation of a member to make a contribution or return. A conditional obligation of a member to make a contribution or return money or other property to a limited liability company may not be enforced unless the conditions of the obligation have been satisfied or waived as to or by such member. Conditional obligations include contributions payable upon a discretionary call of a limited liability company prior to the time the call occurs.

(c) A limited liability company agreement may provide that the interest of any member who fails to make any contribution that [1]*the member* is obligated to make shall be subject to specified penalties for, or specified consequences of, such failure. Such penalty or consequence may take the form of reducing or eliminating the defaulting member's proportionate interest in a limited liability company, subordinating [2]*the member's* limited liability company interest to that of nondefaulting members, a forced sale of [2]*that* limited liability company interest, forfeiture of the defaulting member's limited liability company interest, the lending by other members of the amount necessary to meet [2]*the defaulting member's* commitment, a fixing of the value of the defaulting member's limited liability company interest by appraisal or by formula and redemption or sale of [2]*the* limited liability company interest at such value, or other penalty or consequence. (Last amended by Ch. 186, L. '95, eff. 7-10-95.)

Ch. 186, L. '95, eff. 7-10-95, added matter in italic and deleted [1]"he" and [2]"his".

.1 **Standing to sue other members.**—A member of a limited liability company has standing to bring an action in its own right against other members of the company for breaches of contract, covenant of good faith, fair dealing and fiduciary duty, if the member alleges an injury distinct from other members. Because there was no case law on point, the court analogized a limited liability company to a corporation where members are similar to stockholders. *Taurus Advisory Group, Inc v Sector Management, Inc, No. CV96 015083, 1996 Conn. Super. LEXIS 2272 (Conn. Super. Ct. 8-29-96)* (Delaware law).

.2 **Breach of fiduciary duty.**—When a member of a limited liability company sues other members for breach of fiduciary duty, the complaint must allege that the relationship between the opposing parties is analogous to that of a majority shareholder to a minority shareholder. Because there was no case law on point, the court analogized a limited liability company to a corporation where members are similar to stockholders. *Taurus Advisory Group, Inc v Sector Management, Inc, No. CV96 015083, 1996 Conn. Super. LEXIS 2272 (Conn. Super. Ct. 8-29-96)* (Delaware law).

18-503 ALLOCATION OF PROFITS AND LOSSES.—The profits and losses of a limited liability company shall be allocated among the members, and among classes or groups of members, in the manner provided in a limited liability company agreement. If the limited liability company agreement does not so provide, profits and losses shall be allocated on the basis of the agreed value (as stated in the records of the limited liability company) of the contributions made by each member to the extent they have been received by the limited liability company and have not been returned.

18-504 ALLOCATION OF DISTRIBUTIONS.—Distributions of cash or other assets of a limited liability company shall be allocated among the members, and among classes or groups of members, in the manner provided in a limited liability company agreement. If the limited liability company agreement does not so provide, distributions shall be made on the basis of the agreed value (as stated in the records of the limited liability company) of the contributions made by each member to the extent they have been received by the limited liability company and have not been returned.

18-505 DEFENSE OF USURY NOT AVAILABLE.—No obligation of a member or manager of a limited liability company to the limited liability company arising under the limited liability company agreement or a separate agreement or writing, and no note, instrument or other writing evidencing any such obligation of a member or manager, shall be subject to the defense of usury, and no member or manager shall interpose the defense of usury with respect to any such obligation in any action. (Added by Ch. 260, L. '94, eff. 8-1-94.)

Subchapter VI. Distributions and Resignation

18-601 INTERIM DISTRIBUTION.—Except as provided in this subchapter, to the extent and at the times or upon the happening of the events specified in a limited liability company agreement, a member is entitled to receive from a limited liability company distributions before [1]*the member's* resignation from the limited liability company and before the dissolution and winding up thereof. (Last amended by Ch. 186, L. '95, eff. 7-10-95.)

_{Ch. 186, L. '95, eff. 7-10-95, added matter in italic and deleted [1]"his".}

18-602 RESIGNATION OF MANAGER.—A manager may resign as a manager of a limited liability company at the time or upon the happening of events specified in a limited liability company agreement and in accordance with the limited liability company agreement. A limited liability company agreement may provide that a manager shall not have the right to resign as a manager of a limited liability company. Notwithstanding that a limited liability company agreement provides that a manager does not have the right to resign as a manager of a limited liability company, a manager may resign as a manager of a limited liability company at any time by giving written notice to the members and other managers. If the resignation of a manager violates a limited liability company agreement, in addition to any remedies otherwise available under applicable law, a limited liability company may recover from the resigning manager damages for breach of the limited liability company agreement and offset the damages against the amount otherwise distributable to the resigning manager.

18-603 RESIGNATION OF MEMBER.—A member may resign from a limited liability company *only* at the time or upon the happening of events specified in a limited liability company agreement and in accordance with the limited liability company agreement. [1]*Notwithstanding anything to the contrary under applicable law, unless a limited liability company agreement provides otherwise, a member may not resign from a limited liability company prior to the dissolution and winding up of the limited liability company. Notwithstanding anything to the contrary under applicable law, a limited liability company agreement may provide that a limited liability company interest may not be assigned prior to the dissolution and winding up of the limited liability company.*

Unless otherwise provided in a limited liability company agreement, a limited liability company whose original certificate of formation was filed with the Secretary of State and effective on or prior to July 31, 1996, shall continue to be governed by this section as in effect on July 31, 1996, and shall not be governed by this section. (Last amended by Ch. 360, L. '96, eff. 8-1-96.)

_{Ch. 360, L. '96, eff. 8-1-96, added matter in italic and deleted [1]"If a limited liability company agreement does not specify the time or the events upon the happening of which a member may resign or a definite time for the dissolution and winding up of a limited liability company, a member may resign upon not less than 6 months prior written notice to the limited liability company at its registered office as set forth in the certificate of formation filed in the Office of the Secretary of State and to each member and manager at each member's and manager's address as set forth on the records of the limited liability company. Notwithstanding anything to the contrary under applicable law, a limited liability company agreement may provide that a member may not resign from a limited liability company or assign his limited liability company interest prior to the dissolution and winding up of the limited liability company."}

Ch. 360, L. '96 Synopsis of Section 18-603

This section amends §18-603 of the Act to provide that a member may resign from a limited liability company only in accordance with the terms and provisions, if any, of the limited liability company agreement and to confirm that a limited liability company agreement may prohibit any assignment of a limited liability company interest. Unless otherwise provided in a limited liability company agreement, this section will not, however, apply retroactively to limited liability companies whose original certificate of formation was filed with the Delaware Secretary of State and effective prior to July 31, 1996. Those limited liability companies will instead be governed by 6 Del. C. §18-603 as in effect on July 31, 1996.

18-604 DISTRIBUTION UPON RESIGNATION.—[1]*Except as provided in this subchapter, upon resignation any resigning member is entitled to receive any distribution to which such member is entitled under a limited liability company agreement and, if not otherwise provided in a limited liability company agreement, such member is entitled to receive, within a reasonable time after resignation, the fair value of such member's limited liability company interest as of the date of resignation based upon such member's right to* share in distributions from the limited liability company. (Last amended by Ch. 129, L. '99, eff. 8-1-99.)

Ch. 129, L. '99, eff. 8-1-99, added matter in italic and deleted [1]"Except as provided in this subchapter, a member who resigns or otherwise ceases for any reason to be a member is entitled to receive on the terms and conditions provided in a limited liability company agreement any distribution to which such member is entitled under the limited liability company agreement, and if not otherwise provided in the limited liability company agreement, such member is entitled to receive, within a reasonable time after the date on which such member resigned or otherwise ceased to be a member, the fair value of such member's interest in the limited liability company as of the date on which such member resigned or otherwise ceased to be a member based upon such member's right to share in distributions from the limited liability company."

Ch. 129, L. '99 Synopsis of Section 18-604

This section amends §18-604 of the Act to restore language previously deleted from the Act.

Ch. 341, L. '98 Synopsis of Section 18-604

This section amends §18-604 of the Act by confirming the basis for the valuation of a person's interest in a limited liability company and the timing of payment of the value of that interest regardless of the reason for a person's ceasing to be a member of a limited liability company.

.1 **Oral operating agreements.**—An oral limited liability company operating agreement is enforceable if it is possible for it to be completed within one year, and a limited liability company manager cannot breach his fiduciary duty based on a good faith reliance on such an oral operating agreement. *Olson v Halvorsen*, 2009 Del. Ch. LEXIS 78 (Ch Ct 2009).

18-605 DISTRIBUTION IN KIND.—Except as provided in a limited liability company agreement, a member, regardless of the nature of [1]*the member's* contribution, has no right to demand and receive any distribution from a limited liability company in any form other than cash. Except as provided in a limited liability company agreement, a member may not be compelled to accept a distribution of any asset in kind from a limited liability company to the extent that the percentage of the asset distributed [2]exceeds a percentage of that asset which is equal to the percentage in which [3]*the member* shares in distributions from the limited liability company. Except as provided in the limited liability company agreement, a member may be compelled to accept a distribution of any asset in kind from a limited liability company to the extent that the percentage of the asset distributed [2]*is equal to* a percentage of that asset which is equal to the percentage in which [3]*the member* shares in distributions from the limited liability company. (Last amended by Ch. 186, L. '95, eff. 7-10-95.)

Ch. 186, L. '95, eff. 7-10-95, added matter in italic and deleted [1]"his"; [2]"to him"; and [3]"he".

18-606 RIGHT TO DISTRIBUTION.—Subject to §§18-607 and 18-804 of this title, and unless otherwise provided in a limited liability company agreement, at the time a member becomes entitled to receive a distribution, [1]*the members* has the status of, and is entitled to all remedies available to, a creditor of a limited liability company with respect to the distribution. A limited liability company agreement may provide for the establishment of a record date with respect to allocations and distributions by a limited liability company. (Last amended by Ch. 186, L. '95, eff. 7-10-95.)

Ch. 186, L. '95, eff. 7-10-95, added matter in italic and deleted [1]"he".

18-607 LIMITATIONS ON DISTRIBUTION.—(a) A limited liability company shall not make a distribution to a member to the extent that at the time of the distribution, after giving effect to the distribution, all liabilities of the limited liability company, other than liabilities to members on account of their limited liability company interests and liabilities for which the recourse of creditors is limited to specified property of the limited liability company, exceed the fair value of the assets of the limited liability company, except that the fair value of property that is subject to a liability for which the recourse of creditors is limited shall be included in the assets of the limited liability company only to the extent that the fair value of that property exceeds that liability. *For purposes of this subsection (a), the term "distribution" shall not include amounts constituting reasonable compensation for present or past services or reasonable payments made in the ordinary course of business pursuant to a bona fide retirement plan or other benefits program.*

(b) A member who receives a distribution in violation of subsection (a) of this section, and who knew at the time of the distribution that the distribution violated subsection (a) of this section, shall be liable to a limited liability company for the amount of the distribution. A member who receives a distribution in violation of subsection (a) of this section, and who did not know at the time of the distribution that the distribution violated subsection (a) of this section, shall not be liable for the amount of the distribution. Subject to subsection (c) of this section, this subsection shall not affect any obligation or liability of a member under an agreement or other applicable law for the amount of a distribution.

(c) Unless otherwise agreed, a member who receives a distribution from a limited liability company shall have no liability under this chapter or other applicable law for the amount of the distribution after the expiration of 3 years from the date of the distribution unless an action to recover the distribution from such member is commenced prior to the expiration of the said 3-year period and an adjudication of liability against such member is made in the said action. (Last amended by Ch. 389, L. '00, eff. 8-1-00.)

Ch. 389, L. '00, eff. 8-1-00, added matter in italic.

Ch. 389, L. '00 Synopsis of Section 18-607

This section amends §18-607(a) of the Act to clarify the limitations on distributions by limited liability companies.

Subchapter VII. Assignment of Limited Liability Company Interests

18-701 NATURE OF LIMITED LIABILITY COMPANY INTEREST.—A limited liability company interest is personal property. A member has no interest in specific limited liability company property.

18-702 ASSIGNMENT OF LIMITED LIABILITY COMPANY INTEREST.—
(a) A limited liability company interest is assignable in whole or in part except as provided in a limited liability company agreement. The assignee of a member's limited liability company interest shall have no right to participate in the management of the business and affairs of a limited liability company except as provided in a limited liability company agreement [1] *or, unless otherwise provided in the limited liability company agreement, upon the affirmative vote or written consent* of all of the members of the limited liability company.[2]

(b) Unless otherwise provided in a limited liability company agreement:
(1) An assignment of a limited liability company interest does not entitle the assignee to become or to exercise any rights or powers of a member;
(2) An assignment of a limited liability company interest entitles the assignee to share in such profits and losses, to receive such distribution or distributions, and to receive such allocation of income, gain, loss, deduction, or credit or similar item to which the assignor was entitled, to the extent assigned; and
(3) A member ceases to be a member and to have the power to exercise any rights or powers of a member upon assignment of all of the member's limited liability company interest. Unless otherwise provided in a limited liability company agreement, the pledge of, or granting of a security interest, lien or other encumbrance in or against, any or all of the limited liability company interest of a member shall not cause the member to cease to be a member or to have the power to exercise any rights or powers of a member.

(c) Unless otherwise provided in a limited liability company agreement, a member's interest in a limited liability company may be evidenced by a certificate of limited liability company interest issued by the limited liability company. A limited liability company agreement may provide for the assignment or transfer of any limited liability company interest represented by such a certificate and make other provisions with respect to such certificates. A limited liability company shall not have the power to issue a certificate of limited liability company interest in bearer form.

(d) Unless otherwise provided in a limited liability company agreement and except to the extent assumed by agreement, until an assignee of a limited liability company interest becomes a member, the assignee shall have no liability as a member solely as a result of the assignment.

(e) Unless otherwise provided in the limited liability company agreement, a limited liability company may acquire, by purchase, redemption or otherwise, any limited liability company interest or other interest of a member or manager in the limited liability company. Unless otherwise provided in the limited liability company agreement, any such interest so acquired by the limited liability company shall be deemed canceled. (Last amended by Ch. 287, L. '10, eff. 8-2-10.)

Ch. 287, L. '10, eff. 8-2-10, added matter in italic and deleted [1]"and upon: (1) The approval" and [2]"other than the member assigning the limited liability company interest; or (2) Compliance with any procedure provided for in the limited liability company agreement".

Ch. 287, L. '10 Synopsis of Section 18-702

This section amends §18-702(a) of the Act to confirm the circumstances in which an assignee of a limited liability company interest has the right to participate in the management of the business and affairs of a limited liability company.

Ch. 105, L. '07 Synopsis of Section 18-702

This section amends §18-702(c) of the Act to provide that a limited liability company shall not have the power to issue a certificate of limited liability company interest in bearer form.

Ch. 83, L. '01 Synopsis of Section 18-702

This section amends §18-702(c) of the Act to permit greater flexibility with respect to certificating a limited liability company interest.

Ch. 360, L. '96 Synopsis of Section 18-702

This section amends §18-702 of the Act to confirm that, unless the limited liability company agreement so provides, no assignee shall become a member or have the ability to exercise the rights or powers of a member.

.1 **Operating agreement; remedy for breach.**—Where a limited liability company operating agreement is structured so that a member will not be forced to become a partner with another member not of its choosing, a member that breaches the operating agreement may be divested of its status as an active member, and may be rendered a passive investor with the status and rights of an assignee. *Eureka VIII, LLC v Niagara Falls Holdings, LLC*, 899 A2d 95 (Ch Ct 2006).

18-703 MEMBER'S LIMITED LIABILITY COMPANY INTEREST SUBJECT TO CHARGING ORDER.—(a) On application by a judgment creditor of a member or of a member's assignee, a court having jurisdiction may charge the limited liability company interest of the judgment debtor to satisfy the judgment. [1]*To the extent so charged, the judgment creditor has only the right to receive any distribution or distributions to which the judgment debtor would otherwise have been entitled in respect of such limited liability company interest.*

(b) A charging order constitutes a lien on the judgment debtor's limited liability company interest. [2]

[3]

[4]*(c)* This chapter does not deprive a member of a right *or member's assignee* under exemption laws with respect to the [5]*judgment debtor's* limited liability company interest.

[6]*(d)* [7]*The entry of a charging order is* the exclusive remedy by which a judgment creditor of a member or *of a* member's assignee may satisfy a judgment out of the judgment debtor's limited liability company interest.

[8]*(e)* No creditor of a member *or of a member's assignee* shall have any right to obtain possession of, or otherwise exercise legal or equitable remedies with respect to, the property of the limited liability company.

(f) The Court of Chancery shall have jurisdiction to hear and determine any matter relating to any such charging order. (Last amended by Ch. 51, L. '05, eff. 8-1-05.)

Ch. 51, L. '05, eff. 8-1-05, added matter in italic and deleted [1]"The court may appoint a receiver of the share of the distributions due to or to become due to the judgment debtor in respect of the limited liability company, which receiver shall have only the rights of an assignee, and the court may make all other orders, directions, accounts and inquiries the judgment debtor might have made or which the circumstances of the case may require."; [2]"The court may order a foreclosure of the limited liability company interest subject to the charging order at any time. The purchaser at the foreclosure sale has only the rights of an assignee."; [3]"(c) Unless otherwise provided in a limited liability company agreement, at any time before foreclosure, a limited liability company interest charged may be redeemed:

(1) By the judgment debtor;

(2) With property other than limited liability company property, by 1 or more of the other members; or
(3) By the limited liability company with the consent of all of the members whose interests are not so charged."; [4]"(d)"; [5]"member's"; [6]"(e)"; [7]"This section provides"; and [8]"(f)".

Ch. 51, L. '05 Synopsis of Section 18-703

These sections amend §18-703 to clarify the nature of a charging order and provide that a charging order is the sole method by which a judgment creditor may satisfy a judgment out of the limited liability company interest of a member or a member's assignee. Attachment, garnishment, foreclosure or like remedies are not available to the judgment creditor and a judgment creditor does not have any right to become or to exercise any rights or powers of a member (other than the right to receive the distribution or distributions to which the member would otherwise have been entitled, to the extent charged).

Ch. 389, L. '00 Synopsis of Section 18-703

This section amends §18-703 to clarify the rights of a judgment creditor of a member or a member's assignee with respect to a judgment debtor's limited liability company interest.

18-704 RIGHT OF ASSIGNEE TO BECOME MEMBER.—(a) An assignee of a limited liability company interest may become a member [1]:
 (1) [2] *As provided in the limited liability company agreement; or*
 (2) [3] *Unless otherwise provided in the limited liability company agreement, upon the affirmative vote or written consent of all of the members of the limited liability company.*
 (b) An assignee who has become a member has, to the extent assigned, the rights and powers, and is subject to the restrictions and liabilities, of a member under a limited liability company agreement and this chapter. Notwithstanding the foregoing, unless otherwise provided in a limited liability company agreement, an assignee who becomes a member is liable for the obligations of the assignor to make contributions as provided in §18-502 of this title, but shall not be liable for the obligations of the assignor under subchapter VI of this chapter. However, the assignee is not obligated for liabilities, including the obligations of the assignor to make contributions as provided in §18-502 of this title, unknown to the assignee at the time the assignee became a member and which could not be ascertained from a limited liability company agreement.
 (c) Whether or not an assignee of a limited liability company interest becomes a member, the assignor is not released from liability to a limited liability company under subchapters V and VI of this chapter. (Last amended by Ch. 287, L. '10, eff. 8-2-10.)

Ch. 287, L. '10, eff. 8-2-10, added matter in italic and deleted [1]"as provided in a limited liability company agreement and upon"; [2]"The approval of all of the members of the limited liability company other than the member assigning limited liability company interest"; and [3]"Compliance with any procedure provided for in the limited liability company agreement".

Ch. 287, L. '10 Synopsis of Section 18-704

This section amends §18-704(a) of the Act to confirm the circumstances in which an assignee of a limited liability company interest may become a member.

18-705 POWERS OF ESTATE OF DECEASED OR INCOMPETENT MEMBER.—If a member who is an individual dies or a court of competent jurisdiction adjudges the member to be incompetent to manage the member's person or property, the member's [1]*personal representative* may exercise all of the member's rights for the purpose of settling the member's estate or administering the member's property, including any power under a limited liability company agreement of an assignee to become a member. If a member is a corporation, trust or other entity and is dissolved or terminated, the powers of that member may be exercised by its [2]*personal representative.* (Last amended by Ch. 77, L. '97, eff. 8-1-97.)

Ch. 77, L. '97, eff. 8-1-97, added matter in italic and deleted [1]"executor, administrator, guardian, conservator or other legal representative" and [2]"legal representative or successor".

Ch. 77, L. '97 Synopsis of Section 18-705

This section amends §18-705 of the Act to use a definition that has been added to the Act.

Ch. 360, L. '96 Synopsis of Section 18-705

This section amends §18-705 of the Act to use as a definition that has been added to the Act.

Subchapter VIII. Dissolution

18-801 DISSOLUTION.—(a) A limited liability company is dissolved and its affairs shall be wound up upon the first to occur of the following:

(1) At the time specified in a limited liability company agreement, but if no such time is set forth in the limited liability company agreement, then the limited liability company shall have a perpetual existence;

(2) Upon the happening of events specified in a limited liability company agreement;

(3) Unless otherwise provided in a limited liability company agreement, upon the *affirmative vote or* written consent of the members of the limited liability company or, if there is more than 1 class or group of members, then by each class or group of members, in either case, by members who own more than two-thirds of the then-current percentage or other interest in the profits of the limited liability company owned by all of the members or by the members in each class or group, as appropriate;

(4) [1]*At any time there are no members; provided that the limited liability company is not dissolved and is not required to be wound up if:*

a. *Unless otherwise provided in a limited liability company agreement, within 90 days or such other period as is provided for in the limited liability company agreement after the occurrence of the event that terminated the continued membership of the last remaining member, the personal representative of the last remaining member agrees in writing to continue the limited liability company and to the admission of the personal representative of such member or its nominee or designee to the limited liability company as a member, effective as of the occurrence of the event that terminated the continued membership of the last remaining member; provided that a limited liability company agreement may provide that the personal representative of the last remaining member shall be obligated to agree in writing to continue the limited liability company and to the admission of the personal representative of such member or its nominee or designee to the limited liability company as a member, effective as of the occurrence of the event that terminated the continued membership of the last remaining member, or*

b. *A member is admitted to the limited liability company in the manner provided for in the limited liability company agreement, effective as of the occurrence of the event that terminated the continued membership of the last remaining member, within 90 days or such other period as is provided for in the limited liability company agreement after the occurrence of the event that terminated the continued membership of the last remaining member, pursuant to a provision of the limited liability company agreement that specifically provides for the admission of a member to the limited liability company after there is no longer a remaining member of the limited liability company.*

(5) The entry of a decree of judicial dissolution under §18-802 of this title.

(b) Unless otherwise provided in a limited liability company agreement, the death, retirement, resignation, expulsion, bankruptcy or dissolution of any member or the occurrence of any other event that terminates the continued membership of any member shall not cause the limited liability company to be dissolved or its affairs to be wound up, and upon the occurrence of any such event, the limited liability company shall be continued without dissolution [2]. (Last amended by Ch. 129, L. '99, eff. 8-1-99.)

Ch. 129, L. '99, eff. 8-1-99, added matter in italic and deleted [1]"At any time there are no members; provided, that, unless otherwise provided in a limited liability company agreement, the limited liability company is not dissolved and is not required to be wound up if, within 90 days or such other period as is provided for in the limited liability company agreement after the occurrence of the event that terminated the continued membership of the last remaining member, the personal representative of the last remaining member agrees in writing to continue the limited liability company and to the admission of the personal representative of such member or its nominee or designee to the limited liability company as a member, effective as of the occurrence of the event that terminated the continued membership of the last remaining member; or"; and [2]", unless within 90 days following the occurrence of such event, members of the limited liability company or, if there is more than 1 class or group of members, then each class or group of members, in either case, by members who own more than 50 percent of the then-current percentage or other interest in the profits of the limited liability company owned by all of the members or by the members in each class or group, as appropriate, agree in writing to dissolve the limited liability company."

Ch. 129, L. '99 Synopsis of Section 18-801

This section amends §18-801(a)(3) of the Act to confirm that dissolution may be approved by a vote in addition to a consent.

This section amends §18-801(a) of the Act by increasing the flexibility that can be used in connection with the continuation of a limited liability company upon the loss of the last remaining member.

This section amends §18-801(b) of the Act to delete an unnecessary provision from the Act.

Ch. 77, L. '97 Synopsis of Section 18-801

This section amends §18-801 of the Act to (1) designate the existing text of the section as a separate subsection, (2) provide that, in the absence of a provision in a limited liability company agreement addressing the term of the limited liability company, a limited liability company shall have a perpetual existence, (3) provide that, in the absence of a relevant provision in a limited liability company agreement, two-thirds in interest of the members of a limited liability company (measured by their then-current percentage or other interest in the profits of the limited liability company) may elect to dissolve the limited liability company, (4) provide that members may agree to continue a limited liability company upon the loss of the last member of the limited liability company, and (5) provide that, unless otherwise provided in a limited liability company agreement, a limited liability company will not dissolve upon the occurrence of listed events, unless the members of the limited liability company agree to dissolve the limited liability company.

Ch. 360, L. '96 Synopsis of Section 18-801

This section amends §18-801(4) of the Act to confirm that a limited liability agreement may identify which members, if any, shall cause the limited liability company to dissolve by virtue of an event that causes the termination of such members' membership in the limited liability company. This section also amends §18-801(4) of the Act to confirm that a limited liability company agreement may specify any percentage in interest of members the written consent or vote of which shall be required to approve the continuation of the business of the limited liability company upon an event that would otherwise cause the dissolution of the limited liability company under this subsection of the Act. Furthermore, this section amends §18-801(4) of the Act by changing the default rule of this subsection of the Act from requiring a unanimous vote or written consent of the members in order to continue the business of the limited liability company upon an event under this subsection of the Act that may cause dissolution of the limited liability company to requiring a majority in interest vote or written consent of the members in order to continue the business of the limited liability company upon an event under this subsection of the Act that may cause dissolution of the limited liability company.

Ch. 75, L. '95 Synopsis of Section 18-801

This Section confirms that a limited liability company agreement may provide that a limited liability company may be dissolved upon the written consent of less than all of its members.

18-802 JUDICIAL DISSOLUTION.—[1]On application by or for a member or manager the Court of Chancery may decree dissolution of a limited liability company whenever it is not reasonably practicable to carry on the business in conformity with a limited liability company agreement. [2](Last amended by Ch. 75, L. '95, eff. 8-1-95.)

Ch. 75, L. '95, eff. 8-1-95, deleted [1]"(a)" and [2]"(b) If a limited liability company has any publicly traded limited liability company interests and such limited liability company is treated as a corporation for purposes of United States income taxation, then, on application by or for a member or manager, the Court of Chancery shall grant such relief as may be appropriate to cause the limited liability company not to have any publicly traded limited liability company interests or decree dissolution of the limited liability company."

Ch. 75, L. '95 Synopsis of Section 18-802

This Section eliminates a restriction on the ability to use a Delaware limited liability company if the limited liability company has publicly traded limited liability company interests and is treated as a corporation for purposes of United States income taxation.

.1 Judicial dissolution.—A limited liability company will be dissolved where its owners are deadlocked, the limited liability company's purpose is moot, and it appears limited liability company was formed as a part of a scheme to deceive innocent investors. *In re Silver Leaf, LLC, 2005 Del. Ch. LEXIS 119 (Ch Ct 2005).*

A limited liability company will not be dissolved where its members are not in deadlock and it is not impracticable to carry on the limited liability company's business, even where the limited liability company is merely a passive investment vehicle. *In re Seneca Investments, LLC, 970 A2d 259 (Ch Ct 2008).*

Where a limited liability company has no office, no employees, no operating revenue, no prospects of equity or debt infusion, and when the company's board has a long history of deadlock as a result of its governance structure, it is not "reasonably practicable" for it to continue to operate and it may be dissolved. *Fisk Ventures, LLC v Segal, 2009 Del. Ch. LEXIS 7 (Ch Ct 2009).*

.2 Liquidating trustee.—A liquidating trustee will be appointed to wind up the affairs of a limited liability company whose members are deadlocked where the limited liability company's agreement already provides for dissolution. *Spellman v Katz, 2009 Del. Ch. LEXIS 18 (Ch Ct 2009).*

.3 Counterclaims.—Where limited liability company members seek its dissolution based on deadlock, counterclaims for indemnification and for injunctive relief based on breaches of fiduciary duties and breaches of the implied covenant of good faith and fair dealing, will be permitted to proceed to trial where none of the claims seeks immediate relief and must be determined at the hearing for dissolution. *In re ECH Management, LLC, 2009 Del. Ch. LEXIS 39 (Ch Ct 2009).*

.4 Dissolution.—A limited liability company will not be dissolved where it cannot be shown that the limited liability company is not operating in accordance with the broad purposes set forth in the limited liability company agreement, and where it is merely alleged that the limited liability company has failed to meet performance projections or that management's exercise of discretion is poor. *In re Arrow Investment Advisors, LLC, 2009 Del. Ch. LEXIS 66 (Ch Ct 2009).*

When two coequal owners and managers of a limited liability company whose mutual agreement is required for any company action are deadlocked as to the future direction and management of the enterprise and the limited liability company agreement provides no mechanism by which to break the deadlock, it is not reasonably practicable for the limited liability company to operate consistently with its operating agreement and a judicial dissolution will be ordered. *Vila v BVWebTies LLC, 2010 Del. Ch. LEXIS 202 (Ch Ct 2010).*

18-803 WINDING UP.—(a) Unless otherwise provided in a limited liability company agreement, a manager who has not wrongfully dissolved a limited liability company or, if none, the members or a person approved by the members or, if there is more than 1 class or group of members, then by each class or group of members, in either case, by members who own more than 50 percent of the then current percentage or other interest in the profits of the limited liability company owned by all of the members or by the members in each class or group, as appropriate, may wind up the limited liability company's affairs; but the Court of Chancery, upon cause shown, may wind up the limited liability company's affairs upon application of any member or manager, the member's or manager's [1]*personal* representative or assignee, and in connection therewith, may appoint a liquidating trustee.

(b) Upon dissolution of a limited liability company and until the filing of a certificate of cancellation as provided in §18-203 of this chapter, the persons winding up the limited liability company's affairs may, in the name of, and for and on behalf of, the limited liability company, prosecute and defend suits, whether civil, criminal or administrative, gradually settle and close the limited liability company's business, dispose of and convey the limited liability company's property, discharge or make reasonable provision for the limited liability company's liabilities, and distribute to the members any remaining assets of the limited liability company, all without affecting the liability of members and managers and without imposing liability on a liquidating trustee. (Last amended by Ch. 77, L. '97, eff. 8-1-97.)

Ch. 77, L. '97, eff. 8-1-97, added matter in italic and deleted [1]"legal".

Ch. 77, L. '97 Synopsis of Section 18-803

This section amends §18-803(a) of the Act to use a definition that has been added to the Act.

.1 Liquidating trustee.—A liquidating trustee will be appointed to wind up the affairs of a limited liability company whose members are deadlocked where the limited liability company's agreement already provides for dissolution. *Spellman v Katz, 2009 Del. Ch. LEXIS 18 (Ch Ct 2009).*

18-804 DISTRIBUTION OF ASSETS.—(a) Upon the winding up of a limited liability company, the assets shall be distributed as follows:

(1) To creditors, including members and managers who are creditors, to the extent otherwise permitted by law, in satisfaction of liabilities of the limited liability company (whether by payment or the making of reasonable provision for payment thereof) other than liabilities for which reasonable provision for payment has been made and liabilities for distributions to members and former members under §18-601 or §18-604 of this title;

(2) Unless otherwise provided in a limited liability company agreement, to members and former members in satisfaction of liabilities for distributions under §18-601 or §18-604 of this title; and

(3) Unless otherwise provided in a limited liability company agreement, to members first for the return of their contributions and second respecting their limited liability company interests, in the proportions in which the members share in distributions.

(b) A limited liability company which has dissolved:

(1) Shall pay or make reasonable provision to pay all claims and obligations, including all contingent, conditional or unmatured contractual claims, known to the limited liability company;

(2) Shall make such provision as will be reasonably likely to be sufficient to provide compensation for any claim against the limited liability company which is the subject of a pending action, suit or proceeding to which the limited liability company is a party; and

(3) Shall make such provision as will be reasonably likely to be sufficient to provide compensation for claims that have not been made known to the limited liability company or that have not arisen but that, based on facts known to the limited liability company, are likely to arise or to become known to the limited liability company within 10 years after the date of dissolution.

If there are sufficient assets, such claims and obligations shall be paid in full and any such provision for payment made shall be made in full. If there are insufficient assets, such claims and obligations shall be paid or provided for according to their priority and, among claims of equal priority, ratably to the extent of assets available therefor. Unless otherwise provided in the limited liability company agreement, any remaining assets shall be distributed as provided in this chapter. Any liquidating trustee winding up a limited liability company's affairs who has complied with this section shall not be personally liable to the claimants of the dissolved limited liability company by reason of such person's actions in winding up the limited liability company.

(c) A member who receives a distribution in violation of subsection (a) of this section, and who knew at the time of the distribution that the distribution violated subsection (a) of this section, shall be liable to the limited liability company for the amount of the distribution. *For purposes of the immediately preceding sentence, the term "distribution" shall not include amounts constituting reasonable compensation for present or past services or reasonable payments made in the ordinary course of business pursuant to a bona fide retirement plan or other benefits program.* A member who receives a distribution in violation of subsection (a) of this section, and who did not know at the time of the distribution that the distribution violated subsection (a) of this section, shall not be liable for the amount of the distribution. Subject to subsection (d) of this section, this subsection shall not affect any obligation or liability of a member under an agreement or other applicable law for the amount of a distribution.

(d) Unless otherwise agreed, a member who receives a distribution from a limited liability company to which this section applies shall have no liability under this chapter or other applicable law for the amount of the distribution after the expiration of 3 years from the date of the distribution unless an action to recover the distribution from such member is commenced prior to the expiration of the said 3-year period and an adjudication of liability against such member is made in the said action.

(e) Section 18-607 of this title shall not apply to a distribution to which this section applies. (Last amended by Ch. 389, L. '00, eff. 8-1-00.)

Ch. 389, L. '00, eff. 8-1-00, added matter in italic.

Ch. 389, L. '00 Synopsis of Section 18-804

This section amends §18-804(c) of the Act to clarify the limitations on distributions by limited liability companies.

Ch. 341, L. '98 Synopsis of Section 18-804

This section amends §18-804 to clarify the provisions of the Act relating to the liquidation of a limited liability company following dissolution. In connection with the liquidation of a limited liability company, paragraph (b) clarifies how liabilities, including contingent liabilities, are to be paid or otherwise dealt with, and, in connection with certain types of possible claims, establishes a 10 year period in connection with which reasonable provision is to be made. Paragraphs (c), (d) and (e) adopt rules upon dissolution similar to rules currently existing in §18-607 of the Act relating to distributions made by a limited liability company prior to dissolution.

18-805 TRUSTEES OR RECEIVERS FOR LIMITED LIABILITY COMPANIES; APPOINTMENT; POWERS; DUTIES.—When the certificate of formation of any limited liability company formed under this chapter shall be canceled by the filing of a certificate of cancellation pursuant to §18-203 of this chapter, the Court of Chancery, on application of any creditor, member or manager of the limited liability company, or any other person who shows good cause therefor, at any time, may either appoint 1 or more of the managers of the limited liability company to be trustees, or appoint 1 or more persons to be receivers, of and for the limited liability company, to take charge of the limited liability company's property, and to collect the debts and property due and belonging to the limited liability company, with the power to prosecute and defend, in the name of the limited liability company, or otherwise, all such suits as may be necessary or proper for the purposes aforesaid, and to appoint an agent or agents under them, and to do all other acts which might be done by the limited liability company, if in being, that may be necessary for the final settlement of the unfinished business of the limited liability company. The powers of the trustees or receivers may be continued as long as the Court of Chancery shall think necessary for the purposes aforesaid. (Added by Ch. 85, L. '03, eff. 8-1-03.)

Ch. 85, L. '03 Synopsis of Section 18-805

This section amends the Act to add a new §18-805 to provide, under certain circumstances, for the appointment of trustees and receivers for limited liability companies after the cancellation of the certificate of formation upon the application of a creditor, a person who was a member or manager at the time of the cancellation of the certificate of formation or any person who shows good cause.

18-806 REVOCATION OF DISSOLUTION.—Notwithstanding the occurrence of an event set forth in Section 18-801(a)(1), (2), (3) or (4) of this title, the limited liability company shall not be dissolved and its affairs shall not be wound up if, prior to the filing of a certificate of cancellation in the office of the Secretary of State, the limited liability company is continued, effective as of the occurrence of such event, pursuant to the affirmative vote or written consent of all remaining members of the limited liability company or the personal representative of the last remaining member of the limited liability company if there is no remaining member (and any other person whose approval is required under the limited liability company agreement to revoke a dissolution pursuant to this section), provided, however, if the dissolution was caused by a vote or written consent, the dissolution shall not be revoked unless each member and other person (or their respective personal representatives) who voted in favor of, or consented to, the dissolution has voted or consented in writing to continue the limited liability company. If there is no remaining member of the limited liability company and the personal representative of the last remaining member votes in favor of or consents to the continuation of the limited liability company, such personal representative shall be required to agree in writing to the admission of the personal representative of such member or its nominee or designee to the limited liability company as a member, effective as of the occurrence of the event that terminated the continued membership of the last remaining member. (Added by Ch. 51, L. '05, eff. 8-1-05.)

Ch. 51, L. '05 Synopsis of Section 18-806

This section amends the Act to add a new §18-806 to provide, under certain circumstances, for the revocation of the dissolution of a limited liability company.

Subchapter IX. Foreign Limited Liability Companies

18-901 LAW GOVERNING.—(a) Subject to the Constitution of the State of Delaware:

(1) The laws of the state, territory, possession, or other jurisdiction or country under which a foreign limited liability company is organized govern its organization and internal affairs and the liability of its members and managers; and

(2) A foreign limited liability company may not be denied registration by reason of any difference between those laws and the laws of the State of Delaware.

(b) A foreign limited liability company shall be subject to §18-106 of this title.

18-902 REGISTRATION REQUIRED; APPLICATION.—Before doing business in the State of Delaware, a foreign limited liability company shall register with the Secretary of State. In order to register, a foreign limited liability company shall submit to the Secretary of State:

(1) A copy executed by an authorized person of an application for registration as a foreign limited liability company, setting forth:

    a. The name of the foreign limited liability company and, if different, the name under which it proposes to register and do business in the State of Delaware;

    b. The state, territory, possession or other jurisdiction or country where formed, the date of its formation and a statement from an authorized person that, as of the date of filing, the foreign limited liability company validly exists as a limited liability company under the laws of the jurisdiction of its formation;

    c. The nature of the business or purposes to be conducted or promoted in the State of Delaware;

    d. The address of the registered office and the name and address of the registered agent for service of process required to be maintained by §18-904(b) of this title;

    e. A statement that the Secretary of State is appointed the agent of the foreign limited liability company for service of process under the circumstances set forth in §18-910(b) of this title; and

    f. The date on which the foreign limited liability company first did, or intends to do, business in the State of Delaware.

(2) A certificate, as of a date not earlier than 6 months prior to the filing date, issued by an authorized officer of the jurisdiction of its formation evidencing its existence. If such certificate is in a foreign language, a translation thereof, under oath of the translator, shall be attached thereto.

[1] *(3)* A fee as set forth in §18-1105(a)(6) of this title shall be paid. (Last amended by Ch. 287, L. '10, eff. 8-2-10.)

Ch. 287, L. '10, eff. 8-2-10, added matter in italic and deleted [1]"(2)".

Ch. 287, L. '10 Synopsis of Section 18-902

This sections amends §18-902 of the Act to require that a foreign limited liability company registering with the Secretary of State must file a certificate, as of a date not earlier than 6 months prior to the filing date, issued by an authorized officer of the jurisdiction of its formation evidencing its existence, along with, if applicable, a translation thereof under oath.

Ch. 51, L. '05 Synopsis of Section 18-902

These sections amend the Act to add a new §18-912 to identify the activities of a foreign limited liability company in the State of Delaware that will not constitute doing business for purposes of Subchapter IX of the Act and move former subsection (b) of §18-902 of the Act to new §18-912.

18-903 ISSUANCE OF REGISTRATION.—(a) If the Secretary of State finds that an application for registration conforms to law and all requisite fees have been paid, the Secretary shall:

(1) Certify that the application has been filed by endorsing upon the original application the word "Filed", and the date and hour of the filing. This endorsement is conclusive of the date and time of its filing in the absence of actual fraud;

(2) File and index the endorsed application.

(b) The Secretary of State shall prepare and return to the person who filed the application or [1]*the person's* representative a copy of the original signed application, similarly endorsed, and shall certify such copy as a true copy of the original signed application.

(c) The filing of the application with the Secretary of State shall make it unnecessary to file any other documents under Chapter 31 of this title. (Last amended by Ch. 186, L. '95, eff. 7-10-95.)

Ch. 186, L. '95, eff. 7-10-95, added matter in italic and deleted [1]"his".

18-904 NAME; REGISTERED OFFICE; REGISTERED AGENT.—(a) A foreign limited liability company may register with the Secretary of State under any name (whether or not it is the name under which it is registered in the jurisdiction of its formation) that includes the words "Limited Liability Company" or the abbreviation "L.L.C." or the designation "LLC" and that could be registered by a domestic limited liability company;

provided however, that a foreign limited liability company may register under any name which is not such as to distinguish it upon the records in the office of the Secretary of State from the name on such records of any domestic or foreign corporation, partnership, statutory trust, limited liability company or limited partnership reserved, registered, formed or organized under the laws of the State of Delaware with the written consent of the other corporation, partnership, statutory trust, limited liability company or limited partnership, which written consent shall be filed with the Secretary of State.

(b) Each foreign limited liability company shall have and maintain in the State of Delaware:

(1) A registered office which may but need not be a place of its business in the State of Delaware; and

(2) A registered agent for service of process on the foreign limited liability company, *having a business office identical with such registered office,* which agent may be [1]*any of:*

a. An individual resident in the State of Delaware,

b. A domestic limited liability company, a domestic corporation, a domestic partnership (whether general (including a limited liability partnership) or limited (including a limited liability limited partnership)), or a domestic statutory trust, or

c. A foreign corporation, a foreign partnership (whether general (including a limited liability partnership) or limited (including a limited liability limited partnership)), a foreign limited liability company (other than the foreign limited liability company itself), or a foreign statutory trust.

(c) A registered agent may change the address of the registered office of the foreign limited liability companies for which the agent is registered agent to another address in the State of Delaware by paying a fee as set forth in §18-1105(a)(7) of this title and filing with the Secretary of State a certificate, executed by such registered agent, setting forth the address at which such registered agent has maintained the registered office for each of the foreign limited liability companies for which it is a registered agent, and further certifying to the new address to which each such registered office will be changed on a given day, and at which new address such registered agent will thereafter maintain the registered office for each of the foreign limited liability companies for which it is registered agent. Upon the filing of such certificate, the Secretary of State shall furnish to the registered agent a certified copy of the same under the Secretary's hand and seal of office, and thereafter, or until further change of address, as authorized by law, the registered office in the State of Delaware of each of the foreign limited liability companies for which the agent is a registered agent shall be located at the new address of the registered agent thereof as given in the certificate. In the event of a change of name of any person acting as a registered agent of a foreign limited liability company, such registered agent shall file with the Secretary of State a certificate, executed by such registered agent, setting forth the new name of such registered agent, the name of such registered agent before it was changed and the address at which such registered agent has maintained the registered office for each of the foreign limited liability companies for which it is registered agent, and shall pay a fee as set forth in §18-1105(a)(7) of this title. Upon the filing of such certificate, the Secretary of State shall furnish to the registered agent a certified copy of the same under the Secretary's own hand and seal of office. A change of name of any person acting as a registered agent of a foreign limited liability company as a result of the merger or consolidation of the registered agent with or into another person which succeeds to its assets and liabilities by operation of law shall be deemed a change of name for purposes of this section. Filing a certificate under this section shall be deemed to be an amendment of the application of each foreign limited liability company affected thereby and each such foreign limited liability company shall not be required to take any further action with respect thereto to amend its application under §18-905 of this title. Any registered agent filing a certificate under this section shall promptly, upon such filing, deliver a copy of any such certificate to each foreign limited liability company affected thereby.

(d) The registered agent of 1 or more foreign limited liability companies may resign and appoint a successor registered agent by paying a fee as set forth in §18-1105(a)(7) of this title and filing a certificate with the Secretary of State stating that it resigns and the name and address of the successor registered agent. There shall be attached to such certificate a statement of each affected foreign limited liability company ratifying and approving such

§18-904

change of registered agent. Upon such filing, the successor registered agent shall become the registered agent of such foreign limited liability companies as have ratified and approved such substitution and the successor registered agent's address, as stated in such certificate, shall become the address of each such foreign limited liability company's registered office in the State of Delaware. The Secretary of State shall then issue a certificate that the successor registered agent has become the registered agent of the foreign limited liability companies so ratifying and approving such change and setting out the names of such foreign limited liability companies. Filing of such certificate of resignation shall be deemed to be an amendment of the application of each foreign limited liability company affected thereby and each such foreign limited liability company shall not be required to take any further action with respect thereto to amend its application under §18-905 of this title.

(e) The registered agent of 1 or more foreign limited liability companies may resign without appointing a successor registered agent by paying a fee as set forth in §18-1105(a)(7) of this title and filing a certificate of resignation with the Secretary of State, but such resignation shall not become effective until 30 days after the certificate is filed. The certificate shall contain a statement that written notice of resignation was given to each affected foreign limited liability company at least 30 days prior to the filing of the certificate by mailing or delivering such notice to the foreign limited liability company at its address last known to the registered agent and shall set forth the date of such notice. After receipt of the notice of the resignation of its registered agent, the foreign limited liability company for which such registered agent was acting shall obtain and designate a new registered agent to take the place of the registered agent so resigning. If such foreign limited liability company fails to obtain and designate a new registered agent as aforesaid prior to the expiration of the period of 30 days after the filing by the registered agent of the certificate of resignation, such foreign limited liability company shall not be permitted to do business in the State of Delaware and its registration shall be [2]canceled. After the resignation of the registered agent shall have become effective as provided in this section and if no new registered agent shall have been obtained and designated in the time and manner aforesaid, service of legal process against each foreign limited liability company for which the resigned registered agent had been acting shall thereafter be upon the Secretary of State in accordance with §18-911 of this title. (Last amended by Ch. 105, L. '07, eff. 8-1-07.)

Ch. 105, L. '07, eff. 8-1-07, added matter in italic and deleted [1]"either an individual resident of the State of Delaware whose business office is identical with the foreign limited liability company's registered office, or a domestic corporation, or a domestic limited partnership, or a domestic limited liability company, or a domestic statutory trust, or a foreign corporation, or a foreign limited partnership, or a foreign limited liability company authorized to do business in the State of Delaware having a business office identical with such registered office, which is generally open during normal business hours to accept service of process and otherwise perform the functions of a registered agent" and [2]"deemed to be".

Ch. 105, L. '07 Synopsis of Section 18-904

This section amends §18-904(b)(2) of the Act to conform such subsection to §18-104 regarding the types of entities that may serve as registered agents and confirm that the business office of a foreign limited liability company's registered agent shall be identical to the registered office of the foreign limited liability company in the State of Delaware.

This section amends §18-904(e) of the Act to make a technical change.

Ch. 295, L. '02 Synopsis of Section 18-904

This section amends §18-904(a) of the Act to clarify the intended meaning of the section.

This section amends §18-904 of the Act to clarify procedures relating to the change in the address of a registered office, the change in the name of a registered agent and the resignation of a registered agent for foreign limited liability companies. It parallels the amendments previously made for registered agents for domestic limited liability companies.

Ch. 329, L. '02 Synopsis of Section 18-904

The amendments set forth are made for the purpose of avoiding any implication that a trust formed under Chapter 38, Title 12 of the Delaware Code constitutes a "business trust" within the meaning of Title 11 of the United States Code. Such amendments are not intended to result in any substantive change in Delaware law. These amendments are made solely for the purpose of conforming the Delaware Code to the amendments set forth above.

Ch. 77, L. '97 Synopsis of Section 18-904

This Section amends §18-904(b)(2) of the Act to expand the types of entities that may act as a registered agent for a foreign limited liability company.

This Section amends §18-904(b)(2) of the Act to add a requirement that a registered agent for a foreign limited liability company must be generally open during normal business hours to perform its functions as a registered agent.

Ch. 75, L. '95 Synopsis of Section 18-904

This Section permits the use of the designation "LLC" without periods as part of the name of a foreign limited liability company.

18-905 AMENDMENTS TO APPLICATION.—If any statement in the application for registration of a foreign limited liability company was false when made or any arrangements or other facts described have changed, making the application false in any respect, the foreign limited liability company shall promptly file in the office of the Secretary of State a certificate, executed by an authorized person, correcting such statement, together with a fee as set forth in §18-1105(a)(6) of this title.

18-906 CANCELLATION OF REGISTRATION.—A foreign limited liability company may cancel its registration by filing with the Secretary of State a certificate of cancellation, executed by an authorized person, together with a fee as set forth in §18-1105(a)(6) of this title. The registration of a foreign limited liability company shall be canceled as provided in §§18-104(i)(4) [1], 18-904(e) *and 18-1107(h)* of this title. A cancellation does not terminate the authority of the Secretary of State to accept service of process on the foreign limited liability company with respect to causes of action arising out of the doing of business in the State of Delaware. (Last amended by Ch. 105, L. '07, eff. 8-1-07.)

Ch. 105, L. '07, eff. 8-1-07, added matter in italic and deleted [1]"and".

Ch. 105, L. '07 Synopsis of Section 18-906

This section amends §18-906 of the Act to make a technical change

Ch. 317, L. '06 Synopsis of Section 18-906

This Section amends §18-906 of the Act to conform to the provisions of §18-904(e) and new §18-104(i)(4) of the Act which provide for the cancellation of the registration of a foreign limited liability company under the circumstances therein provided.

18-907 DOING BUSINESS WITHOUT REGISTRATION.—(a) A foreign limited liability company doing business in the State of Delaware may not maintain any action, suit or proceeding in the State of Delaware until it has registered in the State of Delaware, and has paid to the State of Delaware all fees and penalties for the years or parts thereof, during which it did business in the State of Delaware without having registered.

(b) The failure of a foreign limited liability company to register in the State of Delaware does not impair:

(1) The validity of any contract or act of the foreign limited liability company;

(2) The right of any other party to the contract to maintain any action, suit or proceeding on the contract; or

(3) Prevent the foreign limited liability company from defending any action, suit or proceeding in any court of the State of Delaware.

(c) A member or a manager of a foreign limited liability company is not liable for the obligations of the foreign limited liability company solely by reason of the limited liability company's having done business in the State of Delaware without registration.

(d) Any foreign limited liability company doing business in the State of Delaware without first having registered shall be fined and shall pay to the Secretary of State $200 for each year or part thereof during which the foreign limited liability company failed to register in the State of Delaware.

18-908 FOREIGN LIMITED LIABILITY COMPANIES DOING BUSINESS WITHOUT HAVING QUALIFIED; INJUNCTIONS.—The Court of Chancery shall have jurisdiction to enjoin any foreign limited liability company, or any agent thereof, from doing any business in the State of Delaware if such foreign limited liability company has failed to register under this subchapter or if such foreign limited liability company has secured a certificate of the Secretary of State under §18-903 of this title on the basis of false or misleading representations. Upon the motion of the Attorney General or upon the relation of proper parties, the Attorney General shall proceed for this purpose by complaint in any county in which such foreign limited liability company is doing or has done business. (Last amended by Ch. 186, L. '95, eff. 7-10-95.)

18-909 EXECUTION; LIABILITY.—Section 18-204(c) of this chapter shall be applicable to foreign limited liability companies as if they were domestic limited liability companies.

18-910 SERVICE OF PROCESS ON REGISTERED FOREIGN LIMITED LIABILITY COMPANIES.—(a) Service of legal process upon any foreign limited liability company shall be made by delivering a copy personally to any managing or general agent or manager of the foreign limited liability company in the State of Delaware or the registered agent of the foreign limited liability company in the State of Delaware, or by leaving it at the dwelling house or usual place of abode in the State of Delaware of any such managing or general agent, manager or registered agent (if the registered agent be an individual), or at the registered office or other place of business of the foreign limited liability company in the State of Delaware. If the registered agent be a corporation, service of process upon it as such may be made by serving, in the State of Delaware, a copy thereof on the president, vice-president, secretary, assistant secretary or any director of the corporate registered agent. Service by copy left at the dwelling house or usual place of abode of any managing or general agent, manager or registered agent, or at the registered office or other place of business of the foreign limited liability company in the State of Delaware, to be effective must be delivered thereat at least 6 days before the return date of the process, and in the presence of an adult person, and the officer serving the process shall distinctly state the manner of service in the officer's return thereto. Process returnable forthwith must be delivered personally to the managing or general agent, manager or registered agent.

(b) [1] *In case the officer whose duty it is to serve legal process cannot by due diligence serve the process in any manner provided for by subsection (a) of this section, it shall be lawful to serve the process against the foreign limited liability company upon the Secretary of State, and such service shall be as effectual for all intents and purposes as if made in any of the ways provided for in subsection (a) of this section. Process may be served upon the Secretary of State under this subsection by means of electronic transmission but only as prescribed by the Secretary of State. The Secretary of State is authorized to issue such rules and regulations with respect to such service as the Secretary of State deems necessary or appropriate. In the event that service is effected through the Secretary of State in accordance with this subsection, the Secretary of State shall forthwith notify the foreign limited liability company by letter, directed to the foreign limited liability company at its last registered office. Such letter shall be sent by a mail or courier service that includes a record of mailing or deposit with the courier and a record of delivery evidenced by the signature of the recipient.* Such letter shall enclose a copy of the process and any other papers served on the Secretary of State pursuant to this subsection. It shall be the duty of the plaintiff in the event of such service to serve process and any other papers in duplicate, to notify the Secretary of State that service is being effected pursuant to this subsection, and to pay to the Secretary of State the sum of $50 for the use of the State of Delaware, which sum shall be taxed as a part of the costs in the proceeding if the plaintiff shall prevail therein. The Secretary of State shall maintain an alphabetical record of any such service setting forth the name of the plaintiff and defendant, the title, docket number and nature of the proceeding in which process has been served upon the Secretary, the fact that service has been effected pursuant to this subsection, the return date thereof and the day and hour when the service was made. The Secretary of State shall not be required to retain such information for a period longer than 5 years from the Secretary's receipt of the service of process. (Last amended by Ch. 287, L. '10, eff. 8-2-10.)

Ch. 287, L. '10, eff. 8-2-10, added matter in italic and deleted [1] *"In case the officer whose duty it is to serve legal process cannot by due diligence serve the process in any manner provided for by subsection (a) of this section, it shall be lawful to serve the process against the foreign limited liability company upon the Secretary of State, and such service shall be as effectual for all intents and purposes as if made in any of the ways provided for in subsection (a) of this section. In the event service is effected through the Secretary of State in accordance with this subsection, the Secretary of State shall forthwith notify the foreign limited liability company by letter, certified mail, return receipt requested, directed to the foreign limited liability company at its last registered office."*

Ch. 287, L. '10 Synopsis of Section 18-910

Sections 2, 26, 27 and 28 amend §§18-105(b), 18-910(b), 18-911(a) and 18-911(c) of the Act to allow for service of process upon the Secretary of State thereunder by means of electronic transmission but only as prescribed by the Secretary of State, to authorize the Secretary of State to issue such rules and regulations with respect to such service as the Secretary of State deems necessary or appropriate, and to enable the Secretary of State, in the event that service is effected through the Secretary of State in accordance therewith, to provide notice of service by letter sent by a mail or courier service that includes a record of mailing or deposit with the courier and a record of delivery evidenced by the signature of the recipient.

18-911 SERVICE OF PROCESS ON UNREGISTERED FOREIGN LIMITED LIABILITY COMPANIES.—(a) Any foreign limited liability company which shall do business in the State of Delaware without having registered under §18-902 of this title shall be deemed to have thereby appointed and constituted the Secretary of State of the State of Delaware its agent for the acceptance of legal process in any civil action, suit or proceeding against it in any state or federal court in the State of Delaware arising or growing out of any business done by it within the State of Delaware. The doing of business in the State of Delaware by such foreign limited liability company shall be a signification of the agreement of such foreign limited liability company that any such process when so served shall be of the same legal force and validity as if served upon an authorized manager or agent personally within the State of Delaware. *Process may be served upon the Secretary of State under this subsection by means of electronic transmission but only as prescribed by the Secretary of State. The Secretary of State is authorized to issue such rules and regulations with respect to such service as the Secretary of State deems necessary or appropriate.*

(b) Whenever the words "doing business", "the doing of business" or "business done in this State," by any such foreign limited liability company are used in this section, they shall mean the course of practice of carrying on any business activities in the State of Delaware, including, without limiting the generality of the foregoing, the solicitation of business or orders in the State of Delaware.

(c) In the event of service upon the Secretary of State in accordance with subsection (a) of this section, the Secretary of State shall forthwith notify the foreign limited liability company thereof by letter, [1] directed to the foreign limited liability company at the address furnished to the Secretary of State by the plaintiff in such action, suit or proceeding. *Such letter shall be sent by a mail or courier service that includes a record of mailing or deposit with the courier and a record of delivery evidenced by the signature of the recipient.* Such letter shall enclose a copy of the process and any other papers served upon the Secretary of State. It shall be the duty of the plaintiff in the event of such service to serve process and any other papers in duplicate, to notify the Secretary of State that service is being made pursuant to this subsection, and to pay to the Secretary of State the sum of $50 for the use of the State of Delaware, which sum shall be taxed as part of the costs in the proceeding, if the plaintiff shall prevail therein. The Secretary of State shall maintain an alphabetical record of any such process setting forth the name of the plaintiff and defendant, the title, docket number and nature of the proceeding in which process has been served upon the Secretary, the return date thereof, and the day and hour when the service was made. The Secretary of State shall not be required to retain such information for a period longer than 5 years from the receipt of the service of process. (Last amended by Ch. 287, L. '10, eff. 8-2-10.)

Ch. 287, L. '10, eff. 8-2-10, added matter in italic and deleted [1] "certified mail, return receipt requested,".

Ch. 287, L. '10 Synopsis of Section 18-911

Sections 2, 26, 27 and 28 amend §§18-105(b), 18-910(b), 18-911(a) and 18-911(c) of the Act to allow for service of process upon the Secretary of State thereunder by means of electronic transmission but only as prescribed by the Secretary of State, to authorize the Secretary of State to issue such rules and regulations with respect to such service as the Secretary of State deems necessary or appropriate, and to enable the Secretary of State, in the event that service is effected through the Secretary of State in accordance therewith, to provide notice of service by letter sent by a mail or courier service that includes a record of mailing or deposit with the courier and a record of delivery evidenced by the signature of the recipient.

18-912 ACTIVITIES NOT CONSTITUTING DOING BUSINESS.—(a) Activities of a foreign limited liability company in the State of Delaware that do not constitute doing business for the purpose of this subchapter include:

(1) Maintaining, defending or settling an action or proceeding;

(2) Holding meetings of its members or managers or carrying on any other activity concerning its internal affairs;

(3) Maintaining bank accounts;

(4) Maintaining offices or agencies for the transfer, exchange or registration of the limited liability company's own securities or maintaining trustees or depositories with respect to those securities;

(5) Selling through independent contractors;

(6) Soliciting or obtaining orders, whether by mail or through employees or agents or otherwise, if the orders require acceptance outside the State of Delaware before they become contracts;

(7) Selling, by contract consummated outside the State of Delaware, and agreeing, by the contract, to deliver into the State of Delaware, machinery, plants or equipment, the construction, erection or installation of which within the State of Delaware requires the supervision of technical engineers or skilled employees performing services not generally available, and as part of the contract of sale agreeing to furnish such services, and such services only, to the vendee at the time of construction, erection or installation;

(8) Creating, as borrower or lender, or acquiring indebtedness with or without a mortgage or other security interest in property;

(9) Collecting debts or foreclosing mortgages or other security interests in property securing the debts, and holding, protecting and maintaining property so acquired;

(10) Conducting an isolated transaction that is not 1 in the course of similar transactions;

(11) Doing business in interstate commerce; and

(12) Doing business in the State of Delaware as an insurance company.

(b) A person shall not be deemed to be doing business in the State of Delaware solely by reason of being a member or manager of a domestic limited liability company or a foreign limited liability company.

(c) This section does not apply in determining whether a foreign limited liability company is subject to service of process, taxation or regulation under any other law of the State of Delaware. (Added by Ch. 51, L. '05, eff. 8-1-05.)

Ch. 51, L. '05 Synopsis of Section 18-912

These sections amend the Act to add a new §18-912 to identify the activities of a foreign limited liability company in the State of Delaware that will not constitute doing business for purposes of Subchapter IX of the Act and move former subsection (b) of §18-902 of the Act to new §18-912.

Subchapter X. Derivative Actions

18-1001 RIGHT TO BRING ACTION.—A member *or an assignee of a limited liability company interest* may bring an action in the Court of Chancery in the right of a limited liability company to recover a judgment in its favor if managers or members with authority to do so have refused to bring the action or if an effort to cause those managers or members to bring the action is not likely to succeed. (Last amended by Ch. 341, L. '98, eff. 8-1-98.)

Ch. 341, L. '98, eff. 8-1-98, added matter in italic.

Ch. 341, L. '98 Synopsis of Section 18-1001

These sections amend §18-1001 and §18-1002 of the Act to provide that an assignee of a limited liability company interest has the right to bring a derivative action.

.1 Standing to bring derivative suit.—Under §18-1001 and §18-1003, a member of a limited liability company could not bring a derivative suit because the member failed to state in the complaint what efforts were made to get managers to bring the suit or why such efforts would be unlikely to succeed. *Taurus Advisory Group, Inc v Sector Management, Inc, No. CV96 015083, 1996 Conn. Super. LEXIS 2272 (Conn. Super. Ct. 8-29-96)* (Delaware law).

18-1002 PROPER PLAINTIFF.—In a derivative action, the plaintiff must be a member *or an assignee of a limited liability company interest* at the time of bringing the action and:

(1) At the time of the transaction of which the plaintiff complains; or

(2) The plaintiff's status as a member *or an assignee of a limited liability company interest* had devolved upon the plaintiff by operation of law or pursuant to the terms of a limited liability company agreement from a person who was a member *or an assignee of a limited liability company interest* at the time of the transaction. (Last amended by Ch. 341, L. '98, eff. 8-1-98.)

Ch. 341, L. '98, eff. 8-1-98, added matter in italic.

Ch. 341, L. '98 Synopsis of Section 18-1002

These sections amend §18-1001 and §18-1002 of the Act to provide that an assignee of a limited liability company interest has the right to bring a derivative action.

.1 Operating agreement; remedy for breach.—Where a limited liability company operating agreement is structured so that a member will not be forced to become a partner with another member not of its choosing, a member that breaches the operating agreement may be divested of its status as an active member, and may be rendered a passive investor with the status and rights of an assignee. *Eureka VIII, LLC v Niagara Falls Holdings, LLC, 899 A2d 95 (Ch Ct 2006).*

.2 Creditors of insolvent LLCs; standing to bring derivative action—A creditor of an insolvent limited liability company does not have standing under the Delaware Limited Liability Company Act to bring a derivative action against the limited liability company. *CML V, LLC v Bax, 6 A3d 238 (Ch Ct 2010).*

18-1003 COMPLAINT.—In a derivative action, the complaint shall set forth with particularity the effort, if any, of the plaintiff to secure initiation of the action by a manager or member or the reasons for not making the effort.

.1 Requirements.—Under §18-1001 and §18-1003, a complaint must allege what efforts were made to get managers to bring a derivative suit or why such efforts would be unlikely to succeed. *Taurus Advisory Group, Inc v Sector Management, Inc, No. CV96 015083, 1996 Conn. Super. LEXIS 2272 (Conn. Super. Ct. 8-29-96)* (Delaware law).

18-1004 EXPENSES.—If a derivative action is successful, in whole or in part, as a result of a judgment, compromise or settlement of any such action, the court may award the plaintiff reasonable expenses, including reasonable attorney's fees, from any recovery in any such action or from a limited liability company.

Subchapter XI. Miscellaneous

18-1101 CONSTRUCTION AND APPLICATION OF CHAPTER AND LIMITED LIABILITY COMPANY AGREEMENT.—(a) The rule that statutes in derogation of the common law are to be strictly construed shall have no application to this chapter.

(b) It is the policy of this chapter to give the maximum effect to the principle of freedom of contract and to the enforceability of limited liability company agreements.

(c) To the extent that, at law or in equity, a member or manager or other person has duties (including fiduciary duties) to a limited liability company or to another member or manager or to another person that is a party to or is otherwise bound by a limited liability company agreement, the member's or manager's or other person's duties may be expanded or restricted or eliminated by provisions in the limited liability company agreement; provided that the limited liability company agreement may not eliminate the implied contractual covenant of good faith and fair dealing.

(d) Unless otherwise provided in a limited liability company agreement, a member or manager or other person shall not be liable to a limited liability company or to another member or manager or to another person that is a party to or is otherwise bound by a limited liability company agreement for breach of fiduciary duty for the member's or manager's or other person's good faith reliance on the provisions of the limited liability company agreement.

(e) A limited liability company agreement may provide for the limitation or elimination of any and all liabilities for breach of contract and breach of duties (including fiduciary duties) of a member, manager or other person to a limited liability company or to another member or manager or to another person that is a party to or is otherwise bound by a limited liability company agreement; provided, that a limited liability company agreement may not limit or eliminate liability for any act or omission that constitutes a bad faith violation of the implied contractual covenant of good faith and fair dealing.

(f) Unless the context otherwise requires, as used herein, the singular shall include the plural and the plural may refer to only the singular. The use of any gender shall be applicable to all genders. The captions contained herein are for purposes of convenience only and shall not control or affect the construction of this chapter.

(g) Sections 9-406 and 9-408 of this title do not apply to any interest in a limited liability company, including all rights, powers and interests arising under a limited liability company agreement or this chapter. This provision prevails over §§9-406 and 9-408 of this title.

(h) Action validly taken pursuant to 1 provision of this chapter shall not be deemed invalid solely because it is identical or similar in substance to an action that could have been taken pursuant to some other provision of this chapter but fails to satisfy 1 or more requirements prescribed by such other provision.

(i) *A limited liability company agreement that provides for the application of Delaware law shall be governed by and construed under the laws of the State of Delaware in accordance with its terms.* (Last amended by Ch. 287, L. '10, eff. 8-2-10.)

Ch. 287, L. '10, eff. 8-2-10, added matter in italic.

Ch. 287, L. '10 Synopsis of Section 18-1101

This section amends §18-1101 of the Act to provide that a limited liability company agreement that provides for the application of Delaware law shall be governed by and construed under the laws of the State of Delaware in accordance with its terms. This amendment is not intended to negate the application of Delaware law to the interpretation and enforcement of a limited liability company agreement that does not explicitly provide for the application of Delaware law or to negate the application of the internal affairs doctrine to Delaware limited liability companies.

Ch. 58, L. '09 Synopsis of Section 18-1101

This section amends §18-1101 of the Act to clarify that the doctrine of independent legal significance, as developed in Delaware corporation law, applies in the context of Delaware limited liability companies. The amendment is not intended to limit development or application, with respect to Delaware limited liability companies, of the doctrine of independent legal significance as developed in cases arising under Delaware corporation law.

Ch. 275, L. '04 Synopsis of Section 18-1101(c), (d), and (e)

This amendment clarifies that duties (including fiduciary duties) may be expanded, restricted and eliminated in a limited liability company agreement. This amendment confirms that a limited liability company agreement may not eliminate the implied contractual covenant of good faith and fair dealing.

The amendment in new Subsection 18-1101(d) of the Act clarifies the default exculpation provision in the Act by providing that it only applies with respect to breaches of fiduciary duties. The amendment in new Subsection 18-1101(e) of the Act confirms the flexibility permitted in the Act regarding exculpation.

Ch. 221, L. '02 Synopsis of Section 18-1101

This section amends §18-1101 of the Act to confirm the principle of freedom of contract that exists regarding the ability to restrict assignments of interests in a limited liability company.

Ch. 389, L. '00 Synopsis of Section 18-1101

This section amends §18-1101(c) of the Act to confirm that provisions found in a limited liability company agreement relating not only to duties and liabilities owed to members and managers, but also to other persons that are parties to, or that are otherwise bound by, a limited liability company agreement, are enforceable.

.1 Manager liability and exculpation.—Where a derivative action is brought on behalf of a limited liability company and the limited liability company's managers are contractually and/or statutorily exculpated from certain claims, demand will not be excused unless non-exculpated claims are pleaded with particularity. *Wood v Baum,* 953 A2d 136 (2008).

.2 Modification of fiduciary duties.—Where a limited liability company agreement purports to modify common law fiduciary duties, but creates ambiguity in doing so, an action will not be dismissed for failure to state a claim where the court would be forced to choose between reasonable interpretations of ambiguous provisions in the limited liability company agreement. *Kahn v Portnoy,* 2008 Del. Ch. LEXIS 184 (Ch Ct 2008).

.3 Statute of frauds.—The statute of frauds applies to limited liability company operating agreements, so that multi-year provisions in an unsigned operating agreement will not be binding. *Olson v Halvorsen,* 982 A2d 286 (Ch Ct 2008).

.4 Managers' and members' duties during merger; derivative actions.—Where an LLC agreement authorizes mergers, and a merger complies with the requirements of the agreement, a member whose interest is eliminated by the merger does not have standing to bring derivative claims arising out of the merger. The former member may, however, maintain direct claims, such as for breach of fiduciary duty. In the absence of a provision explicitly altering fiduciary duties owed by managers to the LLC and its members and by members to each other, an LLC's managers and controlling members in a manager-managed LLC owe the traditional fiduciary duties that directors and controlling shareholders in a corporation would. Consequently, where managers willfully violate their duty of loyalty or care, the former member may bring a direct claim for such a breach, as well as for the aiding and abetting of such breach. *Kelly v Blum, 2010 Del. Ch. LEXIS 31 (Ch Ct 2010).*

18-1102 SHORT TITLE.—This chapter may be cited as the "Delaware Limited Liability Company Act".

18-1103 SEVERABILITY.—If any provision of this chapter or its application to any person or circumstances is held invalid, the invalidity does not affect other provisions or applications of the chapter which can be given effect without the invalid provision or application, and to this end, the provisions of this chapter are severable.

18-1104 CASES NOT PROVIDED FOR IN THIS CHAPTER.—In any case not provided for in this chapter, the rules of law and equity, including the law merchant, shall govern.

18-1105 FEES.—(a) No document required to be filed under this chapter shall be effective until the applicable fee required by this section is paid. The following fees shall be paid to and collected by the Secretary of State for the use of the State of Delaware:

(1) Upon the receipt for filing of an application for reservation of name, an application for renewal of reservation or a notice of transfer or cancellation of reservation pursuant to §18-103(b) of this title, a fee in the amount of $75.

(2) Upon the receipt for filing of a certificate under §18-104(b) of this title, a fee in the amount of $200, upon the receipt for filing of a certificate under §18-104(c) of this title, a fee in the amount of $200, and upon the receipt for filing of a certificate under §18-104(d) of this title, a fee in the amount of $2.00 *for each limited liability company whose registered agent has resigned by such certificate.*

(3) Upon the receipt for filing of a certificate of formation under §18-201 of this title, a fee in the amount of $70 and upon the receipt for filing of a certificate of limited liability company domestication under §18-212 of this title, a certificate of transfer or a certificate of transfer and domestic continuance under §18-213 of this title, a certificate of conversion to limited liability company under §18-214 of this title, a certificate of conversion to a non-Delaware entity under §18-216 of this title, a certificate of amendment under §18-202 of this title *(except as otherwise provided in paragraph (a)(11) of this section),* a certificate of cancellation under §18-203 of this title, a certificate of merger or consolidation or a certificate of ownership and merger under §18-209 of this title, a restated certificate of formation under §18-208 of this title, a certificate of amendment of a certificate with a future effective date or time under §18-206(c) of this title, a certificate of termination of a certificate with a future effective date or time under §18-206(c) of this title, a certificate of correction under §18-211 of this title, or a certificate of revival under §18-1109 of this title, a fee in the amount of $180.

(4) For certifying copies of any paper on file as provided for by this chapter, a fee in the amount of $50 for each copy certified.

(5) The Secretary of State may issue photocopies or electronic image copies of instruments on file, as well as instruments, documents and other papers not on file, and for all such photocopies or electronic image copies, whether certified or not, a fee of $10 shall be paid for the 1st page and $2 for each additional page. The Secretary of State may also issue microfiche copies of instruments on file as well as instruments, documents and other papers not on file, and for each such microfiche a fee of $2 shall be paid therefor. Notwithstanding the State of Delaware's Freedom of Information Act [Chapter 100 of Title 29] or other provision of this Code granting access to public records, the Secretary of State shall issue only photocopies, microfiche or electronic image copies of records in exchange for the fees described above.

(6) Upon the receipt for filing of an application for registration as a foreign limited liability company under §18-902 of this title, a certificate under §18-905 of this title or a certificate of cancellation under §18-906 of this title, a fee in the amount of $200.

(7) Upon the receipt for filing of a certificate under §18-904(c) of this title, a fee in the amount of $200, upon the receipt for filing of a certificate under §18-904(d) of this title, a fee

in the amount of $200, and upon the receipt for filing of a certificate under §18-904(e) of this title, a fee in the amount of $2.00 *for each foreign limited liability company whose registered agent has resigned by such certificate.*

(8) For preclearance of any document for filing, a fee in the amount of $250.

(9) For preparing and providing a written report of a record search, a fee in the amount of $50.

(10) For issuing any certificate of the Secretary of State, including but not limited to a certificate of good standing, other than a certification of a copy under paragraph (4) of this subsection, a fee in the amount of $50, except that for issuing any certificate of the Secretary of State that recites all of a limited liability company's filings with the Secretary of State, a fee of $175 shall be paid for each such certificate.

(11) For receiving and filing and/or indexing any certificate, affidavit, agreement or any other paper provided for by this chapter, for which no different fee is specifically prescribed, a fee in the amount of $200. For filing any instrument submitted by a limited liability company or foreign limited liability company that only changes the registered office or registered agent *and is specifically captioned as a certificate of amendment changing only the registered office or registered agent*, a fee in the amount of $50 provided that no fee shall be charged pursuant to *§18*-206(e) of this title.

(12) The Secretary of State may in the Secretary of State's own discretion charge a fee of $60 for each check received for payment of any fee that is returned due to insufficient funds or the result of a stop payment order.

(b) In addition to those fees charged under subsection (a) of this section, there shall be collected by and paid to the Secretary of State the following:

(1) For all services described in subsection (a) of this section that are requested to be completed within 30 minutes on the same day as the day of the request, an additional sum of up to $7,500 and for all services described in subsection (a) of this section that are requested to be completed within 1 hour on the same day as the day of the request, an additional sum of up to $1,000 and for all services described in subsection (a) of this section that are requested to be completed within 2 hours on the same day of the request, an additional sum of up to $500;

(2) For all services described in subsection (a) of this section that are requested to be completed within the same day as the day of the request, an additional sum of up to $300; and

(3) For all services described in subsection (a) of this section that are requested to be completed within a 24-hour period from the time of the request, an additional sum of up to $150.

The Secretary of State shall establish (and may from time to time amend) a schedule of specific fees payable pursuant to this subsection.

(c) The Secretary of State may in his or her discretion permit the extension of credit for the fees required by this section upon such terms as the secretary shall deem to be appropriate.

(d) The Secretary of State shall retain from the revenue collected from the fees required by this section a sum sufficient to provide at all times a fund of at least $500, but not more than $1,500, from which the secretary may refund any payment made pursuant to this section to the extent that it exceeds the fees required by this section. The funds shall be deposited in a financial institution which is a legal depository of State of Delaware moneys to the credit of the Secretary of State and shall be disbursable on order of the Secretary of State.

(e) Except as provided in this section, the fees of the Secretary of State shall be as provided in §2315 of Title 29. (Last amended by Ch. 95, L. '11, eff. 8-1-11.)

Ch. 95, L. '11, eff. 8-1-11, added matter in italic.

Ch. 95, L. '11 Synopsis of Section 18-1105

These sections amend §§18-1105(a)(2) and (a)(7) of the Act to clarify that a registered agent filing a single certificate of resignation to resign from more than one limited liability company or foreign limited liability company must pay a $2.00 fee to the Secretary of State for each limited liability company or foreign limited liability company from which the registered agent is resigning.

These sections amend §§18-1105(a)(3) and (a)(11) of the Act to clarify the type of instrument to be filed by a limited liability company that changes only the registered office or registered agent of the limited liability company for a fee of $50.

Ch. 287, L. '10 Synopsis of Section 18-1105

Sections 4, 6, 7, 8, 9, 10, 11, 13, 14, 15, 16, 17, 20 and 30 amend §§18-203, 18-206(a), 18-206(b), 18-206(d), 18-209(a), 18-209(b), 18-209(c), 18-209(d), 18-209(e), 18-209(f), 18-209, 18-210, 18-301(b) and 18-1105(a) of the Act to provide a mechanism to implement a short form merger under new Section 267 of Title 8 where a domestic limited liability company is the parent Entity (as defined in new Section 267(e)(2) of Title 8).

Ch. 78, L. '09 Synopsis of Section 18-1105

This Act increases various fees and taxes assessed by the Delaware Secretary of State.

Ch. 105, L. '07 Synopsis of Section 18-1105

Sections 11, 12, 13, 14, and 35 amend §§18-206 and 18-1105 of the Act to make technical changes.

Ch. 85, L. '03 Synopsis of Section 18-1105

These amendments permit conversion of a Delaware limited liability company to a non-Delaware entity.

Ch. 52, L. '03 Synopsis of Section 18-1105

Amends the Delaware Limited Liability Company Act as follows:

1. Increases the fees related to forming a domestic limited liability company from $50 to $90, eliminates the $50 fee for restoring a limited liability company to good standing, and increases the fees for most other domestic certificates from $50 to $100.
2. Increases the fee for certifying copies from $20 to $30.
3. Increases the fee for copies from $5 for the first page and $1 for each additional page to $10 for the first page and $2 for each additional page.
4. Increases certain fees for foreign limited liability companies from $50 to $100.
5. Increases the fee for a short form certificate of good standing from $20 to $30 and increases the fee for a long form certificate of good standing from $100 to $125.
6. Increases the fee for miscellaneous filings from $25 to $50.
7. Increases the amount the Secretary of State may charge for each check received for payment of fees or taxes that is returned for insufficient funds or as a result of a stop payment order from $25 to $60.
8. Enables the Secretary of State to offer a new "1 hour" expedited service to complement the Secretary of State's existing "2 hour" service offering.

Ch. 83, L. '01 Synopsis of Section 18-1105

These sections amend §18-206, §18-209(d) and §18-1105(a)(3) of the Act to provide for the amendment or termination, prior to an effective time or date, of any certificate with a future effective date or time (including a certificate of merger or consolidation) that may be filed pursuant to the Act."

Ch. 129, L. '99 Synopsis of Section 18-1105

This Section amends §18-1105(a)(3) of the Act to delete a requirement relating to a certificate of restoration.

Ch. 77, L. '97 Synopsis of Section 18-1105

This Section amends §18-1105(a)(3) of the Act to add a fee in connection with the filing of a certificate of transfer and continuance.

Ch. 360, L. '96 Synopsis of Section 18-1105

This Section amends §18-1105(a)(3) of the Act to provide for a filing fee for a certificate of limited liability company domestication, a certificate of transfer and a certificate of conversion to limited liability company.

Ch. 75, L. '95 Synopsis of Section 18-1105

This Section modifies the fee relating to the reservation of a name for a limited liability company.

This Section amends §18-1105(a)(3) of the Act to provide for a filing fee for a certificate of revival. This Section provides for a fee in connection with the use of a certificate of amendment of a certificate of merger or consolidation.

This Section modifies certain fees charged by the Secretary of State.

This Section provides for a fee in connection with two-hour service by the Secretary of State.

18-1106 RESERVED POWER OF STATE OF DELAWARE TO ALTER OR REPEAL CHAPTER.—All provisions of this chapter may be altered from time to time or repealed and all rights of members and managers are subject to this reservation. *Unless expressly stated to the contrary in this chapter, all amendments of this chapter shall apply to limited liability companies and members and managers whether or not existing as such at the time of the enactment of any such amendment.* (Last amended by Ch. 129, L. '99, eff. 8-1-99.)

Ch. 129, L. '99, eff. 8-1-99, added matter in italic.

Ch. 129, L. '99 Synopsis of Section 18-1106

This section amends §18-1106 of the Act to confirm the intended retroactive effect of amendments of the Act heretofore, now and hereafter enacted.

18-1107 TAXATION OF LIMITED LIABILITY COMPANIES.—(a) For purposes of any tax imposed by the State of Delaware or any instrumentality, agency or political subdivision of the State of Delaware, a limited liability company formed under this chapter or qualified to do business in the State of Delaware as a foreign limited liability company shall be classified as a partnership unless classified otherwise for federal income tax purposes, in which case the limited liability company shall be classified in the same manner as it is classified for federal income tax purposes. For purposes of any tax imposed by the State of Delaware or any instrumentality, agency or political subdivision of the State of Delaware, a member or an assignee of a member of a limited liability company formed under this chapter or qualified to do business in the State of Delaware as a foreign limited liability company shall be treated as either a resident or nonresident partner unless classified otherwise for federal income tax purposes, in which case the member or assignee of a member shall have the same status as such member or assignee of a member has for federal income tax purposes.

(b) Every domestic limited liability company and every foreign limited liability company registered to do business in the State of Delaware shall pay an annual tax, for the use of the State of Delaware, in the amount of $250.

(c) The annual tax shall be due and payable on the first day of June following the close of the calendar year or upon the cancellation of a certificate of formation. The Secretary of State shall receive the annual tax and pay over all taxes collected to the Department of Finance of the State of Delaware. If the annual tax remains unpaid after the due date, the tax shall bear interest at the rate of 1 and one-half percent for each month or portion thereof until fully paid.

(d) The Secretary of State shall, at least 60 days prior to the first day of June of each year, cause to be mailed to each domestic limited liability company and each foreign limited liability company required to comply with the provisions of this section in care of its registered agent in the State of Delaware an annual statement for the tax to be paid hereunder.

(e) In the event of neglect, refusal or failure on the part of any domestic limited liability company or foreign limited liability company to pay the annual tax to be paid hereunder on or before the 1st day of June in any year, such domestic limited liability company or foreign limited liability company shall pay the sum of [1]*$200* to be recovered by adding that amount to the annual tax and such additional sum shall become a part of the tax and shall be collected in the same manner and subject to the same penalties.

(f) In case any domestic limited liability company or foreign limited liability company shall fail to pay the annual tax due within the time required by this section, and in case the agent in charge of the registered office of any domestic limited liability company or foreign limited liability company upon whom process against such domestic limited liability company or foreign limited liability company may be served shall die, resign, refuse to act as such, remove from the State of Delaware or cannot with due diligence be found, it shall be lawful while default continues to serve process against such domestic limited liability company or foreign limited liability company upon the Secretary of State. Such service upon the Secretary of State shall be made in the manner and shall have the effect stated in §18-105 of this title in the case of a domestic limited liability company and §18-910 of this title in the case of a foreign limited liability company and shall be governed in all respects by said sections.

(g) The annual tax shall be a debt due from a domestic limited liability company or foreign limited liability company to the State of Delaware, for which an action at law may be maintained after the same shall have been in arrears for a period of 1 month. The tax shall also be a preferred debt in the case of insolvency.

(h) A domestic limited liability company or foreign limited liability company that neglects, refuses or fails to pay the annual tax when due shall cease to be in good standing as a domestic limited liability company or registered as a foreign limited liability company in the State of Delaware.

(i) A domestic limited liability company that has ceased to be in good standing or a foreign limited liability company that has ceased to be registered by reason of the failure to pay an annual tax shall be restored to and have the status of a domestic limited liability company in good standing or a foreign limited liability company that is registered in the State of Delaware upon the payment of the annual tax and all penalties and interest thereon for each year for which such domestic limited liability company or foreign limited liability company neglected, refused or failed to pay an annual tax.

(j) On the motion of the Attorney General or upon request of the Secretary of State, whenever any annual tax due under this chapter from any domestic limited liability company or foreign limited liability company shall have remained in arrears for a period of 3 months after the tax shall have become payable, the Attorney General may apply to the Court of Chancery, by petition in the name of the State of Delaware, on 5 days' notice to such domestic limited liability company or foreign limited liability company, which notice may be served in such manner as the Court may direct, for an injunction to restrain such domestic limited liability company or foreign limited liability company from the transaction of any business within the State of Delaware or elsewhere, until the payment of the annual tax, and all penalties and interest due thereon and the cost of the application which shall be fixed by the Court. The Court of Chancery may grant the injunction, if a proper case appears, and upon granting and service of the injunction, such domestic limited liability company or foreign limited liability company thereafter shall not transact any business until the injunction shall be dissolved.

(k) A domestic limited liability company that has ceased to be in good standing by reason of its neglect, refusal or failure to pay an annual tax shall remain a domestic limited liability company formed under this chapter. The Secretary of State shall not accept for filing any certificate (except a certificate of resignation of a registered agent when a successor registered agent is not being appointed) required or permitted by this chapter to be filed in respect of any domestic limited liability company or foreign limited liability company which has neglected, refused or failed to pay an annual tax, and shall not issue any certificate of good standing with respect to such domestic limited liability company or foreign limited liability company, unless or until such domestic limited liability company or foreign limited liability company shall have been restored to and have the status of a domestic limited liability company in good standing or a foreign limited liability company duly registered in the State of Delaware.

(l) A domestic limited liability company that has ceased to be in good standing or a foreign limited liability company that has ceased to be registered in the State of Delaware by reason of its neglect, refusal or failure to pay an annual tax may not maintain any action, suit or proceeding in any court of the State of Delaware until such domestic limited liability company or foreign limited liability company has been restored to and has the status of a domestic limited liability company or foreign limited liability company in good standing or duly registered in the State of Delaware. An action, suit or proceeding may not be maintained in any court of the State of Delaware by any successor or assignee of such domestic limited liability company or foreign limited liability company on any right, claim or demand arising out the transaction of business by such domestic limited liability company after it has ceased to be in good standing or a foreign limited liability company that has ceased to be registered in the State of Delaware until such domestic limited liability company or foreign limited liability company, or any person that has acquired all or substantially all of its assets, has paid any annual tax then due and payable, together with penalties and interest thereon.

(m) The neglect, refusal or failure of a domestic limited liability company or foreign limited liability company to pay an annual tax shall not impair the validity on any contract, deed, mortgage, security interest, lien or act or such domestic limited liability company or foreign limited liability company or prevent such domestic limited liability company or foreign limited liability company from defending any action, suit or proceeding with any court of the State of Delaware.

(n) A member or manager of a domestic limited liability company or foreign limited liability company is not liable for the debts, obligations or liabilities of such domestic limited liability company or foreign limited liability company solely by reason of the neglect, refusal or failure of such domestic limited liability company or foreign limited liability company to pay an annual tax or by reason of such domestic limited liability company or foreign limited liability company ceasing to be in good standing or duly registered. (Last amended by Ch. 78, L. '09, eff. 8-1-09.)

Ch. 78, L. '09, eff. 8-1-09, added matter in italic and deleted [1]"$100".

Ch. 78, L. '09 Synopsis of Section 18-1107

This Act increases various fees and taxes assessed by the Delaware Secretary of State.

Ch. 287, L. '08 Synopsis of Section 18-1107

This Act increases the annual tax assessed on partnerships, limited partnerships and limited liability companies on file with the Secretary of State from $200 to $250.

Ch. 52, L. '03 Synopsis of Section 18-1107

Eliminates the requirement to pay a fee to restore a limited liability company to good standing.

Ch. 129, L. '99 Synopsis of Section 18-1107

This section amends §18-1107(i) of the Act to delete the requirement of the filing of a certificate of restoration.

Ch. 341, L. '98 Synopsis of Section 18-1107

This section amends §18-1107(k) of the Act to correct a typographical error.

Ch. 75, L. '95 Synopsis of Section 18-1107

This Section eliminates an ambiguity in existing law by making it clear that the classification of a limited liability company for federal income tax purposes will govern its classification for not only any tax imposed by the State of Delaware but also any tax imposed by any instrumentality, agency or political subdivision of the State of Delaware.

.1 **Restoration of good standing.**—Once a limited liability company has lost its good standing for nonpayment of its taxes and a member who attempts to restore good standing represents less than a majority of the voting power of the limited liability company and knows that there is a dispute as to whether the company should continue and where another co-equal member of the limited liability company has initiated litigation to dissolve the company, the member with that knowledge cannot unilaterally restore the limited liability company to good standing. *In re Grupo Dos Chiles, LLC*, 2006 Del. Ch. LEXIS 54 (Ch Ct 2006).

18-1108 CANCELLATION OF CERTIFICATE OF FORMATION FOR FAILURE TO PAY TAXES.—(a) The certificate of formation of a domestic limited liability company shall be [1]canceled if the domestic limited liability company shall fail to pay the annual tax due under §18-1107 of this title for a period of 3 years from the date it is due, such cancellation to be effective on the third anniversary of such due date.

(b) A list of those domestic limited liability companies whose certificates of formation were canceled on June 1 of such calendar year pursuant to Section 18-1108(a) of this title shall be filed in the office of the Secretary of State. On or before October 31 of each calendar year, the Secretary of State shall publish such list on the Internet or on a similar medium for a period of 1 week and shall advertise the website or other address where such list can be accessed in at least 1 newspaper of general circulation in the State of Delaware. (Last amended by Ch. 105, L. '07, eff. 8-1-07.)

Ch. 105, L. '07, eff. 8-1-07, deleted [1]"deemed to be".

Ch. 105, L. '07 Synopsis of Section 18-1108

This section amends §18-1108(a) of the Act to make a technical change.

Ch. 295, L. '02 Synopsis of Section 18-1108

This section amends §18-1108 of the Act to permit the Delaware Secretary of State to carry out its obligation to provide notice of canceled domestic limited liability companies through the use of electronic communication.

Ch. 75, L. '95 Synopsis of Section 18-1108

This Sections adds a new §18-1108 to the Act to provide for the cancellation of the certificate of formation of a domestic limited liability company upon failure to pay the annual tax due the State of Delaware. In the case of nonpayment of the annual tax, cancellation occurs on the third anniversary of the due date of the unpaid annual tax. The Secretary of State's office is required to publish annually a list of the domestic limited liability companies whose certificates of formation have been canceled due to nonpayment of taxes.

.1 Waiver of dissolution rights.—A member of a limited liability company may contractually waive the statutory right to seek dissolution. *R&R Capital, LLC v Buck and Doe Run Valley Farms, LLC, 2008 Del. Ch. LEXIS 115 (Ch Ct 2008).*

18-1109 REVIVAL OF DOMESTIC LIMITED LIABILITY COMPANY.—
(a) A domestic limited liability company whose certificate of formation has been canceled pursuant to §18-104(d) or §18-104(i)(4) or §18-1108(a) of this title may be revived by filing in the office of the Secretary of State a certificate of revival accompanied by the payment of the fee required by §18-1105(a)(3) of this title and payment of the annual tax due under §18-1107 of this title and all penalties and interest thereon [1]*due at the time of the cancellation of its certificate of formation.* The certificate of revival shall set forth:

(1) The name of the limited liability company at the time its certificate of formation was canceled and, if such name is not available at the time of revival, the name under which the limited liability company is to be revived;

(2) The date of filing of the original certificate of formation of the limited liability company;

(3) The address of the limited liability company's registered office in the State of Delaware and the name and address of the limited liability company's registered agent in the State of Delaware;

(4) A statement that the certificate of revival is filed by 1 or more persons authorized to execute and file the certificate of revival to revive the limited liability company; and

(5) Any other matters the persons executing the certificate of revival determine to include therein.

(b) The certificate of revival shall be deemed to be an amendment to the certificate of formation of the limited liability company, and the limited liability company shall not be required to take any further action to amend its certificate of formation under §18-202 of this title with respect to the matters set forth in the certificate of revival.

(c) Upon the filing of a certificate of revival, a limited liability company shall be revived with the same force and effect as if its certificate of formation had not been canceled pursuant to §18-104(d) or §18-104(i)(4) or §18-1108(a) of this title. Such revival shall validate all contracts, acts, matter and things made, done and performed by the limited liability company, its members, managers, employees and agents during the time when its certificate of formation was canceled pursuant to §18-104(d) or §18-104(i)(4) or §18-1108(a) of this title, with the same force and effect and to all intents and purposes as if the certificate of formation had remained in full force and effect. All real and personal property, and all rights and interests, which belonged to the limited liability company at the time its certificate of formation was canceled pursuant to §18-104(d) or §18-104(i)(4) or §18-1108(a) of this title or which were acquired by the limited liability company following the cancellation of its certificate of formation pursuant to §18-104(d) or §18-104(i)(4) or §18-1108(a) of this title, and which were not disposed of prior to the time of its revival, shall be vested in the limited liability company after its revival as fully as they were held by the limited liability company at, and after, as the case may be, the time its certificate of formation was canceled pursuant to §18-104(d) or §18-104(i)(4) or §18-1108(a) of this title. After its revival, the limited liability company shall be as exclusively liable for all contracts, acts, matters and things made, done or performed in its name and on its behalf by its members, managers, employees and agents prior to its revival as if its certificate of formation had at all times remained in full force and effect. (Last amended by Ch. 78, L. '09, eff. 8-1-09.)

Ch. 78, L. '09, eff. 8-1-09, added matter in italic and deleted [1]"for each year for which such domestic limited liability company neglected, refused or failed to pay such annual tax, including each year between the cancellation of its certificate of formation and its revival".

Ch. 78, L. '09 Synopsis of Section 18-1109

This Act increases various fees and taxes assessed by the Delaware Secretary of State.

Ch. 317, L. '06 Synopsis of Section 18-1109

These Sections amend §18-1109 of the Act to permit the revival of a certificate of formation of a limited liability company whose certificate of formation has been cancelled pursuant to new §18-104(i)(4).

Ch. 75, L. '95 Synopsis of Section 18-1109

This Section adds a new §18-1109 to the Act to permit a domestic limited liability company whose certificate of formation has been canceled pursuant to §18-104(d) or §18-1108(a) to be revived by filing a certificate of revival together with payment of all unpaid taxes, interest and penalties.

[The page following this is DSTA-i]

2011 AMENDMENTS TO THE DELAWARE STATUTORY TRUST ACT—ANALYSIS

By Eric A. Mazie
Richards, Layton & Finger, P.A.
Wilmington, Delaware

I. Introduction

The Delaware Statutory Trust Act, 12 *Del. C.* § 3801, *et seq.* (the "Act"), was amended on July 13, 2011 in order to address several technical issues. The amendments to the Act (the "2011 Amendments") are set forth in House Bill No. 115.

II. Registered Agents

—Resignation of a Registered Agent and Appointment of a Successor [12 Del. C. § 3807(f), and 12 Del. C. § 3813(a)(5)].

The 2011 Amendments amend Section 3807 and Section 3813 of the Act to provide for the resignation of a registered agent of one or more statutory trusts upon the appointment of a successor registered agent upon the filing of a certificate of resignation with the Secretary of State that provides the name and address of the successor registered agent, and the payment to the Secretary of State of a filing fee of $200. Attached to the certificate shall be a statement of each affected statutory trust ratifying and approving the change in registered agent. The filing of such certificate of resignation and appointment will constitute an amendment to the certificate of trust of the affected trusts, and no additional filings will be required.

—Resignation of a Registered Agent Without Appointment of a Successor [12 Del. C. § 3807(g) and 12 Del. C. § 3813(a)(5)].

The 2011 Amendments amend Section 3807 and Section 3813 of the Act to provide for the resignation of a registered agent of one or more statutory trusts without the appointment of a successor registered agent upon filing of a certificate of resignation with the Secretary of State and the payment to the Secretary of State of a filing fee of $2.00 per affected trust. Such resignation will not become effective until 30 days after filing. Affected trusts must designate a replacement registered agent, or appoint a Delaware trustee. The Secretary of State will act as a default agent for the service of legal process if no new registered agent or Delaware trustee is designated by an affected statutory trust.

—Address of a Trustee and Registered Agent [12 Del. C. § 3807(h) and 12 Del. C. § 3812(g)].

The 2011 Amendments amend Section 3807 of the Act to require that in documents filed with the Secretary of State under the Act, address details of any trustee or registered agent include the street, number, city and postal code. The 2011 Amendments also amend Section 3812 of the Act to clarify that only certificates filed after August 1, 2011 will be subject to the new Section 3807(h) of the Act.

III. Certificate Filings

—Post-filing Effective Dates [12 Del. C. § 3812(b)].

The 2011 Amendments amend Section 3808(b) of the Act to provide that any certificate filed with the Secretary of State under the Act on or after January 1, 2012 may have a post-filing effective date not to exceed 180 days after filing.

IV. Trust Names

—Distinguishing Trust Names [12 Del. C. § 3814(a)].

The 2011 Amendments amend Section 3814(a) of the Act to provide that, after July 31, 2011, no domestic statutory trust may register under a name not sufficient to distinguish it from any other domestic statutory trust then registered upon the records of the Secretary of State unless its certificate of trust was filed on or before July 31, 2011, and it has obtained the consent of the other domestic statutory trust and such consent was filed with the Secretary of State. The 2011 Amendments also amend Section 3814(a) of the Act to clarify, however, that domestic statutory trusts may continue to register under names not sufficient to distinguish themselves from foreign statutory trusts provided they have obtained the consents of such foreign statutory trusts and filed such consents with the Secretary of State.

V. Merger or Consolidation

—Amendment of Governing Instrument [12 Del. C. § 3815(f)].

The 2011 Amendments amend Section 3815(f) to correct a typographical error in last year's amendment to the same section. That amendment was intended to provide that notwithstanding anything to the contrary contained in the governing instrument of a statutory trust, an agreement of merger or consolidation approved in accordance with subsection (a) of this section may (1) effect any amendment to the governing instrument of the statutory trust or (2) effect the adoption of a new governing instrument of the statutory trust if it is the surviving or resulting statutory trust in the merger or consolidation. Prior to the amendment, such activities must have been specifically provided for in the governing instrument of the statutory trust.

VI. Conversion

—Filing a Certificate of Conversion [12 Del. C. § 3820(a)].
The 2011 Amendments amend Section 3820 of the Act to provide that whenever a business entity converts into a statutory trust the certificate of conversion must be filed simultaneously with, and if applicable, filed with the same post-filing effective date as, the corresponding certificate of trust, both of which must be filed with the Secretary of State in order to effectuate a conversion of another business entity into a statutory trust.

VII. Domestication

—Filing a Certificate of Domestication [12 Del. C. § 3822(b)].

The 2011 Amendments amend Section 3822 of the Act to provide that whenever a non-United States entity converts into a statutory trust the certificate of domestication must be filed simultaneously with, and if applicable, filed with the same post-filing effective date as, the corresponding certificate of trust, both of which must be filed with the Secretary of State in order to effectuate a domestication of a non-United States entity into a statutory trust.

VIII. Registered Agent of a Foreign Statutory Trust

—Fees [12 Del. C. § 3862].

The 2011 Amendments amend Section 3862 of the Act to revise the fees such that a registered agent shall pay a fee to the Secretary of State of (a) $200 when filing a certificate under § 3854(c) to change its name or address, (b) $200 when filing a certificate under § 3854(d) to resign with the appointment of a successor and (c) $2.00 for each statutory trust whose registered agent resigns when it files a certificate under § 3854(e) to resign without the appointment of a successor.

[The page following this is Corp.—701]

STATUTORY TRUSTS

Title 12. Decedents' Estates and Fiduciary Relations

Chapter 38. Treatment of Delaware Statutory Trusts

Subchapter I. Domestic Statutory Trusts

(Added by Ch. 279, L. '88, eff. 10-1-88. The amendments by Ch. 329, L. '02, eff. 9-1-02, were made for the purpose of avoiding any implication that a trust formed under Chapter 38, Title 12 of the Delaware Code constitutes a "business trust" within the meaning of Title 11 of the United States Code. Such amendments are not intended to result in any substantive change in Delaware law.)

T. 12, 3801 DEFINITIONS.—(a) "Beneficial owner" means any owner of a beneficial interest in a statutory trust, the fact of ownership to be determined and evidenced (whether by means of registration, the issuance of certificates or otherwise) in conformity to the applicable provisions of the governing instrument of the statutory trust.

(b) "Foreign statutory trust" means a business trust or statutory trust formed under the laws of any state or under the laws of any foreign country or other foreign jurisdiction and denominated as such under the laws of such state or foreign country or other foreign jurisdiction.

(c) "Governing instrument" means any instrument (whether referred to as a trust agreement, declaration of trust or otherwise) which creates a statutory trust or provides for the governance of the affairs of the statutory trust and the conduct of its business. A governing instrument:

(1) May provide that a person shall become a beneficial owner or a trustee if such person (or, in the case of a beneficial owner, a representative authorized by such person orally, in writing or by other action such as payment for a beneficial interest) complies with the conditions for becoming a beneficial owner or a trustee set forth in the governing instrument or any other writing and, in the case of a beneficial owner, acquires a beneficial interest;

(2) May consist of 1 or more agreements, instruments or other writings and may include or incorporate bylaws containing provisions relating to the business of the statutory trust, the conduct of its affairs and its rights or powers or the rights or powers of its trustees, beneficial owners, agents or employees; and

(3) May contain any provision that is not inconsistent with law or with the information contained in the certificate of trust.

A statutory trust is not required to execute its governing instrument. A statutory trust is bound by its governing instrument whether or not it executes the governing instrument. A beneficial owner or a trustee is bound by the governing instrument whether or not such beneficial owner or trustee executes the governing instrument.

(d) "Independent trustee" means, solely with respect to a statutory trust that is registered as an investment company under the Investment Company Act of 1940, as amended (15 U.S.C. §80a-1 et seq.), or any successor statute thereto (the "1940 Act"), any trustee who is not an "interested person" (as such term is defined below) of the statutory trust; provided that the receipt of compensation for service as an independent trustee of the statutory trust and also for service as an independent trustee of 1 or more other investment companies managed by a single investment adviser (or an "affiliated person" (as such term is defined below) of such investment adviser) shall not affect the status of a trustee as an independent trustee under this chapter. An independent trustee as defined hereunder shall be deemed to be independent and disinterested for all purposes. For purposes of this definition, the terms "affiliated person" and "interested person" have the meanings set forth in the 1940 Act or any rule adopted thereunder.

(e) "Other business entity" means a corporation, a partnership (whether general or limited), a limited liability company, a common-law trust, a foreign statutory trust or any other unincorporated business *or entity*, excluding a statutory trust.

(f) "Person" means a natural person, partnership (whether general or limited), limited liability company, trust *(including a common law trust, business trust, statutory trust, voting trust or any other form of trust)* estate, association (including any group, organization, cotenancy, plan, board, council or committee), corporation, government (including a country, state, county or any other governmental subdivision, agency or instrumentality), custodian, nominee or any other individual or entity (or series thereof) in its own or any representative capacity, in each case, whether domestic or foreign, and a statutory trust or foreign statutory trust.

(g) "Statutory trust" means an unincorporated association which:

(1) Is created by a governing instrument under which property is or will be held, managed, administered, controlled, invested, reinvested and/or operated, or business or professional activities for profit are carried on or will be carried on, by a trustee or trustees or as otherwise provided in the governing instrument for the benefit of such person or persons as are or may become beneficial owners or as otherwise provided in the governing instrument, including but not limited to a trust of the type known at common law as a "business trust," or "Massachusetts trust," or a trust qualifying as a real estate investment trust under §856 et seq. of the United States Internal Revenue Code of 1986 [26 U.S.C. §856 et seq.], as amended, or under any successor provision, or a trust qualifying as a real estate mortgage investment conduit under §860D of the United States Internal Revenue Code of 1986 [26 U.S.C. §860D], as amended, or under any successor provision; and

(2) Files a certificate of trust pursuant to §3810 of this title.

Any such association heretofore or hereafter organized shall be a statutory trust and a separate legal entity. The term "statutory trust" shall be deemed to include each trust formed under this chapter prior to September 1, 2002, as a "business trust" (as such term was then defined in this subsection). A statutory trust may be organized to carry on any lawful business or activity, whether or not conducted for profit, and/or for any of the purposes referred to paragraph (g)(1) of this section (including, without limitation, for the purpose of holding or otherwise taking title to property, whether in an active or custodial capacity). Neither use of the designation "business trust" nor a statement in a certificate of trust or governing instrument executed prior to September 1, 2002, to the effect that the trust formed thereby is or will qualify as a Delaware business trust within the meaning of or pursuant to this chapter, shall create a presumption or an inference that the trust so formed is a "business trust" for purposes of Title 11 of the United States Code.

(h) "Trustee" means the person or persons appointed as a trustee in accordance with the governing instrument of a statutory trust, and may include the beneficial owners or any of them. (Last amended by Ch. 403, L. '10, eff. 8-1-10.)

Ch. 403, L. '10, eff. 8-1-10, added matter in italic.

T. 12, 3802 CONTRIBUTIONS BY BENEFICIAL OWNERS.—(a) A contribution of a beneficial owner to the [1]*statutory trust* may be in cash, property or services rendered, or a promissory note or other obligation to contribute cash or property or to perform services; provided however, that a person may become a beneficial owner of a [1]*statutory trust* and may receive a beneficial interest in a [1]*statutory trust* without making a contribution or being obligated to make a contribution to the [1]*statutory trust*.

(b) Except as provided in the governing instrument, a beneficial owner is obligated to the [1]*statutory trust* to perform any promise to contribute cash, property or to perform services, even if the beneficial owner is unable to perform because of death, disability or any other reason. If a beneficial owner does not make the required contribution of property or services, the beneficial owner is obligated at the option of the [1]*statutory trust* to contribute cash equal to that portion of the agreed value (as stated in the records of the [1]*statutory trust*) of the contribution that has not been made. The foregoing option shall be in addition to, and not in lieu of, any other rights, including the right to specific performance, that the [1]*statutory trust* may have against such beneficial owner under the governing instrument of applicable law.

(c) A governing instrument may provide that the interest of any beneficial owner who fails to make any contribution that the beneficial owner is obligated to make shall be subject to specific penalties for, or specified consequences of, such failure. Such penalty or consequence may take the form of reducing or eliminating the defaulting beneficial owner's proportionate interest in the [1]*statutory trust*, subordinating the beneficial interest to that of nondefaulting beneficial owners, a forced sale of the beneficial interest, forfeiture of the beneficial interest, the lending by other beneficial owners of the amount necessary to meet the beneficiary's commitment, a fixing of the value of the defaulting beneficial owner's beneficial interest by appraisal or by formula and redemption or sale of the beneficial interest at such value, or any other penalty or consequence. (Last amended by Ch. 329, L. '02, eff. 9-1-02.)

Ch. 329, L. '02, eff. 9-1-02, added matter in italic and deleted [1]"business trust".

T. 12, 3803 LIABILITY OF BENEFICIAL OWNERS AND TRUSTEES.—

(a) Except to the extent otherwise provided in the governing instrument of the [1]*statutory trust*, the beneficial owners shall be entitled to the same limitation of personal liability extended to stockholders of private corporations for profit organized under the general corporation law of the State.

(b) Except to the extent otherwise provided in the governing instrument of a [1]*statutory trust*, a trustee, when acting in such capacity, shall not be personally liable to any person other than the [1]*statutory trust* or a beneficial owner for any act, omission or obligation of the [1]*statutory trust* or any trustee thereof.

(c) Except to the extent otherwise provided in the governing instrument of a [1]*statutory trust*, an officer, employee, manager or other person acting pursuant to §3806(b)(7) of this title, when acting in such capacity, shall not be personally liable to any person other than the [1]*statutory trust* or a beneficial owner for any act, omission or obligation of the [1]*statutory trust* or any trustee thereof.

(d) No obligation of a beneficial owner or trustee of a [1]*statutory trust* to the [1]*statutory trust* arising under the governing instrument or a separate agreement in writing, and no note, instrument or other writing evidencing any such obligation of a beneficial owner or trustee, shall be subject to the defense of usury, and no beneficial owner or trustee shall interpose the defense of usury with respect to any such obligation in any action. (Last amended by Ch. 329, L. '02, eff. 9-1-02.)

Ch. 329, L. '02, eff. 9-1-02, added matter in italic and deleted [1]"business trust".

T. 12, 3804 LEGAL PROCEEDINGS.—

(a) A statutory trust may sue and be sued, and service of process upon 1 of the trustees shall be sufficient. In furtherance of the foregoing, a statutory trust may be sued for debts and other obligations or liabilities contracted or incurred by the trustees, or by the duly authorized agents of such trustees, in the performance of their respective duties under the governing instrument of the statutory trust, and for any damages to persons or property resulting from the negligence of such trustees or agents acting in the performance of such respective duties. The property of a statutory trust shall be subject to attachment and execution as if it were a corporation, subject to §3502 of Title 10. Notwithstanding the foregoing provisions of this section, in the event that the governing instrument of a statutory trust, including a statutory trust which is a registered investment company under the Investment Company Act of 1940, as amended (15 U.S.C. §80a-1 et seq.), creates 1 or more series as provided in §3806(b)(2) of this title, and if separate and distinct records are maintained for any such series and the assets associated with any such series are held in such separate and distinct records (directly or indirectly, including through a nominee or otherwise) and accounted for *in such separate and distinct records* separately from the other assets of the statutory trust, or any other series thereof, and if the governing instrument so provides, and notice of the limitation on liabilities of a series as referenced in this sentence is set forth in the certificate of trust of the statutory trust, then the debts, liabilities, obligations and expenses incurred, contracted for or otherwise existing with respect to a particular series shall be enforceable against the assets of such series only, and not against the assets of the statutory trust generally or any other series thereof, and, unless otherwise provided in the governing instrument, none of the debts, liabilities, obligations and expenses incurred, contracted for or otherwise existing with respect to the statutory trust generally or any other series thereof shall be enforceable against the assets of such series.

(b) A trustee of a statutory trust may be served with process in the manner prescribed in subsection (c) of this section in all civil actions or proceedings brought in the State involving or relating to the activities of the statutory trust or a violation by a trustee of a duty to the statutory trust, or any beneficial owner, whether or not the trustee is a trustee at the time suit is commenced. Every resident or nonresident of the State who accepts election or appointment or serves as a trustee of a statutory trust shall, by such acceptance or service, be deemed thereby to have consented to the appointment of the Delaware trustee or registered agent of such statutory trust required by §3807 of this title (or, if there is none, the Secretary of State) as such person's agent upon whom service of process may be made as provided in this section. Such acceptance or service shall signify the consent of such trustee that any process when so served shall be of the same legal force and validity as if served upon such trustee within the State and such appointment of such Delaware trustee or registered agent (or, if there is none, the Secretary of State) shall be irrevocable.

(c) Service of process shall be effected by serving the Delaware trustee or registered agent of such statutory trust required by §3807 of this title (or, if there is none, the Secretary of State) with 1 copy of such process in the manner provided by law for service of writs of summons. In the event service is made under this subsection upon the Secretary of State, the plaintiff shall pay to the Secretary of State the sum of $50 for the use of the State, which sum shall be taxed as part of the costs of the proceeding if the plaintiff shall prevail therein. In addition, the Prothonotary or the Register in Chancery of the court in which the civil action or proceeding is pending shall, within 7 days of such service, deposit in the United States mails, by registered mail, postage prepaid, true and attested copies of the process, together with a statement that service is being made pursuant to this section, addressed to the defendant at the defendant's address last known to and furnished by the party desiring to make such service.

(d) In any action in which any such trustee has been served with process as hereinafter provided, the time in which a defendant shall be required to appear and file a responsive pleading shall be computed from the date of mailing by the Prothonotary or the Register in Chancery as provided in subsection (c) of this section: provided however, the court in which such action has been commenced may order such continuance or continuances as may be necessary to afford such trustee reasonable opportunity to defend the action.

(e) In the governing instrument of the statutory trust or other writing, a trustee or beneficial owner or other person may consent to be subject to the nonexclusive jurisdiction of the courts of, or arbitration in, a specified jurisdiction, or the exclusive jurisdiction of the courts of the State, or the exclusivity of arbitration in a specified jurisdiction of the State, and to be served with legal process in the manner prescribed in such governing instrument of the statutory trust or other writing. Except by agreeing to arbitrate any arbitrable matter in a specified jurisdiction or in the State, a beneficial owner who is not a trustee may not waive its right to maintain a legal action or proceeding in the courts of the State with respect to matters relating to the organization or internal affairs of a business trust.

(f) Nothing herein contained limits or affects the right to serve process in any other manner now or hereafter provided by law. This section is an extension of and not a limitation upon the right otherwise existing of service of legal process upon nonresidents.

(g) The Court of Chancery and the Superior Court may make all necessary rules respecting the form of process, the manner of issuance and return thereof and such other rules which may be necessary to implement this section and are not inconsistent with this section. The Court of Chancery shall have jurisdiction over statutory trusts to the same extent as it has jurisdiction over common law trusts formed under the laws of the State.

[1] (Last amended Ch. 418, L. '06, eff. 8-1-06.)

Ch. 418, L. '06, eff. 8-1-06, deleted [1] "(h) A partnership (whether general or limited), corporation or other non-natural person formed or organized under the laws of any foreign country or other foreign jurisdiction or the laws of any state other than the State of Delaware shall not be deemed to be doing business in the State solely by reason of its being a trustee of a statutory trust."

T. 12, 3805 RIGHTS OF BENEFICIAL OWNERS *AND TRUSTEES* IN TRUST PROPERTY.—(a) Except to the extent otherwise provided in the governing instrument of the [1]*statutory trust*, a beneficial owner shall have an undivided beneficial interest in the property of the [1]*statutory trust* and shall share in the profits and losses of the [1]*statutory trust* in the proportion (expressed as a percentage) of the entire undivided beneficial interest in the [1]*statutory trust* owned by such beneficial owner. The governing instrument of a [1]*statutory trust* may provide that the [1]*statutory trust* or the trustees, acting for and on behalf of the [1]*statutory trust*, shall be deemed to hold beneficial ownership of any income earned on securities of the [1]*statutory trust* issued by any business entities formed, organized, or existing under the laws of any jurisdiction, including the laws of any foreign country.

(b) No creditor of the beneficial owner shall have any right to obtain possession of, or otherwise exercise legal or equitable remedies with respect to, the property of the [1]*statutory trust*.

(c) A beneficial owner's beneficial interest in the [1]*statutory trust* is personal property notwithstanding the nature of the property of the trust. Except to the extent otherwise provided in the governing instrument of a [1]*statutory trust*, a beneficial owner has no interest in specific[1]*statutory trust* property.

(d) A beneficial owner's beneficial interest in the [1]*statutory trust* is freely transferable except to the extent otherwise provided in the governing instrument of the [1]*statutory trust*.

(e) Except to the extent otherwise provided in the governing instrument of a [1]*statutory trust*, at the time a beneficial owner becomes entitled to receive a distribution, the beneficial owner has the status of, and is entitled to all remedies available to, a creditor of the [1]*statutory trust* with respect to the distribution. A governing instrument may provide for the establishment of record dates with respect to allocations and distributions by a [1]*statutory trust*.

(f) Except to the extent otherwise provided in the governing instrument of the [1]*statutory trust*, legal title to the property of the [1]*statutory trust* "or any part thereof" may be held in the name of any trustee of the [1]*statutory trust*, in its capacity as such, with the same effect as if such property were held in the name of the [1]*statutory trust*.

(g) No creditor of the trustee shall have any right to obtain possession of, or otherwise exercise legal or equitable remedies with respect to, the property of the [1]*statutory trust* with respect to any claim against, or obligation of, such trustee in its individual capacity and not related to the [1]*statutory trust*.

(h) *Except to the extent otherwise provided in the governing instrument of the business trust, where the business trust is a registered investment company under the Investment Company Act of 1940, as amended (15 U.S.C. §80a-1 et seq.), any class, group or series of beneficial interests established by the governing instrument with respect to such business trust shall be a class, group or series preferred as to distribution of assets or payment of dividends over all other classes, groups or series in respect to assets specifically allocated to the class, group or series as contemplated by §18 (or any amendment or successor provision) of the Investment Company Act of 1940 [15 U.S.C. §80a-18], as amended, and any regulations issued thereunder, provided that this section is not intended to affect in any respect the provisions of §3804(a) of this title.*

(i) *Unless otherwise provided in the governing instrument of a statutory trust or another agreement, a beneficial owner shall have no preemptive right to subscribe to any additional issue of beneficial interests or another interest in a statutory trust.* (Last amended by Ch. 328, L. '02, eff. 8-1-02 and Ch. 329, L. '02, eff. 9-1-02.)

Ch. 328, L. '02, eff. 8-1-02, added matter in italic in the title and new paragraphs (h) and (i).

Ch. 329, L. '02, eff. 9-1-02, added matter in italic and deleted [1]"business trust".

T. 12, 3806 MANAGEMENT OF STATUTORY TRUST.—(a) Except to the extent otherwise provided in the governing instrument of a statutory trust, the business and affairs of a statutory trust shall be managed by or under the direction of its trustees. To the extent provided in the governing instrument of a statutory trust, any person (including a beneficial owner) shall be entitled to direct the trustees or other persons in the management of the statutory trust. Except to the extent otherwise provided in the governing instrument of a statutory trust, neither the power to give direction to a trustee or other persons nor the exercise thereof by any person (including a beneficial owner) shall cause such person to be a trustee. To the extent provided in the governing instrument of a statutory trust, neither the power to give direction to a trustee or other persons nor the exercise thereof by any person (including a beneficial owner) shall cause such person to have duties (including fiduciary duties) or liabilities relating thereto to the statutory trust or to a beneficial owner thereof.

(b) A governing instrument may contain any provision relating to the management of the business and affairs of the statutory trust, and the rights, duties and obligations of the trustees, beneficial owners and other persons, which is not contrary to any provision or requirement of this subchapter and, without limitation:

(1) May provide for classes, groups or series of trustees or beneficial owners, or classes, groups or series of beneficial interests, having such relative rights, powers and duties as the governing instrument may provide, and may make provision for the future creation in the manner provided in the governing instrument of additional classes, groups or series of trustees, beneficial owners or beneficial interests, having such relative rights, powers and duties as may from time to time be established, including rights, powers and duties senior or subordinate to existing classes, groups or series of trustees, beneficial owners or beneficial interests;

(2) May establish or provide for the establishment of designated series of trustees, beneficial owners, *assets* or beneficial interests having separate rights, powers or duties with respect to specified property or obligations of the statutory trust or profits and losses associated with specified property or obligations, and, to the extent provided in the governing instrument, any such series may have a separate business purpose or investment objective;

(3) May provide for the taking of any action, including the amendment of the governing instrument, the accomplishment of a merger, conversion or consolidation, the appointment of one or more trustees, the sale, lease, exchange, transfer, pledge or other disposition of all or any part of the assets of the statutory trust or the assets of any series, or the dissolution of the statutory trust, or may provide for the taking of any action to create under the provisions of the governing instrument a class, group or series of beneficial interests that was not previously outstanding, in any such case without the vote or approval of any particular trustee or beneficial owner, or class, group or series of trustees or beneficial owners.

(4) May grant to (or withhold from) all or certain trustees or beneficial owners, or a specified class, group or series of trustees or beneficial owners, the right to vote, separately or with any or all other classes, groups or series of the trustees or beneficial owners, on any matter, such voting being on a per capita, number, financial interest, class, group, series or any other basis;

(5) May, if and to the extent that voting rights are granted under the governing instrument, set forth provisions relating to notice of the time, place or purpose of any meeting at which any matter is to be voted on, waiver of any such notice, action by consent without a meeting, the establishment of record dates, quorum requirements, voting in person, by proxy or in any other manner, or any other matter with respect to the exercise of any such right to vote;

(6) May provide for the present or future creation of more than 1 statutory trust, including the creation of a future statutory trust to which all or any part of the assets, liabilities, profits or losses of any existing statutory trust will be transferred, and for the conversion of beneficial interests in an existing statutory trust, or series thereof, into beneficial interests in the separate statutory trust, or series thereof.

(7) May provide for the appointment, election or engagement, either as agents or independent contractors of the statutory trust or as delegatees of the trustees, as officers, employees, managers or other persons who may manage the business and affairs of the statutory trust and may have such titles and such relative rights, powers and duties as the governing instrument shall provide. Except to the extent otherwise provided in the governing instrument of a statutory trust, the trustees shall choose and supervise such officers, managers, employees and other persons;

(8) May provide rights to any person, including a person who is not a party to the governing instrument, to the extent set forth therein; or

(9) May provide for the manner in which it may be amended, including by requiring the approval of a person who is not a party to the governing instrument or the satisfaction of conditions, and to the extent the governing instrument provides for the manner in which it may be amended such governing instrument may be amended only in that manner or as otherwise permitted by law, *including as permitted by §3815(f) of this title* (provided that the approval of any person may be waived by such person and that any such conditions may be waived by all persons for whose benefit such conditions were intended).

(c) To the extent that, at law or in equity, a trustee or beneficial owner or other person has duties (including fiduciary duties) to a statutory trust or to another trustee or beneficial owner or to another person that is a party to or is otherwise bound by a governing instrument, the trustee's or beneficial owner's or other person's duties may be expanded or restricted or eliminated by provisions in the governing instrument; provided, that the governing instrument may not eliminate the implied contractual covenant of good faith and fair dealing.

(d) Unless otherwise provided in a governing instrument, a trustee or beneficial owner or other person shall not be liable to a statutory trust or to another trustee or beneficial owner or to another person that is a party to or is otherwise bound by a governing instrument for breach of fiduciary duty for the trustee's or beneficial owner's or other person's good faith reliance on the provisions of the governing instrument.

(e) A governing instrument may provide for the limitation or elimination of any and all liabilities for breach of contract and breach of duties (including fiduciary duties) of a trustee, beneficial owner or other person to a statutory trust or to another trustee or beneficial owner or to another person that is a party to or is otherwise bound by a governing instrument; provided, that a governing instrument may not limit or eliminate liability for any act or omission that constitutes a bad faith violation of the implied contractual covenant of good faith and fair dealing.

(f) Unless otherwise provided in the governing instrument of a statutory trust, meetings of beneficial owners may be held by means of conference telephone or other communications equipment by means of which all persons participating in the meeting can hear each other, and participation in a meeting pursuant to this subsection shall constitute presence in person at the meeting. Unless otherwise provided in the governing instrument of a statutory trust, on any matter that is to be voted on by the beneficial owners,

(1) The beneficial owners may take such action without a meeting, without a prior notice and without a vote if a consent or consents in writing, setting forth the action so taken, shall be signed by the beneficial owners having not less than the minimum number of votes that would be necessary to authorize or take such action at a meeting at which all interests in the statutory trust entitled to vote thereon were present and voted and

(2) The beneficial owners may vote in person or by proxy, and such proxy may be granted in writing, by means of electronic transmission or as otherwise permitted by applicable law.

Unless otherwise provided in a governing instrument, a consent transmitted by electronic transmission by a beneficial owner or by a person or persons authorized to act for a beneficial owner shall be deemed to be written and signed for purposes of this subsection. For purposes of this subsection, the term "electronic transmission" means any form of communication not directly involving the physical transmission of paper that creates a record that may be retained, retrieved, and reviewed by a recipient thereof and that may be directly reproduced in paper form by such a recipient through an automated process.

(g) Unless otherwise provided in the governing instrument of a statutory trust, meetings of trustees may be held by means of conference telephone or other communications equipment by means of which all persons participating in the meeting can hear each other, and participation in a meeting pursuant to this subsection shall constitute presence in person at the meeting. Unless otherwise provided in the governing instrument of a statutory trust, on any matter that is to be voted on by the trustees,

(1) The trustees may take such action without a meeting, without a prior notice and without a vote if a consent or consents in writing, setting forth the action so taken, shall be signed by the trustees having not less than the minimum number of votes that would be necessary to authorize or take such action at a meeting at which all trustees entitled to vote thereon were present and voted and

(2) The trustee may vote in person or by proxy, and such proxy may be granted in writing, by means of electronic transmission or as otherwise permitted by applicable law.

Unless otherwise provided in a governing instrument, a consent transmitted by electronic transmission by a trustee or by a person or persons authorized to act for a trustee shall be deemed to be written and signed for purposes of this subsection. For purposes of this subsection, the term "electronic transmission" means any form of communication not directly involving the physical transmission of paper that creates a record that may be retained, retrieved and reviewed by a recipient thereof and that may be directly reproduced in paper form by such a recipient through an automated process.

(h) Except to the extent otherwise provided in the governing instrument of a statutory trust, a beneficial owner, trustee, officer, employee or manager may lend money to, borrow money from, act as a surety, guarantor or endorser for, guarantee or assume 1 or more obligations of, provide collateral for, and transact other business with, a business trust and, subject to other applicable law, has the same rights and obligations with respect to any such matter as a person who is not a beneficial owner, trustee, officer, employee or manager.

(i) Except to the extent otherwise provided in the governing instrument of a business trust, a trustee of a business trust has the power and authority to delegate to 1 or more other persons the trustee's rights and powers to manage and control the business and affairs of the business trust, including to delegate to agents, officers and employees of the trustee or the business trust, and to delegate by management agreement or other agreement with, or otherwise to, other persons. Except to the extent otherwise provided in the governing instrument of a business trust, such delegation by a trustee of a business trust shall not cause the trustee to cease to be a trustee of the business trust or cause the person to whom any such rights and powers have been delegated to be a trustee of the business trust.

(j) The governing instrument of a statutory trust may provide that:

(1) A beneficial owner who fails to perform in accordance with, or to comply with the terms and conditions of, the governing instrument shall be subject to specified penalties or specified consequences;

(2) At the time or upon the happening of events specified in the governing instrument, a beneficial owner shall be subject to specified penalties or specified consequences; and

(3) The specified penalties or specified consequences under paragraphs (j)(1) and (j)(2) of this subsection may include and take the form of any penalty or consequence set forth in §3802(c) of this title.

(k) A trustee, beneficial owner or an officer, employee, manager or other person designated in accordance with paragraph (b)(7) of this section shall be fully protected in relying in good faith upon the records of the statutory trust and upon information, opinions, reports or statements presented by another trustee, beneficial owner or officer, employee, manager or other person designated in accordance with paragraph (b)(7) of this section, or by any other person as to matters the trustee, beneficial owner or officer, employee, manager or other person designated in accordance with paragraph (b)(7) of this section reasonably believes are within such other person's professional or expert competence, including information, opinions, reports or statements as to the value and amount of the assets, liabilities, profits or losses of the statutory trust, or the value and amount of assets or reserves or contracts, agreements or other undertakings that would be sufficient to pay claims and obligations of the statutory trust or to make reasonable provision to pay such claims and obligations, or any other facts pertinent to the existence and amount of assets from which distributions to beneficial owners or creditors might properly be paid. (Last amended by Ch. 403, L. '10, eff. 8-1-10.)

Ch. 403, L. '10, eff. 8-1-10, added matter in italic.

T. 12, 3807 TRUSTEE IN STATE; *REGISTERED AGENT.*—(a) Every statutory trust shall at all times have at least 1 trustee which, in the case of a natural person, shall be a person who is a resident of this State or which, in all other cases, has its principal place of business in this State.

(b) Notwithstanding the provisions of subsection (a) of this section, if a statutory trust is, becomes, or will become prior to or within 180 days following the first issuance of beneficial interests, a registered investment company under the Investment Company Act of 1940, as amended (15 U.S.C. §§80a-1 et seq.), such statutory trust shall not be required to have a trustee who is a resident of this State or who has a principal place of business in this State if notice that the statutory trust is or will become an investment company as referenced in this sentence is set forth in the certificate of trust of the statutory trust and if and for so long as such statutory trust shall have and maintain in this State:

(1) A registered office, which may but need not be a place of business in this State; and

(2) A registered agent for service of process on the statutory trust, which agent may be either an individual resident in this State whose business office is identical with such statutory trust's registered office, or a domestic corporation, limited partnership, limited liability company or statutory trust, or a foreign corporation, limited partnership, limited liability company or statutory trust authorized to transact business in this State, having a business office identical with such registered office.

(c) Any statutory trust maintaining a registered office and registered agent in this State under subsection (b) of this section may change the location of its registered office in this State to any other place in this State, or may change the registered agent to any other person or corporation (meeting the requirements contained in subsection (b) of this section), by filing an amendment to its certificate of trust in accordance with the applicable provisions of this subchapter. If a statutory trust which is an investment company registered as aforesaid maintains a registered office and registered agent in this State as herein provided, then the reference in §3810(a)(1)b. of this title to the "name and the business address of at least 1 of the trustees meeting the requirements of §3807 of this title" shall be deemed a reference to the name and the business address of the registered agent and registered office maintained under this section, and the certificate of trust filed under §3810 of this title shall reflect such information in lieu of the information otherwise required by §3810(a)(1)b. of this title.

(d) Service of process upon a registered agent maintained by a statutory trust pursuant to subsection (b) of this section shall be as effective as if served upon one of the trustees of the statutory trust pursuant to §3804 of this title.

(e) A trustee or registered agent of a statutory trust whose address, as set forth in a certificate of trust pursuant to §3810(a)(1)b. of this title, has changed may change such address in the certificates of trust of all statutory trusts for which such trustee or registered agent is appointed to another address in the State by paying a fee as set forth in §3813(a)(5) of this title and filing with the Secretary of State a certificate, executed by such trustee or registered agent, setting forth the address of such trustee or registered agent before it was changed, and further certifying as to the new address of such trustee or registered agent for each of the statutory trusts for which it is trustee or registered agent. Upon the filing of such certificate, the Secretary of State shall furnish to the trustee or registered agent a certified copy of the same under the Secretary's hand and seal of office, and thereafter, or until further change of address, as authorized by law, the address of such trustee or registered agent in the State for each of the statutory trusts for which it is trustee or registered agent shall be located at the new address of the trustee or registered agent thereof as given in the certificate. A trustee or registered agent of a statutory trust whose name, as set forth in a certificate of trust pursuant to §3810(a)(1)b. of this title, has changed may change such name in the certificates of trust of all statutory trusts for which such trustee or registered agent is appointed to its new name by paying a fee as set forth in §3813(a)(5) of this title and filing with the Secretary of State a certificate, executed by such trustee or registered agent, setting forth the name of such trustee or registered agent before it was changed and further certifying as to the new name of such trustee or registered agent for each of the statutory trusts for which it is a trustee or registered agent. Upon the filing of such certificate and payment of such fee, the Secretary of State shall furnish to the trustee or registered agent a certified copy of the certificate under the Secretary's hand and seal of office. A change of name of any person acting as a trustee or registered agent of a statutory trust as a result of a merger or consolidation of the trustee or registered agent with another person who succeeds to its assets and liabilities by operation of law shall be deemed a change of name for purposes of this section. Filing a certificate under this section shall be deemed to be an amendment of the certificate of trust of each statutory trust affected thereby, and no further action with respect thereto to amend its certificate of trust under §3810 of this title shall be required. Any trustee or registered agent filing a certificate under this section shall promptly, upon such filing, deliver a copy of any such certificate to each statutory trust affected thereby.

(f) The registered agent of 1 or more statutory trusts may resign and appoint a successor registered agent by paying a fee as set forth in §3813(a)(5) of this title and filing a certificate with the Secretary of State stating that it resigns and providing the name and address of the successor registered agent. There shall be attached to such certificate a statement of each affected statutory trust ratifying and approving such change of registered agent. Upon such filing, or upon the future effective date or time of such certificate if it is not to be effective upon filing, the successor registered agent shall become the registered agent of such statutory trusts as have ratified and approved such succession, and the successor registered agent's address, as stated in such certificate, shall become the address of each such statutory trust's registered office in the State of Delaware. The Secretary of State shall then issue a certificate that the successor registered agent has become the registered agent of the statutory trusts so ratifying and approving such change and setting out the names of such statutory trusts. Filing of such certificate of resignation shall be deemed to be an amendment to the certificate of trust of each statutory trust affected thereby, and no further action with respect thereto to amend its certificate of trust under § 3810 of this title shall be required.

(g) The registered agent of 1 or more statutory trusts may resign without appointing a successor registered agent by paying a fee as set forth in §3813(a)(5) of this title and filing a certificate of resignation with the Secretary of State, but such resignation shall not become effective until 30 days after the certificate is filed. The certificate shall contain a statement that written notice of resignation was given to each affected statutory trust at least 30 days prior to the filing of the certificate by mailing or delivering such notice to each statutory trust at its address last known to the registered agent and shall set forth the date of such notice. After receipt of the notice of the resignation of its registered agent, each statutory trust for which such registered agent was maintaining a registered office and registered agent in this State under subsection (b) of this section shall obtain and designate a new registered agent, to take the place of the registered agent so resigning, or shall appoint a trustee meeting the requirements of subsection (a) of this section. After the resignation of the registered agent shall have become effective as provided in this section and if no new registered agent shall have been obtained and designated in the time and manner aforesaid, service of legal process against each statutory trust for which the resigned registered agent had been acting shall thereafter be upon the Secretary of State in accordance with §3804 of this title.

(h) As contained in any certificate of trust, application for registration as a foreign statutory trust, or other document filed in the office of the Secretary of State under this chapter, the address of a trustee and a registered agent or registered office shall include the street, number, city and postal code. (Last amended by Ch. 114, L. '11, eff. 7-13-11.)

Ch. 114, L. '11, eff. 7-13-11, added matter in italic.

T. 12, 3808 EXISTENCE OF STATUTORY TRUST.—(a) Except to the extent otherwise provided in the governing instrument of the statutory trust, a statutory trust shall have perpetual existence, and a statutory trust may not be terminated or revoked by a beneficial owner or other person except in accordance with the terms of its governing instrument.

(b) Except to the extent otherwise provided in the governing instrument of a statutory trust, the death, incapacity, dissolution, termination or bankruptcy of a beneficial owner *or a trustee* shall not result in the termination or dissolution of a statutory trust.

(c) In the event that a statutory trust does not have perpetual existence, a statutory trust is dissolved and its affairs shall be wound up at the time or upon the happening of events specified in the governing instrument. Notwithstanding the happening of events specified in the governing instrument, the statutory trust shall not be dissolved and its affairs shall not be wound up if, prior to the filing of a certificate of cancellation as provided in §3810 of this title, the statutory trust is continued, effective as of the happening of such event, pursuant to the affirmative vote or written consent of all remaining beneficial owners of the statutory trust (and any other person whose approval is required under the governing instrument to revoke a dissolution pursuant to this section), provided, however, if the dissolution was caused by a vote or written consent, the dissolution shall not be revoked unless each beneficial owner and other person (or their respective personal representatives) who voted in favor of, or consented to, the dissolution has voted or consented in writing to continue the statutory trust.

(d) Upon dissolution of a statutory trust and until the filing of a certificate of cancellation as provided in §3810 of this title, the persons who, under the governing instrument of the statutory trust, are responsible for winding up the statutory trust's affairs may, in the name of and for and on behalf of the statutory trust, prosecute and defend suits, whether civil, criminal or administrative, gradually settle and close the statutory trust business, dispose of and convey the statutory trust property, discharge or make reasonable provision for the statutory trust liabilities and distribute to the beneficial owners any remaining assets of the statutory trust.

(e) A statutory trust which has dissolved shall pay or make reasonable provision to pay all claims and obligations, including all contingent, conditional or unmatured claims and obligations, known to the statutory trust and all claims and obligations which are known to the statutory trust but for which the identity of the claimant is unknown and claims and obligations that have not been made known to the statutory trust or that have not arisen but that, based on the facts known to the statutory trust, are likely to arise or to become known to the statutory trust within 10 years after the date of dissolution. If there are sufficient assets, such claims and obligations shall be paid in full and any such provision for payment shall be made in full. If there are sufficient assets, such claims and obligations shall be paid or provided for according to their priority and, among claims and obligations of equal priority, ratably to the extent of assets available therefor. Unless otherwise provided in the governing instrument of a statutory trust, any remaining assets shall be distributed to the beneficial owners. Any person, including any trustee, who under the governing instrument of the statutory trust is responsible for winding up a statutory trust's affairs who has complied with this subsection shall not be personally liable to the claimants of the dissolved statutory trust by reason of such person's actions in winding up the statutory trust.

(f) Except to the extent otherwise provided in the governing instrument of the statutory trust, a series established in accordance with §3804(a) of this title may be dissolved and its affairs wound up without causing the dissolution of the statutory trust or any other series thereof. Unless otherwise provided in the governing instrument of the statutory trust, the dissolution, winding up, liquidation or termination of the statutory trust or any series thereof shall not affect the limitation of liability with respect to a series established in accordance with §3804(a) of this title. A series established in accordance with §3804(a) of this title is dissolved and its affairs shall be wound up at the time or upon the happening of events specified in the governing instrument of the statutory trust. Except to the extent otherwise provided in the governing instrument of a statutory trust, the death, incapacity, dissolution, termination or bankruptcy of a beneficial owner of such series shall not result in the termination or dissolution of such series and such series may not be terminated or revoked by a beneficial owner of such series or other person except in accordance with the terms of the governing instrument of the statutory trust.

(g) Upon dissolution of a series of a statutory trust, the persons who under the governing instrument of the statutory trust are responsible for winding up such series' affairs may, in the name of the statutory trust and for and on behalf of the statutory trust and such series, take all actions with respect to the series as are permitted under subsection (d) of this section and shall provide for the claims and obligations of the series and distribute the assets of the series as provided under subsection (e) of this section. Any person, including any trustee, who under the governing instrument is responsible for winding up such series' affairs who has complied with subsection (e) of this section shall not be personally liable to the claimants of the dissolved series by reason of such person's actions in winding up the series. (Last amended by Ch. 403, L. '10, eff. 8-1-10.)

Ch. 403, L. '10, eff. 8-1-10, added matter in italic.

T. 12, 3809 APPLICABILITY OF TRUST LAW.—Except to the extent otherwise provided in the governing instrument of a [1]*statutory trust* or in this subchapter, the laws of this State pertaining to trusts are hereby made applicable to [2]*statutory trusts*; provided however, that for purposes of any tax imposed by this State or any instrumentality, agency or political subdivision of this State a [1]*statutory trust* shall be classified as a corporation, an association, a partnership, a trust or otherwise, as shall be determined under the United States Internal Revenue Code of 1986 [26 U.S. Code §1 et seq.], as amended, or under any successor provision. (Last amended by Ch. 329, L. '02, eff. 9-1-02.)

Ch. 329, L. '02, eff. 9-1-02, added matter in italic and deleted [1]"business trust" and [2]"business trusts".

T. 12, 3810 CERTIFICATE OF TRUST; AMENDMENT; RESTATEMENT; CANCELLATION.—(a)(1) Every statutory trust shall file a certificate of trust in the office of the Secretary of State. The certificate of trust shall set forth:
   a. The name of the statutory trust;
   b. The name and [1] address *in this State* of at least 1 of the trustees meeting the requirements of §3807 of this title;
   c. The future effective date or time (which shall be a date or time certain) of effectiveness of the certificate if it is not to be effective upon the filing of the certificate; and

d. Any other information the trustees determine to include therein.

(2) A statutory trust is formed at the time of the filing of the initial certificate of trust in the office of the Secretary of State or at any later date or time specified in the certificate of trust if, in either case, there has been substantial compliance with the requirements of this section. A statutory trust formed under this chapter shall be a separate legal entity, the existence of which as a separate legal entity shall continue until cancellation of the statutory trust's certificate of trust.

(3) The filing of a certificate of trust in the office of the Secretary of State shall make it unnecessary to file any other documents under Chapter 31 of Title 6.

(b)(1) A certificate of trust may be amended by filing a certificate of amendment thereto in the office of the Secretary of State. The certificate of amendment shall set forth:

a. The name of the statutory trust;
b. The amendment to the certificate; and
c. The future effective date or time (which shall be a date or time certain) of effectiveness of the certificate if it is not to be effective upon the filing of the certificate.

(2) Except to the extent otherwise provided in the certificate of trust or in the governing instrument of a statutory trust, a certificate of trust may be amended at any time for any purpose as the trustees may determine. A trustee who becomes aware that any statement in a certificate of trust was false when made or that any matter described has changed making the certificate false in any material respect shall promptly file a certificate of amendment.

(c)(1) A certificate of trust may be restated by integrating into a single instrument all the provisions of the certificate of trust which are then in effect and operative as a result of there having been theretofore filed one or more certificates of amendment pursuant to subsection (b) of this section, and the certificate of trust may be amended or further amended by the filing of a restated certificate of trust. The restated certificate of trust shall be specifically designated as such in its heading and shall set forth:

a. The present name of the statutory trust, and if it has been changed, the name under which the statutory trust was originally formed;
b. The date of filing of the original certificate of trust with the Secretary of State;
c. The information required to be included pursuant to subsection (a) of this section; and
d. Any other information the trustees determine to include therein.

(2) A certificate of trust may be restated at any time for any purpose as the trustees may determine. A trustee who becomes aware that any statement in a restated certificate of trust was false when made or that any matter described has changed making the restated certificate false in any material respect shall promptly file a certificate of amendment or a restated certificate of trust.

(d) A certificate of trust shall be cancelled upon the dissolution and the completion of winding up of a statutory trust, or [2] upon the filing of a certificate of merger or consolidation if the statutory *trust is not the surviving or resulting entity in a merger or consolidation, or upon the future effective date or time of a certificate of merger or consolidation if the* trust is not the surviving or resulting entity in a merger or consolidation, or upon the filing *of a certificate of transfer, or upon the future effective date or time* of a certificate of transfer, or upon the filing of a certificate of conversion to [3] non-Delaware other business *entity or upon the future effective date or time of a certificate of conversion to non-Delaware* entity. A certificate of cancellation shall be filed in the office of the Secretary of State and set forth;

(1) The name of the statutory trust;
(2) The date of filing of its certificate of trust;
(3) The future effective date or time (which shall be a date or time certain) of cancellation if it is not to be effective upon the filing of the certificate; and
(4) Any other information the trustee determines to include therein.

The Secretary of State shall not issue a certificate of good standing with respect to a statutory trust if its certificate of trust is cancelled.

(e) Whenever any certificate authorized to be filed with the office of the Secretary of State under this subchapter has been so filed and is an inaccurate record of the action therein referred to or was defectively or erroneously executed, such certificate may be corrected by filing with the office of the Secretary of State a certificate of correction of such certificate. The certificate of correction shall specify the inaccuracy or defect to be corrected, shall set forth the portion of the certificate in corrected form and shall be executed and filed as required by this subchapter. *The certificate of correction shall be effective as of the date the original certificate was filed, except as to those persons who are substantially and adversely affected by the correction, and as to those persons the certificate of correction shall be effective from the filing date.* In lieu of filing a certificate of correction, the certificate may be corrected by filing with the office of the Secretary of State a corrected certificate which shall be executed and filed in accordance with this subchapter. The corrected certificate shall be specifically designated as such in its heading, shall specify the inaccuracy or defect to be corrected and shall set forth the entire certificate in corrected form. The corrected certificate shall be effective as of the date the original certificate was filed, except as to those persons who are substantially and adversely affected by the corrections, and as to those persons the corrected certificate shall be effective from the filing date.

(f) If any certificate filed in accordance with this subchapter provides for a future effective date or time and if the transaction is terminated or amended to change the future effective date or time prior to the future effective date or time, the certificate shall be terminated or amended by the filing, prior to the future effective date or time set forth in such original certificate, of a certificate of termination or amendment of the original certificate, executed and filed in accordance with this subchapter, which shall identify the original certificate which has been terminated or amended and shall state that the original certificate has been terminated or amended. (Last amended by Ch. 403, L. '10, eff. 8-1-10.)

Ch. 403, L. '10, eff. 8-1-10, added matter in italic and deleted [1]"the business"; [2]"shall be deemed to be cancelled"; and [3]"a".

T. 12, 3811 EXECUTION OF CERTIFICATE.—(a) Each certificate required by this subchapter to be filed in the office of the Secretary of State shall be executed in the following manner:

(1) A certificate of trust must be signed by all of the trustees;

(2) A certificate of amendment, a certificate of correction, a corrected certificate, a certificate of termination or amendment, and a restated certificate of trust must be signed by at least one of the trustees;

(3) A certificate of cancellation must be signed by all of the trustees or as otherwise provided in the governing instrument of the statutory trust; and

(4) If a statutory trust is filing a certificate of merger or consolidation, certificate of conversion, certificate of transfer, certificate of transfer and continuance, certificate of statutory trust domestication or certificate of termination or amendment to any such certificate, the certificate of merger or consolidation, certificate of conversion, certificate of transfer, certificate of transfer and continuance, certificate of statutory trust domestication or certificate of termination or amendment to any such certificate must be signed by all of the trustees or as otherwise provided in the governing instrument of the statutory trust, or if the certificate of merger or consolidation, certificate of conversion [1], certificate of statutory trust domestication or certificate of termination or amendment to any such certificate is being filed by another business entity *or non-United States entity (as such term is defined in §3822 of this title thereof)*, the certificate of merger or consolidation, certificate of conversion [1], certificate of statutory trust domestication or certificate of termination or amendment to any such certificate must be signed by a person authorized to execute the certificate on behalf of the other business entity *or non-United States entity (as such term is defined in §3822 of this title hereof)*.

(b) Unless otherwise provided in the governing instrument, any person may sign any certificate or amendment thereof or enter into a governing instrument or amendment thereof by any agent, including any attorney-in-fact. An authorization, including a power of attorney, to sign any certificate or amendment thereof or to enter into a governing instrument or amendment thereof need not be in writing, need not be sworn to, verified or acknowledged and need not be filed in the office of the Secretary of State, but if in writing, must be retained by the statutory trust or a trustee or other person authorized to manage the business and affairs of the statutory trust.

(c) The execution of a certificate by a trustee, *or other person authorized pursuant to subsection (a) of this section above,* constitutes an oath or affirmation, under the penalties of perjury in the third degree, that, to the best of the trustee's, *or other person authorized pursuant to subsection (a) of this section above,* knowledge and belief, the facts stated therein are true. (Last amended by Ch. 403, L. '10, eff. 8-1-10.)

Ch. 403, L. '10, eff. 8-1-10, added matter in italic and deleted [1]", certificate of transfer, certificate of transfer and continuance".

T. 12, 3812 FILING OF CERTIFICATE.—(a) Any certificate authorized to be filed with the office of the Secretary of State under this subchapter (or any judicial decree of amendment or cancellation) shall be delivered to the office of the Secretary of State for filing. A person who executes a certificate as an agent or fiduciary need not exhibit evidence of the person's authority as a prerequisite to filing. Unless the Secretary of State finds that any certificate does not conform to law, upon receipt of all filing fees required by law the Secretary of State shall:

(1) Certify that the certificate (or any judicial decree of amendment or cancellation) has been filed in the Secretary of State's office by endorsing upon the filed certificate (or judicial decree) the word "filed", and the date and hour of the filing. This endorsement is conclusive of the date and time of its filing in the absence of actual fraud;

(2) File and index the endorsed certificate (or judicial decree);

(3) Prepare and return to the person who filed it or the person's representative a copy of the filed certificate (or judicial decree), similarly endorsed, and shall certify such copy as a true copy of the filed certificate (or judicial decree); and

(4) Enter such information from the certificate as the Secretary of State deems appropriate into the Delaware Corporation Information System or any system which is a successor thereto in the office of the Secretary of State, and such information shall be permanently maintained as a public record. A copy of each certificate shall be permanently maintained on optical disk or by other suitable medium.

[1] *(b) Notwithstanding any other provision of this chapter, any certificate filed in the office of the Secretary of State under this chapter shall be effective at the time of its filing with the Secretary of State or at any later date or time (not later than a time on the 180th day after the date of its filing if such date of filing is on or after January 1, 2012) specified in the certificate. Upon the effective time of a certificate of amendment (or judicial decree of amendment), certificate of correction, corrected certificate, or restated certificate, the certificate of trust shall be amended or restated as set forth therein. Upon the effective time of a certificate of cancellation (or a judicial decree thereof) or a certificate of merger or consolidation which acts as a certificate of cancellation or a certificate of transfer or a certificate of conversion to a non-Delaware entity, as provided for therein, the certificate of trust shall be canceled. Upon the effective time of a certificate of termination or amendment, the original certificate identified in the certificate of termination or amendment shall be terminated or amended, as the case may be.*

(c) A fee as set forth in §3813(a)(2) of this title shall be paid at the time of the filing of a certificate of trust, a certificate of amendment, a certificate of correction, a corrected certificate, a certificate of termination or amendment, a certificate of cancellation, a certificate of merger or consolidation, a certificate of conversion, a certificate of transfer, a certificate of transfer and continuance, a certificate of statutory trust domestication or a restated certificate.

(d) A fee as set forth in §3813(a)(3) of this title shall be paid for a certified copy of any certificate on file as provided for by this subchapter, and a fee as set forth in §3813(a)(4) of this title shall be paid for each page copied.

(e) Any signature on any certificate authorized to be filed with the Secretary of State under any provision of this subchapter may be a facsimile, a conformed signature or an electronically transmitted signature. Any such certificate may be filed by telecopy, fax or similar electronic transmission; provided, however, that the Secretary of State shall have no obligation to accept such filing if such certificate is illegible or otherwise unsuitable for processing.

(f) The fact that a certificate of trust is on file in the office of the Secretary of State is notice that the entity formed in connection with the filing of the certificate of trust is a statutory trust formed under the laws of the State and is notice of all other facts set forth therein which are required to be set forth in a certificate of trust by §3810(a)(1) of this title and is notice of the limitation on liability of a series of a statutory trust which is permitted to be set forth in a certificate of trust by §3804(a) of this title.

(g) Notwithstanding any other provision of this chapter, it shall not be necessary for any statutory trust or foreign statutory trust to amend its certificate of trust, its application for registration as a foreign statutory trust, or any other document that has been filed in the office of the Secretary of State prior to August 1, 2011, to comply with §3807(h) of this chapter; notwithstanding the foregoing, any certificate or other document filed under this

chapter on or after August 1, 2011 and changing the address of a trustee or registered agent or registered office shall comply with §3807(h) of this chapter. (Last amended by Ch. 114, L. '11, eff. 7-13-11.)

Ch. 114, L. '11, eff. 7-13-11, added matter in italic and deleted [1]"Upon the filing of a certificate of trust in the office of the Secretary of State, or upon the future effective date or time of a certificate of trust as provided for therein, the certificate of trust shall be effective. Upon the filing of a certificate of amendment (or judicial decree of amendment), certificate of correction, corrected certificate or restated certificate in the office of the Secretary of State, or upon the future effective date or time of a certificate of amendment (or judicial decree of amendment) or restated certificate as provided for therein, the certificate of trust shall be amended or restated as set forth therein. Upon the filing of a certificate of cancellation (or a judicial decree thereof) or a certificate of merger or consolidation which acts as a certificate of cancellation or a certificate of transfer or a certificate of conversion to a non-Delaware entity in the office of the Secretary of State, or upon the future effective date or time of a certificate of cancellation (or a judicial decree thereof) or a certificate of merger or consolidation which acts as a certificate of cancellation or a certificate of transfer or a certificate of conversion to a non-Delaware entity, as provided therein, the certificate of trust shall be canceled. Upon the filing of a certificate of termination or amendment, the original certificate identified in the certificate of termination or amendment shall be terminated or amended, as the case may be."

T. 12, 3813 FEES.—(a) No documents required to be filed under this subchapter shall be effective until the applicable fee required by this section is paid. The following fees shall be paid to and collected by the Secretary of State for the use of this State:

(1) Upon the receipt for filing of an application for reservation of name, and application for renewal of reservation, or notice of transfer or cancellation of reservation pursuant to §3814 of this title, a fee in the amount of $75.

(2) Upon the receipt for filing of a certificate of trust, a certificate of amendment, a certificate of cancellation or a certificate of merger or consolidation, a certificate of correction, a corrected certificate, a certificate of conversion, a certificate of transfer, a certificate of transfer and continuance, a certificate of statutory trust domestication, a certificate of termination or amendment or a restated certificate, a fee in the amount of up to $300.

(3) For certifying copies of any paper on file as provided for by this subchapter, a fee in the amount of $50 for each copy certified.

(4) For issuing further copies of instruments on file, whether certified or not, a fee in the amount of $10 for the first page and $2 for each additional page.

(5) Upon the receipt for filing of a certificate under §3807(e) of this title, a fee in the amount of $200, *upon the receipt for filing of a certificate under §3807(f) of this title, a fee in the amount of $200, and upon the receipt for filing of a certificate under §3807(g) of this title, a fee in the amount of $2.00 for each statutory trust whose registered agent has resigned by such certificate.*

(6) For issuing any certificate of the Secretary of State, including but not limited to a certificate of good standing, other than a certification of a copy under paragraph (a)(3) of this section, a fee in the amount of $50, except that for issuing any certificate of the Secretary of State that recites all of a statutory trust's filings with the Secretary of State, a fee of $175 shall be paid for each such certificate.

(b) In addition to those fees charged under subsection (a) of this section, there shall be collected by and paid to the Secretary of State the following:

(1) For all services described in subsection (a) of this section that are requested to be completed within 30 minutes on the same day as the day of the request, an additional sum of up to $7,500 and for all services described in subsection (a) of this section that are requested to completed within 1 hour on the same day as the day of the request, an additional sum of up to $1,000 and for all services described in subsection (a) of this section that are requested to be completed within 2 hours on the same day as the day of the request, an additional sum of up to $500; and

(2) For all services described in subsection (a) of this section that are requested to be completed within the same day as the day of the request, an additional sum of up to $300; and

(3) For all services described in subsection (a) of this section that are requested to be completed within a 24-hour period from the time of the request, an additional sum of up to $150.

The Secretary of State shall establish (and may from time to time alter or amend) a schedule of specific fees payable pursuant to this subsection.

(c) Except as provided by this section, all other fees for the Secretary of State shall be as provided for in §2315 of Title 29. (Last amended by Ch. 114, L. '11, eff. 7-13-11.)

Ch. 114, L. '11, eff. 7-13-11, added matter in italic.

T. 12, 3814 USE OF NAMES REGULATED.—(a) The name of each statutory trust as set forth in its certificate of trust must be such as to distinguish it upon the records of the office of the Secretary of State from the name of any corporation, partnership, limited partnership, statutory trust or limited liability company reserved, registered, formed or organized under the laws of this State or qualified to do business or registered as a foreign corporation, foreign partnership, foreign limited partnership, foreign statutory trust or foreign limited liability company in this State; provided, however, that a statutory trust may register under any name which is not such as to distinguish it upon the records of the office of the Secretary of State from the name of any domestic or foreign corporation, partnership, limited partnership, *or foreign* statutory trust or limited liability company reserved, registered, formed or organized under the laws of this State with the written consent of the other corporation, partnership, limited partnership, *foreign* statutory trust or limited liability company, which written consent shall be filed with the Secretary of State; *provided further, that, if on July 31, 2011 a statutory trust is registered (with the consent of another statutory trust) under a name which is not such as to distinguish it upon the records in the office of the Secretary of State from the name on such records of such other domestic statutory trust, it shall not be necessary for any such statutory trust to amend its certificate of trust to comply with this subsection.*

(b) The name of each statutory trust as set forth in its Certificate of Trust may contain the name of a beneficial owner, a trustee or any other person.

(c) The name of each statutory trust as set forth in its Certificate of Trust may contain the following words: "Company", "Association", "Club", "Foundation", "Fund", "Institute", "Society", "Union", "Syndicate", "Limited", or "Trust" (or abbreviations of like import).

(d) The exclusive right to the use of a name may be reserved by:

(1) Any person intending to form a statutory trust and to adopt that name; and

(2) Any statutory trust registered in this State which proposes to change its name.

(e) The reservation of a specified name shall be made by filing with the Secretary of State an application, executed by the applicant, together with a duplicate copy, which may either be a signed or conformed copy, specifying the name to be reserved and the name and address of the applicant. If the Secretary of State finds that the name is available for use by a statutory trust, the Secretary shall reserve the name for the exclusive use of the applicant for a period of 120 days. Once having so reserved a name, the same applicant may again reserve the same name for successive 120-day periods. The right to the exclusive use of a reserved name may be transferred to any other person by filing in the Office of the Secretary of State a notice of the transfer, executed by the applicant for whom the name was reserved, together with a duplicate copy, which may be either a signed or conformed copy, specifying the name to be transferred and the name and address of the transferee. The reservation of a specified name may be cancelled by filing with the Secretary of State a notice of cancellation, executed by the applicant or transferee, together with a duplicate copy, which may be either a signed or conformed copy, specifying the name reservation to be cancelled and the name and address of the applicant or transferee. Any duplicate copy filed with the Secretary of State, as required by this subsection, shall be returned by the Secretary of State to the person who filed it or that person's representative with a notation thereon of the action taken with respect to the original copy thereof by the Secretary of State.

(f) Fees as set forth in §3813 of this title shall be paid at the time of the initial reservation of any name, at the time of the renewal of any such reservation and at the time of the filing of a notice of the transfer or cancellation of any such reservation. (Last amended by Ch. 114, L. '11, eff. 7-13-11.)

Ch. 114, L. '11, eff. 7-13-11, added matter in italic.

T. 12, 3815 MERGER AND CONSOLIDATION.—(a) Pursuant to an agreement of merger or consolidation, a statutory trust may merge or consolidate with or into 1 or more statutory trusts or other business entities formed or organized or existing under the laws of the State or any other state or the United States or any foreign country or other foreign jurisdiction, with such statutory trust or other business entity as the agreement shall provide being the surviving or resulting statutory trust or other business entity. Unless otherwise provided in the governing instrument of a statutory trust, a merger or consolidation shall be approved by each statutory trust which is to merge or consolidate by all of the trustees and the beneficial owners of such statutory trust. In connection with a merger or consolidation hereunder, rights or securities of, or interests in, a statutory trust or other business entity which is a constituent party to the merger or consolidation may be exchanged for or converted into cash, property, rights or securities of, or interests in, the surviving or resulting statutory trust or other business entity or, in addition to or in lieu thereof, may be exchanged for or converted into cash, property, rights or securities of, or interests in, a statutory trust or other business entity which is not the surviving or resulting statutory trust or other business entity in the merger or consolidation. Notwithstanding prior approval, an agreement of merger or consolidation may be terminated or amended pursuant to a provision for such termination or amendment contained in the agreement of merger or consolidation or may be cancelled. Notwithstanding prior approval, an agreement of merger or consolidation may be terminated or amended pursuant to a provision for such termination or amendment contained in the agreement of merger or consolidation.

(b) If a statutory trust is merging or consolidating under this section, the statutory trust or other business entity surviving or resulting in or from the merger or consolidation shall file a certificate of merger or consolidation in the office of the Secretary of State. The certificate of merger or consolidation shall state:

(1) The name and jurisdiction of formation or organization of each of the statutory trust or other business entities which is to merge or consolidate;

(2) That an agreement of merger or consolidation has been approved and executed by each of the statutory trusts or other business entities which is to merge or consolidate;

(3) The name of the surviving or resulting statutory trust or other business entity;

(4) In the case of a merger in which a statutory trust is the surviving entity, such amendments, if any, to the certificate of trust of the surviving statutory trust to change its name, registered office or registered agent as are desired to be effected by the merger;

(5) The future effective date or time (which shall be a date or time certain) of the merger or consolidation if it is not to be effective upon the filing of the certificate of merger or consolidation;

(6) That the executed agreement of merger or consolidation is on file at the principal place of business of the surviving or resulting statutory trust or other business entity, and shall state the address thereof;

(7) That a copy of the agreement of merger or consolidation will be furnished by the surviving or resulting statutory trust or other business entity, on request and without cost, to any beneficial owner of any statutory trust or any person holding an interest in any other business entity which is to merge or consolidate; and

(8) If the surviving or resulting entity is not a statutory trust or other business entity formed or organized or existing under the laws of the State of Delaware, a statement that such surviving or resulting other business entity agrees that it may be served with process in the State in any action, suit or proceeding for the enforcement of any obligation of any statutory trust which is to merge or consolidate, irrevocably appointing the Secretary of State as its agent to accept service of process in any such action, suit or proceeding and specifying the address to which a copy of such process shall be mailed to it by the Secretary of State. Process may be served upon the Secretary of State under this subsection by means of electronic transmission but only as prescribed by the Secretary of State. The Secretary of State is authorized to issue such rules and regulations with respect to such service as the Secretary of State deems necessary or appropriate. In the event of service hereunder upon the Secretary of State, the plaintiff in any such action, suit or proceeding shall furnish the Secretary of State with the address specified in the certificate of merger or consolidation provided for in this section and any other address which the plaintiff may elect to furnish, together with copies of such process as required by the Secretary of State, and the Secretary of State shall notify such surviving or resulting other business entity thereof at all such addresses furnished by the plaintiff by letter. Such letter shall be sent by a mail or courier service that includes a record of mailing or deposit with the courier and a record of delivery evidenced by the signature of the recipient. Such letter shall enclose a copy of the process and any other papers served upon the Secretary of State. It shall be the duty of the plaintiff in the event of such service to serve process and any other papers in duplicate, to notify the Secretary of State that service is being made pursuant to this subsection, and to pay the Secretary of State the sum of $50 for use of the State, which sum shall be taxed as part of the

costs in the proceeding, if the plaintiff shall prevail therein. The Secretary of State shall maintain an alphabetical record of any such process setting forth the name of the plaintiff and defendant, the title, docket number and nature of the proceedings in which process has been served upon the Secretary, the return date thereof, and the day and hour when the service was made. The Secretary of State shall not be required to retain such information for a period longer than 5 years from the Secretary's receipt of the service of process.

(c) Any failure to file a certificate of merger or consolidation in connection with a merger or consolidation which was effective prior to July 5, 1990 shall not affect the validity or effectiveness of any such merger or consolidation.

(d) Unless a future effective date or time is provided in a certificate of merger or consolidation, in which event a merger or consolidation shall be effective at any such future effective date or time, a merger or consolidation shall be effective upon the filing in the office of the Secretary of State of a certificate of merger or consolidation.

(e) A certificate of merger or consolidation shall act as a certificate of cancellation for a statutory trust which is not the surviving or resulting entity in the merger or consolidation. A certificate of merger that sets forth any amendment in accordance with subsection (b)(4) of this section shall be deemed to be an amendment to the certificate of trust of the statutory trust, and the statutory trust shall not be required to take any further action to amend its certificate of trust under §3810 of this title with respect to such amendments set forth in the certificate of merger. Whenever this section requires the filing of a certificate of merger or consolidation, such requirement shall be deemed satisfied by the filing of an agreement of merger or consolidation containing the information required by this section to be set forth in the certificate of merger or consolidation.

(f) Notwithstanding anything to the contrary contained in the governing instrument of a statutory trust, [1] an agreement of merger or consolidation approved in accordance with subsection (a) of this section may:

(1) Effect any amendment to the governing instrument of the statutory trust; or

(2) Effect the adoption of a new governing instrument of the statutory trust if it is the surviving or resulting statutory trust in the merger or consolidation.

Any amendment to the governing instrument of a statutory trust or adoption of a new governing instrument of the statutory trust made pursuant to the foregoing sentence shall be effective at the effective time or date of the merger or consolidation and shall be effective notwithstanding any provision of the governing instrument relating to amendment or adoption of a new governing instrument, other than a provision that by its terms applies to an amendment to the governing instrument or the adoption of a new governing instrument, in either case, in connection with a merger or consolidation. The provisions of this subsection shall not be construed to limit the accomplishment of a merger or consolidation or of any of the matters referred to herein by any other means provided for in the governing instrument of a statutory trust or other agreement or as otherwise permitted by law, including that the governing instrument of any constituent statutory trust to the merger or consolidation (including a statutory trust formed for the purpose of consummating a merger or consolidation) shall be the governing instrument of the surviving or resulting statutory trust. Unless otherwise provided in a governing instrument, a statutory trust whose original certificate of trust was filed with the Secretary of State and effective on or prior to July 31, 2010, shall continue to be governed by this subsection as in effect on July 31, 2010.

(g) When any merger or consolidation shall have become effective under this section, for all purposes of the laws of the State, all of the rights, privileges and powers of each of the statutory trusts and other business entities that have merged or consolidated, and all property, real, personal and mixed, and all debts due to any of said statutory trusts and other business entities, as well as all other things and causes of action belonging to each of such statutory trusts and other business entities, shall be vested in the surviving or resulting statutory trust or other business entity, and shall thereafter be the property of the surviving or resulting statutory trust or other business entity as they were of each of the statutory trusts and other business entities that have merged or consolidated, and the title to any real property vested by deed or otherwise, under the laws of the State, in any of such statutory trusts and other business entities, shall not revert or be in any way impaired by reason of this subchapter; but all rights of creditors and all liens upon any property of any of said statutory trusts and other business entities shall be preserved unimpaired, and all debts, liabilities and duties of each of the said statutory trusts and other business entities that have merged or consolidated shall thenceforth attach to the surviving or resulting statutory trust or other business entity, and may be enforced against it to the same extent as if said debts, liabilities and duties had been incurred or contracted by it. Unless otherwise agreed, a merger or consolidation of a statutory trust, including a statutory trust which is not the surviving or resulting entity in the merger or consolidation, shall not require such statutory trust to wind up its affairs under §3808(d) of this title or pay any of its liabilities and distribute its assets under §3808(e) of this title, and the merger or consolidation shall not constitute the dissolution of such statutory trust.

(h) A governing instrument or an agreement of merger or consolidation may provide that contractual appraisal rights with respect to a beneficial interest or another interest in a statutory trust shall be available for any class, group or series of beneficial owners or beneficial interests in connection with any amendment of a governing instrument, any merger or consolidation in which the statutory trust is a constituent party to the merger or consolidation or the sale of all or substantially all of the statutory trust's assets. The Court of Chancery shall have jurisdiction to hear and determine any matter relating to any such appraisal rights.

(i) A governing instrument may provide that a statutory trust shall not have the power to merge or consolidate as set forth in this section. (Last amended by Ch. 114, L. '11, eff. 7-13-11.)

Ch. 114, L. '11, eff. 7-13-11, added matter in italic and deleted [1]"a governing instrument of a statutory trust may provide that".

T. 12, 3816 DERIVATIVE ACTIONS.—(a) A beneficial owner may bring an action in the Court of Chancery in the right of a [1]*statutory trust* to recover a judgment in its favor if trustees with authority to do so have refused to bring the action or if an effort to cause those trustees to bring the action is not likely to succeed.

(b) In a derivative action, the plaintiff must be a beneficial owner at the time of bringing the action and:

(1) At the time of the transaction of which the plaintiff complains; or

(2) Plaintiff's status as a beneficial owner had devolved upon plaintiff by operation of law or pursuant to the terms of the governing instrument of the [1]*statutory trust* from a person who was a beneficial owner at the time of the transaction.

(c) In a derivative action, the complaint shall set forth with particularity the effort, if any, of the plaintiff to secure initiation of the action by the trustees, or the reasons for not making the effort.

(d) If a derivative action is successful, in whole or in part, or if anything is received by a [1]*statutory trust* as a result of a judgment, compromise or settlement of any such action, the Court may award the plaintiff reasonable expenses, including reasonable attorney's fees. If anything is so received by the plaintiff, the Court shall make such award of plaintiff's expenses payable out of those proceeds and direct plaintiff to remit to the [1]*statutory trust* the remainder thereof, and if those proceeds are insufficient to reimburse plaintiff's reasonable expenses, the Court may direct that any such award of plaintiff's expenses or a portion thereof be paid by the [1]*statutory trust*.

(e) A beneficial owner's right to bring a derivative action may be subject to such additional standards and restrictions, if any, as are set forth in the governing instrument of the [1]*statutory trust*, including, without limitation, the requirement that beneficial owners owning a specified beneficial interest in the [1]*statutory trust* join in the bringing of the derivative action. (Last amended by Ch. 329, L. '02, eff. 9-1-02.)

Ch. 329, L. '02, eff. 9-1-02, added matter in italic and deleted [1]"business trust".

T. 12, 3817 INDEMNIFICATION.—(a) Subject to such standards and restrictions, if any, as are set forth in the governing instrument of a [1]*statutory trust*, a [1]*statutory trust* shall have the power to indemnify and hold harmless any trustee or beneficial owner or other person from and against any and all claims and demands whatsoever.

(b) The absence of a provision for indemnity in the governing instrument of a [1]*statutory trust* shall not be construed to deprive any trustee or beneficial owner or other person of any right to indemnity which is otherwise available to such person under the laws of this State. (Last amended by Ch. 329, L. '02, eff. 9-1-02.)

Ch. 329, L. '02, eff. 9-1-02, added matter in italic and deleted [1]"business trust".

T. 12, 3818 TREASURY INTERESTS.—Except to the extent otherwise provided in the governing instrument of a *statutory trust*, a *statutory trust* may acquire, by purchase, redemption or otherwise, any beneficial interest in the *statutory trust* held by a beneficial owner of the *statutory trust*. Except to the extent otherwise provided in the governing instrument of a *statutory trust*, any such interest so acquired by a *statutory trust* shall be deemed canceled. (Last amended by Ch. 329, L. '02, eff. 9-1-02.)

Ch. 329, L. '02, eff. 9-1-02, added matter in italic and deleted [1]"business trust".

T. 12, 3819 ACCESS TO AND CONFIDENTIALITY OF INFORMATION; RECORDS.—(a) Except to the extent otherwise provided in the governing instrument of a *statutory trust*, each beneficial owner of a *statutory trust* has the right, subject to such reasonable standards (including standards governing what information and documents are to be furnished at what time and location and at whose expense) as may be established by the trustees, to obtain from the *statutory trust* from time to time upon reasonable demand for any purpose reasonably related to the beneficial owner's interest as a beneficial owner of the *statutory trust*:

(1) A copy of the governing instrument and certificate of trust and all amendments thereto, together with copies of any written powers of attorney pursuant to which the governing instrument and any certificate and any amendments thereto have been executed;

(2) A current list of the name and last known business, residence or mailing address of each beneficial owner and trustee;

(3) Information regarding the business and financial condition of the *statutory trust*; and

(4) Other information regarding the affairs of the *statutory trust* as is just and reasonable.

(b) Except to the extent otherwise provided in the governing instrument of a *statutory trust*, each trustee shall have the right to examine all the information described in subsection (a) of this section for any purpose reasonably related to the trustee's position as a trustee.

(c) Except to the extent otherwise provided in the governing instrument of a *statutory trust*, the trustees of a *statutory trust* shall have the right to keep confidential from the beneficial owners, for such period of time as the trustees deem reasonable, any information that the trustees reasonably believe to be in the nature of trade secrets or other information, the disclosure of which the trustees in good faith believe is not in the best interest of the *statutory trust* or could damage the *statutory trust* or its business or which the *statutory trust* is required by law or by agreement with a third party to keep confidential.

(d) A *statutory trust* may maintain its records in other than a written form if such form is capable of conversion into a written form within a reasonable time.

(e) Any demand by a beneficial owner or trustee under this section shall be in writing and shall state the purpose of such demand. (Last amended by Ch. 329, L. '02, eff. 9-1-02.)

Ch. 329, L. '02, eff. 9-1-02, added matter in italic and deleted [1]"business trust".

T. 12, 3820 CONVERSION OF OTHER BUSINESS ENTITIES TO A STATUTORY TRUST.—(a) Any other business entity formed or organized or existing under the laws of the State or any other state or the United States or any foreign country or other foreign jurisdiction may convert to a statutory trust by complying with subsection (g) of this section and filing in the Office of the Secretary of State in accordance with §3812 of this title:

(1) A certificate of conversion to statutory trust that has been executed in accordance with §3811 of this title; and

(2) A certificate of trust that complies with §3810 of this title and has been executed in accordance with §3811 of this title.

(b) The certificate of conversion to statutory trust shall state:

(1) The date on which and jurisdiction where the other business entity was first formed or organized or otherwise came into being and, if it has changed, its jurisdiction immediately prior to its conversion to a statutory trust;

(2) The name of the other business entity immediately prior to the filing of the certificate of conversion to statutory trust;

(3) The name of the statutory trust as set forth in its certificate of trust filed in accordance with subsection (a) of this section; and

(2) The name of the other business entity immediately prior to the filing of the certificate of conversion to statutory trust;

(3) The name of the statutory trust as set forth in its certificate of trust filed in accordance with subsection (a) of this section; and

(4) The future effective date or time (which shall be a date or time certain) of the conversion to a statutory trust if it is not to be effective upon the filing of the certificate of conversion to statutory trust and the certificate of trust.

(c) Upon the filing in the Office of the Secretary of State of the certificate of conversion to statutory trust and the certificate of trust or upon the future effective date or time of the certificate of conversion to statutory trust and the certificate of trust, the other business entity shall be converted into a statutory trust and the statutory trust shall thereafter be subject to all of the provisions of this title, except that notwithstanding §3810(a)(2) of this title, the existence of the statutory trust shall be deemed to have commenced on the date the other business entity commenced its existence in the jurisdiction in which the other business entity was first formed or organized or otherwise came into being.

(d) The conversion of any other business entity into a statutory trust shall not be deemed to affect any obligations or liabilities of the other business entity incurred prior to its conversion to a statutory trust, or the personal liability of any person incurred prior to such conversion.

(e) When any conversion shall have become effective under this section, for all purposes of the laws of the State, all of the rights, privileges and powers of the other business entity that has converted, and all property, real, personal and mixed, and all debts due to such other business entity, as well as all other things and causes of action belonging to such other business entity, shall remain vested in the statutory trust to which such other business entity has converted and shall be the property of such statutory trust, and the title to any real property vested by deed or otherwise in such other business entity shall not revert or be in any way impaired by reason of this chapter; but all rights of creditors and all liens upon any property of such other business entity shall be preserved unimpaired, and all debts, liabilities and duties of the other business entity that has converted shall remain attached to the statutory trust to which such other business entity has converted, and may be enforced against it to the same extent as if said debts, liabilities and duties had been incurred or contracted by it in its capacity as a statutory trust. The rights, privileges, powers and interests in property of the other business entity, as well as the debts, liabilities and duties of the other business entity, shall not be deemed, as a consequence of the conversion, to have been transferred to the statutory trust to which such other business entity has converted for any purpose of the laws of the State.

(f) Unless otherwise agreed, for all purposes of the laws of the State of Delaware, the converting other business entity shall not be required to wind up its affairs or pay its liabilities and distribute its assets, and the conversion shall not be deemed to constitute a dissolution of such other business entity and shall constitute a continuation of the existence of the converting other business entity in the form of a statutory trust. When the other business entity has been converted to a statutory trust pursuant to this section, the statutory trust shall, for all purposes of the laws of the State, be deemed to be the same entity as the converting other business entity.

(g) Prior to filing a certificate of conversion to statutory trust with the Office of the Secretary of State, the conversion shall be approved in the manner provided for by the document, instrument, agreement or other writing, as the case may be, governing the internal affairs of the other business entity and the conduct of its business or by applicable law, as appropriate, and a governing instrument shall be approved by the same authorization required to approve the conversion.

(h) This section shall not be construed to limit the accomplishment of a change in the law governing, or the domicile of, any other business entity to the State by any other means provided for in an agreement governing the internal affairs of the other business entity or as otherwise permitted by law, including by the amendment of an agreement governing the internal affairs of the other business entity.

(i) In connection with a conversion hereunder, rights or securities of or interests in the other business entity which is to be converted to a statutory trust may be exchanged for or converted into cash, property, rights or securities of, or interests in, such statutory trust or, in addition to or in lieu thereof, may be exchanged for or converted into cash, property, rights or securities of, or interests in, another statutory trust or other business entity or may be cancelled. (Last amended by Ch. 114, L. '11, eff. 7-13-11.)

> Ch. 114, L. '11, eff. 7-13-11, added matter in italic.

T. 12, 3821 CONVERSION OF A STATUTORY TRUST.—(a) Upon compliance with this section, a statutory trust may convert to an other business entity.

(b) If the governing instrument specifies the manner of authorizing a conversion of the statutory trust, the conversion shall be authorized as specified in the governing instrument. If the governing instrument does not specify the manner of authorizing a conversion of the statutory trust and does not prohibit a conversion of the statutory trust, the conversion shall be authorized in the same manner as is specified in the governing instrument for authorizing a merger or consolidation that involves the statutory trust as a constituent party to the merger or consolidation. If the governing instrument does not specify the manner of authorizing a conversion of the statutory trust or a merger or consolidation that involves the statutory trust as a constituent party and does not prohibit a conversion of the statutory trust, the conversion shall be authorized by the approval by all of the beneficial owners and all of the trustees.

(c) Unless otherwise agreed, the conversion of a statutory trust to an other business entity pursuant to this section shall not require such statutory trust to wind up its affairs under §3808 of this title or pay its liabilities and distribute its assets under §3808 of this title.

(d) In connection with a conversion of a statutory trust to an other business entity pursuant to this section, rights or securities of, or interests in, the statutory trust which is to be converted may be exchanged for or converted into cash, property, rights or securities of, or interests in, the other business entity into which the statutory trust is being converted or, in addition to or in lieu thereof, may be exchanged for or converted into cash, property, rights or securities of, or interests in, any other business entity or may be cancelled.

(e) If a statutory trust shall convert in accordance with this section to an other business entity organized, formed or created under the laws of a jurisdiction other than the State of Delaware, a certificate of conversion to a non-Delaware entity executed in accordance with §3811 of this title, shall be filed in the Office of the Secretary of State in accordance with §3812 of this title. The certificate of conversion to a non-Delaware entity shall state:

(1) The name of the statutory trust and, if it has been changed, the name under which its certificate of trust was originally filed;

(2) The date of filing of its original certificate of trust with the Secretary of State;

(3) The jurisdiction in which the other business entity, to which the statutory trust shall be converted, is organized, formed or created;

(4) The future effective date or time (which shall be a date or time certain) of the conversion if it is not to be effective upon the filing of the certificate of conversion to a non-Delaware entity;

(5) That the conversion has been approved in accordance with this section;

(6) The agreement of the statutory trust that it may be served with process in the State of Delaware in any action, suit or proceeding for enforcement of any obligation of the statutory trust arising while it was a statutory trust of the State of Delaware, and that it irrevocably appoints the Secretary of State as its agent to accept service of process in any such action, suit or proceeding;

(7) The address to which a copy of the process referred to in subsection (e)(6) of this section shall be mailed to it by the Secretary of State. *Process may be served upon the Secretary of State under paragraph (e)(6) of this section by means of electronic transmission but only as prescribed by the Secretary of State. The Secretary of State is authorized to issue such rules and regulations with respect to such service as the Secretary of State deems necessary or appropriate.* In the event of service under this section upon the Secretary of State, the procedures set forth in §3861(c) of this title shall be applicable, except that the plaintiff in any such action, suit or proceeding shall furnish the Secretary of State with the address specified in this subsection and any other address that the plaintiff may elect to furnish, together with copies of such process as required by the Secretary of State, and the Secretary of State shall notify the statutory trust that has converted out of

the State of Delaware at all such addresses furnished by the plaintiff in accordance with the procedures set forth in §3861(c) of this title.

(f) Upon the filing in the Office of the Secretary of State of the certificate of conversion to a non-Delaware entity or upon the future effective date or time of the certificate of conversion to a non-Delaware entity and payment to the Secretary of State of all fees prescribed in this chapter, the Secretary of State shall certify that the statutory trust has filed all documents and paid all fees required by this chapter, and thereupon the statutory trust shall cease to exist as a statutory trust of the State of Delaware. Such certificate of the Secretary of State shall be prima facie evidence of the conversion by such statutory trust out of the State of Delaware.

(g) The conversion of a statutory trust out of the State of Delaware in accordance with this section and the resulting cessation of its existence as a statutory trust of the State of Delaware pursuant to a certificate of conversion to a non-Delaware entity shall not be deemed to affect any obligations or liabilities of the statutory trust incurred prior to such conversion or the personal liability of any person incurred prior to such conversion, nor shall it be deemed to affect the choice of law applicable to the statutory trust with respect to matters arising prior to such conversion.

(h) When a statutory trust has been converted to an other business entity pursuant to this section, the other business entity shall, for all purposes of the laws of the State of Delaware, be deemed to be the same entity as the statutory trust. When any conversion becomes effective under this section, for all purposes of the laws of the State of Delaware, all of the rights, privileges and powers of the statutory trust that has converted, and all property, real, personal and mixed, and all debts due to such statutory trust, as well as all other things and causes of action belonging to such statutory trust, shall remain vested in the other business entity to which such statutory trust has converted and shall be the property of such other business entity, and the title to any real property vested by deed or otherwise in such statutory trust shall not revert or be in any way impaired by reason of this chapter; but all rights of creditors and all liens upon any property of such statutory trust shall be preserved unimpaired, and all debts, liabilities and duties of the statutory trust that has converted shall remain attached to the other business entity to which such statutory trust has converted, and may be enforced against it to the same extent as if said debts, liabilities and duties had originally been incurred or contracted by it in its capacity as such other business entity. The rights, privileges, powers and interests in property of the statutory trust that has converted, as well as the debts, liabilities and duties of such statutory trust, shall not be deemed, as a consequence of the conversion, to have been transferred to the other business entity to which such statutory trust has converted for any purpose of the laws of the State of Delaware.

(i) A governing instrument may provide that a statutory trust shall not have the power to convert as set forth in this section. (Last amended by Ch. 403, L. '10, eff. 8-1-10.)

Ch. 403, L. '10, eff. 8-1-10, added matter in italic.

T. 12, 3822 DOMESTICATION OF NON-UNITED STATES ENTITIES.— (a) As used in this section, "non-United States entity" means a foreign statutory trust (other than one formed under the laws of a state), or a corporation, a limited liability company, a business trust or association, a real estate investment trust, a common-law trust, or any other unincorporated business, including a partnership (whether general (including a limited liability partnership) or limited (including a limited liability limited partnership)), formed, incorporated, created or that otherwise came into being under the laws of any foreign country or other foreign jurisdiction (other than any state).

(b) Any non-United States entity may become domesticated as a statutory trust in the State of Delaware by complying with subsection (g) of this section and filing in the Office of the Secretary of State in accordance with §3812 of this title:

(1) A certificate of statutory trust domestication that has been executed in accordance with §3811 of this title; and

(2) A certificate of trust that complies with §3810 of this title and has been executed in accordance with §3811 of this title.

Each of the certificates required by this subsection (b) shall be filed simultaneously in the office of the Secretary of State and, if such certificates are not to become effective upon their filing as permitted by §3812(b) of this title, then each such certificate shall provide for the same effective date or time in accordance with §3812(b) of this title.

(c) The certificate of statutory trust domestication shall state:

(1) The date on which and jurisdiction where the non-United States entity was first formed, incorporated, created or otherwise came into being;

(2) The name of the non-United States entity immediately prior to the filing of the certificate of statutory trust domestication;

(3) The name of the statutory trust as set forth in the certificate of trust filed in accordance with subsection (b) of this section;

(4) The future effective date or time (which shall be a date or time certain) of the domestication as a statutory trust if it is not to be effective upon the filing of the certificate of statutory trust domestication and the certificate of trust; and

(5) The jurisdiction that constituted the seat, siege social, or principal place of business or central administration of the non-United States entity, or any other equivalent thereto under applicable law, immediately prior to the filing of the certificate of statutory trust domestication.

(d) Upon the filing in the Office of the Secretary of State of the certificate of statutory trust domestication and the certificate of trust or upon the future effective date or time of the certificate of statutory trust domestication and the certificate of trust, the non-United States entity shall be domesticated as a statutory trust in the State of Delaware and the statutory trust shall thereafter be subject to all of the provisions of this chapter, except that notwithstanding §3810(a)(2) of this title, the existence of the statutory trust shall be deemed to have commenced on the date the non-United States entity commenced its existence in the jurisdiction in which the non-United States entity was first formed, incorporated, created or otherwise came into being.

(e) The domestication of any non-United States entity as a statutory trust in the State of Delaware shall not be deemed to affect any obligations or liabilities of the non-United States entity incurred prior to its domestication as a statutory trust in the State of Delaware, or the personal liability of any person therefor.

(f) The filing of a certificate of statutory trust domestication shall not affect the choice of law applicable to the non-United States entity, except that from the effective date or time of the domestication, the law of the State of Delaware, including the provisions of this chapter, shall apply to the non-United States entity to the same extent as if the non-United States entity had been formed as a statutory trust on that date.

(g) Prior to filing a certificate of statutory trust domestication with the Office of the Secretary of State, the domestication shall be approved in the manner provided for by the document, instrument, agreement or other writing, as the case may be, governing the internal affairs of the non-United States entity and the conduct of its business or by applicable non-Delaware law, as appropriate, and a governing instrument shall be approved by the same authorization required to approve the domestication.

(h) When any domestication shall have become effective under this section, for all purposes of the laws of the State of Delaware, all of the rights, privileges and powers of the non-United States entity that has been domesticated, and all property, real, personal and mixed, and all debts due to such non-United States entity, as well as all other things and causes of action belonging to such non-United States entity, shall remain vested in the domestic statutory trust to which such non-United States entity has been domesticated and shall be the property of such domestic statutory trust, and the title to any real property vested by deed or otherwise in such non-United States entity shall not revert or be in any way impaired by reason of this chapter; but all rights of creditors and all liens upon any property of such non-United States entity shall be preserved unimpaired, and all debts, liabilities and duties of the non-United States entity that has been domesticated shall remain attached to the domestic statutory trust to which such non-United States entity has been domesticated, and may be enforced against it to the same extent as if said debts, liabilities and duties had originally been incurred or contracted by it in its capacity as a domestic statutory trust. The rights, privileges, powers and interests in property of the non-United States entity, as well as the debts, liabilities and duties of the non-United States entity, shall not be deemed, as a consequence of the domestication, to have been transferred to the domestic statutory trust to which such non-United States entity has domesticated for any purpose of the laws of the State of Delaware.

(i) When a non-United States entity has become domesticated as a statutory trust pursuant to this section, the statutory trust shall, for all purposes of the laws of the State of Delaware, be deemed to be the same entity as the domesticating non-United States entity. Unless otherwise agreed, for all purposes of the laws of the State of Delaware, the domesticating non-United States entity shall not be required to wind up its affairs or pay its liabilities and distribute its assets, and the domestication shall not be deemed to constitute a dissolution of such non-United States entity and shall constitute a continuation of the existence of the domesticating non-United States entity in the form of a domestic statutory trust. If, following domestication, a non-United States entity that has become domesticated as a statutory trust continues its existence in the foreign country or other foreign jurisdiction in which it was existing immediately prior to domestication, the statutory trust and such non-United States entity shall, for all purposes of the laws of the State of Delaware, constitute a single entity formed, incorporated, created or otherwise having come into being, as applicable, and existing under the laws of the State of Delaware and the laws of such foreign country or other foreign jurisdiction.

(j) In connection with a domestication hereunder, rights or securities of, or interests in, the non-United States entity that is to be domesticated as a domestic statutory trust may be exchanged for or converted into cash, property, rights or securities of, or interests in, such domestic statutory trust or, in addition to or in lieu thereof, may be exchanged for or converted into cash, property, rights or securities of, or interests in, an other domestic statutory trust or other entity or may be cancelled. (Last amended by Ch. 114, L. '11, eff. 7-13-11.)

Ch. 114, L. '11, eff. 7-13-11, added matter in italic.

T. 12, 3823 TRANSFER OR CONTINUANCE OF DOMESTIC STATUTORY TRUSTS.—(a) Upon compliance with the provisions of this section, any statutory trust may transfer to or domesticate in any jurisdiction, other than any state, and, in connection therewith, may elect to continue its existence as a statutory trust in the State of Delaware.

(b) If the governing instrument specifies the manner of authorizing a transfer or domestication or continuance described in (a) of this section, the transfer or domestication or continuance shall be authorized as specified in the governing instrument. If the governing instrument does not specify the manner of authorizing a transfer or domestication or continuance described in (a) of this section and does not prohibit such a transfer or domestication or continuance, the transfer or domestication or continuance shall be authorized in the same manner as is specified in the governing instrument for authorizing a merger or consolidation that involves the statutory trust as a constituent party to the merger or consolidation. If the governing instrument does not specify the manner of authorizing a transfer or domestication or continuance described in (a) of this section or a merger or consolidation that involves the statutory trust as a constituent party and does not prohibit such a transfer or domestication or continuance, the transfer or domestication or continuance shall be authorized by the approval by all of the beneficial owners and all of the trustees. If a transfer or domestication or continuance described in (a) of this section shall be approved as provided in this subsection (b) of this section, a certificate of transfer if the statutory trust's existence as a statutory trust of the State of Delaware is to cease, or a certificate of transfer and continuance if the statutory trust's existence as a statutory trust in the State of Delaware is to continue, executed in accordance with §3811 of this title, shall be filed in the Office of the Secretary of State in accordance with §3812 of this title. The certificate of transfer or the certificate of transfer and continuance shall state:

(1) The name of the statutory trust and, if it has been changed, the name under which its certificate of trust was originally filed;

(2) The date of the filing of its original certificate of trust with the Secretary of State;

(3) The jurisdiction to which the statutory trust shall be transferred or in which it shall be domesticated;

(4) The future effective date or time (which shall be a date or time certain) of the transfer or domestication to the jurisdiction specified in subsection (b)(3) of this section if it is not to be effective upon the filing of the certificate of transfer or the certificate of transfer and continuance;

(5) That the transfer or domestication or continuance of the statutory trust has been approved in accordance with the provisions of this section;

(6) In the case of a certificate of transfer:

a. That the existence of the statutory trust as a statutory trust of the State of Delaware shall cease when the certificate of transfer becomes effective; and

b. The agreement of the statutory trust that it may be served with process in the State of Delaware in any action, suit or proceeding for enforcement of any obligation of the statutory trust arising while it was a statutory trust of the State of Delaware, and that it irrevocably appoints the Secretary of State as its agent to accept service of process in any such action, suit or proceeding;

(7) The address to which a copy of the process referred to in paragraph (b)(6) of this section shall be mailed to it by the Secretary of State. *Process may be served upon the Secretary of State under paragraph (b)(6) of this section by means of electronic transmission but only as prescribed by the Secretary of State. The Secretary of State is authorized to issue such rules and regulations with respect to such service as the Secretary of State deems necessary or appropriate.* In the event of service under this section upon the Secretary of State, the procedures set forth in §3861(c) of this title shall be applicable, except that the plaintiff in any such action, suit or proceeding shall furnish the Secretary of State with the address specified in this subsection and any other address that the plaintiff may elect to furnish, together with copies of such process as required by the Secretary of State, and the Secretary of State shall notify the statutory trust that has transferred or domesticated out of the State of Delaware at all such addresses furnished by the plaintiff in accordance with the procedures set forth in §3861(c) of this title; and

(8) In the case of a certificate of transfer and continuance, that the statutory trust will continue to exist as a statutory trust of the State of Delaware after the certificate of transfer and continuance becomes effective.

(c) Upon the filing in the Office of the Secretary of State of the certificate of transfer or upon the future effective date or time of the certificate of transfer and payment to the Secretary of State of all fees prescribed in this chapter, the Secretary of State shall certify that the statutory trust has filed all documents and paid all fees required by this chapter, and thereupon the statutory trust shall cease to exist as a statutory trust of the State of Delaware. Such certificate of the Secretary of State shall be prima facie evidence of the transfer or domestication by such statutory trust out of the State of Delaware.

(d) The transfer or domestication of a statutory trust out of the State of Delaware in accordance with this section and the resulting cessation of its existence as a statutory trust of the State of Delaware pursuant to a certificate of transfer shall not be deemed to affect any obligations or liabilities of the statutory trust incurred prior to such transfer or domestication or the personal liability of any person incurred prior to such transfer or domestication, nor shall it be deemed to affect the choice of law applicable to the statutory trust with respect to matters arising prior to such transfer or domestication. Unless otherwise agreed, the transfer or domestication of a statutory trust out of the State of Delaware in accordance with this section shall not require such statutory trust to wind up its affairs or pay its liabilities and distribute its assets under §3808 of this title.

(e) If a statutory trust files a certificate of transfer and continuance, after the time the certificate of transfer and continuance becomes effective, the statutory trust shall continue to exist as a statutory trust of the State of Delaware, and the laws of the State of Delaware, including the provisions of this chapter, shall apply to the statutory trust, to the same extent as prior to such time. So long as a statutory trust continues to exist as a statutory trust of the State of Delaware following the filing of a certificate of transfer and continuance, the continuing statutory trust and the other business entity formed, incorporated, created or that otherwise came into being as a consequence of the transfer of the statutory trust to, or its domestication in, a foreign country or other foreign jurisdiction shall, for all purposes of the laws of the State of Delaware, constitute a single entity formed, incorporated, created or otherwise having come into being, as applicable, and existing under the laws of the State of Delaware and the laws of such foreign country or other foreign jurisdiction.

(f) In connection with a transfer or domestication of a statutory trust to or in another jurisdiction pursuant to subsection (a) of this section, rights or securities of, or interests in, such statutory trust may be exchanged for or converted into cash, property, rights or securities of, or interests in, the other business entity in which the statutory trust will exist in such other jurisdiction as a consequence of the transfer or domestication or, in addition to or in lieu thereof, may be exchanged for or converted into cash, property, rights or securities of, or interests in, any other business entity or may be cancelled.

(g) When a statutory trust has transferred or domesticated out of the State of Delaware pursuant to this section, the transferred or domesticated other business entity shall, for all purposes of the laws of the State of Delaware, be deemed to be the same entity as the statutory trust. When any transfer or domestication of a statutory trust out of the State of Delaware shall have become effective under this section, for all purposes of the laws of the State of Delaware, all of the rights, privileges and powers of the statutory trust that has transferred or domesticated, and all property, real, personal and mixed, and all debts due to such statutory trust, as well as all other things and causes of action belonging to such statutory trust, shall remain vested in the transferred or domesticated other business entity and shall be the property of such transferred or domesticated other business entity, and the title to any real property vested by deed or otherwise in such statutory trust shall not revert or be in any way impaired by reason of this chapter; but all rights of creditors and all liens upon any property of such statutory trust shall be preserved unimpaired, and all debts, liabilities and duties of the statutory trust that has transferred or domesticated shall remain attached to the transferred or domesticated other business entity, and may be enforced against it to the same extent as if said debts, liabilities and duties had originally been incurred or contracted by it in its capacity as the transferred or domesticated other business entity. The rights, privileges, powers and interests in property of the statutory trust that has transferred or domesticated, as well as the debts, liabilities and duties of such statutory trust, shall not be deemed, as a consequence of the transfer or domestication out of the State of Delaware, to have been transferred to the transferred or domesticated other business entity for any purpose of the laws of the State of Delaware.

(h) A governing instrument may provide that a statutory trust shall not have the power to transfer, domesticate or continue as set forth in this section. (Last amended by Ch. 403, L. '10, eff. 8-1-10.)

Ch. 403, L. '10, eff. 8-1-10, added matter in italic.

T. 12, 3824 RESERVED POWER OF STATE TO AMEND OR REPEAL CHAPTER.—All provisions of this subchapter may be altered from time to time or repealed and all rights of statutory trusts, trustees, beneficial owners and other persons are subject to this reservation. Unless expressly stated to the contrary in this chapter, all amendments of this chapter shall apply to business trusts, trustees, beneficial owners and other persons whether or not existing as at the time of the enactment of any such amendment. (Last amended by Ch. 353, L. '04, eff. 8-1-04.)

Ch. 353, L. '04, eff. 8-1-04, renumbered section 3822 as section 3824.

T. 12, 3825 CONSTRUCTION AND APPLICATION OF CHAPTER AND GOVERNING INSTRUMENT.—(a) The rule that statutes in derogation of the common law are to be strictly construed shall have no application to this subchapter.

(b) It is the policy of this subchapter to give maximum effect to the principle of freedom of contract and to the enforceability of governing instruments.

(c) Action validly taken pursuant to 1 provision of this chapter shall not be deemed invalid solely because it is identical or similar in substance to an action that could have been taken pursuant to some other provision of this chapter but fails to satisfy 1 or more requirements prescribed by such other provision. (Last amended by Ch. 403, L. '10, eff. 8-1-10.)

Ch. 403, L. '10, eff. 8-1-10, added matter in italic.

T. 12, 3826 SHORT TITLE.—This subchapter may be cited as the "Delaware Statutory Trust Act." (Last amended Ch. 353, L. '04, eff. 8-1-04.)

Ch. 353, L. '04, eff. 8-1-04, renumbered section 3824 as section 3826.

Subchapter II. Foreign Statutory Trusts

(Added by Ch. 335, L. '98, eff. 6-29-98. The amendments by Ch. 329, L. '02, eff. 9-1-02 were made for the purpose of avoiding any implication that a trust formed under Chapter 38, Title 12 of the Delaware Code constitutes a "business trust" within the meaning of Title 11 of the United States Code. Such amendments are not intended to result in any substantive change in Delaware law.)

T. 12, 3851 LAW GOVERNING.—Subject to the Constitution of the State:

(1) The laws of the state, territory, possession or other jurisdiction or country under which a foreign [1]*statutory trust* is organized govern its organization and internal affairs and the liability of its beneficial owners and trustees; and

(2) A foreign [1]*statutory trust* may not be denied registration by reason of any difference between those laws and the laws of the State. (Last amended by Ch. 329, L. '02, eff. 9-1-02.)

Ch. 329, L. '02, eff. 9-1-02, added matter in italic and deleted [1]"business trust".

T. 12, 3852 REGISTRATION REQUIRED; APPLICATION.—(a) Before doing business in the State, a foreign statutory trust shall register with the Secretary of State. In order to register, a foreign statutory trust shall submit to the Secretary of State:

(1) A copy executed by a trustee or other authorized person of an application for registration as a foreign statutory trust, setting forth:

a. The name of the foreign statutory trust and, if different, the name under which it proposes to register and do business in the State;

b. The state, territory, possession or other jurisdiction or country where formed, the date of its formation and a statement from a trustee or other authorized person that, as of the date of filing, the foreign statutory trust validly exists as a statutory trust under the laws of the jurisdiction of its formation;

c. The nature of the business or purposes to be conducted or promoted in the State;

d. The address of the registered office and the name and address of the registered agent for service of process required to be maintained by §3854(b) of this title;

e. A statement that the Secretary of State is appointed the agent of the trust for service of process under the circumstances set forth in §3860(b) of this title; and

f. The date on which the foreign statutory trust first did, or intends to do, business in the State.

(2) *A certificate, as of a date not earlier than 6 months prior to the filing date, issued by an authorized officer of the jurisdiction of its formation evidencing its existence. If such certificate is in a foreign language, a translation thereof, under oath of the translator, shall be attached thereto.*

[1] *(3)* A fee as set forth in §3862 of this title shall be paid.

(b) If a foreign statutory trust that is registering to do business in the State of Delaware in accordance with §3852(a) of this title is governed by a governing instrument that establishes or provides for the establishment of designated series of trustees, beneficial owners, beneficial interests or assets having separate rights, powers or duties with respect to specified property or obligations of the foreign statutory trust or profits and losses associated with specified property or obligations, that fact shall be so stated on the application for registration as a foreign statutory trust. In addition, the foreign statutory trust shall state on such application whether the debts, liabilities and obligations incurred, contracted for or otherwise existing with respect to a particular series, if any, shall be enforceable against the assets of such series only, and not against the assets of the foreign statutory trust generally or any other series thereof, and whether any of the debts, liabilities, obligations and expenses incurred, contracted for or otherwise existing with respect to the foreign statutory trust generally or any series thereof shall be enforceable against the assets of such series. (Last amended by Ch. 403, L. '10, eff. 8-1-10.)

Ch. 403, L. '10, eff. 8-1-10, added matter in italic and deleted [1]"(2)".

T. 12, 3853 ISSUANCE OF REGISTRATION.—(a) If the Secretary of State finds that an application for registration conforms to law and all requisite fees have been paid, the Secretary of State shall:

(1) Certify that the application has been filed in the Secretary of State's office by endorsing upon the original application the word "Filed", and the date and hour of the filing. This endorsement is conclusive of the date and time of its filing in the absence of actual fraud;

(2) File and index the endorsed application.

(b) The Secretary of State shall prepare and return to the person who filed the application or the person's representative a copy of the original signed application, similarly endorsed, and shall certify such copy as a true copy of the original signed application.

(c) The filing of the application with the Secretary of State shall make it unnecessary to file any other documents under Chapter 31 of this title. (Last amended by Ch. 186, L. '95, eff. 7-10-95.)

T. 12, 3854 NAME; REGISTERED OFFICE; REGISTERED AGENT.—(a) A foreign statutory trust may register with the Secretary of State under any name (whether or not it is the name under which it is registered in the jurisdiction of its formation) that could be registered by a domestic statutory trust; provided, however, that a foreign statutory trust may register under any name which is not such as to distinguish it upon the records in the Office of the Secretary of State from the name on such records of any domestic or foreign corporation, partnership, statutory trust, limited liability company or limited partnership reserved, registered, formed or organized under the laws of the State with the written consent of the other corporation, partnership, statutory trust, limited liability company or limited partnership, which written consent shall be filed with the Secretary of State.

(b) Each foreign statutory trust shall have and maintain in the State:

(1) A registered office which may but need not be a place of its business in the State; and

[1](2) *A registered agent for service of process on the foreign statutory trust, having a business office identical with such registered office which agent may be any of:*

a. *An individual resident of the State of Delaware,*

b. *A domestic limited liability company, a domestic corporation, a domestic partnership (whether general (including a limited liability partnership) or limited (including a limited liability limited partnership)), or a domestic statutory trust; or*

c. *A foreign corporation, a foreign partnership (whether general (including a limited liability partnership) or limited (including a limited liability limited partnership)), a foreign limited liability company or a foreign statutory trust (other than the foreign statutory trust itself).*

(c) A registered agent may change the address of the registered office of the foreign statutory trust or trusts for which [2] *the agent* is registered agent to another address in the State by paying a fee as set forth in §3862 of this title and filing with the Secretary of State a certificate, executed by such registered agent, setting forth the address at which such registered agent has maintained the registered office for each of the foreign statutory trusts for which it is a registered agent and further certifying to the new address to which each such registered office will be changed on a given day and at which new address such registered agent will thereafter maintain the registered office for each of the foreign statutory trusts for which it is registered agent. Upon the filing of such certificate, the Secretary of State shall furnish to the registered agent a certified copy of the same under the Secretary's hand and seal of office, and thereafter, or until further change of address, as authorized by law the registered offices in the State each of the foreign statutory trusts for which the agent is registered agent shall be located at the new address of the registered agent thereof as given in the certificate. In the event of a change of name of any person acting as a registered agent of a foreign statutory trust, such registered agent shall file with the Secretary of State a certificate, executed by such registered agent, setting forth the new name of such registered agent, the name of such registered agent before it was changed, and the address at which such registered agent has maintained the registered office for each of the foreign statutory trusts for which it is registered agent, and shall pay a fee as set forth in §3862 of this title. Upon the filing of such certificate, the Secretary of State shall furnish to the registered agent a certified copy of the same under the Secretary's hand and seal of office. A change of name of any person acting as a registered agent of a foreign statutory trust as a result of the merger or consolidation of the registered agent, with or into another person which succeeds to its assets and liabilities by operation of law, shall be deemed a change of name for purposes of this section. Filing a certificate under this section shall be deemed to be an amendment of the application of each foreign statutory trust affected thereby, and each foreign statutory trust shall not be required to take any further action with respect thereto to amend its application under §3855 of this title.

Any registered agent filing a certificate under this section shall promptly, upon such filing, deliver a copy of any such certificate to each foreign statutory trust affected thereby.

(d) The registered agent of 1 or more foreign statutory trusts may resign and appoint a successor registered agent by paying a fee as set forth in §3862 of this chapter and filing a certificate with the Secretary of State, stating that it resigns and the name and address of the successor registered agent. There shall be attached to such certificate a statement of each affected foreign statutory trust ratifying and approving such change of registered agent. Upon such filing, the successor registered agent shall become the registered agent of such foreign statutory trust as has ratified and approved such substitution and the successor registered agent's address, as stated in such certificate, shall become the address of each such foreign statutory trust's registered office in the State. The Secretary of State shall then issue a certificate that the successor registered agent has become the registered agent of the foreign statutory trusts so ratifying and approving such change and setting out the names of such foreign statutory trusts. Filing of such certificate of resignation shall be deemed to be an amendment of the application of each foreign statutory trust affected thereby and each such foreign statutory trust shall not be required to take any further action with respect thereto, to amend its application under §3855 of this title.

(e) The registered agent of one or more foreign statutory trusts may resign without appointing a successor registered agent by paying a fee as set forth in §3862 of this title and filing a certificate of resignation with the Secretary of State, but such resignation shall not become effective until 30 days after the certificate is filed. The certificate shall contain a statement that written notice of resignation was given to each affected foreign statutory trust at least 30 days prior to the filing of the certificate by mailing or delivering such notice to the foreign statutory trust at its address last known to the registered agent and shall set forth the date of such notice. After receipt of the notice of the resignation of its registered agent, the foreign statutory trust for which such registered agent was acting shall obtain and designate a new registered agent, to take the place of the registered agent so resigning. If such foreign statutory trust fails to obtain and designate a new registered agent as aforesaid prior to the expiration of the period of 30 days after the filing by the registered agent of the certificate of resignation, such foreign statutory trust shall not be permitted to do business in the State and its registration [3] to be canceled. After the resignation of the registered agent shall have become effective as provided in this section and if no new registered agent shall have been obtained and designated in the time and manner aforesaid, service of legal process against the foreign statutory trust for which the resigned registered agent had been acting shall thereafter be upon the Secretary of State in accordance with §3861 of this title. (Last amended by Ch. 403, L. '10, eff. 8-1-10.)

Ch. 403, L. '10, eff. 8-1-10, added matter in italic and deleted [1]"A registered agent for service of process on the foreign statutory trust, which agent may be either an individual resident of the State whose business office is identical with the foreign statutory trust's registered office, or a domestic corporation, or a domestic limited partnership, or a statutory trust, or a domestic limited liability company, or a foreign corporation, or a foreign limited partnership, or a foreign statutory trust, or a foreign limited liability company authorized to do business in the State having a business office identical with such registered office, which is generally open during normal business hours to accept service of process and otherwise perform the functions of a registered agent."; [2]"he"; and [3]"shall be deemed".

T. 12, 3855 AMENDMENTS TO APPLICATION.—If any statement in the application for registration of a foreign [1]*statutory trust* was false when made or any arrangements or other facts described have changed, making the application false in any respect, the foreign [1]*statutory trust* shall promptly file in the Office of the Secretary of State a certificate, executed by a trustee or other authorized person, correcting such statement, together with a fee as set forth in §3862 of this title. (Last amended by Ch. 329, L. '02, eff. 9-1-02.)

Ch. 329, L. '02, eff. 9-1-02, added matter in italic and deleted [1]"business trust".

T. 12, 3856 CANCELLATION OF REGISTRATION.—A foreign [1]*statutory trust* may cancel its registration by filing with the Secretary of State a certificate of cancellation, executed by a trustee or other authorized person, together with a fee as set forth in §3862 of this title. A cancellation does not terminate the authority of the Secretary of State to accept service of process on the foreign [1]*statutory trust* with respect to causes of action arising out of the doing of business in the State. (Last amended by Ch. 329, L. '02, eff. 9-1-02.)

Ch. 329, L. '02, eff. 9-1-02, added matter in italic and deleted [1]"business trust".

T. 12, 3857 DOING BUSINESS WITHOUT REGISTRATION.—(a) A foreign ¹*statutory trust* doing business in the State may not maintain any action, suit or proceeding in the State until it has registered in the State, and has paid to the State all fees and penalties for the years or parts thereof, during which it did business in the State without having registered.

(b) The failure of a foreign ¹*statutory trust* to register in the State does not:
(1) Impair the validity of any contract or act of the foreign ¹ *statutory trust*;
(2) Impair the right of any other party to the contract to maintain any action, suit or proceeding on the contract; or
(3) Prevent the foreign ¹*statutory trust* from defending any action, suit or proceeding in any court of the State.

(c) A beneficial owner or a trustee of a foreign ¹*statutory trust* is not liable for the obligations of the foreign ¹*statutory trust* solely by reason of the ²*statutory trust's* having done business in the State without registration.

(d) Any foreign ¹*statutory trust* doing business in the State without first having registered shall be fined and shall pay to the Secretary of State $200 for each year or part thereof during which the foreign ¹*statutory trust* failed to register in the State. (Last amended by Ch. 329, L. '02, eff. 9-1-02.)

Ch. 329, L. '02, eff. 9-1-02, added matter in italic and deleted ¹"business trust" and ²"business trust's".

T. 12, 3858 FOREIGN STATUTORY TRUSTS DOING BUSINESS WITHOUT HAVING QUALIFIED; INJUNCTIONS.—The Court of Chancery shall have jurisdiction to enjoin any foreign ¹*statutory trust*, or any agent thereof, from doing any business in the State if such foreign ¹*statutory trust* has failed to register under this subchapter or if such foreign ¹*statutory trust* has secured a certificate of the Secretary of State under §3853 of this title on the basis of false or misleading representations. The Attorney General shall, upon the Attorney General's own motion or upon the relation of proper parties, proceed for this purpose by complaint in any county in which such foreign ¹*statutory trust* is doing or has done business. (Last amended by Ch. 329, L. '02, eff. 9-1-02.)

Ch. 329, L. '02, eff. 9-1-02, added matter in italic and deleted ¹"business trust".

T. 12, 3859 EXECUTION; LIABILITY.—Section 3811(c) of this title shall be applicable to foreign ¹*statutory trusts* as if they were domestic ¹*statutory trusts*. (Last amended by Ch. 329, L. '02, eff. 9-1-02.)

Ch. 329, L. '02, eff. 9-1-02, added matter in italic and deleted ¹"business trusts".

T. 12, 3860 SERVICE OF PROCESS ON REGISTERED FOREIGN STATUTORY TRUSTS.—(a) Service of legal process upon any foreign statutory trust shall be made by delivering a copy personally to any trustee of the foreign statutory trust in the State or the registered agent of the foreign statutory trust in the State, or by leaving it at the dwelling house or usual place of abode in the State of any such trustee or registered agent (if the registered agent be an individual), or at the registered office or other place of business of the foreign statutory trust in the State. If the registered agent be a corporation, service of process upon it as such may be made by serving, in the State, a copy thereof on the president, vice-president, secretary, assistant secretary or any director of the corporate registered agent. Service by copy left at the dwelling house or usual place of abode of any trustee or registered agent, or at the registered office or other place of business of the foreign statutory trust in the State, to be effective must be delivered thereat at least 6 days before the return date of the process, and in the presence of an adult person, and the officer serving the process shall distinctly state the manner of service in the officer's return thereto. Process returnable forthwith must be delivered personally to the trustee or registered agent.

(b) ¹ *In case the officer whose duty it is to serve legal process cannot by due diligence serve the process in any manner provided for by subsection (a) of this section, it shall be lawful to serve the process against the foreign statutory trust upon the Secretary of State, and such service shall be as effectual for all intents and purposes as if made in any of the ways provided for in subsection (a) of this section. Process may be served upon the Secretary of State under this subsection by means of electronic transmission but only as prescribed by the Secretary of State. The Secretary of State is authorized to issue such rules and regulations with respect to such service as the Secretary of State deems necessary or appropriate. In* the event that service is effected through the Secretary of State in accordance with this subsection, the Secretary of State shall forthwith notify the foreign statutory trust by letter, directed to the foreign statutory trust at its last registered office. Such letter shall be sent by a mail or courier service that includes a record of mailing or deposit with the courier and a record of delivery evidenced by the signature of the recipient. Such letter shall enclose a copy of the process and any other papers served on the Secretary of State pursuant to this subsection. It shall be the duty of the plaintiff in the event of such service to serve process and any other papers in duplicate, to notify the Secretary of State that service is being effected pursuant to this subsection, and to pay to the Secretary of State the sum of $50 for the use of the State, which sum shall be taxed as a part of the costs in the proceeding if the plaintiff shall prevail therein. The Secretary of State shall maintain an alphabetical record of any such service setting forth the name of the plaintiff and defendant, the title, docket number and nature of the proceeding in which process has been served upon the Secretary of State, the fact that service has been effected pursuant to this subsection, the return date thereof and the day and hour when the service was made. The Secretary of State shall not be required to retain such information for a period longer than 5 years from receipt of the service of process. (Last amended by Ch. 403, L. '10, eff. 8-1-10.)

Ch. 403, L. '10, eff. 8-1-10, added matter in italic and deleted [1]"In case the officer whose duty it is to serve legal process cannot by due diligence serve the process in any manner provided for by subsection (a) of this section, it shall be lawful to serve the process against the foreign statutory trust upon the Secretary of State, and such service shall be as effectual for all intents and purposes as if made in any of the ways provided for in subsection (a) of this section. In the event service is effected through the Secretary of State in accordance with this subsection, the Secretary of State shall forthwith notify the foreign statutory trust by letter, certified mail, return receipt requested, directed to the foreign statutory trust at its last registered office."

T. 12, 3861 SERVICE OF PROCESS ON UNREGISTERED FOREIGN STATUTORY TRUSTS.—(a) Any foreign statutory trust which shall do business in the State without having registered under §3852 of this title shall be deemed to have thereby appointed and constituted the Secretary of State of the State its agent for the acceptance of legal process in any civil action, suit or proceeding against it in any state or federal court in the State arising or growing out of any business done by it within the State. The doing of business in the State by such foreign statutory trust shall be a signification of the agreement of such foreign statutory trust that any such process when so served shall be of the same legal force and validity as if served upon an authorized manager or agent personally within the State. *Process may be served upon the Secretary of State under this subsection by means of electronic transmission but only as prescribed by the Secretary of State. The Secretary of State is authorized to issue such rules and regulations with respect to such service as the Secretary of State deems necessary or appropriate.*

(b) Whenever the words "doing business," "the doing of business" or "business done in this State" by any such foreign statutory trust are used in this section, they shall mean the course or practice of carrying on any business activities in the State, including, without limiting the generality of the foregoing, the solicitation of business or orders in the State; provided, however such words shall be deemed to have the same meaning as similar words of like import in §371 of Title 8, but the requirement of such foreign statutory trust to register under §3852 of this title shall be subject to the same exceptions as are set forth in §373 of Title 8.

(c) In the event of service upon the Secretary of State in accordance with subsection (a) of this section, the Secretary of State shall forthwith notify the foreign statutory trust thereof by letter, [1] directed to the foreign statutory trust at the address furnished to the Secretary of State by the plaintiff in such action, suit or proceeding. *Such letter shall be sent by a mail or courier service that includes a record of mailing or deposit with the courier and a record of delivery evidenced by the signature of the recipient.* Such letter shall enclose a copy of the process and any other papers served upon the Secretary of State. It shall be the duty of the plaintiff in the event of such service to serve process and any other papers in duplicate, to notify the Secretary of State that service is being made pursuant to this subsection, and to pay to the Secretary of State the sum of $50 for the use of the State, which sum shall be taxed as part of the costs in the proceeding, if the plaintiff shall prevail therein. The Secretary of State shall maintain an alphabetical record of any such process setting forth the name of the plaintiff and defendant, the title, docket number and nature of the proceeding in which process has been served upon the Secretary of State, the return date thereof, and the day and hour when the service was made.

The Secretary of State shall not be required to retain such information for a period longer than 5 years from receipt of the service of process. (Last amended by Ch. 403, L. '10, eff. 8-1-10.)

Ch. 403, L. '10, eff. 8-1-10, added matter in italic and deleted [1]"certified mail, return receipt requested,".

T. 12, 3862 FEES.—No document required to be filed under this subchapter shall be effective until the applicable fee required by this section is paid. The following fees shall be paid to and collected by the Secretary of State for the use of the State:

(1) Upon receipt for filing of an application for registration as a foreign statutory trust under §3852 of this title, a certificate under §3855 of this title or a certificate of cancellation under §3856 of this title, a fee in amount of up to $300 together with such fees for services as may be authorized pursuant to §3813(b) of this title.

[1] *(2) Upon the receipt for filing of a certificate under §3854(c) of this title, a fee in the amount of $200, upon the receipt for filing of a certificate under §3854(d) of this title, a fee in the amount of $200, and upon the receipt for filing of a certificate under §3854(e) of this title, a fee in the amount of $2.00 for each statutory trust whose registered agent has resigned by such certificate.* (Last amended by Ch. 114, L. '11, eff. 7-13-11.)

Ch. 114, L. '11, eff. 7-13-11, added matter in italic and deleted [1]"(2) Upon the receipt for filing of a certificate under §3854(c) of this title, a fee in the amount of $50, upon the receipt for filing of a certificate under §3854(d) of this title, a fee in the amount of $50 and a further fee of $2 for each foreign statutory trust affected by such certificate, and upon the receipt for filing of a certificate under §3854(e) of this title, a fee in the amount of $2.50."

T. 12, 3863 ACTIVITIES NOT CONSTITUTING DOING BUSINESS.—
(a) Activities of a foreign statutory trust in the State of Delaware that do not constitute doing business for the purpose of this chapter include:

(1) Maintaining, defending or settling an action or proceeding;

(2) Holding meetings of its beneficial owners or trustees or carrying on any other activity concerning its internal affairs;

(3) Maintaining bank accounts;

(4) Maintaining offices or agencies for the transfer, exchange or registration of the statutory trust's own securities or maintaining trustees or depositories with respect to those securities;

(5) Selling through independent contractors;

(6) Soliciting or obtaining orders, whether by mail or through employees or agents or otherwise, if the orders require acceptance outside the State of Delaware before they become contracts;

(7) Selling, by contract consummated outside the State of Delaware, and agreeing, by the contract, to deliver into the State of Delaware, machinery, plants or equipment, the construction, erection or installation of which within the State of Delaware requires the supervision of technical engineers or skilled employees performing services not generally available, and as part of the contract of sale agreeing to furnish such services, and such services only, to the vendee at the time of construction, erection or installation;

(8) Creating, as borrower or lender, or acquiring indebtedness with or without a mortgage or other security interest in property;

(9) Collecting debts or foreclosing mortgages or other security interests in property securing the debts, and holding, protecting and maintaining property so acquired;

(10) Conducting an isolated transaction that is not one in the course of similar transactions;

(11) Doing business in interstate commerce; and

(12) Doing business in the State of Delaware as an insurance company.

(b) A person shall not be deemed to be doing business in the State of Delaware solely by reason of being a beneficial owner or trustee of a domestic statutory trust or a foreign statutory trust.

(c) This section does not apply in determining whether a foreign statutory trust is subject to service or process, taxation or regulation under any other law of the State of Delaware. (Added by Ch. 418, L. '06, eff. 8-1-06.)

[The page following this is Corp.—801]

DELAWARE CODE

Below are reproduced selected sections of the law relating to corporations not found in the General Corporation Law.

TITLE 6. COMMERCE AND TRADE

Chapter 21. Antitrust

T. 6, 2103 RESTRAINT OF TRADE UNLAWFUL.—Every contract, combination in the form of trust or otherwise, or conspiracy, in restraint of trade or commerce of this State shall be unlawful. (Added by Ch. 89, L. '79, eff. 1-3-80.)

T. 6, 2107 ACTIONS BY ATTORNEY GENERAL FOR VIOLATIONS; CIVIL PENALTY; EQUITABLE RELIEF.—The Attorney General may bring an action for any violation or threatened violation of this chapter. In any such action, the Court may assess against each defendant a civil penalty for the benefit of the State of not less than $1,000 nor more than $100,000 for each violation, or may award appropriate equitable relief, or may order a combination of civil penalty and equitable relief. (Added by Ch. 89, L. '79, eff. 1-3-80.)

T. 6, 2108 ACTIONS FOR EQUITABLE RELIEF AND DAMAGES; SUITS PARENS PATRIAE.—(a) If the State or any public body thereof is threatened with injury or injured in its business or property by a violation of this chapter, the Attorney General may bring an action for appropriate equitable relief, damages sustained and, as determined by the Court, taxable costs, and reasonable fees for expert witnesses and attorneys, including the Attorney General.

(b) The Attorney General may bring suit as parens patriae on behalf of natural persons residing in this State to secure monetary relief for such persons who are injured in their business or property by a violation of this chapter. The Court may also award taxable costs, and reasonable fees for expert witnesses and attorneys, including the Attorney General.

(c) In actions under this section, the Court may, in its discretion, award as monetary relief up to threefold the total damage sustained, in addition to costs and fees, provided that the Court finds the acts complained of to have been wilful.

(d) Monetary relief awarded under subsection (b) of this section may be payable to the State or may be distributed in such manner as the Court in its discretion may authorize.

(e) In any action brought under subsection (b) of this section, the Attorney General shall, at such times, in such manner, and with such content as the Court may direct, cause notice thereof to be given by publication. If the Court finds that notice given solely by publication would deny due process of law to any person or persons, the Court may direct further notice to such person or persons according to the circumstances of the case.

(f) Any person on whose behalf an action is brought under subsection (b) of this section may elect to exclude from adjudication the portion of the state claim for monetary relief attributable to the person by filing notice of such election with the Court in the manner specified in the notice given pursuant to subsection (e) of this section. The final judgment in any action under subsection (b) of this section shall be res judicata as to any claim under this chapter by any person on behalf of whom such action was brought and who fails to give notice of exclusion in the manner specified in this subsection.

(g) In any action brought under subsection (b) of this section, the Court shall exclude from the amount of any monetary relief awarded any amount which duplicates an award made by any court for the same injury, or which is allocable to persons excluded under subsection (f) of this section. (Last amended by Ch. 186, L. '95, eff. 7-10-95.)

Chapter 23. Interest

T. 6, 2306 DEFENSE OF USURY AS AVAILABLE TO CERTAIN ENTITIES AND ASSOCIATIONS.—No corporation, limited partnership, statutory trust, business trust or limited liability company, and no association or joint stock company having any of the powers and privileges of corporations not possessed by individuals or partnerships, shall interpose the defense of usury in any action. (Last amended by Ch. 329, L. '02, eff. 9-1-02.)

Chapter 27. Contracts

T. 6, 2708 CHOICE OF LAW.—(a) The parties to any contract, agreement or other undertaking, contingent or otherwise, may agree in writing that the contract, agreement or other undertaking shall be governed by or construed under the laws of this State, without regard to principles of conflict of laws, or that the laws of this State shall govern, in whole or in part, any or all of their rights, remedies, liabilities, powers and duties if the parties, either as provided by law or in the manner specified in such writing are, (i) subject to the jurisdiction of the courts of, or arbitration in, Delaware and, (ii) may be served with legal process. The foregoing shall conclusively be presumed to be a significant, material and reasonable relationship with this State and shall be enforced whether or not there are other relationships with this State.

(b) Any person may maintain an action in a court of competent jurisdiction in this State where the action or proceeding arises out of or relates to any contract, agreement or other undertaking for which a choice of Delaware law has been made in whole or in part and which contains the provision permitted by subsection (a) of this section.

(c) This section shall not apply to any contract, agreement or other undertaking, (i) to the extent provided to the contrary in §1-301(c) of this title, or, (ii) involving less than $100,000.

(d) In the event that any provision hereof shall be held to be invalid or unenforceable, such holding shall not invalidate or render unenforceable any other provision hereof. Any provision hereof which is held to be invalid or unenforceable only in part or degree or under specific facts, shall remain in full force and effect to the extent, and with respect to facts in connection with which, it has not been held to be invalid or unenforceable.

(e) This section shall not limit any jurisdiction otherwise existing in a court sitting in the State and shall not affect the validity of any other choice of law provisions in any contract, agreement or other undertaking. (Last amended by Ch. 66, L. '05, eff. 6-28-05.)

Chapter 77. Voluntary Alternative Dispute Resolution
(Added by Ch. 151, L. '95, eff. 10-1-95.)

T. 6, 7701 SHORT TITLE; PURPOSE.—(a) This chapter shall be known and may be cited as the "Delaware Voluntary Alternative Dispute Resolution Act."

(b) The purposes of the Delaware Voluntary Alternative Dispute Resolution Act are to provide a means to resolve business disputes without litigation and to permit parties to agree, prior to any disputes arising between them, to utilize alternative dispute resolution techniques if a dispute occurs. An interpretation of the provisions of this chapter shall seek to achieve these purposes.

T. 6, 7702 DEFINITIONS.—As used in this chapter, unless the context otherwise requires:

(a) "ADR" means the alternative dispute resolution method provided for by this chapter unless the parties to a dispute adopt by written agreement some other method of ADR in which event "ADR" shall refer to the method they adopt.

(b) A "dispute subject to ADR" means any dispute that (1) involves at least $100,000 in contention, and (2) is not a summary proceeding under §§211, 215, 220 or 225 of Title 8.

(c) "ADR Specialist" means an individual who has the qualifications provided for in §7708 of this title to conduct an ADR proceeding.

(d) "Person" means any individual, corporation, association, partnership, statutory trust, business trust, limited liability company or other entity whether or not organized for profit. (Last amended by Ch. 329, L. '02, eff. 9-1-02.)

T. 6, 7703 HOW ADR IS SELECTED.—(a) Any person, by filing the certificate provided for in §7704 of this title, shall be deemed to have agreed to submit all disputes subject to ADR to the ADR provided for by this chapter. Upon the filing of such certificate, the filer shall be bound by the provisions of this chapter until a certificate of revocation has become effective under §7707 of this title.

(b) In addition to persons covered by subsection (a), any person who enter into a written agreement with a person who has filed the certificate provided for in §7704 of this title when such agreement incorporates (by reference or otherwise) the ADR requirements of this chapter, will be bound by the ADR requirements of this chapter with regard to disputes arising out of the subject matter of such written agreement. For purposes of compliance with this provision, it shall be sufficient for such writing to state: "The undersigned hereby agree to be bound by the provisions of the Delaware Voluntary Alternative Dispute Resolution Act with respect to any dispute which arises out of the subject matter of this agreement."

T. 6, 7704 CONTENTS OF CERTIFICATE.—(a) The certificate of agreement to submit to ADR shall set forth (1) the name of the person filing the certificate, (2) the address of such person (which shall include the street, number, city and state) at which it shall be given notice of any dispute, and (3) the agreement of such person that by filing the certificate that person is bound to follow the provisions of this chapter and submits to the power of any court with jurisdiction over it to require it to participate in ADR with any other person who invokes the provisions of this chapter for any dispute subject to ADR.

(b) Any provision in a certificate that purports to limit the disputes that are subject to ADR shall be of no force or effect.

T. 6, 7705 PLACE OF FILING.—(a) The certificate accepting ADR shall be filed with the Secretary of State of the State of Delaware and shall be executed and acknowledged by the chairperson or vice-chairperson of the board of directors or by the president or vice-president of any corporation, by a general partner of any partnership, or by a person with equivalent authority in any other entity.

(b) The Secretary of State shall keep such records as are required to determine who has filed a certificate accepting ADR or revoking such a certificate, together with the date of any such filing. (Last amended by Ch. 186, L. '95, eff. 7-10-95.)

T. 6, 7706 FILING FEE.—No certificate accepting ADR or revoking ADR shall be filed unless it shall be accompanied by the payment of $1,000 to the State, except that the filing fee shall be $100 for every corporation, limited partnership, statutory trust, limited liability company or other entity organized under the laws of the State. (Last amended by Ch. 329, L. '02, eff. 9-1-02.)

T. 6, 7707 REVOCATION OF ADR.—A certificate accepting ADR may be revoked by the filing of a certificate stating that it revokes a previously filed certificate. A certificate of revocation shall be executed and acknowledged in the same manner as a certificate accepting ADR. A certificate of revocation shall be effective upon filing and payment of the filing fee, except with respect to disputes arising under contracts requiring ADR and which were entered into prior to the filing of the certificate of revocation.

T. 6, 7708 QUALIFICATIONS OF ADR SPECIALIST.—The ADR proceedings shall be conducted by any individual meeting one of the following criteria:

(a) Successful completion of 25 hours of training in resolving civil disputes in a course approved by the department or division of the government authority charged with responsibility over adult education in the jurisdiction where that individual resides, or

(b) Admission to the bar of the jurisdiction in which that individual resides, together with a minimum of 5 years experience as a practicing attorney.

T. 6, 7709 SELECTION OF ADR SPECIALIST.—(a) In the case of ADR proceedings that are to be held in the State, the party who initiates the proceedings shall select a panel of 3 ADR Specialists in Delaware to be considered by the parties. Unless the parties otherwise agree in writing, the ADR Specialist shall thereafter be chosen in accordance with the procedures set forth in subsections (c) through (f) below.

(b) In all disputes not to be submitted to ADR in the State and unless the parties otherwise agree in writing, the ADR Specialist shall be selected by the following procedure:

(1) When there are 2 parties to the dispute, the party who initiates the ADR proceedings shall choose a panel of 3 ADR Specialists from those qualified persons who reside or have an office in either (i) the state of incorporation or domicile of the other party to the dispute, or (ii) the jurisdiction where the other party to the dispute resides as determined from the address stated on the ADR certificate on file with the Secretary of State.

(2) When there are more than 2 parties to the dispute, the party who initiates the ADR proceedings shall choose a panel of 3 ADR Specialists from those qualified persons who reside or have an office in the jurisdiction where the greatest number of the other parties to the ADR proceeding (i) are incorporated or domiciled, or (ii) reside as determined from the address stated on any ADR certificate on file with the Secretary of State. If no jurisdiction has the greatest number of parties then the person initiating ADR shall choose panelists from any of the states of incorporation, domicile or residence of the other parties.

(c) The identity of the panel of the ADR Specialists shall be included in the ADR notice provided for in §7710 of this title.

(d) Within 14 days of receiving the ADR notice provided for in §7710 of this title a person receiving such notice shall:

(1) Select one of the members of the panel of ADR Specialists contained in the notice by advising the person initiating the ADR in writing of the selection; or

(2) Advise the party initiating the ADR that none of the members of the panel are acceptable.

When more than 2 persons are involved in the ADR proceedings, the ADR Specialist shall be the person chosen by the greatest number of parties and in the case of a tie in a vote, the person initiating the ADR proceedings shall choose the ADR Specialist from the ADR Specialists who received the same number of votes.

(e) Upon receiving the selection of the ADR Specialist by the other person or persons to the dispute, the person initiating the ADR proceedings shall promptly notify the ADR Specialist of that person's selection and send copies of such notice to the other parties. If a party receiving an ADR notice provided for in §7710 of the title does not select an ADR Specialist in a timely manner, or advise that none of the members of the panel are acceptable, the person sending the ADR notice (1) may select the ADR Specialist, or (2) in the case of more than 2 parties to a dispute, may cast a vote for the ADR Specialist on behalf of the party who failed to respond to the ADR notice.

(f) If none of the ADR Specialists selected by the party initiating the ADR proceedings are acceptable to the other parties to the dispute, in the ADR proceedings that are to be held in Delaware the ADR Specialist shall be selected in accordance with the rules of the Superior Court of the State as may be adopted by that Court and approved by the Delaware Supreme Court. In ADR proceedings to be conducted outside of Delaware, in the case of a failure of the parties to agree on the ADR Specialist the Specialist shall be selected in accordance with such rules as may apply in the jurisdiction where the ADR proceedings are to be conducted or, if no such rules have been adopted, then by the American Arbitration Association. (Last amended by Ch. 186, L. '95, eff. 7-10-95.)

T. 6, 7710 INITIATION OF ADR PROCEEDING.—ADR proceedings are initiated by written notice to the other parties to a dispute who have filed an ADR certificate in accordance with §7704 of this title or who have agreed to be bound by the ADR requirements of this chapter. The notice shall state in summary form: (1) the dispute is subject to the provisions of this chapter, (2) the nature of the dispute to be submitted to ADR and (3) the identities of the members of the panel of ADR Specialists chosen pursuant to §7709 of this title. A failure to send such a notice to a person who has an interest in the dispute shall not prevent the ADR proceedings from going forward between or among parties who did receive such notice.

T. 6, 7711 PARTICIPATION BY OTHER PARTIES.—When not all the parties to a dispute have filed an ADR certificate or have agreed to be bound by the Delaware Voluntary Dispute Resolution Act, such other parties may be given the opportunity to participate in the ADR proceedings by delivering to them the notice provided for in §7710 of this title. Parties to the dispute who are not bound to participate in the ADR proceedings may elect to participate in the ADR by selecting an ADR Specialist in accordance with §7709 of this title. Such selection shall constitute the agreement of the party to be subject to the provisions of this chapter for purposes of the dispute in which the election to participate is made. After the passage of the time for selection of the ADR Specialist, the ADR shall proceed without further notice to or involvement by those parties to the dispute who have not elected ADR.

T. 6, 7712 SCHEDULING OF ADR PROCEEDINGS.—Promptly after notification of appointment, the ADR Specialist shall: (a) advise the parties of a willingness to serve as the ADR Specialist for this dispute, (b) notify the parties of the expected rate of compensation, and (c) set the time and date of the ADR proceedings which shall be within 60 days of notice of appointment unless the parties and the ADR Specialist agree to another date. Unless otherwise agreed, the ADR proceedings shall be held in the offices of the ADR Specialist. (Last amended by Ch. 186, L. '95, eff. 7-10-95.)

T. 6, 7713 COMPENSATION OF ADR SPECIALIST.—(a) The ADR Specialist shall be reimbursed for all reasonable out-of-pocket expenses. The ADR Specialist shall be compensated on the basis of the Specialist's regular hourly fees for professional services for time spent during the day of the actual ADR proceeding and for any subsequent continuation of the proceedings agreed to by parties. In addition to this compensation for the actual ADR proceeding, the ADR Specialist may charge for up to 10 hours spent in preparing for the ADR proceeding, unless the parties agree to additional preparation time.

(b) The ADR Specialist may require the parties, on a pro rata basis, to advance the Specialist's fees for preparation and the actual proceeding within 10 days of the notice of the scheduling of the ADR proceedings.

(c) Unless otherwise agreed, the fees and expenses of the ADR Specialist shall be divided among the parties to the proceedings on a pro rata basis.

(d) The parties and the ADR Specialist may agree on any method or rate of compensation other than as set forth in this section, provided that such agreement is in a writing signed by the parties to the agreement. (Last amended by Ch. 186, L. '95, eff. 7-10-95.)

T. 6, 7714 CONDUCT OF THE ADR PROCEEDINGS.—Subject to any agreement of the parties to adopt different rules of proceeding and the power of the ADR Specialist to modify these procedures in appropriate instances, the ADR shall be conducted as follows:

(a) No later than 7 days prior to the commencement of the ADR, each party shall submit to the ADR Specialist and the other parties a statement of its position in the dispute and such supporting documents as it deems appropriate, provided that such statement of position shall not exceed 25 pages in length.

(b) Upon the commencement of the ADR, each party shall have no more than 1 hour to present its position to the ADR Specialist in the presence of the other parties. This presentation may be made by counsel, by examining witnesses or by any other means that is reasonable under the circumstances. Upon conclusion of any party's presentation, the ADR Specialist may permit the other parties to have up to 1 hour to ask questions of the presenting party, with such hour to be divided among the other parties as determined by the ADR Specialist.

(c) Upon conclusion of the initial presentations of positions by all the parties and such questioning of the parties as thereafter occurs pursuant to subsection (b), the ADR Specialist as soon as possible shall attempt to resolve the dispute by meeting with the parties, either separately or as a group as the Specialist determines is appropriate. Such meetings shall conclude when the dispute is resolved or at the regular close of business on the day the ADR commenced, whichever first occurs.

(d) If the parties thereafter agree, the ADR Specialist may continue to discuss the resolution of the dispute with them, either separately or together, until any party notifies the ADR Specialist that such discussions are at an impasse.

T. 6, 7715 CONCLUSION OF ADR.—Any settlement of the dispute submitted to ADR shall be reduced to writing as soon as possible after the settlement is reached, with such writing to be prepared by the ADR Specialist (unless the parties otherwise agree as part of their settlement that they will prepare the writing) and shall be signed by the parties to be valid and binding upon them. If no settlement is reached at the close of business on the day the ADR is commenced or after further mediation at the parties request until an impasse is declared, the ADR Specialist shall declare the ADR has concluded by advising the parties in writing.

T. 6, 7716 CONFIDENTIALITY.—All ADR proceedings shall be confidential and any memoranda submitted to the ADR Specialist, any statements made during the ADR and any notes or other materials made by the ADR Specialist or any party in connection with the ADR shall not be subject to discovery or introduced into evidence in any proceeding and shall not be construed to be a waiver of any otherwise applicable privilege. Nothing in this section shall limit the discovery or use as evidence of documents that would have otherwise been discoverable or admissible as evidence but for the use of such documents in the ADR proceeding.

T. 6, 7717 IMMUNITY.—The ADR Specialist shall have such immunity as if the Specialist were a judge acting in a court with jurisdiction over the subject matter and the parties involved in the dispute that led to ADR. (Last amended by Ch. 186, L. '95, eff. 7-10-95.)

T. 6, 7718 ATTENDANCE AT ADR.—A person may be represented by counsel in all stages of the ADR proceeding. In addition to its counsel, each party must attend the initial ADR proceeding in which the parties make their presentations and submit to questioning and meet with the ADR Specialist. A person may attend through its chief executive officer (or person holding an equivalent position in such entity) or through any other person authorized in writing by the entity's governing body to so attend, provided such authorized person files a written authorization to attend with the ADR Specialist. The authorization shall state that the representative has the authority to settle the dispute (subject to any limits that are deemed appropriate by the governing body and which limits need not be revealed) and such person is charged with the responsibility of reporting to the party's governing body on what occurred during the ADR proceedings. Any such report shall be confidential in accordance with §7716 of this title. (Last amended by Ch. 186, L. '95, eff. 7-10-95.)

T. 6, 7719 ENFORCEMENT OF ADR RIGHTS.—(a) The right to ADR provided for under this chapter may be enforced by any court with jurisdiction over the parties. Any person who files a certificate under §7704 of this title thereby consents to the jurisdiction of the Court of Chancery of the State for the purpose of enforcing in a summary proceeding the rights provided for by this chapter.

(b) In addition to the right to compel ADR provided by subsection (a), any party to an ADR proceeding to be conducted pursuant to this chapter shall be entitled to reasonable attorneys' fees incurred in compelling ADR.

(c) Any party failing to pay the reasonable fees and expenses of an ADR Specialist shall be subject to suit by the ADR Specialist for 3 times the amount of such fees and expenses, together with the attorneys' fees and other costs incurred in such litigation.

T. 6, 7720 TOLLING OF LIMITATIONS.—The initiation of ADR under §7710 of this title shall suspend the running of the statute of limitations applicable to the dispute that is the subject of the ADR until 14 days after the ADR is concluded in accordance with §7715 of this title.

T. 6, 7721 EFFECT OF COMMENCING LITIGATION.—Other than a proceeding to require ADR under §7719 of this title, this chapter and the procedures provided for herein shall cease to have any force or effect upon the commencement of litigation concerning the dispute that is the subject of the ADR proceedings. The parties to any such litigation shall be exclusively subject to the rules of the tribunal in which such litigation has been commenced and nothing in this chapter shall be construed to infringe upon or otherwise affect the jurisdiction of the courts over such disputes.

TITLE 10. COURTS AND JUDICIAL PROCEDURE
Chapter 3. Court of Chancery
Subchapter III. General Jurisdiction and Powers

T. 10, 346 TECHNOLOGY DISPUTES.—(a) Notwithstanding any other provision in this Code, and without limiting the jurisdiction vested in any court in this State, the Court of Chancery shall have power to mediate and jurisdiction to hear and determine technology disputes as defined herein when:

(1) The parties have consented to the jurisdiction of or mediation by the Court of Chancery by agreement or by stipulation;
(2) At least one party is a "business entity" as defined herein;
(3) At least one party is a business entity formed or organized under the laws of this State or having its principal place of business in this State;
(4) No party is a "consumer", as that term is defined in §2731 of Title 6, with respect to the technology dispute; and
(5) In the case of technology disputes involving solely a claim for monetary damages, the amount in controversy is no less than $1,000,000 or such greater amount as the Court of Chancery determines by rule.

Neither punitive damages nor a jury trial shall be available for a technology dispute heard and determined by the Court of Chancery pursuant to this section. Mediation proceedings shall be considered confidential and not of public record.

(b) A "business entity" means a corporation, statutory trust, business trust or association, a real estate investment trust, a common-law trust, or any other unincorporated business, including a partnership (whether general (including a limited liability partnership) or limited (including a limited liability limited partnership)) or a limited liability company.

(c)(1) A technology dispute" means a dispute arising out of an agreement and relating primarily to: the purchase or lease of computer hardware; the development, use, licensing or transfer of computer software; information, biological, pharmaceutical, agricultural or other technology of a complex or scientific nature that has commercial value, or the intellectual property rights pertaining thereto; the creation or operation of Internet web sites; rights or electronic access to electronic, digital or similar information; or support or maintenance of the above.

(2) The term "technology dispute" does not include a dispute arising out of an agreement:
  a. That is primarily a financing transaction; or
  b. Merely because the parties' agreement is formed by, or contemplates that communications about the transaction will be by, the transmission of electronic, digital or similar information.

(3) The court shall interpret the term "technology dispute" liberally so as to effectuate the intent of this section to provide an expeditious and expert forum for the handling of technology disputes involving parties who have agreed to resolve their disputes in the Court of Chancery, whether the parties are seeking to have the Court of Chancery:
  a. Mediate the dispute only;
  b. Mediate the dispute initially, and if that fails, adjudicate the dispute; or
  c. Adjudicate the dispute.

The Court shall adopt rules to facilitate the efficient processing of technology disputes, including rules to govern the filing of mediation only technology disputes, and to set filing fees and other cost schedules for the processing of technology disputes. (Added by Ch. 36, L. '03, eff. 5-27-03.)

T. 10, 347 MEDIATION PROCEEDINGS FOR BUSINESS DISPUTES.—
(a) Without limiting the jurisdiction of any court of this State, the Court of Chancery shall have the power to mediate business disputes when:

(1) The parties have consented to the mediation by the Court of Chancery by agreement or by stipulation;

(2) At least one party is a business entity as defined in §346 of this title;

(3) At least one party is a business entity formed or organized under the laws of this State or having its principal place of business in this State;

(4) No party is a consumer, as that term is defined in §2731 of Title 6, with respect to the business dispute; and

(5) In the case of disputes involving solely a claim for monetary damages, the amount in controversy is no less than one million dollars or such greater amount as the Court of Chancery determines by rule.

A mediation pursuant to this section shall involve a request by parties to have a member of the Court of Chancery, or such other person as may be authorized under rules of the Court, act as a mediator to assist the parties in reaching a mutually satisfactory resolution of their dispute. Mediation proceedings shall be considered confidential and not of public record.

(b) By rule, the Court of Chancery may define those types of cases that are eligible for submission as a business dispute mediation. This section is intended to encourage the Court of Chancery to include complex corporate and commercial disputes, including technology disputes, within the ambit of the business dispute mediation rules. The Court of Chancery should interpret its rule-making authority broadly to effectuate that intention. (Added by Ch. 36, L. '03, eff. 5-27-03.)

Subchapter IV. Procedure

T. 10, 365 COMPELLING APPEARANCE OF DEFENDANT IN ABSENCE OF PERSONAL SERVICE.—If, after summons or other process issued out of the Court of Chancery, any defendant therein named does not appear in obedience to the process and according to the rules of such Court, the Court may, on affidavit that such defendant is out of the State, or cannot be found to be served with process and that there is just ground to believe that the defendant intentionally avoids such service, make an order for his or her appearance on a certain day and publish such order as the Court directs not less than once a week for 3 consecutive weeks. If the defendant does not appear, after such publication, according to the order, the Court may enter judgment by default against the nonappearing defendant, and may thereupon issue process to compel the performance either by seizure of the real and personal property of such defendant or part thereof, sufficient to satisfy the plaintiff's demand, or by causing possession of the estate, or effects, demanded by the complaint, to be delivered to the plaintiff, or otherwise, as the case requires. The Court may also order the plaintiff to be paid the demand out of any property so seized, upon the plaintiff's giving approved security, in a sufficient sum, to abide any other of the Court for the restitution thereof upon the defendant's appearing to defend the action, and paying such costs as the Court shall order. If such security is not given, the property seized, or whereof possession is ordered to be delivered, shall remain under the direction of the Court in the hands of a receiver or otherwise, until the defendant's appearance, or until such order is made therein as the Court deems is just. (Last amended by Ch. 186, L. '95, eff. 7-10-95.)

.1 **Voting trustee.**—Service by publication upon nonresident trustees of a Delaware voting trust was valid without seizure of the stock constituting the trust provided the suit was against the trustees in their official capacity only. *Smith v The Biggs Boiler Works Co, 85 A2d 365 (Ch Ct 1951)*, aff'd sub nom, *Krizanek v Smith, 87 A2d 871 (1952).*

When Delaware court had declared voting trust void and trustees started action in Ohio to have the trust declared valid, the Delaware court, lacking personal jurisdiction over the trustees and thus unable to punish them for contempt, would consider quo warranto proceedings against the corporation. *Id.*

.2 **Special appearance.**—Although a non-resident defendant in an in rem proceeding may not enter a special appearance, the matters formerly raised in a special appearance have been preserved in the Rules of Court; when a nonresident appears solely in response to in rem process, it would be a constructive fraud to thereby subject him to personal liability. *Abercrombie v Davies, 118 A2d 358 (Ch Ct 1955).*

.3 **In rem jurisdiction.**—Delaware court could not assert in rem jurisdiction over nonresident defendants whose only contact with state was ownership of stock in Delaware corporation even though suit concerned status and ownership rights of this stock. *Arden-Mayfair, Inc v Louart Corp, 385 A2d 3 (Ch Ct 1978).*

Ownership of stock in a Delaware corporation, on its own, is an insufficient basis for a court to exercise personal or in rem jurisdiction where the action does not relate directly to the legal existence, rights, characteristics, or attributes of the stock; does not allege a defect in the corporate process by which the stock was issued; and does not challenge transactions that substantially involve the stock. *OneScreen Inc v Hudgens, 2010 Del. Ch. LEXIS 62 (Ch Ct 2010).*

T. 10, 366 COMPELLING APPEARANCE OF NONRESIDENT DEFENDANT.—(a) If it appears in any complaint filed in the Court of Chancery that the defendant or any one or more of the defendants is a nonresident of the State, the Court may make an order directing such nonresident defendant or defendants to appear by a day certain to be designated. Such order shall be served on such nonresident defendant or defendants by mail or otherwise, if practicable, and shall be published in such manner as the Court directs, not less than once a week for 3 consecutive weeks. The Court may compel the appearance of the defendants by the seizure of all or any part of his property, which property may be sold under the order of the Court to pay the demand of the plaintiff, if the defendant does not appear, or otherwise defaults. Any defendant whose property shall have been so seized and who shall have entered a general appearance in the cause may, upon notice of the plaintiff, petition the Court for an order releasing such property or any part thereof from the seizure. The Court shall release such property unless the plaintiff shall satisfy the Court that because of other circumstances there is a reasonable possibility that such release may render it substantially less likely that plaintiff will obtain satisfaction of any judgment secured. If such petition shall not be granted, or if no such petition shall be filed, such property shall remain subject to seizure and may be sold to satisfy any judgment entered in the cause. The Court may at any time release such property or any part thereof upon the giving of sufficient security.

(b) The Court may make all necessary rules respecting the form of process, the manner of issuance and return thereof, the release of such property from seizure and for the sale of the property so seized, and may require the plaintiff to give approved security to abide any order of the Court respecting the property.

(c) Any transfer or assignment of the property so seized after the seizure thereof shall be void and after the sale of the property is made and confirmed, the purchaser shall be entitled to and have all the right, title and interest of the defendant in and to the property so seized and sold and such sale and confirmation shall transfer to the purchaser all the right, title and interest of the defendant in and to the property as fully as if the defendant had transferred the same to the purchaser in accordance with law.

.1 Application of section.—This section applies only to cases "where a sale is necessary to render effectual the nature of relief which the complainant's bill seeks." *Wightman v San Francisco Bay Toll Bridge Co, 142 A 783 (Ch Ct 1928).*

Nonresident directors' shares in a Delaware corporation cannot be sequestered in a derivative suit in which the prayer for damages would not allow entry of money judgment against the directors. *Steinberg v Shields, 152 A2d 113 (Ch Ct 1959).*

Stock held in joint tenancy can be sequestered as separate property of one tenant, even though they are husband and wife; general appearance after sequestration gives court jurisdiction only as to issues raised in original pleadings. *Townsend Corp v Davidson, 181 A2d 219 (Ch Ct 1962).*

Dividends on stock declared after its sequestration belong to owner, though order gives sequestrator "all the right, title and interest" in the stock; if dividends were to be included, the order could have so provided. *Trans World Airlines, Inc v Hughes, 187 A2d 350 (Ch Ct 1962).*

Absent fraud, a foreign subsidiary's Delaware property cannot be sequestered in a suit against its foreign parent. *Buechner v Farbenfabriken Bayer, AG, 151 A2d 125 (Ch Ct), aff'd, 154 A2d 684 (1959).*

.2 Stockholders' action.—Where property is seized in a derivative action, the chancellor can require a plaintiff to give approved security to abide his order respecting the property. *Cantor v Sachs, 162 A 75 (Ch Ct 1932).*

Stockholder suing nonresident direoctors in a derivative action may compel their appearance by seizing their unrecorded equitable stock interests in a Delaware corporation. However, the stockholder must identify the shares to be seized, including, possibly, the number of shares beneficially owned, the names of the record holders, and the numbers and dates of issuance of the certificates. *Greene v Johnston, 99 A2d 627 (1953).*

Stockholders suing derivatively can sequester property of nonresident directors; they can say directors are not residents in motion to sequester even though they did not in complaint. *Chasin v Gluck, 207 A2d 30 (Ch Ct 1964).*

.3 Creditor's suit.—In action by creditor against debtor (domestic subsidiary) and debtor's transferee (foreign parent) for alleged fraudulent conveyance, jurisdiction over foreign parent was obtained by seizure of stock it held in subsidiary—though suit was not for a money judgment. *EM Fleischmann Lumber Corp v Resources Corp Int'l, 95 A2d 506 (Ch Ct 1953).*

.4 What may be sequestered.—Nonresident defendant whose stock in a Delaware corporation is sequestered may either attack the jurisdiction of the Delaware court or appear generally; he may not contest plaintiff's claim and at the same time limit his liability to the value of the sequestered property. *Leftcourt Realty Corp v Sands, 113 A2d 428 (Ch Ct), aff'd, 117 A2d 365 (1955).*

Stock can be sequestered in a suit for an accounting if a money judgment is possible without an actual accounting. *Lutz v Boas, 156 A2d 96 (Ch Ct 1959), aff'd, 158 A2d 487 (1960).*

Corporation can sequester nonresident's stock in Delaware corporation when it brings him in as third-party defendant though neither he nor stock certificates are in state. *Trans World Airlines, Inc v Hughes, 185 A2d 762 (Ch Ct 1962).*

Court will not sequester nonresident shareholder's shares in instate corporation to compel shareholder's appearance at breach of contract action, when shares had been turned over to voting trust and could not be readily identified or sold without disregarding rights of others in voting trust. *Winitz v Kline,* 288 A2d 456 *(Ch Ct 1971).*

Mail from and telephone calls by nonresident directors of Delaware corporation do not support substituted service of process on them, nor does filing of corporate registration statement in state; even their general appearance does not waive jurisdiction when that appearance is solely under compulsion caused by sequestration of securities. *Bank of America National Trust and Savings Association v GAC Properties Credit,* 389 A2d 1304 *(Ch Ct 1978).*

Sequestration of stock owned by non-resident directors and former directors without notice pending derivative action did not violate due process when it ensured appearance of non-residents at trial of derivative action, since derivative action for benefit of corporation organized instate presented valid governmental interest to compel instate appearance. *Gordon v Michel,* 297 A2d 420 *(Ch Ct 1972).*

Receiver of dissolved Delaware corporation that had claim against Mexican corporation not doing business in Delaware could not sequester debt due Mexican corporation by New York corporation qualified in Delaware, since such debt had no connection with any instate activities. *D'Angelo v Petroleos Mexicanos,* 317 A2d 38, rev'd, 331 A2d 388 *(1974).* See also opinion dated 11-6-73.

Court will not order sequestered stock owned by securities firm released, on ground it was really held in street name, unless and until firm supplied list of true owners. *Life Assurance Co of Pa v Associated Investors International Corp,* 312 A2d 337 *(Ch Ct 1973).*

Court validates instate sequestration of corporate shares for purposes of jurisdiction in derivative action against foreign directors-defendants; Delaware sequestration procedures, as applied to shares of stock, guarantee due process safeguards. *Greyhound Corp v Heitner,* 361 A2d 225 *(1976).*

Court did not have jurisdiction over shareholder and director's husband who allegedly conspired with directors to assist shareholder, without full board's knowledge, in obtaining control of Delaware corporation because court could not obtain quasi in rem jurisdiction over non-directors by sequestering their shareholdings because case is not about ownership rights in stock; stock forms part of case only insofar as it is subject of requested relief. *Aurora Bancshares Corp v Streit,* No. 8357 *(Ch Ct 3-7-86).*

.5 Constitutionality.—Unique Delaware statute providing that site of incorporation is site of corporation's stock and allowing sequestration of shares physically held outside of state ruled unconstitutional for not satisfying due process standards in allowing jurisdiction over out-of-state individual's when statute itself is only contact with Delaware; neither corporation nor shareholder had any other contacts with state (except the instate incorporation)—no relevant transactions occurred there, no property located in Delaware was involved; and no business was conducted there. *US Industries, Inc v Gregg,* 540 F2d 142 *(3d Cir 1976).* To same effect, *Barber-Greene Co v Walco National Corp,* 428 FSupp 567 *(D Del 1977).*

.6 Time in which to raise defense of lack of personal jurisdiction.—Non-resident corporate president whose stock was sequestered waived his valid defense of lack of personal jurisdiction by failing to raise it promptly; he waited 82 days after first learning of the newly available defense to raise it. *Tuckman v Aerosonic Corp,* No. 4094 *(Ch Ct 9-11-78).*

Chapter 5. Superior Court
General Jurisdiction and Powers

1. 10, 546 MEDIATION AND ARBITRATION PROCEEDINGS FOR BUSINESS DISPUTES.—(a) Without limiting the jurisdiction of any court of this State, the Superior Court shall have the power to mediate and arbitrate business disputes when:

 (1) The parties have consented by agreement or by stipulation to the mediation or arbitration by Courts of this State;

 (2) At least one party is a business entity formed or organized under the laws of this State or having its principal place of business in this State, or the business dispute is governed by Delaware law;

 (3) No party is a consumer, as that term is defined in §2731 of Title 6 of the Delaware Code, with respect to the business dispute;

 (4) The amount in controversy is no less than one-hundred thousand dollars ($100,000) or such other amount as the Superior Court determines by rule; and

 (5) The Superior Court, without regard to this Section, would have subject matter jurisdiction to adjudicate the business dispute.

 (b) A mediation pursuant to this section shall involve a request by parties to have a member of the Superior Court act as a mediator to assist the parties in reaching a mutually satisfactory resolution of their business dispute. Mediation proceedings shall be considered confidential and not of public record.

 (c) Arbitration proceedings shall be considered confidential and not of public record until such time, if any, as the proceedings are the subject of an appeal. In the case of an appeal, the record shall be filed by the parties with the Supreme Court in accordance with its rules, and to the extent applicable, the rules of the Superior Court.

810—Corp.   **DELAWARE Code**   8-16-10

(d) The parties in any matter may stipulate that the decision of the Superior Court, or a Commissioner of the Superior Court if they so choose, shall be final and binding and not subject to appeal.

(e) This section is intended to encourage the resolution of business disputes by means of arbitration and mediation. The Superior Court should interpret its rule-making authority broadly to effectuate that intention. (Added by Ch. 439, L. '10, eff. 7-27-10.)

Chapter 31. Process; Commencement of Actions

T. 10, 3104 PERSONAL JURISDICTION BY ACTS OF NONRESIDENTS.—
(a) The term "person" in this section includes any natural person, association, partnership or corporation.

(b) The following acts constitute legal presence within the State. Any person who commits any of the acts hereinafter enumerated thereby submits to the jurisdiction of the Delaware courts.

(c) As to a cause of action brought by any person arising from any of the acts enumerated in this section, a court may exercise personal jurisdiction over any nonresident, or a personal representative, who in person or through an agent:

(1) Transacts any business or performs any character of work or service in the State;

(2) Contracts to supply services or things in this State;

(3) Causes tortious injury in the State by an act or omission in this State;

(4) Causes tortious injury in the State or outside of the State by an act or omission outside the State if the person regularly does or solicits business, engages in any other persistent course of conduct in the State or derives substantial revenue from services, or things used or consumed in the State;

(5) Has an interest in, uses or possesses real property in the State; or

(6) Contracts to insure or act as surety for, or on, any person, property, risk, contract, obligation or agreement located, executed or to be performed within the State at the time the contract is made, unless the parties otherwise provide in writing.

* * * * * * * * * * *

(Last amended by Ch. 329, L. '08, eff. 10-7-08.)

.1 Long-arm jurisdiction.—Commercial marketing activities in Delaware by wholly owned American subsidiary corporation subjected its German manufacturing parent corporation to long-arm jurisdiction of Delaware courts in tort action. *Waters v Deutz Corp, 460 A2d 1332 (1983).*

Court did not have jurisdiction over Wisconsin corporation that received purchase orders from Delaware for asbestos paper and transferred them to affiliated corporation that sold asbestos paper and was subject to Delaware's jurisdiction because: (1) gratuitous referrals not performed in Delaware did not constitute Delaware transactions; (2) corporation was not agent for affiliate; and (3) corporation was not affiliate's alter ego. *O'Neal v Huxley Development Corp, 558 FSupp 462 (D Del 1983).*

Court had jurisdiction over German tractor-manufacturing corporation that had no employees, offices, or showroom in Delaware because corporation was doing business in state through its wholly owned Florida subsidiary, which imported 40% of corporation's tractors in U.S. through Delaware. *Waters v Deutz Corp, 479 A2d 273 (1984).*

Court did not have jurisdiction over Texas corporation charged with breaches of fiduciary duty and contract in connection with formation and management of holding company because: (1) action did not derive from corporation's contract with Delaware Department of Transportation, (2) incorporation of holding company in Delaware did not constitute transaction of business, (3) corporation did not regularly do or solicit business in Delaware when it only advertised there three times and its employees only made isolated visits there, and (4) revenue from Department of Transportation contract was not substantial enough to provide basis for jurisdiction. *J Royal Parker Associates, Inc v Pacro Brown & Root, Inc, No. 7013 (Ch Ct 11-30-84).*

Court had jurisdiction over Italian roofing material manufacturer in action for damages allegedly caused by roofing material when (1) manufacturer's activities in establishing and implementing insured warranty program for its product was persistent course of conduct and "presence" in Delaware and (2) manufacturer's presence in Delaware is intentional and consumer-directed and does not arise simply because product finds its way into Delaware at behest of manufacturer's American distributor's sales efforts. *LaNuova D & B, SpA v Bowe Co, 513 A2d 764 (1986).*

Court had jurisdiction over Virginia corporation in action challenging cash-out merger because (1) corporation was registered to do business in Delaware and had appointed agent there for service of process and (2) corporation incorporated Delaware subsidiary, which it used to effectuate cash-out merger. *Rabkin v Philip A Hunt Chemical Corp, 547 A2d 963 (Ch Ct 1986).*

Nonresident officers of Delaware corporation were subject to personal jurisdiction of Delaware courts under long arm statute despite claim that they were transacting business in Delaware solely as fiduciaries. *Reason:* Fiduciary shield defense did not apply because corporation was found to be shell for defendants when: (1) Plaintiff's complaint alleged that defendants were controlling shareholders; (2) The record did not have any reference to:

nature of business; the number of employees, other than defendants; its assets, other than property that was subject of suit, and purchase money mortgage received on its sale, later assigned to defendants after initiation of suit; and (3) Assignment of mortgage indicated that corporation lacked assets with which to respond to suit. *Plummer & Co Realtors v Crisafi, 533 A2d 1242 (Ch Ct 1987).*

.2 Jurisdiction over alter ego.—Service on subsidiary of Dutch corporation in Delaware was not sufficient to give court jurisdiction over corporation because subsidiary was not corporation's alter ego or agent when subsidiary was independent operating company that maintained separate books and had significant rights and obligations apart from corporation; service by mailing copy of summons and complaint to corporation in Holland and by serving secretary of state was also improper because corporation had no direct connection with Delaware, and its subsidiaries, which did have Delaware connections, were not corporation's alter egos or agents, so their activities could not be attributed to corporation. *Akzona Incorporated v E I Du Pont De Nemours & Co, 607 FSupp 227 (D Del 1984).*

.3 Independent and disinterested directors breached their fiduciary duty of loyalty in unfair merger transaction.—Independent and disinterested directors breached their fiduciary duty of loyalty by acquiescing in a merger which personally benefitted another director to the detriment of other stockholders, and by approving the merger at an unfair price, thereby tainting the entire merger process and stripping the board of business judgment protection, *Crescent/Mach I Partners, L.P. v Turner, C.A. No. 17455 (Ch Ct 9-29-00).*

.4 Attorney liability.—A non-Delaware corporate lawyer and his law firm may be sued in Delaware as to claims arising out of their actions in providing advice and services to a Delaware public corporation, its directors, and its managers regarding matters of Delaware corporate law when the lawyer and law firm: (i) prepared and delivered to Delaware for filing a certificate amendment under challenge in the lawsuit; (ii) advertised themselves as being able to provide coast-to-coast legal services and as experts in matters of corporate governance; (iii) provided legal advice on a range of Delaware law matters at issue in the lawsuit; (iv) undertook to direct the defense of the lawsuit; and (v) face well-pled allegations of having aided and abetted the top managers of the corporation in breaching their fiduciary duties by entrenching and enriching themselves at the expense of the corporation and its public stockholders. *Sample v Morgan, 935 A2d 1046 (Ch Ct 2007).*

.5 Breach of duty of loyalty.—Directors breach their duty of loyalty by engaging in pervasive, diverse and substantial fraud and other illicit activities, thereby knowing that the corporation's internal controls and compliance efforts are inadequate, as well as knowing of the improper conduct, and failing to bring these to the attention of the full board. *American International Group, Inc Consolidated Derivative Litigation, 965 A2d 763 (Ch Ct 2009).*

.6 Implied consent.—Neither merely conferring with members of management on occasion and being involved in a single issue before a company's board nor having a direct role in the formation of a limited liability company and executing documents on its behalf constitutes material participation and management for purposes of implied consent. *Ross Holding and Management Co v Advance Realty Group LLC, 2010 Del. Ch. LEXIS 86 (Ch Ct 2010).*

* * * * * * * * * * *

T. 10, 3111 ACTIONS AGAINST CORPORATIONS; SERVICE OF PROCESS.—(a) Actions may be brought against any corporation, at law or in chancery, by summons. Process may be served on the president, or head officer, if residing in the State, and if not, on any officer, director, or manager of the corporation. When a cause of action arises in this State against any corporation incorporated outside of this State, and there is no president or head officer of such corporation or any officer, director or manager thereof resident in this State, nor any certified agent thereof, for the service of process, resident in this State, process against such corporation may be served upon any agent of such corporation then being in the State. If such corporation appears, the action shall proceed as in other cases, and if it fails to appear, the plaintiff shall have judgment by default, service of the process being first proved. * * * Copies of any rules of court, notice, proceeding, or order, may be served in the same way as original process or upon the attorney of record.

(b) In any action against a corporation whose officers reside out of the State, process may be served by publishing the substance thereof in a newspaper of this State, and of the state where the head officer resides, 20 days before the return thereof, and such service shall be sufficient.

(c) In respect to such corporation, 10 days notice of any motion, rule, order, or other matter or proceeding is sufficient. Such notice may be served personally on the president, any director or manager, or on the attorney of the corporation, or by copy of the rule or other matter sent by mail to the president or head officer at his or her usual place of abode, or by publishing the same in a newspaper near thereto.

(d) Service upon corporations may also be made as provided by §321 of Title 8. (Last amended by Ch. 186, L. '95, eff. 7-10-95.)

.1 Service on vice president.—Under this section, process may be served, upon the vice president (attending a meeting in the state) of a foreign corporation whether or not doing business in the state so long as the cause of action arose in the state. It is not necessary that the cause of action should have arisen out of business done in the state. *Klein v Sunbeam Corp, 95 A2d 460 (1953).*

T. 10, 3114 SERVICE OF PROCESS ON NONRESIDENT DIRECTORS, TRUSTEES, MEMBERS OF THE GOVERNING BODY OR OFFICERS OF DELAWARE CORPORATIONS.

—(a) Every nonresident of this State who after September 1, 1977, accepts election or appointment as a director, trustee or member of the governing body of a corporation organized under the laws of this State or who after June 30, 1978, serves in such capacity, and every resident of this State who so accepts election or appointment or serves in such capacity and thereafter removes residence from this State shall, by such acceptance or by such service, be deemed thereby to have consented to the appointment of the registered agent of such corporation (or, if there is none, the Secretary of State) as an agent upon whom service of process may be made in all civil actions or proceedings brought in this State, by or on behalf of, or against such corporation, in which such director, trustee or member is a necessary or proper party, or in any action or proceeding against such director, trustee or member for violation of a duty in such capacity, whether or not the person continues to serve as such director, trustee or member at the time suit is commenced. Such acceptance or service as such director, trustee or member shall be a signification of the consent of such director, trustee or member that any process when so served shall be of the same legal force and validity as if served upon such director, trustee or member within this State and such appointment of the registered agent (or, if there is none, the Secretary of State) shall be irrevocable.

(b) Every nonresident of this State who after January 1, 2004, accepts election or appointment as an officer of a corporation organized under the laws of this State, or who after such date serves in such capacity, and every resident of this State who so accepts election or appointment or serves in such capacity and thereafter removes residence from this State shall, by such acceptance or by such service, be deemed thereby to have consented to the appointment of the registered agent of such corporation (or, if there is none, the Secretary of State) as an agent upon whom service of process may be made in all civil actions or proceedings brought in this State, by or on behalf of, or against such corporation, in which such officer is a necessary or proper party, or in any action or proceeding against such officer for violation of a duty in such capacity, whether or not the person continues to serve as such officer at the time suit is commenced. Such acceptance or service as such officer shall be a signification of the consent of such officer that any process when so served shall be of the same legal force and validity as if served upon such officer within this State and such appointment of the registered agent (or, if there is none, the Secretary of State) shall be irrevocable. As used in this section, the word "officer" means an officer of the corporation who (i) is or was the president, chief executive officer, chief operating officer, chief financial officer, chief legal officer, controller, treasurer or chief accounting officer of the corporation at any time during the course of conduct alleged in the action or proceeding to be wrongful, (ii) is or was identified in the corporation's public filings with the United States Securities and Exchange Commission because such person is or was one of the most highly compensated executive officers of the corporation at any time during the course of conduct alleged in the action or proceeding to be wrongful, or (iii) has, by written agreement with the corporation, consented to be identified as an officer for purposes of this section.

(c) Service of process shall be effected by serving the registered agent (or, if there is none, the Secretary of State) with 1 copy of such process in the manner provided by law for service of writs of summons. In addition, the Prothonotary or the Register in Chancery of the court in which the civil action or proceeding is pending shall, within 7 days of such service, deposit in the United States mails, by registered mail, postage prepaid, true and attested copies of the process, together with a statement that service is being made pursuant to this section, addressed to such director, trustee, member or officer (i) at the corporation's principal place of business and (ii) at the residence address as the same appears on the records of the Secretary of State, or, if no such residence address appears, at the address last known to the party desiring to make such service; provided, however, that if any such director's, trustee's, member's or officer's address as described in clause (ii) of this subsection (c) shall be the same as the address described in clause (i) of this subsection, then the Prothonotary or Register in Chancery shall be required to make only 1 such mailing to such director, trustee, member or officer, at the address described in clause (i) of this subsection.

(d) In any action in which any such director, trustee, member or officer has been served with process as hereinabove provided, the time in which a defendant shall be required to appear and file a responsive pleading shall be computed from the date of mailing by the Prothonotary or the Register in Chancery as provided in subsection (c) of this section; however, the court in which such action has been commenced may order such continuance or continuances as may be necessary to afford such director, trustee, member or officer reasonable opportunity to defend the action.

(e) Nothing herein contained limits or affects the right to serve process in any other manner now or hereafter provided by law. This section is an extension of and not a limitation upon the right otherwise existing of service of legal process upon nonresidents.

(f) The Court of Chancery and the Superior Court may make all necessary rules respecting the form of process, the manner of issuance and return thereof and such other rules which may be necessary to implement this section and are not inconsistent with this section. (Last amended by Ch. 24, L. '09, eff. 8-1-09.)

.1 **Substituted service not valid.**—Mail from and telephone calls by nonresident directors of Delaware corporation do not support substituted service of process on them, nor does filing of corporate registration statement in state; even their general appearance does not waive jurisdiction when that appearance is solely under compulsion caused by sequestration of securities. *Bank of America National Trust and Savings Association v GAC Properties Credit, Inc, 389 A2d 1304 (Ch Ct 1978).*

Nonresident director of Delaware corporation, who died before suit was filed, could not be made party to suit by substituted service of process on his personal representative because statute covering corporate directors' implied consent to service of process provided no method for giving notice to personal representative; general tort feasor long-arm service of process statute provided method of service on personal representative of deceased non-resident tort feasor but that statute could not be grafted on non-resident directors statute because statutes were dissimilar, served different purposes, and were adopted at different times. *Tabas v Crosby, 444 A2d 250 (Ch Ct 1982).*

.2 **Jurisdiction over directors.**—Court did not have jurisdiction over chief executive officer/director of Delaware brokerage corporation in action asserting that corporation violated contractual and fiduciary duties owed its customers by improperly using their funds because (1) customer is not suing chief executive officer for breach of duty owed to corporation or its shareholders and (2) duty sought to be enforced arises under New York, not Delaware, law. *Steinberg v Prudential-Bache Securities, Inc, No. 8173 (Ch Ct 4-30-86).*

Court may not exercise personal jurisdiction over nonresident director under 10 Delaware Code §3114 for breach of contract claim wholly unrelated to his fiduciary duties as director in Delaware corporation. That statute allows jurisdiction only for those acts performed by nonresident as director.

Actions that are adversarial in nature—actions for breach of fiduciary duty or misappropriation of corporate opportunity—cannot be raised in dissolution proceeding. Issues in dissolution proceeding are narrowly limited to those concerns directly related to dissolution. *In re Cambridge Financial Group, Ltd, No. 9279 (Ch Ct 10-22-87).*

Creditor's action against Delaware corporation's nonresident director did not fall within "corporate directors' long-arm statute" when: (1) statute's language requires more than director status to effect personal jurisdiction and has been construed to permit jurisdiction only when necessary to define, regulate, and enforce fiduciary duties of such individuals to their corporation and shareholders; and (2) creditor, whose rights arose from contract, did not have standing to assert claim for breaches of fiduciary duty. *Prudential-Bache v Franz Mfg Co, 531 A2d 953 (1987).*

Service pursuant to Code Tit. 10, §3114 was effective to give court jurisdiction over nonresident director/officer charged with failure to disclose corporate wrongdoing. Defendant claimed he was being sued for acts in his capacity as officer, so §3114 did not apply. However, director violates duty of loyalty if he knows company has been defrauded and he keeps silent about wrongdoing. Thus, complaint alleged breach of directorial loyalty justifying service under §3114. *Hoover Industries, Inc v Chase, No. 9276 (Ch Ct 7-13-88).*

Under 10 Delaware Code §3114, court had jurisdiction over nonresident directors of Delaware subsidiary. However, court lacked jurisdiction over nonresident directors of Ohio parent. *Sternberg v O'Neil, 550 A2d 1105 (1988).*

In an action for breach of contract and misrepresentation, the Superior Court of Delaware held that it lacked personal jurisdiction over a director of a Delaware corporation (with its principal place of business in Connecticut) where the non-resident director was not a necessary or proper party to the action brought against his corporation and where, even if the director committed tortious acts and breaches of contract vis-a-vis the plaintiffs, it was not alleged that he breached any fiduciary duty as director of his corporation. The contract was not made or performed in Delaware, no tortious act occurred or had impact there, and Delaware law did not apply to the dispute. In short, the only contact between the director and Delaware was his status as director of a Delaware corporation, and under those circumstances, it would be constitutionally impermissible to subject him to personal jurisdiction. *Hirshman v Vendamerica, Inc, 90C-AP-40-ICV (Super Ct 3-9-92).*

In a motion to dismiss for lack of personal jurisdiction over defendant directors, the Court of Chancery granted the motion. Plaintiffs brought a class action pursuant to §11 and 15 of the Securities Act of 1933. The individual nonresident defendants brought this motion to dismiss, alleging lack of personal jurisdiction. Plaintiffs alleged that the non-resident directors were subject to personal jurisdiction in Delaware pursuant to 10 Delaware Code §3114, which provides that nonresidents who accept election or appointment as a director of a corporation organized under Delaware law shall be deemed to have consented to the appointment of the registered agent of such corporation as his agent upon whom service of process may be made. The court rejected this argument, however, asserting that Delaware case law established that nonresident directors were subject to jurisdiction in Delaware where the actions were brought under Delaware law, but not where they were brought under federal law. The court stated that §3114 does not confer personal jurisdiction over nonresident directors merely by virtue of their status as directors of Delaware corporations. Because no claims under Delaware law were alleged against defendants in this case, defendants' motion to dismiss for lack of personal jurisdiction was granted. *Van de Walle v L.F. Rothschild Holdings Inc, C.A. No. 9894 (Ch Ct 8-2-94).*

.3 Jurisdiction over non-directors.—Court did not have jurisdiction over shareholder and director's husband who allegedly conspired with directors to assist shareholder, without full board's knowledge, in obtaining control of Delaware corporation. *Reasons:* (1) Apart from stock ownership, defendant non-directors had no contact with Delaware. (2) Court could not obtain quasi in rem jurisdiction over non-directors by sequestering their shareholdings because case is not about ownership rights in stock; stock forms part of case only insofar as it is subject of requested relief. (3) Non-directors' acts performed outside of Delaware in furtherance of alleged conspiracy had *no* effect, let alone "substantial effect," in Delaware. *Aurora Bancshares Corp v Streit, No. 8357 (Ch Ct 3-7-86).*

Statute providing for substituted service of process on nonresident directors of Delaware corporations applies only to actions in which director is a proper party, or in any action or proceeding against director for violation of his or her duty as director. Corporation's former president was improperly served under statute when complaint did not set forth any claim against him arising from his status as a director, and court was therefore precluded from exercising personal jurisdiction over him. *Goodrich v EF Hutton Group, Inc, No. 8279 (Ch Ct 9-10-87).*

.4 Corporate "zone of insolvency".—Creditors of a corporation do not, as a matter of law, have a direct claim against directors of an insolvent corporation, or one in the zone of insolvency, for breach of fiduciary duty. *North American Catholic Educational Programming Foundation, Inc. v Gheewalla, 2007 Del. LEXIS 227 (2007).*

.5 Winding up.—A corporation's certificate of dissolution will not be nullified, nor its full corporate existence restored or a receiver appointed, where, although the dissolved corporation is a party to ongoing litigation, its management is actively winding up its affairs, and, the company's existence as a body corporate will not end before the conclusion of the litigation. *LeCrenier v Central Oil Asphalt Corp, 2010 Del. Ch. LEXIS 246 (Ch Ct 2010).*

Chapter 35.   Attachments

T. 10, 3501 DOMESTIC ATTACHMENT; WHEN WRIT MAY BE ISSUED.—A writ of domestic attachment may be issued against an inhabitant of this State upon proof satisfactory to the court that the defendant cannot be found, or that the defendant is justly indebted to the plaintiff in a sum exceeding $50, and has absconded from the defendant's usual place of abode or is about to leave the State or has gone out of the State with intent to defraud his or her creditors or to elude process. (Last amended by Ch. 186, L. '95, eff. 7-10-95.)

.1 Attachment of undelivered stock.—In action against its nonresident officers and directors, corporation can attach stock it issued but never delivered to them, since it is permissible to attach others' property it has in its custody to insure their personal appearance in suit. *First Western Financial Corp v Neumeyer, 240 A2d 579 (1968).*

T. 10, 3502 CORPORATIONS SUBJECT TO ATTACHMENT AND GARNISHMENT.—(a) All corporations doing business in this State, except as specified in subsections (b) and (c) of this section, are subject to the operations of the attachment laws of this State, as provided in the case of individuals. A corporation shall be liable to be summoned as garnishee.

* * * * * * * * * * *

(Last amended by Ch. 327, L. '96, eff. 5-2-96.)

T. 10, 3507 FOREIGN ATTACHMENT AGAINST FOREIGN CORPORATIONS.—A writ of foreign attachment may be issued against any corporation, aggregate or sole, not created by or existing under the laws of this State upon proof satisfactory to the court that the defendant is a corporation not created by, or existing under the laws of this State, and that the plaintiff has a good cause of action against the defendant in an amount exceeding $50.

Chapter 39.   Pleading and Practice

T. 10, 3915 PROOF OF INCORPORATION OR CORPORATE EXISTENCE.—In any action by or against any corporation, the plaintiff may specifically require the defendant or defendants to deny the allegation of the incorporation and existence of the corporation by affidavit filed with the answer, by the specific notation of the need for denial by affidavit within the paragraph alleging the corporate existence. Any defendant so answering shall deny the incorporation and existence of the corporation as alleged, and stating to the best of affiant's knowledge whether there is any corporation existing which has a relationship to the subject matter of the action. Such affidavit may be made by the president, secretary, treasurer or any director of any corporate defendant. Where plaintiff has complied with this section, failure of any defendant to file an affidavit with its answer shall be deemed an admission of existence of the corporation as alleged. (Last amended by Ch. 296, L. '86, eff. 7-23-86.)

Chapter 49. Executions

T. 10, 4935 EMPLOYEES OF INSOLVENT CORPORATION.—Employees of insolvent corporations shall have a lien for, and a preference in the payment of, wages due them from such corporation, not exceeding wages for 2 months, as provided in §300 of Title 8.

Chapter 81. Personal Actions

T. 10, 8114 CORPORATE OFFICERS' BONDS.—No action shall be brought upon any bond given to the president, directors and company of any bank, or to any corporation, by any officer of such bank or corporation, with condition for the officer's good behavior, or for the faithful discharge of the duties of the officer's station, or touching the execution of the officer's office, against either the principal or sureties, after the expiration of 2 years from the accruing of the cause of such action. No action shall be brought, and no proceedings shall be had upon any such bond, or upon any judgment thereon, against either the principal or sureties, for any cause of action accruing after the expiration of 6 years from the date of such bond. (Last amended by Ch. 186, L. '95, eff. 7-10-95.)

Chapter 95. Procedure

T. 10, 9525 DEPOSIT FOR COST.—* * * (b) Where the person bringing the action under this subchapter is a corporation, the action may be prosecuted by an officer or employee of the corporation who need not be a duly licensed attorney-at law provided, however, that officer or employee is duly qualified under Delaware Supreme Court Rule 57. (Last amended by Ch. 27, L. '07, eff. 5-23-07.)

TITLE 12. DECEDENTS' ESTATES AND FIDUCIARY RELATIONS

Chapter 11. Escheats

Subchapter IV. Other Unclaimed Property

T. 12, 1197 OTHER PROPERTY ESCHEATED.—Except as otherwise provided elsewhere in the Delaware Code all property, as hereinafter defined and not otherwise subject to escheat in accordance with this chapter, the title to which has failed and the power of alienation suspended by reason of: * * * (2) the owner thereof having disappeared or being missing from the owner's last known place of residence for a continuous period of 5 years or more, leaving no known heirs-at-law; or (3) the same having been abandoned by the owner thereof, as hereinafter defined, shall descend to the State as an escheat in accordance with the Constitution, the general laws of this State or this subchapter. (Last amended by Ch. 186, L. '95, eff. 7-10-95.)

.1 **Application of section.**—State of Delaware had no right to claim escheat of undeliverable stock certificates and uncashed dividend checks when last known address of stockholder was in Massachusetts. *Nellius v Tampax Inc, 394 A2d 233 (Ch Ct 1978).*

T. 12, 1198 DEFINITIONS.—For purposes of this subchapter, the following definitions shall apply:

(1) "Abandoned property" means property against which a full period of dormancy has run.

(2) "Appropriation" means the act of the State, through its duly constituted officers or agencies, in taking or accepting possession or custody of abandoned, unprotected, unclaimed or lost property as conservator thereof for later disposition by descent to the State as an escheat or redemption by the owner as provided in this subchapter.

(3) "Distributions held by financial intermediaries for unknown owners" means property as generally defined in paragraph (11) of this section, which consists of dividends, interest, stock and other distributions made by issuers of securities which are held by

financial intermediaries (including, by way of example and not limitation, banks, transfer agents, brokers and other depositories) for beneficial owners whose identities are unknown.

(4) "Escheat" means the descent or devolution of property to the State under and by virtue of the Constitution of the State, the general laws of this State or this subchapter.

(5) "Escheatable property" means property which is subject to escheat to the State under and by virtue of the Constitution of the State, the general laws of this State or this subchapter.

(6) "Escheated property" means property which has descended to the State as an escheat.

(7) "Holder" means any person having possession, custody or control of the property of another person and includes a post office, a depository, a bailee, a trustee, a receiver or other liquidating officer, a fiduciary, a governmental department, institution or agency, a municipal corporation and the fiscal officers thereof, a public utility, service corporation and every other legal entity incorporated or created under the laws of this State or doing business in this State. For purposes of this subchapter, the issuer of any intangible ownership interest in a corporation, whether or not represented by a stock certificate, which is registered on stock transfer or other like books of the issuer or its agent, shall be deemed a holder of such property. This definition shall be construed as distinguishing the term "holder" of property from the term "owner" of property as hereinbefore defined and as excluding from the term "holder" any person holding or possessing property by virtue of title or ownership.

(8) "Owner," in addition to its commonly accepted meaning, shall be construed to particularly mean and include any person, as hereinbefore defined, having the legal or equitable title to property coming within the purview of this subchapter.

(9) a. "Period of dormancy" means the full and continuous period of 5 years, except a period of 15 years for traveler's checks, during which an owner has ceased, failed or neglected to exercise dominion or control over property or to assert a right of ownership or possession or to make presentment and demand for payment and satisfaction or to do any other act in relation to or concerning such property. Notwithstanding the forgoing, "period of dormancy" means the full and continuous period of 3 years with respect to intangible ownership or indebtedness in a corporation or other entity whether or not represented by a stock certificate or other certificate of membership, bonds and other securities including fractional shares, interest, dividends, cash, coupon interest, liquidation value of stocks and bonds, funds to redeem stocks and bonds, and distributions held by financial intermediaries.

b. A full period of dormancy shall be deemed to have run with respect to any dividends or other distributions held for or owing to an owner at the time a period of dormancy shall have run with respect to the intangible ownership interest in a corporation partnership, statutory or common law trust, limited liability company, or other entity to which such dividend or other distribution attaches. For good cause shown, and upon notice to the State Escheator, the Court of Chancery may, with respect to property over which the court has otherwise assumed jurisdiction, extend the period of dormancy to a specific date by which an owner may exercise a right, make a demand or file a claim, provided each extension is set forth in a separate order of the court referring specifically to this section, and each extension is no longer than 3 years, provided further there shall be no more than 2 extensions under this subsection. Except as provided in §1210 of this title, the period of dormancy shall not commence to run with respect to which claims, demands or other property held by a holder pursuant to a written agreement which contemplates that there shall be a specific period of inactivity, until the expiration of the contemplated period of inactivity. This definition shall be construed as excluding any act or doing of a holder of abandoned property not done at the express request or authorization of the owner. Notwithstanding the foregoing, the "period of dormancy" with regard to gift certificates shall be the shorter of:

1. 5 years, or
2. The expiration period, if any, of the gift certificate less 1 day. In the event the period of dormancy is determined by reference to the expiration period of the gift certificate, the rights of the Escheator shall attach at the time provided in this paragraph (9)b.2. of this section, but the issuer may continue to hold the property and may report and pay over such property as if the period of dormancy were 5 years.

A full period of dormancy shall be deemed to have run with respect to any property that is otherwise reportable and payable to this State that a holder in accordance with the laws of the jurisdiction wherein the holder is located, is obligated or required to report and pay over such property to the other jurisdiction because of a shorter period of dormancy or reporting period.

c. Notwithstanding the foregoing, "period of dormancy" means the full and continuous period of 1 year following the last day of the meet with respect to sums held for the payment of outstanding pari-mutuel tickets from the meet.

(10) "Person" includes a natural person, a corporation organized or created under the laws of this State or a corporation doing business or which has been engaged in business in this State, a copartnership, a voluntary association and every or any other association or organization of individuals, but excludes banking organizations and any life insurance company.

(11) "Property" means personal property, including "distributions held by financial intermediaries for unknown owners" as that phrase is defined in paragraph (3) of this section, of every kind or description, tangible or intangible, in the possession or under the control of a holder, as hereinafter defined, and includes, but not by way of limitation, * * * (iii) intangible ownership interests in corporations, whether or not represented by a stock certificate, bonds and other securities; * * * (v) dividends, cash or stock; (vi) certificates of membership in a corporation or association; * * * (viii) funds deposited by holder with fiscal agents of fiduciaries for payment to owner of dividends, coupon interest and liquidation value of stocks and bonds; (ix) funds to redeem stocks and bonds; * * * (Last amended by Ch. 417, L. '10, eff. 7-23-10.)

T. 12, 1199 REPORT BY HOLDERS OF ABANDONED PROPERTY.—

(a) Every holder of funds or other property, tangible or intangible, deemed abandoned under this subchapter shall file with the State Escheator, on or before March 1 of each year, as of December 31 next preceding, a report with respect to such property. The report shall be verified and shall include:

(1) The name, if known, and last known address, if any, of each person appearing from the records of the holder to be the owner of any property deemed abandoned under this subchapter;

(2) The nature and identifying number, if any, or description of the property and the amount appearing from the records to be due, except that items of value under $50 each may be reported in aggregate;

(3) The date when the property became payable, demandable or returnable and the date of the last transaction with the owner with respect to the property; and

(4) Other information which the State Escheator may prescribe.

(b) Upon written request the State Escheator may grant an extension of time with respect to the date for filing the report.

(c) The requirements of this section for filing an annual report shall not apply to municipal corporations or counties and the fiscal officers thereof.

(d) Verification, if made by a partnership, shall be executed by a partner, if made by an unincorporated association or private corporation, by an officer and if made by a public corporation, by its chief fiscal officer.

(e) If the person holding property deemed abandoned is a successor to other persons who previously held the property for the owner or if the holder has changed his name while holding the property, he shall file with his report all prior known names and addresses of each holder of the property.

(f)(1) With respect to any stock or other certificate of ownership or any dividend, profit, distribution, interest, payment on principal, or other sum held owing by a corporation or other business association for or to a shareholder, certificate holder, member, bondholder, or other security holder, the initial report filed under this section shall include all such items of property deemed abandoned under this subchapter without limitation as to time.

(2) Except as provided in paragraph (1) of this subsection, the initial report shall include all such items of property which, under this subchapter, would have been deemed abandoned on the effective date of this subchapter had this subchapter been in effect on January 1, 1964.

(g) No reporting shall be required solely by virtue of holding property constituting consideration paid for unredeemed gift certificates which, in the aggregate, for the reporting period have a face value of less than $5,000 or for gift certificates having a face value of $5.00 or under issued by a holder whose business is described in §2906 of Title 30 whether or not such firm conducts business in this state. (Last amended by Ch. 45, L. '99, eff. for gift certificates issued on or after 1-1-94.)

T. 12, 1200 NOTICE AND PUBLICATION OF LISTS OF ABANDONED PROPERTY.—(Repealed by Ch. 122, L. '91, eff. 7-8-91.)

T. 12, 1201 PAYMENT OR DELIVERY OF ABANDONED PROPERTY.—(a) On or before the date required for the filing of the report pursuant to §1199 of this title, every holder of abandoned property shall pay or deliver to the State Escheator all abandoned property specified in the report, except that if it appears the reported abandonment is erroneous, the holder need not pay or deliver the property, which will no longer be deemed abandoned, to the State Escheator, but in lieu thereof shall file a verified written explanation of the proof of claim or other reason. The holder of any intangible ownership interest in a corporation deemed abandoned under this subchapter shall, when making the delivery contemplated by this section:

(1) If such interest is a certificated security as defined in §8-102(1) of Title 6 deliver either the original stock certificate evidencing the abandoned property, if such is in its possession or a duly issued replacement certificate evidencing such property in a form suitable for transfer; or

(2) If such interest is an uncertificated security as defined in §8-102(1) of Title 6 cause such uncertificated security to be registered in the name of the State Escheator.

(b) [Deleted.] (Last amended by Ch. 19, L. '05, eff. 4-27-05.)

T. 12, 1202 PERIODS OF LIMITATION NOT A BAR.—The expiration of any period of time specified by statute or court order, during which an action or proceeding may be commenced or enforced to obtain payment of a claim for money or recovery of property, shall not prevent the money or property from being deemed abandoned property nor affect any duty to file a report required by this subchapter or to pay or deliver abandoned property to the State Escheator. (Last amended by Ch. 426, L. '72, eff. 6-15-72.)

T. 12, 1203 EFFECT OF PAYMENT AND DELIVERY.—(a) Unless otherwise addressed in subsection (b) of this section, the payment or delivery of property to the State Escheator by any holder shall terminate any legal relationship between the holder and the owner and shall release and discharge such holder from any and all liability to the owner, the owner's heirs, personal representatives, successors and assigns by reason of such delivery or payment, regardless of whether such property is in fact and in law abandoned property and such delivery and payment may be pleaded as a bar to recovery and shall be a conclusive defense in any suit or action brought by such owner, the owner's heirs, personal representatives, successors and assigns or any claimant against the holder by reason of such delivery or payment. Application of this subsection (a) is mutually exclusive of subsection (b) of this section and, accordingly, shall not be applied in conjunction with subsection (b) of this section.

(b) Upon the delivery in good faith of a duplicate certificated security to the State Escheator or the registration of an uncertificated security to the State Escheator pursuant to §1201 of this title, the holder and any transfer agent, registrar or other person acting for or on behalf of the holder in executing or delivering such duplicate certificate or effectuating such registration, is relieved of all liability of every kind to every person, including any person acquiring the original of a certificated security or the duplicate of a certificated security issued to the State Escheator, for any losses or damages resulting to any person by issuance and delivery to the State Escheator of the duplicate certificated security or the registration to the holder's name of an uncertificated security.

(c) If the holder pays or delivers property to the State Escheator in good faith and thereafter another person claims the property from the holder or another state claims the money or property under its laws relating to escheat or abandoned or unclaimed property, the State Escheator acting on behalf of the State, upon written notice of the claim, shall defend the holder against the claim and indemnify the holder against any liability on the claim.

(d) For the purposes of this section, "good faith" means that:

(1) Payment or delivery was made in a reasonable attempt to comply with this subchapter;

(2) The person delivering the property was not a fiduciary then in breach of trust in respect to the property and had a reasonable basis for believing, based on the facts then known to the person, that the property was abandoned for the purposes of this subchapter; and

(3) There is no showing that the records pursuant to which the delivery was made did not meet reasonable commercial standards of practice in the industry.

(e) The State Escheator at the request of a holder and in his sole discretion, may allow a holder to pay over or deliver property otherwise properly payable to the State but against which a full period of dormancy has not yet run. In the event the State Escheator acquiesces to the request and accepts such property, the holder shall be entitled to the protections of this section as if and the property shall be treated generally as if it had been paid over after a full period of dormancy had run. The provisions of §§1145 and 1206(c) of this title shall not apply to property accepted by the State Escheator under this subsection until a full period of dormancy has run against the property. (Last amended by Ch. 81, L. '11, eff. 7-5-11.)

T. 12, 1204 SALE OF ABANDONED PROPERTY.—(a) All abandoned property, other than money, delivered to the State Escheator under this subchapter shall be sold or disposed of in accordance with §1143 of this title.

(b) All sales of property made by the State Escheator under this subchapter shall pass absolute title to the purchaser. The State Escheator or the Secretary of State shall execute all documents necessary to complete the transfer of title. (Added by Ch. 426, L. '72, eff. 6-15-72.)

T. 12, 1205 DEPOSIT AND DISBURSEMENT OF FUNDS.—(a) All funds received by the State Escheator under this subchapter, including the proceeds of sale under §1204 of this title, shall forthwith be paid and deposited into the General Fund of the State.

(b) All disbursements for expenses, claims, storage, etc., made or authorized by the State Escheator in connection with the administration of this subchapter shall be paid by the Secretary of Finance upon presentation of a signed voucher by the State Escheator. (Added by Ch. 426, L. '72, eff. 6-15-72.)

T. 12, 1206 CLAIMS FOR ABANDONED PROPERTY PAID OR DELIVERED, DETERMINATION OF CLAIMS; APPEALS.—(a) Any person claiming an interest in any property paid or delivered to the State Escheator under this subchapter may file a claim thereto or to the proceeds from the sale thereof with the State Escheator.

(b) The determination of claims and rights of appeal shall be accomplished as prescribed in §1146(b) of this title.

(c) When property is paid or delivered to the State Escheator under this subchapter, the owner is not entitled to receive income or other increments accruing thereafter. (Added by Ch. 426, L. '72, eff. 6-15-72.)

T. 12, 1208 RULES AND REGULATIONS.—The State Escheator may make such rules and regulations as the Escheator may deem necessary to administer and enforce this subchapter. (Last amended by Ch. 186, L. '95, eff. 7-10-95.)

T. 12, 1209 EXAMINATION OF RECORDS.—(Repealed by Ch. 267, L. '90, eff. 7-2-90.)

T. 12, 1210 NO PRIVATE ESCHEATS.—Any provision in a certificate of incorporation, by law, trust agreement, contract or any other writing regulating the relationships between an owner and a holder, relating to property with the exception of non-escheat capital credits as defined in §909 of Title 26, which is or may be subject to the provisions of this chapter, which provides that upon the owner's failure to act or make a claim regarding property in possession of the holder, that such property reverts to or becomes the property of the holder, in contravention of this chapter, shall be void and unenforceable. (Last amended by Ch. 448, L. '98, eff. 7-14-98.)

Chapter 35. Trusts

Subchapter III. General Provisions

T. 12, 3532 TRANSFER OF STOCKS, BONDS OR OTHER CORPORATE SECURITIES BY TRUSTEE; CERTIFICATE OF REGISTER IN CHANCERY.—Upon the transfer by trustees of the stocks, bonds or other securities of any corporation, the certificate of the Register of the Court of Chancery in which such trustee was appointed or other proper public official, according to the form and provisions of §1572 of this title, shall be sufficient authority to the officers of such corporation to transfer or reissue such stocks, bonds or other securities to such person as such trustee in writing directs.

TITLE 15.   ELECTIONS
Chapter 80.   Limits on Campaign Contributions and Expenditures

T. 15, 8012   CONTRIBUTION LIMITS GENERALLY.—* * *   (e) A corporation, partnership or other entity (other than a political committee) which makes a contribution to a political committee shall notify such political committee in writing of the names and addresses of all persons who, directly or otherwise, own a legal or equitable interest of 50 percent or greater (whether in the form of stock ownership, percentage of partnership interest, liability for the debts of the entity, entitlement to the profits from the other entity or other indicia of interest) in such corporation, partnership or other entity, or that no such persons exist. The political committee may rely on such notification, and should the notification provided by the representative of the entity be inaccurate or misleading, the person or persons responsible for the notification, and not the political committee which received the contribution, shall be liable therefor. A ratable portion of the contribution by the corporation, partnership or other entity shall be deemed to be a contribution under this chapter to the political committee by each such person who owns a 50 percent or greater interest in the entity, shall be included within the limit imposed by this section on individual contributions, and shall be so included in the reports filed by the candidate committee with the Commissioner under §8030 of this title.* * *   (Last amended by Ch. 230, L. '92, eff. 4-21-92.)

TITLE 25.   PROPERTY
Chapter 1.   Deeds
Subchapter II.   Form, Acknowledgment and Proof of Deeds and Other Legal Instruments

T. 25, 127   ACKNOWLEDGMENT OF CORPORATE DEEDS; OTHER INSTRUMENTS.—A deed concerning lands or tenements or any other written instrument entitled to be recorded, executed by a corporation, may be executed and acknowledged before any judge of this State, or a judge of the District Court or Court of Appeals of the United States, or a notary public, or 2 justices of the peace of the same county, by the president or other presiding officer or a vice-president or an assistant vice-president, duly authorized by resolution of the directors, trustees or other managers, or by the legally constituted attorney, of such corporation.

Chapter 3.   Titles and Conveyances

T. 25, 305   DEEDS BY FOREIGN CORPORATIONS * * *.—* * * A foreign corporation owning lands in Delaware may exercise all rights and privileges of ownership to the same extent as if such corporation were a corporation lawfully created by and existing under the laws of this State.

TITLE 29.   STATE GOVERNMENT
Chapter 23.   Secretary of State

T. 29, 2311   DISPOSITION OF MONEYS RECEIVED; DIVISION OF CORPORATIONS CORPORATE REVOLVING FUND; SECRETARY OF STATE SPECIAL OPERATIONS FUND.—(a) All fees which are by law taxable by and payable to the Secretary of State, except those fees collected pursuant to §9-525(d)(3) of Title 6, §15-1207(b) of Title 6, §17-1107(b) of Title 6, §18-1105(b) of Title 6, §3813(b) of Title 12, §391(h) of Title 8 and §2318 and §4307 of this title, shall be collected by the Secretary of State and paid into the State Treasury, provided however that an amount equal to 23% of all fees assessed pursuant to §9-525 of Title 6 (excluding any fees assessed pursuant to §9-525(d)(3) of Title 6 and any fees assessed pursuant to §9-525(a)(2) in excess of $15), and an annual amount not to exceed $1 million equal to the sum of:

(1) All fees and taxes collected pursuant to Chapter 69 of Title 18 required by law to be transferred to the General Fund, and

(2) Those fees collected pursuant to §3813(a)(2) and §3862(1) of Title 12, shall be remitted monthly to the treasury of the City of Wilmington. To ensure implementation of

this subsection, the Insurance Commissioner shall, transfer any amounts collected subsequent to June 30, 2007, pursuant to Chapter 69 of Title 18 and required by law to be transferred to the General Fund to the Secretary of State.

(b) There is hereby created, within the Division of Corporations, a special fund to be designated as the Division of Corporations Corporate Revolving Fund which shall be used in the operation of the Division of Corporations in the performance of special requests for services and the funding of appropriated special funds positions.

(c) All fees which are by law payable to the Secretary of State pursuant to §9-525(d)(3) of Title 6, §15-1207(b) of Title 6, §17-1107(b) of Title 6, §18-1105(b) of Title 6, §3813(b) of Title 12, and §391(h) of Title 8 and §4307 of this title shall be deposited in the State Treasury to the credit of said Division of Corporations Corporate Revolving Fund. No other fees or taxes collected by the Secretary of State shall be deposited in said Fund.

(d) Funds in the Division of Corporations Corporate Revolving Fund shall be used by the Division of Corporations in the performance of the functions and duties involved in creating and maintaining the capability to perform services in response to special requests for the same day service and 24-hour turnaround service.

(e) The maximum unencumbered balance which shall remain in the Division of Corporations, Corporate Revolving Fund at the end of Fiscal Year 2001 shall be $1,300,000 and any amount in excess thereof shall be transferred to the General Fund of the State. The maximum unencumbered balance which shall remain in the Division of Corporations, Corporate Revolving Fund at the end of Fiscal Year 2002 and any subsequent fiscal year thereafter shall be $1,000,000 and any amount in excess thereof shall be transferred to the General Fund of the State.

(f) There is hereby created, within the office of the Secretary of State, a special fund to be designated as the Secretary of State Special Operations Fund. Funds deposited in said Special Operations Fund shall be used to maintain and improve the capability to perform the operations, functions and duties of the Secretary of State, including but not limited to maintaining and improving the statewide communications network maintained by the Secretary of State, creating, maintaining and improving electronic files, creating, maintaining and improving the ability to provide remote access to electronic files maintained by the Secretary of State and funding appropriated positions relating to such activities.

(g) All fees which are by law payable to the Secretary of State pursuant to §2318 of this title shall be deposited in the State Treasury to the credit of said Secretary of State Special Operations Fund. No other fees or taxes collected by the Secretary of State shall be deposited in said Fund. (Last amended by Ch. 78, L. '09, eff. 8-1-09.)

T. 29, 2315 FEES.—The fees to be charged by the Secretary of State for the use of the State are as follows. * * *

For receiving, filing and indexing certificates, statements, affidavits, decrees, agreements, surveys, reports and any other papers pertaining to corporations, except as otherwise provided in Title 8 of the Delaware Code	10.00
For receiving, filing and indexing every paper now or hereafter provided by law to be filed with the Secretary of State, except as otherwise provided in Title 8 of the Delaware Code.	10.00
For recording, filing and indexing certificates, articles of association and any other paper required by law to be recorded by the Secretary of State, the same fees as provided by law for the Recorder, except as otherwise provided in Title 8 of the Delaware Code	blank as in statutes
For proceeding for reinstatement, including the receiving, filing and indexing and all necessary certificates	15.00

For filing certificates of foreign corporations including the receiving, filing, indexing and issuing necessary certificates, $13 of which shall be paid to each Prothonotary for filing & c.................................. 30.00

* * * * * * * * * * *

(Last amended by Ch. 52, L. '03, eff. 8-1-03.)

[The page following this is Corp.—901]

DELAWARE COURT OF CHANCERY RULES

Rule 4 PROCESS.—(a) Summons; Issuance. Upon commencement of an action, the plaintiff may present a summons to the Register in Chancery for singnature and seal. If the summons is in proper form,the Rgister in Chacery shall sign, seal and issue it to the plaintiff for service on the defendant. A summons, or a copy of the summons if addressed to multiple defendants, shall be issued for each defendant to be served.

(b) Same; Form. The summons shall be signed by the Register in Chancery, be under the seal of the Court, contain the name of the Court and the names of the parties, state the name of the official or other person to whom it is directed, the name and address of the plaintiff's attorney, if any, otherwise the plaintiff's address, and the time within which these Rules require the defendant to appear and defend, and shall notify the defendant that in case of the defendant's failure to do so judgment by default will be rendered against the defendant for the relief demanded in the complaint.

(c) By Whom Served. Service of summons may be effected by any person who is not a party and who is at least 18 years of age. At the request of the plaintiff, the court may direct that service be affected by the sheriff, the sheriff's deputy or by another person specially appointed by the court for that purpose.

(d) Summons; Personal Service. The summons and complaint shall be served together. The Register in Chancery shall furnish the person making service with such copies as are necessary. Service shall be made as follows:

* * * * * * * * * * * *

(4) Upon a Delaware corporation or a foreign corporation in the manner provided by statute.

(5), (6) Repealed.

(7) An order directing another or an additional mode of service of a summons in a special case may be made by the Court.

(da) Service by Publication. No order shall be entered under 10 Del. C. §365 unless a verified complaint or affidavit accompanying the application for such an order contains an allegation that any defendant is a nonresident of the State and contains a further allegation as to the last known address of such defendant or an allegation that the address of the defendant outside Delaware is unknown and cannot, with due diligence, be ascertained. In addition to the publication of the order for the appearance of a defendant prescribed by 10 Del. C. §365, the order shall provide for sending such defendant by registered or certified mail a copy of such order and a copy of the complaint at the defendant's address outside of Delaware where the verified complaint or affidavit contains such information. The Court may direct the giving of other notice to such defendant in such manner as may be deemed appropriate under the circumstances.

(db) Service by Publication and Seizure. (1) No order shall be entered under 10 Del. C. §366 unless it appears in the complaint that the defendant or any one or more of the defendants is a nonresident of the State of Delaware and the application therefor is accompanied by the affidavit of a plaintiff or other credible person stating:

(a) As to each nonresident defendant whose appearance is sought to be compelled, the defendant's last known address or a statement that such address is unknown and cannot with due diligence be ascertained.

(b) The following information as to the property of each such defendant sought to be seized:

(i) A reasonable description thereof.

(ii) The estimated amount and value thereof.

(iii) The nature of the defendant's title or interest therein; and if such title or interest be equitable in nature, the name of the holder of the legal title.

(iv) The source of affiant's information as to any of the items as to which the affidavit is made on information and belief.

(v) The reason for the omission of any of the required statements.

(2) Within 3 business days after the filing of such bond or bonds as may be required or within such other time as the Court may fix, the Register shall, in addition to making the required publication, send by registered or certified mail to each defendant whose

appearance is sought to be compelled a certified copy of the order and a copy of the pleading asserting the claim.

(3) After the filing of such bond or bonds as may be required by the order, but not later than 10 days after the date of the order of seizure, the sequestrator shall serve a certified copy of the order upon the person, persons or corporation having possession or custody of the property or control of its transfer, and shall seize the property. The sequestrator shall seize property which is, or appears, not to be susceptible of physical seizure within the State by serving a director in writing that the person, persons or corporation having possession or custody of the property or control of its transfer, shall:

(a) Retain the property and recognize no transfer thereof until further notice from the sequestrator or order of the Court;

(b) Forthwith make a notation upon any records pertaining to the property that such property is held pursuant to the order of the Court; and

(c) Within 10 days after the date of such service, deliver a certificate under oath to the sequestrator, specifying (i) Such defendant's property, if any, of which it has possession, custody or control or control of its transfer; (ii) whether the title or interest of each such defendant is legal or beneficial; and (iii) if legal, the name and address of the holder of any equitable title or interest therein, if known, and, if beneficial, the name and address of the holder of the legal title thereto, if known.

(4) Within 20 days after seizure, unless otherwise specially ordered, the sequestrator shall make a return to the Court, therein setting out all proceedings hereunder to the date of said return, including the date and hour or service and seizure pursuant to subparagraph (3) hereof.

(5) The Court may in its discretion and subject to statutory requirements dispense with or modify compliance with the requirements of any part of this rule in any cause upon application to it stating the reasons therefor.

(dc) Service Pursuant to 10 Del. C. §3114 (1)(a) In every action where service of process is sought pursuant to 10 Del. C. §3114 against a nonresident of Delaware by reason of such nonresident's service as director, trustee or member of the governing body of a corporation organized under the laws of this State, the party seeking such service of process shall at the time when such service is applied for file with the Register in Chancery a statement signed by the attorney for the applicant or, if the applicant is not represented by counsel, by the applicant, containing the following information:

(i) The name and principal business address of the corporation upon whose governing body the nonresident serves or has served, which address shall be the principal business address set forth on the most recent annual report filed by the corporation with the Secretary of State of Delaware, unless the statement shall also contain the basis for the applicant's conclusion that the business address set forth on the most recent annual report is not presently the principal business address of the corporation.

(ii) The name and address, including county, of the registered agent in Delaware of said corporation, or a statement that the corporation has no present registered agent.

(iii) The last residence address known to the applicant of each nonresident as to whom service of process is sought, which address shall be the residence address of such nonresident defendant set forth on the most recent annual report filed by the corporation with the Secretary of State of Delaware, unless the statement shall also contain the basis for the applicant's conclusion that the residence address set forth in the most recent annual report filed by the corporation is not presently the residence address of such nonresident.

(b) If any information called for by subparagraph (1)(a) is not known to the applicant, the statement shall so state and shall also state affirmatively that the applicant has made diligent efforts to ascertain such information.

(2)(a) If the summons presented by the plaintiff applying for service pursuant to 10 Del. C. §3114 is in proper form, the Register in Chancery shall sign, seal and issue it to the plaintiff for service upon the registered agent of the corporation upon whose governing board the nonresident serves or has served, or, if the corporation has no registered agent, upon the Secretary of State. The plaintiff shall file a return of service forthwith after effectuation of said service.

(b) The summons issued pursuant to subparagraph (2)(a) hereof shall, in addition to the statements called for under other provisions of law, state that it is issued pursuant to

10 Del. C. §3114 and a copy of that statute shall be appended thereto. The summons shall direct that an answer or other responsive pleading be filed in accordance with the time provisions of the statute.

(3) Within 7 days after service under subparagraph (2)(b) hereof is effected, the Register shall send by registered mail to each nonresident upon whom service is being effected, copies of all of the papers served upon the corporation under subparagraph (2)(a) hereof at: (a) The principal place of business of the corporation and (b) the residence address of such nonresident. The Register shall note on the docket of the cause the date upon which such mailings take place.

IN THE COURT OF CHANCERY OF THE STATE OF
DELAWARE IN AND FOR NEW CASTLE COUNTY

Plaintiff,	CIVIL ACTION NO.
v.	SUMMONS PURSUANT
Defendant.	TO 10 DEL. C. §3114

THE STATE OF DELAWARE
TO THE SHERIFF OF NEW CASTLE COUNTY
YOU ARE COMMANDED:

To Summon the above named individual defendant ( ) by service pursuant to 10 Del. C. §3114 upon the defendant(s)' designated agent for service of process in Delaware, ..., being the registered agent for ...., a Delaware corporation, so that within the time required by law, such defendant ( ) shall serve upon ...., plaintiff's attorney whose address is .... and answer to the complaint.

To serve upon defendant ( ) a copy hereof, of the complaint, and of a statement of plaintiff filed pursuant to Chancery Court Rule 4(dc)(1).

Dated ....

....
Register in Chancery

(e) and (f) Omitted.

(g) Return. The summons provided for in paragraph (a) hereof shall be returnable 20 days after the issuance thereof unless otherwise specially ordered. The person serving the process shall make return thereof to the Court promptly, after service and in any event on the return day thereof. Process which cannot be served before the return day thereof shall be returned on the return day and such return shall set forth the reasons why service could not be had. If service is made by a person other than by an officer or the officer's deputy such person's return shall be verified. Failure to make a return or proof of service shall not affect the validity of service.

(h) Amendment. At any time in its discretion and upon such terms as it deems just, the Court may allow any process or return of proof of service to be amended unless it clearly appears that material prejudice would result to the substantial rights of the party against whom the process issued. (Last amended eff. 2-1-06.)

Rule 23.1 DERIVATIVE ACTIONS BY SHAREHOLDERS.—In a derivative action brought by one or more shareholders or members to enforce a right of a corporation or of an unincorporated association, the corporation or association having failed to enforce a right which may properly be asserted by it, the complaint shall allege that the plaintiff was a shareholder or member at the time of the transaction of which the plaintiff complains or that the plaintiff's share or membership thereafter devolved on the plaintiff by operation of law. The complaint shall also allege with particularity the efforts, if any, made by the plaintiff to obtain the action the plaintiff desires from the directors or comparable authority and the reasons for the plaintiff's failure to obtain the action or for not making the effort.

(b) Each person seeking to serve as a representative plaintiff on behalf of a corporation or unincorporated association pursuant to this Rule shall file with the Register in Chancery an affidavit stating that the person has not received, been promised or offered and will not accept any form of compensation, directly or indirectly, for prosecuting or serving as a representative party in the derivative action in which the person or entity is a named party except (i) such fees, costs or other payments as the Court expressly approves to be paid to or on behalf of such person, or (ii) reimbursement, paid by such person's attorneys, of actual and reasonable out-of-pocket expenditures incurred directly in connection with the prosecution of the action. The affidavit required by this subpart shall be filed within 10 days after the earliest of the affiant filing the complaint, filing a motion to intervene in the action or filing a motion seeking appointment as a representative party in the action. An affidavit provided pursuant to this subpart shall not be construed to be a waiver of the attorney-client privilege.

(c) The action shall not be dismissed or compromised without the approval of the Court, and notice by mail, publication or otherwise of the proposed dismissal or compromise shall be given to shareholders or members in such manner as the Court directs; except that if the dismissal is to be without prejudice or with prejudice to the plaintiff only, then such dismissal shall be ordered without notice thereof if there is a showing that no compensation in any form has passed directly or indirectly from any of the defendants to the plaintiff or plaintiff's attorney and that no promise to give any such compensation has been made. At the time that any party moves or otherwise applies to the Court for approval of a compromise of all or any part of a derivative action, each representative plaintiff in such action shall file with the Register in Chancery a further affidavit in the form required by subpart (b) of this rule.

(d) For purposes of this Rule, and "unincorporated association" includes a statutory trust, business trust, limited liability company and a partnership (whether general or limited), and a "member" includes a person permitted by applicable law to bring a derivative action to enforce a right of such an unincorporated association. (Last amended eff. 1-1-07.)

.1 Pre-suit demand.—Pre-suit demand was not excused where plaintiffs alleged that defendant directors either wittingly or unwittingly permitted the allegedly illegal course of conduct to develop and continue to the point where Merrill Lynch was exposed to enormous legal liability and that, in so doing, they violated their fiduciary duty to monitor Merrill Lynch's corporate affairs. The court found that the law of Delaware, the state of Merrill Lynch's incorporation, was controlling. Under Delaware law, conclusory allegations of recklessness or gross negligence are insufficient to overcome the strong presumption of propriety afforded by the business judgment rule. *Wilson v Tully,* 676 NYS2d 531 *(NY App Div 1998).*

Demand in a derivative suit will not be excused where plaintiff's allegations were based entirely on a newspaper article, which failed to cast doubt upon the directors' independence or showed that the directors had not validly exercised their business judgment. *White v Panic, C.A. No. 16800 (Ch Ct 1-19-00).*

A stockholder is excused from making a demand in derivative litigation when one member of a two-member board of directors cannot impartially consider such demand. *Beneville v York, C.A. No. 17638 (Ch Ct 7-10-00).*

Shareholders meet their burden of showing demand futility where they show that half the directors of a corporation's board, which has an even number of directors, are directly interested or are subject to a reasonable doubt about their independence. *In re The Limited, Inc Shareholders Litigation,* 2002 Del. Ch. LEXIS 28 *(Ch Ct 2002).*

In a derivative action involving a closely-held corporation, demand is excused where there are two opposing director factions and a director whose independence is at issue is consistently allied with the faction that opposes the faction that is bringing the derivative action. *Haseotes v Bentas,* 2002 Del. Ch. LEXIS 106 *(Ch Ct 2002).*

Demand futility is not established where the complaint does not with particularity raise a reasonable doubt that a majority of the directors are interested or dependent—e.g., the complaint fails to state percentage of ownership in various entities by putatively controlling or dominating directors. *Zimmerman v Braddock,* 2002 Del. Ch. LEXIS 145 *(Ch Ct 2002).*

Pre-suit demand is excused for a derivative claim that a corporation's board granted key executives severance packages for the purpose of entrenchment where doubt is cast about the disinterest and independence of a majority of the directors. *California Public Employees' Retirement System v Coulter,* 2002 Del. Ch. LEXIS 144 *(Ch Ct 2002).*

In a case that sends a strong message that in a derivative action, demand excusal must be supported by particularized facts, the Chancery Court dismissed a complaint alleging breach of fiduciary duty where the court found that the plaintiffs did not "come close" to meeting their burden of showing that directors were interested, and admonished the plaintiffs for having failed to seek books and records that could have provided the basis for particularized fact plead-ing. *Guttman v JenHsun-Huang,* 2003 Del. Ch. LEXIS 48 *(Ch Ct 2003).*

Failure to particularize facts that support demand excusal—occurring most likely as the result of a race to the courthouse and a failure to conduct a presuit investigation—will doom a derivative action. *In re Citigroup Inc Shareholders Litigation,* 2003 Del. Ch. LEXIS 61 *(Ch Ct 2003).*

For purposes of demand futility, a director is not interested where a derivative action names the director as a defendant and the plaintiff fails to plead with particularity facts that tend to show that it is substantially likely that the director will face personal liability. *Rattner v Bidzos,* 2003 Del. Ch. LEXIS 103 *(Ch Ct 2003).*

For purposes of determining demand futility, mere friendship between directors who move in the same social circles and who have developed business relationships, even where such friendships have preceded membership on a corporation's board of directors, does not by itself impugn those directors' independence. *Beam v Stewart, 845 A2d 1040 (2004).*

A plaintiff stockholders' failure to bring pre-suit demand is excused and does not jeopardize a derivative action for stock option backdating where over half the board members are not disinterested; however, the stockholder does not have standing to prosecute those elements of the complaint that pre-date her stock ownership. *Conrad v Blank, 2007 Del. Ch. LEXIS 130 (Ch Ct 2007).*

A derivative action must be dismissed where the plaintiffs have not made pre-suit demand on the board, and where no directors are interested or dependent, the directors were adequately informed of the challenged transaction, and the directors do not face a substantial likelihood of personal liability. *In re the Dow Chemical Company Derivative Litigation, 2010 Del. Ch. LEXIS 2 (Ch Ct 2010).*

.2 Merger; breach of duties of loyalty and care.—Where a corporation's former directors negotiated and approved a merger that uniquely benefitted one director and the son of another to the exclusion of the rest of the corporation's stockholders, plaintiffs stated claims for breach of the duties of loyalty and care, and therefore, an exculpatory clause in the corporation's charter barring damages for the breach of duty of care would not bar recovery for the breach of duty and loyalty. *Chaffin v GNI Group, Inc, C.A. No. 16211-NC (Ch Ct 9-3-99).*

An action for breach of fiduciary duty that is brought derivatively will be dismissed for demand failure where all directors of the corporation are named, but a majority of them have no management positions and no evidence is adduced to suggest that the non-management directors were not independent or disinterested. *Akins v Cobb, 2001 Del. Ch. LEXIS 135 (Ch Ct 2001).*

An underwriting agreement that provides for mandatory arbitration for any dispute, controversy, or claim that is "connected to" the agreement, covers well-pled claims for breach of fiduciary duty that do not depend on proof of a breach of the underwriting agreement. *Parfi Holding AB v Mirror Image Internet, Inc, 2001 Del. Ch. LEXIS 154 (Ch Ct 2001).*

Where it is claimed that directors breached their duty of loyalty and care by granting the corporation's chairman a stock option agreement that constituted corporate waste, the independence of the corporation's directors is put into dispute where it is alleged that some of the directors were also executive officers who were beholden to the chairman; some of the directors received excessive compensation and were beholden to the chairman by virtue of fees paid to their firm; some of the directors, albeit outside directors, received excessive compensation; and some of the directors received valuable stock options. *Telxon Corp v Bogomolny, 2001 Del. Ch. LEXIS 131 (Ch Ct 2001).*

A breach of fiduciary claim based on knowing misrepresentation is derivative in nature and will be dismissed with prejudice where the plaintiff has disavowed any intention of bringing a derivative action. *Manzo v Rite Aid Corp, 2002 Del. Ch. LEXIS 147 (Ch Ct 2002).*

The household icon, Martha Stewart (Stewart), a director of Martha Stewart Living Omnimedia, Inc. (MSO), and its founder, chairman, chief executive officer, and by far its majority shareholder, was alleged to have improperly traded shares of ImClone Systems, Inc. (ImClone). These allegations, which subsequently were presented in a formal indictment, were well-publicized. Monica Beam, an MSO shareholder, brought a derivative action against MSO's directors, asserting, *inter alia*, that the director defendants breached their fiduciary duties by failing to ensure that Stewart would not conduct her personal, financial, and legal affairs in a manner that would harm MSO, its intellectual property, or its business. The court concluded that MSO's board had no duty to monitor Stewart's personal affairs. *Beam v Stewart, 2003 Del. Ch. LEXIS 98 (Ch Ct 2003).*

.3 Derivative plaintiff standing in insider sale occurs upon completion of transaction.—A plaintiff has standing to maintain his derivative claims where an insider sale that was part of a merger was authorized when the plaintiff was not a stockholder, was consummated when the shares were issued to the insiders, which occurred after plaintiff became a shareholder. *Leung v Schuler, C.A. No. 17089 (Ch Ct 2-29-00).*

.4 De novo review of Chancery Court's dismissal of derivative suit.—The Delaware Supreme Court will apply a de novo review and not an abuse of discretion review of an appeal from a dismissal of a derivative suit involving the Court of Chancery's ruling on a Chancery Rule 23.1 motion to dismiss. *Brehm v Eisner, 746 A2d 244 (2000).*

.5 Corporate waste.—A board of director's decision to lend corporate funds to its CEO's for settlement of a lawsuit does not constitute corporate waste, and therefore is presumed to be a valid exercise of business judgment, where the CEO provides some collateral for the loan and there is no evidence that at the time of the transaction the transaction was not worthwhile. *White v Panic, 783 A2d 543 (2001).*

.6 Disinterested directors.—For the purpose of determining disinterestedness, several board of directors resolutions may be treated as one interrelated group of transactions where each of the resolutions is a quid pro quo for the others and where the directors who voted for the resolutions, taken together, personally benefit from passage of the resolutions. *In re National Auto Credit, Inc Shareholders Litigation, 2003 Del. Ch. LEXIS 5 (Ch Ct 2003).*

.7 Misleading disclosures.—Allegedly misleading partial disclosures in a proxy statement soliciting shareholder votes for the election of directors is not an injury to the individual voting rights of the shareholders, and, therefore, an action based on those misleading disclosures must be brought derivatively. *Paskowitz v Wohlstadter, 822 A2d 1272 (Md Ct Spec App 2003).*

.8 Class certification.—The rejection of minority shareholders' disclosure claims does not constitute an adequate basis for barring minority shareholders who vote yes on a merger or who later accept the merger consideration from pressing a fairness challenge to the merger, and, therefore, the minority shareholders cannot be denied class certification. *In re JCC Holding Co Shareholders Litigation, 2003 Del. Ch. LEXIS 99 (Ch Ct 2003).*

.9 Demand requirements.—Where a plaintiff's derivative complaint has been dismissed and the plaintiff is given leave to file an amended complaint, the plaintiff must make a demand on the board of directors in place at that time the amended complaint is filed or demonstrate that demand is legally excused as to that board. *Braddock v Zimmerman, 906 A2d 776 (2006).*

.10 Stock option backdating.—A derivative action for backdated stock option grants will be dismissed for lack of standing where the plaintiff shareholder acquired his shares after the stock options were granted, and will also be dismissed for failure to adequately plead demand excusal regarding option grants to employees and officers where the plaintiff cannot show that the board could not exercise an independent and disinterested business judgment in responding to a demand. The complaint will also be dismissed regarding option grants to a majority of the board where the stockholders approve the issuance of the exact number of options to be awarded annually to the outside directors and the date of issuance. *Desimone v Barrows, 2007 Del. Ch. LEXIS 75 (Ch Ct 2007).*

A plaintiff stockholders' failure to bring pre-suit demand is excused and does not jeopardize a derivative action for stock option backdating where over half the board members are not disinterested; however, the stockholder does not have standing to prosecute those elements of the complaint that predate her stock ownership. *Conrad v Blank, 2007 Del. Ch. LEXIS 130 (Ch Ct 2007).*

.11 Demand excusal; excessive executive compensation.—In a derivative action claiming that a board's compensation to a corporation's executive is excessive, demand is excused where sufficient facts are alleged that when taken together show that a majority of the directors were neither sufficiently disinterested nor independent to consider objectively a demand upon the board. *In re InfoUSA, Inc Shareholders Litigation, 2007 Del. Ch. LEXIS 123 (Ch Ct 2007).*

.12 Special litigation committee; discovery.—In connection with a motion to dismiss a derivative action for failure to make demand, a motion to compel discovery of documents relied on by a special litigation committee that investigated the matters alleged in the complaint will be granted where the defendants who are seeking to dismiss the action expressly and repeatedly reference the committee's findings. *Young v Klaassan, 2008 Del. Ch. LEXIS 52 (Ch Ct 2008).*

.13 Demand futility; business judgment rule.—Demand futility is established where directors receive options under a stockholder approved option plan, the directors stand on both sides of the transaction, and particularized allegations support an inference that the directors intended to violate the terms of the plan by fraudulently depressing the value of the options, thus rebutting the business judgment rule presumption. *London v Tyrrell, 2008 Del. Ch. LEXIS 75 (Ch Ct 2008).*

A derivative action must be dismissed where the plaintiffs have not made pre-suit demand on the board, and where no directors are interested or dependent, the directors were adequately informed of the challenged transaction, and the directors do not face a substantial likelihood of personal liability. *In re the Dow Chemical Company Derivative Litigation, 2010 Del. Ch. LEXIS 2 (Ch Ct 2010).*

.14 Stock option claims; direct vs. derivative.—A claim that a shareholder failed to receive adequate merger consideration because of previously issued stock options to which merger consideration was allocated is a derivative claim. *Feldman v Cutaia, 951 A2d 727 (2008).*

.15 Preferred shareholders.—Preferred shareholders have standing to bring derivative claims in the absence of express restrictions or limitations in the articles of incorporation, the preferred share designations, or some other appropriate document. *MCG Capital Corp v Maginn, 2010 Del. Ch. LEXIS 87 (Ch Ct 2010).*

.16 Attorneys' fees; corporate benefit doctrine.—A shareholder whose litigation has resulted in disabling continuing director provisions, thereby promoting the shareholder franchise for all shareholders, has conferred a substantial and significant benefit on the shareholders, and is therefore entitled to a reasonable award of attorneys' fees and expenses. *San Antonio Fire & Police Pension Fund v Bradbury, 2010 Del. Ch. LEXIS 218 (Ch Ct 2010).*

.17 Double derivative actions.—To maintain a double derivative action, a shareholder who was a pre-merger shareholder in the acquired company and who is a current shareholder, by virtue of a stock-for-stock merger, in the post-merger parent company, is not required to demonstrate that, at the time of the alleged wrongdoing at the acquired company, the shareholder owned stock in the acquiring company, and the acquiring company owned stock in the acquired company. *Lambrecht v O'Neal, 3 A3d 277 (2010).*

[The page following this is DRULPA-i]

2011 AMENDMENTS TO THE DELAWARE REVISED UNIFORM LIMITED PARTNERSHIP ACT—ANALYSIS

By Mark V. Purpura
Richards, Layton & Finger, P.A.
Wilmington, Delaware

I. Introduction

Consistent with Delaware's commitment to maintaining statutes that are state-of-the-art with respect to limited partnerships and limited liability limited partnerships, the Delaware Revised Uniform Limited Partnership Act, 6 *Del. C.* § 17-101, *et seq.* (the "Act"), was amended in 2011. The 2011 amendments to the Act (the "2011 Amendments") became effective on August 1, 2011. Some of the 2011 Amendments are technical in nature, but the more substantive aspects of the 2011 Amendments are discussed below.

II. Address of Registered Office and Registered Agent [6 Del. C. §§ 17-104(k) and 17-206(f)]

The 2011 Amendments add a new subsection (k) to Section 17-104 of the Act, which requires the address of the registered agent or the registered office of a limited partnership listed in any certificate or other document filed with the Secretary of State to include the street, number, city and postal code. The 2011 Amendments also amend Section 17-206 of the Act by adding a new subsection (f), which provides that such requirement in Section 17-104(k) does not apply to any document filed with the Secretary of State prior to August 1, 2011, unless a filing is being made to change the address of a registered agent or registered office.

III. Certificate of Correction of Certificate of Cancellation [6 Del. C. § 17-203]

The 2011 Amendments amend Section 17-203 of the Act to confirm that a certificate of cancellation that has been filed prior to the dissolution or the completion of the winding up of a limited partnership may be corrected as an erroneously executed certificate by filing a certificate of correction of such certificate of cancellation. The amendment thus permits the termination of a limited partnership to be negated in certain situations, such as when assets of a terminated limited partnership are later discovered, liabilities or potential liabilities of a terminated limited partnership are threatened or discovered before the statute of limitations has expired, or a certificate of cancellation was inadvertently filed or not duly authorized.

IV. Future Effective Dates [6 Del. C. § 17-206(b)]

The 2011 Amendments amend Section 17-206(b) of the Act to provide that a future effective date or time specified in any certificate filed under the Act on or after January 1, 2012 shall not be later than a time on the 180th day after the date such certificate has been filed with the Secretary of State.

V. Simultaneous Filings for Domestications and Conversions [6 Del. C. §§ 17-215(b) and 17-217(b)]

The 2011 Amendments amend Section 17-215 of the Act to clarify that a certificate of domestication and a certificate of limited partnership for a non-United States entity domesticating to Delaware as a limited partnership must be filed simultaneously in the office of the Secretary of State and, to the extent such certificates have a future effective date or time, such certificates must provide for the same effective date or time. The 2011 Amendments also amend Section 17-217 of the Act to clarify that a certificate of conversion to limited partnership and a certificate of limited partnership for an entity converting to a limited partnership must be filed simultaneously in the office of the Secretary of State and, to the extent such certificates have a future effective date or time, such certificates must provide for the same effective date or time.

VI. Amendments to Limited Partnership Agreements [6 Del. C. § 17-302(f)]

The 2011 Amendments amend Section 17-302(f) of the Act to provide that supermajority amendment provisions in a limited partnership agreement apply only to provisions expressly included in such agreement and do not apply to default voting provisions of the Act unless otherwise provided in the limited partnership agreement. In a 2004 case, *In re LJM2 Co-Investment, L.P. Limited Partners Litigation*, 866 A.2d 762 (Del. Ch. 2004) ("*LJM2*"), the Delaware Court of Chancery considered an amendment provision in a limited partnership agreement prohibiting amendments to any provision of the agreement that affected the vote required in such provision unless the proposed amendment was approved by at least the vote originally required in such provision. The Court of Chancery held that the amendment section applied to amendments to default voting provisions of the Act that became part of the limited partnership agreement in the absence of any specific contractual provision to the contrary. Thus, the amendment to Section 17-302(f) adopts a rule different from the analysis articulated by the Court of Chancery in *LJM2*.

VII. Written and Electronically Transmitted Consents [§§ 17-302(e) and 17-405(d)]

The 2011 Amendments amend Section 17-302(e) of the Act to clarify that actions by limited partners of a limited partnership without a meeting may take the form of a written consent or an electronic transmission. Similarly, the 2011 Amendments amend Section 17-405(d) of the Act to clarify that general partners of a limited partnership may take action without a meeting in the form of a written consent or an electronic transmission. The amendments to Sections 17-302(e) and 17-405(d) make the Act consistent with Section 141(f) of the General Corporation Law of the State of Delaware, which authorizes board action by written consent or electronic transmission.

[The page following this is DE-35]

Part II

DELAWARE REVISED UNIFORM LIMITED PARTNERSHIP ACT

(Effective January 1, 1983, as amended through August 1, 2011)

Delaware Code Annotated, Title 6, Chapter 17

Subchapter I
GENERAL PROVISIONS

§ 17-101.	Definitions.
§ 17-102.	Name set forth in certificate.
§ 17-103.	Reservation of name.
§ 17-104.	Registered office; registered agent.
§ 17-105.	Service of process on domestic limited partnerships.
§ 17-106.	Nature of business permitted; powers.
§ 17-107.	Business transactions of partner with the partnership.
§ 17-108.	Indemnification.
§ 17-109.	Service of process on partners and liquidating trustees.
§ 17-110.	Contested matters relating to general partners; contested votes.
§ 17-111.	Interpretation and enforcement of partnership agreement.

Subchapter II
FORMATION; CERTIFICATE OF LIMITED PARTNERSHIP

§ 17-201.	Certificate of limited partnership.
§ 17-202.	Amendment to certificate.
§ 17-203.	Cancellation of certificate.
§ 17-204.	Execution.
§ 17-205.	Execution, amendment or cancellation by judicial order.
§ 17-206.	Filing.
§ 17-207.	Liability for false statement.
§ 17-208.	Notice.
§ 17-209.	Delivery of certificates to limited partners.
§ 17-210.	Restated certificate.
§ 17-211.	Merger and consolidation.
§ 17-212.	Contractual appraisal rights.
§ 17-213.	Certificate of correction.
§ 17-214.	Limited partnerships as limited liability limited partnerships.
§ 17-215.	Domestication of non-United States entities.
§ 17-216.	Transfer or continuance of domestic limited partnership.
§ 17-217.	Conversion of certain entities to a limited partnership.
§ 17-218.	Series of limited partners, general partners, partnership interests or assets.
§ 17-219.	Approval of conversion of a limited partnership.

Subchapter III
LIMITED PARTNERS

§ 17-301.	Admission of limited partners.
§ 17-302.	Classes and voting.
§ 17-303.	Liability to third parties.
§ 17-304.	Person erroneously believing himself or herself limited partner.
§ 17-305.	Access to and confidentiality of information; records.
§ 17-306.	Remedies for breach of partnership agreement by limited partner.

Subchapter IV
GENERAL PARTNERS

§ 17-401. Admission of general partners.
§ 17-402. Events of withdrawal.
§ 17-403. General powers and liabilities.
§ 17-404. Contributions by a general partner.
§ 17-405. Classes and voting.
§ 17-406. Remedies for breach of partnership agreement by general partner.
§ 17-407. Reliance on reports and information by limited partners, liquidating trustees, and general partners.

Subchapter V
FINANCE

§ 17-501. Form of contribution.
§ 17-502. Liability for contribution.
§ 17-503. Allocation of profits and losses.
§ 17-504. Allocation of distributions.
§ 17-505. Defense of usury not available.

Subchapter VI
DISTRIBUTIONS AND WITHDRAWAL

§ 17-601. Interim distributions.
§ 17-602. Withdrawal of general partner and assignment of general partner's partnership interest.
§ 17-603. Withdrawal of limited partner.
§ 17-604. Distribution upon withdrawal.
§ 17-605. Distribution in kind.
§ 17-606. Right to distribution.
§ 17-607. Limitations on distribution.

Subchapter VII
ASSIGNMENT OF PARTNERSHIP INTERESTS

§ 17-701. Nature of partnership interest.
§ 17-702. Assignment of partnership interest.
§ 17-703. Partner's partnership interest subject to charging order.
§ 17-704. Right of assignee to become limited partner.
§ 17-705. Powers of estate of deceased or incompetent partner.

Subchapter VIII
DISSOLUTION

§ 17-801.   Nonjudicial dissolution.
§ 17-802.   Judicial dissolution.
§ 17-803.   Winding up.
§ 17-804.   Distribution of assets.
§ 17-805.   Trustees or receivers for limited partnerships; appointment; powers; duties.
§ 17-806.   Revocation of dissolution.

Subchapter IX
FOREIGN LIMITED PARTNERSHIPS

§ 17-901.   Law governing.
§ 17-902.   Registration required; application.
§ 17-903.   Issuance of registration.
§ 17-904.   Name; registered office; registered agent.
§ 17-905.   Amendments to application.
§ 17-906.   Cancellation of registration.
§ 17-907.   Doing business without registration.
§ 17-908.   Foreign limited partnerships doing business without having qualified; injunctions.
§ 17-909.   Execution; liability.
§ 17-910.   Service of process on registered foreign limited partnerships.
§ 17-911.   Service of process on unregistered foreign limited partnerships.
§ 17-912.   Activities not constituting doing business.

Subchapter X
DERIVATIVE ACTIONS

§ 17-1001.   Right to bring action.
§ 17-1002.   Proper plaintiff.
§ 17-1003.   Complaint.
§ 17-1004.   Expenses.

Subchapter XI
MISCELLANEOUS

§ 17-1101.	Construction and application of chapter and partnership agreement.
§ 17-1102.	Short title.
§ 17-1103.	Severability.
§ 17-1104.	Effective date and extended effective date.
§ 17-1105.	Cases not provided for in this chapter.
§ 17-1106.	Prior law.
§ 17-1107.	Fees.
§ 17-1108.	Reserved power of the State of Delaware to alter or repeal chapter.
§ 17-1109.	Annual tax of domestic limited partnership and foreign limited partnership.
§ 17-1110.	Cancellation of certificate of limited partnership for failure to pay annual tax.
§ 17-1111.	Revival of domestic limited partnership.

Subchapter I
GENERAL PROVISIONS

§ 17-101. Definitions.

As used in this chapter unless the context otherwise requires:

(1) "Certificate of limited partnership" means the certificate referred to in § 17-201 of this title, and the certificate as amended.

(2) "Contribution" means any cash, property, services rendered or a promissory note or other obligation to contribute cash or property or to perform services, which a partner contributes to a limited partnership in the capacity as a partner.

(3) "Event of withdrawal of a general partner" means an event that causes a person to cease to be a general partner as provided in § 17-402 of this title.

(4) "Foreign limited partnership" includes a partnership formed under the laws of any state or under the laws of any foreign country or other foreign jurisdiction and having as partners 1 or more general partners and 1 or more limited partners.

(5) "General partner" means a person who is named as a general partner in the certificate of limited partnership or similar instrument under which a limited partnership is formed if so required and who is admitted to the limited partnership as a general partner in accordance with the partnership agreement or this chapter.

(6) "Knowledge" means a person's actual knowledge of a fact, rather than the person's constructive knowledge of the fact.

(7) "Limited liability limited partnership" means a limited partnership complying with § 17-214 of this title.

(8) "Limited partner" means a person who is admitted to a limited partnership as a limited partner as provided in § 17-301 of this title or, in the case of a foreign limited partnership, in accordance with the laws of the state or foreign country or other foreign jurisdiction under which the limited partnership is formed.

(9) "Limited partnership" and "domestic limited partnership" mean a partnership formed under the laws of the State of Delaware consisting of 2 or more persons and having 1 or more general partners and 1 or more limited partners, and includes, for all purposes of the laws of the State of Delaware, a limited liability limited partnership.

(10) "Liquidating trustee" means a person, other than a general partner, but including a limited partner, carrying out the winding up of a limited partnership.

(11) "Partner" means a limited or general partner.

(12) "Partnership agreement" means any agreement, written, oral or implied of the partners as to the affairs of a limited partnership and the conduct of its business. A partner of a limited partnership or an assignee of a partnership interest is bound by the partnership agreement whether or not the partner or assignee executes the partnership agreement. A limited partnership is not required to execute its partnership agreement. A limited partnership is bound by its partnership agreement whether or not the limited partnership executes the partnership agreement. A partnership agreement is not subject to any statute of frauds (including Section 2714 of this Title). A partnership agreement may provide rights to any person, including a person who is not a party to the partnership agreement, to the extent set forth therein. A written partnership agreement or another written agreement or writing:

a. May provide that a person shall be admitted as a limited partner of a limited partnership, or shall become an assignee of a partnership interest or other rights or powers of a limited partner to the extent assigned (i) if such person (or a representative authorized by such person orally, in writing or by other action such as payment for a partnership interest) executes the partnership agreement or any other writing evidencing the intent of such person to become a limited partner or assignee, or (ii) without such execution, if such person (or a representative authorized by such person orally, in writing or by other action such as payment for a partnership interest) complies with the conditions for becoming a limited partner or assignee as set forth in the partnership agreement or any other writing; and

b. Shall not be unenforceable by reason of its not having been signed by a person being admitted as a limited partner or becoming an assignee as provided in paragraph a. of this subdivision, or by reason of its having been signed by a representative as provided in this title.

(13) "Partnership interest" means a partner's share of the profits and losses of a limited partnership and the right to receive distributions of partnership assets.

(14) "Person" means a natural person, partnership (whether general or limited), limited liability company, trust (including a common law trust, business trust, statutory trust, voting trust or any other form of trust), estate, association (including any group, organization, co-tenancy, plan, board, council or

committee), corporation, government (including a country, state, county or any other governmental subdivision, agency or instrumentality), custodian, nominee or any other individual or entity (or series thereof) in its own or any representative capacity, in each case, whether domestic or foreign.

(15) "Personal representative" means, as to a natural person, the executor, administrator, guardian, conservator or other legal representative thereof and, as to a person other than a natural person, the legal representative or successor thereof.

(16) "State" means the District of Columbia or the Commonwealth of Puerto Rico or any state, territory, possession, or other jurisdiction of the United States other than the State of Delaware.

ANNOTATIONS

Agreement to be read as a whole — A complex commercial contract such as a limited partnership agreement is best interpreted not by focusing on a single clause, but by considering the parties' language and the context of their entire agreement and, where ambiguity exists, from the context in which the parties contracted. *First Olefins Limited Partnership v. American Olefins, Inc.*, 1996 WL 209719 (Del. Ch. Mar. 1, 1996), petition refused, 676 A.2d 902 (Del. 1996).

Agreement to be read precisely — The language of a limited partnership agreement must be read precisely. Where an ambiguity exists, the agreement must be read as a whole. *In re Mesa Limited Partnership Preferred Unitholders Litigation*, 1991 Del. Ch. LEXIS 214 (Del. Ch. Dec. 10, 1991).

Ambiguity construed against general partner — In the absence of evidence that a limited partnership agreement was the product of meaningful individualized negotiations between the general partner and all other parties to the agreement, the principal of contra proferentem applies. Accordingly, ambiguous terms in a limited partnership agreement should be construed against the general partner as the entity solely responsible for the articulation of the terms. In such a case, extrinsic evidence is irrelevant to the intent of all of the parties at the time they entered into the agreement. *SI Management L.P. v. Wininger*, 707 A.2d 37 (Del. 1998).

Amendment to agreement generally — It is permissible for a partnership agreement to create a mechanism by which the agreement may be amended following dissolution of the partnership. *Boesky v. CX Partners, L.P.*, 1988 Del. Ch. LEXIS 60 (Del. Ch. April 28, 1988).

Analogous corporate law — Cases construing corporate law are not binding precedents as to issues arising under a limited partnership agreement, but such cases may be helpful by analogy. *In re Mesa Limited Partnership Preferred Unitholders Litigation*, 1991 Del. Ch. LEXIS 214 (Del. Ch. Dec. 10, 1991), appeal refused, 608 A.2d 728 (Del. 1992).

Analogous corporate law — As a general rule, in the absence of authority addressing an issue in the limited partnership context, analogues to corporate law may be applied. *Katell v. Morgan Stanley Group, Inc.*, 1993 Del. Ch. LEXIS 92 (Del. Ch. June 8, 1993).

Approval of transaction neither ratification nor amendment — That limited partners voted in favor of a sale transaction did not constitute ratification of the general partner's termination of priority distributions under the partnership agreement nor approval of an amendment to the partnership agreement to permit such termination. Ratification requires that the specific transaction to be ratified be clearly delineated to the limited partners' whose approval is sought and that the approval be put to a vote. Similarly, where no amendment to the partnership agreement is proposed and limited partners are not asked to vote on a amendment, mere approval of transaction did not amend agreement. *In re Cencom Cable Income Partners, L.P. Litigation*, 2000 WL 640676 (Del. Ch. May 5, 2000).

Breach of covenant of good faith and fair dealing — In response to a buy/sell notice from a limited partner, the limited partner to whom the notice was directed (i) refused to perform in accordance with the partnership agreement, (ii) made a non-conforming counteroffer, (iii) threatened litigation, and (iv) engaged in conduct designed to exert economic coercion in order to force the other limited partner to accept a sum for its interest that was far lower than what the limited partner was entitled to receive. Such conduct constituted a breach of the implied contractual covenant of good faith and fair dealing. *PAMI-LEMB I Inc. v. EMB-NHC, L.L.C.*, 2004 WL 1488720 (Del. Ch. June 22, 2004).

Contract provisions control rights and duties — Limited partnership agreement is the operative document governing the rights and responsibilities of the partners, and the statute provides "fall-back" or default provisions where the agreement is silent. Where the provisions defining the rights and responsibilities of the parties are spelled out with particularity, those provisions are accorded significant deference by the court, and the contract provisions, not default fiduciary rules, control whether conduct constitutes a breach of duty. *Cantor Fitzgerald, L.P. v. Cantor*, 2001 WL 1456494 (Del. Ch. Nov. 5, 2001).

Default consent requirement for amending agreement — Absent an express provision in a partnership agreement, the consent of all partners is necessary to amend the partnership agreement. *In re LJM2 Co-Inv., L.P.*, 866 A.2d 762 (Del. Ch. 2004).

Implied contractual obligation — A contractual obligation will not be implied unless the court, by reference to the express terms of the contract, can conclude that the parties to the contract, at the time of its drafting, would have agreed to be bound by the implied obligation. Where a partnership agreement prohibited limited partners from competing with the partnership's "Cellular Service" and defined "Cellular Service" with precision, the parties knew at the time of drafting that other forms of competition might be developed and the partnership agreement expressly permitted limited partners to engage in any other business venture, the court would not imply an obligation not to compete with the partnership through the use of new technology that, while not within the definition of "Cellular Service," enabled limited partners to offer essentially the same service as the partnership. *Cincinnati SMSA Limited Partnership v. Cincinnati Bell Cellular Systems Co.*, 1997 WL 525873 (Del. Ch. Aug. 13, 1997), *aff'd*, 708 A.2d 989 (Del. 1998).

Implied obligations — Implying obligations based on the implied covenant of good faith and fair dealing is a cautious enterprise, and the Court will not imply an obligation on the part of a limited partner not to compete when the partnership agreement clearly, expressly and unambiguously limits prohibited competition and provides generous leeway to partners with respect to other ventures. *Cincinnati SMSA Limited Partnership v. Cincinnati Bell Cellular Systems Company*, 708 A.2d 989 (Del. 1998).

Interpretation of agreement — The provisions of a limited partnership agreement should be interpreted using basic rules of contract law, which require the intention of the parties to be determined from the language of the agreement. The agreement should be read in its entirety and interpreted to reconcile all of its provisions. *In re Cencom Cable Income Partners, L.P. Litigation*, 2000 WL 640676 (Del. Ch. May 5, 2000).

Interpretation of agreement — In interpreting partnership agreement, court will look at the entire agreement to determine intent and existence of ambiguity. If the contract is clear, the court will rely on the literal meaning of the words, will not look to extrinsic evidence, and will not attempt to discern intent of the parties. If ambiguity exists, the court, will consider extrinsic evidence to determine the reasonable shared expectations of the parties at the time of contracting. *Interactive Corp. v. Vivendi Universal, S.A.*, 2004 WL 1572932 (Del. Ch. July 6, 2004).

Latent ambiguity — Where limited partnership agreement defined "Cellular Service" in precise terms as service authorized by the FCC under Part 22 of its cellular rules, and there were no internal inconsistencies within the partnership agreement, later developed technology authorized by the FCC under Part 24 of its cellular rules and which permitted limited partners to compete with the partnership by offering an essentially identical service did not create a latent ambiguity justifying resort to extrinsic evidence to interpret the definition of "Cellular Service." *Cincinnati SMSA Limited Partnership v. Cincinnati Bell Cellular Systems Co.*, 1997 WL 525873 (Del. Ch. Aug. 13, 1997), *aff'd*, 708 A.2d 989 (Del. 1998).

Law governing agreement to form partnership — The interpretation of an agreement to form a limited partnership is governed by the law of the state having the most significant relationship to the transaction. Where one party to the agreement was located in Oregon, performance was to be in Oregon, initial negotiations were conducted in Oregon, and the only contact with Delaware was the fact that all of the parties were Delaware corporations, Oregon law would apply in determining whether the agreement resulted in formation of a limited partnership. *GTE Mobilnet Inc. v. Nehalem Cellular, Inc.*, 1994 Del. Ch. LEXIS 30 (Del. Ch. March 17, 1994).

Mistake — To warrant reformation of a limited partnership agreement based on either mutual mistake or unilateral mistake, the party seeking reformation must allege and prove by clear and convincing evidence that the parties came to a specific prior understanding that differed materially from the written agreement. *Interactive Corp. v. Vivendi Universal, S.A.*, 2004 WL 1572932 (Del. Ch. July 6, 2004).

Oral amendments — Where partnership agreement expressly provided that all amendments were to be in writing signed by all of the partners, party seeking to prove oral amendment must present specific and direct evidence of the oral amendment that leaves no doubt of the intention of the parties to change what was previously solemnized by a formal document. *The Continental Insurance Company v. Rutledge & Company, Inc.*, 2000 WL 62951 (Del. Ch. Jan. 10, 2000).

Partnership agreement incorporates default rules — Where a partnership agreement provided that it could be amended by a majority vote, provided that no amendment could alter the vote necessary for any consent "required hereunder" unless such amendment were approved by the vote necessary at the time of the amendment, the words "required hereunder" incorporated the default statutory provision of Section 502(b)(1), which requires a compromise of capital contributions to be approved by all partners. Accordingly, an amendment purporting to reduce to a majority the consent required to compromise capital contributions was invalid in the absence of unanimous consent to the amendment. *In re LJM2 Co-Inv., L.P.*, 866 A.2d 762 (Del. Ch. 2004).

Partnership agreement need not be amendable during liquidation — Although partners may define the specifics of their partnership within the requirements of law, there is no necessity, legal or practical, that requires that an agreement of limited partnership be amendable during the winding-up phase. *Boesky v. CX Partners, L.P.*, 1988 Del. Ch. LEXIS 60 (Del. Ch. April 28, 1988).

Powers of liquidating partner to amend agreement — Where the partnership agreement conferred upon the liquidating partner all of the rights and powers over the assets and liabilities of the partnership which the general partner had over the assets and liabilities of the partnership during the term of the partnership, such power did not include the general partner's power to consent to an amendment to the agreement of limited partnership following dissolution. *Boesky v. CX Partners, L.P.*, 1988 Del. Ch. LEXIS 60 (Del. Ch. April 28, 1988).

Proxy statement disclosure did not trigger dissolution provision — Where limited partnership agreement provided that the partnership would be dissolved upon a written determination by the general partner that future revenues would be insufficient to pay projected costs and expenses or that continued operation of the partnership was not in the best interest of the partners, the general partner's discussion in a proxy statement that the partnership would not have sufficient revenue to pay distributions in the future and that the general partner was therefore recommending that the limited partnership be converted into a corporation if the conversion were approved by the requisite vote of limited partners did not constitute a written determination resulting in a dissolution of the partnership under the terms of the partnership agreement. *In re Mesa Limited Partnership Preferred Unitholders Litigation*, 1991 Del. Ch. LEXIS 214 (Del. Ch. Dec. 10, 1991).

Repudiation of agreement — Where a limited partner invoked a buy/sell provision, and the limited partner to whom the notice was directed stated that it would perform only on terms different from those provided in the agreement and threatened litigation if its terms were not accepted, it repudiated the agreement, could not act a buyer, and was required to sell its interest pursuant to the terms of the agreement to the limited partner who had sent the buy/sell notice. *PAMI-LEMB I Inc. v. EMB-NHC, L.L.C.*, 2004 WL 1488720 (Del. Ch. June 22, 2004).

Tax losses not within purposes — Where the partnership agreement provided that the purpose of the limited partnership was to invest in, develop and otherwise deal with certain real property "for profit and as an investment," the generation of continuing tax losses was not within the purposes of the limited partnership. *PC Tower Center, Inc. v. Tower Center Dev. Assocs. Limited Partnership*, 1989 Del. Ch. LEXIS 72 (Del. Ch. June 8, 1989).

Unilateral amendment by general partner — Although not deciding the issue, the Chancery Court expressed significant reservation that a general partner could, in response to a threatened takeover bid, unilaterally and without a vote of the limited partners amend the partnership agreement to reduce the compensation level of future or successor general partners. *CRI Insured Mortgage Assoc., Inc. v. AIM Capital Management Corp.*, 1990 Del. Ch. LEXIS 232 (Del. Ch. Dec. 20, 1990).

§ 17-102. Name set forth in certificate.

The name of each limited partnership as set forth in its certificate of limited partnership:

(1) Shall contain the words "Limited Partnership" or the abbreviation "L.P." or the designation "L.P." or, in the case of a limited partnership that is formed as or becomes a limited liability limited partnership, shall contain the words, abbreviation or designation required by § 17-214(a) of this Title;

(2) May contain the name of a partner;

(3) Must be such as to distinguish it upon the records in the office of the Secretary of State from the name on such records of any corporation, partnership, limited partnership, statutory trust or limited liability company reserved, registered, formed or organized under the laws of the State of Delaware or qualified to do business or registered as a foreign corporation, foreign limited partnership, foreign statutory trust, foreign partnership or foreign limited liability company in the State of Delaware; provided, however, that a limited partnership may register under any name which is not such as to distinguish it upon the records in the office of the Secretary of State from the name on such records of any domestic or foreign corporation, partnership, statutory trust, or limited liability company or foreign limited partnership reserved, registered, formed or organized under the laws of the State of Delaware with the written consent of the other corporation, partnership, statutory trust, limited liability company or foreign limited partnership, which written consent shall be filed with the Secretary of State; provided further, that, if on July 31, 2011 a limited partnership is registered (with the consent of another limited partnership) under a name which is not such as to distinguish it upon the records in the office of the Secretary of

State from the name on such records of such other domestic limited partnership, it shall not be necessary for any such limited partnership to amend its certificate of limited partnership to comply with this subsection; and

(4) May contain the following words: "Company", "Association", "Club", "Foundation", "Fund", "Institute", "Society", "Union", "Syndicate", "Limited" or "Trust" (or abbreviations of like import).

§ 17-103. Reservation of name.

(a) The exclusive right to the use of a name may be reserved by:

(1) Any person intending to organize a limited partnership under this chapter and to adopt that name;

(2) Any domestic limited partnership or any foreign limited partnership registered in the State of Delaware which, in either case, proposes to change its name;

(3) Any foreign limited partnership intending to register in the State of Delaware and adopt that name; and

(4) Any person intending to organize a foreign limited partnership and intending to have it register in the State of Delaware and adopt that name.

(b) The reservation of a specified name shall be made by filing with the Secretary of State an application, executed by the applicant, specifying the name to be reserved and the name and address of the applicant. If the Secretary of State finds that the name is available for use by a domestic or foreign limited partnership, the Secretary shall reserve the name for the exclusive use of the applicant for a period of 120 days. Once having so reserved a name, the same applicant may again reserve the same name for successive 120 day periods. The right to the exclusive use of a reserved name may be transferred to any other person by filing in the Office of the Secretary of State a notice of the transfer, executed by the applicant for whom the name was reserved, specifying the name to be transferred and the name and address of the transferee. The reservation of a specified name may be cancelled by filing with the Secretary of State a notice of cancellation, executed by the applicant or transferee, specifying the name reservation to be cancelled and the name and address of the applicant or transferee. Unless the Secretary of State finds that any application, notice of transfer, or notice of cancellation filed with the Secretary of State as required by this subsection does not conform to law, upon receipt of all filing fees required by law, the Secretary shall prepare and return to the person who filed such instrument a copy of the filed instrument with a notation thereon of the action taken by the Secretary of State.

(c) A fee as set forth in § 17-1107(a)(1) of this title shall be paid at the time of the initial reservation of any name, at the time of the renewal of any such reservation and at the time of the filing of a notice of the transfer or cancellation of any such reservation.

§ 17-104. Registered office; registered agent.

(a) Each limited partnership shall have and maintain in the State of Delaware:

(1) A registered office which may but need not be a place of its business in the State of Delaware; and

(2) A registered agent for service of process on the limited partnership, having a business office identical with such registered office, which agent may be any of

　a. the limited partnership itself,

　b. an individual resident in the State of Delaware,

　c. a domestic limited liability company, a domestic corporation, a domestic partnership (whether general (including a limited liability partnership) or limited (other than the limited partnership itself, including a limited liability limited partnership)), or a domestic statutory trust, or

　d. a foreign corporation, a foreign partnership (whether general (including a limited liability partnership) or limited (including a limited liability limited partnership)), a foreign limited liability company, or a foreign statutory trust.

(b) A registered agent may change the address of the registered office of the limited partnership(s) for which it is registered agent to another address in the State of Delaware by paying a fee as set forth in § 17-1107(a)(2) of this title and filing with the Secretary of State a certificate, executed by such registered agent, setting forth the address at which such registered agent has maintained the registered office for each of the limited partnerships for which it is a registered agent, and further certifying to the new address to which each such registered office will be changed on a given day, and at which new address such registered agent will thereafter maintain the registered office for each of the limited partnerships for which it is a registered agent. Upon the filing of such certificate, the Secretary of State shall furnish to the registered agent a certified copy of the same under the Secretary's hand and seal of office, and thereafter, or until further change of address, as authorized by law, the registered office in the State of Delaware of each of the limited partnerships for which the agent is a registered agent shall be located at the new address of the registered agent thereof as given in the certificate. In the event of a change of name of any person acting as a registered agent of a limited partnership, such registered agent shall file with the Secretary of State a certificate, executed by such registered agent, setting forth the new name of such registered agent, the name of such registered agent before it was changed and the address at which such registered agent has maintained the registered office for each of the limited partnerships for which it is a registered agent, and shall pay a fee as set forth in § 17-1107(a)(2) of this title. Upon the filing of such certificate, the Secretary of State shall furnish to the registered agent a certified copy of the certificate under his or her hand and seal of office. A change of name of any person acting as a registered agent of a limited partnership as a result of a merger or consolidation of the registered agent, with or into another person which succeeds to its assets and liabilities by operation of law, shall be deemed a change of name for purposes of this section. Filing a certificate under this section shall be deemed to be an amendment of the certificate of limited partnership of each limited partnership affected thereby and each such limited partnership shall not be required to take any further action with respect thereto, to amend its certificate of limited partnership under § 17-202 of this title. Any registered agent filing a certificate under this section shall promptly, upon such filing, deliver a copy of any such certificate to each limited partnership affected thereby.

(c) The registered agent of 1 or more limited partnerships may resign and appoint a successor registered agent by paying a fee as set forth in § 17-1107(a)(2) of this title and filing a certificate with the Secretary of State, stating that it resigns and the name and address of the successor registered agent. There shall be attached to such certificate a statement of each affected limited partnership ratifying and approving such change of registered agent. Upon such filing, the successor registered agent shall become the registered agent of such limited partnerships as have ratified and approved such substitution and the successor registered agent's address, as stated in such certificate, shall become the address of each such limited partnership's registered office in the State of Delaware. The Secretary of State shall then issue a certificate that the successor registered agent has become the registered agent of the limited partnerships so ratifying and approving such change and setting out the names of such limited partnerships. Filing of such certificate of resignation shall be deemed to be an amendment of the certificate of limited partnership of each limited partnership affected thereby and each such limited partnership shall not be required to take any further action with respect thereto to amend its certificate of limited partnership under § 17-202 of this title.

(d) The registered agent of one or more limited partnerships may resign without appointing a successor registered agent by paying a fee as set forth in § 17-1107(a)(2) of this title and filing a certificate of resignation with the Secretary of State, but such resignation shall not become effective until 30 days after the certificate is filed. The certificate shall contain a statement that written notice of resignation was given to each affected limited partnership at least 30 days prior to the filing of the certificate by mailing or delivering such notice to the limited partnership at its address last known to the registered agent and shall set forth the date of such notice. After receipt of the notice of the resignation of its registered agent, the limited partnership for which such registered agent was acting shall obtain and designate a new registered agent, to take the place of the registered agent so resigning. If such limited partnership fails to obtain and designate a new registered agent as aforesaid prior to the expiration of the period of 30 days after the filing by the registered agent of the certificate of resignation, the certificate of such limited partnership shall be cancelled. After the resignation of the registered agent shall have become effective as provided in this section and if no new registered agent shall have been obtained and designated in the time and manner aforesaid, service of legal process against each limited partnership for which the resigned registered agent had been acting shall thereafter be upon the Secretary of State in accordance with § 17-105 of this title.

(e) Every registered agent shall:

(1) If an entity, maintain a business office in the State of Delaware which is generally open, or if an individual, be generally present at a designated location in the State of Delaware, at sufficiently frequent times to accept service of process and otherwise perform the functions of a registered agent;

(2) If a foreign entity, be authorized to transact business in the State of Delaware;

(3) Accept service of process and other communications directed to the limited partnerships and foreign limited partnerships for which it serves as registered agent and forward same to the limited partnership or foreign limited partnerships to which the service or communication is directed; and

(4) Forward to the limited partnerships and foreign limited partnerships for which it serves as registered agent the statement for the annual tax described in § 17-1109 of this Title or an electronic notification of same in a form satisfactory to the Secretary of State.

(f) Any registered agent, who at any time serves as registered agent for more than fifty entities (a "Commercial Registered Agent"), whether domestic or foreign, shall satisfy and comply with the following qualifications.

(1) A natural person serving as a Commercial Registered Agent shall:

a. Maintain a principal residence or a principal place of business in the State of Delaware;

b. Maintain a Delaware business license;

c. Be generally present at a designated location within the State of Delaware during normal business hours to accept service of process and otherwise perform the functions of a registered agent as specified in subsection (e); and

d. Provide the Secretary of State upon request with such information identifying and enabling communication with such Commercial Registered Agent as the Secretary of State shall require.

(2) A domestic or foreign corporation, a domestic or foreign partnership (whether general (including a limited liability partnership) or limited (including a limited liability limited partnership)), a domestic or foreign limited liability company, or a domestic or foreign statutory trust serving as a Commercial Registered Agent shall:

a. Have a business office within the State of Delaware which is generally open during normal business hours to accept service of process and otherwise perform the functions of a registered agent as specified in subsection (e);

b. Maintain a Delaware business license;

c. Have generally present at such office during normal business hours an officer, director or managing agent who is a natural person; and

d. Provide the Secretary of State upon request with such information identifying and enabling communication with such Commercial Registered Agent as the Secretary of State shall require.

(3) For purposes of this subsection and subsection (i)(2)a., a Commercial Registered Agent shall also include any registered agent which has an officer, director or managing agent in common with any other registered agent or agents if such registered agents at any time during such common service as officer, director or managing agent collectively

served as registered agents for more than fifty entities, whether domestic or foreign.

(g) Every limited partnership formed under the laws of the State of Delaware or qualified to do business in the State of Delaware shall provide to its registered agent and update from time to time as necessary the name, business address and business telephone number of a natural person who is a partner, officer, employee or designated agent of the limited partnership, who is then authorized to receive communications from the registered agent. Such person shall be deemed the communications contact for the limited partnership. Every registered agent shall retain (in paper or electronic form) the above information concerning the current communications contact for each limited partnership and each foreign limited partnership for which he, she, or it serves as registered agent. If the limited partnership fails to provide the registered agent with a current communications contact, the registered agent may resign as the registered agent for such limited partnership pursuant to this Section.

(h) The Secretary of State is authorized to issue such rules and regulations as may be necessary or appropriate to carry out the enforcement of subsections (e), (f) and (g) of this Section, and to take actions reasonable and necessary to assure registered agents compliance with subsections (e), (f) and (g). Such actions may include refusal to file documents submitted by a registered agent.

(i) Upon application of the Secretary of State, the Court of Chancery may enjoin any person or entity from serving as a registered agent or as an officer, director or managing agent of a registered agent.

(1) Upon the filing of a complaint by the Secretary of State pursuant to this Section, the Court may make such orders respecting such proceeding as it deems appropriate, and may enter such orders granting interim or final relief as it deems proper under the circumstances.

(2) Any one or more of the following grounds shall be a sufficient basis to grant an injunction pursuant to this Section:

a. With respect to any registered agent who at any time within one (1) year immediately prior to the filing of the Secretary of State's complaint is a Commercial Registered Agent, failure after notice and warning to comply with the qualifications set forth in subsection (e) and/or the requirements of subsections (f) or (g) above;

b. The person serving as a registered agent, or any person who is an officer, director or managing agent of an entity registered agent, has been convicted of a felony or any crime which includes an element of dishonesty or fraud or involves moral turpitude; or

 c. The registered agent has engaged in conduct in connection with acting as a registered agent that is intended to or likely to deceive or defraud the public.

(3) With respect to any order the Court enters pursuant to this Section with respect to an entity that has acted as a registered agent, the Court may also direct such order to any person who has served as an officer, director or managing agent of such registered agent. Any person who, on or after January 1, 2007, serves as an officer, director or managing agent of an entity acting as a registered agent in the State of Delaware shall be deemed thereby to have consented to the appointment of such registered agent as agent upon whom service of process may be made in any action brought pursuant to this Section, and service as an officer, director or managing agent of an entity acting as a registered agent in the State of Delaware shall be a signification of the consent of such person that any process when so served shall be of the same legal force and validity as if served upon such person within the State of Delaware, and such appointment of the registered agent shall be irrevocable.

(4) Upon the entry of an order by the Court enjoining any person or entity from acting as a registered agent, the Secretary of State shall mail or deliver notice of such order to each general partner of each affected limited partnership at the address of such general partner specified in the affected limited partnership's certificate of limited partnership. If such a limited partnership is a domestic limited partnership and fails to obtain and designate a new registered agent within thirty (30) days after such notice is given, the certificate of limited partnership of such limited partnership shall be cancelled. If such a limited partnership is a foreign limited partnership and fails to obtain and designate a new registered agent within thirty (30) days after such notice is given, such foreign limited partnership shall not be permitted to do business in the State of Delaware and its registration shall be cancelled. If the Court enjoins a person or entity from acting as a registered agent as provided in this Section and no new registered agent shall have been obtained and designated in the time and manner aforesaid by an affected limited partnership, service of legal process against the limited partnership for which the registered agent had been acting shall thereafter be upon the Secretary of State in accordance with § 17-105 or § 17-911 of this Title. The Court of Chancery may, upon application of the Secretary of State on notice

to the former registered agent, enter such orders as it deems appropriate to give the Secretary of State access to information in the former registered agent's possession in order to facilitate communication with the limited partnerships the former registered agent served.

(j) The Secretary of State is authorized to make a list of registered agents available to the public, and to establish such qualifications and issue such rules and regulations with respect to such listing as the Secretary of State deems necessary or appropriate.

(k) As contained in any certificate of limited partnership, application for registration as a foreign limited partnership, or other document filed in the office of the Secretary of State under this chapter, the address of a registered agent or registered office shall include the street, number, city and postal code.

ANNOTATIONS

Diversity in non-derivative actions — Whether a limited partnership's citizenship must be considered for diversity jurisdiction purposes depends on whether the action is derivative or direct in nature. *Nomura Asset Capital v. Overland Company, Inc.*, 2003 WL 138093 (D. Del. Jan. 8, 2003).

Diversity jurisdiction where limited partnership has a partnership as a limited partner — In determining diversity jurisdiction, where a limited partnership has as one of its limited partners a second partnership, the citizenship of the partners in the second partnership must be considered. *Hart v. Terminex International*, 336 F.3d 541 (7th Cir. 2003).

Diversity of citizenship — A limited partnership is a citizen of every state in which its general partner or any of its limited partners is a citizen. *South Port Marine, LLC v. Gulf Oil Limited Partnership*, 1999 U.S. Dist. LEXIS 11743 (D. Me. July 26, 1999). Accord, *Roche v. Lincoln Property Co.*, 373 F.3d 610 (4th Cir. 2004); *Maiden v. North American Stainless, L.P.*, 125 Fed. Appx. 1, 2004 WL 2889919 (6th Cir. 2004); *457 Madison Avenue Corp. v. Amedeo Hotels Limited Partnership*, 2004 WL 1335937 (S.D.N.Y. June 11, 2004); *Provident Pioneer Partners, L.P. v. Electric & Gas Technology, Inc.*, 2002 WL 31319450 (D. Del. Sept. 6, 2002).

Joinder of limited partners — Failure to join limited partners provided no basis for dismissal of suit against general partner on partnership liability because limited partners are not liable for partnership obligations unless limited partners are general partners or participated in the control of the partnership. *Beal Bank, SSB v. Lucks*, 2001 WL 220252 (Del. Ch. 2001).

Joinder of partnership not mandatory; diversity jurisdiction — Because all of the partners of a small limited partnership were parties to a lawsuit alleging breach of the partnership agreement, joinder of the partnership itself was not required. Complete diversity of citizenship existed among the three partners who were parties, which would be destroyed by joinder of the partnership. *HB General Corp. v. Manchester Partners, L.P.*, 95 F.3d 1185 (3rd Cir. 1996).

Limited partnership is a person — A limited partnership formed under the RULPA (1976) may be sued in its own name, and thus is a "person" for purposes of the due process clause of the Fourteenth Amendment. *Hart Holding Co. v. Drexel Burnham Lambert, Inc.*, 1992 Del. Ch. LEXIS 112 (Del. Ch. May 28, 1992).

Limited partnership not a "citizen" — A limited partnership may not be considered in its own right a "citizen" of the state that created it for purposes of determining whether federal diversity jurisdiction exists. *Carden v. Arkoma Assocs.*, 494 U.S. 185, 110 S.Ct. 1015, 108 L.Ed. 2d 157 (1990).

Place of business — Limited partnerships act through their general partners. Accordingly, a limited partnership had a place of business in New York through the presence of the general partner who acted on behalf of the limited partnership. *In re Paper I Partners, L.P.*, 283 B.R. 661 (Bankr. S.D.N.Y. 2002).

§ 17-105. Service of process on domestic limited partnerships.

(a) Service of legal process upon any domestic limited partnership shall be made by delivering a copy personally to any managing or general agent or general partner of the limited partnership in the State of Delaware or the registered agent of the limited partnership in the State of Delaware, or by leaving it at the dwelling house or usual place of abode in the State of Delaware of any such managing or general agent, general partner or registered agent (if the registered agent be an individual), or at the registered office or other place of business of the limited partnership in the State of Delaware. If the registered agent be a corporation, service of process upon it as such may be made by serving, in the State of Delaware, a copy thereof on the president, vice-president, secretary, assistant secretary or any director of the corporate registered agent. Service by copy left at the dwelling house or usual place of abode of an officer, managing or general agent, general partner or registered agent, or at the registered office or other place of business of the limited partnership in the State of Delaware, to be effective, must be delivered there at least 6 days before the return date of the process, and in the presence of an adult person, and the officer serving the process shall distinctly state the manner of service in his or her return thereto. Process returnable forthwith must be delivered personally to the officer, managing or general agent, general partner or registered agent.

(b) In case the officer whose duty it is to serve legal process cannot by due diligence serve the process in any manner provided for by subsection (a) of this section, it shall be lawful to serve the process against the limited partnership upon the Secretary of State, and such service shall be as effectual for all intents and purposes as if made in any of the ways provided for in subsection (a) hereof. Process may be served upon the Secretary of State under this subsection by means of electronic transmission but only as prescribed by the Secretary of State. The Secretary of State is authorized to issue such rules and regulations with respect to such service as the Secretary of State deems necessary or appropriate. In the event that service is effected through the Secretary of State in accordance with this subsection, the Secretary of State shall forthwith notify the limited partnership by letter, directed to the limited partnership at the address of a general partner as it appears on the records relating to such limited partnership on file with the Secretary of State or, if no such address appears, at its last registered office. Such letter shall be sent by a mail or courier service that includes a record of mailing or deposit with the courier and a record of delivery evidenced by the signature of the recipient. Such letter shall enclose a copy of the process and any other papers served on the Secretary of State pursuant to this subsection. It shall be the duty of the plaintiff in the event of such service to serve process and any other papers in duplicate, to notify the Secretary of State that service is being effected pursuant to this subsection, and to pay the Secretary of State the sum of $50 for the use of the State of Delaware, which sum shall be taxed as part of the costs in the proceeding if the plaintiff shall prevail therein. The Secretary of State shall maintain an alphabetical record of any such service setting forth the name of the plaintiff and defendant, the title, docket number and nature of the proceeding in which process has been served upon the Secretary, the fact that service has been effected pursuant to this subsection, the return date thereof, and the day and hour when the service was made. The Secretary of State shall not be required to retain such information for a period longer than 5 years from the receipt of the service of process.

ANNOTATIONS

Service of process — Service on a limited partnership at its record place of business, when the certificate of limited partnership had not been amended to reflect a current place of business, was insufficient service under § 17-105(a) when the plaintiff failed to attempt service at either the dwelling house or usual place of abode of the general partner or registered agent or at any other place of business of the limited partnership. *Webster v. Ferm*, 1986 WL 5874 (Del. Super. Ct. Apr. 24, 1986).

Substituted service ineffective — Where it appeared the plaintiff could have effected service on a limited partnership in accordance with § 17-105(a) and failed to take reasonable steps to do so, the plaintiff could not rely on service on the Secretary of State under § 17-105(b). *Webster v. Ferm*, 1986 WL 5874 (Del. Super. Ct. Apr. 24, 1986).

§ 17-106. Nature of business permitted; powers.

(a) A limited partnership may carry on any lawful business, purpose or activity, whether or not for profit, with the exception of the business of banking as defined in § 126 of Title 8.

(b) A limited partnership shall possess and may exercise all the powers and privileges granted by this chapter or by any other law or by its partnership agreement, together with any powers incidental thereto, including such powers and privileges as are necessary or convenient to the conduct, promotion or attainment of the business, purposes or activities of the limited partnership.

(c) Notwithstanding any provision of this chapter to the contrary, without limiting the general powers enumerated in subsection (b) above, a limited partnership shall, subject to such standards and restrictions, if any, as are set forth in its partnership agreement, have the power and authority to make contracts of guaranty and suretyship, and enter into interest rate, basis, currency, hedge or other swap agreements, or cap, floor, put, call, option, exchange or collar agreements, derivative agreements or other agreements similar to any of the foregoing.

(d) Unless otherwise provided in a partnership agreement, a limited partnership has the power and authority to grant, hold or exercise a power of attorney, including an irrevocable power of attorney.

§ 17-107. Business transactions of partner with the partnership.

Except as provided in the partnership agreement, a partner may lend money to, borrow money from, act as a surety, guarantor or endorser for, guarantee or assume 1 or more specific obligations of, provide collateral for and transact other business with, the limited partnership and, subject to other applicable law, has the same rights and obligations with respect thereto as a person who is not a partner.

§ 17-108. Indemnification.

Subject to such standards and restrictions, if any, as are set forth in its partnership agreement, a limited partnership may, and shall have the power to, indemnify and hold harmless any partner or other person from and against any and all claims and demands whatsoever.

ANNOTATIONS

Advancement of expenses and public policy — The public policy of the indemnification statute is to allow advancement of legal expenses, if the partnership agreement so provides, even in cases in which the plaintiff is a limited partner and the claims are for breach of fiduciary duty. *Delphi Easter Partners Limited Partnership v. Spectacular Partners, Inc.*, 1993 Del. Ch. LEXIS 159 (Del. Ch. August 6, 1993).

Advancement of litigation expenses must be explicitly authorized by agreement — While Section 17-108 appears to grant a limited partnership the discretion to indemnify a general partner even if the agreement is silent on indemnification, that same discretion does not exist with respect to the advancement of litigation expenses. Accordingly, general partners have no right to advance to themselves partnership funds for litigation expenses to defend against an action brought by limited partners unless the partnership agreement explicitly authorizes such an advancement of expenses. *Christman v. Brauvin Realty Advisors, Inc.*, 1997 U.S. Dist. LEXIS 19563 (N.D. Ill. Dec. 3, 1997).

Business judgment rule — Where a general partner elects to advance fees to or indemnify itself or its affiliates, and the partnership agreement does not address the issue, the business judgment rule does not apply to such self-interested decisions, and the general partner must demonstrate the fairness of the advancements or indemnification. *Active Asset Recovery, Inc. v. Real Estate Asset Recovery Services, Inc.*, 1999 WL 743479 (Del. Ch. Sept. 10, 1999).

Entitlement to advancement of expenses — The controlling parent of the general partner is entitled to advancement of expenses when it assumed broad managerial responsibility for the partnership's business pursuant to a contract with the partnership; indemnification for services "on behalf of" the partnership, under the partnership agreement, are not limited to those performed within an agency or partnership relationship. *Delphi Easter Partners Limited Partnership v. Spectacular Partners, Inc.*, 1993 Del. Ch. LEXIS 159 (Del. Ch. August 6, 1993).

Express limitation on advancements overrides discretionary power — Where limited partners initiate action against a general partner, and the partnership agreement makes advancement of litigation expenses mandatory except in cases where the plaintiffs are limited partners, the general partner may not advance litigation expenses to itself in reliance on its more general discretionary authority to manage the partnership's affairs. The provision relating to advancement of expenses by reverse inference precludes advances under such circumstances. *In re Cencom Cable Income Partners, L.P. Litigation*, 2000 WL 130629 (Del. Ch. Jan. 27, 2000).

General intent of the statute — In construing contractual language under the Delaware Revised Uniform Limited Partnership Act conferring rights of indemnification, courts should interpret language so as to achieve where possible the beneficial purposes that indemnification can afford, including the allocation of certain risks at the onset of a contractual relation in order to make the contractual structure feasible or more attractive to participants. *Delphi Easter Partners Limited Partnership v. Spectacular Partners, Inc.*, 1993 Del. Ch. LEXIS 159 (Del. Ch. August 6, 1993).

Indemnification provision creates no duties — Indemnification provision in limited partnership agreement did not create liability for failure to comply with the contractual standard of duty. Rather, the indemnification provision created a safe harbor that insulated persons from liability to which they might otherwise be exposed for violation of duties imposed by other provisions of the partnership agreement or by law as long as they met the contractual standard of duty. *Lazard Debt Recovery GP, LLC v. Weinstock*, 2004 WL 1813286 (Del. Ch. Aug. 6, 2004).

Injunction against advancement of expenses — General partners of four Delaware limited partnerships would be enjoined from advancing out of the partnerships' funds the expenses of defending an action brought against the general partners by limited partners where two of the partnership agreements contained no provisions explicitly authorizing the advancement of litigation expenses and advancements were barred by the plain terms of the remaining two partnership agreements. *Christman v. Brauvin Realty Advisors, Inc.*, 1997 U.S. Dist. LEXIS 19563 (N.D. Ill. Dec. 3, 1997).

Limitation period for indemnification claim by plaintiff — Where plaintiff claimed indemnification for expenses in prosecuting actions, statute of limitations on indemnification claim did not begin to run until after disposition by appellate courts of the actions giving rise to the indemnification claim. *Salovaara v. SSP Advisors, L.P.*, 2003 WL 23190391 (Del. Ch. Dec. 22, 2003).

Power to indemnify or advance expenses — The power of limited partnership under Section 17-108 to indemnify or advance expenses is not dependent on an express provision in the partnership agreement granting such power. The partnership agreement may eliminate or tailor the power to indemnify or advance expenses, but in the absence of such provisions, the partnership retains the power granted by Section 17-108. *Active Asset Recovery, Inc. v. Real Estate Asset Recovery Services, Inc.*, 1999 WL 743479 (Del. Ch. Sept. 10, 1999).

Right to advancement of costs; bankruptcy; "bona fide dispute" — For bankruptcy purposes, a limited partnership's general partner's advancement of costs, obtained in a consent order and judgment in a lawsuit seeking its removal as managing general partner, was not a "bona fide dispute." Thus, the general partner's involuntary bankruptcy petition filed against the partnership was not dismissed on the ground that it was the subject of a "bona fide dispute as to the liability or amount," under Bankruptcy Code § 303 was provided for in The partnership agreement provided for the right to the advancement of costs and distinguished the right from the right to indemnification which depended on the underlying dispute's outcome. The partnership would have the right to seek repayment of the advanced funds; and the partner a duty to repay the advances, if the general partner was not entitled to indemnification. *In re Ransome Group Investors I, LLLP*, 424 B.R. 547 (M.D. Fla. 2009) (DE law applied.).

Statute is broadly enabling — The indemnification provision is broadly enabling and broader than the statutory indemnification provision applicable to Delaware corporations; it defers completely to the contracting parties and itself creates no rights to indemnification. *Delphi Easter Partners Limited Partnership v. Spectacular Partners, Inc.*, 1993 Del. Ch. LEXIS 159 (Del. Ch. August 6, 1993).

Willful misconduct; bad faith — Partnerships have broad power to indemnify persons from claims and demands, and the court defers completely to the indemnification rights and obligations created by contract. Partnership agreement that provided for indemnification except for conduct constituting willful misconduct or bad faith, the agreement imposed a contractual limitation on the right to indemnification. A partner that breached its duty of loyalty necessarily acted in bad faith. Bad faith results from a conscious wrongful act that lacks a reasonable basis for its performance. Willful misconduct involves intentional conduct without justifiable excuse. Where the partnership agreement required partners to use their best efforts to promote the partnership's business, a partner who left his employment with the partnership to work for a competitor consciously elected not to give his best efforts, and thus engaged in willful misconduct. Accordingly, the partner could not be entitled to indemnification from the partnership for the amount of a judgment or litigation expenses. *Salovaara v. Eckert III*, 2002 WL 32396171 (N.J. Super. Ch. Div. Sept. 24, 2002) (applying Delaware law).

§ 17-109. Service of process on partners and liquidating trustees.

(a) A general partner or a liquidating trustee of a limited partnership may be served with process in the manner prescribed in this section in all civil actions or proceedings brought in the State of Delaware involving or relating to the business of the limited partnership or a violation by the general partner or the liquidating trustee of a duty to the limited partnership, or any partner of the limited partnership, whether or not the general partner or the liquidating trustee is a general partner or a liquidating trustee at the time suit is commenced. The filing in the Office of the Secretary of State of a certificate of limited partnership executed, and the execution thereof, by a resident or nonresident of the State of Delaware which names such person as a general partner or a liquidating trustee of a limited partnership, or the acceptance by a general partner or a liquidating trustee after August 1, 1999, of election or appointment as a general partner or a liquidating trustee of a limited partnership, or a general partner or a liquidating trustee of a limited partnership serving in such capacity after August 1, 1999, constitute such person's consent to the appointment of the registered agent of the limited partnership (or, if there is none, the Secretary of State) as such person's agent upon whom service of process may be made as provided in this section. Such execution and filing, or such acceptance or service, shall signify the consent of such general partner or liquidating trustee that any process when so served shall be of the same legal force and validity as if served upon such general partner or liquidating trustee within the State of Delaware and such appointment of the registered agent (or, if there is none, the Secretary of State) shall be irrevocable.

(b) Service of process shall be effected by serving the registered agent (or, if there is none, the Secretary of State) with 1 copy of such process in the manner provided by law for service of writs of summons. In the event service is made under this subsection upon the Secretary of State, the plaintiff shall pay to the Secretary of State the sum of $50 for the use of the State of Delaware, which sum shall be taxed as part of the costs of the proceeding if the plaintiff shall prevail therein. In addition, the Prothonotary or the Register in Chancery of the court in which the civil action or proceeding is pending shall, within 7 days of such service, deposit in the United States mails, by registered mail, postage prepaid, true and attested copies of the process, together with a statement that service is being made pursuant to this section, addressed to such general partner or liquidating trustee at the same address that appears in the certificate of limited partnership of the limited partnership, or, if no such address appears, at his or her address last known to the party desiring to make such service.

(c) In any action in which any such general partner or liquidating trustee has been served with process as hereinabove provided, the time in which a defendant shall be required to appear and file a responsive pleading shall be computed from the date of mailing by the Prothonotary or the Register in Chancery as provided in subsection (b) of this section; however, the court in which such action has been commenced may order such continuance or continuances as may be necessary to afford such general partner or liquidating trustee reasonable opportunity to defend the action.

(d) In a written partnership agreement or other writing, a partner may consent to be subject to the nonexclusive jurisdiction of the courts of, or arbitration in, a specified jurisdiction, or the exclusive jurisdiction of the courts of the State of Delaware, or the exclusivity of arbitration in a specified jurisdiction or the State of Delaware, and to be served with legal process in the manner prescribed in such partnership agreement or other writing. Except by agreeing to arbitrate any arbitrable matter in a specified jurisdiction or in the State of Delaware, a limited partner may not waive its right to maintain a legal action or proceeding in the courts of the State of Delaware with respect to matters relating to the organization or internal affairs of a limited partnership.

(e) Nothing herein contained limits or affects the right to serve process in any other manner now or hereafter provided by law. This section is an extension of and not a limitation upon the right otherwise existing of service of legal process upon nonresidents.

(f) The Court of Chancery and the Superior Court may make all necessary rules respecting the form of process, the manner of issuance and return thereof and such other rules which may be necessary to implement this section and are not inconsistent with this section.

ANNOTATIONS

Advisory board members — Where limited partners serving on advisory board did not participate in management of the partnership, exert control over the partnership, or take actions in Delaware or that had an effect in Delaware, limited partners were not subject to personal jurisdiction under Delaware's long-arm statute. Moreover, where the members of the advisory board did not reside in Delaware, conduct business in Delaware, own real property in Delaware, attend advisory board meetings in Delaware, supply goods or services on behalf of the partnership in Delaware, or do any act in Delaware or any act outside of Delaware that caused injury in Delaware, assertion of personal jurisdiction would violate due process. *Werner v. Miller Technology Management, L.P.*, 831 A.2d 318 (Del. Ch. 2003).

Arbitration — Limited partner settled claims, withdrew arbitration proceeding, and agreed not to initiate any future arbitration proceedings against general partner and its affiliates. Limited partner subsequently commenced arbitration proceedings against general partner and its affiliates based on subsequent actions of the general partner that the limited partner claimed breached fiduciary duties. The arbitrators ruled that the limited partner was bound by the settlement agreement and could not initiate any arbitration proceedings. The arbitration proceeding was dismissed. Limited partner sought to vacate the arbitration award in favor of defendants on the ground that it violated public policy to release future breaches of fiduciary duty. Court held that agreement not to initiate future arbitration proceedings did not violate Connecticut public policy. Court also held that Connecticut law applied, rather than Delaware law, notwithstanding that the limited partnership was formed under Delaware law. *Merrick v. Cummin*, 919 A.2d 495 (Conn. App. 2007).

Consent — res judicata — Where partners had in the partnership agreement consented to jurisdiction in the State of Delaware, and prior judgment by England's High Court did not clearly address claims specifically grounded in the partnership agreement, the prior judgment would not under the doctrine of *res judicata* bar plaintiff's claims. *Cantor Fitzgerald, L.P. v. Chandler*, 1998 WL 442440 (Del. Ch. July 20, 1998).

Consent to jurisdiction — General partner of partnership formed in 1994 consented to personal jurisdiction in Delaware as to claims relating to the general partner's actions as general partner and to the business of the partnership. *RJ Associates, Inc. v. Health Payors' Organization Limited Partnership*, 1999 Del. Ch. LEXIS 161 (July 16, 1999).

Directors of corporate general partner — Delaware courts have personal jurisdiction over directors of a Delaware corporation serving as general partner of a Delaware limited partnership in an action against the directors for breach of fiduciary duties owed to limited partners. The fiduciary duties owed by directors to the partnership and to limited partners are duties owed by the directors in their capacity as directors of the corporate general partner, thus subjecting them to personal jurisdiction under the Delaware director consent statute, 10 Del. C. § 3114. *In re USACafes, L.P. Litigation*, 600 A.2d 43 (Del. Ch. 1991).

Enforcement, vacation or modification of arbitration award — The Court of Chancery's inherent equity jurisdiction confers subject matter jurisdiction to hear a motion to enforce, vacate or modify an arbitration award rendered under the Federal Arbitration Act in another jurisdiction. *SBC Interactive, Inc. v. Corporate Media Partners*, 1998 WL 749446 (Del. Ch. Oct. 7, 1998) (involving general partnership).

No retroactive application — Section 17-109 is an implied consent statute and will not be applied retroactively. Accordingly, where a certificate of limited partnership was filed prior to the September 1, 1988 effective date of Section 17-109, and the plaintiff asserted jurisdiction over nonresident general partners solely on the basis of Section 17-109, the Court lacked personal jurisdiction over the defendant nonresident general partners. *CRI Liquidating REIT, Inc. v. A.F. Evans Company, Inc.*, 1997 WL 689486 (Del. Ch. Oct. 30, 1997).

Tort claim — Where limited partners had consented in the partnership agreement to jurisdiction in the Court of Chancery for breach of fiduciary duty and breach of contract claims arising out of the partnership agreement, the Court of Chancery would exercise personal jurisdiction over limited partners with respect to a claim for alleged tortious interference with a contract where the facts giving rise to the claim of tortious interference were either the same or closely related to the acts and factual circumstances underlying the breach of duty and breach of contract claims. *Fitzgerald v. Chandler*, 1999 WL 1022065 (Del. Ch. Oct. 14, 1999).

§ 17-110. Contested matters relating to general partners; contested votes.

(a) Upon application of any partner, the Court of Chancery may hear and determine the validity of any admission, election, appointment or removal or other withdrawal of a general partner of a limited partnership, and the right of any person to become or continue to be a general partner of a limited partnership, and, in case the right to serve as a general partner is claimed by more than 1 person, may determine the person or persons entitled to serve as general partners; and to that end make such order or decree in any such case as may be just and proper, with power to enforce the production of any books, papers and records of the limited partnership relating to the issue. In any such application, the limited partnership shall be named as a party and service of copies of the application upon the registered agent of the limited partnership shall be deemed to be service upon the limited partnership and upon the person or persons whose right to serve as a general partner is contested and upon the person or persons, if any, claiming to be a general partner or claiming the right to be a general partner; and the registered agent shall forward immediately a copy of the application to the limited partnership and to the person or persons whose right to serve as a general partner is contested and to the person or persons, if any, claiming to be a general partner or the right to be a general partner, in a postpaid, sealed, registered letter addressed to such limited partnership and such person or persons at their post-office addresses last known to the registered agent or furnished to the registered agent by the applicant partner. The Court may make such order respecting further or other notice of such application as it deems proper under the circumstances.

(b) Upon application of any partner, the Court of Chancery may hear and determine the result of any vote of partners upon matters as to which the partners of the limited partnership, or any class or group of partners, have the right to vote pursuant to the partnership agreement or other agreement or this chapter (other than the admission, election, appointment or removal or other withdrawal of general partners). In any such application, the limited partnership shall be named as a party and service of the application upon the registered agent of the limited partnership shall be deemed to be service upon the limited partnership, and no other party need be joined in order for the Court to adjudicate the result of the vote. The Court may make such order respecting further or other notice of such application as it deems proper under the circumstances.

(c) Nothing herein contained limits or affects the right to serve process in any other manner now or hereafter provided by law. This section is an extension of and not a limitation upon the right otherwise existing of service of legal process upon nonresidents.

ANNOTATIONS

Del. Code Ann. tit. 6, § 17-110 is the partnership analogue to Del. Code. Ann. tit. 8, § 225; however, plaintiff's challenge to a corporate general partner's right to continue as general partner following alleged failure to meet its obligations under funding and partnership agreements does not fit within provisions of § 17-110, but within the provisions of § 17-111. *Adirondack GP, Inc. v. American Power Corp.*, 1996 WL 684376 (Del. Ch. Nov. 13, 1996).

§ 17-111. Interpretation and enforcement of partnership agreement.

Any action to interpret, apply or enforce the provisions of a partnership agreement, or the duties, obligations or liabilities of a limited partnership to the partners of the limited partnership, or the duties, obligations or liabilities among partners or of partners to the limited partnership, or the rights or powers of, or restrictions on, the limited partnership or partners, or any provision of this chapter, or any other instrument, document, agreement or certificate contemplated by any provision of this chapter, may be brought in the Court of Chancery.

ANNOTATIONS

Enforcement and interpretation — No court is better suited to enforce fiduciary obligations of partners in a Delaware limited partnership or to interpret the meaning of the limited partnership agreement than Delaware's Court of Chancery. *Cantor Fitzgerald, L.P. v. Chandler*, 1998 WL 442440 (Del. Ch. July 20, 1998).

Scope of § 17-111 — Del. Code Ann. tit. 6, § 17-110 is the partnership analogue to Del. Code Ann. tit. 8, § 225; however, plaintiff's challenge to a corporate general partner's right to continue as general partner following alleged failure to meet its obligations under funding and partnership agreements does not fit within provisions of § 17-110, but within the provisions of § 17-111. *Adirondack GP, Inc. v. American Power Corp.*, 1996 WL 684376 (Del. Ch. Nov. 13, 1996).

Statute's precedence over agreement — Delaware statute took precedence over a limited partnership agreement that was never signed, in determining whether certain arbitration awards were "irrational." For example, the agreement provided that any change in the general partner's status (other than a transfer of his partnership interest) would convert his interest into a limited partnership interest; the arbitration panel, relying on Delaware law, held that the general partner had reverted from a general partner to a limited partner when he was removed. The panel also found that certain actions by the general partner effected a dissolution of the partnership under Delaware law, although this result may have conflicted with the agreement which provided that no general or limited partners had the right to terminate or dissolve the partnership. In addition, the limited partners contended that the panel disregarded the terms of the agreement by finding that the general partner was entitled to an accounting since the agreement stated that no partner was entitled to demand or receive the return of his capital contribution, while the panel found that the general partner was entitled to an accounting under Delaware law. Similarly, the panel found that, under Delaware law, the general partner's actions terminated the partnership. The agreement provided that Delaware law controlled. *Arbitration between Bosack v. Soward*, 573 F.3d 891 (9th Cir. 2009).

Statutory rights — Jurisdiction conferred by § 17-111 on the Court of Chancery is not limited solely to actions involving rights and obligations created by the partnership agreement itself but includes actions involving enforcement of any statutory rights under the Delaware Revised Uniform Limited Partnership Act, including statutory rights of general partners arising under the Uniform Partnership Act and incorporated by § 17-403 of the limited partnership act. *Schwartzberg v. CRITEF Associates Limited Partnership*, 685 A.2d 365, 373 n.13 (Del. Ch. 1996).

Subject matter jurisdiction — Section 17-111 maintains the former rule that the Court of Chancery has sole jurisdiction over internal partnership affairs except after some event has occurred that obviates equity's superior ability to resolve outstanding matters between the parties. Thus, where negligence and fraud claims were more aptly stated as duty of care, duty of disclosure and duty of loyalty claims, the equitable nature of the claims bore on the internal partnership, the Superior Court lacked subject matter jurisdiction, and the matter would be transferred to the Court of Chancery. *Albert v. Alex. Brown Management Services, Inc.*, 2004 WL 2050527 (Del. Super. Sept. 15, 2004).

Subchapter II
FORMATION; CERTIFICATE OF LIMITED PARTNERSHIP

§ 17-201. Certificate of limited partnership.

(a) In order to form a limited partnership, 1 or more persons (but not less than all of the general partners) must execute a certificate of limited partnership. The certificate of limited partnership shall be filed in the Office of the Secretary of State and set forth:

(1) The name of the limited partnership;

(2) The address of the registered office and the name and address of the registered agent for service of process required to be maintained by § 17-104 of this title;

(3) The name and the business, residence or mailing address of each general partner; and

(4) Any other matters the partners determine to include therein.

(b) A limited partnership is formed at the time of the filing of the initial certificate of limited partnership in the Office of the Secretary of State or at any later date or time specified in the certificate of limited partnership if, in either case, there has been substantial compliance with the requirements of this section. A limited partnership formed under this chapter shall be a separate legal entity, the existence of which as a separate legal entity shall continue until cancellation of the limited partnership's certificate of limited partnership.

(c) The filing of the certificate of limited partnership in the Office of the Secretary of State shall make it unnecessary to file any other documents under Chapter 31 of this title.

(d) A partnership agreement shall be entered into or otherwise existing either before, after or at the time of the filing of a certificate of limited partnership and, whether entered into or otherwise existing before, after or at the time of such filing, may be made effective as of the formation of the limited partnership or at such other time or date as provided in or reflected by the partnership agreement.

ANNOTATIONS

Contribution specified in certificate — The fact that certain partners contribute less than other partners to a limited partnership is not grounds for a derivative action when the limited partners who contribute less nevertheless contribute the amount specified under the certificate of limited partnership and no legal obligation to make a greater contribution exists. *Murphy v. Bay Shores Six, Ltd. Partnership*, 1987 WL 5776 (Del. Ch. Jan. 26, 1987).

Contributions generally — Each partner is obligated to make contributions to a limited partnership to the extent stated in the certificate of limited partnership, in the partnership agreement or in any other contractual undertaking. *Murphy v. Bay Shores Six, Ltd. Partnership*, 1987 WL 5776 (Del. Ch. Jan. 26, 1987).

Diversity in non-derivative actions — Whether a limited partnership's citizenship must be considered for diversity jurisdiction purposes depends on whether the action is derivative or direct in nature. *Nomura Asset Capital v. Overland Company, Inc.*, 2003 WL 138093 (D. Del. Jan. 8, 2003).

Diversity jurisdiction where limited partnership has a partnership as a limited partner — In determining diversity jurisdiction, where a limited partnership has as one of its limited partners a second partnership, the citizenship of the partners in the second partnership must be considered. *Hart v. Terminex International*, 336 F.3d 541 (7th Cir. 2003).

Diversity of citizenship — A limited partnership is a citizen of every state in which its general partner or any of its limited partners is a citizen. *South Port Marine, LLC v. Gulf Oil Limited Partnership*, 56 F. Supp. 104 (D. Me. 1999). *Accord, Roche v. Lincoln Property Co.*, 373 F.3d 610 (4th Cir. 2004); *457 Madison Avenue Corp. v. Amedeo Hotels Limited Partnership*, 2004 WL 1335937 (S.D.N.Y. June 11, 2004); *Provident Pioneer Partners, L.P. v. Electric & Gas Technology, Inc.*, 2002 WL 31319450 (D. Del. Sept. 6, 2002).

Immunity from workers' compensation claims—Under New Hampshire law, a Delaware limited partnership was held to be entitled to the same immunity from workers' compensation claims that the general partner of the limited partnership enjoyed under New Hampshire law. *Currier v. Amerigas Propane, L.P.*, 1999 N.H. LEXIS 82 (N.H. Supr. Aug. 6, 1999).

Limited partnership is a person—A limited partnership formed under the RULPA (1976) may be sued in its own name, and thus is a "person" for purposes of the due process clauses of the Fourteenth Amendment. *Hart Holding Co. v. Drexel Burnham Lambert, Inc.*, 1992 Del. Ch. LEXIS 112 (May 28, 1992).

Decisions under prior law

"Member" defined—The term "member" in section 1702 of the Delaware Limited Partnership Act, which requires that the name and address of "each member" of the limited partnership be included in the certificate of limited partnership, and which also applies to any amended certificate, includes existing limited partners evidenced by interests in the partnership and new limited partners to be added by amendment, but may not reasonably be construed to include former limited partners no longer maintaining an enforceable interest in the limited partnership. *Weltman v. Silna*, 739 F. Supp. 477 (E.D. Mo. 1990), *aff'd* 936 F.2d 358 (8th Cir.), *cert. denied*, 502 U.S. 941, 112 S. Ct. 377 (1991).

§ 17-202. Amendment to certificate.

(a) A certificate of limited partnership is amended by filing a certificate of amendment thereto in the Office of the Secretary of State. The certificate of amendment shall set forth:

(1) The name of the limited partnership; and

(2) The amendment to the certificate.

(b) A general partner who becomes aware that any statement in a certificate of limited partnership was false when made, or that any matter described has changed making the certificate false in any material respect, shall promptly amend the certificate.

(c) Notwithstanding the requirements of subsection (b) of this section, no later than 90 days after the happening of any of the following events an amendment to a certificate of limited partnership reflecting the occurrence of the event or events shall be filed by a general partner:

(1) The admission of a new general partner;

(2) The withdrawal of a general partner; or

(3) A change in the name of the limited partnership or, except as provided in § 17-104(b) and (c) of this title, a change in the address of the registered office or a change in the name or address of the registered agent of the limited partnership.

(d) A certificate of limited partnership may be amended at any time for any other proper purpose the general partners may determine.

(e) Unless otherwise provided in this chapter or in the certificate of amendment, a certificate of amendment, a certificate of amendment shall be effective at the time of its filing with the Secretary of State.

(f) If after the dissolution of a limited partnership but prior to the filing of a certificate of cancellation as provided in § 17-203 of this title:

(1) A certificate of limited partnership has been amended to reflect the withdrawal of all general partners of a limited partnership, the certificate of limited partnership shall be amended to set forth the name and the business, residence or mailing address of each person winding up the limited partnership's affairs, each of whom shall execute and file such certificate of amendment, and each of whom shall not be subject to liability as a general partner by reason of such amendment; or

(2) A person shown on a certificate of limited partnership as a general partner is not winding up the limited partnership's affairs, the certificate of limited partnership shall be amended to add the name and the business, residence or mailing address of each person winding up the limited partnership's affairs, each of whom shall execute and file such certificate of amendment, and each of whom shall not be subject to liability as a general partner by reason of such amendment. A person shown on a certificate of limited partnership as a general partner who is not winding up a limited partnership's affairs need not execute a certificate of amendment which is being executed and filed as required under this subsection.

ANNOTATIONS

Amendment to authorize redemption plan; partners treated differently; bad faith — An amendment of the limited partnership agreement fostered by the corporate general partner to authorize a plan to redeem partnership units at different prices was a breach of the agreement and a breach of fiduciary duty. The general partner and its affiliates controlled the votes for the amendment. The plan favored current management and employees. Redemption of units was at book value, which was far less than their fair market value, and the redemption schedule provided longer periods of time for unit holders who were current employees, including management. The process by which the partnership agreement was amended also did not comply with conflict of interest requirements in the agreement and, therefore, was not done in good faith. *Gelfman v. Weeden Investors, L.P.*, 859 A.2d 89 (Del. Ch. 2004).

Applicability of Act — Under § 17-1104(b), the Revised Uniform Limited Partnership Act applies only to acts performed after January 1, 1985, by limited partnerships formed after July 1, 1973, so that when, as president of the corporate general partner of a limited partnership, a limited partner signed a 1975 amendment to the partnership agreement that added several new limited partners but omitted his own name as a limited partner, the issue of whether that limited partner technically withdrew from the partnership is governed by Del. Code Ann. tit. 6. § 1725, the predecessor to § 17-204, *Weltman v. Silna*, 879 F.2d 425 (8th Cir. 1989).

Authority to create new class of preferred limited partners; authority to amend agreement — The general partner could not unilaterally amend the limited partnership agreement to create a new class of preferred limited partners. Although the general partner had discretion to issue additional limited partner units that could dilute the interests of existing limited partners, if a new issuance subordinated the rights of existing limited partners, the general partner was required to obtain their consent to amend the partnership agreement to allow this. In addition, the authority to create a new class of limited partners should be spelled out explicitly in the partnership agreement. *In re Nantucket Island Associates Ltd. Partnership Unitholders Litigation*, 810 A.2d 351 (Del. Ch. 2002).

Service of process — The failure to amend the certificate of limited partnership to reflect the partnership's current address will not stop the partnership from showing ineffective service of process under § 17-105(b) where the plaintiff fails to take reasonable steps to serve the partnership under § 17-105(a) either by delivering a copy of the complaint personally to the general partner or leaving a copy at the dwelling or usual place of abode of the general partner or the registered agent or at any other place of business of the limited partnership. *Webster v. Ferm*, 1986 WL 5874 (Del. Super. Apr. 24, 1986).

Decisions under prior law

Existing limited partner omitted — The validity of a limited partnership amendment, where an existing limited partner is not included in the amended version of the limited partnership membership composition, is not covered by the Delaware Limited Partnership Act, and, where also not covered by the original partnership agreement, the question should be resolved under section 1730 of the Act and the general presumptions and rules governing statutory construction. *Weltman v. Silna*, 739 F. Supp. 477 (E.D. Mo. 1990), *aff'd on other grounds*, 936 F.2d 358 (8th Cir. 1991), *cert. denied*, 112 S. Ct. 377 (1991).

Former limited partner; assignment of interest — Pursuant to section 1725(a)(2) of the Delaware Limited Partnership Act, a former limited partner is required to sign an amendment to the certificate of limited partnership only where such limited partner assigns his/her interest to another to be substituted in his/her place. *Weltman v. Silna*, 739 F. Supp. 477 (E.D. Mo. 1990), *aff'd on other grounds*, 936 F.2d 358 (8th Cir. 1991), *cert. denied*, 112 S. Ct. 377 (1991).

"Member" defined — The term "member" in section 1702 of the Delaware Limited Partnership Act, which requires that the name and address of "each member" of the limited partnership be included in the certificate of limited partnership, and which also applies to any amended certificate, includes existing limited partners evidenced by interests in the partnership and new limited partners to be added by amendment, but may not reasonably be construed to include former limited partners no longer maintaining an enforceable interest in the limited partnership. *Weltman v. Silna*, 739 F. Supp. 477 (E.D. Mo. 1990), *aff'd on other grounds*, 936 F.2d 358 (8th Cir. 1991), *cert. denied*, 502 U.S. 941, 112 S. Ct. 377 (1991).

Withdrawal of limited partner — Under § 1724 of the Delaware limited partnership law (repealed in 1982), there were no conditions precedent to a limited partner effectively withdrawing from the limited partnership, so that amendment of the limited partnership certificate was not required for a limited partner to withdraw from the partnership. *Weltman v. Silna*, 936 F.2d 358 (8th Cir. 1991), *cert. denied*, 112 S. Ct. 377 (1991).

Withdrawn limited partner — An amended certificate of limited partnership does not require the signature of a former limited partner who had already withdrawn from the partnership. *Weltman v. Silna*, 936 F.2d 358 (8th Cir. 1991), *cert. denied*, 112 S. Ct. 377 (1991).

§ 17-203. Cancellation of certificate.

(a) A certificate of limited partnership shall be cancelled upon the dissolution and the completion of winding up of the limited partnership, or as provided in § 17-104(d) or § 17-104(i)(4) or § 17-1110 of this title, or upon the filing of a certificate of merger or consolidation or a certificate of ownership and merger if the limited partnership is not the surviving or resulting entity in a merger or consolidation or upon the future effective date or time of a certificate of merger or consolidation or a certificate of ownership and merger if the limited partnership is not the surviving or resulting entity in a merger or consolidation, or upon the filing of a certificate of transfer or upon the future effective date or time of a certificate of transfer, or upon the filing of a certificate of conversion to non-Delaware entity or upon the future effective date or time of a certificate of conversion to non-Delaware entity. A certificate of cancellation shall be filed in the Office of the Secretary of State to accomplish the cancellation of a certificate of limited partnership upon the dissolution and the completion of winding up a limited partnership and shall set forth:

(1) The name of the limited partnership;
(2) The date of filing of its certificate of limited partnership;

(3) The future effective date or time (which shall be a date or time certain) of cancellation if it is not to be effective upon the filing of the certificate; and

(4) Any other information the person filing the certificate of cancellation determines.

(b) A certificate of cancellation that is filed in the office of the Secretary of State prior to the dissolution or the completion of winding up of a limited partnership may be corrected as an erroneously executed certificate of cancellation by filing with the office of the Secretary of State a certificate of correction of such certificate of cancellation in accordance with § 17-213 of this title.

(c) The Secretary of State shall not issue a certificate of good standing with respect to a limited partnership if its certificate of limited partnership is cancelled.

ANNOTATIONS

Certificate of cancellation; right to bring derivative action — Limited partners of a Delaware limited partnership could not bring a derivative action in Massachusetts when the partnership had never registered as a foreign limited partnership there. Since a certificate of cancellation had been filed in Delaware, before the partnership could register in Massachusetts, it would have to revive its existence as a limited partnership in Delaware. The certificate of cancellation terminated the existence of the partnership; partners could not bring a derivative action. *Smyth v. Marshall Field Fifth*, 40 Mass. Ct. App. 625, 666 N.E.2d 1008 (1996) (applying Delaware law).

Nullification — Plaintiff limited partners were entitled to a judicial nullification of a certificate of cancellation filed by the general partner where the general partner failed to demonstrate that the limited partnership had been properly dissolved in accordance with the terms of the agreement of limited partnership and that the limited partnership's affairs had been wound up as required by Section 17-804. *In re CC&F Fox Hill Associates Limited Partnership*, 1997 WL 349236 (Del. Ch. June 13, 1997), *reh'g denied*, 1997 WL 525841 (Del. Ch. July 7, 1997).

§ 17-204. Execution.

(a) Each certificate required by this subchapter to be filed in the Office of the Secretary of State shall be executed in the following manner:

(1) An initial certificate of limited partnership, a certificate of limited partnership domestication, a certificate of conversion to limited partnership,

a certificate of conversion to a non-Delaware entity, a certificate of transfer and a certificate of transfer and domestic continuance must be signed by all general partners or, in the case of a certificate of limited partnership domestication or certificate of conversion to limited partnership, by any person authorized to execute such certificate on behalf of the non-United States entity or other entity, respectively;

(2) A certificate of amendment or a certificate of correction must be signed by at least 1 general partner and by each other general partner designated in the certificate of amendment or a certificate of correction as a new general partner, but if the certificate of amendment or a certificate of correction reflects the withdrawal of a general partner as a general partner, it need not be signed by that former general partner;

(3) A certificate of cancellation must be signed by all general partners or, if the general partners are not winding up the limited partnership's affairs, then by all liquidating trustees; provided, however, that if the limited partners are winding up the limited partnership's affairs, a certificate of cancellation shall be signed by the limited partners or, if there is more than 1 class or group of limited partners, then by each class or group of limited partners, in either case, by limited partners who own more than 50 percent of the then current percentage or other interest in the profits of the limited partnership owned by all of the limited partners or by the limited partners in each class or group, as appropriate;

(4) If a domestic limited partnership is filing a certificate of merger or consolidation or a certificate of ownership and merger, the certificate of merger or consolidation or a certificate of ownership and merger must be signed by at least 1 general partner of the domestic limited partnership, or if the certificate of merger or consolidation is being filed by another business entity (as defined in § 17-211(a) of this title), the certificate of merger or consolidation must be signed by a person authorized by such other business entity;

(5) A certificate of revival must be signed by at least 1 general partner; and

(6) A certificate of termination of a certificate with a future effective date or time or a certificate of amendment of a certificate with a future effective date or time being filed in accordance with § 17-206(c) of this chapter shall be signed in the same manner as the certificate with a future effective date or time being amended or terminated is required to be signed under this chapter.

(b) Unless otherwise provided in the partnership agreement, any person may sign any certificate or amendment thereof or enter into a partnership agreement or amendment thereof by an agent, including an attorney-in-fact. An authorization, including a power of attorney, to sign any certificate or amendment thereof or to enter into a partnership agreement or amendment thereof need not be in writing, need not be sworn to, verified or acknowledged, and need not be filed in the Office of the Secretary of State, but if in writing, must be retained by a general partner.

(c) For all purposes of the laws of the State of Delaware, a power of attorney with respect to matters relating to the organization, internal affairs or termination of a limited partnership or granted by a person as a partner or an assignee of a partnership interest or by a person seeking to become a partner or an assignee of a partnership interest shall be irrevocable if it states that it is irrevocable and it is coupled with an interest sufficient in law to support an irrevocable power. Such irrevocable power of attorney, unless otherwise provided therein, shall not be affected by subsequent death, disability, incapacity, dissolution, termination of existence or bankruptcy of, or any other event concerning, the principal. A power of attorney with respect to matters relating to the organization, internal affairs or termination of a limited partnership or granted by a person as a partner or an assignee of a partnership interest or by a person seeking to become a partner or an assignee of a partnership interest and, in either case, granted to the limited partnership, a general partner or limited partner thereof, or any of their respective officers, directors, managers, members, partners, trustees, employees or agents shall be deemed coupled with an interest sufficient in law to support an irrevocable power.

(d) The execution of a certificate by a person who is authorized by this Chapter to execute such certificate constitutes an oath or affirmation, under the penalties of perjury in the third degree, that, to the best of such person's knowledge and belief, the facts stated therein are true.

ANNOTATIONS

Applicability of Act — Under § 17-1104(b), the Revised Uniform Limited Partnership Act applies only to acts performed after January 1, 1985 by limited partnerships formed after July 1, 1973, so that when, as president of the corporate general partner of a limited partnership, a limited partner signed a 1975 amendment to the partnership agreement that added several new limited partners but omitted his own name as a limited partner, the issue of whether that limited partner technically withdrew from the partnership is governed by Del. Code Ann., tit. 6, § 1725, the predecessor to § 17-204. *Weltman v. Silna*, 879 F.2d 425 (8th Cir. 1989).

§ 17-205. Execution, amendment or cancellation by judicial order.

(a) If a person required by § 17-204 of this title to execute any certificate fails or refuses to do so, any other person who is adversely affected by the failure or refusal may petition the Court of Chancery to direct the execution of the certificate. If the Court finds that the execution of the certificate is proper and that any person so designated has failed or refused to execute the certificate, it shall order the Secretary of State to record an appropriate certificate.

(b) If a person required to execute a partnership agreement or amendment thereof fails or refuses to do so, any other person who is adversely affected by the failure or refusal may petition the Court of Chancery to direct the execution of the partnership agreement or amendment thereof. If the Court finds that the partnership agreement or amendment thereof should be executed and that any person so designated has failed or refused to do so, it shall enter an order granting appropriate relief.

ANNOTATIONS

Agreement to form limited partnership — An agreement providing that the parties agreed to enter into a limited partnership agreement or otherwise support the parties in a specific venture did not appear clearly to require the formation of a limited partnership, or even if it did, that the limited partnership had to be a Delaware limited partnership. Under such circumstances, it did not appear that Section 17-205(b) applied so as to authorize the Court to compel execution of a partnership agreement. *GTE Mobilnet Inc. v. Nehalem Cellular, Inc.*, 1994 Del. Ch. LEXIS 30 (Del. Ch. Mar. 17, 1994).

§ 17-206. Filing.

(a) The signed copy of the certificate of limited partnership and of any certificates of amendment, correction, amendment of a certificate with a future effective date or time, termination of a certificate with a future effective date or time or cancellation (or of any judicial decree of amendment or cancellation), and of any certificate of merger or consolidation, any certificate of ownership and merger any restated certificate, any corrected certificate, any certificate of conversion to limited partnership, any certificate of conversion to a non-Delaware entity, any certificate of transfer, any certificate of transfer and domestic continuance, any certificate of limited partnership domestication, and any certificate of revival shall be delivered to the Secretary of State. A person who executes a certificate as an agent or fiduciary need not exhibit evidence of that person's authority as a prerequisite to filing. Any signature on any certificate authorized to be filed with the Secretary of State under any provision of this chapter may be a facsimile, a conformed signature or an electronically transmitted signature. Upon delivery of any certificate, the Secretary of State shall record the date and time of its delivery. Unless the Secretary of State finds that any certificate does not conform to law, upon receipt of all filing fees required by law the Secretary of State shall:

(1) Certify that the certificate of limited partnership, the certificate of amendment, the certificate of correction, the certificate of amendment of a certificate with a future effective date or time, the certificate of termination of a certificate with a future effective date or time, the certificate of cancellation (or of any judicial decree of amendment or cancellation), the certificate of merger or consolidation, the certificate of ownership and merger, restated certificate, the corrected certificate, the certificate of conversion to limited partnership, the certificate of conversion to a non-Delaware entity, the certificate of transfer, the certificate of transfer and domestic continuance, the certificate of limited partnership domestication or certificate of revival has been filed in the Secretary of State's office by endorsing upon the signed certificate the word "Filed," and the date and time of the filing. This endorsement is conclusive of the date and time of its filing in the absence of actual fraud. Except as provided in subdivision (a)(5) or (a)(6) of this section, such date and time of filing of a certificate shall be the date and time of delivery of the certificate;

(2) File and index the endorsed certificate;

(3) Prepare and return to the person who filed it or that person's representative a copy of the signed certificate, similarly endorsed, and shall certify such copy as a true copy of the signed certificate; and

(4) Cause to be entered such information from the certificate as the Secretary of State deems appropriate into the Delaware Corporation

Information System or any system which is a successor thereto in the office of the Secretary of State, and such information and a copy of such certificate shall be permanently maintained as a public record on a suitable medium. The Secretary of State is authorized to grant direct access to such system to registered agents subject to the execution of an operating agreement between the Secretary of State and such registered agent. Any registered agent granted such access shall demonstrate the existence of policies to ensure that information entered into the system accurately reflects the content of certificates in the possession of the registered agent at the time of entry.

(5) Upon request made upon or prior to delivery, the Secretary of State may, to the extent deemed practicable, establish as the date and time of filing of a certificate a date and time after its delivery. If the Secretary of State refuses to file any certificate due to an error, omission or other imperfection, the Secretary of State may hold such certificate in suspension, and in such event, upon delivery of a replacement certificate in proper form for filing and tender of the required fees within 5 business days after notice of such suspension is given to the filer, the Secretary of State shall establish as the date and time of filing of such certificate the date and time that would have been the date and time of filing of the rejected certificate had it been accepted for filing. The Secretary of State shall not issue a certificate of good standing with respect to any limited partnership with a certificate held in suspension pursuant to this subsection. The Secretary of State may establish as the date and time of filing of a certificate the date and time at which information from such certificate is entered pursuant to subdivision (a)(4) of this section if such certificate is delivered on the same date and within 4 hours after such information is entered.

(6) If:

a. Together with the actual delivery of a certificate and tender of the required fees, there is delivered to the Secretary of State a separate affidavit (which in its heading shall be designated as an affidavit of extraordinary condition) attesting, on the basis of personal knowledge of the affiant or a reliable source of knowledge identified in the affidavit, that an earlier effort to deliver such certificate and tender such fees was made in good faith, specifying the nature, date and time of such good faith effort and requesting that the Secretary of State establish such date and time as the date and time of filing of such certificate; or

b. Upon the actual delivery of a certificate and tender of the required fees, the Secretary of State in his or her discretion provides a written waiver of the requirement for such an affidavit stating that it appears to the Secretary of State that an earlier effort to deliver such certificate and tender such fees was made in good faith and specifying the date and time of such effort; and

    c. The Secretary of State determines that an extraordinary condition existed at such date and time, that such earlier effort was unsuccessful as a result of the existence of such extraordinary condition, and that such actual delivery and tender were made within a reasonable period (not to exceed 2 business days) after the cessation of such extraordinary condition, then the Secretary of State may establish such date and time as the date and time of filing of such certificate. No fee shall be paid to the Secretary of State for receiving an affidavit of extraordinary condition. For purposes of this subsection, an extraordinary condition means: any emergency resulting from an attack on, invasion or occupation by foreign military forces of, or disaster, catastrophe, war or other armed conflict, revolution or insurrection, or rioting or civil commotion in, the United States or a locality in which the Secretary of State conducts its business or in which the good faith effort to deliver the certificate and tender the required fees is made, or the immediate threat of any of the foregoing; or any malfunction or outage of the electrical or telephone service to the Secretary of State's office, or weather or other condition in or about a locality in which the Secretary of State conducts its business, as a result of which the Secretary of State's office is not open for the purpose of the filing of certificates under this chapter or such filing cannot be effected without extraordinary effort. The Secretary of State may require such proof as it deems necessary to make the determination required under this subparagraph c. of this subdivision, and any such determination shall be conclusive in the absence of actual fraud. If the Secretary of State establishes the date and time of filing of a certificate pursuant to this subsection, the date and time of delivery of the affidavit of extraordinary condition or the date and time of the Secretary of State's written waiver of such affidavit shall be endorsed on such affidavit or waiver and such affidavit or waiver, so endorsed, shall be attached to the filed certificate to which it relates. Such filed certificate shall be effective as of the date and time established as the date and time of filing by the Secretary of State pursuant to this subsection, except as to those persons who are substantially and adversely affected by such establishment and, as to those persons, the certificate shall be effective from the date and time endorsed on the affidavit of extraordinary condition or written waiver attached thereto.

(b) Notwithstanding any other provision of this chapter, any certificate filed under this chapter shall be effective at the time of its filing with the Secretary of State or at any later date or time (not later than a time on the one hundred and eightieth day after the date of its filing if such date of filing is on or after January 1, 2012) specified in the certificate. Upon the filing of a certificate of amendment (or judicial decree of amendment), certificate of correction, corrected certificate or restated certificate in the Office of the Secretary of State, or upon the future effective date or time of a certificate of amendment (or judicial decree thereof) or restated certificate, as provided for therein, the certificate of limited partnership shall be amended, corrected or restated as set forth therein. Upon the filing of a certificate of cancellation (or a judicial decree thereof), or a certificate of merger or consolidation or a certificate of ownership and merger which acts as a certificate of cancellation, or a certificate of transfer, or a certificate of conversion to a non-Delaware entity, or upon the future effective date or time of a certificate of cancellation (or a judicial decree thereof) or of a certificate of merger or consolidation or a certificate of ownership and merger which acts as a certificate of cancellation, or a certificate of transfer, or a certificate of conversion to a non-Delaware entity, as provided for therein, or as specified in § 17-104(d), § 17-104(i)(4) or § 17-1110(a) of this title, the certificate of limited partnership is canceled. Upon the filing of a certificate of limited partnership domestication, or upon the future effective date or time of a certificate of limited partnership domestication, the entity filing the certificate of limited partnership domestication is domesticated as a limited partnership with the effect provided in § 17-215 of this title. Upon the filing of a certificate of conversion to limited partnership, or upon the future effective date or time of a certificate of conversion to limited partnership, the entity filing the certificate of conversion to limited partnership is converted to a limited partnership with the effect provided in § 17-217 of this title. Upon the filing of a certificate of revival, the limited partnership shall be revived with the effect provided in § 17-1111 of this title. Upon the filing of a certificate of transfer and domestic continuance, or upon the future effective date or time of a certificate of transfer and domestic continuance, as provided for therein, the limited partnership filing the certificate of transfer and domestic continuance shall continue to exist as a limited partnership of the State of Delaware with the effect provided in § 17-216 of this title.

(c) If any certificate filed in accordance with this chapter provides for a future effective date or time and if, prior to such future effective date or time set forth in such certificate, the transaction is terminated or its terms are amended to change the future effective date or time or any other matter described in such certificate so as to make such certificate false or inaccurate in any respect, such certificate shall, prior to the future effective date or time set forth in such certificate, be terminated or amended by the filing of a certificate of termination or certificate of amendment of such certificate, executed in accordance with § 17-204 of this title, which shall identify the certificate which has been terminated or amended and shall state that the certificate has been terminated or the manner in which it has been amended. Upon the filing of a certificate of amendment of a certificate with a future effective date or time, the certificate identified in such certificate of amendment is amended. Upon the filing of a certificate of termination of a certificate with a future effective date or time, the certificate identified in such certificate of termination is terminated.

(d) A fee as set forth in § 17-1107(a)(3) of this title shall be paid at the time of the filing of a certificate of limited partnership, a certificate of amendment, a certificate of correction, a certificate of amendment of a certificate with a future effective date or time, a certificate of termination of a certificate with a future effective date or time, a certificate of termination of a merger or consolidation, a certificate of cancellation, a certificate of merger or consolidation, a certificate of ownership and merger, a restated certificate, a corrected certificate, a certificate of conversion to limited partnership, a certificate of conversion to a non-Delaware entity, a certificate of transfer, certificate of transfer and domestic continuance, a certificate of limited partnership domestication or a certificate of revival.

(e) A fee as set forth in § 17-1107(a)(4) of this title shall be paid for a certified copy of any paper on file as provided for by this chapter, and a fee as set forth in § 17-1107(a)(5) of this title shall be paid for each page copied.

(f) Notwithstanding any other provision of this chapter, it shall not be necessary for any limited partnership or foreign limited partnership to amend its certificate of limited partnership, its application for registration as a foreign limited partnership, or any other document that has been filed in the office of the Secretary of State prior to August 1, 2011, to comply with § 17-104(k) of this title; notwithstanding the foregoing, any certificate or other document filed under this chapter on or after August 1, 2011 and changing the address of a registered agent or registered office shall comply with § 17-104(k) of this title.

ANNOTATIONS

Filing as basis for jurisdiction — A Delaware court did not have jurisdiction over the parent of the corporate general partner of a Delaware limited partnership in a suit brought by the limited partners alleging breach of the partnership agreement, where the parent had no contacts with Delaware other than the filing of the limited partnership documents, the parent was not a party to the partnership agreement, did not transact any business in Delaware and did no act in Delaware related to the transaction at issue. *Red Sail Easter Limited Partners v. Radio City Music Hall Productions, Inc.*, 1991 Del. Ch. LEXIS 113 (Del. Ch. July 10, 1991).

§ 17-207. Liability for false statement.

(a) If any certificate of limited partnership or certificate of amendment, correction, revival or cancellation or certificate of conversion to limited partnership, or certificate of conversion to a non-Delaware entity, certificate of transfer, certificate of transfer and domestic continuance, or certificate of limited partnership domestication contains a materially false statement, one who suffers loss by reasonable reliance on the statement may recover damages for the loss from:

(1) Any general partner who executes the certificate and knew or should have known the statement to be false in any material respect at the time the certificate was executed; and

(2) Any general partner who thereafter knows that any arrangement or other fact described in the certificate is false in any material respect or has changed, making the statement false in any material respect, if that general partner had sufficient time to amend, correct or cancel the certificate, or to file a petition for its amendment, correction or cancellation, before the statement was reasonably relied upon.

(b) No general partner shall have any liability for failing to cause the amendment, correction or cancellation of a certificate to be filed or failing to file a petition for its amendment, correction or cancellation pursuant to subsection (a) of this section if the certificate of amendment, certificate of correction, certificate of cancellation or petition is filed within 90 days of when that general partner knew or should have known to the extent provided in subsection (a) of this section that the statement in the certificate was false in any material respect.

§ 17-208. Notice.

The fact that a certificate of limited partnership is on file in the Office of the Secretary of State is notice that the partnership is a limited partnership and is notice of all other facts set forth therein which are required to be set forth in a certificate of limited partnership by § 17-201(a)(1)-(3) and by § 17-202(f) of this title and which are permitted to be set forth in a certificate of limited partnership by § 17-218(b) of this title.

§ 17-209. Delivery of certificates to limited partners.

Upon the return by the Secretary of State pursuant to § 17-206 of this title of a certificate marked "Filed," the general partners shall promptly deliver or mail a copy of the certificate to each limited partner if the partnership agreement so requires.

§ 17-210. Restated certificate.

(a) A limited partnership may, whenever desired, integrate into a single instrument all of the provisions of its certificate of limited partnership which are then in effect and operative as a result of there having theretofore been filed with the Secretary of State 1 or more certificates or other instruments pursuant to any of the sections referred to in this subchapter and it may at the same time also further amend its certificate of limited partnership by adopting a restated certificate of limited partnership.

(b) If the restated certificate of limited partnership merely restates and integrates but does not further amend the initial certificate of limited partnership, as theretofore amended or supplemented by any instrument that was executed and filed pursuant to any of the sections in this subchapter, it shall be specifically designated in its heading as a "Restated Certificate of Limited Partnership" together with such other words as the partnership may deem appropriate and shall be executed by a general partner and filed as provided in § 17-206 of this title in the Office of the Secretary of State. If the restated certificate restates and integrates and also further amends in any respect the certificate of limited partnership, as theretofore amended or supplemented, it shall be specifically designated in its heading as an "Amended and Restated Certificate of Limited Partnership" together with such other words as the partnership may deem appropriate and shall be executed by at least 1 general partner and by each other general partner designated in the restated certificate of limited partnership as a new general partner, but if the restated certificate reflects the withdrawal of a general partner as a general partner, such restated certificate of limited partnership need not be signed by that former general partner, and filed as provided in § 17-206 of this title in the Office of the Secretary of State.

(c) A restated certificate of limited partnership shall state, either in its heading or in an introductory paragraph, the limited partnership's present name, and, if it has been changed, the name under which it was originally filed, and the date of filing of its original certificate of limited partnership with the Secretary of State, and the future effective date or time (which shall be a date or time certain) of the restated certificate if it is not to be effective upon the filing of the restated certificate. A restated certificate shall also state that it was duly executed and is being filed in accordance with this section. If the restated certificate only restates and integrates and does not further amend the limited partnership's certificate of limited partnership as theretofore amended or supplemented and there is no discrepancy between those provisions and the restated certificate, it shall state that fact as well.

(d) Upon the filing of the restated certificate of limited partnership with the Secretary of State, or upon the future effective date or time of a restated certificate of limited partnership as provided for therein, the initial certificate of limited partnership, as theretofore amended or supplemented, shall be superseded; thenceforth, the restated certificate of limited partnership, including any further amendment or changes made thereby, shall be the certificate of limited partnership of the limited partnership, but the original effective date of formation shall remain unchanged.

(e) Any amendment or change effected in connection with the restatement and integration of the certificate of limited partnership shall be subject to any other provision of this chapter, not inconsistent with this section, which would apply if a separate certificate of amendment were filed to effect such amendment or change.

§ 17-211. Merger and consolidation.

(a) As used in this section, "other business entity" means a corporation, a statutory trust, a business trust, an association, a real estate investment trust, a common-law trust, a limited liability company, or an unincorporated business or entity, including a partnership (whether general (including a limited liability partnership) or limited (including a foreign limited liability limited partnership), but excluding a domestic limited partnership). As used in this section and in § § 17-212 and 17-301 of this title, "plan of merger" means a writing approved by a domestic limited partnership, in the form of resolutions or otherwise, that states the terms and conditions of a merger under subsection (l) of this section.

(b) Pursuant to an agreement of merger or consolidation, 1 or more domestic limited partnerships may merge or consolidate with or into 1 or more domestic limited partnerships or 1 or more other business entities formed or organized under the laws of the State of Delaware or any other state or the United States or any foreign country or other foreign jurisdiction, or any combination thereof, with such domestic limited partnership or other business entity as the agreement shall provide being the surviving or resulting domestic limited partnership or other business entity. Unless otherwise provided in the partnership agreement, an agreement of merger or consolidation or a plan of merger shall be approved by each domestic limited partnership which is to merge or consolidate (1) by all general partners, and (2) by the limited partners or, if there is more than 1 class or group of limited partners, then by each class or group of limited partners, in either case, by limited partners who own more than 50 percent of the then current percentage or other interest in the profits of the domestic limited partnership owned by all of the limited partners or by the limited partners in each class or group, as appropriate. In connection with a merger or consolidation hereunder, rights or securities of, or interests in, a limited partnership or other business entity which is a constituent party to the merger or consolidation may be exchanged for or converted into cash, property, rights or securities of, or interests in, the surviving or resulting limited partnership or other business entity or, in addition to or in lieu thereof, may be exchanged for or converted into cash, property, rights or securities of, or interests in, a limited partnership or other business entity which is not the surviving or resulting limited partnership or other business entity in the merger or consolidation or may be cancelled. Notwithstanding prior approval, an agreement of merger or consolidation or a plan of merger may be terminated or amended pursuant to a provision for such termination or amendment contained in the agreement of merger or consolidation or plan of merger.

(c) Except in the case of a merger under subsection (l) of this section, if a domestic limited partnership is merging or consolidating under this section, the domestic limited partnership or other business entity surviving or resulting in or from the merger or consolidation shall file a certificate of merger or consolidation executed by at least 1 general partner on behalf of the domestic limited partnership when it is the surviving or resulting entity in the office of the Secretary of State. The certificate of merger or consolidation shall state:

(1) The name and jurisdiction of formation or organization of each of the domestic limited partnerships and other business entities which is to merge or consolidate;

(2) That an agreement of merger or consolidation has been approved and executed by each of the domestic limited partnerships and other business entities which is to merge or consolidate;

(3) The name of the surviving or resulting domestic limited partnership or other business entity;

(4) In the case of a merger in which a domestic limited partnership is the surviving entity, such amendments, if any, to the certificate of limited partnership of the surviving domestic limited partnership (and in the case of a surviving domestic limited partnership that is a limited liability limited partnership, to the statement of qualification of such surviving domestic limited partnership filed under § 15-1001 of this title) to change its name, registered office or registered agent as are desired to be effected by the merger;

(5) The future effective date or time (which shall be a date or time certain) of the merger or consolidation if it is not to be effective upon the filing of the certificate of merger or consolidation;

(6) That the agreement of merger or consolidation is on file at a place of business of the surviving or resulting domestic limited partnership or other business entity, and shall state the address thereof;

(7) That a copy of the agreement of merger or consolidation will be furnished by the surviving or resulting domestic limited partnership or other business entity, on request and without cost, to any partner of any domestic limited partnership or any person holding an interest in any other business entity which is to merge or consolidate; and

(8) If the surviving or resulting entity is not a domestic limited partnership (including a limited liability limited partnership), or a corporation, limited liability company, partnership (including a limited liability partnership) or statutory trust organized under the laws of the State of Delaware, a

statement that such surviving or resulting other business entity agrees that it may be served with process in the State of Delaware in any action, suit or proceeding for the enforcement of any obligation of any domestic limited partnership which is to merge or consolidate, irrevocably appointing the Secretary of State as its agent to accept service of process in any such action, suit or proceeding and specifying the address to which a copy of such process shall be mailed to it by the Secretary of State. Process may be served upon the Secretary of State under this subsection by means of electronic transmission but only as prescribed by the Secretary of State. The Secretary of State is authorized to issue such rules and regulations with respect to such service as the Secretary of State deems necessary or appropriate. In the event of service hereunder upon the Secretary of State, the procedures set forth in § 17-911(c) of this title shall be applicable, except that the plaintiff in any such action, suit or proceeding shall furnish the Secretary of State with the address specified in the certificate of merger or consolidation provided for in this section and any other address which the plaintiff may elect to furnish, together with copies of such process as required by the Secretary of State, and the Secretary of State shall notify such surviving or resulting other business entity at all such addresses furnished by the plaintiff in accordance with the procedures set forth in § 17-911(c) of this title.

(d) Any failure to file a certificate of merger or consolidation in connection with a merger or consolidation pursuant to this section which was effective prior to September 1, 1988, shall not affect the validity or effectiveness of any such merger or consolidation.

(e) Unless a future effective date or time is provided in a certificate of merger or consolidation, or in the case of a merger under subsection (l) of this section in a certificate of ownership and merger, in which event a merger or consolidation shall be effective at any such future effective date or time, a merger or consolidation shall be effective upon the filing in the Office of the Secretary of State of a certificate of merger or consolidation or a certificate of ownership and merger.

(f) A certificate of merger or consolidation or a certificate of ownership and merger shall act as a certificate of cancellation for a domestic limited partnership which is not the surviving or resulting entity in the merger or consolidation. A certificate of merger that sets forth any amendment in accordance with subsection (c)(4) of this section shall be deemed to be an amendment to the certificate of limited partnership (and if applicable to the statement of qualification) of the limited partnership, and the limited partnership shall not be required to take any further action to amend its certificate of limited partnership under § 17-202 of this title (or if applicable its statement of qualification under § 15-105 of this title) with respect to such amendments set forth in the certificate of merger. Whenever this section requires the filing of a certificate of merger or consolidation, such requirement shall be deemed satisfied by the filing of an agreement of merger or consolidation containing the information required by this section to be set forth in the certificate of merger or consolidation.

(g) An agreement of merger or consolidation or a plan of merger approved in accordance with subsection (b) of this section may (1) effect any amendment to the partnership agreement or (2) effect the adoption of a new partnership agreement for a limited partnership if it is the surviving or resulting limited partnership in the merger or consolidation. Any amendment to a partnership agreement or adoption of a new partnership agreement made pursuant to the foregoing sentence shall be effective at the effective time or date of the merger or consolidation and shall be effective notwithstanding any provision of the partnership agreement relating to amendment or adoption of a new partnership agreement, other than a provision that by its terms applies to an amendment to the partnership agreement or the adoption of a new partnership agreement, in either case, in connection with a merger or consolidation. The provisions of this subsection shall not be construed to limit the accomplishment of a merger or of any of the matters referred to herein by any other means provided for in a partnership agreement or other agreement or as otherwise permitted by law, including that the partnership agreement of any constituent limited partnership to the merger or consolidation (including a limited partnership formed for the purpose of consummating a merger or consolidation) shall be the partnership agreement of the surviving or resulting limited partnership. Unless otherwise provided in a partnership agreement, a limited partnership whose original certificate of limited partnership was filed with the Secretary of State and effective on or prior to July 31, 2005, shall continue to be governed by this subsection as in effect on July 31, 2005.

(h) When any merger or consolidation shall have become effective under this section, for all purposes of the laws of the State of Delaware, all of the rights, privileges and powers of each of the domestic limited partnerships and other business entities that have merged or consolidated, and all property, real, personal and mixed, and all debts due to any of said domestic limited partnerships and other business entities, as well as all other things and causes of action belonging to each of such domestic limited partnerships and other business entities, shall be vested in the surviving or resulting domestic limited partnership or other business entity, and shall thereafter be the property of the surviving or resulting domestic limited partnership or other business entity as they were of each of the domestic limited partnerships and other business entities that have merged or consolidated, and the title to any real property vested by deed or otherwise, under the laws of the State of Delaware, in any of such domestic limited partnerships and other business entities, shall not revert or be in any way impaired by reason of this chapter; but all rights of creditors and all liens upon any property of any of said domestic limited partnerships and other business entities shall be preserved unimpaired, and all debts, liabilities and duties of each of the said domestic limited partnerships and other business entities that have merged or consolidated shall thenceforth attach to the surviving or resulting domestic limited partnership or other business entity, and may be enforced against it to the same extent as if said debts, liabilities and duties had been incurred or contracted by it. Unless otherwise agreed, a merger or consolidation of a domestic limited partnership, including a domestic limited partnership which is not the surviving or resulting entity in the merger or consolidation, shall not require such domestic limited partnership to wind up its affairs under § 17-803 of this title or pay its liabilities and distribute its assets under § 17-804 of this title, and the merger or consolidation shall not constitute a dissolution of such limited partnership.

(i) Except as provided by agreement with a person to whom a general partner of a limited partnership is obligated, a merger or consolidation of a limited partnership that has become effective shall not affect any obligation or liability existing at the time of such merger or consolidation of a general partner of a limited partnership which is merging or consolidating.

(j) If a limited partnership is a constituent party to a merger or consolidation that shall have become effective, but the limited partnership is not the surviving or resulting entity of the merger or consolidation, then a judgment creditor of a general partner of such limited partnership may not levy execution against the assets of the general partner to satisfy a judgment based on a claim against the surviving or resulting entity of the merger or consolidation unless:

(1) A judgment based on the same claim has been obtained against the surviving or resulting entity of the merger or consolidation and a writ of execution on the judgment has been returned unsatisfied in whole or in part;

(2) The surviving or resulting entity of the merger or consolidation is a debtor in bankruptcy;

(3) The general partner has agreed that the creditor need not exhaust the assets of the limited partnership that was not the surviving or resulting entity of the merger or consolidation;

(4) The general partner has agreed that the creditor need not exhaust the assets of the surviving or resulting entity of the merger or consolidation;

(5) A court grants permission to the judgment creditor to levy execution against the assets of the general partner based on a finding that the assets of the surviving or resulting entity of the merger or consolidation that are subject to execution are clearly insufficient to satisfy the judgment, that exhaustion of the assets of the surviving or resulting entity of the merger or consolidation is excessively burdensome, or that the grant of permission is an appropriate exercise of the court's equitable powers; or

(6) Liability is imposed on the general partner by law or contract independent of the existence of the surviving or resulting entity of the merger or consolidation.

(k) A partnership agreement may provide that a domestic limited partnership shall not have the power to merge or consolidate as set forth in this section.

(l) In any case in which (i) at least 90% of the outstanding shares of each class of the stock of a corporation or corporations (other than a corporation which has in its certificate of incorporation the provision required by § 251(g)(7)(i) of Title 8), of which class there are outstanding shares that, absent § 267(a) of Title 8, would be entitled to vote on such merger, is owned by a domestic limited partnership, (ii) 1 or more of such corporations is a corporation of the State of Delaware, and (iii) any corporation that is not a corporation of the State of Delaware is a corporation of any other state or the District of Columbia or another jurisdiction, the laws of which do not forbid such merger, the domestic limited partnership having such stock ownership may either merge the corporation or corporations into itself and assume all of its or their obligations, or merge itself, or itself and 1 or more of such corporations, into 1 of the other corporations, pursuant to a plan of merger. If a domestic limited partnership is causing a merger under this subsection, the domestic limited partnership shall file a certificate of ownership and merger executed by at least 1 general partner on behalf of the domestic limited partnership in the office of the Secretary of State. The certificate of ownership and merger shall certify that such merger was authorized in accordance with the domestic limited partnership's partnership agreement and this chapter, and if the domestic limited partnership shall not own all the outstanding stock of all the corporations that are parties to the merger, shall state the terms and conditions of the merger, including the securities, cash, property, or rights to be issued, paid, delivered or granted by the surviving domestic limited partnership or corporation upon surrender of each share of the corporation or corporations not owned by the domestic limited partnership, or the cancellation of some or all of such shares. The terms and conditions of the merger may not result in a holder of stock in a corporation becoming a general partner in a surviving domestic limited partnership (other than a limited liability limited partnership). If a corporation surviving a merger under this subsection is not a corporation organized under the laws of the State of Delaware, then the terms and conditions of the merger shall obligate such corporation to agree that it may be served with process in the State of Delaware in any proceeding for enforcement of any obligation of the domestic limited partnership or any obligation of any constituent corporation of the State of Delaware, as well as for enforcement of any obligation of the surviving corporation, including any suit or other proceeding to enforce the right of any stockholders as determined in appraisal proceedings pursuant to § 262 of Title 8, and to irrevocably appoint the Secretary of State as its agent to accept service of process in any such suit or other proceedings, and to specify the address to which a copy of such process shall be mailed by the Secretary of State. Process may be served upon the Secretary of State under this subsection by means of electronic transmission but only as prescribed by the Secretary of State. The Secretary of State is authorized to issue such rules and regulations with respect to such service as the Secretary of State deems necessary or appropriate. In the event of such service upon the Secretary of State in accordance with this subsection, the Secretary of State shall forthwith notify such surviving corporation thereof by letter, directed to such surviving corporation at its address so specified, unless such surviving corporation shall have designated in writing to the Secretary of State a different address for such purpose, in which case it shall be mailed to the last address so designated. Such letter shall be sent by a mail or courier service that includes a record of mailing or deposit with the courier and a record of delivery evidenced by the signature of the recipient. Such letter shall enclose a copy of the process and any other papers served on the Secretary of State pursuant to this subsection. It shall be the duty of the plaintiff in the event of such service to serve process and any other papers in duplicate, to notify the

Secretary of State that service is being effected pursuant to this subsection and to pay the Secretary of State the sum of $50 for the use of the State of Delaware, which sum shall be taxed as part of the costs in the proceeding, if the plaintiff shall prevail therein. The Secretary of State shall maintain an alphabetical record of any such service setting forth the name of the plaintiff and the defendant, the title, docket number and nature of the proceeding in which process has been served, the fact that service has been effected pursuant to this subsection, the return date thereof, and the day and hour service was made. The Secretary of State shall not be required to retain such information longer than 5 years from receipt of the service of process.

ANNOTATIONS

Conversion of limited partnership; applicable law — New York law, not Delaware law, applied to an attempt to convert a New York limited partnership into a Delaware limited liability company. The purported conversion was ineffective because the sole member of an entire class of ownership interest had voted against it, and the statutory mechanism requiring the consent of that class was the sole manner authorized to make the entity change without a merger or consolidation. *Miller v. Ross*, 43 A.D.3d 730, 841 N.Y.S.2d 586 (1st Dep't 2007).

Fairness of merger — Where a general partner receives different consideration in a merger than the limited partners, merger will not be enjoined on grounds of unfairness where there is a valid business purpose for the disparate treatment and the value of the consideration to be received by the general partner is not disproportionate to the value of the general partner's interest. *In re Mesa Limited Partnership Preferred Unitholders Litigation*, 1991 Del. Ch. LEXIS 214 (Del. Ch. Dec. 10, 1991), appeal refused, 608 A2d. 728 (Del. 1992).

Modification of fiduciary duties — merger — Unless limited by the partnership agreement, a general partner has the fiduciary duty to manage the partnership in the interests of the partnership and its limited partners. However, principles of contract preempt fiduciary principles where the parties to a limited partnership have plainly intended to do so. Only when the partnership agreement is silent or ambiguous will the Court turn for guidance to the statutory default rules, traditional notions of fiduciary duties or other extrinsic evidence. Where the partnership agreement gave general partner sole discretion to structure a merger of the partnership, discretion was defined in a manner that did not require the general partner to consider the interests of the partnership of limited partners, and limited partners had the right under the agreement to accept or reject the merger by a two-thirds vote, complaint alleging that the general partner breached its fiduciary duties by proposing an unfair merger or unfairly manipulating its timing would be dismissed for failure to state a claim. *Sonet v. Timber Company, L.P.*, 1998 WL 749445 (Del. Ch. Dec. 16, 1998).

Rights of successor partnership; enforcement of note; choice of law — A limited partnership arising out of a merger with another limited partnership had standing to enforce a note held by the older limited partnership. Under Virginia choice of law rules, the substantive law applied in interpreting the merger agreement was the law of the place of making, namely that place where the last act giving rise to the agreement was completed. The merger agreement was completed in Delaware and certified by Delaware authorities. Therefore, Delaware substantive law applied to determine the rights and obligations transferred under the merger agreement. Under Delaware law, the new limited partnership inherited all the rights and obligations of the old partnership including the right to enforce the note it held. Accordingly, it had standing to seek relief from the automatic stay resulting from the bankruptcy filing of an obligee under the note. However, the enforcement of the note was governed by the note's choice of law provision that required Maryland law be applied. Under Maryland law, the holder of the note was entitled to enforce it, in this case the limited partnership that arose from the merger. *In re Ebersole,* 440 B.R. 690 (W.D. Va. 2010).

Standards governing proposed merger; fiduciary duty eliminated; covenant of good faith and fair dealing — A proposed merger between a master limited partnership and another non-party limited partnership, sought to be enjoined by a limited partner, did not violate the covenant of good faith and fair dealing owed to the limited partner by the partnership. The partnership agreement specifically eliminated the fiduciary duty that would otherwise be owed by the general partner to a limited partner leaving the agreement as the sole basis for the obligations between the two. The covenant of good faith and fair dealing arising from the agreement was not a substitute for a fiduciary duty, the court's most powerful remedial and gap-filling power. The partnership agreement established a contractual standard of review of transactions that supplanted fiduciary duty analysis, which was followed in the merger process. This standard did not require a search for alternative transactions to prevent an alleged undervaluation of the limited partner interest, as claimed by the limited partner. Instead, it provided a "Special Approval" process outlined in the agreement. Nor did the covenant of good faith and fair dealing require that the merger be conditioned on approval of a majority of the minority voting rights, also as claimed by the challenging limited partner. *Lonergan v. EPE Holdings, LLC,* 5 A.3d 1008 (Del. Ch. 2010).

§ 17-212. Contractual appraisal rights.

A partnership agreement or an agreement of merger or consolidation or a plan of merger may provide that contractual appraisal rights with respect to a partnership interest or another interest in a limited partnership shall be available for any class or group or series of partners or partnership interests in connection with any amendment of a partnership agreement, any merger or consolidation in which the limited partnership is a constituent party to the merger or consolidation, any conversion of the limited partnership to another business form, any transfer to or domestication or continuance in any jurisdiction by the limited partnership, or the sale of all or substantially all of the limited partnership's assets. The Court of Chancery shall have jurisdiction to hear and determine any matter relating to any such appraisal rights.

ANNOTATION

Appraisal; individual or aggregate valuation of assets — Where partnership agreement called for assets to be valued on a going concern basis in conformity with standard appraisal techniques, the agreement did not provide for a specific method of valuation and, accordingly, limited partners could not be said to have agreed on one specific method of valuation. Summary judgment could not be granted where appraiser valued assets individually, another valued the assets as a whole, and the evidence was not sufficient for the court to determine the basis for valuation of assets individually rather than as a whole or the impact of the general partner's right of first refusal on "standard appraisal techniques." *In re Cencom Cable Income Partners, L.P. Litigation*, 1997 WL 666970 (Del. Ch. Oct. 15, 1997), *reargument denied*, 1997 WL 770158 (Del. Ch. Dec. 3, 1997).

§ 17-213. Certificate of correction.

(a) Whenever any certificate authorized to be filed with the office of the Secretary of State under any provision of this chapter has been so filed and is an inaccurate record of the action therein referred to, or was defectively or erroneously executed, such certificate may be corrected by filing with the office of the Secretary of State a certificate of correction of such certificate. The certificate of correction shall specify the inaccuracy or defect to be corrected, shall set forth the portion of the certificate in corrected form and shall be executed and filed, as required by this chapter. The certificate of correction shall be effective as of the date the original certificate was filed except as to those persons who are substantially and adversely affected by the correction, and as to those persons, the certificate of correction shall be effective from the filing date.

(b) In lieu of filing a certificate of correction, a certificate may be corrected by filing with the Secretary of State a corrected certificate which shall be executed and filed as if the corrected certificate were the certificate being corrected, and a fee equal to the fee payable to the Secretary of State if the certificate being corrected were then being filed shall be paid to and collected by the Secretary of State for the use of the State of Delaware in connection with the filing of the corrected certificate. The corrected certificate shall be specifically designated as such in its heading, shall specify the inaccuracy or defect to be corrected and shall set forth the entire certificate in corrected form. A certificate corrected in accordance with this section shall be effective as of the date the original certificate was filed except as to those persons who are substantially and adversely affected by the correction and, as to those persons, the certificate as corrected shall be effective from the filing date.

§ 17-214. Limited partnerships as limited liability limited partnerships.

(a) A limited partnership may be formed as, or may become, a limited liability limited partnership pursuant to this Section. A limited partnership may become a limited liability limited partnership as permitted by the limited partnership's partnership agreement or, if the limited partnership's partnership agreement does not provide for the limited partnership's becoming a limited liability limited partnership, with the approval (i) by all general partners, and (ii) by the limited partners, or, if there is more than one (1) class or group of limited partners, then by each class or group of limited partners, in either case, by limited partners who own more than 50 percent of the then current percentage or other interest in the profits of the limited partnership owned by all of the limited partners or by the limited partners in each class or group, as appropriate. To be formed or to become, and to continue as, a limited liability limited partnership, a limited partnership shall, in addition to complying with the requirements of this Chapter;

(1) File a statement of qualification as provided in § 15-1001 of this Title and thereafter an annual report as provided in § 15-1003 of this Title; and

(2) Have as the last words or letters of its name the words "Limited Liability Limited Partnership", or the abbreviation "L.L.L.P.", or the designation "LLLP".

(b) In applying the Delaware Revised Uniform Partnership Act to a limited liability limited partnership for purposes of subsections (a) and (c) of this section:

(1) Any statement shall be executed by at least 1 general partner of the limited partnership; and

(2) All references to partners mean general partners only.

(c) If a limited partnership is a limited liability limited partnership, (i) its partners who are liable for the debts, liabilities and other obligations of the limited partnership shall have the limitation on liability afforded to partners of limited liability partnerships under the Delaware Revised Uniform Partnership Act and (ii) no limited partner of the limited partnership shall have any liability for the obligations of the limited partnership under § 17-303(a) of this title.

(d) Except as provided in subsections (a), (b) and (c) of this section, a limited liability limited partnership shall be governed by this chapter, including, without limitation, § 17-1105 of this chapter.

(e) Notwithstanding anything in this chapter to the contrary, a limited partnership having, on December 31, 1999, the status of a registered limited liability limited partnership under predecessor law, shall have the status of a limited liability limited partnership under this chapter as of January 1, 2000, and, to the extent such limited partnership has not filed a statement of qualification pursuant to Section 15-1001 of the Delaware Revised Uniform Partnership Act, the latest application or renewal application filed by such limited partnership under such predecessor law shall constitute a statement of qualification filed under Section 15-1001 of the Delaware Revised Uniform Partnership Act.

ANNOTATIONS

Diversity Jurisdiction — For purposes of diversity jurisdiction, a limited liability partnership is a citizen of every state in which one of its partners resides. *Reisman v. KPMG Peat Marwick LLP*, 965 F. Supp. 165 (D. Mass. 1997).

§ 17-215. Domestication of non-United States entities.

(a) As used in this section and in § 17-204, "non-United States entity" means a foreign limited partnership (other than one formed under the laws of a state) (including a foreign limited liability limited partnership (other than one formed under the laws of a state)), or a corporation, a statutory trust, a business trust, an association, a real estate investment trust, a common-law trust or any other unincorporated business or entity, including a general partnership (including a limited liability partnership) or a limited liability company, formed, incorporated, created or that otherwise came into being under the laws of any foreign country or other foreign jurisdiction (other than any state).

(b) Any non-United States entity may become domesticated as a limited partnership in the State of Delaware by complying with subsection (g) of this section and filing in the office of the Secretary of State in accordance with § 17-206 of this title:

Each of the certificates required by this subsection (b) shall be filed simultaneously in the office of the Secretary of State and, if such certificates are not to become effective upon their filing as permitted by § 17-206(b) of this title, then each such certificate shall provide for the same effective date or time in accordance with § 17-206(b) of this title.

(1) A certificate of limited partnership domestication that has been executed in accordance with § 17-204 of this title; and

(2) A certificate of limited partnership that complies with § 17-201 of this title and has been executed in accordance with § 17-204 of this title.

(c) The certificate of limited partnership domestication shall state:

(1) The date on which and jurisdiction where the non-United States entity was first formed, incorporated, created or otherwise came into being;

(2) The name of the non-United States entity immediately prior to the filing of the certificate of limited partnership domestication;

(3) The name of the limited partnership as set forth in the certificate of limited partnership filed in accordance with subsection (b) of this section;

(4) The future effective date or time (which shall be a date or time certain) of the domestication as a limited partnership if it is not to be effective upon the filing of the certificate of limited partnership domestication and the certificate of limited partnership;

(5) The jurisdiction that constituted the seat, siege social, or principal place of business or central administration of the non-United States entity, or any other equivalent thereto under applicable law, immediately prior to the filing of the certificate of limited partnership domestication; and

(6) That the domestication has been approved in the manner provided for by the document, instrument, agreement or other writing, as the case may be, governing the internal affairs of the non–United States entity and the conduct of its business or by applicable non–Delaware law, as appropriate.

(d) Upon the filing in the office of the Secretary of State of the certificate of limited partnership domestication and the certificate of limited partnership or upon the future effective date or time of the certificate of limited partnership domestication and the certificate of limited partnership, the non–United States entity shall be domesticated as a limited partnership in the State of Delaware and the limited partnership shall thereafter be subject to all of the provisions of this chapter, except that notwithstanding § 17-201 of this title, the existence of the limited partnership shall be deemed to have commenced on the date the non–United States entity commenced its existence in the jurisdiction in which the non–United States entity was first formed, incorporated, created or otherwise came into being.

(e) The domestication of any non–United States entity as a limited partnership in the State of Delaware shall not be deemed to affect any obligations or liabilities of the non–United States entity incurred prior to its domestication as a limited partnership in the State of Delaware, or the personal liability of any person therefor.

(f) The filing of a certificate of limited partnership domestication shall not affect the choice of law applicable to the non–United States entity, except that from the effective date or time of the domestication, the law of the State of Delaware, including the provisions of this chapter, shall apply to the non–United States entity to the same extent as if the non–United States entity had been formed as a limited partnership on that date.

(g) Prior to the filing of a certificate of limited partnership domestication with the office of the Secretary of State, the domestication shall be approved in the manner provided for by the document, instrument, agreement or other writing, as the case may be, governing the internal affairs of the non–United States entity and the conduct of its business or by applicable non-Delaware law, as appropriate, and a partnership agreement shall be approved by the same authorization required to approve the domestication; provided, that in any event, such approval shall include the approval of any person who, at the effective date or time of the domestication, shall be a general partner of the limited partnership.

(h) When any domestication shall have become effective under this section, for all purposes of the laws of the State of Delaware, all of the rights, privileges and powers of the non–United States entity that has been domesticated, and all property, real, personal and mixed, and all debts due to such non–United States entity, as well as all other things and causes of action belonging to such non-United States entity, shall remain vested in the domestic limited partnership to which such non–United States entity has been domesticated (and also in the non–United States entity, if and for so long as the non–United States entity continues its existence in the foreign jurisdiction in which it was existing immediately prior to the domestication) and shall be the property of such domestic limited partnership (and also to the non–United States entity, if and for so long as the non–United States entity continues its existence in the foreign jurisdiction in which it was existing immediately prior to the domestication), and the title to any real property vested by deed or otherwise in such non–United States entity shall not revert or be in any way impaired by reason of this chapter; but all rights of creditors and all liens upon any property of such non–United States entity shall be preserved unimpaired, and all debts, liabilities and duties of the non–United States entity that has been domesticated shall remain attached to the domestic limited partnership to which such non–United States entity has been domesticated, (and also to the non–United States entity, if and for so long as the non–United States entity continues its existence in the foreign jurisdiction in which it was existing immediately prior to the domestication) and may be enforced against it to the same extent as if said debts, liabilities and duties had originally been incurred or contracted by it in its capacity as a domestic limited partnership. The rights, privileges, powers and interests in property of the non–United States entity, as well as the debts, liabilities and duties of the non–United States entity, shall not be deemed, as a consequence of the domestication, to have been transferred to the domestic limited partnership to which such non–United States entity has domesticated for any purpose of the laws of the State of Delaware.

(i) When a non–United States entity has become domesticated as a limited partnership pursuant to this section, for all purposes of the laws of the State of Delaware, the limited partnership shall be deemed to be the same entity as the domesticating non–United States entity and the domestication shall constitute a continuation of the existence of the domesticating non–United States entity in the form of a domestic limited partnership. Unless otherwise agreed, for all purposes of the laws of the State of Delaware, the domesticating non–United States entity shall not be required to wind up its affairs or pay its liabilities and distribute its assets, and the domestication shall not be deemed to constitute a dissolution of such non–United States entity. If, following domestication, a non–United States entity that has become domesticated as a limited partnership continues its existence in the foreign country or other foreign jurisdiction in which it was existing immediately prior to domestication, the limited partnership and such non–United States entity shall, for all purposes of the laws of the State of Delaware, constitute a single entity formed, incorporated, created or otherwise having come into being, as applicable, and existing under the laws of the State of Delaware and the laws of such foreign country or other foreign jurisdiction.

(j) In connection with a domestication hereunder, rights or securities of, or interests in, the non-United States entity that is to be domesticated as a domestic limited partnership may be exchanged for or converted into cash, property, rights or securities of, or interests in, such domestic limited partnership or, in addition to or in lieu thereof, may be exchanged for or converted into cash, property, rights or securities of, or interests in, another domestic limited partnership or other entity or may be cancelled.

§ 17-216. Transfer or continuance of domestic limited partnerships.

(a) Upon compliance with the provisions of this section, any limited partnership may transfer to or domesticate or continue in any jurisdiction, other than any state, and, in connection therewith, may elect to continue its existence as a limited partnership in the State of Delaware.

(b) If the partnership agreement specifies the manner of authorizing a transfer or domestication or continuance described in subsection (a) of this section, the transfer or domestication or continuance shall be authorized as specified in the partnership agreement. If the partnership agreement does not specify the manner of authorizing a transfer or domestication or continuance described in subsection (a) of this section and does not prohibit such a transfer or domestication or continuance, the transfer or domestication or continuance shall be authorized in the same manner as is specified in the partnership agreement for authorizing a merger or consolidation that involves the limited partnership as a constituent party and to the merger or consolidation. If the partnership agreement does not specify the manner of authorizing a transfer or domestication or continuance described in subsection (a) of this section or a merger or consolidation that involves the limited partnership as a constituent party and does not prohibit such a transfer or domestication or continuance, the transfer or domestication or continuance shall be authorized by the approval by (1) all general partners and (2) the limited partners or, if there is more than 1 class or group of limited partners, then by each class or group of limited partners, in either case, by limited partners who own more than 50 percent of the then current percentage or other interest in the profits of the domestic limited partnership owned by all of the limited partners or by the limited partners in each class or group, as appropriate. If a transfer or domestication described in subsection (a) of this section shall be authorized as provided in this subsection (b), a certificate of transfer if the limited partnership's existence as a limited partnership of the State of Delaware is to cease or a certificate of transfer and domestic continuance if the limited partnership's existence as a limited partnership in the State of Delaware is to continue, executed in accordance with § 17-204 of this title, shall be filed in the office of the Secretary of State in accordance with § 17-206 of this title. The certificate of transfer or the certificate of transfer and domestic continuance shall state:

(1) The name of the limited partnership and, if it has been changed, the name under which its certificate of limited partnership was originally filed;

(2) The date of the filing of its original certificate of limited partnership with the Secretary of State;

(3) The jurisdiction to which the limited partnership shall be transferred or in which it shall be domesticated or continued and the name of the entity or business form formed, incorporated, created or that otherwise comes into being as a consequence of the transfer of the limited partnership to, or its domestication or continuance in, such foreign jurisdiction;

(4) The future effective date or time (which shall be a date or time certain) of the transfer to or domestication or continuance in the jurisdiction specified in subsection (b)(3) of this section if it is not to be effective upon the filing of the certificate of transfer or the certificate of transfer and domestic continuance;

(5) That the transfer or domestication or continuance of the limited partnership has been approved in accordance with the provisions of this section;

(6) In the case of a certificate of transfer, (i) that the existence of the limited partnership as a limited partnership of the State of Delaware shall cease when the certificate of transfer becomes effective and (ii) the agreement of the limited partnership that it may be served with process in the State of Delaware in any action, suit or proceeding for enforcement of any obligation of the limited partnership arising while it was a limited partnership of the State, and that it irrevocably appoints the Secretary of State as its agent to accept service of process in any such action, suit or proceeding;

(7) The address to which a copy of the process referred to in subsection (b)(6) of this section shall be mailed to it by the Secretary of State. Process may be served upon the Secretary of State under paragraph (b)(6) of this

section by means of electronic transmission but only as prescribed by the Secretary of State. The Secretary of State is authorized to issue such rules and regulations with respect to such service as the Secretary of State deems necessary or appropriate. In the event of service hereunder upon the Secretary of State, the procedures set forth in § 17-911(c) of this title shall be applicable, except that the plaintiff in any such action, suit or proceeding shall furnish the Secretary of State with the address specified in this subsection and any other address that the plaintiff may elect to furnish, together with copies of such process as required by the Secretary of State, and the Secretary of State shall notify the limited partnership that has transferred or domesticated or continued out of the State of Delaware at all such addresses furnished by the plaintiff in accordance with the procedures set forth in § 17-911(c) of this title; and

(8) In the case of a certificate of transfer and domestic continuance, that the limited partnership will continue to exist as a limited partnership of the State of Delaware after the certificate of transfer and domestic continuance becomes effective.

(c) Upon the filing in the office of the Secretary of State of the certificate of transfer or upon the future effective date or time of the certificate of transfer and payment to the Secretary of State of all fees prescribed in this chapter, the Secretary of State shall certify that the limited partnership has filed all documents and paid all fees required by this chapter and thereupon the limited partnership shall cease to exist as a limited partnership of the State of Delaware. Such certificate of the Secretary of State shall be *prima facie* evidence of the transfer or domestication or continuance by such limited partnership out of the State of Delaware.

(d) The transfer or domestication or continuance of a limited partnership out of the State of Delaware in accordance with this section and the resulting cessation of its existence as a limited partnership of the State of Delaware pursuant to a certificate of transfer shall not be deemed to affect any obligations or liabilities of the limited partnership incurred prior to such transfer or domestication or continuance or the personal liability of any person incurred prior to such transfer or domestication or continuance, nor shall it be deemed to affect the choice of law applicable to the limited partnership with respect to matters arising prior to such transfer or domestication or continuance. Unless otherwise agreed, the transfer or domestication or continuance of a limited partnership out of the State of Delaware in accordance with this section shall not require such limited partnership to wind up its affairs under § 17-803 of this title or pay its liabilities and distribute its assets under § 17-804 of this title and shall not be deemed to constitute a dissolution of such limited partnership.

(e) If a limited partnership files a certificate of transfer and domestic continuance, after the time the certificate of transfer and domestic continuance becomes effective, the limited partnership shall continue to exist as a limited partnership of the State of Delaware, and the laws of the State of Delaware, including the provisions of this chapter, shall apply to the limited partnership, to the same extent as prior to such time. So long as a limited partnership continues to exist as a limited partnership of the State of Delaware following the filing of a certificate of transfer and domestic continuance, the continuing domestic limited partnership and the entity or business form formed, incorporated, created or that otherwise came into being as a consequence of the transfer of the limited partnership to, or its domestication or continuance in, a foreign country or other foreign jurisdiction shall, for all purposes of the laws of the State of Delaware, constitute a single entity formed, incorporated, created or otherwise having come into being, as applicable, and existing under the laws of the State of Delaware and the laws of such foreign country or other foreign jurisdiction.

(f) In connection with a transfer or domestication or continuance of a domestic limited partnership to or in another jurisdiction pursuant to subsection (a) of this section, rights or securities of, or interests in, such limited partnership may be exchanged for or converted into cash, property, rights or securities of, or interests in, the entity or business form in which the limited partnership will exist in such other jurisdiction as a consequence of the transfer or domestication or continuance or, in addition to or in lieu thereof, may be exchanged for or converted into cash, property, rights or securities of, or interests in, another entity or business form or may be cancelled.

(g) When a limited partnership has transferred or domesticated or continued out of the State of Delaware pursuant to this section, the transferred or domesticated or continued entity or business form shall, for all purposes of the laws of the State of Delaware, be deemed to be the same entity as the limited partnership and shall constitute a continuation of the existence of such limited partnership in the form of the transferred or domesticated or continued entity or business form. When any transfer or domestication or continuance of a limited partnership out of the State of Delaware shall have become effective under this section, for all purposes of the laws of the State of Delaware, all of the rights, privileges and powers of the limited partnership that has transferred or domesticated or continued, and all property, real, personal and mixed, and all debts due to such limited partnership, as well as all other things and causes of action belonging to such limited partnership, shall remain vested in the transferred or domesticated or continued entity or business form (and also in the limited partnership that has transferred, domesticated or continued, if and for so long as such limited partnership continues its existence as a domestic limited partnership), and shall be the property of such transferred or domesticated or continued entity or business form (and also of the limited partnership that has transferred, domesticated or continued, if and for so long as such limited partnership continues its existence as a domestic limited partnership), and the title to any real property vested by deed or otherwise in such limited partnership shall not revert or be in any way impaired by reason of this chapter; but all rights of creditors and all liens upon any property of such limited partnership shall be preserved unimpaired, and all debts, liabilities and duties of the limited partnership that has transferred or domesticated or continued shall remain attached to the transferred or domesticated or continued entity or business form (and also to the limited partnership that has transferred, domesticated or continued, if and for so long as such limited partnership continues its existence as a domestic limited partnership), and may be enforced against it to the same extent as if said debts, liabilities and duties had originally been incurred or contracted by it in its capacity as the transferred or domesticated or continued entity or business form. The rights, privileges, powers and interests in property of the limited partnership that has transferred or domesticated or continued, as well as the debts, liabilities and duties of such limited partnership, shall not be deemed, as a consequence of the transfer or domestication or continuance out of the State of Delaware, to have been transferred to the transferred or domesticated or continued entity or business form for any purpose of the laws of the State of Delaware.

(h) A partnership agreement may provide that a domestic limited partnership shall not have the power to transfer, domesticate or continue as set forth in this section.

§ 17-217. Conversion of certain entities to a limited partnership.

(a) As used in this section and in § 17-204, the term "other entity" means a corporation, a statutory trust, a business trust, an association, a real estate investment trust, a common-law trust, or any other unincorporated business or entity, including a general partnership (including a limited liability partnership) or a foreign limited partnership (including a foreign limited liability limited partnership) or a limited liability company.

(b) Any other entity may convert to a domestic limited partnership (including a limited liability limited partnership) by complying with subsection (h) of this section and filing in the office of the Secretary of State in accordance with § 17-206 of this title:

(1) A certificate of conversion to limited partnership that has been executed in accordance with § 17-204 of this title; and

(2) A certificate of limited partnership that complies with § 17-201 of this title and has been executed in accordance with § 17-204 of this title.

(3) In the case of a conversion to a limited liability limited partnership, a statement of qualification in accordance with subsection (c) of § 15-1001 of this Title.

Each of the certificates (and, as applicable, the statement) required by this subsection (b) shall be filed simultaneously in the office of the Secretary of State and, if such certificates (and, as applicable, such statement) are not to become effective upon their filing as permitted by § 17-206(b) of this title, then each such certificate (and, as applicable, such statement) shall provide for the same effective date or time in accordance with § 17-206(b) of this title.

(c) The certificate of conversion to limited partnership shall state:

(1) The date on which and jurisdiction where the other entity was first created, incorporated, formed or otherwise came into being and, if it has changed, its jurisdiction immediately prior to its conversion to a domestic limited partnership;

(2) The name of the other entity immediately prior to the filing of the certificate of conversion to limited partnership;

(3) The name of the limited partnership as set forth in its certificate of limited partnership filed in accordance with subsection (b) of this section; and

(4) The future effective date or time (which shall be a date or time certain) of the conversion to a limited partnership if it is not to be effective upon the filing of the certificate of conversion to limited partnership and the certificate of limited partnership.

(d) Upon the filing in the office of the Secretary of State of the certificate of conversion to limited partnership, the certificate of limited partnership and the statement of qualification (if applicable), or upon the future effective date or time of the certificate of conversion to limited partnership and the statement of qualification (if applicable), the certificate of limited partnership, the other entity shall be converted into a domestic limited partnership (including a limited liability limited partnership, if applicable) and the limited partnership shall thereafter be subject to all of the provisions of this chapter, except that notwithstanding § 17-201 of this title, the existence of the limited partnership shall be deemed to have commenced on the date the other entity commenced its existence in the jurisdiction in which the other entity was first created, formed, incorporated or otherwise came into being.

(e) The conversion of any other entity into a domestic limited partnership (including a limited liability limited partnership) shall not be deemed to affect any obligations or liabilities of the other entity incurred prior to its conversion to a domestic limited partnership, or the personal liability of any person incurred prior to such conversion.

(f) When any conversion shall have become effective under this section, for all purposes of the laws of the State of Delaware, all of the rights, privileges and powers of the other entity that has converted, and all property, real, personal and mixed, and all debts due to such other entity, as well as all other things and causes of action belonging to such other entity, shall remain vested in the domestic limited partnership to which such other entity has converted and shall be the property of such domestic limited partnership, and the title to any real property vested by deed or otherwise in such other entity shall not revert or be in any way impaired by reason of this chapter; but all rights of creditors and all liens upon any property of such other entity shall be preserved unimpaired, and all debts, liabilities and duties of the other entity that has converted shall remain attached to the domestic limited partnership to which such other entity has converted, and may be enforced against it to the same extent as if said debts, liabilities and duties had originally been incurred or contracted by it in its capacity as a domestic limited partnership. The rights, privileges, powers and interests in property of the other entity, as well as the debts, liabilities and duties of the other entity, shall not be deemed, as a consequence of the conversion, to have been transferred to the domestic limited partnership to which such other entity has converted for any purpose of the laws of the State of Delaware.

(g) Unless otherwise agreed, for all purposes of the laws of the State of Delaware, the converting other entity shall not be required to wind up its affairs or pay its liabilities and distribute its assets and the conversion shall not be deemed to constitute a dissolution of such other entity. When an other entity has been converted to a limited partnership pursuant to this section, for all purposes of the laws of the State of Delaware the limited partnership shall be deemed to be the same entity as the converting other entity and the conversion shall constitute a continuation of the existence of the converting other entity in the form of a domestic limited partnership.

(h) Prior to filing a certificate of conversion to limited partnership with the office of the Secretary of State, the conversion shall be approved in the manner provided for by the document, instrument, agreement or other writing, as the case may be, governing the internal affairs of the other entity and the conduct of its business or by applicable law, as appropriate, and a partnership agreement shall be approved by the same authorization required to approve the conversion; provided, that in any event, such approval shall include the approval of any person who, at the effective date or time of the conversion, shall be a general partner of the limited partnership.

(i) In connection with a conversion hereunder, rights or securities of, or interests in, the other entity which is to be converted to a domestic limited partnership may be exchanged for or converted into cash, property, rights or securities of, or interests in, such domestic limited partnership or, in addition to or in lieu thereof, may be exchanged for or converted into cash, property, rights or securities of, or interests in, another domestic limited partnership or other entity or may be cancelled.

(j) The provisions of this section shall not be construed to limit the accomplishment of a change in the law governing, or the domicile of, another entity to the State of Delaware by any other means provided for in a partnership agreement or other agreement or as otherwise permitted by law, including by the amendment of a partnership agreement or other agreement.

§ 17-218. Series of limited partners, general partners, partnership interests or assets.

(a) A partnership agreement may establish or provide for the establishment of 1 or more designated series of limited partners, general partners, partnership interests or assets. Any such series may have separate rights, powers or duties with respect to specified property or obligations of the limited partnership or profits and losses associated with specified property or obligations, and any such series may have a separate business purpose or investment objective.

(b) Notwithstanding anything to the contrary set forth in this chapter or under other applicable law, in the event that a partnership agreement establishes or provides for the establishment of 1 or more series or states that the liabilities of a general partner are limited to the liabilities of a designated series, and if the records maintained for any such series account for the assets associated with such series separately from the other assets of the limited partnership, or any other series thereof, and if the partnership agreement so provides, and if notice of the limitation on liabilities of a series or a general partner as referenced in this subsection is set forth in the certificate of limited partnership, then the liabilities, obligations, and expenses incurred, contracted for or otherwise existing with respect to a particular series or general partner shall be enforceable only against the assets of such series or a general partner associated with such series and not against the assets of the limited partnership generally, any other series thereof, or any general partner not associated with such series, and, unless otherwise provided in the partnership agreement, none of the debts, liabilities, obligations and expenses incurred, contracted for or otherwise existing with respect to the limited partnership generally or any other series thereof shall be enforceable against the assets of such series or a general partner associated with such series. Assets associated with a series may be held directly or indirectly, including in the name of such series, in the name of the limited partnership, through a nominee or otherwise. Records maintained for a series that reasonably identify its assets, including by specific listing, category, type, quantity, computational or allocational formula or procedure (including a percentage or share of any asset or assets) or by any other method where the identity of such assets is objectively determinable, will be deemed to account for the assets associated with such series separately from the other assets of the limited partnership, or any other series thereof.

(c) A series established in accordance with subsection (b) of this section may carry on any lawful business, purpose or activity, whether or not for profit, with the exception of the business of banking as defined in § 126 of Title 8. Unless otherwise provided in a partnership agreement, a series established in accordance with subsection (b) of this section shall have the power and capacity to, in its own name, contract, hold title to assets (including real, personal and intangible property), grant liens and security interests, and sue and be sued.

(d) Notice in a certificate of limited partnership of the limitation on liabilities of a series as referenced in subsection (b) of this section shall be sufficient for all purposes of subsection (b) of this section whether or not the limited partnership has established any series when such notice is included in the certificate of limited partnership, and there shall be no requirement that any specific series of the limited partnership be referenced in such notice. The fact that a certificate of limited partnership that contains the notice of the limitation on liabilities of a series or a general partner as referenced in subsection (b) of this section is on file in the office of the Secretary of State shall constitute notice of such limitation on liabilities.

(e) A limited partner may possess or exercise any of the rights and powers or act or attempt to act in 1 or more of the capacities as permitted under to § 17-303 of this title, with respect to any series, without participating in the control of the business of the limited partnership or with respect to any series thereof within the meaning of § 17-303(a) of this title. A partnership agreement may provide for classes or groups of general partners or limited partners associated with a series having such relative rights, powers and duties as the partnership agreement may provide, and may make provision for the future creation in the manner provided in the partnership agreement of additional classes or groups of general partners or limited partners associated with the series having such relative rights, powers and duties as may from time to time be established, including rights, powers and duties senior to existing classes and groups of general partners or limited partners associated with the series. A partnership agreement may provide for the taking of an action, including the amendment of the partnership agreement, without the vote or approval of any general partner or limited partner or class or group of general partners or limited partners, including an action to create under the provisions of the partnership agreement a class or group of the series of partnership interests that was not previously outstanding.

(f) A partnership agreement may grant to all or certain identified general partners or limited partners or a specified class or group of the general partners or limited partners associated with a series the right to vote separately or with all or any class or group of the general partners or limited partners associated with the series, on any matter. Voting by general partners or limited partners associated with a series may be on a per capita, number, financial interest, class, group or any other basis.

(g) Section 17-603 of this title shall apply to a limited partner with respect to any series with which the limited partner is associated. Except as otherwise provided in a partnership agreement, any event under this subsection or in a partnership agreement that causes a limited partner to cease to be associated with a series shall not, in itself, cause such limited partner to cease to be associated with any other series or to be a limited partner of the limited partnership or cause the termination of the series, regardless of whether such limited partner was the last remaining limited partner associated with such series. A limited partner shall cease to be a limited partner with respect to a series and to have the power to exercise any rights or powers of a limited partner with respect to such series upon the happening of either of the following events:

(1) The limited partner withdraws with respect to the series in accordance with § 17-603 of this title; or

(2) Except as otherwise provided in the partnership agreement, the limited partner assigns all of his or her partnership interest with respect to the series.

(h) Section 17-602 of this title shall apply to a general partner with respect to any series with which the general partner is associated. A general partner shall cease to be a general partner with respect to a series and to have the power to exercise any rights or powers of a general partner with respect to such series upon an event of withdrawal of the general partner with respect to such series. Except as otherwise provided in a partnership agreement, either of the following events or any event in a partnership agreement that causes a general partner to cease to be associated with a series shall not, in itself, cause such general partner to cease to be associated with any other series or to be a general partner of the limited partnership:

(1) The general partner withdraws with respect to the series in accordance with § 17-602 of this title; or

(2) The general partner assigns all of the general partner's partnership interest with respect to the series.

(i) Notwithstanding § 17-606 of this title, but subject to subsections (j) and (l) of this section, and unless otherwise provided in a partnership agreement, at the time a partner associated with a series that has been established in accordance with subsection (b) of this section becomes entitled to receive a distribution with respect to such series, the partner has the status of, and is entitled to all remedies available to, a creditor of the series, with respect to the distribution. A partnership agreement may provide for the establishment of a record date with respect to allocations and distributions with respect to a series.

(j) Notwithstanding § 17-607(a) of this title, a limited partnership may make a distribution with respect to a series that has been established in accordance with subsection (b) of this section. A limited partnership shall not make a distribution with respect to a series that has been established in accordance with subsection (b) of this section to a partner to the extent that at the time of the distribution, after giving effect to the distribution, all liabilities of such series, other than liabilities to partners on account of their partnership interests with respect to such series and liabilities for which the recourse of creditors is limited to specified property of such series, exceed the fair value of the assets associated with such series, except that the fair value of property of the series that is subject to a liability for which the recourse of creditors is limited shall be included in the assets associated with such series only to the extent that the fair value of that property exceeds that liability. For purposes of the immediately preceding sentence, the term "distribution" shall not include amounts constituting reasonable compensation for present or past services or reasonable payments made in the ordinary course of business pursuant to a bona fide retirement plan or other benefits program. A limited partner who receives a distribution in violation of this subsection, and who knew at the time of the distribution that the distribution violated this subsection, shall be liable to a series for the amount of the distribution. A limited partner who receives a distribution in violation of this subsection, and who did not know at the time of the distribution that the distribution violated this subsection, shall not be liable for the amount of the distribution. Subject to § 17-607(c) of this title, which shall apply to any distribution made with respect to a series under this subsection, this subsection shall not affect any obligation or liability of a limited partner under an agreement or other applicable law for the amount of a distribution.

(k) Subject to § 17-801 of this title, except to the extent otherwise provided in the partnership agreement, a series may be terminated and its affairs wound up without causing the dissolution of the limited partnership. The termination of a series established in accordance with subsection (b) of this section shall not affect the limitation on liabilities of such series provided by subsection (b) of this section.

A series is terminated and its affairs shall be wound up upon the dissolution of the limited partnership under § 17-801 of this chapter or otherwise upon the first to occur of the following:

(1) At the time specified in the partnership agreement;

(2) Upon the happening of events specified in the partnership agreement;

(3) Unless otherwise provided in the partnership agreement, upon the affirmative vote or written consent of (i) all general partners associated with such series and (ii) the limited partners associated with such series or, if there is more than 1 class or group of limited partners associated with such series, then by each class or group of limited partners associated with such series, in either case, by limited partners associated with such series who own more than two-thirds of the then-current percentage or other interest in the profits of the limited partnership associated with such series owned by all of the limited partners associated with such series or by the limited partners in each class or group associated with such series, as appropriate;

(4) An event of withdrawal of a general partner associated with the series unless at the time there is at least 1 other general partner associated with the series and the partnership agreement permits the business of the series to be carried on by the remaining general partner and that partner does so, but the series is not terminated and is not required to be wound up by reason of any event of withdrawal if (i) within 90 days or such other period as is provided for in the partnership agreement after the withdrawal either (A) if provided for in the partnership agreement, the then-current percentage or other interest in the profits of the series specified in the partnership agreement owned by the remaining partners associated with the series agree, in writing or vote, to continue the business of the series and to appoint, effective as of the date of withdrawal, 1 or more additional general partners for the series if necessary or desired, or (B) if no such right to agree or vote to continue the business of the series of the limited partnership and to appoint 1 or more additional general partners for such series is provided for in the partnership agreement, then more than 50% of the then-current percentage or other interest in the profits of the series owned by the remaining partners associated with the series or, if there is more than one class or group of remaining partners associated with the series, then more than 50% of the then-current percentage or other interest in the profits of the series owned by each class or classes or group or groups of remaining partners associated with the series agree, in writing or vote, to continue the business of the series and to appoint, effective as of the date of withdrawal, 1 or more additional general partners for the series if necessary or desired, or (ii) the business of the series is continued pursuant to a right to continue stated in the partnership agreement and the appointment, effective as of the date of withdrawal, of 1 or more additional general partners to be associated with the series if necessary or desired; or

(5) The termination of such series under subsection (m) of this section.

(l) Notwithstanding § 17-803(a) of this title, unless otherwise provided in the partnership agreement, a general partner associated with a series who has not wrongfully terminated the series or, if none, the limited partners associated with the series or a person approved by the limited partners associated with the series or, if there is more than one class or group of limited partners associated with the series, then by each class or group of limited partners associated with the series, in either case, by limited partners who own more than 50 percent of the then current percentage or other interest in the profits of the series owned by all of the limited partners associated with the series or by the limited partners in each class or group associated with the series, as appropriate, may wind up the affairs of the series; but, if the series has been established in accordance with subsection (b) of this section, the Court of Chancery, upon cause shown, may wind up the affairs of the series upon application of any partner associated with the series, the person's personal representative or assignee, and in connection therewith, may appoint a liquidating trustee. The persons winding up the affairs of a series may, in the name of the limited partnership and for and on behalf of the limited partnership and such series, take all actions with respect to the series as are permitted under § 17-803(b) of this title. The persons winding up the affairs of a series shall provide for the claims and obligations of the series and distribute the assets of the series as provided in § 17-804 of this title, which section shall apply to the winding up and distribution of assets of a series. Actions taken in accordance with this subsection shall not affect the liability of limited partners and shall not impose liability on a liquidating trustee.

(m) On application by or for a partner associated with a series established in accordance with subsection (b) of this section, the Court of Chancery may decree termination of such series whenever it is not reasonably practicable to carry on the business of the series in conformity with a partnership agreement.

(n) If a foreign limited partnership that is registering to do business in the State of Delaware in accordance with § 17-902 of this chapter is governed by a partnership agreement that establishes or provides for the establishment of designated series of limited partners, general partners, partnership interests or assets having separate rights, powers or duties with respect to specified property or obligations of the foreign limited partnership or profits and losses associated with specified property or obligations, that fact shall be so stated on the application for registration as a foreign limited partnership. In addition, the foreign limited partnership shall state on such application whether the debts, liabilities and obligations incurred, contracted for or otherwise existing with respect to a particular series, if any, or general partner associated with such series shall be enforceable only against the assets of such series or any general partner associated with such series and not against the assets of the foreign limited partnership generally, any other series thereof, or any general partner not associated with such series and, whether any of the debts, liabilities, obligations and expenses incurred, contracted for or otherwise existing with respect to the foreign limited partnership generally or any other series thereof shall be enforceable against the assets of such series or a general partner associated with such series.

§ 17-219. Approval of conversion of a limited partnership.

(a) Upon compliance with this section, a domestic limited partnership may convert to a corporation, a statutory trust, a business trust, an association, a real estate investment trust, a common-law trust or any other unincorporated business or entity, including a general partnership (including a limited liability partnership) or a foreign limited partnership (including a foreign limited liability limited partnership) or a limited liability company.

(b) If the partnership agreement specifies the manner of authorizing a conversion of the limited partnership, the conversion shall be authorized as specified in the partnership agreement. If the partnership agreement does not specify the manner of authorizing a conversion of the limited partnership and does not prohibit a conversion of the limited partnership, the conversion shall be authorized in the same manner as is specified in the partnership agreement for authorizing a merger or consolidation that involves the limited partnership as a constituent party to the merger or consolidation. If the partnership agreement does not specify the manner of authorizing a conversion of the limited partnership or a merger or consolidation that involves the limited partnership as a constituent party and does not prohibit a conversion of the limited partnership, the conversion shall be authorized by the approval (1) by all general partners, and (2) by the limited partners or, if there is more than one class or group of limited partners, then by each class or group of limited partners, in either case, by limited partners who own more than 50 percent of the then current percentage or other interest in the profits of the domestic limited partnership owned by all of the limited partners or by the limited partners in each class or group, as appropriate.

(c) Unless otherwise agreed, the conversion of a domestic limited partnership to another entity or business form pursuant to this section shall not require such limited partnership to wind up its affairs under § 17-803 of this title or pay its liabilities and distribute its assets under § 17-804 of this title, and the conversion shall not constitute a dissolution of such limited partnership. When a limited partnership has converted to another entity or business form pursuant to this Section, for all purposes of the laws of the State of Delaware, the other entity or business form shall be deemed to be the same entity as the converting limited partnership and the conversion shall constitute a continuation of the existence of the limited partnership in the form of such other entity or business form.

(d) In connection with a conversion of a domestic limited partnership to another entity or business form pursuant to this section, rights or securities of or interests in the domestic limited partnership which is to be converted may be exchanged for or converted into cash, property, rights or securities of or interests in the entity or business form into which the domestic limited partnership is being converted or, in addition to or in lieu thereof, may be exchanged for or converted into cash, property, rights or securities of or interests in another entity or business form or may be cancelled.

(e) If a limited partnership shall convert in accordance with this section to another entity or business form organized, formed or created under the laws of a jurisdiction other than the State of Delaware, a certificate of conversion to non-Delaware entity executed in accordance with § 17-204 of this title shall be filed in the office of the Secretary of State in accordance with § 17-206 of this title. The certificate of conversion to non-Delaware entity shall state:

(1) The name of the limited partnership and, if it has been changed, the name under which its certificate of limited partnership was originally filed;

(2) The date of filing of its original certificate of limited partnership with the Secretary of State;

(3) The jurisdiction in which the entity or business form, to which the limited partnership shall be converted, is organized, formed or created, and the name of such entity or business form;

(4) The future effective date or time (which shall be a date or time certain) of the conversion if it is not to be effective upon the filing of the certificate of conversion to non-Delaware entity;

(5) That the conversion has been approved in accordance with this section;

(6) The agreement of the limited partnership that it may be served with process in the State of Delaware in any action, suit or proceeding for enforcement of any obligation of the limited partnership arising while it was a limited partnership of the State of Delaware, and that it irrevocably appoints the Secretary of State as its agent to accept service of process in any such action, suit or proceeding;

(7) The address to which a copy of the process referred to in subsection (e)(6) of this section shall be mailed to it by the Secretary of State. Process may be served upon the Secretary of State under subdivision (e)(6) of this section by means of electronic transmission but only as prescribed by the Secretary of State. The Secretary of State is authorized to issue such rules and regulations with respect to such service as the Secretary of State deems necessary or appropriate. In the event of service hereunder upon the Secretary of State, the procedures set forth in § 17-911(c) of this title shall be applicable, except that the plaintiff in any such action, suit or proceeding shall furnish the Secretary of State with the address specified in this subsection (e)(7) and any other address that the plaintiff may elect to furnish, together with copies of such process as required by the Secretary of State, and the Secretary of State shall notify the limited partnership that has converted out of the State of Delaware at all such addresses furnished by the plaintiff in accordance with the procedures set forth in § 17-911(c) of this title.

(f) Upon the filing in the office of the Secretary of State of the certificate of conversion to non-Delaware entity or upon the future effective date or time of the certificate of conversion to non-Delaware entity and payment to the Secretary of State of all fees prescribed in this chapter, the Secretary of State shall certify that the limited partnership has filed all documents and paid all fees required by this chapter, and thereupon the limited partnership shall cease to exist as a limited partnership of the State of Delaware. Such certificate of the Secretary of State shall be prima facie evidence of the conversion by such limited partnership out of the State of Delaware.

(g) The conversion of a limited partnership out of the State of Delaware in accordance with this section and the resulting cessation of its existence as a limited partnership of the State of Delaware pursuant to a certificate of conversion to non-Delaware entity shall not be deemed to affect any obligations or liabilities of the limited partnership incurred prior to such conversion or the personal liability of any person incurred prior to such conversion, nor shall it be deemed to affect the choice of law applicable to the limited partnership with respect to matters arising prior to such conversion.

(h) When any conversion shall have become effective under this section, for all purposes of the laws of the State of Delaware, all of the rights, privileges and powers of the limited partnership that has converted, and all property, real, personal and mixed, and all debts due to such limited partnership, as well as all other things and causes of action belonging to such limited partnership, shall remain vested in the other entity or business form to which such limited partnership has converted and shall be the property of such other entity or business form, and the title to any real property vested by deed or otherwise in such limited partnership shall not revert or be in any way impaired by reason of this chapter; but all rights of creditors and all liens upon any property of such limited partnership shall be preserved unimpaired, and all debts, liabilities and duties of the limited partnership that has converted shall remain attached to the other entity or business form to which such limited partnership has converted, and may be enforced against it to the same extent as if said debts, liabilities and duties had originally been incurred or contracted by it in its capacity as such other entity or business form. The rights, privileges, powers and interests in property of the limited partnership that has converted, as well as the debts, liabilities and duties of such limited partnership, shall not be deemed, as a consequence of the conversion, to have been transferred to the other entity or business form to which such limited partnership has converted for any purpose of the laws of the State of Delaware.

(i) A partnership agreement may provide that a domestic limited partnership shall not have the power to convert as set forth in this section.

ANNOTATION

Approval of conversion — Attempted conversion of limited partnership without the consent of the general partner was invalid. *Greenwich Global, LLC v. Clairvoyant Capital, LLC*, 2002 WL 31168715 (Conn. Super. Ct. Aug. 22, 2002).

Subchapter III
LIMITED PARTNERS

§ 17-301. Admission of limited partners.

(a) In connection with the formation of a limited partnership, a person is admitted as a limited partner of the limited partnership upon the later to occur of:

(1) The formation of the limited partnership; or

(2) The time provided in and upon compliance with the partnership agreement or, if the partnership agreement does not so provide, when the person's admission is reflected in the records of the limited partnership.

(b) After the formation of a limited partnership, a person is admitted as a limited partner of the limited partnership:

(1) In the case of a person who is not an assignee of a partnership interest, including a person acquiring a partnership interest directly from the limited partnership and a person to be admitted as a limited partner of the limited partnership without acquiring a partnership interest in the limited partnership, at the time provided in and upon compliance with the partnership agreement or, if the partnership agreement does not so provide, upon the consent of all partners and when the person's admission is reflected in the records of the limited partnership;

(2) In the case of an assignee of a partnership interest, as provided in § 17-704(a) of this title and at the time provided in and upon compliance with the partnership agreement or, if the partnership agreement does not so provide, when any such person's permitted admission is reflected in the records of the limited partnership; or

(3) In the case of a person being admitted as a partner of a surviving or resulting limited partnership pursuant to a merger or consolidation approved in accordance with § 17-211(b) of this title, as provided in the partnership agreement of the surviving or resulting limited partnership or in the agreement of merger or consolidation or plan of merger, and in the event of any inconsistency, the terms of the agreement of merger or consolidation or plan of merger shall control; and in the case of a person being admitted as a partner of a limited partnership pursuant to a merger or consolidation in which such limited partnership is not the surviving or resulting limited partnership in the merger or consolidation, as provided in the partnership agreement of such limited partnership.

(c) In connection with the domestication of a non-United States entity (as defined in § 17-215 of this title) as a limited partnership in the State of Delaware in accordance with § 17-215 of this title or the conversion of another entity (as defined in § 17-217 of this title) to a domestic limited partnership in accordance with § 17-217 of this title, a person is admitted as a limited partner of the limited partnership as provided in the partnership agreement.

(d) A person may be admitted to a limited partnership as a limited partner of the limited partnership and may receive a partnership interest in the limited partnership without making a contribution or being obligated to make a contribution to the limited partnership. Unless otherwise provided in a partnership agreement, a person may be admitted to a limited partnership as a limited partner of the limited partnership without acquiring a partnership interest in the limited partnership. Unless otherwise provided in a partnership agreement, a person may be admitted as the sole limited partner of a limited partnership without making a contribution or being obligated to make a contribution to the limited partnership or without acquiring a partnership interest in the limited partnership.

(e) Unless otherwise provided in a partnership agreement or another agreement, a limited partner shall have no preemptive right to subscribe to any additional issue of partnership interests or another interest in a limited partnership.

ANNOTATIONS

Admission of transferee as substitute limited partner — A plaintiff was held to have been admitted as a substitute limited partner where the NASD forms used by the partnership for registering transfers of interests constituted a request for admission as a substitute limited partner, the general partner was found to have delegated to the partnership's transfer agent the general partner's authority to consent not only to assignments but to admission of a transferee as a substituted limited partner and the transfer agent had confirmed to the plaintiff its status as a limited partner. *In re American Tax Credit Limited Partnerships*, 1997 WL 770717 (Del. Ch. Dec. 5, 1997), *aff'd*, 707 A.2d 765 (Del. 1998).

Conversion to limited partner — The general partner who was removed by unanimous written consent of the limited partners could not convert his capital contribution into a limited partnership interest. The limited partnership agreement permitted a general partner who left voluntarily, for example through retirement, to convert his capital contribution into a limited partnership interest. But, a general partner who was ousted involuntarily did not have this privilege. *Hillman v. Hillman*, 903 A.2d 798 (Del. Ch. 2006).

§ 17-302. Classes and voting.

(a) A partnership agreement may provide for classes or groups of limited partners having such relative rights, powers and duties as the partnership agreement may provide, and may make provision for the future creation in the manner provided in the partnership agreement of additional classes or groups of limited partners having such relative rights, powers and duties as may from time to time be established, including rights, powers and duties senior to existing classes and groups of limited partners. A partnership agreement may provide for the taking of an action, including the amendment of the partnership agreement, without the vote or approval of any limited partner or class or group of limited partners, including an action to create under the provisions of the partnership agreement a class or group of partnership interests that was not previously outstanding.

(b) Subject to § 17-303 of this title, the partnership agreement may grant to all or certain identified limited partners or a specified class or group of the limited partners the right to vote separately or with all or any class or group of the limited partners or the general partners, on any matter. Voting by limited partners may be on a per capita, number, financial interest, class, group or any other basis.

(c) A partnership agreement may set forth provisions relating to notice of the time, place or purpose of any meeting at which any matter is to be voted on by any limited partners, waiver of any such notice, action by consent without a meeting, the establishment of a record date, quorum requirements, voting in person or by proxy, or any other matter with respect to the exercise of any such right to vote.

(d) Any right or power, including voting rights, granted to limited partners as permitted under § 17-303 of this title shall be deemed to be permitted by this section.

(e) Unless otherwise provided in a partnership agreement, meetings of limited partners may be held by means of conference telephone or other communications equipment by means of which all persons participating in the meeting can hear each other, and participation in a meeting pursuant to this subsection shall constitute presence in person at the meeting. Unless otherwise provided in a partnership agreement, on any matter that is to be voted on, consented to or approved by limited partners, the limited partners may take such action without a meeting, without prior notice and without a vote if consented to, in writing or by electronic transmission, by limited partners having not less than the minimum number of votes that would be necessary to authorize or take such action at a meeting at which all limited partners entitled to vote thereon were present and voted. Unless otherwise provided in a partnership agreement, on any matter that is to be voted on by limited partners, the limited partners may vote in person or by proxy, and such proxy may be granted in writing, by means of electronic transmission or as otherwise permitted by applicable law. Unless otherwise provided in a partnership agreement, a consent transmitted by electronic transmission by a limited partner or by a person or persons authorized to act for a limited partner shall be deemed to be written and signed for purposes of this subsection. For purposes of this subsection, the term "electronic transmission" means any form of communication not directly involving the physical transmission of paper that creates a record that may be retained, retrieved and reviewed by a recipient thereof and that may be directly reproduced in paper form by such a recipient through an automated process.

(f) If a partnership agreement provides for the manner in which it may be amended, including by requiring the approval of a person who is not a party to the partnership agreement or the satisfaction of conditions, it may be amended only in that manner or as otherwise permitted by law, including as permitted by Section 17-211(g) of this title (provided that the approval of any person may be waived by such person and that any such conditions may be waived by all persons for whose benefit such conditions were intended). If a partnership agreement does not provide for the manner in which it may be amended, the partnership agreement may be amended with the approval of all the partners or as otherwise permitted by law, including as permitted by Section 17-211(g) of this title. A limited partner and any class or group of limited partners have the right to vote only on matters as specifically set forth in this chapter, on matters specifically provided by agreement, including a partnership agreement, and on any matter with respect to which a general partner may determine in its discretion to seek a vote of a limited partner or a class or group of limited partners if a vote on such matter is not contrary to a partnership agreement or another agreement to which a general partner or the limited partnership is a party. A limited partner and any class or group of limited partners have no other voting rights. A partnership agreement may provide that any limited partner or class or group of limited partners shall have no voting rights. Unless otherwise provided in a partnership agreement, a supermajority amendment provision shall only apply to provisions of the partnership agreement that are expressly included in the partnership agreement. As used in this section, "'supermajority amendment provision" means any amendment provision set forth in a partnership agreement requiring that an amendment to a provision of the partnership agreement be adopted by no less than the vote or consent required to take action under such latter provision.

ANNOTATIONS

Amendment to agreement — An amendment to the limited partnership agreement intended to "compromise" a capital call made by the former general partner was not validly adopted. The amendment purported to reduce the requirement in the partnership agreement that all partners had to unanimously consent to any change in the obligation of a partner to make a contribution, to a requirement that only a simple majority of the partners could change an obligation to make a contribution. But, the amendment itself, under the default provision of the Delaware Revised Uniform Limited Partnership Act, required unanimous consent, which was not met. *In re LJM2 Co-Investment, L.P.*, 866 A.2d 762 (Del. Ch. 2004).

Authority to create new class of preferred limited partners; authority to amend agreement — The general partner could not unilaterally amend the limited partnership agreement to create a new class of preferred limited partners. Although the general partner had discretion to issue additional limited partner units that could dilute the interests of existing limited partners, if a new issuance subordinated the rights of existing limited partners, the general partner was required to obtain their consent to amend the partnership agreement to allow this. In addition, the authority to create a new class of limited partners should be spelled out explicitly in the partnership agreement. *In re Nantucket Island Associates Ltd. Partnership Unitholders Litigation*, 810 A.2d 351 (Del. Ch. 2002).

Consent required to compromise contribution — Where a partnership agreement provided that it could be amended by a majority vote, provided that no amendment could alter the vote necessary for any consent "required hereunder" unless such amendment were approved by the vote necessary at the time of the amendment, the words "required hereunder" incorporated the default statutory provision of Section 502(b)(1), which requires a compromise of capital contributions to be approved by all partners. Because the partnership agreement contained no express provision altering the unanimous vote requirement of Section 502(b)(1), the partnership agreement could not be amended to permit a majority vote of partners to compromise capital commitments without the unanimous consent of the partners. *In re LJM2 Co-Inv., L.P.*, 866 A.2d 762 (Del. Ch. 2004).

Consents effective when given — Absent contrary provision in the partnership agreement, written consents by limited partners to removal of general partner were effective to remove the general partner when the requisite percentage of limited partners had executed consents, not when consents were delivered to the partnership or the general partner. *Alpine Investment Partners v. LJM2 Capital Management, L.P.*, 794 A.2d 1276 (Del. Ch. 2002).

Default consent requirement for amending agreement — Absent an express provision in a partnership agreement, the consent of all partners is necessary to amend the partnership agreement. *In re LJM2 Co-Inv., L.P.*, 866 A.2d 762 (Del. Ch. 2004).

Partnership agreement incorporates default rules — Where a partnership agreement provided that it could be amended by a majority vote, provided that no amendment could alter the vote necessary for any consent "required hereunder" unless such amendment were approved by the vote necessary at the time of the amendment, the words "required hereunder" incorporated the default statutory provision of Section

502(b)(1), which requires a compromise of capital contributions to be approved by all partners. Accordingly, an amendment purporting to reduce to a majority the consent required to compromise capital contributions was invalid in the absence of unanimous consent to the amendment. *In re LJM2 Co-Inv., L.P.*, 866 A.2d 762 (Del. Ch. 2004).

Sufficiency of proxies — Proxies need not be in any particular form. Absent evidence of fraud or other misconduct, all that is required for a valid proxy is a document authenticated by a signature, stamp or characteristic authorizing someone to vote the limited partnership units together with a sufficient indication of how the vote is to be cast. *In re Mesa Limited Partnership Preferred Unitholders Litigation*, 1991 Del. Ch. LEXIS 216 (Del. Ch. Dec. 31, 1991).

Supermajority vote required for amendment — Where a partnership agreement required a two-thirds vote of limited partners to approve a merger, the two-thirds vote requirement could not be amended by a majority vote even though the agreement provided that it could be amended by the vote of only a majority in interest of limited partners. To permit a majority to amend the two-thirds vote would render the two-thirds vote requirement illusory. *Wurtzel v. Park Towne Place Apartments Limited Partnership, 2001* WL 1807405 (Pa. Ct. Com. Pleas Sept. 11, 2001) (applying Delaware law).

Tabulation by independent tabulator presumptively valid — Absent evidence that an independent tabulator of votes acted unreasonably or improperly, the result of the vote as certified by the independent tabulator is presumed valid. *In re Mesa Limited Partnership Preferred Unitholders Litigation*, 1991 Del. Ch. LEXIS 216 (Del. Ch. Dec. 31, 1991).

Vote buying — No impermissible vote buying or coercion by a general partner was involved where the general partner conditioned distribution of assets through an exchange offer on the approval by the limited partners of various amendments to the partnership agreement. *Cantor Fitzgerald, L.P. v. Cantor*, 2001 WL 1456494 (Del. Ch. Nov. 5, 2001).

Voting by proxy prohibited by agreement — Where the partnership agreement provided that limited partners were to vote by written ballot (which could be distributed and returned by mail) and did not include any provisions for voting by proxy, the agreement controlled and general partner could not vote proxies obtained from limited partners. *Christman v. Brauvin Realty Advisors, Inc.*, 1998 U.S. Dist. LEXIS 12614 (E.D. Ill. Aug. 12, 1998).

Voting; solicitation of new votes — Where general partner supplemented a disclosure statement to correct an error in the calculation of the expected distribution to limited partners and gave limited partners approximately three weeks within which to change their votes, limited partners were sufficiently informed and had sufficient time to consider the information presented. Resolicitation of votes was not required. *In re Cencom Cable Income Partners, L.P. Litigation*, 1997 WL 666970 (Del. Ch. Oct. 15, 1997), *reargument denied*, 1997 WL 770158 (Del. Ch. Dec. 3, 1997).

§ 17-303. Liability to third parties.

(a) A limited partner is not liable for the obligations of a limited partnership unless he or she is also a general partner or, in addition to the exercise of the rights and powers of a limited partner, he or she participates in the control of the business. However, if the limited partner does participate in the control of the business, he or she is liable only to persons who transact business with the limited partnership reasonably believing, based upon the limited partner's conduct, that the limited partner is a general partner.

(b) A limited partner does not participate in the control of the business within the meaning of subsection (a) of this section by virtue of possessing or, regardless of whether or not the limited partner has the rights or powers, exercising or attempting to exercise 1 or more of the following rights or powers or having or, regardless of whether or not the limited partner has the rights or powers, acting or attempting to act in 1 or more of the following capacities:

(1) To be an independent contractor for or to transact business with, including being a contractor for, or to be an agent or employee of, the limited partnership or a general partner, or to be an officer, director or stockholder of a corporate general partner, or to be a partner of a partnership that is a general partner of the limited partnership, or to be a trustee, administrator, executor, custodian or other fiduciary or beneficiary of an estate or trust which is a general partner, or to be a trustee, officer, advisor, stockholder or beneficiary of a statutory trust which is a general partner or to be a member, manager, agent or employee of a limited liability company which is a general partner;

(2) To consult with or advise a general partner or any other person with respect to any matter, including the business of the limited partnership, or to act or cause a general partner or any other person to take or refrain from taking any action, including by proposing, approving, consenting or disapproving, by voting or otherwise, with respect to any matter, including the business of the limited partnership;

(3) To act as surety, guarantor or endorser for the limited partnership or a general partner, to guaranty or assume 1 or more obligations of the limited partnership or a general partner, to borrow money from the limited partnership or a general partner, to lend money to the limited partnership or a general partner, or to provide collateral for the limited partnership or a general partner;

(4) To call, request, or attend or participate at a meeting of the partners or the limited partners;

(5) To wind up a limited partnership pursuant to § 17-803 of this title;

(6) To take any action required or permitted by law to bring, pursue or settle or otherwise terminate a derivative action in the right of the limited partnership;

(7) To serve on a committee of the limited partnership or the limited partners or partners or to appoint, elect or otherwise participate in the choice of a representative or another person to serve on any such committee, and to act as a member of any such committee directly or by or through any such representative or other person;

(8) To act or cause the taking or refraining from the taking of any action, including by proposing, approving, consenting or disapproving, by voting or otherwise, with respect to 1 or more of the following matters:

a. The dissolution and winding up of the limited partnership or an election to continue the limited partnership or an election to continue the business of the limited partnership.

b. The sale, exchange, lease, mortgage, assignment, pledge or other transfer of, or granting of a security interest in, any asset or assets of the limited partnership.

c. The incurrence, renewal, refinancing or payment or other discharge of indebtedness by the limited partnership.

d. A change in the nature of the business.

e. The admission, removal or retention of a general partner.

f. The admission, removal or retention of a limited partner.

g. A transaction or other matter involving an actual or potential conflict of interest.

h. An amendment to the partnership agreement or certificate of limited partnership.

i. The merger or consolidation of a limited partnership.

j. In respect of a limited partnership which is registered as an investment company under the Investment Company Act of 1940 as amended [15 U.S.C. 81a-1 et seq.], any matter required by the Investment Company Act of 1940, as amended, or the rules and regulations of the Securities and Exchange Commission thereunder, to be approved by the holders of beneficial interests in an investment company, including the electing of directors or trustees of the investment company, the approving or terminating of investment advisory or underwriting contracts and the approving of auditors.

k. The indemnification of any partner or other person.

l. The making of, or calling for, or the making of other determinations in connection with, contributions.

m. The making of, or the making of other determinations in connection with or concerning, investments, including investments in property, whether real, personal or mixed, either directly or indirectly, by the limited partnership.

n. The nomination, appointment, election or other manner of selection or removal of an independent contractor for, or an agent or employee of, the limited partnership or a general partner, or an officer, director or stockholder of a corporate general partner, or a partner of a partnership which is a general partner, or a trustee, administrator, executor, custodian or other fiduciary or beneficiary of an estate or trust which is a general partner, or a trustee, officer, advisor, stockholder or beneficiary of a business trust or a statutory trust which is a general partner, or a member or manager of a limited liability company which is a general partner, or a member of a governing body of, or a fiduciary for, any person, whether domestic or foreign, which is a general partner; or

o. Such other matters as are stated in the partnership agreement or in any other agreement or in writing.

(9) To serve on the board of directors or a committee of, to consult with or advise, to be an officer, director, stockholder, partner, member, manager, trustee, agent or employee of, or to be a fiduciary or contractor for, any person in which the limited partnership has an interest or any person providing management, consulting, advisory, custody or other services or products for, to or on behalf of, or otherwise having a business or other relationship with, the limited partnership or a general partner of the limited partnership; or

(10) Any right or power granted or permitted to limited partners under this chapter and not specifically enumerated in this subsection.

(c) The enumeration in subsection (b) of this section does not mean that the possession or exercise of any other powers or having or acting in other capacities by a limited partner constitutes participation by him or her in the control of the business of the limited partnership.

(d) A limited partner does not participate in the control of the business within the meaning of subsection (a) of this section by virtue of the fact that all or any part of the name of such limited partner is included in the name of the limited partnership.

(e) This section does not create rights or powers of limited partners. Such rights and powers may be created only by a certificate of limited partnership, a partnership agreement or any other agreement or in writing, or other sections of this chapter.

(f) A limited partner does not participate in the control of the business within the meaning of subsection (a) of this section regardless of the nature, extent, scope, number or frequency of the limited partner's possessing or, regardless of whether or not the limited partner has the rights or powers, exercising or attempting to exercise 1 or more of the rights or powers or having or, regardless of whether or not the limited partner has the rights or powers, acting or attempting to act in 1 or more of the capacities which are permitted under this section.

ANNOTATIONS

Attributes of limited partner — The attributes of a limited partner are: (1) inability to control the business of the partnership, and (2) limited liability for the obligations incurred in the business of the partnership. *Harper v. Delaware Valley Broadcasters, Inc.*, 743 F. Supp. 1076 (D. Del. 1990), *aff'd* 932 F.2d 959 (3rd Cir. 1991).

Citizenship for diversity jurisdiction — The citizenship of the limited partners (as well as the citizenship of the general partners) of a limited partnership must be taken into account in determining whether there is complete diversity among the parties in a suit brought in federal court based on diversity jurisdiction. *Carden v. Arkoma Assocs.*, 494 U.S. 185, 110 S.Ct. 1015, 108 L.Ed. 2d 157 (1990).

Control by limited partner — The limited partner could be held liable for damages caused by the partnership if she "assumed control and domination" of the partnership's business. The limited partner liability initially introduced herself as the "landlord" during lease negotiations, negotiated the sublease on behalf of the partnership and acted as its attorney, alone met with the sublessee's representatives during a dispute concerning overcharges, and was the sole representative of the partnership who collected the rent and arranged for repairs on the premises. *Tapps of Nassau Supermarkets Inc. v. Linden Boulevard L.P.*, 661 N.Y.S. 2d 223 (A.D. 1st Dept. 1997) (applying Delaware law).

Execution sale — Although lacking subject matter jurisdiction, the court stated that execution sale of a limited partnership interest is probably unavailable as a remedy to satisfy the payment of spousal support arising from a foreign decree of divorce. *MacDonald v. MacDonald*, 1986 WL 5480 (Del. Ch. May 9, 1986).

Fiduciary duty of limited partner — All partners owe each other fiduciary obligations, and to the extent that a partnership agreement empowers a limited partner to take actions affecting the governance of the partnership, the limited partner may be subject to the obligations of a fiduciary, including the obligation to act in good faith as to the other partners. *KE Property Management Inc. v. 275 Madison Management Corp.*, 1993 Del. Ch. LEXIS 147 (July 21, 1993).

Fiduciary duty of limited partner — Unless expressly modified by the partnership agreement, a limited partner owes to other partners the fiduciary duties set forth in Section 1521 of the Delaware Uniform Partnership Act, specifically the duty to account to the partnership for any benefit, and to hold as trustee for it any profits derived by the limited partner without the consent of the other partners from any transaction connected with the conduct of the partnership or from any use of partnership property, *RJ Associates, Inc. v. Health Payors' Organization Limited Partnership*, 1999 Del. Ch. LEXIS 161 (July 16, 1999).

Fiduciary duty of limited partner — In the absence of a provision in the partnership agreement imposing fiduciary duties on limited partners, a limited partner who has no power to manage or control the partnership property owes no fiduciary duty to other partners in connection with making a mini-tender offer for limited partnership interests. *Bond Purchase, L.L.C. v. Patriot Tax Credit Properties, L.P.*, 1999 Del. Ch. LEXIS 159 (July 23, 1999), motion to stay denied, 1999 Del. Ch. LEXIS 170 (Aug. 16, 1999).

Joinder of limited partners — Failure to join limited partners provided no basis for dismissal of suit against general partner on partnership liability because limited partners are not liable for partnership obligations unless limited partners are general partners or participated in the control of the partnership. *Beal Bank, SSB v. Lucks*, 2001 WL 220252 (Del. Ch. 2001).

Knowledge of status — Even where a third party knew that a company had only been designated as a limited partner, the conduct of the limited partner by participating in the control of the business could result in a reasonable belief that it was a *de facto* general partner. The company was listed as a limited partner in the Certificate filed with the Secretary of State and in the partnership agreement, and the third party knew of its status. But, under Section 17-303, the limited partner's "conduct" would control whether it had acted like a *de facto* general partner, which required a factual determination. *In re Adelphia Communications Corp.*, 376 B.R. 87 (S.D.N.Y. 2007).

Limited partnership interest not an investment contract where limited partner retained material control — Where a limited partner retained substantial control over its investment through provisions in the partnership agreement, the partnership agreement was not an investment contract for federal securities laws purposes. The limitation on liability to third parties afforded by Section 17-303(b) does not equate with the limited partner's being a passive investor for purposes of federal securities laws. *Steinhardt Group, Inc. v. Citicorp*, 126 F.3d 144 (3rd Cir. 1997).

Limited partner who acts individually and not solely in capacity as agent of the general partner may be liable — A person who is both a limited partner and an officer of the general partner and who participates in the control of the limited partnership must prove that any relevant actions taken were performed solely in the capacity of an officer of the general partner. Thus, summary judgment in favor of a defendant limited partner was denied where the limited partner was a shareholder and officer of the general partner named in the certificate of limited partnership, controlled a purported substituted corporate general partner, the certificate of limited partnership was never amended to substitute the purported general partner, and the limited partner participated in negotiations without disclosing that the limited partner was acting in a representative capacity. Such facts precluded a finding that as a matter of law the limited partner did not participate in control and that the plaintiff's belief that the limited partner was acting as the partner and could appoint four of the general partner's seven directors, received 49.5 percent of distributions and benefited directly from Delaware law through the operation of the partnership's business, controlled management of the partnership through control of the general partner, caused the partnership agreement to be amended to change the agreed-upon distributions to limited partners and agreed to a Delaware choice of law provision in the partnership agreement, the limited partner had sufficient contacts to be subject to personal jurisdiction in Delaware. *RJ Associates, Inc., v. Health Payors' Organization Limited Partnership*, 1999 Del. Ch. LEXIS 161 (July 16, 1999).

Limited partners not bound by obligations of general partner — Individuals signing limited partnership agreement as limited partners did not bind themselves to the contractual obligations applicable to the general partner. *Lazard Debt Recovery GP, LLC v. Weinstock*, 2004 WL 1813286 (Del. Ch. Aug. 6, 2004).

Personal jurisdiction; out-of-state limited partner — The "usual contacts" of an out-of-state limited partner with the partnership do not establish sufficient contacts with the partnership's home state to justify personal jurisdiction over the out-of-state limited partner. Simply being a limited partner, a passive investor, does not establish sufficient contacts. Nor does sending subscription payments, or receiving distributions from, the home state of the partnership. *Marriott PLP Corporation v. Tuschman*, 904 F. Supp. 461 (D. Md. 1995), *aff'd*, 1996 U.S. App. LEXIS 24677 (4th Cir. Sept. 19, 1996).

Removal of general partner; delivery of votes of limited partners — The written vote of limited partners in favor of removing the general partner did not have to be delivered to the general partner by the voting deadline to be effective. Neither the limited partnership agreement nor the limited partnership statute required such delivery for a vote to remove the general partner to be effective. Thus, the removal of the general partner based on votes not delivered by the voting deadline was effective. *Alpine Investment Partners v. LJM2 Capital Management, L.P.*, 794 A.2d 1276 (Del. Ch. 2002).

§ 17-304. Person erroneously believing himself or herself limited partner.

(a) Except as provided in subsection (b) of this section, a person who makes a contribution to a partnership and erroneously but in good faith believes that he or she has become a limited partner in the partnership is not a general partner in the partnership and is not bound by its obligations by reason of making the contribution, receiving distributions from the partnership or exercising any rights of a limited partner, if, within a reasonable time after ascertaining the mistake:

(1) In the case of a person who wishes to be a limited partner, he or she causes an appropriate certificate to be executed and filed; or

(2) In the case of a person who wishes to withdraw from the partnership, that person takes such action as may be necessary to withdraw.

(b) A person who makes a contribution under the circumstances described in subsection (a) of this section is liable as a general partner to any third party who transacts business with the partnership prior to the occurrence of either of the events referred to in subsection (a) of this section:

(1) If such person knew or should have known either that no certificate has been filed or that the certificate inaccurately refers to the person as a general partner; and

(2) If the third party actually believed in good faith that such person was a general partner at the time of the transaction, acted in reasonable reliance on such belief and extended credit to the partnership in reasonable reliance on the credit of such person.

§ 17-305. Access to and confidentiality of information; records.

(a) Each limited partner has the right, subject to such reasonable standards (including standards governing what information and documents are to be furnished, at what time and location and at whose expense) as may be set forth in the partnership agreement or otherwise established by the general partners, to obtain from the general partners from time to time upon reasonable demand for any purpose reasonably related to the limited partner's interest as a limited partner:

(1) True and full information regarding the status of the business and financial condition of the limited partnership;

(2) Promptly after becoming available, a copy of the limited partnership's federal, state and local income tax returns for each year;

(3) A current list of the name and last known business, residence or mailing address of each partner;

(4) A copy of any written partnership agreement and certificate of limited partnership and all amendments thereto, together with executed copies of any written powers of attorney pursuant to which the partnership agreement and any certificate and all amendments thereto have been executed;

(5) True and full information regarding the amount of cash and a description and statement of the agreed value of any other property or services contributed by each partner and which each partner has agreed to contribute in the future, and the date on which each became a partner; and

(6) Other information regarding the affairs of the limited partnership as is just and reasonable.

(b) A general partner shall have the right to keep confidential from limited partners for such period of time as the general partner deems reasonable, any information which the general partner reasonably believes to be in the nature of trade secrets or other information the disclosure of which the general partner in good faith believes is not in the best interest of the limited partnership or could damage the limited partnership or its business or which the limited partnership is required by law or by agreement with a third party to keep confidential.

(c) A limited partnership may maintain its records in other than a written form if such form is capable of conversion into written form within a reasonable time.

(d) Any demand under this section shall be in writing and shall state the purpose of such demand.

(e) Any action to enforce any right arising under this section shall be brought in the Court of Chancery. If a general partner refuses to permit a limited partner to obtain from the general partner the information described in subsection (a) of this section or does not reply to the demand that has been made within 5 business days (or such shorter or longer period of time as is provided for in a partnership agreement but not longer than 30 business days) after the demand has been made, the limited partner may apply to the Court of Chancery for an order to compel such disclosure. The Court of Chancery is hereby vested with exclusive jurisdiction to determine whether or not the person seeking such information is entitled to the information sought. The Court of Chancery may summarily order the general partner to permit the limited partner to obtain the information described in subsection (a) of this section and to make copies or abstracts therefrom, or the Court of Chancery may summarily order the general partner to furnish to the limited partner the information described in subsection (a) of this section on the condition that the limited partner first pay to the limited partnership the reasonable cost of obtaining and furnishing such information and on such other conditions as the Court of Chancery deems appropriate. When a limited partner seeks to obtain the information described in subsection (a) of this section, the limited partner shall first establish (1) that the limited partner has complied with the provisions of this section respecting the form and manner of making demand for obtaining such information, and (2) that the information the limited partner seeks is reasonably related to the limited partner's interest as a limited partner. The Court of Chancery may, in its discretion, prescribe any limitations or conditions with reference to the obtaining of information, or award such other or further relief as the Court of Chancery may deem just and proper. The Court of Chancery may order books, documents and records, pertinent extracts therefrom, or duly authenticated copies thereof, to be brought within the State of Delaware and kept in the State of Delaware upon such terms and conditions as the order may prescribe.

(f) The rights of a limited partner to obtain information as provided in this section may be restricted in an original partnership agreement or in any subsequent amendment approved or adopted by all of the partners or in compliance with any applicable requirements of the partnership agreement. The provisions of this subsection shall not be construed to limit the ability to impose restrictions on the rights of a limited partner to obtain information by any other means permitted under this chapter.

ANNOTATIONS

Applicable corporate precedent — Case law under Section 220 of the Delaware general corporation law provides the most logical and meaningful source of precedent relative to Section 17-305. *Gotham Partners, L.P. v. Hallwood Realty Partners, L.P.*, 714 A.2d 96 (Del. Ch. 1998).

Books and records may include list of limited partners — The term "books and records" as used in the partnership agreement was held to include the list of partners, although the Court cautioned that its finding did not mean that the term "books and records" always includes a list of partners or other investors. *Bond Purchase, L.L.C. v. Patriot Tax Credit Properties, L.P.*, 1999 Del. Ch. LEXIS 159, at *2 (Del Ch. July 23, 1999), motion to stay denied, 1999 Del. Ch. LEXIS 170 (Aug. 16, 1999).

Books and records of subsidiary — Right to inspect books and records of a limited partnership does not ordinarily include the right to inspect books and records maintained by the partnership's subsidiary limited partnerships. *Madison Avenue Investment Partners, LLC v. America First Real Estate Investment Partners, L.P.*, 806 A.2d 165 (Del. Ch. 2002).

Conditions on use of list of partners — Where partner had contractual right to the list of partners, the Court refused to condition access to and use of list on limiting minitender offer to 3% of units, inclusion in offer of disclosure, withdrawal and proration rights, allowing partnership to mail the offer and requiring indemnification of partnership, the general partner and other investors for any harm caused by the mini-tender offer. *Bond Purchase, L.L.C. v. Patriot Tax Credit Properties, L.P.*, 1999 Del. Ch. LEXIS 159 (July 23, 1999), motion to stay denied, 1999 Del. Ch. LEXIS 170 (Aug. 16, 1999).

Contractual right to list of limited partners — Plaintiffs have a contractual right to the list of limited partners under the terms of the partnership agreement that provided for an unconditional right to the list and that did not imply an "improper purpose defense." *In re Paine Webber Limited Partnerships*, 1996 WL 535403 (Del. Ch. Sept. 17, 1996); see also, *Paine Webber Qualified Plan Property Fund Three, L.P. Litigation*, 1997 WL 89092 (Del. Ch. Feb. 24, 1997).

Expedited proceedings — The Court of Chancery routinely accelerates summary proceedings brought pursuant to Section 17-305. *Solena Inc. v. Magic Sliders Inc.*, 1999 WL 669369 (Del. Ch. Aug. 18, 1999).

General partner's good faith denial of list; burden of proof — Where general partner believed in good faith that use of list of limited partners to conduct a mini-tender offer might jeopardize limited partnership's tax status (even though it was not clear that such an adverse effect would in fact result), general partner had statutory right under Section 17-305(b) to deny access to the list in response to a request pursuant to Section 17-305(a). The general partner must prove only that a basis exists for its good faith belief, and not that actual damage would occur. *Bond Purchase, L.L.C. v. Patriot Tax Credit Properties*, L.P., 1999 Del. Ch. LEXIS 159, at *2 (July 23, 1999), motion to stay denied, 1999 Del. Ch. LEXIS 170 (Aug. 16, 1999).

Implied improper purpose defense to contract right; burden of proof — Under the "improper purpose defense," the Court may deny access to partnership records despite a contractual right to the records when (i) no contract or statutory provision expressly negates the notion that a partner must have a proper purpose for obtaining records and (ii) the partner denying access can prove that the partner seeking access does so for a purpose personal to that partner and adverse to the interests of the partnership considered jointly. The partner denying access must prove that it is more likely than not that the adverse effect would in fact occur. *Bond Purchase, L.L.C. v. Patriot Tax Credit Properties, L.P.*, 1999 Del. Ch. LEXIS 159, *2 (July 23, 1999), motion to stay denied, 1999 Del. Ch. LEXIS 170 (Aug. 16, 1999).

Injunction against access to list of limited partners — Limited partners' request after trial for injunction so that plaintiffs could not exercise their right to access list of limited partners under partnership agreement denied. *Paine Webber Limited Partnership Litigation*, 1997 WL 118401 (Del. Ch. Mar. 4, 1997).

Inspection of books and records of affiliates — Generally, a limited partner may inspect only records of the partnership itself, and not those of other entities. Bare allegation that another entity is the alter ego of the partnership is insufficient to permit inspection of books and records of the other entity. *Forsythe v. CIBC Employee Private Equity Fund (U.S.) I, L.P.*, 2005 WL 1653963 (Del. Ch. July 7, 2005).

List of BUC holders — Where all partnership investors, except the general partner and the Assignor Limited Partner, hold beneficial unit certificates ("BUCs"), a list of the names and addresses of BUC holders falls within Section 17-305(a)(6) as "other information regarding the affairs of the limited partnership as is just and reasonable." *Bond Purchase, L.L.C. v. Patriot Tax Credit Properties, L.P.*, 1999 Del. Ch. LEXIS 159, *16 (July 23, 1999), motion to stay denied, 1999 Del. Ch. LEXIS 170 (Aug. 16, 1999).

Name and address of partners; disclosure to other partners — A limited partnership was ordered to disclose to one limited partner the names and addresses of the other limited partners. After the partnership suffered large losses that wiped out investor capital, a limited partner sought the names and addresses of other limited partners to investigate its claims of mismanagement and breach of fiduciary duty by the general partner, among other things. Privacy notices sent to the limited partners by the general partner did not bar the disclosure because the partnership agreement granted limited partners the right of access to a list of the names and addresses of each partner which the general partner could not eliminate through the privacy notices or through its right to establish reasonable standards to access such information. Nor did federal privacy regulations prevent such access because they did not conflict with the Delaware limited partnership law that allowed the disclosure. *Parkcentral Global v. Brown Inv. Mgmt., L.P.*, 1 A.3d 291 (Del. 2010).

Partnership failed to prove purpose adverse to partnership as a whole — Where list of partners was sought for purpose of making a mini-tender offer, the partnership failed to prove that disclosure of the list would in fact be adverse to the partnership. The Court rejected as insufficient the partnership's claims that the mini-tender offer would (1) cause the partnership to fall outside the Internal Revenue Service's 5% safe harbor provision relating to transfers, (2) depress the marketability of partnership interests, (3) violate federal securities laws or, (4) be a breach of fiduciary duty by the tendering partner. *Bond Purchase, L.L.C. v. Patriot Tax Credit Properties, L.P.*, 1999 Del. Ch. LEXIS 159, *44-59 (July 23, 1999), motion to stay denied, 1999 Del. Ch. LEXIS 170 (Aug. 16, 1999).

Proper purpose — Desire to obtain list of limited partners to communicate minitender offer is a legally sufficient purpose. *Bond Purchase, L.L.C. v. Patriot Tax Credit Properties, L.P.*, 1999 Del. Ch. LEXIS 159, *1 (Del. Ch. July 23, 1999), motion to stay denied, 1999 Del. Ch. LEXIS 170 (Aug. 16, 1999).

Proper purpose — Valuing an investment in a limited partnership and considering whether to acquire additional units are proper purposes for inspection of books and records, and the magnitude of the limited partner's investment in the partnership is not relevant. *Madison Avenue Investment Partners, LLC v. America First Real Estate Investment Partners, L.P.*, 806 A.2d 165 (Del. Ch. 2002).

Proper purpose — In determining existence of proper purpose, court may look to decisions under Section 220 of the general corporation law, the corporate analogue to Section 17-305. *Forsythe v. CIBC Employee Private Equity Fund (U.S.) I, L.P.*, 2005 WL 1653963 (Del. Ch. July 7, 2005).

Proper purpose required — A limited partner seeking to enforce a right of inspection under § 17-305 bears the burden of proving a proper purpose in requesting access to information. *Schwartzberg v. Critef Associates Limited Partnership*, 685 A.2d 365 (Del. Ch. 1996).

Proper purpose to investigate mismanagement — Limited partner may inspect books and records to investigate possible mismanagement upon showing a credible basis to warrant a suspicion of mismanagement. *Forsythe v. CIBC Employee Private Equity Fund (U.S.) I, L.P.*, 2005 WL 1653963 (Del. Ch. July 7, 2005).

Proper purpose to investigate mismanagement — Limited partner may inspect books and records to investigate possible mismanagement. However, limited partner must prove existence of some credible evidence of possible wrongdoing sufficient to warrant continued investigation. *Holman v. Northwest Broadcasting, L.P.*, 2007 WL 1074770 (Del. Ch. Mar. 29, 2007).

Proper purpose to value interest — Valuation of a limited partner's interest in a limited partnership is a proper purpose for inspection of partnership books and records. Inspection is limited to books and records essential and sufficient to accomplish the limited partner's stated purpose. Executive compensation in the context of a privately held limited partnership is relevant to a limited partner's valuation of its interest. Limited partner was thus entitled to a schedule of compensation received by the partnership's three most highly paid officers and employees, separated into cash and non-cash consideration, as well as performance-based payments. *Holman v. Northwest Broadcasting, L.P.*, 2007 WL 1074770 (Del. Ch. Mar. 29, 2007).

Proper purpose to value units — Purpose to value interest in partnership is generally a proper purpose. Where limited partners showed that nature of investments made valuing plaintiffs' interest difficult and that partnership's overall value had declined by 75 percent, limited partners had a proper purpose to inspect books and records to assist in valuing their interests. *Forsythe v. CIBC Employee Private Equity Fund (U.S.) I, L.P.*, 2005 WL 1653963 (Del. Ch. July 7, 2005).

Purpose personal to partner — Where a list of partners was requested to permit the making of a mini-tender offer, the purpose of the request was personal to the requesting partner. *Bond Purchase, L.L.C. v. Patriot Tax Credit Properties, L.P.*, 1999 Del. Ch. LEXIS 159, *44, 45 (July 23, 1999), motion to stay denied, 1999 Del. Ch. LEXIS 170 (Aug. 16, 1999).

Right of access to books and records — The corporate general partner of a limited partnership and its president breached their fiduciary duties to the limited partners by failing to provide access to the limited partners to inspect the books and records of the partnership. *Curley v. Brignoli Curley and Roberts Assocs.*, 746 F. Supp. 1208 (S.D.N.Y. 1989) *aff'd*, 915 F.2d 81 (2d Cir. 1990), *cert. denied*, 499 U.S. 955 (1991) (applying Delaware law).

Right to list of limited partners under statute or agreement — Limited partners did not have a statutory right to obtain a list of all limited partners because the request was to assist a third party (their affiliate) to decide whether to launch a tender offer for interests in the partnership. *In re Paine Webber Qualified Plan Property Fund Three, L.P. Litigation*, 698 A.2d 389 (Del. Ch. 1997).

Scope of inspection — Some limited partners who filed an action against other limited partners and the general partner claiming partnership property was sold for an inadequate price had a right to inspect records of "transactions" consummated by the partnership, but no right to a full discovery of matters that did not involve partnership "transactions." The partnership agreements conferred a right of inspection consistent with that under Delaware's Revised Uniform Limited Partnership Act, 17-305. *Trump v. Cheng*, 63 A.D.3d 623, 882 N.Y.S. 2d 87 (N.Y. App. Div. 1st Dept. 2009).

Scope of inspection — Fact that limited partner had valued its investment based on publicly available information did not preclude inspection of non-public information in order to perform a more accurate valuation. *Madison Avenue Investment Partners, LLC v. America First Real Estate Investment Partners, L.P.*, 806 A.2d 165 (Del. Ch. 2002).

Scope of proceeding — Denying a motion to amend a complaint brought under Section 17-305 to add claims of breach of contract and breach of fiduciary duty unrelated to the Section 17-305 issues, the Court held that as a general rule the Court will not entertain outside claims or collateral issues but will hear only those matters that pertain to the limited partner's demand to inspect the books. *Gotham Partners, L.P. v. Hallwood Realty Partners, L.P.*, 714 A.2d 96 (Del. Ch. 1998).

Standing — A plaintiff was held to have been admitted as a limited partner, and thus entitled to demand to inspect the list of limited partners, because the NASD forms used by the partnership for registering transfers of interests constituted a request for admission as a substitute limited partner, the general partner was found to have delegated to the partnership's transfer agent the general partner's authority to consent not only to assignments but to admission of a transferee as a substituted limited partner and the transfer agent had confirmed to the plaintiff its status as a limited partner. *In re American Tax Credit Limited Partnerships*, 714 A.2d 87 (Del. Ch. 1997), *aff'd*, 707 A.2d 765 (Del. 1998).

Standing — Where transfer documents made no distinction between an assignee and a substituted unit holder, and partnership agreement clearly distinguished between assignees and substituted unit holders and delineated requirements and procedures for obtaining limited partner status, the partnership agreement rather than the transfer documents control the status of the transferee as an assignee or limited partner. *Monterey Investments, Inc. v. Healthcare Properties, L.P.*, 1997 Del. Ch. LEXIS 98 (June 20, 1997).

Statutory right to list of limited partners — Plaintiffs did not have a statutory right to the list of limited partners because they did not establish a proper statutory purpose where a yet-to-be-created investment fund would conduct any tender offer and plaintiffs were to participate in any such tender offer only on a de minimis basis. *In re Paine Webber Limited Partnerships*, 1996 WL 535403 (Del. Ch. Sept. 17, 1996); *see also, Paine Webber Qualified Plan Property Fund Three, L.P. Litigation*, 698 A.2d 389 (Del. Ch. 1997).

What constitutes books and records — Where agreement provided that books and records "shall include" certain enumerated items, but did not otherwise clearly restrict access to information, the agreement did not limit "books and records" to those items specifically enumerated, and thus did not curtail a limited partner's right to access to other documents. *Madison Avenue Investment Partners, LLC v. America First Real Estate Investment Partners, L.P.*, 806 A.2d 165 (Del. Ch. 2002).

§ 17-306. Remedies for breach of partnership agreement by limited partner.

A partnership agreement may provide that (1) a limited partner who fails to perform in accordance with, or to comply with the terms and conditions of, the partnership agreement shall be subject to specified penalties or specified consequences, and (2) at the time or upon the happening of events specified in the partnership agreement, a limited partner shall be subject to specified penalties or specified consequences. Such specified penalties or specified consequences may include and take the form of any penalty or consequence set forth in § 17-502(c) of this chapter.

Subchapter IV
GENERAL PARTNERS

§ 17-401. Admission of general partners.

(a) A person may be admitted to a limited partnership as a general partner of the limited partnership and may receive a partnership interest in the limited partnership without making a contribution or being obligated to make a contribution to the limited partnership. Unless otherwise provided in a partnership agreement, a person may be admitted to a limited partnership as a general partner of the limited partnership without acquiring a partnership interest in the limited partnership. Unless otherwise provided in a partnership agreement, a person may be admitted as the sole general partner of a limited partnership without making a contribution or being obligated to make a contribution to the limited partnership or without acquiring a partnership interest in the limited partnership. Nothing contained in this subsection shall affect the first sentence of § 17-403(b) of this title.

(b) After the filing of a limited partnership's initial certificate of limited partnership, unless otherwise provided in the partnership agreement, additional general partners may be admitted only with the written consent of each partner.

(c) Unless otherwise provided in a partnership agreement or another agreement, a general partner shall have no preemptive right to subscribe to any additional issue of partnership interests or another interest in a limited partnership.

§ 17-402. Events of withdrawal.

(a) A person ceases to be a general partner of a limited partnership upon the happening of any of the following events:

(1) The general partner withdraws from the limited partnership as provided in § 17-602 of this title;

(2) The general partner ceases to be a general partner of the limited partnership as provided in § 17-702 of this title;

(3) The general partner is removed as a general partner in accordance with the partnership agreement;

(4) Unless otherwise provided in the partnership agreement, or with the written consent of all partners, the general partner:

　　a. Makes an assignment for the benefit of creditors;

　　b. Files a voluntary petition in bankruptcy;

　　c. Is adjudged a bankrupt or insolvent, or has entered against him or her an order for relief in any bankruptcy or insolvency proceeding;

　　d. Files a petition or answer seeking for himself or herself any reorganization, arrangement, composition, readjustment, liquidation, dissolution or similar relief under any statute, law or regulation;

　　e. Files an answer or other pleading admitting or failing to contest the material allegations of a petition filed against him or her in any proceeding of this nature; or

　　f. Seeks, consents to or acquiesces in the appointment of a trustee, receiver or liquidator of the general partner or of all or any substantial part of his properties;

(5) Unless otherwise provided in the partnership agreement, or with the written consent of all partners, 120 days after the commencement of any proceeding against the general partner seeking reorganization, arrangement, composition, readjustment, liquidation, dissolution or similar relief under any statute, law or regulation, the proceeding has not been dismissed, or if within 90 days after the appointment without the general partner's consent or acquiescence of a trustee, receiver or liquidator of the general partner or of all or any substantial part of his or her properties, the appointment is not vacated or stayed, or within 90 days after the expiration of any such stay, the appointment is not vacated;

(6) In the case of a general partner who is a natural person:

　　a. The general partner's death; or

　　b. The entry by a court of competent jurisdiction adjudicating the general partner's incompetent to manage his or her person or property;

(7) In the case of a general partner who is acting as a general partner by virtue of being a trustee of a trust, the termination of the trust (but not merely the substitution of a new trustee);

(8) In the case of a general partner that is a separate partnership, the dissolution and commencement of winding up of the separate partnership;

(9) In the case of a general partner that is a corporation, the filing of a certificate of dissolution, or its equivalent, for the corporation or the revocation of its charter and the expiration of 90 days after the date of

notice to the corporation of revocation without a reinstatement of its charter;

(10) Unless otherwise provided in the partnership agreement, or with the written consent of all partners, in the case of a general partner that is an estate, the distribution by the fiduciary of the estate's entire interest in the limited partnership;

(11) In the case of a general partner that is a limited liability company, the dissolution and commencement of winding up of the limited liability company; or

(12) In the case of a general partner who is not an individual, partnership, limited liability company, corporation, trust or estate, the termination of the general partner.

(b) A general partner who suffers an event that with the passage of the specified period becomes an event of withdrawal under subsection (a)(4) or (5) of this section shall notify each other general partner, or in the event that there is no other general partner, each limited partner, of the occurrence of the event within 30 days after the date of occurrence of the event of withdrawal.

ANNOTATIONS

Delivery of votes of limited partners — The written vote of limited partners in favor of removing the general partner did not have to be delivered to the general partner by the voting deadline to be effective. Neither the limited partnership agreement nor the limited partnership statute required such delivery for a vote to remove the general partner to be effective. Thus, the removal of the general partner based on votes not delivered by the voting deadline was effective. *Alpine Investment Partners v. LJM2 Capital Management, L. P.*, 794 A.2d 1276 (Del. Ch. 2002).

Good faith and reasonable determination to remove general partner — Limited partners' determination that general partner's performance was unsatisfactory and that, therefore, it should be removed because (1) the partnership made no cash distributions, (2) the partnership continued to incur excessive overhead expenses; (3) the partnership never concluded any significant number of transactions; and (4) the limited partners had lost confidence and trust in the chairman of the corporate general partner was made reasonably and in good faith; thus, the removal of the general partners was proper. *Wilmington Leasing, Inc. v. Parrish Leasing Company, L.P.*, 1996 WL 752364 (Del. Ch. Dec. 23, 1996).

Power to remove general partner — Limited partners' contractual power to remove general partner under partnership agreement is not absolute, but is subject to the implied condition that the removal determination be reasonable and made in good faith; such a determination is factual. *Wilmington Leasing, Inc. v. Parrish Leasing Company, L.P.*, 1996 WL 560190 (Del. Ch. Sept. 25, 1996).

Removal and appointment of receiver — Where a court concludes that the general partner of a limited partnership could not continue in that capacity because of gross misconduct and arbitrary management, it could grant the limited partners the more limited relief of removal of the general partner and appointment of a receiver until such time as a successor general partner could be named rather than resort to the more drastic remedy of dissolving the partnership. *Curley v. Brignoli Curley and Roberts Assoc.*, 746 F. Supp. 1208 (S.D.N.Y. 1989), *aff'd*, 915 F.2d. 81 (2d Cir. 1990), *cert. denied*, 499 U.S. 955 (1991) (applying Delaware law).

Removal by arbitrator and reduction of interest — The replacement of the general partner with an independent property manager, and reduction of his partnership interest to reflect the change in management duties, were not only within the scope of the authority of the arbitrator assigned to hear the dispute, but, given the "extreme animosity" between the limited and general partners, was the only practical way the partnership could continue. *Malekzadeh v. Wyschock*, 611 A.2d 18 (Del. Ch. 1992).

Removal of general partner — A court may remove the general partner of a limited partnership for breach of fiduciary duties and self-dealing because the partnership depends on the good faith and fair dealing of the general partner. *Curley v. Brignoli Curley and Roberts Assoc.*, 746 F. Supp. 1208 (S.D.N.Y. 1989), *aff'd*, 915 F.2d. 81 (2d Cir. 1990), *cert. denied*, 499 U.S. 955 (1991) (applying Delaware law).

Removal of general partner — A limited partnership's management company's use of transaction fees to pay salaries and bonuses contrary to the terms of an approved service agreement constitutes a breach of the limited partnership agreement. Even though the general partner delegated administrative management authority to the management company, it breached the limited partnership agreement by permitting the management company to use the transaction fees for purposes other than the service agreement allowed and, thus, the general partner's conduct formed an appropriate basis for the limited partners' removal of the general partner. *Davenport Group MG, L.P. v. Strategic Investment Partners, Inc.*, 685 A.2d 715 (Del. Ch. 1996).

Removal of general partner — Where partnership agreement does not provide for removal of the general partner, Delaware law does not provide for the removal of a general partner by limited partners without a court order. *Greenwich Global, LLC v. Clairvoyant Capital, LLC*, 2002 WL 31168715 (Conn. Super. Ct. Aug. 22, 2002).

Removal of general partner for cause — Where a general partner loaned to an affiliate $1.3 million in violation of a provision in the partnership agreement expressly prohibiting loans to the general partner or its affiliates without the prior consent of the limited partners, and the general partner concealed the loan from limited partners, the general partner's action was a material breach of its fiduciary duty and thus lawful ground to remove the general partner under a provision in the partnership agreement authorizing removal by limited partners for material breach of fiduciary duty. *Knetzger v. Centre City Corp.*, 1999 Del. Ch. LEXIS 145 (June 30, 1999).

Unanimous removal of general partner — The general partner who was removed by unanimous written consent of the limited partners could not convert his capital contribution into a limited partnership interest. The limited partnership agreement permitted a general partner who left voluntarily, for example through retirement, to convert his capital contribution into a limited partnership interest. But, a general partner who was ousted involuntarily did not have this privilege. *Hillman v. Hillman*, 903 A.2d 798 (Del. Ch. 2006).

§ 17-403. General powers and liabilities.

(a) Except as provided in this chapter or in the partnership agreement, a general partner of a limited partnership has the rights and powers and is subject to the restrictions of a partner in a partnership that is governed by the Delaware Uniform Partnership Law (6 Del. C. § 1501, *et seq.*).

(b) Except as provided in this chapter, a general partner of a limited partnership has the liabilities of a partner in a partnership that is governed by the Delaware Uniform Partnership Law (6 Del. C. § 1501, *et seq.*) to persons other than the partnership and the other partners. Except as provided in this chapter or in the partnership agreement, a general partner of a limited partnership has the liabilities of a partner in a partnership that is governed by the Delaware Uniform Partnership Law (6 Del. C. § 1501, *et seq.*) to the partnership and to the other partners.

(c) Unless otherwise provided in the partnership agreement, a general partner of a limited partnership has the power and authority to delegate to 1 or more other persons the general partner's rights and powers to manage and control the business and affairs of the limited partnership, including to delegate to agents, officers and employees of the general partner or the limited partnership, and to delegate by a management agreement or another agreement with, or otherwise to, other persons. Unless otherwise provided in the partnership agreement, such delegation by a general partner of a limited partnership shall not cause the general partner to cease to be a general partner of the limited partnership or cause the person to whom any such rights and powers have been delegated to be a general partner of the limited partnership.

(d) A judgment creditor of a general partner of a limited partnership may not levy execution against the assets of the general partner to satisfy a judgment based on a claim against the limited partnership unless:

(1) A judgment based on the same claim has been obtained against the limited partnership and a writ of execution on the judgment has been returned unsatisfied in whole or in part;

(2) The limited partnership is a debtor in bankruptcy;

(3) The general partner has agreed that the creditor need not exhaust the assets of the limited partnership;

(4) A court grants permission to the judgment creditor to levy execution against the assets of the general partner based on a finding that the assets of the limited partnership that are subject to execution are clearly insufficient to satisfy the judgment, that exhaustion of the assets of the limited partnership is excessively burdensome, or that the grant of permission is an appropriate exercise of the court's equitable powers; or

(5) Liability is imposed on the general partner by law or contract independent of the existence of the limited partnership.

ANNOTATIONS

Agreement requirements vs. fiduciary duty — Where a limited partnership agreement unambiguously provided that the general partner had sole discretion to propose a merger and the unitholders had the power to veto the transaction, common law fiduciary duties did not apply in deciding a limited partner's claim that the merger was unfair. The scheme for mergers was unambiguously set forth in the partnership agreement; therefore, there was no requirement that it be "fair and reasonable." *Sonet v. Timber Co., L.P.*, 722 A.2d 319 (Del. Ch. 1998).

Aiding and abetting breach of contractually created fiduciary duty — A claim for aiding and abetting a breach of fiduciary duty may be predicated on a fiduciary duty created by contract. Because the existence of a fiduciary relationship does not depend on the origin of the fiduciary relationship, the origin of the relationship is immaterial to a claim for aiding and abetting a breach of fiduciary duty. Moreover, because Section 17-1101(d) permits partners to define their fiduciary duties in the partnership agreement, it would be inconsistent with Section 17-1101(d) to preclude claims for aiding and abetting breaches of fiduciary duties for which the partners contracted. *Fitzgerald v. Cantor*, 1999 Del. Ch. LEXIS 52 (Mar. 25, 1999).

Attorney-client communications — Privileged communications between general partners and counsel to the limited partnership are entitled to qualified protection. Requiring limited partner plaintiffs to show good cause in order to discover such communications protects the purposes of the attorney-client privilege while allowing for disclosure of privileged communications where necessary to ensure that fiduciaries such as general partners act in the best interests of their beneficiaries. *In re ML-Lee Acquisition Fund II, L.P. and ML-Lee Acquisition Fund (Retirement Accounts) II, L.P. Securities Litigation*, 848 F. Supp. 527 (D. Del. 1994).

Attorney-client privilege — A limited partner's access to privileged information given to the board of directors of a corporate general partner is comparable to the contingent right of a stockholder in a derivative suit to demand privileged documents from the corporation's board of directors. Thus, for a limited partner to obtain access to privileged documents provided to the general partner, the burden is on the limited partner to show good cause, the elements of which are: the assertion of a colorable claim, the necessity of the information sought and its unavailability elsewhere, a specific as opposed to a broad request fishing for information and that requested documents do not disclose litigation strategies or theories protected by the work product doctrine. *Gotham Partners, L.P. v. Hallwood Realty Partners, L.P.*, 1999 Del. Ch. LEXIS 66 (Mar. 31, 1999).

Attorney-client privilege — In limited partner's direct and derivative action against the general partner, mutuality of interest lapses at least by the time the general partner and the limited partner can reasonably anticipate litigation over an identified dispute. At that point, the interests of the parties are sufficient adverse that the general partner may communicate with the partnership's counsel without fear that the fiduciary duty exception to the attorney-client privilege may be invoked. *Metropolitan Bank & Trust Co. v. Dovenmuehle Mortgage, Inc.*, 2001 WL 1671445 (Del. Ch. Dec. 20, 2001).

Attorney-client relation — Although mere status as a general partner does not automatically entitle a general partner access to all advice rendered by counsel to the partnership, where a managing general partner had a reasonable expectation that counsel to the partnership was representing the general partner's interests, the general partner was entitled to obtain discovery from counsel for the partnership with respect to partnership transactions prior to the time that the general partner's position as managing general partner came into dispute and the general partner could no longer have reasonably expected that the partnership's counsel was representing the general partner's interests. *Fitzgerald v. Cantor*, 1998 Del. Ch. LEXIS 198 (Oct. 28, 1998).

Authority to engage in projects similar to partnership business — A general partner could engage in projects in other states similar to the partnership project where authorized by the limited partnership agreement. The agreement authorized the general partner to engage in ventures similar to the partnership business anywhere without offering the opportunity either to the partnership or other partners. *Whalen v. Connelly*, 545 N.W. 2d 284 (Iowa 1996).

Bad faith — General partner acted in bad faith when it knowingly deprived limited partners of partnership interests for less than its fair market value without a preexisting contractual right to do so while simultaneously securing favorable treatment for its own interests and those of others. *Gelfman v. Weeden Investors, L.P.*, 2004 WL 1587571 (Del. Ch. July 12, 2004).

Bad faith "excusal" of limited partner from investments — A complaint by a limited partner alleging that the general partner acted in bad faith in "excusing" the limited partner from participating in various investment opportunities of the limited partnership in retaliation for the limited partner's filing of an earlier suit against the general partner should not have been dismissed on the pleadings. Giving the limited partner the benefit of every inference, its allegation that the "excusals" took place after its initial lawsuit was adequate to raise a question of fact (or a mixed question of law and fact) as to whether the general partner's actions were reasonable or retaliatory. Furthermore, the plaintiff did not have to plead bad faith on the part of the general partner with particularity. *Desert Equities v. Morgan Stanley Leveraged*, 624 A.2d 1199 (Del. 1993).

Books and records — A general partner may be justified in denying another general partner access to partnership books and records where the general partner can show that the requested access is for an improper purpose (a purpose personal to the requesting party) and that would be detrimental to the economic interests of the partnership or all partners considered as a whole, notwithstanding that the partnership agreement itself conferred a contractual right to access to books and records without a showing of a proper purpose. *Schwartzberg v. CRITEF Associates Limited Partnership*, 685 A.2d 365 (Del. Ch. 1996).

Breach of contract and fiduciary duty; issuing new units; unequal pricing of units — The corporate general partner breached its fiduciary duty to certain limited partners and breached the partnership agreement by permitting some directors on its board to purchase partnership units at a price more favorable than the price to certain limited partners. This decision was not made in good faith but to obtain approval from the directors of the general partner to the issuance of a large number of new partnership units to management and employees of the partnership. These directors were enriched at the expense of the limited partners. *Gelfman v. Weeden Investors. L.P.*, 859 A.2d 89 (Del. Chan. 2004).

Breach of duty; future damages — Limited partners are entitled to offer proof of future damages arising from an alleged failure or refusal by the general partner to exploit partnership assets. *Red Sail Easter Limited Partners, L.P. v. Radio City Music Hall Prod., Inc.* 1992 Del. Ch. LEXIS 224 (Oct. 6, 1992).

Breach of duty in conversion to corporate form — Complaint by limited partner stated claim for breach of fiduciary duties of loyalty and fair dealing in connection with the conversion of a limited partnership to a corporation when the limited partner alleged (1) the individual general partner increased his holdings in the enterprise from 25 percent to 61 percent at the expense of other unitholders, (2) an independent committee of the board of the corporate general partner was selected by the individual general partner, who was the controlling stockholder of the corporate general partner, and members of the committee had a personal interest in the transaction, and (3) the financial and legal advisors to the board committee had long-standing relations with the individual general partner. *Trustees of General Elec. Pension Trust v. Levinson*, 1992 Del. Ch. LEXIS 43 (Mar. 3, 1992).

Breach of duty in conversion to corporate form; remedy — Where a general partner breached its duties of due care and fair dealing in converting a limited partnership to a corporation, limited partners were entitled to the fair value of their units. *MacLane Gas Co., L.P. v. Enserch Corp.*, 1992 Del. Ch. LEXIS 255 (Dec. 9, 1992), *aff'd*, 633 A.2d 369 (Del. 1993).

Breach of duty of care requires gross negligence — A claim for breach of duty of care requires allegations of conduct amounting to gross negligence. Allegation that committee of board of corporate general partner breached duty of care by relying on advice of investment bankers who had relied on financial information furnished to them without independent review or evaluation failed to state a claim for gross negligence on the part of the committee. *Trustees of General Elec. Pension Trust v. Levinson*, 1992 Del. Ch. LEXIS 43 (Mar. 3, 1992).

Breach of duty of loyalty — General partner breached its duty of loyalty by unilaterally imposing profit sharing terms favorable to itself at the expense of the limited partner. *Active Asset Recovery, Inc. v. Real Estate Asset Recovery Services, Inc.*, 1999 WL 743479 (Del. Ch. Sept. 10, 1999).

Breach of fiduciary duty; agreement not to arbitrate — An agreement not to arbitrate future disputes, reached in an arbitration of a dispute between a limited and two general partners of a Delaware limited partnership, did not violate Connecticut public policy. The limited partner claimed (unsuccessfully) that the general partners breached their fiduciary duty by usurping a business opportunity, that public policy favored the enforcement of a fiduciary duty, and that this public policy prohibited a person from agreeing to waive future claims stemming from another person's breach of fiduciary duty. *Merrick v. Cummin*, 100 Conn. App. 664, 919 A.2d 495 (2007) (applying Delaware law).

Breach of fiduciary duty; agreement prevails over statute — A limited partner who claimed to have been the general partner may have breached its fiduciary duty to the partnership by allegedly refusing to participate in discussions relating to the funding of the partnership project. Absent a contrary provision in the limited partnership agreement, the general partner owed the traditional duties of loyalty and care to the partnership and its partners. The claim for breach of fiduciary duty had to first be analyzed under the terms of the partnership agreement; only when the agreement was silent or ambiguous, could a court look for guidance from the statutory default rules, traditional notions of fiduciary duties or other extrinsic evidence. *SJ Properties Suites v. STJ, P.C.*, 2010 WL 5300541 (E.D. Wis. Dec. 17, 2010).

Breach of fiduciary duty; allegations of bad faith — In a suit by a limited partner against a general partner for breach of fiduciary duty, it was essential to allege that the general partner acted in bad faith. A general partner acting in good faith reliance on the partnership agreement (which appeared to allow the general partner to compete with the partnership for business) was shielded from liability for breach of fiduciary duty. Allegations that the general partner "willfully failed to share the right to provide cellular services [to the partnership]" did not meet the requirement of alleging "bad faith." *United States Cellular Investment Company of Allentown v. Bell Atlantic Mobile Systems, Inc.*, 677 A.2d 497 (Del. 1996).

Breach of fiduciary duty; change in circumstances — Although the terms of a partnership agreement did not preclude a general partner from taking certain action, the contours of the general partner's fiduciary duties at the time it seeks to exercise its rights may be affected by changed and unforeseen circumstances. *U.S. West, Inc. v. Time Warner Inc.*, 1996 WL 307445 (Del. Ch. June 6, 1996).

Breach of fiduciary duty; competition — As a matter of statutory law, traditional fiduciary duties among and between partners are default rules that may be modified by the partnership agreement. Where the partnership agreement expressly provided that any partner could compete directly or indirectly with the business of the partnership, the partnership could have no legitimate expectancy to be informed of or to participate in investments made by the general partner or its affiliates. In the absence of a showing that the investment opportunity came to the general partner in its capacity as such and was diverted to the general partner or its affiliates, there was no usurpation of partnership opportunity. *Kahn v. Icahn*, 1998 WL 832629 (Del. Ch. Nov. 12, 1998).

Breach of fiduciary duty; denying access to books and records — The corporate general partner of a limited partnership and its president breached their fiduciary duties to the limited partners by failing to permit the limited partners to inspect the books and records of the partnership. *Curley v. Brignoli Curley and Roberts Assocs.*, 746 F. Supp. 1208 (S.D.N.Y. 1989), *aff'd*, 915 F.2d 81 (2d Cir. 1990), *cert. denied*, 499 U.S. 955 (1991) (applying Delaware law).

Breach of fiduciary duty; failure to market assets — Where the partnership agreement expressly provided that the general partner could sell assets to affiliates at an appraised value, the general partner had no fiduciary duty to "test the market" by marketing the assets to third parties before the sale to an affiliate. *In re Cencom Cable Income Partners, L.P. Litigation*, 1997 WL 666970 (Del. Ch. Oct. 15, 1997), *reargument denied*, 1997 WL 770158 (Del. Ch. Dec. 3, 1997).

Breach of fiduciary duty; fraud — While alleged conduct of general partners in failing to disclose and subsequently concealing the structure of the limited partnership may give rise to a common law claim of fraud, such conduct does not amount to breach of a fiduciary duty to the limited partnership where a limited partner's expected contribution is clearly set forth and adhered to by the general partners. *Murphy v. Bay Shores Six, Ltd. Partnership*, 1987 WL 5776 (Del. Ch. Jan. 26, 1987).

Breach of fiduciary duty; improper borrowing — A general partner may breach its duty of loyalty by borrowing solely to enhance management fees at the expense of limited partners. *In re Cencom Cable Income Partners, L.P. Litigation*, 1997 WL 666970 (Del. Ch. Oct. 15, 1997), *reargument denied*, 1997 WL 770158 (Del. Ch. Dec. 3, 1997).

Breach of fiduciary duty; information furnished appraisers — General partner had no duty to cooperate with any appraiser other than those appraisers appointed pursuant to the appraisal process contemplated by the partnership agreement. However, where general partner nonetheless undertook to provide information to an additional appraiser, failure to provide equal information to each of the appraisers in order to minimize the valuation would be a breach of the general partner's fiduciary duty of loyalty. *In re Cencom Cable Income Partners, L.P. Litigation*, 1997 WL 666970 (Del. Ch. Oct. 15, 1997), *reargument denied*, 1997 WL 770158 (Del. Ch. Dec. 3, 1997).

Breach of fiduciary duty; lack of arms-length negotiations — Where partnership agreement contained express provisions for the sale of partnership assets to affiliates of the general partner, the written terms of the sale process are not subject to an "entire fairness" standard, and general partner had no obligation to include in the sale agreement terms that might have been included in an agreement negotiated at arms-length. *In re Cencom Cable Income Partners, L.P. Litigation*, 1997 WL 666970 (Del. Ch. Oct. 15, 1997), *reargument denied*, 1997 WL 770158 (Del. Ch. Dec. 3, 1997).

Breach of fiduciary duty; misappropriating assets — The president of the corporate general partner of a limited partnership misappropriated partnership assets, and thereby breached his fiduciary duty to the partnership, by using a CD owned by the partnership to secure a bank loan for another entity in which he was interested, for his and its benefit but to the detriment of the limited partnership. *Curley v. Brignoli Curley* *and Roberts Assocs.*, 746 F. Supp. 1208 (S.D.N.Y. 1989), *aff'd*, 915 F.2d 81 (2d. Cir. 1990) *cert. denied*, 499 U.S. 955 (1991) (applying Delaware law).

Breach of fiduciary duty; partnership opportunity — The principals of fiduciary duty upon which the "corporate opportunity" doctrine is based apply analogously to partnership fiduciaries. *U.S. West, Inc. v. Time Warner Inc.*, 1996 WL 307445 (Del. Ch. June 6, 1996).

Breach of fiduciary duty; standard set by agreement — A limited partnership agreement may provide for contractually created fiduciary duties substantially mirroring traditional fiduciary duties that apply in corporation law. A limited partnership agreement provided for such fiduciary duties by requiring the general partner and its controlling entity to treat the limited partners in accordance with the "entire fairness" standard. The general partner and its corporate parent breached this fiduciary duty owed to a limited partner. An audit committee never reviewed certain transactions between the general partner and the partnership as required by the partnership agreement. *Gotham Partners, L.P. v. Hallwood Realty Partners, L.P.*, 817 A.2d 160 (Del. 2002).

Breach of general partner's fiduciary duties — Refusal of general partner (and majority owner) to sell the limited partnership's business did not breach its fiduciary duties of care and loyalty just because such a sale would profit one limited partner that was a minority investor. *Cincinnati Bell Cellular Systems Co. v. Ameritech Mobile Phone Service of Cincinnati, Inc.*, 1996 Del. Ch. LEXIS 116 (Sept. 3, 1996), *aff'd.* 1997 Del. LEXIS 58 (Feb. 11, 1997).

Breach of partnership agreement — laches — Limited partner's breach of contract claim was barred by laches because limited partner's delay was unreasonable and general partner was materially prejudiced as a result of delay in filing suit. *U.S. Cellular Inv. Co. of Allentown v. Bell Atlantic Mobile Systems, Inc.*, 677 A.2d 497 (Del. 1996).

Breach of voluntarily assumed duty — Where general partner represented that independent counsel would oversee compliance by the partnership and the general partner with the terms of the partnership agreement in connection with a sale of assets to an affiliate of the general partner, the general partner voluntarily assumed a duty to ensure that independent counsel would fulfill such obligations and limited partners were entitled to rely on the general partner's representations that independent counsel would do so. *In re Cencom Cable Income Partners, L.P. Litigation*, 1997 WL 666970 (Del. Ch. Oct. 15, 1997), *reargument denied*, 1997 WL 770158 (Del. Ch. Dec. 3, 1997).

Business judgment — The actions of a general partner are protected by the business judgment rule, which affords the general partner a presumption that it acted on an informed basis and in the honest belief that it acted in the best interest of the partnership and the limited partners. A plaintiff bears the burden of rebutting the presumption by sufficiently pleading that the general partner stood on both sides of the transaction or derived a personal benefit in the sense of self-dealing. *In re Boston Celtics Limited Partnership Shareholders Litigation*, 1999 Del. Ch. LEXIS 166 (Aug. 6, 1999).

Business judgment rule — A corporate general partner and the directors of the general partner own a fiduciary duty of loyalty to the limited partnership and its partners. However, the corporate general partner and its directors are entitled to the protections of the business judgment rule, including the presumption that the general partner acted on an informed basis and in the honest belief that it was acting in the best interests of the partnership and its limited partners. A complaint that fails to allege sufficient facts showing that the corporate general partner or its directors stood on both sides of a transaction or engaged in self-dealing fails to state a claim. *Zoren v. Genesis Energy, L.P.*, 836 A.2d 521 (Del. Ch. 2003).

"Change in control" of limited partnership — When the limited partnership agreement recognizes a right in the general partner to veto any transfer of limited partnership interests "in its absolute discretion," the general partner does not have a fiduciary obligation to the limited partners to solicit possible alternatives prior to commencing its own tender offer for at least 50.1% of the limited partnership units. *In re Marriott Hotel Properties II Limited Partnership Unitholders Litigation*, 1996 WL 342040 (Del. Ch. June 12, 1996).

Coercive nature of offer for limited partnership units — For purposes of a preliminary injunction, the general partner's tender offer for at least 50.1% of limited partnership units is not coercive because the limited partners have a choice whether or not to tender their units and there appears to be no consequence that compels limited partners to tender. *In re Marriott Hotel Properties II Limited Partnership Unitholders Litigation*, 1996 WL 342040 (Del. Ch. June 12, 1996).

Co-investments not breach of duty of loyalty — A general partner that used partnership funds to co-invest in projects with either the general partner or affiliates of the general partner did not give rise to a breach of duty of loyalty absent any showing that the investments were not potentially advantageous to the partnership and the general partner or its affiliates alike. *Miller v. American Real Estate Partners, L.P.*, 2001 WL 1045643 (Del. Ch. Sept. 6, 2001).

Conduct inconsistent with partnership purposes — A conscious decision by a corporate general partner to enrich its outside directors in order to obtain their support for issuances of large numbers of new partnership interests to employees, and thereby avoid dilution of interests of the outside directors, was conduct inconsistent with the purposes of the partnership. Consequently, general partner did not satisfy contractual standards of conduct, and default fiduciary duties would apply. *Gelfman v. Weeden Investors, L.P.*, 2004 WL 1587571 (Del. Ch. July 12, 2004)

Conduct may be both breach of contract and of fiduciary duty — Conduct by a general partner may be the basis of both a contract and a breach of fiduciary duty claim. *RJ Associates, Inc. v. Health Payors' Organization Limited Partnership*, 1999 Del. Ch. LEXIS 161 (July 16, 1999).

Conflict of interests — Contract provisions preempt fiduciary principles. Thus, where in accordance with the provisions of the partnership agreement, the general partner submitted transaction in which the general partner had a conflict of interest to the limited partnership's Conflicts and Audit Committee for approval, and the committee gave its approval, compliance with the partnership agreement barred any challenge based on default principals of law or equity. *Brickell Partners v. Wise*, 794 A.2d 1 (Del. Ch. 2001).

Consent to transfer; duty of good faith and fair dealing — A general partner with sole and absolute discretion under the partnership agreement to withhold consent to a transfer of shares of a corporate limited partner cannot withhold consent out of self-interest, or to advance the interests of other partners that are unrelated to the partnership. Such conduct implicates the covenant of good faith and fair dealing implied in every limited partnership agreement and the general partner's duty of loyalty. *Fitzgerald v. Cantor*, 1999 Del. Ch. LEXIS 55 (Mar. 23, 1999).

Contract may modify fiduciary duties — Under Delaware law, in the limited partnership context the tension between contract principles and fiduciary duties is resolved in favor of contract law, rendering fiduciary duties default rules. Thus, parties to a limited partnership agreement can enter into a contract that diminishes the general partner's fiduciary duties. Where the contract amends the fiduciary duties a general partner owes to limited partners, the court will give full force to the terms of the contract. *The Continental Insurance Company v. Rutledge & Company, Inc.*, 2000 WL 62951 (Del. Ch. Jan. 10, 2000).

Contract provisions control rights and duties — Limited partnership agreement is the operative document governing the rights and responsibilities of the partners, and the statute provides "fall-back" or default provisions where the agreement is silent. Where the provisions defining the rights and responsibilities of the parties are spelled out with particularity, those provisions are accorded significant deference by the court, and the contract provisions, not default fiduciary rules, control whether conduct constitutes a breach of duty. *Cantor Fitzgerald, L.P. v. Cantor*, 2001 WL 1456494 (Del. Ch. Nov. 5, 2001).

Delay in disclosing "bail out" from partnership; direct claim — The general partner's delay in disclosing to the limited partners that the general partner had "bailed out" of the partnership deprived the limited partners of the opportunity to "cut their losses" promptly. The limited partners' allegation that a statement which the general partner was required to prepare for the limited partners was misleading of materially false stated a direct, as opposed to a derivative, claim. (The claimants had withdrawn from the partnership and could no longer bring a derivative claim.) *Anglo American Security Fund, L.P. v. S.R. Global International Fund, L.P.*, 829 A.2d 143 (Del. Ch. 2003).

Delegation to special committee — Board of directors of corporate general partner of a Delaware limited partnership had authority to delegate to a special committee of the board the investigation of a demand on the general partner to pursue partnership claims. A partnership agreement provision granting the general partner authority to "take any action of any kind and to do anything and everything they [sic] deem necessary with respect [to the business of the partnership]" was sufficiently broad to include the appointment of a special committee to investigate the limited partner's demand. Section 17-403(c) also provided authority for the delegation. *Whalen v. Connelly*, 593 N.W.2d 147 (Iowa Supr. 1999) (applying Delaware law).

Disclosure duty of fiduciary — Fiduciaries of a limited partnership have the burden of demonstrating that all material facts were disclosed. Where the lone source of disclosure is a fiduciary having a conflict of interest, the materiality standard remains unchanged, but the scrutiny of the disclosures made in that context is more exacting. *Sonet v. Plum Creek Timber Co.*, 1999 Del. Ch. LEXIS 49 (Mar. 18, 1999).

Duties of control persons — Entity controlling the board of directors of a general partner owed a duty of loyalty to the partnership and other partners by virtue of such control.

James River-Pennington Inc. v. CRSS Capital, Inc., 1995 WL 106554 (Del. Ch. Mar. 6, 1995); *U.S. West, Inc. v. Time Warner, Inc.*, 1996 WL 307445 (Del. Ch. June 6, 1996).

Duties of directors of corporate general partner — Directors of a Delaware corporation acting as general partner of a Delaware limited partnership owe fiduciary duties of loyalty and due care directly to the limited partnership and to limited partners when such directors take action that affects partnership property or the partnership's business. *In re USACafes, L.P. Litigation*, 600 A.2d 43, (Del. Ch. 1991). *James River-Pennington Inc. v. CRSS Capital, Inc.*, 1995 WL 106554 (Del. Ch. Mar. 6, 1995).

Duties of loyalty and care — In the absence of a partnership agreement making plain the parties' intention to preempt the fundamental fiduciary duties of loyalty and care, a general partner remains obligated to act fairly toward limited partners and to prove fairness when it makes self-interested decisions. *Active Asset Recovery, Inc. v. Real Estate Asset Recovery Services, Inc.*, 1999 WL 743479 (Del. Ch. Sept. 10, 1999).

Duty of disclosure — In extending an offer to limited partners to purchase their limited partnership units, the general partner owes a duty of full disclosure of material information which is in its possession respecting the business and value of the partnership. *In re Marriott Hotel Properties II Limited Partnership Unitholders Litigation*, 1996 WL 342040 (Del. Ch. June 12, 1996).

Duty of disclosure — It is well settled that a general partner making an offer to limited partners to buy their limited partnership interests owes a duty of full disclosure of material information respecting the business and value of the partnership. Where the lone source of disclosure is a fiduciary having a conflict of interest, there is an obligation of complete candor and judicial scrutiny of the disclosure is more exacting. *In re Marriott Hotel Properties II Limited Partnership*, 2000 WL 128875 (Del. Ch. Jan. 24, 2000).

Duty of disclosure; magazine article — Failure to disclose views of executive officer of a corporate general partner was not misleading. In an interview published in a magazine, the officer made comments inconsistent with the views of the general partner stated in the partnership's disclosure statement to limited partners. The officer was not obligated to share the views of the general partner, and a magazine article cannot be an official comment on behalf of the partnership. No reasonable person would conclude that the officer's "puffing" about future performance is a material fact that a prudent investor would rely on in determining how to vote. *In re Cencom Cable Income Partners, L.P. Litigation*, 1997 WL 666970 (Del. Ch. Oct. 15, 1997), *reargument denied*, 1997 WL 770158 (Del. Ch. Dec. 3, 1997).

Duty of disclosure; reserve — Disclosure that a reserve would be created to pay obligations and contingencies of the partnership was not misleading simply because the reserve would be used to pay litigation costs or to indemnify the general partner. *In re Cencom Cable Income Partners, L.P. Litigation*, 1997 WL 666970 (Del. Ch. Oct. 15, 1997), *reargument denied*, 1997 WL 770158 (Del. Ch. Dec. 3, 1997).

Duty of disclosure; tender offer — A general partner owes limited partners a fiduciary duty to disclose with entire candor all relevant material facts in the possession of or known to the general partner when making a tender offer for limited partnership interests. *Wurtzel v. Park Towne Place Associates Limited Partnership*, 2002 WL 373041 (Pa. Ct. Com. Pleas Jan. 11, 2002) (applying Delaware law).

Duty of loyalty not modified — A provision in a limited partnership agreement expressly providing that the general partner could engage in other business ventures altered the general partner's duty of loyalty so as to permit the general partner to take for itself what would otherwise constitute partnership opportunities. However, such a provision does not alter the duty of loyalty's prohibition against self-dealing. *The Continental Insurance Company v. Rutledge & Company, Inc.*, 2000 WL 62951 (Del. Ch. Jan. 10, 2000).

Duty to remain as employees of general partner — Two employees of the general partner of a limited partnership did not owe a fiduciary duty to the general or limited partners to remain as employees of the general partner. The two employees ran an investment fund and resigned under circumstances that gave the general partner no choice but to close the fund or transfer it to a competing business started by these employees. Their departure without adequate notice to find replacements could have been addressed by contract but did not implicate any fiduciary duty on the part of the two employees. *Lazard Debt Recovery GP, LLC v. Weinstock*, 864 A.2d 955 (Del. Ch. 2004).

Employees of general partner as limited partners; duties — Two employees of the general partner were not bound by contractual duties to which the general partner was bound. The employees ran an investment fund and resigned under circumstances that gave the general partner no choice but to close the fund or transfer it to a competing business started by these employees. In addition, by signing a subscription agreement to invest in the partnership personally, these employees did not have the same obligations of the general partner. In the subscription agreement, they only agreed to be bound by the partnership agreement as limited partners. Nor did the employees violate the obligation of good faith barring limited partners from competing with the partnership since their behavior did not constitute bad faith failure to inform the partnership of investment opportunities. *Lazard Debt Recovery GP LLC v. Weinstock*, 864 A.2d 955 (Del. Ch. 2004).

Entire fairness — In challenging the fairness of a transaction, such as a cash-out merger of minority limited partners by a majority limited partner, the plaintiff must allege specific items of misconduct that demonstrate unfairness. If the plaintiff meets this burden, then the burden shifts to the general partner to establish to the Court's satisfaction that the transaction was the product of both fair dealing and fair price. *In re Boston Celtics Limited Partnership Shareholders Litigation*, 1999 Del. Ch. LEXIS 166 (Aug. 6, 1999).

Entrenchment — Complaint stated a claim for unlawful entrenchment by general partner where plaintiff alleged a scheme pursuant to which the general partner used a reverse split of units, an odd-lot buy back, open market purchases and grant of options to obtain a *de facto* veto over any vote to remove the general partner, thereby injuring the partnership through unnecessary purchases of units and limited partners by adversely affecting their voting rights. *Gotham Partners, L.P. v. Hallwood Realty Partners*, 1998 WL 832631 (Del. Ch. Nov. 10, 1998).

Equitable tolling of limitation period for breach of partnership agreement — The analogous period of limitations is not equitably tolled because limited partner had a duty of reasonable inquiry and, if such inquiry had been made, limited partners would have realized well within the 3-year period that general partner was acting inconsistently with its obligation under the partnership agreement. *U.S. Cellular Inv. Co. of Allentown v. Bell Atlantic Mobile Systems, Inc.*, 677 A.2d 497 (Del. 1996).

Equitable tolling of limitations — In action for breach of fiduciary duty by general partners, the limitations period may be tolled even without allegations of affirmative acts of concealment by the defendants, where a fiduciary relation exists and plaintiff alleges self-dealing. Absent self-dealing, equitable tolling operates in much the same way as the doctrine of fraudulent concealment. *Litman v. Prudential-Bache Properties, Inc.*, 1994 Del. Ch. LEXIS 3 (Jan. 14, 1994), *aff'd*, 642 A.2d 837 (Del. 1994).

Exclusive jurisdiction of the Court of Chancery — When a claim is entirely derived from and dependent upon allegations of fiduciary duties owed by a general partner to limited partners of a Delaware limited partnership and none of the allegations states a cause of action independent of equitable theories, the claim is within the exclusive jurisdiction of the Court of Chancery. *Snyder v. Butcher & Co.*, 1992 WL 240344 (Del. Super. Sept. 15, 1992).

Failure to meet contractual standard of conduct — Even where restrictions on fiduciary duties are clearly stated in the partnership agreement, the general partner must comply with the substitute contractual standard of conduct as a prerequisite to taking advantage of the contractual modification of its fiduciary duties. The partnership jurisdiction of the Court of Chancery. *Snyder v. Butcher & Co.*, 1992 WL 240344 (Del. Super. Sept. 15, 1992).

Failure to meet contractual standard of conduct — Even where restrictions on fiduciary duties are clearly stated in the partnership agreement, the general partner must comply with the substitute contractual standard of conduct as a prerequisite to taking advantage of the contractual modification of its fiduciary duties. The partnership agreement excused fiduciary duties so long as general partner's actions were not grossly negligent, in bad faith or inconsistent with the overall purposes of the partnership. Where general partner was grossly negligent and acted in bad faith in implementing a self-interested transaction, general partner did not meet the standards of conduct called for by the agreement. Accordingly, default standards of fiduciary duty applied to general partner's conduct. *Gelfman v. Weeden Investors, L.P.*, 2004 WL 1587571 (Del. Ch. July 12, 2004).

Fiduciary duty — Unless limited by the partnership agreement, a general partner and directors of a corporate general partner, have a fiduciary duty to manage the partnership in the best interests of the partnership and the limited partners, and to deal fairly with the limited partners. *In re Boston Celtics Limited Partnership Shareholders Litigation*, 1999 Del. Ch. LEXIS 166 (Aug. 6, 1999).

Fiduciary duty and personal liability of directors of general partner to limited partners — The directors of the general partner have a fiduciary duty to the limited partners, and are personally liable for a breach of such duty. *In re: USACafes, L.P. Litigation*, 600 A.2d 43 (Del. Ch. 1991).

Fiduciary duty claim; statute of limitations; partnership agreement — The statute of limitations in a limited partnership agreement stating that a limited partner may not commence an action "under this Agreement" unless "brought within six months after the actions or circumstances giving rise to such course of action occurred," did not apply to a breach of fiduciary duty claim brought by a limited partner against the general partner and others. Among other reasons, the curtailment of the statute of limitations applied only to claims brought under the partnership agreement, and did not extend to actions for breach of fiduciary duty. *Werner v. Miller Technology Management, L.P.*, 831 A.2d 318 (Del. Ch. 2003).

Fiduciary duty of controlling persons — Mere ownership, direct or indirect, of the general partner of a limited partnership does not by itself create a fiduciary relation. Affiliates of a general partner who exercise control over the limited partnership's property may owe fiduciary duties to the partnership and its limited partners. *Bigelow/Diversified Secondary Partnership Fund 1990 v. Damson/Birtcher Partners*, 2001 WL 1641239 (Del. Ch. Dec. 4, 2001).

Fiduciary duties of employees — Employees of limited partnership and partnership investment manager did not breach any fiduciary duty when they terminated their employment. Absent any employment contract provisions that limited manner or timing of resignation, employees were free to resign at will. Their fiduciary duties as agents were limited by the scope of their agency relation. Thus, absent allegations of a breach of duties relating to management of fund assets, employees were free to resign in order to work for a competitor, and did not breach any duty in planning for their departure or in not providing advance notice of their plans. *Lazard Debt Recovery GP, LLC v. Weinstock*, 2004 WL 1813286 (Del. Ch. Aug. 6, 2004).

Fiduciary duty of parent and affiliates — Complaint alleging that a parent corporation of a corporate general partner and entities affiliated with the general partner controlled the affairs of a limited partnership, including the creation of and distribution of partnership assets for their own benefit, stated a claim for breach of fiduciary duty by the parent and affiliates of the general partner. *Wallace v. Wood*, 1999 WL 893577 (Del. Ch. Oct. 12, 1999).

Fiduciary exception to attorney-client privilege — Court may look to corporate cases to determine the application in the limited partnership context of the fiduciary exception to the attorney-client privilege. Once limited partners made their intention to withdraw known to the general partner, there was no longer mutuality of interest between the general partner and the limited partners. Mutuality of interest is a prerequisite to the fiduciary exception. Thus, advice of counsel rendered after there was no longer a mutuality of interest between the general and the limited partners was privileged and not subject to discovery. Advice of counsel rendered prior to the formation of the partnership was privileged because there was no fiduciary relation until the partnership was formed, and thus the fiduciary exception has no application. *The Continental Ins. Co. v. Rutledge & Co., Inc.*, 1999 Del. Ch. LEXIS 12 (Jan. 26, 1999).

General partner owes duty of care and loyalty — Duties of a general partner include both the duty of care and the duty of loyalty. A general partner who purchases units from limited partners owes a duty of loyalty to the limited partners. *MacLane Gas Co., L.P. v. Enserch Corp.*, 1992 Del. Ch. LEXIS 255 (Dec. 9, 1992).

General partners accountable for partnership's violation of Fair Debt Collection Practices Act — General partners of a limited partnership are jointly and severally liable for everything chargeable to the partnership, and thus where a limited partnership engaged in debt collection violates the Fair Debt Collection Practices Act, the general partners themselves may be held liable under the FDCPA. *Randle v. GC Services, L.P.*, 25 F. Supp. 2d 849 (N.D. Ill. 1998); *Peters v. AT&T Corporation*, 179 F.R.D. 564 (N.D. Ill. 1998); *Peters v. AT&T Corporation*, 43 F. Supp. 2d 926 (E.D. Ill. 1999).

Gross negligence — General partner that consciously structured a transaction that would deprive certain limited partners of their interests at book value, which was far below fair market value, but made no inquiry into how far below fair market value the book value was, acted with gross negligence. *Gelfman v. Weeden Investors, L.P.*, 2004 WL 1587571 (Del. Ch. July 12, 2004).

Gross negligence and mismanagement — General partner's conduct does not rise to the level of gross negligence or gross mismanagement where decisions about partnership's business were made in good faith and based on informed judgment, even if particular decisions ultimately proved mistaken or less advantageous than originally conceived. *Cincinnati Bell Cellular Systems Co. v. Ameritech Mobile Phone Service of Cincinnati, Inc.*, 1996 Del. Ch. LEXIS 116 (Sept. 3, 1996), *aff'd*, 1997 Del. LEXIS 58 (Feb. 11, 1997).

Implied covenant of good faith and fair dealing; agreement takes precedence over statute — A limited partner may have breached its duty of good faith and fair dealing by engaging in "closed door discussions" with a third-party regarding the partnership project. The limited partnership agreement provided that only the general partner could conduct the affairs of the partnership. Section 17-403 could not be construed to support a conclusion to the contrary because that would contravene Delaware's policy regarding freedom of contract, as expressed in the limited partnership agreement in this case. Delaware courts have employed the covenant of good faith and fair dealing sparingly when parties have crafted detailed complex agreements, although they have occasionally recognized the necessity of implying contract terms to ensure the parties' reasonable expectations are fulfilled. *SJ Properties Suites v. STJ, P.C.*, 2010 WL 5300541 (E.D. Wis. Dec. 17, 2010).

Jurisdiction over directors of corporate general partner — Delaware courts have personal jurisdiction over directors of a Delaware corporation serving as general partner of a Delaware limited partnership in an action against the directors for breach of fiduciary duties owed to limited partners. The fiduciary duties owed by directors to the partnership and to limited partners are duties owed by the directors in their capacity as directors of the corporate general partner, thus subjecting them to personal jurisdiction under the Delaware director consent statute, 8 Del. C § 3114. *In re USACafes, L.P. Litigation*, 600 A.2d 43, (Del. Ch. 1991).

Knowledge of general partner's conflict — Limited partners would be precluded from claiming that the general partner's actions on behalf of the partnership were compromised by a conflict of interest, if the limited partners knew of this conflict when they invested in the partnership (and therefore acquiesced in it). *Seaford Funding Limited Partnership v. M&M Associates II, L.P.*, 672 A.2d 66 (Del. Ch. 1995). *Accord, Cabaniss v. Deutsche Bank Securities, Inc.*, 611 S.E.2d 878 (N.C. Ct. App. 2005).

Lack of procedural safeguards and timing evidence unfair dealing — Lack of procedural safeguards in conversion of limited partnership to corporation, such as absence of independent representation of limited partners, is persuasive of unfair dealing. A transaction timed to serve the general partner's interests and undertaken at a time when the general partner expected major improvements in the market, and decreased distributions to unitholders, was evidence of unfair dealing in the structure and timing of the transaction. *MacLane Gas Co., L.P. v. Enserch Corp.*, 1992 Del. Ch. LEXIS 255 (Del. Ch., Dec. 9, 1992), *aff'd*, 633 A.2d 369 (Del. 1993).

Liability — A general partner of a limited partnership is liable to third parties as is a partner in a partnership without limited partners. *Council of the Wilmington Condominium v. Wilmington Avenue Associates, L.P.*, 1997 WL 817843 (Del. Super. Oct. 24, 1997).

Liability for debts — A general partner of a limited partnership is liable for the debts of the limited partnership. Complaint alleging breach of contract by a limited partnership signatory to the contract stated a claim against the corporate general partner. *Sandyik v. Advent International Corp.*, 83 F. Supp. 442 (D. Del. 1999).

Liability of parent corporation — To hold parent corporation of corporate general partner liable for breach of fiduciary duty by general partner, plaintiff must raise material facts to support a conclusion that parent corporation personally participated in the alleged wrongs and used partnership assets under their control to enrich itself at the expense of the limited partners. *Niki Development Corp. v. HOB Hotel Chicago Partners, L.P.*, 2003 WL 1712563 (N.D. Ill. Mar. 31, 2003).

Limited partner's promise to advance funds; standing to sue; receiver — The general partner had standing to pursue a claim against a limited partner who allegedly promised to advance funds for a partnership transaction and failed to do so, even though a receiver had been appointed for the partnership, and became the general partner, and might be "the more proper proponent" of the claim. *SJ Properties Suites v. STJ, P.C.*, 2010 WL 5300541 (E.D. Wis. Dec. 17, 2010).

Mismanagement and diversion claims — The plaintiffs, a group of limited partners in a Delaware public limited partnership, lacked standing, under both New York and Delaware law, to assert individual or class action claims for breach of contract and breach of fiduciary duty against the partnership, the general partner and the entities controlling the general partner, for the wrongful deferral of management fees and payment of such fees out of the proceeds of the sale of partnership assets. The claims were derivative in nature, in that they alleged the mismanagement and diversion of assets, and did not implicate any injury to the plaintiffs distinct from the harm to the partnership. *Broome v. ML Media Opportunity Partnerships, L.P.*, 709 N.Y.S.2d 59 (1st Dept. 2000).

Misrepresentation claim — Limited partners who concede in pretrial depositions that they were unaware of defendant general partner's connection with the limited partnership could not bring suit for misrepresentation and concealment against that general partner without alleging any actual participation in wrongdoing. *Murphy v. Bay Shores Six, Ltd. Partnership*, 1987 WL 5776 (Del. Ch. Jan. 26, 1987).

Misrepresentations — Generalized statements by employees of partnership and partnership investment manager of contentment with employment, as opposed to statements that they were bound by contract and committed to remain employed for a defined period of time, did not amount to a material misrepresentation on which potential investors would have reasonably relied. *Lazard Debt Recovery GP, LLC v. Weinstock*, 2004 WL 1813286 (Del. Ch. Aug. 6, 2004).

Modification of default fiduciary duties — Where application of default fiduciary duties can be reconciled with the practical operation of the terms of the partnership agreement, default fiduciary duties will apply absent clear contractual language disclaiming their applicability. If use of default fiduciary duties would intrude on the contractual rights or expectations of the general partner, or be insensible in view of the contractual mechanisms governing the transaction under consideration, default fiduciary duties will not be applied. *R.S.M., Inc. v. Alliance Capital Management Holdings L.P.*, 790 A.2d 478 (Del. Ch. 2001).

Modification of fiduciary duties — Limited partnership agreement expressly provided that the standard of conduct contained in the partnership agreement superseded any other standards, including standards under the Delaware RULPA or other applicable law. Accordingly, the agreement effectively modified the general partner's fiduciary duties such that the general partner would not be liable for breach of contract or of fiduciary duty simply because the result of its actions was not entirely fair. Rather, liability would exist only on a showing of violation of the contractual standards of gross negligence, wanton or willful misconduct, or actions taken in bad faith. Where actions of general partner would deprive certain limited partners of their investment at a book value materially below fair value and place heavy concentration of ownership in affiliates of the general partner, plaintiffs raised a litigable issue of bad faith sufficient to withstand a motion to dismiss for failure to state a claim. *Gelfman v. Weeden Investors, L.P.*, 792 A.2d 977 (Del. Ch. 2001).

Modification of fiduciary duties — merger — Unless limited by the partnership agreement, a general partner has the fiduciary duty to manage the partnership in the interests of the partnership and its limited partners. However, principles of contract preempt fiduciary principles where the parties to a limited partnership have plainly intended to do so. Only when the partnership agreement is silent or ambiguous will the Court turn for guidance to the statutory default rules, traditional notions of fiduciary duties or other extrinsic evidence. Where the partnership agreement gave general partner sole discretion to structure a merger of the partnership, discretion was defined in a manner that did not require the general partner to consider the interests of the partnership or limited partners, and limited partners had the right under the agreement to accept or reject the merger by a two-thirds vote, complaint alleging that the general partner breached its fiduciary duties by proposing an unfair merger or unfairly manipulating its timing would be dismissed for failure to state a claim. *Sonet v. Timber Company, L.P.*, 1998 WL 749445 (Del. Ch. Dec. 16, 1998).

Modification of fiduciary duty by private placement memorandum — A limited partner of a Delaware limited partnership could not sue the partnership and its general partner for breach of fiduciary duty when the specific activity complained of was disclosed and allowed in the private placement memorandum. The Delaware Revised Uniform Limited Partnership Act permitted a limited partnership to order its own affairs including the modification of fiduciary duties. *Nolan v. Virginia Inv. Fund L.P.*, 833 So.2d 853 (Fla. Ct. App. 2002) (applying Delaware law).

Necessary Parties — A limited partnership was not a necessary party in an action brought by its general partner to recover moneys owed to the partnership by a corporation. The corporation had allegedly made payments to its principal before making payments to the partnership, in violation of a subordination agreement. Among other things, joinder of the partnership as a party did not appear necessary for complete relief because the interests of the partnership and the general partner were identical, and the partnership could only act through the general partner which was authorized to bring suit on the partnership's behalf in its own name. *In re Olympic Mills Corporation*, 333 B.R. 540 (B.A.P. 1st Cir. 2005).

Negligence vs. gross negligence — A provision in the limited partnership agreement providing for indemnification of the general partner except for instances of the general partner's gross negligence, willful misconduct, or recklessness would not prevent the limited partners from recovering against the general partner for misconduct that was merely negligent, where the agreement only exempted from liability conduct performed in "good faith" and within the general partner's scope of authority. *Curley v. Brignoli Curley and Roberts Assocs.*, 746 F. Supp. 1208 (S.D.N.Y. 1989) (applying Delaware law).

New general partner; compromise of capital call; breach of contract and fiduciary duty — Allegations (by the trustee in bankruptcy for the debtor limited partnership) that appointment of a new general partner by the limited partners was for the purpose of having the new general partner rescind a capital call issued by the former general partner, stated a claim for breach of contract and breach of fiduciary duty by the new general partner. Thus, a court could enforce the capital call issued by the former general partner. The failure to comply with the capital call in the original commitment by the limited partners to the partnership had rendered the partnership insolvent. *In re LJM2 Co-Investment, L.P.*, 866 A.2d 762 (Del. Ch. 2004).

No breach of duty where general partner received different merger consideration — Receipt by the general partner of a general partner interest in subsidiary partnerships rather than stock upon conversion of a master limited partnership to corporate form was not unfair where there was a valid business reason for such treatment rather than conversion of the general partner's interest into stock. *In re Mesa Limited Partnership Preferred Unitholders Litigation*, 1991 Del. Ch. LEXIS 214 (Dec. 10, 1991) *appeal refused*, 608 A.2d 728 (Del. 1992).

No breach of fiduciary duty where partners rely on terms of partnership agreement — When partnership agreement of Delaware limited partnership provided for termination of a partner's interest at the sole discretion of the other partners, remaining partners in the limited partnership did not breach their fiduciary duty of good faith by forfeiting and reallocating the general partner's interest upon his termination as general partner because they relied in good faith on the provisions of the partnership agreement. *Rothmeier v. Investment Advisers, Inc.*, 556 N.W.2d 590 (Minn. Ct. App. 1996), *review denied*, 1997 Minn. LEXIS 148 (Minn. Feb. 26, 1997).

Non pro rata distributions — Where a partnership agreement expressly provided that the general partner could make distributions in kind, and that distributions did not have to be made pro rata to all classes of partnership interests, but did have to be made pro rata within any one class, a pro rata distribution of assets to one class did not involve a breach of duty. *Cantor Fitzgerald, L.P. v. Cantor,* 2001 WL 1456494 (Del. Ch. Nov. 5, 2001).

Outside majority approval may extinguish fiduciary duty claims — Where a limited partnership agreement requires a transaction between the partnership and the general partner to be approved by a majority of the limited partners unaffiliated with the general partner, such approval extinguishes any breach of fiduciary duty claim unless the general partner has failed to comply with its duty of disclosure in connection with obtaining limited partner approval. *R.S.M., Inc. v. Alliance Capital Management Holdings, L.P.,* 790 A.2d 478 (Del. Ch. 2001).

Personal jurisdiction over parent of general partner — A Delaware court did not have jurisdiction over the parent of the corporate general partner of a Delaware limited partnership in a suit brought by the limited partners, alleging breach of the partnership agreement, where the parent had no contacts with Delaware other than the filing of the limited partnership documents, the parent was not a party to the partnership agreement, did not transact any business in Delaware and did not act in Delaware related to the transaction at issue. *Red Sail Easter Limited Partners v. Radio City Music Hall Prod., Inc.,* 1991 Del. Ch. LEXIS 113 (July 10, 1991).

Place of business — Limited partnerships act through their general partners. Accordingly, a limited partnership had a place of business in New York through the presence of the general partner who acted on behalf of the limited partnership. *In re Paper I Partners, L.P.,* 283 B.R. 661 (Bankr. S.D.N.Y. 2002).

Power of attorney; consent for limited partners — The power of attorney granted to the general partner by the partnership agreement did not give the general partner the power to consent to an amendment to the agreement on behalf of limited partners who had not given their consent to the amendment. The amendment would have reduced the requirement for "compromising" a capital call issued by the former general partner from unanimous approval of all partners to approval by a simple majority. Execution by the new general partner of this amendment, therefore, was not evidence of the required unanimous approval of the amendment. *In re LJM2 Co-Investment, L.P.,* 866 A.2d 762 (Del. Ch. 2004).

Power to enter binding contracts — A managing general partner who signs a contract on behalf of a limited partnership binds the partnership where (1) the general partner is carrying on partnership business "in the usual way" and (2) there are no limitations on the partner's authority to enter the contract or, if any such limitations exist, the other party to the contract is unaware of them. *Harper v. Delaware Valley Broadcasters, Inc.,* 743 F. Supp. 1076 (D. Del. 1990), *aff'd,* 932 F.2d 959 (3d Cir. 1991).

Power to rescind capital call — As a general matter, the power to rescind a capital call is implicit in a general partner's power to make such a call in the first instance. The power to rescind is not the same as the power to compromise and thus is not subject to the unanimous consent requirement of Section 17-502(b)(1). *In re LJM2 Co-Inv., L.P.,* 866 A.2d 762 (Del. Ch. 2004).

Powers of general partner — General partner of a limited partnership possesses essentially the same powers as a partner in a partnership without limited partners. *Currier v. Amerigas Propane, L.P.,* 1999 N.H. LEXIS 82 (N.H. Supr. Aug. 6, 1999).

Removal of general partner — A limited partnership's management company's use of transaction fees to pay salaries and bonuses contrary to the terms of an approved service agreement constitutes a breach of the limited partnership agreement. Even though the general partner delegated administrative management authority to the management company, it breached the limited partnership agreement by permitting the management company to use the transaction fees for purposes other than the service agreement allowed and thus, the general partner's conduct formed an appropriate basis for the limited partners' removal of the general partner. *Davenport Group MG, L.P. v. Strategic Investment Partners, Inc.*, 685 A.2d 715 (Del. Ch. Jan. 23, 1996).

Reliance on provisions of agreement — Absent allegations of facts from which an inference of bad faith can be drawn, a complaint fails to state a cause of action for breach of fiduciary duty by a general partner where the general partner has relied on the provisions of the partnership agreement as authority for the conduct alleged to be a breach of fiduciary duty. *United States Cellular Investment Co. of Allentown v. Bell Atlantic Mobile Systems, Inc.*, 1994 Del. Ch. LEXIS 37 (March 11, 1994), *aff'd*, 677 A.2d 497 (Del. 1996).

Restriction of fiduciary duties — Restrictions on fiduciary duties must be set forth clearly and unambiguously. Where partnership agreement gave the general partner sole discretion to determine certain matters, provided that in exercising its sole discretion the general partner did not have to consider the interests of the partnership or its limited partners, and provided that the general partner was not subject to any different standard of conduct imposed by the partnership agreement or other agreements, the general partner remained subject to default fiduciary duties in exercising its discretion. The agreement was ineffective to limit application of default fiduciary duties because it did not expressly provide that default fiduciary duties did not apply if they would hinder the general partner's discretion, but only provided that other standards set out in the agreement would give way. *Miller v. American Real Estate Partners, L.P.*, 2001 WL 1045643 (Del. Ch. Sept. 6, 2001).

Self-dealing prohibited — Although the limited partnership agreement gave the general partner broad authority to engage in "other business activity" with partnership portfolio companies, it did not permit self-dealing. Therefore, the general partner could not use its position as general partner, and its ability to control the terms of transactions, to invest limited partnership funds for its own gain, as opposed to investing for the benefit of the limited partnership. And, if the general partner engaged in self-dealing, the limited partners could recover from the general partner fees paid by partnership portfolio companies to the general partner. *Continental Insurance Company v. Rutledge & Company, Inc.*, 750 A.2d 1219 (Del. Ch. 2000).

Special litigation committees — Where the partnership agreement was duly amended to authorize the general partners to delegate handling of derivative litigation to a special litigation committee, a special litigation committee could be validly created, and corporate law doctrines relating to special litigation committees would apply. *Katell v. Morgan Stanley Group, Inc.*, 1993 Del. Ch. LEXIS 236 (Sept. 27, 1993).

Special litigation committees — The general partners' authority to manage the partnership affairs includes the right to determine whether derivative actions should proceed.

Delaware law does not contain an express provision allowing general partners to delegate their authority to a special litigation committee; therefore, such rights and responsibilities are determined by the parties' particular partnership agreement. *Katell v. Morgan Stanley Group, Inc.*, 1993 Del. Ch. LEXIS 92 (June 8, 1993).

Special litigation committees — Where a special litigation committee had been duly created in accordance with the partnership agreement, the independence of the committee will not be considered by the Court until after the committee determines whether to pursue the derivative litigation, and proceedings will be stayed for a reasonable period of time to permit the committee to conduct its investigation. *Katell v. Morgan Stanley Group, Inc.*, 1993 Del. Ch. LEXIS 236 (Sept. 27, 1993).

Standards governing proposed merger; fiduciary duty eliminated; covenant of good faith and fair dealing — A proposed merger between a master limited partnership and another non-party limited partnership, sought to be enjoined by a limited partner, did not violate the covenant of good faith and fair dealing owed to him by the partnership. The partnership agreement specifically eliminated the fiduciary duty that would otherwise be owed by the general partner to a limited partner leaving the agreement as the sole basis for the obligations between the two. The covenant of good faith and fair dealing arising from the agreement was not a substitute for a fiduciary duty, the court's most powerful remedial and gap-filling power. The partnership agreement established a contractual standard of review of transactions that supplanted fiduciary duty analysis, which was followed in the merger process. This standard did not require a search for alternative transactions to prevent an alleged undervaluation of the limited partner interest, as claimed by the limited partner. Instead, it provided a "Special Approval" process outlined in the agreement. Nor did the covenant of good faith and fair dealing require that the merger be conditioned on approval of a majority of the minority voting rights, also as claimed by the challenging limited partner. *Lonergan v. EPE Holdings, LLC*, 5 A.3d 1008 (Del. Ch. 2010).

Suit among partners; accounting as prerequisite — An accounting was a condition precedent to a suit between limited partners which alleged fraudulent conveyance. (The partnership agreement provided for the application of Delaware law in disputes concerning the agreement. The court stated that New York law should be applied to a tort suit.) New York and Delaware both require a pre-suit accounting before maintaining an action at law between partners. The RULPA allows a direct action by a limited partner against the limited partnership or another partner, with or without an accounting, if the partner can plead and prove an actual or threatened injury that is not solely the result of an injury suffered or threatened to be suffered by the limited partnership. While Delaware allows direct action by one partner against another in a general partnership, it has not adopted a similar exception to the accounting rule in actions between limited partners. *Drenis v. Haligiannis*, 452 F. Supp. 2d 418 (S.D.N.Y. 2006).

Suit by limited partner against general partner as derivative suit — A suit by limited partners against the general partners for breach of fiduciary duty with respect to choice of investments was a derivative claim; the alleged injuries were to the partnership and not direct to the limited partners, even though the breach resulted in diminished income to the limited partners. *Litman v. Prudential-Bache Properties*, 611 A.2d 12 (Del. Ch. 1992).

Termination of distributions not a breach of duty of loyalty — A general partner's decision to terminate customary distributions to limited partners was not a breach of duty of loyalty where the partnership agreement gave the general partner express authority to determine whether or not to make distributions and no facts were alleged that would show that the general partner used undistributed partnership cash solely for the benefit of the general partner or its affiliates. *Miller v. American Real Estate Partners, L.P.*, 2001 WL 1045643 (Del. Ch. Sept. 6, 2001).

Termination of partner as employee — Agreement by two of three partners that the third partner would be terminated as an employee of the partnership if either of the two partners so requested was not a breach of fiduciary duty to the third partner. Partner/employee injured in his capacity as an employee has a remedy under his employment contract, but not a remedy for breach of fiduciary duty by the controlling partners. *Juran v. Bron*, 2000 WL 1521478 (Del. Ch. Oct. 6, 2000).

Time-barred claims — breach of fiduciary duty — While statute of limitations do not apply directly, equity will apply a statute of limitations by analogy where appropriate. The statute of limitations for breach of fiduciary duty is three years. Where information in limited partnerships' annual reports, if pursued, would have lead to the discovery by plaintiffs of their alleged injury, plaintiffs were on inquiry notice such that statute of limitations was not tolled, and claims made more than three years after plaintiffs were on inquiry notice of alleged breaches of fiduciary duties were time barred. *In re Dean Witter Partnership Litigation*, 1998 WL 442456 (Del. Ch. July 17, 1998).

Time-barred claims for breach of partnership agreement — Where limited partner sought a legal remedy in a court of equity and a statute of limitations exists for an analogous action at law, the statutory period created a presumptive time period for application of laches to bar a claim. *See* Del. Code Ann. tit. 10, § 8106; *U.S. Cellular Inv. Co. of Allentown v. Bell Atlantic Mobile Systems, Inc.*, 677 A.2d 497 (Del. 1996).

Tolling of statute of limitations — Equitable tolling of statute of limitations was appropriate with respect to breach of contract and breach of fiduciary duty claims against a general partner where the general partner had failed to refund investments, concealed fact that partnership was not fully subscribed, failed to advance cash to the partnership, and concealed facts essential to limited partners' cause of action. *Niehoff v. Maynard*, 299 F.3d 41 (1st Cir. 2002).

Unclean hands defense available against general partner — In a declaratory judgment action by a general partner against a limited partner for a declaration that the exercise of a buyout provision in the limited partnership agreement would not be a breach of fiduciary duty to the limited partner, who would suffer adverse tax consequences, the limited partner could raise the defense of unclean hands based on alleged misrepresentations of the value of assets contributed by the general partner to the partnership and alleged self-dealing that artificially decreased the income of the partnership. *Rhone-Poulenc Surfactants and Specialties, Inc. v. GAF Chemicals Corp.*, 1993 Del. Ch. LEXIS 38 (Feb. 26, 1993), dismissed, 1993 Del. Ch. LEXIS 59 (Apr. 6, 1993).

Unfair process — Plaintiff adequately alleged unfair process by alleging that the majority partner and the general partner set the terms of a reorganization, the general partner had admitted conflicts of interest, minority limited partners had no opportunity to vote on the reorganization, no independent party represented the minority limited partners, the general partner did not employ any special committee or financial advisor to assess the fairness of the reorganization, and the sole basis for the determination that the reorganization was fair was the pro rata allocation of net assets between entities based on partnership interests. *In re Boston Celtics Limited Partnership Shareholders Litigation*, 1999 Del. Ch. LEXIS 166 (Aug. 6, 1999).

Unfair terms — Plaintiff adequately alleged unfair reorganization terms by alleging that holders of less than 100 limited partnership units would be cashed out, the general partner would be allowed to collect management fees that it could not collect prior to the reorganization, and the partnership would incur substantial debt in connection with the reorganization. Allowing limited partners owning less than 100 shares to buy additional shares to round up to 100 units did not cure unfairness. For a reorganization to be fair, it must be fair to all limited partners given their status at the time the reorganization is announced, without requiring them to make a further investment. *In re Boston Celtics Limited Partnership Shareholders Litigation*, 1999 Del. Ch. LEXIS 166 (Aug. 6, 1999).

Vote buying — No impermissible vote buying or coercion by a general partner was involved where the general partner conditioned distribution of assets through an exchange offer on the approval by the limited partners of various amendments to the partnership agreement. *Cantor Fitzgerald, L.P. v. Cantor*, 2001 WL 1456494 (Del. Ch. Nov. 5, 2001).

Work product doctrine — Work product doctrine applies only to documents created for or in anticipation of litigation. Work product doctrine is more limited in its effect than the mutuality of interest requirement. Thus, lack of mutuality of interest could arise and preclude production of counsels' advice long before the work product doctrine would become effective. *Continental Insurance Company v. Rutledge & Company, Inc.*, 1999 Del. Ch. LEXIS 12 (Jan. 26, 1999).

Decisions under prior law

Fiduciary duty owed to limited partners — The liabilities imposed on general partners by former 6 Del. Code § 1709, ensured that a general partner in a limited partnership owed a fiduciary duty to the limited partners, providing the basis for chancery jurisdiction over an action by limited partners who challenged the sale of their partnership interests to the general partner's corporate owner at an allegedly inadequate price. *Boxer v. Husky Oil Co.*, 429 A.2d 995 (Del. Ch. 1981).

§ 17-404. Contributions by a general partner.

A general partner of a limited partnership may make contributions to the limited partnership and share in the profits and losses of, and in distributions from, the limited partnership as a general partner. A general partner also may make contributions to and share in profits, losses and distributions as a limited partner. A person who is both a general partner and a limited partner has the rights and powers, and is subject to the restrictions and liabilities, of a general partner and, except as provided in the partnership agreement, also has the rights and powers, and is subject to the restrictions, of a limited partner to the extent of his or her participation in the partnership as a limited partner.

§ 17-405. Classes and voting.

(a) A partnership agreement may provide for classes or groups of general partners having such relative rights, powers and duties as the partnership agreement may provide, and may make provision for the future creation in the manner provided in the partnership agreement of additional classes or groups of general partners having such relative rights, powers and duties as may from time to time be established, including rights, powers and duties senior to existing classes and groups of general partners.

A partnership agreement may provide for the taking of an action, including the amendment of the partnership agreement, without the vote or approval of any general partner or class or group of general partners, including an action to create under the provisions of the partnership agreement a class or group of partnership interests that was not previously outstanding.

(b) The partnership agreement may grant to all or certain identified general partners or a specified class or group of the general partners the right to vote, separately or with all or any class or group of the limited partners or the general partners, on any matter. Voting by general partners may be on a per capita, number, financial interest, class, group or any other basis.

(c) A partnership agreement may set forth provisions relating to notice of the time, place or purpose of any meeting at which any matter is to be voted on by any general partner, waiver of any such notice, action by consent without a meeting, the establishment of a record date, quorum requirements, voting in person or by proxy, or any other matter with respect to the exercise of any such right to vote.

(d) Unless otherwise provided in a partnership agreement, meetings of general partners may be held by means of conference telephone or other communications equipment by means of which all persons participating in the meeting can hear each other, and participation in a meeting pursuant to this subsection shall constitute presence in person at the meeting. Unless otherwise provided in a partnership agreement, on any matter that is to be voted on, consented to or approved by general partners, the general partners may take such action without a meeting, without prior notice and without a vote if consented to, in writing or by electronic transmission, by general partners having not less than the minimum number of votes that would be necessary to authorize or take such action at a meeting at which all general partners entitled to vote thereon were present and voted. Unless otherwise provided in a partnership agreement, on any matter that is to be voted on by general partners, the general partners may vote in person or by proxy, and such proxy may be granted in writing, by means of electronic transmission or as otherwise permitted by applicable law. Unless otherwise provided in a partnership agreement, a consent transmitted by electronic transmission by a general partner or by a person or persons authorized to act for a general partner shall be deemed to be written and signed for purposes of this subsection (d). For purposes of this subsection (d), the term "electronic transmission" means any form of communication not directly involving the physical transmission of paper that creates a record that may be retained, retrieved and reviewed by a recipient thereof and that may be directly reproduced in paper form by such a recipient through an automated process.

ANNOTATION

Approval of conversion — Attempted conversion of limited partnership without the consent of the general partner was invalid. *Greenwich Global, LLC v. Clairvoyant Capital, LLC,* 2002 WL 31168715 (Conn. Super. Ct. Aug. 22, 2002).

§ 17-406. Remedies for breach of partnership agreement by general partner.

A partnership agreement may provide that (1) a general partner who fails to perform in accordance with, or to comply with the terms and conditions of, the partnership agreement shall be subject to specified penalties or specified consequences, and (2) at the time or upon the happening of events specified in the partnership agreement, a general partner shall be subject to specified penalties or specified consequences. Such specified penalties or specified consequences may include and take the form of any penalty or consequence set forth in § 17-502(c) of this chapter.

§ 17-407. Reliance on reports and information by limited partners, liquidating trustees, and general partners.

(a) A limited partner or liquidating trustee of a limited partnership shall be fully protected in relying in good faith upon the records of the limited partnership and upon information, opinions, reports or statements presented by a general partner of the limited partnership, an officer or employee of a general partner of the limited partnership, another liquidating trustee, or committees of the limited partnership, limited partners or partners, or by any other person as to matters the limited partner or liquidating trustee reasonably believes are within such other person's professional or expert competence, including information, opinions, reports or statements as to the value and amount of the assets, liabilities, profits or losses of the limited partnership, or the value and amount of assets or reserves or contracts, agreements or other undertakings that would be sufficient to pay claims and obligations of the limited partnership or to make reasonable provision to pay such claims and obligations, or any other facts pertinent to the existence and amount of assets from which distributions to partners or creditors might properly be paid.

(b) A general partner of a limited liability limited partnership shall be fully protected in relying in good faith upon the records of the limited partnership and upon information, opinions, reports or statements presented by another general partner of the limited partnership, an officer or employee of the limited partnership, a liquidating trustee, or committees of the limited partnership, limited partners or partners, or by any other person as to matters the general partner reasonably believes are within such other person's professional or expert competence, including information, opinions, reports or statements as to the value and amount of the assets, liabilities, profits or losses of the limited partnership, or the value and amount of assets or reserves or contracts, agreements or other undertakings that would be sufficient to pay claims and obligations of the limited partnership or to make reasonable provision to pay such claims and obligations, or any other facts pertinent to the existence and amount of assets from which distributions to partners or creditors might properly be paid.

(c) A general partner of a limited partnership that is not a limited liability limited partnership shall be fully protected from liability to the limited partnership, its partners or other persons party to or otherwise bound by the partnership agreement in relying in good faith upon the records of the limited partnership and upon information, opinions, reports or statements presented by another general partner of the limited partnership, an officer or employee of the limited partnership, a liquidating trustee, or committees of the limited partnership, limited partners or partners, or by any other person as to matters the general partner reasonably believes are within such other person's professional or expert competence, including information, opinions, reports or statements as to the value and amount of the assets, liabilities, profits or losses of the limited partnership, or the value and amount of assets or reserves or contracts, agreements or other undertakings that would be sufficient to pay claims and obligations of the limited partnership or to make reasonable provision to pay such claims and obligations, or any other facts pertinent to the existence and amount of assets from which distributions to partners or creditors might properly be paid.

Subchapter V
FINANCE

§ 17-501. Form of contribution.

The contribution of a partner may be in cash, property or services rendered, or a promissory note or other obligation to contribute cash or property or to perform services.

§ 17-502. Liability for contribution.

(a)(1) Except as provided in the partnership agreement, a partner is obligated to the limited partnership to perform any promise to contribute cash or property or to perform services, even if that partner is unable to perform because of death, disability or any other reason. If a partner does not make the required contribution of property or services, he or she is obligated at the option of the limited partnership to contribute cash equal to that portion of the agreed value (as stated in the records of the limited partnership) of the contribution that has not been made.

(2) The foregoing option shall be in addition to, and not in lieu of, any other rights, including the right to specific performance, that the limited partnership may have against such partner under the partnership agreement or applicable law.

(b)(1) Unless otherwise provided in the partnership agreement, the obligation of a partner to make a contribution or return money or other property paid or distributed in violation of this chapter may be compromised only by consent of all the partners. Notwithstanding the compromise, a creditor of a limited partnership who extends credit, after the entering into of a partnership agreement or an amendment thereto which, in either case, reflects the obligation, and before the amendment thereof to reflect the compromise, may enforce the original obligation to the extent that, in extending credit, the creditor reasonably relied on the obligation of a partner to make a contribution or return.

(2) A conditional obligation of a partner to make a contribution or return money or other property to a limited partnership may not be enforced unless the conditions to the obligation have been satisfied or waived as to or by such partner. Conditional obligations include contributions payable upon a discretionary call of a limited partnership or a general partner prior to the time the call occurs.

(c) A partnership agreement may provide that the interest of any partner who fails to make any contribution that he or she is obligated to make shall be subject to specified penalties for, or specified consequences of, such failure. Such penalty or consequence may take the form of reducing or eliminating the defaulting partner's proportionate interest in the limited partnership, subordinating the partnership interest to that of nondefaulting partners, a forced sale of his or her partnership interest, forfeiture of that partnership interest, the lending by other partners of the amount necessary to meet his or her commitment, a fixing of the value of that partnership interest by appraisal or by formula and redemption or sale of the partnership interest at such value, or other penalty or consequence.

ANNOTATIONS

Capital call; reasonable reliance of creditors — A bank which advanced credit to a limited partnership could have reasonably relied on the commitment of the limited partners to contribute additional funds to the partnership when called by the general partner to do so. The section of the limited partnership agreement discussing this future financial commitment by the limited partners was attached to the documentation provided to the bank indicating that such future contributions by limited partners would be one of the sources available to repay the bank loan. *In re LJM2 Co-Investment, L.P.*, 866 A.2d 762 (Del. Ch. 2004).

Consent required to compromise contribution — Where a partnership agreement provided that it could be amended by a majority vote, provided that no amendment could alter the vote necessary for any consent "required hereunder" unless such amendment were approved by the vote necessary at the time of the amendment, the words "required hereunder" incorporated the default statutory provision of Section 502(b)(1), which requires a compromise of capital contributions to be approved by all partners. Because the partnership agreement contained no express provision altering the unanimous vote requirement of Section 502(b)(1), the partnership agreement could not be amended to permit a majority vote of partners to compromise capital commitments without the unanimous consent of the partners. *In re LJM2 Co-Inv., L.P.*, 866 A.2d 762 (Del. Ch. 2004).

Contribution specified in certificate — The fact that certain partners contribute less than other partners to a limited partnership is not grounds for a derivative action when the limited partners who contribute less nevertheless contribute the amount specified under the certificate of limited partnership and no legal obligation to make a greater contribution exists. *Murphy v. Bay Shores Six, Ltd. Partnership*, 1987 WL 5776 (Del. Ch. Jan. 26, 1987).

Contributions generally — Each partner is obligated to make contributions to a limited partnership to the extent stated in the certificate of limited partnership, in the partnership agreement or in any other contractual undertaking. *Murphy v. Bay Shores Six, Ltd. Partnership*, 1987 WL 5776 (Del. Ch. Jan. 26, 1987).

Failure to make capital contribution — If a limited partner fails to make a capital contribution that he is legally obligated to make the limited partnership may sue to force that payment to be made. *Murphy v. Bay Shores Six, Ltd. Partnership*, 1987 WL 5776 (Del. Ch. Jan. 26, 1987).

Obligation to contribute; loan vs. capital; resetting partnership interests; loss of voting rights — A limited partner did not establish, as a matter of law, that it had made an additional $6.1 million equity contribution to the partnership justifying the resetting of his partnership interest at greater than 67%. The partnership agreement distinguished between capital contributions and loans to the partnership and the limited partner failed to establish that the $6.1 million was a capital contribution rather than a loan. This limited partner also alleged that another limited partner, who became the general partner, lost its voting rights by failing to contribute additional capital. However, the limited partner did not establish that a proper capital call was made. The partnership agreement provided that all partners had a right to make capital contributions but that none had an obligation to do so. Any argument to the contrary based on § 17-502 was rejected because a court would look for guidance from the statutory default rules, as well as from traditional rules governing fiduciary duties or other extrinsic evidence, only where the partners have not made provisions in the partnership agreement for the issue involved or the agreement was inconsistent with mandatory statutory provisions. *SJ Properties Suites v. STJ, P.C.*, 2010 WL 5300541 (E.D. Wis. Dec. 17, 2010).

Partnership agreement incorporates default rules — Where a partnership agreement provided that it could be amended by a majority vote, provided that no amendment could alter the vote necessary for any consent "required hereunder" unless such amendment were approved by the vote necessary at the time of the amendment, the words "required hereunder" incorporated the default statutory provision of Section 502(b)(1), which requires a compromise of capital contributions to be approved by all partners. Accordingly, an amendment purporting to reduce to a majority the consent required to compromise capital contributions was invalid in the absence of unanimous consent to the amendment. *In re LJM2 Co-Inv., L.P.*, 866 A.2d 762 (Del. Ch. 2004).

Power to rescind capital call — As a general matter, the power to rescind a capital call is implicit in a general partner's power to make such a call in the first instance. The power to rescind is not the same as the power to compromise and thus is not subject to the unanimous consent requirement of Section 17-502(b)(1). *In re LJM2 Co-Inv., L.P.*, 866 A.2d 762 (Del. Ch. 2004).

Promise to advance funds; general partner's standing to sue; receiver — The general partner had standing to pursue a claim against a limited partner who allegedly promised to advance funds for a partnership transaction and failed to do so, even though a receiver had been appointed for the partnership, and became the general partner, and might be "the more proper proponent" of the claim. *SJ Properties Suites v. STJ, P.C.*, 2010 WL 5300541 (E.D. Wis. Dec. 17, 2010).

§ 17-503. Allocation of profits and losses.

The profits and losses of a limited partnership shall be allocated among the partners, and among classes of partners, in the manner provided in writing in the partnership agreement. If the partnership agreement does not so provide, profits and losses shall be allocated on the basis of the agreed value (as stated in the records of the limited partnership) of the contributions made by each partner to the extent they have been received by the limited partnership and have not been returned.

ANNOTATIONS

Bad faith "excusal" of limited partner from investments — A complaint by a limited partner alleging that the general partner acted in bad faith in "excusing" the limited partner from participating in various investment opportunities of the limited partnership in retaliation for the limited partner's filing of an earlier suit against the general partner should not have been dismissed on the pleadings. Giving the limited partner the benefit of every inference, its allegation that the "excusals" took place after its initial lawsuit was adequate to raise a question of fact (or a mixed question of law and fact) as to whether the general partner's actions were reasonable or retaliatory. Furthermore, the plaintiff did not have to plead bad faith on the part of the general partner with particularity. *Desert Equities v. Morgan Stanley Leveraged*, 624 A.2d 1199 (Del. 1993).

§ 17-504. Allocation of distributions.

Distributions of cash or other assets of a limited partnership shall be allocated among the partners, and among classes or groups of partners, in the manner provided in the partnership agreement. If the partnership agreement does not so provide, distributions will be made on the basis of the agreed value (as stated in the records of the limited partnership) of the contributions made by each partner to the extent they have been received by the limited partnership and have not been returned.

ANNOTATIONS

Amendment to authorize redemption plan; partners treated differently; bad faith — An amendment of the limited partnership agreement fostered by the corporate general partner to authorize a plan to redeem partnership units at different prices was a breach of the agreement and a breach of fiduciary duty. The general partner and its affiliates controlled the votes for the amendment. The plan favored current management and employees. Redemption of units was at book value, which was far less than their fair market value, and the redemption schedule provided longer periods of time for unit holders who were current employees, including management. The process by which the partnership agreement was amended also did not comply with conflict of interest requirements in the agreement and, therefore, was not done in good faith. *Gelfman v. Weeden Investors, L.P.*, 859 A.2d 89 (Del. Ch. 2004).

Non-pro rata distribution to partners — Where a liquidating partner proposed a non-pro-rata distribution to partners, excluding from the distribution those partners against whom the liquidating partner believed the partnership had a valid claim, the proposed non-pro rata distribution did not constitute a breach of fiduciary duty because it was proposed in good faith and in pursuit of what the liquidating partner believed to be the best interests of the partnership; however, the liquidating partner could not affect the non-pro rata distribution in violation of provisions in the agreement of limited partnership which precluded any limited partner from having a priority over any other limited partner in respect of distributions. *Boesky v. CX Partners, L.P.*, 1988 Del. Ch. LEXIS 60 (Del. Ch. April 28, 1988).

§ 17-505. Defense of usury not available.

No obligation of a partner of a limited partnership to the limited partnership arising under the partnership agreement or a separate agreement or writing, and no note, instrument or other writing evidencing any such obligation of a partner, shall be subject to the defense of usury, and no partner shall interpose the defense of usury with respect to any such obligation in any action.

Subchapter VI
DISTRIBUTIONS AND WITHDRAWAL

§ 17-601. Interim distributions.

Except as provided in this subchapter, to the extent and at the times or upon the happening of the events specified in the partnership agreement, a partner is entitled to receive from a limited partnership distributions before his withdrawal from the limited partnership and before the dissolution and winding up thereof.

ANNOTATIONS

Appointment of receiver to insure distribution — The appointment of a receiver for a Delaware limited partnership was not justified where one limited partner claimed that another partner was collecting monies on behalf of the partnership but failing to remit loan repayments and partnership distributions to that limited partner. The partnership was not insolvent and the limited partner who sought the receiver did not show any fraud that would pose an imminent danger of loss of partnership assets or threaten the existence of the partnership. Only the distributions of one limited partner were at issue and there was an adequate remedy at law. *Sharon Gardens Associates, L.P. v. Florescue*, 629 So.2d 1002 (Fla. Ct. App. 4 Dist. 1993).

Mandatory tax distributions — Where limited partnership agreement expressly provided for a mandatory annual distribution to partners based on the amount of taxable income allocated to each partner, a limited partner holding both preferred and common limited partnership interests was entitled to a tax distribution based on the income allocated to its preferred and common interests. Tax distributions would not be computed based only on holdings of common interests in the absence of any express provision limiting tax distributions to allocations of income based on holdings of common interests or any provision making tax distributions discretionary. *Interactive Corp. v. Vivendi Universal, S.A.*, 2004 WL 1572932 (Del. Ch. July 6, 2004).

Non-pro rata distributions — Where a partnership agreement expressly provided that the general partner could make distributions in kind, and that distributions did not have to be made pro rata to all classes of partnership interests, but did have to be made pro rata within any one class, a pro rata distribution of assets to one class did not involve a breach of duty. *Cantor Fitzgerald, L.P. v. Cantor*, 2001 WL 1456494 (Del. Ch. Nov. 5, 2001).

Termination of distributions — Where limited partners claimed that the general partner of a dissolved limited partnership had improperly terminated priority distributions, the general partner was not entitled to summary judgment in its favor where it failed to provide any evidence that the partnership agreement allowed priority distributions to be terminated before termination of the partnership, cancellation of the partnership agreement or the winding up, liquidation or distribution of assets. *In re Cencom Cable Income Partners, L.P. Litigation,* 1997 WL 666970 (Del. Ch. Oct. 15, 1997), *reargument denied,* 1997 WL 770158 (Del. Ch. Dec. 3, 1997).

Termination of distributions not a breach of duty of loyalty — A general partner's decision to terminate customary distributions to limited partners was not a breach of duty of loyalty where the partnership agreement gave the general partner express authority to determine whether or not to make distributions and no facts were alleged that would show that the general partner used undistributed partnership cash solely for the benefit of the general partner or its affiliates. *Miller v. American Real Estate Partners, L.P.,* 2001 WL 1045643 (Del. Ch. Sept. 6, 2001).

Withdrawal of funds by general partner in excess of capital account — Limited partners' claim that the general partner withdrew funds from the partnership in excess of its capital account and in violation of the partnership agreement were direct, not derivative claims. Injuries from a direct reduction of the partnership's assets effected an almost immediate reduction in each existing partner's capital accounts. The injury to the partnership was immediately and irrevocably passed to the limited partners through a diminution of their capital accounts' value. *Anglo American Security Fund, L.P. v. S.R. Global International Fund, L.P.,* 829 A.2d 143 (Del. Ch. 2003).

§ 17-602. Withdrawal of general partner and assignment of general partner's partnership interest.

(a) A general partner may withdraw from a limited partnership at the time or upon the happening of events specified in the partnership agreement and in accordance with the partnership agreement. A partnership agreement may provide that a general partner shall not have the right to withdraw as a general partner of a limited partnership. Notwithstanding that a partnership agreement provides that a general partner does not have the right to withdraw as a general partner of a limited partnership, a general partner may withdraw from a limited partnership at any time by giving written notice to the other partners. If the withdrawal of a general partner violates a partnership agreement, in addition to any remedies otherwise available under applicable law, the limited partnership may recover from the withdrawing general partner damages for breach of the partnership agreement and offset the damages against the amount otherwise distributable to the withdrawing general partner.

(b) Notwithstanding anything to the contrary set forth in this chapter, a partnership agreement may provide that a general partner may not assign a partnership interest in a limited partnership prior to the dissolution and winding up of the limited partnership.

§ 17-603. Withdrawal of limited partner.

A limited partner may withdraw from a limited partnership only at the time or upon the happening of events specified in the partnership agreement and in accordance with the partnership agreement. Notwithstanding anything to the contrary under applicable law, unless a partnership agreement provides otherwise, a limited partner may not withdraw from a limited partnership prior to the dissolution and winding up of the limited partnership. Notwithstanding anything to the contrary under applicable law, a partnership agreement may provide that a partnership interest may not be assigned prior to the dissolution and winding up of the limited partnership.

Unless otherwise provided in a partnership agreement, a limited partnership whose original certificate of limited partnership was filed with the Secretary of State and effective on or prior to July 31, 1996, shall continue to be governed by this section as in effect on July 31, 1996, and shall not be governed by this section.

ANNOTATIONS

Applicability of Act — Under § 17-1104(b), the Revised Uniform Limited Partnership Act applies only to acts performed after January 1, 1985 by limited partnerships formed after July 1, 1973, so that when, as president of the corporate general partner of a limited partnership, a limited partner signed a 1975 amendment to the partnership agreement that added several new limited partners but omitted his own name as a limited partner, the issue of whether that limited partner technically withdrew from the partnership is governed by Del. Code Ann. tit. 6, § 1725, the predecessor to § 17-204. *Weltman v. Silna*, 879 F.2d 425 (8th Cir. 1989).

Suspension of right to withdraw — A limited partnership agreement which provided that it could be amended by written consent of all the partners was not orally modified to amend the agreement to suspend the power of a limited partner to withdraw from the partnership. *Continental Insurance Company v. Rutledge & Company, Inc.*, 750 A.2d 1219 (Del. Ch. 2000).

Decisions under prior law

Existing limited partner omitted — The validity of a limited partnership amendment, where an existing limited partner is not included in the amended version of the limited partnership membership composition, is not covered by the Delaware Limited Partnership Act, and, where also not covered by the original partnership agreement, the question should be resolved under section 1730 of the Act and the general presumptions and rules governing statutory construction. *Weltman v. Silna*, 739 F. Supp. 477 (E.D. Mo. 1990) *aff'd on other grounds*, 936 F.2d 358 (8th Cir. 1991), *cert. denied*, 502 U.S. 941, 112 S. Ct. 377 (1991).

Former limited partner; amendment of certificate — An amended certificate of limited partnership does not require the signature of a former limited partner who had already withdrawn from the partnership. *Weltman v. Silna*, 936 F.2d 358 (8th Cir. 1991), *cert. denied*, 112 S. Ct. 377 (1991).

Former limited partner; assignment of interest — Pursuant to section 1725(a)(2) of the Delaware Limited Partnership Act, a former limited partner is required to sign an amendment to the certificate of limited partnership only where such limited partner assigns his/her interest to another to be substituted in his/her place. *Weltman v. Silna*, 739 F. Supp. 477 (E.D. Mo. 1990), *aff'd on other grounds*, 936 F.2d 358 (8th Cir. 1991), *cert. denied*, 112 S. Ct. 377 (1991).

Withdrawal of limited partner — Under § 1724 of the Delaware limited partnership law (repealed in 1982), there were no conditions precedent to a limited partner effectively withdrawing from the limited partnership, so that amendment of the limited partnership certificate was not required for a limited partner to withdraw from the partnership. *Weltman v. Silna*, 936 F.2d 358 (8th Cir. 1991), *cert. denied*, 112 S. Ct. 377 (1991).

Withdrawal pursuant to agreement — Where limited partnership shifted its strategy from investing in publicly traded equities to investing in private equity, a limited partner's exercise of a right to withdraw from a limited partnership by giving timely notice of intent to withdraw did not violate implied covenant of good faith and fair dealing. Withdrawal was not in bad faith where at the time the partnership was formed the parties expected the partnership would invest in private equity and the withdrawal provisions were nonetheless agreed upon. *Continental Insurance Company v. Rutledge & Company, Inc.*, 750 A.2d 1219 (Del. Ch. 2000).

§ 17-604. Distribution upon withdrawal.

Except as provided in this subchapter, upon withdrawal any withdrawing partner is entitled to receive any distribution to which such partner is entitled under a partnership agreement and, if not otherwise provided in a partnership agreement, such partner is entitled to receive, within a reasonable time after withdrawal, the fair value of such partner's partnership interest in the limited partnership as of the date of withdrawal based upon such partner's right to share in distributions from the limited partnership.

ANNOTATIONS

Payment to removed general partner — Where general partner was removed by the limited partners, and the partnership agreement did not give the general partner any right to convert its interest to that of a limited partner, the removed general partner had no standing to bring claims based on contractual or fiduciary obligations. By its terms, Section 17-604 does not apply to a general partner who is involuntarily removed. However, looking to general partnership law, the removed general partner was entitled to receive the fair value of its interest, based on the net value of the interest as though the partnership had been liquidated. *Hillman v. Hillman*, 910 A.2d 262 (Del. Ch. 2006).

Payment to withdrawn partners — Former limited partners commenced involuntary bankruptcy proceeding against limited partnership. Partnership agreement obligated partnership to pay limited partners the value of their interest either in cash or securities within 30 days after notice of their expulsion from the partnership. "Securities" meant the investment securities held by the partnership, and thus general partner lacked authority to create new obligations of the partnership itself with later maturity date, denominate them "securities" and substitute them for the existing obligation to pay former limited partners. Thus, former limited partners held non-contingent bona fide claims and had standing under Section 303(b) of the Bankruptcy Code to commence involuntary bankruptcy proceeding. *In re Paper I Partners, L.P.*, 283 B.R. 661 (Bankr. S.D.N.Y. 2002).

§ 17-605. Distribution in kind.

Except as provided in the partnership agreement, a partner, regardless of the nature of the partner's contribution, has no right to demand and receive any distribution from a limited partnership in any form other than cash. Except as provided in the partnership agreement, a partner may not be compelled to accept a distribution of any asset in kind from a limited partnership to the extent that the percentage of the asset distributed to him exceeds a percentage of that asset which is equal to the percentage in which he shares in distributions from the limited partnership. Except as provided in the partnership agreement, a partner may be compelled to accept a distribution of any asset in kind from a limited partnership to the extent that the percentage of the asset distributed to him is equal to a percentage of that asset which is equal to the percentage in which the partner shares in distributions from the limited partnership.

§ 17-606. Right to distribution.

(a) Subject to § § 17-607 and 17-804 of this title, and unless otherwise provided in the partnership agreement, at the time a partner becomes entitled to receive a distribution, he or she has the status of, and is entitled to all remedies available to, a creditor of the limited partnership with respect to the distribution.

A partnership agreement may provide for the establishment of a record date with respect to allocations and distributions by a limited partnership.

ANNOTATIONS

Suit by limited partner against general partner as derivative claim — A suit by limited partners against the general partners for breach of fiduciary duty with respect to choice of investments was a derivative claim; the alleged injuries were to the partnership and not direct to the limited partners, even though the breach resulted in diminished income to the limited partners. *Litman v. Prudential-Bache Properties*, 611 A.2d 12 (Del. Ch. 1992).

§ 17-607. Limitations on distribution.

(a) A limited partnership shall not make a distribution to a partner to the extent that at the time of the distribution, after giving effect to the distribution, all liabilities of the limited partnership, other than liabilities to partners on account of their partnership interests and liabilities for which the recourse of creditors is limited to specified property of the limited partnership, exceed the fair value of the assets of the limited partnership, except that the fair value of property that is subject to a liability for which the recourse of creditors is limited shall be included in the assets of the limited partnership only to the extent that the fair value of that property exceeds that liability. For purposes of this subsection (a), the term "distribution" shall not include amounts constituting reasonable compensation for present or past services or reasonable payments made in the ordinary course of business pursuant to a bona fide retirement plan or other benefits program.

(b) A limited partner who receives a distribution in violation of subsection (a) of this section, and who knew at the time of the distribution that the distribution violated subsection (a) of this section, shall be liable to the limited partnership for the amount of the distribution. A limited partner who receives a distribution in violation of subsection (a) of this section, and who did not know at the time of the distribution that the distribution violated subsection (a) of this section, shall not be liable for the amount of the distribution. Subject to subsection (c) of this section, this subsection shall not affect any obligation or liability of a limited partner under an agreement or other applicable law for the amount of a distribution.

(c) Unless otherwise agreed, a limited partner who receives a distribution from a limited partnership shall have no liability under this chapter or other applicable law for the amount of the distribution after the expiration of 3 years from the date of the distribution.

ANNOTATIONS

Claim to recover excess distributions; statute of repose — Limited partners did not have to return alleged overpayment of distributions because claims to recover any such overpayments were barred by a Delaware three year statute of repose. The limited partners were residents of Illinois and under Illinois' five year statute of limitations such claims would not have been barred. But under the partnership agreement Delaware law applied and specifically referenced Section 17-607 (c) of the Delaware RULPA, which contained the three year statute of repose for claims challenging the amount of distributions. The distributions were allegedly made during a period when the partnership's assets were overvalued resulting in distributions that were, likewise, overvalued. *Freeman v. Williamson*, 383 Ill. App. 3d 993, 890 N.E.2d 1127 (2008).

Distribution date — Where limited partner exercised right to withdraw, and in lieu of cash distribution provided for in partnership agreement entered into a contract permitting payment at a later date, the "distribution" was the contract itself and occurred on the date the contract was entered into, not on the date that payments were made to the limited partner under the contract. *Pomeranz v. Museum Partners, L.P.*, 2005 WL 217039 (Del. Ch. Jan. 24, 2005).

Equitable tolling — Where defendants did not argue that the three-year limitations period in Section 17-607(c) could not be tolled, the court would assume (without deciding) that the three-year limitations period in Section 17-607(c) may be tolled under Delaware jurisprudence developed under other statutes of limitation. *Pomeranz v. Museum Partners, L.P.*, 2005 WL 217039 (Del. Ch. Jan. 24, 2005).

Subchapter VII
ASSIGNMENT OF PARTNERSHIP INTERESTS

§ 17-701. Nature of partnership interest.

A partnership interest is personal property. A partner has no interest in specific limited partnership property.

ANNOTATIONS

Limited partnership interest not an investment contract where limited partner retained material control — Where a limited partner retained substantial control over its investment through provisions in the partnership agreement, the partnership agreement was not an investment contract for federal securities laws purposes. The limitation on liability to third parties afforded by Section 17-303(b) does not equate with the limited partner's being a passive investor for purposes of federal securities laws. *Steinhardt Group, Inc. v. Citicorp*, 126 F.3d 144 (3d Cir. 1997).

Put right is equity security — A limited partner's right to require either the partnership or an affiliated corporation to purchase the limited partner's interest for cash, shares of the affiliate's stock, or a combination of both did not constitute a claim but was a form of equity security as defined in Section 101(16) of the Bankruptcy Code. *In re Einstein/Noah Bagel Corp.*, 257 B.R. 499 (U.S.B.C. D. Ariz. 2000).

§ 17-702. Assignment of partnership interest.

(a) Unless otherwise provided in the partnership agreement:

(1) A partnership interest is assignable in whole or in part;

(2) An assignment of a partnership interest does not dissolve a limited partnership or entitle the assignee to become or to exercise any rights or powers of a partner;

(3) An assignment of a partnership interest entitles the assignee to share in such profits and losses, to receive such distribution or distributions, and to receive such allocation of income, gain, loss, deduction, or credit or similar item to which the assignor was entitled, to the extent assigned; and

(4) A partner ceases to be a partner and to have the power to exercise any rights or powers of a partner upon assignment of all of his partnership interest. Unless otherwise provided in a partnership agreement, the pledge of, or granting of a security interest, lien or other encumbrance in or against, any or all of the partnership interest of a partner shall not cause the partner to cease to be a partner or to have the power to exercise any rights or powers of a partner.

(b) Unless otherwise provided in a partnership agreement, a partner's interest in a limited partnership may be evidenced by a certificate of partnership interest issued by the limited partnership. A partnership agreement may provide for the assignment or transfer of any partnership interest represented by such a certificate and make other provisions with respect to such certificates. A limited partnership shall not have the power to issue a certificate of partnership interest in bearer form.

(c) Unless otherwise provided in a partnership agreement and except to the extent assumed by agreement, until an assignee of a partnership interest becomes a partner, the assignee shall have no liability as a partner solely as a result of the assignment.

(d) Unless otherwise provided in the partnership agreement, a limited partnership may acquire, by purchase, redemption or otherwise, any partnership interest or other interest of a partner in the limited partnership. Unless otherwise provided in the partnership agreement, any such interest so acquired by the limited partnership shall be deemed canceled.

ANNOTATIONS

Consent to transfer; duty of good faith and fair dealing — A general partner with sole and absolute discretion under the partnership agreement to withhold consent to a transfer of shares of a corporate limited partner cannot withhold consent out of self-interest, or to advance the interests of other partners that are unrelated to the partnership. Such conduct implicates the covenant of good faith and fair dealing implied in every limited partnership agreement and the general partner's duty of loyalty. *Fitzgerald v. Cantor*, 1999 Del. Ch. LEXIS 55 (Mar. 23, 1999).

Merger of corporate general partner — Merger of a corporate general partner into another wholly-owned corporation of the same parent does not violate an anti-transfer clause of the partnership agreement; absent contract language expressly treating the point, the law should not conclusively presume that a general partner's identity is invariably a factor so inherently material that under no circumstances would the parties have intended to permit any change in that identity, especially where the transaction did not materially increase the risks to or otherwise harm the limited partners. *Star Cellular Telephone Company, Inc. v. Baton Rouge CGSA, Inc.*, 1993 Del. Ch. LEXIS 158 (July 30, 1993), *aff'd*, 647 A.2d 382 (Del. 1994).

Sale of partnership or partnership interest; bankruptcy; payoff of secured creditor — The Chapter 11 plan of two debtors, limited partners, was confirmed because they would be able to sell the limited partnership within a year, reasonable time, as required under the Bankruptcy Code. The prompt sale of the partnership (DE law governed) would generate sufficient resources for the debtor limited partners to pay off their secured creditors that opposed the confirmation of the plan. The plan would maximize the value to the limited partners by selling the partnership assets as a going concern. The debtor limited partners also had a fall-back plan to sell their interests if the partnership itself could not be sold, which enhanced the feasibility of the plan. *In re South Canaan Cellular Invs., Inc.*, 2010 WL 1257747 (Bankr. E.D. Pa. 2010) (DE law applied).

Sale of stock of corporate general partner — Sale of all of the stock of a corporate general partner does not constitute a sale or transfer of the corporate general partner's interest as a general partner in a limited partnership, and thus does not violate a provision in a partnership agreement that any sale or transfer by the general partner of its interest in the partnership must be approved in advance by limited partners. *In re Integrated Resources, Inc.*, Case No. 90-B-10411 (CB) 1990 WL 325414 (Bankr. S.D.N.Y. Oct. 22, 1990).

Standing of assignee — Where a partnership agreement provided that an assignee of a limited partnership interest had no right to vote until admitted as a substituted limited partner, assignee who had not been so admitted in accordance with the provisions of the partnership agreement lacked standing to bring a claim for breach of fiduciary duty relating to the exercise of his right to vote by written consent. *U-H Acquisition Co. v. Barbo*, 1994 Del. Ch. LEXIS 9 (Jan. 28, 1994, revised January 31, 1994).

Transfer in breach of contract — Allegation by general partner that limited partner transferred limited partnership interests without general partner's consent in violation of the partnership agreement stated a claim for breach of contract where the partnership agreement expressly provided that interests could be transferred only with the consent of the general partner. *Fitzgerald v. Cantor*, 1998 Del. Ch. LEXIS 218 (Nov. 6, 1998).

Voting rights of assignees — Where the partnership agreement, assignment agreement and instrument of assignment provided by the limited partnership are ambiguous and do not expressly state whether subsequent assignees have voting rights, the agreements must be construed according to the reasonable expectations of investors who purchase additional limited partnership interests; subsequent assignees that acquired their limited partnership interests pursuant to a tender offer have a right to vote because they could read the agreements as providing for such voting rights. *Arvida/JMB Partners, L.P. v. Vanderbilt Income and Growth Assoc., L.L.C.*, 1997 Del. Ch. LEXIS 79 (May 23, 1997), *appeal dismissed*, 700 A.2d 735 (Del. 1997); *see also, Vanderbilt Income and Growth Assoc., L.L.C. v. Arvida/JMB Managers, Inc.*, 691 A.2d 609 (Del. 1996) (trial court cannot resolve ambiguity in documents on a motion to dismiss) (reversing *Vanderbilt Income and Growth Assoc., L.L.C. v. Arvida/JBM Managers, Inc.*, 1996 WL 652773 (Del. Ch. Nov. 4, 1996, revised Nov. 7, 1996).

§ 17-703. Partner's partnership interest subject to charging order.

(a) On application by a judgment creditor of a partner or of a partner's assignee, a court having jurisdiction may charge the partnership interest of the judgment debtor to satisfy the judgment. To the extent so charged, the judgment creditor has only the right to receive any distribution or distributions to which the judgment debtor would otherwise have been entitled in respect of such partnership interest.

(b) A charging order constitutes a lien on the judgment debtor's partnership interest.

(c) This chapter does not deprive a partner or partner's assignee of a right under exemption laws with respect to the judgment debtor's partnership interest.

(d) The entry of a charging order is the exclusive remedy by which a judgment creditor of a partner or of a partner's assignee may satisfy a judgment out of the judgment debtor's partnership interest.

(e) No creditor of a partner or of a partner's assignee shall have any right to obtain possession of, or otherwise exercise legal or equitable remedies with respect to, the property of the limited partnership.

(f) The Court of Chancery shall have jurisdiction to hear and determine any matter relating to any such charging order.

ANNOTATIONS

Decisions under prior law

Divorced spouse as judgment creditor — Although lacking subject matter jurisdiction, the court stated that, to be considered a "judgment creditor" in order to obtain an order under § 17-703 charging a partner's interest in a limited partnership with payment of amounts owing that partner's former spouse for support, the partner's spouse would have to reduce her foreign decree of divorce to a domestic judgment bearing an "amount." *MacDonald v. MacDonald*, 1986 WL 5480 (Del. Ch. May 9, 1986).

Execution sale — Although lacking subject matter jurisdiction, the court stated that execution sale of a limited partnership interest is probably unavailable as a remedy to satisfy the payment of spousal support arising from a foreign decree of divorce. *MacDonald v. MacDonald*, 1986 WL 5480 (Del. Ch. May 9, 1986).

Partnership not liable for capital contribution loan — Creditor who loaned a general partner money for the general partner's capital contribution to a limited partnership was not a creditor of the limited partnership where the partnership had not signed the note, no facts supported the claim that the general partner was acting as an agent of the limited partnership in borrowing the money, and the creditor knew it was dealing with an individual who was making a capital contribution to an entity, and not dealing with the entity itself. *Clapp. v. Fields*, 1992 Del. Ch. LEXIS 79 (Apr. 3, 1992).

Partnership not liable to creditor of general partner — A third party with notice that a transaction entered into by a general partner of a limited partnership in the general partner's individual capacity and which was outside the partnership's business cannot rely on the limited partnership's credit. *Abt v. Harmony Mill Limited Partnership*, 1992 Del. Ch. LEXIS 267 (Del. Ch. Dec. 18, 1992).

§ 17-704. Right of assignee to become limited partner.

(a) An assignee of a partnership interest, including an assignee of a general partner, may become a limited partner:

(1) As provided in the partnership agreement; or

(2) Unless otherwise provided in the partnership agreement, upon the affirmative vote or written consent of all partners.

(b) An assignee who has become a limited partner has, to the extent assigned, the rights and powers, and is subject to the restrictions and liabilities, of a limited partner under the partnership agreement and this chapter. Notwithstanding the foregoing, unless otherwise provided in the partnership agreement, an assignee who becomes a limited partner is liable for the obligations of his assignor to make contributions as provided in § 17-502 of this title, but shall not be liable for the obligations of his assignor under subchapter VI of this chapter. However, the assignee is not obligated for liabilities, including the obligations of his assignor to make contributions as provided in § 17-502 of this title, unknown to the assignee at the time he became a limited partner and which could not be ascertained from the partnership agreement.

(c) Whether or not an assignee of a partnership interest becomes a limited partner, the assignor is not released from his liability to the limited partnership under subchapters V and VI of this chapter.

ANNOTATIONS

Admission of transferee as substitute limited partner — A plaintiff was held to have been admitted as a substitute limited partner where the NASD forms used by the partnership for registering transfers of interests constituted a request for admission as a substitute limited partner, the general partner was found to have delegated to the partnership's transfer agent the general partner's authority to consent not only to assignments but to admission of a transferee as a substituted limited partner and the transfer agent had confirmed to the plaintiff its status as a limited partner. *In re American Tax Credit Limited Partnerships*, 714 A.2d 87 (Del. Ch. 1997), *aff'd*, 707 A.2d 765 (Del. 1998).

Voting rights of assignees — Where the partnership agreement, assignment agreement and instrument of assignment provided by the limited partnership are ambiguous and do not expressly state whether subsequent assignees have voting rights, the agreements must be construed according to the reasonable expectations of investors who purchase additional limited partnership interests; subsequent assignees that acquired their limited partnership interest pursuant to a tender offer have a right to vote because they could read the agreements as providing for such voting rights. *Arvida/JMB Partners, L.P. v. Vanderbilt Income and Growth Assoc., L.L.C.*, 1997 Del. Ch. LEXIS 79 (Del. Ch. May 23, 1997), *appeal dismissed*, 700 A.2d 735 (Del. 1997); *see also, Vanderbilt Income and Growth Assoc., L.L.C. v. Arvida/JMB Managers, Inc.*, 691 A.2d 609 (Del. 1996) (trial court cannot resolve ambiguity in documents on a motion to dismiss) (reversing *Vanderbilt Income and Growth Assoc., L.L.C. v. Arvida/JMB Managers, Inc.*, 1996 WL 652773 (Del. Ch. Nov. 4, 1996, revised Nov. 7, 1996).

§ 17-705. Powers of estate of deceased or incompetent partner.

If a partner who is an individual dies or a court of competent jurisdiction adjudges him to be incompetent to manage his person or his property, the partner's personal representative may exercise all of the partner's rights for the purpose of settling his estate or administering his property, including any power under the partnership agreement of an assignee to become a limited partner. If a partner is a corporation, trust or other entity and is dissolved or terminated, the powers of that partner may be exercised by its personal representative.

Subchapter VIII
DISSOLUTION

§ 17-801. Nonjudicial dissolution.

A limited partnership is dissolved and its affairs shall be wound up upon the first to occur of the following:

(1) At the time specified in a partnership agreement, but if no such time is set forth in the partnership agreement, then the limited partnership shall have a perpetual existence.

(2) Unless otherwise provided in a partnership agreement, upon the affirmative vote or written consent of (a) all general partners and (b) the limited partners of a limited partnership or, if there is more than one class or group of limited partners, then by each class or group of limited partners, in either case, by limited partners who own more than two-thirds of the then current percentage or other interest in the profits of the limited partnership owned by all of the limited partners or by the limited partners in each class or group, as appropriate;

(3) An event of withdrawal of a general partner unless at the time there is at least 1 other general partner and the partnership agreement permits the business of the limited partnership to be carried on by the remaining general partner and that partner does so, but the limited partnership is not dissolved and is not required to be wound up by reason of any event of withdrawal if (i) within 90 days or such other period as is provided for in a partnership agreement after the withdrawal either (A) if provided for in the partnership

agreement, the then-current percentage or other interest in the profits of the limited partnership specified in the partnership agreement owned by the remaining partners agree, in writing or vote, to continue the business of the limited partnership and to appoint, effective as of the date of withdrawal, 1 or more additional general partners if necessary or desired, or (B) if no such right to agree or vote to continue the business of the limited partnership and to appoint one or more additional general partners is provided for in the partnership agreement, then more than 50% of the then-current percentage or other interest in the profits of the limited partnership owned by the remaining partners or, if there is more than 1 class or group of remaining partners, then more than 50% of the then-current percentage or other interest in the profits of the limited partnership owned by each class or classes or group or groups of remaining partners agree, in writing or vote, to continue the business of the limited partnership and to appoint, effective as of the date of withdrawal, 1 or more additional general partners if necessary or desired, or (ii) the business of the limited partnership is continued pursuant to a right to continue stated in the partnership agreement and; the appointment, effective as of the date of withdrawal, of 1 or more additional general partners if necessary or desired;

(4) At the time there are no limited partners; provided that the limited partnership is not dissolved and is not required to be wound up if:

a. Unless otherwise provided in a partnership agreement, within 90 days or such other period as is provided for in the partnership agreement after the occurrence of the event that caused the last remaining limited partner to cease to be a limited partner, the personal representative of the last remaining limited partner and all of the general partners agree, in writing or by vote, to continue the business of the limited partnership and to the admission of the personal representative of such limited partner or its nominee or designee to the limited partnership as a limited partner, effective as of the occurrence of the event that caused the last remaining limited partner to cease to be a limited partner; provided, that a partnership agreement may provide that the general partners or the personal representative of the last remaining limited partner shall be obligated to agree in writing to continue the business of the limited partnership and to the admission of the personal representative of such limited partner or its nominee or designee to the limited partnership as a limited partner, effective as of the occurrence of the event that caused the last limited partner to cease to be a limited partner; or

b. A limited partner is admitted to the limited partnership in the manner provided for in the partnership agreement, effective as of the occurrence of the event that caused the last remaining limited partner to cease to be a limited partner, within 90 days or such other period as is provided for in the partnership agreement after the occurrence of the event that caused the last remaining limited partner to cease to be a limited partner, pursuant to a provision of the partnership agreement that specifically provides for the admission of a limited partner to the limited partnership after there is no longer a remaining limited partner of the limited partnership.

(5) Upon the happening of events specified in a partnership agreement; or

(6) Entry of a decree of judicial dissolution under § 17-802 of this title.

ANNOTATIONS

Appointment of a receiver: dissolution not imminent — The appointment of a receiver for a Delaware limited partnership was not justified where one limited partner claimed that another partner was collecting monies on behalf of the partnership but failing to remit loan repayments and partnership distributions to that limited partner. The partnership was not insolvent and the limited partner who sought the receiver did not show any fraud that would pose an imminent danger of loss of partnership assets or threaten the existence of the partnership. Only the distributions of one limited partner were at issue and there was an adequate remedy at law. *Sharon Gardens Associates, L.P. v. Florescue*, 629 So.2d 1002 (Fla. Ct. App. 4 Dist. 1993).

Dissolution by express will — Where a limited partnership agreement contained no provisions limiting the dissolution rights of the partners, the partners retained the right to dissolve the partnership by the express will of any partner. *Active Asset Recovery, Inc. v. Real Estate Asset Recovery Services, Inc.*, 1999 WL 743479 (Del. Ch. Sept 10, 1999).

Proxy statement disclosure did not trigger dissolution provision — Where limited partnership agreement provided that the partnership would be dissolved upon a written determination by the general partner that future revenues would be sufficient to pay projected costs and expenses or that continued operation of the partnership was not in the best interest of the partners, the general partner's discussion in a proxy statement that the partnership would not have sufficient revenue to pay distributions in the future and that the general partner was therefore recommending that the limited partnership be converted into a corporation if the conversion were approved by the requisite vote of limited partners did not constitute a written determination resulting in a dissolution of the partnership under the terms of the partnership agreement. *In re Mesa Limited Partnership Preferred Unitholders Litigation*, 1991 Del. Ch. LEXIS 214 (Del. Ch. Dec. 10, 1991), *appeal refused*, 608 A.2d 728 (Del. 1992).

Withdrawal of all limited partners — A limited partnership is dissolved as a matter of law after all limited partners have withdrawn. *The Continental Insurance Company v. Rutledge & Company, Inc.*, 2000 WL 62951 (Del. Ch. Jan 10, 2000).

§ 17-802. Judicial dissolution.

On application by or for a partner the Court of Chancery may decree dissolution of a limited partnership whenever it is not reasonably practicable to carry on the business in conformity with the partnership agreement.

ANNOTATIONS

Arbitration of dissolution claims — Where one of three relevant partnership agreements required arbitration of dissolution claims and two of the three relevant partnership agreements do not, given the burden involved in the simultaneous litigation of the same basic controversy with the same witnesses and attorneys in two different fora, the Delaware Chancery action is stayed pending a decision in the arbitration proceeding. *Salzman v. Canaan Capital Partners, L.P.*, 1996 WL 422341 (Del. Ch. July 23, 1996).

Breach of duty may justify dissolution — Material breaches of a fiduciary duty that make continuation of business, as contemplated by the partnership agreement, impractical may justify dissolution. *Red Sail Easter Limited Partners, L.P. v. Radio City Music Hall Prods., Inc.*, 1992 Del. Ch. LEXIS 224 (Del. Ch. Oct. 6, 1992).

Date of dissolution — The date of entry of a decree of dissolution under Section 17-802 does not necessarily fix the date of dissolution. Where an event of dissolution under Section 17-801 had occurred prior to the entry of a decree of dissolution under Section 17-802, the limited partnership was dissolved on the earlier date. *Active Asset Recovery, Inc. v. Real Estate Asset Recovery Services, Inc.*, 1999 WL 743479 (Del. Ch. Sept 10, 1999).

Dissolution of limited partnership — Limited partnership will not be dissolved where the limited partner failed to point to specific facts to demonstrate that the business of the limited partnership was no longer reasonably practicable to continue. *Cincinnati Bell Cellular Systems Co. v. Ameritech Mobile Phone Service of Cincinnati, Inc.*, 1996 Del. Ch. LEXIS 116 (Del. Ch. Sept. 3, 1996), *aff'd*, 1997 Del. LEXIS 58 (Del. Feb. 11, 1997).

Dissolution is denied — Dissolution is denied after trial when the general partner competently and in good faith managed the principal business of the partnership and the partnership's business remains a viable economic prospect: efforts to develop a specific business of the partnership were pursued in good faith, reasonably and with no material failure, although failure to pursue the specific business would not have constituted a material breach of the partnership agreement. *Red Sail Easter Limited Partners, L.P. v. Radio City Music Hall Productions, Inc.*, 1993 Del. Ch. LEXIS 154 (Del. Ch. July 28, 1993).

Impracticality under original agreement — Judicial dissolution under Section 17-802 was appropriate where the limited partnership could not carry on its business under the terms of the original partnership agreement, and substantial and material amendments to the original agreement would be necessary to enable the partnership to carry out the general purpose for which it was formed. *Sriram v. Preferred Income Fund III Limited Partnership*, 22 F.3d 498 (2d Cir. 1994).

Insolvency — For purposes of Section 17-802, it was not reasonably practicable to carry on the business of the limited partnership were the value of the partnership's property was less than the debt and liens encumbering the property, the partnership had no equity in its property, the principal tenant was insolvent, redevelopment of the property was highly unlikely, and the partnership lacked capital to make the financial concessions and renovations necessary to attract new tenants. The generation of continued tax losses that might benefit limited partners was not in conformity with the partnership agreement, which stated that the partnership's purposes were to invest in and develop real estate "for profit and as an investment." *PC Tower Center, Inc. v. Tower Center Development Assocs. Limited Partnership*, 1989 Del. Ch. LEXIS 72 (Del. Ch. June 8, 1989).

Removal and appointment of receiver — Where a court concluded that the general partner of a limited partnership could not continue in that capacity because of gross misconduct and arbitrary management, it could grant the limited partners the more limited relief of removal of the general partner and appointment of a receiver until such time as a successor general partner could be named rather than dissolving the partnership. *Curley v. Brignoli Curley and Roberts Assocs.*, 746 F. Supp. 1208 (S.D.N.Y. 1989), *aff'd*, 915 F.2d 81 (2d Cir. 1990), *cert. denied*, 499 U.S. 955 (1991) (applying Delaware law).

Standard is exclusive — The legal standard for judicial dissolution of a limited partnership is established by Section 17-802 and not by any broader standard derived from general partnership law. *Red Sail Easter Limited Partners, L.P. v. Radio City Music Hall Productions, Inc.*, 1992 Del. Ch. LEXIS 224 (Del. Ch. Oct. 6, 1992).

Standard is reasonable practicability — The standard for judicial dissolution under Section 17-802 is one of reasonable practicability, not impossibility or complete frustration of the purposes for which the limited partnership was formed. *PC Tower Center, Inc. v. Tower Center Development Assocs. Limited Partnership*, 1989 Del. Ch. LEXIS 72 (Del. Ch. June 8, 1989).

§ 17-803. Winding up.

(a) Unless otherwise provided in the partnership agreement, the general partners who have not wrongfully dissolved a limited partnership or, if none, the limited partners, or a person approved by the limited partners or, if there is more than 1 class or group of limited partners, then by each class or group of limited partners, in either case, by limited partners who own more than 50 percent of the then current percentage or other interest in the profits of the limited partnership owned by all of the limited partners or by the limited partners in each class or group, as appropriate may wind up the limited partnership's affairs; but the Court of Chancery, upon cause shown, may wind up the limited partnership's affairs upon application of any partner, the partner's personal representative or assignee, and in connection therewith, may appoint a liquidating trustee.

(b) Upon dissolution of a limited partnership and until the filing of a certificate of cancellation as provided in § 17-203 of this title, the persons winding up the limited partnership's affairs may, in the name of, and for and on behalf of, the limited partnership, prosecute and defend suits, whether civil, criminal or administrative, gradually settle and close the limited partnership's business, dispose of and convey the limited partnership's property, discharge or make reasonable provision for the limited partnership's liabilities, and distribute to the partners any remaining assets of the limited partnership, all without affecting the liability of limited partners and without imposing the liability of a general partner on a liquidating trustee.

ANNOTATIONS

Appointment of liquidating trustee — Appointment of an independent liquidating trustee under Section 17-803(a) was proper in connection with a judicial dissolution where the general partner had material conflicts of interest. Where the same person was general partner of a borrower partnership and a lender partnership, and in winding up the two partnerships the lender partnership might be advantaged by foreclosure on properties owned by the borrower partnership, and the borrower partnership might be disadvantaged by foreclosure and loss of equity, the general partner faced a conflict of interest that constituted ample "cause shown" for purposes of Section 17-803(a). *Sriram v. Preferred Income Fund III Limited Partnership*, 22 F.3d 498 (2d Cir. 1994).

§ 17-804. Distribution of assets.

(a) Upon the winding up of a limited partnership, the assets shall be distributed as follows:

(1) To creditors, including partners who are creditors, to the extent otherwise permitted by law, in satisfaction of liabilities of the limited partnership (whether by payment or the making of reasonable provision for payment thereof) other than liabilities for which reasonable provision for payment has been made and liabilities for distributions to partners and former partners under § 17-601 or § 17-604 of this title;

(2) Unless otherwise provided in the partnership agreement, to partners and former partners in satisfaction of liabilities for distributions under § 17-601 or § 17-604 of this title; and

(3) Unless otherwise provided in the partnership agreement, to partners first for the return of their contributions and second respecting their partnership interests, in the proportions in which the partners share in distributions.

(b) A limited partnership which has dissolved:

(1) Shall pay or make reasonable provision to pay all claims and obligations, including all contingent, conditional or unmatured contractual claims, known to the limited partnership;

(2) Shall make such provision as will be reasonably likely to be sufficient to provide compensation for any claim against the limited partnership which is the subject of a pending action, suit or proceeding to which the limited partnership is a party; and

(3) Shall make such provision as will be reasonably likely to be sufficient to provide compensation for claims that have not been made known to the limited partnership or that have not arisen but that, based on facts known to the limited partnership, are likely to arise or to become known to the limited partnership within 10 years after the date of dissolution. If there are sufficient assets, such claims and obligations shall be paid in full and any such provision for payment made shall be made in full. If there are insufficient assets, such claims and obligations shall be paid or provided for according to their priority and, among claims of equal priority, ratably to the extent of assets available therefor. Unless otherwise provided in the partnership agreement, any remaining assets shall be distributed as provided in this chapter. Any liquidating trustee winding up a limited partnership's affairs who has complied with this section shall not be personally liable to the claimants of the dissolved limited partnership by reason of such person's actions in winding up the limited partnership.

(c) A limited partner who receives a distribution in violation of subsection (a) of this section, and who knew at the time of the distribution that the distribution violated subsection (a) of this section, shall be liable to the limited partnership for the amount of the distribution. For purposes of the immediately preceding sentence, the term "distribution" shall not include amounts constituting reasonable compensation for present or past services or reasonable payments made in the ordinary course of business pursuant to a bona fide retirement plan or other benefits program. A limited partner who receives a distribution in violation of subsection (a) of this section, and who did not know at the time of the distribution that the distribution violated subsection (a) of this section, shall not be liable for the amount of the distribution. Subject to subsection (d) of this section, this subsection shall not affect any obligation or liability of a limited partner under an agreement or other applicable law for the amount of a distribution.

(d) Unless otherwise agreed, a limited partner who receives a distribution from a limited partnership to which this section applies shall have no liability under this chapter or other applicable law for the amount of the distribution after the expiration of 3 years from the date of distribution.

(e) Section 17-607 of this title shall not apply to a distribution to which this section applies.

ANNOTATIONS

Calculation of liquidating distributions — Where partnership agreement provided that the partnership's balance sheet was to be prepared in accordance with generally accepted accounting practices, the general partner was not entitled to base liquidating distributions on the general partner's unilateral determination that distributions should be calculated using a hypothetical adjustment based on what the general partner believed the partnership's balance sheet would look like if a limited partner had not taken certain actions that the general partner believed breached the partnership agreement. Nor was general partner entitled to recoupment with respect to alleged violations as to which the statute of limitations had run. *TIFD III-X LLC v. Fruehauf Production Company, L.L C.*, 2004 WL 1517135 (Del. Ch. June 29, 2004).

Claims of limited partners for equitable relief — Section 17-804 establishes a process by which the rights of parties to which the limited partnership is (or may be) obligated are protected. The claims encompassed by Section 17-804(b) are not limited to those of creditors against the limited partnership, but include claims of derivative claimants. Equitable rights as well as monetary claims are protected. *In re CC&F Fox Hill Associates Limited Partnership*, 1997 WL 349236 (Del. Ch. June 13, 1997), *reh'g denied*, 1997 WL 525841 (Del. Ch. July 7, 1997).

Dissolution; accounting — Pursuant to the Delaware Revised Uniform Limited Partnership Act (DRULPA) Section 17-1105, courts apply the provisions of the Delaware Uniform Partnership Law (DUPL) to determine the rules governing accounting for a limited partnership in the event of dissolution. DRULPA did not include provisions concerning dissolution. DUPL states that each partner is entitled to a settlement of all partnership accounts in the event of dissolution (applying Delaware law). *Mizrahi v. Chanel, Inc.*, 746 N.Y.S.2d 808 (Sup. Ct. 2001).

Distribution of assets; recoupment claims — In an action to distribute partnership assets after the limited partner exercised its right to cause the partnership's dissolution, the general partner could not seek recoupment for alleged breaches by the limited partner of the partnership agreement where these claims were already time-barred. These claims were not only already time-barred but also derivative (i.e., they belonged to the partnership). They were based on allegations of interference by the limited partner in the management of the partnership causing loss of partnership profits. These claims did not have the required transactional nexus with the distribution of the partnership's assets upon its dissolution to overcome the fact that they were time-barred, and did not spring back into life when interpreting the payout provisions upon dissolution. *TIFD III - X LLC v. Fruehauf Production Company, Ltd.*, 883 A.2d 854 (Del. Ch. 2004).

Distribution of intellectual property; priority of creditors — Although a limited partnership agreement may modify the distribution of assets of the partnership following a voluntary dissolution, it may not modify the priority given to creditors. Intellectual property — a partnership asset — would be distributed to creditors to satisfy outstanding liabilities before it would be distributed to a limited partner (applying Delaware law). *Mizrahi v. Chanel, Inc.*, 746 N.Y.S.2d 808 (Sup. Ct. 2001).

Distributions — Distributions of capital and earnings to partners in respect of the partnership interest are authorized even if all creditors have not yet been paid, provided that an adequate reserve is established for all such creditors. *Boesky v. CX Partners, L.P.*, 1988 Del. Ch. LEXIS 60 (Del. Ch. April 28, 1988).

Duties of liquidating partner — The duties of a liquidating partner are to gather the firm's assets, to pay creditors or make adequate provisions for the payment of valid claims, and to distribute the remaining funds to the firm's partners in the manner provided for in the firm's governing instrument. *Boesky v. CX Partners, L.P.*, 1988 Del. Ch. LEXIS 60 (Del. Ch. April 28, 1988).

Non-pro rata distribution to partners — Where a liquidating partner proposed a non-pro rata distribution to partners, excluding from the distribution those partners against whom the liquidating partner believed the partnership had a valid claim, the proposed non-pro rata distribution did not constitute a breach of fiduciary duty because it was proposed in good faith and in pursuit of what the liquidating partner believed to be the best interests of the partnership; however, the liquidating partner could not effect the non-pro rata distribution in violation of provisions in the agreement of limited partnership that precluded any limited partner from having a priority over any other limited partner in respect of distributions. *Boesky v. CX Partners, L.P.*, 1988 Del. Ch. LEXIS 60 (Del. Ch. April 28, 1988).

Powers of liquidating partner to amend agreement — Where the partnership agreement conferred upon the liquidating partner all of the rights and powers over the assets and liabilities of the partnership which the general partner had over the assets and liabilities of the partnership during the term of the partnership, such power did not include the general partner's power to consent to an amendment to the agreement of limited partnership following dissolution. *Boesky v. CX Partners, L.P.*, 1988 Del. Ch. LEXIS 60 (Del. Ch. April 28, 1988).

Reimbursement for litigation expense in winding up — General partner that incurs reasonable litigation expenses necessary to the winding up of the partnership may recover such expenses. The general partner has the rights of a partner in a general partnership, which include the right to receive reasonable compensation for the task of winding up. That right includes the right to recover reasonable litigation expenses incurred in winding up. *Active Asset Recovery, Inc. v. Real Estate Asset Recovery Services, Inc.*, 1999 WL 743479 (Del. Ch. Sept. 10, 1999).

Request for accounting — Request by limited partners for an accounting falls within the category of "contingent, conditional or unmatured claims and obligations" and general partners must make reasonable provisions to cover the claim in connection with winding up the partnership. *In re CC&F Fox Hill Associates Limited Partnership*, 1997 WL 349236 (Del. Ch. June 13, 1997), *reh'g denied*, 1997 WL 525841 (Del. Ch. July 7, 1997).

Reserves for contingent claims — A person claiming to be a creditor of a partnership in dissolution is entitled to adequate security before distributions are made to partners pursuant to § 17-804. Such security may, in appropriate cases, be afforded by the general assets left in the partnership, even if not set up in discreet reserve accounts. Where the claim is unliquidated or contingent, what constitutes adequate security is a question of judgment. A liquidating trustee's judgment as to what constitutes adequate security, even when made in good faith and advisedly, is not entitled to the benefits of the business judgment rule. It is inescapably the function of the court that supervises the liquidation to make an independent judgment of the adequacy of such security when it is challenged. Where a liquidating trustee elects to distribute assets to partners in respect of the partnership interest before either all creditors have been paid or actually funded (i.e., dollar for dollar) and segregated reserves for their claims have been established, it is the burden of the liquidating trustee to persuade the court that adequate security for the payment of such claims has been provided. In appropriate circumstances, adequate security for contingent, unliquidated claims may be provided by an enforceable undertaking by partners to whom early liquidating distributions are to be made requiring each distributee to submit to the jurisdiction of the court and to return part or all of any distribution to the partnership to the extent necessary to satisfy any judgment or settled claim against it. *Boesky v. CX Partners, L.P.*, 1988 Del. Ch. LEXIS 60 (Del. Ch. April 28, 1988).

Termination of distributions — Where limited partners claimed that the general partner of a dissolved limited partnership had improperly terminated priority distributions, the general partner was not entitled to summary judgment in its favor where it failed to provide any evidence that the partnership agreement allowed priority distributions to be terminated before termination of the partnership, cancellation of the partnership agreement or the winding up, liquidation or distribution of assets. *In re Cencom Cable Income Partners, L.P. Litigation*, 1997 WL 666970 (Del. Ch. Oct. 15, 1997), *reargument denied*, 1997 WL 770158 (Del. Ch. Dec. 3, 1997).

Valuation of assets for distribution — Section 17-804 provides for the distribution of assets to partners. A going concern valuation of the partnership is not relevant. Limited partners receive their proportionate share of assets, not the value of their proportionate ownership interests in the limited partnership as a going concern. *Active Asset Recovery, Inc. v. Real Estate Asset Recovery Services, Inc.*, 1999 WL 743479 (Del. Ch. Sept. 10, 1999).

§ 17-805. Trustees or receivers for limited partnerships; appointment; powers; duties.

When the certificate of limited partnership of any limited partnership formed under this chapter shall be canceled by the filing of a certificate of cancellation pursuant to § 17-203 of this chapter, the Court of Chancery, on application of any creditor or partner of the limited partnership, or any other person who shows good cause therefor, at any time, may either appoint one or more of the general partners of the limited partnership to be trustees, or appoint one or more persons to be receivers, of and for the limited partnership, to take charge of the limited partnership's property, and to collect the debts and property due and belonging to the limited partnership, with the power to prosecute and defend, in the name of the limited partnership, or otherwise, all such suits as may be necessary or proper for the purposes aforesaid, and to appoint an agent or agents under them, and to do all other acts which might be done by the limited partnership, if in being, that may be necessary for the final settlement of the unfinished business of the limited partnership. The powers of the trustees or receivers may be continued as long as the Court of Chancery shall think necessary for the purposes aforesaid.

§ 17-806. Revocation of dissolution.

Notwithstanding the occurrence of an event set forth in § 6/17-801(1), (2), (3), (4) or (5) of this title, the limited partnership shall not be dissolved and its affairs shall not be wound up if, prior to the filing of a certificate of cancellation in the office of the Secretary of State, the business of the limited partnership is continued, effective as of the occurrence of such event, pursuant to the affirmative vote or written consent of (1) all remaining general partners and all remaining limited partners of the limited partnership, (2) all remaining general partners and the personal representative of the last remaining limited partner of the limited partnership if there is no remaining limited partner, (3) all remaining limited partners if there is no remaining general partner or (4) the personal representative of the last remaining limited partner if there is no remaining limited partner and no remaining general partner (and, in each instance, any other person whose approval is required under the partnership agreement to revoke a dissolution pursuant to this section), provided, however, if the dissolution was caused by a vote or written consent, the dissolution shall not be revoked unless each general partner and limited partner and other person (or their respective personal representatives) who voted in favor of, or consented to, the dissolution has voted or consented in writing to continue the business of the limited partnership. If there is no remaining general partner of the limited partnership and all remaining limited partners or, if there is no remaining limited partner, the personal representative of the last remaining limited partner, vote in favor of or consent to the continuation of the business of the limited partnership, such limited partners or personal representative, as applicable, shall be required to agree in writing to appoint 1 or more general partners effective as of the date of withdrawal of the last general partner, and if there is no remaining limited partner of the limited partnership and the personal representative of the last remaining limited partner votes in favor of or consents to the continuation of the business of the limited partnership, such personal representative shall be required to agree in writing to the admission of the personal representative of such limited partner or its nominee or designee to the limited partnership as a limited partner, effective as of the occurrence of the event that caused the last remaining limited partner to cease to be a limited partner.

Subchapter IX
FOREIGN LIMITED PARTNERSHIPS

§ 17-901. Law governing.

(a) Subject to the Constitution of the State of Delaware:

(1) The laws of the State of Delaware, territory, possession, or other jurisdiction or country under which a foreign limited partnership is organized govern its organization and internal affairs and the liability of its limited partners; and

(2) A foreign limited partnership may not be denied registration by reason of any difference between those laws and the laws of the State of Delaware.

(b) A foreign limited partnership shall be subject to § 17-106 of this title.

ANNOTATIONS

Choice of law; Delaware limited partnership, New York court — Delaware law applied to a lawsuit brought in a New York court relating to a Delaware limited partnership. According to the partnership agreement, the laws of New York applied, including the state's conflict of laws principles. In New York, the laws under which a foreign limited partnership was organized governed its organization, internal affairs, and the liability of its partners. *Mizrahi v. Chanel, Inc.*, 746 N.Y.S.2d 808 (Sup. Ct. 2001).

Diversity jurisdiction — For purposes of diversity jurisdiction, a limited liability partnership is a citizen of every state in which one of its partners resides. *Reisman v. KPMG Peat Marwick LLP*, 965 F. Supp. 165 (D. Mass. 1997).

Jurisdiction—Delaware courts lack personal jurisdiction over a California limited partnership whose only contact with Delaware is ownership of shares of stock of a Delaware corporation and the passive receipt of income from such investment. *Hart Holding Co. v. Drexel Burnham Lambert, Inc.*, 1992 Del. Ch. LEXIS 112 (Del. Ch. May 28, 1992).

Law of state of organization applies—California law applies in determining whether a court will ignore distinctions between a corporation and a limited partnership organized under California law and find the entities to be mere alter egos. *Hart Holding Co. v. Drexel Burnham Lambert, Inc.*, 1992 Del. Ch. LEXIS 112 (Del. Ch. May 28, 1992).

§ 17-902. Registration required; application.

Before doing business in the State of Delaware, a foreign limited partnership shall register with the Secretary of State. In order to register, a foreign limited partnership shall submit to the Secretary of State:

(1) A copy executed by a general partner of an application for registration as a foreign limited partnership, setting forth:

a. The name of the foreign limited partnership and, if different, the name under which it proposes to register and do business in the State of Delaware;

b. The State, territory, possession or other jurisdiction or country where organized, the date of its organization and a statement from a general partner that, as of the date of filing, the foreign limited partnership validly exists as a limited partnership under the laws of the jurisdiction of its organization;

c. The nature of the business or purposes to be conducted or promoted in the State of Delaware;

d. The address of the registered office and the name and address of the registered agent for service of process required to be maintained by § 17-904(b) of this title;

e. A statement that the Secretary of State is appointed the agent of the foreign limited partnership for service of process under the circumstances set forth in § 17-910(b) of this title;

f. The name and business, residence or mailing addresses of each of the general partners; and

g. The date on which the foreign limited partnership first did, or intends to do, business in the State of Delaware.

(2) A certificate, as of a date not earlier than 6 months prior to the filing date, issued by an authorized officer of the jurisdiction of its formation evidencing its existence. If such certificate is in a foreign language, a translation thereof, under oath of the translator, shall be attached thereto.

(3) A fee as set forth in § 17-1107(a)(6) of this title shall be paid.

§ 17-903. Issuance of registration.

(a) If the Secretary of State finds that an application for registration conforms to law and all requisite fees have been paid, the Secretary shall:

(1) Certify that the application has been filed in the Secretary's office by endorsing upon the original application the word "Filed," and the date and hour of the filing. This endorsement is conclusive of the date and time of its filing in the absence of actual fraud;

(2) File and index the endorsed application.

(b) The Secretary of State shall prepare and return to the person who filed the application or the person's representative a copy of the original signed application, similarly endorsed, and shall certify such copy as a true copy of the original signed application.

(c) The filing of the application with the Secretary of State shall make it unnecessary to file any other documents under Chapter 31 of this title.

§ 17-904. Name; registered office; registered agent.

(a) A foreign limited partnership may register with the Secretary of State under any name (whether or not it is the name under which it is registered in the jurisdiction of its organization) that includes the words "Limited Partnership" or the abbreviation "L.P." or the designation "LP" and that could be registered by a domestic limited partnership; provided, however, that a foreign limited partnership may register under any name which is not such as to distinguish it upon the records in the office of the Secretary of State from the name on such records of any domestic or foreign corporation, partnership, statutory trust, limited liability company or limited partnership reserved, formed, registered or organized under the laws of the State of Delaware with the written consent of the other corporation, partnership, statutory trust, limited liability company or limited partnership, which written consent shall be filed with the Secretary of State.

(b) Each foreign limited partnership shall have and maintain in the State of Delaware:

(1) A registered office which may but need not be a place of its business in the State of Delaware; and

(2) A registered agent for service of process on the limited partnership, having a business office identical with such registered office, which agent may be any of:

a. An individual resident in the State of Delaware,

b. A domestic limited liability company, a domestic corporation, a domestic partnership (whether general (including a limited liability partnership) or limited (including a limited liability limited partnership)), or a domestic statutory trust, or

c. A foreign corporation, a foreign partnership (whether general (including a limited liability partnership) or limited (including a limited liability limited partnership)) (other than the foreign limited partnership itself), a foreign limited liability company or a foreign statutory trust.

(c) A registered agent may change the address of the registered office of the foreign limited partnership(s) for which the agent is registered agent to another address in the State of Delaware by paying a fee as set forth in § 17-1107(a)(7) of this title and filing with the Secretary of State a certificate, executed by such registered agent, setting forth the address at which such registered agent has maintained the registered office for each of the foreign limited partnerships for which it is a registered agent, and further certifying to the new address to which each such registered office will be changed on a given day, and at which new address such registered agent will thereafter maintain the registered office for each of the foreign limited partnerships for which it is a registered agent. Upon the filing of such certificate, the Secretary of State shall furnish to the registered agent a certified copy of the same under the Secretary's hand and seal of office, and thereafter, or until further change of address, as authorized by law, the registered office in the State of Delaware of each of the foreign limited partnerships for which the agent is a registered agent shall be located at the new address of the registered agent thereof as given in the certificate. In the event of a change of name of any person acting as a registered agent of a foreign limited partnership, such registered agent shall file with the Secretary of State a certificate, executed by such registered agent, setting forth the new name of such registered agent, the name of such registered agent before it was changed and the address at which such registered agent has maintained the registered office for each of the foreign limited partnerships for which it is a registered agent, and shall pay a fee as set forth in § 17-1107(a)(7) of this title. Upon the filing of such certificate, the Secretary of State shall furnish to the registered agent a certified copy of the certificate under the Secretary of State's own hand and seal of office. A change of name of any person acting as a registered agent of a foreign limited partnership as a result of a merger or consolidation of the registered agent, with or into another person which succeeds to its assets and liabilities by operation of law, shall be deemed a change of name for purposes of this section. Filing a certificate under this section shall be deemed to be an amendment of the application of each foreign limited partnership affected thereby and each such foreign limited partnership shall not be required to take any further action with respect thereto, to amend its application under § 17-905 of this title. Any registered agent filing a certificate under this section shall promptly, upon such filing, deliver a copy of any such certificate to each foreign limited partnership affected thereby.

(d) The registered agent of 1 or more foreign limited partnerships may resign and appoint a successor registered agent by paying a fee as set forth in § 17-1107(a)(7) of this title and filing a certificate with the Secretary of State, stating that it resigns and the name and address of the successor registered agent. There shall be attached to such certificate a statement of each affected foreign limited partnership ratifying and approving such change of registered agent. Upon such filing, the successor registered agent shall become the registered agent of such foreign limited partnerships as have ratified and approved such substitution and the successor registered agent's address, as stated in such certificate, shall become the address of each such foreign limited partnership's registered office in the State of Delaware. The Secretary of State shall then issue a certificate that the successor registered agent has become the registered agent of the foreign limited partnerships so ratifying and approving such change and setting out the names of such foreign limited partnerships. Filing of such certificate of resignation shall be deemed to be an amendment of the application of each foreign limited partnership affected thereby and each such foreign limited partnership shall not be required to take any further action with respect thereto to amend its application under § 17-905 of this title.

(e) The registered agent of one or more foreign limited partnerships may resign without appointing a successor registered agent by paying a fee as set forth in § 17-1107(a)(7) of this title and filing a certificate of resignation with the Secretary of State, but such resignation shall not become effective until 30 days after the certificate is filed. The certificate shall contain a statement that written notice of resignation was given to each affected foreign limited partnership at least 30 days prior to the filing of the certificate by mailing or delivering such notice to the foreign limited partnership at its address last known to the registered agent and shall set forth the date of such notice. After receipt of the notice of the resignation of its registered agent, the foreign limited partnership for which such registered agent was acting shall obtain and designate a new registered agent to take the place of the registered agent so resigning. If such foreign limited partnership fails to obtain and designate a new registered agent as aforesaid prior to the expiration of the period of 30 days after the filing by the registered agent of the certificate of resignation, such foreign limited partnership shall not be permitted to do business in the State of Delaware and its registration shall be cancelled. After the resignation of the registered agent shall have become effective as provided in this section and if no new registered agent shall have been obtained and designated in the time and manner aforesaid, service of legal process against each foreign limited partnership for which the resigned registered agent had been acting shall thereafter be upon the Secretary of State in accordance with § 17-911 of this title.

§ 17-905. Amendments to application.

If any statement in the application for registration of a foreign limited partnership was false when made or any arrangements or other facts described have changed, making the application false in any respect, the foreign limited partnership shall promptly file in the office of the Secretary of State a certificate, executed by a general partner, correcting such statement, together with a fee as set forth in § 17-1107(a)(6) of this title.

§ 17-906. Cancellation of registration.

A foreign limited partnership may cancel its registration by filing with the Secretary of State a certificate of cancellation executed by a general partner, together with a fee as set forth in § 17-1107(a)(6) of this title. The registration of a foreign limited partnership shall be cancelled as provided in § 17-104(i)(4), § 17-904(e) and § 17-1109(g), of this Title. A cancellation does not terminate the authority of the Secretary of State to accept service of process on the foreign limited partnership with respect to causes of action arising out of the doing of business in the State of Delaware.

§ 17-907. Doing business without registration.

(a) A foreign limited partnership doing business in the State of Delaware may not maintain any action, suit or proceeding in the State of Delaware until it has registered in the State of Delaware, and has paid to the State of Delaware all fees and penalties for the years or parts thereof during which it did business in the State of Delaware without having registered.

(b) The failure of a foreign limited partnership to register in the State of Delaware does not impair:

(1) The validity of any contract or act of the foreign limited partnership;

(2) The right of any other party to the contract to maintain any action, suit or proceeding on the contract; or

(3) Prevent the foreign limited partnership from defending any action, suit or proceeding in any court of the State of Delaware.

(c) A limited partner of a foreign limited partnership is not liable as a general partner of the foreign limited partnership solely by reason of the foreign limited partnership's having done business in the State of Delaware without registration.

(d) Any foreign limited partnership doing business in the State of Delaware without first having registered shall be fined and shall pay to the Secretary of State $200 for each year or part thereof during which the foreign limited partnership failed to register in the State of Delaware.

§ 17-908. Foreign limited partnerships doing business without having qualified; injunctions.

The Court of Chancery shall have jurisdiction to enjoin any foreign limited partnership, or any agent thereof, from doing any business in the State of Delaware if such foreign limited partnership has failed to register under this subchapter or if such foreign limited partnership has secured a certificate of the Secretary of State under § 17-903 of this title on the basis of false or misleading representations. The Attorney General shall, upon the Attorney General's own motion or upon the relation of proper parties, proceed for this purpose by complaint in any county in which such foreign limited partnership is doing or has done business.

§ 17-909. Execution; liability.

Sections 17-204(c) and 17-207 of this title shall be applicable to foreign limited partnerships as if they were domestic limited partnerships.

§ 17-910. Service of process on registered foreign limited partnerships.

(a) Service of legal process upon any foreign limited partnership shall be made by delivering a copy personally to any managing or general agent or general partner of the foreign limited partnership in the State of Delaware or the registered agent of the foreign limited partnership in the State of Delaware, or by leaving it at the dwelling house or usual place of abode in the State of Delaware of any such managing or general agent, general partner or registered agent (if the registered agent be an individual), or at the registered office or other place of business of the foreign limited partnership in the State of Delaware. If the registered agent be a corporation, service of process upon it as such may be made by serving, in the State of Delaware, a copy thereof on the president, vice-president, secretary, assistant secretary or any director of the corporate registered agent. Service by copy left at the dwelling house or usual place of abode of any officer, managing or general agent, general partner or registered agent, or at the registered office or other place of business of the foreign limited partnership in the State of Delaware, to be effective must be delivered there at least 6 days before the return date of the process, and in the presence of an adult person, and the officer serving the process shall distinctly state the manner of service in the return thereto. Process returnable forthwith must be delivered personally to the officer, managing or general agent, general partner or registered agent.

(b) In case the officer whose duty it is to serve legal process cannot by due diligence serve the process in any manner provided for by subsection (a) of this section, it shall be lawful to serve the process against the foreign limited partnership upon the Secretary of State, and such service shall be as effectual for all intents and purposes as if made in any of the ways provided for in subsection (a) hereof. Process may be served upon the Secretary of State under this subsection by means of electronic transmission but only as prescribed by the Secretary of State. The Secretary of State is authorized to issue such rules and regulations with respect to such service as the Secretary of State deems necessary or appropriate. In the event that service is effected through the Secretary of State in accordance with this subsection, the Secretary of State shall forthwith notify the foreign limited partnership by letter, directed to the foreign limited partnership at the address of a general partner as it appears on the records relating to such foreign limited partnership on file with the Secretary of State or, if no such address appears, at its last registered office. Such letter shall be sent by a mail or courier service that includes a record of mailing or deposit with the courier and a record of delivery evidenced by the signature of the recipient. Such letter shall enclose a copy of the process and any other papers served on the Secretary of State pursuant to this subsection. It shall be the duty of the plaintiff in the event of such service to serve process and any other papers in duplicate, to notify the Secretary of State that service is being effected pursuant to this subsection, and to pay to the Secretary of State the sum of $50 for the use of the State of Delaware, which sum shall be taxed as a part of the costs in the proceeding if the plaintiff shall prevail therein. The Secretary of State shall maintain an alphabetical record of any such service setting forth the name of the plaintiff and defendant, the title, docket number and nature of the proceeding in which process has been served upon the Secretary, the fact that service has been effected pursuant to this subsection, the return date thereof and the day and hour when the service was made. The Secretary of State shall not be required to retain such information for a period longer than 5 years from receipt of the service of process.

§ 17-911. Service of process on unregistered foreign limited partnerships.

(a) Any foreign limited partnership which shall do business in the State of Delaware without having registered under § 17-902 of this title shall be deemed to have thereby appointed and constituted the Secretary of State of the State of Delaware its agent for the acceptance of legal process in any civil action, suit or proceeding against it in any state or federal court in the State of Delaware arising or growing out of any business done by it within the State of Delaware. The doing of business in the State of Delaware by such foreign limited partnership shall be a signification of the agreement of such foreign limited partnership that any such process when so served shall be of the same legal force and validity as if served upon an authorized general partner or agent personally within the State of Delaware. Process may be served upon the Secretary of State under this subsection by means of electronic transmission but only as prescribed by the Secretary of State. The Secretary of State is authorized to issue such rules and regulations with respect to such service as the Secretary of State deems necessary or appropriate.

(b) Whenever the words "doing business", "the doing of business" or "business done in this State", by any such foreign limited partnership are used in this section, they shall mean the course or practice of carrying on any business activities in the State of Delaware, including, without limiting the generality of the foregoing, the solicitation of business or orders in the State of Delaware.

(c) In the event of service upon the Secretary of State in accordance with subsection (a) of this section, the Secretary of State shall forthwith notify the foreign limited partnership thereof by letter, directed to the foreign limited partnership at the address furnished to the Secretary of State by the plaintiff in such action, suit or proceeding. Such letter shall be sent by a mail or courier service that includes a record of mailing or deposit with the courier and a record of delivery evidenced by the signature of the recipient. Such letter shall enclose a copy of the process and any other papers served upon the Secretary of State. It shall be the duty of the plaintiff in the event of such service to serve process and any other papers in duplicate, to notify the Secretary of State that service is being made pursuant to this subsection, and to pay to the Secretary of State the sum of $50 for the use of the State of Delaware, which sum shall be taxed as part of the costs in the proceeding, if the plaintiff shall prevail therein. The Secretary of State shall maintain an alphabetical record of any such process setting forth the name of the plaintiff and defendant, the title, docket number and nature of the proceeding in which process has been served upon the Secretary, the return date thereof, and the day and hour when the service was made. The Secretary of State shall not be required to retain such information for a period longer than 5 years from receipt of the service of process.

ANNOTATIONS

Consent to jurisdiction constitutes doing business — Where a foreign limited partnership consented to personal jurisdiction in Delaware pursuant to a contractual forum selection clause, the partnership was "doing business" in Delaware for purposes of Section 17-911 and could be served with process through the Delaware Secretary of State. *Alstom Power Inc. v. Duke/Fluor Daniel Carribbean S.E.*, 2005 WL 407206 (Del. Super. Jan. 31, 2005).

Doing business — An unregistered foreign limited partnership that purposefully elected to use a Delaware corporation as its general partner and the common and statutory law of Delaware governing the operation of the general partner as an integral part of the total transaction out of which the plaintiff's cause of action arose was "doing business" in Delaware within the meaning of Section 17-911, and thus service on the general partner was effective. Such activity also satisfied minimum contact due process standards for exercising personal jurisdiction. *Macklowe v. Planet Hollywood, Inc.*, 1994 Del. Ch. LEXIS 179 (Del. Ch., Oct. 13, 1994).

Forum selection clause implies consent to jurisdiction — Where foreign limited partnership entered into a contract providing that the contract was subject to the law and jurisdiction of Delaware, the limited partnership consented to personal jurisdiction in Delaware. *Alstom Power Inc. v. Duke/Fluor Daniel Carribbean S.E.*, 2005 WL 407206 (Del. Super. Jan. 31, 2005).

Service on Delaware general partner — Section 17-911 governs service of process for the purpose of exercising personal jurisdiction over an unregistered foreign limited partnership. The test for jurisdiction is a "doing business" test. The statute does not address the significance of the Delaware residency of a general partner of an unregistered foreign limited partnership. Section 17-911 does not address the situation of an unregistered foreign limited partnership having a Delaware corporation as its general partner. Thus, under Section 17-1105, rules relating to general partnerships apply. The general rule is that service of process on a foreign general partnership is effective when served on a resident partner. Thus, an unregistered foreign limited partnership having a Delaware resident corporation as its general partner may reasonably expect its general partner to be served with process in the event the limited partnership was doing business in Delaware. *Macklowe v. Planet Hollywood, Inc.*, 1994 Del. Ch. LEXIS 179 (Del. Ch., Oct. 13, 1994).

§ 17-912. Activities not constituting doing business.

(a) Activities of a foreign limited partnership in the State of Delaware that do not constitute doing business for the purpose of this subchapter include:

(1) Maintaining, defending or settling an action or proceeding;

(2) Holding meetings of its partners or carrying on any other activity concerning its internal affairs;

(3) Maintaining bank accounts;

(4) Maintaining offices or agencies for the transfer, exchange or registration of the limited partnership's own securities or maintaining trustees or depositories with respect to those securities;

(5) Selling through independent contractors;

(6) Soliciting or obtaining orders, whether by mail or through employees or agents or otherwise, if the orders require acceptance outside the State of Delaware before they become contracts;

(7) Selling, by contract consummated outside the State of Delaware, and agreeing, by the contract, to deliver into the State of Delaware, machinery, plants or equipment, the construction, erection or installation of which within the State of Delaware requires the supervision of technical engineers or skilled employees performing services not generally available, and as part of the contract of sale agreeing to furnish such services, and such services only, to the vendee at the time of construction, erection or installation;

(8) Creating, as borrower or lender, or acquiring indebtedness with or without a mortgage or other security interest in property;

(9) Collecting debts or foreclosing mortgages or other security interests in property securing the debts, and holding, protecting and maintaining property so acquired;

(10) Conducting an isolated transaction that is not one in the course of similar transactions;

(11) Doing business in interstate commerce; and

(12) Doing business in the State of Delaware as an insurance company.

(b) A person shall not be deemed to be doing business in the State of Delaware solely by reason of being a partner of a domestic limited partnership or a foreign limited partnership.

(c) This section does not apply in determining whether a foreign limited partnership is subject to service of process, taxation or regulation under any other law of the State of Delaware.

Subchapter X
DERIVATIVE ACTIONS

§ 17-1001. Right to bring action.

A limited partner or an assignee of a partnership interest may bring an action in the Court of Chancery in the right of a limited partnership to recover a judgment in its favor if general partners with authority to do so have refused to bring the action or if an effort to cause those general partners to bring the action is not likely to succeed.

ANNOTATIONS

Breaches of fiduciary duty and contract; injury to partnership—Claims for breach of fiduciary duty and breach of contract brought by a limited partner against the administrator of a hedge fund partnership (controlled by the law of Delaware) which invested in a Ponzi scheme by serving as a "feeder fund" to Bernie Madoff were derivative claims and could not be brought as individual claims. The limited partner alleged the administrator failed to adequately carry out its duties to him and the fund which, in turn, led to the maintenance of the fund's position with Madoff and induced the limited partner to invest in the fund causing the loss of his investment, and that this behavior constituted a breach of the administrator's fiduciary duty to him. If, as alleged, the administrator breached a fiduciary duty by not discovering that the funds accounts were invested in a Ponzi scheme, it "necessarily" injured the fund in doing so. Therefore, the limited partner could not prevail without showing injury to the partnership and, accordingly, was derivative. Similarly, the limited partner did not allege an independent injury or breach of contractual obligation specific to him but a general breach applicable to the partnership at large and, accordingly, could not show his own injury without showing that the partnership was injured so that this claim, too, was derivative. *Stephenson v. Citgo Group Ltd.*, 700 F. Supp. 2d 599 (S.D.N.Y. 2010).

Claim of asset sale at inadequate price is derivative—Limited partners have no individual claim where they allege damage resulting from the general partner's causing the partnership to dispose of assets at an inadequate price. *Katell v. Morgan Stanley Group. Inc.*, 1993 Del. Ch. LEXIS 5 (Del. Ch. Jan. 14, 1993).

Claim of diminished distributions is derivative — A claim that the general partner's misconduct resulted in diminished distributions to limited partners is a derivative claim because it flows from a direct injury to the partnership (i.e., lower income) and is not a direct injury to the limited partners or one that exists independently of the partnership. *Litman v. Prudential-Bache Properties. Inc.*, 611 A.2d 12 (Del. Ch. 1992).

Claim of mismanagement is derivative—A claim that general partners have mismanaged the partnership and wasted partnership assets is derivative in nature because limited partners are not injured directly or independently of the partnership. *Whalen v. Connelly*, 545 N.W.2d 284 (Iowa 1996) (applying Delaware law).

Claims over liquidation may be individual, not derivative—Where the only two parties in interest are the class of limited partners and the general partner, and the business of the partnership is over except for winding up, and the class of limited partners and the general partner oppose each other in a dispute over the liquidation, the claims of limited partners are direct claims, not derivative. Superimposing derivative pleading requirements upon such claims needlessly delays resolution and serves no useful or meaningful public policy. *In re Cencom Cable Income Partners, L.P. Litigation*, 2000 WL 130629 (Del. Ch. Jan. 27, 2000).

Complaint must allege particularized facts to excuse demand — To excuse demand on general partners, limited partners must either rebut by particular facts the threshold presumption of the general partners' disinterestedness or independence, or must plead particular facts sufficient to create reasonable doubt that the challenged transaction was the product of a valid exercise of business judgment. *Katell v. Morgan Stanley Group. Inc.*, 1993 Del. Ch. LEXIS 5 (Jan. 14, 1993).

Conversion to class action; diversity jurisidiction — Where a derivative suit brought in federal court was based on an invalid theory of a diversity jurisdiction in light of *Carden v. Arkoma Assocs.*, 110 S. Ct. 1015 (1990), the court recharacterized the derivative claim as a class action and dismissed the limited partnership, itself, to establish complete diversity. *Curley v. Brignoli, Curley and Roberts Assocs.*, 915 F.2d 81 (2d Cir. 1990), *cert. denied*, 499 U.S. 955 (1991).

Demand on general partner — The exception to the requirement that prior to instituting a derivative suit the limited partners demand relief from the general partners for situations where such a demand would be futile applied where such a demand would have included access to the partnership's books and records and the general partner had already refused to provide such access. *Curley v. Brignoli, Curley and Roberts Assocs.*, 746 F. Supp. 1208 (S.D.N.Y. 1989), *aff'd* 915 F.2d 81 (2d Cir. 1990), *cert. denied*, 499 U.S. 955 (applying Delaware law).

Derivative action standards — Even though demand letter was signed by only one limited partner, it clearly stated that signor represented all limited partners; corporate standards apply to limited partnerships in "demand excused" and "demand refused" analyses; limited partners did not concede the general partner was disinterested by making pre-suit demand; failure to present matters to the general partner when making a demand results in a waiver of the claims not presented; and a conflict of interest disclosed in a prospectus or partnership agreement and a limited partner's acceptance of those terms precludes the limited partner from bringing a derivative claim based on facts disclosed in these documents. *Seaford Funding Limited Partnership v. M&M Assoc. II, L.P.*, 672 A.2d 66 (Del. Ch. 1995).

Determination of claim as derivative — Whether limited partner's claim is direct or derivative turns on whether the alleged harm was suffered by partnership or the limited partners individually, and whether the benefit of any remedy would be received by the partnership or the limited partners individually. *In re BCP Management, Inc. v. PricewaterhouseCoopers LLP*, 320 B.R. 265 (Bankr. D. Del. 2005); *Cabaniss v. Deutsche Bank Securities, Inc.*, 611 S.E.2d 878 (N.C. Ct. App. 2005).

Evenly divided general partners excused demand — Where one general partner was interested in a transaction, and another disinterested, and commencement of an action would require the consent of both general partners, demand would be excused. *Katell v. Morgan Stanley Group, Inc.*, 1993 Del. Ch. LEXIS 5 (Jan. 14, 1993).

Facts insufficient to excuse demand — That general partner earned fees is not sufficient by itself to excuse demand. Conclusory allegation that general partners cannot be expected to sue themselves is insufficient as a matter of law to excuse demand. In the absence of self-dealing, the fact that a general partner owes divided loyalties to the partnership and limited partners on the one hand, and to the general partner's parent company on the other hand, does not excuse demand. A limited partner cannot predicate a derivative claim on a general partner's divided loyalties where the divided loyalties were described in the prospectus and the limited partner knew and accepted the terms described in the prospectus. *Litman v. Prudential-Bache Properties, Inc.*, 1993 Del. Ch. LEXIS 13 (Jan. 4, 1993).

Failure to make demand or explain — A claim by a limited partner that the general partners were mismanaging the partnership and wasting its assets was derivative because the limited partner was not injured "directly or independently" of the partnership. Therefore, the limited partner was required to make a demand on the general partners to bring the litigation or explain in the pleadings why such a demand was not made. Failure to take either of these steps deprived the limited partner of standing to bring the claim. *Whalen v. Connelly*, 545 N.W.2d 284 (Iowa 1996).

Fiduciary exception to attorney-client privilege — Court may look to corporate cases to determine the application in the limited partnership context of the fiduciary exception to the attorney-client privilege. Once limited partners made their intention to withdraw known to the general partner, there was no longer mutuality of interest between the general partner and the limited partners. Mutuality of interest is a prerequisite to the fiduciary exception. Thus, advice of counsel rendered after there was no longer a mutuality of interest between the general and the limited partners was privileged and not subject to discovery. Advice of counsel rendered prior to the formation of the partnership was privileged because there was no fiduciary relation until the partnership was formed, and thus the fiduciary exception has no application. *The Continental Ins. Co. v. Rutledge & Co., Inc.*, 1999 Del. Ch. LEXIS 12 (Jan. 26, 1999).

Fraud; direct claims; diminution in value of interest — The court dismissed limited partners fraud claim against a limited partnership hedge fund. The claims stated derivative, not direct claims. The limited partners sued the partnership's auditors claiming that inaccurate financial statements fraudulently induced them to invest in the fund. However, the partners pleaded no injury distinct from those that affected, and was the subject of a suit on behalf of, all limited partners. Diminution of in the value of their limited partnership interests was the only asserted injury. *Continental Cas. Co. v. PricewaterhouseCoopers, LLP*, 2010 WL 2569187 (N.Y. Ct. App. June 29, 2010) (DE law applied).

General partners control derivative suits — General partners have control over derivative suits, and thus demand futility under Sections 17-1001 and 17-1003 is identical to demand futility under corporation law. *Litman v. Prudential-Bache Properties, Inc.*, 1993 Del. Ch. LEXIS 13 (Jan. 4, 1993).

Individual claim — Individual claim for breach of duty is stated by allegations that general partners wrongfully amended partnership agreement to adversely affect a limited partner's contractual right to vote by written consent and refused to rescind such amendments. *U-H Acquisition Co. v. Barbo*, 1994 Del. Ch. LEXIS 9 (Jan. 28, 1994, revised Jan. 31, 1994).

Intervention by limited partners—Where limited partners sought to intervene in a declaratory judgment action brought by the general partner against third parties, intervention was denied where the limited partners' claims were identical to claims already raised and where the limited partners' interests were adequately represented by the general partner. *South Street Corporation Recovery Fund I v. Salovaara*, 1999 Del. Ch. LEXIS 144 (July 9, 1999).

Joinder of parties—Where all three partners of a small limited partnership are before the court, joinder of the partnership entity is not required because the exclusion of the partnership entity causes no prejudice to the defendant limited partner or the partnership; further, under Delaware law, which is the source of any cause of action plaintiffs (the general partner and one of the limited partners) have for breach of the partnership agreement, they are the real parties in interest within the meaning of Fed. R. Civ. P. 17 and thus can proceed without the partnership, whether or not the action is derivative. *HB General Corp. v. Manchester Partners, L.P.*, 95 F.3d 1185 (3d Cir. 1996).

Laches may bar derivative claim—Limited partners are not required to delve aggressively into internal affairs to assure that a non-public self-dealing transaction is not barred by the statute of limitations, but when facts are disclosed that give rise to inquiry, applicable statute of limitations requires timely action by limited partners to preserve their rights to pursue derivative claims against directors of a corporate general partner. *In re USACafes L.P. Litigation*, 1993 Del. Ch. LEXIS 12 (Jan. 21, 1993).

Loss in market value states derivative claim—Mismanagement that diminishes the market value of limited partnership units gives rise to a derivative and not an individual claim because the diminution in value flows from damage inflicted directly on the partnership. *Litman v. Prudential-Bache Properties, Inc.*, 611 A.2d 12 (Del. Ch. 1992).

Loss of value of partnership interest states individual claim—Claim for an alleged loss in value to partnership interests as a result of breaches of fiduciary duty by defendants was both a derivative claim and a direct or individual claim. Plaintiffs alleged that they were deprived of their contractual equity interests by the breaches of fiduciary duty. The injury was not only to the partnership but also to the limited partners. *Sturm v. Marriott Marquis Corp.*, 85 F. Supp. 1356 (N.D. Ga. 2000).

Mismanagement and diversion claims—The plaintiffs, a group of limited partners in a Delaware public limited partnership, lacked standing, under both New York and Delaware law, to assert individual or class action claims for breach of contract and breach of fiduciary duty against the partnership, the general partner and the entities controlling the general partner, for the wrongful deferral of management fees and payment of such fees out of the proceeds of the sale of partnership assets. The claims were derivative in nature, in that they alleged the mismanagement and diversion of assets, and did not implicate any injury to the plaintiffs distinct from the harm to the partnership. *Broome v. ML Media Opportunity Partnerships, L.P.*, 709 N.Y.S.2d 59 (1st Dept. 2000).

Mismanagement states derivative claim—A claim that the general partner's misconduct in investigating and monitoring investments resulted in limited partners receiving less income states a derivative claim because the injury is inflicted directly on the partnership, limited partners are damaged only to the extent of their proportionate interests, and the claim does not exist independently of the partnership. *Litman v. Prudential-Bache Properties, Inc.*, 611 A.2d 12 (Del. Ch. 1992).

Must allege facts raising reasonable doubt as to general partner's disinterestedness — A limited partner must demonstrate with particularity facts showing why an effort to cause a general partner to bring an action is not likely to succeed, and thus must allege with particularity facts showing a conflict affecting the general partner's conduct which raise a reasonable question as to the general partner's disinterestedness, independence or business judgment. *Litman v. Prudential-Bache Properties, Inc.*, 1993 Del. Ch. LEXIS 13 (Jan. 4, 1993).

Nature of derivative claim generally — Injuries that do not exist independently of the limited partnership or that are not directly inflicted on the limited partners are derivative claims. *Litman v. Prudential-Bache Properties, Inc.*, 611 A.2d 12 (Del. Ch. 1992).

Nature of derivative claim generally — Limited partnership law follows corporation law for test of derivative claims, and to have an individual action, a limited partner must have been injured directly or independently of the partnership. *Katell v. Morgan Stanley Group, Inc.*, 1993 Del. Ch. LEXIS 5 (Jan. 14, 1993).

Negligent preparation of tax returns — Limited partners have no derivative cause of action for negligent preparation of federal tax returns against partnership accountants, where the complaint alleges only exposure to additional tax liabilities but does not allege any present injury. *Murphy v. Bay Shores Six, Ltd. Partnership*, 1987 WL 5776 (Del. Ch. Jan. 26, 1987).

Presumption of exercise of business judgment — General partners are presumed to exercise business judgment, and a limited partner must allege otherwise with particularity to establish demand futility and state a valid derivative claim. To rebut the presumption of the exercise of business judgment, a limited partner must allege with particularity facts rising to the level of gross negligence or broad overreaching. *Litman v. Prudential-Bache Properties, Inc.*, 1993 Del. Ch. LEXIS 13 (Jan. 4, 1993).

Proper analysis for distinguishing between direct and derivative claims — The Delaware Supreme Court has determined in the corporate context that whether claims are derivative or individual is to be determined solely on the basis of (1) who suffered the alleged harm, the corporation or the suing stockholder individually and (2) who would receive the benefit of the recovery or other remedy? The court expressly disapproved both "the concept of 'special injury' and the concept that a claim is necessarily derivative if it affects all stockholders equally." *Tooley v. Donaldson, Lufkin, & Jenrette, Inc.*, 845 A.2d 1031 (Del. 2004). Although decided in the corporate context, the court's shift in the analysis of individual and derivative claims will likely be applicable to distinguishing individual and derivative claims in the limited partnership context because the courts have consistently looked to corporate law principles when determining whether claims are individual or derivative.

Refusal to bring action — A limited partner may bring a derivative action if the general partner refuses to bring the action or if any demand to that effect would not be likely to succeed. *Murphy v. Bay Shores Six, Ltd. Partnership*, 1987 WL 5776 (Del. Ch. Jan. 26, 1987).

Reliance on corporate law — In determining whether asserted claim is derivative or individual, the court may rely on corporate as well as partnership case law to determine the nature of the claim. *Litman v. Prudential-Bache Properties, Inc.*, 611 A.2d 12 (Del. Ch. 1992).

Representation by attorney required — A limited liability company may not be represented in court by a member or manager, but must be represented by a member of the Delaware bar. A corporation may not represent itself in court, but a partnership may. Although a limited liability company is treated as a partnership for federal income tax purposes, it is largely a creature of contract and the interests of a member are analogous to the interests of a shareholder in a corporation. *Poore v. Fox Hollow Enterprises*, 1994 Del. Super. LEXIS 193 (Mar. 29, 1994).

Special litigation committees — Where the partnership agreement was duly amended to authorize the general partners to delegate handling of derivative litigation to a special litigation committee, a special litigation committee could be validly created, and corporate law doctrines relating to special litigation committees would apply. *Katell v. Morgan Stanley Group, Inc.*, 1993 Del. Ch. LEXIS 236 (Sept. 27, 1993).

Special litigation committees — Unless the constitution of a special litigation committee gives rise to a conclusive presumption of lack of independence, a challenge to the committee's independence is premature if it comes before the committee has made a recommendation of dismissal to the proper judicial authority. *Katell v. Morgan Stanley Group, Inc.*, 1993 Del. Ch. LEXIS 236 (Sept. 27, 1993).

Special litigation committees — The general partners' authority to manage the partnership affairs includes the right to determine whether derivative actions should proceed. Delaware law does not contain an express provision allowing general partners to delegate their authority to a special litigation committee, therefore, such rights and responsibilities are determined by the parties' particular partnership agreement. *Katell v. Morgan Stanley Group, Inc.*, 1993 Del. Ch. LEXIS 92 (June 8, 1993).

Special litigation committees — Where a special litigation committee had been duly created in accordance with the partnership agreement, the independence of the committee will not be considered by the Court until after the committee determines whether to pursue the derivative litigation, and proceedings will be stayed for a reasonable period of time to permit the committee to conduct its investigation. *Katell v. Morgan Stanley Group, Inc.*, 1993 Del. Ch. LEXIS 236 (Sept. 27, 1993).

Standing — Absent either a demand on the general partner to institute action or allegations in the complaint explaining with particularity why a demand was not made on the general partners, a limited partner lacks standing to prosecute a derivative action. *Litman v. Prudential-Bache Properties, Inc.*, 611 A.2d 12 (Del. Ch. 1992).

Standing — Limited partner who fails to make a demand or plead facts sufficient to excuse a demand lacks standing to pursue derivative claims. Demand was not excused merely because the demand would in essence ask managers of the general partner to sue themselves. *Cabaniss v. Deutsche Bank Securities, Inc.*, 611 S.E.2d 878 (N.C. Ct. App. 2005).

Standing to sue; general partner's conflict affecting independent business judgment — The limited partners had standing to file a derivative action after making demand on the sole general partner to enforce a note against another limited partnership which the general partner refused to do. There was reasonable doubt as to whether the general partner's refusal to take action was a valid exercise of the general partner's disinterested and independent business judgment. He was sole general partner of the other limited partnership. Not only did the general partner control both the lender and debtor partnerships, but he had personally guaranteed the note as well. *Seaford Funding Limited Partnership v. M&M Associates II, L.P.*, 672 A.2d 66 (Del. Ch. 1995).

Suit by limited partner against general partner as derivative suit — A suit by limited partners against the general partners for breach of fiduciary duty with respect to choice of investments was a derivative claim; the alleged injuries were to the partnership and not direct to the limited partners, even though the breach resulted in diminished income to the limited partners. *Litman v. Prudential-Bache Properties*, 611 A.2d 12 (Del. Ch. 1992).

Timely demand for internal redress — Limited partners' failure to make timely and complete demand upon the general partners to seek internal redress for a general partner's negligent conduct would bar a derivative suit by the limited partners. *Murphy v. Bay Shores Six, Ltd. Partnership*, 1987 WL 5776 (Del. Ch. Jan. 26, 1987).

Unregistered foreign limited partnership — Limited partners of a Delaware limited partnership could not bring a derivative action in Massachusetts when the partnership had never registered as a foreign limited partnership there. Since a certificate of cancellation had been filed in Delaware before the partnership could register in Massachusetts, the entity would have to revive its existence as a limited partnership in Delaware before it could register as a foreign limited partnership in Massachusetts because the certificate of cancellation terminated the existence of the partnership. *Smyth v. Marshall Field Fifth*, 40 Mass. Ct. App. 625, 666 N.E.2d 1008 (1996) (applying Delaware law).

Voting rights of assignees — Where the partnership agreement, assignment agreement and instrument of assignment provided by the limited partnership are ambiguous and do not expressly state whether subsequent assignees have voting rights, the agreements must be construed according to the reasonable expectations of investors who purchase additional limited partnership interests; subsequent assignees that acquired their limited partnership interests pursuant to a tender offer have a right to vote because they could read the agreements as providing for such voting rights. *Arvida/JMB Partners, L.P. v. Vanderbilt Income and Growth Assoc., L.L.C.*, 1997 Del. Ch. LEXIS 79 (May 23, 1997), *appeal dismissed*, 700 A.2d 735 (Del. 1997); *see also, Vanderbilt Income and Growth Assoc., L.L.C. v. Arvida/JMB Managers, Inc.*, 691 A.2d 609 (Del. 1996) (trial court cannot resolve ambiguity in documents on a motion to dismiss) (reversing *Vanderbilt Income and Growth Assoc., L.L.C. v. Arvida/JMB Managers, Inc.*, 1996 WL 652773 (Del. Ch. Nov. 4, 1996, revised Nov. 7, 1996).

Work product doctrine — Work product doctrine applies only to documents created for or in anticipation of litigation. Work product doctrine is more limited in its effect than the mutuality of interest requirement. Thus, lack of mutuality of interest could arise and preclude production of counsels' advice long before the work product doctrine would become effective. *The Continental Ins. Co. v. Rutledge & Co., Inc.*, 1999 Del. Ch. LEXIS 12 (Jan. 26, 1999).

§ 17-1002. Proper plaintiff.

In a derivative action, the plaintiff must be a partner or an assignee of a partnership interest at the time of bringing the action and:

(1) At the time of the transaction of which the plaintiff complains; or

(2) His status as a partner or an assignee of a partnership interest had devolved upon the plaintiff by operation of law or pursuant to the terms of the partnership agreement from a person who was a partner or an assignee of a partnership interest at the time of the transaction.

ANNOTATIONS

Appropriation of goodwill and fees; waste; diverting opportunity; breach of fiduciary duty — A limited partner may bring derivative claims in a New York court on behalf of a Delaware limited partnership, alleging that the general partner and another limited partner appropriated the partnership's good will and asset management fees, and committed waste, by spending the partnership's money on another business entity. However, a claim that the defendant partners diverted an opportunity from the partnership was dismissed because the partnership agreement permitted partners to engage in "other business" including business opportunities that might have gone to the partnership. Nevertheless, this "other business" clause did not permit "self-dealing or self-interested transactions" because a partnership agreement may limit, but not eliminate, a general partner's fiduciary duties. *Barrett v. Toroyan*, 813 N.Y.S.2d 415 (App. Div. 1st Dept. 2006) (applying N.Y. law).

Attorney's fees; settlement of suits; merger — A $10 million fee was granted to the attorneys representing the plaintiff limited partners in a derivative suit which was settled. The suit alleged the limited partnership and another entity, controlled by the partnership's controlling partner, entered into a transaction that constituted a breach of fiduciary duty. The controlling partner unfairly favored the other party to the transaction over the partnership by undervaluing the partnership's assets. The suit also alleged that a merger between the partnership and the other entity intended to extinguish the plaintiff's standing to pursue the derivative suit. The fee represented 10% of the settlement to the partnership and constituted compensation for 10,000 hours of work. Attorneys representing limited partners who objected to the settlement of the derivative suit were granted $80,000. *Brinckerhoff v. Texas Eastern Products Pipeline Co.*, 986 A.2d 370 (Del. Ch. 2010).

Citizenship for diversity jurisdiction — The citizenship of the limited partners (as well as the citizenship of the general partners) of a limited partnership must be taken into account in determining whether there is complete diversity among the parties in a suit brought in federal court based on diversity jurisdiction. *Carden v. Arkoma Assocs.*, 494 U.S. 185, 110 S. Ct. 1015, 108 L.Ed. 2d 157 (1990). *Accord, Roche v. Lincoln Property Co.*, 373 F.3d 610 (4th Cir. 2004); *457 Madison Avenue Corp. v. Amedeo Hotels Limited Partnership*, 2004 WL 1335937 (S.D.N.Y. June 11, 2004); *Provident Pioneer Partners, L.P. v. Electric & Gas Technology, Inc.*, 2002 WL 31319450 (D. Del. Sept. 6, 2002).

Conversion; partnership opportunity; fees; choice of law — New York law applied in a derivative suit brought in a New York court to determine whether the general partner and a limited partner converted a Delaware limited partnership's opportunity because the suit did not involve questions of internal partnership governance. This conversion claim was dismissed because it did not involve tangible personal property. However, a claim for conversion of management fees by another limited partner should not have been dismissed. *Barrett v. Toroyan*, 813 N.Y.S.2d 415 (App. Div. 1st Dept. 2006).

Delay in disclosing "bail out" from partnership; direct claim — The general partner's delay in disclosing to the limited partners that the general partner had "bailed out" of the partnership deprived the limited partners of the opportunity to "cut their losses" promptly. The limited partners' allegation that a statement which the general partner was required to prepare for the limited partners was misleading or materially false stated a direct, as opposed to a derivative, claim. (The claimants had withdrawn from the partnership and could no longer bring a derivative claim.) *Anglo American Security Fund, L.P. v. S.R. Global International Fund, L.P.*, 829 A.2d 143 (Del. Ch. 2003).

Diversity in non-derivative actions — Whether a limited partnership's citizenship must be considered for diversity jurisdiction purposes depends on whether the action is derivative or direct in nature. *Nomura Asset Capital v. Overland Company, Inc.*, 2003 WL 138093 (D. Del. Jan. 8, 2003).

Diversity jurisdiction where limited partnership has a partnership as a limited partner — In determining diversity jurisdiction, where a limited partnership has as one of its limited partners a second partnership, the citizenship of the partners in the second partnership must be considered. *Hart v. Terminex International*, 336 F.3d 541 (7th Cir. 2003).

Intervention — A limited partner who was a partner at the time a derivative action was commenced but was not a partner at the time of the alleged wrongs, and who failed to allege that it had acquired its limited partnership interest pursuant to the terms of the partnership agreement from a person who was a partner at the time of the alleged wrongs, lacked standing to have commenced the derivative action and thus could not intervene as a plaintiff in the action. However, the limited partner could intervene as to a cause of action that accrued after the limited partner had become a partner. *Flynn v. Bachow*, 1998 WL 671273 (Del. Ch. Sept. 18, 1998).

Joinder of parties — Where all three partners of a small limited partnership are before the court, joinder of the partnership entity is not required because the exclusion of the partnership entity causes no prejudice to the defendant limited partner or the partnership; further, under Delaware law, which is the source of any cause of action plaintiffs (the general partner and one of the limited partners) have for breach of the partnership agreement, they are the real parties in interest within the meaning of Fed. R. Civ. P. 17 and thus can proceed without the partnership, whether or not the action is derivative. *HB General Corp. v. Manchester Partners, L.P.*, 95 F.3d 1185 (3d Cir. 1996).

Standing — A limited partner who had terminated his interest in the limited partnership prior to commencing a derivative action lacked standing to bring the action. *Flynn v. Bachow*, 1998 WL 671273 (Del. Ch. Sept. 18, 1998).

Standing — Plaintiffs seeking declaratory judgment declaring certain amendments to the partnership agreement null and void, and alleging breach of duty by general partners in adopting amendments lacked standing to maintain action where neither plaintiff was a limited partner at the time the agreement was amended or at the time suit was commenced. *U-H Acquisition Co. v. Barbo*, 1994 Del. Ch. LEXIS 9 (Jan. 28, 1994, revised Jan. 31, 1994).

Standing of assignee — Where partnership agreement provided that an assignee of a limited partnership interest had no right to vote until admitted as a substituted limited partner, assignee who had not been so admitted in accordance with the provisions of the partnership agreement lacked standing to bring a claim for breach of fiduciary duty relating to the exercise of his right to vote by written consent. *U-H Acquisition Co. v. Barbo*, 1994 Del. Ch. LEXIS 9 (Jan. 28, 1994, revised Jan. 31, 1994).

§ 17-1003. Complaint.

In a derivative action, the complaint shall set forth with particularity the effort, if any, of the plaintiff to secure initiation of the action by a general partner or the reasons for not making the effort.

ANNOTATIONS

Complaint must allege particularized facts to excuse demand — To excuse demand on general partners, limited partners must either rebut by particular facts the threshold presumption of the general partners' disinterestedness or independence, or must plead particular facts sufficient to create reasonable doubt that the challenged transaction was the product of a valid exercise of business judgment. *Katell v. Morgan Stanley Group, Inc.*, 1993 Del. Ch. LEXIS 5 (Jan. 14, 1993).

Demand excused — Where the general partner was 100% owned by one person, and the general partner would be required to bring suit against that person, there was doubt as to the disinterest of the general partner. Accordingly, pre-suit demand was excused. *Dean v. Dick*, 1999 Del. Ch. LEXIS 121 (June 10, 1999).

Demand excused where corporate general partner conflicted, even though majority of board of directors is disinterested — A demand on a corporate general partner is sufficient, and a limited partner need not also make a demand on the board of directors of the corporate general partner. Thus, where the corporate general partner has conflicts of interests that excuse demand, no demand need be made on the board of directors even if a majority of the board is free of conflicts of interests. *Gotham Partners, L.P. v. Hallwood Realty Partners,* 1998 WL 832631 (Del. Ch. Nov. 10, 1998).

Demand on general partner — The exception to the requirement that prior to instituting a derivative suit the limited partners demand relief from the general partners for situations where such a demand would be futile applied where such a demand would have included access to the partnership's books and records and the general partner had already refused to provide such access. *Curley v. Brignoli, Curley and Roberts Assocs.,* 746 F. Supp. 1208 (S.D.N.Y. 1989), *aff'd,* 915 F.2d 81 (2d Cir. 1990), *cert. denied,* 499 U.S. 955 (1991) (applying Delaware law).

Derivative action standards — Even though demand letter was signed by only one limited partner, it clearly stated that signor represented all limited partners; corporate standards apply to limited partnerships in "demand excused" and "demand refused" analyses; limited partners did not concede the general partner was disinterested by making pre-suit demand; failure to present matters to the general partner when making a demand results in a waiver of the claims not presented; and a conflict of interest disclosed in a prospectus or partnership agreement and a limited partner's acceptance of those terms precludes the limited partner from bringing a derivative claim based on facts disclosed in these documents. *Seaford Funding Limited Partnership v. M&M Assoc. II, L.P.,* 672 A.2d 66 (Del. Ch. 1995).

Derivative action standards — Section 17-1003 is the limited partnership parallel to the corporate law demand requirement. According, corporate case law concerning demand futility is applicable in the limited partnership context. *Dean v. Dick,* 1999 Del. Ch. LEXIS 121 (June 10, 1999).

Entrenchment claim both derivative and individual — Where plaintiff alleged an unlawful scheme involving a reverse split of units, odd-lot buy backs, open market purchases and grant of options for the purpose of entrenching the general partner by giving it a *de facto* veto over its removal by limited partners, the complaint stated a derivative claim for harm to the partnership by reason of the use of partnership assets to acquire units and an individual claim for harm to unit holders by reason of the adverse consequences to their voting rights. *Gotham Partners, L.P. v. Hallwood Realty Partners,* 1998 WL 832631 (Del. Ch. Nov. 10, 1998).

Evenly divided general partners excuses demand — Where one general partner was interested in a transaction, and another disinterested, and commencement of an action would require the consent of both general partners, demand would be excused. *Katell v. Morgan Stanley Group, Inc.,* 1993 Del. Ch. LEXIS 5 (Jan. 14, 1993).

Facts insufficient to excuse demand — That general partner earned fees is not sufficient by itself to excuse demand. Conclusory allegation that general partners cannot be expected to sue themselves is insufficient as a matter of law to excuse demand. In the absence of self-dealing, the fact that a general partner owes divided loyalties to the partnership and limited partners on the one hand, to the general partner's parent company on the other hand, does not excuse demand. A limited partner cannot predicate a derivative claim on a general partner's divided loyalties where the divided loyalties were described in the prospectus and the limited partner knew and accepted the terms described in the prospectus. *Litman v. Prudential-Bache Properties, Inc.*, 1993 Del. Ch. LEXIS 13 (Jan. 4, 1993).

General partners control derivative suites — General partners have control over derivative suites, and thus demand futility under Sections 17-1001 and 17-1003 is identical to demand futility under corporation law. *Litman v. Prudential-Bache Properties. Inc.*, 1993 Del. Ch. LEXIS 13 (Jan. 4, 1993).

Must allege facts raising reasonable doubt as to general partner's disinterestedness — A limited partner must demonstrate with particularity facts showing why an effort to cause a general partner to bring an action is not likely to succeed, and thus must allege with particularity facts showing a conflict affecting the general partner's conduct which raise a reasonable question as the general partner's disinterestedness, independence or business judgment. *Litman v. Prudential-Bache* Properties, Inc., 1993 Del. Ch. LEXIS 13 (Jan. 4, 1993).

No pre-suit demand — Several derivative claims brought by some limited partners against other limited partners and the general partners were dismissed because they did not allege "with particularity" the reasons why a pre-suit demand on the general partners was not "likely to succeed." The plaintiffs did not create a reasonable doubt either as to whether the defendants were disinterested and independent or whether the transaction at issue resulted from a valid exercise of business judgment. In addition, purported direct claims alleging that the partnership property was sold for an inadequate price were really derivative claims and also dismissed. *Trump v. Cheng*, 63 A.D.3d 623, 882 N.Y.S. 2d 87 (N.Y. App. Div. 1st Dept. 2009).

Pre-suit demand concedes independence of general partner — A limited partner's pre-suit demand on a corporate general partner waived any contention that the corporate general partner was incapable of acting on the demand. "Capable of acting" means that the board of directors of the general partner could properly appoint a special committee to investigate the demand and make recommendations to the board. *Whalen v. Connelly*, 593 N.W.2d 147 (Iowa Supr. 1999) (applying Delaware law).

Presumption of exercise of business judgment — General partners are presumed to exercise business judgment, and a limited partner must allege otherwise with particularity to establish demand futility and state a valid derivative claim. To rebut the presumption of the exercise of business judgment, a limited partner must allege with particularity facts rising to the level of gross negligence or broad overreaching. *Litman v. Prudential-Bache Properties, Inc.*, 1993 Del. Ch. LEXIS 13 (Jan. 4, 1993).

Proper analysis for distinguishing between direct and derivative claims — The Delaware Supreme Court has determined in the corporate context that whether claims are derivative or individual is to be determined solely on the basis of (1) who suffered the alleged harm, the corporation or the suing stockholder individually and (2) who would receive the benefit of the recovery or other remedy? The court expressly disapproved both "the concept of 'special injury' and the concept that a claim is necessarily derivative if it affects all stockholders equally." *Tooley v. Donaldson, Lufkin, & Jenrette, Inc.*, 845 A.2d 1031 (Del. 2004). Although decided in the corporate context, the court's shift in the analysis of individual and derivative claims will likely be applicable to distinguishing individual and derivative claims in the limited partnership context because the courts have consistently looked to corporate law principles when determining whether claims are individual or derivative.

Standing — Absent either a demand on the general partner to institute action or allegations in the complaint explaining with particularity why a demand was not made on the general partners, a limited partner lacks standing to prosecute a derivative action. *Litman v. Prudential-Bache Properties, Inc.*, 611 A.2d 12 (Del. Ch. 1992).

Standing — In asserting a derivative claim, a plaintiff must either make a demand on the general partners or plead an explanation of why a demand was not made. Accordingly, a plaintiff who failed to make a demand or plead any thing explaining the failure to do so, lacked standing to bring a derivative claim. *Whalen v. Connelly*, 545 N.W.2d 284 (Iowa 1996) (applying Delaware law).

Timely demand for internal redress — Limited partners' failure to make timely and complete demand upon the general partners to seek internal redress for a general partner's negligent conduct would bar a derivative suite by the limited partners. *Murphy v. Bay Shores Six, Ltd. Partnership*, 1987 WL 5776 (Del. Ch. Jan. 26, 1987).

Voluntary dismissal without costs — Limited partners who filed suit in Delaware against the general partner, the general partner's parent corporation, an affiliate corporation and directors and officers of the general partner were allowed to dismiss this suit voluntarily without the imposition of costs. Other limited partners had also filed a similar suit in Florida. *In re Marriott Hotel Properties II Limited Partnership Unitholders Litigation*, 1997 WL 589028 (Del. Ch. Sept. 17, 1997).

§ 17-1004. Expenses.

If a derivative action is successful, in whole or in part, as a result of a judgment, compromise or settlement of any such action, the court may award the plaintiff reasonable expenses, including reasonable attorney's fees, from any recovery in any such action or from a limited partnership.

ANNOTATIONS

Attorney's fees; settlement of suits; merger — A $10 million fee was granted to the attorneys representing the plaintiff limited partners in a derivative suit which was settled. The suit alleged the limited partnership and another entity, controlled by the partnership's controlling partner, entered into a transaction that constituted a breach of fiduciary duty. The controlling partner unfairly favored the other party to the transaction over the partnership by undervaluing the partnership's assets. The suit also alleged that a merger between the partnership and the other entity intended to extinguish the plaintiff's standing to pursue the derivative suit. The fee represented 10% of the settlement to the partnership and constituted compensation for 10,000 hours of work. Attorneys representing limited partners who objected to the settlement of the derivative suit were granted $80,000. *Brinckerhoff v. Texas Eastern Products Pipeline Co.*, 986 A.2d 370 (Del. Ch. 2010).

Subchapter XI
MISCELLANEOUS

§ 17-1101. Construction and application of chapter and partnership agreement.

(a) This chapter shall be so applied and construed to effectuate its general purpose to make uniform the law with respect to the subject of this chapter among states enacting it.

(b) The rule that statutes in derogation of the common law are to be strictly construed shall have no application to this chapter.

(c) It is the policy of this chapter to give maximum effect to the principle of freedom of contract and to the enforceability of partnership agreements.

(d) To the extent that, at law or in equity, a partner or other person has duties (including fiduciary duties) to a limited partnership or to another partner or to another person that is a party to or is otherwise bound by a partnership agreement, the partner's or other person's duties may be expanded or restricted or eliminated by provisions in the partnership agreement; provided that the partnership agreement may not eliminate the implied contractual covenant of good faith and fair dealing.

(e) Unless otherwise provided in a partnership agreement, a partner or other person shall not be liable to a limited partnership or to another partner or to another person that is a party to or is otherwise bound by a partnership agreement for breach of fiduciary duty for the partner's or other person's good faith reliance on the provisions of the partnership agreement.

(f) A partnership agreement may provide for the limitation or elimination of any and all liabilities for breach of contract and breach of duties (including fiduciary duties) of a partner or other person to a limited partnership or to another partner or to another person that is a party to or is otherwise bound by a partnership agreement; provided that a partnership agreement may not limit or eliminate liability for any act or omission that constitutes a bad faith violation of the implied contractual covenant of good faith and fair dealing.

(g) Sections 9-406 and 9-408 of this Title do not apply to any interest in a limited partnership, including all rights, powers and interests arising under a partnership agreement or this chapter. This provision prevails over Sections 9-406 and 9-408 of this Title.

(h) Action validly taken pursuant to one provision of this chapter shall not be deemed invalid solely because it is identical or similar in substance to an action that could have been taken pursuant to some other provision of this chapter but fails to satisfy one or more requirements prescribed by such other provision.

(i) A partnership agreement that provides for the application of Delaware law shall be governed by and construed under the laws of the State of Delaware in accordance with its terms.

ANNOTATIONS

Absent ambiguity, extrinsic evidence is not to be considered — Where the terms of a limited partnership agreement were found not to be ambiguous, extrinsic evidence would not be considered. *Cantera v. Marriott Senior Living Servs., Inc.*, 1999 Del. Ch. LEXIS (Feb. 18, 1999).

Aiding and abetting breach of contractually created fiduciary duty — A claim for aiding and abetting a breach of fiduciary duty may be predicated on a fiduciary duty created by contract. Because the existence of a fiduciary relationship does not depend on the origin of the fiduciary relationship, the origin of the relationship is immaterial to a claim for aiding and abetting a breach of fiduciary duty. Moreover, because Section 17-1101(d) permits partners to define their fiduciary duties in the partnership agreement, it would be inconsistent with Section 17-1101(d) to preclude claims for aiding and abetting breaches of fiduciary duties for which the partners contracted. *Fitzgerald v. Cantor*, 1999 Del. Ch. LEXIS 52 (Mar. 25, 1999).

Ambiguity construed against general partner — In the absence of evidence that a limited partnership agreement was the product of meaningful individualized negotiations between the general partner and all other parties to the agreement, the principal of contra proferentem applies. Accordingly, ambiguous terms in a limited partnership agreement should be construed against the general partner as the entity solely responsible for the articulation of the terms. In such a case, extrinsic evidence is irrelevant to the intent of all of the parties at the time they entered into the agreement. *SI Management L.P. v. Wininger*, 707 A.2d 37 (Del. 1998).

Applicability of principles of contract interpretation; ambiguity — It is well-settled that Delaware courts apply principles of contract interpretation to limited partnership agreements. A contract provision is ambiguous only when the provisions in controversy are reasonably or fairly susceptible of different interpretations or may have two or more different meanings. A contract is to be construed as it would be understood by an objective reasonable third party. *Cantera v. Marriott Senior Living Servs., Inc.*, 1999 Del. Ch. LEXIS (Del. Ch. Feb. 18, 1999).

Approval of transaction neither ratification nor amendment — That limited partners voted in favor of a sale transaction did not constitute ratification of the general partner's termination of priority distributions under the partnership agreement nor approval of an amendment to the partnership agreement to permit such termination. Ratification requires that the specific transaction to be ratified be clearly delineated to the limited partners' whose approval is sought and that the approval be put to a vote. Similarly, where no amendment to the partnership agreement is proposed and limited partners are not asked to vote on a amendment, mere approval of transaction did not amend agreement. *In re Cencom Cable Income Partners, L.P. Litigation*, 2000 WL 640676 (Del. Ch. May 5, 2000).

Breach of covenant of good faith and fair dealing — In response to a buy/sell notice from a limited partner, the limited partner to whom the notice was directed (i) refused to perform in accordance with the partnership agreement, (ii) made a non-conforming counteroffer, (iii) threatened litigation, and (iv) engaged in conduct designed to exert economic coercion in order to force the other limited partner to accept a sum for its interest that was far lower than what the limited partner was entitled to receive. Such conduct constituted a breach of the implied contractual covenant of good faith and fair dealing. *PAMI-LEMB I Inc. v. EMB-NHC, L.L.C.*, 2004 WL 1488720 (Del. Ch. June 22, 2004).

Breach of fiduciary duty; competition — As a matter of statutory law, traditional fiduciary duties among and between partners are default rules that may be modified by the partnership agreement. Where partnership agreement expressly provided that any partner could compete directly or indirectly with the business of the partnership, the partnership could have no legitimate expectancy to be informed of or to participate in investments made by the general partner or its affiliates. In the absence of a showing that the investment opportunity came to the general partner in its capacity as such and was diverted to the general partner or its affiliates, there was no usurpation of partnership opportunity. *Kahn v. Icahn*, 1998 WL 832629 (Del. Ch. Nov. 12, 1998).

Breach of fiduciary duty; standard set by agreement — A limited partnership agreement may provide for contractually created fiduciary duties substantially mirroring traditional fiduciary duties that apply in corporation law. A limited partnership agreement provided for such fiduciary duties by requiring the general partner and its controlling entity to treat the limited partners in accordance with the "entire fairness" standard. The general partner and its corporate parent breached this fiduciary duty owed to a limited partner. An audit committee never reviewed certain transactions. *Gotham Partners, L.P. v. Hallwood Realty Partners, L.P.*, 817 A.2d 160 (Del. 2002).

Conflict of interests — Contract provisions preempt fiduciary principles. Thus, where in accordance with the provisions of the partnership agreement, the general partner submitted transaction in which the general partner had a conflict of interest to the limited partnership's Conflicts and Audit Committee for approval, and the committee gave its approval, compliance with the partnership agreement barred any challenge based on default principals of law or equity. *Brickell Partners v. Wise*, 794 A.2d 1 (Del. Ch. 2001).

Contract may modify fiduciary duties — Under Delaware law, in the limited partnership context the tension between contract principles and fiduciary duties is resolved in favor of contract law, rendering fiduciary duties default rules. Thus, parties to a limited partnership agreement can enter into a contract that diminishes the general partner's fiduciary duties. Where the contract amends the fiduciary duties a general partner owes to limited partners, the court will give full force to the terms of the contract. *The Continental Insurance Company v. Rutledge & Company, Inc.*, 2000 WL 62951 (Del. Ch. Jan. 10, 2000).

Contract provisions control rights and duties — Limited partnership agreement is the operative document governing the rights and responsibilities of the partners, and the statute provides "fall-back" or default provisions where the agreement is silent. Where the provisions defining the rights and responsibilities of the parties are spelled out with particularity, those provisions are accorded significant deference by the court, and the contract provisions, not default fiduciary rules, control whether conduct constitutes a breach of duty. *Cantor Fitzgerald, L.P. v. Cantor*, 2001 WL 1456494 (Del. Ch. Nov. 5, 2001).

Contractual fiduciary duty — Where a fiduciary duty of loyalty is expressly written into a limited partnership agreement, the court will conclude that the parties bargained for the provision. It is crucial to the orderly management of, and the related economic success of, limited partnerships that the Delaware courts uphold bargained-for fiduciary duties contained in limited partnership agreements. *Cantor Fitzgerald, L.P. v. Cantor*, 1998 WL 409371 (Del. Ch. July 12, 1998).

Contractual fiduciary duty governs obligations — Claims that competitive activity breached a fiduciary duty of loyalty expressly created by the partnership agreement would not be dismissed for failure to state a claim. However, because a claim for unjust enrichment does not lie when a contract determines the obligations between the parties, a claim of unjust enrichment from competitive activity alleged to breach a limited partner's implied duty of loyalty would be dismissed. Whether an implied duty of loyalty applies to limited partners generally need not be addressed where the limited partnership agreement itself expressly creates such a duty. The parties had pursuant to Section 17-1101(d) addressed the fiduciary duty of loyalty, and it may be assumed that the parties intended the nature and scope of the fiduciary duties adopted by them in the agreement. Consistent with the policy expressed in Section 17-1101(c), Delaware law favors allowing parties to an agreement to pursue their own aims in the absence of underlying fraud or innocent misrepresentations that taints the agreement actually reached. *Cantor Fitzgerald, L.P. v. Cantor*, 1998 Del. Ch. LEXIS 97 (June 16, 1998).

Creation of fiduciary duties by contract — Partnership agreement of a Delaware limited partnership may provide that all partners, including limited partners who neither manage, operate nor govern the partnership, are subject to a fiduciary duty of loyalty. Section 17-1101(d), which permits duties to be expanded or restricted, does not by implication preclude a limited partnership from creating duties that do not exist separately at law or in equity. *Cantor Fitzgerald, L.P. v. Cantor*, 2000 WL 307370 (Del. Ch. Mar. 17, 2000).

Duties of loyalty and care — In the absence of a partnership agreement making plain the parties' intention to preempt the fundamental fiduciary duties of loyalty and care, a general partner remains obligated to act fairly toward limited partners and to prove fairness when it makes self-interested decisions. *Active Assets Recovery, Inc. v. Real Estate Asset Recovery Services, Inc.*, 1999 WL 743479 (Del. Ch. Sept. 10, 1999).

Duty of loyalty not modified — A provision in a limited partnership agreement expressly providing that the general partner could engage in other business ventures altered the general partner's duty of loyalty so as to permit the general partner to take for itself what would otherwise constitute partnership opportunities. However, such a provision does not alter the duty of loyalty's prohibition against self-dealing. *The Continental Insurance Company v. Rutledge & Company, Inc.*, 2000 WL 62951 (Del. Ch. Jan. 10, 2000).

Enforceability of agreement — Explicitly negotiated and validly adopted provisions of a partnership agreement will be enforced in the absence of any defect in process, such as fraud, non-disclosure or manipulation by a fiduciary. *U.S. West, Inc. v. Time Warner Inc.*, 1996 WL 307445 (Del. Ch. June 6, 1996).

Fiduciary duty of limited partner — In the absence of a provision in the partnership agreement imposing fiduciary duties on limited partners, a limited partner who has no power to manage or control the partnership property owes no fiduciary duty to other partners in connection with making a mini-tender offer for limited partnership interests. *Bond Purchase, L.L.C. v. Patriot Tax Credit Properties, L.P.*, 1999 Del. Ch. LEXIS 159 (July 23, 1999), motion to stay denied, 1999 Del. Ch. LEXIS 170 (Aug. 16, 1999).

Freedom of contract — The limited partnership act permits partners to have the broadest possible discretion in drafting their agreement. The partnership agreement is the cornerstone of a Delaware limited partnership, and effectively constitutes the entire agreement among the partners with respect to the admission of partners and the creation, operation and termination of the limited partnership. Once partners exercise their contractual freedom, they have a great deal of certainty that their partnership agreement will be enforced in accordance with its terms. *Elf Atochem North America, Inc. v. Jaffari*, 727 A.2d 286 (Del. 1999) (dicta, comparing limited partnership law and limited liability company law).

Freedom of contract — The Delaware limited partnership act is designed to provide the contracting parties with the maximum level of contracting freedom. *Active Assets Recovery, Inc. v. Real Estate Asset Recovery Services, Inc.*, 1999 WL 743479 (Del. Ch. Sept. 10, 1999).

General partner under no duty to protect against unfairly priced offer by affiliate — Where an affiliate of the general partner made a tender offer, the general partner had no duty to protect limited partners from an unfair price. Unlike a third party tender offer, the affiliate of the general partner had a fiduciary obligation to make is offer non-coercive and with complete disclosure. Such duties adequately protect the interests of limited partners. *In re Marriott Hotel Properties II Limited Partnership*, 2000 WL 128875 (Del. Ch. Jan. 24, 2000).

Good faith reliance on agreement requires ambiguity — For a general partner to be protected from liability based on good faith reliance on the provisions of a limited partnership agreement, the provision allegedly relied on must be ambiguous. If the agreement is not ambiguous, then Section 1101(d)(1) does not apply. A general partner cannot wrongly rely in good faith on a misinterpretation of a contract clause if it is subject to only one plausible interpretation. *The Continental Insurance Company v. Rutledge & Company, Inc.*, 2000 WL 62951 (Del. Ch. Jan. 10, 2000).

Implied contractual obligation — A contractual obligation will not be implied unless the court, by reference to the express terms of the contract, can conclude that the parties to the contract, at the time of its drafting, would have agreed to be bound by the implied obligation. Where a partnership agreement prohibited limited partners from competing with the partnership's "Cellular Service" and defined "Cellular Service" with precision, the parties knew at the time of drafting that other forms of competition might be developed and the partnership agreement expressly permitted limited partners to engage in any other business venture, the court would not imply an obligation not to compete with the partnership through the use of new technology that, while not within the definition of "Cellular Service," enabled limited partners to offer essentially the same service as the partnership. *Cincinnati SMSA Limited Partnership v. Cincinnati Bell Cellular Systems Co.*, 1997 WL 525873 (Del. Ch. Aug. 13, 1997), *aff'd*, 1998 Del. LEXIS 175 (Apr. 30, 1998).

Implied obligations — Implying obligations based on the implied covenant of good faith and fair dealing is a cautious enterprise, and the Court will not imply an obligation on the part of a limited partner not to compete when the partnership agreement clearly, expressly and unambiguously limits prohibited competition and provides generous leeway to partners with respect to other ventures. *Cincinnati SMSA Limited Partnership v. Cincinnati Bell Cellular Systems Company*, 708 A.2d 989 (Del. 1998).

Interpretation of agreement — The provisions of a limited partnership agreement should be interpreted using basic rules of contract law, which require the intention of the parties to be determined from the language of the agreement. The agreement should be read in its entirety and interpreted to reconcile all of its provisions. *In re Cencom Cable Income Partners, L.P. Litigation*, 2000 WL 640676 (Del. Ch. May 5, 2000).

Interpretation of agreement — In interpreting partnership agreement, court will look at the entire agreement to determine intent and existence of ambiguity. If the contract is clear, the court will rely on the literal meaning of the words, will not look to extrinsic evidence, and will not attempt to discern intent of the parties. If ambiguity exists, the court will consider extrinsic evidence to determine the reasonable shared expectations of the parties at the time of contracting. *Interactive Corp. v. Vivendi Universal, S.A.*, 2004 WL 1572932 (Del. Ch. July 6, 2004).

Latent ambiguity — Where limited partnership agreement defined "Cellular Service" in precise terms as service authorized by the FCC under Part 22 of its cellular rules, and there were no internal inconsistencies within the partnership agreement, later developed technology authorized by the FCC under Part 24 of its cellular rules and which permitted limited partners to compete with the partnership by offering an essentially identical service did not create a latent ambiguity justifying resort to extrinsic evidence to interpret the definition of "Cellular Service." *Cincinnati SMSA Limited Partnership v. Cincinnati Bell Cellular Systems Co.*, 1997 WL 525873 (Del. Ch. Aug. 13, 1997), *aff'd*, 1998 Del. LEXIS 175 (Del. Apr. 30, 1998).

Limited partner's fiduciary duty — Unless expressly modified by the partnership agreement, a limited partner owes to other partners the fiduciary duties set forth in Section 1521 of the Delaware Uniform Partnership Act, specifically the duty to account to the partnership for any benefit, and to hold as trustee for it any profits, derived by the limited partner without the consent of the other partners from any transaction connected with the conduct of the partnership or from any use of partnership property. *RJ Associates, Inc. v. Health Payors' Organization Limited Partnership*, 1999 Del. Ch. LEXIS 161 (July 16, 1999).

Mistake — To warrant reformation of a limited partnership agreement based on either mutual mistake or unilateral mistake, the party seeking reformation must allege and prove by clear and convincing evidence that the parties came to a specific prior understanding that differed materially from the written agreement. *Interactive Corp. v. Vivendi Universal, S.A.*, 2004 WL 1572932 (Del. Ch. July 6, 2004).

Modification of default fiduciary duties — Where application of default fiduciary duties can be reconciled with the practical operation of the terms of the partnership agreement, default fiduciary duties will apply absent clear contractual language disclaiming their applicability. If use of default fiduciary duties would intrude on the contractual rights or expectations of the general partner, or be insensible in view of the contractual mechanisms governing the transaction under consideration, default fiduciary duties will not be applied. *R.S.M., Inc. v. Alliance Capital Management Holdings L.P.*, 790 A.2d 478 (Del. Ch. 2001).

Modification of fiduciary duties — Limited partnership agreement expressly provided that the standard of conduct contained in the partnership agreement superseded any other standards, including standards under the Delaware RULPA or other applicable law. Accordingly, the agreement effectively modified the general partner's fiduciary duties such that the general partner would not be liable for breach of contract or of fiduciary duty simply because the result of its actions was not entirely fair. Rather, liability would exist only on a showing of violation of the contractual standards of gross negligence, wanton or willful misconduct, or actions taken in bad faith. Where actions of general partner would deprive certain limited partners of their investment at a book value materially below fair value and place heavy concentration of ownership in affiliates of the general partner, plaintiffs raised a litigable issue of bad faith sufficient to withstand a motion to dismiss for failure to state a claim. *Gelfman v. Weeden Investors, L.P.*, 792 A.2d 977 (Del. Ch. 2001).

Modification of fiduciary duties — Partners may modify fiduciary duties through contract. General partner who exercised right under the partnership agreement to purchase assets at appraised value rather than seek a third party purchaser did not breach its fiduciary duty to limited partners. *In re Cencom Cable Income Partners LP Litigation*, 1996 WL 74726 (Del. Ch. Feb. 15, 1996); *James River-Pennington Inc. v. CRSS Capital, Inc.*, 1995 WL 106554 (Del. Ch. Mar. 6, 1995).

Modification of fiduciary duties — merger — Unless limited by the partnership agreement, a general partner has the fiduciary duty to manage the partnership in the interests of the partnership and its limited partners. However, principles of contract preempt fiduciary principles where the parties to a limited partnership have plainly intended to do so. Only when the partnership agreement is silent or ambiguous will the Court turn for guidance to the statutory default rules, traditional notions of fiduciary duties or other extrinsic evidence. Where the partnership agreement gave general partner sole discretion to structure a merger of the partnership, discretion was defined in a manner that did not require the general partner to consider the interests of the partnership or limited partners, and limited partners had the right under the agreement to accept or reject the merger by a two-thirds vote, complaint alleging that the general partner reached its fiduciary duties by proposing an unfair merger or unfairly manipulating its timing would be dismissed for failure to state a claim. *Sonet v. Timber Company, L.P.*, 1998 WL 749445 (Del. Ch. Dec. 16, 1998).

No breach of fiduciary duty where partners rely on terms of partnership agreement — When partnership agreement of Delaware limited partnership provided for termination of a partner's interest at the sole discretion of the other partners, remaining partners in the limited partnership did not breach their fiduciary duty of good faith by forfeiting and reallocating the general partner's interest upon his termination as general partner because they relied in good faith on the provisions of the partnership agreement. *Rothmeier v. Investment Advisers, Inc.*, 556 N.W. 2d 590 (Minn Ct. App. 1996), *review denied*, 1997 Minn. LEXIS 148 (Minn. Feb. 26, 1997).

No implied obligation to establish a fair price in a tender offer — Where the partnership agreement contained provisions protecting limited partners in the event of certain transactions between the partnership and the general partner or its affiliates, but did not provide for any protective provisions in the event of a tender offer by an affiliate of the general partner, and because acceptance of a tender offer is essentially voluntary in nature, the court would not imply an intention to subject a tender offer to an independent appraisal process. *In re Marriott Hotel Properties II Limited Partnership*, 2000 WL 128875 (Del. Ch. Jan. 24, 2000).

Non-conforming capital contribution breached agreement — Partnership's acceptance of a capital contribution made by one partner in response to a non-conforming capital call was a breach of contract, and the capital contribution could not be used to justify a modification to a non-contributing limited partner's capital account in connection with the purchase of the limited partner's interest upon exercise of put option by the limited partner. *Telstra Corporation, Ltd. v. Dynegy, Inc.*, 2003 WL 1016984 (Del. Ch. Mar. 4, 2003).

Oral amendments — Where partnership agreement expressly provided that all amendments were to be in writing signed by all of the partners, party seeking to prove oral amendment must present specific and direct evidence of the oral amendment that leaves no doubt of the intention of the parties to change what was previously solemnized by a formal document. *The Continental Insurance Company v. Rutledge & Company, Inc.*, 2000 WL 62951 (Del. Ch. Jan. 10, 2000).

Outside majority approval may extinguish fiduciary duty claims — Where a limited partnership agreement requires a transaction between the partnership and the general partner to be approved by a majority of the limited partners unaffiliated with the general partner, such approval extinguishes any breach of fiduciary duty claim unless the general partner has failed to comply with its duty of disclosure in connection with obtaining limited partner approval. *R.S.M., Inc. v. Alliance Capital Management Holdings, L.P.*, 790 A.2d 478 (Del. Ch. 2001).

Partnership opportunities — When partnership agreement allowed general partner to engage in similar ventures without offering the opportunity to the limited partnership or other partners, such a provision did not violate the Delaware law and a general partner was free to engage in such conduct without breach of the partnership agreement. *Whalen v. Connelly*, 545 N.W.2d 284 (Iowa 1996) (applying Delaware Law).

Reliance on provisions of agreement — Absent allegations of facts from which an inference of bad faith can be drawn, a complaint fails to state a cause of action for breach of fiduciary duty by a general partner where the general partner has relied on the provisions of the partnership agreement as authority for the conduct alleged to be a breach of fiduciary duty. *United States Cellular Investment Company of Allentown v. Bell Atlantic Mobile Systems, Inc.*, 1994 Del. Ch. LEXIS 37 (Del. Ch. March 11, 1994), *aff'd*, 677 A.2d 497 (Del. 1996).

Repudiation of agreement — Where a limited partner invoked a buy/sell provision, and the limited partner to whom the notice was directed stated that it would perform only on terms different from those provided in the agreement and threatened litigation if its terms were not accepted, it repudiated the agreement, could not act a buyer, and was required to sell its interest pursuant to the terms of the agreement to the limited partner who had sent the buy/sell notice. *PAMI-LEMB I Inc. v. EMB-NHC, L.L.C.*, 2004 WL 1488720 (Del. Ch. June 22, 2004).

Restriction of fiduciary duties — Restrictions on fiduciary duties must be set forth clearly and unambiguously. Where partnership agreement gave the general partner sole discretion to determine certain matters, provided that in exercising its sole discretion the general partner did not have to consider the interests of the partnership or its limited partners, and provided that the general partner was not subject to any different standard of conduct imposed by the partnership agreement or other agreements, the general partner remained subject to default fiduciary duties in exercising its discretion. The agreement was ineffective to limit application of default fiduciary duties because it did not expressly provide that default fiduciary duties did not apply if they would hinder the general partner's discretion, but only provided that other standards set out in the agreement would give way. *Miller v. American Real Estate Partners, L.P.*, 2001 WL 1045643 (Del. Ch. Sept. 6, 2001).

Safe harbor against breach of fiduciary duty claims — Limited partner did not plead that general partner acted in bad faith, so a general partner acting in good faith reliance on the provisions of the partnership agreement is shielded from liability for breach of fiduciary duty. *U.S. Cellular Inv. Co. of Allentown v. Bell Atlantic Mobile Systems, Inc.*, 677 A.2d 497 (Del. 1996).

Special litigation committees — The general partners' authority to manage the partnership affairs includes the right to determine whether derivative actions should proceed. Delaware law does not contain an express provision allowing general partners to delegate their authority to a special litigation committee; therefore, such rights and responsibilities are determined by the parties' particular partnership agreement. *Katell v. Morgan Stanley Group, Inc.*, 1993 Del. Ch. LEXIS 92 (Del. Ch. June 8, 1993).

Standards governing proposed merger; fiduciary duty eliminated; covenant of good faith and fair dealing — A proposed merger between a master limited partnership and another non-party limited partnership, sought to be enjoined by a limited partner, did not violate the covenant of good faith and fair dealing owed to him by the partnership. The partnership agreement specifically eliminated the fiduciary duty that would otherwise be owed by the general partner to a limited partner leaving the agreement as the sole basis for the obligations between the two. The covenant of good faith and fair dealing arising from the agreement was not a substitute for a fiduciary duty, the court's most powerful remedial and gap-filling power. The partnership agreement established a contractual standard of review of transactions that supplanted fiduciary duty analysis, which was followed in the merger process. This standard did not require a search for alternative transactions to prevent an alleged undervaluation of the limited partner interest, as claimed by the limited partner. Instead, it provided a "Special Approval" process outlined in the agreement. Nor did the covenant of good faith and fair dealing require that the merger be conditioned on approval of a majority of the minority voting rights, also as claimed by the challenging limited partner. *Lonergan v. EPE Holdings, LLC,* 5 A.3d 1008 (Del. Ch. 2010).

Tender offer did not violate implied covenant of good faith and fair dealing — Tender offer by affiliate of general partner did not result in a breach by the general partner of the implied covenant of good faith and fair dealing. Nothing in the partnership agreement precluded such a tender offer, and the tender offer was voluntary. Accordingly, the tender offer was not a device to circumvent protections in the partnership agreement relating to a sale of assets to an affiliate. *In re Marriott Hotel Properties II Limited Partnership,* 2000 WL 128875 (Del. Ch. Jan. 24, 2000).

Tender offer not a sale of assets — A tender offer by an affiliate of a general partner was not a sale of assets to the affiliate so as to trigger provisions in the partnership agreement requiring an appraisal process in connection with a sale of assets to an affiliate of the general partner. *In re Marriott Hotel Properties II Limited Partnership,* 2000 WL 128875 (Del. Ch. Jan. 24, 2000).

Decisions under prior law

Policy of prior act — Although the provisions of the Delaware Limited Partnership Act were intended to govern all questions arising out of the formation and operation of limited partnerships formed after 1973, when that act is silent as to a particular right or obligation it should be construed, under section 1730 thereof, "so as to flesh out the parties' agreement consistent with promoting the policy of that act, of creating and maintaining certainty in business relationships." *Weltman v. Silna,* 739 F. Supp. 477 (E.D. Mo. 1990), *aff'd on other grounds,* 936 F.2d 358 (8th Cir. 1991), *cert. denied,* 502 U.S. 941, 112 S. Ct. 377 (1991).

Statutory construction; general presumptions and rules — The validity of a limited partnership amendment, where an existing limited partner is not included in the amended version of the limited partnership membership composition, is not covered by the Delaware Limited Partnership Act, and also is not covered by the original partnership agreement, should be resolved under section 1730 of that act and the general presumptions and rules governing statutory construction. *Weltman v. Silna,* 739 F. Supp. 477 (E.D., Mo. 1990), *aff'd on other grounds,* 936 F.2d 358 (8th Cir. 1991), *cert. denied,* 112 S. Ct. 377 (1991).

§ 17-1102. Short title.

This chapter may be cited as the "Delaware Revised Uniform Limited Partnership Act."

§ 17-1103. Severability.

If any provision of this chapter or its application to any person or circumstances is held invalid, the invalidity does not affect other provisions or applications of the chapter which can be given effect without the invalid provision or application, and to this end the provisions of this chapter are severable.

§ 17-1104. Effective date and extended effective date.

(a) All limited partnerships formed on or after January 1, 1983, the "effective date," shall be governed by this chapter.

(b) Except as provided in subsections (e) and (f) of this section, all limited partnerships formed on or after July 1, 1973, and prior to the effective date, under chapter 17 of this title as hereby repealed, shall continue to be governed by that chapter until January 1, 1985, the "extended effective date," at which time such limited partnerships shall be governed by this chapter.

(c) Except as provided in subsection (e) of this section, a limited partnership formed prior to July 1, 1973, shall continue to be governed by Chapter 17 of this title in effect prior to the adoption of Chapter 17 of this title as hereby repealed, except that such limited partnership shall not be renewed except under this chapter.

(d) Except as provided in subsection (e) of this section, subchapter IX of this chapter, dealing with foreign limited partnerships, is not effective until the extended effective date.

(e) Any limited partnership formed prior to the effective date, and any foreign limited partnership, may elect to be governed by this chapter before the extended effective date by filing with the Secretary of State a certificate of limited partnership or an application for registration as a foreign limited partnership which complies with this chapter or a certificate of amendment which would cause its certificate of limited partnership to comply with this chapter and which specifically states that it is electing to be so bound.

(f) With respect to a limited partnership formed on or after July 1, 1973, and prior to the effective date:

(1) On and after the extended effective date, such limited partnership need not file with the Secretary of State a certificate of amendment which would cause its certificate of limited partnership to comply with this chapter until the occurrence of an event which, under this chapter, requires the filing of a certificate of amendment;

(2) Sections 17-501 and 17-502 of this title shall apply only to contributions and distributions made after the effective date; and

(3) Section 17-704 of this title shall apply only to assignments made after the effective date.

ANNOTATIONS

Applicability of Act — Under § 17-1104(b), the Revised Uniform Limited Partnership Act (effective January 1, 1983) applies only to acts performed after January 1, 1985 by limited partnerships formed after July 1, 1973, rather than applying after January 1, 1985 to acts performed at any time by limited partnerships formed after July 1, 1973. *Weltman v. Silna*, 879 F.2d 425 (8th Cir. 1989).

Applicability of Act to 1975 amendment to partnership agreement — Under § 17-1104(b), the Revised Uniform Limited Partnership Act applies only to acts *performed after* January 1, 1985 by limited partnerships formed after July 1, 1973, so that when, as president of the corporate general partner of a limited partnership, a limited partner signed a 1975 amendment to the partnership agreement that added several new limited partners but omitted his own name as a limited partner, the issue of whether that limited partner technically withdrew from the partnership is governed by Del. Code Ann., tit. 6, § 1725, the predecessor to § 17-204. *Weltman v. Silna*, 879 F.2d 425 (8th Cir. 1989).

§ 17-1105. Cases not provided for in this chapter.

In any case not provided for in this chapter the Delaware Uniform Partnership Law (6 Del. C. § 1501, *et seq.*) and the rules of law and equity, including the Law Merchant, shall govern.

ANNOTATIONS

Claims after removal — The general partner removed by the limited partners was entitled to fair value for his capital contribution. Although this eventuality was not covered in the limited partnership agreement, the removal of the general partner was an "event of withdrawal," under DRULPA Section 17-402(a)(3); however, the removed general partner was not a "withdrawing partner," under DRULPA Section 17-604, entitled to the remedies in that section. Turning to the DUPA, as provided in DRULPA Section 17-1105, the removed general partner was only entitled to receive fair value for his partnership capital interest. In addition, the removed general partner did not have standing to pursue claims against the new general partner and the limited partners based on events which occurred after his removal (e.g., alleged breach of fiduciary duty and breach of the limited partnership agreement). Once removed as general partner, he became only a contract claimant with fixed rights (i.e., to receive fair value for his partnership interest). *Hillman v. Hillman*, 903 A.2d 798 (Del. Ch. 2006).

Dissolution by express will — Where a limited partnership agreement contained no provisions limiting the dissolution rights of the partners, the partners implicitly retain the right to dissolve the partnership by the express will of any partner. Section 17-1105 of the Delaware limited partnership act makes the Delaware uniform partnership act applicable to matters not provided for in the limited partnership act, and Section 15-1531(2) of the uniform partnership act permits a partnership to be dissolved by the express will of any partner. Thus, in the absence of an agreement to the contrary, the partners retained the right to dissolve the partnership by the express will of any partner. *Active Asset Recovery, Inc. v. Real Estate Asset Recovery Services, Inc.*, 1999 WL 743479 (Del. Ch. Sept 10, 1999).

Service of process — Section 17-911 dealing with service of process on unregistered foreign limited partnerships doing business in Delaware does not address service of process on an unregistered foreign limited partnership having a Delaware corporation as its general partner. In such a case, it is appropriate to look to general partnership law relating to service of process on foreign general partnerships and to extend such law to limited partnerships. *Macklowe v. Planet Hollywood, Inc.*, 1994 Del. Ch. LEXIS 179 (Del. Ch., Oct. 13, 1994).

§ 17-1106. Prior law.

Except as set forth in § 17-1104 of this title, Chapter 17 of this title is hereby repealed.

§ 17-1107. Fees.

(a) No document required to be filed under this chapter shall be effective until the applicable fee required by this section is paid. The following fees shall be paid to and collected by the Secretary of State for the use of the State of Delaware:

(1) Upon the receipt for filing of an application for reservation of name, an application for renewal of reservation or a notice of transfer or cancellation of reservation pursuant to § 17-103(b) of this title, a fee in the amount of $75.

(2) Upon the receipt for filing of a certificate under § 17-104(b) of this title, a fee in the amount of $200, upon the receipt for filing of a certificate under § 17-104(c) of this title, a fee in the amount of $200, and upon the receipt for filing of a certificate under § 17-104(d) of this title, a fee in the amount of $2.00 for each limited partnership whose registered agent has resigned by such certificate.

(3) Upon the receipt for filing of a certificate of limited partnership domestication under § 17-215 of this title, a certificate of transfer or a certificate of transfer and domestic continuance under § 17-216 of this title, a certificate of conversion to limited partnership under § 17-217 of this title, a certificate of conversion to a non-Delaware entity under § 17-219 of this title, a certificate of limited partnership under § 17-201 of this title, a certificate of amendment under § 17-202 of this title, (except as otherwise provided in paragraph (a)(11) of this section) a certificate of cancellation under § 17-203 of this title, a certificate of merger or consolidation or a certificate of ownership and merger under § 17-211 of this title, a restated certificate of limited partnership under § 17-210 of this title, a certificate of amendment of a certificate with a future effective date or time under § 17-206(c) of this title, a certificate of termination of a certificate with a future effective date or time under § 17-206(c) of this title, a certificate of correction under § 17-213 of this title, or a certificate of revival under § 17-1111 of this title, a fee in the amount of $200.

(4) For certifying copies of any paper on file as provided for by this chapter, a fee in the amount of $50 for each copy certified.

(5) The Secretary of State may issue photocopies or electronic image copies of instruments on file, as well as instruments, documents and other papers not on file, and for all such photocopies or electronic image copies, whether certified or not, a fee of $10 shall be paid for the first page and $2 for each additional page. The Secretary of State may also issue microfiche copies of instruments on file as well as instruments, documents and other papers not on file, and for each such microfiche a fee of $2 shall be paid therefor. Notwithstanding the State of Delaware's Freedom of Information Act or other provision of this Code granting access to public records, the Secretary of State shall issue only photocopies, microfiche or electronic image copies of records in exchange for the fees described above.

(6) Upon the receipt for filing of an application for registration as a foreign limited partnership under § 17-902 of this title, a certificate under § 17-905 of this title or a certificate of cancellation under § 17-906 of this title, a fee in the amount of $200.

(7) Upon the receipt for filing of a certificate under § 17-904(c) of this title, a fee in the amount of $200, upon the receipt for filing of a certificate under § 17-904(d) of this title, a fee in the amount of $200, and upon the receipt for filing of a certificate under § 17-904(e) of this title, a fee in the amount of $2.00 for each foreign limited partnership whose registered agent has resigned by such certificate.

(8) For preclearance of any document for filing, a fee in the amount of $250.

(9) For preparing and providing a written report of a record search, a fee in the amount of $50.

(10) For issuing any certificate of the Secretary of State, including but not limited to a certificate of good standing, other than a certification of a copy under paragraph (4) of this subsection, a fee in the amount of $50, except that for issuing any certificate of the Secretary of State that recites all of a limited partnership's filings with the Secretary of State, a fee of $175 shall be paid for each such certificate.

(11) For receiving and filing and/or indexing any certificate, affidavit, agreement or any other paper provided for by this chapter, for which no different fee is specifically prescribed, a fee in the amount of $100. For filing any instrument submitted by a limited partnership or foreign limited partnership that only changes the registered office or registered agent and is specifically captioned as a certificate of amendment changing only the registered office or registered agent, a fee in the amount of $50.

(12) The Secretary of State may in his or her discretion charge a fee of $60 for each check received for payment of any fee that is returned due to insufficient funds or the result of a stop payment order.

(b) In addition to those fees charged under subsection (a) of this section, there shall be collected by and paid to the Secretary of State the following:

(1) For all services described in subsection (a) of this section that are requested to be completed within 30 minutes on the same day as the day of the request, an additional sum of up to $7,500 and for all services described in subsection (a) of this section that are requested to be completed within one (1) hour on the same day as the day of the request, an additional sum of up to $1,000 and for all services described in subsection (a) of this section that are requested to be completed within 2 hours on the same day as the day of the request, an additional sum of $200.

(2) For all services described in subsection (a) of this section that are requested to be completed within the same day as the day of the request, an additional sum of up to $300; and

(3) For all services described in subsection (a) of this section that are requested to be completed within a 24-hour period from the time of the request, an additional sum of up to $150.

The Secretary of State shall establish (and may from time to time amend) a schedule of specific fees payable pursuant to this subsection.

(c) The Secretary of State may in his or her discretion permit the extension of credit for the fees required by this section upon such terms as the Secretary shall deem to be appropriate.

(d) The Secretary of State shall retain from the revenue collected from the fees required by this section a sum sufficient to provide at all times a fund of at least $500, but not more than $1,500, from which the secretary may refund any payment made pursuant to this section to the extent that it exceeds the fees required by this section. The funds shall be deposited in a financial institution which is a legal depository of State of Delaware moneys to the credit of the Secretary of State and shall be disbursable on order of the Secretary of State.

(e) Except as provided in this section, the fees of the Secretary of State shall be as provided in § 2315 of Title 29.

§ 17-1108. Reserved power of State of Delaware to alter or repeal chapter.

All provisions of this chapter may be altered from time to time or repealed and all rights of partners are subject to this reservation. Unless expressly stated to the contrary in this chapter, all amendments of this chapter shall apply to limited partnerships and partners whether or not existing as such at the time of the enactment of any such amendment.

§ 17-1109. Annual tax of domestic limited partnership and foreign limited partnership.

(a) Every domestic limited partnership and every foreign limited partnership registered to do business in the State of Delaware shall pay an annual tax, for the use of the State of Delaware, in the amount of $200.

(b) The annual tax shall be due and payable on the 1st day of June following the close of the calendar year or upon the cancellation of a certificate of limited partnership. The Secretary of State shall receive the annual tax and pay over all taxes collected to the Department of Finance of the State of Delaware. If the annual tax remains unpaid after the due date established by subsection (d) of this section, the tax shall bear interest at the rate of 1½% for each month or portion thereof until fully paid.

(c) The Secretary of State shall, at least 60 days prior to the 1st day of June of each year, cause to be mailed to each domestic limited partnership and foreign limited partnership required to comply with the provisions of this section in care of its registered agent in the State of Delaware an annual statement for the tax to be paid hereunder.

(d) In the event of neglect, refusal or failure on the part of any domestic limited partnership or foreign limited partnership to pay the annual tax to be paid hereunder on or before the 1st day of June in any year, such domestic limited partnership or foreign limited partnership shall pay the sum of $200 to be recovered by adding that amount to the annual tax, and such additional sum shall become a part of the tax and shall be collected in the same manner and subject to the same penalties.

(e) In case any domestic limited partnership or foreign limited partnership shall fail to pay the annual tax due within the time required by this section, and in case the agent in charge of the registered office of any domestic limited partnership or foreign limited partnership upon whom process against such domestic limited partnership or foreign limited partnership may be served shall die, resign, refuse to act as such, remove from the State of Delaware or cannot with due diligence be found, it shall be lawful while default continues to serve process against such domestic limited partnership or foreign limited partnership upon the Secretary of State. Such service upon the Secretary of State shall be made in the manner and shall have the effect stated in § 17-105 of this title in the case of a domestic limited partnership and § 17-910 of this title in the case of a foreign limited partnership and shall be governed in all respects by said sections.

(f) The annual tax shall be a debt due from a domestic limited partnership or foreign limited partnership to the State of Delaware, for which an action at law may be maintained after the same shall have been in arrears for a period of 1 month. The tax shall also be a preferred debt in the case of insolvency.

(g) A domestic limited partnership or foreign limited partnership that neglects, refuses or fails to pay the annual tax when due shall cease to be in good standing as a domestic limited partnership or registered as a foreign limited partnership in the State of Delaware.

(h) A domestic limited partnership that has ceased to be in good standing or a foreign limited partnership that has ceased to be registered by reason of the failure to pay an annual tax shall be restored to and have the status of a domestic limited partnership in good standing or a foreign limited partnership that is registered in the State of Delaware upon the payment of the annual tax and all penalties and interest thereon for each year for which such domestic limited partnership or foreign limited partnership neglected, refused or failed to pay an annual tax. A fee as set forth in § 17-1107(a)(3) of this title shall be paid at the time of restoration.

(i) The Attorney General, either on the Attorney General's own motion or upon request of the Secretary of State, whenever any annual tax due under this chapter from any domestic limited partnership or foreign limited partnership shall have remained in arrears for a period of 3 months after the tax shall have become payable, may apply to the Court of Chancery, by petition in the name of the State of Delaware, on 5 days' notice to such domestic limited partnership or foreign limited partnership, which notice may be served in such manner as the Court may direct, for an injunction to restrain such domestic limited partnership or foreign limited partnership from the transaction of any business within the State of Delaware or elsewhere, until the payment of the annual tax, and all penalties and interest due thereon and the cost of the application, which shall be fixed by the Court. The Court of Chancery may grant the injunction, if a proper case appears, and upon granting and service of the injunction, such domestic limited partnership or foreign limited partnership thereafter shall not transact any business until the injunction shall be dissolved.

(j) A domestic limited partnership that has ceased to be in good standing by reason of its neglect, refusal or failure to pay an annual tax shall remain a domestic limited partnership formed under this chapter. The Secretary of State shall not accept for filing any certificate (except a certificate of resignation of a registered agent when a successor registered agent is not being appointed) required or permitted by this chapter to be filed in respect of any domestic limited partnership or foreign limited partnership which has neglected, refused or failed to pay an annual tax, and shall not issue any certificate of good standing with respect to such domestic limited partnership or foreign limited partnership, unless and until such domestic limited partnership or foreign limited partnership shall have been restored to and have the status of a domestic limited partnership in good standing or a foreign limited partnership duly registered in the State of Delaware.

(k) A domestic limited partnership that has ceased to be in good standing or a foreign limited partnership that has ceased to be registered in the State of Delaware by reason of its neglect, refusal or failure to pay an annual tax may not maintain any action, suit or proceeding in any court of the State of Delaware until such domestic limited partnership or foreign limited partnership has been restored to and has the status of a domestic limited partnership or foreign limited partnership in good standing or duly registered in the State of Delaware. An action, suit or proceeding may not be maintained in any court of the State of Delaware by any successor or assignee of such domestic limited partnership or foreign limited partnership on any right, claim or demand arising out of the transaction of business by such domestic limited partnership after it has ceased to be in good standing or a foreign limited partnership that has ceased to be registered in the State of Delaware until such domestic limited partnership or foreign limited partnership, or any person that has acquired all or substantially all of its assets, has paid any annual tax then due and payable, together with penalties and interest thereon.

(l) The neglect, refusal or failure of a domestic limited partnership or foreign limited partnership to pay an annual tax shall not impair the validity of any contract, deed, mortgage, security interest, lien or act of such domestic limited partnership or foreign limited partnership or prevent such domestic limited partnership or foreign limited partnership from defending any action, suit or proceeding in any court of the State of Delaware.

(m) A limited partner of a domestic limited partnership or foreign limited partnership is not liable as a general partner of such domestic limited partnership or foreign limited partnership solely by reason of the neglect, refusal or failure of such domestic limited partnership or foreign limited partnership to pay an annual tax or by reason of such domestic limited partnership or foreign limited partnership ceasing to be in good standing or duly registered.

§ 17-1110. Cancellation of certificate of limited partnership for failure to pay annual tax.

(a) The certificate of limited partnership of a domestic limited partnership shall be canceled if the limited partnership shall fail to pay the annual tax due under § 17-1109 of this title for a period of 3 years from the date it is due, such cancellation to be effective on the 3rd anniversary of such due date.

(b) A list of those domestic limited partnerships whose certificates of limited partnership were canceled on June 1 of such calendar year pursuant to Section 17-1110(a) of this title shall be filed in the office of the Secretary of State. On or before October 31 of each calendar year, the Secretary of State shall publish such list on the Internet or on a similar medium for a period of 1 week and shall advertise the website or other address where such list can be accessed in at least 1 newspaper of general circulation in the State of Delaware.

§ 17-1111. Revival of domestic limited partnership.

(a) A domestic limited partnership whose certificate of limited partnership has been canceled pursuant to § 17-104(d) or § 17-104(i)(4) or § 17-1110(a) of this title may be revived by filing in the office of the Secretary of State a certificate of revival accompanied by the payment of the fee required by § 17-1107(a)(3) of this title and payment of the annual tax due under § 17-1109 of this title and all penalties and interest thereon due at the time of the cancellation of its certificate of limited partnership.

(1) The name of the limited partnership at the time its certificate of limited partnership was canceled and, if such name is not available at the time of revival, the name under which the limited partnership is to be revived;

(2) The date of filing of the original certificate of limited partnership of the limited partnership;

(3) The address of the limited partnership's registered office in the State of Delaware and the name and address of the limited partnership's registered agent in the State of Delaware;

(4) A statement that the certificate of revival is filed by 1 or more general partners of the limited partnership authorized to execute and file the certificate of revival to revive the limited partnership; and

(5) Any other matters the general partner or general partners executing the certificate of revival determine to include therein.

(b) The certificate of revival shall be deemed to be an amendment to the certificate of limited partnership of the limited partnership, and the limited partnership shall not be required to take any further action to amend its certificate of limited partnership under § 17-202 of this title with respect to the matters set forth in the certificate of revival.

(c) Upon the filing of a certificate of revival, a limited partnership shall be revived with the same force and effect as if its certificate of limited partnership had not been canceled pursuant to § 17-104(d) or § 17-104(i)(4) or § 17-1110(a) of this title. Such revival shall validate all contracts, acts, matters and things made, done and performed by the limited partnership, its partners, employees and agents during the time when its certificate of limited partnership was canceled pursuant to § 17-104(d) or § 17-104(i)(4) or § 17-1110(a) of this title, with the same force and effect and to all intents and purposes as if the certificate of limited partnership had remained in full force and effect. All real and personal property, and all rights and interests, which belonged to the limited partnership at the time its certificate of limited partnership was canceled pursuant to § 17-104(d) or § 17-104(i)(4) or § 17-1110(a) of this title, or which were acquired by the limited partnership following the cancellation of its certificate of limited partnership pursuant to § 17-104(d) or § 17-104(i)(4) or § 17-1110(a) of this title, and which were not disposed of prior to the time of its revival, shall be vested in the limited partnership after its revival as fully as they were held by the limited partnership at, and after, as the case may be, the time its certificate of limited partnership was canceled pursuant to § 17-104(d) or § 17-104(i)(4) or § 17-1110(a) of this title. After its revival, the limited partnership and its partners shall have the same liability for all contracts, acts, matters and things made, done or performed in the limited partnership's name and on its behalf by its partners, employees and agents as the limited partnership and its partners would have had if the limited partnership's certificate of limited partnership had at all times remained in full force and effect.

2011 AMENDMENTS TO THE DELAWARE REVISED UNIFORM PARTNERSHIP ACT—ANALYSIS

By Mark V. Purpura
Richards, Layton & Finger, P.A.
Wilmington, Delaware

I. Introduction

Consistent with Delaware's commitment to maintaining statutes that are state-of-the-art with respect to general partnerships and limited liability partnerships, the Delaware Revised Uniform Partnership Act, 6 *Del. C.* § 15-101, *et seq.* (the "Act"), was amended in 2011. The 2011 amendments to the Act (the "2011 Amendments") became effective on August 1, 2011. Some of the 2011 Amendments are technical in nature, but the more substantive aspects of the 2011 Amendments are discussed below.

II. Statements of Cancellation [6 Del. C. §§ 15-105(d), 15-902(f) and 15-1001(d)]

The 2011 Amendments amend various sections of the Act to clarify that separate statements of cancellation must be filed with the Secretary of State to cancel a statement of partnership existence and a statement of qualification, respectively. The amendments to Section 15-105(d) of the Act also clarify that a statement of qualification of a limited liability partnership shall be cancelled upon the dissolution and the completion of winding up of a limited liability partnership by filing a statement of cancellation setting forth the information required by the Act.

III. Future Effective Dates [6 Del. C. § 15-105(h)]

The 2011 Amendments amend Section 15-105(h) of the Act to provide that a future effective date or time specified in a statement or certificate filed on or after January 1, 2012 shall not be later than a time on the 180th day after the date such certificate has been filed with the Secretary of State.

IV. Address of Registered Office and Registered Agent [6 Del. C. §§ 15-111(k) and 15-105(l)]

The 2011 Amendments add a new subsection (k) to Section 15-111 of the Act, which requires the address of the registered agent or the registered office of a partnership listed in any statement or other document filed with the Secretary of State to include the street, number, city and postal code. The 2011 Amendments also amend Section 15-105 of the Act by adding a new subsection (l), which provides that such requirement in Section 15-111(k) does not apply to any document filed with the Secretary of State prior to August 1, 2011, unless a filing is being made to change the address of a registered agent or registered office.

V. Personal Liability of Partners of Limited Liability Partnership [6 Del. C. § 15-306(c)]

The 2011 Amendments amend Section 15-306(c) of the Act to clarify that an obligation of a partnership arising out of or relating to circumstances or events occurring while the partnership is a limited liability partnership is solely the obligation of the partnership and that partners are not personally liable for such an obligation that arose out of or related to circumstances or events occurring while the partnership was a limited liability partnership. In a recent non-Delaware case involving a Texas partnership, the United States Court of Appeals for the Fifth Circuit affirmed a district court holding that partners of a Texas partnership were personally liable for a judgment against the partnership rendered after the partnership ceased to be a limited liability partnership, which judgment related to conduct occurring while the partnership was a limited liability partnership.

VI. Written and Electronically Transmitted Consents [6 Del. C. § 15-407(d)]

The 2011 Amendments amend Section 15-407(d) of the Act to clarify that actions by partners of a partnership without a meeting may take the form of a written consent or an electronic transmission. The amendment to Section 15-407(d) makes the Act consistent with Section 141(f) of the General Corporation Law of the State of Delaware, which authorizes board action by written consent or electronic transmission

VII. Amendments to Partnership Agreements [6 Del. C. § 15-407(e)]

The 2011 Amendments amend Section 15-407(e) of the Act to provide that supermajority amendment provisions in a partnership agreement apply only to provisions expressly included in such agreement and do not apply to default voting provisions of the Act unless otherwise provided in the partnership agreement. In a 2004 case, *In re LJM2 Co-Investment, L.P. Limited Partners Litigation*, 866 A.2d 762 (Del. Ch. 2004) ("*LJM2*"), the Delaware Court of Chancery considered an amendment provision in a limited partnership agreement prohibiting amendments to any provision of the agreement that affected the vote required in such provision unless the proposed amendment was approved by at least the vote originally required in such provision. The Court of Chancery held that the amendment section applied to amendments to default voting provisions of the Delaware Revised Uniform Limited Partnership Act that became part of the limited partnership agreement in the absence of any specific contractual provision to the contrary. Thus, the amendment to Section 15-407(e) of the Act adopts a rule different from the analysis articulated by the Court of Chancery in *LJM2*.

VIII. Simultaneous Filings for Conversions and Domestications [6 Del. C. §§ 15-901 and 15-904]

The 2011 Amendments amend Section 15-901 of the Act to clarify that a certificate of conversion to partnership, a statement of partnership existence and, if applicable, a statement of qualification for an entity converting to a partnership or a limited liability partnership must be filed simultaneously in the office of the Secretary of State and, to the extent such certificate and statements have a future effective date or time, such certificate and statements must provide for the same effective date or time. The 2011 Amendments also amend Section 15-904 of the Act to clarify that a certificate of domestication and a statement of partnership existence for a non-United States entity domesticating to Delaware as a partnership must be filed simultaneously in the office of the Secretary of State and, to the extent such certificate and statement have a future effective date or time, such certificate and statement must provide for the same effective date or time.

DELAWARE
(DEL. CODE TIT. 6, CH. 15, § 101-1210)

DELAWARE REVISED UNIFORM PARTNERSHIP ACT

SUBCHAPTER I.
GENERAL PROVISIONS

§ 15-101. Definitions

As used in this chapter unless the context otherwise requires:

(1) "Business" includes every trade, occupation and profession, the holding or ownership of property and any other activity for profit.

(2) "Certificate" means a certificate of conversion to partnership under § 15-901 of this title, a certificate of conversion to a non-Delaware entity under § 15-903 of this title, a certificate of merger or consolidation or a certificate of ownership and merger under § 15-902 of this title, a certificate of partnership domestication under § 15-904 of this title, a certificate of transfer and a certificate of transfer and domestic continuance under § 15-905 of this title, a certificate of correction and a corrected certificate under § 15-118 of this title, and a certificate of termination of a certificate with a future effective date or time and a certificate of amendment of a certificate with a future effective date or time under § 15-105(i) of this title.

(3) "Debtor in bankruptcy" means a person who is the subject of:

(i) an order for relief under Title 11 of the United States Code or a comparable order under a successor statute of general application; or

(ii) a comparable order under State of Delaware federal, state or foreign law governing insolvency.

(4) "Distribution" means a transfer of money or other property from a partnership to a partner in the partner's capacity as a partner or to a transferee of all or a part of a partner's economic interest.

(5) "Domestic partnership" means an association of two or more persons formed under § 15-202 of this title or predecessor law to carry on any lawful business, purpose or activity.

(6) "Economic interest" means a partner's share of the profits and losses of a partnership and the partner's right to receive distributions.

(7) "Foreign limited liability partnership" means a partnership that:

(i) is formed under laws other than the laws of the State of Delaware; and

(ii) has the status of a limited liability partnership under those laws.

(8) "Limited liability partnership" means a domestic partnership that has filed a statement of qualification under § 15-1001 of this title.

(9) "Liquidating Trustee" means a person, other than a partner, carrying out the winding up of a partnership.

(10) "Partner" means a person who is admitted to a partnership as a partner of the partnership.

(11) "Partnership" means an association of two or more persons formed under § 15-202 of this title, predecessor law or comparable law of another jurisdiction to carry on any business, purpose or activity.

(12) "Partnership agreement" means the agreement, whether written, oral or implied, among the partners concerning the partnership, including amendments to the partnership agreement. A partnership is not required to execute its partnership agreement. A partnership is bound by its partnership agreement whether or not the partnership executes the partnership agreement. A partnership agreement is not subject to any statute of frauds (including Section 2714 of

this Title). A partnership agreement may provide rights to any person, including a person who is not a party to the partnership agreement, to the extent set forth therein. A partner of a partnership or a transferee of an economic interest is bound by the partnership agreement whether or not the partner or transferee executes the partnership agreement.

(13) "Partnership at will" means a partnership that is not a partnership for a definite term or particular undertaking.

(14) "Partnership for a definite term or particular undertaking" means a partnership in which the partners have agreed to remain partners until the expiration of a definite term or the completion of a particular undertaking.

(15) "Partnership interest" or "partner's interest in the partnership" means all of a partner's interests in the partnership, including the partner's economic interest and all management and other rights.

(16) "Person" means a natural person, partnership, (whether general or limited), limited partnership, trust (including a common law trust, business trust, statutory trust, voting trust or any other form of trust), limited liability company, trust, estate, association (including any group, organization, co-tenancy, plan, board, council or committee), corporation, government (including a country, state, county or any other governmental subdivision, agency or instrumentality), custodian, nominee or any other individual or entity (or series thereof) in its own or any representative capacity, in each case, whether domestic or foreign.

(17) "Property" means all property, real, personal or mixed, tangible or intangible, or any interest therein.

(18) "State" means the District of Columbia or the Commonwealth of Puerto Rico or any state, territory, possession or other jurisdiction of the United States other than the State of Delaware.

(19) "Statement" means a statement of partnership existence under § 15-303 of this title, a statement of denial under § 15-304 of this title, a statement of dissociation under § 15-704 of this title, a statement of dissolution under § 15-805 of this title, a statement of qualification under § 15-1001 of this title, a statement of foreign qua-

lification under § 15-1102 of this title, and an amendment or cancellation of any of the foregoing under § 15-105 of this title and a statement of correction and a corrected statement under § 15-118 of this title.

(20) "Transfer" includes an assignment, conveyance, lease, mortgage, deed, and encumbrance.

§ 15-102. Knowledge and Notice

(a) A person knows a fact if the person has actual knowledge of it.

(b) A person has notice of a fact:

(1) if the person knows of it;

(2) if the person has received a notification of it;

(3) if the person has reason to know it exists from all of the facts known to the person at the time in question; or

(4) by reason of a filing or recording of a statement or certificate to the extent provided by and subject to the limitations set forth in this chapter.

(c) A person notifies or gives a notification to another by taking steps reasonably required to inform the other person in the ordinary course, whether or not the other person obtains knowledge of it.

(d) A person receives a notification when the notification:

(1) comes to the person's attention; or

(2) is received at the person's place of business or at any other place held out by the person as a place for receiving communications.

(e) Except as otherwise provided in subsection (f), a person other than an individual knows, has notice, or receives a notification of a fact for purposes of a particular transaction when the individual conducting the transaction knows, has notice, or receives a notification of the fact, or in any event when the fact would have been brought to the individual's attention if the person had exercised reasonable diligence. The person exercises reasonable diligence if it maintains reasonable routines for communicating significant information to the individual conducting the transaction and there is reasonable compliance with the routines. Reasonable diligence does not require an individual acting for the person to communicate information unless the communication is part of the individual's regular duties or the individual has reason to know of the transaction and that the transaction would be materially affected by the information.

(f) A partner's knowledge, notice or receipt of a notification of a fact relating to the partnership is effective immediately as knowledge by, notice to or receipt of a notification by the partnership, except in the case of a fraud on the partnership committed by or with the consent of that partner.

§ 15-103. Effect of Partnership Agreement; Nonwaivable Provisions

(a) Except as otherwise provided in subsection (b), relations among the partners and between the partners and the partnership are governed by the partnership agreement. To the extent the partnership agreement does not otherwise provide, this chapter governs relations among the partners and between the partners and the partnership.

(b) The partnership agreement may not:

(1) Vary the rights and duties under Section 15-105 except to eliminate the duty to provide copies of statements to all of the partners;

(2) Restrict a partner's rights to obtain information as provided in § 15-403 of this title, except as permitted by § 15-403(f) of this title;

(3) Eliminate the implied contractual covenant of good faith and fair dealing;

(4) Vary the power to dissociate as a partner under Section 15-602(a), except to require the notice under Section 15-601(1) to be in writing;

(5) Vary the right of a court to expel a partner in the events specified in Section 15-601(5);

(6) Vary the requirement to wind up the partnership business in cases specified in Section 15-801(4), (5) or (6) or

(7) Vary the law applicable to a limited liability partnership under Section 15-106(b); or

(8) Vary the denial of partnership power to issue a certificate of partnership interest in bearer form under Section 15-503(h).

(c) Notwithstanding anything to the contrary contained in this section, §§ 15-201, 15-203 and 15-501 of this title may be modified only to the extent provided in a statement of partnership existence or a statement of qualification and in a partnership agreement.

(d) It is the policy of this chapter to give maximum effect to the principle of freedom of contract and to the enforceability of partnership agreements.

(e) A partner or other person shall not be liable to a partnership or to another partner or to another person that is a party to or is otherwise bound by a partnership agreement for breach of fiduciary duty for the partner's or other person's good faith reliance on the provisions of the partnership agreement.

(f) A partnership agreement may provide for the limitation or elimination of any and all liabilities for breach of contract and breach of duties (including fiduciary duties) of a partner or other person to a partnership or to another partner or to another person that is a party to or is otherwise bound by a partnership agreement; provided, that a partnership agreement may not limit or eliminate liability for any act or omission that constitutes a bad faith violation of the implied contractual covenant of good faith and fair dealing.

§ 15-104. Supplemental Principles of Law

(a) In any case not provided for in this chapter, the rules of law and equity, including the law merchant, shall govern.

(b) No obligation of a partner to a partnership arising under a partnership agreement or a separate agreement or writing, and no note, instruction or other writing evidencing any such obligation of a partner, shall be subject to the defense of usury, and no partner shall interpose the defense of usury with respect to any such obligation in any action. If an obligation to pay interest arises under this chapter and the rate is not specified, the rate is that specified in § 2301 of this title.

(c) Sections 9-406 and 9-408 of this title do not apply to any interest in a domestic partnership, including all rights, powers and interests arising under a partnership agreement or this chapter. This provision prevails over §§ 9-406 and 9-408 of this title.

§ 15-105. Execution, Filing and Recording of Statements and Certificates

(a) A statement or certificate may be filed with the Secretary of State by delivery to the Secretary of State of the signed copy of the statement or of the certificate. A certified copy of a statement that is filed in an office in another state may be filed with the Secretary of State. Either filing in the State of Delaware has the effect provided in this chapter with respect to partnership property located in or transactions that occur in the State of Delaware.

(b) Only a certified copy of a filed statement recorded in the office for recording transfers of real property has the effect provided for recorded statements in this chapter.

(c) A statement or certificate filed by a partnership must be executed by at least one partner or by one or more authorized persons. Other statements or certificates must be executed by a partner or 1 or more authorized persons or, in the case of a certificate of conversion to partnership or a certificate of partnership domestication, by any person authorized to execute such certificate on behalf of the other entity or non-United States entity, respectively, except that a certificate of merger or consolidation filed by a surviving or resulting other business entity shall be executed by any person authorized to execute such certificate on behalf of such other business entity. The execution of a statement or certificate by a person who is authorized by this chapter to execute such statement or certificate constitutes an oath or affirmation, under the penalties of perjury in the third degree, that, to the best of such person's knowledge and belief, the facts stated therein are true. A person who executes a statement or a certificate as an agent or fiduciary need not exhibit evidence of his authority as a prerequisite to filing. Any signature on any statement or certificate authorized to be filed with the Secretary of State under any provision of this chapter may be a facsimile, a conformed signature or an electronically transmitted signature. Upon delivery of any statement or certificate, the Secretary of State shall record the date and time of its delivery. Unless the Secretary of State finds that any statement or certificate does not conform to law, upon receipt of all filing fees required by law the Secretary of State shall:

(1) Certify that the statement or certificate has been filed with the Secretary of State by endorsing upon the original statement or certificate the word "Filed", and the date and time of the filing. This endorsement is conclusive of the date and time of its filing in the absence of actual fraud. Except as provided in subdivision (c)(5) or (c)(6) of this section, such date and time of filing of a statement or certificate shall be the date and time of delivery of the statement or certificate;

(2) File and index the endorsed statement or certificate;

(3) Prepare and return to the person who filed it or the person's representative a copy of the signed statement or certificate similarly endorsed, and shall certify such copy as a true copy of the signed statement or certificate; and

(4) Cause to be entered such information from the statement or certificate as the Secretary of State deems appropriate into the Delaware Corporation Information System or any system which is a successor thereto in the office of the Secretary of State, and such information and a copy of such statement or certificate shall

be permanently maintained as a public record on a suitable medium. The Secretary of State is authorized to grant direct access to such system to registered agents subject to the execution of an operating agreement between the Secretary of State and such registered agent. Any registered agent granted such access shall demonstrate the existence of policies to ensure that information entered into the system accurately reflects the content of statements or certificates in the possession of the registered agent at the time of entry.

(5) Upon request made upon or prior to delivery, the Secretary of State may, to the extent deemed practicable, establish as the date and time of filing of a statement or certificate a date and time after its delivery. If the Secretary of State refuses to file any statement or certificate due to an error, omission or other imperfection, the Secretary of State may hold such statement or certificate in suspension, and in such event, upon delivery of a replacement statement or certificate in proper form for filing and tender of the required fees within 5 business days after notice of such suspension is given to the filer, the Secretary of State shall establish as the date and time of filing of such statement or certificate the date and time that would have been the date and time of filing of the rejected statement or certificate had it been accepted for filing. The Secretary of State shall not issue a certificate of good standing with respect to any partnership with a statement or certificate held in suspension pursuant to this subsection. The Secretary of State may establish as the date and time of filing of a statement or certificate the date and time at which information from such statement or certificate is entered pursuant to subdivision (c)(4) of this section if such statement or certificate is delivered on the same date and within 4 hours after such information is entered.

(6) If:

a. Together with the actual delivery of a statement or certificate and tender of the required fees, there is delivered to the Secretary of State a separate affidavit (which in its heading shall be designated as an affidavit of extraordinary condition) attesting, on the basis of personal knowledge of the

DRUPA–9

affiant or a reliable source of knowledge identified in the affidavit, that an earlier effort to deliver such statement or certificate and tender such fees was made in good faith, specifying the nature, date and time of such good faith effort and requesting that the Secretary of State establish such date and time as the date and time of filing of such statement or certificate; or

b. Upon the actual delivery of a statement or certificate and tender of the required fees, the Secretary of State in his or her discretion provides a written waiver of the requirement for such an affidavit stating that it appears to the Secretary of State that an earlier effort to deliver such statement or certificate and tender such fees was made in good faith and specifying the date and time of such effort; and

c. The Secretary of State determines that an extraordinary condition existed at such date and time, that such earlier effort was unsuccessful as a result of the existence of such extraordinary condition, and that such actual delivery and tender were made within a reasonable period (not to exceed 2 business days) after the cessation of such extraordinary condition, then the Secretary of State may establish such date and time as the date and time of filing of such statement or certificate. No fee shall be paid to the Secretary of State for receiving an affidavit of extraordinary condition. For purposes of this subsection, an extraordinary condition means: any emergency resulting from an attack on, invasion or occupation by foreign military forces of, or disaster, catastrophe, war or other armed conflict, revolution or insurrection or rioting or civil commotion in, the United States or a locality in which the Secretary of State conducts its business or in which the good faith effort to deliver the statement or certificate and tender the required fees is made, or the immediate threat of any of the foregoing; or any malfunction or outage of the electrical or telephone service to the Secretary of State's office, or weather or other condition in or about a locality in which the Secretary of State conducts its business, as a result of which the Secretary of State's office is not open for the purpose of the filing of statements and certificates under this chapter or such filing cannot be effected without extraordinary effort. The Secretary of State may require such proof as it deems necessary to make the determination required under this subparagraph c. of this subdivision, and any such determination shall be conclusive in the absence of actual fraud. If the Secretary of State establishes the date and time of filing of a statement or certificate pursuant to this subsection, the date and time of delivery of the affidavit of extraordinary condition or the date and time of the Secretary of State's written waiver of such affidavit shall be endorsed on such affidavit or waiver and such affidavit or waiver, so endorsed, shall be attached to the filed statement or certificate to which it relates. Such filed statement or certificate shall be effective as of the date and time established as the date and time of filing by the Secretary of State pursuant to this subsection, except as to those persons who are substantially and adversely affected by such establishment and, as to those persons, the statement or certificate shall be effective from the date and time endorsed on the affidavit of extraordinary condition or written waiver attached thereto.

(d)(1) A person authorized by this chapter to file a statement or certificate may amend or cancel the statement or certificate by filing an amendment or cancellation that names the partnership, identifies the statement or certificate, and states the substance of the amendment or cancellation. A person authorized by this chapter to file a statement or certificate who becomes aware that such statement or certificate was false when made, or that any matter described in the statement or certificate has changed, making the statement or certificate false in any material respect, shall promptly amend the statement or certificate. Upon the filing of a statement or a certificate amending or correcting a statement or a certificate (or judicial decree of amendment) with the Secretary of State, or upon the future effective date or time of a statement or a certificate amending or correcting a statement or a certificate (or judicial decree thereof), as provided for therein, the statement or the certificate being corrected or amended shall be corrected or amended as set forth therein. Upon the filing of a statement of cancellation of a statement of partnership existence (or judicial decree thereof), or a certificate of merger or consolidation or a certificate of ownership and merger which acts as a statement of cancellation of a statement of partnership existence, or a certificate of transfer, or a certificate of conversion to a non-Delaware entity, or upon the future effective date or time of a statement of cancellation of a statement of partnership existence (or a judicial decree thereof) or of a certificate of merger or consolidation or a certificate of ownership and merger which acts as a statement of cancellation of a statement of partnership existence, or a certificate of transfer, or a certificate of conversion to a non-Delaware entity, as provided for therein, or as specified in § 15-111(d), § 15-111(i)(4) or § 15-1209(a) of this title, the statement of partnership existence is canceled. Neither the filing of a statement of cancellation to accomplish the cancellation of a statement of qualification nor the revocation of a statement of qualification pursuant to § 15-1003 of this title cancels a statement of partnership existence for such partnership. A statement of partnership existence shall be canceled upon the dissolution and the completion of winding up of the partnership, or as provided in § 15-111(d), § 15-111(i)(4) or § 15-1209(a) of this title, or upon the filing of a certificate of merger or consolidation or a certificate of ownership and merger if the domestic partnership is not the surviving or resulting entity in a merger or consolidation, or upon the filing of a certificate of transfer, or upon the filing of a certificate of conversion to a non-Delaware entity. A statement of cancellation shall be filed with the Secretary of State to accomplish the cancellation of a statement of partnership existence upon the dissolution and the completion of winding up of a domestic partnership and shall set forth:

    a. The name of the partnership;

    b. The date of filing of its statement of partnership existence; and

Delaware Revised Uniform Partnership Act

c. Any other information the person filing the statement of cancellation determines.

(2) The Secretary of State shall not issue a certificate of good standing with respect to a domestic partnership if its statement of partnership existence is canceled.

(3) Upon the filing of a statement of cancellation of a statement of qualification (or judicial decree thereof), or a certificate of merger or consolidation or a certificate of ownership and merger which acts as a statement of cancellation of a statement of qualification, or a certificate of transfer, or a certificate of conversion to a non-Delaware entity, or upon the future effective date or time of a statement of cancellation of a statement of qualification (or a judicial decree thereof) or of a certificate of merger or consolidation or a certificate of ownership and merger which acts as a statement of cancellation of a statement of qualification, or a certificate of transfer, or a certificate of conversion to a non-Delaware entity, as provided for therein, or as specified in § 15-111(d) or § 15-111(i)(4) of this title, the statement of qualification is canceled. Neither the filing of a statement of cancellation to accomplish the cancellation of a statement of partnership existence nor the cancellation of a statement of partnership existence pursuant to § 15-1209(a) of this title cancels a statement of qualification for such partnership. A statement of qualification shall be canceled upon the dissolution and the completion of winding up of the limited liability partnership, or as provided in § 15-111(d) or § 15-111(i)(4) of this title, or upon the filing of a certificate of merger or consolidation or a certificate of ownership and merger if the limited liability partnership is not the surviving or resulting entity in a merger or consolidation, or upon the filing of a certificate of transfer, or upon the filing of a certificate of conversion to a non-Delaware entity. A statement of cancellation shall be filed with the Secretary of State to accomplish the cancellation of a statement of qualification upon the dissolution and the completion of winding up of a limited liability partnership and shall set forth:

a. The name of the limited liability partnership;

b. The date of filing of its statement of qualification; and

DRUPA-13

c. Any other information the person filing the statement of cancellation determines.

(4) Upon the filing of a certificate of partnership domestication, or upon the future effective date or time of a certificate of partnership domestication, the entity filing the certificate of partnership domestication is domesticated as a partnership with the effect provided in § 15-904 of this title. Upon the filing of a certificate of conversion to partnership, or upon the future effective date or time of a certificate of conversion to partnership, the entity filing the certificate of conversion to partnership is converted to a partnership with the effect provided in § 15-901 of this title. Upon the filing of a certificate of transfer and domestic continuance, or upon the future effective date or time of a certificate of transfer and domestic continuance, as provided for therein, the partnership filing the certificate of transfer and domestic continuance shall continue to exist as a partnership of the State of Delaware with the effect provided in § 15-905 of this title.

(e) A person who files a statement or certificate pursuant to this section shall promptly send a copy of the statement or certificate to every nonfiling partner and to any other person named as a partner in the statement or certificate. Failure to send a copy of a statement or certificate to a partner or other person does not limit the effectiveness of the statement or certificate as to a person not a partner.

(f) The filing of a statement of partnership existence under § 15-303, a statement of qualification under § 15-1001 or a statement of foreign qualification under § 15-1102 with the Secretary of State shall make it unnecessary to file any other document under Chapter 31 of this Title.

(g) A statement or certificate filed with the Secretary of State shall be effective if there has been substantial compliance with the requirements of this chapter.

(h) Notwithstanding any other provision of this chapter, any statement or certificate filed under this chapter shall be effective at the time of its filing with the Secretary of State or at any later date or time (not later than a time on the one hundred and eightieth day after the date of its filing if such date of filing is on or after January 1, 2012) specified in the statement or certificate.

(i) If any certificate filed in accordance with this chapter provides for a future effective date or time and if, prior to such future effective date or time set forth in such certificate, the transaction is terminated or its terms are amended to change the future effective date or time or any other matter described in such certificate so as to make such certificate false or inaccurate in any respect, such certificate shall, prior to the future effective date or time set forth in such certificate, be terminated or amended by the filing of a certificate of termination or certificate of amendment of such certificate, executed in the same manner as the certificate being terminated or amended is required to be executed in accordance with this section, which shall identify the certificate which has been terminated or amended and shall state that the certificate has been terminated or the manner in which it has been amended. Upon the filing of a certificate of amendment of a certificate with a future effective date or time, the certificate identified in such certificate of amendment is amended. Upon the filing of a certificate of termination of a certificate with a future effective date or time, the certificate identified in such certificate of termination is terminated.

(j) A fee as set forth in § 15-1207 of this title shall be paid at the time of the filing of a statement or a certificate.

(k) A fee as set forth in § 15-1207 of this title shall be paid for a certified copy of any paper on file as provided for by this chapter, and a fee as set forth in § 15-1207 of this title shall be paid for each page copied.

(l) Notwithstanding any other provision of this chapter, it shall not be necessary for any partnership (including a limited liability partnership) or foreign partnership to amend its statement of partnership existence, its statement of qualification (as applicable), its statement of foreign qualification, or any other document that has been filed with the Secretary of State prior to August 1, 2011, to comply with § 15-111(k) of this title; notwithstanding the foregoing, any statement or other document filed under this chapter on or after August 1, 2011, and changing the address of a registered agent or registered office shall comply with § 15-111(k) of this title.

§ 15-106. Governing Law

(a) Except as otherwise provided in subsection (b), the law of the jurisdiction governing a partnership agreement governs relations among the partners and between the partners and the partnership.

(b) The law of the State of Delaware governs relations among the partners and between the partners and the partnership and the liability of partners for an obligation of a limited liability partnership.

(c) If (i) a partnership agreement provides for the application of the laws of the State of Delaware, and (ii) the partnership files with the Secretary of State a statement of partnership existence or a statement of qualification, then the partnership agreement shall be governed by and construed under the laws of the State of Delaware.

§ 15-107. Reserved Power of State of Delaware to Alter or Repeal Chapter

All provisions of this chapter may be altered from time to time or repealed and all rights of partners are subject to this reservation. Unless expressly stated to the contrary in this chapter, all amendments of this chapter shall apply to partnerships and partners whether or not existing at the time of the enactment of any such amendment.

§ 15-108. Name of Partnership

(a) The name of a partnership: (i) may contain the name of a partner and (ii) may contain the following words: "Company," "Association," "Club," "Foundation," "Fund," "Institute," "Society," "Union," "Syndicate," "Trust" (or abbreviations of like import).

(b) The name of a limited liability partnership shall contain as the last words or letters of its name the words "Limited Liability Partnership," the abbreviation "L.L.P." or the designation "LLP."

(c) The name of a partnership to be included in the statement of partnership existence, statement of qualification or statement of foreign qualification filed by such partnership must be such as to distinguish it upon the records in the office of the Secretary of State from the name on such records of any corporation, partnership (including a limited liability partnership), limited partnership (including a limited liability limited partnership), statutory trust or limited liability company organized under the laws of the State of Delaware and reserved, registered, formed or organized with the Secretary of State or qualified to do business and registered as a foreign corporation, foreign limited liability partnership, foreign limited partnership, foreign statutory trust or foreign limited liability company in the State of Delaware; provided, however, that a domestic partnership may be registered under any name which is not such as to distinguish it upon the records of the Secretary of State from the name on such records of any domestic or foreign corporation, limited partnership (including a limited liability limited partnership), statutory trust or limited liability company or foreign limited liability partnership reserved, registered, formed or organized under the laws of the State of Delaware with the written consent of the other corporation, limited partnership (including a limited liability limited partnership), statutory trust, limited liability company, or foreign limited liability partnership which written consent shall be filed with the Secretary of State; provided further, that, if on July 31, 2011, a domestic partnership is registered (with the consent of another domestic partnership) under a name which is not such as to distinguish it upon the records in the office of the Secretary of State from the name on such records of such other domestic partnership, it shall not be necessary for any such domestic partnership to amend its statement of partnership existence or statement of qualification to comply with this subsection.

§ 15-109. Reservation of Name

(a) The exclusive right to use of a specified name in a statement using the specified name may be reserved by: (1) any person intending to organize a partnership under this chapter and to adopt that name; (2) any partnership or any foreign limited liability partnership registered in the State of Delaware which, in either case, proposes to change its name; (3) any foreign limited liability partnership intending to register in the State of Delaware and adopt that name; and (4) any person intending to organize a foreign limited liability partnership and intending to have it register in the State of Delaware and adopt that name.

(b) The reservation of a specified name shall be made by filing with the Secretary of State an application, executed by the applicant, specifying the name to be reserved and the name and address of the applicant. If the Secretary of State finds that the name is available for use, the Secretary shall reserve the name for exclusive use of the applicant in a statement using the specified name for a period of 120 days. Once having so reserved a name, the same applicant may again reserve the same name for successive 120 day periods. The right to the exclusive use of a reserved name in a statement using the specified name may be transferred to any other person by filing with the Secretary of State a notice of the transfer, executed by the applicant for whom the name was reserved, specifying the name to be transferred and the name and address of the transferee. The reservation of a specified name may be canceled by filing with the Secretary of State a notice of cancellation, executed by the applicant or transferee, specifying the name reservation to be canceled and the name and address of the applicant or transferee. Unless the Secretary of State finds that any application, notice of transfer or notice of cancellation filed with the Secretary of State as required by this subsection does not conform to law, upon receipt of all filing fees required by law, the Secretary shall prepare and return to the person who filed such instrument a copy of the filed instrument with a notation thereon of the action taken by the Secretary of State.

(c) A fee as set forth in Section 15-1207 of this chapter shall be paid at the time of the initial reservation of any name, at the time of the renewal of any such reservation and at the time of the filing of a notice of the transfer or cancellation of any such reservation.

§ 15-110. Indemnification

Subject to such standards and restrictions, if any, as are set forth in its partnership agreement, a partnership may, and shall have the power to, indemnify and hold harmless any partner or other person from and against any and all claims and demands whatsoever.

§ 15-111. Registered Office; Registered Agent

(a) Each partnership that files a statement of partnership existence, a statement of qualification or a statement of foreign qualification shall have and maintain in the State of Delaware:

(1) A registered office, which may but need not be a place of its business in the State of Delaware; and

(2) A registered agent for service of process on the partnership, having a business office identical with such registered office, which agent may be any of

a. the partnership itself,

b. an individual resident in the State of Delaware,

c. a domestic limited liability company, a domestic corporation, a domestic partnership (other than the partnership itself) (whether general (including a limited liability partnership) or limited (including a limited liability limited partnership)), or a domestic statutory trust, or

d. a foreign corporation, a foreign partnership (whether general (including a limited liability partnership) or limited (including a limited liability limited partnership)), a foreign limited liability company, or a foreign statutory trust.

(b) A registered agent may change the address of the registered office of the partnership(s) for which it is registered agent to another address in the State of Delaware by paying a fee as set forth in § 15-1207 of this title and filing with the Secretary of State a certificate, executed by such registered agent, setting forth the address at which such registered agent has maintained the registered office for each of the partnerships for which it is a registered agent, and further certifying to the new address to which each such registered office will be changed on a given day, and at which new address such registered agent will thereafter maintain the registered office for each of the partnerships for which it is a registered agent. Upon the filing of such certificate, the Secretary of State shall furnish to the registered agent a certified copy of the same under the Secretary's hand and seal of office, and thereafter, or until further change of address as authorized by law, the registered office in the State of Delaware of each of the partnerships for which the agent is a registered agent shall be located at the new address of the registered agent thereof as given in the certificate. In the event of a change of name of any person acting as a registered agent of a partnership, such registered agent shall file with the Secretary of State a certificate, executed by such registered agent, setting forth the new name of such registered agent, the name of such registered agent before it was changed and the address at which such registered agent has maintained the registered office for each of the partnerships for which it is a registered agent, and shall pay a fee as set forth in § 15-1207 of this title. Upon the filing of such certificate, the Secretary of State shall furnish to the registered agent a certified copy of the certificate under his or her hand and seal of office. A change of name of any person acting as a registered agent of a partnership as a result of a merger or consolidation of the registered agent, with or into another person which succeeds to its assets and liabilities by operation of law, shall be deemed a change of name for purposes of this section. Filing a certificate under this section shall be deemed to be an amendment of the statement of partnership existence, statement of qualification or statement of foreign qualification of each partnership affected thereby and each such partnership shall not be required to take any further action, with respect thereto, to amend its statement of partnership existence, statement of qualification or statement of foreign qualification under § 15-105(d) of this title. Any registered agent filing a certificate under this section shall promptly, upon such filing, deliver a copy of any such certificate to each partnership affected thereby.

(c) The registered agent of 1 or more partnerships may resign and appoint a successor registered agent by paying a fee as set forth in § 15-1207 of this title and filing a certificate with the Secretary of State, stating the name and address of the successor registered agent. There shall be attached to such certificate a statement of each affected partnership ratifying and approving such change of registered agent. Upon such filing, the successor registered agent shall become the registered agent of such partnerships as have ratified and approved such substitution and the successor registered agent's address, as stated in such certificate, shall become the address of each such partnership's registered office in the State of Delaware. The Secretary of State shall then issue a certificate that the successor registered agent has become the registered agent of the partnerships so ratifying and approving such change and setting out the names of such partnerships. Filing of such certificate of resignation shall be deemed to be an amendment of the statement of partnership existence, statement of qualification or statement of foreign qualification of each partnership affected thereby and each such partnership shall not be required to take any further action with respect thereto to amend its statement of partnership existence, statement of qualification or statement of foreign qualification under § 15-105(d) of this title.

(d) The registered agent of 1 or more partnerships may resign without appointing a successor registered agent by paying a fee as set forth in § 15-1207 of this title and filing a certificate of resignation with the Secretary of State, but such resignation shall not become effective until 30 days after the certificate is filed. The certificate shall contain a statement that written notice of resignation was given to each affected partnership at least 30 days prior to the filing of the certificate by mailing or delivering such notice to the partnership at its address last known to the registered agent and shall set forth the date of such notice. After receipt of the notice of the resignation of its registered agent, the partnership for which such registered agent was acting shall obtain and designate a new registered agent to take the place of the registered agent so resigning. If such partnership fails to obtain and designate a new registered agent as aforesaid prior to the expiration of the period of 30 days after the filing by the registered agent of the certificate of resignation, the statement of partnership existence, statement of qualification or statement of foreign qualification of such partnership shall be canceled. After the resignation of the registered agent shall have become effective as provided in this section and if no new registered agent shall have been obtained and designated in the time and manner aforesaid, service of legal process against each partnership for which the resigned registered agent had been acting shall thereafter be upon the Secretary of State in accordance with § 15-113 of this title.

(e) Every registered agent shall:

(1) If an entity, maintain a business office in the State of Delaware which is generally open, or if an individual, be generally present at a designated location in the State of Delaware, at sufficiently frequent times to accept service of process and otherwise perform the functions of a registered agent;

(2) If a foreign entity, be authorized to transact business in the State of Delaware;

(3) Accept service of process and other communications directed to the partnerships for which it serves as registered agent and forward same to the partnership to which the service or communication is directed; and

(4) Forward to the partnerships for which it serves as registered agent the statement for the annual tax described in § 15-1208 of this title or an electronic notification of same in a form satisfactory to the Secretary of State.

(f) Any registered agent who at any time serves as registered agent for more than fifty entities (a "Commercial Registered Agent"), whether domestic or foreign, shall satisfy and comply with the following qualifications.

(1) A natural person serving as a Commercial Registered Agent shall:

a. Maintain a principal residence or a principal place of business in the State of Delaware;

b. Maintain a Delaware business license;

c. Be generally present at a designated location within the State of Delaware during normal business hours to accept service of process and otherwise perform the functions of a registered agent as specified in subsection (e); and

d. Provide the Secretary of State upon request with such information identifying and enabling communication with such Commercial Registered Agent as the Secretary of State shall require.

(2) A domestic or foreign corporation, a domestic or foreign partnership (whether general (including a limited liability partnership) or limited (including a limited liability limited partnership)), a domestic or foreign limited liability company, or a domestic or foreign statutory trust serving as a Commercial Registered Agent shall:

a. Have a business office within the State of Delaware which is generally open during normal business hours to accept service of process and otherwise perform the functions of a registered agent as specified in subsection (e);

b. Maintain a Delaware business license;

c. Have generally present at such office during normal business hours an officer, director or managing agent who is a natural person; and

d. Provide the Secretary of State upon request with such information identifying and enabling communication with such Commercial Registered Agent as the Secretary of State shall require.

(3) For purposes of this subsection and subsection (i)(2)a., a Commercial Registered Agent shall also include any registered agent which has an officer, director or managing agent in common with any other registered agent or agents if such registered agents at any time during such common service as officer, director or managing agent collectively served as registered agents for more than fifty entities, whether domestic or foreign.

(g) Every partnership formed under the laws of the State of Delaware or qualified to do business in the State of Delaware that has and maintains a registered agent pursuant to § 15-111 of this title shall provide to its registered agent and update from time to time as necessary the name, business address and business telephone number of a natural person who is a partner, officer, employee or designated agent of the partnership, who is then authorized to receive communications from the registered agent. Such person shall be deemed the communications contact for the partnership. Every registered agent shall retain (in paper or electronic form) the above information concerning the current communications contact for each partnership for which he, she, or it serves as registered agent. If the partnership fails to provide the registered agent with a current communications contact, the registered agent may resign as the registered agent for such partnership pursuant to this Section.

(h) The Secretary of State is authorized to issue such rules and regulations as may be necessary or appropriate to carry out the enforcement of subsections (e), (f) and (g) of this Section, and to take actions reasonable and necessary to assure registered agents' compliance with subsections (e), (f) and (g). Such actions may include refusal to file documents submitted by a registered agent.

(i) Upon application of the Secretary of State, the Court of Chancery may enjoin any person or entity from serving as a registered agent or as an officer, director or managing agent of a registered agent.

(1) Upon the filing of a complaint by the Secretary of State pursuant to this Section, the Court may make such orders respecting such proceeding as it deems appropriate, and may enter such orders granting interim or final relief as it deems proper under the circumstances.

(2) Any one or more of the following grounds shall be a sufficient basis to grant an injunction pursuant to this Section:

a. With respect to any registered agent who at any time within one year immediately prior to the filing of the Secretary of State's complaint is a Commercial Registered Agent, failure after notice and warning to comply with the qualifications set forth in subsection (e) and/or the requirements of subsections (f) or (g) above;

b. The person serving as a registered agent, or any person who is an officer, director or managing agent of an entity registered agent, has been convicted of a felony or any crime which includes an element of dishonesty or fraud or involves moral turpitude; or

c. The registered agent has engaged in conduct in connection with acting as a registered agent that is intended to or likely to deceive or defraud the public.

(3) With respect to any order the Court enters pursuant to this Section with respect to an entity that has acted as a registered agent, the Court may also direct such order to any person who has served as an officer, director or managing agent of such registered agent. Any person who, on or after January 1, 2007, serves as an officer, director or managing agent of an entity acting as a registered agent in the State of Delaware shall be deemed thereby to have consented to the appointment of such registered agent as agent upon whom service of process may be made in any action brought pursuant to this Section, and service as an officer, director or managing agent of an entity acting as a registered agent in the State of Delaware shall be a signification of the consent of such person that any process when so served shall be of the same legal force and validity as if served upon such person within the State of Delaware, and such appointment of the registered agent shall be irrevocable.

(4) Upon the entry of an order by the Court enjoining any person or entity from acting as a registered agent, the Secretary of State shall mail or deliver notice of such order to each affected partnership.

a. that has specified the address of a place of business in a record of the Secretary of State, to the address specified, or

b. an address of which the Secretary of State has obtained from the partnership's former registered agent, to the address obtained.

If such a partnership is a domestic partnership and fails to obtain and designate a new registered agent within thirty (30) days after such notice is given, the statement of partnership existence and statement of qualification of such partnership (in each case as applicable) shall be cancelled. If such a partnership is a foreign limited liability partnership and fails to obtain and designate a new registered agent within thirty (30) days after such notice is given, such foreign limited liability partnership shall not be permitted to do business in the State of Delaware and its statement of foreign qualification shall be cancelled. If any other affected partnership is a domestic partnership and fails to obtain and designate a new registered agent within sixty (60) days after entry of an order by the Court enjoining such partnership's registered agent from acting as a registered agent, the statement of partnership existence and statement of qualification of such partnership (in each case as applicable) shall be cancelled. If any other affected partnership is a foreign limited liability partnership and fails to obtain and designate a new registered agent within sixty (60) days after entry of an order by Court enjoining such partnership's registered agent from acting as a registered agent, such foreign limited liability partnership shall not be permitted to do business in the State of Delaware and its statement of foreign qualification shall be cancelled. If the Court enjoins a person or entity from acting as a registered agent as provided in this Section and no new registered agent shall have been obtained and designated in the time and manner aforesaid, service of legal process against the partnership for which the registered agent had been acting shall thereafter be upon the Secretary of State in accordance with Section 15-113 of this title. The Court of Chancery may, upon application of the Secretary of State on notice to the former registered agent, enter such orders as it deems appropriate to give the Secretary of State access to information in the former registered agent's possession in order to facilitate communication with the partnerships the former registered agent served.

(j) The Secretary of State is authorized to make a list of registered agents available to the public, and to establish such qualifications and issue such rules and regulations with respect to such listing as the Secretary of State deems necessary or appropriate.

Delaware Revised Uniform Partnership Act

(k) As contained in any statement of partnership existence, statement of qualification, statement of foreign qualification, or other document filed with the Secretary of State under this chapter, the address of a registered agent or registered office shall include the street, number, city and postal code.

§ 15-112. Service of Process on Partnership Filing a Statement

(a) Service of legal process upon any partnership which has filed a statement of partnership existence, a statement of qualification or a statement of foreign qualification shall be made by delivering a copy personally to any partner of the partnership in the State of Delaware or any partner who signed a statement of partnership existence, a statement of qualification or a statement of foreign qualification or the registered agent of the partnership in the State of Delaware or by leaving it at the dwelling house or usual place of abode in the State of Delaware of any such partner or registered agent (if the registered agent be an individual), or at the registered office or any place of business of the partnership in the State of Delaware. Service by copy left at the dwelling house or usual place of abode of a partner, registered agent, or at the registered office or any place of business of the partnership in the State of Delaware, to be effective, must be delivered thereat at least 6 days before the return date of the process, and in the presence of an adult person, and the officer serving the process shall distinctly state the manner of service in the return thereto. Process returnable forthwith must be delivered personally to the partner or registered agent.

(b) In case the officer whose duty it is to serve legal process cannot by due diligence serve the process in any manner provided for by subsection (a) of this section, it shall be lawful to serve the process against the partnership upon the Secretary of State, and such service shall be as effectual for all intents and purposes as if made in any of the ways provided for in subsection (a) hereof. Process may be served upon the Secretary of State under this subsection by means of electronic transmission but only as prescribed by the Secretary of State. The Secretary of State is authorized to issue such rules and regulations with respect to such service as the Secretary of State deems necessary or appropriate. In the event that service is effected through the Secretary of State in accordance with this subsection, the Secretary of State shall forthwith notify the partnership by letter, directed to the partnership at the address of any partner as it appears on the records relating to such partnership on file with the Secretary of State or, if no such address appears, at the last registered office. Such letter shall be sent by a mail or courier service that includes a record of mailing or deposit with the courier and a record of delivery evidenced by the signature of the recipient. Such letter shall enclose a copy of the process and any other papers served on the Secretary of State pursuant to this subsection. It shall be the duty of the plaintiff in the event of such service to serve process and any other papers in duplicate, to notify the Secretary of State that service is being effected pursuant to this subsection, and to pay the Secretary of State the sum of $50 for the use of the State of Delaware, which sum shall be taxed as part of the costs in the proceeding if the plaintiff shall prevail therein. The Secretary of State shall maintain an alphabetical record of any such service setting forth the name of the plaintiff and defendant, the title, docket number and nature of the proceeding in which process has been served upon him, the fact that service has been effected pursuant to this subsection, the return date thereof, and the day and hour when the service was made. The Secretary of State shall not be required to retain such information for a period longer than 5 years from receipt of the service of process.

§ 15-113. Service of Process on a Partnership Not Filing a Statement

(a) Service of legal process upon any partnership which has not filed a statement of partnership existence, a statement of qualification or a statement of foreign qualification and which is formed under the laws of the State of Delaware or doing business in the State of Delaware shall be made by delivering a copy personally to any partner doing business in the State of Delaware or by leaving it at the dwelling house or usual place of abode in the State of Delaware of a partner or at a place of business of the partnership in the State of Delaware. Service by copy left at the dwelling house or usual place of abode of a partner or at a place of business of the partnership in the State of Delaware, to be effective, must be delivered thereat at least 6 days before the return date of the process, and in the presence of an adult person, and the officer serving the process shall distinctly state the manner of service in the return thereto. Process returnable forthwith must be delivered personally to the partner.

(b) In case the officer whose duty it is to serve legal process cannot by due diligence serve the process in any manner provided for by subsection (a) of this section, it shall be lawful to serve the process against the partnership upon the Secretary of State, and such service shall be as effectual for all intents and purposes as if made in any of the ways provided for in subsection (a) hereof. Process may be served upon the Secretary of State under this subsection by means of electronic transmission but only as prescribed by the Secretary of State. The Secretary of State is authorized to issue such rules and regulations with respect to such service as the Secretary of State deems necessary or appropriate. In the event that service is effected through the Secretary of State in accordance with this subsection, the Secretary of State shall forthwith notify the partnership by letter, directed to the partnership at the address of any partner or the partnership as it is furnished to the Secretary of State by the person desiring to make service. Such letter shall be sent by a mail or courier service that includes a record of mailing or deposit with the courier and a record of delivery evidenced by the signature of the recipient. Such letter shall enclose a copy of the process and any other papers served on the Secretary of State pursuant to this subsection. It shall be the duty of the plaintiff in the event of such service to serve process and any other papers in duplicate, to notify the Secretary of State that service is being effected pursuant to this subsection, and to pay the Secretary of State the sum of $50 for the use of the State of Delaware, which sum shall be taxed as part of the costs on the proceeding if the plaintiff shall prevail therein. The Secretary of State shall maintain an alphabetical record of any such service setting forth the name of the plaintiff and defendant, the title, docket number and nature of the proceeding in which process has been served upon the Secretary of State, the fact that service has been effected pursuant to this subsection, the return date thereof, and the day and hour when the service was made. The Secretary of State shall not be required to retain such information for a period longer than 5 years from the Secretary of State's receipt of the service of process.

§ 15-114. Service of Process on a Partner and Liquidating Trustee

(a) A partner or a liquidating trustee of a partnership which is formed under the laws of the State of Delaware or doing business in the State of Delaware may be served with process in the manner prescribed in this section in all civil actions or proceedings brought in the State of Delaware involving or relating to the business of the partnership or a violation by the partner or the liquidating trustee of a duty to the partnership or any partner of the partnership, whether or not the partner or the liquidating trustee is a partner or a liquidating trustee at the time suit is commenced. A person who is at the time of the effectiveness of this section or who becomes a partner or a liquidating trustee of a partnership thereby consents to the appointment of the registered agent of the partnership (or, if there is none, the Secretary of State) as such person's agent upon whom service of process may be made as provided in this section. Any process when so served shall be of the same legal force and validity as if served upon such partner or liquidating trustee within the State of Delaware and such appointment of the registered agent (or, if there is none, the Secretary of State) shall be irrevocable.

(b) Service of process shall be effected by serving the registered agent (or, if there is none, the Secretary of State) with 1 copy of such process in the manner provided by law for service of writs of summons. In the event service is made under this subsection upon the Secretary of State, the plaintiff shall pay to the Secretary of State the sum of $50 for the use of the State of Delaware, which sum shall be taxed as part of the costs of the proceeding if the plaintiff shall prevail therein. In addition, the Prothonotary or the Register in Chancery of the court in which the civil action or proceeding is pending shall, within 7 days of such service, deposit in the United States mails, by registered mail, postage prepaid, true and attested copies of the process, together with a statement that service is being made pursuant to this section, addressed to such partner or liquidating trustee at the partner's or liquidating trustee's address furnished to the Prothonotary or Register in Chancery by the person desiring to make service, which address shall be the partner's or the liquidating trustee's address as the same appears in any statement of the partnership or, if no such address appears, the partner's or the liquidating trustees's last known address.

(c) In any action in which any such partner or liquidating trustee has been served with process as hereinabove provided, the time in which a defendant shall be required to appear and file a responsive pleading shall be computed from the date of mailing by the Prothonotary or the Register in Chancery as provided in subsection (b) of the section; however, the court in which such action has been commenced may order such continuance or continuances as may be necessary to afford such partner or liquidating trustee reasonable opportunity to defend the action.

(d) In a written partnership agreement or other writing, a partner may consent to be subject to the nonexclusive jurisdiction of the courts of, or arbitration in, a specified jurisdiction, or the exclusive jurisdiction of the courts of the State of Delaware, or the exclusivity of arbitration in a specified jurisdiction or the State of Delaware, and to be served with legal process in the manner prescribed in such partnership agreement or other writing.

(e) Nothing herein contained limits or affects the right to serve process in any other manner now or hereafter provided by law. This section is an extension of and not a limitation upon the right otherwise existing of service of legal process upon nonresidents.

(f) The Court of Chancery and the Superior Court may make all necessary rules respecting the form of process, the manner of issuance and return thereof and such other rules which may be necessary to implement this section and are not inconsistent with this section.

§ 15-115. Doing Business

A limited partnership, a partnership, a limited liability company, a business or other trust or association, or a corporation formed or organized under the laws of any foreign country or other foreign jurisdiction or the laws of any state shall not be deemed to be doing business in the State of Delaware solely by reason of its being a partner in a domestic partnership.

§ 15-116. Restated Statement of Partnership Existence

(a) A statement of partnership existence may be restated by integrating into a single instrument all of the provisions of the statement of partnership existence which are then in effect and operative as a result of there having been theretofore filed 1 or more amendments pursuant to Section 15-105(d) or other instruments having the effect of amending a statement of partnership existence and the statement of partnership existence may be amended or further amended by the filing of a restated statement of partnership existence. The restated statement of partnership existence shall be specifically designated as such in its heading and shall set forth:

(1) The present name of the partnership, and if it has been changed, the name under which the partnership was originally formed;

(2) The date of filing of the original statement of partnership existence with the Secretary of State;

(3) The information required to be included pursuant to Section 15-303(a); and

(4) Any other information desired to be included therein.

(b) Upon the filing of the restated statement of partnership existence with the Secretary of State, or upon the future effective date or time of a restated statement of partnership existence as provided for therein, the initial statement of partnership existence, as theretofore amended, shall be superseded; thenceforth, the restated statement of partnership existence, including any further amendment made thereby, shall be the statement of partnership existence of the partnership, but the original date of formation of the partnership shall remain unchanged.

(c) Any amendment effected in connection with the restatement of the statement of partnership existence shall be subject to any other provision of this chapter, not inconsistent with this section, which would apply if a separate amendment were filed to effect such amendment.

§ 15-117. Execution, Amendment or Cancelation by Judicial Order

(a) If a person required by this chapter to execute any statement or certificate fails or refuses to do so, any other person who is adversely affected by the failure or refusal, may petition the Court of Chancery to direct the execution of the statement or certificate. If the Court finds that the execution of the statement or certificate is proper and that any person so designated has failed or refused to execute the statement or certificate, the Court shall order the Secretary of State to file an appropriate statement or certificate.

(b) If a person required to execute a partnership agreement or amendment thereof fails or refuses to do so, any other person who is adversely affected by the failure or refusal may petition the Court of Chancery to direct the execution of the partnership agreement or amendment thereof. If the Court finds that the partnership agreement or amendment thereof should be executed and that any person so designated has failed or refused to do so, the Court shall enter an order granting appropriate relief.

§ 15-118. Statement or Certificate of Correction; Corrected Statement or Certificate

(a) Whenever any statement or certificate authorized to be filed with the Secretary of State under any provision of this chapter has been so filed and is an inaccurate record of the action therein referred to, or was defectively or erroneously executed, such statement or certificate may be corrected by filing with the Secretary of State a statement or certificate of correction of such statement or certificate. The statement or certificate of correction shall specify the inaccuracy or defect to be corrected, shall set forth the portion of the statement or certificate in corrected form and shall be executed and filed as required by this chapter. The statement or certificate of correction shall be effective as of the date the original statement or certificate was filed, except as to those persons who are substantially and adversely affected by the correction, and as to those persons the statement or certificate of correction shall be effective from the filing date.

(b) In lieu of filing a statement or certificate of correction, a statement or certificate may be corrected by filing with the Secretary of State a corrected statement or certificate which shall be executed and filed as if the corrected statement or certificate were the statement or certificate being corrected, and a fee equal to the fee payable to the Secretary of State if the statement or certificate being corrected were then being filed shall be paid to and collected by the Secretary of State for the use of the State of Delaware in connection with the filing of the corrected statement or certificate. The corrected statement or certificate shall be specifically designated as such in its heading, shall specify the inaccuracy or defect to be corrected, and shall set forth the entire statement or certificate in corrected form. A statement or certificate corrected in accordance with this section shall be effective as of the date the original statement or certificate was filed, except as to those persons who are substantially and adversely affected by the correction and as to those persons the statement or certificate as corrected shall be effective from the filing date.

§ 15-119. Business Transactions of Partner with the Partnership

Except as provided in the partnership agreement, a partner may lend money to, borrow money from, act as a surety, guarantor or endorser for, guarantee or assume 1 or more specific obligations of, provide collateral for and transact other business with, the partnership and, subject to other applicable law, has the same rights and obligations with respect thereto as a person who is not a partner.

§ 15-120. Contractual Appraisal Rights

A partnership agreement or an agreement of merger or consolidation or a plan of merger may provide that contractual appraisal rights with respect to a partnership interest or another interest in a partnership shall be available for any class or group of partners or partnership interests in connection with any amendment of a partnership agreement, any merger or consolidation in which the partnership is a constituent party to the merger or consolidation, any conversion of the partnership to another business form, any transfer to or domestication or continuance in any jurisdiction by the partnership, or the sale of all or substantially all of the partnership's assets. The Court of Chancery shall have jurisdiction to hear and determine any matter relating to any such appraisal rights.

§ 15-121. Contested Matters Relating to Partners; Contested Votes

(a) Upon application of any partner of a partnership which is formed under the laws of the State of Delaware or doing business in the State of Delaware, the Court of Chancery may hear and determine the validity of any admission, election, appointment or dissociation of a partner of the partnership, and the right of any person to become or continue to be a partner of the partnership, and to that end make such order or decree in any such case as may be just and proper, with power to enforce the production of any books, papers and records relating to the issue. In any such application, the partnership shall be named as a party, and service of copies of the application upon the partnership shall be deemed to be service upon the partnership and upon the person or persons whose right to be a partner is contested and upon the person or persons, if any, claiming to be a partner or claiming the right to be a partner; and the person upon whom service is made shall forward immediately a copy of the application to the partnership and to the person or persons whose right to be a partner is contested and to the person or persons, if any, claiming to be a partner or the right to be a partner, in a postpaid, sealed, registered letter addressed to such partnership and such person or persons at their post-office addresses last known to the person upon whom service is made or furnished to the person upon whom service is made by the applicant partner. The Court may make such order respecting further or other notice of such application as it deems proper under the circumstances.

(b) Upon application of any partner of a partnership which is formed under the laws of the State of Delaware or doing business in the State of Delaware, the Court of Chancery may hear and determine the result of any vote of partners upon matters as to which the partners of the partnership, or any class or group of partners, have the right to vote pursuant to the partnership agreement or other agreement or this chapter (other than the admission, election, appointment or dissociation of partners). In any such application, the partnership shall be named as a party, and service of the application upon the person upon whom service is made shall be deemed to be service upon the partnership, and no other party need be joined in order for the Court to adjudicate the result of the vote. The Court may make such order respecting further or other notice of such application as it deems proper under the circumstances.

(c) Nothing herein contained limits or affects the right to serve process in any other manner now or hereafter provided by law. This section is an extension of and not a limitation upon the right otherwise existing of service of legal process upon nonresidents.

§ 15-122. *Interpretation and Enforcement of Partnership Agreement*

Any action to interpret, apply or enforce the provisions of a partnership agreement of a partnership which is formed under the laws of the State of Delaware or doing business in the State of Delaware, or the duties, obligations or liabilities of such partnership to the partners of the partnership, or the duties, obligations or liabilities among partners or of partners to such partnership, or the rights or powers of, or restrictions on, such partnership or partners or any provision of this chapter, or any other instrument, document, agreement or certificate contemplated by any provision of this chapter, including actions authorized by Section 15-405, may be brought in the Court of Chancery.

§ 15-123. Irrevocable Power of Attorney

For all purposes of the laws of the State of Delaware, a power of attorney with respect to matters relating to the organization, internal affairs or termination of a partnership or granted by a person as a partner or a transferee of an economic interest or by a person seeking to become a partner or a transferee of an economic interest shall be irrevocable if it states that it is irrevocable and it is coupled with an interest sufficient in law to support an irrevocable power. Such irrevocable power of attorney, unless otherwise provided therein, shall not be affected by subsequent death, disability, incapacity, dissolution, termination of existence or bankruptcy of, or any other event concerning, the principal. A power of attorney with respect to matters relating to the organization, internal affairs or termination of a partnership or granted by a person as a partner or a transferee of an economic interest or by a person seeking to become a partner or a transferee of an economic interest and, in either case, granted to the partnership, a partner thereof, or any of their respective officers, directors, managers, members, partners, trustees, employees or agents shall be deemed coupled with an interest sufficient in law to support an irrevocable power.

SUBCHAPTER II.
NATURE OF PARTNERSHIP

§ 15-201. Partnership as Entity

(a) A partnership is a separate legal entity which is an entity distinct from its partners unless otherwise provided in a statement of partnership existence or a statement of qualification and in a partnership agreement.

(b) A limited liability partnership continues to be the same partnership that existed before the filing of a statement of qualification under Section 15-1001.

§ 15-202. Formation of Partnership; Powers

(a) Except as otherwise provided in subsection (b), the association of two or more persons (i) to carry on as co-owners a business for profit forms a partnership, whether or not the persons intend to form a partnership, and (ii) to carry on any purpose or activity not for profit, forms a partnership when the persons intend to form a partnership. A limited liability partnership is for all purposes a partnership.

(b) Subject to § 15-1206 of this title, an association formed under a statute other than (i) this chapter, (ii) a predecessor statute or (iii) a comparable statute of another jurisdiction, is not a partnership under this chapter.

(c) In determining whether a partnership is formed under Section 15-202(a)(i), the following rules apply:

(1) Joint tenancy, tenancy in common, tenancy by the entireties, joint property, common property or part ownership does not by itself establish a partnership, even if the co-owners share profits made by the use of the property.

(2) The sharing of gross returns does not by itself establish a partnership, even if the persons sharing them have a joint or common right or interest in property from which the returns are derived.

(3) A person who receives a share of the profits of a business is presumed to be a partner in the business, unless the profits were received in payment:

(i) of a debt by installments or otherwise;

(ii) for services as an independent contractor or of wages or other compensation to an employee;

(iii) of rent;

(iv) of an annuity or other retirement or health benefit to a beneficiary, representative or designee of a deceased or retired partner;

(v) of interest or other charge on a loan, even if the amount of payment varies with the profits of the business, including a direct or indirect present or future ownership of the collateral, or rights to income, proceeds or increase in value derived from the collateral; or

(vi) for the sale of the goodwill of a business or other property by installments or otherwise.

(d) A partnership shall possess and may exercise all the powers and privileges granted by this chapter or by any other law or by its partnership agreement, together with any powers incidental thereto, including such powers and privileges as are necessary or convenient to the conduct, promotion or attainment of the business, purposes or activities of the partnership.

(e) Notwithstanding any provision of this chapter to the contrary, without limiting the general powers enumerated in subsection (d) of this section, a partnership shall, subject to such standards and restrictions, if any, as are set forth in its partnership agreement, have the power and authority to make contracts of guaranty and suretyship and enter into interest rate, basis, currency, hedge or other swap agreements or cap, floor, put, call, option, exchange or collar agreements, derivative agreements, or other agreements similar to any of the foregoing.

(f) Unless otherwise provided in a partnership agreement, a partnership has the power and authority to grant, hold or exercise a power of attorney, including an irrevocable power of attorney.

§ 15-203. Partnership Property

Unless otherwise provided in a statement of partnership existence or a statement of qualification and in a partnership agreement, property acquired by a partnership is property of the partnership and not of the partners individually.

§ 15-204. When Property is Partnership Property

(a) Property is partnership property if acquired in the name of:

(1) the partnership; or

(2) one or more persons with an indication in the instrument transferring title to the property of the person's capacity as a partner or of the existence of a partnership but without an indication of the name of the partnership.

(b) Property is acquired in the name of the partnership by a transfer to:

(1) the partnership in its name; or

(2) one or more persons in their capacity as partners in the partnership, if the name of the partnership is indicated in the instrument transferring title to the property.

(c) Property is presumed to be partnership property if purchased with partnership assets, even if not acquired in the name of the partnership or of one or more persons with an indication in the instrument transferring title to the property of the person's capacity as a partner or of the existence of a partnership.

(d) Property acquired in the name of one or more persons, without an indication in the instrument transferring title to the property of the person's capacity as a partner or of the existence of a partnership and without use of partnership assets, is presumed to be separate property, even if used for partnership purposes.

§ 15-205. Admission without Contribution or Partnership Interest

Each person to be admitted as a partner to a partnership formed under either § 15-202(a)(i) or § 15-202(a)(ii) of this title may be admitted as a partner and may receive a partnership interest in the partnership without making a contribution or being obligated to make a contribution to the partnership. Each person to be admitted as a partner to a partnership formed under either § 15-202(a)(i) or § 15-202(a)(ii) of this title may be admitted as a partner without acquiring an economic interest in the partnership. Nothing contained in this section shall affect a partner's liability under § 15-306 of this title.

§ 15-206. Form of Contribution

The contribution of a partner may be in cash, property or services rendered, or a promissory note or other obligation to contribute cash or property or to perform services.

§ 15-207. Liability for Contribution

(a) A partner is obligated to the partnership to perform any promise to contribute cash or property or to perform services, even if the partner is unable to perform because of death, disability or any other reason. If a partner does not make the required contribution of property or services, the partner is obligated at the option of the partnership to contribute cash equal to that portion of the value of the contribution that has not been made. The foregoing option shall be in addition to, and not in lieu of, any other rights, including the right to specific performance, that the partnership may have against such partner under the partnership agreement or applicable law.

(b) A partnership agreement may provide that the partnership interest of any partner who fails to make any contribution that the partner is obligated to make shall be subject to specified penalties for, or specified consequences of, such failure. Such penalty or consequence may take the form of reducing or eliminating the defaulting partner's interest in the partnership, subordinating the partner's partnership interest to that of nondefaulting partners, a forced sale of the partner's partnership interest, forfeiture of the partner's partnership interest, the lending by other partners of the amount necessary to meet the partner's commitment, a fixing of the value of the partner's partnership interest by appraisal or by formula and redemption or sale of the partner's partnership interest at such value, or other penalty or consequence.

SUBCHAPTER III.
RELATIONS OF PARTNERS TO PERSONS DEALING WITH PARTNERSHIP

§ 15-301. Partner Agent of Partnership

Subject to the effect of a statement of partnership existence under Section 15-303:

(1) Each partner is an agent of the partnership for the purpose of its business, purposes or activities. An act of a partner, including the execution of an instrument in the partnership name, for apparently carrying on in the ordinary course the partnership's business, purposes or activities or business, purposes or activities of the kind carried on by the partnership binds the partnership, unless the partner had no authority to act for the partnership in the particular matter and the person with whom the partner was dealing had notice that the partner lacked authority.

(2) An act of a partner which is not apparently for carrying on in the ordinary course the partnership's business, purposes or activities or business, purposes or activities of the kind carried on by the partnership binds the partnership only if the act was authorized by the other partners.

§ 15-302. Transfer of Partnership Property

(a) Partnership property may be transferred as follows:

(1) Subject to the effect of a statement of partnership existence under Section 15-303, partnership property held in the name of the partnership may be transferred by an instrument of transfer executed by a partner in the partnership name.

(2) Partnership property held in the name of one or more partners with an indication in the instrument transferring the property to them of their capacity as partners or of the existence of a partnership, but without an indication of the name of the

partnership, may be transferred by an instrument of transfer executed by the persons in whose name the property is held.

(3) Partnership property held in the name of one or more persons other than the partnership, without an indication in the instrument transferring the property to them of their capacity as partners or of the existence of a partnership, may be transferred by an instrument of transfer executed by the persons in whose name the property is held.

(b) A partnership may recover partnership property from a transferee only if it proves that execution of the instrument of initial transfer did not bind the partnership under Section 15-301 and:

(1) as to a subsequent transferee who gave value for property transferred under Section 15-302(a)(1) and (2), proves that the subsequent transferee had notice that the person who executed the instrument of initial transfer lacked authority to bind the partnership; or

(2) as to a transferee who gave value for property transferred under subsection (a)(3), proves that the transferee had notice that the property was partnership property and that the person who executed the instrument of initial transfer lacked authority to bind the partnership.

(c) A partnership may not recover partnership property from a subsequent transferee if the partnership would not have been entitled to recover the property, under Section 15-302(b), from any earlier transferee of the property.

(d) If a person holds all of the partners' interests in the partnership, all of the partnership property vests in that person. The person may execute a document in the name of the partnership to evidence vesting of the property in that person and may file or record the document.

§ 15-303. Statement of Partnership Existence

(a) A partnership may file a statement of partnership existence, which:

(1) must include:

(i) the name of the partnership; and

(ii) the address of the registered office and the name and address of the registered agent for service of process required to be maintained by Section 15-111 of this title; and

(2) may state (i) the names of the partners authorized to execute an instrument transferring real property held in the name of the partnership, (ii) the authority, or limitations on the authority, of some or all of the partners to enter into other transactions on behalf of the partnership and (iii) any other matter.

(b) A statement of partnership existence supplements the authority of a partner to enter into transactions on behalf of the partnership as follows:

(1) Except for transfers of real property, a grant of authority contained in a statement of partnership existence is conclusive in favor of a person who gives value without knowledge to the contrary, so long as and to the extent that a limitation on that authority is not then contained in another statement. A filed cancellation of a limitation on authority revives the previous grant of authority.

(2) A grant of authority to transfer real property held in the name of the partnership contained in a certified copy of a statement of partnership existence recorded in the office for recording transfers of that real property is conclusive in favor of a person who gives value without knowledge to the contrary, so long as and to the extent that a certified copy of a statement containing a limitation on that authority is not then of record in the office for recording transfers of that real property. The recording in the office for recording transfers of that real property of a certified

copy of a cancellation of a limitation on authority revives the previous grant of authority.

(c) A person not a partner is deemed to know of a limitation on the authority of a partner to transfer real property held in the name of the partnership if a certified copy of the statement containing the limitation on authority is of record in the office for recording transfers of that real property.

(d) Except as otherwise provided in subsections (b) and (c) and Sections 15-704 and 15-805, a person not a partner is not deemed to know of a limitation on the authority of a partner merely because the limitation is contained in a statement.

§ 15-304. Denial of Status as Partner

If a person named in a statement of partnership existence is or may be adversely affected by being so named, the person may petition the Court of Chancery to direct the correction of the statement. If the Court finds that correction of the statement is proper and that an authorized person has failed or refused to execute and file a certificate of correction or a corrected statement, the Court shall order the Secretary of State to file an appropriate correction.

§ 15-305. Partnership Liable for Partner's Actionable Conduct

(a) A partnership is liable for loss or injury caused to a person, or for a penalty incurred, as a result of a wrongful act or omission, or other actionable conduct, of a partner acting in the ordinary course of business of the partnership or with authority of the partnership.

(b) If, in the course of the partnership's business or while acting with authority of the partnership, a partner receives or causes the partnership to receive money or property of a person not a partner, and the money or property is misapplied by a partner, the partnership is liable for the loss.

§ 15-306. Partner's Liability

(a) Except as otherwise provided in subsections (b) and (c), all partners are liable jointly and severally for all obligations of the partnership unless otherwise agreed by the claimant or provided by law.

(b) A person admitted as a partner into an existing partnership is not personally liable for any obligation of the partnership incurred before the person's admission as a partner.

(c) An obligation of a partnership arising out of or related to circumstances or events occurring while the partnership is a limited liability partnership or incurred while the partnership is a limited liability partnership, whether arising in contract, tort or otherwise, is solely the obligation of the partnership. A partner is not personally liable, directly or indirectly, by way of indemnification, contribution, assessment or otherwise, for such an obligation solely by reason of being or so acting as a partner.

(d) The ability of an attorney-at-law, admitted to the practice of law in the State of Delaware, to practice law in Delaware in a limited liability partnership, shall be determined by the Rules of the Supreme Court of the State of Delaware.

(e) Notwithstanding the provisions of subsection (c) of this section, under a partnership agreement or under another agreement, a partner may agree to be personally liable, directly or indirectly, by way of indemnification, contribution, assessment or otherwise, for any or all of the obligations of the partnership incurred while the partnership is a limited liability partnership.

§ 15-307. Actions By and Against Partnership and Partners

(a) A partnership may sue and be sued in the name of the partnership.

(b) An action may be brought against the partnership and, to the extent not inconsistent with Section 15-306, any or all of the partners in the same action or in separate actions.

Delaware Revised Uniform Partnership Act

(c) A judgment against a partnership is not by itself a judgment against a partner. A judgment against a partnership may not be satisfied from the assets of a partner liable as provided in Section 15-306 for a partnership obligation unless there is also a judgment against the partner for such obligation.

(d) A judgment creditor of a partner may not levy execution against the assets of the partner to satisfy a judgment based on a claim against the partnership unless:

(1) the claim is for an obligation of the partnership for which the partner is liable as provided in Section 15-306 and either:

(i) a judgment based on the same claim has been obtained against the partnership and a writ of execution on the judgment has been returned unsatisfied in whole or in part;

(ii) the partnership is a debtor in bankruptcy;

(iii) the partner has agreed that the creditor need not exhaust partnership assets; or

(iv) a court grants permission to the judgment creditor to levy execution against the assets of a partner based on a finding that partnership assets subject to execution are clearly insufficient to satisfy the judgment, that exhaustion of partnership assets is excessively burdensome, or that the grant of permission is an appropriate exercise of the court's equitable powers; or

(2) liability is imposed on the partner by law or contract independent of the existence of the partnership.

(e) This section applies to any obligation of the partnership resulting from a representation by a partner or purported partner under Section 15-308.

§ 15-308. Liability of Purported Partner

(a) If a person, by words or conduct, purports to be a partner, or consents to being represented by another as a partner, in a partnership or with one or more persons not partners, the purported partner is liable to a person to whom the representation is made, if that person, relying on the representation, enters into a transaction with the actual or purported partnership. If the representation, either by the purported partner or by a person with the purported partner's consent, is made in a public manner, the purported partner is liable to a person who relies upon the purported partnership even if the purported partner is not aware of being held out as a partner to the claimant. If a partnership obligation results, the purported partner is liable with respect to that obligation as if the purported partner were a partner. If no partnership obligation results, the purported partner is liable with respect to that obligation jointly and severally with any other person consenting to the representation. In the case of a limited liability partnership, a person's liability under Section 15-308(a) is subject to Section 15-306 as if the person were a partner in the limited liability partnership.

(b) If a person is thus represented to be a partner in an existing partnership, or with one or more persons not partners, the purported partner is an agent of persons consenting to the representation to bind them to the same extent and in the same manner as if the purported partner were a partner, with respect to persons who enter into transactions in reliance upon the representation. If all of the partners of the existing partnership consent to the representation, a partnership act or obligation results. If fewer than all of the partners of the existing partnership consent to the representation, the person acting and the partners consenting to the representation are jointly and severally liable.

(c) A person is not liable as a partner merely because the person is named by another in a statement of partnership existence.

(d) A person does not continue to be liable as a partner merely because of a failure to file a statement of dissociation or to amend a statement of partnership existence to indicate the partner's dissociation from the partnership.

(e) Except as otherwise provided in subsections (a) and (b), persons who are not partners as to each other are not liable as partners to other persons.

§ 15-309. Limitations on Distribution

(a) A limited liability partnership shall not make a distribution to a partner to the extent that at the time of the distribution, after giving effect to the distribution, all liabilities of the limited liability partnership, other than liabilities to partners on account of their economic interests and liabilities for which the recourse of creditors is limited to specified property of the limited liability partnership, exceed the fair value of the assets of the limited liability partnership, except that the fair value of property that is subject to a liability for which the recourse of creditors is limited shall be included in the assets of the limited liability partnership only to the extent that the fair value of that property exceeds that liability. For purposes of this subsection, the term "distribution" shall not include amounts constituting reasonable compensation for present or past services or reasonable payments made in the ordinary course of business pursuant to a bona fide retirement plan or other benefits program.

(b) A partner of a limited liability partnership who receives a distribution in violation of subsection (a) of this section, and who knew at the time of the distribution that the distribution violated subsection (a) of this section, shall be liable to the partnership for the amount of the distribution. A partner of a limited liability partnership who receives a distribution in violation of subsection (a) of this section, and who did not know at the time of the distribution that the distribution violated subsection (a) of this section, shall not be liable for the amount of the distribution. Subject to subsection (c) of this section, this subsection (b) shall not affect any obligation or liability of a partner of a limited liability partnership under an agreement or other applicable law for the amount of a distribution.

(c) Unless otherwise agreed, a partner of a limited liability partnership who receives a distribution from a partnership shall have no liability under this chapter or other applicable law for the amount of the distribution after the expiration of three years from the date of the distribution.

SUBCHAPTER IV.
RELATIONS OF PARTNERS TO EACH OTHER AND TO PARTNERSHIP

§ 15-401. *Partner's Rights and Duties*

(a) Each partner is deemed to have an account that is:

(1) credited with an amount equal to the money plus the value of any other property, net of the amount of any liabilities, the partner contributes to the partnership and the partner's share of the partnership profits; and

(2) charged with an amount equal to the money plus the value of any other property, net of the amount of any liabilities, distributed by the partnership to the partner and the partner's share of the partnership losses.

(b) Each partner is entitled to an equal share of the partnership profits and is chargeable with a share of the partnership losses in proportion to the partner's share of the profits.

(c) In addition to indemnification under Section 15-110, a partnership shall reimburse a partner for payments made and indemnify a partner for liabilities incurred by the partner in the ordinary course of the business of the partnership or for the preservation of its business or property; however, no person shall be required as a consequence of any such indemnification to make any payment to the extent that the payment is inconsistent with Sections 15-306(b) or (c).

(d) A partnership shall reimburse a partner for an advance to the partnership beyond the amount of capital the partner agreed to contribute.

(e) A payment or advance made by a partner which gives rise to a partnership obligation under subsection (c) or (d) constitutes a loan to the partnership which accrues interest from the date of the payment or advance.

(f) Each partner has equal rights in the management and conduct of the partnership business and affairs.

(g) A partner may use or possess partnership property only on behalf of the partnership.

(h) A partner is not entitled to remuneration for services performed for the partnership, except for reasonable compensation for services rendered in winding up the partnership.

(i) A person may become a partner only with the consent of all of the partners.

(j) A difference arising as to a matter in the ordinary course of business of a partnership may be decided by a majority of the partners. An act outside the ordinary course of business of a partnership may be undertaken only with the consent of all of the partners.

(k) This section does not affect the obligations of a partnership to other persons under Section 15-301.

(l) A partner has the power and authority to delegate to one or more other persons the partner's rights and powers to manage and control the business and affairs of the partnership, including to delegate to agents, officers and employees of the partner or the partnership, and to delegate by a management agreement or other agreement with, or otherwise to, other persons. Such delegation by a partner shall not cause the partner to cease to be a partner of the partnership or cause the person to whom any such rights and powers have been delegated to be a partner of the partnership.

(m) Unless otherwise provided in a partnership agreement or another agreement, a partner shall have no preemptive right to subscribe to any additional issue of partnership interests or another interest in a partnership.

§ 15-402. Distributions in Kind

A partner, regardless of the nature of the partner's contribution, has no right to demand and receive any distribution from a partnership in kind. A partner may not be compelled to accept a distribution of any asset in kind from a partnership to the extent that the percentage of the asset distributed to the partner exceeds a percentage of that asset which is equal to the percentage in which the partner shares in distributions from the partnership. A partner may be compelled to accept a distribution of any asset in kind from a partnership to the extent that the percentage of the asset distributed to the partner is equal to a percentage of that asset which is equal to the percentage in which the partner shares in distributions from the partnership.

§ 15-403. *Partner's Rights and Duties with Respect to Information*

(a) Each partner and the partnership shall provide partners, former partners and the legal representative of a deceased partner or partner under a legal disability and their agents and attorneys, access to the books and records of the partnership and other information concerning the partnership's business and affairs (in the case of former partners, only with respect to the period during which they were partners) upon reasonable demand, for any purpose reasonably related to the partner's interest as a partner in the partnership. The right of access shall include access to:

(1) True and full information regarding the status of the business and financial condition of the partnership;

(2) Promptly after becoming available, a copy of the partnership's federal, state and local income tax returns for each year;

(3) A current list of the name and last known business, residence or mailing address of each partner;

(4) A copy of any statement and written partnership agreement and all amendments thereto, together with executed copies of any written powers of attorney pursuant to which the statement or the partnership agreement and any amendments thereto have been executed;

(5) True and full information regarding the amount of cash and a description and statement of the agreed value of any other

property or services contributed by each partner and which each partner has agreed to contribute in the future, and the date on which each partner became a partner; and

(6) Other information regarding the affairs of the partnership as is just and reasonable.

The right of access includes the right to examine and make extracts from books and records and other information concerning the partnership's business and affairs. The partnership agreement may provide for, and in the absence of such provision in the partnership agreement, the partnership or the partner from whom access is sought may impose, reasonable standards (including standards governing what information and documents are to be furnished at what time and location and at whose expense) with respect to exercise of the right of access.

(b) A partnership agreement may provide that the partnership shall have the right to keep confidential from partners for such period of time as the partnership deems reasonable, any information which the partnership reasonably believes to be in the nature of trade secrets or other information the disclosure of which the partnership in good faith believes is not in the best interest of the partnership or could damage the partnership or its business or affairs or which the partnership is required by law or by agreement with a third party to keep confidential.

(c) A partnership and its partners may maintain the books and records and other information concerning the partnership in other than a written form if such form is capable of conversion into written form within a reasonable time.

(d) Any demand by a partner under this section shall be in writing and shall state the purpose of such demand.

(e) Any action to enforce any right arising under this section shall be brought in the Court of Chancery. If the partnership or a partner refuses to permit access as described in subsection (a) of this section or does not reply to a demand that has been made within 5 business days (or such shorter or longer period of time as is provided for in a partnership agreement but not longer than 30 business days) after the demand has been made, the demanding partner, former partner, or legal representative of a deceased partner or partner under a legal disability may apply to the Court of Chancery for an order to compel such disclosure. The Court of Chancery is hereby vested with exclusive jurisdiction to determine whether or not the person making the demand is entitled to the books and records or other information concerning the partnership's business and affairs sought. The Court of Chancery may summarily order the partnership or partner to permit the demanding partner, former partner or legal representative of a deceased partner or partner under a legal disability and their agents and attorneys to provide access to the information described in subsection (a) of this section and to make copies or extracts therefrom; or the Court of Chancery may summarily order the partnership or partner to furnish to the demanding partner, former partner or legal representative of a deceased partner or partner under a legal disability and their agents and attorneys the information described in subsection (a) of this section on the condition that the partner, former partner or legal representative of a deceased partner or partner under a legal disability first pay to the partnership or to the partner from whom access is sought the reasonable cost of obtaining and furnishing such information and on such other conditions as the Court of Chancery deems appropriate. When a demanding partner, former partner or legal representative of a deceased partner or partner under a legal disability seeks to obtain access to information described in subsection (a) of this section, the demanding partner, former partner or legal representative of a deceased partner or partner under a legal disability shall first establish (1) that the demanding partner, former partner or legal representative of a deceased partner or partner under a legal disability has complied with the provisions of this section respecting the form and manner of making demand for obtaining access to such information and (2) that the information the demanding partner, former partner or legal representative of a deceased partner or partner under a legal disability seeks is reasonably related to the partner's interest as a partner in the partnership. The Court of Chancery may, in its discretion, prescribe any limitations or conditions with reference to the access to information, or award such other or further relief as the Court of Chancery may deem just and proper. The Court of Chancery may order books, documents and records, pertinent extracts therefrom, or duly authenticated copies thereof, to be brought within the State of Delaware and kept in the State of Delaware upon such terms and conditions as the order may prescribe.

(f) The rights of a partner to obtain information as provided in this section may be restricted in an original partnership agreement or in any subsequent amendment approved or adopted by all of the partners or in compliance with any applicable requirements of the partnership agreement.

§ 15-404. *General Standards of Partner's Conduct*

(a) The only fiduciary duties a partner owes to the partnership and the other partners are the duty of loyalty and the duty of care set forth in subsections (b) and (c).

(b) A partner's duty of loyalty to the partnership and the other partners is limited to the following:

(1) to account to the partnership and hold as trustee for it any property, profit or benefit derived by the partner in the conduct or winding up of the partnership business or affairs or derived from a use by the partner of partnership property, including the appropriation of a partnership opportunity;

(2) to refrain from dealing with the partnership in the conduct or winding up of the partnership business or affairs as or on behalf of a party having an interest adverse to the partnership; and

(3) to refrain from competing with the partnership in the conduct of the partnership business or affairs before the dissolution of the partnership.

(c) A partner's duty of care to the partnership and the other partners in the conduct and winding up of the partnership business or affairs is limited to refraining from engaging in grossly negligent or reckless conduct, intentional misconduct, or a knowing violation of law.

(d) A partner does not violate a duty or obligation under this chapter or under the partnership agreement solely because the partner's conduct furthers the partner's own interest.

(e) A partner may lend money to, borrow money from, act as a surety, guarantor or endorser for, guarantee or assume 1 or more specific obligations of, provide collateral for and transact other business with, the partnership and, subject to other applicable law, has the same rights and obligations with respect thereto as a person who is not a partner.

(f) This section applies to a person winding up the partnership business or affairs as the personal or legal representative of the last surviving partner as if the person were a partner.

§ 15-405. Actions by Partnership and Partners; Derivative Actions

(a) A partnership may maintain an action against a partner for a breach of the partnership agreement, or for the violation of a duty to the partnership, causing harm to the partnership.

(b) A partner may maintain an action against the partnership or another partner for legal or equitable relief, with or without an accounting as to partnership business, to:

(1) enforce the partner's rights under the partnership agreement;

(2) enforce the partner's rights under this chapter, including:

(i) the partner's rights under Sections 15-401, 15-403 or 15-404;

(ii) the partner's right on dissociation to have the partner's interest in the partnership purchased pursuant to Section 15-701 or enforce any other right under Subchapter VI or VII; or

(iii) the partner's right to compel a dissolution and winding up of the partnership business under Section 15-801 or enforce any other right under Subchapter VIII; or

(3) enforce the rights and otherwise protect the interests of the partner, including rights and interests arising independently of the partnership relationship.

(c) The accrual of, and any time limitation on, a right of action for a remedy under this section is governed by other law. A right to an accounting upon a dissolution and winding up does not revive a claim barred by law.

(d) A partner may bring a derivative action in the Court of Chancery in the right of a partnership to recover a judgment in the partnership's favor.

(e) In a derivative action, the plaintiff must be a partner at the time of bringing the action and:

(1) At the time of the transaction of which the partner complains; or

(2) The partner's status as a partner had devolved upon the partner by operation of law or pursuant to the terms of the partnership agreement from a person who was a partner at the time of the transaction.

(f) In a derivative action, the complaint shall set forth with particularity the effort, if any, of the plaintiff to secure initiation of the action by the partnership or the reason for not making the effort.

(g) If a derivative action is successful, in whole or in part, as a result of a judgment, compromise or settlement of any such action, the court may award the plaintiff reasonable expenses, including reasonable attorney's fees, from any recovery in any such action or from a partnership.

§ 15-406. Continuation of Partnership Beyond Definite Term or Particular Undertaking

(a) If a partnership for a definite term or particular undertaking is continued, without an express agreement, after the expiration of the term or completion of the undertaking, the rights and duties of the partners remain the same as they were at the expiration or completion, so far as is consistent with a partnership at will.

(b) If the partners, or those of them who habitually acted in the business or affairs during the term or undertaking, continue the business or affairs without any settlement or liquidation of the partnership, they are presumed to have agreed that the partnership will continue.

§ 15-407. Classes and Voting

(a) A partnership agreement may provide for classes or groups of partners having such relative rights, powers and duties as the partnership agreement may provide, and may make provision for the future creation in the manner provided in the partnership agreement of additional classes or groups of partners having such relative rights, powers and duties as may from time to time be established, including rights, powers and duties senior to existing classes and groups of partners. A partnership agreement may provide for the taking of an action, including the amendment of the partnership agreement, without the vote or approval of any partner or class or group of partners, including an action to create under the provisions of the partnership agreement a class or group of partnership interests that was not previously outstanding. A partnership agreement may provide that any partner or class or group of partners shall have no voting rights.

(b) The partnership agreement may grant to all or certain identified partners or a specified class or group of the partners the right to vote separately or with all or any class or group of the partners on any matter. Voting by partners may be on a per capita, number, financial interest, class, group or any other basis.

(c) A partnership agreement may set forth provisions relating to notice of the time, place or purpose of any meeting at which any matter is to be voted on by any partners, waiver of any such notice, action by consent without a meeting, the establishment of a record date, quorum requirements, voting in person or by proxy, or any other matter with respect to the exercise of any such right to vote.

Delaware Revised Uniform Partnership Act

(d) Unless otherwise provided in a partnership agreement, meetings of partners may be held by means of conference telephone or other communications equipment by means of which all persons participating in the meeting can hear each other, and participation in a meeting pursuant to this subsection shall constitute presence in person at the meeting. On any matter that is to be voted on, consented to or approved by partners, the partners may take such action without a meeting, without prior notice and without a vote if consented to, in writing or by electronic transmission, by partners having not less than the minimum number of votes that would be necessary to authorize or take such action at a meeting at which all partners entitled to vote thereon were present and voted. On any matter that is to be voted on by partners, the partners may vote in person or by proxy, and such proxy may be granted in writing, by means of electronic transmission or as otherwise permitted by applicable law. Unless otherwise provided in a partnership agreement, a consent transmitted by electronic transmission by a partner or by a person or persons authorized to act for a partner shall be deemed to be written and signed for purposes of this subsection (d). For purposes of this subsection (d), the term "electronic transmission" means any form of communication not directly involving the physical transmission of paper that creates a record that may be retained, retrieved and reviewed by a recipient thereof and that may be directly reproduced in paper form by such a recipient through an automated process.

(e) If a partnership agreement provides for the manner in which it may be amended, including by requiring the approval of a person who is not a party to the partnership agreement or the satisfaction of conditions, it may be amended only in that manner or as otherwise permitted by law, including as permitted by § 15-902(g) of this title (provided that the approval of any person may be waived by such person and that any such conditions may be waived by all persons for whose benefit such conditions were intended). If a partnership agreement does not provide for the manner in which it may be amended, the partnership agreement may be amended with the approval of all the partners or as otherwise permitted by law, including as permitted by § 15-902(g) of this title. Unless otherwise provided in a partnership agreement, a supermajority amendment provision shall only apply to provisions of the partnership agreement that are expressly included in the partnership agreement. As used in this section, "supermajority amendment provision" means any amendment provision set forth in a partnership agreement requiring that an amendment to a provision of the partnership agreement be adopted by no less than the vote or consent required to take action under such latter provision.

§ 15-408. Remedies for Breach of Partnership Agreement

A partnership agreement may provide that (i) a partner who fails to perform in accordance with, or to comply with the terms and conditions of, the partnership agreement shall be subject to specified penalties or specified consequences, and (ii) at the time or upon the happening of events specified in the partnership agreement, a partner shall be subject to specified penalties or specified consequences. Such specified penalties or specified consequences may include and take the form of any penalty or consequence set forth in § 15-207(b) of this title.

§ 15-409. Reliance on Reports and Information by Partner or Liquidating Trustee

(a) A liquidating trustee of a partnership (including a limited liability partnership) shall be fully protected in relying in good faith upon the records of the partnership and upon information, opinions, reports or statements presented by a partner of the partnership, an officer or employee of the partnership, another liquidating trustee, or committees of the partnership or partners, or by any other person as to matters the liquidating trustee reasonably believes are within such other person's professional or expert competence, including information, opinions, reports or statements as to the value and amount of assets, liabilities, profits or losses of the partnership, or the value and amount of assets or reserves or contracts, agreements or other undertakings that would be sufficient to pay claims and obligations of the partnership or to make reasonable provision to pay such claims and obligations, or any other facts pertinent to the existence and amount of assets from which distributions to partners or creditors might properly be paid.

(b) A partner of a limited liability partnership shall be fully protected in relying in good faith upon the records of the partnership and upon information, opinions, reports or statements presented by another partner of the partnership, an officer or employee of the partnership, a liquidating trustee, or committees of the partnership or partners, or by any other person as to matters the partner reasonably believes are within such other person's professional or expert competence, including information, opinions, reports or statements as to the value and amount of assets, liabilities, profits or losses of the partnership, or the value and amount of assets or reserves or contracts, agreements or other undertakings that would be sufficient to pay claims and obligations of the partnership or to make reasonable provision to pay such claims and obligations, or any other facts pertinent to the existence and amount of assets from which distributions to partners or creditors might properly be paid.

(c) A partner of a partnership that is not a limited liability partnership shall be fully protected from liability to the partnership, its partners or other persons party to or otherwise bound by the partnership agreement in relying in good faith upon the records of the partnership and upon information, opinions, reports or statements presented by another partner of the partnership, an officer or employee of the partnership, a liquidating trustee, or committees of the partnership or partners, or by any other person as to matters the partner reasonably believes are within such other person's professional or expert competence, including information, opinions, reports or statements as to the value and amount of assets, liabilities, profits or losses of the partnership, or the value and amount of assets or reserves or contracts, agreements or other undertakings that would be sufficient to pay claims and obligations of the partnership or to make reasonable provision to pay such claims and obligations, or any other facts pertinent to the existence and amount of assets from which distributions to partners or creditors might properly be paid.

SUBCHAPTER V.
TRANSFEREES AND CREDITORS OF PARTNER

§ 15-501. Partner Not Co-Owner of Partnership Property

Unless otherwise provided in a statement of partnership existence or a statement of qualification and in a partnership agreement, a partner is not a co-owner of partnership property and has no interest in specific partnership property.

§ 15-502. Partner's Economic Interest in Partnership; Personal Property

A partnership interest is personal property. Only a partner's economic interest may be transferred.

§ 15-503. Transfer of Partner's Economic Interest

(a) A transfer, in whole or in part, of a partner's economic interest in the partnership:

(1) is permissible;

(2) does not by itself cause the partner's dissociation or a dissolution and winding up of the partnership business or affairs; and

(3) does not entitle the transferee to participate in the management or conduct of the partnership business or affairs, to require access to information concerning partnership transactions, or to inspect or copy the partnership books or records.

(b) A transferee of a partner's economic interest in the partnership has a right:

(1) to receive, in accordance with the transfer, distributions to which the transferor would otherwise be entitled;

(2) to receive upon the dissolution and winding up of the partnership business or affairs, in accordance with the transfer, the net amount otherwise distributable to the transferor; and

(3) to seek under Section 15-801(6) a judicial determination that it is equitable to wind up the partnership business or affairs.

(c) In a dissolution and winding up, a transferee is entitled to an account of partnership transactions only from the date of the latest account agreed to by all of the partners.

(d) Upon transfer, the transferor retains the rights and duties of a partner other than the economic interest transferred.

(e) A partnership need not give effect to a transferee's rights under this section until it has notice of the transfer. Upon request of a partnership or a partner, a transferee must furnish reasonable proof of a transfer.

(f) A transfer of a partner's economic interest in the partnership in violation of a restriction on transfer contained in a partnership agreement is ineffective.

(g) Notwithstanding anything to the contrary under applicable law, a partnership agreement may provide that a partner's economic interest may not be transferred prior to the dissolution and winding up of the partnership.

(h) A partnership interest in a partnership may be evidenced by a certificate of partnership interest issued by the partnership. A partnership agreement may provide for the transfer of any partnership interest represented by such a certificate and make other provisions with respect to such certificates. A partnership shall not have the power to issue a certificate of partnership interest in bearer form.

(i) Except to the extent assumed by agreement, until a transferee of a partnership interest becomes a partner, the transferee shall have no liability as a partner solely as a result of the transfer.

(j) A partnership may acquire, by purchase, redemption or otherwise, any partnership interest or other interest of a partner in the partnership. Any such interest so acquired by the partnership shall be deemed canceled.

§ 15-504. Partner's Economic Interest Subject to Charging Order

(a) On application by a judgment creditor of a partner or of a partner's transferee, a court having jurisdiction may charge the economic interest of the judgment debtor to satisfy the judgment. To the extent so charged, the judgment creditor has only the right to receive any distribution or distributions to which the judgment debtor would otherwise have been entitled in respect of such economic interest.

(b) A charging order constitutes a lien on the judgment debtor's economic interest in the partnership.

(c) This chapter does not deprive a partner or a partner's transferee of a right under exemption laws with respect to the judgment debtor's economic interest in the partnership.

(d) The entry of a charging order is the exclusive remedy by which a judgment creditor of a partner or of a partner's transferee may satisfy a judgment out of the judgment debtor's economic interest in the partnership.

(e) No creditor of a partner or of a partner's transferee shall have any right to obtain possession of, or otherwise exercise legal or equitable remedies with respect to, the property of the partnership.

(f) The Court of Chancery shall have jurisdiction to hear and determine any matter relating to any such charging order.

SUBCHAPTER VI.
PARTNER'S DISSOCIATION

§ 15-601. Events Causing Partner's Dissociation

A partner is dissociated from a partnership upon the occurrence of any of the following events:

(1) the partnership's having notice of the partner's express will to withdraw as a partner on a later date specified by the partner in the notice or, if no later date is specified, then upon receipt of notice;

(2) an event agreed to in the partnership agreement as causing the partner's dissociation;

(3) the partner's expulsion pursuant to the partnership agreement;

(4) the partner's expulsion by the unanimous vote of the other partners if:

    (i) it is unlawful to carry on the partnership business or affairs with that partner; or

    (ii) there has been a transfer of all or substantially all of that partner's economic interest, other than a transfer for security purposes, or a court order charging the partner's interest which, in either case, has not been foreclosed;

(5) on application by or for the partnership or another partner to the Court of Chancery, the partner's expulsion by determination by the Court of Chancery because:

    (i) the partner engaged in wrongful conduct that adversely and materially affected the partnership business or affairs;

    (ii) the partner willfully or persistently committed a material breach of either the partnership agreement or of a duty owed to the partnership or the other partners; or

(iii) the partner engaged in conduct relating to the partnership business or affairs which makes it not reasonably practicable to carry on the business or affairs in partnership with the partner;

(6) The partner's:

a. Making an assignment for the benefit of creditors;

b. Filing a voluntary petition in bankruptcy;

c. Being adjudged a bankrupt or insolvent, or having entered against that partner an order for relief in any bankruptcy or insolvency proceeding;

d. Filing a petition or answer seeking for that partner any reorganization, arrangement, composition, readjustment, liquidation, dissolution or similar relief under any statute, law or regulation;

e. Filing an answer or other pleading admitting or failing to contest the material allegations of a petition filed against that partner in any proceeding of this nature;

f. Seeking, consenting to or acquiescing in the appointment of a trustee, receiver or liquidator of that partner or of all or any substantial part of that partner's properties; or

g. Failing, within 120 days after its commencement, to have dismissed any proceeding against that partner seeking reorganization, arrangement, composition, readjustment, liquidation, dissolution or similar relief under any statute, law or regulation, or failing, within 90 days after the appointment without that partner's consent or acquiescence, to have vacated or stayed the appointment of a trustee, receiver or liquidator of that partner or of all or any substantial part of that partner's properties, or failing, within 90 days after the expiration of any such stay, to have the appointment vacated;

(7) in the case of a partner who is an individual:

(i) the partner's death;

(ii) the appointment of a guardian or general conservator for the partner; or

(iii) a judicial determination that the partner has otherwise become incapable of performing the partner's duties under the partnership agreement;

(8) in the case of a partner that is a trust or is acting as a partner by virtue of being a trustee of a trust, distribution of the trust's entire economic interest, but not merely by reason of the substitution of a successor trustee;

(9) in the case of a partner that is an estate or is acting as a partner by virtue of being a personal representative of an estate, distribution of the estate's entire economic interest, but not merely by reason of the substitution of a successor personal representative;

(10) the expiration of 90 days after the partnership notifies a corporate partner that it will be expelled because it has filed a certificate of dissolution or the equivalent, its existence has been terminated or its certificate of incorporation has been revoked, or its right to conduct business has been suspended by the jurisdiction of its incorporation, if there is no revocation of the certificate of dissolution or no reinstatement of its existence, its certificate of incorporation or its right to conduct business;

(11) a partnership, a limited liability company, a trust or a limited partnership that is a partner has been dissolved and its business is being wound up; or

(12) termination of a partner who is not an individual, partnership, corporation, trust, limited partnership, limited liability company or estate.

§ 15-602. *Partner's Power to Dissociate; Wrongful Dissociation*

(a) A partner has the power to dissociate at any time, rightfully or wrongfully, by express will pursuant to Section 15-601(1).

(b) A partner's dissociation is wrongful only if any of the following apply:

(1) it is in breach of an express provision of the partnership agreement; or

(2) in the case of a partnership for a definite term or particular undertaking, before the expiration of the term or the completion of the undertaking if any of the following apply:

(i) the partner withdraws by express will, unless the withdrawal follows within 90 days after another partner's dissociation by death or otherwise under Section 15-601(6) through (12) or wrongful dissociation under this subsection;

(ii) the partner is expelled by judicial determination under Section 15-601(5);

(iii) the partner is dissociated under Section 15-601(6); or

(iv) in the case of a partner who is not an individual, trust (other than a statutory trust), or estate, the partner is expelled or otherwise dissociated because it willfully dissolved or terminated.

(c) A partner who wrongfully dissociates is liable to the partnership and to the other partners for damages caused by the dissociation. Such liability is in addition to any other obligation of the partner to the partnership or to the other partners.

§ 15-603. *Effect of Partner's Dissociation*

(a) If a partner's dissociation results in a dissolution and winding up of the partnership business, Subchapter VIII applies; otherwise, Subchapter VII applies.

(b) Upon a partner's dissociation:

(1) the partner's right to participate in the management and conduct of the partnership business terminates, except as otherwise provided in Section 15-803;

(2) the partner's duty of loyalty under Section 15-404(b)(3) terminates; and

(3) the partner's duty of loyalty under Section 15-404(b)(1) and (2) and duty of care under Section 15-404(c) continue only with regard to matters arising and events occurring before the partner's dissociation, unless the partner participates in winding up the partnership's business pursuant to Section 15-803.

SUBCHAPTER VII.
PARTNER'S DISSOCIATION WHEN BUSINESS OR AFFAIRS NOT WOUND UP

§ 15-701. Purchase of Dissociated Partner's Partnership Interest

(a) If a partner is dissociated from a partnership without resulting in a dissolution and winding up of the partnership business or affairs under Section 15-801, the partnership shall cause the dissociated partner's interest in the partnership to be purchased for a buyout price determined pursuant to subsection (b).

(b) The buyout price of a dissociated partner's partnership interest is an amount equal to the fair value of such partner's economic interest as of the date of dissociation based upon such partner's right to share in distributions from the partnership. Interest must be paid from the date of dissociation to the date of payment.

(c) Damages for wrongful dissociation under Section 15-602(b), and all other amounts owing, whether or not presently due, from the dissociated partner to the partnership, must be offset against the buyout price. Interest must be paid from the date the amount owed becomes due to the date of payment.

(d) A partnership shall indemnify a dissociated partner whose partnership interest is being purchased against all partnership obligations, whether incurred before or after the dissociation, except partnership obligations incurred by an act of the dissociated partner under Section 15-702.

(e) If no agreement for the purchase of a dissociated partner's partnership interest is reached within 120 days after a written demand for payment, the partnership shall pay, or cause to be paid, in cash to the dissociated partner the amount the partnership estimates to be the buyout price and accrued interest, reduced by any offsets and accrued interest under subsection (c).

(f) If a deferred payment is authorized under subsection (h), the partnership may tender a written offer to pay the amount it estimates to be the buyout price and accrued interest, reduced by any offsets under subsection (c), stating the time of payment, the amount and type of security for payment, and the other terms and conditions of the obligation.

(g) The payment or tender required by subsection (e) or (f) of this section must be accompanied by the following:

(1) a written statement of partnership assets and liabilities as of the date of dissociation;

(2) the latest available partnership balance sheet and income statement, if any;

(3) a written explanation of how the estimated amount of the payment was calculated; and

(4) written notice which shall state that the payment is in full satisfaction of the obligation to purchase unless, within 120 days after the written notice, the dissociated partner commences an action in the Court of Chancery under (i) to determine the buyout price of that partner's partnership interest, any offsets under subsection (c) or other terms of the obligation to purchase.

(h) A partner who wrongfully dissociates before the expiration of a definite term or the completion of a particular undertaking is not entitled to payment of any portion of the buyout price until the expiration of the term or completion of the undertaking, unless the partner establishes to the satisfaction of the Court of Chancery that earlier payment will not cause undue hardship to the business of the partnership. A deferred payment must bear interest and, to the extent it would not cause undue hardship to the business of the partnership, be adequately secured.

(i) A dissociated partner may maintain an action against the partnership, pursuant to Section 15-405(b)(2)(ii), to determine the buyout price of that partner's partnership interest, any offsets under subsection (c), or other terms of the obligation to purchase. The action must be commenced within 120 days after the partnership has tendered payment or an offer to pay or within one year after written demand for payment if no payment or offer to pay is tendered. The Court of Chancery shall determine the buyout price of the dissociated partner's partnership interest, any offset due under subsection (c), and accrued interest, and enter judgment for any additional payment or refund. If deferred payment is authorized under subsection (h), the Court of Chancery shall also determine the security, if any, for payment and other terms of the obligation to purchase. The Court of Chancery may assess reasonable attorney's fees and the fees and expenses of appraisers or other experts for a party to the action, in amounts the Court of Chancery finds equitable, against a party that the Court of Chancery finds acted arbitrarily, vexatiously or not in good faith. The finding may be based on the partnership's failure to tender payment or an offer to pay or to comply with subsection (g).

§ 15-702. Dissociated Partner's Power to Bind and Liability to Partnership

(a) For one year after a partner dissociates without resulting in a dissolution and winding up of the partnership business, the partnership, including a surviving partnership under Subchapter IX, is bound by an act of the dissociated partner which would have bound the partnership under Section 15-301 before dissociation only if at the time of entering into the transaction the other party:

(1) reasonably believed that the dissociated partner was then a partner and reasonably relied on such belief in entering into the transaction;

(2) did not have notice of the partner's dissociation; and

(3) is not deemed to have had knowledge under Section 15-303(c) or notice under Section 15-704(c).

(b) A dissociated partner is liable to the partnership for any damage caused to the partnership arising from an obligation incurred by the dissociated partner after dissociation for which the partnership is liable under subsection (a).

§ 15-703. Dissociated Partner's Liability to Other Persons

(a) A partner's dissociation does not of itself discharge the partner's liability for a partnership obligation incurred before dissociation. A dissociated partner is not liable for a partnership obligation incurred after dissociation, except as otherwise provided in subsection (b).

(b) A partner who dissociates without resulting in a dissolution and winding up of the partnership business is liable as a partner to the other party in a transaction entered into by the partnership, or a surviving partnership under Subchapter IX, within one year after the partner's dissociation, only if the partner is liable for the obligation under Section 15-306 and at the time of entering into the transaction the other party:

(1) reasonably believed that the dissociated partner was then a partner and reasonably relied on such belief in entering into the transaction;

(2) did not have notice of the partner's dissociation; and

(3) is not deemed to have had knowledge under Section 15-303(c) or notice under Section 15-704(c).

(c) By agreement with the partnership creditor and the partners continuing the business, a dissociated partner may be released from liability for a partnership obligation.

(d) A dissociated partner is released from liability for a partnership obligation if a partnership creditor, with notice of the partner's dissociation but without the partner's consent, agrees to a material alteration in the nature or time of payment of a partnership obligation.

§ 15-704. Statement of Dissociation

(a) A dissociated partner or, after the filing by the partnership of a statement of partnership existence, the partnership may file a statement of dissociation stating the name of the partnership and that the partner is dissociated from the partnership.

(b) A statement of dissociation is a limitation on the authority of a dissociated partner for the purposes of Section 15-303(b) and (c).

(c) For the purposes of Sections 15-702(a)(3) and 15-703(b)(3), a person not a partner is deemed to have notice of the dissociation 60 days after the statement of dissociation is filed.

§ 15-705. Continued Use of Partnership Name

Continued use of a partnership name, or a dissociated partner's name as part thereof, by partners continuing the business does not of itself make the dissociated partner liable for an obligation of the partners or the partnership.

SUBCHAPTER VIII.
WINDING UP PARTNERSHIP BUSINESS OR AFFAIRS

§ 15-801. Events Causing Dissolution and Winding Up of Partnership Business or Affairs

A partnership is dissolved, and its business must be wound up, only upon the occurrence of any of the following events:

(1) In a partnership at will, the partnership's having notice from a partner, other than a partner who is dissociated under Section 15-601(2) through (12), of that partner's express will to withdraw as a partner, on a later date specified by the partner in the notice or, if no later date is specified, then upon receipt of notice;

(2) In a partnership for a definite term or particular undertaking:

(i) Within 90 days after a partner's dissociation by death or otherwise under Section 15-601(6) through (12) or wrongful dissociation under Section 15-602(b), at least half of the remaining partners express the will to wind up the partnership business, for which purpose a partner's rightful dissociation pursuant to Section 15-602(b)(2)(i) of this title constitutes the expression of that partner's will to wind up the partnership business;

(ii) The express will of all of the partners to wind up the partnership business or affairs; or

(iii) The expiration of the term or the completion of the undertaking;

(3) An event agreed to in the partnership agreement resulting in the winding up of the partnership business or affairs;

(4) An event that makes it unlawful for all or substantially all of the business or affairs of the partnership to be continued, but a cure of such illegality within 90 days after the partnership has notice of the event is effective retroactively to the date of the event for purposes of this section;

(5) On application by or for a partner to the Court of Chancery, the entry of a decree of dissolution of a partnership by the Court of Chancery upon a determination by the Court of Chancery that it is not reasonably practicable to carry on the partnership business, purpose or activity in conformity with the partnership agreement; or

(6) On application by a transferee of a partner's economic interest to the Court of Chancery, a determination by the Court of Chancery that it is equitable to wind up the partnership business or affairs:

(i) After the expiration of the term or completion of the undertaking, if the partnership was for a definite term or particular undertaking at the time of the transfer or entry of the charging order that gave rise to the transfer; or

(ii) At any time, if the partnership was a partnership at will at the time of the transfer or entry of the charging order that gave rise to the transfer.

§ 15-802. Partnership continues after dissolution

(a) Subject to subsection (b), a partnership continues after dissolution only for the purpose of winding up its business or affairs. The partnership is terminated when the winding up of its business or affairs is completed.

(b) At any time after the dissolution of a partnership and before the winding up of its business or affairs is completed, all of the partners, including any dissociating partner other than a wrongfully dissociating partner, may waive the right to have the partnership's business or affairs wound up and the partnership terminated. In that event:

(1) the partnership resumes carrying on its business or affairs as if dissolution had never occurred, and any liability incurred by the partnership or a partner after the dissolution and before the waiver is determined as if dissolution had never occurred; and

(2) the rights of a third party accruing under Section 15-804(1) or arising out of conduct in reliance on the dissolution before the third party knew or received a notification of the waiver may not be adversely affected.

§ 15-803. Right to Wind Up Partnership Business or Affairs

(a) A partner at the time of dissolution, including a partner who has dissociated but not wrongfully, may participate in winding up the partnership's business or affairs, but on application of any partner or a partner's legal representative or transferee, the Court of Chancery for good cause shown, may order judicial supervision of the winding up.

(b) The legal representative of the last surviving partner may wind up a partnership's business or affairs.

(c) The persons winding up the partnership's business or affairs may, in the name of, and for and on behalf of, the partnership, prosecute and defend suits, whether civil, criminal or administrative, gradually settle and close the partnership's business or affairs, dispose of and convey the partnership's property, discharge or make reasonable provision for the partnership's liabilities, distribute to the partners pursuant to Section 15-807 any remaining assets of the partnership, and perform other acts which are necessary or convenient to the winding up of the partnership's business or affairs.

§ 15-804. Partner's Power to Bind Partnership After Dissolution

Subject to Section 15-805, a partnership is bound by a partner's act after dissolution that:

(1) is appropriate for winding up the partnership business or affairs; or

(2) would have bound the partnership under Section 15-301 before dissolution, if the other party to the transaction did not have notice of the dissolution.

§ 15-805. Statement of Dissolution

(a) After dissolution, a partnership may file a statement of dissolution stating the name of the partnership and that the partnership has dissolved and is winding up its business or affairs.

(b) A statement of dissolution cancels a filed statement of partnership existence for the purposes of Section 15-303(b) and is a limitation on authority for the purposes of Section 15-303(c).

(c) For the purposes of Sections 15-301 and 15-804, a person not a partner is deemed to have notice of the dissolution and the limitation on the partners' authority as a result of a statement of dissolution 60 days after it is filed.

(d) After filing a statement of dissolution, a dissolved partnership may file a statement of partnership existence which will operate with respect to a person not a partner as provided in Section 15-303(b) and (c) in any transaction, whether or not the transaction is appropriate for winding up the partnership business or affairs.

(e) If a partnership which has dissolved fails or refuses to file a statement of dissolution, any partner or dissociated partner who is or may be adversely affected by the failure or refusal may petition the Court of Chancery to direct the filing. If the Court finds that the statement of dissolution should be filed and that the partnership has failed or refused to do so, it shall enter an order granting appropriate relief.

§ 15-806. Partner's Liability to Other Partners After Dissolution

(a) Except as otherwise provided in subsection (b) and Section 15-306, after dissolution a partner is liable to the other partners for the partner's share of any partnership obligation incurred under Section 15-804.

(b) A partner who, with knowledge of the dissolution, causes the partnership to incur an obligation under Section 15-804(2) by an act that is not appropriate for winding up the partnership business or affairs is liable to the partnership for any damage caused to the partnership arising from the obligation.

§ 15-807. Settlement of Accounts and Contributions Among Partners

(a) In winding up a partnership's business or affairs, the assets of the partnership, including the contributions of the partners required by this section, must be applied to pay or make reasonable provision to pay the partnership's obligations to creditors, including, to the extent permitted by law, partners who are creditors. Any surplus must be applied to pay in cash the net amount distributable to partners in accordance with their right to distributions under subsection (b).

(b) Each partner is entitled to a settlement of all partnership accounts upon winding up the partnership business or affairs. In settling accounts among the partners, profits and losses that result from the liquidation of the partnership assets must be credited and charged to the partners'' accounts. The partnership shall make a distribution to a partner in an amount equal to any excess of the credits over the charges in the partner's account. A partner shall contribute to the partnership an amount equal to any excess of the charges over the credits in the partner's account but excluding from the calculation charges attributable to an obligation for which the partner is not personally liable under Section 15-306.

(c) After the settlement of accounts, each partner shall contribute, in the proportion in which the partner shares partnership losses, the amount necessary to pay or make reasonable provision to pay partnership obligations that were not known at the time of the settlement and for which the partner is personally liable under Section 15-306.

(d) If a partner fails to contribute, all of the other partners shall contribute, in the proportions in which those partners share partnership losses, the additional amount necessary to pay or make reasonable provision to pay the partnership obligations for which they are personally liable under Section 15-306.

(e) A partner or partner's legal representative may recover from the other partners any contributions the partner makes to the extent the amount contributed exceeds that partner's share of the partnership obligations for which the partner is personally liable under Section 15-306.

(f) The estate of a deceased partner is liable for the partner's obligation to contribute to the partnership.

(g) An assignee for the benefit of creditors of a partnership or a partner, or a person appointed by a court to represent creditors of a partnership or a partner, may enforce a partner's obligation to contribute to the partnership.

(h) A limited liability partnership which has dissolved (i) shall pay or make reasonable provision to pay all claims and obligations, including all contingent, conditional or unmatured contractual claims, known to the limited liability partnership, (ii) shall make such provision as will be reasonably likely to be sufficient to provide compensation for any claim against the limited liability partnership which is the subject of a pending action, suit or proceeding to which the limited liability partnership is a party and (iii) shall make such provision as will be reasonably likely to be sufficient to provide compensation for claims that have not been made known to the limited liability partnership or that have not arisen but that, based on facts known to the limited liability partnership, are likely to arise or to become known to the limited liability partnership within 10 years after the date of dissolution. If there are sufficient assets, such claims and obligations shall be paid in full and any such provision for payment made shall be made in full. If there are insufficient assets, such claims and obligations shall be paid or provided for according to their priority and, among claims of equal priority, ratably to the extent of assets available therefor. Unless otherwise provided in the partnership agreement, any remaining assets shall be distributed as provided in this chapter. Any liquidating trustee winding up a limited liability partnership's affairs who has complied with this section shall not be personally liable to the claimants of the dissolved limited liability partnership by reason of such person's actions in winding up the limited liability partnership.

(i) A partner of a limited liability partnership who receives a distribution in violation of subjection (h) of this section, and who knew at the time of the distribution that the distribution violated subsection (h) of this section, shall be liable to the limited liability partnership for the amount of the distribution. For purposes of the immediately preceding sentence, the term "distribution" shall not include amounts constituting reasonable compensation for present or past services or reasonable payments made in the ordinary course of business pursuant to a bona fide retirement plan or other benefits program. A partner of a limited liability partnership who receives a distribution in violation of subsection (h) of this section, and who did not know at the time of the distribution that the distribution violated subsection (h) of this section, shall not be liable for the amount of the distribution. Subject to subsection (j) of this section, this subsection shall not affect any obligation or liability of a partner of a limited liability partnership under an agreement or other applicable law for the amount of a distribution.

(j) Unless otherwise agreed, a partner of a limited liability partnership who receives a distribution from a limited liability partnership shall have no liability under this chapter or other applicable law for the amount of the distribution after the expiration of 3 years from the date of the distribution.

(k) Section 15-309 of this chapter shall not apply to a distribution to which this section applies.

SUBCHAPTER IX.
CONVERSION; MERGER; DOMESTICATION; AND TRANSFER

§ 15-901. Conversion of Certain Entities to a Domestic Partnership

(a) As used in this section and in § 15-105, the term "other entity" means a corporation, a statutory trust, a business trust or association, a real estate investment trust, a commonlaw trust or any other unincorporated business, including a limited partnership (including a limited liability limited partnership), a foreign partnership or a limited liability company.

(b) Any other entity may convert to a domestic partnership (including a limited liability partnership) by complying with subsection (h) of this section and filing with the Secretary of State in accordance with § 15-105 of this chapter:

(1) A certificate of conversion to partnership that has been executed in accordance with § 15-105 of this chapter;

(2) A statement of partnership existence that complies with § 15-303 of this chapter and has been executed in accordance with § 15-105 of this chapter; and

(3) In the case of a conversion to a limited liability partnership, a statement of qualification in accordance with subsection (c) of § 15-1001 of this title.

Each of the certificate and statements required by this subsection (b) shall be filed simultaneously with the Secretary of State and, if such certificate and statements are not to become effective upon their filing as permitted by § 15-105(h) of this title, then such certificate and each such statement shall provide for the same effective date or time in accordance with § 15-105(h) of this title.

(c) The certificate of conversion to partnership shall state:

(1) The date on which and jurisdiction where the other entity was first created, formed or otherwise came into being and, if it has changed, its jurisdiction immediately prior to its conversion to a domestic partnership;

(2) The name of the other entity immediately prior to the filing of the certificate of conversion to partnership;

(3) The name of the partnership as set forth in its statement of partnership existence filed in accordance with subsection (b) of this section;

(4) The future effective date or time (which shall be a date or time certain) of the conversion to a partnership if it is not to be effective upon the filing of the certificate of conversion to partnership and the statement of partnership existence; and

(5) In the case of a conversion to a limited liability partnership, that the partnership agreement of the partnership states that the partnership shall be a limited liability partnership.

(d) Upon the filing with the Secretary of State of the certificate of conversion to partnership, the statement of partnership existence and the statement of qualification (if applicable), or upon the future effective date or time of the certificate of conversion to partnership, the statement of partnership existence and the statement of qualification (if applicable), the other entity shall be converted into a domestic partnership (including a limited liability partnership, if applicable) and the partnership shall thereafter be subject to all of the provisions of this chapter, except that the existence of the partnership shall be deemed to have commenced on the date the other entity commenced its existence in the jurisdiction in which the other entity was first created, formed, incorporated or otherwise came into being.

(e) The conversion of any other entity into a domestic partnership (including a limited liability partnership) shall not be deemed to affect any obligations or liabilities of the other entity incurred prior to its conversion to a domestic partnership, or the personal liability of any person incurred prior to such conversion.

(f) When any conversion shall have become effective under this section, for all purposes of the laws of the State of Delaware, all of the rights, privileges and powers of the other entity that has converted, and all property, real, personal and mixed, and all debts due to such other entity, as well as all other things and causes of action belonging to such other entity, shall remain vested in the domestic partnership to which such other entity has converted and shall be the property of such domestic partnership, and the title to any real property vested by deed or otherwise in such other entity shall not revert or be in any way impaired by reason of this chapter; but all rights of creditors and all liens upon any property of such other entity shall be preserved unimpaired, and all debts, liabilities and duties of the other entity that has converted shall remain attached to the domestic partnership to which such other entity has converted, and may be enforced against it to the same extent as if said debts, liabilities and duties had originally been incurred or contracted by it in its capacity as a domestic partnership. The rights, privileges, powers and interests in property of the other entity, as well as the debts, liabilities and duties of the other entity, shall not be deemed, as a consequence of the conversion, to have been transferred to the domestic partnership to which such other entity has converted for any purpose of the laws of the State of Delaware.

(g) Unless otherwise agreed, for all purposes of the laws of the State of Delaware, the converting other entity shall not be required to wind up its affairs or pay its liabilities and distribute its assets, the conversion shall not be deemed to constitute a dissolution of such other entity, and the conversion shall constitute a continuation of the existence of the converting other entity in the form of a domestic partnership. When another entity has been converted to a domestic partnership pursuant to this section, the domestic partnership shall, for all purposes of the laws of the State of Delaware, be deemed to be the same entity as the converting other entity and the conversion shall constitute a continuation of the existence of the converting other entity in the form of a domestic partnership.

(h) Prior to filing a certificate of conversion to partnership with the Secretary of State, the conversion shall be approved in the manner provided for by the document, instrument, agreement or other writing, as the case may be, governing the internal affairs of the other entity and the conduct of its business or by applicable law, as appropriate, and a partnership agreement shall be approved by the same authorization required to approve the conversion; provided, that in the event the continuing domestic partnership is not a limited liability partnership, such approval shall include the approval of any person who, at the effective date or time of the conversion, shall be a partner of the partnership.

(i) In connection with a conversion hereunder, rights or securities of, or interests in, the other entity which is to be converted to a domestic partnership may be exchanged for or converted into cash, property, rights or securities of or interests in such domestic partnership or, in addition to or in lieu thereof, may be exchanged for or converted into cash, property, rights or securities of or interests in another domestic partnership or other entity or may be cancelled.

(j) In connection with the conversion of any other entity to a domestic partnership (including a limited liability partnership), a person is admitted as a partner of the partnership as provided in the partnership agreement. For the purpose of subsection (b) of § 15-306 of this title, a person who, at the effective time or date of the conversion of any other entity to a domestic partnership (including a limited liability partnership), is a partner of the partnership, shall be deemed admitted as a partner of the partnership at the effective date or time of such conversion.

(k) The provisions of this section shall not be construed to limit the accomplishment of a change in the law governing, or the domicile of, an other entity to the State of Delaware by any other means provided for in a document, instrument, agreement or other writing, including by the amendment of any such document, instrument, agreement or other writing, or by applicable law.

§ 15-902. Merger or Consolidation

(a) As used in this section and in § 15-105, "other business entity" means a corporation, a statutory trust, a business trust, an association, a real estate investment trust, a common-law trust, or an unincorporated business or entity, including a limited liability company, a limited partnership (including a limited liability limited partnership) and a foreign partnership, but excluding a domestic partnership. As used in this section and in § 15-120 of this title, "plan of merger" means a writing approved by a domestic partnership, in the form of resolutions or otherwise, that states the terms and conditions of a merger under subsection (m) of this section.

(b) Pursuant to an agreement of merger or consolidation, 1 or more domestic partnerships may merge or consolidate with or into 1 or more domestic partnerships or 1 or more other business entities formed or organized under the laws of the State of Delaware or any other state or the United States or any foreign country or other foreign jurisdiction, or any combination thereof, with such domestic partnership or other business entity as the agreement shall provide being the surviving or resulting domestic partnership or other business entity. Unless otherwise provided in the partnership agreement, an merger or consolidation or a plan of merger shall be approved by each domestic partnership which is to merge or consolidate by all of its partners. In connection with a merger or consolidation hereunder, rights or securities of, or interests in, a domestic partnership or other business entity which is a constituent party to the merger or consolidation may be exchanged for or converted into cash, property, rights or securities of, or interests in, the surviving or resulting domestic partnership or other business entity or, in addition to or in lieu thereof, may be exchanged for or converted into cash, property, rights or securities of, or interests in a domestic partnership or other business entity which is not the surviving or resulting domestic partnership or other business entity in the merger or consolidation or may be cancelled. Notwithstanding prior approval, an agreement of merger or consolidation or a plan of merger may be terminated or amended pursuant to a provision for such termination or amendment contained in the agreement of merger or consolidation or a plan of merger.

(c) Except in the case of a merger under subsection (m) of this section, if, a domestic partnership is merging or consolidating under this section, (i) if the domestic partnership has not filed a statement of partnership existence, then the domestic partnership shall file a statement of partnership existence and (ii) the domestic partnership or other business entity surviving or resulting in or from the merger or consolidation shall file a certificate of merger or consolidation executed by at least 1 partner or by 1 or more authorized persons on behalf of the domestic partnership when it is the surviving or resulting entity with the Secretary of State. The certificate of merger or consolidation shall state:

(1) The name and jurisdiction of formation or organization of each of the domestic partnerships and other business entities which is to merge or consolidate;

(2) That an agreement of merger or consolidation has been approved and executed by each of the domestic partnerships and other business entities which is to merge or consolidate;

(3) The name of the surviving or resulting domestic partnership or other business entity;

(4) In the case of a merger in which a domestic partnership is the surviving entity, such amendments, if any, to the statement of partnership existence of the surviving domestic partnership (and in the case of a surviving domestic partnership that is a limited liability partnership, to the statement of qualification of such surviving domestic partnership) to change its name, registered office or registered agent as are desired to be effected by the merger;

(5) The future effective date or time (which shall be a date or time certain) of the merger or consolidation if it is not to be effective upon the filing of the certificate of merger or consolidation;

(6) That the agreement of merger or consolidation is on file at a place of business of the surviving or resulting domestic partnership or other business entity, and shall state the address thereof;

(7) That a copy of the agreement of merger or consolidation will be furnished by the surviving or resulting domestic partnership or other business entity, on request and without cost, to any partner of any domestic partnership or any person holding an interest in any other business entity which is to merge or consolidate; and

(8) If the surviving or resulting entity is not formed, organized or created under the laws of the State of Delaware, a statement that such surviving or resulting entity agrees that it may be served with process in the State of Delaware in any action, suit or proceeding for the enforcement of any obligation of any domestic partnership which is to merge or consolidate, irrevocably appointing the Secretary of State as its agent to accept service of process in any such action, suit or proceeding and specifying the address to which a copy of such process shall be mailed to it by the Secretary of State. In the event of service hereunder upon the Secretary of State, the procedures set forth in Section 15-113(b) of this chapter shall be applicable, except that the plaintiff in any such action, suit or proceeding shall furnish the Secretary of State with the address specified in the certificate of merger or consolidation provided for in this section and any other address which the plaintiff may elect to furnish, together with copies of each process as required by the Secretary of State, and the Secretary of State shall notify such surviving or resulting entity at all such addresses furnished by the plaintiff in accordance with the procedures set forth in Section 15-113(b) of this chapter.

(d) Any failure to file a certificate of merger or consolidation in connection with a merger or consolidation which occurred prior to the effective date of this chapter shall not affect the validity or effectiveness of any such merger or consolidation.

(e) Unless a future effective date or time is provided in a certificate of merger or consolidation or in the case of a merger under subsection (m) of this section in a certificate of ownership and merger, in which event a merger or consolidation shall be effective at any such future effective date or time, a merger or consolidation shall be effective upon the filing with the Secretary of State of a certificate of merger or consolidation or a certificate of ownership and merger.

(f) A certificate of merger or consolidation or a certificate of ownership and merger shall act as a certificate of cancellation of the statement of partnership existence for a domestic partnership which is not the surviving or resulting entity in the merger or consolidation. A certificate of merger that sets forth any amendment in accordance with paragraph (c)(4) of this section shall be deemed to be an amendment to the statement of partnership existence (and if applicable to the statement of qualification) of the domestic partnership, and the domestic partnership shall not be required to take any further action to amend its statement of partnership existence (or if applicable its statement of qualification) under § 15-105 of this title with respect to such amendments set forth in the certificate of merger. Whenever this section requires the filing of a certificate of merger or consolidation, such requirement shall be deemed satisfied by the filing of an agreement of merger or consolidation containing the information required by this section to be set forth in the certificate of merger or consolidation.

(g) An agreement of merger or consolidation or a plan of merger approved in accordance with subsection (b) of this section may (1) effect any amendment to the partnership agreement or (ii) effect the adoption of a new partnership agreement for a domestic partnership if it is the surviving or resulting partnership in the merger or consolidation. Any amendment to a partnership agreement or adoption of a new partnership agreement made pursuant to the foregoing sentence shall be effective at the effective time or date of the merger or consolidation and shall be effective notwithstanding any provision of the partnership agreement relating to amendment or adoption of a new partnership agreement, other than a provision that by its terms applies to an amendment to the partnership agreement or the adoption of a new partnership agreement, in either case, in connection with a merger or consolidation. The provisions of this subsection shall not be construed to limit the accomplishment of a merger or of any of the matters referred to herein by any other means provided for in a partnership agreement or other agreement or as otherwise permitted by law, including that the partnership agreement of any constituent domestic partnership to the merger or consolidation (including a domestic partnership formed for the purpose of consummating a merger or consolidation) shall be the partnership agreement of the surviving or resulting domestic partnership.

(h) When any merger or consolidation shall have become effective under this section, for all purposes of the laws of the State of Delaware, all of the rights, privileges and powers of each of the domestic partnerships and other business entities that have merged or consolidated, and all property, real, personal and mixed, and all debts due to any of said domestic partnerships and other business entities, as well as all other things and causes of action belonging to each of such domestic partnerships and other business entities, shall be vested in the surviving or resulting domestic partnership or other business entity, and shall thereafter be the property of the surviving or resulting domestic partnership or other business entity as they were of each of the domestic partnerships and other business entities that have merged or consolidated, and the title to any real property vested by deed or otherwise, under the laws of the State of Delaware, in any of such domestic partnerships and other business entities, shall not revert or be in any way impaired by reason of this chapter; but all rights of creditors and all liens upon any property of any of said domestic partnerships and other business entities shall be preserved unimpaired, and all debts, liabilities and duties of each of the said domestic partnerships and other business entities that have merged or consolidated shall thenceforth attach to the surviving or resulting domestic partnership or other business entity, and may be enforced against it to the same extent as if said debts, liabilities and duties had been incurred or contracted by it. Unless otherwise agreed, a merger or consolidation of a domestic partnership, including a domestic partnership which is not the surviving or resulting entity in the merger or consolidation, shall not require such domestic partnership to wind up its affairs under Subchapter VIII or pay its liabilities and distribute its assets under Subchapter VIII, and the merger or consolidation shall not constitute a dissolution of such partnership.

(i) Except as provided by agreement with a person to whom a partner of a domestic partnership is obligated, a merger or consolidation of a domestic partnership that has become effective shall not affect any obligation or liability existing at the time of such merger or consolidation of a partner of a domestic partnership which is merging or consolidating.

(j) If a domestic partnership is a constituent party to a merger or consolidation that shall have become effective, but the domestic partnership is not the surviving or resulting entity of the merger or consolidation, then a judgment creditor of a partner of such domestic partnership may not levy execution against the assets of the partner to satisfy a judgment based on a claim against the surviving entity of the merger or consolidation unless:

(1) The claim is for an obligation of the domestic partnership for which the partner is liable as provided in Section 15-306 and either:

(i) A judgment based on the same claim has been obtained against the surviving or resulting entity of the merger or consolidation and a writ of execution on the judgment has been returned unsatisfied in whole or in part;

(ii) The surviving or resulting entity of the merger or consolidation is a debtor in bankruptcy;

(iii) The partner has agreed that the creditor need not exhaust the assets of the domestic partnership that was not the surviving or resulting entity of the merger or consolidation;

(iv) The partner has agreed that the creditor need not exhaust the assets of the surviving or resulting entity of the merger or consolidation; or

(v) A court grants permission to the judgment creditor to levy execution against the assets of the partner based on a finding that the assets of the surviving or resulting entity of the merger or consolidation that are subject to execution are clearly insufficient to satisfy the judgment, that exhaustion of the assets of the surviving or resulting entity of the merger or consolidation is excessively burdensome, or that the grant of permission is an appropriate exercise of the court's equitable powers; or

(2) Liability is imposed on the partner by law or contract independent of the existence of the surviving or resulting entity of the merger or consolidation.

(k) A person is admitted as a partner of a surviving or resulting domestic partnership pursuant to a merger or consolidation approved in accordance with subsection (b) of this section as provided in the partnership agreement of the surviving or resulting domestic partnership or in the agreement of merger or consolidation or the plan of merger, and in the event of any inconsistency, the terms of the agreement of merger or consolidation or the plan of merger shall control. A person is admitted as a partner of a domestic partnership pursuant to a merger or consolidation in which such domestic partnership is not the surviving or resulting domestic partnership in the merger or consolidation as provided in the partnership agreement of such domestic partnership.

(l) A partnership agreement may provide that a domestic partnership shall not have the power to merge or consolidate as set forth in this section.

(m) In any case in which (x) at least 90% of the outstanding shares of each class of the stock of a corporation or corporations (other than a corporation which has in its certificate of incorporation the provision required by § 251(g)(7)(i) of Title 8), of which class there are outstanding shares that, absent § 267(a) of Title 8, would be entitled to vote on such merger, is owned by a domestic partnership, (y) 1 or more of such corporations is a corporation of the State of Delaware, and (z) any corporation that is not a corporation of the State of Delaware is a corporation of any other state or the District of Columbia or another jurisdiction, the laws of which do not forbid such merger, the domestic partnership having such stock ownership may either merge the corporation or corporations into itself and assume all of its or their obligations, or merge itself, or itself and 1 or more of such corporations, into 1 of the other corporations, pursuant to a plan of merger. If a domestic partnership is causing a merger under this subsection, the domestic partnership shall file a certificate of ownership and merger executed by at least 1 partner or by 1 or more authorized persons on behalf of the domestic partnership in the office of the Secretary of State. The certificate of ownership and merger shall certify that such merger was authorized in accordance with the domestic partnership's partnership agreement and this chapter, and if the domestic partnership shall not own all the outstanding stock of all the corporations that are parties to the merger, shall state the terms and conditions of the merger, including the securities, cash, property, or rights to be issued, paid, delivered or granted by the surviving domestic partnership or corporation upon surrender of each share of the corporation or corporations not owned by the domestic partnership, or the cancellation of some or all of such shares. The terms and conditions of the merger may not result in a holder of stock in a corporation becoming a partner in a surviving domestic partnership (other than a limited liability partnership). If a corporation surviving a merger under this subsection is not a corporation organized under the laws of the State of Delaware, then the terms and conditions of the merger shall obligate such corporation to agree that it may be served with process in the State of Delaware in any proceeding for enforcement of any obligation of the domestic partnership or any obligation of any constituent corporation of the State of Delaware, as well as for enforcement of any obligation of the surviving corporation, including any suit or other proceeding to enforce the right of any stockholders as determined in appraisal proceedings pursuant to § 262 of Title 8, and to irrevocably appoint the Secretary of State as its agent to accept service of process in any such suit or other proceedings, and to specify the address to which a copy of such process shall be mailed by the Secretary of State. Process may be served upon the Secretary of State under this subsection by means of electronic transmission but only as prescribed by the Secretary of State. The Secretary of State is authorized to issue such rules and regulations with respect to such service as the Secretary of State deems necessary or appropriate. In the event of such service upon the Secretary of State in accordance with this subsection, the Secretary of State shall forthwith notify such surviving corporation thereof by letter, directed to such surviving corporation at its address so specified, unless such surviving corporation shall have designated in writing to the Secretary of State a different address for such purpose, in which case it shall be mailed to the last address so designated. Such letter shall be sent by a mail or courier service that includes a record of mailing or deposit with the courier and a record of delivery evidenced by the signature of the recipient. Such letter shall enclose a copy of the process and any other papers served on the Secretary of State pursuant to this subsection. It shall be the duty of the plaintiff in the event of such service to serve process and any other papers in duplicate, to notify the Secretary of State that service is being effected pursuant to this subsection and to pay the Secretary of State the sum of $50 for the use of the State of Delaware, which sum shall be taxed as part of the costs in the proceeding, if the plaintiff shall prevail therein. The Secretary of State shall maintain an alphabetical record of any such service setting forth the name of the plaintiff and the defendant, the title, docket number and nature of the proceeding in which process has been served, the fact that service has been effected pursuant to this subsection, the return date thereof, and the day and hour service was made. The Secretary of State shall not be required to retain such information longer than 5 years from receipt of the service of process.

§ 15-903. *Approval of Conversion of a Domestic Partnership*

(a) Upon compliance with this section, a domestic partnership may convert to a corporation, a statutory trust, a business trust or association, a real estate investment trust, a common-law trust or any other unincorporated business, including a limited partnership (including a limited liability limited partnership), a foreign partnership or a limited liability company. If a domestic partnership is converting under this section to another business form organized, formed or created under the laws of a jurisdiction other than the State of Delaware and has not filed a statement of partnership existence, then the domestic partnership shall file a statement of partnership existence prior to or at the time of the filing of the certificate of conversion to non-Delaware entity.

(b) If the partnership agreement specifies the manner of authorizing a conversion of the partnership, the conversion shall be authorized as specified in the partnership agreement. If the partnership agreement does not specify the manner of authorizing a conversion of the partnership and does not prohibit a conversion of the partnership, the conversion shall be authorized in the same manner as is specified in the partnership agreement for authorizing a merger or consolidation that involves the partnership as a constituent party to the merger or consolidation. If the partnership agreement does not specify the manner of authorizing a conversion of the partnership or a merger or consolidation that involves the partnership as a constituent party and does not prohibit a conversion of the partnership, the conversion shall be authorized by the approval by all the partners.

(c) Unless otherwise agreed, the conversion of a domestic partnership to another business form pursuant to this section shall not require such partnership to wind up its affairs under Subchapter VIII of this chapter, and the conversion shall not constitute a dissolution of such partnership. When a partnership has converted to another entity or business form pursuant to this Section, for all purposes of the laws of the State of Delaware, the other entity or business form shall be deemed to be the same entity as the converting partnership and the conversion shall constitute a continuation of the existence of the partnership in the form of such other entity or business form.

(d) In connection with a conversion of a domestic partnership to another business form pursuant to this section, rights or securities of or interests in the domestic partnership which is to be converted may be exchanged for or converted into cash, property, rights or securities of or interests in the business form into which the domestic partnership is being converted or, in addition to or in lieu thereof, may be exchanged for or converted into cash, property, rights or securities of or interests in another business form or may be cancelled.

(e) If a partnership shall convert in accordance with this section to another business form organized, formed or created under the laws of a jurisdiction other than the State of Delaware, a certificate of conversion to non-Delaware entity executed in accordance with § 15-105 of this title shall be filed in the office of the Secretary of State in accordance with § 15-105 of this title. The certificate of conversion to non-Delaware entity shall state:

(1) The name of the partnership and, if it has been changed, the name under which its statement of partnership existence was originally filed;

(2) The date of the filing of its original statement of partnership existence with the Secretary of State;

(3) The jurisdiction in which the business form, to which the partnership shall be converted, is organized, formed or created, and the name of such entity or business form;

(4) The future effective date or time (which shall be a date or time certain) of the conversion if it is not to be effective upon the filing of the certificate of conversion to non-Delaware entity;

(5) That the conversion has been approved in accordance with this section;

(6) The agreement of the partnership that it may be served with process in the State of Delaware in any action, suit or proceeding for enforcement of any obligation of the partnership arising while it was a partnership of the State of Delaware, and that it irrevocably appoints the Secretary of State as its agent to accept service of process in any such action, suit or proceeding;

(7) The address to which a copy of the process referred to in subdivision (e)(6) of this section shall be mailed to it by the Secretary of State. In the event of service hereunder upon the Secretary of State, the procedures set forth in § 15-112(b) of this title shall be applicable, except that the plaintiff in any such action, suit or proceeding shall furnish the Secretary of State with the address specified in this subdivision and any other address that the plaintiff may elect to furnish, together with copies of such process as required by the Secretary of State, and the Secretary of State shall notify the partnership that has converted out of the State of Delaware at all such addresses furnished by the plaintiff in accordance with the procedures set forth in § 15-112(b) of this title.

(f) Upon the filing in the office of the Secretary of State of the certificate of conversion to non-Delaware entity or upon the future effective date or time of the certificate of conversion to non-Delaware entity and payment to the Secretary of State of all fees prescribed in this chapter, the Secretary of State shall certify that the partnership has filed all documents and paid all fees required by this chapter, and thereupon the partnership shall cease to exist as a partnership of the State of Delaware. Such certificate of the Secretary of State shall be prima facie evidence of the conversion by such partnership out of the State of Delaware.

(g) The conversion of a partnership out of the State of Delaware in accordance with this section and the resulting cessation of its existence as a partnership of the State of Delaware pursuant to a certificate of conversion to non-Delaware entity shall not be deemed to affect any obligations or liabilities of the partnership incurred prior to such conversion or the personal liability of any person incurred prior to such conversion, nor shall it be deemed to affect the choice of law applicable to the partnership with respect to matters arising prior to such conversion.

(h) When a domestic partnership has been converted to another business form pursuant to this section, the other business form shall, for all purposes of the laws of the State of Delaware, be deemed to be the same entity as the domestic partnership. When any conversion shall have become effective under this section, for all purposes of the laws of the State of Delaware, all of the rights, privileges and powers of the domestic partnership that has converted, and all property, real, personal and mixed, and all debts due to such partnership, as well as all other things and causes of action belonging to such partnership, shall remain vested in the other business form to which such partnership has converted and shall be the property of such other business form, and the title to any real property vested by deed or otherwise in such partnership shall not revert or be in any way impaired by reason of this chapter; but all rights of creditors and all liens upon any property of such partnership shall be preserved unimpaired, and all debts, liabilities and duties of the domestic partnership that has converted shall remain attached to the other business form to which such partnership has converted, and may be enforced against it to the same extent as if said debts, liabilities and duties had originally been incurred or contracted by it in its capacity as such other business form. The rights, privileges, powers and interests in property of the domestic partnership that has converted, as well as the debts, liabilities and duties of such partnership, shall not be deemed, as a consequence of the conversion, to have been transferred to the other business form to which such partnership has converted for any purpose of the laws of the State of Delaware.

(i) A partnership agreement may provide that a domestic partnership shall not have the power to convert as set forth in this section.

§ 15-904. Domestication of Non-United States Entities

(a) As used in this section and in § 15-105, "non-United States entity" means a foreign limited partnership (other than one formed under the laws of a state) (including a foreign limited liability limited partnership (other than one formed under the laws of a state)), or a corporation, a business trust or association, a real estate investment trust, a common-law trust or any other unincorporated business, including a general partnership (including a limited liability partnership) or a limited liability company, formed, incorporated, created or that otherwise came into being under the laws of any foreign country or other foreign jurisdiction (other than any state).

(b) Any non-United States entity may become domesticated as a partnership in the State of Delaware by complying with subsection (g) of this section and filing with the Secretary of State in accordance with Section 15-105 of this chapter:

(1) A certificate of partnership domestication that has been executed in accordance with Section 15-105 of this chapter; and

(2) A statement of partnership existence that complies with Section 15-303 of this chapter and has been executed in accordance with Section 15-105 of this chapter.

The certificate and the statement required by this subsection (b) shall be filed simultaneously with the Secretary of State and, if such certificate and such statement are not to become effective upon their filing as permitted by § 15-105(h) of this title, then such certificate and such statement shall provide for the same effective date or time in accordance with § 15-105(h) of this title.

(c) The certificate of partnership domestication shall state:

(1) The date on which and jurisdiction where the non-United States entity was first formed, incorporated, created or otherwise came into being;

(2) The name of the non-United States entity immediately prior to the filing of the certificate of partnership domestication;

(3) The name of the partnership as set forth in the statement of partnership existence filed in accordance with subsection (b) of this section;

(4) The future effective date or time (which shall be a date or time certain) of the domestication as a partnership if it is not to be effective upon the filing of the certificate of partnership domestication and the statement of partnership existence; and

(5) The jurisdiction that constituted the seat, siege social, or principal place of business or central administration of the non-United States entity, or any other equivalent thereto under applicable law, immediately prior to the filing of the certificate of partnership domestication.

(6) That the domestication has been approved in the manner provided for by the document, instrument, agreement or other writing, as the case may be, governing the internal affairs of the non-United States entity and the conduct of its business or by applicable non-Delaware law, as appropriate.

(d) Upon the filing with the Secretary of State of the certificate of partnership domestication and the statement of partnership existence or upon the future effective date or time of the certificate of partnership domestication and the statement of partnership existence, the non-United States entity shall be domesticated as a partnership in the State of Delaware and the partnership shall thereafter be subject to all of the provisions of this chapter, provided that the existence of the partnership shall be deemed to have commenced on the date the non-United States entity commenced its existence in the jurisdiction in which the non-United States entity was first formed, incorporated, created or otherwise came into being.

(e) The domestication of any non-United States entity as a partnership in the State of Delaware shall not be deemed to affect any obligations or liabilities of the non-United States entity incurred prior to its domestication as a partnership in the State of Delaware, or the personal liability of any person therefor.

(f) The filing of a certificate of partnership domestication shall not affect the choice of law applicable to the non-United States entity, except that from the effective date or time of the domestication, the laws of the State of Delaware, including the provisions of this chapter, shall apply to the non-United States entity to the same extent as if the non-United States entity had been formed as a partnership on that date.

(g) Prior to filing a certificate of partnership domestication with the Secretary of State, the domestication shall be approved in the manner provided for by the document, instrument, agreement or other writing, as the case may be, governing the internal affairs of the non-United States entity and the conduct of its business or by applicable non-Delaware law, as appropriate, and a partnership agreement shall be approved by the same authorization required to approve the domestication; provided that, in the event the continuing domestic partnership is not a limited liability partnership, such approval shall include the approval of any person who, at the effective date or time of the domestication, shall be a partner of the partnership.

(h) When any domestication shall have become effective under this section, for all purposes of the laws of the State of Delaware, all of the rights, privileges and powers of the non-United States entity that has been domesticated, and all property, real, personal and mixed, and all debts due to such non-United States entity, as well as all other things and causes of action belonging to such non-United States entity, shall remain vested in the domestic partnership to which such non-United States entity has been domesticated (and also in the non-United States entity, if and for so long as the non-United States entity continues its existence in the foreign jurisdiction in which it was existing immediately prior to the domestication) and shall be the property of such domestic partnership (and also of the non-United States entity, if and for so long as the non-United States entity continues its existence in the foreign jurisdiction in which it was existing

Delaware Revised Uniform Partnership Act

immediately prior to the domestication), and the title to any real property vested by deed or otherwise in such non-United States entity shall not revert or be in any way impaired by reason of this chapter; but all rights of creditors and all liens upon any property of such non-United States entity shall be preserved unimpaired, and all debts, liabilities and duties of the non-United States entity that has been domesticated shall remain attached to the domestic partnership to which such non-United States entity has been domesticated (and also to the non-United States entity, if and for so long as the non-United States entity continues its existence in the foreign jurisdiction in which it was existing immediately prior to the domestication), and may be enforced against it to the same extent as if said debts, liabilities and duties had originally been incurred or contracted by it in its capacity as a domestic partnership. The rights, privileges, powers and interests in property of the non-United States entity, as well as the debts, liabilities and duties of the non-United States entity, shall not be deemed, as a consequence of the domestication, to have been transferred to the domestic partnership to which such non-United States entity has domesticated for any purpose of the laws of the State of Delaware.

(i) When a non-United States entity has become domesticated as a domestic partnership pursuant to this section, the domestic partnership shall, for all purposes of the laws of the State of Delaware, be deemed to be the same entity as the domesticating non-United States entity and the domestication shall constitute a continuation of the existence of the domesticating non-United States entity in the form of a domestic partnership. Unless otherwise agreed, for all purposes of the laws of the State of Delaware, the domesticating non-United States entity shall not be required to wind up its affairs or pay its liabilities and distribute its assets, the domestication shall not be deemed to constitute a dissolution of such non-United States entity, and the domestication shall constitute a continuation of the existence of the domesticating non-United States entity in the form of a domestic partnership. If, following domestication, a non-United States entity that has become domesticated as a domestic partnership continues its existence in the foreign country or other foreign jurisdiction in which it was existing immediately prior to domestication, the domestic partnership and such non-United States entity shall, for all purposes of the laws of the State of Delaware, constitute a single entity formed, incorporated, created or otherwise having come into being, as applicable, and existing under the laws of the State of Delaware and the laws of such foreign country or other foreign jurisdiction.

(j) In connection with a domestication hereunder, rights or securities of, or interests in, the non-United States entity that is to be domesticated as a domestic partnership may be exchanged for or converted into cash, property, rights or securities of, or interests in, such domestic partnership or, in addition to or in lieu thereof, may be exchanged for or converted into cash, property, rights or securities of, or interests in, another domestic partnership or other entity or may be cancelled.

(k) In connection with the domestication of a non-United States entity as a domestic partnership (including a limited liability partnership), a person is admitted as a partner of the partnership as provided in the partnership agreement. For the purpose of subsection (b) of § 15-306 of this title, a person who, at the effective time or date of the domestication of any non-United States entity as a domestic partnership (including a limited liability partnership), is a partner of the partnership, shall be deemed admitted as a partner of the partnership at the effective date or time of such domestication.

§ 15-905. Transfer or Continuance of Domestic Partnerships

(a) Upon compliance with the provisions of this section, any domestic partnership may transfer to or domesticate in any jurisdiction, other than any state, and, in connection therewith, may elect to continue its existence as a partnership in the State of Delaware. If a domestic partnership is transferring or domesticating or continuing under this section and has not filed a statement of partnership existence, then the domestic partnership shall file a statement of partnership existence prior to or at the time of the filing of the certificate of transfer or certificate of transfer and continuance.

(b) If the partnership agreement specifies the manner of authorizing a transfer or domestication described in subsection (a) of this section, the transfer or domestication shall be authorized as specified in the partnership agreement. If the partnership agreement does not specify the manner of authorizing a transfer or domestication described in subsection (a) of this section and does not prohibit such a transfer or domestication, the transfer or domestication shall be authorized in the same manner as is specified in the partnership agreement for authorizing a merger or consolidation that involves the partnership as a constituent party to the merger or consolidation. If the partnership agreement does not specify the manner of authorizing a transfer or domestication described in subsection (a) of this section or a merger or consolidation that involves the partnership as a constituent party and does not prohibit such a transfer or domestication, the transfer or domestication shall be authorized by the approval by all the partners. If a transfer or domestication described in subsection (a) of this section shall be authorized as provided in this subsection (b), a certificate of transfer if the partnership's existence as a partnership of the State of Delaware is to cease, or a certificate of transfer and continuance if the partnership's existence as a partnership in the State of Delaware is to continue, executed in accordance with Section 15-105 of this chapter, shall be filed with the Secretary of State in accordance with Section 15-105 of this chapter. The certificate of transfer or the certificate of transfer and continuance shall state:

(1) The name of the partnership and, if it has been changed, the name under which its statement of partnership existence was originally filed;

(2) The date of the filing of its original statement of partnership existence with the Secretary of State;

(3) The jurisdiction to which the partnership shall be transferred or in which it shall be domesticated or continued and the name of the entity or business form formed, incorporated, created or that otherwise comes into being as a consequence of the transfer of the partnership to, or its domestication or continuance in, such foreign jurisdiction;

(4) The future effective date or time (which shall be a date or time certain) of the transfer or domestication to the jurisdiction specified in subsection (b)(3) of this section if it is not to be effective upon the filing of the certificate of transfer or the certificate of transfer and continuance;

(5) That the transfer or domestication or continuance of the partnership has been approved in accordance with the provisions of this section;

(6) In the case of a certificate of transfer, (i) that the existence of the partnership as a partnership of the State of Delaware shall cease when the certificate of transfer becomes effective and (ii) the agreement of the partnership that it may be served with process in the State of Delaware in any action, suit or proceeding for enforcement of any obligation of the partnership arising while it was a partnership of the State of Delaware, and that it irrevocably appoints the Secretary of State as its agent to accept service of process in any such action, suit or proceeding;

(7) The address to which a copy of the process referred to in subsection (b)(6) of this section shall be mailed to it by the Secretary of State. In the event of service hereunder upon the Secretary of State, the procedures set forth in Section 15-113(b) of this chapter shall be applicable, except that the plaintiff in any such action, suit or proceeding shall furnish the Secretary of State with the address specified in this subsection and any other address that the plaintiff may elect to furnish, together with copies of such process as required by the Secretary of State, and the Secretary of State shall notify the partnership that has transferred or domesticated out of the State of Delaware at all such addresses furnished by the plaintiff in accordance with the procedures set forth in Section 15-113(b) of this chapter; and

(8) In the case of a certificate of transfer and continuance, that the partnership will continue to exist as a partnership of the State of Delaware after the certificate of transfer and continuance becomes effective.

(c) Upon the filing with the Secretary of State of the certificate of transfer or upon the future effective date or time of the certificate of transfer and payment to the Secretary of State of all fees prescribed in this chapter, the Secretary of State shall certify that the partnership has filed all documents and paid all fees required by this chapter, and thereupon the partnership shall cease to exist as a partnership of the State. Such certificate of the Secretary of State shall be *prima* facie evidence of the transfer or domestication by such partnership out of the State of Delaware.

(d) The transfer or domestication of a partnership out of the State of Delaware in accordance with this section and the resulting cessation of its existence as a partnership of the State of Delaware pursuant to a certificate of transfer shall not be deemed to affect any obligations or liabilities of the partnership incurred prior to such transfer or domestication or the personal liability of any person incurred prior to such transfer or domestication, nor shall it be deemed to affect the choice of law applicable to the partnership with respect to matters arising prior to such transfer or domestication. Unless otherwise agreed, the transfer or domestication of a partnership out of the State of Delaware in accordance with this section shall not require such partnership to wind up its affairs under subchapter VIII of this chapter or pay its liabilities and distribute its assets under subchapter VIII and shall not be deemed to constitute a dissolution of such partnership.

(e) If a partnership files a certificate of transfer and continuance, after the time the certificate of transfer and continuance becomes effective, the partnership shall continue to exist as a partnership of the State of Delaware, and the laws of the State of Delaware, including the provisions of this chapter, shall apply to the partnership, to the same extent as prior to such time. So long as a partnership continues to exist as a partnership of the State of Delaware following the filing of a certificate of transfer and continuance, the continuing domestic partnership and the entity formed, incorporated, created or that otherwise came into being as a consequence of the transfer of the partnership to, or its domestication in, a foreign country or other foreign jurisdiction shall, for all purposes of the laws of the State of Delaware, constitute a single entity formed, incorporated, created or otherwise having come into being, as applicable, and existing under the laws of the State of Delaware and the laws of such foreign country or other foreign jurisdiction.

(f) In connection with a transfer or domestication of a domestic partnership to or in another jurisdiction pursuant to subsection (a) of this section, rights or securities of, or interests in, such partnership may be exchanged for or converted into cash, property, rights or securities of, or interests in, the business form in which the partnership will exist in such other jurisdiction as a consequence of the transfer or domestication or, in addition to or in lieu thereof, may be exchanged for or converted into cash, property, rights or securities of, or interests in, another business form or may be cancelled.

(g) When a domestic partnership has transferred or domesticated or continued out of the State of Delaware pursuant to this section, the transferred or domesticated or continued entity or business form shall, for all purposes of the laws of the State of Delaware, be deemed to be the same entity as the domestic partnership. When any transfer or domestication of a domestic partnership out of the State of Delaware shall have become effective under this section, for all purposes of the laws of the State of Delaware, all of the rights, privileges and powers of the domestic partnership that has transferred or domesticated or continued, and all property, real, personal and mixed, and all debts due to such partnership, as well as all other things and causes of action belonging to such partnership, shall remain vested in the transferred or domesticated or continued entity or business form (and also in the domestic partnership that has transferred, domesticated or continued, if and for so long as such domestic partnership continues its existence as a domestic partnership), and shall be the property of such transferred or domesticated or continued entity or business form (and also of the domestic partnership that has transferred, domesticated or continued, if and for so long as such domestic partnership continues its existence as a domestic partnership), and the title to any real property vested by deed or otherwise in such partnership shall not revert or be in any way impaired by reason of this chapter; but all rights of creditors and all liens upon any property of such partnership shall be preserved unimpaired, and all debts, liabilities and duties of the domestic partnership that has transferred or domesticated shall remain attached to the transferred or domesticated or continued entity or business form (and also to the domestic partnership that has transferred, domesticated or continued, if and for so long as such domestic partnership continues its existence as a domestic partnership), and may be enforced against it to the same extent as if said debts, liabilities and duties had originally been incurred or contracted by it in its capacity as the transferred or domesticated or continued entity or business form. The rights, privileges, powers and interests in property of the domestic partnership that has transferred or domesticated or continued, as well as the debts, liabilities and duties of such partnership, shall not be deemed, as a consequence of the transfer or domestication or continuance out of the State of Delaware, to have been transferred to the transferred or domesticated or continued entity or business form for any purpose of the laws of the State of Delaware.

(h) A partnership agreement may provide that a domestic partnership shall not have the power to transfer, domesticate or continue as set forth in this section.

SUBCHAPTER X.
LIMITED LIABILITY PARTNERSHIP

§ 15-1001. Statement of Qualification of a Domestic Partnership

(a) A domestic partnership may be formed as, or may become, a limited liability partnership pursuant to this section.

(b) In order to form a limited liability partnership, the original partnership agreement of the partnership shall state that the partnership is formed as a limited liability partnership, and the partnership shall file a statement of qualification in accordance with subsection (c) of this section. In order for an existing partnership to become a limited liability partnership, the terms and conditions on which the partnership becomes a limited liability partnership must be approved by the vote necessary to amend the partnership agreement and, in the case of a partnership agreement that expressly considers obligations to contribute to the partnership, also the vote necessary to amend those provisions, and after such approval, the partnership shall file a statement of qualification in accordance with subsection (c) of this section.

(c) The statement of qualification must contain:

(1) The name of the partnership;

(2) The address of the registered office and the name and address of the registered agent for service of process required to be maintained by Section 15-111 of this chapter;

(3) The number of partners of the partnership at the time of the effectiveness of the statement of qualification;

(4) A statement that the partnership elects to be a limited liability partnership; and

(5) The future effective date or time (which shall be a date or time certain) of the statement of qualification if it is not to be effective upon the filing of the statement of qualification.

(d) The status of a partnership as a limited liability partnership is effective on the later of the filing of the statement of qualification or a future effective date or time specified in the statement of qualification. The status as a limited liability partnership remains effective, regardless of changes in the partnership and regardless of cancellation of a statement of partnership existence for such partnership pursuant to the filing of a statement of cancellation to accomplish the cancellation of such statement of partnership existence or pursuant to § 15-1209(a) of this title, until the statement of qualification is canceled pursuant to § 15-105(d), § 15-111(d), or § 15-111(i)(4) of this chapter or revoked pursuant to § 15-1003 of this chapter.

(e) A partnership is a limited liability partnership if there has been substantial compliance with the requirements of this subchapter. The status of a partnership as a limited liability partnership and the liability of its partners is not affected by errors or later changes in the information required to be contained in the statement of qualification under subsection (c).

(f) The filing of a statement of qualification establishes that a partnership has satisfied all conditions precedent to the qualification of the partnership as a limited liability partnership.

(g) An amendment or cancellation of a statement of qualification is effective when it is filed or on a future effective date or time specified in the amendment or cancellation.

(h) If a person is included in the number of partners of a limited liability partnership set forth in a statement of qualification, a statement of foreign qualification or an annual report, the inclusion of such person shall not be admissible as evidence in any action, suit or proceeding, whether civil, criminal, administrative or investigative, for the purpose of determining whether such person is liable as a partner of such limited liability partnership. The status of a partnership as a limited liability partnership and the liability of a partner of such limited liability partnership shall not be adversely affected if the number of partners stated in a statement of qualification, a statement of foreign qualification or an annual report is erroneously stated provided that the statement of qualification, the statement of foreign qualification or the annual report was filed in good faith.

(i) Notwithstanding anything in this chapter to the contrary, a domestic partnership having, or that but for its election in accordance with § 15-1206(c) of this chapter, would have had, on December 31, 2001, the status of a registered limited liability partnership under predecessor law, shall have the status of a limited liability partnership under this chapter as of January 1, 2002, and to the extent such partnership has not filed a statement of qualification pursuant to this section, the latest application or renewal application filed by such partnership under such predecessor law shall constitute a statement of qualification filed under this section.

§ 15-1002. Name

The name of a limited liability partnership shall comply with Section 15-108 of this chapter.

§ 15-1003. Annual Report

(a) A limited liability partnership, and a foreign limited liability partnership authorized to transact business in the State of Delaware, shall file an annual report with the Secretary of State which contains:

(1) the name of the limited liability partnership and the state or other jurisdiction under whose laws the foreign limited liabili-

ty partnership is formed and the number of partners of the partnership; and

(2) the address of the registered office and the name and address of the registered agent for service of process required to be maintained by Section 15-111 of this chapter.

(b) An annual report must be filed by June 1 of each year following the calendar year in which a statement of qualification filed by a partnership becomes effective or a foreign partnership becomes authorized to transact business in the State of Delaware.

(c) On or before March 31 of each year, the Secretary of State shall mail to each partnership at its registered office set forth in the last filed statement of qualification or statement of foreign qualification or annual report a notice specifying that the annual report together with applicable fees shall be due on June 1 of the current year and stating that the statement of qualification or statement of foreign qualification of the partnership shall be revoked unless such report is filed and such filing fee is paid on or before June 1 of the following year. The Secretary of State shall not issue a certificate of good standing with respect to any limited liability partnership or foreign limited liability partnership which has not filed an annual report and paid the required filing fee pursuant to this section or with respect to any limited liability partnership or foreign limited liability partnership if its statement of qualification or statement of foreign qualification (as applicable) is canceled or revoked. The statement of qualification or statement of foreign qualification of any such partnership that fails to file such annual report or pay such required filing fee on or before June 1 of the following year shall be revoked.

(d) A revocation under subsection (c) only affects a partnership's status as a limited liability partnership and is not an event of dissolution of the partnership.

(e) A partnership whose statement of qualification or statement of foreign qualification has been revoked pursuant to subsection (c) may apply to the Secretary of State for reinstatement after the effective date of the revocation. The application must state:

(1) the name of the partnership and the effective date of the revocation; and

(2) that the ground for revocation either did not exist or has been corrected.

(f) A reinstatement under subsection (e) relates back to and takes effect as of the effective date of the revocation, and the partnership's status as a limited liability partnership continues as if the revocation had never occurred.

§ 15-1004. Reinstatement of Statement of Qualification or Statement of Foreign Qualification

(a) A partnership whose statement of qualification or statement of foreign qualification has been canceled pursuant to Section 15-111(d) or Section 15-111(i)(4) of this chapter may apply to the Secretary of State for reinstatement after the effective date of the cancellation. The application must state:

(1) The name of the partnership and the effective date of the cancellation and, if such name is not available at the time of reinstatement, the name under which the statement of qualification or statement of foreign qualification is to be reinstated; and

(2) That the partnership has obtained and designated a new registered agent as required by § 15-111(a) of this chapter and the name and address of such new registered agent and the address of the partnership's registered office in the State of Delaware.

(b) A cancellation of a partnership's statement of qualification or statement of foreign qualification pursuant to Section 15-111(d) or Section 15-111(i)(4) of this chapter only affects a partnership's status as a limited liability partnership or a foreign limited liability partnership and is not an event of dissolution of the partnership.

(c) A reinstatement under subsection (a) relates back to and takes effect as of the effective date of the cancellation, and the partnership's status as a limited liability partnership or a foreign limited liability partnership continues as if the cancellation had never occurred.

SUBCHAPTER XI.
FOREIGN LIMITED LIABILITY PARTNERSHIP

§ 15-1101. Law Governing Foreign Limited Liability Partnership

(a) The law under which a foreign limited liability partnership is formed governs relations among the partners and between the partners and the partnership and the liability of partners for obligations of the partnership.

(b) A foreign limited liability partnership may not be denied a statement of foreign qualification by reason of any difference between the law under which the partnership was formed and the law of the State of Delaware.

(c) A statement of foreign qualification does not authorize a foreign limited liability partnership to engage in any business or exercise any power that a partnership may not engage in or exercise in the State of Delaware as a limited liability partnership.

§ 15-1102. Statement of Foreign Qualification

(a) Before doing business in the State of Delaware, a foreign limited liability partnership shall register with the Secretary of State by filing:

(1) a statement of foreign qualification must contain:

(A) the name of the foreign limited liability partnership which satisfies the requirements of the State or other jurisdiction under whose law it is formed and ends with the words "Registered Limited Liability Partnership'' or ''Limited Liability Partnership,'' the abbreviation ''R.L.L.P.'' or ''L.L.P.'' or the designation ''RLLP'' or ''LLP'';

(B) the address of the registered office and the name and address of the registered agent for service of process required to be maintained by Section 15-111 of this chapter;

(C) the number of partners of the partnership; and

(D) the future effective date or time (which shall be a date or time certain) of the statement of foreign qualification if it is not to be effective upon the filing of the statement of foreign qualification.

(2) a certificate, as of a date not earlier than 6 months prior to the filing date, issued by an authorized officer of the jurisdiction of its formation evidencing its existence. If such certificate is in a foreign language, a translation thereof, under oath of the translator, shall be attached thereto.

(b) The status of a partnership as a foreign limited liability partnership is effective on the later of the filing of the statement of foreign qualification or the future effective date or time specified in the statement of foreign qualification. The status remains effective, regardless of changes in the partnership, until it is canceled pursuant to Section 15-105(d) of this chapter or revoked pursuant to Section 15-1003 of this chapter.

(c) An amendment or cancellation of a statement of foreign qualification is effective when it is filed or on the future effective date or time specified in the amendment or cancellation.

§ 15-1103. *Effect of Failure to Qualify*

(a) A foreign limited liability partnership doing business in the State of Delaware may not maintain an action or proceeding in the State of Delaware until it has in effect a statement of foreign qualification and has paid to the State of Delaware all fees and penalties for the years or parts thereof during which it did business in the State of Delaware without such qualification.

(b) The failure of a foreign limited liability partnership to have in effect a statement of foreign qualification does not impair the validity of a contract or act of the foreign limited liability partnership or preclude it from defending an action or proceeding in the State of Delaware or does not impair the right of any other party to a contract to maintain any action, suit or proceeding on the contract.

(c) A limitation on personal liability of a partner is not waived solely by doing business in the State of Delaware without a statement of foreign qualification having been filed.

(d) If a foreign limited liability partnership does business in the State of Delaware without a statement of foreign qualification having been filed, the Secretary of State is its agent for service of process with respect to a right of action arising out of the doing of business in the State of Delaware and service of process may be made in accordance with the procedures set forth in Section 15-113 of this chapter.

§ 15-1104. Activities Not Constituting Doing Business

(a) Activities of a foreign limited liability partnership in the State of Delaware which do not constitute doing business for the purpose of this subchapter include:

(1) Maintaining, defending or settling an action or proceeding;

(2) Holding meetings of its partners or carrying on any other activity concerning its internal affairs;

(3) Maintaining bank accounts;

(4) Maintaining offices or agencies for the transfer, exchange or registration of the partnership's own securities or maintaining trustees or depositories with respect to those securities;

(5) Selling through independent contractors;

(6) Soliciting or obtaining orders, whether by mail or through employees or agents or otherwise, if the orders require accep-

tance outside the State of Delaware before they become contracts;

(7) Selling, by contract consummated outside the State of Delaware, and agreeing, by the contract, to deliver into the State of Delaware, machinery, plants or equipment, the construction, erection or installation of which within the State of Delaware requires the supervision of technical engineers or skilled employees performing services not generally available, and as part of the contract of sale agreeing to furnish such services, and such services only, to the vendee at the time of construction, erection or installation;

(8) Creating, as borrower or lender, or acquiring indebtedness with or without a mortgage or other security interest in property;

(9) Collecting debts or foreclosing mortgages or other security interests in property securing the debts, and holding, protecting and maintaining property so acquired;

(10) Conducting an isolated transaction that is not one in the course of similar transactions;

(11) Doing business in interstate commerce; and

(12) Doing business in the State of Delaware as an insurance company.

(b) A person shall not be deemed to be doing business in the State of Delaware solely by reason of being a partner in a partnership.

(c) This section does not apply in determining whether a foreign limited liability partnership is subject to service of process, taxation or regulation under any other law of the State of Delaware.

§ 15-1105. Foreign Limited Liability Partnerships Doing Business Without Having Qualified; Injunctions

(a) The Court of Chancery shall have jurisdiction to enjoin any foreign limited liability partnership, or any agent thereof, from doing any business in the State of Delaware if such foreign limited liability partnership has failed to register under this subchapter or if such foreign limited liability partnership's statement of foreign qualification contains false or misleading representations. The Attorney General shall, upon his own motion or upon the relation of proper parties, proceed for this purpose by complaint in any county in which such foreign limited liability partnership is doing or has done business.

(b) Any foreign limited liability partnership doing business in the State of Delaware without first having registered shall pay to the Secretary of State a fee of $200 for each year or part thereof during which the foreign limited liability partnership failed to register in the State of Delaware.

SUBCHAPTER XII.
MISCELLANEOUS PROVISIONS

§ 15-1201. Uniformity of Application and Construction

This chapter shall be applied and construed to effectuate its general purpose to make uniform the law with respect to the subject of this chapter among states enacting it. The rule that statutes in derogation of the common law are to be strictly construed shall have no application to this chapter. Action validly taken pursuant to one provision of this chapter shall not be deemed invalid solely because it is identical or similar in substance to an action that could have been taken pursuant to some other provision of this chapter but fails to satisfy one or more requirements prescribed by such other provision.

§ 15-1202. Short Title

This chapter may be cited as the Delaware Revised Uniform Partnership Act.

§ 15-1203. Severability Clause

If any provision of this chapter or its application to any person or circumstance is held invalid, the invalidity does not affect other provisions or applications of this chapter which can be given effect without the invalid provision or application, and to this end the provisions of this chapter are severable.

§ 15-1204. Effective Date

This chapter takes effect January 1, 2000.

§ 15-1205. Repeals

Except with respect to limited partnerships (see 6 Del. C. § 17-1105), effective January 1, 2002, the Delaware Uniform Partnership Law, 6 Del. C. § 1501 - § 1553 is repealed.

§ 15-1206. Applicability

(a) Before January 1, 2002, this chapter governs only a partnership formed:

(1) after the effective date of this chapter, except a partnership that is continuing the business of a dissolved partnership under 6 Del. C. § 1541; and

(2) before the effective date of this chapter, that elects, as provided by subsection (c), to be governed by this chapter.

(b) On and after January 1, 2002, this chapter governs all partnerships.

(c) Before January 1, 2002, a partnership voluntarily may elect, in the manner provided in its partnership agreement or by law for amending the partnership agreement, to be governed by this chapter. The provisions of this chapter relating to the liability of the partnership's partners to third parties apply to limit those partners' liability to a third party who had done business with the partnership within one year before the partnership's election to be governed by this chapter only if the third party knows or has received a notification of the partnership's election to be governed by this chapter.

§ 15-1207. Fees

(a) No document required to be filed under this chapter shall be effective until the applicable fee required by this section is paid. The following fees shall be paid to and collected by the Secretary of State for the use of the State of Delaware:

(1) Upon the receipt for filing of any statement or certificate, a fee in the amount of $200.00.

(2) Upon the receipt for filing of an application for reservation of name, an application for renewal of reservation or a notice of transfer or cancellation of reservation pursuant to Section 15-109 of this chapter, a fee in the amount of $75.

(3) Upon the receipt for filing of a statement of qualification, a statement of foreign qualification or an annual report for a limited liability partnership or a foreign limited liability partnership, a fee in the amount of $200 for each partner, but in no event shall the fee payable for any year with respect to a limited liability partnership or a foreign limited liability partnership under this section be more than $120,000.

(4) For certifying copies of any paper on file as provided for by this chapter, a fee in the amount of $50 for each copy certified.

(5) The Secretary of State may issue photocopies or electronic image copies of instruments on file, as well as instruments, documents and other papers not on file, and for all such photocopies or electronic image copies, whether certified or not, a fee of $10 shall be paid for the first page and $2 for each additional

page. The Secretary of State may also issue microfiche copies of instruments on file as well as instruments, documents and other papers not on file, and for each such microfiche a fee of $2 shall be paid therefor. Notwithstanding the State of Delaware's Freedom of Information Act [Chapter 100 of Title 29] or other provision of this Code granting access to public records, the Secretary of State shall issue only photocopies, microfiche or electronic image copies of records in exchange for the fees described above.

(6) Upon the receipt for filing of a certificate under Section 15-111(b) of this chapter, a fee in the amount of $200, upon the receipt for filing of a certificate under Section 15-111(c) of this chapter, a fee in the amount of $200, and upon the receipt for filing of a certificate under Section 15-111(d) of this chapter, a fee in the amount of $20 for each partnership whose registered agent has resigned by such certificate.

(7) For preclearance of any document for filing, a fee in the amount of $250.

(8) For preparing and providing a written report of a record search, a fee in the amount of $50.

(9) For issuing any certificate of the Secretary of State, including but not limited to a certificate of good standing, other than a certification of a copy under paragraph (2) of this subsection, a fee in the amount of $50, except that for issuing any certificate of the Secretary of State that recites all of a partnership's filings with the Secretary of State, a fee of $175 shall be paid for each such certificate.

(10) For receiving and filing and/or indexing any certificate, affidavit, agreement or any other paper provided for by this chapter, for which no different fee is specifically prescribed, a fee in the amount of $100. For filing any instrument submitted by a partnership that only changes the registered office or registered agent and is specifically captioned as a certificate or statement of amendment changing only the registered office or registered agent, a fee in the amount of $50.

(11) The Secretary of State may in the Secretary of State's discretion charge a fee of $60 for each check received for payment of any fee that is returned due to insufficient funds or the result of a stop payment order.

(b) In addition to those fees charged under subsection (a) of this section, there shall be collected by and paid to the Secretary of State the following:

(1) For all services described in subsection (a) of this section that are requested to be completed within 30 minutes on the same day as the day of the request, an additional sum of up to $7,500 and for all services described in subsection (a) of this section that are requested to be completed within 1 hour on the same day as the day of the request, an additional sum of up to $1,000 and for all services described in subsection (a) of this section that are requested to be completed within 2 hours on the same day as the day of the request, an additional sum of up to $500;

(2) For all services described in subsection (a) of this section that are requested to be completed within the same day as the day of the request, an additional sum of up to $500; and

(3) For all services described in subsection (a) of this section that are requested to be completed within a 24-hour period from the time of the request, an additional sum of up to $150.

The Secretary of State shall establish (and may from time to time amend) a schedule of specific fees payable pursuant to this subsection.

(c) The Secretary of State may in the Secretary of State's discretion permit the extension of credit for the fees required by this section upon such terms as the Secretary of State shall deem to be appropriate.

(d) The Secretary of State shall retain from the revenue collected from the fees required by this section a sum sufficient to provide at all times a fund of at least $500, but not more than $1,500, from which the Secretary of State may refund any payment made pursuant to this section to the extent that it exceeds the fees required by this section. The funds shall be deposited in a financial institution which is a legal depository of State of Delaware moneys to the credit of the Secretary of State and shall be disbursable on order of the Secretary of State.

(e) Except as provided in this section, the fees of the Secretary of State shall be as provided in Section 2315 of Title 29.

§ 15-1208. Annual Tax of Partnership

(a) Every partnership that has filed a statement of partnership existence shall pay an annual tax, for the use of the State of Delaware, in the amount of $250.

(b) The annual tax shall be due and payable on the first day of June following the close of the calendar year or upon the cancellation of a statement of partnership existence. The Secretary of State shall receive the annual tax and pay over all taxes collected to the Department of Finance of the State of Delaware. If the annual tax remains unpaid after the due date established by subsection (d) of this section, the tax shall bear interest at the rate of 1 1/2% for each month or portion thereof until fully paid.

(c) The Secretary of State shall, at least 60 days prior to the first day of June of each year, cause to be mailed to each partnership required to comply with the provisions of this section in care of its registered agent in the State of Delaware an annual statement for the tax to be paid hereunder.

(d) In the event of neglect, refusal or failure on the part of any partnership to pay the annual tax to be paid hereunder on or before the first day of June in any year, such partnership shall pay the sum of $200 to be recovered by adding that amount to the annual tax, and such additional sum shall become a part of the tax and shall be collected in the same manner and subject to the same penalties.

(e) In case any partnership shall fail to pay the annual tax due within the time required by this section, and in case the agent in charge of the registered office of any partnership upon whom process against such partnership may be served shall die, resign, refuse to act as such, remove from the State of Delaware or cannot with due diligence be found, it shall be lawful while default continues to serve process against such partnership upon the Secretary of State. Such service upon the Secretary of State shall be made in the manner and shall have the effect stated in Section 15-113 of this chapter in the case of a partnership and shall be governed in all respects by said sections.

(f) The annual tax shall be a debt due from a partnership to the State of Delaware, for which an action at law may be maintained after the same shall have been in arrears for a period of one month. The tax shall also be a preferred debt in the case of insolvency.

(g) A partnership that neglects, refuses or fails to pay the annual tax when due shall cease to be in good standing as a partnership in the State of Delaware.

(h) A partnership that has ceased to be in good standing by reason of the failure to pay an annual tax shall be restored to and have the status of a partnership in good standing in the State of Delaware upon the payment of the annual tax and all penalties and interest thereon for each year for which such partnership neglected, refused or failed to pay an annual tax.

(i) The Attorney General, either on his own motion or upon request of the Secretary of State, whenever any annual tax due under this chapter from any partnership shall have remained in arrears for a period of 3 months after the tax shall have become payable, may apply to the Court of Chancery, by petition in the name of the State of Delaware, on 5 days' notice to such partnership, which notice may be served in such manner as the Court may direct, for an injunction to restrain such partnership from the transaction of any business within the State of Delaware or elsewhere, until the payment of the annual tax, and all penalties and interest due thereon and the cost of the application, which shall be fixed by the Court. The Court of Chancery may grant the injunction, if a proper case appears, and upon granting and service of the injunction, such partnership thereafter shall not transact any business until the injunction shall be dissolved.

(j) A partnership that has ceased to be in good standing by reason of its neglect, refusal or failure to pay an annual tax shall remain a partnership formed under this chapter. The Secretary of State shall not accept for filing any certificate (except a certificate of resignation of a registered agent when a successor registered agent is not being appointed) required or permitted by this chapter to be filed in respect of any partnership which has neglected, refused or failed to pay an annual tax, and shall not issue any certificate of good standing with respect to such partnership, unless and until such partnership shall have been restored to and have the status of a partnership in good standing in the State of Delaware.

(k) A partnership that has ceased to be in good standing in the State of Delaware by reason of its neglect, refusal or failure to pay an annual tax may not maintain any action, suit or proceeding in any court of the State of Delaware until such partnership has been restored to and has the status of a partnership in good standing in the State of Delaware. An action, suit or proceeding may not be maintained in any court of the State of Delaware by any successor or assignee of such partnership on any right, claim or demand arising out of the transaction of business by such partnership after it has ceased to be in good standing in the State of Delaware until such partnership, or any person that has acquired all or substantially all of its assets, has paid any annual tax then due and payable, together with penalties and interest thereon.

(l) The neglect, refusal or failure of a partnership to pay an annual tax shall not impair the validity of any contract, deed, mortgage, security interest, lien or act of such partnership or prevent such partnership from defending any action, suit, or proceeding in any court of the State of Delaware.

§ 15-1209. Cancelation of Statement of Partnership Existence for Failure to Pay Annual Tax

(a) The statement of partnership existence of a partnership shall be canceled if the partnership shall fail to pay the annual tax due under Section 15-1208 of this chapter for a period of three years from the date it is due, such cancellation to be effective on the third anniversary of such due date.

(b) A list of those partnerships whose statement of partnership existence were canceled on June 1 of such calendar year pursuant to

§ 15-1209(a) of this title shall be filed in the office of the Secretary of State. On or before October 31 of each calendar year, the Secretary of State shall publish such list on the Internet or on a similar medium for a period of 1 week and shall advertise the website or other address where such list can be accessed in at least 1 newspaper of general circulation in the State of Delaware.

(c) A partnership whose statement of partnership existence has been canceled and has not been revived pursuant to § 15-1210 of this title shall be deemed, from the date such cancellation became effective, to be a partnership that has not filed a statement of partnership existence.

§ 15-1210. Revival of Statement of Partnership Existence

(a) A statement of partnership existence that has been canceled pursuant to Section 15-111(d) or Section 15-1209(a) of this chapter may be revived by filing in the office of the Secretary of State a certificate of revival accompanied by the payment of the fee required by Section 15-1207 of this chapter and payment of the annual tax due under Section 15-1208 of this chapter and all penalties and interest thereon due at the time of the cancellation of its statement of partnership existence. The certificate of revival shall set forth:

(1) The name of the partnership at the time its statement of partnership existence was canceled and, if such name is not available at the time of revival, the name under which the partnership is to be revived;

(2) The date of filing of the original statement of partnership existence of the partnership;

(3) The address of the partnership's registered office in the State of Delaware and the name and address of the partnership's registered agent in the State of Delaware;

(4) A statement that the certificate of revival is filed by one or more partners of the partnership authorized to execute and file the certificate of revival to revive the partnership; and

(5) Any other matters the partner or partners executing the certificate of revival determine to include therein.

(b) The certificate of revival shall be deemed to be an amendment to the statement of partnership existence of the partnership, and the partnership shall not be required to take any further action to amend its statement of partnership existence under Section 15-105 of this chapter with respect to the matters set forth in the certificate of revival.

(c) Upon the filing of a certificate of revival, the statement of partnership existence of the partnership shall be revived with the same force and effect as if its statement of partnership existence had not been canceled pursuant to Section 15-111(d) or Section 15-1209(a) of this chapter.

TITLE 6.
COMMERCE AND TRADE
CHAPTER 19. DELAWARE UNIFORM UNINCORPORATED NONPROFIT ASSOCIATION ACT

Sec.
- 1901. Definitions.
- 1902. Supplementary general principles of law and equity.
- 1903. Territorial application.
- 1904. Real and personal property; nonprofit association as legatee, devisee or beneficiary.
- 1905. Statement of authority as to real property.
- 1906. Liability in tort and contract.
- 1907. Capacity to assert and defend; standing
- 1908. Effect of judgment or order.
- 1909. Disposition of personal property of inactive nonprofit association.
- 1910. Appointment of agent to receive service of process.
- 1911. Claim not abated by change of members or officers.
- 1912. Venue.
- 1913. Summons and complaint; service on whom.
- 1914. Uniformity of application and construction.
- 1915. Short title.
- 1916. Transition concerning real and personal property.

§ 1901. Definitions.

In this chapter:

(1) "Member" means a person who, under the rules or practices of a nonprofit association, may participate in the selection of persons author-

ized to manage the affairs of the nonprofit association or in the development of policy of the nonprofit association.

(2) "Nonprofit association" means an unincorporated organization consisting of 2 or more members joined by mutual consent for a common, nonprofit purpose. However, joint tenancy, tenancy in common or tenancy by the entireties does not by itself establish a nonprofit association, even if the co-owners share use of the property for a nonprofit purpose.

(3) "Person" means an individual, corporation, statutory trust, estate, trust, partnership, limited liability company, association, joint venture, government, governmental subdivision, agency or instrumentality or any other legal or commercial entity.

(4) "State" means a state of the United States, the District of Columbia, the Commonwealth of Puerto Rico or any territory or insular possession subject to the jurisdiction of the United States. (71 Del. Laws, c. 79, § 1.)

§ 1902. Supplementary general principles of law and equity.

Principles of law and equity supplement this chapter unless displaced by a particular provision of it. (71 Del. Laws, c. 79, § 1.)

§ 1903. Territorial application.

Real and personal property in this State may be acquired, held, encumbered and transferred by a nonprofit association, whether or not the nonprofit association or a member has any other relationship to this State. (71 Del. Laws, c. 79, § 1.)

§ 1904. Real and personal property; nonprofit association as legatee, devisee or beneficiary.

(a) A nonprofit association in its name may acquire, hold, encumber or transfer an estate or interest in real or personal property.

(b) A nonprofit association may be a legatee, devisee or beneficiary of a trust or contract.

(71 Del. Laws, c. 79, § 1.)

§ 1905. Statement of authority as to real property.

(a) A nonprofit association may execute and file a statement of authority to transfer an estate or interest in real property in the name of the nonprofit association.

(b) An estate or interest in real property in the name of a nonprofit association may be transferred by a person so authorized in a statement of authority filed in the office in the county in which a transfer of the property would be recorded.

(c) A statement of authority must set forth:

(1) The name of the nonprofit association;

(2) The address in this State, including the street address, if any, of the nonprofit association or, if the nonprofit association does not have an address in this State, its address out of state;

(3) The name or title of a person authorized to transfer an estate or interest in real property held in the name of the nonprofit association; and

(4) The action, procedure or vote of the nonprofit association which authorizes the person to transfer the real property of the nonprofit association and which authorizes the person to execute the statement of authority

(d) A statement of authority must be executed in the same manner as a deed by a person who is not the person authorized to transfer the estate or interest.

(e) A filing officer may collect a fee for filing a statement of authority in the amount authorized for recording a transfer of real property.

(f) An amendment, including a cancellation, of a statement of authority must meet the requirements for execution and filing of an original statement. Unless canceled earlier, a filed statement of authority or its most recent amendment is canceled by operation of law 5 years after the date of the most recent recording.

(g) If the record title to real property is in the name of a nonprofit association and the statement of authority is filed in the office of the county in which a transfer of real property would be recorded, the authority of the person named in a statement of authority is conclusive in favor of a person who gives value without notice that the person lacks authority. (71 Del. Laws, c. 79, § 1.)

§ 1906. Liability in tort and contract.

(a) A nonprofit association is a legal entity separate from its members for the purposes of determining and enforcing rights, duties and liabilities in contract and tort.

(b) A person is not liable for a breach of a nonprofit association's contract merely because the person is a member, is authorized to participate in the management of the affairs of the nonprofit association or is a person considered to be a member by the nonprofit association.

(c) A person is not liable for a tortious act or omission for which a nonprofit association is liable merely because the person is a member, is authorized to participate in the management of the affairs of the nonprofit association or is a person considered as a member by the nonprofit association.

(d) A tortious act or omission of a member or other person for which a nonprofit association is liable is not imputed to a person merely because the person is a member of the nonprofit association, is authorized to participate in the management of the affairs of the nonprofit association or is a person considered as a member by the nonprofit association.

(e) A member of, or a person considered to be a member by, a nonprofit association may assert a claim against the nonprofit association. A nonprofit association may assert a claim against a member or a person considered to be a member by the nonprofit association. (71 Del. Laws, c. 79, § 1.)

§ 1907. Capacity to assert and defend; standing.

(a) A nonprofit association, in its name, may institute, defend, intervene or participate in a judicial, administrative or other governmental proceeding or in an arbitration, mediation or any other form of alternative dispute resolution.

(b) A nonprofit association may assert a claim in its name on behalf of its members if 1 or more members of the nonprofit association have standing to assert a claim in their own right, the interests the nonprofit association seeks to protect are germane to its purposes and neither the claim asserted nor the relief requested requires the participation of a member. (71 Del. Laws, c. 79, § 1.)

§ 1908. Effect of judgment or order.

A judgment or order against a nonprofit association is not by itself a judgment or order against a member. (71 Del. Laws, c. 79, § 1.)

§ 1909. Disposition of personal property of inactive nonprofit association.

If a nonprofit association has been inactive for 3 years or longer, a person in possession or control of personal property of the nonprofit association may transfer the property:

(1) If a document of a nonprofit association specifies a person to whom transfer is to be made under these circumstances, to that person; or

(2) If no person is so specified, to a nonprofit association or nonprofit corporation pursuing broadly similar purposes or to a government or governmental subdivision, agency or instrumentality. (71 Del. Laws, c. 79, § 1.)

§ 1910. Appointment of agent to receive service of process.

(a) A nonprofit association may file in the office of the Secretary of State a statement appointing an agent authorized to receive service of process.

(b) A statement appointing an agent must set forth:

(1) The name of the nonprofit association;

(2) The address in this State, including the street address, if any, of the nonprofit association or, if the nonprofit association does not have an address in this State, its address out of state; and

(3) The name of the person in this State authorized to receive service of process and the person's address, including the street address, in this State.

(c) A statement appointing an agent must be signed and acknowledged by a person authorized to manage the affairs of a nonprofit association. The statement must also be signed and acknowledged by the person appointed agent, who thereby accepts the appointment. The appointed agent may resign by filing a resignation in the office of the Secretary of State and giving notice to the nonprofit association.

(d) A filing officer may collect a fee for filing a statement appointing an agent to receive service of process, an amendment or a resignation in the amount charged for filing similar documents.

(e) An amendment to a statement appointing an agent to receive service of process must meet the requirements for execution of an original statement. (71 Del. Laws, c. 79, § 1.)

§ 1911. Claim not abated by change of members or officers.

A claim for relief against a nonprofit association does not abate merely because of a change in its members or persons authorized to manage the affairs of the nonprofit association. (71 Del. Laws, c. 79, § 1.)

§ 1912. Venue.

For purposes of venue, a nonprofit association is a resident of a city or county in which it has an office. (71 Del. Laws, c. 79, § 1.)

§ 1913. Summons and complaint; service on whom.

In an action or proceeding against a nonprofit association, a summons and complaint must be served on an agent authorized by appointment to receive service of process, an officer, managing or general agent, or a person authorized to participate in the management of its affairs. If none of them can be served, service may be made on a member. (71 Del. Laws, c. 79, § 1.)

§ 1914. Uniformity of application and construction.

This chapter shall be applied and construed to effectuate its general purpose to make uniform the law with respect to the subject of this chapter among states enacting it. (71 Del. Laws, c. 79, § 1.)

§ 1915. Short title.

This chapter shall be known as and may be cited as the "Delaware Uniform Unincorporated Nonprofit Association Act." (71 Del. Laws, c. 79, § 1.)

§ 1916. Transition concerning real and personal property.

(a) If, before June 25, 1997, an estate or interest in real or personal property was purportedly transferred to a nonprofit association, on June 25, 1997, the estate or interest vests in the nonprofit association unless the parties have treated the transfer as ineffective.

(b) If, before June 25, 1997, the transfer vested the estate or interest in another person to hold the estate or interest as a fiduciary for the benefit of the nonprofit association, its members, or both, on or after June 25, 1997, the fiduciary may transfer the estate or interest to the nonprofit association in its name, or the nonprofit association, by appropriate proceedings, may require that the estate or interest be transferred to it in its name. (71 Del. Laws, c. 79, § 1.)

SELECTED TAXES AND FEES FOR DELAWARE CORPORATIONS

Upon the receipt for filing of an original certificate of incorporation, the tax shall be computed on the basis of:

2 cents for each share of authorized capital stock *having a par value* up to and including 20,000 shares,

1 cent for each share of authorized capital stock *having a par value* in excess of 20,000 shares up to and including 200,000 shares, and

2/5 of a cent for each share of authorized capital stock *having a par value* in excess of 200,000 shares;

1 cent for each share of authorized capital stock *without par value* up to and including 20,000 shares,

1/2 of a cent for each share of authorized capital stock *without par value* in excess of 20,000 shares up to and including 2,000,000 shares, and

2/5 of a cent for each share of authorized capital stock *without par value* in excess of 2,000,000 shares.

In no case shall the amount paid be less than $15. For the purpose of computing the tax on par value stock each $100 unit of the authorized capital stock shall be counted as one taxable share. *(See 8 Del. C. § 391(a)(1).)*

ANNUAL CORPORATE FRANCHISE TAX

All corporations incorporated in the State of Delaware are required to file an Annual Franchise Tax report and to pay a franchise tax. Religious and charitable non-stock corporations are exempt from the tax but must file an annual report. Taxes and annual reports are to be received no later than March 1st of each year. The minimum tax is $75.00 with a maximum tax of $180,000.00. Taxpayers owing more than $5,000.00 pay taxes in quarterly installments with 40% due June 1, 20% due by September 1, 20% due by December 1, and the remainder due March 1.

Methods Used to Calculate Franchise Taxes

—Authorized Shares Method

- 5,000 shares or less (minimum tax) **$75.00**

- 5,001 – 10,000 shares — **$150.00**

- each additional 10,000 shares or portion thereof add **$75.00**

- maximum yearly tax is **$180,000.00**.

—Assumed Par Value Capital Method

To use this method, a company must provide figures for **all issued shares** (including treasury shares) and **total gross assets** in the spaces provided in its Annual Franchise Tax report. Total Gross Assets shall be those "total assets" reported on the U.S. Form 1120, Schedule L (Federal Return) relative to the company's fiscal year ending the calendar year of the report. The tax rate under this method is $350.00 per million or portion of a million of the assumed par value capital, which is calculated as described below, if the assumed par value capital is greater than $1,000,000. If the assumed par value capital is less than $1,000,000, the tax is calculated by dividing the assumed par value capital by $1,000,000 then multiplying that result by $350.00. If an amendment changing a company's stock or par value was filed with the Division of Corporations during the year, issued shares and total gross assets within **30 days** of the amendment must be given for **each portion** of the year during which each distinct authorized amount of capital stock or par value was in effect. The tax is then prorated for each portion of the year dividing the number of days the stock/par value was in effect by 365 days (366 leap year), then multiplying this result by the tax calculated for that portion of the year. The total tax for the year is the sum of all the prorated taxes for each portion of the year. *(See 8 Del. C. § 501 et seq.)*

Filing Fees

—Corporate Annual Report

Annual reports for corporations are sent to the registered agents in December of each year. A $25.00 filing fee is required for the annual report. Annual reports or reprints may be requested through your registered agent.

DELAWARE TAXES & FEES

Calculations for Franchise Tax due are done using the Authorized Share Method on the annual report.

—*LP/LLC/GP*

All Limited Partnerships, Limited Liability Companies and General Partnerships formed in the State of Delaware are required to pay an annual tax of $250.00. Taxes for these entities are to be received no later than June 1st of each year.

For a more detailed list of corporate fees, see the Delaware Department of State Division of Corporations Fee Schedule located at: http://www.state.de.us/corp/fee.shtml.